Webster's New Dictionary

LONGMEADOW
PRESS

Photography: IMTEK IMAGINEERING
Masterfile

Copyright © 1994 by Promotional Sales Books

Published by Longmeadow Press, 201 High Ridge Road, Stamford, CT 06904.
All rights reserved. No part of this book may be reproduced or utilized in any form or by any means, electronic or mechanical, including photocopying, recording or by any information storage and retrieval system, without permission in writing from the Publisher. Longmeadow Press and the colophon are registered trademarks.

ISBN: 0-681-00782-6 Hardcover
0-681-00781-8 Paperback

Printed in the United States of America

First Longmeadow Press Edition

0 9 8 7 6 5 4 3 2 1 Hardcover
0 9 8 7 6 5 4 3 2 1 Paperback

This book is not published by the original publishers of **WEBSTER'S DICTIONARY** or by their successors.

Contents

Preface

What do you do when you encounter a new word while you are reading a book, a magazine, or a newspaper? Do you ask someone else what it means? Do you try to figure out its meaning based on the context in which it appears? Or do you use the dictionary?

Years ago, the maxim in school was, "Look it up and you'll never forget it." In fact, that is still true today. Using this, or any other dictionary, will help you remember the word long after you first discovered it. Why? Because once you've had a chance to see it in writing, along with its definition, it will stick in your mind. You will get a visual image of the word, so when you encounter it again, it triggers that visual memory.

When you hear a new word, the dictionary is your answer, once again. You will not only understand its meaning, but you will also learn how to spell the word correctly. Most of the words in this dictionary include the derivation of the words, so that you can more fully understand the word and associated words.

This dictionary has been created for easy use. It features dozens of "new" words that have appeared in the English language throughout the last decade. Furthermore, no modern dictionary would be complete without featuring the language of computers. You will find those significant, contemporary computer terms throughout. The type is set in a clear face, the root words and associated words are set in bold type in order to help you identify them quickly. Wherever necessary, brief pronunciation guides are provided. Finally, the derivation of the word(s) appears at the end of each entry.

Take this book with you wherever you are. Use it while you are reading, use it to help solve crossword puzzles. Most of all, it will help you understand and discover the nuances of the English language.

About This Dictionary

In order to make this dictionary a valuable "tool" for anyone concerned with the English language, the lexicographers who have compiled this book have tried to make it easy-to-use as well as contemporary. It would be of little use to you to have a dictionary that featured thousands of foreign, obscure, and antiquated terms. Thus, these words have been trimmed down to the basics — words that may still be in use after hundreds of years as well as those foreign words that you may encounter on a steady basis (**du jour**). In addition, we have included many of the more contemporary words that have come into use throughout the last several years, especially in the fields of science and computers. Words and terms such as **desktop publishing** and acronyms such as **ASCII** and **DOS** are important inclusions that assure the contemporary nature of this dictionary.

To use this dictionary, it is necessary for you to understand how it is organized. We've organized the words in paragraphs, featuring the root word in a larger, bold typeface. The words that are derived from this root word, or those that are related to it, are also in bold type. Thus, the word **execute** will include derivative words such as **execution, executioner**, and **executive.** If there are alternative spellings for the words, they are included. If there are unique plural forms of the word, these are included also.

In the next section is a list of abbreviations which appear throughout this dictionary. This includes the parts of speech, in order for you to recognize how the entry word is used. (Since this is not a grammar book, you will have to look elsewhere to determine what a *noun* is in contrast to a *verb transitive.*) You will find the word **lady** as a *noun* (*n.*) and the word **lag** as a *verb intransitive* (*v.i.*). However, the word **laggard** is a *noun* and an *adjective*, and the differing definitions are provided.

For many of the words where there may be a question of how to pronounce them, there are accent marks (ʹ) to show syllable emphasis as well as pronunciation guides. For example, look at the word **banquet.**

banq'uet (bang'-kwet) *n.* feast. -*v.i.* feast. -*v.t.* give a feast to -**banq'ueter** *n.* [F., dim of *banc*, bench]

This is a complete entry. First you are provided with the root word; **banquet**. In order for you to know that the accent is on the first syllable, there is an accent mark ('). Following the root word is a pronunciation guide in parentheses. The first syllable is pronounced like the word ***bang***; the second sounds like ***kwet***. The parts of speech follow. This word can be used in several ways: as a *noun, verb intransitive, verb transitive*. The associated word is **banqueter,** which is a *noun* . Finally, the derivation of the word is given, the diminutive (dim) of the French word *banc*.

We do not provide the accent marks with words of one syllable, or those with a silent *e* at the end of the word.

Most pronunciation guides are self-explanatory. For example, the second syllable in the word **baroque** is pronounced as a *k*, and the pronunciation guide provides the letter (-k-). As a guide for you, following are the common pronunciations that we use:

ch	chip	ng	ring
CH	chord	s	sweet
g	go	th	thing
hw	where	TH	this
j	juice, gene	y	yes
ng	Franch nasal sound	zh	measure

As you saw from the example above, the derivation or etymology of the main word is provided at the end of most entries in square brackets. Like the rest of this dictionary, we've tried to make it easy to use and in most cases have given the primary origin for a word, usually the Latin or Anglo-Saxon derivation. From time to time, where it would enhance your understanding of the derivation of the word, a somewhat more detailed explanation is provided.

Finally, when entries contain prefixes, we have offered only a handful of the words that can be created by the use of the prefix. A prefix such as **anti-** can be used to create hundreds of words. We have offered only a few, but suggest that you see the words without the prefix.

Abbreviations Used In This Book

a.	adjective
abbrev.	abbreviation
adv.	adverb
alg.	algebra
arch.	archaic
archit.	architecture
astron.	astronomy
avoir.	avoirdupois
bot.	botany
cap.	capital
cp.	compare
char.	character
chem.	chemistry
colloq.	colloquial
comp.	comparative
compute.	computers
conj.	conjunction
contr.	contraction
const.	construction
corrupt.	corruption, corrupted
dial.	dialect, dialectal
dem. pron.	demonstrative pronoun
dim.	diminutive
e.g.	for instance
elec.	electricity
esp.	especially
euph.	euphemism
fem.	feminine
fig.	figuratively
fort.	fortification
fr.	from
gen.	generally
geog.	geography
geol.	geology
gram.	grammar
hist.	history
ident.	identical
i.e.	that is
imit.	imitation, imitative
impers.	impersonal
infin.	infinitive
intens.	intensive
interj.	interjection
lang.	language
lit.	literally
maths.	mathematics
med.	medicine
mil.	military
mod.	modern
mus.	music
myth.	mythology
n.	noun
n. masc.	noun masculine
naut.	nautical
obj.	objective
obs.	obsolete
opp.	opposite
orig.	origin (-ally)
p.p.	past participle
p.t.	past tense
perh.	perhaps
pert.	pertaining to
philos.	philosophy
phot.	photography
phys.	physics
pl.	plural
poet.	poetry, poetical
polit.	politics
poss.	possessive
pref.	prefix
prep.	preposition
pres. p.	present participle
print.	printing
prob.	probably
pron.	pronoun
pros.	prosody
prov.	provincial
psych.	psychology
q.v.	which see
redupl.	reduplication
reflex.	reflexive
rhet.	rhetoric
rel. pron.	relative pronoun
sing.	singular
sl.	slang
superl.	superlative
surg.	surgery
trans.	transitive
trig.	trigonometry
ult.	ultimately

usu.	usually	*v.s.*	(*vide supra*) see above
v.	verb	*v.t.*	verb transitive
var.	variant, variation	*zool.*	zoology
v. aux.	auxiliary verb		
v.i.	verb intransitive		

Word Derivations

AF.	Anglo-French	ME.	Middle English
Afr.	African	Med. L.	Medieval Latin
Am. Amer.	American	Mex.	Mexican
Arab.	Arabic	Mod. L.	Modern Latin
Aram.	Aramaic	Mongol.	Mongolian
Austr.	Australian	N.	North
Braz.	Brazilian	Norw.	Norwegian
Can. F.	Canadian French	O.	Old
Carib.	Caribbean	OE.	Old English
Celt.	Celtic	OF.	Old French
Chin.	Chinese	OHG.	Old High German
Dan.	Danish	ON.	Old Norse
Du.	Dutch	ONF.	Old North French
E.	English	Pers.	Persian
F.	French	Peruv.	Peruvian
Flem.	Flemish	Port.	Portuguese
G.	Greek	Rom.	Romany
Gael.	Gaelic	Russ.	Russian
Ger.	German	S.	South
Heb.	Hebrew	Sans.	Sanskrit
Hind.	Hindustani	Sc.	Scottish, Scots
Hung.	Hungarian	Scand.	Scandinavian
Ice.	Icelandic	Slav.	Slavonic
Ind.	Indian	Sp.	Spanish
Ir.	Irish	Sw.	Swedish
It.	Italian	Teut.	Teutonic
Jap.	Japanese	Tibet.	Tibetan
L.	Latin	Turk.	Turkish
LL.	Low or Late Latin	U.S.	United States
M.	Middle	VL.	Vulgar Latin
Malay	Malay	W.	Welsh, West

A

a, an *a.* one; any. [OE, an, one]
aard'vark *n.* S. African ant-bear. [Du. *aarde,* earth, *Larken*, pig]
aard'wolf *n.* S. African earth-wolf, kind of hyena. [Du. = *earth-wolf*]
A-bomb *n.* atomic bomb.
ab'aca *n.* Indian plantain, Manila hemp. [Malay]
aback' *adv.* backwards (of sails blown back against the mast). **-ta'ken aback'**, surprised, abashed. [OE. *on baec*]
ab'acus *n.* flat piece at the top of a column; frame with parallel wires on which slide beads for counting. [L. -G. *abax,* tablet, reckoning board]
Abad'don *n.* Apollyon, the Devil. [Heb. *abad*, be lost]
abaft' *adv.* and *prep.* behind; in or to the aft. [OE. *on* and *baeftan,* by aft]
abalo'ne (-one) *n.* shellfish yielding mother-of-pearl. [Sp. Amer.]
aban'don *v.t.* give up altogether.
aban'doned *pp.* and *a.* given up, *esp.* to evil. **-aban'donment** *n.* [F. *abandonner*]
abase' *v.t.* lower, humiliate. **-abase'-ment** *n.* [F. *abaiser.* See **base**]
abash' *v.t.* confuse, make ashamed. **-abash'ment** *n.* [F. *ébahir*, astound]
abate' *v.t.* lessen. *-v.i.* become less. **abate'ment.** [F. *abatire*, beat off]
ab'atis, ab'attis *n.* barricade of felled trees for defense. [F. *abatis*]
abattoir' (-war') *n.* slaughter-house. [F.]
ab'ature *n.* trail of an animal. [F.]
ab'bey *n.* monastery or nunnery under an abbot, abbess. [abbot]
abb'ot *n.* head of a monastery. **-abb'ess** *fem.* **-abb'acy** *n.* office of abbot. [OE. *abbod*, fr. L. *abbas*, father]
abbreviate *v.t.* shorten or abridge. **-abbrevia'tion** *n.* [L. *abbreviate*]
ab'dicate *v.t.* give up formally. *-v.i.* give up power or office, *esp.* the throne. **abdica'tion** *n.* [L. *abdicate*]
abdo'men *n.* belly. **-abdom'inal** *a.* [L.]
abduce' *v.t.* (anatomy) draw from natural position, *e.g.* limb. **-abduc'ent** *a.* [L. *abducere,* lead away]
abduct' *v.t.* carry off, kidnap. **-abduc-tion** *n.* [L *abducere*, lead away]
abeam' *adv.* abreast, in line. [*beam*]
abed' *adv.* in bed. [*bed*]
abele' *n.* white poplar. [L. *albus*, white]
aberration *n.* wandering, *esp.* mental disorder, 'wandering of wits.' —
aberr'ant *a.* [L. *aberrare*, wander away]
abet' *v.t.* help in something bad. **-abett'er, abett'or** *n.* [OF. *abeter*, egg on]
abey'ance *n.* suspension from use or action. [OF. *abéance*, fr. *aboer,* gape at]
abhor' *v.t.* dislike very strongly; loathe, detest. **-abhorr'ence** *n.* **-abho'ent** *a,* [L. *abhorrere*, shrink from]
abide' *v.i.* stay, reside; await. *-v.t.* endure, put up with. [OE. *abidan*]
ab'igail *n.* lady's maid. [Biblical character]
abil'ity *n.* capacity, power, skill. [L. *habilis*, easy to hold]
abiogen'esis *n.* starting of life from non-living matter. **-abio'genist** *n.* one who believes in this. [G. *a*, not, *bios*, life, *genesis*, birth]
ab'ject *a.* mean, despicable. *-n.* outcast. [L. *abicere*, cast away]
abjure' *v.t.* give up by oath, renounce; deny solemnly. **-abjura'tion** *n.* [L. *abjurare*, swear off]
ab'lative *a.* and *n.* Latin case of nouns, primarily meaning 'away from.' [L. *ablativus*, borne away]
ab'laut *n.* change, modification in root vowel of word, *e.g.*, *ring*, *rang*, *rung*. [Ger. *ah*, off, *laut,* loud]
ablaze' *a.* burning. [*blaze*]
a'ble *a.* capable, clever, having power or skill. **-a'bly** *adv.* [L. *habilis*, fit]
ablu'tion *n.* washing; ceremonial cleansing. [L. *abluere*, wash away]
ab'negate *v.t.* give up, renounce. **abnega'tion** *n.* [L. *abnegare*, deny]
abnorm'al *a.* irregular; not usual; not according to type; exceptional. **-abnormal'ity, abnorm'ity** *n.* **-abnorm'ally** *adv.* [L. *ab*, from, *norma*, rule]
aboard' *adv.* on board, on a ship, train or plane. *-prep.* on board of. [board]
abode' *n.* home, dwelling. [*abide*]
abolish *v.t.* do away with. **-aboli'tion** *n.* **-aboli'tionism** *n.* **-aboli'tionist** *n.* one who wishes to do away with, *esp.* an evil, *e.g.*, slavery. [F. *abolir*]
abom'inate *v.t.* hate strongly. **-abom'inable** *a.* **-abom'inably** *adv.* **abomina'tion** *n.* (object of) detestation. [L. *abominari*, shrink from as a bad omen]
aborigines (-ji-nez) *n. pl.* original inhabitants of a country. **-aborig'inal** *a.* [L. *ab origine*, from the beginning]
abort' *v.t.* miscarry-**abor'tion** *n.* something misshapen or unnatural. **abor'tive** *a.* prematurely born; come to nothing. [L.

aboriri, miscarry]

abou'lia (-bow'-) *n.* loss of will-power. - **aboul'ic** *a.* -also **abu'lia, abu'lic.** [G. *a,* not, *boule*, will]

abound' *v.t.* be plentiful. [F. *abonder* L. *abundare*, overflow]

about' *adv.* on all sides; nearly; up and down; out, astir. *-prep.* round; near; dealing with. [OE. *onbutan*]

above' *adv.* in a higher place. *-prep.* on top of, higher; more than. [OE. *abufan*]

abracadabra *n.* cabbalistic word used as a charm; magic formula; gibberish. [First found in 2nd c. poem]

abrade' *v.t.* rub off, scrape away. - **abra'sion** *n.* [L. *abradere*]

abreast' *adv.* side by side. [*breast*]

abridge' *v.t.* cut short, abbreviate. - **abridg'ment** *n.* [F. *abreger*]

abroad' *adv.* out of house or country; at large. [ME. *on brede*, on breadth]

ab'rogate *v.t.* cancel, put an end to. **-abroga'tion** *n.* [L. *abrogare,* call ofl]

abrupt' *a.* hasty; steep; sudden; blunt. **-abrupt'ly** *adv.* **-abrupt'ness** *n.* [L. *abrumpere*, break off]

ab'scess (-ses) *n.* collection of pus in the tissues. [L. *abscedere*, go away]

abscind' (-sind') *v.t.* cut off. **abscission** *n.* [L. abscindere, cut away]

abscis'sa (-sis'-) *n.* (*maths.*) distance of a point from the axis of ordinates. [L. abscissa (linea), cut off (line)]

abscond' (-sk-) *v.i.* withdraw; decamp. [L. *abscondere*, hide away]

ab'sent *a.* away, not present. -(**absent'**) *v.t.* keep away. **-ab'sence** *n.* **-absentee'** *n.* one away; one who habitually stays away. -absentee'ism *n.* practise of a landlord living away from his estate, or a man absenting himself from his work. **ab'sently** *adv.* **-ab'sent-mind'ed** *a.* inattentive, preoccupied. -**ab'sent-mindedness** *n.* [L. *absens,* away]

ab'sinthe (ab'sinth) *n.* wormwood; liqueur flavored with wormwood. [F.]

ab'solute *a.* not limited, unconditional; entire, pure (as absolute alcohol). **ab'solutely** *adv.* -**ab'soluteness** *n.* [L. *absolvere*, set free]

absolve' *v.t.* free from, pardon. - **absolu'tion** *n.* [L. *absolvere*, set free]

absorb' *v.t.* suck up, drink in; engage the whole attention **of-absorb'ent** *a.* and *n.* **-absorp'tion** *n.* **-absorp'tive** *a.* [L. *absorbers*, suck away]

abstain *v.i.* keep from, refrain, *esp.* fromstrong drink. **-abstain'er** *n.* **abstention** *n.* **-ab'stinence** *n.* **-abstinent** *a.* [L. *abstenere*, hold from]

abstem'ious *a.* sparing in food or *esp.* in alcoholic drink. **-abste'miously** *adv.* - **abste'miousness** *n.* [L. *abstemious*, fr. *temetum*, strong drink]

absterge' *v.t.* clean by wiping. • **abster'gent** *a.* **-abster'sion** *n.* • **abster'sive** *a.* [L. *abstergere*, wipe away]

ab'stract *a.* separate; existing only in the mind, not concrete. *-n.* summary, abridgment. **-abstract'** *v.t.* draw from, remove. **-abstract'ed** *a.* absent-minded. **-abstraction** *n.* **-abstract'ly** *adv.* [L. *abstrahere,* draw away]

abstruse' *a.* obscure, hard to understand. **-abstruse'ly** *adv.* **-abstruse'ness** *n.* [L. *abstrudere*, push away]

absurd' *a.* silly, contrary to reason. • **absurd'ity** *n.* **-absurd'ly** *adv.* [L. *absurdus,* fr. *surdus*, deaf]

abundance *n.* great plenty. **-abun'dant** *a.* plentiful. **-abun'dantly** *adv.* [F. *abondance*]

abuse' *v.t.* misuse; miscall, address in rude language. *n.* **abu'sive** *a.* **-abu'sively** *adv.* **-abu'siveness** *n.* (L. *ab*, away from, *uti,* use]

abut' *v.i.* end on, border on. **-abut'ment** *n.* support, *esp.* for the end of a bridge. [OF. *abouter*, join at the end]

abu'tilon *n.* flowering plant of the mallow family. [Arab. *aubutilum*]

abyss' *n.* very deep gulf or pit. **-abys'mal** (-z-) *a.* **-abys'mally** *adv.* **-abyss'al** *a.* [G. *abyssos*, bottomless]

aca'cia *n.* thorny tropical shrub yielding gum arabic. [G. *akakia*]

acad'emy *n.* higher school; society to advance arts or sciences. **-academ'ic** *a.* of an academy; theoretical. **-academ'ically** *adv.* **-academi'cian** *n.* [G. *akademeia*, garden where Plato taught]

acan'thus *n.* prickly plant, the 'bear's breech'; architectural ornament like its leaf on Corinthian pillar. [L.]

accede' (aks-) *v.i.* enter on an office; agree, consent. **-acces'sion** (*ak-se'-shun*) *n.* [L. *accedere*, approach]

accelerando *a.* and *adv.* (*mus.*) with increasing speed. [It.]

accel'erate (aks-) *v.t.* and *i.* increase speed. **-accelera'tion** *n.* **-accel'erative** *a.* **-accel'erator** *n.* mechanism to increase speed, *esp.* in an automobile. [L. *accelerate*, fr. *celer*, swift]

ac'cent (aks-) *n.* stress of the voice; mark to show such stress; manner of speech peculiar to a district or individual. -(sent′) *v.t.* **-accen′tual** *a.* **-accen′tuate** *v.t.* **-accentua′tion** *n.* [F., fr. L. accentual note or tone]

accept′ (aks-) *v.t.* take, receive; admit, believe; agree to. **-acceptabil′ity** *n.* **accep′table** *a.* **-accep′tably** *adv.* **accep′tance** *n.* **acceptation** *n.* **- accep′ter** *n.* [L. *acceptare*, take]

ac′cess (-ks-) *n.* admission; entrance; attack; liberty to approach; means of approach. **-accessibil′ity** *n.* **-access′ible** *a.* easy to approach. **-access′ibly** *adv.* [L. *accedere*, go near to]

accessary *n.* helper, *esp.* in a crime.[*access*]

accessory *a.* additional. *-n.* added or non-essential item of dress or equipment; accomplice, aid in crime (*access*]

ac′cidence (-ks-) *n.* part of grammar dealing with changes in the form of words, *e.g.*, plurals. [for accidents]

ac′cident (-ks-) *n.* something happening by chance; mishap; quality not essential. **-acciden′tal** *a.* happening by chance. *-n.* (*mus.*) sharp, flat or natural, not of the key. **-acciden′tally** *adv.* [F.]

accip′itrine *a.* of, like, a hawk. [L. *accipiter*, hawk]

acclaim′ *v.t.* applaud, receive with applause. **-acclama′tion** *n.* **-acclam′a-tory** *a.* [L. *acclamare*, shout to]

accli′matize *v.t.* accustom to a new climate. **-acclimatiza′tion** *n.* [F. *acclimater*]

accliv′ity *n.* upward slope. [L. *acclivitas*]

accolade′ *n.* part of the ceremony of conferring knighthood, a light stroke with a flat of the sword. [F.]

accomm′odate *v.t.* fit; harmonize; supply. **-accomm′odating** *a.* obliging. **accommoda′tion** *n.* lodgings; loan; adjustment or compromise; obligingness. [L. *accommodate*, fit]

accom′pany *v.t.* go with; join with. **accom′paniment** *n.* something which accompanies, *esp.* (*mus.*) the instrumental part which goes with, *e.g.*, a vocal solo. **-accom′panist** *n.* one who plays an accompaniment. [F. *accompagner*]

accom′plice *n.* companion in evil deeds. [Earlier *complice*, fr. L. *complex*, woven together]

accom′plish *v.t.* carry out; finish. **accom′plished** *a.* complete, perfect; socially talented. **-accom′plishment** *n.* completion; a personal ability, talent. [F. *accomplir*]

accord′ *v.t.* compose, settle. *-v.i.* agree. *-n.* agreement, harmony. **-accord′-ance** *n.* **-accord′ant** *a.* **-accord′ing** *adv.* **-accord′ingly** *adv.* as the circumstances suggest. [L. *ad*, to, *cor, cordis*, heart]

accord′ion *n.* wind instrument worked by a bellows in the hands, a concertina. [See **accord**]

accost′ *v.t.* speak to, approach. [F. *accoster*, fr. L. *costa*, rib]

accouche′ment *n.* delivery in childbed. [F.]

account′ *v.t.* reckon, judge. *-v.i.* give a reason; make a statement of money. *-n.* statement of monies; report, description. **-accountabil′ity** *n.* **-account′able** *a.* responsible. **-account′ant** *n.* professional reckoner, one skilled in accounts. [OF. *aconter*, reckon]

accountancy *n.* the office or work of an accountant. [OF. *acconter*-L. *ad*, to, *computare*, to reckon]

accou′tre, accouter *v.t.* equip. **-accou′trements, accouterments** *n. pl.* equipment, *esp.* military. [F. *accoutrer*]

accred′it *v.t.* recommend; vouch for. [F. *accréditer*]

accre′tion *n.* growth; increase; something added on. (L. *accretio*]

accrue′ *v.t.* result; come as an addition. [F., pp. of *accroitre*, grow]

accumulate *v.t.* amass. *-v.i.* grow into a mass, increase. **-accumula′tion** *v.* **-accu′mulator** *n.* electrical storage battery. [L. *cumulare*, heap up]

ac′curate *a.* exact, correct. **-ac′curacy** *n.* **-ac′curately** *adv.* **-ac′curateness** *n.* [L. *accurare*, give care to]

accurs′ed, accurst′ *a.* under a curse; hateful. [*a-*, intens. and *cursed*]

accuse′ *v.t.* charge with wrongdoing; blame. **-accusa′tion** *n.* **-accu′sative** *n.* Latin case of nouns indicating an object. **-accu′satory** *a.* **-accu′ser** *n.* [L. *accusare*, call to account]

accus′tom *v.t.* make used to, familiarize. **-accus′tomed** *a.* [OF. *acostumer*]

ace *n.* the one at dice, cards, dominoes; single point; (*sl.*) very successful fighting airman; star performer in any sphere. [F. *as*, fr. L. *as*, unit]

acer′bity *n.* sour bitterness; severity of manner. [L. *acerbitas*]

ace′tic *a.* derived from or having the nature of vinegar. **-acetose′** *a.* -ac′**etous** (as-) *a.* **-ace′tic ac′id**, sour principle of vinegar. [L. *acetum*, vinegar]

ac′etone *n.* carbon compound used as a

solvent. [*acetic*]

acet'ylene *n.* gas made from calcium carbide and water, burning with a bright flame. [*acetic*]

ache (ak) *n.* continuous pain. -*v.i.* be in pain. -**ach'ing** *a.* [OE. *acan*]

achieve' *v.t.* finish, accomplish, perform successfully. -**achieve'ment** *n.* something accomplished; high exploit; coat of arms. [F. *achever*]

achromat'ic *a.* free from or not showing color, as of a lens. -**achro'matism** *n.* [G. *achrom, atos*]

ac'id *a.* sharp, sour. -*n.* sour substance; (*chem.*) one of a class of compounds which combine with bases (alkalis, oxides, *etc.*) to form salts. -**acid'ify** *v.t.* -**acid'ity** *n.* **acid rain** *n.* rain that contains a high concentration of pollutants, chiefly sulfur dioxide and nitrogen oxide, released into the atmosphere by the burning of fossil fuels such as coal or oil. -**acid'ulate** *v.t.* make slightly acid. -**acid'ulated** *a.* **acid'ulous** *a.* [L. *acidus-acere*, be sour]

ack-ack *a.* anti-aircraft. [abbrev. -*ack* = formerly 'a' in signalling code]

acknow'ledge (-nol' -) *v.t.* admit, own, recognize. -**acknow'ledgment** *n.* [ME. *knowlechen*, perceive]

ac'me *n.* highest point. [G. *akme*, point]

ac'ne *n.* skin disease; pimple. [G. *akme*, point]

ac'olyte *n.* lesser church officer; attendant on a priest; assistant. [G. *akolouthos*, following]

ac'onite *n.* poisonous plant, wolf's-bane or monk'shood. [L. *aconitum*]

a'corn *n.* fruit of the oak. [OE. *æcern*, fruit of the open country]

acous'tic *a.* pertaining to hearing. **acous'tics** *n. pl.* science of sounds. -**acoustic guitar** *n.* one not amplified by electronic means. [G. *akoustikos*]

acquaint' *v.t.* make to know, inform. -**acquaint'ance** *n.* personal knowledge; person known. -**acquaint'anceship** *n.* [OF. *acointier* -L. *ad*, to, *cognitus*, known]

acquiesce' *v.i.* agree in silence; consent. -**acquiescence** *n.* -**acquiescent** *a.* [L. *acquiescere*, rest]

acquire' *v.t.* gain, get. -**acquire'ment** *n.* -**acquisi'tion** *n.* act of getting; thing gained. -**acquis'itive** *a.* desirous of gaining. -**acquis'itiveness** *n.* [L. *acquirere*]

acquit' *v.t.* settle, discharge, as a debt; behave (oneself); declare innocent. **acquitt'al** *n.* act of declaring innocent in a court. -**acquitt'ance** *n.* discharge of a debt. [F. *acquitter*]

a'cre (*a'*-ker) *n.* measure of land, 4840 square yards. -*pl.* lands, estates, **a'creage** *n.* number of acres in a piece of land. [OE. *wer*, field]

ac'rid *a.* bitter and hot to the taste; irritating. -**acrid'ity** *n.* -**ac'ridness** *n.* [irreg. formation fr. L. *acer*, sharp]

ac'rimony *n.* bitterness of feelings or language. -**acrimo'nious** *a.* sharp, biting, severe. [L. *acrimonia*]

acritochro'macy *n.* colorblindness. [G. *a*, not, *krinein*, separate, *chroma*, color]

ac'robat *n.* performer of skilled gymnastic feats. -**acrobat'ic** *a.* -**acrobat'ics** *n. pl.* his art- [G. *akrobatos*, tiptoe walking]

acrophobia *n.* fear of heights. [G. *akron*, point, *phobos*, fear]

acropolis *n.* citadel, *esp.* that at Athens. [G. *akros*, topmost, *polis*, city]

across' *adv.* and *prep.* crosswise; from side to side. [For on or in cross]

acros'tic *n.* poem in which the first or last letters of the lines, in order, spell a word or words. [G. *akros*, extreme, and *stichos*, row or verse]

act *n.* thing done, deed; process of doing; law or decree; section of a play. -*v.t.* perform, as in a play. -*v.i.* exert force; work, as a mechanism; behave. -**ac'ting** *n.* performance of a part; working. -**ac'tion** *n.* -**activity**; operation; gesture; battle; lawsuit. -**action stations**, positions assumed before action or attack;-**ac'tionable** *a.* subject to a lawsuit. -**ac'tive** *a.* brisk, energetic. **activ'ity** *n.* -**ac'tively** *adv.* -**ac'tor** *n.* performer in plays (*fem.* **ac'tress**). [F. *acte* fr. L. *agere*, do]

ac'tinism *n.* chemical action of radiant energy.-**actin'ic** *a.* -**actinother'apy** *n.* treatment of disease by radiation, *esp.* sunlight. [G. *aktis*, ray]

actin'ium *n.* radioactive element found in pitchblende. (G. *aktis*, ray]

act'ual *adv.* real; existing in the present; not imaginary or bygone. -**actual'ity** *n.* **ac'tually** adv. [l. *actualis*]

ac'tuary *n.* registrar; one who makes calculations for insurance companies. -**actua'rial** *a.* [L. *actuarius*, recorder]

ac'tuate *v.t.* move, impel. [act]

ac'umen *n.* sharpness of wit. [L.]

acute' *a.* sharp; sensitive; keen, shrewd; critical. -**acute'ly** *adv.* -**acute'ness** *n.* [L. *acutus*, sharpened]

ADA *n.* a high-level computer programming language designed for dealing with real-time processing problems: used for military and other systems. [fr. Ada, Lady Lovelace (1815-52) who worked with Charles Babbage and whose description of his computing machines preserved them for posterity]

ad'age *n.* old saying, proverb. [F.]

ada'gio *a.* and *adv.* (*mus.*) slowly. -*n.* slow movement. [It. *ad agio*, at ease]

ad'amant *n.* very hard stone; diamond. -*a.* very hard, unbreakable; unyielding. -**adamant'ine** *a.* [G. *adamas*, invincible, not to be broken or tamed]

Adam's ap'ple *n.* projecting part of a man's throat, thyroid cartilage. [allusion to the forbidden fruit supposed to have stuck in Adam's throat]

adapt' *v.t.* fit; modify; alter for a new use. -**adaptabil'ity** *n.* -**adapt'able** *a.* **adapta'tion** *n.* -**adaptéive** *a.* -**adapt'iveness** *n.* [L. *adaptare*]

add *v.t.* and *i.* join; put something on; say further. -**adden'dum** (*pl.* -a) something to be added. -**addi'tion** *n.* -**addi'tional** *a.* [L. *addere*, put to]

ad'dax *n.* large African antelope with twisted horns. [local name]

add'er *n.* small poisonous snake, viper. [OE. *naedre*, snake. A *nadde*r became an *adder* in ME.]

ad'dict *n.* one given up to something, usually an evil, *e.g.*, drug-addict. **addict'ed** *a.* -**addic'tion** *n.* [L. *addictus;-addicere*, make over]

ad'dle *v.t.* and *i.* make or become rotten, muddled. [OE. *adela*, mud]

address' *v.t.* speak to; direct; dispatch; mark a destination, as on an envelope. *n.* skill; bearing; a speech; direction on a letter. -**addressee'** *n.* person to whom a letter *etc.* is directed. -**address'es** *n. pl.* courtship. [F. *adresser*, make straight]

adduce' *v.t.* bring forward; cite. -**addu'cible** *a.* -**adduc'tion** *n.* [L. *adducere*]

ad'enoids *n.pl.* small growths at the back of the nasal passage. [G. *aden*, acorn]

adept' *a.* skilled. *n.* expert; alchemist. [L. *adeptus*, having attained]

ad'equate *a.* sufficient, suitable; equal to. -**ad'equacy** *n.* -**ad'equately** *adv.* [L. *adæquatus*, made equal to]

adhere' *v.i.* stick to; become or remain firm, in an opinion *etc.* -**adhe'rent** *n.* and *a.* -**adhe'sion** *n.* -**adhe'sive** *a.* [L. *adhærere*, stick]

adhib'it *v.t.* use, attach, apply. [L. *adhibere*, to have, hold, employ]

adieu' *int.* farewell. -*n.* act of taking leave. [OF. *à Dieu*, to God]

ad'ipose *a.* fatty. [L. *adeps*, fat]

ad'it *n.* horizontal entrance into a pit or mine. [L. *adire*, go in]

adja'cent *a.* lying close to; contiguous. -**adja'cency** *n.* [L. *adjacere*]

adjective *n.* word added to a noun to show quality or circumstance. -**adjecti'val** *a.* [L. *adjectivus*, added]

adjoin' *v.t.* and *i.* add; be next to. **adjoin'ing** *a.* [F. *adjoindre*]

adjourn' (a-jurn') *v.t.* and *i.* put off, postpone; end a meeting; move to another place. -**adjourn'ment** *n.* [F. *ajourner*, fr. OF. *journ*, day]

adjudge' *v.t.* decide; award; give sentence. [F. *adjuger* -L. *adjudicate*]

adjudicate *v.t.* and *i.* try, judge; sit in judgment. -**adjudica'tion** *n.* -**adju'dicator** *n.* [L. *adjudicate*]

a'junct *a.* joined, added. -*n.* person or thing added. [L. *adjungere*, add to]

adjure' *v.t.* beg, entreat; charge on oath. -**adjura'tion** *n.* [L. *adjurare*, swear]

adjust' *v.t.* set right; make exact or suitable; **arrange.** -**adjust'able** *a.* -**adjust'ment** *n.* [F. *ajuster*, fr. *juste*, right]

ad'jutant *n.* military officer who assists the commanding officer of a unit. -**ad'jutancy** *n.* [L. adjutare, help]

admin'ister *v.t.* manage; look after; dispense, as justice *etc.*; supply. **admin'istra'tion** *n.* -**admin'istrative.** *a.* -**admin'istrator** *n.* [L. *administrate*]

ad'miral *n.* naval officer of very high or great rank. -**ad'miralty** *n.* board which controls the British Navy; buildings of that board. [F. *amiral*, fr. Arab. *amir-al* (*bahr*), prince of the (sea)]

admire' *v.t.* look on with wonder and pleasure; respect highly; love or esteem. **admirable** *a.* -**ad'mirably** *adv.* **admiration** *n.* -**admir'er** *n.* -**admir'ingly** *adv.* [L. *admirari*, wonder at]

admit' *v.t.* let in; allow; accept as true; grant. -**admissibil'ity** *n.* -**admiss'ible** *a.* -**admiss'ibly** *adv.* -**admis'sion** *n.* -**admitt'ance** *n.* [L. *admittere*, send to]

admix'ture *n.* act of mixing; blend, alloy or compound. [*mixture*]

admon'ish *v.t.* warn; reprove gently; advise. -**admoni'tion** *n.* -**admon'itory** *a.* [earlier *amonest*, OF. *amonester*, advise]

ado' *n.* fuss. [infin. *at do*]

ado'be (-bi) *n.* sun-dried brick. [U. S. fr. Mex Sp. *adobar*, plaster]

adoles'cent *a.* growing to manhood; not fully adult. -*n.* youth. -**adoles'cence** *n.* [L.

adolescere, grow up]

adopt′ *v.t.* take into relationship, *esp.* as one's child; take up, as a principle, resolution, idea. **-adop′tion** *n.* **-adoptive** *a.* that adopts or is adopted. [L. *adoptare*, choose for oneself]

adore′ *v.t.* and *i.* worship; love intensely. **-ador′able** *a.* **-adora′tion** *n.* **-ador′er** *n.* (L. *adorare*, worship, pray to]

adorn′ *v.t.* beautify, embellish, deck. **-adorn′ment** *n.* [L. adornare]

adre′nal *a.* near the kidneys. **-adre′nal glands′**, two small ductless glands over the kidneys. **-adre′nalin** *n.* secretion of these glands, taken from animals for use in medicine; powerful astringent drug. [L. *ad*, to, *renes*, kidneys]

adrift′ *a.* and *adv.* floating free; loose; without aim or direction. [*on drift*]

adroit′ *a.* skillful, expert, clever; dexterous. **-adroit′ly** *adv.* **-adroitness** *n.* [F., orig. *àd droit*, rightly]

ad′ulate *v.t.* flatter. **-adula′tion** *n.* **ad′uiator** *n.* **-ad′ulatory** *a.* [L. *adulari*]

ad′ult *a.*-grown-up, mature. -*n.* grownup person. [L. *adolescere, adult-*, grow]

adul′terate *v.t.* corrupt; make impure by mixture. **-adul′terant** *n.* **-adul′terated** *a.* **-adultera′tion** *n.* **-adul′terator** *n.* [L. *adulterate*, corrupt]

adul′tery *n.* sexual intercourse of two persons, either of whom is married to a third. **-adul′terer** *n. masc.* **-adul′teress** *n. fem.* **-adul′terous** *a.* [L. *adulterum*]

adum′brate *v.t.* outline, indicate; foreshadow. **-adum′brant** *n.* **-adumbra′tion** *n.* **-adum′brative** *a.* [L. *adumbrare*, foreshadow]

advance′ *v.t.* bring forward; promote; encourage; pay beforehand. -*v.i.* go forward; improve in rank or value. -*n.* movement forward; promotion; improvement; loan. **-advance′ment** *n.* [F. *avancer,* put forward]

advantage *n.* gain; superiority. -*v.t.* benefit, promote. **-advanta′geous** *a.* **-advanta′geously** *adv.* [F. *avantage*]

ad′vent *n.* coming, arrival; the first or second coming of Christ; season of four weeks before Christmas. **-adven′tual** *a.* [L. *adventus–ad*, to, *venire*, come]

adventi′tious (-shus) *a.* added; accidental; casual. [L. *adventicius*, coming from abroad]

adven′ture *n.* remarkable happening; enterprise; risk; bold exploit; commercial speculation. -*v.t.* and *i.* risk; take a risk. **-adven′turer** *n. masc.* **-adven′turess** *n. fem.* one who seeks adventures; one who lives on her wits. **-adven′turous** *a.* **-adven′turously** *adv.* **-adven′turousness** *n.* [F. *aventure*]

ad′verb *n.* word added to a verb, adjective or other adverb to modify the meaning. **-adverb′ial** *a.* [L. *adverbium*, fr. *ad*, to, *verbum*, word]

ad′verse *a.* opposed to; hostile; contrary to desire. **-ad′versary** *n.* enemy-**advers′ative** *a.* **-ad′versely** *adv.* **-advers′ity** *n.* distress, misfortune. [L. *advertere*, turn against]

advert′ *v.i.* turn the mind or attention to; refer. **-advert′ence** *n.* **-advert′ency** *n.* **-advert′ent** *a.* **-advert′ently** *adv.* [L. *advertere*, turn to]

advertise *v.t.* and *i.* make known; give notice of, *esp.* in newspapers, bills, *etc.* **-advert′isement** *n.* **-ad′vertiser** *n.* **ad′vertising** *n.* and *a.* [F. *avertir*, warn]

advice′ *n.* opinion given; counsel; information, news (*esp.* in *pl.*). [F. *avis*]

advise *v.t.* and *i.* give an opinion to; recommend a line of conduct; inform. **advis′able** *a.* expedient. **-advised′** (-zd) *a.* considered, deliberate, as in **well-advised. -advi′sedly** *adv.* **-advi′ser, advisor** *n.* **-advi′sory** *a.* [F. *avis*]

ad′vocate *n.* defender; one who pleads the cause of another, *esp.* in a court of law. -*v.t.* uphold, recommend. **ad′vocacy** *n.* **-advoca′tion** *n.* [L. *advocatus*, called in]

advow′son *n.* right of patronage or presentation to a church benefice. **-advow′ee** *n.* one who has that right. [OF. *avöeson*, fr. L. *advocate*, call in]

adyna′mia (-a′-) *n.* morbid lack of power. **-adynam′ic** *a.* [G.]

adze (adz) *n.* carpenter's tool with a curved blade set with the edge at right angles to the handle. [OE. *adesa*]

ae′gis *n.* shield given by Zeus; anything that protects. [G. *aigis*]

ae′grotat *n.* in an English university, certificate of illness preventing attendance at class. [L. = he is sick]

Aeo′lian *a.* acted on by the wind, as Aeolian harp. [L. *Aeolus*, god of winds]

ae′on *n.* age, or series of ages; period of time; eternity. [G. *aion*, age]

aepyor′nis *n.* large wingless fossil bird of Madagascar. [G. *aipys*, tall, *ornis*, bird]

a′erate *v.t.* expose to, or mix with, air; charge with carbonic acid or other gas. **-a′erator** *n.* apparatus to do this. **aera′tion** *n.* [L. *aer*, air]

aer′ial *a.* belonging to the air; ethereal:

-*n.* elevated wire to send out or receive radio signals. [L. *aer,* air]

a'erie, a'ery, ey'rie *n.* nest of a bird of prey, *esp.* an eagle. [F. *aire*]

aero- *prefix* having to do with air or aircraft. [L. *aer*, air] **-aerobat'ics** *n.* 'stunts' in aviation. **-a'erodrome** *n.* **airfield. -a'erogram** *n.* **air letter. a'erolite** *n.* meteoric stone. **-a'eronaut** *n.* 'air-sailor', *esp.* one who flies in airships or balloons. **-aeronaut'ics** *n. pl.* science of air navigation. **-aero'optics** *n.* the study of the effect of aircraft-induced and atmospheric disturbances on the efficiency of laser weapons. **-a'eroplane** *n.* airplane. **-a'erostat** *n.* balloon. **-a'erostatics,** science treating the behaviour of objects suspended in gases.

aero'bia *n. pl.* bacteria that cannot live without air, [G. *aer*, air, *bios*, life]

aero'bics *n.* any system of sustained exercises designed to increase the amount of oxygen in the blood and strengthen the heart and lungs.

aer'obieist *n. See* **aerobia.**

a'erosol *n.* suspension of fine solid or liquid particles in a gas; container for dispensing such.

Aescula'pian *a.* relating to the practice of medicine. [*Aesculapius*, Roman god of medicine]

aesthetic, esthetic *a.* relating to the principles of beauty and taste, and of art. **-aes'thete, es'thete** *a.* one who affects an extravagant love of art. **aesthetically, esthetically** *adv.* **aestheticism, esthet'icism** *n.* cult of beauty, *esp.* a much-ridiculed movement of the late 19th c. in England. **aesthet'ics, esthetics** *n.* [G. *aisthesthai*, perceive]

aes'tival. *See* **estival.**

ae'ther. *See* **ether.**

aetiol'ogy. *See* **etiology.**

afar' *adv.* from, at, or to a distance. [M. E. *on fer* and *offer,* becoming *a fer*]

af'fable *a.* easy to speak to, polite and friendly. **-affabil'ity** *n.* **-affably** *adv.* [F]

affair' *n.* business operation; any small matter; romantic attachment. *-pl.* mattersin general; public business. [F. *affaire*, fr. *faire*, do]

affect' *v.t.* acton, influence; move the feelings of, make a show of, make pretense; assume. **-affecta'tion** *n.* show, pretense. **-affec'ted** *a.* making a pretense. **affec'tedly** *adv.* **-affec'ting** *a.* moving the feelings, pathetic. **-affec'tingly** *adv.* **-affec'tion** *n.* fondness, love. **affec'tionate** *a.* loving. **-affec'tionately** *adv.* [L. *affectare*, aim at, fr. *afficere*, apply oneself to]

af'ferent *a.* bringing to, *esp.* describing nerves which carry sensation to the brain. [pres. p. of L. *affere*, bring to]

affi'ance *v.t.* betroth. -*n.* trust; pledged faith. [OF. *afiance*, trust]

affida'vit *n.* written statement on oath. [Late L. = he has sworn]

affiliate *v.t.* adopt; attach, as a society to a federation, *etc.* ; attribute to, father on. **-affilia'tion** *n.* [L. *affiliate*]

affinity *n.* relationship; structural resemblance; attraction, *esp.* chemical attraction. **-affin'itive** *a.* [L. *affinitas*]

affirm *v.t.* assert positively; maintain a statement. -*v.i.* make a solemn declaration, *esp.* without oath in a court of law. **-affirma'tion** *n.* **-affirm'ative** *a.* asserting. -*n.* word of assent. **affirmatively** *adv.* [L, *affirmare*, make firm]

affix' *v.t.* fasten to, attach. **-affix** *n.* addition, *esp.* to a word, as a suffix or prefix. [L. *affigere, affix-*, fix to]

affla'tus *n.* inspiration, as of a poet, orator; religious inspiration, the divine afflatus. [L. *afflare, afflat-*, inspire]

afflict' *v.t.* give pain or grief, vex. **-afflic'tion** *n.* distress, that which afflicts. **-afflic'tive** *a.* [L. *affligere*]

af'fluent *a.* wealthy. -*n.* tributary stream. **-af'fluence** *n.* wealth, abundance. [L. *affluere,* flow towards]

afford' *v.t.* be able to buy, or. to sustain the expense of-, produce, yield. [earlier *aforth*, OE. *geforthian*, fr. *forth*, forward]

affor'est *v.t.* turn land into forest, plant trees. **-afforesta'tion** *n.* [*forest*]

affray' *n.* fight, brawl. [OF. verb *esfreier,* frighten. Verb in E. survives only in p.p. *afraid = affrayed*]

affright' *v.t.* terrify. -*n.* sudden panic. [fr. p.p. of OE. *afyrhtan*, terrify]

affront' *v.t.* insult openly; meet face to face. -*n.* insult; contemptuous treatment. [F. *affronter*, confront]

afield' *adv.* in or on the field; away from home. [*field*]

afire' *adv.* on fire; in an inflamed condition. [*fire*]

aflame' *adv.* burning; in a blaze. [*blaze*]

afloat' *adv.* floating; at sea. [*float*]

afoot' *adv.* on foot; astir. [*foot*]

afore' *prep.* and *adv.* before, *usu.* in compounds, as **aforesaid, afore'-thought, afore'time.** [OE. *on foran*]

afiraid' *a.* in fear; timid. [See *affray*]

afresh' *adv.* again, anew. [*fresh*]

aft *adv.* towards or near the stern of a ship.

[OE. *æftan*]

af'ter *adv.* behind; later. -*prep.* like or in imitation of, behind; later than. -*a.* behind; later; nearer to the stem of a ship. [OE. *æfter*, farther away]

af'ter- as *prefix* makes compounds, as **afterbirth** *n.* membrane expelled after a birth. -**af'terclap** *n.* brief, dramatic recrudescence of an affair apparently closed. -**artercrop** *n.* -**afterdamp** *n.* gas left after an explosion in a coalmine. -**af'terglow** *n.* light after sunset. -**af'termath** *n.* second mowing of grass; sequel, later or secondary results. **af'ternoon** *n.* -**af'terthought** *n.* **af'terwards, af'terward** *adv.* later. [OE. *Eeftanweard*]

a'ga *n.* Turkish commander. [Turk *agha*]

again' *adv.* once more; back, in return; besides. [OE. *ongean*]

against' *prep.* opposite; in opposition to; in contact with; in exchange for. [*again*, with *gen.* -*es*, and -*t* added]

a'gar, a'gar-a'gar *n.* kind of gelatin extracted from seaweed. [Malay.]

ag'aric *n.* mushroom; family of fungi. [G. *agarikon*]

ag'ate *n.* precious stone composed of layers of quartz in different colors. [F.]

aga've n. plant of the amaryllis family. [G.]

age *n.* length of time a person or thing has existed; period of time; period of history; maturity; a long time. -*v.t.* make old. *v.i.* grow old. -**a'ged** *a.* old. -*n. pl.* old people. -**age'less** *a.* -**age'long** *a.* [OF. *edage*, fr. L. *a!tas*, age]

age'ism, ag'ism *n.* discrimination against people on the grounds of age; specifically, discrimination against the elderly. -**age'ist, ag'ist** *a.* [See **age**]

agen'da *n.* things to be done; program of a business meeting. [L.]

a'gent *n.* person or thing producing an effect; cause; natural force; person authorised to carry on business or affairs for another. -**a'gency** *n.* instrumentality; business or place of business of an agent. [L. *agere*, do]

agglomerate *v.t.* and *i.* gather into a mass. -*n.* rock consisting of volcanic fragments. -*a.* -**agglom'erated** *a.* **agglomeration** *n.* -**agglom'erative** *a.* [L. *agglomerate*]

agglutinate *v.t.* cause to adhere, as by glue. -**agglu'tinant** *a.* -**agglutina'tion** *n.* -**agglu'tinative** *a.* [L. *agglutinate*]

aggrandize *v.t.* make greater in size, power or rank. -**aggrand'izement** *n.* [F. *agrundir*-L. *ad*, to, *grandis*, large]

aggravate *v.t.* make worse; [colloq.] annoy. -**ag'gravating** *a.* -**aggrava'tion** *n.* [L. *aggravate*, make heavy]

aggregate *v.t.* gather into a mass. -*n.* sum total. -**aggrega'tion** *n.* -**ag'gregative** *a.* [L. *aggregate*, form into a rock]

aggres'sion *n.* unprovoked attack. **aggress'** *v.i.* -**aggress'ive** *a.* quarrelsome. -**aggress'iveness** *n.* -**aggress'or** *n.* [L. *aggredi, aggress-*, advance towards]

aggrieve' *v.t.* pain or injure. **aggrieved'** *a.* [OF. *agrever*, fr. L. *gravis*, heavy.] See **grieve.**

aghast' *a.* terrified; horror-stricken. [earlier *agast*, fr. OE. *æmstan*, terrify]

ag'ile (-j-) *a.* active, nimble. -**ag'ilely** *adv.* -**agil'ity** *n.* [F., fr. L. *agere*, do]

ag'itate (-j-) *v.t.* keep in motion; disturb, excite; keep in discussion. -**agita'tion** *n.* -**ag'itator** *n.* [L. *agitare*]

aglow' *a.* in a glow; eager. [glow]

ag'nate *a.* related on the father's side; allied. [L. *agnatus*]

ag'nosia *n.* loss or diminution of the power to recognize familiar objects or people, usually as a result of brain damage. -**ag'nosic** *a.* [G. *agnosa*, a, without, *gnosis* knowledge]

agnos'tic *n.* one who holds that we know nothing of things outside the material world. -**agnos'ticism** *n.* [G. *a*, not, *gnostos*, knowing]

ago' *adv.* gone; since; past. [earlier *agone*, p.p. of OE. *agan*, pass]

agog' *a.* and *adv.* eager, astir. [OF. *en gogues*, of which the orig. is unknown]

ag'ony *n.* extreme suffering; violent struggle; death struggle. -**ag'onize** *v.i.* suffer great pain or sorrow. -**ag'onizing** *a.* [G. *agonia*, struggle for victory]

agorapho'bia *n.* morbid fear of crossing open spaces. [G. *agora*, market-place, *phobos*, fear]

agou'ti *n.* small S. American rodent like the guinea-pig. [native name]

agra'rian *a.* relating to land or its management. -**agra'rianism** *n.* political movement for the redistribution of land. [L. *agrarius*, fr. *ager*, field]

agree' *v.i.* be of one mind; consent; harmonize; determine, settle; suit. **agreeabil'ity** *n.* -**agree'able** *a.* **agreeableness** *n.* -**agree'ably** *adv.* **agree'ment** *n.* [F. *agréer*, fr. L. *gratus*, pleasing]

ag'riculture *n.* art or practise of cultivating the ground. -**agricult'ural** *a.*

agricult'uralist, agriculturist *n.* [L. *agricultural*, tillage of the field]

ag'rimony *n.* plant of the rose group, with small yellow flowers and bitter taste. [L. *agrimonia*]

agron'omy *n.* scientific study of land and cultivation of crops. [G. *agros*, field, *nemein*, deal out]

aground' *adv.* stranded. [on ground]

a'gue *n.* fever in periodic fits, with shivering; quaking. [F. *aigu*, sharp]

ah *int.* of joy, surprise, pity *etc.* [perh. OF. *a*]

aha' *int.* of triumph or contempt [*ah, ha*]

ahead' *adv.* in front of. [*a* and *head*]

ahoy' *int.* shout used at sea for hailing, calling attention. [ME. hoy]

a'i *n.* Brazilian three-toed sloth. [fr. its cry]

aid *v.t.* help. *-n.* help, support; something helpful. [F. *aider* -L. *adjutare*]

aide-de-camp' *n.* (*pl.* **aides-de-camp'**) officer who attends a general, conveys his orders, *etc.* [P. = camp assistant]

AIDS *n.* acronym for acquired immune (or immuno-) deficiency syndrome: a condition thought to be caused by a virus, in which the body's white cells lose their ability to protect against infections.

aigrette' *n.* tuft of feathers; spray-shaped ornament of jewelery. [F. = lesser white heron; its crest]

aiguille' *n.* needle-like peak of rock. [F. -L. *acus*, needle]

ail *v.t.* trouble, afflict. *-v.i.* be ill. **-ail'ing** *a.* **-ail'ment** *n.* [OE. *eglan*]

ail'eron *n.* steadying flap on wing-tip of airplane. [F. -L. *ala*, wing]

aim *v.t.* and *i* . direct effort towards; try to; give direction to a weapon; strike or throw. *-n.* direction; endeavor; object, purpose. **-aim'less** *a.* without object. [OF. *esmer*, estimate]

air *n.* mixture of gases we breathe, the atmosphere; breeze; tune; manner; affected manner. *-pl.* affected manners. *v.t.* expose; dry or warm. **-air'ity** *adv.* **air'iness** *n.* **-air'ing** *n.* exposure to air; exposure to public consideration. **air'less** *a.* **-air'y** *a.* [G. *aer*, fr. *aein*, blow]

air- as a *prefix* makes compounds denoting things in, of, or having to do with the air, as **air'balloon** *n.*, including broadcasting by radiowaves, as **air'time. -air' base** *n.* **-air' brake** *n.* **air' chamber** *n.* **-air'-condition** *v.t.* fit with system to keep the interior air atrequisite temperature, *etc.* **-aircraft** *n.* **-air'craft carrier** *n.* **-air'crew** *n.* **air'duct** *n.* **-air' force** *n.* national organization dealing with military aircraft. **-airgun** *n.* gun discharged by force of compressed air. **-air' hole** *n.* **-air' lane** *n.* aircraft route. **-air' lift** *n.* organized air transport operation. **-air'line** *n.* organization dealing with transport by airplanes. **-air'man** *n.*. **-air'plane** *n.* heavier-than-air flying machine **-air'pocket** *n.* part of the air where an airplane drops suddenly. **-air'port** *n.* station for passenger aircraft. **air'power** *n.* **-air' pump** *n.* machine to draw air from a vessel. **-air' raid** *n.* attack by aircraft. **-air' screw** *n.* propeller. **air'ship** *n.* **-air'sickness** *n.* **-air'ship** *n.* (temporary) runway. **-air'tight** *a.* not allowing the passage of air. **-air' valve** *n.* **-air'way** *n.* regular aircraft route. **air'worthy** *a.* fit for service in the air. **airwor'thiness** *n.*

Aire'dale *n.* large terrier dog. [fr. valley of the *Aire*, Yorks.]

aisle *n.* wing of a church, or lateral division of any part of a church; walk between seats in a church. [bad spelling of F. *aile*-fr. L. *ala*, wing]

ait, eyot *n.* small island in river or take. [OE. *iggath, igeoth*]

aitch'bone *n.* bone of the rump; cut of beef over this bone. [ME. *nache*, buttock (fr. OF.); a *nache* became an *aitch*. cp. **adder**]

ajar' *adv.* partly open. [ME. *on char*, on the turn]

akim'bo *adv.* with arm bent and hand on hip. tME. in kenebowe, for can bow, the bow, curved handle, of a can, vessel. Other languages use the same metaphor of 'standing like a pot with two handles']

akin' *a.* related by blood; like, having the same qualities. [of kin]

alabaster *n.* kind of soft, white, semi-transparent stone. [G. *alabastros*]

alack' *int.* cry of sorrow. **-alack'-a-day** *int.* [prob. change of *alas*, by association with lack, failure or shame]

alac'rity *n.* quickness, briskness. [L. *alacritas*]

ala'lia *n.* loss of speech. [G. *a.*, not, *lalein*, speak]

a'lar *a.* winged. **-a'late** *a.* [L. *alatus* -*ala*, wing]

alarm' *n.* notice of danger; sudden fright; call to arms. *-v.t.* warn of danger; frighten. **-alarm'ing** *a.* **-alarm'ist** *n.* one given to prophesying danger. **-alarm-clock'** *n.* clock which rings a bell at a set hour to give warning of the time. **-alarum'** (alarm') *n.* variant of alarm. [OF. *à l'arme*, fr. It. *all' arme,* to arms (cp. *alert*). With the *r* rolled it gives also *alarum.*]

alas' *int.* cry of grief. [OF. *a las, ah,* weary]

alb *n.* long white priestly vestment worn at Mass. [L. *albus,* white]

al'bacore *n.* large kind of tunny fish. [Port.]

albatross *n.* large, long-winged seabird, remarkable for its flying powers. [fr. obs. *alcatras,* frigate-bird, influenced by L. *albus,* white]

albe'it *conj.* although. [all be it]

albi'no *n.* person or animal with unusually white skin and hair and pink eyes, due to lack of pigment in the skin. **al'binism** *n.* [Sp., fr. L. *albus,* white]

al'bum *n.* book of blank leaves, for collecting portraits, stamps, autographs. *etc.* [L. *albus,* white]

albu'men *n.* constituent of animal and vegetable matter, found nearly pure in white of egg. **-albu'minoid** *a.* **albuminous** *a.* [L., fr. *albus,* white]

al'chemy (-k-) *n.* earlier stage of chemistry, its main aims the turning of base metals into gold and the finding of an elixir of life. **-al'chemist** *n.* [Arab. *alkimiya,* transmutation]

al'cohol *n.* liquid made in fermenting sugar *etc.*, and forming the intoxicating part of fermented drinks. **-alcohol'ic** *a.* **alcoholiza'tion** *n.* **-al'coholize** *v.t.* **al'coholism** *n.* a disease, alcohol poisoning. [Arab. *al koh'l,* fine powder used to darken the eyelids]

al'cove *n.* recess; arbor, bower. [Arab. *al qobbah,* the vault]

al'dehyde *n.* volatile fluid produced by oxidation of alcohol. [L. *alcohol dehydrogenatum,* alcohol deprived of hydrogen]

al'der (awl'-) *n.* tree related to the birch. [OE. *aln*-L. *ainus*]

al'derman (awl'-) *n.* town councellor appointed for life or a long period and not elected like the ordinary councillors. [OE. *ealdormann,* elder, chief]

ale *n.* fermented malt beverage, beer. **ale'-house** *n.* [OE. *ealu*]

alert' *a.* watchful; brisk. *-n.* sudden attack or surprise; alarm signal. **alert'ness** *n.* [OF. *à l'érte,* fr. It. *all' erta,* to the height (watch-tower). cp. *alarm*]

ale'wife *n.* fish of the herring family. [N. Amer. Ind. *aloofe*]

alexan'drine *n.* rhyming verse of twelve syllables. [used in F. poems on Alexander the Great]

alex'in *n.* disease-resisting body in blood serum. [G. *alexein,* ward off]

alfal'fa *n.* fodder plant, lucerne. [Sp.]

al fres'co *adv.* in the open air. [It.]

al'gae *n.pl.* seaweed. **-al'gous** *a.* [L. *alga*]

al'gebra *n.* method of calculating, using letters to represent the numbers and signs to show relations between them, making a kind of abstract arithmetic. **-algebra'ic, algebra'ical** *a.* **-al'gebraist** *n.* [Arab. *al-jebr,* joining of broken parts]

al'gesia *n.* the capacity to feel pain. [G. *algesis,* sense of pain]

al'gid (-j-) *a.* cold, chilled, *esp.* as a symptom of disease. [L. *algere,* be cold]

AL'GOL *n.* computer programming language designed for mathematical and scientific purposes. (fr. *algo*rithmic language]

a'lias *adv.* otherwise. *-n.* assumed name. [L.]

al'ibi *n.* plea that a person charged with a crime was somewhere else when it was conunitted. [L. = other-where]

a'lien *a.* foreign; different in nature; adverse. *-n.* foreigner. **-alienabil'ity** *n.* **-a'lienable** *a.* capable of being transferred, as property not entailed. **a'lienate** *v.t.* transfer; estrange. **alienation** *n.* **-a'lienism** *n.* **-a'lienist** *n.* doctor who specializes in treatment of mental disease. [L. *alienus,* foreign]

alight' *v.i.* get down, descend (from a vehicle *etc.*). [OE *alihtan,* spring down]

alight' *a.* on fire. [OE. *onlichtan*]

align', aline' *v.t.* bring into line. **-align'ment, aligne'ment** *n.* [F. *ligne,* line]

alike' *a.* like, similar. [ME. yliche]

al'iment *n.* food. *-v.t.* feed, support. **aliment'ary** *a.* **-alimenta'tion** *n.* [L. *alimentu-alere,* nourish]

al'imony *n.* income allowed to a man or woman legally separated from his or her spouse. [L. *alimonia,* maintenance]

al'iquot *a.* such part of a number as will divide it without remainder. [L. *alius,* other, *quot,* how many]

allve' *a.* living; in life or activity; lively, brisk. [OE. on life]

al'kali *n.* substance which combines with acid and neutralizes it, forming a salt. Potash, soda *etc.* are **alkalis. -al'kaline** *a.* **-alkalin'ity** *n.* **-al'kalize** *v.t.* **-al'kaloid** *n.* [Arab. *al-qali,* burnt ashes of certain plants]

all (awl) *a.* the whole of, every one of. *adv.* wholly, entirely. *-n.* the whole, everything.

[OE. *all, eall*]
Al'lah *n.* Arabic name of God. [Arab.]
allay' *v.t.* lighten, relieve, calm. [OE. *alecgan*, put down]
allege' *v.t.* and *i.* plead, bring forward as an argument; assert. -**allega'tion** *n.* [L. *allegare*, quote]
alle'giance *n.* duty of a subject to his government or superior; loyalty. [*See* liege]
al'legory *n.* story with a meaning other than the literal one; description of one thing under the image of another. -**allegorical** *a.* -**al'legorize** *v.t.* -**al'legorist** *n.* [G. *allegoria*]
alleg'ro *adv.* (*mus.*) briskly. [It.]
allel'opathy *n.* the effect of one living plant upon another, either harmful, as by exuding toxic substances, or beneficial, as by assisting the intake of nutrients. [G. *alle-*, one another, *pathos*, suffering]
al'lem *n.* abnormal reaction of the body against certain foods, *etc.* ; antipathy. **aller'gic** *a.* [G.]
alleviate *v.t.* make light, ease, lessen. **allevia'tion** *n.* -**alle'viator** *n.* (Late L. *alleviate*, fr. *levis*, light]
al'ley *n.* walk, path; narrow lane; enclosure for bowling. *-pl.* **al'leys.** [Fr. *allée*, fr. *aller*, go]
al'ley *n.* fine marble (in the game). [prob. abbrev. of *alabaster*]
allia'ceous *a.* of, or like, garlic. [L. *allium*, garlic]
alli'ance *n.* union, *esp.* by marriage **or** treaty. [*See* **ally**]
alligator *n.* reptile of the crocodile family. [Sp. *el lagarto*, the lizard]
allitera'tion *n.* beginning of two or more words in close succession with the same sound, as *e.g.*, Sing a Song of Sixpence. -**allit'erate** *v.i.* -**allit'erative** *a.* [L. *ad*, to, and *littera*, letter]
al'locate *v.t.* place; assign as a share. -**allocation** *n.* apportionment [VL. *allocare*, fr. *locus* place]
allocution *n.* formal speech or address. [L. *allocution* fr. *loqui*, speak]
allo'dial *a.* freehold. *n.* freehold estate. [Law L.]
al'lograft *n.* a tissue graft from a donor genetically unrelated to the recipient. (G. *allos*, other, F. *greffe*]
al'lograph *n.* writing made on behalf of another. [G. *allos*, other, *graphein*, write]
allop'athy *n.* orthodox practise of medicine, applying treatment to produce a condition incompatible with the disease; opposite of homeopathy. [G. *allos*, other, *pathos*, suffering]
allot' *v.t.* give out; distribute as shares. **allot'ment** *n.* -**allott'ee** *n.* [OF. *aloter. See* **lot**]
allotropy *n.* property of some elements of existing in several forms, as, *e.g.*, carbon in the form of coal, diamond and charcoal. -**allotrop'ic** *a.* -**allot'ropism** *n.* [G. *allos*, other, *tropos*, manner]
allow' *v.t.* acknowledge; permit; give, grant. -**allow'able** *a.* -**allow'ably** *adv.* -**allow'ance** *n.* [OF. *allouer*]
alloy' *v.t.* mix metals; debase. *-n.* mixture of two or more metals. **alloy'age** *n.* [F. *aloi*, fr. L. *alligare*, bind]
all'spice (awl'-) *n.* pimento or Jamaica pepper, supposed to combine the flavors of various spices, *e.g.*, cinnamon, nutmeg. [*all* and *spice*]
allude' *v.i.* mention lightly, make indirect reference to; refer to. -**all'usion** *n.* -**allu'sive** *a.* -**allu'sively** *adv.* [L. *alludere, allus-*, play on]
allure' *v.t.* entice, win over; fascinate. **allure'ment** *n.* -**allu'ring** *a.* -**allu'r-ingly** *adv.* [*lure*]
allu'vial *a.* deposited by rivers. -**allu'vion** *n.* land formed by washed-up earth and sand. -**allu'vium** *n.* water-borne matter deposited on lower lands. [L. *alluvius*, washed against]
ally' *v.t.* join in relationship by treaty, marriage or friendship. -**allied'** *a.* -**al'ly** *n.* confederate; state or sovereign bound to another by treaty. *-pl.* **al'lies.** [F. *allier*]
al'magest *n.* Ptolemy's great treatise on thematics and astronomy; any similar treatise. (G. *megistos*, greatest]
alma ma'ter *n.* the college or school which one has graduated; the song that college or school. [L. *almus*, nourishing, *mater*, mother]
almanac (awl'-) *n.* table of days and months *etc.* [Sp. Arab]
almighty (awl-mi'ti) a. having all power, supreme. -**The Almighty** *n.* God. [OE. *allmeahtig*]
almond (am'-) *n.* kernel of the fruit of a tree related to the peach; the tree. [OF. *alamande*]
almost (awl'-) *adv.* nearly, all but. [OE. *eallmæst*]
alms (amz) *n.* gifts to the poor. -**alm'oner** *n.* distributor of alms. -**alm'onry** *n.* place of distribution of alms. -**alms'house** *n.* house endowed for poor persons to live in. [OE. *aelmesse*, fr. G. *eleemosyne*, pity; al-

moner through OF. *almosnier*]

aloe *n.* genus of plants of medicinal value, found chiefly in S. Africa. *-pl.* bitter drug made from the plants; American plant of the amaryllis family [G.]

aloft' *adv.* on high; overhead; (*naut.*) at the masthead. [ON, *a lopt*, in the air]

alone' *a.* single, solitary. *-adv.* separately. [all one]

along' *adv.* lengthwise; forward; together (with). [OE. *andlang*]

aloof *adv.* at a distance; apart; with reserve. **-aloof'ness** *n.* [fr. Du. *to loef*, to windward]

alope'cia *n.* baldness. [G.]

aloud' *adv.* with loud voice; audibly; not in a whisper. [*loud*]

alp *n.* high mountain; mountain pasture. *-pl.* **Alps**, *esp.* the mountains of Switzeriand. **-al'pen, al'pine** *a.* **-al'pinist** *n.* mountain climber. [L. *Alpes*, pl.]

alpac'a *n.* llama-like Peruvian sheep; cloth made from its wool. [Sp.]

alp'enstock *n.* long iron-shod staff for mountaineering. [Ger. = *Alpine stick*]

al'phabet *n.* set of letters used in writing a language. **-alphabet'ic, alphabetical** *a.* in the order of the letters. **-alphabet'ically** *adv.* [G. *alpha beta*, A, B, the first two letters]

al'pha-rays *n. pl.* streams of heliumparticles given off by radium *etc.* [G. letter *alpha*]

alread'y (awl-red'i) *adv.* before, previously. [all ready, prepared]

Alsa'tian (al-sa'-shan) a. of Alsatia, *i.e.*, Alsace. *-n.* large dog of wolf-like breed. [Latinization of *Alsace*]

al'so (awl'-) *adv.* further, too; in addition; besides. [OE. *eallswa*]

al'tar (awl'-) *n.* raised place, stone, etc. on which sacrifice may be offered; in a Christian Church, table on which the priest consecrates the Eucharist. -Forms compounds, as **al'tar-cloth** *n.* **-al'tar-piece** *n.* **-al'tar-rails** *n.* **-al'tarstone** *n.* [L. *altare*]

al'ter (awl'-) *v.t.* change, make different. *-v.i.* become different. **-alterabil'ity** *n.* **-al'terable** *a.* **-al'terably** *adv.* **-altera'tion** *n.* **-al'terative** *a.* (F. *altirer*, fr. L. *alter*, other]

alterca'tion (awl-) *n.* dispute, wrangling. **-al'tercate** *v.i.* **-al'tercative** *a.* [L. *altercari*, disputer]

al'ternate *v.t.* cause to occur by turns. *v.i.* happen by turns-**alter'nate** *a.* one after the other, by turns. **-alter'nately** *adv.* **-alterna'tion** *n.* **-alter'native** *a.* and *n.* **-alter'natively** *adv.* [L. *alternate*, fr. *alter*, other]

al'ternator *n.* generator of alternating current. **-al'ternating current**, electric current which flows in alternate directions. [L. *alter*, other]

although' *conj.* notwithstanding that. [all though]

altim'eter *n.* instrument for measuring heights. [L. *altos*, high, and *meter*]

al'titude *n.* height. [L. *altitudo*]

al'to *n.* (*mus.*) male voice of highest pitch or female of the lowest; part written for it; contralto part. [It., fr. L. *altus*, high]

altogeth'er (awl-) *adv.* entirely. [three words in OE. *See* **together**]

al'truism *n.* principle of living and acting for the good of others. **-altruist'ic** *a.* **-altruist'ically** *adv.* [F. *altruisme*]

al'um *n.* mineral salt, double sulfate of alumina and potash. [L. *alumen*]

alum'inum *n.* metal like silver, very light. [fr. *alum*]

alum'nus *n.* graduate or pupil of a school or college. *-pl.* **alum'ni.** [L. *alere*, nourish]

al'ways (awl'-) *adv.* at all times; for ever. -also **always** [*all* and *ways*]

alyss'um *n.* rock-garden plant with white or yellow flowers. [G. *alysdon*]

amal'gam *n.* compound of mercury and another metal; soft mixture; combination of elements. **-amal'gamate** *v.t.* mix mercury with another metal; compound. *-v.i.* unite, *esp.* of two companies, societies *etc.* ; blend. **-amalgama'tion** *n.* [F, *amalgams*]

amanuen'sis *n.* one who takes dictation; copyist; secretary. [L. *a. manu*, by hand]

am'aranth *n.* imaginary purple flower which never fades; love-lies-bleeding; purple color. **-amaranth'ine** *a.* unfading. [G. *amaratos*, unfailing]

amass' *v.t.* collect in quantity. **-amass'able** *a.* [F. *amasser*]

am'ateur (-ur) *n.* one who carries on an art, study, game, *etc.* for the love of it, not for money. *-a.* imperfect, like the work of an amateur; not professional. **-amateur'ish** *a.* **-amateur'ishly** *adv.* **am'at-eurism** *n.* [F. fr. L. *amator*, lover]

am'atol *n.* high explosive. [*am*monium nitrate, trinitro*tol*ume]

am'atory *a.* relating to love or lovers. [L. *amatorius-amare*, love]

amauro'sis *n.* blindness from disease of the optic nerve. **-amaurot'ic** *a.* [G. *amauros*, dark]

amaw' *v.t.* surprise, greatly astound. **-amazement** *n.* **-ama'zing** *a.* **-amazingly**

adv. [OE. *amasian*]

am'azon *n.* female warrior; masculine woman. -**amazo'nian** *a.* [G.]

ambassador *n.* representative of the highest rank sent by one state to another. -**ambassado'rial** *a.* -**ambass'adress** *n. fem.* -**am'bassage** now *usu.* **em'bassage** *n.* [F. *ambassadeur*]

am'batch *n.* tropical African tree, growing in marshes. [native name]

am'ber *n.* yellowish fossil resin. -*a.* made of, or colored like, amber. [Arab. *anbar*, ambergris]

am'bergris *n.* gray substance secreted by the spermaceti whale, and used in perfumery. [F. *ambre gris*, gray amber]

ambidex'ter, ambidex'trous *a.* able to use both hands with equal ease. **ambidexter'ity** *n.* [Late L., fr. *ambi*, both, and *dexter*, right hand]

am'bient *a.* surrounding, encompassing. -*n.* air, sky. [L. *ambi*, about, *iens, ient-*, going]

ambiguous *a.* of double meaning; doubtful. -**ambigu'ity** *n.* [L., fr. *amb* and *agere*, lit., drive both ways]

am'bit *n.* circuit; space around; sphere of action. [L. *ambitus*, going round]

ambi'tion *n.* desire of power, fame, honor; object of that desire. -**ambi'tious** *a.* -**ambi'tiously** *adv.* -**ambi'tiousness** *n.* [L. *ambitio*, going about for votes -*ambire*, go round]

ambivalence, ambiv'alency *n.* in one person, opposite emotional reactions to the same thing; -**ambiv'alent** *a.* [L. *ambi*, both, *valere*, be strong]

am'ble *v.i.* of a horse, move with both legs together one side, then the other; move at an easy pace. -*n.* this movement. **am'bler** *n.* [L. *ambulate*, walk]

amblyo'pia *n.* partial blindness. **amblyop'sis** *n.* 'blind' fish of the Mammoth Cave of Kentucky. [G. *amblys* dull, *ops*, eye]

ambro'sia *n.* food of the gods. -**ambro'sial** *a.* fragrant, delicious. [G.]

ambulance *n.* special carriage for the sick or wounded; movable hospital. [F. earlier *hôpital ambulant*, fr. L. *ambulate*, walk]

ambuscade' *n.* ambush, hiding to attack by surprise. [F. *ambuscade*]

am'bush *n.* a lying in wait. -*v.t.* waylay, attack from hiding. [OF. *embusche*, hiding in the woods]

ame'liorate *v.t.* and *i.* make better, improve. -**ameliora'tion** *n.* -**ame'liorative** *a.* [L. *ad*, to, *melior*, better]

amen' *interj.* surely, so let it be. [Heb. *amen*, truly, certainly]

ame'nable *a.* easy to be led or controlled. -**amenabil'ity, ame'nableness** *n.* -**ame'nably** *adv.* [F. *amener*, lead]

amend' *v.i.* grow better. -*v.t.* make better, improve; alter in detail, **amendment** *n.* -**amends'** *n. pl. reparation. [F. amender* -L. *ex* and *mendum*, fault]

amen'ity *n.* pleasantness. -*pl.* pleasant ways, civilities. [F. *amenité*]

amen'tia (-sh-) *n.* mental deficiency. [L.]

amerce' *v.t.* punish by fine. [OF. *amercier*, fine]

American *a.* of pert. to the United States of America or the American continents. *n.* a native of America. [fr. *Amerigo Vespucci*, Italian navigator]

americanize *v.t.* express in American English, turn into (U. S.) American form. -**americanism** *n.* American idiomor peculiarity. [*See* **American**]

Ames'lan *n.* American sign language: a communications systemin which meaning is conveyed by hand gestures and their position in relation to the upper part of the body. (fr. *Ame*rican *s*ign *lan*guage]

Ames test *n.* a method of preliminary screening for carcinogens, based on their ability to cause mutations in bacteria. [Bruce *Ames* (b. 1928), U. S. biochemist who invented the test]

am'ethyst *n.* bluish-violet precious stone. [G. *amethystos, a-*, not, *methyein*, be drunken. The stone was supposed to be a charm against drunkenness]

a'miable *a.* friendly, kindly. -**amiabil'ity** *n.* -**a'miableness** *n.* -**a'miably** *adv.* [F. *aimable*, lovable, fr. L. *amare*, love]

am'icable *a.* friendly. -**amicabil'ity** *n.* -**am'icably** *adv.* [Late L. *amicabilis*]

am'ice (am'-is) *n.* square of white linen worn by celebrant priest at Mass; furred cape worn by religious orders. [L. *amictus*, dress]

amid', amidst' *prep.* in the middle of, among. [OE. *on middan*]

amidships *adv.* half-way between stem and stern of a ship. [*amid* and pass. of *ship*]

amiss' *a.* wrong. -*adv.* faultily. [*miss*, failure]

am'ity *n.* friendship. [F. *amitio*]

am'meter *n.* instrument for measuring electric currents. [fr. *ampere* and *meter*]

am'monal *n.* high explosive used in bombs. [fr. *ammon*ium nitrate and *al*uminum]

ammo'nia *n.* pungent alkaline gas. **ammo'niac** *a.* **-ammo'niated** *a.* **-ammo'nium** *n.* hypothetical base of ammonia. [fr. *sal ammoniac*, salt said to have been first obtained in a region named after the god (Jupiter) *Ammon*]

am'monite *n.* fossil spiral shell of extinct mollusk. [fr. horn of (Jupiter) *Ammon*]

ammuni'tion *n.* cartridges, powder *etc.* for firearms; formerly, all military stores [F. *l'ammunition*, for *in munition. See* **munition**]

amne'sia *n.* loss of memory. [G.]

am'nesty *n.* general pardon. [G. *amnesia*, oblivion]

amoeb'a *n.* simplest microscopic animal, a unit mass which constantly changes its shape. [G. *amoibe*, change]

amok'. See **amuck'**.

among' (-mu-), amongst' *prep.* mixed with, or the number of [OE. *on gemang*, fr. *gemang*, crowd]

amor'al *a.* non-moral. [*a-*, *neg.*, and *moral*]

am'orous *a.* easily moved to love; in love. **-am'orously** *adv.* **-am'orousness** *n.* [F. *amoreux*]

amorph'ous *a.* shapeless; uncrystallized. **-amorph'ism** *n.* [G. *amorphos*]

amort'ize *v.t.* reduce or pay a debt through a sinking fund; convey to a corporation. [L. *ad*, to, *mortem*, death]

amount' *v.i.* come to, be equal to. *-n.* sum total; result; quantity. [OF. *amonter*, mount up]

amour' *n.* love intrigue or illicit love affair. **-amour' propre'** (-pr), self-esteem. [F., fr. L. *amor*, love]

am'père *n.* unit of current of electricity, the amount one volt can send through one ohm. [fr. *Ampère*, F. physicist]

am'persand *n.* character &. [and per se, '*land*' by itself]

amphib'ious *a.* living both on land and in water. **-amphib'ian** *n.* (G. *amphi*, on both sides, *bios*, life]

amphi'pathic, amphi'path *a.* of or relating to a molecule that possesses both hydrophobic and hydrophilic elements, such as are found in detergents, or phospholipids of biological membranes. [G. *amphi*, on both sides, *pathos*, feeling]

amphithe'ater *n.* building with tiers of seats round an arena. [G. *amphi*, both sides, *theatron*, theater]

am'phora *n.* ancient Greek two-handled jar. **-am'phoric** *a.* (G. *amphi*, on both sides, *pherein*, bear]

am'ple *a.* big enough, full, spacious. **am'pleness** *n.* **-amplifica'tion** *n.* **amplica'tory** *a.* **-am'plifier** *n.* thermionic valve to increase power level of electric currents; apparatus to augment the output of sound. **-am'plify** *v.t.* make bigger, louder *etc.* **-am'plitude** *n.* spaciousness. **-am'ply** *adv.* fully. [F.]

ampoule' *n.* small glass container for hypodermic dose. [L. *ampulla*, two-handled flask]

am'putate *v.t.* cut off (a limb *etc.*) **amputation** *n.* [L. amputate]

amuck', amok' *adv.* used only in phrase **run amuck'**, run in sudden frenzy to murder indiscriminately. [Malay. *amoq*]

am'ulet n. something carried, worn, as a charm against evil *etc.* [F. *amulette*]

amuse' *v.t.* divert; occupy pleasantly; excite a sense of fun. **-amu'sement** *n.* **amu'sing** *a.* **-amu'singly** *adv.* [F. *amuser*, make to muse. *See* **muse**]

amyg'darn *n.* crystalline principle of bitter almonds. **-amyg'dalate** *a.* of or like almonds. **-amyg'daloid** *a.* almond-shaped. [G. *amygdate*, almond]

am'yl *n.* an alcohol radical. **-amyla'ceous** *a.* starchy. [G. *amylon*, starch]

an. *See* **a.**

anabap'tist *n.* one who holds that baptism should be adult only, and that those baptized in infancy should be baptized again. [G. *ana*, again, *baptizein*, baptise]

an'abas *n.* E. Indian fish that climbs trees, climbing perch. [G. = *climbing*]

anab'olism *n.* series of chemical changes by which food *etc.* becomes living matter. [G. *anabole*, rising]

an'abranch *n.* stream that flows from a river and re-enters it lower down [for *anastomosing branch*]

anach'ronism (-k-) *n.* mistake of time, by which something is put in the wrong period; something out of keeping with the time. **-anach'ronize** *v.t.* **- anachronist'ic** *a.* [G. *ana*, backwards, *chronos*, time]

anacolu'thon *n.* sentence or words faulty in grammatical sequence. [G. *anakolouthos*, not following]

anacon'da *n.* large water-snake of S. America. [orig. uncertain]

anad'romous *a.* of fish, ascending rivers to spawn. (G. *ana*, up, *dromos*, run]

anaero'bia *n. pl.* bacteria able to live without air. **anerob'ic** *a.* [G. *a.* without, *aer*, air, *bios*, life]

anaesthetic *See* **anesthetic.**

an'agram *n.* word or sentence made by arranging in different order the letters of another word or sentence, *e.g.*, *ant* from *tan*. -**anagrammat'ical,** *a.* -**anagram-m'atist** *n.* (G. *anagramma*]
analge'sic *n.* anodyne, pain-killer. **analge'sia** *n.* painlessness. [G. *an*, not, *al-gein*, feel pain]
anal'ogy *n.* agreement or likeness in certain respects; correspondence. **analo'gical** *a.* -**analog'ically** *adv.* **anal'ogize** *v.t.* -**anal'ogist** *n.* **analogous** *a.* having similarity or correspondence. -**anal'ogously** *adv.* (G. *analogia*]
anal'ysis *n.* separation or breaking up of anything into its elements or component parts. -*pl.* **anal'yses** -**an'alyze** *v.t.* **an'alyst** *n.* -**analyt'ical** *a.* **analytically** *adv.* [G., fr. *lyein*, loose]
an'apest, an'apaest *n.* (*prosody*) foot of three syllables, short-short-long, reverse of dactyl. [G. *anapaistos*, reversed]
anaphylax'is *n.* abnormal sensitivity in some persons to substances introduced into the body as food, *e.g.* egg, or serumin the treatment of disease. [G. *phylaxis*, guarding]
an'archy *n.* lack of government in a state; lawlessness; confusion. **anarch'al** *a.* -**anarch'ically** *adv.* **an'archism** *n.* system of certain revolutionaries, aiming at a society with no government, in which each man should be a law to himself. -**an'arch, an'archist** *n.* [G. *anarchia*]
anath'ema *n.* solemn curse; anything accursed. -**anath'ematize** *v.t.* [G. offering; later, something devoted to evil]
anat'omy *n.* dissection of a body; science of the structure of the body; detailed analysis or examination. -**anatom'ical** *a.* -**anatom'icatly** *adv.* -**anat'omize** *v.t.* -**anat'omist** *n.* [G. *ena*, up, *temnein*, cut]
an'cestor *n.* forefather. -**ances'tral** *a.* -**an'cestry** *n.* [L. *ante*, before, *cedere*, go]
anch'or (-k-) *n.* implement for chaining a ship to the bottom of the sea. -*v.t.* fasten by an anchor. -*v.i.* cast anchor. **anch'orage** *n.* suitable place for anchoring. [L. *ancoral*]
anchorite, anchéoret *n.* hermit; one who has retired from the world, *esp.* for religion. [F., fr. G. *anachoretes*]
ancho'vy (-ch-) *n.* small fish of the herring family. [Sp. *anchova*]
anchylo'sis, *n.* stiffening of a joint, by thickening of the fibrous tissue *etc.* [G. *angkylos*, crooked]
an'cient *a.* old; belonging to a former age; time-worn. -*n.* old man; one who lived in an earlier age (*esp.* in *pl*) **anciently** *adv.* [F. *ancien*]
an'cilary *a.* subordinate; subservient. [L. *ancilla*, maidservant]
and *conj.* in addition, used to join words and sentences, to introduce a consequence, *etc.* [OE. *and, end*]
andan'te *adv.* (*mus.*) moderately slow, at an easy pace. [It. *andante*, going]
and'iron *n.* iron bar or bracket for supporting logs in a wood fire. [OF. *andier*. The ending is due to popular confusion with E. *iron*]
androcen'tric *a.* having or regarding man or the male sex as central or primary. -**androcen'trism** *n.* [G. *andros*, man, L. *centrum, centre*]
androceph'alous *a.* having a human head, as the Sphinx. (G. *andros*, man, *kephale*, head]
an'ecdote *n.* very short story, dealing with a single incident. -**an'ecdotage** *n.* collection of anecdotes; chattering old age. -**anecdot'al** *a.* [G. = *unpublished*]
anele', aneal' *v.t.* give extreme unction to. [fr. OE. *ele*, oil. (Archaic, *See* **Hamlet** v.)]
anem'ia *n.* lack of blood. -**anem'ic** *a.* [G. *an-*, not, *hainia*, blood]
anemom'eter *n.* instrument to measure the strength of wind, a wind-gauge. **anemomet'ric** a. -**anemom'etry** *n.* [G. *anemos*, wind, and meter]
anem'one (-ni) *n.* wind-flower. -**sea-anem'one** *n.* plant-like marine animal. [G., fr. *anemos*, wind]
anencephalic *a.* born with no or only a partial brain. [G. *an-*, without, *kephale*, head]
anent' *prep.* concerning. [OE. *on-efen*, on even with]
an'eroid *a.* denoting a barometer which measures atmospheric pressure without the use of mercury or other liquid. [G. *a-*, not, *neros*, damp]
anesthet'ic *a.* causing insensibility. -*n.* drug that does this. -**anesthe'sia** *n.* state of insensibility. -**anesthet'ically** adv. **anes'thetize** *v.t.* -**anes'thetist** *n.* [G. *anais-thetos*, without feeling]
an'eurism *n.* swelling out of a part of an artery. [G. *aneurysma*]
anew' *adv.* afresh. [earlier of new]
ang'ary *n.* belligerent's right to seize and use neutral territory, under indemnity. [G. *angaros*, courier]
an'gel (anj-) *n.* divine messenger; mini-

stering spirit; person with the qualities of such a spirit, as gentleness, purity *etc.* **-angel'ic** *a.* **-angel'ically** *adv.* [G. *angelos*, messenger]

angel-fish *n.* fish allied to the shark, with wing-like pectoral fins; also tropical American river-fish. [*angel* and *fish*]

angel'ica *n.* genus of aromatic plants; their stalks, candied and used in confectionery, *etc.* [Med. L. *herba angelica*]

An'gelus *n.* (R. C.) prayer to the Virgin; bell calling to Angelus at morning, noon and sunset. [fr. first word, *Angelus*]

ang'er *n.* wrath, strong emotion including a sense of injury and a desire to retaliate. *-v.t.* rouse this emotion in. **-ang'rily** *adv.* **ang'ry** *a.* [ON. *angr*]

angi'na *n.* severe inflammation of the throat; quinsy. **-angi'na pec'toris,** heart disease marked by spasms of severe pain. [L., fr. *anguere*, strangle]

angiogen'esis *n.* the induction of blood vessel growth, often in radiation with a particular organ or tissue or with a tumor. **-angiog'raphy** *n.* a method of obtaining an x-ray of blood vessels by injecting into them a substance, such as iodine, that shows up as opaque on an x-ray picture. **-an'gioplasty** *n.* a surgical technique for restoring normal blood flow through a narrowed or blocked artery, either by inserting a balloon into the narrowed section and inflating it or by using a laser beam. **-angioten'sin** *n.* a peptide of physiological importance that is capable of causing constriction of blood vessels, which raises blood pressure. [G. *angeion*, (blood) vessel]

ang'le (ang'gl) *v.t.* fish. *-n.* book. **ang'ler** *n.* **angling** *n.* [OE. *angel*]

ang'le *n.* corner; meeting of two lines. **ang'ular** *a.* **-angular'ity** *n.* [F., fr. L. *angulus*, corner]

Ang'lican *a.* of the Church of England. **Ang'licanism** *n.* [Med. L. *anglicanus*]

ang'licize *v.t.* express in English, turn into English form. **-ang'licism** *n.* English idiom or peculiarity. [L. *Anglicus*]

Anglo- *prefix* English. [fr. the Angles] **Anglo-American, Anglo-Catholic, Anglo-Indian, Anglo-Saxon,** *etc.* **-ang'lophile** *n.* lover of England and things English -also *a.* **-anglopho'bia** *n.* dislike of England.

ango'ra *n.* goat with long, white, silky hair; cat with long silky fur; rabbit with long, white, fine fur; cloth or wool made from the hair of the goat or rabbit. [*Angora*, city in Asia Minor, famed for its breed of goats]

angostu'ra *n.* bitter aromatic bark used as a febrifuge and tonic. [Venezuelan town]

ang'uine (-gwi-) *a.* snake-like. [L. *anguis*, snake]

ang'uish (-ng-gw-) *n.* great pain, mental or bodily. [L. *anguere*, strangle]

an'harmonic *a.* of or concerned with an oscillation whose frequency is not an integral factor or multiple of the base frequency. [G. *an-*, without, *harmonia*, agreement]

anhela'tion *n.* shortness of breath. (L. *anhelare -halare*, breathe]

anhy'drous *a.* of chemical substances, free from water. [G. *an*, not, *hydor*, water]

an'il *n.* indigo plant. [Arab. *an-nil*]

an'ile *a.* old-womanish, senile. (L. *anus*, old woman]

an'iline *n.* product of coal-tar which yields dyestuffs. [F. *anil*, fr. Arab, *al-nil*, the indigo. Aniline was first gotten from indigo]

animadvert' *v.i.* criticize, pass censure. **-animadver'sion** *n.* [L. *animadvertere*, turn the mind *(animum)* to]

an'imal *n.* being having life, feeling, power of voluntary motion; beast. *-a.* of or belonging to animals; sensual. **an'imalism** *n.* **-an'imally** *adv.* [L. *animale*, having breath of life]

animal'cule *n.* very small animal, *esp.* one which cannot be seen with the naked eye. **-animal'cular** *a.* [L. dim. *animalculum*]

an'imate *v.t.* to give life to; enliven; actuate. **-an'imated** *a.* **-anima'tion** *n.* [L. *animare*]

an'imism *n.* primitive religion, the belief that natural effects are due to spirits, that inanimate things have spirits. **-an'imist** *n.* **-animist'ic** *a.* [L. *animus*, spirit]

animos'ity *n.* hatred. enmity. **-an'imus** *n.* actuating spirit; enmity. [L. *animus*, spirit]

an'ise *n.* plant with aromatic seeds used for flavoring. **-an'iseed** *n.* liqueur or preparation of the seeds. [F. *anis*]

an'kle (ang-kl) *n.* joint between the foot and the leg. **-ank'let** *n.* ornament or ring for the ankle. [OE. *ancleow*]

ankylosaur *n.* any plant-eating dinosaur of the Cretaceous period of the suborder ankylosauria which has short legs and an armor of bony plate.

an'kylosis. See **anchylosis.**

an'na *n.* Indian coin, sixteenth part of a rupee. [Hind. *ana*]

an'nals *n. pl.* record of events set down year by year. **-an'nalist** *n.* [L. *annales* (*libri*), year-(books)]

annat'to *n.* bright orange dye used for cloth, foodstuffs, *etc.* -also **anat'ta.** [native S. American word]

anneal' *v.t.* toughen metal or glass by heating and slow cooling. **-anneal'ing** *n.* [OE. *anælan*, set on fire, bake]

annex' *v.t.* add, attach; take possession of, *esp.* territory. **-annexa'tion** *n.* **an'nexe** *n.* something added; supplementary building. [F. *annexer*, fr. L. *nectere*, bind]

anni'hilate *v.t.* reduce to nothing, destroy. **-annihila'tion** *n.* **anni'hilative** *a.* **-anni'hilator** *n.* [Late L. *annihilate*, fr. *nihil*, nothing]

anniversary *a.* yearly. *-n.* day on which an event happened or is celebrated. [L. *annus*, year, *vertere*, turn]

an'notate *v.t.* make notes upon. **annota'tion** *n.* **-an'notator** *n.* [earlier *annote*; F. *annoter*. *See* **note**]

announce' *v.t.* make known, proclaim. **-announce'ment** *n.* **-announ'cer** *n.* one who announces, *esp.* a broadcasting official who reads out the news and announces items in the program. [F. *annoncer*, fr. L. *nuntius*, messenger]

annoy' *v.t.* trouble, vex; tease. **annoy'ance** *n.* [OF. *enoier*, fr. L. *in odio*, in hatred]

ann'ual *a.* yearly. *-n.* plant which lives only a year; book published every year. **-annualize** *v.t.* to calculate for a shorter period as though on the basis of a full year. **-ann'ually** *adv.* [Late L. *annualis*, fr. *annus*, year]

annu'ity *n.* sum paid every year. **annu'itant** *n.* one who receives such a sum. [F. *annuité*-L. *annus*, year]

annul' *v.t.* reduce to nothing, abolish. **annul'ment** *n.* [L. *annulare*, reduce to naught, *nullum*]

an'nular *a.* ring-shaped. **-an'nulated** *a.* formed in rings. **-annula'tion** *n.* **an'nulet** *n.* a small ring. [L. *annularis*, fr. *annulus*, ring]

annuncia'tion *n.* an announcing; the angel's announcement to the Virgin Mary. [*See* **announce**]

an'ode *n.* (*elec.*) positive pole, or point of entry of a current-opposite to **cathode.** [G. *anodos*, way up]

an'odyne *a.* relieving pain. *-n.* drug to allay pain. [G. *anodynos*, painless]

anoint' *v.t.* smear with oil or ointment; consecrate with oil. **-anoint'ment** *n.* **The Anoint'ed** *n.* the Messiah. [OF. *enoindre* -L. *ungere*]

anom'alous *a.* irregular. **-anom'aly** *n.* irregularity; something showing irregularity. [G. *anomalos*, uneven]

anon' *adv.* in a short time; by and by. [OE. *on* an, *in* one]

anon'ymous *a.* nameless, *esp.* without an author's name. **anonym'ity** *n.* **anon'ymously** *adv.* [G. *anonymos*]

anoph'eles *n.* germ-carrying mosquito. [G. *anophelis*, hurtful]

anorex'ia, anorex'y *n.* loss of appetite. [G. *an*, not, *orexis*, longing]

anoth'er (-u-) *pron.* one other, a different one. [for another]

An'schluss (-shloos) *n.* union, *esp.* that of Austria with Germany. [Ger.]

an'serine *a.* of, like, a goose; silly. [L. *anser*, goose]

an'swer *v.t.* reply to; pay, meet; satisfy; suit. *-v.i.* reply, prove suitable; *n.* reply; solution; acknowledgment. **-an'swerable** *a.* that can be answered; accountable. **-an'swerer** *n.* [OE. *andswarian*, swear back]

ant *n.* small social insect, proverbial for industry, the emmet. **-ant'eater** *n.* S. American animal which feeds on ants by means of a long sticky tongue. **-ant'hill** *n.* mound raised by ants in building their home [OE. *aemette*]

ant *prefix* for **anti-** before a vowel, as **antacids antal'akli.** *See* words in **anti-. antagonist** *n.* opponent. **-antag'onize** *v.t.* **-antag'onism** *n.* **-antagonis'tic** *a.* hostile. **-antagonis'tically** *adv.* [G. *agonizesthai*, contend]

antarctic *a.* of the south polar regions. *-n.* these regions [G. *anti-* and *arctic*]

ante- *prefix* before [L. *ante*] found in compound words, as **antechamber** *n.* room leading to a chief apartment. **antedate'** *v.t.* date before the true time; assign to an earlier date; anticipate. **antemerid'ian** (*abbrev.* A. M.) *a.* before noon; between midnight and noon. **antena'tal, antenup'tial, antepenult'imate,** *etc., etc.*.

antece'dent *a.* going before. *-n.* (*gram.*) noun *etc.* to which a relative pronoun refers. *-n. pl.* one's past history, record. [L. *antecedere*, go before]

antedilu'vian *a.* before the flood; out of date, primitive. [L. *diluvium*, deluge]

an'telope *n.* deer-like ruminant animal, remarkable for grace and speed. [Late G. *antholops*]

antenì'cene (-ni-) *a.* before the (Christian) Nicene Conference of 325 A. D. [*Nicaea* (Nice) in Bithynia]
antenn'a *n.* (*pl.* **antenn'ae**) insect's feeler; (*radio*) elevated conducting wire, an aerial. [L. = *sail-yard*]
ante'rior a. before; earlier; in front. [L. *compar*. fr. *ante*, before]
an'teroom. *See* **ante-** **[antechamber]**
an'them *n.* piece of Scripture set to music for singing in churches; piece of sacred music (originally sung in alternate parts by two choirs). [OE. *antefu*, fr. G. *anti-*, against, *phone*, sound]
an'ther *n.* top of the pollen-bearing stamen in a flower. (G. *anthos*, flower]
anthol'ogy *n.* collection of choice poems, literary extracts *etc*. **-anthol'ogist** *n.* maker of such. [G. *anthologia*, gathering of flowers]
an'thracite *n.* hard, carbonaceous coat burning almost without flame or smoke. [G. *anthrakites*, coal-like]
an'thrax *n.* infectious disease of sheep and cattle, which can be transmitted to man. [G. = *carbuncle*]
anthropog'eny *n.* study of man's origin. [G. *anthropos*, man, *genes*, birth]
anthropography *n.* the branch of anthropology that deals with the geographical distribution of humans by skin color, language, customes, etc. -anthropographic. *adj.*
an'thropoid *a.* like man (of certain apes). [G. *anthropos*, man]
anthropol'ogy *n.* scientific study of the human race. **-anthropolog'ical** *a.* **anthropol'ogist** *n.* [G. *anthropos*, *logos*, word]
anthropomorph'ism *n.* ascription of human form and qualities to the Deity. [G. *anthropos*, man, *morphe*, form]
anti- *prefix* against; **ant-** before a vowel. [G. *anti*] Makes compounds as **anti-air'craft** *a.* **-anticath'olic** *a.* **An'tichrist** *n.* **-anticli'max** *n.* **anticli'nal** *a.* sloping in opposite directions. **-anticy'clone** *n.* **an'tidote** *n.* counter-poison **-antidumping** *adj.* pertaining to laws or practices that discourage importing of goods, often by imposition of customs duties or tariffs and selling below cost. **-antilog'arithm** *n.* **antimacassar** *n.* cover to protect chairs from macassar (hair-) oil. **-an'timasque** *n.* grotesque interlude in a masque. **antimonarch'ical** (-k-) a. **-antinuclear** *a.* opposed to nuclear weapons. **-antiphlogistic** *a.* counteracting inflammation. - **an'tipope** *n.* pope elected in opposition to the one regularly chosen. **-antirachit'ic** *a.* **-antiscorbu'tic** *n.* **-antisep'tic** *a.* and *n.* **antispasmod'ic** *a.* and *n.* **-antitox'in** *n.* **an'titrade** *n.* wind contrary to trade wind. *etc.* (see word without prefix]
an'tibody *n.* protective substance forming in the blood in response to the presence of toxins *etc.* [*body*]
an'tic *a.* odd, grotesque. *-n.* grotesque figure or movement, an odd trick. [It. *antico* -L. *antiquus*, ancient]
antici'pate *v.t.* be beforehand; take or consider before the due time; foresee; enjoy in advance; expect. **-anticipa'tion** *n.* **-anti'cipative, anticipatory** *a.* [L. *anticipare*, take beforehand]
antil'ogy *n.* contradiction. [G. *antilogia*]
an'timony *n.* brittle, bluish-white metal. [Med. L. *antimonia*]
antin'omy *n.* contradiction in a law, or between authorities or apparently logical conclusions. [G. *nomos*, law]
antioxidant *n.* substance that inhibits or slows oxidation and, therefore, checking the deterioration it causes to tissue.
antip'athy *n.* dislike. **-antipathetic** *a.* [G. *antipatheia*, fr. *pathos*, feeling]
an'tiphon *n.* anthem *etc.*, in which alternate lines or verses are alternately sung by two choirs. [G. *anti*, in return, *phone*, voice]
antip'odes *n. pl.* region of the globe exactly opposite ours. **-antip'odal** *a.* [G., fr. *pous, pod-*, foot. Originally the people on the other side of the world, whose feet are opposite ours]
antipyret'ic *a.* remedial against fever. *n.* drug with this property. **-antipy'rin** *n.* one such drug, got from coal-tar. [G. *pyretos*, fever, fr. *pyr*, fire]
antique' *a.* ancient; old-fashioned *-n.* relic of former times. **-antiqua'rian, antiquary** *n.* student or collector of old things. **-an'tiquated** *a.* out of date. **anti'quity** *n.* great age; former times. [F., fr. L. *ante*, before]
antirrhi'num *n.* snapdragon, a flowering garden plant. [G. *anti*, against, *rhis, rhin-*, nose]
anti-Semitism *n.* hostility or prejudice against the Jews. **-an'ti-Sem'itic** *a.* **an'ti-Sem'ite** *n.* [*See* **Semitic**]
anitiso'cial *a.* acting against the common good, or the customs, *etc.* of society. [social]
antith'esis *n.* contrast; opposite; opposition of ideas. **-antithet'ical** *a.* **antithe'tically** *adv.* [G. fr. *tithenai*, place]

antitox'in *n.* substance formed in the body to counteract a disease or poison; appropriate serum injected into the bloodstream for the prevention of certain diseases. (G. *anti-, toxicon*, poison]

an'titype *n.* that which a type symbolizes. [*type*]

ant'ler *n.* deer's horn; branch of that horn. **-ant'lered** *a.* [VL. *ante ocularis ramus* branch before the eye]

antonoma'sia *n.* figure of speech substituting a common for a proper noun and vice versa. [G.]

an'tonym *n.* word of which the meaning is the opposite of another. [G. *anti*, against, *and onyma*, name]

an'trum *n.* cavity, *esp.* in the upper jawbone. [L. = *cave*]

a'nus (a'-) *n.* lower opening of the bowel. [L. = *ring*]

an'vil *n.* iron block on which a smith hammers metal. [OE. *anfilte*]

anxiolytic *n.* drug that relieves tension or anxiety; tranquilizer.

anx'ious (angk'-shus) *a.* troubled, uneasy, *esp.* about something doubtful or in the future. **-anxi'ety** *n.* **anxiously** *adv.* [L. *anxius*, fr. *angere*, compress]

an'y *a.* and *pron.* one indefinitely; some. **-an'ybody** *n.* **-an'yhow** *adv.* **an'ything** *n.* **-an'yway** *adv.* **-an'ywhere** *adv.* [OE. *aenig*, fr. *an*, one]

a'orist *n.* (G. *gram.*) indefinite past tense. [G. *a.* without, *horos*, limit]

aort'a *n.* great artery which rises from the left ventricle of the heart and sends its branches all through the body. **-aort'al** *a.* [G. *aorte*, what is hung up]

apace' *adv.* swiftly. [*a-* and *pace*, walk]

Apach'e *n.* group of American Indians; member of that group.

apache' *n.* desperado, *esp.* a Parisian one. [name of American Indian tribe]

apagog'ic *a.* proving indirectly by reduction to absurdity. [G. *apagoge*, leading away]

apart' *adv.* separately; aside. [F. *à part*]

apart'heid (a-part-had) *n.* idea of segregation of races. [*Afrikaans*]

apart'ment *n.* room, or suite of rooms, in a house, *usu.* rented as a self-contained lodging. (F. *appartement*, orig. *separation*]

ap'athy *n.* want of feeling; indifference- **apathet'ic** *a.* **-apathet'ically** *adv.* [G. *apatheia*]

ape *n.* monkey; monkey with no tail; imitator. *-v.t.* imitate. **-a'pish** *a.* **-a'pishly** *adv.* [OE. *apa*]

apercu' *n.* brief survey, outline. [F. pp. of *apercevoir*, to perceive]

ape'rient *a.* opening; mildly laxative. *-n.* any such medicine. [L. *aperire*, open]

apéritif *n.* drink to whet the appetite. [F. -L. *aperire*, open]

ap'erture *n.* opening. [L. *aperture*]

a'pex *n.* (*pl.* **a'pexes, a'pices**] top or peak of anything. [L. = *summit*]

apha'sia *n.* dumbness due to brain disease. [G. *a-*, not, *phasis*, speech]

aphe'lion *n.* point of a planet's orbit farthest from the sun. [G. *apo*, off, *helios*, sun]

aph'esis *n.* (*gram.*) gradual loss of an unaccented vowel beginning a word. **aphet'ic** *a.* [G.]

a'phis *n.* (*pl.* **aph'ides)** family of small insects parasite on roots, leaves *etc.* of plants, the greenfly, aphid. [orig. unknown]

aphorism *n.* maxim, pithy saying **aph'orist** *n.* **-aphoris'tic** *a.* [G. *aphorismos*, definition]

aphrodisiac *a.* exciting to sexual intercourse. *-n.* that which so excites. [G. *Aphrodite*, goddess of love]

a'piary *n.* place where bees are kept. - **a'pian, apiar'ian** *a.* **-a'piarist** *n.* beekeeper. **-a'piculture** *n.* [L. *apiarium*, fr. *apis*, bee]

apiece' *adv.* for each. [orig. two words]

aplenty *a., adv.* abundant, enough; in supply.

aplomb' *n.* self-possession, coolness. [F. phrase *à plomb*, perpendicular, fr. *plomb*, lead, plummet]

apocalypse *n.* Revelation of St. John; any revelation. **-apocalyp'tic** *a.* - **apocalyp'tically** *adv.* [G. *apokalypsis*]

apocrypha *n.* religious writing of doubtful authenticity, or excluded from the Canon, *esp.* the fourteen books or parts of books known as the Apocrypha of the Old Testament, found in the Septuagint but not in the Hebrew Canon. **apoc'ryphal** *a.* [L. fr. G. *apokryphos*, hidden away]

ap'odal *a.* (of animal, bird *etc.*) without feet. [G. *apodos*, footless]

apod'osis *n.* (*gram.*) consequent clause in a conditional sentence, as distinct from the protasis, or 'if' clause. [G., fr. *apodidonai*, give back]

ap'ogee *n.* point of the sun's or moon's orbit farthest from the earth; the highest point. [F., fr. G. *apo*, off, *ge*, earth]

Apol'lyon *n.* the destroyer, Satan. [G. *destroying*]

ap'ologue *n.* moral fable or parable; allegory. [G. *apologos*, fable]

apol'ogy *n.* something spoken in defense; acknowledgment of an offence and expression of regret; poor substitute (with for). **-apologet'ic** *a.* **-apologetically** *adv.* **-apologet'ics** *n.* branch of theology charged with the defence of Christianity. **-apol'ogize** *v.i.* **-apol'ogist** *n.* [G. *apologia*, speaking away]

ap'ophthegm, ap'othegm (-o-them) *n.* terse saying. [G. *apophthegnia*]

ap'oplexy *n.* sudden stroke, causing loss of sensation and motion, usually through haemorrhage in the brain. **-apoplec'tic** *a.* [G. *apoplexia*, disablement]

aposiope'sis *n.* (*rhet.*) sudden breaking off for effect. [G. *siope*, silence]

aposi'tia *n.* aversion to food. [G. *apo*, away from, *sitos*, food]

apos'tasy *n.* abandonment of one's religious or other faith. **-apos'tate** *n.* [G. *apostates*, one who stands away]

apos'tle (-sl) *n.* one sent to preach the Gospel, *esp.* one of the first disciples of Jesus; founder of the Christian church in a country; chief champion of any new system. **-apos'tleship** *n.* **-apostol'ic, apostol'ical** *a.* **-apostolic'ity** *n.* [G. *apostolos*, messenger]

apos'trophe *n.* a turning away from the subject of a speech to address some person present or absent; mark (') showing the omission of a letter or letters in a word. **-apos'trophize** *v.t.* [G., fr. *strephein*, turn]

apoth'ecary *n.* old name for one who prepares and sells drugs, druggist. [G. *apotheke*, storehouse]

apotheo'sis *n.* deification, the act of raising any person or thing into a god. [G., fr. theos, god]

appall' (-awl') *v.t.* dismay, terrify. **appall'ing** *a.* (OF. *apalir*, make pale]

ap'panage, ap'anage *n.* provision for younger sons, *esp.* of kings; dependency; perquisite. [F. -L. *ad*, to, *panis*, bread]

apparatchik *n.* a member of a Communist party organization; a bureaucrat in any organization. [Russ.]

appara'tus *n.* equipment, instruments, for performing any experiment or operation. [L. fr. *apparare*, make ready]

appa'rel (-a-) *v.t.* clothe. *-n.* clothing. [F. *appareiller*, orig. put like to like]

appa'rent *a.* seeming; obvious. **appa'rently** *adv.* [L. *apparere*, appear]

appari'tion (-i'-shun) *n.* appearance, esp. of a ghost or other remarkable thing. [L. *apparere*, appear]

appeal' *v.i.* call upon, make earnest request; refer to, have recourse to; refer to a higher court. *-n.* request, reference, supplication. **-appeal'able** *a.* **-appeal'- ing** *a.* **-appeal'ingly** *adv.* **-appell'ant** *n.* one who appeals to a higher court. **-appell'ate** *a.* [F. *appeler*]

appear' *v.i.* become visible; come before; see, be plain. **-appear'ance** *n.* (OF. *apareir* -L. *apparere*]

appease' *v.t.* pacify, quiet, allay. **-appease'able** *a.* **-appease'ment** *n.* policy of conciliation by concessions to avoid war *etc.* [OF. *a pais*, at peace]

appell'ant. *See* **appeal.**

appella'tion *n.* name. **-appell'ative** *n.* generic name. *-a.* [*See* **appeal**]

append' *v.t.* join on, add. **-appen'dage** *n.* **-appen'dix** (*pl.*) **appendices'ixes** *n.* [L. *appendere*, hang on]

appendici'tis *n.* inflammation of the vermiform appendix, a prolongation of the intestine. [*append*]

appertain' *v.i.* belong, relate to. [L. *ad*, to, *pertinere*, belong]

ap'petite *n.* desire, inclination, *esp.* desire for food. **-ap'petize** *v.t.* **-appeti'zer** *n.* **-appeti'zing** a. **-appeti'zingly** *adv.* [F. *apetit*, fr. L. *petere*, seek]

applaud' *v.t.* praise by handclapping; praise loudly. **-applaud'er** *n.* **applauding** *a.* **-applaud'ingly** *adv.* **-applause'** *n.* [L. *applaudere*, clap]

ap'ple *n.* familiar round, firm, fleshy fruit. [OE. *æppel*]

applied' *a.* used for a practical or utilitarian purpose, as **applied art, sci'ence.** [*apply*]

appli'qué *n.* ornamentation laid on surface of material. [F. *appliquer*, apply]

apply' *v.t.* lay or place on; administer; bring into operation; devote, employ. **appli'ance** *n.* **-applicabil'ity** *n.* **applicable** *a.* **-ap'plicably** *adv.* **-applicant** *n.* **-apptica'tion** *n.* [L. *applicare*, bend to]

appoggiatu'ra *n.* (*mus.*) grace-note. [It.]

appoint' *v.t.* fix, settle; name to an office; equip. **-appoint'ment** *n.* *-n.pl.* equipment. (F., fr. *à point*, fitly]

apport' *n.* supernatural transport of a material object, *esp.* at a spiritualistic seance; object transported. [L. *portare*, carry]

appor'tion *v.t.* divide out in shares. **appor'tionment** *n.* [*See* **portion**]

ap'posite *a.* suitable, apt. **-ap'positely** *adv.* **-ap'positeness** *n.* **-apposi'tion** *n.* proximity; placing of one word beside another in explanation. **-appos'itive** *a.* [L. *appositus*, put against]

appraise' *v.t.* set a price on, value. **-apprais'able** *a.* **-apprais'al** *n.* **appraise'ment** *n.* **-apprais'er** *n.* [F. *approcier*, fr. L. *pretium*, price]

appre'ciate (-shi-) *v.t.* estimate justly; be sensible of good qualities in the thing judged. *-v.i.* rise in price. **-appre'ciable** *a.* **-appre'ciably** *adv.* **-apprecia'tion** *n,* **-appre'ciative** a. **-appre'ciator** *n.* [Late L. *appretiare*, fr. *pretium*, price]

apprehend' *v.t.* take hold of, seize by authority; recognize, understand; fear. **-apprehensibil'ity** *n.* **-apprehen'sible** *a.* **-apprehen'sion** *n.* **-apprehen'sive** *a.* **-apprehen'siveness** *n.* [L. *apprehendere*, take hold of]

appren'tice *n.* one bound to a master to learn an art or trade; novice. *-v.t.* bind as an **apprentice.** **-appren'ticeship** *n.* [F. *apprenti*, fr. *apprendre*, learn]

apprise' *v.t.* inform; acquaint. [F. appris, p. p. of *apprendre*, learn, teach]

approach' *v.i.* draw near; come near in quality, condition, *etc.* *-v.t.* come near to; *n.* a drawing near; means of reaching; approximation. **-approachabil'ity** *n.* **approach'able** *a.* [F. *approcher*, fr. L. *proprius*, nearer]

approba'tion *n.* sanction, approval. [L. *approbate*, test, try]

appro'priate *v.t.* take to oneself *-a.* suitable, fitting. **-appro'priately** *adv.* **-appro'priateness** *n.* **-appro'pria'tion** *n.* **-appro'priative** *a.* **-appro'priator** *n.* [Late L. *appropriate*, fr. *proprius*, own]

approve' *v.t.* think well of, commend. **-approv'al** *n.* **-approv'er** *n.* **approv'ingly** *adv.* [F. *approuver*]

approx'imate *a.* nearly resembling; nearing correctness. *-v.t.* bring close. *v.i.* come near. **-approx'imately** *adv.* **-approxima'tion** *n.* **-approx'imative** *a.* [L. *proximus*, nearest]

appui' (-we') *n.* defense; support. *-v.t.* place in a strong position. [OF. *apuyer*, fr. *puy*, hill; Low L. *appodiare*, support]

appur'tenance *n.* thing which appertains to; accessory. **-appur'tenant** *n.* and *a.* [F. *appartenir*, belong]

après *prep.* after, following; used in hyphenated compounds. **après-ski** *adv., adj.* after skiing; pertaining to the time after skiing used for eating, drinking, and socializing.

ap'ricate *v.i.* sunbathe. **-aprica'tion.** [L. *apricari*, expose to sun]

a'pricot *n.* orange-colored fruit of the plum kind. *-a.* of the color of the fruit. [F. *abricot*, fr. Port. *albricoque*, which gave obs. *apricock*]

A'pril *n.* fourth month of the year. [L. *aprilis*]

a prio'ri *a.* of knowledge gained without actual experience; of reasoning from cause to effect. [L. *a*, from, *priori*, preceding]

a'pron (a'-) *n.* piece of cloth, leather, *etc.* worn in front to protect the clothes, or as part of an official dress. [an *apron* was a *napron*, fr. F. *napperon*, fr. *nappe*, cloth. cp. *adder*]

apropos' *adv.* to the purpose; appropriately; in reference (to). [F. *à propos*]

apse *n.* arched recess at the end of a church. **-ap'sidal** *a.* [earlier *apsis*, G. *felloe* of a wheel]

apt *a.* suitable; prompt, quick-witted, likely. **-apt'itude** *n.* **-apt'ly** *adv.* **-apt'ness** *n.* [L. *aptus*, fr. *apere*, fasten]

ap'teryx *n.* kiwi, tailless and almost wingless bird of New Zealand. [G. *a-*, without, *ptetyx*, wing]

a'qua-for'tis *n.* nitric acid, a powerful solvent. [L. = *strong water*]

aquamarine' *n.* precious stone, the beryl. *-a.* pale blue, sea-colored. [L. *aqua marina*, sea water]

aquarelle' *n.* water-color painting. [F.]

aqua'rium *n.* (*pl.* **aqua'riums, aqua'ria**) tank or pond for keeping water animals or plants, usually in a natural setting. [L. *aqua*, water]

Aqua'rius *n.* the Water-bearer, llth sign of the zodiac, which sun enters on 21st January. [constellation *Aquarius* -L. *aqua*, water]

aquat'ic *a.* living or growing in water, or having to do with water, **-aquat'ics** *n. pl.* water-sports. [L. *aqua*, water]

aq'ueduct *n.* artificial channel for water, *esp.* a bridge to carry water across a valley, a canal across an obstacle *etc.* [L. *aquae ductus*, water conduit]

a'queous *a.* watery. [L. *aqua*, water]

aq'uiline *a.* relating to an eagle; hooked like an eagle's beak. [L. *aquila*, eagle]

Ar'ab *n.* native of Arabia; Arabian horse. **-Ar'abic** *n.* language of the Arabs. **-street' ar'ab**, neglected, homeless child. [L. *arabs*]

arabesque' *n.* painted or carved ornament of Arabian design. *-a.* in this style, fantastic. [F.]

ar'abis *n.* kinds of low-growing rock-plant; the rock cress. [Low L. = *Arabian*]
ar'able *a.* fit for plowing. [L. *arabilis*, fr. *arare*, plough]
arach'nida (-k-) *n.* class including spiders, scorpions, mites. **-arach'nid** *n.* one of these. [G. *arachna*, spider]
arauca'ria *n.* tall evergreen tree, the monkey-puzzle. [*Arauco*, S. Chili]
ar'balest, ar'blast *n.* strong crossbow with catapult action. [OF., fr. Late L. *arcuballista*, bow-sling]
ar'biter *n.* (**ar'bitress** *fem.*) judge; umpire. **-arbit'rament** *n.* **-ar'bitrary** *a.* not bound by rules; despotic. **-arbitrarily** *adv.* **-ar'bitrate** *v.i.* act as arbiter,, decide a dispute. **-arbitra'tion** *n.* **-ar'bitrator** *n.* [L. = *judge*]
ar'bor *n.* garden seat enclosed by branches, plants; shaded walk. [earlier *erber*, fr. OF. *herbier*, herb-garden]
arbo'real, arbo'reous *a.* relating to trees. **-arbore'tum** *n.* place for cultivating specimens of trees. -**ar'boriculture** *n.* forestry, cultivation of trees for timber *etc.* [L. *arbor*, tree]
ar'butus *n.* ornamental evergreen shrub, strawberry-tree. [L.]
arc *n.* part of a circle or other curve. [L. *arcus*, bow]
arc *n.* luminous electrical discharge between two terminals. **-arc'-lamp** *n.* **arc'-light** *n.* [L. *arcus*, bow]
arcade' *n.* row of arches on pillars; covered walk or avenue. [F.]
Arca'dian *a.* rural; ideally simple and artless. [*Arcadia*, district of Greece]
arcane' *a.* being understood only by those who have access to a special knowledge. [*See* **arcanum**]
arca'num *n.* (*pl.* **arca'na**) secret; mystery; (alchemy) elixir of life. [L. *arcana*, secrets, things shut in chests]
arch *n.* curved structure in building, supporting itself over an open space by mutual pressure of the stones. *-v.t.* give, or make into, an arch. **-arched'** *a.* **arch'way** *n.* [L. *arcus*, bow]
arch *a.* chief; roguish, sly. **-arch'ly** *adv.* **-arch'ness** *n.* **-arch**-*prefix* chief, *e.g.*, **archenemy** *n.* **-arch-her'etic** *n.* **arch-rogue'** *n.* [G. *archos*, chief. Meaning of 'roguish' arose from arch-rogue]
archaeol'ogy (-k-) *n.* study of ancient times from remains of art, implements *etc.* **-archaeolog'ical** *a.* **-archaeol'ogist** *n.* [G. *archaiologia*]
archaeop'teryx (-k-) *n.* oldest known fossil bird. [G. *archaios*, ancient, pteryx, wing]
archa'ic (-k-) *a.* old, primitive. **-archa'ically** *adv.* **-ar'chaism** *n.* obsolete word or phrase. [G. *archaios*, old]
archan'gel (-k-) *n.* angel of the highest order. [*angel*]
archbish'op *n.* chief bishop. **-archbish'opric** *n.* [*bishop*]
archdeac'on *n.* chief deacon, clergyman next in rank to a bishop. **-archdeac'onate** *n.* **-archdeac'onry** *n.* **archdeac'onship** *n.* [*deacon*]
archduke' *n.* duke of specially highrank. **-archdu'cal** *a.* **-archduch'ess** *fem.* - **archduch'y** *n.* [*duke*]
arch'er *n.* one who shoots with a bow. **arch'ery** *n.* [L. *arcus*, bow]
arch'etype (-ki-) *n.* original pattern or model. **-arch'etypal** *a.* [G. *typos*, model]
archiepis'copal (-k-) *a.* relating to an archbishop. **-archiepis'copacy** *n.* **archiepis'copate** *n.* [*episcopal*]
ar'chil *n.* lichen yielding a violet dye; dye got from it. [OF. *orchel*]
ar'chimage (-k-) *n.* chief magician. [G. *archi-*, chief, and *magus*]
Archimede'an *a.* pertaining to the Greek mathematician Archimedes
Archimede'an screw' *n.* device for raising water by tube in form of screw wound round cylinder.
archipel'ago (-k-) *n.* sea full of small islands; group of islands. *-pl.* **archipel'agoes. -archipelag'ic** *a.* [G. *archi-*, chief, *pelagos*, sea. The Greek chief sea was the Aegean]
arch'itect (-k-) *n.* master-builder, one who designs buildings; any maker or contriver. **-architecton'ic** *a.* **-architec'tural** *a.* **archi'tecture** *n.* [G. *architekton*, chief builder]
ar'chitrave *n-* in architecture, lowest division of entablature resting immediately on top of column. [L. *trabs*, beam]
archives (-kivz) *n.* place where government records are kept. *-pl.* public records. **-arch'ival** *a.* **-arch'ivist** *n.* [G. *archeion*, public office]
arc'tic *a.* of northern polar regions; extremely cold. *-n.* region round the north pole. [G. *arktikos*, fr. *arktos*, bear, constellation of the Great Bear]
ar'dent a. fiery; passionate. **-ar'dency***n.* **-ar'dor** *n.* [L. *ardere*, burn]
ard'uous *a.* laborious, hard to accomplish. **-ard'uously** *adv.* **arduousness** *n.* [L. *arduus*, steep]

a'rea *n.* open space; superficial contents of a figure: extent, scope. [L. open space]
Ar'eca *n.* genus of palms. **-ar'eca-nut** *n.* betel nut. [Port.]
are'na *n.* space in the middle of an amphitheater; place of public contest; place of action; battlefield. [L. = *sand*]
Areop'agus *n.* supreme court of ancient Athens, on Marsé Hill. [G. *areios pagos*, Mars' Hill]
arête' *n.* sharp ridge (of a mountain). [F., fr. L. *arista*, spine]
ar'gali n. Mongolian wild sheep. [Mongol.]
ar'gent *n.* silver. -*a.* silver, silvery white, *esp.* in heraldry. [L. *argentum*]
ar'gil *n.* potter's clay. **-argillaéceous** *a.* [L. *argilla*-G. *arges*, white]
ar'gol *n.* tartar deposit in wine vessels. [AF. *argoil*, of unknown orig.]
ar'gon *n.* inert gas forming part of the air. [G. *argos*, idle]
ar'gonaut *n.* sailor, *esp.* one who sailed in the Argo in search of the Golden Fleece; an octopod mollusk. [G. *Argo* and *nautes*, sailor]
ar'gosy *n.* richly-laden merchant ship. [earlier *ragusye*, ship of *Ragusa*]
ar'got *n.* slang; thieves' cant. [F.]
ar'gue *v.i.* prove; offer reasons; dispute. *v.t.* prove by reasoning; discuss- **ar'guable** *a.* **-ar'guer** *n.* **-ar'gument** *n.* **argumenta'tion** *n.* **-argumen'tative** *a.* [L- *arguere*, prove]
ar'gus' eyed *a.* sharp-eyed; watchful. [fr. the hundred-eyed *Argus* of G. myth]
a'ria *n.* air or rhythmical song in a cantata, opera *etc.* [It.]
ar'id *a.* parched, dry; empty, uninteresting. **-arid'ity** *n.* [L. *aridus*]
A'ries *a.* the Ram, 1st sign of the zodiac, which sun enters on *c.* 21st March [L.]
aright' *adv.* rightly. [for *on right]*
arise' *v.i.* come up; spring up; ascend; rise up. [OE. *arisan*]
aristoc'racy *n.* government by the best in birth or fortune; nobility of a state; upper classes generally. **-ar'istocrat** *n.* **aristocrat'ic** *a.* **-aristocrat'ically** *adv.* [G. *aristos*, best, *kratos*, power]
arith'metic *n.* science of numbers; art of reckoning by figures. **-arithmet'ical** *a.* **arithmet'ically** *adv.* **-arithmeti'cian** *n.* [G. *arithrnetike* -*arithmos*, number]
ark *n.* box, chest; Noah's vessel; place of refuge. [OE. *earc*, L. *arca*, coffer]
arm *n.* limb extending from shoulder to wrist; anything projecting from the main body, as a branch of the sea, the supporting rail of a chair, *etc.* -*v.t.* give an arm to. -compounds as **arm'chair** *n.* **arm'ful** *n.* **arm'hole** *n.* **-arm'let** *n.* band worn on arm, -*etc.* [OE. *earm*]
arm *n.* weapon; branch of the army. -*pl.* weapons; war:the military profession. *v.t.* supply with weapons. -*v.i.*take up arms. **-arm'ament** *n.* **-armed'** *a.* [L. *arma*, neut. P.]
arma'da (-a'-) *n.* fleet of armed ships. [Sp., p.p. of *armar*, arm]
armadill'o *n.* small American animal protected by bands of bony plates. [Sp., dim. of *armado*, man in armor]
Armaged'don *n.* world-war. [fr. scene of great battle prefigured in Revelation]
ar'mature *n.* apparatus for defense; piece of iron across the ends of a magnet; revolving part of a dynamo or motor. [F., fr. L. *armatura*, armor]
arm'istice *n.* truce, suspension of fighting. [F., fr. Mod. L. *armistitium*]
armo'rial *a.* relating to heraldic arms. [*arm*]
arm'or *n.* defensive covering or dress; plating of warships. **-arm'ored** *a.* protected by armour, as armored car, armored train. **-arm'orer** *n.* **-arm'ory** *n.* [L. *armare*, arm]
arm'y *n.* large body of men armed for warfare and under military command; host; great number. [F. *armée*, p.p. of *armer*, fr. L. *armare*, arm]
ar'nica *n.* kinds of plant including mountain tobacco, used as a remedy in apoplexy and (externally) for bruises. [Mod. L., orig. unknown]
aro'ma *n.* sweet smell; peculiar charm. **-aromat'ic** *a.* **-aroma'therapy** *n.* the massaging of the skin with oils or creams containing fragrant plant extracts: a treatment in alternative medicine designed to relieve tension and cure certain skin disorders. (G. = *spice*]
around' *adv.* on every side; in a circle. *prep.* on all sides of. [*round*]
arouse' *v.t.* awaken. [*rouse*]
arpe'ggio (-j-) *n.* chord of which the notes are sounded in quick succession. [It., fr. *arpeggiare*, play the harp]
ar'quebus, harquebus *n.* antiquated hand-gun fired from a forked rest. [F., Du. *haak*, hood, *bus*, gun-barrel]
ar'rack *n.* potent Eastern spirit made from grapes or rice or the juice of the cocapalm- also **ar'ak.** [Arab. '*araq*, juice]
arraign' (-an') *v.t.* accuse, indict, put on

trial; call to account. **-arraign′er** *n.* **-arraign′ment** *n.* [OF. *arainer*; Low L. *arrationare*, reason]

arrange′ *v.t.* set in order; settle, adjust; plan. *-v.i.* make agreement. **-arrange′-ment** *n.* [F. *arranger*, fr. *rang*, rank]

ar′rant *a.* downright, notorious. **-ar′rantly** *adv.* [var. of *errant*, q.v. Errant (wandering), associated with thief, vagabond, *etc.* lost its meaning and came to be just an intensive epithet]

ar′ras *n.* tapestry. [*Arras*, France]

array′ *v.t.* set in order; dress; equip. adorn. *-n.* order, *esp.* military order; dress. [OF. *aréer*]

arrear′ *n.* state of being behind; anything unpaid or undone (*usu.* in *pl.*). [fr. *adv. arrear*, backward]

arrest′ *v.t.* stop; catch the attention; apprehend by legal authority. *-n.* seizure by warrant; making prisoner. **-arrestément** *n.* detention of a person arrested pending bail *etc.* [OF. *arester*]

arr′is *n.* sharp edge, or ridge. [OF. *arris*, sharp edge]

arrive′ *v.i.* reach a destination; (with *at*) attain an object, achieve success. **arri′val** *n.* [F. *arriver*]

ar′rogate *v.t.* claim as one's own; claimproudly or unjustly. **-ar′rogance** *n.* aggressive conceit. **-ar′rogant** *a.* **-arrogantly** *adv.* [L. *arrogare*, claim]

ar′row *n.* pointed weapon to be shot with a bow. **-ar′rowy** *a.* **-ar′row-head** *n.* metal part of an arrow. [OE. *arwe*]

ar′rowroot *n.* W. Indian plant fromwhich is prepared a nutritious starch. [orig. uncertain]

ar′senal *n.* magazine of stores for warfare, guns, ammunition, *etc.* [It. *arsenale*, fr. Arab. *al-sina'ah*, workshop]

ar′senic *n.* one of the chemical elements, a soft, gray metal; its oxide, a powerful poison. **-ar′senate** *n.* **-arsen′ical** *a.* **-arse′nious** *a.* [G. *arsenikon*]

ar′son *n.* crime of intentionally setting on fire houses, ships or other property. [OF., fr. L. *ardere*, bum]

art *n.* skill; human skill as opposed to nature; skill applied to music, painting, poetry *etc.*; any one of the subjects of this skill; system of rules; profession or craft; contrivance, cunning, trick; *-pl.* certain branches of learning, languages, history, *etc.*, as distinct from natural science. **art′ful** *a.* cunning, clever. **-art′fully, -artfulness** *n.* **-art′ist** *n.* one who practises a fine art, *esp.* painting; one who makes his craft a fine art. **-artiste′** *n.* singer or other entertainer. **-artis′tically** *adv.* **-art′istry** *n.* **-art′less** *a.* simple, unaffected. **-art′lessly** *adv.* **-art′less-ness** *n.* [F., fr. L. *ars*, fr. a root meaning 'fit together']

arterio′gram *n.* x-ray of an artery that has been injected with dye; also **arterio′graph.**

arteriosclero′sis *n.* hardening of the arteries. [G. *arterial* artery, *skleros*, hard]

ar′tery *n.* tube carrying blood from the heart; any main channel of commonications. **-arte′rial** *a.* [G. *arterial*]

arte′sian *a.* describes a well bored down until water is reached which rises by itself. [F. *artesien*, of Artois, where such a well was first bored]

arthri′tis *n.* inflammation of a joint, gout. **-arthrit′ic** *a.* [G. *arthron*, joint]

art′ichoke *n.* thistle-like, perennial, eatable plant. **jerusalem artichoke**, a different plant, a sunflower with tubers like the potato. [It. *articiocco*, of Arab. origin. Jerusalem here is corrupt. of It. *girasole*, sunflower]

art′icle *n.* clause, head, paragraph, section; literary composition in a journal *etc.*; rule or condition; commodity or object. *-v.t.* bind as an apprentice. [L. *artus*, joint]

artic′ulate *v.t.* joint; utter distinctly; form into words or syllables. *-v.i.* speak. *a.* jointed; (of speech) clear, distinct. **artic′ulately** *adv.* **-artic′ulateness** *n.* **articula′tion** *n.* [L. *articulate*, joint]

art′ifice *n.* contrivance, trick; cunning, skill. **-artif′icer** *n.* craftsman. [L. *artificiurn-ars*, art, *facere*, make]

artificial (-sh-) *a.* synthetic; made by art, not natural; affected; feigned. **-artificial′ity** *n.* **-artifi′cially** *adv.* **artificial silk′**, *See rayon.* [*artifice]*

artill′ery *n.* cannon; troops who use them. [OF. *artillerie—artiller*, arm]

artisan′ *n.* craftsman, mechanic. [F.]

a′rum *n.* genus of plants including the cuckoo-pint. **-a′rum lil′y,** large sheath-like white lily. [G. *aron*]

A′ryan *a.* relating to the family of nations and languages also called Indo-European. [Sans. *arya*, noble]

as *adv. conj.* in that degree, so far, since, because, when, while, in like manner. [worn-down form of *also*]

asafet′ida, asafoet′ida *n.* medicinal resin, with a pungent smell, also used for culinary purposes in the East. [Pers. *aza*, mastic; L. *fetida*, stinking]

asap, ASAP (*sl.*) as soon as possible.

asbes′tos *n.* fibrous mineral which does

not burn. [G. = *unquenchable*]

ascend' *v.i.* climb, mount up; rise; go back in time. -*v.t.* walk, climb, mount up. -**ascend'ancy** *n.* control, domination. -**ascend'ant** *a.* rising; above the horizon. -*n.* superiority. -**aseen'sion** *n.* -**ascent'** *n.* rise. [L. *ascendere*, climb up]

ascertain' *v.t.* and *i.* get to know, find out. -**ascertain'able** *a.* -**ascertain'ment** *n.* [earlier *acertaine*, OF. *acertener*]

ascet'ic *n.* strict permit; one who denies himself pleasures for the sake of conscience or religion. -a. rigidly abstinent, austere. -**ascet'ically** *adv.* - **asceticism** *n.* [G. *asketikos*]

ASCII *n.* (*compute.*) computer code standardized to allow transmission of data between various hardware and software. [*A*merican *S*tandard *C*ode for *I*nformation *I*nterchange]

ascid'ians *n. pl.* sea-squirts. [G. *askidiom-askos*, wine-skin (fr. their flask-like shape)]

ascor'bic *n.* chemical substance identified with vitamin C. [G. *a*-, and *scorbutic*]

ascot *n.* broad neck scarf; cravat [E. *placename*]

ascribe' *v.t.* attribute, assign. **ascribable** *a.* -**ascrip'tion** *n.* [L. *ad*, to, *scribere*, write]

as'dic *n.* device for detecting submarines. [acrostic of *A*nti-*S*ubmarine *D*etection *I*nvestigation *C*ommittee]

asep'tic *a.* not liable to decay, or to blood-poisoning. -**asep'sis** *n.* [G. *a*, not, *septikos*, decaying]

ash *n.* familiar timber tree; its tough, white wood. -**ash'en** *a.* -**mount'ain ash**, rowan. [OE. *æsc*}

ash *n.* dust or remains of any-thing burnt. -*pl.* dead body. -**ash'y, ash'en** *a.*, of ashes; pale. -**ash'-tray** *n.* tray for tobacco-ash. [OE. *æsc*]

ashamed' *a.* affected with shame. [*See* **shame**]

ash'lar *n.* hewn or squared stone for building. [F. *aisselier*, boarding]

ashore' *adv.* on shore. [*a.* on, and *shore*]

aside' *adv.* to, or on, one side; privately; apart. -*n.* words spoken in an under-tone not to be heard by someone present. [on side]

as'inine *a.* of or like an ass; silly, stupid. -**asinin'ity** *n.* [L. *asinus*, ass]

asi'tia (-sha) *n.* distaste for food. [G. *a*-, and *sitos*, food]

ask *v.t.* request, require, question, invite. -*v.i.* make enquiry; make request. [OE. *ascian* or *acsian*]

askance' *adv.* sideways, awry; with a side look or meaning. -**look askance'**, look at with suspicion. [orig. uncertain, perh. *cog.* with *askew*]

askew' *a. adv.* aslant, awry. [*a.* and *skew*]

aslant' (-ant') *adv.* on the slant, obliquely. -*prep.* athwart, across. [on slant]

asleep' *a.* and *adv.* sleeping; at rest. [earlier on sleep]

asp *n.* small venomous snake, vipera aspis of S. Europe. [G. *aspis*]

aspar'agus *n.* plant cultivated for its young shoots, esteemed as a delicacy. [G. *asparagos*]

as'pect *n.* look, view, appearance. [L. *aspecere*, look at]

as'pen *n.* trembling poplar tree. -*a.* of or like aspen; tremulous [*a.* which has replaced the *n.* asp, OE. *æsp*]

aspe'rity *n.* roughness; harshness, coldness. [L. *asperitas*, fr. *asper*, rough]

asperse' *v.i.* besprinkle; slander, calumniate. -**asper'sion** *n.* slander, calumny. -**asper'sive** *a.* [L. *aspergere, aspers*-, sprinkle]

as'phalt, asphaltum *n.* black, hard, bituminous substance, a mineral pitch, used for paving *etc.* -*v.t.* pave with asphalt. -**asphal'tic** *a.* [G. *asphaltos*]

as'phodel *n.* kind of lily; (G. *myth.*) plant of the dead; fadeless flower of Elysium. [G. *asphodelos*]

asphyx'ia *n.* suffocation. -**asphyx'iate** *v.t.* -**asphyx'iated** *a.* -**asphyxia'tion** *n.* [G. *asphygia*, pulse stoppage]

as'pic *n.* savory jelly containing game, fish, *etc.* [F. = *asp* (fr. its coldness)]

aspidist'ra *n.* common pot-plant with broad leaves. [G. *aspis*, shield]

as'pirate *n.* letter 'h' -*v.t.* pronounce with full breathing as 'h'. [*See* **aspire**]

aspire' *v.i.* desire eagerly; aim at high things; tower up. -**as'pirant** *n.* **aspiration** *n.* -**aspi'ring** a. -**aspi'ringly** *adv.* [L. *aspirate*, breathe towards]

as'pirin *n.* drug used to relieve theumatic and neuralgic pains. [Trademark]

ass *n.* familiar quadruped of the horse family; stupid fellow. (OE. *assa*]

as'sagai, as'segai *n.* slender spear tipped with iron by S. African tribes. [Arab. *az-zaghayah*]

assail' *v.t.* attack, assault. -**assail'ant** *n.* [L. *ad salire*, jump at]

assas'sin *n.* one who kills by treacherous violence, usually for reward. -**assassinate** *v.t.* -**assassina'tion** *n.* [fr. Arab. *hash-*

shashin, eaters of hashish, an intoxicant made from hemp; assassins were orig. followers of the Old Man of the Mountains (Syria), who intoxicated themselves before attempting murder at his orders]

assault' *n.* sudden attack; attack of any kind. -*v.t.* make an attack on. [F. *assaut*, VL. *adsaltus*.]

assay' *v.i.* test the proportions of metals in an alloy or ore; test the fineness of a metal *etc.* -*n.* **-assay'er** *n.* **-assay'ing** *n.* [*See* **essay**, of which this is a variant]

assem'ble *v.t.* bring together, collect; put together, as machinery. -*v.i.* meet together. **-assem'blage** *n.* **-assem'bly** *n.* [F. *assembler*-Late L. *assimulare*, bring together]

assent' *v.i.* concur, agree. -n. acquiescence, agreement. [F. *assentir*]

assert' *v.t.* declare strongly, insist upon. **-asser'tion** *n.* **-asser'tive** *a.* **-asser'tively** *adv.* [L. asserere, claim]

assess' *v.t.* fix the amount (of a tax or fine); tax or fine; fix the value, estimate, *esp.* for taxation. **-assess'able** *a.* **assess'ment** *n.* **-assess'or** *n.* [fr. L. *assidere, assess-*, sit by as judge]

as'sets *n. pl.* property available to pay debts, *esp.* of an insolvent debtor. -*n. sing.* item of such property; thing of value. (F. *assez*, enough]

asseverate *v.t.* and *i.* assert positively, solemnly. **-assevera'tion** *n.* (L. *asseverare*, fr. *severus*, serious]

assiduous *a.* persevering. **-assidu'ity** *n.* tireless application. **-assid'uously** *adv.* [fr. L. *assidere*, sit down to]

assign' *v.t.* allot, apportion, fix; transfer; ascribe. **-assign'able** *a.* **asignation** *n.* appointment to meet, tryst. **-assignee', assign'** *n.* **-assign'ment** *n.* **-assign'or** *n.* [L. *assignare*, allot by sign, *signum*]

assim'ilate *v.t.* make similar; convert into like substance; absorb into the system. **-assim'ilable** *a.* **-assimila'tion** *n.* **-assim'ilative** *a.* [L. *assimilate*, make like, fr. *similis*, like]

assist' *v.t.* help, support. -*v.i.* be present. **-assis'tance** *n.* help, relief

assis'tant *n.* [L. *assistere*, stand by]

assize' *n.* regulation of price; standard. *pl.* sittings of a court of justice. [F. *assise*, judicial assembly]

asso'ciate *v.t.* join with, unite. -*v.i.* combine, unite. -*n.* companion, partner, ally, friend. -*a.* joined, connected. **-associa'tion** *n.* **-asso'ciative** *a.* [L. *associare*, fr. *socius*, companion]

assoil' *v.t.* loose from; absolve; acquit. **assoil'ment** *n.* [L. *ab*, from, *solvere*, loose]

as'sonance *n.* likeness in round. **as'sonant** *a.* [L. *ad*, and *sonere*, sound]

assort' *v.t.* classify, arrange. -*v.i.* match, agree with. **-assort'ed** *a.* varied **assortment** *n.* variety. [OF. *asorter*, see sort]

assuage' (-sw-) *v.t.* soften, allay. **assuage'ment** *n.* **-assua'sive** *a.* [OF. *assouagier*, fr. L. *suavis*, mild]

assume' *v.t.* take for granted; put on; claim, arrogate; pretend. -*v.i.* be arrogant. **-assump'tion** *n.* supposition; arrogance. **-assump'tive** *a.* [L. *assumere*, take to oneself]

assure' *v.t.* make safe; insure; tell positively; give confidence. **-assu'rance** *n.* **assured'** *a.* **-assu'redly** *adv.* [F. *assurer*, make sure, fr. L. *securus*]

assur'gent *a.* rising, up-sweeping. **assur'gency** *n.* [*See* **surge**]

as'ter *n.* perennial plant with late blooming star-like flowers. (G. = *star*]

aster'ias *n.* genus of echinoderms including the common starfish. [G. aster, star]

as'terisk *n.* star (*) used in printing. [G. *asterikos*, little star]

astern' *adv.* at the stern; behind; backwards. [*See* **stern**]

as'teroid *n.* small planet. [G. *aster*, star, *eidos*, form]

astheni'a *n.* debility, weakness. [G. *a-*, without, *sthenos*, strength]

astheno'pia *n.* weakness or fatigue of the eyes, often accompanied by headache, dizziness, and dimming of vision.

asth'ma (-sm-) *n.* chronic disease entailing difficulty in breathing, wheezing, tightness in the chest, *etc.* **asthmat'ic** *a.* **-asthmat'ically** *adv.* [G.]

astigmatism *n.* defect of the eye in which the rays are not brought to a proper focus at one point. **-astigmat'ic** *a.* (G. *a-*, not, *stigma*, point]

astir' *adv.* on the move; out of bed; out of doors; in excitement. (on stir]

astom'atous *a.* having no mouth, as *e.g.*, the protozoa. [G. *a-*, without, *stoma*, mouth]

astonish, astound' *v.t.* amaze, surprise greatly. **-aston'ishing** *a.* **astonishment** *n.* [OF. *estoner*, VL. *extonere*, thunderstrike; ME, astoun, later *astound*; fr. p.p. *astoned* came a new verb *astony*, later *astonish*. *See* **stun**]

astound'. *See* **astonish.**

astrakhan *n.* lambskin with curled wool

from the Caspian region; imitation in fabric. [Astrakhan on the Volga]

as'tral *a.* of the stars, starry; belonging to the spirit-world. [L. *astralis*]

astray' *adv.* out of the right way. [F. *estraie-estraier*, stray]

astride' *adv.* with the legs apart; one leg on either side of [See **stride**]

astrin'gent *a.* binding, contracting. -*n.* binding medicine. **-astrin'gency** *n.* [L. *astringere*, tighten]

astro'cyte *n.* star-shaped neuroglial cell found in the brain, spinal cord, and nervous tissue.

astrol'abe *n.* instrument formerly used to measure the altitude of the sun and stars. [G. *astron*, star, *lambanein*, take]

astrol'ogy *n.* science (formerly synonymous with astronomy) pert. to the influence of the stars on human and terrestrial affairs. **-astrol'oger** *n.* **-astrolo'gical** *a.* [G. *astrologia*, knowing of the stars (*aster*, star)]

astron'omy *n.* science or study of the heavenly bodies. **-astron'omer** *n.* **-astronom'ical** *a.* of astronomy; very great. [G. *astron*, star, *nomos*, law]

astrophysics *n.* study of the physical conditions of the heavenly bodies. [G. *astron*, star, and physics]

astuteé *a.* crafty, cunning; shrewd, acute. **-astute'ly** *adv.* **-astute'ness** *n.* [L. *astutus*, fr. *astus*, crafty]

asun'der *adv.* apart, in pieces. [OE. *on sundran. See* **sunder**]

asy'lum *n.* refuge, sanctuary; home for the care of the unfortunate. *esp.* lunatics; formerly a refuge for criminals. [fr. G. *a-*, not, *syle*, right of seizure]

asymmet'rical *a.* lacking in symmetry or balance between parts, lop-sided. [G. *a-*, not, and *symmetry*]

at *prep.* near to, by, in; engaged on; in the direction of [OE. *æt*]

at'avism *n.* appearance of ancestral, not parental, characteristics in an animal or plant; reversion to an earlier type. **atavis'tic** *a.* [L. *atavus*, great-grandfather's - grandfather]

atax'ia, atax'y *n.* impaired co-ordination (through disease) of the muscles controlling voluntary movement. [G. *a-*, not, *taktos*, arrange]

at'elier *n.* studio, workshop. [F.]

a'theism *n.* disbelief in the existence of God. **-a'theist** *n.* **-atheist'ic** *a.* **atheist'ical** *a.* [fr. G. *a-*, not, *theos*, God]

athenaeum *n.* public institution for lectures *etc.* [fr. temple of Athene at Athens, where poets read their works]

atheto'sis *n.* a condition characterized by uncontrolled rhythmical writhing movement, *esp.* of fingers, hands, head, and tongue, caused by cerebral lesion. **ath'etoid** a. [G. *athetos*, not in place]

athirst' *a.* thirsty. [*See* **thirst**]

ath'lete *n.* one trained to physical exercises, feats or contests of strength. **athlet'ic** *a.* **-athlet'icism** *n.* **-athlet'ics** *n. pl.* sports of running, wrestling, *etc.* [G. *athletes*, fr. *athlos*, contest]

athwart *adv.* across, *esp.* obliquely. *prep.* across. (*See* **thwart**]

atlanétes *n. pl.* sculptured figures used as columns. [*Atlas*]

Atlan'tic *n.* the ocean between Europe, Africa and the American Continent; belonging to Atlas (*myth*). [fr. Mount Atlas in N. W. Africa]

atlantosaur'us *n.* huge fossil reptile of the Jurassic period. [*Atlas*]

at'las *n.* book of maps. [G. *Atlas*, a Titan who bore the world on his shoulders and whose image appeared on the title-page of old map books]

ATM *n.* automatic or automated teller machine, operated by customers with magnetized cards to make financial transactions.

atmosphere *n.* mass of gas surrounding a heavenly body, *esp.* the earth. **atmospher'ic** *a.* **-atmospher'ically** *adv.* **-atmospher'ics** *n. pl.* noises in wireless reception due to electrical disturbances from the atmosphere. [G. *atmos*, vapor, *sphaira*, sphere]

at'oll *n.* ring-shaped coral island enclosing a lagoon. [Maldive word]

at'om *n.* smallest particle of matter which enters into chemical combination; any very small particle. **-atom'ic** *a.* **at'om bomb'**, bomb in which the explosion is caused by atomic energy. **atom'ic en'ergy**, energy derived from a sustained neutron chain reaction resulting from nuclear fission of the atom. [G. *atomos*, fr. *a-*, not, *temnein*, cut (it was long supposed to be indivisible)]

atomi'zer *n.* device for ejecting liquids in a fine mist-like spray. [atom]

atone' *v.i.* give satisfaction or make reparation. **-atone'ment** *n.* [orig., to *reconcile*, fr. *adv.* phrase at one]

atrabil'ious, atrabil'iar *a.* melancholy; hypochondriac. (L. *atra*, black, *bilis*, bile, translating G. *melangeholia. See* **melancholy**]

atre'sia *n.* absence of or unnatural narrowing of a body channel. [G. *atretos*, not perforated]

atrocious (-shus) *a.* extremely cruel or wicked. **-atro'ciously** *adv.* **-atro'city** *n.* (L. *atrox*, cruel, fr. *ater*, black]

at'rophy *n.* wasting away in a living body with lessening of size and strength, emaciation. *-v.i.* waste away, become useless. **-at'rophied** *a.* [G. *a-*, not, *trephein*, nourish]

at'ropine *n.* poisonous alkaloid obtained from deadly nightshade. [G. *Atropos*, the Fate who cuts the thread of life]

attach' *v.t.* fasten, seize, connect, join to. *-v.i.* adhere. **-attach'ment** *n.* [F. *attacher*, It. *attaccare*. *See* **attack**]

attach'é (a-tash'a) *n.* member of an ambassadorés staff. **-attach'é-case** *n.* small rectangular handbag for papers. [F. = *attache*d]

attack' *v.t.* fall upon violently; assault, assail; affect (of a disease). *-n.* assault; seizure. [F. *attaquer*, It. *attaccare*, join; F. and E. sense is fr. *attaccare battaglia*, join battle]

attain' *v.t.* arrive at, reach, gain by effort. **-attainabil'ity** *n.* **-attain'able** *a.* **-attainment** *n.* *esp.* a personal accomplishment. [F. *atteindre*]

attainder *n.* loss of rights through conviction of high treason. **-attaint'** *v.t.* convict; deprive of rights; accuse; stain. (F. *atteindre*, used as a *n.*, fr. L. *ad*, and *tangere*, touch]

att'ar, ott'o *n.* very fragrant oil made in Bulgaria and the East, chiefly from roses. [Pers. *atar-gul*, essence of roses]

attempt' *v.t.* try, endeavor, make an effort or attack on. *-n.* trial, effort. [L. *attentare*, try]

attend' *v.t.* wait upon, accompany; wait for; be present at. *-v.i.* give the mind (to). **-attend'ance** *n.* **-attend'ant** *n.* **atten'tion** *n.* **-atten'tive** *a.* **-atten'tively** *adv.* **-atten'tiveness** *n.* [fr. L. *attendere*, stretch towards]

attenuate *v.t.* make thin or slender; weaken, reduce. *-v.i.* become weak or slender. **-atten'uated** *a.* **-attenua'tion** *n.* [L. *attenuate*, make thin, *tenuis*]

attest' *v.t.* bear witness to, certify. **attesta'tion** *n.* [L. *attestari*, bear witness]

at'tic *n.* low story above the cornice of a building; room in the roof. *-a.* of Athens; elegant. [Attica, Athens]

attire' *v.t.* dress, array. *-n.* dress. [OF. *atirer*, put in order]

at'titude *n.* posture, position; behavior, relation of persons expressing thought, feeling *etc.* [L. *aptitudo*, fr. *aptus*, fit]

attorn'ey (-tur'-) *n.* one legally authorized to act for another; a qualified practicioner of law, lawyer. [OF. *atorner* -Low L. *atornare*, appointl]

attract' *v.t.* draw towards, literally or figuratively; entice; cause to approach; charm, fascinate. **-attrac'tion** *n.* **attractive** *a.* **-attrac'tively** *adv.* **- attractiveness** *n.* [L. *attrahere*]

attribute *v.t.* ascribe, assign, refer to. **(at'tribute)** *n.* quality, property or characteristic of anything. **-attrib'utable** *a.* **attribu'tion** *n.* **-attrib'utive** *a.* [L. *attribuere-tribuere*, pay tribute]

attri'tion (-i'-shun) *n.* rubbing away, wearing down by friction. [L. *attritio*, fr. *terere, trit-*, rub]

attune' *v.t.* put in tune, harmonize. [*at* and *tune*]

ATV *n. pl.* **ATVs** vehicle with special sheels or tires for traversing rough terrain [*a*ll-*t*errain *v*ehicle]

aubade' (õ-bad') *n.* sunrise song. [F., fr. *aube*, dawn]

aubergine' (õ-ber-zhen') *n.* egg-plant; its fruit. [F., fr. *auberge*, peach]

aubrie'tia *n.* purple-flowered rock-garden plant. [fr. the painter Claude Aubriet]

aub'urn *a.* reddish-brown. [fr. L. *auburnus*, whitish (the old meaning was light yellow)]

auc'tion *n.* public sale in which the bidder offers increase of price over another, and what is sold goes to the highest bidder. **-auctioneer'** *n.* **auc'tion-bridge'** *n.* card game. **-Dutch auc'tion,** selling in which the seller starts at a high price and comes down until he meets a bidder. [L. *augere*, increase]

audacious *a.* bold, daring; insolent. **auda'city** *n.* [L. *audax–audere*, dare]

aud'ible *a.* able to be heard. **audibil'ity** *n.* **-aud'ibly** *adv.* [L. *audire*, hear]

aud'ience *n.* act of hearing; judicial hearing; formal interview; assembly of hearers. [F., fr. L. *audire*, hear]

aud'it *n.* formal examination of accounts; periodical settlement. *-v.t.* examine (accounts). **-aud'itor** *n.* [L. *auditus audire*, hear]

audition *n.* sense of hearing; hearing, *esp.* test hearing of a performer.

audito'rium *n.* place for hearing.

aud'itory *a.* [L. *audire*, hear]

au'ger *n.* carpenter's tool for boring

holes. [an *auger* was ME. a *nauger* OE. *nafugar*. cp. adder]

aught *n.* anything. *-adv.* to any extent. [OE. *awiht*, fr. a, ever, *wiht*, thing]

augment' *v.t.* and *i.* increase, enlarge. (aug'-) *n.* increase. **-augmenta'tion** *n.* **augment'ative** *a.* [L. *augmentare*, fr. *augere*, grow]

aug'ur *n.* among the Romans, one who predicted the future by observations of birds *etc.* **-aug'ury** *n.* omen. (L.]

august' *a.* majestic, dignified. **-Aug'ust** *n.* eighth month of the year. **-August'an,** of Augustus, the Roman Emperor; hence classic, distinguished, as applied to a period of literature. [L. *augustus*, venerable; **Augustus Caesar,** 31 B.C.-14 A.D.]

auk *n.* northern sea-bird with short wings used only as paddles. [Sw. *alka*]

aul'ic *a.* of a royal court. [L. *aula*; G. *aule*, court]

aunt (ant) *n.* father's or mother's sister; uncle's wife. [OF. *ante*, fr. L. *amita*, paternal aunt]

aur'a *n.* (*occultism*) subtle emanation surrounding a person or thing; distinctive air or character. [L. *aura*]

aur'al *a.* of the ear. **-aur'ally** *adv.* [L. *auris*, ear]

aur'eate a. golden; gilded. [L. *aurum*, gold]

au'reole, aur'eole *n.* gold color or illumination painted round the head or figure of holy persons in Christian art; halo. (L. *aureola* (corona), golden (crown)]

aur'ic *a.* pertaining to gold. [fr. L. *aurum*]

aur'icle *n.* outside ear. *-pl.* upper-cavities of the heart. **—auric'ular** *a.* of the ear; known by ear, told in the ear, *esp.* of confession. [L. auris, ear]

aurif'erous *a.* bearing or yielding gold. [L. *aurum*, gold]

aur'ist *n.* ear-doctor. **-aur'iscope** *n.* instrument for examining the ear. [L. *auris*, ear]

aur'ochs (-oks) *n.* extinct wild ox. [G. *ouros*, ox]

auro'ra *n.* lights in the atmosphere to be seen radiating from the regions of the poles. The northern is called **auro'ra borea'lis,** and the southern **auro'ra austra'lis.** [L. = *dawn*]

ausculta'tion *n.* listening to the movement of the heart and lungs with a stethoscope. **-ausculta'tor** *n.* **-auscul'tatory** *a.* [L. *auscultare*, listen]

aus'pice *n.* omen drawn from the observation of birds (*usu.* in *pl.*). *-pl.* patronage, favor. **-auspi'cious** *a.* of good omen, favorable. **-auspi'ciously** *adv.* [L. *auspicium*, fr. *avis*, bird, *specere*, behold]

austere' *a.* harsh, strict, severe. **austere'ty** *adv.* **-auster'ity** *n.* [G, *austeros*, making the tongue rough]

aus'tral *a.* southern. [L. *austr-alis auster*, south wind]

au'tacoid *n.* internal glandular secretion which either stimulates or slows down the growth of certain tissues. [G. *autos*, self, *akos*, drug]

authentic *a.* trustworthy, real, genuine, true. **-authen'tically** *adv.* **-authen'ticate** *v.t.* **-authentica'tion** *n.* **-authenti'city** *n.* [G. *authentikos*, first-hand, fr. *authentes*, one who does things for himself]

auth'or *n.* originator, constructor; writer of a book; an author's writings. **auth'oress** *n. fem.* **-auth'orship** *n.* [L. *auctor*, fr. *augere*, make grow]

author'ity *n.* legal power or right; delegated power; permission; book, person *etc.* settling a question, entitled to be believed; body or board in control, *esp.* in *pl.* **-authoriza'tion** *n.* **-auth'orize** *v.t.* **author'itative** *a.* **-author'itatively** *adv.* [L. *auctoritas*, fr. *auctor*, *v. s.*]

autobiog'raphy *n.* biography or life of a person written by himself- **autobiog'rapher** *n.* **-autobiograph'ical** *a.* **autobiograph'ically** *adv.* [fr. G. *autos*, self, *bios*, life, *graphein*, write]

autoch'thon (-k-) *n.* aborigine; primitive inhabitant. **-autoch'thonous** *a.* native, indigenous. [G. *autos*, self, *chthonos*, soil]

aut'ocrat *n.* absolute ruler. **-autoc'-racy** *n.* **-autocrat'ic** *a.* **-autocrat'ically** *adv.* [G. *autos*, self, *kratos*, power]

auto da-fe' *n.* public judgment and punishment by the Inquisition in Spain and Portugal, *esp.* the burning of heretics. [Port. = act of faith]

autogi'ro, autogy'ro *n.* kind of airplane able to stabilize itself by revolving planes in the air or to ascend vertically. [G. *autos*, self, *gyros*, circle]

autograph *n.* oneés own handwriting; signature. **-autograph'ic** *a.* [fr. G. *autos*, self, *graphein*, write]

aut'omation *n.* the automatic control of successive production processes by electronic apparatus. [G. *autos*, self]

automa'ton *n.* self-acting machine, *esp.* one simulating a human being; (*fig.*) human being who acts by routine, without intelligence. **-automat'ic** *a.* **-automat'-ically** *adv.* **-autom'atism** *n.* [G.

automatos, self-moving]

automo'bile *n.* a mechanical road vehicle *usu.* with four wheels and for passenger transportation. **-automo'bilist** *n.* [G. *autos*, self, and mobile]

auton'omy *n.* self-government. **-autonomous** *a.* [G. *autonomia*, self-rule]

autoph'anous *a.* self-luminous. [G. *autos*, self, *phanos*, light]

autop'sy *n.* personal inspection; postmortem examination. [G. *autopsia*, seeing for oneself -autos, self, *opsis*, sight]

auto-suggestion *n.* process of influencing the mind (towards health, future action, *etc.*), conducted by the subject himself. [G. *autos*, self, and suggestion]

aut'umn (-um) *n.* third season of the year, season of harvest; fall. **-autum'nal** *a.* **-autum'nary** *adv.* [L. *autumnus*]

auxil'iary *a.* helping, subsidiary. *-n.* helper; something subsidiary, as troops; verb used to form tenses of other verbs. [L. *auxilium*, help]

avail' *v.i.* be of value, of use. *-v.t.* benefit, help. *-n.* benefit, as in be of little avail, *etc.* **-availabil'ity** *n.* **-avail'able** *a.* **-avail' oneself of,** make use of. [F. *valoir*, be worth]

av'alanche (-sh) *n.* mass of snow and ice sliding down a mountain. [F., earlier *lavanche;* Late L. *labina*, landslide, influenced by *avaler*, descend]

av'arice *n.* greediness of wealth. **avari'cious** *a.* **-avari'ciously** *adv.* [F.]

avast' *int.* (*naut.*) enough! stop! [Du. *houd vast*, hold fast]

avatar' *n.* descent of a Hindu god in visible form; incarnation. [Sans. *avatara*, down-passing]

avaunt' *int.* away! [F. *avant*, forward]

avenge' *v.t.* take vengeance on behalf of (a person) or on account of (a thing). **aven'ger** *n.* **-aven'ging** *a.* [OF. *avengier*, fr. L. *vindicate*. *See* **vengeance**]

av'enue *n.* approach; double row of trees, with or without a road; handsome street. [F., fr. *avenir*, come to]

aver' *v.t.* declare true; assert. **aver'ment** *n.* [F. *avérer*, fr. L. *verus*, true]

av'erage *n.* mean value or quantity of a number of values or quantities; (formerly meant charge over and above freight at sea; loss from damage *etc.*). *-a.* medium, ordinary. *-v.t.* fix or calculate a mean. *v.i.* exist in or form a mean. [orig. unknown]

avert' *v.t.* turn away, ward off. **-averse'** *a.* disinclined, unwilling. **-aver'seness** *n.* **-aver'sion** *n.* dislike. [L. *avertere*, turn from]

a'viary *n.* place for keeping birds. **a'viarist** *n.* [L. *aviarium*, fr. *avis*, bird]

avia'tion *n.* art of flying by mechanical means. **-a'viator** *n.* **-av'ion** *n.* French word for airplane. [F., fr. L. *avis*, bird]

avid'ity *n.* eagerness, greediness. **-av'id** *a.* [L. *aviditas*]

avoca'do *n.* pear-shaped edible fruit of a tropical American tree of the laurel family. [Sp.]

avoca'tion *n.* employment, business; (formerly, distraction from business, diversion). [L. *avocatio*, calling away]

av'ocet *n.* snipe-like wading bird. (F. *avocette*]

avoid' *v.t.* keep clear of, escape; (*law*) annul, invalidate. **-avoid'able** *a.* **avoidance** *n.* [OF. *esvuider*, empty out]

avoirdupois' *n.* and *a.* British system of weights. [corrupt. of OF. *avoir de pòis*, goods sold by weight, *i.e.*, not by number]

avow' *v.t.* own, acknowledge. **-avow'able** *a.* **-avow'al** *n.* **-avowed'** *a.* **avow'edly** *adv.* [F. *avouen*-Low *uotare*, vow]

avuncular *a.* of, like, an uncle. [L. *avunculus*, uncle]

AWACS *n.* acronym for *A*irborne *W*arning *A*nd *C*ontrol *S*ystem

await' *v.t.* wait or stay for; be in store for. [ONF. *awatier*. *See* **wait**]

awake', awa'ken *v.t.* rouse from sleep, stir. *-v.i.* cease from sleep; bestir oneself; become aware, not sleeping. **awakening** *n.* [OE. *awæcnan*]

award' *v.t.* adjudge. *-n.* judgment of an arbiter, final decision. [fr. OF. *eswarder*. *See* **guard, ward**]

aware' *a.* informed, conscious. **awareness** *n.* [OE. *sewer*]

awash' *adv.* level with the surface of water, washed over by waves. [*a*-and *wash*]

away' *adv.* absent, apart, at a distance. [OE. *onweg*, on the way]

awe *n.* dread mingled with reverence. *v.t.* fill with **awe. -aw'ful** *a.* inspiring awe; dreadful; very bad. **-aw'fully** *adv.* **awe'some** *a.* [ON. *agi*, fear]

awhile' *adv.* for a time. [*See* **while**]

awk'ward *a.* clumsy, ungainly; difficult to deal with; embarrassed. **-awk'wardly** *adv.* **-awk'wardness** *n.* [orig. *adv.*, with suffix *-ward* on *old awk*, backhanded]

awl *n.* pointed tool for boring small holes, *esp.* in leather. [OE. *æl*]

awn *n.* beard of corn *etc.* (ON. *ögn*]

awn'ing *n.* covering of canvas *etc.* to

shelter from sun. [orig. unknown]

awry′ *adv.* crookedly, perversely. *a.* crooked, distorted; wrong. [earlier *onwry. See* **wry**]

ax, axe *n.* tool with iron blade for hewing or chopping. [OE. *æx*]

axil′la *n.* armpit. **-ax′illary** *a.* [L.]

ax′iom *n.* self-evident truth; received principle. **-axiomat′ic** *a.* [G. *axioma,* fr. *axioein,* take for granted]

ax′is *n.* straight line round which a body revolves; line or column about which parts are arranged; (politics) German-Italian (Nazi-Fascist) alliance in World War II. **-ax′ial** *a.* of, pert. to axis. **-ax′ially** *adv.* [L. =*pivot*]

ax′le, ax′le-tree *n.* rod on which a wheel turns. [ON. *äxul-tre*]

ay, aye *adv.* ever. [ON. *ei*]

a′yah *n.* native Indian maid or nanny. [Hind. *aya*]

ayatollah *n.* one of a class of Iranian Shiite religious leaders. [Pers. and Arab., *aya,* sign, *Allah*, god]

aye *adv.* yes *-n.* affirmative answer or vote. *-pl.* those voting for a motion. [orig. uncertain. *See* **yea**]

aye′-aye *n.* small squirrel-like animal allied to the lemur. (Malagasy *aiay*]

aza′lea *n.* genus of shrubby plants allied to the rhododendron, with fine white, yellow or red flowers. [fr. G. *azaleas*, dry]

az′imuth *n.* arc between zenith and horizon; its angular distance from the meridian. [Arab. *as-sumut*, the way]

az′tec *a.* and *n.* (member) of ruling race (and language) in Mexico before Spanish Conquest. [*Azteca*, native name of tribe]

az′ure *a.* clear blue, sky-colored. *-n.* delicate blue; the sky. [orig. the *lapis lazuli*, fr. Arab. *azward*, Pers. *lajward*, Place in Turkestan, where it was procured]

B

bab′ble *v.i.* speak like a baby; talk idly. *-v.t.* utter idly. *-n.* chatter, idle talk. - **bab′bler** *n.* **-bab′bling, bab′ble ment** *n.* [imit. of infant speech]

babe. *See* **baby.**

ba′bel *n.* confusion of sounds; scene of confusion. [Tower of *Babel* (Gen. xi), understood as confusion, but prob. Assyr. *bab-ilu*, gate of the gods]

baboon′ *n.* species of large monkey, with long face and dog-like tusks. [F. *babouin*]

ba′by *n.* infant child. **-babe** *n.* **ba′byhood** *n.* **-ba′byish** *a.* **-ba′by boom′** large increase in the birth-rate, *esp.* as occurred in the years following the end of World War II. **-ba′by carr′iage** light vehicle for transporting a baby. —**ba′by-sitt′er** *n.* someone who looks after a baby in the temporary absence of its parents. [earlier *baban.* imit. of baby speech]

baccalau′reate *n.* university degree of bachelor. **-baccalau′rean** *a.* [*See* **bachelor**]

bac′carat (-ra) *n.* game of cards. [F.]

bac′chanal (-ka-) *n.* worshipper of Bacchus; reveller. **-bacchana′lian** *a.* [L. *bacchanalis-Bacchus*, god of wine]

bach′elor *n.* unmarried man; one who takes his first degree at a university; young knight. **-bach′elorhood** *n.*— **bach′elorship** *n.* [Low. L. *baccalarius,* cowherd]

bacil′lus *n.* (*pl.* **bacil′li**) microbe, minute organism causing disease. **-bacil′liform** *a.* **-bacill′ar, bacill′ary** *a.* [Late L., dim. of *baculus*, rod]

back *n.* hinder part.; situated behind. *-v.t.* support; make recede. *-v.i.* move away to the rear. *-v.* to the rear; to a former condition; in return. **back′beat** *n.* the second and fourth beats in music written in even time or, in more complex time signatures, the last beat of the bar. **-back′bite** *v.t.* slander an absent person. **-back′biter** *n.* - **back′biting** *n.* **-back′bone** *n.* **spinal column.** **-back′-chat** *n.* retort, impertinence. **-back-cloth, -drop** *n.* painted cloth at back of stage. **-back′er** *n.* one who supports another, *esp.* in a contest. - **back′fire** *v.i.* ignite wrongly, as a gasburner *etc.* **-back-gam′mon** *n.* board game played with pieces and dice. **-back′-ground** *n.* space at the back; space behind the chief figures of a picture *etc.* **-back-hand** *n.* stroke with the hand turned backward; writing that slopes to the left. - **back′hander** *n.* blow with back of hand; (*colloq.*) bribe. **-back′ing** *n.* support. - **back′-number** *n.* (of a person or thing) out of date, outmoded. **-back′slide** *v.i.* fall back in faith or morals. **-back′stays** *n.pl.* ropes to strengthen the mast of a ship. - **back′ talk** *n.* insolent rejoinder. **-back′-ward, back′wards** *adv.* to the rear; to the past; from a better to a worse state. *a.* lagging behindhand. **-back′wardness** *n.* - **back′-wash** *n.* wave in wake of boat. - **back′woods** *pl.* uncleared forest land *etc.* behind newly developed country. **-back-woodsman** *n.* [OE. *bæc*]

ba′con *n.* cured pig's flesh. [OE.]

bacte′rium *n.* microbe, disease-germ -

bact'ria *pl.* **-bacte'rial** *a.* **-bacteri ol'ogist** *n.* **-bacteriol'ogy** *n.* study of bacteria. [G. *bakerion*, little staff]

Bac'trian *a.* of Bactria. *-n.* two-humped camel. [*Bactria*, Asia]

bad *a.* not good; evil, wicked; faulty. **-bad'ly** *adv.* **-bad'ness** *n.* [ME. *badde*]

badge *n.* mark or sign. (ME. *bage*]

badg'er *n.* burrowing night animal, about the size of a fox. *-v.t.* hunt eagerly, worry, as dogs a badger. [orig. uncertain]

badinage' (-azh') *n.* light playful talk, banter, chaff. [F.]

bad'minton *n.* game like lawn-tennis, but played with shuttlecocks. [*Badminton*, Duke of Beaufort's house]

baf'fle *v.t.* check, frustrate. **-baffle plate** *a.* plate for regulating or diverting flow of liquid. **-baffle-wall** *n.* (defense) wall to divert blast, *etc.* or binder enemy transport. [orig. uncertain]

baff'y *n.* golf club with sloping face. [orig. uncertain]

bag *n.* sack, pouch; measure of quantity. *-v.i.* swell out. *-v.t.* put in a bag; kill, seize, as game, *etc.* **-bagg'y** *a.* loosely bulging. [ON. *baggi*]

bagatelle' *n.* trifle; game played with nine balls and cue on a board. [F.]

bagg'age *n.* portable luggage of an army; any luggage; saucy or worthless woman. [F. *bagage*]

bag'pipe *n.* musical wind-instrument consisting of a leather wind-bag and pipes. **-bag'piper** *n.* [*bag* and *pipe*]

bail *n.* (law) security given for a person's reappearance in court; one giving such security. *-v.t.* release on security. [OF., fr. *bailler*, give]

bail *n.* pole separating horses in a stable. [OF., fr. L. *baculum*, stick]

bail *v.t.* empty out water from a boat. **bail' out** *v.i.* drop from an airplane by parachute. **-bail'er** *n.* [obs. *bail*, bucket]

Bai'ley-bridge *n.* portable prefabricated temporary bridge built in sections. [*Bailey*, inventor]

bail'iff *n.* a minor officer in a court of law; sheriffs officer; land steward. **bail'iwick** *n.* jurisdiction of a bailiff. [OF. *bailif*]

bairn *n.* child. [OE. *bearn*, fr. *beran*, bear]

bait *n.* food put on a hook to entice fish; any lure or enticement; refreshment on a journey. *-v.t.* set a lure; feed and water; annoy, persecute. *-v.i.* take refreshment on a journey. [ON. *beita*, cause to bite]

baize *n.* coarse woollen cloth. [earlier haves (*pl.*) fr. color *bay*]

bake *v.t.* cook or harden by dry heat, to cook in oven. *-v.i.* make bread; become scorched. **-ba'ker** *n.* **-ba'kery, bake' - house** *n.* **-ba'king** *n.* **-ba'ker's doz'en,** thirteen. [OE. *bacan*]

Ba'kelite (bā'-) *n.* synthetic resin; plastic made from it. [Protected Trade Name]. [L. H. *Baekeland*, inventor]

bak'sheesh *n.* tip, gratuity, *esp.* in the East. [Pers.]

balalai'ka (-i'-) *n.* Russian musical instrument like a guitar. [Russ.]

bal'ance *n.* pair of scales; equilibrium; surplus; sum due on an account; difference of two sums. *-v.t.* weigh; bring to equilibrium; adjust. *-v.i.* have equal weight; be in equilibrium. **-bal'ance-sheet** *n.* list of assets and liabilities. **-bal'ance-wheel** *n.* regulating wheel of a watch. [L. *bilanx-bis*, twice, and *lanx*, platter]

bal'ata *n.* synthetic rubber made from gum of S. American tree. [Sp.]

balbu'tient (-sh-) *a.* stammering. [L. *balbutire*, stutter]

bal'cony *n.* platform projecting from the wall of a building; second gallery of a theater. **-bal'conied** *a.* [It. *balcone*]

bald (bawld) *a.* hairless (featherless, *etc*); plain, meager. **-bald'head** *n.* **-bald'ly** *a.* **-bald'ness** *n.* [earlier *balled*, fr. Welsh *bal*, white on the brow]

bal'dachin *n.* canopy over throne, altar, *etc.* [It. *baldacchino*]

bal'derdash (bawl-é) *n.* idle, senseless talk. [orig. uncertain. cp. Welsh *baldorrdus -baidorrd*, idle noisy talk]

bal'dric *n.* shoulder-belt for sword, bugle *etc.* [L. *balteus*, belt]

bale *n.* bundle or package. *-v.t.* make into bundles. [OF. = ball]

bale *n.* evil, mischief, woe. **-bale'ful** *a.* **bale'fully** *adv.* **-bale'fulness** *n.* **-bale'fire** *n.* beacon, bonfire. [OE. *bealo*, woe]

baleen' *n.* whalebone, horny plates in palate of whale. [L. *balæna*, whale]

balk (bawk) *n.* strip of land left unploughed; squared timber, beam hindrance. *-v.t.* thwart, hinder. *-v.i.* swerve, pull up. [OE. *balca*, ridge]

ball (bawl) *n.* anything round; globe, sphere; bullet; game played with ball. [ON. *bollr*]

ball (bawl) *n.* assembly for dancing. **-ball'room** *n.* [F. *bal*]

ball'ad *n.* simple spirited narrative poem; simple song. [F. *ballade*, orig. a dancing-song]

ballade' (ädé) *n.* form of poem. [F.]

ball'ast *n.* heavy material put in a ship to give steadiness by added weight. *-v.t.* load thus. [obs. *last*, burden]

balleri'na n. dancer, *esp.* premiere in a ballet, [It.]

ball'et *n.* theatrical dance. [F.]

ballis'tics *n.* science of projectiles. **-ballis'tic** *a.* [L. *ballista*, Roman military engine—G. *ballein*, throw]

balloon' *n.* early form of aircraft, raised by large gas-filled bag; inflated toy. *-v.i.* go up in a balloon; puff out. **-balloon'ist** *n.* [F. *ballon*]

ball'ot *n.* method of voting secretly by putting balls or tickets into a box. *-v.i.* vote by this method. **-ball'ot-box** *n.* [It. *ballotta*, dim. of *balla*, ball]

balm (bam) *n.* aromatic substance; healing or soothing ointment; anything soothing. **-balm'iness** *n.* **-balm'y** *a.* [L. *balsamum.* See **balsam**]

bal'sam (bawlé-) *n.* resinous aromatic substance. **-balsam'ic** *a.* **-Can'ada bal'sam,** kind of turpentine extracted from an oriental tree. [L. *balsamum*]

bal'un *n.* device for coupling two electrical circuit elements, such as an aerial and its feeder cable, where one is balanced and the other is unbalanced. [shortened from *bal*ance to *un*balance transformer]

bal'uster *n.* short pillar. **-bal'ustrade** *n.* ornamental parapet; row of short pillars surmounted by a rail. [G. *balaustion*, flower of wild pomegranate]

bamboo' *n.* large Indian reed, with hard, hollow stem. [Malay orig.]

bamboo'zle *v.t.* confound or mystify, confuse, puzzle. **-bamboo'zlement** *n.* [arbitrary formation]

ban *n.* denunciation, curse; proclamation. *-v.t.* curse, forbid; outlaw. **-banns** *n. pl.* proclamation of marriage. [OE. *bannan*, summon, later curse]

banal', ba'nal *a.* commonplace, trivial. **-banal'ity** *n.* [F.]

bana'na (-an-) *n.* tall tropical or subtropical tree; its fruit. [Sp. or Port. fr. native Guinea name]

ban'co *interj.* call in gambling games such as chemin de fer and baccarat by a player or bystander who wishes to bet against the entire bank. (It. *banco*, bank]

band *n.* strip used to bind; bond. **-ban'dage** *n.* strip of cloth used by surgeons for binding. [*bind*]

band *n.* company, troop; company of musicians. *-v.t.* and *i.* join into a band. **band'master** *n.* **-bands'man** *n-* **. bandstand** *n.* [F. *bande*]

Band Aid *n.* medical dressing with a sticky surface to adhere to skin. [Trademark]

bandann'a *n.* patterned, colored silk or cotton handkerchief [Hind. *bhandknu*, method of dyeing]

band'box *n.* light box for hats, *etc.* [orig. a *box* for *bands*, collars]

ban'dit *n.* outlaw; robber. [It. *bandito. See* **ban**]

ban'dog *n.* chained watch-dog. [*band*, tie, and *dog*]

bandolier', bandoleer' *n.* shoulder-belt with pockets for cartridges. [F. *bandoulière*]

band'y *n.* game like hockey. *-v.t.* beat to and fro, toss from one to another. **-ban'dy, ban'dy-legged** *a.* having crooked legs. [v. fr. F. *bander*; n. orig. the curved stick for playing]

bane *n.* ruin, destruction; poison. **-bane'ful** *a.* **-bane'fully** *adv.* **-bane'-fulness** *n.* [OE. *bana*, murderer]

bang *n.* heavy blow; sudden loud noise, explosion. *-v.t.* beat, strike violently; slam; make a loud noise. [ON. *banga*, beat, of imit. orig.]

bang'le (-ng'-gl) *n.* ring worn on arm or leg [Hind. *bangri*]

ban'ian, ban'yan *n.* far-spreading Indian tree with rooting branches; Indian trader; loose jacket or gown. [Port., fr. Hind. *banya*, merchant]

ban'ish *v.t.* condemn to exile; drive away. **-ban'ishment** *n.* [F. *bannir*, proclaim outlaw. cp. *ban*]

ban'ister *n.* corrupt, of **baluster** (q.v.)

ban'jo *n.* musical instrument, having a body like a flat drum, a long neck and strings played with the fingers. **-ban'joist** *n.* [earlier *banjore*, corrupt. of old bandore; L. *pandura*]

bank *n.* mound or ridge of earth; margin of a river, lake *etc.* ; rising ground in the sea. *-v.t.* and *i.* enclose with a ridge; pile up; of an airplane, tilt inwards in turning. [ME. *banker*]

bank *n.* establishment for keeping, lending, exchanging, *etc.* money. *-v.t.* put in a bank. *-v.i.* keep or deal with a bank. **-bank'er** *n.* **-bank'ing** *n.* [fr. It. *banca*, orig. a money-changer's bench]

bank *n.* bench in a galley; row or rank. [OF. *banc*, bench]

banket' *n.* S. African gold-bearing conglomerate. [Du. *banketje*, almond rock]

bank'rupt *n.* one who fails in business,

cannot pay his debts. -*a.* insolvent. -**bank'ruptcy** *n.* insolvency. [earlier *bankrout*, fr. It. *banca rotta*, broken bank]

banks'ia *n.* flowering shrub. [Sir J. Banks, 1744–1820]

bann'er *n.* flag bearing a device; a country's flag. [F. *bannière*]

bann'ock *n.* flat home-made cake of oatmeal or barley. [Gael. *bannach*]

banns *n. See* **ban.**

banq'uet (bang'-kwet) *n.* feast. -*v.i.* feast. -*v.t.* give a feast to -**banq'ueter** *n.* [F., dim. of *banc*, bench]

ban'shee *n.* Irish fairy who wails to portend a death. [Ir. *bean sidhe*, fairy woman]

ban'tam *n.* dwarf variety of domestic fowl; boxing weight. [place in Java]

ban'ter *v.t.* make fun of -*n.* raillery in fun. [orig. unknown]

bant'ing *n.* slimming dietary. [W. Banting, its inventor]

bant'ling *n.* child; brat. [fr. arch. Ger. *bänkling*, bastard]

Ban'tu *n.* native name for many races and languages of S. and Central Africa. [native word, *people*]

ba'obab (ā'-) *n.* African tree of enormous girth, the monkey-bread. [native name]

baptize' (-iz') *v.t.* immerse in or sprinkle with water ceremonially; christen. -**bap'tism** *n.* -**baptis'mal** (-iz') *a.* **baptis'mally** *adv.* -**bap'tist** *n.* believer in baptism by immersion only. [G. *baptizein*, immerse]

bar *n.* rod of any substance; bank of sand at the mouth of a river; rail in a law-court; body of lawyers; counter where drinks are served; shop where alcoholic drinks are served and consumed. -*v.t.* make fast; obstruct; hinder, shut out (in); except. *prep.* except. -**bar'code'** *n.* a machine-readable arrangement of numbers and parallel lines of different widths printed on a package, which can be electronically scanned at a checkout to give the price of the goods and to activate computer stock-checking and reordering. -**barr'ing** *prep.* excepting. [F. *barre*]

barb *n.* curved jag on the point of a spear, fish-hook *etc.* -*v.t.* furnish with such jags. [fr. L. *barba*, beard]

bar'barous *a.* savage, brutal, uncivilized. -**barba'rian** *n.* -**barbar'ic** *a.* -**bar'barism** *n.* -**barbar'ity** *n.* -**bar'barously** *adv.* [G. *barbaros*, foreign]

bar'bary ape *n.* magot; small, tailless ape of Gibraltar and Africa. [Barbary]

barb'ecue (-kui) *n.* ox *etc.* roasted whole; outdoor party at which food is cooked over charcoal; frame for cooking in this manner. -*v.t.* [Sp. *barbacoa*]

bar'ber *n.* one who shaves beards and cuts hair. [L. *barba*, beard]

bar'berry *n.* thorny shrub with red berries and yellow flowers, frequently cultivated for ornamental hedges. [L. *berberis*]

bar'bican *n.* watch-tower over town or castle gate. [OF. *barbacane*]

bar'bital *n.* an addictive, hypnotic drug, veronal. -**barbitu'ric a'cid,** an acid derived from urea. -**barbitu'rate** *n.* salt or ester of barbit'uric acid; any of a variety of sedative or hypnotic drugs. [fr. *usnea barbata* (lichen) and *uric* acid]

bar'carolle *n.* boat-song, gondolier's song. [It. *barca*, boat]

bard *n.* poet, minstrel, *esp.* among the Celtic races. -**bard'ic** *a.* [Gael.]

bare *a.* uncovered; naked; poor, scanty. -*v.t.* make bare. -**bare'ly** *adv.* -**bare'ness** *n.* -**bare'back** *a.* and *adv.* without a saddle. -**bare'faced** *a.* impudent. -**bare'foot** *a.* -**barefoot doctor** *n.* (*esp.* in China) a worker trained as a medical auxiliary in a rural area who dispenses medicine, gives first aid, assists at childbirth, *etc.*

bar'gain (-gin) *n.* contract or agreement; favorable purchase -*v.*i. make a bargain; chaffer. [OE. *bargagne*]

barge *n.* flat-bottomed freight boat; state or pleasure boat. -**barge'man, bargee'** *n.* [fr. L. *barca*, bark, boat]

baril'la *n.* crude carbonate of soda, used in making glass *etc.* [Sp. *barrilla*]

baritone *n.* voice between tenor and bass. *a.* having such a voice. [G. *barus*, heavy, *tonos*, tone]

ba'rium *n.* metal element. -**bar'ic** *a.* [fr. G. *barus*, heavy]

bark *n.* rind of a tree. -*v.t.* strip the bark from; rub off (skin). [ON. *börkr*]

bark, barque *n.* small ship; three-masted vessel with fore and main masts square-rigged and mizzen mast fore-and-aft rigged. -**barq'uentine** *n.* ship like a barque, but with main mast also fore-and-aft rigged. [F. *barque*]

bark *v.i.* utter a sharp cry, *esp.* of a dog. -*n.* cry of a dog, *etc.* [OE. *beorcan*]

bar'ley *n.* hardy grain used for food and for making malt liquors and spirits. -**bar'leycorn** *n.* grain of barley. -**bar'ley-su'gar** *n.* sweetmeat made with barley. [OE. *bærlic a.*]

barm *n.* yeast. -**barm'y** *a.* (*sl.*) crazy,

flighty. [OE. *beorma*; Dan. *barme*]

barn *n.* building to store grain, hay, *etc.* **-barn'door, barn'yard** *a.* rustic. [OE. *bern* for *bere-ærn*, barley-house]

bar'nacle *n.* shellfish which sticks to rocks and bottoms of ships. **-bar'nacle goose** *n.* species of wild goose. [fr. OF. *bernaque*]

barom'eter *n.* instrument to measure the weight or pressure of the atmosphere, indicate weather changes. **-bar'ograph** *n.* recording barometer. **-baromet'ric** *a.* [G. *baros*, weight]

bar'on *n.* title of nobility, in Britain a peer of the lowest rank. **-bar'oness** *fem.* **-bar'onage** *n.* **-baro'nial** *a.* **-bar'ony** *n.* **-bar'on of beef'**, double sirloin. [F.]

bar'onet *n.* in Britain the lowest heredi tary title, inferior to baron but superior to knight. **-bar'onetage** *n.* **-bar'onetcy** *n.* [dim. of *baron*]

baroque' (-k) *a.* in art, extravagantly ornamented; irregularly shaped. [F.]

barouche' (-oosh') *n.* four-wheeled carriage with folding top or hood. [it. *baroccio*–L. *bis*, twice, *rota*, wheel]

barque, barquentine. *See* **bark.**

barr'ack *n.* building for soldiers; huge bare building. [F. *baraque*, bul]

barr'ack *v.t.* and *i.* jeer at. [orig. uncertain]

barracuda (-ōō-) *n.* voracious W. Indian fish. [orig. unknown]

barr'age (-azh) *n.* dam built across a river; curtain of shellfire (barrage balloons, mines) to cover an attack *etc.* **-barr'age-balloon** *n.* [F.]

barr'atry *n.* fraud on owners by master or crew of a ship; stirring up of suits by lawyers. **-barra'tor** *n.* **-barr'atrous** *a.* [OF. *barat*, fraud]

barr'el *n.* round wooden vessel, made of curved staves bound with hoops; quantity held by such vessel; anything long and hollow, as tube of a gun. *-v.t.* put in a barrel. **-barr'elled** *a.* [F. *baril*]

barr'en *a.* unfruitful, sterile; unprofitable. **-barr'enness** *n.* [OF. *brehaing*]

bar'ricade *n.* improvised fortification against an enemy. *-v.t.* obstruct; fortify. [F., fr. *barrique*, cask]

bar'rier *n.* fence, obstruction; any obstacle. [F. *barrière*, fr. L. *barra*, bar]

bar'rister *n.* in Britain lawyer in the higher law courts. [fr. *bar* of the Inns of Court]

bar'row *n.* small wheeled hand carriage. [OE. *bearwe*, bier]

bar'row *n.* prehistoric burial mound; tumulus. [OE. *beorg*, hill]

bar'ter *v.i.* traffic by exchange of things. *-v.t.* give (one thing) in exchange for another. *-n.* traffic by exchange. [OF. *barater*, haggle]

bar'ton *n.* farmyard. [OE. *beretun*-bere, barley, *tun*, enclosure]

bas'alt (-sawlt) *n.* dark-colored, hard igneous rock. **-basalt'ic** *a.* [L. *basaltes*]

base *n.* bottom, foundation; starting point; fixed point. *-v.t.* found, establish. **-bas'sic** *a.* **-base'less** *a.* **-base'ment** *n.* lowest story of a building; room or rooms in a building which are below ground level. **-ba'sic English,** simplified form of the English language, based on a limited number of root words. **-ba'sic slag,** fertilizer, a by-product of steel manufacture. [G. *basis*, step, pedestal]

base *a.* low, mean; despicable. **-base'ly** *adv.* **-base'ness** *n.* **-base'-born** *a.* **base-mind'ed** *a.* [VL. *bassus*, stumpy]

base'ball *n.* ball game played by two teams of nine players on an open field and in which the runner must complete a circuit of four bases to score; the ball used in this game. [fr. 'prisoners' base', where *base* is for *bars*]

bash *v.t.* smash in. [orig. unknown]

bash'ful *a.* shy, modest, wanting confidence. **-bash'fully** *adv.* **-bash'fulness** *n.* [*abash*]

ba'sic. *See* **base.**

BA'SIC *n.* a computer programming language that uses common English terms. [*fr. B*eginner's *A*ll-purpose *S*ymbolic *I*nstruction *C*ode]

basil'ica *n.* large Roman hall with colonnades and apse; church built in this style. [L. -G. *basilike*, king's house, palace]

bas'ilisk *n.* fabulous small fire-breathing dragon. [G. *basiliskos*, little king, from its crown-like crest]

ba'sin *n.* deep circular dish; a sink; dock; hollow holding water; land drained by a river. [F. *bassin*]

ba'sis *n.* foundation, groundwork. [G.]

bask (-a-) *v.i.* lie in warmth and sunshine. [ON. *bathask*, bathe]

bas'ket *n.* vessel made of interwoven twigs, rushes *etc.* [orig. doubtful]

basque (bask) *n.* short-skirted jacket, bodice. [F. *Basque*]

Basque (bask) *n.* name of people of W. Pyrenees in Spain and France; their non-Aryan language. (F.]

bas-relief' (ba-) *n.* sculpture in which the

figures do not stand out much. [It. *bassorilievo. See* **base** and **relief**]
bass (bas) *n.* lowest part in music; man's lowest voice; one having such a voice. *-a.* low in the scale, deep. [It. *basso*, base]
bass (bas) *n.* sea-fish of the perch family. [OE. *bærs*]
bas'sinet *n.* baby-carriage or cradle. [orig. doubtful]
bassoon' *n.* wood-wind instrument. **-bassoon'ist** *n.* [F. *basson. See* **bass**]
bast *n.* inner bark of trees (*esp.* lime-tree); fibre; matting. [OE. bæst]
bas'tard *n.* child born of parents not married. *-a.* illegitimate; not genuine. -**bas'tardy** *n.* [OF. *bastard*, also *fils de bast*, son of a pack-saddle]
baste *v.t.* beat with a stick. **-ba'sting** *n.* [Jocular use of *v.i.* baste, anoint]
baste *v.t.* drop melted fat over (roasting meat). [OF. *basser*, soak]
baste *v.t.* sew together loosely. [OF. *bastir*, build; OHG. *bestan*, sew]
bastina'do, bastinade' *n.* beating with a stick, *esp.* on the soles of the feet. *-v.t.* beat thus. [Sp. *bastonada*, fr. *baston*, stick]
bas'tion *n.* projecting part of a fortifi cation. [F. -OF. *bastir*, build]
bat *n.* heavy stick; flat club, *esp.* as used in baseball, cricket, *etc.* *-v.i.* use the bat in a game. **-bat'ter** *n.* **-bat'ting** *n.* [OE. *batt*, club]
bat *n.* mouse-like flying animal of nocturnal habits. [ME. *bakke*]
batch *n.* quantity of bread baked at one time; any quantity or number; set. [ME. *bache*, fr. *bake*]
bate *v.* same as **abate.**
bath (-a'-) *n.* water to plunge the body in; act of bathing; vessel for bathing. *-v.t.* wash. **-bath'house** *n.* **-bath'room** *n.* **bath'tub** *n.* [OE. *bæth*]
bathe *v.t.* and *i.* wash. **-ba'ther** *n.* -**ba'thing** *n.* [OE. *bathian*]
ba'thos *n.* ludicrous descent from the elevated to the mean in writing or speech. [G. = depth]
bath'ysphere *n.* sphere for submarine observation. [G. *bathys*, deep, *sphaira*, sphere]
bat'ik *n.* process of dyeing with several colors; fabric so treated; design so produced. [Javanese]
bat'man *n.* officer's servant or groom. [fr. F. *bât*, pack-saddle]
bat'on *n.* staff, *esp.* of a policeman, conductor or marshal. [F. *bâton*]
batra'chia (-ri'-ke-a) *n.pl.* order to which frogs belong. **-batra'chian** *n.* animal of this order. [G. *batrachos*, frog]
battalion (-yun) *n.* division of the army consisting of several companies and units of soldiers; troops in battle array. [F. *bataillon. See* **battle**]
bat'ten *n.* (*naut.*) piece of wood to secure hatches; any narrow strip of wood. (*baton*)
bat'ten *v.i.* grow fat; live luxuriously. [Ice. *batna*, grow better]
bat'ter *v.t.* strike continuously. *-n.* ingredients beaten up with liquid into a paste. **-bat'tering-ram** *n.* former military engine for beating down walls *etc.* [F. *battre*, beat]
bat'tery *n.* number of cannon; place where they are mounted; unit of artillery, men horses and guns; (*law*) assault by beating; (*electr.*) set of voltaic cells in which electric current is stored, [F. *batterie*]
bat'tle *n.* fight between armies. *-v.i.* fight, struggle. [F. *batailie*]
bat'tledore *n.* bat for striking a ball or shuttlecock. [Sp. *batidor*, 'washing-beetle']
bat'tlement *n.* wall on a fortification with openings or embrasures. [OF. *batillement*]
bau'ble *n.* jester's stick; trifle, trinket. [OF. *baubel*, toy]
baulk. *See* **balk.**
baux'ite *n.* aluminum-yielding clay. [F. *les Beaux*, near Arles]
bawd *n.* procurer, procuress; prostitute; keeper of brothel. **-bawd'y** *a.* lewd. **-bawd'y-house** *n.* brothel. [M. E. *bawdstrot*, pander]
bawl *v.i.* shout; speak noisily. *-n.* shout. [orig. uncertain]
bay *a.* reddish-brown. *-n.* horse of this colour. [fr. L. *badius*]
bay *n.* wide inlet of the sea. [Late L. *baia*]
bay *n.* space between two columns; recess. **-bay'-window** *n.* window in a recess. [F. *baie*, fr. *bayer*, gape]
bay *n.* laurel-tree. *-pl.* honorary crown of victory. [F. *baie*, berry]
bay *n.* bark; cry of hounds in pursuit. *v.i.* bark. *v.t.* bark at. [earlier *abay*, OF. *abaier*, bark]
bay'onet *n.* stabbing weapon fixed to a rifle. *-v.t.* stab with a bayonet. [F. *baionette*, perh. fr. *Bayonne*]
bazaar' (-zar') *n.* Eastern market; fancy fair; a sale for charity; a shop, *usu.* selling goods cheaply. [Pers. *bazar*, market]
bazoo'ka *n.* portable anti-tank gun. [orig. uncertain]
be *v.i.* live; exist; have a state or quality. [OE. *beon*, exist]

beach *n.* shore of the sea. *-v.t.* run on the shore. **-beach'head** *n.* strong position on enemy beach. [orig. unknown]

beac'on *n.* signal-fire; sea-mark; radio transmitter to guide ships or aircraft; traffic lights. [OE. *beacn*]

bead *n.* little ball pierced for threading on a string; narrow molding; flange of tire. **-bead'ed** *a.* **-bead'ing** *n.* **-bead'y** *a.* [OE. *gebed*, prayer (*beads* of rosary)]

bea'dle *n.* mace-bearer; parish-officer; church officer. [OF. *bedel*]

beads'man, bedes'man *n.* one endowed to pray for the founder. *[bead]*

bea'gle *n.* small hound. [ME. *begle*]

beak *n.* bill of a bird; anything pointed or projecting. [F. *bec*]

beak'er *n.* large drinking-cup; glass vessel used by chemists. [ON. *bikarr*]

beam *n.* long squared piece of wood; ship's widest part; bar of a balance; shaft of light. *-v.t.* emit in rays. *-v.i.* shine. *-a.* (of radio transmission) in a controlled direction. **-beam-ends** *n. pl.* ship's side. [OE. = *tree*]

bean *n.* any of various kinds of leguminous plants and their seeds. [OE.]

bear *v.t.* carry; support; endure; produce; press (upon). **-born** *p.p.* brought into being. **-borne** *pp.* carried. [OE. *beran*]

bear *n.* heavy, partly-carnivorous quadruped; rough fellow; speculator for a fall in stocks. [OE. *bera*]

beard *n.* hair on the chin; similar growth in plants. *-v.t.* defy. [OE.]

beast *n.* animal; four-footed animal; brutal man; **-beast'liness** *n.* **-beast'ly** *a.* [OF. *beste*]

beat *v.t.* strike repeatedly; overcome. *-v.i.* throb; sail against the wind. *-n.* stroke; pulsation; regularly-trodden course. [OE. *beatan*]

beat'ify (be-at'-) *v.t.* make happy; pronounce in eternal happiness (the first step in canonization). **-beatific** *a.* **-beatifica'tion** *n.* **-beat'itude** *n.* [L. *beatus*, blessed, *facere*, make]

beat'itude *n.* heavenly happiness, bliss; blessing; blessedness. [L. *beatitudo—beatus*, blessed]

beau *n.* lover; fop or dandy. **-bell** *fem.* **-beaux** *n.pl.* **-beau geste**, magnanimous gesture. [F. *beau, bel*-L. *bellus*, beautiful]

Beaune *n.* a Burgundy wine. [*Beaune*, town]

beaut'y *n.* loveliness, grace; beautiful person or thing. **-beaut'eous** *a.* **-beautic'ian** *n.* keeper of a beauty-parlor. **-beaut'iful** *a.* **-beaut'ifully** *adv.* **-beaut'ify** *v.t.* **-beaut'y-parlor** *n.* salon for the skilled application of cosmetics *etc.* [F. *beauté*]

beav'er *n.* amphibious rodent quadruped; its fur; hat made of the fur. **-beav'er-board** *n.* wood-fiber board used in building. [OE. *beofor*]

becalm' (-kam') *v.t.* make calm; deprive of wind. [*calm*]

because' *adv.* and *conj.* by reason of; on account of. [earlier *by cause*]

beck *n.* sign, gesture; nod. [fr. obs. v. *beck*, beckon]

beck *n.* brook. [ON. *bekkr*]

beck'on *v.i.* make a silent signal. *-v.t.* call by a nod, or movement of the finger. [OE. *bicnan*, fr. *beacn*, sign, beacon]

become' (-kum') *v.i.* come to be. *-v.t.* suit. **-becom'ing** *a.* suitable to; graceful. [OE. *becuman*, fr. *come*]

bed *n.* couch or place to sleep on; place in which anything rests, in architecture, *etc.*; bottom of a river; layer, stratum; garden plot. *-v.t.* lay in a bed; plant. **-bed'ding** *n.* **-bed'ridden** *a.* **-bed'rock** *n.* **-bed'room** *n.* **-bed'stead** *n.* [OE. *bedd*]

bedesman. *See* **beadsman.**

bedev'il *v.t.* to torment greatly, to frustrate repeatedly. [*devil*]

bedi'zen *v.t.* dress gaudily. **-bedi'zened** *a.* [for *dizen*, put flax on a distaff]

bed'lam *a.* place of uproar; lunatic asylum. **-bed'lamite** *n.* [*Bethlehem* (Hospital of St. Mary of Bethlehem, London, converted into lunatic asylum)]

Bed'ouin (-ōō-in) *n.* member of nomadic tribe of Arabia; gypsy. [Arab. *badawin*]

bedragg'le *v.t.* dirty by dragging in mud or water, **-bedragg'led** *a.* [*draggle*]

bee *n.* insect that makes honey; bee-like association of persons in some activity, as sewing-bee, spelling-bee. **-bee'hive** *n*-. **beeline** *n.* shortest route. **-bees'wax** *n.* [OE. *beo*]

beech *n.* common tree with smooth silvery bark and small nuts. **-beech'en** *a.* **-beech'mast** *n.* beech nuts. [OE. *bece*]

beef *n.* flesh of an ox or cow. **-beefy** *a.* fleshy, stolid. [F. *boeuf*, ox]

beef'eater *n.* yeoman of the guard; a warder of the Tower of London. [*beef-eater*, well-fed servant]

beer *n.* fermented alcoholic beverage made from malt and hops. **-beer'house** *n.* **-beer'y** *a.* [OE. *beor*]

beet *n.* plant with a carrot-shaped root, used as a vegetable (red variety) or to extract sugar (white variety). [OE. *bete*]

beet'le *n.* coleopterous insect. **-beet'le browed** *a.* with prominent brows. [OE. *bitela-bitan*, bite]

beet'le *n.* heavy wooden mallet; potato masher. [OE. *bietl*, beater]

befall' (-awl') *v.i.* happen. *-v.t.* happen to. [OE. *befeallan*]

befit' *v.t.* be suitable to. **-befitt'ing** *a.* **-befitt'ingly** *adv.* [*fit*]

before' *prep.* in front of, in presence of, in preference to; earlier than. *-adv.* ahead; earlier; in front; in advance. *-conj.* sooner than. [OE. *beforan*]

befoul' (-owl') *v.t.* make dirty. [*foul*]

befriend' (-rend') *v.t.* help. [*friend*]

beg *v.t.* ask earnestly, beseech; take for granted, *esp.* in begging the question, taking for granted what ought to have been proved. *-v.i.* ask for or live on alms. **-beg'gar** *n.* **-beg'garly** *a.* **-beg'gary** *n.* [OF. *begard*, fr. Med. L. *begardus*, member of a certain mendicant order. The *v.* is fr. the *n.*]

beget' *v.t.* produce, generate. **-begett'er** *n.* [OE. *begilan*, fr. *get*]

begin' *v.i.* take rise; commence. *-v.t.* enter on, originate. **-beginn'er** *n.* **beginn'ing** *n.* [OE. *beginnan*]

begone' *int.* away! be off! [lit. *be gone*]

bego'nia *n.* genus of low-growing plants with large, richly colored flowers. [fr. botanist Michael *Begon*]

begrudge' *v.t.* grudge, envy anyone the possession of something; give unwillingly. [*grudge*]

beguile' (-gil') *v.t.* cheat; wile away. **-beguile'ment** *n.* **-begui'ler** *n.* [*guile*]

be'gum *n.* Muslim princess or high-ranking lady. [Urdu, *begam*]

behalf' (-haf') *n.* favor, benefit (in phrases such as *on behalf of*). [fr. *by (the) half*; OE. *healf*, half side]

behave' *v.i.* bear, carry, conduct (oneself). **-beha'vior** (-yer) *n.* conduct. **-beha'viorism** *n.* psychological approach based on the (objective) study of reaction to external stimulus. [*have*]

behead' *v.t.* cut off the head. [*head*]

behest' *n.* charge, command. [OE. *behæs*, vow, promise]

behind' (-hi'-) *prep.* in the rear of. *-adv.* in the rear. **-behind'hand** *a.* in arrears, tardy. *-adv.* [OE. *behiadan*]

behold' *v.t.* watch, see. **-behold'en** *a.* bound in gratitude. **-behold'er** *n.* onlooker. [OE. *behealdan*]

behoof' *n.* use, benefit. **-behove'** *v.i.* be fit, right, necessary; (only impersonal). [OE. *behofian*, need]

beige (-ezh) *n.* fabric of undyed wool; its color. *a.* [F.]

be'ing *n.* existence; creature. [*be*]

bel *n.* 10 transmission units or decibels, *q.v.* [Graham *Bell*, inventor]

bela'bor *v.t.* beat soundly. [*labor*]

bela'ted *a.* tardy, late. [*late*]

belay' *v.t.* (*naut.*) fasten a running rope by coiling it round a cleat. [*lay*]

belch *v.i.* void wind by the mouth. *-v.t.* eject violently; cast up. *-n.* emission of wind, *etc.* [OE. *bealcian*]

bel'dam *n.* old woman, *esp.* an ugly one; hag. [orig. *grandmother*-F. *belle* and *dame*]

beleag'uer (-er) *v.t.* besiege. [Du. *belegeren*, fr. *leger*, camp]

bel'fry *n.* bell-tower. [OHG. *bergfrid*, guard-peace, watchtower]

belie' *v.t.* falsify; counterfeit; speak falsely of [OE. *beleogan*, deceive]

believe' *v.t.* regard as true; trust in. *-v.i.* have faith; suppose. **-belief'** *n.* **believable** *a.* **-believ'er** *n.* **-believ'ing** *a.* [ME. *beleven*]

belit'tle *v.t.* cause to appear small; make small. **-belit'tlement** *n.* [*little*]

bell *n.* hollow metal vessel to give a ringing sound when struck; anything shaped like a bell; sound of a bell. **-bell'buoy** *n.* **-bell'-founder** *n.* **-bell'- man** *n.* town crier. **-bell'ringer** *n* . **bell'weth'er** *n.* leading sheep of flock with bell on its neck. [OE. *belle*]

bel'ladonna *n.* deadly nightshade; narcotic drug made from it. [It. *bella donna*, fair lady (it was used to brighten the eyes by enlarging the pupils)]

belle *n.* beautiful woman; fairest lady (*e.g.* at a ball). [F.]

belles lettres *n. pl.* elegant literature; its aesthetic study. [F. = fine letters]

bel'licose *a.* war-like. [L. *bellicosus*]

belli'gerent (-ij'-) *a.* waging war. *-n.* nation or person taking part in war. [L. *belligerare*, wage war (*bellum*)]

bel'low *v.i.* roar like a bull; shout. *-n.* roar of a bull; any deep cry or shout. [OE. *bylgan*]

bel'lows *n.* instrument for making a blast of air (to blow up a fire, *etc.*). [fr. OE. *bielg*, belly; the full OE. name was *blæst-belg*, blast-bag]

bel'ly *n.* part of the body which contains the bowels; stomach. *-v.t.* and *i.* swell out. [OE. *belg*]

belong′ *v.i.* be the property or attribute of, be connected with. [earlier *long*, as though 'go along with']

belov′ed (-luv′-) *a.* much loved. (fr. obs. v. *belove*]

below′ *adv.* beneath; unworthy of. *-prep.* lower than. [*by low*]

belt *n.* band; girdle. *-v.t.* furnish, surround, or mark, with a belt. [OE.]

belu′ga *n.* white sturgeon; white whale. [Russ.]

bel′vedere *n.* turret room or summer-house with a view. [It.]

bemoan′ *v.t.* lament, show grief by moaning. [*moan*]

bemuse′ *v.t.* stupefy, confuse; **-bemused′** *a.* [*muse*]

bench *n.* long seat; seat or body of judges, *etc.* *-v.t.* place on a bench. [OE. *benc*]

bend *v.t.* curve or bow. -*v.i.* take a curved shape. *-n.* curve. [OE. *bendan*]

beneath′ *prep.* under, lower than. *-adv.* in a lower position. [OE. *beneothan*]

ben′edick, ben′edict *n.* married (*esp.* newly-married) man. [Shakespearian character]

Benedic′tine *n.* monk of the Order of St. Benedict; Black Friar; a liqueur. [St. *Benedict*]

benedic′tion *n.* invocation of the divine blessing. [L. *benedictio*]

ben′efit *n.* advantage, favor, profit, good. *-v.t.* do good to. *-v.i.* receive good. **-benefac′tion** *n.* **-benefac′tor** *n-* **. benefactress** *fem.* **-ben′efice** *n.* ecclesiastical living. **-benef′icence** *n.* **-benef′icent** *a.* **-benefi′cently** *adv.* **benefi′cial** *a.* **- benefi′cially** *adv.* **-benefi′ciary** *n.* [L. *benefactum*, well done]

benev′olent *a.* kindly, charitable. **-benev′olence** *n.* **- benev′olently** *adv.* [L. *bene*, well, *volens*, wishing]

benight′ed *a.* overtaken by night; in mental or moral darkness; ignorant. [*night*]

benign′ (-in) *a.* kindly, mild, gentle; favorable. **-benig′nancy** *n.* **-benig′nant** *a.* **-benig′nantly** *adv.* **-benig′nity** *n.* **- benign′ly** *adv.* [L. *benignus*]

ben′ison *n.* blessing. [L. *benedictionis*]

bent *n.* kind of wiry grass. [OE. *beonot-* (in place-names)]

bent *n.* inclination, turn of mind. [*bend*]

ben′thos *n.* sea-bottom flora and fauna. [G. = depth]

benumb′ (-m) *v.t.* deaden, stupefy. [OE. *beniman*, deprive]

Ben′zedrine *n.* amphetamine, synthetic drug stimulating central nervous system. [Trademark]

ben′zene *n.* tarry liquid distilled from oil; by-product of coal-tar. **-ben′zine** *n.* distillate of petroleum. **-ben′zol** *n.* benzene. **- ben′zoline** *n.* impure benzene or benzine. **-ben′zion** *n.* aromatic gum. [earlier *benjoin*, fr. Arab. *luban jawi*, Java frankincense]

bequeath′ (-th) *v.t.* leave by will. **- bequest′** *n.* act of bequeathing; legacy. [OE. *becwethan* -be- and *cwethan*, say]

becqu′erel *n.* the derived unit of radioactivity equal to one disintegration per second. [fr. A. H. *Bequerel*, physicist]

berceuse′ *n.* lullaby, cradle-song. [F.]

bereave′ *v.t.* rob of **-bereave′ment** *n.* [OE. *bereafian*, plunder]

beret′ (be′-rã) *n.* woolen cap, orig. of the Basques. [F.]

ber′gamot *n.* strongly-flavoured pear; type of orange; oil, perfume extracted from this. [*Bergamo*, Italy or *Bergama* (Pergamum) Asia Minor]

ber′iberi *n.* tropical deficiency disease. [Cingalese]

berr′y *n.* small stoneless fruit. **-berr′ied** *a.* bearing berries. [OE. *berie*]

ber′serk *a.* frenzied with rage; filled with the fighting fury of a berserk. *-n.* Norse worrior. [Ice. *berserkr*]

berth *n.* shipés anchoring place; place to sleep in a ship; employment, situation. *v.t.* moor. [*bear*, in naut., sense of direction]

Bertillonage′ (-azh′) *n.* system of criminal identification by measurements. [*Bertillon*, inventor]

ber′yl *n.* greenish or bluish precious stone; aquamarine. **-beryl′lium** *n.* the white metal glucinium. [G. *beryllos*]

beseech′ *v.t.* entreat, implore. [ME. *sechen*, seek]

beset′ *v.t.* assail, invest. [OE. *besettan*)

beside′ *prep.* by the side of, near; distinct from. **-besides′** *adv.* and *prep.* in addition, otherwise, over and above. [OE. *bi sidan* by the side]

beseige′ *v.t.* invest, beset with armed forces; throng round [*seige*]

be′som *n.* broom, *usu.* of twigs or heather. [OE. *besema*]

besot′ *v.t.* make a sot; infatuate; stupefy. **-besott′ed** *a.* [*sot*]

bespeak′ *v.t.* engage beforehand; stipulate; betoken. [*speak*]

best *a.*, *adv.* superlative of good or well. *v.t.* defeat. **-best-man** *n.* groomsman at a wedding. **-best-sel′ler** *n.* book with large sales. [OE. *bet(e)st. See* **better**]

bes'tial *a.* like a beast; rude; brutal. -**bestial'ity** *n.* [L. *bestialis*]

bestir' *v.t.* rouse to lively action. [*stir*]

bestow' *v.t.* give; put away; accommodate. -**bestow'al** *n.* [*stow*]

bestride' *v.t.* sit or stand over with legs apart. [OE. *bestridan*, sit on a horse]

bet *n.* wager. -*v.t.* and *i.* wager. [prob. shortened fr. *abet*]

betake' *v. refl.* go (to); have recourse (to). [*take*]

be'ta-rays' *n.pl..* streams of electrons given off by radioactive substances. [G. letter *beta*]

be'tel *n.* an evergreen shrub indigenous to the E. Indies; people in Asia chew its leaves; -**betel nut** *n.* the fruit of the Areca palm [through Port. from Malayan-*vettila*]

betide' *v.i.* happen. [*tidings*]

betimes' *adv.* early, in good time; seasonably. [earlier *betime*, by time]

bet'ony *n.* woodland plant yielding a yellow dye, and formerly used in medicine. [F.]

betray' *v.t.* give up treacherously; be disloyal to; mislead; reveal, show signs of. -**betray'al** *n.* -**betray'er** *n.* [L. *tradere*, hand over]

betroth' (-oth') *v.t.* bind to marry, affiance. -**betroth'al** *n.* -**betrothed'** *a.*and *n.* [ME. *bitreuthien*]

bett'er *a.* and *adv.* comparative of good and well. -*v.t.* and *i.* improve. -**bett'er oneself**, improve one's (financial *etc.*) conditions. [OE. *betera*, compar. of a lost stem*bat*-]

between', betwixt' *prep*, in the middle of two, of space, time, *etc.*; in the middle or intermediate space. -*adv.* midway. [OE. *betweonum*, by twain, and OE. *betweox*, fr. *twisc*, twofold]

bev'el *n.* slant, diagonal surface; tool for setting off angles. -*a.* slanted. -*v.t.* cut away to a slope. [cp. F. *biveau*]

bev'erage *n.* liquor for drinking. [OF. *bevrage*, fr. *beivre*, L. *bibere*, drink]

bev'y *n.* flock of birds, *esp.* quails; company, *esp.* of ladies. [AF. *bevee*, further orig. unknown]

bewail' *v.t.* lament. [*wail*]

beware' *v.i.* be on one's guard. [*ware*]

bewil'der *v.t.* puzzle, lead astray. **bewil'dering** *a.* -**bewil'deringly** *adv.* -**bewil'derment** *n.* confusion of mind. [fr. obs. *wildern*, wilderness]

bewitch' *v.t.* affect by witchcraft; charm, fascinate. -**bewitch'ing** *a.* enchanting. -**bewitch'ingly** *adv.* [*witch*]

bewray' *v.t.* reveal unintentionally. [OE. *wregan*, accuse]

bey *n.* Turkish governor. [Turk. *beg*]

beyond' *adv.* farther away. -*prep.* on the farther side of; later than; surpassing, out of reach of. [OE. *begeondan*]

bez'el *n.* part of a setting which holds a precious stone. [OF. *bisel*]

bezique' (-zek') *n.* card game played with 2 or 4 packs from which cards below 7 are removed. [F. *besique*]

bhang *n.* narcotic, leaf and shoot of Indian hemp. [Hind. *bhdng*]

bi'as *n.* slant; one-sided inclination; leaning, bent; swaying impulse. -*v.t.* influence. -**bi'ased** *a.* prejudiced. [F. *biais*]

bib *n.* cloth put under a child's chin. [ME. *bibben*, fr. L. *bibere*, drink]

Bi'ble *n.* Old and New Testaments, the sacred writings of the Christian Church. -**bib'lical** *a.* [G. *biblia*, books]

bibliog'raphy *n.* history and description of books. -**bibliog'rapher** *n.* - **bibliograph'ical** *a.* [G. *biblion*, book, *graphein*, write]

bib'ulous *a.* given to drinking. [L. *bibulus-bibere*, drink]

bi'centennial *n.* the day celebrating an event exactly 200 years previously. [fr. *bi*-, two, L. *centenarius*, century]

bi'ceps (-s-) *n.* two-headed muscle, *esp.* the muscle of the upper arm. [L. *bis*, twice, *caput*, head]

bick'er *v.i.* quarrel; quiver, flash. -**bick'ering** *n.* [orig. uncertain]

bi'cycle *n.* vehicle with two wheels, one in front of the other, propelled by pedals worked by the rider. -**bi'cyclist** *n.* [F. fr. *bi*-, two, and G. *kyklos*, wheel]

bid *v.t.* offer; command. -*n.* offer, *esp.* of a price at an auction sale. -**bid'der** *n.* -**bid'ding** *n.* [confusion of OE. *beodan*, offer, and *biddan*, request]

bide *v.i.* remain. -*v.t.* await. [OE. *bidan*, remain]

bienn'ial (bi-en'-) *a.* happening every two years; lasting two years. -*n.* plant which lives two years. -**bienn'ially** *adv.* [L. *biennium*, two years]

bier *n.* frame of wood for bearing the dead to the grave. [OE. *bær*]

bifo'cal (bi-fō'-) *a.* having two foci, *esp.* of spectacle lenses designed for near and distant vision. [*bi*-, two, and *focal*]

bifur'cate *a.* having two branches; forked. -*v.t.* and *i.* -**bifurca'tion** *n.* [L. *bifurcus*, two-pronged]

big *a.* large, great; pregnant; haughty.

-**big'ness** *n.* [orig. unknown]
big'amy *n.* crime of having two husbands or two wives at once. -**big'amist** *n.* [*bi-*, two, and G. *gamos*, marriage]
big'horn *n.* Rocky Mountain sheep or goat. (*big* and *horn*]
bight (bit) *n.* loop of a rope; bend or curve; bay. [OE. *byht*]
big'ot *n.* one blindly or obstinately devoted to a party or creed. -**big'oted** *a.* -**big'otry** *n.* narrow zeal. [F.]
bilat'eral (bi-) *a.* two-sided. [*lateral*]
bil'berry *n.* whortleberry, a plant with blue berries. [Dan. *böllebær*]
bile *n.* fluid secreted by the liver; (*fig.*) anger, bitter temper. -**bil'ious** *a.* **bil'iousness** *n.* [L. *bilis*]
bilge *n.* bottom of a ship's hull; foulness collecting therein. -*v.i.* spring a leak. -**bilge'-water** *n.* [form of *bulge*]
biling'ual (bi) *a.* having or written in two languages. -**biling'ualism** *n.* [fr. *bi-*, two, and L. *lingua*, tongue]
bilk *v.t.* cheat, evade. [corrupt. of *balk*]
bill *n.* tool for pruning; halberd, an old weapon. [OE. *bil*, sword]
bill *n.* bird's beak. -*v.i.* join bills, as doves; caress. [OE. *bile*]
bill *n.* note of charges; banknote; draft of proposed law; advertisement; commercial document. -*v.t.* announce by advertisement. -**bill'board** *n.* a large surface designed to exhibit bills for advertising **bill'fold** *n.* a folding pouch designed to carry paper money and other small personal belongings. [Late L. *billa*, *bulla*, seal]
bill'et *n.* note; civilian quarters for troops; resting-place; situation, post. -*v.t.* quarter, as troops. [F.]
bilt'et *n.* short thick stick; small log used as fuel. [OF. *billete*]
bill'iards (-ly-) *n.* game played on a table with balls and cues. (F. *bille*, ball, *billard*, cue]
bill'ion *n.* a thousand millions. [F.]
bill'ow *n.* great swelling wave. -*v.i.* rise in waves. [ON. *bylga*]
bill'y, bill'y-can *n.* (Australia) bushman's tin can used as kettle or tea-pot. [*Bill, William*]
bi-met'allism *n.* system using both gold and silver as standards of monetary value. [*bi-* and *metal*]
bimonth'ly (bi-) *a.* and *adv.* every two months; twice a month. [*month*]
bin *n.* receptacle for storing corn, wine, *etc.*, or for refuse. [OE. *binn*, manger]
bi'nary (bi'-) *a.* twofold. -*n.* double star, two stars revolving round the same center of gravity. [L. *bini*, two by two]
bind *v.t.* tie fast; tie round, gird, tie together; unite; put (a book) into a cover. -**bind'er** *n.* -**bind'ery** *n.* - **bind'ing** *a.* obligatory. -*n.* cover of a book. -**bind'weed** *n.* [OE. *bindan*]
bing *n.* pile, heap. [Scand.]
binge (-j-) *n.* (*sl.*) party or celebration, carouse, spree. [origin unknown]
binn'acle *n.* box in which a ship's compass is kept. [earlier *bittacle*, fr. L. *habitaculum*, little dwelling]
binoc'ular *a.* adapted to both eyes. -*n.* telescope made for two eyes (*usu.* in *pl.*). (L. *bini*, two together, *oculus*, eye]
bino'mial *a.* (*alg.*) quantity consisting of two terms, *e.g.*, a + b [L. *bi-*, twice, and *nomen*, a name, a term]
bi'o- *prefix* meaning life. [G. *bios*] forms compounds as **biochemistry** *n.* chemistry of living things. -**biodynam'ics** *n.* -**biogen'esis** *n.* -**biomet'ry** *n.* -**bi'oplasm** *n.* for which see the simple word.
biodegrad'able *a.* capable of decomposition by natural means. [L. *gradus*, degree]
biog'raphy *n.* story of a person's life. **biog'rapher** *n.* -**biograph'ical** *a.* **biograph'icafly** *adv.* (G. *graphein*, write]
biol'ogy *n.* science of life. -**biolog'ical** *a.* -**biolog'ically** *adv.* -**biol'ogist** *n.* [G. *logos*, discourse]
bion'ics *n.* study of relation of biological and electronic processes -**bion'ic** *a.* having physical functions augmented by electronic equipment. [fr. G. *bios*, life, and elect*ronic*]
bio'rhythm *n.* a cyclically recurring pattern of physiological states in an organism or organ, believed by some to affect physical and mental states and behavior. -**bio'rhythmic** *adv.* [G. *rhythmos*, rhythm]
bi'oscope *n.* early cinematograph. [G. *skopeein*, look at]
bipart'ite *a.* composed of two parts or parties. [*part*]
bi'ped (bi'-) *n.* two-footed animal. [L. *bipes-bi-*, two, *pes*, foot]
bi'plane (bi-') *n.* airplane with two planes in each wing. [*bi-*, two, and *plane*]
birch *n.* tree with smooth white bark; rod for punishment, made of birch twigs. -*v.t.* flog. [OE. *birce*]
bird *n.* feathered animal. [OE. *bridd*]
birth *n.* bearing or being born of, offspring; parentage. [ON. *byrth*]

bis'cuit (-kit) *n.* a soft bread in small cakes; pottery clay that has been fired once prior to glazing. *-a.* pale brown. [F., fr. L. *bis coctus*, twice baked]

bisect' (bi-) *v.t.* cut in equal halves. **bisect'or** *n.* [L. *bi-*, two, *secare*, cut]

bish'op *n.* clergyman in charge of a diocese; spiritual overseer. **-bish'opric** *n.* [G. *episkopos*, overseer]

bis'muth *n.* reddish-wbite metal, used in medicine. [Ger. *wismut*]

bi'son (bi'-) *n.* large wild ox, buffalo. [L.]

bissex'tile *n.* leap-year. [L. *bissextus*, twice sixth, the extra day being after the *sixth* before the Calends of March]

bit *n.* fragment, piece, bite; in computing, smallest unit of information. [OE. *bita*]

bit *n.* biting part of a tool; mouthpiece of a horse's bridle. *-v.t.* put the bit in. [OE. *bite*, bite]

bitch *n.* female dog. [OE. *bicce*]

bite *v.t.* cut into with the teeth; cut into generally; corrode. *-n.* act of biting; wound made by biting; mouthful. **-bi'ter** *n.* **-bi'ting** *a.* mordant, sarcastic. [OE. *bitan*]

bitt'er *a.* harsh-tasting; sharp, painful; stinging. **-bitt'erly** *adv.* **-bitt'erness** *n.* **-bitt'ers** *n. pl.* bitter medicines or essences. [OE. *biter*]

bitt'ern *n.* bird like a heron, with a booming cry. [F. *butor*]

bitts *n. pl.* posts on ship's deck to which cables are fastened. [ON. *biti*, crossbeam]

bit'umen *n.* any of various flammable mineral substances, *e.g.*, petroleum, asphalt, *etc.* **-bitu'minous** *a.* [L.]

bi'valve (bi-') *a.* having a double shell. *n.* mollusk with such a shell. [L. *bi-*, two, *valva*, valve]

biv'ouac (-ōō-ak) *n.* temporary resting place of troops, without tents. *-v.i.* pass the night in the open. [F.]

bizarre' *a.* quaint, fantastic. [F.]

blab *v.t.* talk without ceasing; give away secrets; gossip. **-blabb'er** *n.* tattler. [M.E. *blabbe*]

black *a.* without light; dark; of the darkest color. *-n.* darkest color; black paint or fabric; a person of a black-skinned race. **-black'en** *v.t.* and *i.* **-black'ing** *n.* **-black'ball** *v.t.* reject in voting by putting black ball in ballot box. **-black'berry** *n.* **-black'-letter** *n.* Old English or Gothic letter. **-black'-mar'ket** *n.* illicit dealings in rationed (smuggled, *etc.*) goods; scene of such transaction. **-black'out** *n.* temporary loss of memory or consciousness; obscuring or extinguishing of lights to make dark. *-v.t.* and *i.* **-black'shirt** *n.* fascist. **-black widow** *n.* venomous spider. [OE. *blæc*]

black'guard (blag'ard) *n.* scoundrel. *a.* scoundrelly. *-v.t.* revile. **-black'-guardism** *n.* **-black'guardly** *a.* [*black guard*, the lowest menials]

black'mail *n.* money extorted by threats. *-v.t.* extort thus. [*mail*]

black'smith *n.* smith who works in iron, black metal. (*black* and *smith*]

bladd'er *n.* membraneous bag to contain liquid, *esp.* as part of the body; inflated bag. [OE. *blæddre*]

blade *n.* leaf; leaf-like part of anything; edge of a tool; sword; dashing fellow; flat of an oar. [OE. *blæd*, blade (of oar)]

blain *n.* blister, boil. [OE. *blegen*]

blame *v.t.* find fault with; censure. *-n.* censure, culpability. **-bla'mable** *a.* **blame'less** *a.* **-blame'worthy** *a.* [F. *blâmer* - G. *blasphemein*, speak ill of]

blancmange' *n.* shaped milk-jelly. [F. = *white food*]

blanch *v.t.* whiten, drain color from. [F. *blanc*, white]

bland *a.* smooth in manner. **-bland'ish** *v.t.* **-bland'ishment** *n.* [L. *blandus*]

blank *a.* without marks or writing; empty; vacant, confused; (of verse) without rhyme. *-n.* empty space; lottery ticket not drawing a prize; void. *-v.* in sport, to prevent another team from scoring any points. **-blank'ly** *adv.* [F. *blanc*, white]

blank'et *n.* woollen bed-covering. *-v.t.* cover with a blanket; cover. [F. *blanc*]

blare *v.i.* roar; trumpet. *-n.* trumpet sound; roar. [*imit.*]

blar'ney *n.* insincere flattery, deceit. cajolery. *-v.t.* deceive by insincerity. [*Blarney Castle*, Ireland, which embodies the *Blarney Stone*]

bla'sé (bla'zā) *a.* bored; satiated with pleasure. [F.]

blaspheme' *v.i.* talk profanely. *-v.t.* speak irreverently of. **-blasphe'mer** *n.* **-blas'phemous** *a.* **-blas'phemously** *adv.* **-blas'phemy** *n.* [G. *blasphemein*]

blast (-ast) *n.* current of air; gust of wind; explosion. *-v.t.* blow up; blight, ruin. [OE. *blæst*, strong gust]

bla'tant *n.* *a.* noisy, clamorous, loud. **-bla'tantly** *adv.* [coined by Spenser]

blaze *n.* bright flame of fire; brightness; outburst; white mark on animal's face. *v.i.* burn fiercely, brightly; burn with passion etc. [OE. *blæse*, torch]

blaze *v.t.* proclaim, publish (as with trumpet). [ON. *blasa*, blow]

bla'zer *n.* light flannel sports jacket, often colored. [*blaze*]
bla'zon *n.* coat of arms. -*v.t.* describe or depict (arms); make public. -**bla'zonry** *n.* [F. *blason*]
bleach *v.t.* whiten. -*v.i.* become white. [OE. *blæcan*, fr. *blæc*, pale]
bleak *a.* cold and cheerless; exposed; originally pale. [ON. *bleikr*]
blear *a.* sore or inflamed. -**blear'-eyed** *a.* [ME. *bleren*, have sore eyes]
bleat *v.i.* cry, as a sheep. -*n.* sheep's cry. [OE. *blætan*]
bleed *v.i.* lose blood. -*v.t.* draw blood from; extort money from. [OE. *bledan*]
blem'ish *v.t.* mar, spoil. -*n.* disfigurement, stain, defect. (F. *blêmir*, stain]
blench *v.i.* start back. [OE. *blencan*, deceive]
blend *v.t.* mix. -*n.* mixture. -**blend'er** *n.* a machine for cutting food up finely, or reducing it to a liquid pulp. [ON. *blanda*, mix]
bles'bok *n.* antelope with blazed forehead. [Du. = *blazed buck*]
bless *v.t.* consecrate; give thanks to; invoke happiness on; make happy. **bless'edness** *n.* -**bless'ing** *n.* [OE. *bletsian*, consecrate (with blood)]
bleth'er *v.i.* talk nonsense, gossip. -*n.* [Scot.]
blight (blit) *n.* mildew; plant disease; baneful influence. -*v.t.* affect with blight; spoil. [orig. uncertain]
blimp *n.* small non-rigid type of airship; old fogey. [Colonel *Blimp* of David Low's cartoons]
blind (-i-) *a.* lacking sight; heedless, random; dim; closed at one end; concealed, as *blind corner*. -*v.t.* deprive of sight. -*n.* something cutting off light; screen for a window; pretext. -**blinders** *n. pl.* leather covers to prevent a horse from seeing in any direction but straight forward. -**blind'fold** *a.* and *v.* -**blind'ly** *adv.* -**blind'ness** *n.* -**blind'side** *v.t.* to attack or hit someone from an angle whereby they do not detect or anticipate the attack. -**blind'worm** *n.* - **blind'-al'ley** *n.* occupation with no prospects. -**blind'man's buff**, game in which one player is *blindfolded*. [OE.]
blink *v.i.* look with half-closed eyes; wink; shine unsteadily. -*v.t.* shut the eyes to, shirk. -*n.* gleam; glimpse; glance. -**blink'ers** *n. pl.* blinders [OE. *blencan*, deceive]
bliss *n.* perfect happiness. -**bliss'ful** *a.* -**bliss'fully** *adv.* -**bliss'fuliness** *n.* [OE *bliths*, fr. *blithe*]
blis'ter *n.* bubble on the skin; plaster to produce one. -*v.t.* raise a blister. [OF. *blestre*]
blithe *a.* happy, gay. -**blithe'ly** *adv.* -**blithe'some** *a.* [OE.]
blitz *n.* sudden fierce onslaught, *esp.* from the air. [Ger. = *lightning*]
blitz'krieg (-kreg) *n.* lightning attack; raids by heavy bombers. [Ger. *blitz*, lightning, *krieg*, war]
blizz'ard *n.* blinding storm of wind and snow. [orig. uncertain]
bloat'ed *a.* swollen. [fr. ON. *blautr*, soft]
bloat'er *n.* kind of smoked herring. [Scand. *blot*, soft]
blob *n.* spot, globule. [imit. a bubble]
bloc *n.* combination, *e.g.*, of nations, for a common aim. [F.]
block *n.* solid piece of wood, a stump; any compact mass; obstacle; stoppage; pulley with frame; group of houses; stupid person. -*v.t.* obstruct, stop up; shape on a block; sketch. -**blockade** *n.* shutting of a place by siege. -*v.t.* close by siege. -**block'head** *n.* unintelligent person [F. *bloc*]
blond, blonde *a.* light golden-brown; fair. -*n.* one who is fair. [F. *blond*]
blood *n.* (blud) red fluid in the veins of men and animals; race, kindred; good parentage; temperament; passion. -*v.t.* draw blood from; harden to blood-shed. -**blood'ily** *adv.* -**blood'less** *a.* -**blood'y** *a.* -**blood-bank** *n.* classified store of human blood preserved in dried or plasma form for use in transfusion. -**blood count** *n.* amount of red and white corpuscles in given quantity of blood. -**blood'-guiltiness** *n.* -**blood'-guilty** *a.* -**blood'heat** *n.* -**blood'horse** *n.* -**blood'hound** *n.* - **blood'-money** *n.* -**blood'-poisoning** *n.* -**blood'-relation** *n.* -**blood'shed** *n.* - **blood'shot** *a.* -**blood-sport** *n.* hunting in which animal is killed. -**blood-test** *n.* testing of blood sample. **blood'-thirsty** *a.* -**blood-transfusion** *n.* transference of blood of one person to another of same blood group. -**blood'vessel** *n.* [OE. *blod*]
bloom *n.* flower of a plant; blossoming; prime, perfection; glow; powdery deposit on fruit. -*v.i.* be in flower; flourish. -**bloom'ing** *a.* [ON. *blom*]
bloom'er *n.* (*sl.*) blunder; absurd mistake. [from *bloom*, *v.s.*]
bloom'ers *n. pl.* loose trousers gathered at the knee; woman's underpants of the same design. [fr. Mrs *Bloomer*, inventor]

bloop *v.t.* (sports) in baseball, to hit a ball in a low arc so that it falls between the fielders. **-blooper** *n.*

bloss'om *n.* flower; flower-bud. *-v.i.* flower. [OE. *blostm*]

blot *n.* spot, stain; blemish; disgrace. *-v.i.* spot, stain; obliterate; dry with blotting-paper. **-blott'ing-pad** *n.* **-blott'ing-paper** *n.* [orig. uncertain]

blotch *n.* dark spot on the skin. *-v.t.* make spotted. **-blotch'y** *a.* [OF. *bloche*]

blot'ter *n.* a book in which records are held temporarily before being entered into a permanent register. [orig. uncertain]

blouse (-ow-) *n.* light, loose upper garment; woman's loose bodice. **-blouson** *n.* very loose-fitting blouse that gathers at the waist by elastic, drawstring, or other means. [F.]

blow *v.i.* make a current of air; pant; sound a blast. *-v.t.* drive air upon or into; drive by current of air; sound; spout (of whales); boast; fan, *-n.* blast. **-blow-down** *n.* an accident in a nuclear reactor in which a cooling pipe bursts causing the loss of essential coolant. **-blow'er** *n.* - **blow'fly** *n.* - **blow'hole** *n.* - **blow'pipe** *n.* [OE. *blawan*]

blow *v.i.* blossom. [OE. *blowan*]

blow *n.* stroke or knock; sudden calamity, [orig. uncertain]

blubb'er *n.* fat of whales; weeping. *-v.i.* weep [imit. formation, with first meaning of bubble]

blud'geon (-jen) *n.* short thick club. *v.t.* strike with such club. [orig. uncertain]

blue *a.* of the color of the sky or shades of that color; livid; (*sl.*) depressed. *-n.* the color; paint, clothing *etc.* of that color. *-v.t.* make blue; dip in blue liquid. **-blu'ish** *a.* **-blue baby** *n.* baby suffering from congenital eyanosis. **-blue'bell** *n..* **-blue'bird** *n.* symbol of happiness. **-blue'bottle** *n.* blowfly. **-blue'grass** *n..* **-blue'jacket** *n.* naval seaman. **-blue-pen'cil** *v.t.* correct or edit. **-blue'-print** *n.* copy of a drawing made by the action of light on sensitised paper, in which the lines are white on a blue ground; proposal for action. **-blue rib'bon** *a.* of high and respected quality. **-blue'-stocking** *n.* learned or pedantic woman. **-the blues,** (*colloq.*) depression; style of songs and music *orig.* from Southern U. S. *a.*, usually of lamentation, [F. *bleu*]

bluff *a.* steep; abrupt; rough and hearty blunt, frank. *-n.* cliff, high steep bank. [obs. Du. *blaf*]

bluff *v.t.* deceive by pretence of strength. [cp. Du. *verbluffen*]

blun'der *v.i.* flounder; make a stupid mistake. *-n.* gross mistake. [ME. *blondren,* confuse]

blun'derbuss *n.* short gun with wide bore. [cp. Du. *donderbus,* thunder-box]

blunt *a.* having dull edge or point; abrupt of speech. *-v.t.* dull **-blunt'ly** *adv.* - **blunt'ness** *n.* [orig. unknown]

blur *n.* spot, stain. *-v.t.* stain; obscure, dim. [orig. unknown]

blurb *n.* publisher's recommendation on book-jacket. [coined in U.S.A. by Gelett Burgess]

blurt *v.t.* utter suddenly or unadvisedly. [imit.]

blush *v.i.* become red in the face; be ashamed. *-n.* red glow on the face; flush of color. [OE. *blyscan,* shine]

blus'ter *v.i.* of wind, blow boisterously; swagger; bully. *-n.* blast. **-blus'tering** *a.* noisy. bullying. **-blus'tery** *a.* stormy. [orig. uncertain]

bo'a *n.* genus of snakes which kill by crushing; long coil of fur or feathers worn round the neck by ladies. [L.]

boar *n.* male of the swine. **-boar'hound** *n.* **-boar'-spear** *n.* [OE. *bar*]

board *n.* broad, flat piece of wood; table, meals; authorized body of men; thick stiff paper. *-pl.* theater, stage. *-v.t.* cover with planks; supply food daily; enter a ship; attack *-v.i.* take daily meals. **-board'er** *n.* - **board'ing-house** *n.* - **board'ing-pike** *n.* **-board'ing-school** *n.* **-board'-wages** *n.pl.* money allowed to servants in place of food. **-on board',** in or into a ship. [OE. *bord,* plank, table, side of ship]

boast *n.* brag, vaunt. *-v.i.* brag. *-v.t.* brag of, have to show. **-boast'er** *n.* **-boast'ful** *a.* **-boast'fully** *adv.* **-boast'fulness** *n.* [AF. *bost,* clamor]

boat *n.* small open vessel; ship generally. *-v.i.* sail about in a boat. **boat'er** *n.* flat straw hat. **-boat'hook** *n.* **-boat'house** *n.* - **boat'ing** *n.* **-boat'man** *n.* **-boat'swain** (bōs'n) *n.* ship's officer in charge of boats, sails *etc.* [OE. *bat*]

bob *n.* pendant; slight blow; knot of hair, ribbon *etc.*; weight of a plumb-line, *etc.* *v.i.* move up and down. *-v.t.* move jerkily; cut (women's hair) short. **-bobbed** *a.* [orig. uncertain]

bobb'in *n.* small round stick on which thread is wound. [F. *bobine*]

bobb'y sock *n.* (*sl.*) ankle-sock. **bobbysox'er** *n.* girl in her teens. [orig. uncertain]

bobèche *n.* cup, ring, or disk with a center hole placed on a candle below the wick to catch the drippings. [F]

bob'sled, bob'sleigh *n.* sledge made of two smaller ones tied together; racing sled. [*sleigh*]

bode *v.t.* portend, prophesy. **-bode'ful** *a.* ominous. [OE. *bodian*, announce]

bod'ice (-is) *n.* upper part of a woman's dress. [for (*pair of*) bodies, *i.e.*, stays]

bod'kin *n.* small dagger; tool for piercing holes; large blunt needle. [ME. *boidekin*]

bod'y *n.* whole frame of a man or animal; main part of such frame; main part of anything; substance; mass; person; number of persons united or organized; matter, opposed to spirit. *-v.t.* give form to. **-bod'iless** *a.* **-bod'ily** *a.* and *adv.* - **bod'yguard** *n.* **-bod'yservant** *n.* personal attendant. - **bod'ysnatcher** *n.* stealer of corpses from their graves. [OE. *bodig*]

Boer (-ōō-) *n.* Dutch colonist in S. Africa, *esp.* one who farms land. [Du. = *peasant*]

bog *n.* wet, soft ground. *-v.t.* entangle in such ground. **-bogg'y** *a.* [Ir. Gael. *bogach*, fr. *bog*, soft]

bo'gey *n.* goblin, bugbear. (*See* **bogle**]

bo'gey *n.* in golf, score of one over par at a hole. [Colonel *Bogey*, imaginary player]

bogg'le (-gl) *v.i.* stop at, hesitate; make difficulties; bungle, fumble. **-bogg'ler** *n.* [orig. to start with fright, as though at a ghost. *See* **bogle**]

bo'gie *n.* low truck on four wheels; revolving under-carriage, as on a railway engine. [orig. unknown]

bo'gle *n.* spectre; ogre. [Celtic]

bo'gus *a.* sham. [orig. unknown]

Bohe'mian *n.* Czech; unconventional person, *esp.* if artist, actor or the like; [F. *bohemien*, gypsy]

boil *n.* inflamed swelling. [OE. *byl*]

boil *v.i.* bubble up from the action of heat; be agitated, seethe; be cooked by boiling. *-v.t.* cause to bubble up; cook by boiling. **-boil'er** *n.* vessel for heating water or generating steam. **-boil'ing point** *n.* [F. *bouillir*]

bois'terous *a.* wild, noisy; turbulent. - **bois'terously** *adv.* **-bois'terousness** *n.* [ME. *boistous*]

bold *a.* daring, fearless; presumptuous; well-marked, prominent. **-bold'ly** *adv.* - **bold'ness** *n.* [OE. *bald*]

bole *n.* trunk of a tree. [ON. *bolr*]

bole'ro *n.* Spanish dance; short jacket. [Sp.]

boll *n.* seed-vessel or pod. **-boll'-wee'vil** *n.* insect pest ravaging American cotton crops. [OE. *bolla*]

bou'ard *n.* post on quay to which ships are secured. [*bole*]

Bol'shevik *n.* revolutionary. [Russ.]

bol'ster *n.* long pillow; pad, support. *v.t.* support, uphold. [OE.]

bolt *n.* bar or pin; arrow; rush, running away; discharge of lightning. *-v.t.* fasten with a bolt; swallow hastily. *-v.i.* rush away; break from control. **-bolt'-hole** *n.* underground refuge, hide-out. [OE. = heavy arrow]

bo'lus *n.* large pill. [L.-G. *bolos*, lump

bomb (bom) *n.* explosive projectile usually dropped from aircraft; grenade. *v.t.* attack with bombs. **-bombard'** *v.t.* shell. - **bombard'ment** *n.* - **bomb'er** *n.* bomb-dropping airman, airplane. [L. *bombus*, a humming]

bom'bast *n.* inflated language. - **bombas'tic** *a.* (OF. *bombace*, cotton-wool]

bo'na fi'de *a.* true, genuinely. sincerely. **-bona fides** *n.* good faith, sincerity. [L. = good faith]

bonan'za *n.* rich vein of gold; lucky strike. [Sp. = fair weather]

bond *n.* that which binds; link, union; written promise to pay money or carry out a contract. *-v.t.* bind; store goods until duty is paid on them. [*band*]

bon'dage *n.* slavery. **-bond'man** *n.* - **bond'servant.** *n.* [OE. *bonda*, farmer]

bone *n.* hard substance forming the skeleton of animals; piece of this. *-v.t.* take out bone. **-bone'less** *a.* **-bone'meal** *n.* - **bo'ny** *a.* [OE. *ban*]

bon'fire *n.* open-air fire to express joy, burn rubbish, *etc.* [for *bone-fire*]

bonn'et *n.* hat or cap, *usu.* worn by a woman. [F., for *chapeau de bonnet*, perh. some unknown material]

bonn'y *a.* beautiful, handsome. **-bonn'ily** *adv.* [F. *bon*, good]

bo'nus *n.* extra payment. [L. *bonum*, something good]

boob'y *n.* foolish person - **boob'y-prize** *n.* - **boob'y-trap** *n.* [Sp. *bobo*, fool]

boo'gie-woo'gie *n.* jazz piano-playing with variations on simple melody and persistent bass rhythm. [imit.]

book *n.* collection of sheets of paper bound together; literary work; main division of a work. *-v.t.* enter in a book. **-book'ish** *a.* **-book'let** *n.* **-book'binder** *n.* **-book'binding** *n.* **-book'case** *n.* and other compounds. [OE. *boc*, beech, *boc stæf*, beech-staff, letter]

boom *n.* long spar; barrier. [Du.]

boom *v.i.* hum; roar. -*n.* hum or roar. [ME. *bommen*]
boom *n.* sudden commercial activity; prosperity. -*v.i.* become active, prosperous. -*v.t.* push into prominence. [orig. uncertain]
boom'erang *n.* Australian hardwood missile, designed to return to the thrower. [native]
boom'slang *n.* venomous tree-snake. [Du. *boom*, tree, *slang*, snake]
boon *n.* favor; thing asked for. [ON. *bon*, petition]
boon *a.* kind; merry, convivial, as in boon companion. [F. *bon*, good]
boor *n.* rustic; rude fellow. --**boor'ish** *a.* [Du. *boer*, peasant]
boost *v.t.* help forward; push, advertise forcefully. -*n.* help forward; advertisement. [orig. unknown]
boot *n.* covering for the foot and lower leg. - **boot'ed** *a.* -**boot'lace** *n.* -**boot'-last** *n.* - **boot'-tree** *n.* [F. *botte*]
boot *n.* profit, use. -**boot'less** *a.* -**to boot'**, in addition. [OE. *bot*]
booth *n.* hut or stall. [ON. *buth*]
boot'legger *n.* smuggler, *esp.* an illicit importer of alcoholic liquor -**boot'leg** *v.t.* and *i.* smuggle. [fr. smuggling of bottles of liquor in the *leg* of a long *boot*]
boot'y *n.* plunder, spoil. [F. *butin*]
bo'rax *n.* mineral salt used in medicine and industry. -**bora'cic, bo'ric** *a.* -**bora'cic a'cid,** acid obtained from borax. [Arab. *buraq*]
bor'der *n.* margin; frontier; limit, boundary; flowerbed adjoining a walk, lawn, *etc.* -*v.t.* put on a margin, edging; adjoin. -*v.i.* resemble. -*v.i.* resemble (with on); be adjacent (with upon). -**bor'derer** *n.* [F. *bordure*, edge]
bore *v.t.* pierce, making a hole; weary. -*n.* hole; size or cavity of a gun; wearisome person. -**bore'dom** *n.* -**bo'rer** *n.* [OE. *borian*, pierce]
bore *n.* tidal wave in a river. [orig. uncertain]
Bor'eas *n.* North wind personified. - **bo'real** *a.* [L. and G. *Boreas*]
born, borne. *See* **bear.**
bo'ron *n.* non-metallic element found in borax, *etc.* [*borax*]
bor'ough (bur'-è) *n.* town with a corporation. [OE. *burg*, *burh*, fort]
bor'row *v.t.* and *i.* obtain on loan or trust; adopt from abroad. -**bor'rower** *n.* [OE. *borgian*, fr. *borg*, pledge]
bor'zoi *n.* Russian wolf-hound. [Russ.]
bosh *n.* and *int.* nonsense; idle talk. [Turk. = worthless]
bosk'age *n.* leafage; bushy undergrowth. -**bosk'y** *a.* [ME. *busky*, bushy]
bo'som *n.* human breast; dress covering it; seat of the passions and feelings; expanse. [OE. *bosm*]
boss *n.* knob or stud. -*v.t.* ornament with bosses. [F. *bosse*, hump]
boss *n.* employer; person in charge. [Du. *baas*]
bossa nova *n.* Brazilian dance music that blends elements of jazz and samba.
bot'any *n.* science of plants. -**botan'ic, botanical** *a.* -**bot'anize** *v.i* -**bot'anist** *n.* [G. *botane*, plant]
botch *v.t.* patch or put together clumsily; bungle. -*n.* clumsy patch; bungled piece of work. -**botch'er** *n.* [ME. *bocchen*, patch]
both *a.* the two. -*adv.* and *conj.* as well; for the one part. [ME. *bathe*]
both'er (-TH-) *v.t.* pester, perplex. -*v.i.* fuss, be troublesome. -*n.* trouble, fuss. [orig. unknown]
both'y, both'ie *n.* hut, humble dwelling; farm servants' quarters. [Sc.]
bot'tle *n.* vessel for holding liquids; contents of such vessel. -*v.t.* put in a bottle. [F. *bouteille*]
bot'tle *n.* truss of hay. [OF. *botel*]
bot'tleneck *n.* narrow retarding passage; hold-up in traffic or in production of a manufactured good for lack of essential component *etc.* [*bottle-neck*]
bott'om *n.* lowest part; bed of a sea, river *etc.* sitting part of the human body; ship; staying power, stamina. -*v.t.* put a bottom to; base. -**bott'omless** *a.* -**bott'omry** *n.* loan on the security of a ship. [OE. *botm*]
bot'ulism *n.* form of food poisoning. [L. *botulus*, sausage]
bou'doir *n.* lady's private room. [F. *bouder*, pout, sulk]
bougainville'a *n.* tropical climbing plant with large rose or purple bracts. [Louis de *Bougainville*]
bough (bow) *n.* branch of a tree. [OE. *bog*, arm, shoulder]
boul'der *n.* large stone rounded by action of water. [ME. *bulderston*]
boul'evard *n.* broad tree-lined promenade. [F. = *rampart. See* **bulwark**]
bounce *v.i.* bound, like a ball; throw oneself about; boast, exaggerate. -*n.* leap, spring, rebound; boast. - **bounc'er** *n.* - **bounc'ing** *a.* large; swaggering. [ME. *bunsen*, thump]
bound *n.* limit, boundary. -*v.t.* limit. close

in. -**bound'ary** *n.* - **bound'ed** *a.* - **bound'less** *a.* [AF. *bounde*]
bound *v.i.* spring, leap. -*n.* spring or leap. -**bound'er** *n.* boisterous, vulgar fellow. [F. *bondir*]
bound *a.* ready to go, as outward bound, *etc.* [fr. ON. *bua*, get ready]
boun'ty *n.* liberality; gift; premium - **boun'teous, bountiful** *a.* - **boun'tifully** *adv.* [F. *bonté*-L. *bonitatem-bonus*, good]
bouquet' *n.* bunch of flowers; perfume of wine. [F.]
bour'geois (-zhwa) *a.* belonging to the (social) middle-class; mediocre; conventional. -*n.* middle-class person. - **bour'geoisie** *n.* middle classes. [F.]
bourgeois' (-jois') *n.* former name for 9-point printing type. [F.]
bourn *n.* small stream; in Scots, burn. [*burn*]
bourn(e) *n.* boundary, goal. [F. *borne*]
bout *n.* turn, round; attempt; contest. [earlier *bought*, bend. *See* **bight**]
bo'vine *a.* of the ox; oxlike, dull, stolid. [L. *bovinus*]
bow *n.* bend, bent line; rainbow; weapon for shooting arrows; looped knot of ribbon *etc.*; instrument for playing violin. - **bow'man** *n.* archer. -**bow'shot** *n.* distance arrow may be shot from bow. -**bow'string** *n.* string for drawing bow. -**bow'-window** *n.* [OE. *bogs*]
bow *v.i.* bend the body in respect, assent *etc.*; submit. -*v.t.* bend downwards; cause to stoop; crush. -*n.* inclination in respect. [OE. *bugan*]
bow *n.* fore end of a ship; stem. [LG. *bug*, shoulder]
bow'el (-ow'-) *n.* intestines. -*pl.* entrails; interior; seat of emotions; pity, feeling. [OF. *bouel*]
bow'er *n.* shady retreat; inner room; arbour. [OE. *bur*, dwelling]
bow'er, bow'er-anch'or *n.* anchor at the bow of a ship. [fr. *bow*]
bowl *n.* round vessel, a deep basin; drinking-cup; hollow part of anything. [OE. *bolle*]
bowl *n.* wooden ball. -*v.t.* and *i.* roll or throw a ball in various ways. -**bowl'er** *n.* -**bowis** *n.* game. -**bowl'ing green** *n.* [F. *boule*]
bow'sprit (bow'-) *n.* spar projecting from the bow of a ship. [Du. *boegspriet*]
box *n.* tree yielding hard smooth wood; its wood; case, generally with a lid; contents of such case; small house or lodge; driver's seat; compartment. -*v.t.* put in a box; confine. -**box'-iron** *n.* -**box'-pleat** *n.* -**box-wood** *n.* -**box' the Compass**, name the thirty-two points in order and backwards, make a complete turn round. [OE., fr. L.]
box *n.* blow. -*v.t.* cuff. -*v.i.* fight with the fists, *esp.* with gloves on. -**box'er** *n.* one who so fights; a breed of dog. [orig. uncertain]
boy *n.* male child; lad; young man; native servant. [ME. *boi*]
boy'cott *v.t.* refuse to deal with. -*n.* concerted refusal to deal with. [fr. treatment of Capt. *Boycott* by the Irish Land League in 1880]
brace *n.* clasp, clamp; pair, couple; strut, support; carpenter's tool for turning boring instruments. -*pl.* suspenders. -*v.t.* stretch, strain, string up, support, make firm. - **bra'cer** *n.* -**bra'cing** *a.* [OF. *brasse*, *pl.* two arms]
brace'let *n.* wrist-ornament. [F.]
brack'en *n.* kind of fern. [ME. *braken*]
brack'et *n.* support for a shelf -*pl.* in printing, the marks [] used to enclose words. -*v.t.* enclose in brackets; couple, connect; (*artillery*) range by dropping shells nearer and farther than a mark. [earlier *bragget*, fr. F. *brogue*]
brackish *a.* saltish. [fr. Du. *brak*]
brad *n.* small nail. -**brad'awl** *n.* tool to pierce holes. [ON. *broddr*, spike]
brag *v.i.* boast, bluster. -*n.* boastful language. - **braggado'cio** (-shyõ) *n.* - **bragg'art** *n.* [OF. *braguer*]
Brah'min (brah'min) *n.* Hindu of the highest or priestly caste. -**Brahman'ic, Branmin'ic** *a.* [Sans. *brahman*, prayer]
braid *v.t.* plait; trim with braid. -*n.* plaited cord; woven band; plait of hair. [OE. *bregdan*]
brail *n.* one of the ropes used to truss sail. -*v.t.* haul in sail with this. [L. *bracale*, waist-belt)
braille *n.* system of printing for the blind; letters used, consisting of raised dots. [Louis *Braille*, inventor]
brain *n.* nervous matter in the skull; intellect. -*v.t.* dash out the brain. -**brain'less** *a.* -**brain'y** *a.* [OE. *brægen*]
braise *v.t.* stew in covered pan, originally between layers of hot charcoal. [F.]
brake *n.* fern; place overgrown with ferns; thicket. [orig. uncertain]
brake *n.* instrument for retarding the motion of a wheel; wagonette. -*v.t.* apply a brake to. -**brake'van** *n.* [OF. *brac*-L. *brachium*, arm]
bram'ble *n.* prickly shrub, the blackber-

ry. -**bram'bly** *a.* [OE. *bræmbel*]

bran *n.* sifted husks of corn. [F.]

branch (-a-) *n.* limb of a tree; anything like a limb; subdivision, section; subordinate department of a business. -*v.i.* bear branches; divide into branches; diverge. -**branch'y** *a.* [F. *branche*]

brand *n.* burning piece of wood; mark made by a hot iron; trade-mark; sword; class of goods; mark of infamy. -*v.t.* burn with an iron; mark. [OE.]

bran'dish *v.t.* flourish. [F. *brandir*, flourish a *brand*, sword]

bran'dy *n.* spirit distilled from wine. (Du. *brandewijn*, burnt wine]

brash *n.* rash, eruption; belching of acid water from stomach; hedge-clippings; rock, ice fragmental. loud, arrogant, ambitious; brittle. [F. *brèche*]

brass *n.* alloy of copper and zinc; brass memorial tablet in a church; (*sl.*) money; impudence. -**brass'y** *a.* [OE. *bræs*]

brassière' *n.* (*abbrev.* **bra**) woman's undergarment supporting the breasts. [F.]

brat *n.* contemptuous name for a child. (orig. uncertain]

brava'do (-va'-) *n.* boastful display of boldness; swagger. [Sp. *bravado*]

brave *a.* bold, courageous; splendid; finely dressed. -*n.* Indian warrior. -*v.t.* defy, meet boldly. -**brave'ly** *adv.* -**bra'very** *n.* [F.]

bra'vo *n.* desperado; hired assassin. [It.]

bra'vo *int.* well done! [It.]

brawl *v.i.* quarrel noisily; flow noisily. *n.* noisy quarrel. -**brawl'er** *n.* [F. *brailler*, be noisy]

brawn *n.* muscle; thick flesh; strength; preparation of chopped meat. -**brawn'y** *a.* [OF. *braon*, fleshy part]

bray *n.* ass's cry. -*v.i.* utter that cry; give out harsh sounds. [F. *braire*]

braze *n.* solder with alloy of brass. [F. *braser*, solder]

bra'zen *a.* (made) of brass; forward. -*v.t.* (with "out") face accusation, *etc.* with impudence. [*brass*]

bra'zier *n.* pan for burning charcoal. [F. *brasier*, fr. *braise*, hot coals]

breach *n.* break, opening; breaking of rule, duty, law, promise; quarrel. -*v.t.* make a gap in. [F. *breche*]

bread (-ed) *n.* food made of flour or meal baked; food; livelihood. [OE.]

breadth (-edth) *n.* extent across, width; largeness of view, mind. [OE. *brad*]

break *v.t.* part by force; shatter, crush, bruise, burst, destroy, frustrate; make bankrupt; discard; loosen, dissolve; tell with care. -*v.i.* become broken, shattered; divided; open, appear; crack, give way; part, fall out. -*n.* fracture; gap, opening; dawn; separation, interruption. -**break'age** *n.* -**break'down** *n.* -**break'er** *n.* - **break'fast** *n.* first meal of the day. - **break'water** *n.* [OE. *brecan*]

break'er *n.* (*naut.*) small cask. [Sp. *barrica*]

break-even point *n.* point at which profit and loss are equal; point when the return equals the investment.

break-in *n.* burglary; illegal forcible entry into another's home, business, car, *etc.*

bream *n.* small freshwater fish. [F. *brème*]

breast (-est) *n.* human chest; woman's mammary gland; affection; any protuberance. -*v.t.* face, oppose; mount. - **breast'plate** *n.* [OE. *breost*]

breath (-eth) *n.* air taken into and put out from the lungs; life; power of breathing; very slight breeze. -**breathe** (-èTH) *v.i.* inhale and exhale air from the lungs; live; pause, rest. -*v.t.* inhale and exhale; utter softly; exercise. -**brea'ther** (-TH-) *n.* - **brea'thing** (-TH-) *n.* **breath'less** *a.* [OE. *bræth*, exhalation]

breech *n.* lower part of the body behind; hinder part of anything, *esp.* of a gun. - *v.t.* put into breeches. -**breech'es** *n. pl.* britches. -**breech-load'er** *n.* [OE. *brec*]

breed *v.t.* generate, bring forth; give rise to; rear. -*v.i.* be produced, be with young. -*n.* offspring produced; race, kind. - **breed'er** *n.* -**breed'ing** *n.* [OE. *bredan*, keep warm, cherish]

breeze *n.* gentle wind; wind; rumor; quarrel; something easily achieved. -**breez'ily** *adv.* -**breez'y** *a.* windy; bright, lively. [F. *brise*]

breth'ren *n. pl.* brothers. [*brother*]

breve' *n.* musical note equal to two semibreves. [L. *brevis*, short]

brev'et *n.* commission carrying rank without the appropriate rate of pay. -*a.* honorary. -**brev'etcy** *n.* [F.]

bre'viary *n.* book of daily prayers of R.C. Church. [L. *breviarium*, summary]

brev'ier *n.* size of printing type, now 8 point. [OF. *brevier*]

brev'ity *n.* shortness. [L. *brevis*, short]

brew *v.t.* prepare a beverage by fermentation, as beer from malt, *etc.*, or by infusion, as tea *etc.*; plot, contrive. -*v.i.* be in preparation. -**brew'age** *n.* -**brew'er** *n.* -**brew'ery** *n.* [OE. *breowan*]

bri'ar *n. See* **brier.**
bri'ar *a.* only in briar pipe, one made of a heather root. [F. *bruyère*, heather]
bribe *n.* gift to corrupt; allurement. *-v.t.* influence by a bribe; win over; pervert. **-bri'ber** *n.* **-bri'bery** *n.* [F. = fragment, broken meats]
bric'-à-brac *n.* curios, or antique or artistic ornaments, *etc.* collected haphazardly. [F. *de bric et de broc*, by hook or by crook]
brick *n.* oblong mass of hardened clay; any oblong block. *-v.t.* lay or pave with bricks. [F. *brique*]
bri'dal *n.* wedding. *-a.* belonging to a wedding. [OE. *brydealu*, bride-ale, feast]
bride *n.* woman about to be, or just, married. **-bride'groom** *n.* man about to be, or just, married. **-brides'maid** *n.* **bride's attendant. [OE.** *bryd*]
bridge *n.* structure for crossing a river, *etc.*; raised narrow platform on a ship; upper part of the nose; part of a violin supporting the strings. *-v.t.* make a bridge over. [OE. *brycg*]
bridge *n.* card game. [Russ. *biritch*]
bri'dle *n.* headgear of horse-harness; curb or restraint. *-v.t.* put a bridle on; restrain *-v.i.* throw up the head. **-bri'dle-path** *n.* [OE. *bridel*]
brief *a.* short; concise. *-n.* summary of a case for the use of counsel; papal letter. *-n. pl.* underpants. **-brief'less** *a.* **-brief'ly** *adv.* **-brief'ness** *n.* [F. *bref*]
bri'er, bri'ar *a.* prickly shrub, *esp.* the wild rose. [earlier *brere*, OE. *brær*]
brig *n.* two-masted, square-rigged ship. [shortened fr. *brigatine*]
brigade' *n.* sub-division of an army, under a general; organized band. *-v.t.* join units into a brigade. **-brigadier-gen'eral** *n.* [F.]
brig'and *n.* robber. **-brig'andage** *n.* [F.]
brig'antine *n.* two-masted vessel, with square-rigged foremast and fore-and-aft mainmast. [It. *brigantino*, perh. orig. 'pirate-ship.' [*See* **brigand**]
bright (brit) *a.* shining, full of light; lively; cheerful; clever; illustrious. **-bright'en** *v.t.* and *i.* **-bright'ly** *adv.* **-bright'ness** *n.* [OE. *beorht*]
Bright's' disease *n.* disease of the kidneys. [Dr. R. *Bright*, 1789-1858]
brill *n.* white-spotted flat-fish like turbot. [orig. unknown]
brill'iant (-lya-) *a.* and *n.* shining; sparkling; splendid. **-brill'iance, brilliancy** *n.* **-brill'iantly** *adv.* [F. *brillant*]
brim *n.* margin or edge, *esp.* of a river, cup, hat. **-brim'less** *a.* **-brim'ming** *a.* [ME. *brymme*]
brim'stone *n.* sulfur. [ME. *bernston, brinston*, burnt stone]
brin'dled, brin'ded *a.* spotted and streaked. [orig. uncertain]
brine *n.* salt water; pickle. **-bri'ny** *a.* salt. *-n.* (*sl.*) the sea. [OE. *bryne*]
bring *v.t.* fetch; carry with one; cause to come. [OE. *bringan*]
brink *n.* edge of a steep place; utmost edge of anything. [ME. *brenk*]
briquette' *n.* block of compressed coal dust. [F.]
brisk *a.* active, lively, sharp. *-v.t.* enliven. *-v.i.* cheer up **-brisk'ly** *adv.* **-brisk'ness** *n.* [W. *brysg*]
bris'ket *n.* breast of an animal (as a joint). [F. *brechet*]
bris'ling *n.* Norwegian sprat. [Norw.]
bris'tle (-is'l) *n.* short, stiff hair. *-v.i.* stand erect *-v.t.* erect like bristles. **-bris'tliness** *n.* **-bris'tly** *a.* [ME. *brustel*]
brit'ches *n. pl.* short trousers *usu.* for men, gathered and fastened at the knee. [OE. *brec*]
Brit'ish *a.* of pert. to Britain **-Brit'on** *n.* native of Britain [OE. *Brit*, Briton]
britt'le *a.* easily broken, fragile. **-britt'leness** *n.* [OE. *breotan*, break]
broach *n.* boring tool; split. *-v.t.* pierce (a cask); open, begin. [F. *broche*, spit]
broad (-awd) *a.* wide, ample, open; outspoken; coarse; general; tolerant; of pronunciation, dialectal. **-broad'en** *v.t.* and *i.* **-broad'ly** *adv.* **-broad'cast** *a.* scattered freely. *-v.t.* scatter, as seed; send out radio messages, music, *etc.* for general reception. **-broad'cloth** *n.* **-broad'gauge** *n.* and *a.* **-broad'-mind'ed** *a.* tolerant, not narrow in ideas. **-broadness** *n.* **-broad'side** *n.* discharge of all guns on one side; sheet printed on one side. **-broad sword** *n.* [OE. *brad*]
brocade' *n.* silk stuff wrought with figures. **-broca'ded** *a.* [Sp. *brocado*]
broc'coli *n.* hardy kind of cauliflower. [It. = *sprouts*]
brochure' (-shōōr) *n.* pamphlet. [F., fr. *brocher*, stitch]
brogue (-ōg) **Bro'gan** *n.* stout shoe. [Ir. Gael. *brog*, shoe]
brogue (-ōg) *n.* dialectal pronunciation, *esp.* the Irish pronunciation of English. [orig. uncertain]
broil *n.* noisy quarrel, tumult; confusion. [F. *brouiller*, mix up]

broil *v.t.* cook over hot coals or direct heat; grill. -*v.t.* be heated. -**broiler** *n.* apparatus for cooking under direct heat, [F. *broiler*, burn]

bro'ker *n.* one employed to buy and sell for others; dealer; one who values goods distrained for rent. - **bro'kerage** *n.* payment to a broker. [OF. *brocheor*]

bro'mide *n.* photograph printed on paper treated with silver bromide; sedative drug; user of clichés. [G. *brōmos*, stink]

bro'mine *n.* gaseous element allied to chlorine. -**bro'mate** *n.* -**bro'mic** *a.* [G. *brōmos*, stink]

bron'chi (-ng'-ki) *n. pl.* branches of the windpipe. -**bronch'ial** *a.* -**bronchi'tis** *n.* [G. *bronchos*, windpipe]

bronc'o *n.* half-tamed horse. [Sp.]

brontosaur'us *n.* extinct giant lizard. [G. *bronte*, thunder, *sauros*, lizard]

bronze *n.* alloy of copper and tin. -*a.* the appearance of bronze to. -**bronzed** *a.* coated with, or colored bronze; sunburnt. [F.]

brooch *n.* ornamental pin or fastening. [var. of *broach*, pin]

brood *n.* family of young, *esp.* of birds; tribe, race. -*v.t.* sit, as a hen on eggs; meditate, think anxiously about. -**brood'y** *a.* -**brood'ing** *a.* [OE. *brod*]

brook *n.* small stream. -**brook'let** *n.* [OE. *broe*]

brook *v.t.* put up with, endure. [OE. *brucan*, use]

broom *n.* yellow-flowered shrub; brush for sweeping (orig. of twigs), - **broom'stick** *n.* [OE. *brom*]

brose (-z) *n.* dish of oat or pease meal. [Scot.]

broth *n.* decoction of meat, usually with vegetables. [OE.]

broth'el *n.* house of prostitutes. [ME. = vile person, fr. OE. *breothan*, go to ruin. Sense is by confusion of *brothel-house* with *bordel*, F. *bordel*, little house]

broth'er (-uTH'-) *n.* son of the same parents; anyone closely united with another. -**broth'erhood** *n.* relationship; fraternity, company. -**broth'erliness** *n.* - **broth'erly** *a.* -**broth'er-in-law** *n.* brother of a husband or wife; husband of a sister. [OE. *brothor*]

brow *n.* ridge over the eyes; forehead; edge of a hill. -**brow'beat** *v.t.* bully. [OE. *bru*, eye-lid, eyebrow]

brown *a.* of a dark color inclining to red or yellow. -*n.* the color. -*v.t.* or *i.* make or become brown. [OE. *brun*]

brown'ie *n.* household spirit or goblin in Scots folklore; member of a junior formation of the girl scouts; a chocolate cookie. [*brown*]

browse *v.i.* feed on shoots and leaves; study desultoriy, as books. [fr. obs. *n.* *browse*, young shoots]

bruise *v.t.* injure by a blow or pounding; oppress. -*n.* contusion; discolored lump raised on the body by a blow. -**bruis'er** *n.* boxer, prizefighter. [OF. *bruiser*]

bruit *n.* noise; rumor, report. -*v.t.* noise abroad. [F.]

bru'mal *a.* pert. to winter. [L. *bruma*, winter]

brunch *n.* combination of breakfast and lunch. [*br*eakfast, l*unch*]

brunette' *n.* woman with dark hair or of dark complexion, [F.]

brunt *n.* shock of an attack; chief stress of anything. [orig. a blow; orig. uncertain]

brush *n.* small shrubs; thicket; backwoods. -**brush'wood** *n.* -**brush' kangaroo'**, wallaby. [F. *brousse*, faggots]

brush *n.* utensil for sweeping; tool of hair used by painters; bushy tail; skirmish, fight; bundle of wires, or anything like a broom. -*v.t.* remove dust, clean with a brush; touch lightly. -*v.i.* move lightly. - **brush'y** *a.* [F. *brousse*, faggots]

brusque (-sk) *a.* rough in manner. [F.]

brute (-ōō-) *n.* one of the lower animals; man like such animal. -*a.* animal; sensual; stupid. -**bru'tal** *a.* -**bru'talize** *v.t.* - **brutal'ity** *n.* -**bru'tally** *adv.* -**bru'tish** *a.* [L. *brutus*, dull, stupid]

brux'ism *n.* the habit of grinding the teeth, *esp.* unconsciously. [G. *brykein*, to gnash the teeth]

bryol'ogy *n.* study of mosses. [G. *bryon*, moss, *logia*, discourse]

bry'ony *n.* wild climbing plant found in hedgerows. [G. *bryonia*]

bubb'le *n.* hollow globe of liquid, blown out with air; anything empty; swindle. -*a.* deceptive; transient. -*v.i.* form bubbles, rise in bubbles. -**bubb'ly** *a.* [earlier *burble*, of imit. orig.]

bu'bo *n.* inflamed swelling in groin or armpit. -**bubon'ic** *a.* of, characterized by buboes. -**bubon'ic plague** *n.* plague, Black death. [L. *bubo*, groin]

buccaneer' *n.* pirate -**buccaneer'ing** *n.* [French hunters who smoked meat on a *boucan*, framework; Brazilian word]

buck *n.* male deer, or other male animal; dandy. -*v.t.* of a horse, attempt to throw a rider by jumping upwards; to oppose in a direct manner. -**buckjumper** *n.* -**buck'shot** *n.* large shot. -**buck'skin** *n.* [OE. *buce*]

buck'et *n.* vessel, usually round with an arched handle, for water, *etc.* -**buck'etful** *n. [OE. buc*, pitcher]

buck'le *n.* metal instrument with rim and tongue, for fastening straps, bands *etc.* -*v.t.* fasten with a buckle. -*v.i.* warp, bend. [F. *boucle*, boss of shield]

buck'ler *n.* shield. [*buckle*]

buck'ram *n.* coarse cloth stiffened with size. [F. *bougran*]

buck'shee *n.* (*sl.*) windfall. *a.* free, gratuitous. [Pers. *backsheesh*]

bucol'ic *a.* rustic. [L. *bucolicus*]

bud *n.* first shoot of a plant, leaf *etc.*; unopened flower. -*v.i.* begin to grow -*v.t.* graft. [ME. *bodde*]

budd'leia *n.* purple or yellow flowered shrub. [A. *Buddle*, d. 1715]

budge *v.i.* move, stir. [F. *bouger*]

budgerigar' *n.* Australian love-bird. [native, *budgeri*, good, *gar*, cockatoo]

budg'et *n.* bag and its contents; annual financial statement; collection of things. -*v.t.* prepare a financial statement. [OF. *bougette*, wallet]

buff *n.* leather made from buffalo or ox hide; its light yellowish color; bare skin. [*buffalo*]

buff'alo *n.* any of several species of large oxen. [Port. *bufalo* - G. *bous*, bull]

buff'er *n.* contrivance to lessen the shock of concussion. -**buffer-state** *n.* neutral country between two others which may not be friendly. [fr. obs. v. *buff*, imit. of muffled blow]

buff'et *n.* blow, slap; misfortune. -*v.t.* strike with the fist; contend against. -**buff'eting** *n.* [OF.]

buff'et *n.* sideboard; refreshment bar. [F.]

buffoon' *n.* clown; fool. -**buffoon'ery** *n.* [F. *bouffon*]

bug *n.* small blood-sucking insect; any insect. [OE. *budda*, beetle]

bug'bear *n.* object of terror, generally needless terror. [W. *bug*, ghost]

bug'gy *n.* light horse-carriage, gig. [orig. unknown]

bu'gle *n.* hunting-horn; instrument like a trumpet. -**bu'gler** *n.* (for *bugle-horn* fr. L. *buculus*, fr. *bos*, ox]

bu'gle *n.* glass bead, usually black. [*bugle* ox, fr. its horny appearance]

bu'gloss (-u'-) *n.* common weed in cornfields. [G. = ox-tongued]

build (bild) *v.t.* erect, as a house, bridge, *etc.*; form, construct. -*v.i.* depend (on). -*n.* make, form.- **build'er** *n.* -**build'ing** *n.* [OE. *byldan*]

bulb *n.* rounded stem or shoot of the onion and other plants; anything resembling this, as electric light bulb. -*v.i.* form, bulbs. -**bulb'ous** *a.* [L. *bulbus*, onion]

bul'bul *n.* Eastern singing bird. [Arab.]

bulge *n.* swelling, protuberance. -*v.i.* swell out -**bulg'iness** *n.* -**bulg'y** *n.* [L. *bulge*, knapsack]

bulk *n.* size, volume; greater part; cargo. -*v.i.* be of weight or importance. -**bulk'iness** *n.* -**bulk'y** *a.* large; unwieldy. [ON. *bulki*, heap, cargo]

bulk'head *n.* partition in the interior of a ship. [fr. ON. *balkr*, beam]

bull (-ŏŏ-) *n.* male of cattle; male of various other animals; speculator for a rise in stocks. -**bull'ock** *n.* castrated bull -**bull's-eye** *n.* boss in glass; lantern; middle part of a target. [ME. *bole*]

bull (-ŏŏ-) *n.* Papal edict, bearing Pope's seal. [L. *bulla*, seal]

bull (-ŏŏ-) *n.* laughable inconsistency in language. [perh. fr. OF. *boul*, cheat]

bull'ace *n.* shrub with sloe-like edible fruit. [OF. *beloce*]

bull'dog *n.* powerfully-built dog of great courage and tenacity. *a.* brave, tenacious. [*bull* and *dog*]

bull'dozer *n.* powerful machine for leveling ground. [orig. uncertain]

bull'et (-ŏŏ-) *n.* metal ball discharged from a rifle, pistol *etc.* [F. *boulet*, cannon-ball]

bull'etin (-ŏŏ-) *n.* official report; brief official statement reporting on an event; news report. [F. fr. L. *bulla*, seal]

bull'finch *n.* red-breasted finch. [*bull* and *finch*]

bull'ion *n.* uncoined gold or silver, in mass. [F. *bouillon*, boiling]

bull'y *n.* rough, overbearing fellow. -*v.t.* intimidate, overawe; ill-treat. [orig. uncertain]

bul'rush *n.* tall, strong rush. [orig. uncertain]

bul'wark (-ŏŏ-) *n.* raised side of a ship; breakwater; rampart; any defense or means of security. -*v.t.* protect. [orig. *rampart*, fr. *bole*, tree, and work]

bum *n.* buttocks; one who has no fixed occupation and who sponges off others -**bum'boat** *n.* boat carrying provisions to ships. [*bump*]

bum'ble-bee *n.* large bee, the humblebee. [imit.]

bum'bledom *n.* fussy officialdom. [*Bumble*, Dickens character]

bump *n.* heavy blow, dull in sound; swelling caused by a blow; protuberance. *-v.t.* strike against. **-bump'er** *n.* full glass. *a.* full, abundant. [imit.]

bump'kin *n.* rustic. [orig. uncertain]

bump'tious (-shus) *a.* self-assertive and self-conceited to an offensive degree. [prob. humorous formation fr. *bump*]

bun *n.* small sweet cake; round mass of hair. [ME. *bunne*, small loaf]

bunch *n.* number of things tied or growing together; cluster; tuft, knot. *-v.t.* put together in a bunch. *-v.i.* draw together into a cluster. **-bunch'y** *a.* [orig. uncertain]

bun'dle *n.* package; number of things tied together. *-v.t.* tie in a bundle; send (off) without ceremony. *-v.i.* pack and go (with off, *etc.*) [*bind*]

bund'wall *n.* a concrete or earth wall surrounding a storage tank containing crude oil or its refined product, designed to hold the contents of the tank in the event of a rupture or leak. (Hind. *band*, embankment, L. *vallum*, wall]

bung *n.* stopper for a cask; large cork. *-v.t.* stop up. **-bung'-hole** *n.* [obs. Du. *bonghe*]

bung'alow (bung'ga-lō) one storied house. [Hind. *bangla*, or Bengal]

bung'le (bung'gl) *v.t.* do badly for lack of skill, manage awkwardly. *-v.i.* act clumsily, awkwardly. *-n.* blunder, muddle. **-bung'led** *a.* **-bung'ler** *n.* **-bung'ling** *a.* [orig. uncertain]

bun'ion *n.* inflamed swelling on the foot. [perh. It. *bugnone*, swelling]

bunk *n.* box or recess for sleeping in. *esp.* in a ship's cabin [Du. *bank*, bench]

bunk'er *n.* receptacle for coal, *esp.* in a ship; sandy hollow on a golf-course. [perh. ON. *bunke*, ship's hold]

bunk'um *n.* claptrap oratory, bombastic speechmaking. [fr. *Buncombe*, county in Carolina, the member for which place once insisted on "making a speech for Buncombe," *i.e.*, for effect on his constituents, not for the House he was addressing]

bun'ny *n.* pet name for rabbit. [*bun*]

bunt *n.* disease of wheat; the fungus. [orig. unknown]

bunt'ing *n.* bird allied to the lark. [ME. *bountyng*]

bunt'ing *n.* worsted material for flags; flags, *etc.* made from it. [orig. uncertain]

buoy (boi) *n.* floating mark anchored in the sea; something to keep a person afloat. *-v.t.* mark with a buoy; keep from sinking; support. **-buoy'ancy** *n.* **-buoy'ant** *a.* [L. *boia*, chain (by which the buoy was secured)]

bur, burr *n.* prickly head of a plant; rough ridge or edge; accent associated with trilled gutteral r- sound, *esp.* of north of England and Scotland. [ME. *borre*]

burd'en, burth'en (-TH-) *n.* load; weight; cargo; anything difficult to bear. *-v.t.* load, encumber. **-burdlen'some** *a.* [OE. *byrthen*]

burd'en *n.* chorus of a song; chief theme. [F. *bourdon*, humming tone]

bur'dock *n.* rough, biennial weed bearing prickly burs and broad leaves. [fr. *bur q.v.*]

bu'reau *n.* writing-desk; office, *esp.* for public business. [F. = *office*, earlier *desk*, and earlier still its cloth covering; OF. *burel*, a coarse cloth]

bureauc'racy (-ok'-) *n.* government by officials; body of officials. **-bu'reaucrat** *n.* **- bureaucrat'ic** *a.* [F. *bureau* and G. *kratein*, govern]

burette' *n.* graduated glass tube for measuring liquids; cruet bottle. [F.]

bur'gee *n.* yachtsman's flag. [F. *bourgeois*, shipowner]

bur'geon (-jen) *n./v.i.* sprout, bud. [F. *bourgeon*]

bur'glar *n.* one who breaks into a house by night with intent to steal. **-burgla'rious** *a.* **-burgla'riously** *adv.* **-bur'glary** *n.* **-burglarize, burgle** *v.t.* [prob. fr. OE. *burg*, dwelling]

bur'gomaster *n.* civic head of Dutch town. (*borough*]

bur'gundy *n.* red wine of Burgundy.

bur'in *n.* graving tool. [*bore*]

burke *v.t.* stifle. [*Burke*, 19th c. murderer, who stifled his victims and sold their bodies for dissection]

burlesque' (-esk') *n.* travesty, grotesque imitation, mockery. *-v.t.* caricature. *-a.* mocking, derisively imitative. [It. *burlesco*, fr. *burla*, jest]

bur'ly *a.* sturdy, stout. **-bur'liness** *n.* [ME. *borlich*, massive]

burn *n.* small stream. [OE. *burne*]

burn *v.t.* destroy or injure by fire. *-v.i.* be on fire, literally or figuratively; shine; be consumed by fire. *-n.* injury or mark caused by fire. **-burn'er** *n.* **-burn'ing** *a.* [OE. *burnan*]

burn'et *n.* common meadow plant with brown flowers. [*brown*]

burn'ish *v.t.* make bright by rubbing,

polish. -*n*. lustre, polish. -**burn'isher** *n*. [F. *brunir*, make bright]

burr'ow *n*. hole of a rabbit, *etc*. -*v.t.* make holes in the ground, as a rabbit; bore; conceal oneself. (var. of borough; OE. *beorgan*, protect]

burs'ar *n*. treasurer, *esp*. of a college; one who holds a bursary or scholarship. -**burs'ary** *n*. [Med. L. *bursarius*, purse bearer. *See* **purse**]

burst *v.i.* fly asunder; break into pieces; break open violently; break suddenly into some expression of feeling. -*v.t.* shatter; break violently. -*n*. a bursting explosion; outbreak; spurt; (*sl.*) drunken spree. [OE. *berstan*]

bur'y (ber'-i) *v.t.* put underground; put in a grave. -**bur'ial** *n*. [OE. *brygan*]

bus *n*. *See* **omnibus.**

bus'by *n*. fur hat worn by hussars. [orig. uncertain]

bush *n*. shrub; woodland, thicket; backwoods, interior of S. Africa and Australia. - **bush'y** *a*. -**bush'man** *n*. member of nomadic S. African tribe; Australian bushdweller. -**bush-whacker** *n*. one who ranges in bush; guerilla fighter; lout. [ME. *bush, busk*]

bush'el *n*. dry measure of eight gallons. [OF. *boissel*, dim. of *boiste*, box]

busk *n*. strip of steel, whalebone *etc*. to stiffen corsets. [F. *base*]

busk *v.t.* and *i*. dress oneself, get ready. [ON. *buask*]

bus'kin *n*. tragic actor's half-boot. [*buckskin*]

bust *n*. sculpture representing the head and shoulders of the human body; upper part of the body. [F. *buste*]

bus'tard *n*. genus of marsh birds. [L. *avis tarda*, slow bird]

bus'tle (-sl) *v.i.* be noisily busy; be active. -*n*. fuss, stir. -**bus'tier** *n*. [obs. *buskle*, make hurried preparations]

bus'y (biz'-i) *a*. actively employed; diligent; meddling; occupied. -*v.t.* occupy. -**bus'ily** *adv*. -**bus'iness** (biz'-nis) *n*. affairs, work, occupation. -**bus'ybody** *n*. meddler. -**bus'yness** *n*. [OE. *bysig*]

but *prep*. and *conj*. without; except; only; yet; still; besides. [OE. *butan, beutan*, outside]

butch'er *n*. one who kills animals for food, or sells meat; bloody or savage man. -*v.t.* slaughter, murder. -**butch'-ery** *n*. -**butch'er-bird** *n*. shrike. [F. *boucher* fr. *bouc*, goat]

but'ler *n*. servant in charge of the wine cellar; chief servant [OF. *bouteillier*, bottler]

butt *n*. large cask. (F. *botte* - Low L. *butta*]

butt *n*. target; object of ridicule. [F. *but*, end, aim]

butt *n*. thick end of anything; stump. [orig. uncertain]

butt *v.t.* and *i*. strike with the head; push. -*n*. blow with the head, as of a sheep. -**butt'er** *n*. [F. *bouter*, thrust]

butt'er *n*. oily substance produced from cream by churning. -*v.t.* spread with butter; flatter grossly. -**butt'ery** *a*. -**butt'ercup** *n*. meadow plant with goldenyellow flowers. -**butt'erfly** *n*. -**butter'milk** *n*. -**butt'erscotch** *n*. sweetmeat. [OE. *butere*, fr. L. *buty-rum*]

butt'ery *n*. storeroom for provisions, *esp*. liquors. (OF. *boterie*, place for bottles]

butt'ock *n*. rump, protruding hinder part (*usu*. in *pl*.). [prob. dim of *butt*, thick end]

butt'on *n*. knob or stud, *esp*. for fastening dress; badge; bud. -*v.t.* fasten with buttons. [F. *bouton*, bud]

butt'ress *n*. structure to support a wall; prop. -*v.t.* support. [OF. *bouterez*, supports, fr. *bouter*, thrust]

buty'ric *a*. of or derived from butter. -**buty'ric a'cid** *n*. [L. *butyram*, butter]

bux'om *a*. full of health, gay, lively. [orig. 'obedient,' fr. OE. *bugan*, bow]

buy (bi) *v.t.* get by payment; obtain in exchange for something; bribe. -**buy'er** *n*. [OE. *bycgan*]

buzz *v.i.* make a humming sound. -*n*. humming; sound of bees. -**buzz'er** *n*. signalling device. -**buzz word** *n*. a word, often originating in a particular jargon, that becomes a vogue word in the community as a whole or among a particular group. [imit.]

buzz'ard *n*. bird of prey of the falcon family; any of the large birds of prey. [OE. *busard*]

by *prep*. near; beside; with, through. *adv*. near, close; out of the way; beyond. -**by'-and-by,** soon. -**by'gone** *a*. past. -**by'-pass** *n*. road to divert traffic from busy main road. -**by'-product** *n*. -**by'-way** *n*. -**by'word** *n*. common saying; object of general derision. [OE. *bi*]

bye *n*. side issue; passing through to the next round in a tournament without playing a match. [*by*]

by'law, bye'law *n*. local law made by a subordinate authority. [ME. *bilaw*, fr. *bi*, borough]

byre *n*. cow-shed. [OE. = cattle-stall]

byte *n.* (*compute.*) sequence of bits processed as a single unit of information. [perh. *bite*]

C

cab *n.* carriage for public transport; taxicab; covered part of a vehicle or machine (*esp.* a locomotive, truck or tractor) which accommodates the driver. -**cab'man, cab'by** *n.* [F. *cabriolet*, light carriage]

cabal' *n.* secret plot; small body of people engaged in one. -*v.i.* plot, intrigue. -**cabal'ler** *n.* [Heb. *quabbalah*, tradition, mystical interpretation]

cab'aret *n.* small tavern; restaurant entertainment. [F.]

cab'bage *n.* green vegetable with large round head. [fr. L. *caput*, head]

ca'ber *n.* pole, tree-stem, tossed in Scottish Highland sports. [Gael.]

cab'in *n.* hut, small room, *esp.* in a ship. -*v.t.* shut up, confine. **cab'in-boy** *n.* [F. *cabane*, hut]

cabinet *n.* case of drawers for things of value; private room; committee of politicians governing a country. -**cab'inet maker** *n.* maker of cabinets, furniture. [dim. of *cabin*]

ca'ble *n.* strong rope; submarine telegraph line; message sent by such line. -*v.t* .and *i.* telegraph by cable. -**cablegram** *n.* [Late L. *capulum*, halter]

caboose' *n.* ship's galley; guard's van in freight train. [early Du. *cabuse*]

cabriolet *See* **cab.**

caca'o *n.* earlier and correct form of cocoa; tropical tree with seeds from which chocolate and cocoa are made. [Mex. *cacanatt*, cacao tree]

cach'alot *n.* sperm whale. [F.]

cache (-ash) *n.* hidden store; secret hiding-place. [F. *cacher*, hide]

cach'et (-she) *n.* seal, stamp. [F.]

cach'innate (-k-) *v.i* laugh loudly. -**cachinna'tion** *n.* [L. *cachinnare*]

cack'le *v.i.* make a chattering noise, as a hen. -*n.* cackling noise; empty chatter. -**cack'ler** *n.* [*imit.*]

cacophony *n.* disagreeable sound, discord of sounds. -**cacoph'onous** *a.* [G. *kakophonia*, ill sound]

cac'tus *n.* prickly desert plant.[L.]

cad *n.* vulgar fellow; no gentleman [*cadet*]

CAD *v.t.* (*compute.*) use of computers to prepare and test mechanical designs and develop engineering drawings. [*C*omputer *A*ssisted *D*esign]

cadav'erous *a.* corpse-like; sickly-looking. [fr. L. *cadaver*, dead body]

cadd'ie *n.* golfers attendant.[fr. *cadet*]

caddy *n.* small box for tea. [Malay *kati*, weight about a pound]

ca'dence *n.* fall or modulation of voice, music or verses. [F., L. *cadere*, fall]

cadet' *n.* younger son or brother; student in a naval or military college. [F.]

cadge *v.i.* and *t.* bag, sponge, acquire by begging. -**cadg'er** *n.* beggar, hawker. [prop. *catch*]

ca'di *n.* Mohammedan judge. [Arab. *qadi*]

ca'dre (ka-der) *n.* nucleus, framework, *esp.* the permanent skeleton of a regiment; cell of a revolutionary political party; indoctrinated member of that cell or similar organization. [F.]

caesarean, cesarean *n.* (birth) delivery by incision. [confusion of L. *caedre, caes-*, cut, with *Caesar*]

caes'ium. *See* **cesium.**

caesu'ra *n.* natural pause in a line of verse. [L. *cædere, cæs-*, cut off]

caf'e' (kaf'a) *n.* coffee-house; restaurant serving drinks and light meals. [F. *coffee*]

cafetière' *n.* a kind of coffeepot in which boiling water is poured onto ground coffee and a plunger fitted with a metal filter is pressed down, forcing the grounds to the bottom. [Fr. *cafetière*, coffeepot]

cafeteria *n.* restaurant where patrons serve themselves from a counter. [Amer. Sp.]

caffeine *n.* alkaloid in tea and coffee. [F. *cafeine*]

cage *n.* place of confinement; box with bars, *esp.* for keeping animals or birds. -*v.t.* put in a cage, confine. -**cage'bird** *n.* [F., fr. L. *caves*, hollow]

cahoot(s)' *n.pl.* (*sl.*) partnership. [F. *cahute*, cabin]

cairn *n.* heap of stones, *esp.* as a monument or landmark. [Gael, *corn*]

cairngorm' *n.* yellow, brown or wine-colored stone or gem. [*Cairngorm* mountains, Scotland]

caiss'on *n.* ammunition wagon; box for working under water; apparatus for lifting a vessel out of the water. [F.]

cai'tiff *n.* mean, despicable fellow. [OF. *caitif*, fr. L. *captivus*, captive]

cajole' *v.t.* cheat by flattery. -**cajole'ment** *n.* -**cajo'ler** *n.* -**cajo'lery** *n.* [F. *cajoler*]

cake *n.* piece of dough baked; fancy

bread; flattened hard mass. -*v.t.* and *i.* make into a cake. -**cake'-walk** *n.* orig. dance performed by black Americans competing for cake. [ON. *kaka*]

cal'abash *n.* kind of melon or gourd; its shell, used as a cooking, *etc.* vessel. [Pers. *kharbuz*, melon]

calaboose *n.* (*sl.*) prison [Sp. *calabozo*, dungeon]

cal'amine *n.* a zinc ore. [Low L. *calamine*]

calamity *n.* great misfortune; distress, disaster. -**calam'itous** *a.* [L. *calamitas*]

calcareous *a.* like or containing lime. [L. *calx*, lime]

calceola'ria *n.* plant with slipper-like flowers [L. *calceolus*, little shoe]

cal'cine *v.t.*reduce to lime; burn to ashes. -*v.i.* burn to ashes. [L. *caix*, lime]

cal'cium *n.* metal derived from lime compounds. -**cal'cic** *a.* [L. *calx*, lime]

calculate '*v.t.*reckon, compute. -*v.i.* make reckonings. -**cal'culable** *a.* -**calculating** *a.* -**calcula'tion** *n.* -**calculator** *n.* a person who calculates; a machine which carries out calculations. -**cal'culus** *n.* stone in the body; method of mathematical calculation. [L. *calculus*, pebble]

cal'dron, caul'dron *n.* a large kettle or boiler. [fr. L. *calidus*, hot]

cal'endar *n.* table of months and days; list of documents, register. [L. *calendae*, first days of months]

cal'endar *n.* machine with rollers for smoothing cloth, paper *etc.* -*v.t.* smooth or finish in such machine. [Med. L. *calendra*, prob. fr. G. *kylindros*, cylinder, roller]

calf (kaf) *n.* young of the cow, also of various other animals; leather made of calfs skin. -**calves** (kavz) *pl.* -**calve** *v.i.* give birth to a calf. [OE. *cealf*]

calf (kaf) *n.* fleshy hinder part of the leg below the knee. [ON. *kalfi*]

caliber *n.* size of the bore of a gun; capacity; character. [F.]

cal'ico *n.* cotton cloth. [*Calicut*, India]

cal'ipers, call'ipers *n.* instrument for measuring diameters. [same as *calibre*]

cal'iph, cal'if *n.* Muslim ruler, successor of Muhammad. -**cal'iphate** *n.* [Arab. *khalifah*, successor]

calk. *See* **caulk.**

call (kawl) *v.t.* announce; name; summon. -*v.i.* shout; pay a short visit. -*n.* shout; animal's cry; visit; invitation. -**call'er** *n.* visitor. -**call'ing** *n.* vocation, occupation. [ON. *kalla*, cry loudly]

callig'raphy *n.* handwriting; penmanship. [G. *kallos*, beauty, graphein, write]

Calli'ope *n.* muse of epic poetry, American steam-organ. [G.]

callisthen'ics *n.pl.* exercises to promote strength and grace. [G. *kallos*, beauty, *sthenos*, strength]

call'ous *a.* hardened, unfeeling. -**callos'ity** *n.* hard lump on the skin. -**call'ously** *adv.* -**call'ousness** *n.* [L. *callosus*, thick-skinned]

call'ow *a.* unfledged; raw, inexperienced [OE. *calu*, bald]

calm (kam) *n.* stillness, want of wind. -*a.* still, quiet.-*v.t.* and *i.* become, make, still or quiet.-**calm'ly** *adv.* -**calm'ness** *n.* [F. *calme*]

cal'orie, cal'ory *n.* unit of heat; unit expressing the heat or energy potential of food when digested. -**calorific** *a.* heatmaking. -**calorim'eter** *n.* heat-measuring instrument. [fr. L. *color*, heat]

cal'otype *n.* early photographic process; photograph made by this process. [G. *kalos*, beautiful, *typos*, impression]

cal'umet *n.* N. Amer. Indian 'peace pipe.' [F. -*dim.* of L. *calamus*, reed]

cal'umny *n.* slander. -**calum'niate** *v.t.* -**calumnia'tion** *n.* -**calum'niator** *n.* -**calum'nious** *a.* [L. *calumnia*]

ca'lyx *n.* covering of a bud. [G. *kalyx*]

cam *n.* device to change a rotary motion to a reciprocating one. [*comb*]

CAM *v.t.* (*compute.*) application of computers to various manufacturing tasks such as process control, inventory control, work schedules [*C*omputer *A*ided *M*anufacturing]

cam'ber *n.* slight convexity on surface, *esp.* of road. -*v.i.* to arch slightly. [L. *camerare*, vault]

cam'bric (ka'-) *n.* fine white linen. [fr. Cambrai, in France]

cam'el *n.* animal of Asia and Africa, with a hump (or two humps) on its back, used as a beast of burden. [G. *kamelos*]

camell'ia *n.* Eastern evergreen shrub with beautiful rose or white flowers. [G. J. *Kamel*, Jesuit and botanist]

camel'opard *n.* (*arch.*) giraffe. [G. *kamelo-pardalis*, camel-leopard]

cam'eo *n.* stone of two layers cut in ornamental relief. [It. *cammeo*]

cam'era *n.* apparatus used to make photographs; judge's private room. **cam'era-man** *n.* photographer attached to newspaper or film company. -**cam'era obscu'ra** *n.* darkened room in which rotating apparatus reflects pictures of surrounding country on screen. [L. *chamber*]

cam'isole *n.* under-bodice. [F.]

cam'omile *n.* aromatic creeping plant used in medicine. [G. *chamaimelon*, earth appie]

camouflage (-azh) *n.* disguise; means of deceiving enemy observation. -*v.t.* disguise. [F.]

camp *n.* tents of an army; military quarters; travellers' resting-place. -*v.i.* form or lodge in a camp. **-camp'er** *n.* **-camp'ing** *n.* [L. *campus*, field]

campaign' *n.* time in which an army keeps the field; series of operations. -*v.i.* serve in a war. **-campaigner** *n.* [L. *campania*, open country]

campani'le *n.* bell-tower. [It.]

campan'ula *n.* kind of plant with bell shaped flowers, *e.g.* harebell, bluebell. [It.*campana*, bell]

cam'phor *n.* solid essential oil with aromatic taste and smell. **-cam'phor- ated** *a.* [Malay. *kapur*, chalk]

cam'pion *n.* common wild plant with pink or white flowers. [orig. unknown]

camp'us *n.* college grounds. [L. = *field*]

can *v.i.* be able; having the power; be allowed. [pres. of OE. *cunnan*, know]

can *n.* vessel, usually of metal, for holding liquids. -*v.t.* put, or preserve, in a can **-cannery** *n.* factory where foods are canned. [OE. *canne*]

canal' *n.* artificial watercourse, duct in the body. **-canaliza'tion** *n.* **-can'alize** *v.t.* cut canal through; convert into canal; direct (thoughts, *etc.*) into particular channel. [L. *canalis*, water-pipe]

canard' *n.* lying rumour; false report. [F.]

cana'ry *n.* yellow singing-bird; light wine. [*Canary* Islands]

can'cel *v.t.* cross out; annul, abolish, suppress. **-cancella'tion, cancelation** *n.* [L. *cancellare*, mark lattice-wise]

Can'cer *n.* malignant growth or tumor; the Crab, 4th sign of the zodiac, which sun enters about midsummer. [L. = *crab*]

candela'brum (-a-) *n.* branched ornamental candlestick. -*pl.* candelabra. [L.]

candescent *a.* white-hot; glowing. **-candes'cence** *n.* [L. *candere*, glow]

can'did *a.* frank, open, impartial. **-can'didly** *adv.* **-can'didness** *n.* **-can'dor** *n.* [L. *candidus*, white]

candidate *n.* one who seeks an office, appointment, privilege, *etc.* [L. *candidatus*, one wearing a white toga]

can'dle *n.* stick of wax with a wick; light. **-can'dlestick** *n.* **-can'dlepower** *n.* unit, standard for measuring light. [L. *candela*]

Candlemas' *n.* R.C. festival on 2nd February, when candles are blessed. [*candle* and *mass*]

can'dor. *See* **candid.**

can'dy *n.* (sweetmeat of) crystallized sugar. -*v.t.* preserve with sugar. -*v.i.* become encrusted with sugar. **-can'died** *a.* [fr. *silgar*-candy, F. *sucre candi*, fr. Arab. *qand*, sugar]

can'dytuft *n.* low-growing plant with white or pinkish flowers in tufts. [L. *Candia*, Crete]

cane *n.* stem of a small palm or large grass; walking-stick. -*v.i.* beat with a cane. [G. *kanna*, reed]

ca'nine *a.* like or pertaining to the dog. [L. *canes*, dog]

canister *n.* box or case, usually of tin. [L. *canistrum*, bread-basket]

cank'er *n.* eating sore; anything that eats away, destroys, corrupts. -*v.t.* infect, corrupt.-*v.i.* become cankered. **-cank'erworm** *n.* [L. *cancer*, crab]

can'na *n.* cotton-grass. [Gael. *canach*]

cannibal *n.* one who eats human flesh. -*a.* **-cann'ibalism** *n.* [Sp. *canibal*, for *Caribal*, Carib]

cann'on *n.* ancient (unrifled) piece of ordnance; modem weapon used in aircraft.**-cannonade'** *n.* and *v.* **-cannonball** *n.* **-cann'on-bone** *n.* horse's legbone. [F. *canon*, fr. L. *canna*, reed, tube]

cann'y *a.* shrewd; cautious; crafty. **-cann'ily** *adv.* **-cann'iness** *n.* [*See* **can**]

canoe' *n.* boat made of a hollow trunk or of bark or skins; light boat.**canoe'ist** *n.* [orig. *canoa*, Sp. fr. Haiti]

can'on *n.* law, rule, *esp.* of the church; standard; body of books accepted as genuine; list of saints. **-canoniza'tion** *n.* **-can'onize** *v.t.* [G. *kanon*, rule]

can'on *n.* church dignitary, member of a cathedral chapter. **-canon'ical** *a.* [L. *canonicus*, regular priest]

can'opy *n.* covering over a throne, bed, *etc.* -*v.t.* cover with a canopy. [G. *konopeion*, couch with mosquito curtains, fr. *konops*, gnat]

cant *n.* hypocritical speech; whining; language of a sect; technical jargon, slang, *esp.* of thieves. -*v.i.* use such language. [ONF. = singing]

cant *n.* inclination from the level. -*v.t.* and *i.* tilt. [Med. L. *cantus*, edge, corner]

cantaloupe (-loop) *n.* variety of melon. [*Canwupo*, town in Italy]

cantank'erous *a.* cross-grained, ill-natured. [ME. *contak,* strife)

canta'ta *n.* short oratorio. [It.]

canteen' *n.* small tin vessel; shop or refectory in a camp, barracks or factory; case of cutlery *etc.* [F. *cantine*]

can'ter *n.* easy galloping pace. -*v.i.* move at this pace. -*v.t.* make to canter. [short for *Canterbury* pace, pilgrim's pace on the Old Kent Road]

can'ticle *n.* hymn. [L. *canere*, sing]

cantilever *n.* large bracket supporting balcony, *ete.* **-can'tilever bridge'**, bridge built on cantilever principle. [Sp. *can*, support; F. *lever,* raise]

can'tillation *n.* traditional notation representing the various traditional Jewish melodies to which scriptural passages are chanted; chanting or intonation. [L. *canere*, sing]

can'to *n.* division of a poem. [It.]

canuck' *n.* (*sl.*) (French) Canadian. [N. Am. Ind.]

can'vas *n.* coarse cloth of hemp, used for sails, painting on, *etc.*; sails of a ship; picture. [F. *canevas*, fr. L. *cannabis*, hemp]

canvass *v.t.* sift, discuss, examine; solicit votes, contributions *etc.* -*n.* solicitation. -**can'vasser** *n.* [*canvas*]

can'yon *n.* deep gorge, ravine. [Sp. *cafton*]

caou'tchouc *a.* /*n.* india-rubber. [Carib. *Cahuchu*]

cap *n.* covering for the head; lid, top or other covering. -*v.t.* put a cap on; confer a degree upon; outdo; raise the cap in respect. [OE. *ceppe*, hood]

ca'pable *a.* able, gifted; having the capacity, power. **-capabil'ity** *n.* [F.]

capa'city (-as'-) *n.* power of holding or grasping; room; volume; character; ability, power of mind. **-capa'cious** *a.* roomy. [F. *capacité*-L. *capere*, hold]

caparison *n.* ornamental trappings for a horse. [Low L. *capa*, cape]

cape *n.* covering for the shoulders. [F.]

cape *n.* point of land running into the sea. [F. *cap*, fr. L. *caput*, head]

ca'per *n.* pickled flower-bud of a shrub growing in Sicily. [L. *capperis*]

ca'per *v.i.* skip or dance. -*n.* frolic; freak. [It.*capriola*; L. *caper*, goat]

capercaill'ie, capercail'zie *n.* large grouse. [Gael. *capull coille,* horse of the wood]

capillary *a.* hair-like. -*n.* tube with very small bore, *esp.* a small vein. [L. *capillaris*, fr. *capillus*, hair]

cap'ital *n.* headpiece of a column; chief town; large-sized letter; money, stock, funds. *a.* affecting life; serious; chief, leading; excellent.-**cap'italize** *v.t.* **-capitalism** *n.* **-cap'italist** *n.* **-cap'itally** *adv.* **-cap'ital lev'y**, tax levied on capital, for a specific purpose. [L. *capitalis*, fr. *caput*, head]

capita'tion *n.* census; poll-tax. [L. *caput*, head]

Cap'itol *n.* temple of Jupiter in Rome; house of Congress or state legislature in U.S. [L. *Capitolium*]

capitulate *v.i.* surrender on terms. -**capitula'tion** *n.* [Med. L. *capitulate*, draw terms under 'heads'; fr. *caput*, head]

capiz' *n.* the bivalve shell of a mollusk found *esp.* in the Philippines and having a smooth translucent shiny interior, used in jewelery, ornaments, *etc.* [native name]

ca'pon *n.* castrated cock. **-ca'ponize** *v.t.* [G. *kqpon*]

caprice' *n.* whim, freak. **-capricious** *a.* **capri'ciousness** *n.* [F.]

Capricorn *n.* the Goat, 10th sign of zodiac, which sun enters in midwinter. [L. *caper*, goat, *cornu*, hom]

capsize' *v.t.* upset.-*v.i.* be upset over turned. [orig. uncertain]

cap'stan *n.* machine turned by spokes, or power, to wind a cable, *esp.* to hoist an anchor on board ship. [fr. L. *capistrare*, fasten with a rope]

cap'sule *n.* seed vessel of a plant; gelatin case for a dose of medicine. [L. *capsular* dim. of *capsa*, case]

cap'tain *n.* leader, chief; commander of a vessel, company of soldiers. [F. *capitaine*. fr. L. *caput*, head]

cap'tion *n.* title, of an article, picture *etc.* [orig. a law term meaning arrest. fr. L. *capere*, take]

captious (-shus) *a.* ready to catch at faults; critical, peevish. **-cap'tiously** *adv.* **-cap'tiousness** *n.* [L. *captiosus*, fr. *captio*, sophistical argument]

cap'tive *n.* one taken prisoner, kept in bondage.; taken, imprisoned. **-captivate** *v.t.* fascinate. **-cap'tivating** *a.* **-capti'vity** *n.* [L. *captivus*]

cap'ture *n.* seizure, taking. -*v.t.* seize, catch, make prisoner. **-cap'tor** *n.* [L. *captura*, fr. *capere*, take]

car *n.* wheeled vehicle, railroad or tramway carriage; automobile. [L. *carrus*]

car'acal *n.* Persian lynx. [Turk. *qarahqulaq*, black-ear]

carafe' *n.* water jug, decanter. [Ital. *caraffa*, flagon]

car'amel *n.* dark substance obtained

from sugar on heating; sweet-meat. [L. *cunna mellis*, (mel) honey]

car'apace *n.* upper shell of tortoise, *etc.* [F. -Sp. *carapacho*]

car'at *n.* small weight used for gold, diamonds, *etc.*; proportional measure of twenty-fourths used to state the fineness of gold. [G. *keration*, carob fruit, small weight]

car'avan *n.* company of merchants, *etc.* traveling together, *esp.* in the East; covered van or house on wheels, trailer. **caravan'serai** *n.* Eastern inn for the reception of caravans; large hotel. [Pers. *karwan*, company of merchants or ships; *sarai*, mansion, inn]

car'away *n.* plant with aromatic seeds; the seeds. [Sp. *carvi*, for G. *karon*]

car'bide *n.* compound of carbon with an element, *esp.* calcium carbide. [*See* **carbon**]

car'bine, car'abine *n.* short rifle. - **carbineer', carbineer'** *n.* [F. *carabine*]

carbolic a'cid, *n.* acid made from coal-tar and used as a disinfectant. [fr. *carbon*, by analogy with alcoholic]

car'bon *n.* non-metallic element, substance of pure charcoal, found in all organic matter. **-car'bonate** *n.* **-carbon'ic** *a.* **-carbonif'erous** *a.* **-car'bonize** *v.t.* - **car'bon copy** *n.* written duplicate made by interleaving sheets of carbon paper. - **car'bon diox'ide,** gas exhaled from the lungs. **-car'bon monoxides,** odorless poisonous gas from car exhausts, *etc.* - **car'bon paper** *n.* paper coated with lampblack. **-carbon'ic acid** *n.* carbon dioxide, compound formed by combination of carbon dioxide and water. [L. *carbo*]

car'boy *n.* large glass bottle protected by a wicker casing. [Pers. *qarabah*]

carbuncle *n.* fiery-red precious stone; inflamed ulcer or tumor. [L. *carbunculus*, little coal]

car'buretor *n.* apparatus for mixing oil vapor and air in an engine. [*carbon*]

car'canet (kar'-ka-) *n.* jeweled collar or head ornament. [L. *carcannum*]

car'cass, car'case *n.* dead body of an animal; orig. skeleton. [F. *carcasses*]

carcinoma *n.* cancerous growth. - **carcino'sis** *n.* spread of cancer in body. [G. *karkinōma*, crab]

card *n.* pasteboard; small piece of pasteboard with a figure for playing games, or with a name and address, *etc.*; dial of a compass. **-card'board** *n.* pasteboard. [G. *chartes*, leaf of papyrus]

card *n.* instrument for combing wool, *etc.* *-v.t.* comb (wool). **card'er** *n.* [L. *carduus*, thistle]

car'diac *a.* pert.to heart; heart stimulant or cordial. **-car'diograph** *n.* instrument recording heart movements-**car'diogram** *n.* graph of these.**car'dioid** *a.* heart-shaped. **-car'dio-pulmonary** *a.* relating to, or affecting, the heart and lungs. [G. *kardia*, heart]

car'digan *n.* knitted woollen jacket, waistcoat.[7th Earl of *Cardigan*]

car'dinal *a.* chief, principal. *-n.* prince of the R.C. Church; member of the pope's council. **-car'dinalate** *n.* **-cardinal numbers,** the simple numbers 1, 2, 3, *etc.* **-cardinal points,** North, South, East and West. [G. *cardinals*, essential, fr. *cardo*, hinge]

care *n.* anxiety; pains, heed; charge, oversight.*-v.i.* be anxious; be disposed (to); have regard or liking (for). **-care'free** *a.* **-care'ful** *a.* **-care'fully** *adv.* **-care'fulness** *n.* **-care'less** *a.* **-care'lessness** *n.* - **care'taker** *n.* [OE. *caru, n., cearian* v., sorrow]

careen' *v.t.*lay a ship over on her side for cleaning or repair. *-v.i.* heel over. [L. *carina*, keel]

career' *n.* course through life; course of action, height of activity; course, running. *-v.i.* run or move at full speed. [F. *carriare*, racecourse]

caress' *v.t.* fondle, embrace, treat with affection. *-n.* act or expression of affection. [L. *carus*, dear]

car'et *n.* mark inserted to show where something has been omitted. [L. *caret*, there is wanting]

car'go *n.* ship's load. [Sp. *cargar*, load]

caribou' *n.* Amer. reindeer. [Can. F.]

caricature *n.* likeness exaggerated or distorted to appear ridiculous. *-v.t.* portray in this way. [It.*caricatura*, lit. an overloading]

ca'ries *n.* tooth or bone decay. [L.]

carill'on (-il'-yen) *n.* peal of bells; tune played on them. [F.]

carminative *n.* medicine for flatulence. [L. *carminare*, comb out]

car'mine *n.* warm crimson color. *-a.* [L. *carminus*, fr. Arab. *qarmazi*, crimson]

carn'age *n.* slaughter. [L. *caro*, flesh]

car'nal *a.* fleshly, sensual; worldly. - **carnal'ity** *n.* **-car'nally** *adv.* [L. *carnalis*, of the flesh]

carna'tion *n.* flesh color; cultivated flower, double-flowering variety of the clove pink. [fr. L. *caro*, flesh]

car'nival *n.* revel; season of revelry before Lent. [F. *carnaval*]
carnivorous *a.* flesh-eating. **carn'i-vore** *n. -pl.* **carnivore.** [L. *carnivorus*]
car'ob *n.* algaroba or locust-tree. [Arab. *kharrubah*]
car'ol *n.* song ofjoy or praise. -*v.i.* and *t.* sing or warble. **-car'olling** *n.* [OF. *carole*]
car'otin *n.* red coloring matter in carrots. [L. *carota*, carrot]
carouse' *n.* drinking-bout.-*v.i.* hold a drinking bout.**-carous'al** *n.* **-carous'er** *n.* [fr. drink, *carouse*, Ger. *gar aus*, quite out]
carouser. *See* **carrousel.**
carp *n.* freshwater fish. [P. *carpe*]
carp *v.i.* catch at small faults or errors; **cavil. -carp'er** *n.* **-carp'ing** *n.***carpingly** *adv.* [ON. *karpa*, chatter, influenced by L. *carpere*, pluck]
carpenter *n.* worker in timber, as in building, *etc.* **car'pentry** *n.* [L. *carpentari*, *carpentum*, chariot]
car'pet *n.* cloth floor-covering. -*v.t.* cover a floor. **-car'pet-bag** *n.* **carpetbagger** *n.* political adventurer. **car'pet-sweep-er** *n.* [Med. L. *carpita*, patchwork]
carriage *n.* act or cost of carrying; vehicle; bearing, conduct.**-carr'iage-horse** *n.* [ONF. *cariage*, fr. *carier*, carry]
carr'ion *n.* rotting dead flesh. *a.* - **carr'ion-crow** *n.* [ONF. *caroigne*]
carr'ot *n.* plant with a reddish, eatable root. **-carr'oty** *a.* red. [G. *karoton*]
carrousel, carouser *n.* merry-go round; circular belt on which items are placed for collection or distribution, as luggage at an airport, *etc.* [F.]
carr'y *v.t.*convey, transport; capture; effect; behave. -*v.i.* reach, of a projectile, sound. -*n.* range. **-carr'ier** *n.* one who, that which, carries goods; kind of pigeon; (*colloq.*) aircraft carrier; person who transmits disease to others, though himself immune. [ONF. *carier*, fr. *car*, vehicle]
cart *n.* two-wheeled vehicle without springs. -*v.t.* convey in such vehicle; carry. **-cart'age** *n.* **-cart'er** *n.* **-cart'-wright** *n.* [ON. *kartr*]
cartilage *n.* firmelastic tissue in the body of vertebrates; gristle. **cartila'ginous** (-aj-) *a.* [L. *cartilage*]
cartography *n.* map or chartmaking. **cartog'rapher** *n.* [L. *charta*, map; G. *graphein*, describe]
car'ton *n.* pasteboard container. [F.]
cartoon' *n.* design for a painting; satirical illustration in a journal, *esp.* relating to current events. **cartoon'ist** *n.* [F. *carton*]
cartridge *n.* case containing the charge for a gun. [F. *cartouche*, fr. It.*cartoccio*, roll of paper, fr. *carta*, card]
carve *v.t.* cut; hew, sculpture, engrave; cut up (meat). **-carv'er** *n.* **car'very** *n.* an eating establishment at which customers pay a set price and may then have unrestricted helpings of food from a variety of meats, salads, and other vegetables. - **carv'ing** *n.* [OE. *coerfan*, cut]
cascade' *n.* waterfall; anything resembling this. -*v.i.* fall in cascades. [F.]
cas'cara, casca'ra *n.* Californian bitter bark used in medicine as a laxative. [for (Sp.) *cascaéra sagraéda*, sacred bark]
case *n.* instance; state of affairs; condition; lawsuit; grounds for a suit. **-case'law** *n.* [orig. 'what befalls'; F. *cas*, fr. L. *cadere*, fall]
case *n.* box, sheath, covering; any receptacle; box and its contents. -*v.t.* put in a case **-case'harden** *v.t.* a process to harden steel by combining it with carbon. **-case'-hardening** *n.* [ONF. *casse*, fr. L. *capere*, hold]
cas'ein *n.* protein in cheese. [L. *caseus*, cheese]
case'mate *n.* bomb-proof vault. [F.]
case'ment *n.* window frame; window opening on hinges. [for *encaseraent*, OF. *enchassement*. *See* **sash**]
cash *n.* money, coin. -*v.t.* turn into or exchange for money. **-cashier'** *n.* **-cash'book** *n.* **-cash'less** *adv.* functioning, operated, or performed without using coins or banknotes for money transactions but instead using credit cards or electronic transfer of funds. **-cash' register** *n.* recording till. [orig. 'moneybox'; It.*cassa*, fr. L. *capere*, hold]
cashew' *n.* S. American tree with kidney-shaped nuts. [Braz. *acajoba*]
cashier' *v.t.* discharge, dismiss in disgrace. [L. *cassare*, make void]
cash'mere *n.* shawl; soft fabric of goat's hair. [*Kashmir*]
casi'no *n.* building with gaming tables, public dance-halls, *etc.* [It.]
cask *n.* barrel. [Sp. *casco*, pot, helmet]
cask'et *n.* small case or box for jewels, *etc.*; coffin, *usu.* of ornate kind. [F. *cassette*, small case]
cassa'va *n.* W. Indian manioc; its starchy root, yielding tapioca. [*native*]
casserole *n.* fireproof dish for cooking and serving meat *etc.* [F.]
cassette' *n.* plastic container for film, magnetic tape, *etc.* [OF. *casse*, case]
cass'ock *n.* long, black tunic worn by

clergymen. **cass'ocked** *a.* [F. *cassaque*]

cast (-a-) *v.t.* throw or fling; shed; throw down; allot, as parts in a play; found, as metal. *-v.i.* cast about, look around. *-n.* throw; thing thrown; distance thrown; squint; mold; manner, quality, tinge, color, degree; set of actors. **-cast'away** *n.* **cast'ing** *n.* **cast'ing-vote** *n.* [ON. *kasta*]

caste *n.* section of society in India; social rank. [Port. *caste*, race]

castigate *v.t.* chastise; punish or rebuke severely. **-castiga'tion** *n.* **-cas'tigator** *n.* [L. *castigate*]

cas'tle (kas'l) *n.* fortress; country mansion. [L. *castellum*]

cast'or (-a-) *n.* beaver; hat made ofbeaver fur. [G. *kastor*]

cast'or (-a-) *n.* small vessel with perforated top, *e.g.*, sugar-castor. [*cast*]

castor-oil (-a-) *n.* vegetable medicinal oil. [formerly name of a drug obtained from the *castor*, beaver]

cas'trate *v.t.* remove the testicles, deprive of the power of generation. - **castra'tion** *n.* [L. *castrate*]

cas'ual (-zh-) *a.* accidental; unforeseen; occasional; unmethodical. **-cas'ually** *adv.* **-cas'ualty** *n.* accident; loss in war. [L. *casualis*, fr. *cadere*, fall]

cas'uist *n.* one who studies and solves cases of conscience; quibbler. - **casuist'ical** *a.* **caus'uistry** *n.* [F. *casuiste*]

cat *n.* tame or wild animal of the genus Felis; spiteful woman; piece of wood tapered at both ends; nine-lashed whip. - **catt'y** *a.* **-cat'-bird** *n.* Amer. thrush with mewing note. **-cat'-fish** *n.* fish with features like cat.**-cat'gut** *n.* cord made of intestines of animals. **-cat'head** *n.* beam at the bow of a ship. **-cat'kin** *n.* spike of flowers, as of willow *etc.* **cat's'paw** *n.* dupe; breath of wind. **-cat's'whisker** *n.* fig. a very fine margin. [ONF. -Late L. *cattus*]

catabolism, katab'olism *n.* destructive metabolism (*q.v.*). [G. *katabole*, cast down]

cat'aclism *n.* upheaval. [G. *kataklysrnos*]

cat'acomb *n.* underground gallery for burial. [Late L. *Catacumbas*]

catafalque' (-falk) *n.* temporary structure which receives the coffin during a lying-in-state. [Fr., -It., *catafalco*]

catalepsy *n.* state of trance; disease causing it.**-catalep'tic** *a.* [G. *kata*, down, *lepsomai*, I seize]

catalogue, cat'alog (-og) *n.* descriptive list.*-v.t.* make a list of; enter in a catalogue. [G. *katalogos*, fr. *legein*, choose]

catal'pa *n.* Amer. tree with large blossoms. [W. Indian]

catal'ysis *n.* chemical change effected by catalyst.**-cat'alyst** *n.* substance producing chemical change in another sub stance without itself changing. [G. *kata*, down, *luein*, loose]

catamaran' *n.* Indian raft of logs. [*Tamil*]

cat'aplasm *n.* poultice, plaster. [G. *kataplasma*, plaster]

cat'apult *n.* small forked stick with an elastic sling used by boys for throwing stones; formerly an engine of war for hurling arrows, stones, *etc.* [fr. G. *katapeltes*, fr. *pallein*, throw]

cat'aract *n.* waterfall; defect in an eye, causing blindness. [G. *katarhaktes*]

catarrh' *n.* discharge from the nose; common cold. **-catar'rhal** *a.* [fr. G. *katarrhein*, flow down]

catastrophe *n.* climax of a tragedy; great disaster. [G. *katastrophe*]

catch *v.t.* take hold of, seize; understand. *-v.i.* be contagious; get entangled. *-n.* seizure; anything that holds, stops, *etc.*; that which is caught; form of musical composition; advantage taken or to be gained; hidden difficulty or drawback. **-catch'er** *n.* **-catch'ing** *a.* **-catch'ment-basin** *n.* area from which a river is fed. **-catch'penny** *a.* **-catchword** *n.* cue; popular phrase; first word of page printed at foot of preceding page. [ONF. *cachier*]

catechize (-k-) *v.t.* instruct by question and answer; question. **-catechet'ic** *a.* - **catechet'ics** *n.* **-cat'echism** *n.* **-catechist** *n.* **-catechu'men** *n.* one under instruction in Christianity. [G. *katechizein*]

category *n.* class or order; division. - **categorical** *a.* positive; what may be affirmed of a class. **-categor'ically** *adv.* - **cat'egorize** *v.t.* [G. *kategoria*, assertion]

catenation *n.* chain, links in chain. [L. *catena*, chain]

ca'ter *v.i.* provide food, entertainment, *etc.* **-ca'terer** *n.* **-ca'tering** *n.* [ME. *acatour*, buyer, fr. OF. *achater*, buy]

caterpillar *n.* hairy grub of a moth or butterfly. **-cat'erpillar-wheel** *n.* endless band instead of a wheel for vehicles crossing rough ground. [OF. *chatepelose*, hairy cat]

cathedral *n.* principal church of a diocese. *-a.* pertaining to a cathedral. [orig. *a.* in cathedral church, fr. G. *kathedra*, seat (*i.e.*, of the bishop)]

cath'ode *n.* negative pole in electricity.

cath'ode rays, streams of electrons. -**cath'odal** *a.* [G. *kata*, down, *hodos*, way]

cath'olic *a.* universal; including the whole body of Christians; relating to the Roman Catholic Church. -*n.* adherent of the R.C. Church. -**cathol'icize** *v.t* . -**cathol'icism** *n.* -**cathol'city** *n.* [G. *katholikos*, universal]

cat'sup *n.* sauce of tomatoes, mushrooms, *etc.* [Malay *kechap*]

catt'le *n.* beasts of pasture, *esp.* oxen, cows. -sometimes horses, sheep, also. -**catt'leman** *n.* -**catt'le-show** *n.* [L. *capitale*, stock, fr. *caput*, head]

cau'cus *n.* private political meeting or group. [perh. fr. Algonquin *cawcawaasough*, counsellor]

caul *n.* membrane covering head of some infants at birth; openwork head covering. [OF. *cale*, small cap]

cauldrons *See* **caldron.**

cauliflower (kol'-) *n.* cabbage with an eatable white flower-head. [L. *caulis*, cabbage, and *flower*]

caulk, calk (kawk) *v.t.*press oakum into the seams of a ship, to make it watertight.-**caulk'er** *n.* -**caulk'ing** *n.* -**caulking-iron** *n.* [Late L. *calicare*, stop up with lime, *calx*]

cause (-z) *n.* that which produces an effect; reason; origin; motive, purpose; lawsuit; party principle. -*v.t.* bring about, make to exist.-**caus'al** *a.* -**causa'tion** *n.* -**cause'less** *a.* [L. *causa*]

cau'serie *n.* chat; short, informal essay. [F.]

causeways, caus'ey (-z-) *n.* raised way, paved street.[earlier *causey*; Late L. *calciata* (via), *paved* (way)]

caustic *a.* burning; bitter, severe. -*n.* corrosive substance. -**caus'tically** *adv.* [G. *kaustikos*]

cauterize *v.t.* burn with a caustic or hot iron. -**cauteriza'tion** *n.* [G. *kauterion*, hot iron]

ca'ution *n.* heedfulness, care; warning. -*v.t.* warn. -**cau'tionary** *a.* -**cau'tioner** *n.* -**cau'tious** *a.* -**cau'tiously** *adv.* -**cau'tiousness** *n.* [L. *cautio*, fr. *cavere*, beware]

cavalcade' *n.* column or procession of persons on horseback; procession of vehicles. -**cavalier'** *n.* horseman; courtly gentleman; adherent of the King in the English Civil War. -a. careless disdainful. -**cavalier'ly** *adv.* -**cav'alry** *n.* mounted troops. [F., fr. L. *caballus*, horse]

cave *n.* hollow place in the earth; den. -**cav'ern** *n.* deep cave. -**cav'ernous** *a.* -**cav'ernously** *adv.* -**cav'ity** *n.* hollow opening. (L. *cavus*, hollow]

cave in fall in; collapse; submit.[fr. earlier E. dialect *calve in*]

cav'eat (ka'vi-at) *n.* a notice or warning, esp. a notice to suspend proceedings in a court of law. [L.]

caviar' *n.* salted sturgeon roe; (*fig.*) some thing too fine for the vulgar taste. [Turk. *khavyar*]

cav'il *v.i.* find fault without sufficient reason, make trifling objections. -**cav'iller** *n.* -**cav'illing** *n.* (L. *caviar*, argue, scoffingly]

caw *n.* crow's cry. -*v.i.* cry as a crew. -**caw'ing** *n.* [imit.]

cayenne', cayenne'-pep'per *n.* very pungent red pepper. [Braz.]

cay'man *n.* kind of alligator. [Sp. Port.(orig. perh. Carib) *caiman*]

cease *v.i.* stop, give over. -*v.t.* discontinue. -**cease'less** *a.* -**cease'lessly** *adv.* [F. *cesser*- L. *cessare*, give over]

ce'dar *n.* large spreading evergreen tree; its wood. [fr. G. *kedros*]

cede' *v.t.* yield, give up, *esp.* of territory. [L. *cedere*, yield]

cei'ling *n.* inner roof, *usu.* plastered; upper limit.-**ceil** *v.t.* [F. *ceil*, heaven, fr. L. *call*, canopy]

cel'andine *n.* yellow flower, the swallowwort. [fr. G. *chelidon*, swallow]

celebrate *v.t.* make famous; mark by ceremony (event of festival); perform with due rites. -**cel'ebrant** *n.* -**cel'ebrated** *a.* famous. -**celebra'tion** *n.* -**celeb'rity** *n.* fame; famous person. [L. *celebrate*]

ceter'ity *n.* swiftness. [L. *celeritas*]

cel'ery *n.* vegetable with long white eatable stalks. [F. *cgleri*]

celestial *a.* heavenly, divine. [L. *cælestis*, fr. *cxlum*, heaven]

celibacy *n.* single life, unmarried state. -**cel'ibate** *a.* [L. *cælebs*, unmarried]

cell *n.* small room; small cavity; unit-mass of living matter. -**cell'ular** *a.* -**cell'ude** *n.* [L. *cella*]

cell'ar *n.* underground room for storage. -**cell'arage** *n.* -**cell'arer** *n.* **cell'aret** *n.* case for bottles. [L. *cellarium*, set of cells]

cell'o (ch-) *n.* for violoncello (*q.v.*). cellophane -*n.* transparent material chiefly used for wrapping. [Trademark]

celluloid *n.* synthetic substance made from cellulose; substitute for bone, ivory, *etc.* [Trademark] . [L. *cella*]

cell'ulose *n.* cell membrane of plants and wood; group of carbohydrates. *a.* containing cells. [L. *cella*]

Celt (kelt, selt) *n.* member of Indo-Germanic people including Irish, Welsh, Scots, *etc.* -**Celtic** *a.* [L. *Celta*]

cement' *n.* mortar; anything used for sticking together. -*v.t.* unite with cement; unite firmly. [F. *ciment*]

cem'etery *n.* burying-ground. [fr. G. *koimeterion*, sleeping-place]

cen'otaph *n.* empty tomb, monument to someone buried elsewhere. [G. *kenos*, empty, *taphos*, tomb]

cen'ser *n.* pan in which incense is burned. [for *incenser*]

cen'sor *n.* supervisor of morals; one who examines plays, books, news, *etc.* before publication. -**censo'rial** *a.* -**censo'rious** *a.* fault-finding. **censo'riously** *adv.* -**censo'riosness** *n.* -**cen'sorship** *n.* [L. = judge of morals]

cen'sure *n.* blame; reproof. -*v.t.* blame, reprove. cen'surable *a.* -**cen'surably** *adv.* [L. *censure*, judgment]

cen'sus *n.* official counting of the inhabitants of a country; any official counting. [L.]

cent *n.* hundred; hundredth part of a dollar. **per cent'**, in, to, by each hundred. [L. *centum*]

cen'taur *n.* mythical monster, half-man, half-horse. -**cen'taury** *n.* pink-flowered tonic herb. [G. *kentauros*]

centennial *n.* hundred years; celebration of a hundredth anniversary. -*a.* pertaining to a hundred. -**centena'rian** *n.* one a hundred years old. *a.* lasting a, or happening every, hundred years. -**cente'nary** *n.* centennial. (L. *centenarius*]

cen'ter *n.* mid-point of anything; pivot, axis; point to which, or from which, things move or are drawn. -**cen'tral** *a.* -**cent'ral heating** *n.* method of heating buildings by system of hot pipes. -**centralization** *n.* -**cen'tralize** *v.t.*-**central'ity** *n.* -**cen'trally** *adv.* -**cen'tric** *a.* -**centrif'ugal** *a.* tending from a center -**centrip'etal** *a.* tending towards a center. [L. *centrum*]

centigrade *a.* having a hundred degrees. [L. *centum*, hundred, *gradus*, degree]

centigram *n.* one hundredth part of gram. [L. *centum*, hundred]

centimeter *n.* one hundredth part of meter. [L. *centum*, hundred]

centipede *n.* small segmented animal with many legs. [L. *centipeda-centum*, hundred, *pes, ped-*, foot]

centurion *n.* commander of a hundred men. [L. *centurio*]

cen'tury *n.* hundred years; unit of one hundred. [L. *centenarius*]

ceph'alic (-f-) *a.* of the head. -**ceph'alopod** *n.* mollusk with tentacles from the head. -**ceph'alous** *a.* [G. *kephale*, head]

ceram'ics *n. pl.* potter's art. -**ceram'ic** *a.* [G. *keramos*, potter's earth]

ceras'tes *n.* horned viper. [G. *keras*, horn]

cere *n.* wax-like part at base of bird's back. -**cera'ceous** *a.* waxy. -**cere'cloth, cer'ement** *n.* waxed cloth for dead body, shroud. [L. *cera*, wax]

ce'real *a.* pertaining to corn. -*n.* grain used as food (*usu. pl.*). [L. *cerealis*, fr. *Ceres*, goddess of agriculture]

cer'ebral *a.* pertaining to the brain. -**cerebra'tion** *n.* brain action. **cer'ebro-spi'nal** *a.* [fr. L. *cerebrum*, brain]

cer'emony *n.* sacred rite; formal observance; usage of courtesy; formality; -**ceremo'nial** *a.* -**ceremo'nially** adv, -**ceremo'nious** *a.* -**ceremo'niously** *adv.* **ceremoniousness** *n.* [L. *cærimonia*]

cer'tain *a.* sure, settled, fixed, inevitable; some, one; of moderate (quantity, degree *etc.*). **cer'tainly** *adv.* **cer'tainty** *n.* -**cer'titude** *n.* [F., fr. L. *certus*]

cer'tify *v.t.* make known as certain; declare formally. -**certifica'tion** *n.* -**certif'icate** *n.* written declaration. -*v.t.* give a written declaration. -**cer'tifier** *n.* [L. *cerius*, sure, *facere*, make]

ceru'lean *a.* sky-blue. [L. *cæruleus*]

cesa'rian *See* **caesarian.**

cesium, caesium *n.* a silver-white alkaline metal. [L. *caesius*, bluish-gray]

cessation *n.* a ceasing or stopping. [L. *cessatio*. *See* **cease**]

cess'ion *n.* a yielding up. [*See* **cede**]

cess'pool *n.* pit in which filthy water collects, a receptacle for sewage. [orig. uncertain]

ceta'cea (-shi-a) *n. pl.* order of aquatic mammals including the whales. [G. *ketos*, sea-monster]

chafe *v.t.* make hot by rubbing; fret or wear by rubbing; irritate. -**cha'fing-dish** *n.* -**cha'fing-gear** *n.* [F. *chauffer*]

cha'fer *n.* beetle. [OE. *ceafor*]

chaff (-af) *n.* husks of corn; worthless matter; banter, making fun. [OE. *ceaf*]

chaff'er *v.i.* haggle, bargain. -*n.* bargaining. -**chaff'erer** *n.* [orig. 'trade', fr. OE. *ceap*, price, and *faru*, journey]

chaf'finch (-insh) *n.* small song-bird of the finch family. [fr. *chaff n.*]

chag'rin (sh-) *n.* vexation, disappointment.-*v.t.* vex. [F. = sad]

chain *n.* series of links or rings each passing through the next; fetter; anything that binds; connected series of things or events; surveyor's measure, -*v.t.* fasten with a chain; confine. makes compound nouns as **-chain-arm'or, chain'-mail, chain'-shot, chain'stitch** *etc.* [F. *chatne*, fr. L. *catena*]

chair *n.* movable seat; seat of authority; professor's seat, or his office; iron support for a rail on a railway. -*v.t.* carry in triumph. **-chair'man** *n.* one who presides. **chair'manship** *n.* [F. *chaire*, fr. G. *kathedra*]

chaise (shaz) *n.* light carriage. [F.]

chalcedony (kal'-) *n.* precious stone, white or bluish-white. [G. chalkedon]

chal'dron (kawl'-) *n.* measure for coals, 36 bushels. [orig. uncertain]

chal'et (shal'-, i) *n.* Swiss Alpine wooden hut; wooden villa. [F.]

chalice *n.* cup, *esp.* Communion Cup. -**chal'iced** *a.* cup-shaped. [L. *colix*, cup]

chalk (chawk) *n.* white substance, carbonate of lime. -*v.t.* rub or mark with chalk. -*v.i.* mark with chalk; keep a reckoning. **chalk'iness** *n.* **-chalk'y** *a.* [OE. *cealc*, L. *calx*, lime]

challenge *v.t.* call to fight; call to account; dispute; claim; object to. -**chall'engeable** *a.* **chall'enger** *n.* [L. *calumnia*, false accusation]

chalyb'eate (ka-lib'-iat) *a.* containing iron. [L. *chakvbs*, steel]

cha'mber *n.* room; room for an assembly; assembly or body of men; compartment; cavity. **-cha'mberlain** *n.* officer appointed by a king, *etc.* for domestic and ceremonial duties. **-cha'mber-maid** *n.* servant with care of bedrooms. -**cha'mber-pot, cha'mber** *n.* vessel for urine. [F. *chambre*, fr. L. *camera*, vault]

chameleon (ka-) *n.* small lizard famous for its power of changing color. [G. *chamaileon*, dwarf lion]

cham'fer *n.* bevel; groove; fluting. -*v.t.* [OF. *chanfraindre*]

cham'ois (sham'-wa) *n.* goat-like mountain animal; soft leather. [F.]

champagne' (sham-pan) *n.* sparkling white wine of Champagne, France.

cham'pion *n.* one who fights for another; one who defends a cause; in sport, *etc.*, one who excels all others; hero. -*v.t.* fight for, maintain. **-cham'pionship** *n.* [F., fr. Late. L. *campio*, fighter in the arena]

chance (-a-) *n.* that which happens; fortune; risk; opportunity; possibility; probability. -*v.t.* risk. -*v.i.* happen- *a.* casual, unexpected. [F., fr. OF. *cheoir*, fall; orig. 'fall' of dice]

chan'cel *n.* eastern part of a church. [L. *cancelli*, lattice between choir and nave]

chancellor *n.* high officer of state; head of university. **-chan'celtery** *n.* -**chan'cellorship** *n.* [F. chancelier, (*orig.*) keeper of a barrier. *See* **chancel**]

chan'cery *n.* office of a chancellor; court of equity. [orig, a court presided over by the Lord *Chancellor*, a chancellery]

chand'ler *n.* retail dealer. **-chandelier'** (sh-) *n.* frame with branches for holding lights. [F. *chandelier*, candlestick. candlemaker, fr. L. *candela*]

change *v.t.* alter or make different; put for another; exchange, interchange. -*v.i.* alter; put on different clothes. -*n.* alteration, variation; variety; conversion of money; small money; balance received on payment. **-changeabil'ity** *n.* **-change'-able** *a.* **-change'ableness** *n.* **-change'ably** *adv.* -**change'ful** *a.* **-change'less** *a.* -**change'ling** *n.* child substituted for another by the fairies. [F. *changer*]

chann'el *n.* bed of a stream; deeper part of a strait, bay, harbor; groove; means of passing or conveying. -*v.t.* groove, furrow. [L. *canalis*]

chant *v.t.* and *i.* sing. -*n.* song; church melody. **-chant'er** *n.* **-chant'ry** *n.* -endowment or chapel for singing masses. -**chant'y** (sh-) *n.* sailor's song. [F. *chanter*, fr. L. *cantare*, sing]

chanticleer *n.* cock. [OF. *chantecler*, 'sing-clear,' the name of the cock in the epic-fable of Reynard the Fox]

Chan'ukah. *See* **Han'ukkah.**

cha'os (ka) *n.* disorder, confusion; state of the universe before the Creation. [G.]

chap *v.t.* crack; strike. -*v.i.* fissure. -*n.* crack in the skin. **-chapped** *a.* [related to *chip*, *chop*]

chap *n.* fellow. [for *chapman*, pedlar]

chap'book *n.* book sold by a chapman. [*See* **chap**]

chap'el *n.* subordinate place of worship, as one attached to a garrison, house, prison, *etc.*, and not a cathedral or parish church; division of a church with its own altar; Dissenters' or Nonconformists' place of worship; association of printers. [orig. sanctuary where was deposited the *cappella*, or sacred cloak, of St.Martin]

chap'eron (sh-) *n.* one who attends a young unmarried lady in public as a protector. -*v.t.* [F. = hood]

chap'lain *n.* clergyman attached to a chapel, regiment, ship of war, institution *etc.* **-chap'laincy** *n.* [F. *chapelain. See* chapel]

chap'let *n.* garland for the head; circlet of gold *etc.*; part of a rosary. [F. *chapelet*, headdress]

chaps *n. pl.* protective leather leggings worn by cowboys. [fr. Mex. Sp. *chaparejos*]

chap'ter *n.* division of a book; section, heading; assembly of the clergy of a cathedral, *etc.* organized branch of a society, fraternity. **chap'ter-house** *n.* [F. *chapitre*-L. *capitulum*, dim. of *caput*, head; the church chapter was a meeting at which a chapter was read]

char *v.t.* scorch, burn, reduce to charcoal. [fr. *charcoal*]

char, chore *n.* odd job. *-pl.* household tasks. *-v.i.* **-char'woman** *n.* domestic cleaner, scrub-woman. [OE. *cierran*, turn]

char'abanc (shar'a-bang) *n.* open coach with seats all facing forward. [F. *char à bancs*]

character (ka-) *n.* letter, sign, or any distinctive mark; essential feature; nature; total of qualities making up an individuality; moral qualities; reputation of possessing them; statement of the qualities of a person who has been in one's service; person noted for eccentricity; personality in a play or novel. **-characteriza'tion** *n.* **characterize** *v.t.* **characteristic** *a.* **characteris'tically** *adv.* **char'acterless** *a.* [G. *character*, tool for stamping]

charade' (shar-ad) *n.* riddle, often acted, on the syllables of a word. [F.]

char'coal *n.* black residue ofwood, bones, *etc.* by smothered burning; charred wood. **char'coal-burner** *n.* [orig. uncertain]

charge *v.t.* fill; load; lay a task on, enjoin, command; deliver an injunction; bring an accusation against; ask as a price; fill with electricity. *-v.i.* make an onset.*-n.* that which is laid on; cost, price; load for a gun, *etc.*; command, exhortation; accusation; accummulation of electricity. *-pl.* expenses. **-charge'able** *a.* **char'ger** *n.* officer's horse. [F. *charger*, Low L. *carricare*, load]

char'iot *n.* two-wheeled war vehicle drawn by horses; state carriage. -**charioteer'** *n.* [F., fr. *char*, car]

charity *n.* love, kindness; disposition to think kindly of others; practical kindliness, alms-giving. **char'itable** *a.* **-charitably** *adv.* [F. *charitg*, fr. L. *caritas-carus*, dear]

char'ivari (sh-) *n.* uproar, noisy tumult, as an expression of protest or disapproval. [F.]

charlatan (sh-) *n.* quack. **-charl'atanry** *n.* [It. *ciarlatano*, prattler]

Charleston *n.* orig. a black American dance, adaptation of this as ballroom dance. [*Charleston*, S. Carolina]

char'lock *n.* yellow-flowered weed in cornfields. [OE. *cerlic*]

charlotte (sh-) *n.* stewed fruit covered with breadcrumbs. **-char'lotte russe'**, fruit, custard, enclosed in spongecake. [F.]

charm *n.* magic spell; thing worn to avert evil; anything that fascinates; attractiveness. *-v.t.* bewitch; delight, attract.-charmed *a.* **-charm'er** *n.* **-charm'ing** *a.* **-charm'ingly** *adv.* [F. *charme*, fr. L. *carmen*, song, incantation]

char'nel-house *n.* place where the bones of the dead are put. (earlier *charnel*, fr. Late L. *carme*, fr. *caro*, flesh)]

chart *n.* map of the sea; diagram or tabulated statement. **-chart'-house** *n.* (Nautical). [L. *charta*, paper]

chart'er *n.* writing in evidence of a grant of privileges, *etc.*; patent. *-v.t.* establish by charter; let or hire. [L. *chartula*, dim. of *charta*, paper]

Chartreuse' *n.* Carthusian monastery; famous liquor made by the monks. [La Grande *Chartreuse*, Grenoble]

chart'ulary, cart'ulary *n.* monastic register, record-keeper. [Low L. *chartularius*, fr. *charta*, paper]

cha'ry *a.* cautious, sparing. **-cha'rily** *adv.* **-cha'riness** *n.* [OE, *cearig*]

chase *v.t* hunt, pursue; drive from, into, *etc.* *-n.* pursuit, hunting; thing hunted; hunting-ground. [F. *chasser*]

chase *v.t* decorate with engraving. -**cha'ser** *n.* **cha'sing** *n.* [for *enchase*, F. *enchdsser*, enshrine]

chasm (kazm) *n.* deep cleft; abyss. [G. *chasma*]

chas'sé *n.* gliding step used in dancing. *-v.i.* perform the step. [F.]

chassis *n.* framework, wheels and machinery of a motor-car; underframe of an airplane. [F.]

chaste *a.* pure; modest; virtuous; (*art*) in good taste. **-chaste'ly** *adv.* **-chas'tity** *n.* [L. *castus*, pure]

cha'sten (-an-) *v.t* free from faults by punishment; restrain, moderate. **-chastened** *a.* [*chaste*]

chastise' *v.t* inflict punishment on; reduce to order. **chas'tisement** *n.* [*chaste*]

chat *v.t* talk idly or familiarly. *-n.*

familiar talk; idle talk; genus of small birds, as stonechat, whinchat *etc.* -**chatt'ily** *adv.* **chatt'y** *a.* [*chatter*]

chatt'el *n.* any movable property (*usu.* in *pl.*). [fr. Late L. *capitale*, goods, property. *See*cattle]

chatt'er *v.i.* talk idly or rapidly; rattle the teeth. -*n.* idle talk. -**chatt'erbox** *n.* -**chatt'erer** *n.* -**chatt'ering** *n.* [imit.]

chauffeur' *n.* professional automobile driver. [F. = *stoker*]

chauvinism *n.* noisy patriotism; smug sense of superiority; jingoism. [*Chauvin*, French soldier]

cheap *a.* low in price; inexpensive; easily obtained; of little value or estimation. -**cheap'en** *v.t.* -**cheap'ly** *adv.* -**cheap'nes** *n.* [OE. *ceap*, a bargain]

cheat *v.t.* deprive of by deceit, defraud; impose upon. -*v.i.* practice deceit.-*n.* fraud. [for *escheat*, confiscate]

check *v.t.* stop; restrain; hinder; repress; control; examine. -*n.* threatening the king at chess; repulse; stoppage; restraint; token, ticket; order for money; bill; a mark (√) indicating approval of the affirmative. -**check'er** *n.* marking like a chess-board. -*pl.* squares like those of a chess-board. -*v.t.* mark in squares; variegate. -**checkered** *a.* marked in squares; uneven, varied. -**check'ers** *pl.* (dial) boardgame using the same board as for chess. -**check'mate** *n.* in chess, the final winning move; any overthrow, defeat.-*v.t.* make the movement ending the game; defeat.-**check'out** *n.* time at which a hotel guest must vacate a room on departure; the settling of accounts on departure; the counter at which payments are made. -*a.* -**check'room** *n.* place where articles (*e.g.*, clothing, *etc.*) may be left temporarily in the care of others. [F. *échec*, fr Pers. *shah*, king (in danger); checkmate fr. F. *échec et mat*, fr. *shah mat*, the king is dead]

Ched'dar *n.* kind of cheese. [first made at *Cheddar*, Somerset]

cheek *n.* side of the face below the eye; impudence. -*v.t.* address impudently. -**cheek'ily** *adv.* -**cheek'y** *a.* [OE. *ceace*, cheek, jaw]

cheer *n.* mood; mirth, joy; food; shout of approval. -*v.t.* comfort; gladden; encourage, *esp.* by shouts. -*v.i.* shout applause. -**cheer'ful** *a.* -**cheer'fully** *adv.* -**cheer'fulness** *n.* -**cheer'ily** *adv.* -**cheer'less** *a.* -**cheer'lessness** *n.* -**cheer'ly** *a.* [F. (*bonne*) *chère*-Low L. *cara*, face]

cheese *n.* curd of milk coagulated, separated from the whey and pressed. **cheese'monger** *n.* -**cheese'paring** *a.* mean. [OE. *ciese*, fr. L. *caseus*]

chee'tah *n.* Indian leopard. [Hind. *chita*]

chef (*sl.*) *n.* head cook. [F. *chef de cuisine*]

chemise' (-ez') *n.* woman's undergarment or underslip. [F., fr. Low L. *cam isia*]

chemistry (k-) *n.* science which treats of the properties of substances and their combinations and reactions. -**chem'ical** *a.* -**chem'ically** *adv.* -**chem'ist** *n.* [*See* **alchemy**]

chenille' *n.* velvety cord used in embroidery *etc.* [F. = *caterpillar*]

cheque' (-ek) *n.* order on a banker. -**cheque'-book** *n.* [earlier *check*]

chequer. *See* **checker.**

cher'ish *v.t.* treat with affection; protect; encourage. [F. *chérir*]

cheroot' (sh-) *n.* open-ended cigar. [Tamil *shuruttu*, roll]

cher'ry *n.* small red stone-fruit; the tree. -*a.* ruddy. [fr. G. *kerasion*]

cher'ub *n.* winged child, angel. -**cherubim, cher'ubs** *pl.* -**cheru'bic** *a.* [Heb. *krub*, pl. *krubim*]

chess *n.* game of skill played by two persons with 32 'pieces' on a board of 64 squares. -**chess'board** *n.* -**chess'men** *n.pl.* the pieces used in chess. [F. of *echec. See* **check**]

chest *n.* box; coffer; upper part of the trunk of the body. [OE. *cist*, fr. L. *cista*]

chest'erfield *n.* long overcoat; padded coouch. [Earl of *Chesterlield*]

chest'nut (-an-) *n.* large reddish-brown nut growing in a prickly husk; tree earing it; (*sl.*) hoary joke. -*a.* reddishbrown. [for *chesteine*-nut, fr. OF. *chastaigne*, G. *kastanea*]

chevalier' (sh-) *n.* cavalier; knight. [F.]

che'viot *n.* breed of sheep; cloth made from its wool. [*Cheviot* Hills, England]

chev'ron (sh-) *n.* V-shaped band of braid used as a badge in the armed forces. [F.]

chew *v.t.* grind with the teeth. -**chew'ing-gum** *n.* [OE. *ceowan*]

chiaroscu'ro (k-) *n.* (art) treatment of light and shade. [It.]

chic *n.* style, elegance. -*a.* [F.]

chicane', chicanery *a.* quibbling trick, artifice. -**chicane'**-*v.i.* quibble, use tricks. [F.]

chican'o *n.* an American citizen of Mexican descent. [fr. Sp. *Mejicano*]

chick *n.* short for chicken; young of birds, *esp.* of the domestic fowl. -**chick'enheart'ed** *a.* -**chick'en-pox** *n.* mild contagious fever. [OE. *cicen*]

chic'le *n.* gum extracted from sapodilla, main ingredient of chewing-gum. [Mex. *tzictli*]
chic'ory *n.* salad plant of which the root is ground and mixed with coffee. [fr. G. *kichora*, endive]
chide *v.t.* scold, reprove. [OE. *cidan*]
chief *n.* head or principal person. -*a.* principal, foremost, leading. -**chiefly** *adv.* [F. *chef*, fr. L. *caput*, head]
chieftain *n.* leader or chief of a clan or tribe. [OF. *chevetain*, another form of *capitaine*, captain]
chiff'-chaff *n.* bird of Warbler family. [imit.]
chiff'on (sh-) *n.* gauzy material. -**chiffonier'** *n.* ornamental cupboard. fF.]
chi'gnon *n.* back-hair twisted into roll or bun. [F.]
chilblain *n.* inflamed sore due to cold. [*chill* and obs. *brain*, sore]
child (-i-) *n.* infant; boy or girl; son or daughter. **child'ren** *n.pl.* **child'bed** *n.* state of a woman giving birth to a child. -**child'birth** *n.* -**child'hood** *n.* -**child'ish** *a.* -**child'ishly** *adv.* -**child'less** *a.* -**child'like** *a.* [OE. *cild*]
chil'i, chil'e, chilli *n.* hot pepper, fruit of the capsicum. [Mex. fr. *Nanuati*, chilli]
chill *n.* coldness; cold with shivering; anything that damps, discourages. -**chilled** *a.* -**chill'iness** *n.* -**chill'ing** *a.* -**chill'y** *a.* [OE. *ciele*, cold]
chime *n.* sound of bells in harmony; set of bells. -*v.i.* ring harmoniously; agree. *v.t.* strike (bells). -**chime in'**, come into a conversation with agreement. [L. *cymbalum*, cymbal]
chime'ra, chimae'ra *n.* fabled monster, made up of parts of various animals; wild fancy. -**chimer'ical** *a.* fanciful. [G. *chimaira*, she-goat]
chim'ney *n.* passage for smoke. -**chim'ney-sweep** *n.* [L. *caminus*, furnace]
chimpanzee' *n.* African anthropoid ape, [native]
chin *n.* part of the face below the mouth. [OE. *cin*]
chi'na *n.* fine earthenware. [fr. *China*]
chinchilla *n.* small S. American rodent; its soft grey fur. [Sp.]
chine *n.* ravine. [OE. *cinu*, cleft]
chink *n.* cleft, crack. [OE. *cinu*]
chink *n.* sound of pieces of metal knocking together. -*v.i.* make this sound. -*v.t.* cause to do so. [*imit.*]
chinook' *n.* warm, dry wind of eastern side of Rocky Mountains; name of native tribe on Columbia river. [name of a N. Am. Ind. people]
chintz *n.* cotton cloth printed in colors. [*pl.* of Hind. *chint*, spotted cotton]
chip *v.t.* chop or cut into small pieces; break little pieces from; shape by cutting off pieces. -*v.i.* break off. -*n.* small piece broken off, thin fried slices of potato; counter used as a token in gambling and games; tiny wafer of silicon forming an integrated circuit in a computer. [related to *chop*]
chipmunk *n.* small squirrel of N. Amer. [Indian name *achitamon*]
Chipp'endale *n.* light drawing-room furniture made by *Chippendale* (18th c.); furniture in this style.
chirography *a.* art of (hand-) writing. [G. *cheir*, hand]
chiropody *n.* skilled treatment of hands and feet.**chirop'odist** *n.* [G. *cheir*, hand, *pous, pod-*, foot]
chiropractic *n.* and *a.* treatment of diseases by manipulating joints, *esp.* ofthe spine. -**chiroprac'tor** *n.* [G. *cheir*, hand, *praktikos*, concerned with action]
chirp, chir'rup *n.* short, sharp cry of a bird. -*v.i.* make this sound. [imit.]
chis'el (-zl) *n.* cutting tool, usually a bar of steel with an edge across the main axis. -*v.t.* cut or carve with a chisel. [ONF., fr. L. *cmdere*, cut]
chit *n.* brat, young girl. [for *kit*, kitten]
chit *n.* note; order, pass. [Hind. *chitthi*]
chi'tin *n.* substance forming hard outer covering of beetles *etc.* [G. *chiton*, tunic]
chiv'alry (sh-) *n.* bravery and courtesy; feudal system of knighthood. -**chivalrous** *a.* -**chiv'alrously** *adv.* [F. *chevaterie*, fr. *cheval*, L. *caballus*, horse]
chlo'rine *n.* yellowish-green gas with a suffocating action on the lungs. **chlo'rate** *n.* -**chlo'ride** *n.* -**chlo'rinate** *v.t.* [G. *chlaros*, yellowish-green]
chloroform (kl-) *n.* liquid used as an anaesthetic. -*v.t.* put to sleep with this drug. [fr. *chlor*ine and *form*ic acid]
chlorophyll (kl-) *n.* coloring matter of plants. [G. *chloros*, green, *phyllon* leaf]
chock *n.* block, wedge. [ONF. *choque*]
chock'-full *a.* quite full. [ME. *choke*, jawbone]
chocolate *n.* paste of cacao-tree seeds; sweetmeat or drink made from it.-*a.* dark brown. [Mex. *chocolatl*]
choice n. act or power of choosing; alternative; something chosen. -*a.* select, fine, worthy of being chosen. -**choice'ly** *adv.* [F.

choisir, choose]

choir *n.* band of singers, *esp.* in a church; part of a church set aside for them. [F. *chœur*-L. *chorus*]

choke *v.t.* throttle; stop up; smother, stifle; obstruct.-*v.i.* suffer choking. -*n.* act or noise of choking; device to regulate flow of gas, *etc.* -**choked** *a.* -**choke'-bore** *n.* gun narrowed towards the muzzle, to concentrate the shot.-**choke'-damp** *n.* carbonic gas in coal-mines. [OE. *aceocian*]

chol'er (k-) *n.* bile; anger. -**chol'eric** *a.* [G. *cholera*, biliousness, fr. *chole*, bile]

chol'era (k-) *n.* deadly disease marked by vomiting and purging. [*See* **choler**]

choose *v.t.* take one thing rather than another; select.-*v.i.* will, think fit. **choos'er** *n.* [OE. *ceosan*]

chop *v.t.* cut with a blow; cut in pieces. *n.* hewing blow; slice of meat containing a rib. -**chop'-house** *n.* **chopper** *n.* [ME., related to *chap* and *chip*]

chop *v.t.* exchange, bandy, *e.g.* chop logic, chop and change. [OE. *ceapian*, barter]

chop, chap *n.* jaw (*usu.* in *pl.*). -**chop'-fallen** *a.* dejected. [orig. uncertain]

chord (k-) *n.* string of a musical instrument; straight line joining the ends of an arc. [G. *chorde*, intestine]

chord (k-) *n.* harmonious simultaneous union of musical notes. [*accord*]

chore *See* **char**

choreography *n.* art, notation of (ballet-) dancing; arrangement of ballets. [G. *choros*, dance]

chorog'raphy *n.* geography, topography. -**chorol'ogy** *n.* science of geographic distribution. [G. *chdra*, region]

chort'le *v.i.* chuckle; laugh in triumph. [coined by Lewis *Carroll*]

chor'us *n.* band of singers; combination of voices singing together; refirain. -*v.t.* sing or say together. -**cho'ral** *a.* -**cho'ric** *a.* -**chor'ister** *n.* [L., fr. G. *choros*, band of singers]

chough (chuf) *n.* red-legged crew. [imit.]

chow *n.* Chinese breed of dog.

chrism *n.* holy oil; unction; confirmation. **chrismal** *a.* -*n.* pyx; christening veil. [G. *chrisma*]

Christian (krisétyan) *n.* follower of Christ.-*a.* following Christ; relating to Christ or his religion. -**chris'ten** *v.t.* baptize, give a name to. **chris'tendom** (-an-) *n.* all Christian countries. -**chris'tianize** *v.t* -**Christian'ity** *n.* religion of Christ. -**Christ'mas** *n.* festival of the birth of Christ. -**Chris'tian name**, name given at christening, individual name. -**Chris'tian Sci'ence**, religious system founded by Mary Baker Eddy, in America. -**Chris'tmas-box** *n.* tip given at Christmas. -**Chris'tmas-card** *n.* [G. *christos*, anointed]

Christinas. *See* **Christian.**

chromatic (k-) *a.* relating to color; (*mus.*) of a scale proceeding by semi-tones. [G. *chrome*, color]

chrome (k-) *n.* chromium or compound of it; chrome-yellow. **chro'mium** *n.* metallic element. [L. *chrome*, color]

chromosome *n.* microscopic body found in cell during division. [G. *chrome*, color]

chron'ic (k-) *a.* lasting a long time. -**chron'icle** *n.* record of events in order of time. -*v.t.* record. -**chron'icler** *n.* -**chronological** *a.* -**chronolo'gically** *adv.* **chronol'ogist** *n.* -**chronol'ogy** *n.* -**chronom'eter** *n.* instrument for measuring time exactly. -**chronomet'rical** *a.* -**chronom'etry** *n.* [G. *chronos*, time]

chrysalis *n.* resting state of an insect between grub and fly; case from which it emerges. [G. *chrysallis*, fr. *chrysos*, gold (fr. the gold-colored sheath of butterflies)]

chrysanthemum *n.* autumn-blooming plant with large handsome flowers. [G. *chrysos*, gold, *anthemon*, flower]

chub *n.* small plump river-fish. -**chubb'y** *a.* plump. [orig. uncertain]

chuck *v.t.* tap, as under the chin; throw. -*n.* tap; throw. [F. *choquer*, shock]

chuck'le *v.i.* laugh in a quiet manner -*n.* such laugh. [*imit.*]

chum *n.* room-mate; friend; mate. [fr. *chamber*-fellow]

chump *n.* block of wood; blockhead, dolt. [*See* **chock**]

chunk *n.* lump; thick piece. [*See* **chock**]

church *n.* building for Christian worship; whole body of Christians; clergy; body or mind of Christians. -*v.t.* give thanks on behalf of (a woman) after childbirth, *etc.* -**church'man** *n.* **church-ward'en** *n.* **church'woman** *n.* **churchy** *n.* [OE. *eirice*, fr. G. *kyriakon*, of the Lord]

churl *n.* rustic; ill-bred fellow **churl'ish** *a.* surly. **churl'ishly** *adv.* -**churl'ish ness** *n.* [OE. *ceorl*, countryman]

churn *n.* vessel for making butter. -*v.t.* shake up (a liquid). [OE. *cyrin*]

chute *n.* waterfall; channel for logs, rubbish *etc.* [F. = *fall*]

chut'ney *n.* condiment of fruits, spices, *etc.* [Hind. *chatni*]
cica'da *n.* chirping insect. [L. = *cricket*]
cicatrix, cic'atrice *n.* scar of a wound. [L.]
cicero'ne *n.* guide. [*cicero*]
ci'der *n.* drink made from apples. [F. *cidre*-G. *sikera*, strong drink]
cigar' *n.* roll of tobacco-leaves for smoking. **cigarette', cigaret'** *n.* finely cut tobacco rolled in paper for smoking. [Sp. *cigarro*; F. *cigarette*]
cinch *n.* saddle girth; (*sl.*) firm grip; walkover; certainty. [Sp. *cincha*]
cinc'ture *n.* girdle, belt.-**cinc'tured** *a.* [L. *cinctura-cingere*, gird]
cin'der *n.* piece of glowing coal; partlyburnt coal. [OE. *sinder*, slag]
cin'ema *n.* motion pictures; building where these are shown. [for *cinematograph*]
cinemat'ograph *n.* apparatus for throwing moving pictures on a screen by means of light. -**cinematograph'ic** *a.* **cinematog'raphy** *n.* **cine-cam'era** *n.* camera for taking moving pictures. [G. *kiaema*, motion]
cinera'ria *n.* plant of aster family, with richly colored flowers. [L. *cinerarius*]
cinnamon *n.* spicy bark of a tree in Ceylon; the tree. -*a.* of a light brown color. [Heb. *qinnamon*]
ci'pher, cy'pher *n.* arithmetical symbol 0; figure; person of no importance; monogram; secret writing. -*v.i.* work at arithmetic. [Arab. *sifr*, empty]
cir'cle (ser-kl) *n.* perfectly round figure; ring; company of persons gathered round another, or round an object of interest; seance; class or division of society. -*v.t.* surround. -*v.i.* move round. -**cir'cular** *a.* round; moving round. -*n.* letter sent to several (a circle of) persons. **circ'ulate** *v.i.* move round; pass from place to place; come to readers. -*v.t.* send round. **circula'tion** *n.* [L. *circulus*, dim. of *circus*, ring]
cir'cuit (-kit) *n.* a moving round; area; round of visitation, *esp.* ofjudges; district; path of an electric current. -**circu'itous** *a.* -**circu'itously** *adv.* [L. *circuitus*, a going round]
circumcise *v.t.* cut off the foreskin of **circumcis'ion** *n.* [L. *circumcidere*, cut round]
circumference *n.* boundary line, *esp.* of a circle. [L. *circumferential* periphery]
circumflex *n.* accent (^) on a vowel or syllable -*a.* bending or winding round. [L. *flectere, flexum*, to bend]
circumlocution *n.* roundabout speech. [L. *circumlocution* a talking round]
circumnav'igate *v.t.* sail round. -**circumnaviga'tion** *n.* **circumnav'igator** *n.* [*See* **navigate**]
circumscribe' *v.t.* confine, bound, limit, hamper. [L. *circumscribere*, write (draw lines) round]
circumspect *a.* watchful, prudent. **circumspec'tion** *n.* -**cir'cumspectly** *adv.* [L. *circumspicere*, look around]
circumstance *n.* detail; event, matter of fact.-*pl.* state of affairs; condition in life; surroundings or things accompanying a certain action. **cir'cumstanced** *a.* situated. -**circumstan'tial** *a.* depending on details; particular as to details; indirect. -**circumstantial'ity** *n.* -**circumstan'tially** adj. -**circumstan'tiate** *v.t.* prove by details; describe exactly. [L. *cir-cumstare*, stand round]
circumvent' *v.t.* outwit. **circumven'tion** *n.* [L. *circumvenire*, come round]
cir'cus *n.* circular building for public shows; entertainment of horse-riding, clowning, *etc.*; group of houses built in a circle. [L.]
cirr'us *n.* high fleecy cloud. [L. = *curl*]
cist (sist) *n.* prehistoric stone coffin or tombs. [L. *cista*, box]
cis'tern *n.* water-tank. [L. *cisterns*]
cit'adel *n.* fortress in or near a city [fr. It.*citadella*, dim. of *citta*, city]
cite *v.t.* summon; quote; bring forward as proof -**cita'tion** *n.* [L. *citare*, call]
cit'izen *n.* inhabitant of a city; townsman; member of a state. -**citizenship** *n.* [fr. OF. *citeain*]
cit'ron *n.* fruit like a lemon; the tree. -**citrus** *a.* -**cit'ric** *a.* of the acid of the lemon and citron. [F., fr. L. *citrus*, citrontree]
cit'y *n.* large town; (properly) town made city by charter. [F. *cite*, fr. L. *civitas*, fr. *civis*, citizen]
civ'ic *a.* pertaining to a city or citizen. -**civics** *n.* science of municipal and national life of service. [L. *civicus*, citizen]
civ'il *a.* relating to citizens or the state; refined, polite, not barbarous; not military; (*law*) not criminal. -**civil'ian** *n.* non-military person. -**civiliza'tion** *n.* **civ'ilize** *v.t.* refine, bring out barbarism. -**civ'ilized** *a.* -**civil'ity** *n.* politeness. -**civ'illy** *adv.* [L. *civilis*]
clack *n.* sharp sound as of wood on wood; chattering of tongues. -*v.t.* [imit.]

clad *See* **clothe**

claim *v.t.* call for; demand as a right.-*n.* demand for a thing supposed due; right; thing **claimed. -claim'ant** *n.* **-clam'ant** *a.* demanding attention. [L. *clamare*, shout]

clairvoy'ancy *n.* second sight, super-sensory vision. **-clairvoy'ant** *n.* and *a.* [F. *clair*, clear, *voir*, see]

clam *n.* bivalve shellfish. [OE. = fetter]

clam'ber *v.i.* climb with hands and feet with difficulty. [orig. uncertain]

clamm'y *a.* moist and sticky. -**clamm'iness** *n.* [earlier *claymy*]

clam'or *n.* loud shouting; outcry, noise. *v.i.* shout; call noisily (for). **-clam'orous** *a.* **clam'orously** *adv.* [L. *clam*or. *See* **claim**]

clamp *n.* tool for holding or pressing. *v.t.* fasten with clamps. [Du. *clamp*]

clan *n.* tribe or collection of families under a chief, and of supposed common ancestry; sect, group. **-clann'ish** *a.* -**clann'ishly** *adv.* **-clann'ishness** *n.* [Gael. *clann*]

clandestine *a.* secret; sly. **-clandestine-ly** *adv.* [L. *clandestinus*]

clang *n.* loud ringing sound. -*v.i.* make such sound. -*v.t.* strike together with a clang. **clang'or** *n.* [L. *clangere*; imit.orig.]

clank *n.* short sound as of pieces of metal struck together. -*v.t.* and *i.* cause, or move with, such a sound. [imit.]

clap *n.* hard, explosive sound; slap. -*v.i.* strike with this noise; strike the open hands together; applaud. -*v.t.* strike together; pat; applaud; thrust suddenly, impose abruptly. **-clapp'er** *n.* one who claps; tongue of a bell. **clapp'ing** *n.* **-clap'trap** *n.* empty words. [imit.]

clar'et *n.* red Bordeaux wine. [OF. (*vin*) claret, clear (wine)]

clar'ify *v.t.* make clear; purify **clarifica-tion** *n.* [L. *clarificare*]

clar'ion *n.* clear-sounding trumpet. **clar'ionet, clar'inet** *n.* wood wind instrument. [L. *clarus*, clear]

clar'ity *n.* clearness. [L. *claritas*]

clash *n.* loud noise, as of weapons striking together; conflict, collision. -*v.i.* make a clash; come into conflict.-*v.t.* strike together to make a clash. [imit.]

clasp *n.* hook or other means of fastening; embrace; military decoration. -*v.t.* fasten; embrace, grasp. **-clasp-knife** *n.* [orig. uncertain]

class *n.* rank of society; division of pupils; division by merit; quality; any division, order, kind, sort.-*v.t.* assign to the proper division. **-classifica'tion** *n.* **-class'ify** *v.t.* arrange methodically in classes. [L. *classes*, division of the Roman people]

class'ic, classical *a.* of the first rank of Greek and Roman authors; of the highest rank generally, but *esp.* of literature; resembling in style the Greek writers; refined, chaste; famous. **-class'ically** *adv.* **-class'icism** *n.* **-class'icist** *n.* [*See* **class**]

clatt'er *n.* rattling noise; noisy conversation. -*v.i.* make a rattling noise; chatter. -*v.t.* make rattle. [imit.]

clause (-z) *n.* part of a sentence; article ; n a formal document. [F., fr. L. *clausa*]

claustrophobia *n.* morbid fear of enclosed spaces. [L. *clausus-claudere*, shut; G. *phobos*, fear]

clavichord (-k-) *n.* obsolete musical instrument like a spinet. [Mod. L. *clavichordium*, key string]

clav'icle *n.* collar-bone. **-clavic'ular** *a.* [L. *clavicula*, dim. of *clavis*, key]

claw *n.* hooked nail of a bird or beast; foot of an animal with hooked nails; anything like a claw. -*v.t.* tear with claws; grip. [OE. *clawu*]

clay *n.* stiff viscous earth; earth generally; human body. **clay'ey** *a.* [OE. *clæg*]

claymore' *n.* Highland sword. [Gael. *claidheamh*, sword, *mor*, great]

clean *a.* free from dirt, stain or any defilement; pure; guiltless; trim, shapely. *adv.* so as to leave no dirt; entirely. -*v.t.* free from dirt.-**clean'er** *n.* **-clean'liness** (klen-) *n.* -**clean'ly** *a.* **-clean'ly** *adv.* **cleanness** *n.* -**cleanse** (klenz) *v.t.* [OE. *claene*]

clear *a.* free from cloud; pure, undimmed, bright; free from obstruction or difficulty; plain, distinct; without defect or draw-back; transparent. -*adv.* wholly, quite. *v.t.* make clear; acquit; pass over or through; make as profit; free from cloud; obstruction, difficulty; free by payment of dues. -*v.i.* become clear, bright, free, transparent. **-clear'ance** *n.* **-clear'ing** *n.* **-clear'ly** *adv.* **-clear'ness** *n.* **-clearinghouse** *n.* place where cheques are exchanged. **-clear'ing-station** *n.* place from which wounded are removed; place where items are kept prior to being removed. **clear-sight'ed** *a.* [F. *clair*, fr. L. *clarus*]

cleat *n.* wedge; (*naut.*) block to which ropes are made fast; porcelain insulation. [*See* **clod, clot**]

cleave *v.t.* split assunder. -*v.i.* crack, part assunder. **-cleav'age** *n.* **-cleav'er** *n.* [OE. *cleofan*]

cleave *v.i.* adhere. [OE. *cliftan*]

cleek *n.* large hook used in fishing; golf

club with iron head. [ME. = clutch]

clef *n.* mark to show the pitch in music. [F., fr. L. *clavis*, key]

cleft *n.* opening made by cleaving; crack, fissure. [*cleave*]

cleg *n.* horse-fly. [ON. *klegg]*

clem'atis *n.* climbing perennial plant with white or purple flowers. [G.]

clem'ent *a.* merciful; gentle; kidd. -**clem'ency** *n.* [L. *clemens*]

clench *v.t.* make fast; set firmly together; grasp; drive home. [OE. *-clencan*, in *beclencan*, make to cling]

clere'story *n.* upper part of a church with a row of windows. [*clear* ('lighted') *storey*]

clergy *n.* appointed m; nisters of the Christian church. -**cler'gyman** *n.* [L. *clericus*. *See* **clerk**]

cler'ic *n.* belonging to the clergyman. clergyman. -**cler'ical** *a.* [*See* **clerk**]

clerk (-ark) *n.* clergyman or priest; one who leads the responses in church; an officer in charge of records, correspon dence *etc.* of a department or corporation; subordinate in an office; salesperson. -**clerk'ly** *a.* -**clerk'ship** *n.* [L. *clericus*, fr. G. *kleros*, heritage, used in 2nd c. of the priestly order; other senses fr. priestly ability to write]

clev'er *a.* able, skillful, adroit.**clev'erly** *adv.* -**clev'erness** *n.* [orig. uncertain]

clew. *See* **clue.**

cli'ché *n.* stereotyped hackneyed phrase. [F., fr. *clicher*, click, sound made in stereotyping]

click *n.* short, sharp sound, as of a latch in the door. -*v.i.* [imit.]

cli'ent *n.* customer, one who employs a professional man. -**clientele'** *n.* body of clients. [L. *cliens*]

cliff *n.* steep rock face. [OE. *clil*]

climacter'ic, climac'teric *n.* critical period in human life. -a. -**climacter'ical** *a.* [G. *klimakter*, rung of a ladder]

climate *n.* the average weather conditions of a region. [G. *klinw, klimatos*, slope]

cli'max *n.* highest point, culmination; arrangement of language to rise in dignity and force; point of greatest excitement, tension, in a play, story, *etc.* [G. *klimax*, ladder]

climb (klim) *v.t* and *i.* mount by clutching, grasping, pulling; creep up, mount, ascend. **climb'er** *n.* -**climb'ing** *n.* [OE. *climban*]

clime *n.* climate (*q.v.*).

clinch *v.* clench (*q.v.*).

cling *v.i.* stick fast, be attached; remain by. -**cling'film** *n.* thin Polythene material that clings closely to any surface around which it is placed, used *esp.* for wrapping food. **cling'stone** *a.* with pulp clinging to stone (of peach). [OE. *clingan*]

clinic *n.* relating to practical instruction in medicine in hospitals. -*n.* place or meeting for medical examination or teaching (also *clinique'*). -**clin'ical** *a.* **clin'ically** *adv.* -**clin'ical thermometer** is used for taking the temperature of patients. [G. *kline*, bed]

clink *n.* sharp metallic sound. -*v.t.* and *i.* make or cause to make such sound. [imit.]

clink'er *n.* hard slag. -**clink'er-built** *a.* of ships, built with overlapping outer planks. [Du. *blinker*]

Cli'o *n.* muse of epic poetry and history. [G. *kleein*, call]

clip *v.t.* grip, clutch, hug. -*n.* device for gripping. [OE. *clyppan*]

clip *v.t.* cut with scissors or shears; cut short.-*n.* the wool shorn at a place or in a season. -**clip'ping** *n.* something clipped off, *esp.* article cut out of a publication. **clipp'er** *n.* [ON. *kappa*]

clipp'er *n.* fast sailing-ship formerly employed to carry tea, wool, *etc.*; fast transworld airplane. [*clip*, shear]

clique (ik) *n.* small exclusive set; faction, gang. **cliq'uy, cliq'uish** *a.* [F.]

cloak *n.* loose outer garment; disguise, pretext.-*v.t.* cover with a cloak; disguise, conceal. -**cloak'room** *n.* place for keeping coats, hats, luggage, *etc.* [earlier *cloke*, fr. Late L. *clocca*, bell (shape of garment)]

cloche (klosh) *n.* bell-shaped glass for growing vegetables, *etc.*; bell-shaped, closefitting hat. [F. *cloche*, bell]

clock *n.* instrument for measuring time; ornament on the side of a stocking. [orig. 'bell;' fr. Late. L. *clocca*]

clod *n.* lump of earth; blockhead. [*clot*]

clog *n.* obstruction, impediment, wooden soled shoe; *v.t.* gather in a mass and cause stoppage; choke up. -**clog'-dance** *n.* [orig. unknown]

clois'ter *n.* covered arcade; convent-*v.t.* confine in a cloister, or within walls. -**clois'tered** *a.* -**clois'tral** *a*, [L- *claudere, claus-*, close]

close (-a) *a.* shut up; confined; secret; unventilated, stifling; reticent; niggardly; compact; crowded; strict, searching. *adv.* nearly, tightly. -*n.* shut-in place; precinct of a cathedral. -**close'ly** *adv.* -**close'ness** *n.*

-**close'-corpora'tion** *n.* -**close'fist'ed** *a.* mean -**close'-seas'on, closed' seas'on** *n.* season when it is illegal to kill (a particular kind of game or fish). -**close'-up** *n.* photograph or film sequence taken at short range. [L. *claudere*, close]

close (-z) *v.t.* shut; stop up; finish. -*v.i.* come together, grapple. -*n.* end. [L. *claudere*]

closed' shop *n.* trade in which all workers belong to trade union; establishment boycotted by trade unions. [fr. *close*, *v.s.*]

clos'et (-z-) *n.* small private room; a cabinet, recess or cupboard for storage of *e.g.*, household utensils or clothes. -*v.t.* shut up in a closet; conceal. [OF. dim. of *clas*, fr. L. *claudere*]

clo'sure (-zh-) *n.* ending of a debate by vote or other authoritative means. [F., fr. L. *clausura*, fr. *claudere*]

clot *n.* mass or lump. -*v.t.* form into lumps. [OE. *clod-*, in compounds]

cloth (-th) *n.* woven fabric. clothes (-TH-) *n. pl.* dress; bed-coverings. -**clothe** *v.t.* put clothes on. **clo'thier** *n.* **clo'thing** *n.* [OE. *clath*]

cloud *n.* vapor floating in the air; state of gloom; great number or mass. -*v.t.* overshadow, dim, darken. -*v.i.* become cloudy. -**cloud'less** *a.* -**cloud'y** *a.* [OE. *clud*, mass]

clout *n.* piece of cloth; blow, cuff. -*v.t.* patch. [OE. *clut*]

clove *n.* dried flower-bud of an Eastern tree, used as a spice. -**clove'-pink** *n.* clove-scented pink. [L. *clavus*, nail]

clo'ven *a.* split. -**clo'ven hoof**, divided hoof of cattle, *etc.*; (*fig.*) sign of the devil's agency. [*cleave*]

clo'ver *n.* low-growing forage plant, trefoil. [OE. *clafre*]

clown *n.* rustic; jester. **clown'ish** *a.* [perh. fr. Du. *kloen*, clew, hoyden]

cloy *v.t.* weary by sweetness, sameness, *etc.* [earlier *accloy*, fr. F. *enclouer, prick*, spike with a nail]

club *n.* thick stick; bat; one of the suits at cards; association for a common object.-*v.t.* strike with a club; put together. -*v.i.* join for a common object. [ON. *klubba*]

cluck *n.* noise of a hen. -*v.i.* make that noise. [OE. *cloccian*]

clue, clew *n.* ball of thread; thread used as a guidance, trail; indication, *esp.* of the solution of a mystery. [OE. *cliwen*, ball of thread]

clum'ber *n.* kind of spaniel. [*Clumber*, Nottinghamshire, England]

clump *n.* cluster of trees or plants; compact mass; lump; thick additional sole. -*v.i.* walk heavily. [Du. *klomp*]

clum'sy (-z-) *a.* awkward, unwieldy, badly made or arranged. -**clum'sily** *adv.* -**clum'siness** *n.* [earlier *clumsed*, ME. *clumsen*, benumb]

clus'ter *n.* group, bunch. -*v.t.* and *i.* gather, grow in a cluster. [OE. *clyster*]

clutch *v.t.* grasp eagerly, snatch. -*v.i.* make a snatch at.-*n.* grasp, tight grip; device for connecting and disconnecting parts of machinery, *e.g.*, a motor engine. [OE. *clyccan*]

clutch *n.* brood of chickens; 'setting' of eggs for hatching. [fr. obs. v. *clerk*, ON. *klekja*, hatch]

clutt'er *n.* litter, confusion. -*v.t.* and *i.* [*clot*]

coach *n.* large four-wheeled carriage; passenger car on a railroad; a class of travel in air transportation which is lower than first class; tutor; trainer in rowing, *etc.* -*v.i.* ride in a coach. -*v.t.* tutor; train. -**coach'man** *n.* [F. *coche*]

coadjutor *n.* helper, associate. -**coadju'tant** *a.* [L. *co*, with, *adjuvare*, help]

coagulate *v.t.* and *i.* curdle, form into a mass. **coag'ulant** *n.* -**coag'ulated** *a.* -**coagula'tion** *n.* [L. *coagulate*]

coal *n.* glowing ember; mineral consisting of carbonized vegetable matter, used as fuel. -*v.t.* supply with coal. -*v.i.* take in coal. [OE. *col*]

coalesce' *v.i.* unite. -**coales'cence** *n.* **coali'tion** *n.* alliance, *esp.* of parties. [L. *coalescere*, grow together]

coam'ings *n. pl.* (*naut.*) erection round hatches to keep out water. [orig. unknown]

coarse *a.* rough, harsh; unrefined; indecent; gross. **coarse'ly** *adv.* -**coarse'ness** *n.* [ME. *cars*, fr. AF. *cros*, F. *gros*]

coast *n.* sea-shore. -*v.i.* and *t.*sail by the coast. -**coast'er** *n.* [L. *costa*, rib]

coat *n.* outer garment; animal's fur or feathers; covering; layer. -*v.t.* clothe, cover with a layer. -**coat-of-arms** *n.* heraldic bearings. [OF. *cote* fr. L. L. *cotta*]

coa'ti *n.* American mammal allied to raccoon. [Tupi]

coax *v.t.* wheedle, cajole, persuade fearlier cokes, cox *n.* [*fool*]

cob *n.* short-legged stout horse; lump; head of maize; male swan. [orig. uncertain]

co'balt *n.* a metal; blue pigment made from it.(Ger. *kobalt*, fr. *kobold*, demon]

cob'ble *v.t.* patch roughly, as shoes. -

cobb'ler *n.* [orig. uncertain]
cobb'le *n.* round stone. [dim. of *cob*]
cob'le, cobb'le *n.* fishing-boat. [W. *ceubal*, skiff]
COB'OL *n.* computer programming language for general commercial use. [fr. *C*ommon *B*usiness *O*riented *L*anguage]
co'bra *n.* poisonous hooded snake. [Port., fr. L. *colubra*, snake]
cob'web *n.* spider's web. [ME. *coppeweb*, fr. *coppe*, spider]
C'oca-Co'la *n.* carbonated soft drink. [Trademark]
cocaine' *n.* alkaloid drug used as an anaesthetic. [*coca*, American shrub]
coch'ineal *n.* scarlet dye got from a Mexican insect. [fr. G. *kokkos*, grain]
cock *n.* male bird; tap for liquids; hammer of a gun; its position drawn back; upward turn. -*v.t.* set or turn assertively; draw back (gun hammer). -**cock'sure** *a.* quite sure; over-confident. -**cock'tail** *n.* drink of spirits with added flavors. [OE. *cocc*]
cock *n.* conical heap, *esp.* of hay. -*v.t.* put up in heaps. [ON. *kokkr*, lump]
cockade' (kok-ad') *n.* a bow of ribbons worn on the hat as a badge. [F. *cocarde* fr. *coq*, cock]
cockatoo' *n.* crested parrot. [Malay *kakatua*; imit.of cry]
cockatrice *n.* mythical reptile resembling basilisk. [OF. *cocatris*]
cock'boat *n.* small ship's boat. [perh. fr. *cog*-OF. *cogue*, ship]
cock'chafer *n.* large flying beetle which destroys vegetation. [*chafer*]
coc'kle *n.* kind of shellfish. [F. *coquille*]
cock'ney *n.* native Londoner; his dialect. [ME. *cokenay*, townsman]
cock'pit *n.* the place where game-cocks fought; the pilot's space in an airplane. [*cock* and *pit*]
cockroach *n.* a black or brown beetle known particularly for its habit of infesting houses and associated with insanitary conditions. [Sp. *cucaracha*]
co'co *n.* tropical palm. -**co'conut** *n.* very large hard nut from the cocopalm. [Sp. = ugly-face, bogey (fr. marks at end of the shell)]
co'coa *n.* powder made from the seed of the cacao, a tropical tree; drink made from the powder. [corrupt.of *cacao.* fr. Mex. *cacauatl*]
cocoon' *n.* sheath of an insect in the chrysalis stage. [F. *cocon*, L. *concha*, shell]
cod *n.* large sea fish. [orig. uncertain]
co'da *n.* passage completing and rounding off a musical composition. [L. *canda*, tail]
cod'dle *v.t.* nurse excessively, take too great care of. [orig. uncertain]
code *n.* collection of laws; system of signals. -**codifica'tion** *n.* -**co'dify** *v.t* [F. fr. L. *cortex*, set of tablets; book]
co'dex *n.* manuscript volume or papyrus, *e.g.* of Bible. -**co'dices** *n. pl.* [L. *codex*, tree-trunk, set of tablets, book]
cod'icil *n.* addition to a will. [L. *codicillus*, dim. of *codex. See* **code**]
coeducation *n.* education of boys and girls together. [L. *co*, with, and *education*]
coefficient *n.* joint agent or factor. [fr. L. *coefficere. See* **effect**]
coerce' *v.t.* force. -**coer'cion** *n.* **coer'cive** *a.* [L. *coercere*, fr. *arcere*, restrain]
coeta'neous *a.* contemporary, of same age. [L. *aetas*, age]
coe'val *a.* equally old; lasting to the same time. [L. *aeuum*, age]
coexist' *v.i.* exist together. -**coexistence** *n.* -**coexist'ent** *a.* [*See* **exist**]
coff'ee *n.* seeds of a shrub originally from Arab; drink made from these seeds. [Turk, *qahveh*, Arab. *qahweh*, wine]
coff'er *n.* chest for valuables. [L. *cophinus*, *See* **coffin**]
coff'in *n.* box for a dead body. -*v.t.* put into a coffin. [L. *cophinus*, G. *kophinos*, basket]
cog *n.* one of a series of teeth on a wheel. [ME. *cogge*]
co'gent *a.* forcible, convincing. -**co'gency** *n.* -**co'gently** *adv.* [L. *cogere*, constrain-*co*, together, *agere*, drive]
cog'itate *v.i.* think, reflect. -*v.t.* plan. -**cogita'tion** *n.* [L. *cogitare*]
cogn'ac *n.* fine French brandy. [made in *Cognac*, Charente]
cog'nate *a.* of the same stock, related. [L. *gnatus*, borne]
cogni'tion *n.* perception; act of knowing. [L. *cognoscere, cognit-*, know]
cognizance *n.* knowledge, awareness, observation. -**cog'nizable** *a.* -**cog'nizant** *a.* [L. *cognoscere*, know]
cogno'men *n.* surname; nickname. [L. *nomen*, name]
cohab'it *v.i.* live together as husband and wife. [L. *co* and *habitare*, dwell]
cohere' *v.i.* stick together; be consistent.-**cohe'rance** *n.* **cohe'rent** *a.* sticking together, making sense. -**cohe'rently** *adv.* -**cohe'sion** *n.* [L. *haerere*, stick]
co'hort *n.* troop; tenth of a legion. [L. *cohors*, company of soldiers]

coif *n.* close-fitting cap or hood. [F. *coif-fecap*]

coiffure' *n.* style of hairdressing. -**coiffeur'** *n.* hairdresser. -**coiffeuse'** fem. [F.]

coign (koin) *n.* quoin. of vantage *n.* good position. [*coin*]

coil *v.t.* lay in rings; twist into a winding shape. -*v.i.* twist; take up a winding shape. -*n.* series of rings. [OF. *coiner*, collect]

coin *n.* piece of money; money. -*v.t.* make into money, stamp; invent.-**coin'age** *n.* [L. *cuneus*, wedge (a stamping die being like a wedge)]

coincide' *v.i.* happen together; agree exactly. -coin'cidence *n.* coincident; coincidental *a.* [Med. *coincidere*, fall together. *See* **incident**]

coir *n.* outer fiber of the coconut. [Malay *kayar*, cord]

coi'tion *n.* sexual intercourse. [L. *coitio*]

coke *n.* popular name for the beverage *Coca-Cola.*

coke *n.* residue left from the distillation of coal. [orig. uncertain]

col'ander *n.* sieve. [L. *colare*, strain]

cold *a.* lacking heat; indifferent, apathetic; dispiriting. -*n.* lack of heat; common ailment marked by nasal catarrh, *etc.* -**cold'ly** *adv.* -**cold'ness** *n.* -**cold feet,** (*sl.*) fear, timidity. -**cold stor'age** *n.* storing perishable goods at artificially reduced temperatures. **cold war,** diplomatic, economic but non-military hostility. [OE. *ceald*]

coleop'tera *n.pl.* order of winged insects, the beetles. [G. *koleos*, sheath, *pteron*, wing]

col'ibri *n.* humming bird. [Sp., fr. Carib.]

col'ic *n.* severe intestinal pain. [fr. G. *kolon*, lower intestine]

collaborate *v.i.* work with another, *esp.* in literature. -**collabora'tion** *n.* -**collaborator** *n.* one who works thus; native who collaborates with the enemy in an occupied country. [L. *collaborare*, fr. *laborare*, work]

collapse' *v.i.* fall together, give way; lose strength, fail. -*n.* act of collapsing. **collaps'ible** *a.* [L. *labi, laps-*, slip]

coll'ar *n.* band worn round the neck. *v.t.* seize, capture. [L. *collum*, neck]

collate' *v.t.* compare carefully; appoint to a benefice. -**colia'tion** *n.* bringing together for comparison; light repast. [L. *collatus*, fr. *conferre*, bring together]

collateral *a.* accompanying; subordinate; of the same stock but a different line. -*n.* kinsman. [L. *latus*, side]

colleague' *n.* associate, companion in an office, employment. [L. *college*]

collect' *v.t.* gather, bring together. -*v.i.* come together. -**collec'ted** *a.* gathered; calm. **collec'tion** *n.* -**collec'tive** *a.* **collect'ively** *adv.* **collect'ivism** *n.* theory that the State should own all means of production. -**collec'tor** *n.* [L. *colligere, collect-*, gather together]

coll'een *n.* girl. [Ir. *cailin*]

coll'ege *n.* society of scholars; place of higher education; association. -**colle'gian** *n.* -**colle'giate** *a.* [L. *collegium*, fr. *legere*, gather]

collide' *v.i.* strike or dash together; come into conflict. -**colli'sion** *n.* [L. *collidere*, fr. *laedere*, hurt]

coll'ie *n.* Scottish sheep-dog. [orig. uncertain]

coll'ier *n.* coal-miner; coal-ship. -**coll'iery** *n.* coal mine. [*coal*]

collo'dion *n.* gummy solution of guncotton in alcohol and ether, and used in surgery. [see *colloid*]

coll'oid *n.* gummy substance. **colloidal** *a.* gummy. [G. *kolla*, glue, *eidos*, form]

coll'op *n.* slice of meat; (Scot.) minced meat. [orig. unknown]

coll'oquy *n.* conversation. -**collo'quial** *a.* conversational, informal. -**collo'quialism** *n.* [L. *colloqui*, converse]

collu'sion *n.* arrangement, action in secret with another. -**collu'sive** *a.* [L. *colludere, collus-*, play together]

colobo'ma *n.* structural defect of the eye. [G. *kolobos*, cut short]

co'lon *n.* mark (:) indicating a division of a sentence. [G. *kolon*, limb, part of a sentence]

co'lon *n.* lower intestine. [*See* **colic**]

colonel (kur'-nel) *n.* commander of a regiment; rank between lieutenant colonel and brigadier general. -**coloneley** (kur'-) *n.* [It. *colonello*, column (*i.e.*, 'support' of regiment)]

colonnade' *n.* row of columns. [F.]

col'ony *n.* body of people who settle in a new country; country so settled. -**colo'nial** *a.* **coloniza'tion** *n.* -**col'on ize** *v.t.* **col'onist** *n.* [L. *colonia*, fr. *colere*, till]

col'ophon *n.* publisher's imprint or device. [G. *kolophen*, summit, finishing touch]

Colora'do bee'tle *n.* black-striped yellow beetle, a wide-spread potato pest. [Colorado, U.S.A.]

coluss'us *n.* huge statue; very big man. -**coloss'al** *a.* huge. [L.]

col'or *n.* hue, tint; complexion; paint or anything giving color; race, when associated with skin-color. *-pl.* flags. *-v.t.* stain, dye, paint, give color to; disguise; misrepresent.*-v.i.* become colored; blush. **-col'orable** *a.* apparently valid and genuine; intended to deceive. **-colorat'ion** *n.* the state ofbeing colored or imposing color; the arrangement of colors exhibited by something. **-col'or bar** *n.* a social barrier which prevents people of different colors mixing freely. **-col'orblind'ness** *n.* the inability to distinguish between certain colors. **-col'ored** *a.* having color; of a race other than white; black. **-col'orful** *a.* of bright colors; exaggerated. **-col'oring** *n.* act of applying color; natural color. [L. *color*]

colporteur' *n.* hawker of religious books. [F. from L. *collum*, neck, *portare*, carry]

colt *n.* young of the horse. **-colts'foot** *n.* yellow-flowered plant formerly used in medicine, [OE.]

col'umbine *a.* of, like, a dove. *-n.* flowering plant with petals resembling doves. [L. *columba*, dove]

col'umn (-um) *n.* long vertical cylinder, pillar; division of a page; body of troops; anything like these. **-colum'nar** *a.* - **col'umnist** (-um-ist) *n.* writer of a periodical column. [L. *columna*-G. *kolone*, hill]

col'za *n.* kind of cabbage; its seeds, yielding oil. [Du. *koolzaad*, cabbage seed]

co'ma *n.* stupor, unnatural sleep. - **co'matose** *a.* [G. *koma*]

comb *n.* toothed instrument for arranging hair, or ornamenting it; cock's crest; mass of honey-cells. *-v.t.* apply a comb to. [OE. *comb*, Ice. *kambri*]

com'bat *v.t.* fight.*-n.* a fight. **com'batant** *n.* **-com'bative** *a.* [F.]

combine' *v.t.* and *i.* join together; ally. **-com'bine** *n.* group of companies or political associates. **-com'bine, com'bine har'vester** *n.* machine for reaping grain. - **combina'tion** *n.* [Late L. *combinare*, put two-and-two (*bini*) together]

combustion *n.* burning. **combustibil'ity** *n.* **-combus'tible** *a.* [Late L. *combustion* fr. *comburere*, burn]

come (kum) *v.i.* approach, arrive, move towards; reach; happen (to); originate (from); get to be, become; turn out to be. [OE. *cuman*]

com'edy *n.* drama dealing with the lighter side of life, ending happily, or treating its subject humorously; play of this kind. **-come'dian** *n.* player in comedy. [I. *comoedia*]

come'ly (kum'-) *a.* fair, pretty; seemly. **come'liness** *n.* [OE. *cymlic*]

comestibles *n. pl.* eatables. [L. *comedere, comes-*, eat up]

com'et *n.* heavenly body like a star or planet w i th a tail of light. **com'etary** *a.* [G. *kome*, head of hair]

com'fit (kum'-) *n.* sweetmeat. [L. *conficere*, put together]

com'fort (kum'-) *v.t.* console, cheer, gladde *-n.* consolation; well-being, ease; means of consolation or ease. **-comfortable** *a.* **-com'fortably** *adv.* **com'forter** *n.* one who comforts; baby's 'dummy'. [Late L. *confortare*, strengthen]

com'frey *n.* tall ditch-growing herb. [OF. *confirie*]

com'ic *a.* relating to comedy; funny, laughable. **-com'ical** *a.* **-com'ically** *adv.* [G. *komikos*]

com'ity *n.* courtesy, friendliness. [L. *comitas-comis*, courteous]

comm'a *n.* mark (,) separating short parts of a sentence. [G. *komma*, piece cut off, short clause]

command' *v.t.* order; rule; compel; have in oneés power; overlook; dominate. *-v.i.* exercise rule. *-n.* order, rule; power of controlling, ruling, dominating, overlooking; post of one commanding; his district. **commandant'** *n.* **-commandeer'** *v.t.* seize for military service. **-command'er** *n.* - **command'ment** *n.* [L. *mandare*, enjoin]

command'o *n.* military body detailed for special or dangerous service; member of this body. [Port.]

commemorate *v.t.* celebrate, keep in memory by ceremony. **-commemora'tion** *n.* **-commem'orative** *a.* [L. *commemorate. See* **memory**]

commence' *v.t.* and *i.* begin. - **commence'ment** *n.* the act of commencing; ceremony at which degrees or diplomas are conferred. [F. *commencer*-L. *com* and *initiare*, begin]

commend' *v.t.* praise; commit, entrust. **-commendable** *a.* praiseworthy. - **commend'ably** *adv.* **-commenda'tion** *n.* **-commend'atory** *a.* [L. *commendare*]

commensurate *a.* in proportion, adequate; equal in size or length of time. [L. *mensurare*, measure]

comm'ent *n.* note, collection of notes; remark; criticism. *-v.i.* make remarks, notes, criticisms. **-comm'entator** *n.* [L. *commentari*]

comm'entary *n.* series of comments; book of notes or comments on another book. -**runn'ing commentary,** comments on a game, *etc.* as it proceeds. [*comment*]

comm'erce *n.* buying and selling; dealings, intercourse. -**commer'cial** *a.* -**commercialize** *n.* [L. *commercium,* fr. *merx,* merchandise]

commina'tion *n.* a threatening with divine wrath. -**com'minatory** *a.* threatening. [L. *comminatio,* strong threatening]

comminute *v.t.* pulverize. -**comminu'tion** *n.* [L. *comminuere,* break into pieces]

commiserate (-z-) *v.t.* pity, condole with. **commisera'tion** *n.* [L. *commiserari,* bewail with]

commissar' *n.* head of a government department in former U.S.S.R. (commit) -**commissariat** *n.* military department in charge of supplies and transport. [F., fr. Low L. *commissarius*]

commission *n.* doing, committing; something entrusted to be done; payment by a percentage for doing something; delegate -d authority; body entrusted with some special duty. -*v.t.* give an order for; authorize, give power to. -**commis'sioner** *n.* [L. *commission* fr. *committere,* entrust]

commit' *v.t.* entrust, give in charge; perpetrate, be guilty of, compromise, entangle. -**committee'** *n.* person to whom something is committed. -**commit'ment** *n.* -**committ'al** *n.* [L. *committere,* entrust]

committee *n.* body appointed or elected for some special business, usually from some large body. [orig. one person entrusted with a duty, *etc.* (fr. L. *committere,* entrust)]

commode' *n.* chest of drawers; stool containing a chamber-pot. [L. *commodus,* fit]

commodious *a.* roomy, convenient. -**commo'diously** *adv.* [L. *commodus,* fit]

commodity *n.* article of trade, anything meeting a need. [L. *commodus, fit]*

Commodore *n.* naval officer ranking between captain and rear-admiral; senior captain in shipping line; president of a yacht club. [orig. uncertain]

comm'on *a.* shared by or belonging to all, or several; public, general; ordinary, usual, frequent; inferior, vulgar. -*n.* land belonging to a community, unenclosed land not belonging to a private owner. *pl.* ordinary people; the lower house of the British Parliament; rations, food provided daily. -**comm'onality** *n.* general body of the people. -**comm'oner** *n.* -**comm'only** *adv.* **comm'onplace** *a.* ordinary, trivial. -*n.* -**comm'onwealth** *n.* state. [L. *communis*]

commotion *n.* stir, disturbance, tumult. [L. *movere, mot-,* move]

commune' *v.i.* have intimate intercourse. - **commu'nicable** *a.* - **commu'nicant** *n.* one who receives Communion. -**commu'nicate** *v.t.* impart, give a share. *v.i.* give or exchange information; receive Communion. -**communica'tion** *n.* act of giving, *esp.* information; information, letter, message; passage (road, railway, *etc.*) or means of exchanging messages (telegraph, post, *etc.*) between places; connection between military base and front. **commu'nicative** *a.* free with information. -**commu'nion** *n.* fellowship; body with a common faith; sharing. -**Commu'nion** *n.* participation in the sacrament of the Lordés Supper; that sacrament, Eucharist. [L. *communes,* common]

communiqué' *n.* an official announcement; news bulletin. [F. fr. L. *communicate*]

communism. *See* **community.**

community *n.* state; body of people with something in common, *e.g.,* district of residence, religion; joint ownership. -**comm'une** *n.* small administrative district; organization where property and responsibilities are shared in common. -**commu'nal** *a.* common, shared by a number. **comm'unism** *n.* doctrine that all goods, means of production, *etc.* should be the property of the community. -**comm'unist** *n.* -**commu'nity singing,** conducted but unpracticed singing by large crowds. [L. *communes,* common]

commute' *v.t.* exchange; change (a punishment, *etc.*) into something less; change (a duty *etc.*) for a money payment; (*elec.*) reverse current.**commuta'tion** *n.* [L. *mutare,* change]

com'pact *n.* agreement, covenant. [L. *compacisci,* agree together]

compact' *a.* neatly arranged or packed; solid, concentrated; terse. **com'pact** *n.* pocket-sized vanity case. -**compact'ly** *adv.* -**compact'ness** *n.* [L. *compingere, compact-,* join together]

compact disc, disk *n.* digital disc used to record music or data, read by a laser device.

compan'ion *n.* mate, follow, comrade, associate. **compan'ionable** *a* . **compan'ionship** *n.* [L. *companio,* mess mate, fr. *panes,* bread]

compan'ion *n.* raised cover over a staircase from the deck to the cabin of a ship;

deck skylight. [Du. *kampanje*]

com′pany *n.* assembly; society; association of people for trade *etc.*; ship's crew; part of a battalion. [*companion*]

compare′ *v.t.* notice or point out the likenesses and differences of anything; liken or contrast; make the comparative and superlative of an adjective or adverb. - *v.i.* be like; compete with. **-com′parable** *a.* - **compar′ative** *a.* that may be compared; not absolute; relative, partial. - **compar′atively** *adv*. **-compar′ison** *n.* [L. *comparare*]

compartment *n.* division or part divided off, a section; division of a railway car, *etc* . **-compartmental** *a.* **-compartmentalize** *v.t.* [L. *com* and *partiri*, share, fr. *pars*, share]

com′pass (kum′-) *n.* instrument for showing the north; instrument for describing circles (*usu.* in *pl.*); circumference, measurement round; space, area, scope, reach. -*v.t.* contrive; surround; attain. [VL. *compassare*, go round, fr. *passus*, step]

compassion (-shun) *n.* pity, sympathy. **compassionate** *a.* **-compas′sionately** *adv.* [L. *com*, with, *pati*, *pass-*, suffer]

compatible *a.* consistent, agreeing with. **-compatibil′ity** *n.* **compat′ibly** *adv.* [Med. L. *compatibilis*, sharing in suffering, fr. *pati*, suffer]

compatriot *n.* fellow-countryman. -*a.* of the same country. [*See* **patriot**]

com′peer *n.* equal; associate. (L. *com-*, together, *par*, equal]

compel′ *v.t.* force, oblige, bring about by force. **-compul′sion** *n.* **compul′sory** *a.* [L. *compellere*, drive together]

compendium *n.* abridgment or summary; epitome. **-compen′dious** *a.* brief but inclusive. **-compen′diously** *adv* . [L. = what is weighed together]

com′pensate *v.t.* make up for; counterbalance. **-compensa′tion** *n.* [L. *compensate*, weigh together]

compère (kong-per) *n.* one who introduces and joins up items in an entertainment program. [F. = gossip]

compete′ *v.i.* strive, vie (with). - **competi′tion** *n.* **-compet′itive** *a.* **compet′itor** *n.* [L. *competere*, seek in common]

competent *a.* able, skillful; properly qualified; proper, due, legitimate, suitable, sufficient.**-com′petence, com′petency** *n.* **-com′petently** *adv.* [L. *competere*, be convenient]

compile′ *v.t.* make up (*e.g.*, a book) from various sources or materials; put together. **-compila′tion** *n.* **-compi′ler** *n.* [L. *compilare*, plunder]

compiler *n.* (*compute.*) computer program that converts a program written in a high-level lanugage into machine language.

complacent *a.* self-satisfied. - **compla′cence, complacency** *n.* - **compla′cently** *adv.* **-com′plaisance** *n.* obligingness, willingness to please. **com′plaisant** *a.* [L. *complacere*, please greatly]

complain′ *v.i.* grumble; bring a charge, make known a grievance; (with of) make known that one is suffering from. - **complain′ant** *n.* **-complaint′** *n.* statement of a wrong, a grievance; an illness. [L. *plangere*, beat the breast]

complaisance. *See* **complacent.**

com′plement. *See* **complete.**

complete *a.* full, finished, ended, perfect.-*v.t.* finish; make whole, full, perfect. **-complement** *n.* something completing a whole; full allowance, equipment, *etc.* - **complement′ary** *a.* **-complete′ly** *adv.* - **complete′ness** *n.* **-comple′tion** *n.* [L. *cornplere*, complete, fill up]

com′plex *a.* intricate, compound, involved-*n.* psychological abnormality, obsession. **-complex′ity** *n.* [L. *complectere*, plait together]

complexion (-ek′-shun) *n.* look, color, *esp.* of the skin. [F., fr. L. *complexio*]

compliant. *See* **comply.**

complicate *v.t.* make intricate, involved, difficult. **-complica′tion** *n.* [L. *eomplicare*, fold together]

complicity *n.* partnership in wrongdoing. [*See*accomplice]

compliment *n.* remark neatly expressing praise. -*pl.* expression of courtesy, formal greetings. -*v.t.* praise, congratulate. - **complement′ary** *a* . [Sp. *cumplimiento*, a 'fulfilling' of an act of courtesy; same word as *complement*]

com′plin(e) seventh and last service of day (9 P.M.) in R.C. church. [L. *plere*, fill]

comply′ *v.i.* consent, yield, do as asked. **-compli′ance** *n.* **compli′ant** *a.* [It.*complire*, fr. Sp. *cumplir*, satisfy requirements, fr. L. *complere*, fill up]

component *n.* part, elemental. composing, making up. [L. *componere*, put together]

comport′ *v.t.* conduct or carry (oneself). - *v.i.* agree, accord (with). [L. *portare*, carry]

compose′ *v.t.* make up; write, invent; arrange, put in order; settle, adjust; calm.

-**composed'** *a.* calm. **compo'ser** *n.* author of a musical work. -**com'posite** *a.* compound, not simple. -**composi'tion** *n.* -**compos'itor** *n.* typesetter, one who arranges type for printing. -**compo'sure** *n.* calmness. [F. *composer*]

com'pote *n.* fruit preserved in syrup. [F.]

compound' *v.t.* mix, make up, put together; compromise, make a settlement of debt by partial payment; condone. -*v.i.* come to an arrangement, make terms. -**com'pound** *a.* not simple; composite, mixed. -*n.* mixture, joining; substance, word, *etc.* made up of parts. [L. *componere*, put together]

com'pound *n.* in the East, an enclosure containing houses. [Malay *kampung*, perh. fr. Port. *campo*, field]

comprehend' *v.t.* understand, take in; include, comprise. -**comprehen'sible** *a.* -**comprehension** *n.* -**comprehen'sive** *a.* -**comprehen'sively** *adv.* -**comprehen'siveness** *n.* [L. *comprehendere*, grasp]

compress' *v.t.* squeeze together; make smaller in size, bulk. -**com'press** *n.* pad of wet lint *etc.* applied to a wound, inflamed part, *etc.* **compress'ible** *a.* **compres'sion** *n.* [L. *premere, press-*, press]

comprise' *v.t.* include, contain. [F. *compris, pp.* of *comprendre*, comprehend]

compromise *n.* meeting halfway, coming to terms by giving up part of a claim. -*v.t.* expose to risk or suspicion. *v.i.* come to terms. [L. *compromittere*, put before an arbiter]

comptroller (kon-tro'-) *n.* controller (in some titles). [bad spelling variant due to mistaken association with F. *compte*, account]

compulsion. *See* **compel.**

compunction *n.* regret for wrongdoing; uneasy scruple; pity. [L. *compunction* prick of conscience]

compute' *v.t.* reckon, estimate. -**computa'tion** *n.* -**comput'er** *n.* a machine, *usu.* electronic, capable of carrying out calculations and other complex functions at high speeds. -**comput'erize** *v.t.* equip with, perform by a computer. [L. *computare*]

com'rade (kom'-rid or kum'rid) *n.* mate, companion, friend. -**com'radeship** *n.* [Sp. *camorada*, roomful, later room-mate; fr. L. *camera*, room]

con *v.t.* learn as a lesson, pore over. [OE. *cunnian*, test, examine]

con *v.t.* direct the steering of a ship. -**conn'ing-tower** *n.* [earlier *cond, condy*, fr. F. *conduire*, guide]

con *v.t.* trick, swindle. -*n.* [fr. *confidence* trick]

cona'tion *n.* impulse to directive effort. -**cona'tive** *a.* [L. *conari, conat-*, attempt]

concatenation *n.* series of links; chain (of events, *etc.*). -**concat'enate** *v.t.* [L. *con*, together, *catena*, chain]

con'cave *a.* hollow, rounded inwards. -**concav'ity** *a.* [L. *cavus*, hollow]

conceal' *v.t.* hide, keep secret. -**concealment** *n.* [L. *celare*, hide]

concede' *v.t.* admit, grant; yield. -**conces'sion** *n.* -**concess'ive** *a.* [L. *cedere, cess-*, give away]

conceit' *n.* vanity, overweening opinion of oneself; far-fetched comparison. -**conceit'ed** *a.* conceive **conceive'** *v.t.* become pregnant with; take into the mind, think of, imagine; understand. -**conceiv'able** *a.* -**conceiv'ably** *adv.* [F. *concevoir*, fr. L. *concipere*]

concentrate *v.t.* reduce to small space; increase in strength; gather to one point. -*v.i.* come together; devote all attention. -**concentra'tion** *n.* -**concentra'tion camp,** camp for political prisoners, *etc.* [L. *concentrum*]

concentric *a.* having a common center. [L. *cum* and *centrum*, center]

con'cept *n.* idea, abstract notion. -**concep'tual** *a.* -**concep'tion** *n.* conceiving, idea [L. *concipere*, conceive]

concern' *v.t.* to relate or belong to; to interest, affect, trouble, involve. -*n.* affair, importance, business, establishment. **concern'ing** *prep.* respecting. [L. *cernere*, have regard to]

concert' *v.t.* arrange, plan together. -**con'cert** *n.* musical entertainment; harmony, agreement. **concert'ed** *a.* mutually arranged. **concer'to** (cher-) *n.* musical composition for solo instrument and orchestra. **concerti'na** *n.* musical instrument with bellows and keys. [F. *concerted*]

concessions *See* **concede.**

concet'to (-chet'-) *n.* ingenious fancy; conceit. -*pl.* **concet'ti.** [It.]

conchol'ogy *n.* study of shells and shellfish. [L. *concha*, shell]

con'chy *n.* (*sl.*) *abbrev.* of conscientious objector.

concierge' (kong-si-erzh) *n.* French doorkeeper, porter, caretaker. [F.]

conciliate *v.t.* pacify, gain friendship. -**concila'tion** *n.* **concil'iatory** *a* . [L. *conciliate*, bring together in council]

concinn'ity *n.* elegance; harmony. -**concinn'ous** *a.* [L. *concinnus*, well adjusted]

concise′ *a.* brief, in few words. -**concise′ly** *adv.* -**concise′ness** *n.* **concision** (-sizhn) *n.* [L. *concisus*, fr. *cædere*, cut]

con′clave *n.* private meeting; assembly for the election of a Pope. [L. *conclave*, inner room, fr. *clavis*, key]

conclude′ *v.t.* end, finish; settle; *v.i.* come to an end; infer, deduce; decide. **conclu′sion** (-oo′shn) *n.* -**conclu′sive** *a.* decisive, convincing. -**conclu′sively** *adv.* [L. *concludere*]

concoct′ *v.t.* make a mixture, prepare with various ingredients; make up; devise, as a plan. -**concoc′tion** *n.* [L. *concoquere*, boil together]

concomitant *a.* accompanying. [L. *concomitari*, go with as companion]

conc′ord *n.* agreement. -**concord′ance** *n.* agreement; an index to the words of a book. **concord′ant** *a.* [L. *Concordia*]

concourse *n.* crowd; a flocking together. [L. *concurrere*, concur, run together]

con′crete *a.* solid; consisting of matter, facts, practice, *etc.*; not abstract.-*n.* mixture of sand, cement, *etc.*, used in building -**concrete′ly** *adv.* [L. *concrescere, concretum*, grow together]

concubine *n.* woman living with a man as his wife, but not married to him. **concu′binage** *n.* [fr. L. *con*, together, and *cubare*, lie]

concu′piscence *n.* lust. [L. *concupiscere*, con and *cupere*, desire]

concur′ *v.i.* agree, express agreement; happen together. -**concur′rence** *n.* **concur′rently** *adv.* [L. *concurrere*, run together]

concussion (-shn) *n.* violent shock; injury by blow, fall, *etc.* [L. *concussion*, shaking together]

condemn′ *v.t.* blame; find guilty; doom; find unfit for use. **condem′natory** *a.* **condemna′tion** *n.* [L. *condemnare*]

condense′ *v.t.* concentrate, make more solid; turn from gas into liquid; compress. - *v.i.* turn from gas to liquid. **condensa′tion** *n.* **conden′ser** *n.* (*elec.*) apparatus for storing electrical energy for reducing vapors to liquid form; lens, mirror for focusing light. [L. *condensare*]

condescend′ *v.i.* stoop, deign; be gracious; patronize. **condecen′sion** *n.* [Late L. *condescendere*, come down]

condign′ *a.* adequate, sufficient. [L. *dignus*, worthy]

condiment *n.* relish, seasoning. [L. *condimentumcondire*, pickle]

condition *n.* thing on which a statement or happening or existing depends; stipulation; state of circumstances of anything. -*v.t.* be essential to the happening or existence of; stipulate; make fit (for). -**condi′tional** *a.* -**condi′tion powder** *n.* powder to improve dogs' health. -**condi′tioned reflex** *n.* response automatically produced by stimulus repeatedly applied. [L. *condicio*, discussion]

condole′ *v.i.* grieve with, offer sympathy. **condo′lence** *n.* [L. *condolere*, suffer with]

condominium *n.* joint rule; an apartment in a house consisting of individually owned apartments; an apartment in such a house. *abbrev.* **con′do.** [L]

condone′ *v.t.* overlook, forgive, treat as not existing. [L. *condonare*, remit]

con′dor *n.* S. Ameriran vulture. [Sp., fr. Peruvian *cuntur*]

conduce′ *v.i.* help to bring about; promote. **conduc′ive** *a.* [L. *conducere, conductum*, lead]

conduct′ *v.t.* lead, direct, manage. -**con′duct** *n.* behavior; management. -**conduc′tor** *n.* **conduc′tion** *n.* **conduc′tive** *a.* -**conductiv′ity** *n.* power to conduct heat, electricity. [L. *conducere*]

con′duit (-dit) *n.* channel or pipe for water. [F., fr. L. *conducere*, lead]

cone *n.* solid figure with a circular base and tapering to a point; any object in this shape; fruit of the pine, fir, *etc.* -**con′ic, con′ical** *a.* **co′nifer** *n.* tree bearing cones. **conif′erous** *a.* [G. *konos*, peak]

confabula′tion (colloq. *abbrev.* **confab**) *n.* chat; familiar talk. **confab′utate** *v.i.* [L. *confabulari*, chat together]

confection *n.* prepared delicacy, sweetmeat; made-up millinery, *etc.* -**confectioner** *n.* dealer in cake, pastry, sweets, *etc.* -**confec′tionery** *n.* [L. *conficere*, make up]

confederate *a.* united in a league-*n.* ally; accomplice. -*v.t.* and *i.* unite. -**confed′eracy** *n.* **confedera′tion** *n.* [L. *confœderatus*, fr. *fœdus, fœderis*, treaty, league]

confer′ *v.t.* grant, give. - *v.i.* talk with, take advice. -**confer′ment** *n.* -**con′ference** *n.* [L. *conferre*, bring together]

confess′ *v.t.* admit, own, acknowledge, declare; (of a priest) to hear the sins of. *v.i.* acknowledge; declare one's sins orally to a priest. -**confes′sion** *n.* -**confes′sional** *n.* confessor's stall or box. -**confes′sor** *n.* priest who hears confessions; person who keeps his faith under pesecution, but without martyrdom; one who confesses. [L. *confiteri, confessus*, acknowledge]

confetti *n.* small shaped pieces of colored paper for throwing at carnivals and weddings [It.]

confide' *v.i.* trust (in). *v.t.* entrust. -**confidant'** *n.* one entrusted with secrets. -**con'fidence** *n.* trust; boldness, assurance; intimacy. **con'fident** *a.* -**con'fidently** *adv.* [L. *fidere*, trust]

configuration *n.* shape, aspect; outline. [L. *figurare*, fashion]

confine' *v.t.* shut up, imprison; keep within bounds; keep in house, bed. -**con'fines** *n.pl.* boundaries. -**confine'ment** *n.* restraint, imprisonment; child bed. [L. *confinis*, bordering]

confirm' *v.t.* make strong, settle; make valid, ratify; make sure, verify; administer confirmation to. -**confirma'tion** *n.* making strong, valid, certain, *etc.*; rite administered by a bishop to confirm baptized persons in the vows made for them at baptism. -**confirm'ative, confirm'atory** *a.* [L. *confirmare*]

con'fiscate *v.t.* seize by authority. -**confisca'tion** *n.* confiscatory *a.* [L. *confiscare*, seize for the treasury, *liscus.* cp. *fiscal*]

conflagration *n.* great fire. [L. *confl agration*, burn up]

con'flict *n.* struggle, trial of strength; variance. -**conflict'** *v.t.* be at odds with, inconsistent with; clash. [L. *conflictusfligere*, strike]

con'fluence *n.* union of streams; meeting place. **con'fluent** *a.* [L. *confluere*, flow together]

conform' *v.t.* and *i.* comply, adapt to rule, pattern, custom, *etc.* -**conform'able** *a.* -**conform'ably** *adv.* -**conforma'tion** *n.* structure; adaptation. -**conform'ity** *n.* [L. conformare, give same shape]

confound' *v.t.* baffle, bring to confusion, defeat; mix up. [F. *confondre*-L. *confundere, confusum*, pour together]

confratern'ity *n.* brotherhood; clan. [L. *frater*, brother]

confront' (-unt') *v.t.* face; bring face to face with. -**confronta'tion** *n.* [F. *confronter*, fr. front, brow]

Confu'cian *a.* of, or pertaining to, the Chinese philosopher Confucius (d. 478 B.C.)

confuse' *v.t.* disorder, mix mentally. -**confu'sion** *n.* [*See* **confound**]

confute' *v.t.* prove wrong. -**confuta'tion** *n.* [L. *confutare*]

congeal' *v.t.* and *i.* solidify by freezing or otherwise. -**congela'tion** *n.* [L. *congelare*, freeze together]

con'gener (-j-) *n.* thing or person of the same kind. [L. of the same]

congen'ial *a.* suitable, to one's liking; of kindred disposition. -**conge' nially** *adv.* -**congenial'ity** *n.* [Mod. L. *congenialis*, suiting one's genius]

congen'ital (-je-) *a.* bom with one, dating from birth. [L. *congenitus*]

cong'er (kong'er), **con'ger-eel**, *n.* large sea eel. [F. *congre*-G. *gonggros*]

conges'tion *n.* abnormal accumulation of blood, population, *etc.*; over-crowding. -**conges'ted** *a.* [L. *congestio*]

conglom'erate *a.* gathered into a ball. -*v.t.* and *i.* -*n.* rock of rounded pebbles cemented together-puddingstone. **conglomera'tion** *n.* confused mass. [L. *conglomerate*]

congrat'ulate *v.t.* felicitate, offer expression of pleasure at another's good fortune, success, *etc.* -**congratula'tion** *n.* **congratulatory** *a.* [L. *congratulari*]

cong'regate (-ng-g-) *v.i.* flock together; assemble. -**congrega'tion** *n.* assembly, *esp.* for religious worship. -**congrega'tional** *a.* of a congregation or Congregationalism. -**Congrega'tionalism** *n.* system in which each separate church is self-governing. -**Congrega'tionalist** *n.* [L. *grex, gregis*, herd]

cong'ress (-ng-g-) *n.* meeting; a formal assembly for discussion; a legislative body. **congres'sional** *a.* [L. *congredi*, congresses, go together]

con'gruent (-ng-groo-) *a.* fitting together; suitable, accordant. -**cong'ruence** *n.* **cong'ruous** *a.* -**congru'ity** *n.* [L. *congruere*, rush together]

con'ic, co'nifer. *See* **cone.**

co'nine *n.* poisonous alkaloid principle of hemlock. [G. *koneion*, hemlock]

conjec'ture *n.* guess. -*v.t.* and *i.* guess. -**conjec'tural** *a.* [L. *conjecture*, fr. *conjicere*, conjecture, throw together]

con'jugal *a.* of marriage; between married persons. -**conjugal'ity** *n.* [L. *conjunx*, spouse, *lit.* joined together]

con'jugate *v.t.* inflect a verb in its various forms (past, present, *etc.*). -**conjuga'tion** *n.* [L. *conjugate*]

conjunc'tion *n.* part of speech joining words, phrases, *etc.*; union; simultaneous happening. -**conjunc'ture** *n.* combination of circumstances, decisive point. [L. *conjungere*, join together]

conjunctiv'a *n.* membrane joining

eyeball and eyelid. -**conjunctivi′tis** *n.* inflammation of the conjunctiva. [L. *conjungere*]

conjure′ *v.t.* implore solemnly. -**con′jure** (kunjer) *v.t.* and *i.* produce magic effects by secret natural means; invoke devils. -**conjura′tion** *n.* **con′jurer, conjuror** *n.* [L. *conjurare*, swear together]

connote′ *a.* innate, congenital. -**conna′tion** *n.* **connat′ural** *a.* of the same nature. [L. *nasci, natus*, be born]

connect′ *v.t.* and *i.* join together, unite; associate -**connec′tion, conne′xion** *n.* -**connect′ive** *a.* [L. *nectere*, bind]

conn′ing-tower. *See* **con.**

connive′ *v.i.* wink at, refrain from preventing, or forbidding, an offense. -**conni′vance** *n.* [L. *connivers*, wink]

connoisseur′ (kon-e-ser′) *n.* critical expert in matters of taste. [OF. *conoisseur*, fr. L. *cognoscere*, know]

connote′ *v.t.* imply, mean in addition to the chief meaning. **connota′tion** *n.* [Med. L. *connotare*]

connub′ial *a.* connected with marriage. [L. *conubium*, marriage]

con′quer (-ker) *v.t.* win by war; overcome, defeat.- *v.i.* be victorious. -**conqueror** (-ke) *n.* -**con′quest** *n.* [L. *quæxrere*, seek]

consangu′inity *n.* kinship. -**consanguin′eous** *a.* [fr. L. *sanguis*, blood]

con′science (-shens) *n.* mental sense of right and wrong. **conscien′tious** *a.* -**conscien′tious objector** one who, for conscience sake, refuses to serve with the armed forces. -**conscien′tiously** *adv.* [L. *conscientia*, knowledge within oneself]

con′scious (-shus) *a.* aware, awake to one's surroundings and identity, in one's senses. -**con′sciously** *adv.* **con′sciousness** *n.* [L. *conscius*, aware]

con′script *n.* one compulsorily enlisted for military service. -**conscrip′tion** *n.* [L. *conscribere*, write together, enroll]

con′secrate *v.t.* make sacred. -**consecration** *n.* [L. *consecrate*]

consec′utive *a.* orderly; in unbroken succession; expressing consequence. -**consec′utively** *adv.* [L. *consequi*, con and *sequi, secutus*, follow]

consen′sus *n.* agreement (of opinion *etc.*); general trend. [*consent*]

consent′ *v.i.* agree to, comply. -*n.* agreement, acquiescence. [L. *consentire*, feel together]

con′sequence *n.* result, effect, what follows on a cause. **con′sequent** *a.* -**consequen′tial** *a.* self-important. **con′sequently** *adv.* [L. *consequential* fr. *consequi*, follow]

conserve′ *v.t.* keep from change or decay. **conser′vancy** *n.* board controlling a river or port, its fisheries *etc.* -**conserva′tion** *n.* -**conser′vative** *a.* and *n.* -**conser′vatory** *n.* greenhouse. [L. *conservare*, protect]

consid′er *v.t.* think over; examine; make allowance for; esteem; be of opinion that. -**considera′tion** *n.* -**consid′erable** *a.* important; somewhat large. **consid′erably** *adv.* -**consid′erate** *a.* thoughtful for others; careful. **consid′erately** *adv.* [L. *considerate*]

consign′ *v.t.* commit or hand over to; entrust to a carrier. -**consign′er** *n.* **consignee′** *n.* **consign′ment** *n.* [L. *corwignare*, fr. *signum*, sign]

consist′ *v.i.* be composed of, agree with, be compatible. **consist′ent** *a.* agreeing (with); constant.-**consist′ently** *adv.* -**consist′ency** *n.* **consist′ence** *n.* degree of density. -**con′sistory** *n.* ecclesiastical court or council, *esp.* of the Pope and Cardinals. [L. *consistere*, stand firm]

console′ *v.t.* comfort in distress. -**consola′tion** *n.* -**consol′atory** *a.* [L. *consolari*, comfort]

con′sole *n.* supporting bracket; unit comprising the keyboards, stops, *etc.* of an organ; electrical equipment. [F.]

consol′idate *v.t.* make firm; combine into a connected whole. -**consolida′tion** *n.* [L. *consolidate*, fr. *solidus*, solid]

consommé *n.* kind of meat soup. [F.]

con′sonant *n.* sound making a syllable only with a vowel, a non-vowel. -*a.* agreeing with, in accord. -**con′sonance** *n.* [L. *consonare*, sound with]

con′sort *n.* ship sailing with another; husband or wife, *esp.* of a queen or king. -**consort′** *v.i.* associate, keep company with. [L. *consors*, fr. *sors*, fate]

consor′tium (-shi-) *n.* society; fellowship; international banking combine. [L. = *partnership*]

conspecific′ *a.* of, or belinging to, the same species.

conspec′tus *n.* general view, synopsis. [L. *conspicere*, look at]

conspic′uous *a.* striking to the eye, very noticeable; eminent. -**conspic′uously** *adv.* [L. *conspicere*, see clearly]

conspire′ *v.i.* combine for an evil purpose, plot. **conspir′ator** *n.* -**conspir′acy** *n.* -**conspirator′ial** *a.* [L. *conspirare*, lit. breathe together]

con'stable *n.* officer of the peace; governor of a royal fortress; British policeman. **constab'ulary** *n.* [Late L. *comes stabuli,* count of the stable, marshal (a chief officer of a Frankish king)]

con'stant *a.* fixed, unchanging; steadfast; always duly happening or continuing. -**con'stantly** *adv.* **con'stancy** *n.* [L. *constare*, stand together]

constella'tion *n.* group of stars. [L. *constellation,* cluster of stars. -*stellar*, star]

consterna'tion *n.* terrifying sense of disaster; dismay. [L. *cowternatio*]

constipa'tion *n.* difficulty in emptying the bowels. **con'stipate** *v.t.* affect with this disorder. [L. *constipare*, press together]

con'stitute *v.t.* set up, establish, make into, found, give form to. **constitu'tion** *n.* make, composition; basic physical condition; disposition; body of principles on which a state is governed. -**constitu'tional** *a.* relating to a constitution; in harinony with a political **constitution.** -*n.* walk taken for health. -**constitu'tionally** *adv.* - **constit'uent** *a.* going towards making up a whole; electing a representative. -*n.* component part; elector. -**constituency** *n.* a body of people entitled to elect a representative in government; the geographical location of this body. [L. *constituere*, place together]

constrain' *v.t.* force, compel; urge. - **constraint'** *n.* compulsion; restraint; embarrassment. [L. *constringere*, tighten]

constric'tion *n.* compression, squeezing together. -**constrict'** *v.t.* -**constrict'ive** *a.* [L. constriction pressing together]

construct' *v.t.* to make, build, form, put together. -**construc'tion** *n.* -**construc'tive** *a.* -**construc'tively** *adv.* [L. *con struere, constructum*, pile together, build]

construe' *v.t.* interpret, analyze, grammatically; translate. [L. *construere*, pile together]

con'suetude (-swe-) *n.* custom; use. - **consuetu'dinary** *a.* -*n.* unwritten law based on ancient usage. [L. *consuetudo*, custom]

con'sul *n.* state agent residing in a foreign town; in ancient Rome, one of the chief magistrates. **con'sular** *a.* -**con'sulate** *n.* - **con'sulship** *n.* [L]

consuit' *v.t.* and *i.* seek counsel, advice or information (from). -**consul'tant** *n.* one who consults or advises; specialist (in medicine *etc.*). **consulta'tion** *n.* [L. *consultare*]

consume' *v.t.* make away with; use up; eat or drink up; destroy. -**consump'tion** *n.* using up; destruction; wasting of the body by tuberculosis. -**consump'tive** *a.* [L. *consumers*, use up]

con'summate *v.t.* complete, finish. - **consumm'ate** *a.* of the greatest perfection or completeness. -**consumm'ately** *adv.* - **consumma'tion** *n.* [L. *summus*, highest]

contabes'cence *n.* wasting away, atrophy. [L. *contabescere*, waste away]

con'tact *n.* touching; being in touch; person contacted. -*v.t.* get into touch with. **conta'gion** (-jn) *a.* passing on of disease by touch, contact; physical or moral pestilence. -**conta'gious** *a.* [L. *tangere*, touch]

contain' *v.t.* hold; have room for; include; restrain (oneself). **contain'er** *n.* [L. *tenere*, hold]

contam'inate *v.t.* stain, sully, infect. - **contamina'tion** *n.* -**contaminant** *n.* substance of thing that infects. [L. *contamen*, contagion]

contemn' *v.t.* scorn, despise. -**contempt'** *n.* scorn; disgrace. -**contemp'tible** *a.* despicable. **contemp'tibly** *adv.* - **contemp'tuous** *a.* scornful. - **contemp'tuously** *adv.* [L. *temnere*, despise]

con'template *v.t.* gaze upon; meditate on; intend, purpose. -**contempla'tion** *n.* **contem'plative** *a.* [L. *contemplari*; orig. of *augurs* viewing a templum in the sky. cp. *templo*]

contem'porary *a.* existing at, or lasting, the same time; of the same age. -*n.* one existing at the same time. - **contempora'neous** *a.* - **contempora'neously** *adv.* [L. *tempus, tempor*, time]

contend' *v.i.* strive, fight, dispute. **con ten'tion** *n.* -**conten'tious** *a.* - **conten'tiously** *adv.* [L. *tendere*, stretch]

content' *a.* satisfied. -*v.t.* satisfy. -*n.* satisfaction. -**con'tent** *n.* holding capacity; *pl.* that contained. -**content'ment** *n.* [L. *continere*, contain]

conterminous *a.* adjacent, with common boundary. -**conter'minal** *a.* [L. *conterminno*, neighboring]

contest' *v.t.* dispute, debate, fight for. - **con'test** *n.* debate; conflict, strife; competition. -**contes'tant** *n.* -**contes'table** *a.* [L. *contestari*, call to witness]

con'text *n.* what comes before and after a passage, words, *esp.* as fixing meaning. [L. *contexere*, weave together]

contiguous *a.* touching; adjoining; neighboring. -**contigu'ity** *n.* [L. *contiguus*, fr. *contingere*, touch]

cont'inent *a.* self-restraining; sexually

chaste. -**con'tinence** *n.* [L. *continere*, hold together]

continent *n.* large continuous mass of land, a main division of the earth. -**The Con'tinent,** European mainland. **continen'tal** *a.* [L. *continere*, hold together]

contingent (-j-) *a.* uncertain; depending for occurrence (on); accidental. -*n.* quota of troops supplied by an ally, an organization, *etc.* -**contin'gency** *n.* [L. *contingere*, relate to]

contin'ue *v.t.* and *i.* go on, carry on, last, remain, keep in existence, prolong, resume. -**contin'ual** *a.* -**contin'ually** *adv.* **continuance** *n.* -**continua'tion** *n.* -**contin'uity** *n.* **contin'uous** *a.* -**contin'uously** *adv.* [L. *continuare*]

contort' *v.t.* twist out of normal shape; writhe. **contor'tion** *n.* [L. *contorquere, contortum*, twist together]

con'tour (-oor) *n.* outline of shape of anything, esp. mountains, coast, *etc.* -**contour** (line) *n.* line on a map showing uniform elevation. [F., fr. *contourner*, follow the outline]

con'traband *n.* forbidden traffic; smuggling; smuggled goods. -**con'trabandist** *n.* [It. *contrabbando*, against law. cp. *ban*]

contracep'tion *n.* birth-control; prevention of conception, *usu.* by artificial means. -**contracep'tive** *a.* and *n.* [L. *contra* and *conception*]

con'tract *n.* bargain, agreement; formal writing recording an agreement; agreement enforceable by law. -**con'tract** (bridge), variation of auction bridge. -**contract'** *v.i.* enter into an agreement; become smaller. -*v.t.* agree upon; incur, become involved in; make smaller; shorten. -**contrac'tile** *a.* -**contrac'tion** *n.* -**contrac'tor** *n.* one making a contract, *esp.* a builder working to a contract. [L. *contrahere*, draw together]

contradict' *v.t.* deny; be at variance with. -**contradic'tory** *a.* -**contradic'tion** *n.* [L. *contradicere*, speak against]

contradistinc'tion *n.* difference marked by contrasting opposite qualities. [L. *contra*, opposite, and *distinction*]

contral'to *n.* voice, or part, next above alto; singer of that voice. [It.]

contrap'tion *n.* (*sl.*) contrivance; odd device or appliance. [orig. uncertain]

contrapunt'al. *See* **counterpoint.**

con'trary *a.* opposed; opposite, other. *n.* something the exact opposite of another. *adv.* in opposition. -**con'trarily** *adv.* -**contrari'ety** *n.* -**con'trariwise** *adv.* [L. *contraries*]

contrast' (-a-) *v.t.* bring out differences; set in opposition for comparison. - *v.i.* show great difference. -**con'trast** *n.* striking difference; something showing a marked difference; placing, comparison, to bring out differences. [Late L. *contrastare*, stand against]

contravene' *v.t.* transgress, infringe; conflict with, contradict. -**contraven'tion** *n.* [L. *contravenire*, come against]

contretemps (kong-tr-tong) *n.* hitch, inopportune happening. [F. = ill-timed]

contribute *v.t.* give or pay to a common fund; help to a common result.- *v.i.* give or pay or help in a common fund or effort. -**contribu'tion** *n.* -**contrib'utor** *n.* **contrib'utory** *a.* **contrib'utive** *a.* [L. *contribuere. See* **tribute**]

con'trite *a.* sorrowing for wrong-doing. -**contri'tion** *n.* -**con'tritely** *adv.* [L. *conterere, contrit-*, bruise]

contrive' *v.t.* devise, invent, design; succeed in bringing about. -**contri'ver** *n.* -**contri'vance** *n.* [F. *controuver*]

control' *v.t.* command, dominate, regulate; direct, check, test.-*n.* domination; restraint; direction; check; (spiritualism) medium's spirit-guide. -*pl.* controlling levers *etc.* of car, plane; -**control'lable** *a.* -**control'ler** *n.* [OF. *contre-rolle*, duplicate register]

controlled' sub'stance *n.* drug whose possession and use is restricted by law.

con'troversy *n.* dispute, debate, *esp.* a dispute in the press and of some duration. **controvert'** *v.t.* **controver'sial** *a.* -**controver'sialist** *n.* **controvert'ible** *a.* [L. *controversus*, turned against]

con'tumacy (-to, -) *n.* stubborn or contemptuous, disobedience. -**contuma'cious** *a.* [L. *contumacia*]

contume'ly (-e-li) *n.* insulting language or treatment; disgrace. -**contume'lious** *a.* [L. *contumec*]

contuse' *v.t.* bruise. -**contu'sion** *n.* [L. *tundere, tusum*, beat, bruise]

conun'drum *n.* riddle, *esp.* one with a punning answer. [orig. uncertain]

convales'cent *a.* recovering from illness. -*n.* person recovering from sickness. **convales'cence** *n.* [L. *convalescere*, grow strong]

convec'tion *n.* (*elec.*) transmission of heat through liquid or gases. -**convective** *a.* [L. *convectio-vehere*, carry]

convenances' *n.pl.* proprieties; social conventions. [F.]

convene′ *v.t.* call together. - *v.i.* assemble. -**conven′er** *n.* one who calls a meeting; chairman of a committee. [L. *convenire*, come together]

convenient *a.* handy; favorable to needs, comfort; well-adapted to one's purpose. -**conve′niently** *adv.* -**conve′nience** *n.* [L. *convenire*, come together]

con′vent *n.* community of monks or nuns; their building. -**conven′tual** *a.* [*convene*]

conventicle *n.* meeting, *esp.* of dissenters when dissent was illegal. [*convene*]

convention *n.* a calling together; assembly; treaty, agreement; rule or practice based on agreement; accepted usage, *esp.* one grown quite formal; deadening. -**conven′tional** *a.* -**conven′tionally** *adv.* -**conventionality** *n.* [*convene*]

converge′ *v.i.* approach, tend to meet. -**conver′gent** *a.* **conver′gence** *n.* (Late L. *convergere*, incline together]

converse′ *v.i.* talk (with). -**con′verse** *n.* talk. -**conversa′tion** *n.* -**conversa′tional** *a.* -**con′versant** *a.* familiar with, versed in. [L. *conversari*, dwell with]

conversazio′ne *n.* gathering, meeting for talk esp. on learned topics. [It.]

con′verse *a.* opposite, turned round. *n.* opposite, statement with the terms of another interchanged or turned round. [L. *conversus*, turned about]

convert′ *v.t.* apply to another purpose; change, transform; cause to adopt a religion, an opinion. -**con′vert** *n.* converted person. -**convert′ible** *a.* being capable of transformation. -*n.* automobile with a collapsible roof. [L. *converters*, turn about]

con′vex *a.* curved outwards, like any part of the surface of an egg; opposite of concave. -**convex′ity** *n.* [L. *conuexus*]

convey′ *v.t.* carry, transport; impart, communicate; make over, transfer. -**convey′ance** *n.* carriage, vehicle; (law) transfer of property. -**convey′ancer** *n.* one skilled in the legal forms of transferring property. -**convey′ancing** *n.* [OF. *conveier*, fr. L. *via*, way; orig. *escort*]

convict′ *v.t.* prove or declare guilty. -**con′vict** *n.* criminal undergoing penal servitude. **convic′tion** *n.* a convicting, verdict of guilty; a being convinced, firm belief, state of being sure. -**convince′** *v.t.* bring to a belief, satisfy by evidence or argument. [L. *convincere*, fr. *vincere*, vanquish]

convivial *a.* festive, jovial. -**convivial′ity** *n.* [L. *convivium*, feast]

convoke′ *v.t.* call together. -**convocation** *n.* a calling together; assembly, *esp.* of clergy, college graduates, *etc.* [L. *convocare*, call together]

convol′vulus *n.* genus of plants with twining stems; bind-weed. [L. *convoluere*, *conuolut-*, roll together]

convolution *n.* state of being coiled; turn of a coil or spiral. **convolu′ted** *a.* spiral, rolled. [L. *convolvere*]

convoy *v.t.* escort for protection, as ships, war supplies, *etc.* -**con′voy** *n.* party (of ships, troops, *etc.*) conveying or convoyed. [same as *convey*]

convulse′ *v.t.* shake violently; affect with violent involuntary contractions of the musdes. -**convul′sive** *a.* -**convul′sively** *adv.* -**convul′sion** *n.* [L. *convel- lere*, fr. *vellere, vulsum*, pluck]

co′ny, co′ney *n.* rock-badger; rabbit. [OF. *conil, -cuniculus*, rabbit]

coo *n.* cry of doves. -*v.i.* make such cry. [imit.orig.]

cook *n.* one who prepares food for the table. - *v.i.* act as cook; undergo cooking. - *v.t.* prepare (food) for the table, *esp.* by heat; (*sl.*) falsify accounts, *etc.*, cookbooks book of cooking recipes. - **cook′-shop,** eating-house. **cook′ery** *n.* -**cook′er** *n.* cooking-stove. [OE *coc*, fr. L. *coquus*]

cook′ie, cooky *n.* plain bun; one of many kinds of sweet, flat baked cakes, *usu.* hard or semi-hard. [*cook*]

cool *a.* moderately cold; unexcited, calm; lacking friendliness or interest.-*v.t.* and *i.* make or become cool. -*n.* cool time, place, *etc.*-**cool′ness** *n.* -**cool′er** *n.* **coolness.** [OE. *col*]

cool′ie *n.* native laborer in India or China. [prob. *kuli*, name of tribe]

coomb *n.* small wooded ravine. [OE. *cumb*, hollow]

coop *n.* cage or pen for fowls. -*v.t.* shut up in a coop; confine. -**coop′er** *n.* one who makes casks. **coop′erage** *n.* [L. *cupa*, vat, cask]

coop′erate *v.i.* work together. -**co′operation** *n.* working together; production or distribution by cooperators who share the profits. -**co′operative** *a.* -**co′operator** *n.* [fr. L. *co-*, together, and *opus*, work]

co-opt′ *v.t.* bring on (a committee, *etc.*) as a member, colleague, by vote of its existing members. [L. *optare*, choose]

coor′dinate *a.* equal in degree, status, *etc.* -*v.t.* place in the same rank; bring into order as parts of a whole. -*n.* coordinate thing;

any set of numbers defining the location of a point. -**co'ordination** *n.* [L. *ordo, ordin-*, order]

coot *n.* water-fowl with white mark on face. [ME. *cote*]

cop *n.* conical ball of thread or spindle. [OE. *cop, copp*]

cop *v.t.* (*sl.*) catch. -*n.* capture. -**copper, cop** *n.* (sl.) policeman. [orig. unknown]

co'pal *n.* kind of resin used in varnish. [Sp., Mex. *copalli*, resin]

cope *n.* ecclesiastical vestment like a long cloak. -*v.t.* cover the top of a wall. **co'ping** *n.* top course of a wall, usually sloping to throw off rain. [ME. *cape*]

cope *v.i.* contend, deal with. [perh. fr. F. *coupler*, grapple]

co'per *n.* dealer. (chiefly in horse-coper). [Du. *koopen*, buy]

copho'sis *n.* total deafness. [G.]

co'pious *a.* plentiful, full, abundant, -**copiously** *adv.* **co'piousness** *n.* [L. *copia*, plenty]

copp'er *n.* reddish malleable ductile metal; bronze money, bronze coin; large vessel for boiling clothes. -*v.t.* cover with copper. -**copp'er-bott'omed** *a.* reliable, *esp.* financially reliable. (from the former practice of coating the bottoms of ships with copper to prevent the timbers rotting). **copp'erplate** *n.* plate or copper for engraving or etching; print from such plate; copybook writing. -**copp'ersmith** *n.* one who works in copper. [L. *Cyprium aes*, bronze from Cyprus, G. *Kypros*]

copp'eras *n.* sulfate of iron, used in making ink. [F. *couperose*-L. *cupri rosa*, rose of copper]

copper'head *n.* venomous snake of *n.* America. [*See* **copper**]

copp'ice, copse *n.* grove of small trees grown for periodical cutting. [OF. *coper*, cut]

cop'ra *n.* dried coconut kernels. [Malay. *koppara*, coconut]

cop'ula *n.* word acting as a connecting link in a sentence; connection. -**cop'ulate** *v.i.* unite sexually. -**copula' tion** *n.* -**cop'ulative** *a.* [L. *copula bond*, couple, fr. *co-*, together, *apere*, fit]

cop'y *n.* imitation; single specimen of a book; piece of writing for a learner to imitate; matter for printing. -*v.t.* make a copy of, imitate. -**cop'yhold** *n.* form of land-tenure with copy of the manor courtroll as title. **cop'yright** *n.* legal exclusive right to print and publish a book, article, work of art, *etc.* -*a.* protected by copyright *v.t.* protect by copyright. -**cop'yist** *n.* [L. *copia*, abundance]

coquette' *n.* woman who plays with men's affections. -**coquett'ish** *a.* -**coquet'** *v.i.* **co'quetry** *n.* [F.]

coquim'bo (-ki'-) S. American burrowing owl. [fr. *Coquimbo*, Chile]

coqui'to *n.* Chilean palm. [Sp. dim of coco, coconut]

cor'acle *n.* boat or wicker covered with skins. [Welsh *cwrwg*; Gael, *curach*]

cor'al *n.* hard substance made by sea polyps and forming pink or red or white growths, islands, reefs; ornament or toy of coral. -**cor'alline** *a.* [L. *corallum*]

coranglais' *n.* tenor oboe. [F.]

corb'el *n.* stone or timber projection from a wall to support something. [OF. *corbel*, raven]

cord *n.* thin rope or thick string; rib on cloth, ribbed fabric; electrical wire with protective coating; measure of cut wood, usually 128 cub. ft.-*v.t.* fasten or bind with cord. -**cord'age** *n.* **cord'uroy** *n.* ribbed cotton stuff. -*a.* -**cord'uroy road'**, swamp road of transverse logs. [G. *chortle*, gut; *corduroy* is of unknown origin]

cordial *a.* hearty, sincere, warm. -*n.* stimulating medicine or drink cordially *adv.* -**cordial'ity** n. [L. *car, cordis*, heart]

cordille'ra (-rd'-ra) *n.* a system of mountain-chains. [Sp., fr. L. *chorda*, cord]

cord'ite *n.* cord-like smokeless explosive. [fr. *cord*]

cord'on *n.* a chain of troops or police; ornamental cord; fruit-tree grown as a single stem. [F. dim of *corde*, cord]

cord'uroy. *See* **cord.**

core *n.* horny seed-case of apple and other fruits; central or innermost part of anything. [perh. fr. L. *car*, heart]

co-respondent *n.* person proceeded against together with the respondent in a divorce suit. [*respondent*]

cor'gi, cor'gy *n.* Welsh breed of dog. [Welsh, *corr*, dwarf, *ci*, dog]

Corin'thian (-th-) *a.* of Corinth; of the Corinthian order of architecture, ornate Greek. -*n.* native of Corinth; man of fashion. [*Corinth*]

cork *n.* bark of cork-oak; piece of it, *esp.* a round piece used as a stopper. -*v.t.* stop up with a cork; stop up generally. **cork'y** *a.* light, buoyant. -**cork'screw** *n.* tool for pulling out corks. -**cork'age** *n.* charge for opening bottles. [Sp. *alcorque*, cork-shoe, slipper; of Arab. orig.]

corm *n.* bulbous underground stem, as of

crocus. [G. *kormos*, lopped-off tree-trunk]
cor'morant *n.* large and voracious seabird. [F. *cormoran*, sea-crow]
corn *n.* grain, fruit or cereals; a grain; maize. -*v.t.* preserve (meat) with salt. - **corn'ball** *n.* person given to mawkish or unsophisticated behavioral. another word for corny. **corn'crake** *n.* bird, the landrail. -**corn'flower** *n.* blue flower growing in cornfields. -**corn'starch** *n.* maize flour. [OE. *corn*]
corn *n.* horny growth on foot or toe. [OF., fr. L. *cornu*, horn]
corn row *n.* hairstyle of narrow braids plaited in rows close to the scalp. -*v.* to arrange as narrow braids.
corn'ea *n.* horny membrane covering the front of the eye. [for L. *cornea tela*, horny web]
corne'lian *n.* precious stone, a reddish chalcedony. [L. *cornu*, horn]
cor'ner *n.* part of a room where two sides meet; remote or humble place; point where two walls, streets, *etc.* meet; angle, projection; buying up of the whole existing stock of a commodity. -*v.t.* drive into a position of difficulty, or one leaving no escape; establish a monopoly- [L. *cornu*, horn]
corn'et *n.* trumpet with valves; formerly lowest-grade cavalry officer, sub-lieutenant. [L. *cornu*, horn]
corn'ice *n.* projecting source near the top of a wall; ornamental molding at junction of wall and ceiling. [F. *corniche*]
cornucopia *n.* symbol of plenty, a goat's horn overflowing with fruit and flowers. [L. *cornu copice*, horn of plenty]
cor'ny *a.* (*sl.*) out-of-date; stale. [orig. uncertain]
corolla *n.* flower's inner envelope of petals. [L. dim. of *corona*, crown]
corollary *n.* proposition that follows without proof from another proved; natural consequence. [L. *corolla*, a garland]
coro'na *n.* crown, top; top part of a cornice; sun's luminous envelope; moon's halo during a solar eclipse. -**cor'onary** *a.* of a crown; of the crown of the head; as a circle; relating to the arteries which supply blood to the heart. [L. *corona*, crown]
cor'onach *n.* dirge, lament. [Gael. *corranach*]
coronation *n.* ceremony of crowning a sovereign. [OF. *coroner*, crown]
cor'oner *n.* officer who holds inquests on bodies of persons supposed killed by violence, accident, *etc.* -**cor'onership** *n.* [A.F. *corouner*, fr. *coroune*, crown]
coroner *n.* small crown. [OF. *coronete*, dim. of *corone*, crown]
corp'oral *n.* non-commissioned officer below a sergeant. [OF. *corporal*, fr. L. *corpus*, body]
corp'oral *a.* of the body; material, as opposed to spiritual. -**corporal'ity** *n.* [L. *corporalis*, fr. *corpus*, body]
corporation *n.* body of persons legally authorised to act as an individual; authorities of a town or city; (*colloq.*) rotundity of figure. -**cor'porate** *a.* [fr. L. *corporate*, to embody]
corporeal *a.* of the body, material. [fr. L. *corpus*, body]
corps *n.* military force, body of troops. [F. = body; L. *corpus*]
corpse *n.* dead body of human being. [L. *corpus*]
corpulent *a.* bulky of body, fat. - **cor'pulence** *n.* [L. *corpulentus*, fr. *corpus*]
corpuscle (-usl) *n.* minute organism or particle, *esp.* the red and white corpuscles of the blood. [L. *corpusculum*, dim. of *corpus*, body]
corral' *n.* enclosure for cattle. -*v.t.* enclose in a corral. [Sp., fr. *correr* - L. *currere*, run. *See* **kraal**]
correct' *v.t.* set right; rebuke, punish; counteract; neutralize. -*a.* right, exact, accurate, in accordance with facts or a standard. **correct'ly** *adv.* -**correc'tion** *n.* - **correct'ive** *n.* and *a.* -**correct'ness** *n.* [L. *corrigere, correct-*, fr. *regere*, rule]
correlate *v.t.* bring into mutual relation. -*n.* either of two things or words necessarily implying the other. -**correlation** *n.* [*relate*]
correspond' *v.i.* exchange letters; answer or agree with in some respect. - **correspond'ence** *n.* **correspon'dent** *n.* [*respond*]
corr'idor *n.* a passage in a building, railyway-train, *etc.* [It. *corridore*, fr. correre, L. *currere*, run]
cor'rie *n.* semicircular hollow in mountain. [Gael. *coire*, cauldron]
corrigen'dum *n.* thing to he corrected *pl.* -**corrigen'da.** [L.]
corrigible *a.* able to be corrected. [L. *corrigere*, correct]
corroborate *v.t.* confirm, support (a statement, *etc.*). -**corrobora'tion** *n.* - **corrob'orative** *a.* [L. *corroborate*, strengthen]
corrode' *v.t.* eat away, eat into the surface of (by chemical action, disease, *etc.*). -

corro'sive *a.* -**corro'sion** *n.* [L. *rodere, ros*, gnaw]

cor'rugated *a.* wrinkled, bent into ridges. -**corruga'tion** *n.* [L. *corrugatus*, fr. *ruga*, wrinkle]

corrupt' *v.t.* make rotten; pervert, make evil; bribe. - *v.i.* rot. *a.* tainted with vice or sin; influenced by bribery; spoilt by mistakes, altered for the worse (of words, literary passages, etc.) -**corrupt'ly** *adv.* - **corruptible** *a.* -**corruptibil'ity** *n.* - **corrup'tion** *n.* [L. *corrumpere, corrupt, lit.break up]*

cor'sage *n.* bodice of a woman's dress; flowers, *etc.* to wear on it.[OF.]

corsair *n.* pirate; pirate ship. [It. *corsare*, fr. L. *cursus*, raid]

corse *n.* poet, corpse (*q.v.*).

cors'et *n.* stiffened inner bodice; stays. [F., dim of OF. *cars*, body]

cors'let *n.* piece of armor to cover the trunk. [F. *corselet*, double dim. of OF. *cars*, body]

cortège' (-ezh') *n.* funeral procession. [F.]

cor'tex *n.* -(**cor'tices** *pl.*) bark. -**cor'tical** *a.* pertaining to the bark or outer skin. - **cor'ticate, -cor'ticated,** having bark. [L.]

cortisone *n.* synthetic hormone, used *esp.* in treatment of rheumatoid arthritis. [fr. L. *cortex*, covering (of the kidneys)]

corundum *n.* aluminous minerals of great weight and hardness. [Tamil *kurundum*]

coruscate *v.i.* sparkle. -**corusca'tion** *n.* [L. *coruscate*, coruscate]

corvette' *n.* small naval escort ship. fF.]

cor'vine *a.* of, or like, a crow. [L. *corvinus-corvus*, crow]

cory'za *n.* common cold. [G.]

cosh *n.* and *v.t.* (*sl.*) bludgeon. [orig. unknown]

cosine *abbrev.* **cos** (kos) *n.* (*trigonometry*) in a right-angled triangle, the cosine of an acute angle is the ratio of its adjacent side to the hypotenuse. [*co*- for complement, and L. *sinus*, a bay]

cosmetic *n.* a preparation to beautify the skin. [G. *kosmos*, order, adornment]

cos'mic (kos'-) *a.* relating to the universe; of the vastness of the universe. -**cos'mic rays'**, shortest known electromagnetic waves. -**cosmog'ony** *n.* theory of the universe and its creation. -**cosmol'ogy** *n.* the science or the study of the universe. -**cosmolog'ical** *a.* -**cosmol'ogist** *n.* - **cosmog'raphy** *n.* description or mapping of the universe. -**cosmog'rapher** *n.* - **cosmograph'ic** *a.* -**cosmopol'itan** *a.* relating to all parts of the world; having the world as one's country; free from national prejudice. -*n.* cosmopolitan person. - **cosmopol'itanism** *n.* -**cosmop'olite** *n.* - **cos'mos** *n.* universe; ordered system, as opposed to chaos. [G. *kosmos*, order (the name given by Pythagoras to the universe)]

Coss'acks *n. pl.* a people of S.E. Russia, famed for horsemanship. [Turk *quzzaq*, adventurer]

coss'et *v.t.* pamper, pet. [fr. *cosset*, young child, or animal fed by hand]

cost *v.t.* entail the payment, or loss, or sacrifice of; have as price. -*n.* price; expenditure of time, labor, *etc.* -*pl.* expenses of a lawsuit. -**cost'ing** *n.* system of calculating cost of production. -**cost'ly** *a.* of great price or value; involving much expenditure, loss, *etc.* -**cost'liness** *n.* [L. *constare*, fr. *stare*, stand]

cos'tal *a.* of, pert. to ribs. -**cos'tate** *a.* ribbed. [L. *costa*, rib]

cos'tard *n.* large ribbed apple. [perh. fr. L. *costa*, rib]

cos'tive *a.* constipated. [L. *constipatus*]

cost'mary *n.* fragrant garden herb. [G. *kostos*, an aromatic plant, and St. *Mary*]

cos'tume *n.* style of dress; outer clothes; set ofouter clothes for a woman; theatrical clothes. -**costu'mier** *n.* [It.*costume*, custom, fashion]

cot *n.* small house. -**cott'ar** *n.* [OE. *cot*]

cot *n.* swinging bed on board ship; light or folding bed. [Hind. *khat*]

cote *n.* shelter for animals. [OE. *cot*]

co'terie *n.* literary or social, *etc.* circle or clique. [F.]

cotillion (-lyon), **cotillion** *n.* dance. [F. *cotillon*, petticoat]

cotoneas'ter *n.* flowering shrub. [L. *cotonea*, quince]

cott'age *n.* small house. -**cott'ager** *n.* [AF. *cotage*, fr. OE. *cot*]

cott'on *n.* plant; the white downy fibrous covering of its seeds; thread, cloth made of this fibre. -**cott'on-wool** *n.* wadding of raw cotton. [Arab, *qutn*]

cott'on *v.i.* take (to); agree (with). [orig. unknown]

cotyledon *n.* primary leaf of plant embryos; seed-leaf. [G. *kotyledon*, cup-shaped cavity]

couch *v.t.* put into (words); lower (a lance) for action; cause to lie down. -*v.i.* lie down, crouch. -*n.* piece of furniture for reclining on by day, sofa; bed, or what serves for one. [F. *coucher*, OF. *colchier*, fr.

L. *collocare*, place together]

cou'gar *n.* large cat-like American beast of prey; puma. [native name]

cough (kof) *v.i.* expel air from the lungs with sudden effort and noise, often to remove an obstruction. -*n.* act of coughing; ailment or affection of coughing. [imit.origin]

coulée *n.* water-worn gully. [F.]

couloir' (-war) *n.* snow-filled gully. [F.]

coulomb' (-om) *n.* unit of measurement of electric current.[C.A. de *Coulomb*]

coul'ter *n.* blade in front of ploughshare. [OE. *culter*-L. *culter* knife]

council *n.* any deliberative or administrative body; one of its meetings. -**coun'cilor, councillor** *n.* [L. *concilium*, assembly]

coun'sel *n.* deliberation or debate; advice; intentions; barrister or barristers. -*v.t.* advise, recommend. -**coun'selor, counsellor** *n.* [L. *consilium*, plan]

count *v.t.* reckon, calculate, number; include; consider to be. - *v.i.* be reckoned in; depend or rely (on); be of importance. *n.* reckoning; item in a list of charges or indictment; act of counting. -**count'less** *a.* -**count'ing-house** *n.* room or building or actions. [L. *computare*, reckon]

count *n.* European nobleman of rank corresponding to British earl. -**count'ess** *n. fem.* wife or widow of a count or earl. [L. *comes, commit-*, a companion]

countenance *n.* face; its expressions support, patronage. -*v.t.* give support, approval. [L. *continentia*, demeanor]

count'er *n.* table of a bank, shop, *etc.*, on which money is paid, *etc.* ; disk or other object used for counting, *esp.* in card games; token. [F. *comptoir,* fr. L. *computare*, count]

count'er *n.* curved part of the stern of a ship. [orig. uncertain]

count'er *adv.* in the opposite direction; contrary. - *v.t.* oppose, contradict.[*See* **counter-** *prefix*]

count'er *n.* fencing, *etc.*, parry. - *v.t.* and *i.* parry. [for *counter-parry*]

counter- *prefix* used to make compounds with meaning of reversed, opposite, rival, retaliatory. [L. *contra*, against]. -**counteract'** *v.t.* neutralize or hinder. -**counterac'tion** *n.* -**count'er-attack** *v.t.* and *i.* and *n.* attack after an enemy's advance. -**count'er-attraction** *n.* -**counterbal'ance** *n.* weight balancing or neutralizing another. -**count'er-blast** *n.* energetic declaration in answer- -**count'er-claim** *n.* (*esp.* in *law*) claim to off-set an opponent's -**count'er-clock'wise** *adv.* and *a.* -**count'er culture** *n.* alternative culture and lifestyle. -**count'er-irr'itant** *n.* -irritant applied to the skin to relieve internal congestion, *etc.* -**count'er-march** *v.i.* -**count'ermine** *v.i.* -**count'erplot** *n.* -**count'erpoise** *n.* weight *etc.* which balances another, equilibrium. - *v.t.* -**count'er-reforma'tion** *n.* -**count'errevolution** *n.* -**count'er-terr'orism** *n. etc.* etc. **counterfeit (-fet)** *a.* sham, forged false. -*n.* imitation, forgery. -*v.t.* imitate with intent to deceive; forge. -**counterfeiter** *n.* [F. *fait*, made]

count'erfoil *n.* part of a check receipt, *etc.*, kept as a record. [*foil*]

countermand' *v.t.* cancel (an order); revoke. [L. *rnandare*, order]

counterpane *n.* coverlet or quilt for a bed. [earlier *counter-point*, OF. *coutepointe*, Late L. *culcita puncta*, stitched quilt, fr. *pungere*, prick]

counterpart *n.* something so like another as to be mistaken for it; something complementary or correlative of another. [*counter* and *part*]

counterpoint *n.* melody added as accompaniment to another; art of so adding melodies. -**contrapun'tal** *a.* [It.*contrappunto*, accompaniment 'pricked against' notes of melody. *See* **puncture**]

countersign (-sin) *n.* signal or password used in answer to another. - *v.t.* sign a document already signed by another; ratify. [*sign*]

count'ess. *See* **count.**

coun'try *n.* region, district; territory of a nation, land of birth, residence, *etc.*; rural districts as opposed to town; nation. -**coun'tryside** *n.* any rural district or its inhabitants. -**coun'trified** *a.* rural in manner or appearance. [F. *controe*, Late L. *contrata*, (land) spread before one, *contra*]

country music *n.* folk music of S.E. and S.W. United States accompanied by guitar, banjor, or other stringed instruments; based on music of cowboys.

coun'ty *n.* division of a country or state. [F. *comté*, fr. *comte*, count]

coup *n.* successful stroke. [F.]

coupé *n.* closed two-seated car or carriage. [F.]

coup'le *n.* two, a pair; leash for two hounds. -*v.t.* tie (hounds) together; connect, fasten together; associate, connect in the mind. -*v.i.* join, associate. -**coup'ler** *n.* -**coup'ling** *n.* **coup'let** *n.* pair of lines of verse, *esp.* rhyming and of equal length. [F., fr. L. *copula*, bond]

cou'pon *n.* detachable ticket entitling the holder to something, *e.g.*, periodical payment of interest, entrance to a competition, share of rationed goods, *etc.* [F., fr. *couper*, cut]

cou'rage *n.* bravery, boldness. couraégeous (ku-ra'jus) *a.* -**coura'geously** *adv.* [F., fr. L. *cor*, heart]

cou'rier (koo'-) *n.* express messenger; attendant on travelers. [F. *courrier*, fr. L. *currere*, run]

course *n.* movement or run in space or time; direction of movement; successive development, sequence; line of conduct or action; series of lectures, exercises, *etc.*; any of the successive parts of a dinner; continuous line of masonry at a level in a building; match between greyhounds pursuing a hare. - *v.t.* hunt. *v.i.* run swiftly, gallop about -**cours'er** *n.* swift horse. [F. *cours*, fr. L. *currere*, run]

court *n.* space enclosed by buildings, yard; number of houses enclosing a yard opening on to a street; section of a museum, *etc.* ; area marked offer enclosed for playing various games; retinue and establishment of a sovereign; assembly held by a sovereign; body with judicial powers, place where they sit, one of their sittings; attention, homage, flattery. - *v.t.* seek; woo, try to win or attract. **cour'teous** *a.* polite. -**cour'teously** *adv.* -**cour'tesy** *n.* - **cour'tier** *n.* one who frequents a royal court. -**court'ly** *a.* ceremoniously polite; characteristic of a court. -**court'liness** *n.* -**court-mar'tial** *n.* court of naval or military officers for trying naval or military offenses. -**courts'-mar'tial** *pl.* - **court'ship** *n.* wooing. -**court'yard** *n.* space enclosed by buildings. -**courtesan'** (kor ti-zan') *n.* prostitute, *esp.* highly-placed or refined. [L. *cohors, cohort-*; cognate with *hortus*, garden]

court-card *n.* king, queen, or knave at cards. [earlier *coat-card*, fr. the heraldic pictures]

cous'in (kuz'-) *n.* sons or daughter of an uncle or aunt; person related to another by descent from one ancestor through two of his or her children. [Med. L. *cosinus*]

coutit', coutille *n.* strong cotton fabric. [F.]

cove *n.* small inlet of coast, sheltered small bay. [OE. *cofa*, recess]

cove *n.* (*sl.*) fellow, chap. [prob. fr. Se. *cofe*, hawker. cp. *chap*]

cov'en (kuv'-) *n.* muster of witches. [*convention*]

cov'enant (ku-) *n.* contract, mutual agreement; compact.- *v.t.* agree to by a covenant.- *v.i.* enter into a covenant. **cov'enanter, covenanter** *n.* [L. *convenire*, come together]

cov'er (ku-) *v.t.* be over the whole top of, enclose; include; shield; protect, screen; counterbalance. -*n.* lid, wrapper, envelope, binding, screen, anything which covers. -**cov'ert** *a.* secret, veiled. -*n.* thicket, place sheltering game. -**cov'ertly** *adv.* [F. *coucrir*, L. *cooperire*]

cov'erlet (ku-) *n.* top covering of a bed. [AF. *coverlet*, cover bed]

cov'et (ku-) *v.t.* long to possess, *esp.* what belongs to another. -**co'vetous** *a.* - **co'vetousness** *n.* [L. *cupiditare*, desire]

cov'ey (ku-) *n.* brood of partridges or quail, *esp.* flying together. [F. *couvée*, fr. *couver*, brood. -L. *cubare*]

cow *n.* female ox; female of elephant, whale, *etc.* -**cow'bane** *n.* water hemlock. -**cow'boy** *n.* cattleman on a ranch. -**cow'-catcher** *n.* fender on locomotive for clearing line. -**cow-par'sley** *n.* -**cowpar'snip** *n.* -**cow'pox** *n.* disease of cows, the source of vaccine. [OE. *cu*]

cow *v.t.* frighten into submission, overawe. [ON. *kuga*, oppress]

cow'ard *n.* one given to fear, fainthearted. -**cow'ardly** *a.* -**cow'ardice** *n.* [F. *couard*, fr. L. *cauda*, tail]

cow'er *v.i.* crouch, shrinking, in fear or cold. [cp, Ger. *kauern*]

cowl *n.* monk's hooded cloak; its hood; hooded top for chimney; (engine) bonnet. [L. *cucullus*, hood of a cloak]

cow'rie *n.* small shell used as money in parts of Africa and Asia. [Hind.]

cow'stip *n.* yellow-flowered meadow primula. [OE. *cuslyppe*, cow-dung]

cowrie-pine. *See* **kauri.**

cox'comb *n.* one given to showing off. [for *cock's-comb* on a jester's headdress]

cox'swain (kok'sn), **cox** n. steers-man of a boat, *esp.* one in permanent charge of a boat. -**cox** *v.t.* and *i.* act as coxswain. [earlier *cock-swain. See* **cockboat** and **swain**]

coy *a.* shy; slow to respond, *esp.* to lovemaking. -**coy'ly** *adv.* -**coy'ness** *n.* [F. *coi*, fr. L. *quietus*]

coyo'te *n.* N. American prairiewolf. [Mex. *coyote*]

coz'en (ku-) *v.t.* cheat. -**coz'enage** *n.* [fr. It. *cozzonare*, 'to breake horses, to plaie the horse-courses, or knavish knave' (Florio's It. Dictionary, 1598)]

co'zy *a.* warm, comfortable, sheltered. - **co'zily** *adv.* [origin uncertain]

CPU *n.* (*compute.*) portion of computer that performs calculations, controls its operations, and contains primary memory. [*C*entral *P*rocessing *U*nit]

crab *n.* edible crustacean with ten legs, of which the front pair are armed with strong pincers, noted for sidelong and backward walk. - *v.i.* (of aircraft) fly sideways. - **crabb'ed** *a.* perverse; bad-tempered, irritable; of writing, hard to read. [OE. *crabba*; the *a.* fr. the crooked walk of the creature]

crab *v.t.* and *i.* carp at; hinder. [*crab*]

crabapple *n.* wild apple of sour taste. [perh. fr. Gael, *craobh*]

crack *v.t.* break, split partially; break with sharp noise; cause to make a sharp noise, as of whip, rifle, *etc.* - *v.i.* make a sharp noise; split; of the voice, lose clearness when changing from boy's to man's *n.* sharp explosive noise; split, fissure; flaw. -(*sl.*) sharp witty retort, **wisecrack.** -*a.* special, smart, of great reputation for skill or fashion. **-crack'er** *n.* explosive firework; a thin dry cake. **-crac'kle** *n.* sound of repeated small cracks, *e.g.*, of distant rifle-fire, crumpled stiff paper, *etc.* -*v.i.* make this sound. **-crack'ling** *n.* crackle; crisp skin of roast pork. - **crack'nel** *n.* crisp biscuit. [OE. *cracian*; of imit.orig.]

cracker. *See* **crack.**

cra'dle *n.* infant's bed on rockers; *fig.* earliest resting-place or home; supporting framework. - *v.t.* lay in, or hold as in, a cradle; cherish in early stages. [OE. *cradol*]

craft *n.* skill, cunning; manual art; skilled trade; members of a trade. **-crafts'man** *n.* **-crafts'manship** *n.* **-crafty** *a.* cunning. - **craf'tily** *adv.* [OE. *cræft*]

craft *n.* vessel of any kind for carriage by water or air; ship; ships collectively. [fr. small craft for vessels of small craft, power]

crag *n.* steep rugged rock. -**cragg'y** *a.* - **crags'man** *n.* rock-climber. [*Celt.*]

crake *n.* bird of the rail kind, comcrake; crow. - *v.i.* cry like a crow. [imit. orig.]

cram *v.t.* fill quite full; stuff, force; pack tightly; feed to excess; prepare quickly for examination. -*n.* close-packed state; rapid preparation for examination; information so got; (*sl.*) lie. **cramm'er** *n.* [OE. *crammian*, fr. *crimman*, insert]

cramp' *n.* painful muscular contraction; clamp for holding masonry, timber, *etc.*, together. - *v.t.* hem in, keep within too narrow limits. [OF. *crampe*]

cranberry *n.* red berry of a dwarf shrub. [Ger. *kranbeere*, crane berry]

crane *n.* large wading bird with long legs, neck and bill; machine for moving heavy weights. -*v.i.* stretch the neck for better seeing. [OE. *cran*]

cra'nium *n.* skull **-cra'nial** *a.* [Low L. G. *kranion*, skull]

crank *n.* arm at right angles to an axis, for turning a main shaft, changing reciprocal into rotary motion, *etc.* ; fanciful turn of speech; fad; faddist. - *v.t.* and *i.* turn, wind. **-crank'y** *a.* shaky; crotchety. [OE. *crane*]

crank *a.* of a ship, easily capsized; rickety, needing care. [Du. *krengen*, to push over, careen a ship]

crann'y *n.* small opening, chink. - **crann'ied** *a.* [F. *cran*, notch]

crap(s) *n.* gambling game played with two dice. [orig. unknown]

crape *n.* gauzy wrinkled fabric, *usu.* of black silk for mourning. [F. *crépe*, fr. L. *crispa*, curly]

crap'ulence *n.* sickness due to intemperance. [L. *crapula*, intoxication]

crash *n.* violent fall or impact with loud noise; burst of mixed loud sound, *e.g.*, of thunder, breaking crockery; sudden collapse or downfall. -*v.i.* make a crash: fall, come with, strike with, a crash; collapse; of an airplane, come to earth by, or with, an accident. [imit. origin]

crash *n.* coarse linen for towels. [Russ. *krashenina*, colored linen]

cra'sis *n.* contraction of two vowels into one, or into a diphthong. [G. *krasis*, mixture]

crass *a.* grossly stupid; gross. [L. *crassus*, thick, fat]

crate' *n.* open-work case of wooden bars or wicker. [Du. *krat*, basket]

cra'ter *n.* mouth of a volcano; bowshaped cavity, *esp.* one made by the explosion of a large shell, a mine, *etc.* [G. *krater*, mixingbowl]

cravat' *n.* neckcloth; necktie; ascot. [F. *cravate*, Croatian (scarf); fr. the scarf wom by *Croats* in Thirty Years' War]

crave *v.t.* and *i.* have a very strong desire for, long for; ask. **-cra'ving** *n.* [OE. *crafi, an*, demand as a right]

cra'ven *a.* cowardly, abject. -*n.* coward. [OF. *craventer*, overthrow]

craw *n.* bird's first stomach or crop. [ME. *crawe*]

craw'fish, cray'fish *n.* crustacean like a small lobster. [corrupt. of ME. *crevesse*, F. *crevisse*]

crawl *v.i.* move along the ground on the belly or on the hands and knees; move very slowly; move stealthily or abjectly; swim with the crawl-stroke. -*n.* crawling motion; very slow walk; racing stroke at swimming. -**crawl'er** *n.* [ON. *krafla*, claw]

cray'on *n.* stick or pencil of colored chalk; picture made with crayons. [F. *crayon*, pencil, fr. *craie*, chalk]

cra'zy *a.* rickety, failing to pieces; full of cracks; insane, extremely foolish; madly eager (for). -**craze** *v.t.* make crazy. -*n.* general or individual mania. [F. *craser*, break]

creak *n.* harsh grating noise. - *v.i.* make a creak. [imit. orig.]

cream *n.* oily part of milk; best part of anything. - *v.i.* form cream. -*v.t.* take cream from; take the best part from. -**cream'y** *a.* -**cream'ery** *n.* butter and cheese factory; shop for milk and cream. [L. *chrisma*, fr. G. *chrism*, anoint]

crease *n.* line made by folding; wrinkle- *v.t.* and *i.* make, develop, creases. [L. *crista*, ridge]

create' *v.t.* bring into being; give rise to; make. -**crea'tion** *n.* -**creative** *a.* -**crea'tor** *n.* -**crea'ture** *n.* anything created; living being; dependent, tool. [L. *create*]

crèche (kresh, krash) *n.* public nursery for babies and young children. [F.]

cre'dence *n.* belief, credit; side-table for the elements of the Eucharist before consecration. -**creden'tials** *n. pl.* letters of introduction, *esp.* those given to an ambassador. [L. *credere*, believe]

cred'it *n.* belief, trust; good name; influence or honor or power based on the trust ofothers; trust in another's ability to pay; allowing customers to take goods for later payment; money at one's disposal in a bank, *etc.*; side of a book on which such sums are entered, - *v.t.* believe; put on the credit side of an account; attribute, believe that a person has. -**cred'ible** *a.* worthy of belief. -**cred'ibly** *adv.* -**credibil'ity** *n.* -**cred'itable** *a.* bringing honor. -**cred'itably** *adv.* -**cred'itor** *n.* one to whom a debt is due. -**credit'worthy** *a.* (of an individual or business enterprise) adjudged as meriting credit on the basis of such factors as earning power previous record of debt repayment, *etc.* -**cred'ulous** *a.* too ready to believe. -**credu'lity** *n.* [L. *credere*, believe]

cree *v.t.* soften (grain) by boiling, soaking. [F. *crever*, burst]

creed *n.* a system of religious belief; summary of Christian doctrine; system of beliefs, opinions, principles, *etc.* [L. *credo*, I believe]

creek *n.* narrow inlet on the sea-coast. [ON. *kriki*, bend, nook]

creel *n.* basket, *esp.* angler's fishhawker's basket. [origin uncertain. cp. OF. *creil*, hurdle; *crates*, wickerwork]

creep *v.i.* make way along the ground, as a snake; move with stealthy, slow movements; go about abjectly; of skin or flesh, to feel a shrinking, shivering sensation, due to fear or repugnance. **creep'er** *n.* creeping or climbing plant. -**creep'y** *a.* uncanny, unpleasant; causing the flesh to creep. [OE. *creopan*]

cremation *n.* burning as a means of disposing of corpses; this process. -**cremate'** *v.t.* -**crem'atory, cremator'ium** *n.* place for cremation. [L. *cremare*, burn]

crerno'na *n.* superior type of violin. [*Cremona*, Italy]

cren'ellated *a.* indented; embattled. [F. fr. Low L. *crena*, notch]

Cre'ole *n.* native of the West Indies or Sp. America descended from European ancestors; a person descended from French or Spanish ancestors settled in the U.S. Gulf states; languages associated with these cultures. [F. *croole*]

cre'osote *n.* oily antiseptic liquid distilled from coal-tar. -*v.t.* coat or impregnate with creosote. [fr. G. *kreas*, flesh, *sozein*, save, fr. its antiseptic properties]

crèpe (krap) *n.* fabric with a crimped surface; a light, thin pancake. **crèp'erie** *n.* eating establishment that specializes in making pancakes; pancake house. -**crèpe-de-chine'** *n.* fine silk crape. -**crèpe rubb'er** *n.* rough-surfaced rubber for soles of shoes, *etc.* [*See* **crepe**]

crep'itate *v.i.* crackle. -**crep'itant** *a.* -**crepita'tion** *n.* [L. *crepitare*]

crepus'cular *a.* of the twilight. [L. *crepusculum*, twilight]

crescendo (-sh-) *a.*, *adv.* and *n.* increase of loudness. [L. *crescere*, grow]

cres'cent *n.* moon as seen on the first or last quarter; any figure of this shape; row of houses on a curve. -*a.* growing, increasing. [L. *crescere*, grow]

cre'sol *n.* antiseptic product of coal-tar distillation. [*creosote* and *alcohol*]

cress *n.* various plants with eatable pungent leaves. [OE. *cerse*, cresse]

cress'et *n.* fire-basket slung as a beacon. [OF. *craisset*, lantern-*craisse*, grease (contents of the *cresset*)]

crest *n.* comb or tuft on an animal's head; plume or top of a helmet; top of mountain, ridge, wave, *etc.* ; badge above the shield of a coat of arms, also used separately on seals, plate, *etc.* - *v.i.* crown. -*v.t.* reach the top of. -**crest'fallen** *a.* cast down by defeat or failure. [L. *crest*]

cretaceous (-shus) *a.* chalky; (*geol.*) of the upper Mesozoic rocks. [L. *creta*, chalk]

cret'in *n.* deformed idiot. -**cret'inism** *n.* -**cret'inous** *a.* [Swiss *crestin*, Christ ian]

cretonne' *n.* unglazed cotton cloth printed in colors. [*Creton*, France]

crev'ice (-is) *n.* cleft, fissure. -**crevasse'** *n.* deep open chasm in a glacier. [F. *crevasse*]

crew *n.* ship's or boat's company, excluding passengers; gang or set. [earlier *crue*, accrue, reinforcement. [fr. L. *crescere*, grow]

crew neck *n.* rounded, close-fitting neckline on a sweater, shirt, or other top.

crew'el *n.* woolen embroidery yarn. [orig. uncertain]

crib *n.* barred rack for fodder; child's bed *usu.* with high or with barred sides; cards thrown out at cribbage; a plagiarism; a translation. -*v.t.* confine in small space; copy unfairly. -**cribb'age** *n.* card game. [OE. *cribb*, ox-stall]

crick *n.* spasm or cramp, *esp.* in the neck. [orig. uncertain]

crick'et *n.* chirping insect. [F. *criquet*, fr. *criquer*, creak, crackle]

crick'et *n.* open-air game played with bats, ball, and wickets. -**crick'eter** *n.* -**crick'et-match** *n.* [orig. uncertain]

crime *n.* violation of the law (*usu.* of a serious offense): wicked or forbidden act; (military) offence against regulations. -*v.t.* charge (in army) with an offence against the regulations. -**crim'inal** *a.* and *n.* -**crim'inally** *adv.* -**criminal'ity** *n.* -**criminol'ogy** *n.* study of crime and criminals. [L. *crimen*]

crimp *v.t.* pinch with tiny parallel pleats. [Du. *krimpen*]

crimp *n.* agent who procures men for service as sailors or soldiers by decoying or force. -*v.t.* [orig. uncertain]

crim'son (-z-) *a.* of rich deep red. -*n.* the color. -*v.t.* and *i.* turn crimson. [O. Sp. *cremesin*, fr. Arab. *qirmiz*, *kermes*, cochineal insect]

crin'al (kri-) *a.* of or like the hair. -**cri'nate** *a.* -**cri'nose** *a.* [L. *crinis*, hair]

cringe *v.i.* shrink, cower; behave obsequiously. [ME. *crengen*, succumb]

crin'kle *v.t.* wrinkle, make a series of bends, windings or twists in a line or surface. -*v.i.* wrinkle. -*n.* wrinkle, winding. -**crin'kly** *a.* [OE. *crincan*]

crinloid *n.* kind of sea-urchin; sea-lily or feather-star. [G. *krinon*, lily]

crinoline (-len) *n.* hooped petticoat. orig. a stiff fabric of thread and horsehair. [F., fr. *crin*, horsehair, and *lin*, flax]

cripp'le *n.* one not having a normal use of the limbs, a disabled or deformed person. -*v.t.* maim or disable; diminish the resources of. [OE. *crypel*]

cri'sis *n.* turning point or decisive moment, *esp.* in illness; time of acute danger or suspense. [G. *krisis*, decision]

crisp *a.* brittle, but of firm consistence; brisk, decided; clear-cut; crackling; of hair, curly. [L. *crispus*, curled]

cris'tate *a.* crested. [L. *crista*, crest]

criterion (kri-) *n.* -(**crite'ria** *pl*). standard of judgment; standard; rule. [G.]

crit'ic *n.* one who passes judgment; writer expert in judging works of literature, art, *etc.* -**crit'ical** *a.* skilled in, or given to, judging; fault-finding; of great importance, decisive. -**crit'icism** *n.* -**crit'ically** *adv.* -**crit'icize** *v.t.* -**critique'** *n.* critical essay, carefully written criticism. [G. *kritikos*, *krinein*, judge]

croak *v.t.* utter a deep hoarse cry, as a raven, frog; talk dismally. -*n.* such cry. -**croak'er** *n.* [imit. origin]

cro'ceous (-shi-) *a.* saffron colored. [G. *krokos*, saffron]

cro'chet (-she) *n.* kind of knitting done with a hooked needle. -*v.t.* and *i.* do such work. [F. dim. of *croc*, hook]

crocid'olite *n.* fibrous mineral, kind of asbestos. [G. *krokis*, cloth, *lithos*, stone]

crock *n.* earthenware jar or pot; broken piece of earthenware; old broken-down horse. -(*sl.*) broken-down or unfit person. -**crock'ery** *n.* earthenware. [OE. *crocc*, pot]

croc'odile (krok'-) *n.* large amphibious reptile. -**croc'odile-tears**, hypocritical pretense of grief, the crocodile being fabled to shed tears while devouring human victims. [G. *krokodeilos*, lizard]

cro'cus *n.* small bulbous plant with yellow, white or purple flowers. [G. *krokos*]

Croe'sus *n.* very wealthy man. [*Crcesus*, king of Lydia]

croft *n.* small farm; small-holding, *esp.* in Scotland. -**crof'ter** *n.* [OE.]

crom'lech (-lek) *n.* prehistoric structure of a flat stone resting on two upright ones.

[*Welsh*]

crone *n.* withered old woman. [perh. fr. Ir. *crion*, withered]

cro'ny *n.* intimate friend (earlier **chrony**), contemporary. [G. *chronos*, time]

crook *n.* hooked staff, any hook, bend, sharp turn; (*sl.*) cheat; criminal. - *v.t.* bend into a hook or curve. -**crook'ed** *a.* bent, twisted; deformed; dishonest. [ON. *krokr*]

croon *v.t.* sing in an undertone; hum. - **croo'ner** *n.* entertainer who croons sentimental songs. [cp. Du. *kreunen*, groan]

crop *n.* year's produce of cultivation of any plant or plants, in a farm, field, country, *etc.*; harvest, *lit.* or *lig.*; pouch in a birdés gullet; stock of a whip; hunting whip; cutting of the hair short, closely-cut head of hair. - *v.t.* and *i.* poll or clip; bite or eat down; raise produce or occupy land with it. -**crop'eared** *a.* with clipped ears; with hair short to show the ears. -**cropp'er** *n.* fall on the head; heavy fall. [OE. *cropp*, head of herb, ear of corn, *etc.*]

cro'quet *n.* lawn game played with balls, mallets and hoops. [Breton dial. *croquet*, ident. with *crochet* (*q.v.*)]

croquette' *n.* meat or fish ball, cake; rissole. [F.]

cro'sier, cro'zier (-zhyer) *n.* bishop's staff. [for *crosier-staff*, the *crosier* being the bearer of a staff. (OF. *crosse*, crook)]

cross *n.* stake with a transverse bar, used for crucifixion. -**the Cross**, that on which Christ suffered; model or picture of this; symbol of the Christian faith; affliction, misfortune, annoyance; any thing or mark in the shape of a cross; intermixture of breeds, hybrid. -*v.t.* place so as to intersect; make the sign of the cross on or over; pass across, over; meet and pass; mark with lines across, thwart, oppose; modify breed of animals or plants by intermixture. - *v.i.* intersect, pass over. -*a.* transverse; intersecting; contrary; adverse; out of temper. -**cross'ly** *adv.* -**cross'-bill** *n.* bird whose mandibles cross when closed. -**cross'bow** *n.* bow fixed across a wooden shoulder-stock. -**cross'coun'try** *a.* across fields or land. **cross'eyed** *a.* squinting. -**cross-exam'ine** *v.t.* examine a witness already examined by the other side. -**cross'ing** *n.* intersection of roads, rails, *etc.*; part of street kept clean for foot passengers to come. -**cross'ing-sweeper** *n.* person who cleaned a crossing in a street. -**cross'wise** *adv.* -**cross'-word puzzle** *n.* puzzle built up of intersecting words, of which some letters are common to two or more words, the words being indicated by clues. [L. *crux*]

crot'al *n.* lichen used for dyeing. [*Gael.*]

crotch'et *n.* musical note, fad. - **crotch'ety** *a.* bad-tempered. [F. *crochet*, little hook]

cro'ton *n.* tropical plant yielding a pungent oil. -**croton-oil.** [G. *kroton*, tick, from the shape of its seeds]

crouch *v.i.* bend low for hiding, or to spring, or servilely. [orig. uncertain]

croup *n.* throat disease of children. [Sc. orig. *croak*]

croup *n.* hindquarters of a horse. [F. *croupe*]

croupier *n.* raker-in of the money on a gaming-table; vice-chairman of a dinner. [F. orig. one who rode on the *croupe*, behind another]

crow *n.* large black carrion-eating bird. [OE. *crawe*, imit. of *cry*]

crow, crow'bar *n.* iron bar, usually beaked at one end, for levering. [OF. *cros*, pl. of *croc*, crook]

crow *v.i.* utter the cock's cry; utter joyful sounds; exult. -*n.* cry of the cock. [OE. *crawan*]

crowd *v.i.* flock together. -*v.t.* cram, force, thrust, pack; fill with people. - **crowd out,** exclude by excess already in. -*n.* throng, large number, mass. [OE. *crudan*, press, push]

crown *n.* monarch's headdress; wreath for the head; royal power; formerly, British coin of five shillings; various foreign coins; top of the head; summit or topmost part; completion or perfection of anything. -**crown'-jew'els**, jewels of regalia. - *v.t.* put a crown on. [L. *corona*]

CRT *n.* (*compute.*) output device that converts electric signals into visual form by means of a controlled electron beam; computer monitor. [cathode *r*ay *t*ube]

cru'cial *a.* decisive, critical. [fr. L. *crux*, cross, in the sense of fingerpost at cross-roads, decision-point]

cru'cible *n.* melting-pot for ores, metal, *etc.* [Med. L. *crucibuium*]

crucif'erous *a.* (*bot.*) having four petals in the form of a cross. [L. *crux, crucis*, cross, *ferre*, bear]

cru'cify *v.t.* put to death on a cross. - **crucifix'ion** *n.* **cru'cifix** *n.* image of Christ on the cross. [L. *crucifigere* (*p.p. fixus*) fix on a cross]

crude *a.* in the natural or raw state; rough, unfinished, rude. -**crude'ly** *adv.* -**cru'dity** *n.* [L. *crudus*, raw]

cru'el *a.* delight in or callous to others' pain; merciless. **-cru'elty** *n.* **-cruelly** *adv.* [F. *cruel*, L. *crudetis*]

cru'et *n.* small stoppered bottle for vinegar, oil, *etc.* ; stand holding such bottles, mustard-pots, *etc.* [OF. *cruie*, pot, F. *cruche*, jar]

cruise (-ooz) *v.i.* sail about without precise destination. *-n.* cruising voyage. **-cruise control** *n.* device that maintains the speed of a vehicle at a setting chosen by the driver. **-cruis'er** *n.* warship of less displacement and greater speed than a battleship. [Du. *kruisen*, fr. *kruis*, cross]

crumb *n.* small particle, fragment; soft part of bread. *-v.t.* reduce to, or cover with crumbs. **-crum'ble** *v.t.* and *i.* break into small fragments; decay. [OE. *cruma*]

crum'pet *n.* flat soft batter-cake, eaten with much butter. [fr. obs. *crump*, curl up]

crum'ple *v.t.* and *i.* make or become crushed, wrinkled, creased. **crum'pled** *a.* crushed, creased; bent, curled. [fr. obs. *crump*, curl up]

crunch *n.* sound made by chewing crisp food, treading on gravel, hard snow, *etc.* *-v.t.* and *i.* chew, tread, *etc.* with this sound. [earlier *craunch*, perhaps imit.]

crupp'er *n.* strap holding back a saddle by passing round a horse's tail; horse's croup. [F. *croupière*]

crusad'e *n.* medieval Christian war to recover the Holy Land; campaign against evil. - *v.i.* engage in a crusade. **-crusa'der** *n.* [F. *croisade*, and Sp. *cruzada*, marked with a cross]

cruse (-ooz) *n.* small earthen pot. [ON. *krus*, F. *cruche*, jar]

cru'set *n.* goldsmith's crucible. [F. *creuset*]

crush *v.t.* compress so as to break, bruise, crumple; break to small pieces; defeat utterly, overthrown. act of crushing; crowded mass of persons, *etc.* [OF. *cruissir*]

crust *n.* hard outer part of bread; similar hard outer casing on anything. - *v.t.* and *i.* cover with or form a crust. **-crust'y** *a.* having or like a crust, short-tempered. - **crust'ily** *adv.* [L. *crusta*, rind]

crustacean (-shn) *n.* hard-shelled animal, *e.g.*, crab, lobster shrimp. - **crusta'ceous** (-shus) *a.* [L. *crusta*, rind]

crutch *n.* staff with a cross-piece to go under the armpit for the use of cripples; forked support. [OE. *crycc*]

crux (kruks) *n.* the most important point; (*fig.*) a cause of extreme difficulty or perplexity. [L. *crux, crucis*, a cross]

cry *v.i.* utter a call; shout; weep, wail. *-v.t.* utter loudly, proclaim. *-n.* loud utterance; scream, wail, shout; the characteristic call of an animal; watch-word; fit of weeping. [F. *crier*]

cryonics *n.* preservation of a dead body by deep freezing.

crypt *n.* vault, *esp.* under a church. - **cryp'tic** *a.* secret, mysterious. - **cryp'togram** *n.* piece of cipher-writing. [G. *krypte*, vault; *cryptein*, hide]

crys'tal *n.* clear transparent mineral; very clear glass; cut-glass vessels; form assumed by many substances with a defi nite internal structure and external shape of symmetrically arranged plane surfaces. - **crys'tal-set'**, wireless set in which a small crystal rectifies current. **-crystalline** *a.* - **crys'tal** *v.t.* and form into crystals; become definite. **-crystauiza'tion** *n.* (G. *krystallos*, clear ice]

cte'noid (tca'-) *a.* comb-shaped, as the fins of some fishes. [G. *kteis, ktenos*, comb, *eidos*, form]

cub *n.* young of the fox and other animals; junior Boy Scout. - *v.t.* and *i.* bring forth (cubs). [perh. fr. Ir. *cuib*, whelp]

cube *n.* regular solid figure contained by six equal squares; cubemultiplying a number by itself twice. *-v.t.* multiply thus. - **cu'bic** *a.* three-dimensional; of the third power. **-cu'bical** *a.* cube-shaped. **-cu'bism** *n.* style of art in which objects are presented to give the appearance of an assemblage of geometrical shapes. **-cu'bist** *n.* (G. *kybos*, a die]

cu'bicle *n.* small separate sleeping compartment in a dormitory. [L. *cubare*, lie]

cu'bit *n.* an old measure of length, about 18 inches. [L. *cubitus*, forearm, from elbow to finger-tips]

cuck'old *n.* husband of unfaithful wife. [OF. *eucu*, cuckoo)

cu'ckoo *n.* migratory bird named from its call. **-cuck'oo-clock,** clock chiming hours with cuckoo-call. **-cuck'oo-flow'er,** lady's smock. **cuck'oo-pint,** wild arum. **-cuck'oo-spit**, blob of froth on leaves, stems 'nest' of insect larvae. [imit. orig.]

cu'cumber *n.* creeping plant with long fleshy green fruit, usually eaten as salad; the fruit. [L. *eucumis*]

cud *n.* food which a ruminant (*e.g.*, cow) brings back into its mouth to chew. [OE. *cudu*]

cud'dle *v.t.* hug. *-v.i.* lie close and snug, nestle. [orig. uncertain]

cudd'y *n.* cabin of a half-decked boat.

[Du. *kajuit*]

cud'gel *n.* short thick stick. -*v.t.* beat with a cudgel. [OE. *cycgel*]

cue *n.* pigtail; long tapering stick used by a billiard player. -**cue'ist** *n.* [F. *queue*, tail]

cue *n.* last words of an actor's speech as signal to another to act or speak; hint or example for action. [earlier 'q.,' for L. *quando*, when (to come in)]

cuff *n.* ending of a sleeve; wristband. [ME. *cuffe*]

cuff *v.t.* strike with the hand. -*n.* blow with the hand. [F. *coiffer*]

cuirass' (kwi-) *n.* metal or leather armo of breastplate and backplate. -**cuirassier'** *n.* [F. cuir, leather]

cuisine' *n.* cookery; kitchen department. [F.]

cul-de-sac *n.* street closed at one end; blind alley. [F.]

culinary *a.* of, or for, cooking. [L. *culinarius*, fr. *culina*, kitchen]

cull *v.t.* gather, select. [L. *colligere*, collect]

culm *n.* stalk of grains or grasses. -**culmif'erous** *a.* [L. *culmns*, stalk]

culminate *v.i.* reach the highest point; come to a climax. -**culmina'tion** *n.* [L. *culmen*, summit]

culpable *a.* blameworthy. -**culpabil'ity** *n.* -**cul'pably** *adv.* [L. *culpa*, fault]

culprit *n.* offender, one guilty of an offense; (*law*) prisoner about to be tried. [fr. OF. *cul. prest*, contr. of *culpable prest*, ready (to be proved) guilty]

cult *n.* system of religious worship; pursuit of, or devotion to, some object. [L. *cultus*, fr. *colere*, cultivate]

cultivate *v.t.* raise (*crops*) on land; develop, improve, refine; devote attention to, practice, frequent. -**cultiva'tion** *n.* -**cultivator** *n.* [L. *cultura*]

culture *n.* cultivation; state of manners, taste, and intellectual development at a time or place. **cul'tured pearl'**, artificially grown real pearl. -**cul'tured** *a.* refined, showing culture. -**cul'tural** *a.* [Late L. *cultivate*, fr. *colere*, till]

cul'verin *n.* ancient long cannon. [F. *couleuvrine*, fr. *couleuvre*, snake]

culvert *n.* tunneled drain for the passage of water, under a road, *etc.* [orig. unknown]

cum'ber *v.t.* block up, be in the way of, hamper. -**cum'bersome**, -**cumbrous** *a.* [Late L. *combrus*, barrier, heap]

cum'in *n.* eastern plant with seeds like caraway. [Heb. *kammon*]

cummerbund *n.* broad sash worn round waist. [Pers. *kamarband*, loin-band]

cumulative (-iv) *a.* representing the sum of items added by degrees; of shares, entitled to arrears of interest before other shares receive current interest. [L. *cumulus*, heap]

cu'mulus *n.* cloud shaped in rounded white masses. -**cu'muli** *pl.* [L. *cumulus*, heap]

cuneiform *a.* wedge-shaped, *esp.* of ancient Persian and Assyrian writing. [L. *cuneus*, wedge]

cunn'ing *n.* skill, dexterity; selfish cleverness; skill in deceit or evasion; -*a.* having such qualities, crafty, sly. -**cunn'ingly** *adv.* [OE. *cunnan*, know]

cup *n.* small drinking vessel of china or earthenware with a handle at one side; any small drinking vessel; contents of a cup; various cup-shaped formations. cavities, sockets, *etc.*; prize in the shape of a cup of gold or other precious material; portion or lot; iced drink of wine and other ingredients *v.t.* bleed surgically; to form a cup, as with one's hands, *etc.* -**cup'ful** *n.* -**cup'board** *n.* closed cabinet, recess, or case with shelves, *esp.* one for crockery or provisions. [OE. *cuppe*; a cupboard was originally a table or sideboard]

Cu'pid *n.* Roman god of love. [L.]

cupidity *n.* greed of gain. [L. *cupere*, desire]

cu'pola *n.* dome; armored gunturret. [It. fr. L. *cupa*, cask]

cu'preous, cu'pric, cu'prous *a.* of, or containing, -**cu'pro-nick'el**, alloy of copper and nickel-material of British 'silver' coins. [L. *cuprum*, copper]

cur *n.* worthless dog; surly, ill-bred, or cowardly fellow. -**curr'ish** *a.* [earlier *curdog*, prob. fr. ON. *kurra*, grumble]

cu'raçao *n.* liqueur flavored with orange peel. [*Curaqao*, W. Indies]

cura're, cura'ri *n.* arrow poison of S. American Indians. -**cura'rine** *n.* poisonous alkaloid of curare. [native]

cu'rassow *n.* S. American wild turkey. [island of *Curagao*]

cur'ate *n.* clergyman who is a parish priest's appointed assistant. -**cur'acy** *n.* fone with a cure of souls. [fr. L. *cura*, care]

curative *a.* tending to cure disease. [fr. L. *curate*, care]

curator *n.* person in charge of something, *esp.* a museum, library, *etc.* -**cura'torship** *n.* [L. fr. *curare*, care]

curb *n.* chain or strap passing under a horse's lower jaw and giving powerful control with reins; any check or means of restraint; stone edging to a footpath or sidewalk. -*v.t.* apply a curb to (a horse); restrain. -**curb'stone** *n.* [F. *courber*, fr. L. *curvare*, bend]

cur'cuma *n.* kind of plant yielding Turmeric; saffron. [Arab. *kurkum*, saffron]

curd *n.* coagulated milk. -**curd'le** *v.t.* and *i.* turn into curd, coagulate; of blood, to shrink with horror, *etc.* -**curd'y** *a.* (ME. *crudde*, prob. fr. OE. *crudan*, press]

cure *v.t.* heal, restore to health; remedy; preserve (fish, skins, *etc.*). -*n.* remedy; course of medical treatment; successful treatment, restoration to health. cure of souls, care of a parish or congregation. -**cu'rable** *a.* -**curabil'ity** *n.* -**cu'rative** *a.* [L. *curate*, fr. *cura*, care]

curé *n.* French parish priest. [L. *cura*, care, cure (of souls)]

cur'few *n.* ringing of a bell at a fixed evening hour, orig. as a signal to put out fires, now, under martial law, to mark the time for everyone to be indoors. [F. *couvrefew*, cover fire]

cu'rious *a.* eager to know, inquisitive; prying; puzzling, strange, odd; minutely accurate. **cu'riously** *adv.* -**curios'ity** *n.* eagerness to know; inquisitiveness; strange or rare thing. -**cu'rio** *n.* curiosity of the kind sought for collections. [L. *curiosus*, inquisitive caring for, fr. *cura*, care]

cu'rium *n.* radioactive inert gaseous element. [Marie and Pierre *Curie*]

curl *v.t.* bend into spiral or curved shape. - *v.i.* take spiral or curved shape or path. -*n.* spiral lock of hair; spiral or curved state or form or motion. -**cur'ly** *a.* -**curl'ing** *n.* game like bowls played with large rounded stones on ice. [ME. *crul*, curly]

curl'ew *n.* long-billed wading bird. (F. *courlieu*, prob. imit. of cry]

curmudgeon (-jn) *n.* miser or churlish fellow. [orig. unknown]

curr'ant *n.* dried fruit of a Levantine grape; fruit of various plants allied to the gooseberry; plants. [orig. F. *raisins de Coraunte*, Corinth]

curr'ent *a.* in circulation or general use; going on, not yet superseded; fluent, running. -*n.* body of water or air in motion; flow of a river, *etc.*; tendency, drift, transmission of electricity through a conductor. -**curr'ently** *adv.* -**curr'ency** *n.* time during which anything is current; money in use; state of being in use. [L. *currere*, run]

curriculum *n.* (**curricula** *pl.*) course of study at school, college, *etc.* [L., fr. *currere*, run]

curr'y *v.t.* rub down (a horse) with a comb; dress (leather); -**curry favor,** originally to *curry 'favel,'* 'the fawn-colored horse', a type of hypocrisy in an old allegory, hence to try to win favor unworthily, to ingratiate oneself -**curr'ier** *n.* leather dresser. [OF. *correer*, prepare, fr. root of *ready*; for *favel. See* **fallow**]

curr'y *n.* preparation of a mixture of spices; dish flavored with it. -*v.t.* prepare a dish with curry. [Tamil *kari*, relish]

curse *n.* utterance intended to send a person or thing to destruction or punishment; expletive in the form of a curse; affliction, bane, scourge. - *v.t.* and *i.* utter a curse, swear at, afflict. [OE. *curs*]

cur'sitor *n.* clerk of the Court of Chancery. [Med. L.]

curs'ive *a.* written in running script. -**curs'ory** *a.* rapid, hasty, without attention to details. -**curs'orily** *adv.* [L. *cursivus*, fr. *currere*, run]

curs'or *n.* (*compute.*) flashing ponter that can be moved about on the face of the computer screen.

curso'rial *a.* (of birds) adapted for running. [L. *currere, cursum*, run]

curt *a.* short, brief, rudely brief. **curt'ness** *n.* -**curt'ly** *adv.* [L. *curtus*, short]

curtail' *v.t.* cut short, diminish. -**curtail'ment** *n.* [L. *curtus*, short]

cur'tain (-tin) *n.* cloth hung as a screen; screen separating audience and stage in a theater; end to an act or scene. -*v.t.* provide or cover with a curtain. -**curt'ain-fire** *n.* barrage. -**curt'ain raiser** *n.* short play coming before the main one. [Late L. *cortina*]

curt'ilage *n.* area of ground attached to a dwelling-house. [OF. *courtil*, court, enclosure]

curt'sy *n.* woman's bow or respectful gesture made by bending the knees and lowering the body. [var. of *courtesy*]

curve *n.* line of which no part is straight, bent line. -*v.t.* bend into a curve. - *v.i.* have or assume a curved form or direction. -**curv'ature** *n.* a bending; a bent shape. -**curvet'** *n.* horse's trained movement like a short leap over nothing. -*v.i.* to make this movement; frisk. -**curvilin'ear** *a.* of bent lines. [L, *curvus*, bent, *curvare*, bend]

cus'cus *n.* Indian grass. [Pers. *khas khas*]

cush'at *n.* wood-pigeon, ringdove. [orig. uncertain]

cu'shion (koo'shn) *n.* bag filled with soft stuffing or air, to support or ease the body; pad, elastic lining ofthe sides of a billiard table. -*v.t.* provide or protect with a cushion. [F. *coussin*]

cu'shy (koo'-) *a.* (*sl.*) soft, comfortable, pleasant, light and well-paid. [Pers. *khush*, pleasant]

cusp *n.* point; horn of the moon; crown of a tooth; the meeting-point of two intersecting curves; the point of change; small architectural ornament. **-cusp'idate, -cusp'idated** *a.* [L. *cuspis*, point]

cus'pidor *n.* spittoon. [*Port.*]

cuss *v.t.* and *i.* (*sl.*) curse, swear. **-cuss'ed** *a.* **-cuss'edness** *n.* contrariness. [*curse*]

cuss *n.* (*sl.*) fellow; creature. [*customer*]

cus'tard *n.* preparation of eggs and milk, flavored and cooked. [ME. *crustade*, pie with a crust]

cus'tody *n.* safe-keeping, guardianship, imprisonment. **-custo'dian** *n.* keeper, caretaker, curator. [L. *custodial* fr. *custos*, keeper]

cus'tom *n.* fashion, usage, habit; business patronage; *pl.* duties levied on imports. **-cus'tomary** *a.* **-cus'tomarily** *adv.* **-cus'tomer** *n.* one who enters a shop to buy, *esp.* one who deals regularly with it. **-cus'tomize** *v.t.* to build or alter to particular specifications. [OF. *coustume*, fr. L. *consuetudo*]

cut *v.t.* sever or penetrate or wound or divide or separate with pressure of an edge or edged instrument; pare or detach or trim or shape by cutting; divide; intersect; reduce, abridge; ignore (a person); strike (with a whip, *etc.*) -*n.* act of cutting; stroke, blow (of knife, whip, *etc.*); fashion, shape; incision; engraving; piece cut off, division. **-draw cuts,** draw lots. **-cutt'er** *n.* one who or that which cuts; warship's rowing and sailing boat; small slooprigged vessel with straight running bowsprit. **-cutt'ing** *n.* act of cutting or a thing cut off or out; *esp.* excavation (for a road, canal, *etc.*) through high ground; piece cut out from a newspaper, *etc.* - **cutting edge** *n.* lead or forefront of a field; state of the art. [orig. uncertain]

cutaneous *a.* of the skin. **-cu'ticle** *n.* outer skin. [L. *cutis*, skin]

cute *a.* (*sl.*) shrewd; cunning; engaging, attractive. [*acute*]

cut'las, cut'lass *n.* sailor's short, broad sword. [OF. *coutelas*, fr. *coutel*, knife]

cut'ler *n.* one who makes, repairs or deals in knives and cutting implements. - **cut'lery** *n.* knives, scissors, **-cutier's wares.** [OF. *coutelier*, fr. *coutel*, knife]

cut'let *n.* small piece of meat broiled or fried. [F. *cotelette*, double dim. of *cote*, rib, L. *costa*]

cutt'er. *See* **cut.**

cut'tle, cuttlefish *n.* ten-armed sea mollusk which ejects an inky fluid when pursued. [OE. *cudele*]

cyan'ogen *n.* poisonous gas, compound of carbon and nitrogen. **-cy'anide** *n.* compound of cyanogen. **-cyano'sis** *n.* blue jaundice. [G. *kyanos*, dark blue]

cyc'lamen (sik'-) *n.* flowering plant of primrose family. (G. *kyklamis*]

cy'cle (si'-) *n.* recurrent series or period; rotation of events; complete series or period; development following a course of stages; series of poems, *etc.*; **bicycle.** -*v.i.* move in cycles; use a bicycle. **-cy'clic, cy'clical** *a.* **-cy'clist** *n.* bicycle-rider. **cyclom'eter** *n.* instrument for measuring circles or recording distance travelled by a wheel, *esp.* of a bicycle. [G. *kyklos*, circle]

cy'clone *n.* a system of winds moving round a center of low pressure; a circular storm. **-cyclon'ic** *a.* [G. *kyklos*, circle]

cycloped'ia. *See* **encyclopedia.**

cy'clops *n.* mythical race of one-eyed giants. **-cyclope'an** *a.* gigantic. [G.]

cyder. *See* **cider.**

cyg'net (sig'-) *n.* young swan. [dim. of F. *cygn*, swan]

cyl'inder (sil'-) *n.* roller-shaped solid or hollow body, of uniform diameter; piston chamber of an engine. **-cylin'drical** *a.* [G. *kylindein*, roll]

cym'bal (sim'-) *n.* one of a pair of cymbals. -*pl.* musical instrument consisting of two round brass plates struck together to produce a ringing or clashing sound. [G. *kymbalon*]

cyn'ic (sin'-) *n.* one of a sect of Greek philosophers affecting contempt of luxury and bluntness of speech; cynical person. **-cyn'ical** *a.* skeptical of or sneering at goodness; given to showing up human weakness, seeing the more unworthy motive in others; shameless in showing or admitting motives more commonly concealed. **-cyn'icism** *n.* [G. *kynikos*, doglike]

cyn'osure (sin'-o-shor) *n.* center of attraction. [G. *kynosoura*, dog's tail, constellation containing Polar Star]

cy'pher. *See* **cipher.**

cy'press *n.* coniferous tree with very dark foliage; its wood; its foliage as a symbol of mourning. [L. *cupressus*]

cyst (si-) *n.* bladder or sac containing morbid matter. [G. *kystis*, bladder]

cytochem'istry *n.* study of the chemical

composition of cells.

Czar, Tzar, Tsar (zar) *n.* emperor or king *esp.* of Russia 1547-1917, or of Bulgaria in the Middle Ages and after 1908. **-Czari'na, Czarit'sa, Tsari'na, Tzarit'sa** *n. fem.*, the wife of a Russian Czar. [L. *Cæsar*]

Czech' (check) *n.* member, language of western branch of Slavs. [*Polish*]

D

dab *v.t.* strike feebly; apply with momentary pressure, *esp.* anything wet and soft. *-n.* slight blow or tap; smear; small flat roundish mass; small flat fish. [orig. uncertain]

dab *n.* (*sl.*) adept. [orig. uncertain]

dab'ble *v.i* splash about; be a desultory student or amateur (in). **-dab'bler** *n.* [obs. Du. *dabbelen*]

dab'chick *n.* small diving bird, kind of grebe. [earlier also dipchick]

da ca'po (da ka'po) (*mus.*) 'return to the beginning' (of movement, *etc.*). -also written D. C. [It.]

dace *n.* freshwater fish. [ME. *darce*]

dachshund (daks'hoont) *n.* short-legged long-bodied dog. [Ger. = badgerhound]

dacoit' *n.* a Burmese bandit. **-dacoit'y** *n.* brigandage. [Hind. *dakait,* robber belonging to an armed band]

dac'tyl *n.* (*pros.*) foot of three syllables, long-short-short. [L. *dactylus*, finger]

dad, daddy *n.* child's name for father. daddy-long-legs *n.* insect or spider with long, ungainly legs, *esp.* the crane-fly or harvestman. [child's speech]

da'do *n.* lower part of a room wall when lined or painted separately. [It.]

dae'mon *n.* familiar spirit; genius. **-daemon'ic** *a.* supernatural. [L.]

daff'odil *n.* a yellow narcissus. [for earlier *affodil,* F. *aspodéle*]

daft *a.* foolish, crazy; fey; feeble-minded. [OE. *gedoefte,* meek, gentle]

dagg'er *n.* short, edged, stabbing weapon. [Med. L. *daggarius*]

daguerreotype *n.* early photographic process; portrait by it. [*Daguerre,* F. inventor, 1839]

dahl'ia (dal'-) *n.* garden plant with large, handsome flowers. [*Dahl*, Sw. botanist]

dail'y *a.* done, occurring, published, *etc.*, every day. *-adv.* every day, constantly. *n.* daily newspaper. [*day*]

dain'ty *n.* choice morsel, delicacy. *-a.* choice, delicate; pretty and neat; hard to please, fastidious. **-dain'tily** *adv.* **-daintiness** *n.* [OF. *deintie*, fr. L. *dignitas*, worthiness]

dair'y *n.* place for dealing with milk and its products. **-dair'yman** *n.* **-dair'ymaid** *n.* **dair'ying** *n.* [ME. *dey*, a woman, servant]

da'is (da-is) *n.* low platform, usually at one end of a hall. [F. fr. L. *discus*, table]

dais'y (-z-) *n.* small wild flower with yellow center and white petals. [OE. *dæges eage*, day's eye]

dais'ywheel *n.* a component of a computer printer in the shape of a wheel with many spokes that prints characters using a disk with characters around the circumference as the print element. [*daisy* and *wheel*]

Dalai' Lam'a head of Buddhist priesthood of Tibet. [Mongol. *datai*, ocean, *lama*, high-priest]

dale *n.* valley. [OE. *dæl*]

dall'y *v.i.* spend time in idleness or amusement or love-making; loiter. **-dalléiance** *n.* [OF. *dallier,* chaft]

Dalma'tian *n.* large spotted coach dog. [*Dalmatia*]

dam *n.* mother, usually of animals. [var. of *dame*]

dam *n.* barrier to hold back a flow of waters. *-v.t.* supply, or hold with a dam. [Du.]

dam'age *n.* injury, harm *-pl.* sum claimed or adjudged in compensation for harm or injury. *-v.t.* do harm to, injure. [L. *damnum*, hurt, loss]

dam'ask *n.* figured woven material of silk or linen, *esp.* white table linen with design shown up by the light; color of the damask-rose, a velvety red. *a.* made of damask; colored like damask-rose. *-v.t.* weave with figured designs. **-damaskeen', damascene'** *v.t.* decorate (steel, *etc.*) with inlaid gold or silver. [*Damascus*]

dame *n.* noble lady; **womandame' school** *n.* elementary school of the kind formerly kept as private ventures by old women. [F., fr. L. *domina, fem.* of *dominus*, lord]

damn (-in) *v.t.* condemn to hell; be the ruin of, give a hostile reception to. *-v.i.* curse. *-interj.* expression of annoyance, impatience, *etc.* **dam'nable** *a.* deserving damnation, hateful, annoying. **-damna'tion,** *n.* **-dam'natory** *a.* [L. *damnare,* condemn to a penalty]

Dam'ocles (-kles) Sword of, symbol of suspense, imminent danger. [*name*]

dam'osel *See* **damsel.**

damp *a.* moist; slightly moist. *-n.* diffused moisture; in coal-mines, a dangerous gas. *-v.t.* make damp; deaden, discourage. -**damp'er** *n.* anything that discourages or depresses; silencing-pad in a piano; plate in a flue to control draught. -**damp'ing** *n.* in electronics, the introduction of resistance into a resonant circuit with the result that the sharpness of response at the peak of a frequency is reduced; in engineering, any method of dispersing energy in a vibrating system. [Du. *damp*, steam]

dam'sel (-z-) *n.* girl. [Fr. *demoiselle*, dim. of *dame*]

dam'son (-z-) *n.* small dark-purple plum; its color. [fr. *Damascus*]

dance (-a-) *v.i.* move with rhythmic steps, leaps, gestures, *etc.*, usually to music; be in lively movement, bob up and down. *v.t.* perform (a dance); cause to dance. *n.* rhythmical movement; arrangement of such movements; tune for them; dancing party. -**dan'cer** *n.* [F. *danser*]

dandelion *n.* yellow-flowered wild plant. [F. *dent de lion*, lion's tooth, from the edge of the leaf]

dan'dle *v.t.* jog (child) on one's knee. [F. *dandiner*, sway, as a *belle*]

dand'ruff, dand'riff *n.* dead skin in small scales among the hair. [ON, *hrufa*, scab]

dan'dy *n.* a man who pays undue attention to dress; fashion; fop. **dan'dyish** *a.* -**dan'dyism** *n.* [orig. uncertain]

dan'ger (dan'-j-) *n.* liability or exposure to injury or harm; risk, peril; originally meaning, subjection. -**dan'gerous** *a.* -**dan'gerously** *adv.* [F. fr. L. *dominium*, rule]

dan'gle (dang'gl) *v.t.* and i. hang loosely and swaying. [related to *ding*]

dank *a.* oozy, unwholesomely damp. [orig. uncertain]

dap *v.t.* and *i.* drop bait gently into the water. [orig. uncertain]

dapp'er *a.* neat and precise, *esp.* in dress. [Du. *dapper*, brave, sprightly]

dapp'le *v.t.* and *i.* mark with rounded spots. -**dap'ple-gray'** *a.* gray marked with darker spots. [v. fr. *dapple-grey* for apple -grey]

dare *v.t.* venture, have the courage (to); defy. **dar'ing** *a.* bold. *-n.* adventurous courage. **dare'devil** *a.* reckless. *-n.* reckless person. [OE. *dearr*]

dark *a.* having little or no light; gloomy; deep in tint; dim, secret, mysterious, unenlightened; wicked. *-n.* absence of light or color or knowledge. -**dark lan'tern** *n.* lantern whose light can be wholly or partly obscured. -**dark'en** *v.t.* and *i.* **dark'ly** *adv.* -**dark'ness** *n.* -**dark'ling** *a.* and *adv.* in the dark. -**dark'some** *a.* [OE. *deorc*]

dar'ling *n.* one much loved or very lovable. *-v.* beloved or prized. [OE. *deorling*, dim. of *dear*]

darn *v.t.* mend by filling (hole, *etc.*) with interwoven yarn. *-n.* place so mended. -**darn'ing** *n.* [orig. uncertain]

dar'nel *n.* tares; kind of rye-grass. [orig. uncertain]

dart *n.* light javelin or other pointed missile: darting motion. *-pl.* indoor game, throwing darts at target. *v.t.* cast, throw rapidly (a dart, glance, *etc.*). *-v.i.* go rapidly or abruptly, like a missile. [F. *dard*]

Darwin'ian *a.* of, pert. to Darwin and his theory of evolution. [Charles *Darwin*]

dash *v.t.* smash, throw, thrust, send with violence; cast down; tinge, flavor. *-v.i.* move or go with great speed or violence. *n.* rush, onset; vigor; smartness; small quantity, tinge; stroke (-) between words. -**dash'ing** *a.* spirited, showy. -**dash'board** *n.* a mudscreen; instrument board in airplane, automobile, *etc.* [prob. imit. orig.]

dash *interj.* euph. for **damn**.

das'tard *n.* base coward, *esp.* one who commits a brutal act without danger to himself. -**das'tardly** *a.* [*daze*]

data. *See* **datum.**

date *n.* stone-fruit of a date palm. IG. *daktylos*, finger]

date *n.* statement on a document of its time, or time and place of writing, time of an occurrence; period of a work of art, *etc.*; season, time; appointment. *-v.t.* mark with a date; refer to a date; court. *-v.i.* exist (from); betray time or period of origin. -**date'less** *a.* without date; immemorial. -**date'-stamp** *n.* [L. *data.* given]

da'tive (-tiv) *n.* noun-case indicating the indirect object, *etc.* [L. *dativus*]

da'tum *n.* **da'ta** *pl.* thing given, known, or assumed as the basis for a reckoning, reasoning, *etc.* *-n. pl.* collection of information, statistics, *etc.* on a given subject. -**da'ta base** *n.* a systematized collection of data that can be accessed immediately and manipulated by a data-processing system for a specific purpose. **da'ta pro'cessing** *n.* the process of converting information into a form that can be machine-read so that it can be stored, used and updated by a computer. [L.]

datu'ra *n.* genus of plants including the

thorn-apple. -**datu'rine** *n.* poisonous alkaloid derived from it. [Hind. *dhatura*]

daub *v.t.* coat, plaster, paint roughly. *n.* smear; rough picture. -**daub'er** *n.* one who daubs; bad painter. [F. *dauber*, fr. L. *dealbare*, plaster, fr. *albus*, white]

daught'er (dawt'-) *n.* female child, female descendant. -**daught'er-in-law** *n.* wife of a son. -**daught'erly** *a.* [OE. *dohtor*]

daunt *v.t.* frighten, *esp.* into giving up a purpose. -**daunt'less** *a.* not to be daunted. [F. *dompter*, L. *domitare*, tame]

dauphin (daw'-fin) *n.* formerly (1349-1830) eldest son of the King of France. [province of *Dauphiné*]

davenport *n.* small writing-table with drawers. [orig. uncertain]

dav'it *n.* crane, usually one of a pair for lowering ship's boats. [OF. *daviet*]

Da'vy-lamp *n.* miner's safety lamp. [invented (1815) by Sir Humphry *Davy*]

Da'vy Jone''s lock'er *n.* the sea as a grave. [orig. obscure]

daw *n.* bird like a crow. [ME. *dawe*]

daw'dle *v.i.* idle, waste time, loiter. [orig. uncertain]

dawn *v.i.* begin to grow light; to appear, begin. -*n.* first light, daybreak, first gleam or beginning of anything. -**dawn'ing** *n.* [earliest is *dawning*, fr. ON. *daga*, become day]

day *n.* time during which the sun is above the horizon; period of 24 hours; point or unit of time; daylight; time, period. -**dail'y** *a.*, *adv.* and *n.* (see also under **daily**). -**day'book** *n.* book in which the sales, *etc.* of a day are entered for later transfer to ledger. **day'-dream,** *n.* reverie. **day'light** *n.* natural light, dawn; (*fig.*) publicity, enlightenment. -**day'light-sa'ving** *n.* system of regulating the clock to maximize the daylight hours. [OE. *dæg*]

daze *v.t.* stupefy, stun, bewilder. -*n.* stupefied or bewildered state. [ON. *dasa*]

daz'zle *v.t.* blind or confuse or overpower with brightness, light, brilliant display or prospects. -*n.* brightness that dazzles the vision. [*daze*]

DBMS *n.* (*compute.*) computer programs that construct, maintain, manipulate, and provide access to a database [*data*base *m*anagement *s*ystem]

deac'on *n.* one in the lowest degree of holy orders; official of a free church. -**deac'oness** *n. fem.* churchwoman appointed to perform charitable works. [G. *diakonos*, servant]

dead (ded) *a.* no longer alive; benumbed; obsolete; extinguished; lacking luster or movement or vigor; sure, complete. -*n.* dead person or persons (gen. in *pl.*, **the dead**). -**dead'-alive'** *a.* dull. -**dead' beat** *a.* exhausted -*n.* one who consistently fails to pay debts; loafer. -**dead'en** *v.t.* -**dead'-end** *n.* blind alley; cul-de sac. -**dead'eye** *n.* pulley. -**dead'heat** *n.* race in which competitors finish exactly even. -**dead let'ter** n. law no longer observed; letter which the post office cannot deliver -**dead let'ter box or drop** *n.* a place where messages and other material can be left and collected secretly without the sender and the recipient meeting. **dead'-lock** *n.* standstill. -**dead'ly** *a.* fatal; death-like. -**dead of night,** time of greatest sillness and darkness. -**dead'reck'oning** *n.* reckoning of ship's position by log and compass alone. [OE.]

deaf (def) *a.* wholly or partly without hearing; unwilling to hear. **deaf'ness** *n.* -**deaf'en** *v.t.* [OE.]

deal *n.* plank of fir or pine; fir or pine wood. [Du. *deel*]

deal *v.t.* to distribute, give out. -*v.i.* to do business (with, in), deal with, handle, act in regard to. -*n.* a share; distribution; quantity. -**deal'er** *n.* one who deals; a trader. [OE. *n. dæl*]

dean *n.* head of a cathedral chapter; university or college official. **dean'ery** *n.* dean's house or appointment. -**decan'al,** of a dean or deanery. [OF. *deien*, fr. L. *decanus;* orig. chief of ten monks]

dear *a.* beloved; costly, expensive. -*n.* beloved one. *adv.* at a high price. -**dear'ly** *adv.* -**dear'ness** *n.* -dearth (derth) *n.* scarcity. [OE. *deore*]

death (deth) *n.* dying; end of life; end, extinction; annihilation; personified power that annihilates, kills. -**death'less** *a.* immortal or destined to be immortal. -**death'ly** *a.* and *adv.* like death. -**death'mask,** plaster-cast of face after death. -**death'-rate,** annual proportion of deaths to population. **death' tax** *n.* tax payable on the transfer of property after someone's death. -**death'-trap,** unsafe place, vessel, mine *etc.* -**death-warrant,** execution order. **death'watch** *n.* ticking beetle. [OE.]

debacle' (di-bakl') *n.* utter collapse, rout, disaster. [F.]

debar' *v.t.* shut out from, stop. [*bar*]

debark' *v.t.* disembark. -**debarka'tion** *n.* [F. *debarquer*]

debar'rass *v.t.* disembarrass; disencumber. [F. *dobarrasser*]

debate′ *v.t.* discuss, dispute about. -*v.i.* engage in discussion; consider; reason out (with oneself). -*n.* discussion, controversy. **deba′table** *a.* -**deba′ter** *n.* [F. *débattre*]

debauch′ (-tsh) *v.t.* lead away from virtue; spoil, vitiate; seduce. -*n.* bout of sensual indulgence. **debauchee′** (-osh-) *n.* -**debauch′ery** *n.* [F. *dobaucher*]

deben′ture *n.* bond of a company or corporation. [L. debere, owe]

debil′ity *n.* feebleness, *esp.* of health. -**debil′itate** *v.t.* [L. *debilitas*, weakness]

deb′it *n.* entry in an account of a sum owed; side of the book in which such sums are entered. -*v.t.* charge, enter as due. [L. *debere*, owe]

debonair′ *a.* genial, pleasant. [F. *débon naire*. orig. (of hawks) well-bred]

debouch′ *v.i.* move out from a narrow place to a wider one. -**debouch′ment** *n.* [F. *débouclier*, fr. *bouche*, mouth]

dèb′ris *n.* fragments, rubbish. [F. *débris*, fr. *briser*, break]

debt (det) *n.* what is owed; state of owing. -**debt′or** *n.* [L. *debere*, owe]

debug′ *v.t.* (*compute.*) detect, trace, and eliminate mistakes in computer software.

debunk′ *v.t.* (*sl.*) show up, deprive of glamor, humbug. [L. *de*, from, and *bunk*]

debut′ *n.* first appearance in public. **de′butant** *n.* (-ante fem.). [F.]

dec′ade *n.* period often years; set often. [G. *dekas*, group of ten]

dec′adent *a.* declining, failing away. -**dec′adence** (or de-ca′) *n.* [F. *decadent*]

dec′agon *n.* figure of ten angles. -**decag′onal** *a.* -**dec′agram** *n.* ten grams. -**decahedron** *n.* solid of ten faces. -**decahe′dral** *a.* -**dec′aliter** *n.* ten liters. -**dec′alogue** *n.* the ten commandments. **dec′ameter** *n.* ten meters. [G. *deka*, ten]

decal′cify *v.t.* (of teeth, bones) deprive of lime. **decalcifica′tion** *n.* [fr. L. *calx, calcis*, lime]

decamp′ *v.i.* make off, abscond. [F. *décamper*, orig, break up camp]

decant′ *v.t.* pour off (liquid, wine, *etc.*) to leave sediment behind. -**decant′er** *n.* stoppered bottle for wine or spirits. [L. *canthus*, lip of jug]

decap′itate *v.t.* behead. -**decapita′tion** *n.* [L. *caput*, head]

decar′bonize *v.t.* deprive of carbon. -**decarboniza′tion** *n.* [*carbon*]

decasyll′able *n.* word or line of ten syllables. -**decasyllab′ic** *a.* [G. *deka*, ten and syllable]

decay′ *v.t.* and *i.* rot, decompose; fall off, decline. -*n.* rotting; a falling away, break up. [OF. *decair*, fr. *de* and L. *cadere*, fall]

decease′ *n.* death. -*v.i.* die. -**deceased′** *a.* dead. -*n.* person lately dead. [L. *decessus*, departure]

deceive′ *v.t.* mislead, persuade of what is false. **deceiv′er** *n.* **deceit′** *n.* -**deceit′ful** *a.* [F. décevoir]

decelerate *v.t.* and *i.* retard the speed of; slow down. [L. *de*, away from, *celer*, speed]

Decem′ber *n.* twelfth month. [L. *decem* (formerly) = tenth month]

decennial *a.* of a period often years. [L. *decennium*, ten years]

de′cent *a.* seemly, not immodest; respectable; passable. -**de′cency** *n.* -**de′cently** *adv.* [L. *decere*. be fitting]

decen′tralize *v.t.* transfer (government functions *etc.*) from main center to local centers. -**decen′tralized** processing *n.* in computer technology, the use of word processing or data processing units in stand-alone or localized situations. [L. *de*, away from, and center]

decep′tion *n.* deceiving; being deceived; trick. -**decep′tive** *a.* misleading, apt to mislead. [F. *deception*]

dec′ibel *n.* 1/10th of bel; approx. smallest change in sound detectable by human ear. [*bel*]

decide′ *v.t.* settle, determine, bring to resolution; give judgment. -*v.i.* determine, resolve. -**deci′ded** *a.* settled; resolute. -**deci′dedly** *adv.* certainly, undoubtedly. **decis′ion** (-zhn) *n.* -**deci′sive** *a.* -**deci′sively** *adv.* [L. *decidere*]

decid′uous *a.* of leaves, horns, *etc.*, falling periodically; of trees, losing leaves annually. [L. *decidere*, fall down]

dec′imal (des-) *a.* relating to tenths; proceeding by tens. -*n.* decimal fraction. -**dec′imal system**, system of weights and measures in which the value of each denomination is ten times the one below it. -**dec′igram** *n.* tenth of a gram. -**dec′iliter** *n.* tenth of a liter. -**dec′imeter** *n.* tenth of a meter. -**dec′imalize** *v.t.* convert into decimal fractions or system. [L. *decem*, ten]

dec′imate *v.t.* kill a tenth or large proportion of. -**decima′tion** *n.* [L. *decem*, ten]

deci′pher *v.t.* turn from cipher into ordinary writing; make out the meaning of -**deci′pherable** *a.* [*cipher*]

deck *n.* platform covering the whole or part of a ship's hull; pack of cards. -*v.t.* array, decorate. **deck′-chair** *n.* light folding chair of wood and canvas. -**deck′**

house *n.* house or shelter, on deck. -**deck'-quoits** *n.* -**deck'-tenn'is** *n.* [Du. *dek*, roof, covering]

deck'le-edge *n.* rough edge of handmade paper, untrimmed. [Ger.]

declaim' *v.i.* and *t.* speak in oratorical style. -**declama'tion** *n.* **declam'atory** *a.* [L. *declamare*, cry out]

declare' *v.t.* announce formally; state emphatically; show; name (as liable to customs duty). -*v.i.* take sides (for). -**declara'tion** *n.* -**declar'atory** *a.* [L. *declarare*, make clear]

decline' *v.i.* slope or bend or sink downward; decay; refuse; make the caseendings of nouns. -*n.* gradual decay, loss of vigor; wasting disease. -**declen'sion** *n.* a falling off, a declining; group of nouns. -**declinable** *a.* -**declina'tion** *n.* downward slope or angle. [L. *declinare*, bend away]

declivity *n.* downward slope. [L. *declivitas*, fr. *declivus*, downward slope]

decoction *n.* extraction of an essence by boiling down; essence or whatever results from a boiling down. -**decoct'** *v.t.* (L. *decoquere*, boil down]

decode' *v.t.* decipher a code message. [L. *de*, from, and *code*]

décolletté *a.* low-cut (dress); wearing low-cut dress. [F.]

de'colorize *v.t.* to remove color from something. **decolorization** *n.* [*color*]

decommission *v.t.* to dismantle (an industrial plant or a nuclear reactor that is no longer required for use) to an extent such that it can be safely abandoned; to remove (a warship or military aircraft from service.) [*commit*]

decompose' (de-, -oz) *v.t.* separate into elements. -*v.i.* rot. -**decompos'able** *a.* -**decomposi'tion** *n.* [*compose*]

decon'centrate *v.t.* scatter. [*de* and *concentrate*]

decontrol' *v.t.* free from control (of Government restrictions, *etc.*) [*control*]

décor' *n.* scenery on stage. [F.]

dec'orate *v.t.* beautify by additions; invest (with an order, medal, *etc.*). -**decora'tion** *n.* -**dec'orative** *a.* -**dec'orator** *n. esp.* a tradesman who paints and papers houses [L. *decorare*, make fitting]

decor'ticate *v.t.* peel; remove bark from. [L. *decorticare-cortex*, bark]

decor'um *n.* seemly behavior, usage required by decency or good manners. -**deco'rous** *a.* -**deco'rously** *adv.* [L.]

de'couple *v.t.* to separate (joined or coupled subsystems) thereby enabling them to exist and operate separately. [*couple*]

decoy' *n.* bird or person trained or used to entrap others; bait, enticement. -**decoy** (or **coy**) **pond**, pond with appliances for catching ducks. [first in *decay-duck; coy* fr. Du. *kooi*, cage]

decrease' *v.t.* and *i.* diminish, make or grow less. -**de'crease** *n.* a lessening. [L. *decrescere-de*, from, *crescere*, grow]

decree' *n.* authoritative order; edict. *v.t.* order with authority, [L. *decretum*]

decrement *n.* decreasing. [L. *decrementum*]

decrepit *a.* old and feeble. -**decrepitude** *n.* [L. *decrepitus*, fr. *crepare* creak]

decre'tal *a.* of a decree. -*n.* decree, *esp.* papal decree; volume of such. -*pl.* papal decrees as part of the canon law. [L. *decretum*]

decriminalize *v.t.* to remove the legal penalties from (some previously illegal act or practice); make no longer illegal. -**decriminali'zation** *n.* [*crime*]

decry' *v.t.* cry down, disparage. [*cry*]

decumbent *a.* lying flat on ground. -**decum'bance, decumbency** *n.* [L. *de*, down, *cumbere*, lie]

dedicate *v.t.* devote to God's service; set aside entirely for some purpose; inscribe or address (a book, *etc.*) -**dedication** *n.* -**ded'icatory** *a.* **ded'icator** *n.* [L. *dedicare*]

deduce' *v.t.* draw as a conclusion from facts. **deduct'** *v.t.* take away, subtract. -**deduction** *n.* deducting; amount subtracted; deducing; conclusion deduced; inference from general to particular. -**deduc'tive** *a.* -**deduc'tively** *adv.* [L. *deducere*, lead down]

deed *n.* act; action or fact; legal document. [OE. *deed*]

deem *v.t.* judge, consider, hold to be true. [OE. *deman*]

deep *a.* extending far down or in or back; at or of a given depth; far down or back; profound; heartfelt; hard to fathom; cunning; engrossed, immersed; of color, dark and rich; of sound, low and full. -*n.* deep place. -*adv.* far down, *etc.* -**deep'en** *v.t.* -**deep'ly** *adv.* [OE. *deop*]

deer *n.* family of ruminant animals with deciduous horns in the male. -**deerhound** *n.* large rough-coated greyhound; -**deer'stalker** *n.* one who stalks deer; pattern of cloth hat, [OE. *deor*, wild animal]

deface' *v.t.* mar the appearance of; blot out. -**deface'ment** *n.* [*face*]

defalca'tion *n.* misappropriation of funds; the resulting shortage. **de'falcate** *v.i.* **-de'falcator** *n.* [Med. L. *defacare*, lop off]

defame' *v.t.* speak ill of, dishonor by slander or rumor. **-defama'tion** *n.* **defam'atory** *a.* [L. *diffamare*]

default' *n.* failure to act or appear or pay. **-in default of,** in the absence of *v.t.* and *i.* fail to pay. **-default'er** *n. esp.* a soldier punished for failure to comply with regulations. [*fault*]

defeas'ible *a.* able to be annulled. - **defeasibil'ity** *n.* [OF. *desfaire*, undo]

defeat' *n.* overthrow; lost battle or encounter; frustration. *-v.t.* overcome. - **defeat'ism** *n.* conduct tending to bring about acceptance of defeated **-defeat'ist** *n.* [F. *dofait,* undone]

def'ecate *v.t.* clear of impurities. **-defeca-tion** *n.* [L. *defcecare*]

defect' *n.* lack, falling short, blemish, failing. **-defec'tion** *n.* abandonment of a leader or cause. **defect'ive** *a.* incomplete, faulty. *-n.* one mentally or physically lacking. [L. *deficere*, undo]

defend *v.t.* protect, guard, uphold. - **defense'** *n.* **-defend'er** *n.* **-defens'ible** *a.* **-defensibil'ity** *n.* **-defens'ive** *a.* serving for defense. *-n.* position or attitude of defense. [L. *defenders*, ward off]

defer' *v.t.* put off. *-v.i.* procrastinate. **defer'ment** *n.* [L. *differre*, set aside]

defer' *v.i.* submit in opinion or judgment (to another). **-def'erence** *n.* respect for another inclining one to accept his views, *etc.* **-deferen'tial** (-shl) *a.* **-deferen'tially** *adv.* (L. *deferrer*, submit]

deferves'cence *n.* coolness; abatement of fever. [L. *defervescere*, cease boiling]

defi'ance. *See* **defy.**

defi'cient (-ish'nt) *a.* wanting or falling short in something. **-defi'ciency** *n.* **defi'ciency diseas'es,** diseases of malnutrition. **-def'icit** *n.* amount by which a sum of money is too small, excess of liabilities over assets, or expenditure over income. [L. *deficere*, fail]

de'file *n.* narrow pass; march in file. *-v.i.* march in file. [F. *déliler*, march past]

defile' *v.t.* make dirty, pollute. defilement *n.* [OE. *fylan*, foul]

define' *v.t.* mark out, show clearly the form; lay down clearly, fix the bounds or limits of, state contents or meaning of **defi'nable** *a.* **-defini'tion** *n.* **def'inite** (-it) *a.* exact, precise, defined. **def'initely** *adv.* **-defin'itive** *a.* conclusive, to be looked on as final. **-defin'itively** *adv.* [F. *dgfinir*]

deflate' *v.t.* release air from (something inflated); remove excess of paper money in circulation. **-defla'tion** *n.* **-defla'tor** *n.* [coinage fr. *inflate*]

deflect' *v.i.* and *i.* make to turn, or turn, from a straight course. **-deflec'tion** *n.* [L. *deflectere*, bend aside]

deflow'er *v.t.* deprive of flowers, beauty, virginity; ravish. [L. *de*, from, *flos*, flower]

defor'est *v.t.* clear (region) of forest. [*forest*]

deform' *v.t.* spoil the shape of, make ugty. **-deform'ity** *n.* **-deforma'tion** *n.* [L. *deformis*, ill-formed, ugly]

defraud' *v.t.* cheat. [*fraud*]

defray' *v.t.* provide the money for (expenses, *etc.*). [F. *defrayer*]

deft *a.* skillful, neat-handed. **-deft'ly** *adv.* **-deft'ness** *n.* [OE. *gedxfte*, gentler]

defunct' *a.* dead. [L. *defungi*, accomplish, one's duty, finish]

defy' *v.t.* set at naught; challenge to do, *esp.* something beyond expected power; offer insuperable difficulties. **defi'ance** *n.* **-defi'ant** *a.* **-defi'antly** *adv.* [F. *défier* - Low L. *deffidare*, renounce faith]

dégagé (da-ga-zha) *a.* easy, open, unembarrassed. [F. = *disentangled*]

degauss' (-gows') *v.t.* fit (ship) with electrical device to counteract magnetic mines. [*Gauss*, German scientist]

degenerate *v.i.* fall away from the qualities proper to race or kind. *a.* fallen away in quality. *-n.* **-degenerate person.** **-degenera'tion** *n.* **-degen'eracy** *n.* [L. *degenerate*]

degluti'tion *n.* swallowing. [L. *de*, down, *glutire*, swallow]

degrade' *v.t.* reduce to a lower rank; dishonor; debase. **degrada'tion** *n.* - **degra'ded** *a.* [L. *gradus*, degree, step]

degree' *n.* step or stage in a process or scale or series; relative rank, order, condition, manner, way; university rank; unit of measurement of angles or temperature; form in the comparison of *a.* and *adv.* [F. *degré,* fr. L. *de* and *gradus*, step]

dehort' *v.t.* dissuade. **dehorta'tion** *n.* - **dehort'ative,** *a.* **dehort'atory** *a.* [L. *dehortari*]

dehydrate *v.t.* deprive of water; dry by chemical means, as certain food-stuffs. - **dehydra'tion** *n.* [L. *de,* not, G. *hvdor,* water]

de-ice' *v.t.* remove ice (from aircraft *etc.*) **-de'-ic'er** *n.* [*ice*]

de'ify *v.t.* make a god of, treat as a god.

-deifica'tion *n.* [fr. L. *deus*, god, and *facere*, make]
deign *v.i.* condescend, think fit. [F. *daigner*, fr. L. *dignari*, think fit]
deindustrializa'tion *n.* the decline in importance of manufacturing industry in the economy of a nation or area. **-deindustrialize** *v.* [*industry*]
de'ism *n.* belief in a god but not in revelation. **-de'ist** *n.* **-deis'tic** *a.* [L. *deus*, god]
de'ity *n.* divine status or attributes, a god; the Supreme Being. [L. *deus*, god]
deject' *v.t.* dispirit, cast down. **-deject'ed** *a.* **-dejec'tion** *n.* [L. *dejicere*]
delaine' *n.* light wool muslin. [F. = of wool]
delay' *v.t.* postpone, hold back. *-v.i.* be tardy, linger. *-n.* act of delaying; fact of being delayed. [F. *délai*]
de'le *v.t.* direction to printer to delete something written. [L.]
delectable *a.* delightful. **-delecta'tion** *n.* [L. *delectabilis*]
del'egate *v.t.* send as deputy; commit (authority, business, *etc.*) to a deputy. **-delega'tion** *n.* **-del'egate** *n.* **-del'egacy** *n.* [L. *delegate*]
delete' *v.t.* strike out. **-dele'tion** *n.* **-delen'da** *n. pl.* things to be deleted. [L. *delere, deletunt*, destroy]
deleterious *a.* harmful. [G. *deleterios*]
delf, delft*n.* glazed earthenware. [*Delft*, in Holland]
deliberate *v.t.* and *i.* consider, debate. *a.* done on purpose; well-considered: without haste, slow. **delib'erately** *adv.* **-deliberation** *n.* **-delib'erative** *a.* [L. *deliberate*, weigh]
delicate *a.* dainty; tender; fastidious; exquisite; deft; ticklish; sensitive, modest. **-del'icately** *adv.* **-del'icacy** *n.* [L. *delicatus*, fr. *lacere*, entice]
delicatessen *n.* food that is sold ready-prepared, such as cooked meats, salads, *etc.*; the store where such food is sold. **-del'i** *abbrev.* [Ger.]
delicious (-ish'us) *a.* very delightful or pleasing. **-deli'ciously** *adv.* **-deli' ciousness** *n.* [L. *delicix*, delight]
delight' (-lit') *v.t.* please highly. *-v.i.* take great pleasure (in). *-n.* great pleasure. **-delight'ful** *a.* [L. *delectare*]
delimitation *n.* assigning of boundaries. **delim'it** *v.t.* [*limit*]
delineate *v.t.* portray by drawing or description. **-delin'eator** *n.* **-delinea'tion** *n.* [L. *delineate*, fr. *linea*, line]
delinquent *n.* offender. **-delin'quency** *n.* [L. *delinquere*, fr. *linquere*, leave]
deliquesce' (-es') *v.i.* change into liquid form. **deliques'cence** *n.* **-deliques'cent** *a.* [L. *deliquescere*]
delirium *n.* disorder of the mind; raving, as in fever. **-delir'ious** *a.* **-delir'iously** *adv.* with wild excitement. [L.]
deliv'er *v.t.* set free; hand over; launch, send in, deal; give forth; disburden, as a woman at childbirth. **-deliv'ery** *n.* **-deliv'erance** *n.* [fr. L. *liberare*, set free]
dell *n.* wooded hollow. [OE.]
Del'phic *a.* of Delphi (Ancient Greece) or its famous oracle.
delphinium *n.* tall border plant allied to larkspur. [G. *delphinion*, larkspur]
del'ta *n.* tract of alluvial land at the mouth of a river. [fr. its usual shape, the Greek fourth letter, *delta*, Δ]
delude' (-a-) *v.t.* deceive. **-delu'sion** *n.* false belief; hallucination. **-delu'sive** *a.* [L. *deludere*, play false]
del'uge *n.* flood, great flow, rush, downpour. *-v.t.* flood. [F. *deluge*]
delve *v.t.* and *i.* dig. [OE. *delfan*]
demagogue (-og) *n.* mob leader or agitator. **-demagog'ic** (-oj'-) *a.* **-dem'agogy** (-jy) *n.* [G. *dernagogos*, fr. *demos*, people, and *agogos*, leader]
demand' (-a-) *v.t.* ask as by right, ask as giving an order; call for as due or right or necessary*-n.* urgent request, claim, requirement; call for (a commodity). [L. *dem, andare*, entrust)
demarcation *n.* boundary line, its marking out. [Sp. *demarcacin*]
demean' (-men') *v.t.* conduct oneself, behave, show specified bearing. **-demean'or** (-er) *n.* conduct, bearing. [F. *dérnener*, conduct]
demean' *v.t.* lower, degrade (oneself). [mean, in sense of low, base]
dement'ed *a.* mad; beside oneself [L. *dementare*, send out of one's mind]
démen'ti *n.* diplomatic denial, contradiction. [F. *dementir*, give the lie to]
demerit *n.* bad point; undesirable quality. [L. *demeritum*, desert]
demesne' *n.* estate kept in the owner's hands, possession of land with unrestricted rights; sovereign's or state's territory; landed estate. [OF. *demeine*, fr. L. *dominium*, rule]
dem'igod *n.* being half divine, half human. [F. *demi*, half]
dem'ijohn *n.* large wicker-cased bottle. [corrupt. of F. *dome-jeanne*, 'Lady Jane']
dem'irep *n.* woman of doubtful reputa-

tion. [*demi-reputable*]

demise′ (-z) *n.* death; conveyance by will or lease; transfer of sovereignty on death or abdication. *-v.t.* convey to another. [F. *ettre*, put off]

demit′ *v.t./i.* send down; resign, abdicate. **demiss′ion** *n.* [L. *dis-*, apart, *rnittire*, send]

dem′iurge (-uri) *n.* being (other than The Supreme Being) credited with the creation of the world. [G. *demiourgos*]

demo′bilize *v.t.* disband (troops). -**demobiliza′tion** *n.* [*mobilise*]

democ′racy *n.* government by the people; state so governed. -**dem′ocrat** *n.* advocate of democracy. **democrat′ic** *a.* -**democrat′ically** *adv.* -**democ′ratize** *v.t.* -**democratiza′tion** *n.* [G. *demokratia, demos*, the people, *Kratein*, rule]

demog′raphy *n.* study of human population with emphasis on statistical analysis. -**demograph′ics** *n.pl.* data resulting from the science of demography; population statistics. [G. *demos*, people, *graphein*, draw]

demolish *v.t.* knock to pieces, destroy, overthrow. **demoli′tion** *n.* [L. *demoliri*, fr. *moles*, mass, building]

de′mon *n.* devil, evil spirit; person of prenatural cruelty or evil character or energy. -**demo′niac** *n.* one possessed by a demon. -**demoni′acal** *a.* -**demon′ic** *a.* of the nature of a devil, or of genius. **demonol′ogy** *n.* study of demons. -**demonol′atry** *n.* worship of demons. [G. *daimon*]

demonstrate *v.t.* show by reasoning, prove; describe or explain by specimens or experiment. *-v.i.* make exhibition of political sympathy; make a show of armed force. -**demon′strable** *a.* -**demon′strably** *adv.* -**demonstra′tion** *n.* -**dem′onstrator** *n.* -**demon′strative** *a.* conclusive; needing outward expression, unreserved; pointing out. [L. *demonstrate*]

demoralize *v.t.* deprave morally; deprive of courage and discipline, morale. -**demoraliza′tion** *n.* **demoraliz′ing** *a.* [F. *démoratiser*]

De′mos *n.* the people. -**Demot′ic** *a.* popular; of the Ancient Egyptian script of the laity. [G.]

demote′ *v.t.* reduce in rank; grade downwards. -**demo′tion** *n.* [*motion*]

demul′cent *a.* soothing. [*pp.* of L. *demulcere*]

demur′ (-mer) *v.i.* raise objections, make difficulties. *-n.* hesitation, pause. [AF. *demurer*, stay]

demure′ *a.* reserved, quiet, staid; affecting to be grave or decorous. -**demure′ly** *adv.* [AF. *demurer*, stay]

demurrage *n.* undue retention; charge for keeping a ship, truck, *etc.*, beyond the time agreed for unloading. -**demur′rer** *n.* one who demurs; law, an exception taken to an opponent's point. [AF. *demurer*, stay]

den *n.* cave or hole of a wild beast; lurking place; small room. [OE. *denn*]

dena′ture *v.t.* deprive of essential qualities. -**dena′tured al′cohol,** spirit made undrinkable. [*nature*]

dene *n.* dell; small valley. [cp. *den*]

den′dral *a.* of trees. -**den′droid** *a.* tree shaped. -**dendrol′atry** *n.* tree-worship. -**dendrol′ogy** *n.* study of trees. [G. *dendron*, tree]

deng′ue (deng′-gee) *n.* acute tropical fever. [Swahili *dinga*, seizure]

deni′al. *See* **deny.**

denigrate *v.t.* blacken, defame. -**denigra′tion** *n.* [L. *nigrare*, blacken]

denizen *n.* inhabitant. [AF. *deinz*, fr. L. *de intus*, from within]

denominate *v.t.* give a name to -**denomina′tion** *n.* name, *esp.* one applicable to each individual of a class; distinctively named church or sect. -**denomina′tional** *a.* -**denom′inator** *n.* number written below the line in a fraction, the divisor. [L. *denominate*]

denote′ *v.t.* stand for, be the name of, mark, indicate, show. -**denota′tion** *n.* [L. *denotare*]

denouement *n.* unravelling of a dramatic plot; final solution of a mystery. [F.]

denounce′ *v.t.* speak violently against; accuse; give notice to withdraw from (a treaty, *etc.*) **denuncia′tion** *n.* -**denun′ciatory** *a.* [F. *dononcer*]

dense *a.* thick, compact; stupid. -**dense′ly** *adv.* -**dens′ity** *n.* [L. *densus*]

dent *n.* hollow or mark left by a blow or pressure. *-v.t.* make a dent in. [*dint*]

dent′al *a.* of or relating to teeth or dentistry; pronounced by applying the tongue to the teeth. —**dent′ate** *a.* toothed. -**dent′ifrice** (-is) *n.* powder, paste, or wash for cleaning the teeth. -**dent′ist** *n.* doctor who attends to teeth. -**dent′istry** *n.* art of a dentist. -**denti′tion** *n.* teething; arrangement of teeth. -**dent′ure** *n.* set of teeth, *esp.* artificial. [L. *dens*, tooth]

denude′ *v.t.* strip, make bare. -**denuda′tion** *n.* *esp.* removal of forest or surface soil by natural agency; erosion. [L. *denudare*]

denunciation See **denounce.**

deny′ *v.t.* declare untrue or non-existent; contradict, reject; disown; refuse to give; refuse. **deni′al** *n.* **deni′able** *a.* [F. *denier;* L. *denegare*]

deodar′ *n.* Himalayan cedar. [Hind. *deodéar*]

deodorize *v.t.* rid of smell. -**deodoriza′tion** *n.* -**deo′dorizer** *n.* [*odour*]

depart′ *v.i.* go away; start; die; diverge, stray from. **depart′ure** *n.* [F. *dopartir*]

department *n.* division, branch province. -**department′al** *a.* -**department′ally** *adv.* [*depart*]

depend′ *v.i.* rely entirely; live (on); be contingent, await settlement or decision (on); hand down. -**depend′able** *a.* reliable. -**depend′ant** *n.* one for whose maintenance another is responsible. -**depend′ent** *a.* -**depend′ence** *n.* -**depend′ency** *n.* country or province controlled by another. [L. *dependere,* hang from]

depict′ *v.t.* give a picture of. -**depic′tion** *n.* -**depict′or** *n.* [L. *depingere,* depict]

depil′atory *a.* removing hair. -*n.* substance that does this. -**depila′tion** *n.* [L. *depilare,* fr. *pilus,* hair]

deplane′ *v.i.* disembark from aircraft. [*airplane*]

deplete′ *v.t.* empty, exhaust, or nearly. -**deple′tion** *n.* [L. *deplere,* deplete]

deplore′ *v.t.* lament, regret. -**deplor′able** *a.* -**deplor′ably** *adv.* [L. *deplorare*]

deploy′ *v.i.* of troops, ships, *etc.*, to spread out from column into line. -**deploy′ment** *n.* [F. *déployer*]

depo′larize *v.t.* deprive of polarity. [*polarize*]

depo′nent *n.* one who makes a statement on oath, a deposition. [L. *deponere,* put down]

depop′ulate *v.t.* deprive of, reduce, population. -**depopula′tion** *n.* [*populate*]

deport′ *v.t.* remove into exile; transport. -**deporta′tion** *n.* [F. *deporter*]

deport′ment *n.* behavior, hearing. -**deport′** *v. refl.* [OE. *desporter*]

depose′ *v.t.* remove from office, *esp.* of a sovereign. -*v.i.* make a statement on oath, give evidence. -**deposi′tion** *n.* [F. *doposer,* set down]

depos′it (-z-) *v.t.* set down; give into safe keeping, *esp.* in a bank; pledge for the carrying out of a contract. -*n.* act of depositing; thing deposited; pledge; sediment. -**depositor** *n.* -**depos′itory** *n.* place for safe keeping. -**depos′itary** *n.* person with whom a thing is deposited. [L. *depositum,* laid down]

dep′ot *n.* railroad or bus station; storage place for supplies, *esp.* military. [F. *dépôt*]

deprave′ *v.t.* make bad, corrupt, pervert. -**deprav′ity** *n.* wickedness. [L. *pravus,* crooked, wrong]

dep′recate *v.t.* express disapproval of, advise against. -**dep′recatory** *a.* [L. *deprecari,* pray against]

depre′ciate (-shi-) *v.t.* lower the price or value or purchasing power of; belittle. *v.i.* fall in value. -**deprecia′tion** *n.* -**depreciator** *n.* -**depre′ciatory** *a.* [L. *depretiare*]

depreda′tion *n.* plundering, ravage. -**dep′redator** *n.* [L. *prævda,* prey]

depress′ *v.t.* lower, in level or activity; affect with low spirits. -**depres′sion** (-shn) *n.* depressing; hollow; center of low barometric pressure; low spirits; low state of trade. -**depress′ible** *a.* [L. *deprimere, depress-,* press down]

deprive′ *v.t.* strip, dispossess (of). -**depriva′tion** *n.* [L. *privare,* deprive]

depth *n.* deepness; degree of deepness; deep place, abyss; profundity; intensity. **depth′charge** *n.* bomb for dropping on a submerged submarine, exploding at a set depth. [*deep*]

depute′ *v.t.* commit to (a substitute); point as substitute. -**dep′uty** *n.* substitute, delegate. -**deputa′tion** *n.* persons sent to speak for others. -**dep′utize** *v.i.* act for another. [L. *deputare,* choose - *lit.* cut off]

derac′inate *v.t.* uproot. [L. *radix, radicis,* root]

derail′ *v.t.* make (a train) leave the ails. -**derail′ment** *n.* [*rail*]

derange′ *v.t.* throw into confusion or isorder; disturb; disorder the mind at; -**deranged′** *a.* disordered; out of one's mind, insane. -**derange′ment** *n.* [F. *ranger*]

derate′ *v.t.* relive from local rates (whole part). [*rate*]

derby *n.* a man's hat with dome-shaped crown and narrow brim; horse-race, *usu.* restricted to three-year-olds; race or competition in any sport, *usu.* with specific qualifications. [Earl of *Derby*]

der′elict *a.* abandoned, forsaken, *esp.* of ship. -*n.* thing forsaken, *esp.* a ship; son who has become unable to look after himself *usu.* as a result of alcoholism. -**derelic′tion** *n.* neglect (of duty). [L. *derelictus,* forsaken]

deride′ *v.t.* laugh to scorn. -**deris′ion, derisive** *a.* -**deris′ory** *a.* futile. [L. *ridere,* laugh at]

derive′ *v.t.* get from; deduce; show the gin of. *-v.i.* issue (from), be descended from). **-deriva′tion** *n.* **-deriv′ative** *a.* traceable back to something else. *-n.* thing or word derived from another. [L. *care*, lead water]

dermatol′ogy *n.* (*phys.*) science of the kin. **-dermati′tis** *n.* inflammation of the skin. [G. *derma,* skin]

der′ogate *v.i.* detract (from); degenerate. **deroga′tion** *n.* **-derog′atory** *a.* involving discredit, loss of dignity. [L. *dere*, repeal partly]

derr′ick *n.* hoisting-machine. [*Derrick*, hangman at Tyburn, London, c. 1600]

derr′ing-do′ *n.* desperate valor. [In Chaucer, *durring don*, 'daring to do,' mistaken by Spenser for an abstract noun used in present form by him]

derr′inger (-j-) *n.* small pistol. [Henry *Derringer,* gunsmith]

derr′is (powder) *n.* insecticide derived tropical plant. [G. = leather coat]

der′vish *n.* member of Islamic sect noted for the swirling motions of devotional trances. [*turk.*]

des′cant *n.* sung accompaniment to plainsong. **-descant′** *v.i.* talk at large; dwell on *esp.*, with enthusiasm. [OF. *deschant*, Med. L. *diseantus*, part song]

descend′ *v.i.* come or go down; slope down; swoop on or attack; stoop, condescend; spring from (ancestor, *etc.*); pass to an heir, be transmitted-*v.t.* go or come down. **-descend′ant** *n.* one descended from another. **-descent′** *n.* [L. *descendere*, climb down]

describe′ *v.t.* give a detailed account of, trace out (a geometrical figure, *etc.*); pass along (a course, *etc.*). **-descrip′tive** *a.* **-descrip′tion** *n.* detailed account; marking out; kind, sort, species. [L. *describere,* write down]

descry′ *v.t.* make out, catch sight of, *esp.* at a distance. [OF. *descrier*, to shout; orig. on seeing something]

desecrate *v.t.* violate the sanctity of, profane; convert to evil uses. **-desecra′tion** *n.* **-des′ecrator** *n.* [opposite of *consecrate*]

desert′ (-z-) *n.* (*usu. pl.*) conduct or qualities deserving reward or punishment; what is due as reward or punish ment; merit, virtue. [OF.]

desert′ (-z-) *v.t.* abandon, leave. *-v.i.* run away from service, *esp.* of soldiers and sailors. **-deser′tion** *n.* **-desert′er** *n.* [L. *deserere*, abandon]

des′ert (-z-) *n.* uninhabited and barren region. *-a.* barren, uninhabited, desolate. **-desertification** *n.* a process by which fertile land turns into barren land or desert. [L. *deserere, desert-*, abandon]

deserve′ (-z-) *v.t.* show oneself worthy of, have by conduct a claim to. *-v.i.* be worthy (of reward, *etc.*). **-deserv′edly** *adv.* **-deserv′ing** *a.* meritorious. [L. *deservire*, serve well]

déshabille′ (das-a-bel′) *n.* undress, negligé costume. [F.]

desiccate *v.t.* to dry up. **desicca′tion** *n.* [L. *desiccate*, fr. *siccus*, dry]

desid′erate *v.t.* feel as missing. **-desidera′tum** *n.*; **-ata** *pl.* felt want. [L. *desiderare*, long for, desire]

design′ (-zin) *v.t.* plan out; purpose; set apart for a purpose; make working drawings for; sketch. *-n.* project, purpose, mental plan; outline, sketch, working plan; art of making decorative patterns, *etc.* **-design′edly** *adv.* on purpose. **-design′ing** *a.* crafty, scheming. **-design′, designer** *n. esp.* one who draws designs for manufacturers. **-des′ignate** (dez′-ig-) *v.t.* name, pick out, appoint to office. *-a.* appointed but not yet installed in office. **-designa′tion** *n.* name. [L. *designare*, mark out]

desire′ (-z-) *v.t.* wish for, long for; ask for, entreat. *-n.* longing; expressed wish; wish or felt lack; request; thing wished or requested. **-desi′rable** *a.* **-desirabil′ity** *n.* **-desi′rous** *a.* [F. *dosirer*, fr. L. *desider-are*, long for]

desist′ *v.i.* cease, give over. [L. *desistere*, stand back]

desk *n.* sloped board on which a writer rests his paper, a reader his book; table or other piece of furniture designed for the use of a writer or reader. **-desk′-top** *a.* of a size or scale that can fit on the top of a desk. [It. *desco* - L. *discus*, disk, table]

desk′top pub′lishing *n.* (*compute.*) use of computers in the preparation of typeset-quality publications *e.g.*, newsletters, reports, books, magazines, *etc.*

de′skill *v.t.* mechanize or computerize (a job or process) to such an extent that little human skill is required to do it; to cause (skilled persons or a labor force) to work at a job that does not utilize their skills. [*skill*]

des′olate *n.* solitary; neglected, barren, ruinous; dreary, dismal, forlorn. *-v.t.* depopulate, lay waste; overwhelm with grief. **desola′tion** *n.* [L. *desolare*, leave alone, fr. *solus*, alone]

despair *v.i.* lose all hope. -*n.* loss of all hope; something causing this. -**despairing** *a.* [L. *desperare,* give up hope]
despatch'. *See* **dispatch.**
des'perate *a.* leaving no room for hope; hopelessly bad or difficult or dangerous; reckless from despair. -**despera'tion** *n.* -**des'perately** *adv.* -**despera'do** *n.* one ready for any lawless deed. [*despair*]
despise' (-z) *v.t.* look down on. -**des'picable** *a.* base, contemptible, vile. -**des'picably** *adv.* -**despite'** *n.* scorn; ill-will, malice, spite. -*prep.* in spite of. -**despite'ful** *a.* -**despite'fully** *adv.* [L. *despicere,* look down]
despoil' *v.t.* plunder, rib, strip of **despolia'tion** *n.* [L. *despoliare,* spoil]
despond' *v.t.* lose heart or hope. -**despond'ent** *a.* -**despond'ency** *n.* -**despond'ently** *adv.* [L. *despondere* (*animum*) give up (heart)]
des'pot *n.* tyrant, oppressor. -**despot'ic** *a.* -**despot'ically** *adv.* -**des'potism** *n.* tyranny; autocracy. [G. *despotes*]
des'quamate *v.i.* come off in scales. -**desquama'tion** *n.* [L. *squama,* scale]
dessert' (-z-) *n.* fruit, *etc., served after dinner. [F., fr. desseruir,* clear away]
destabilize *v.t.* to undermine or subvert (a government, economy, *etc.*) so as to cause unrest or collapse. -**de'stabilization** *n.* (L. *stabilis,* stable]
des'tine (-tin) *v.t.* predetermine, ordain or fix in advance; set apart, devote. -**des'tiny** *n.* power which foreordains; course of events or person's fate, *etc.,* regarded as fixed by this power. -**destina'tion** *n.* place to which a person or thing is bound; intended end of a journey. [L. *destinare,* make fast.]
des'titute *a.* in absolute want, in great need of food, clothing, *etc.* **destitu'tion** *n.* [L. *destitutus,* abandoned]
destroy' *v.t.* make away with, put an end to, reduce to nothingness or uselessness. -**destruct'ible** *a.* -**destruc'tion** *n.* -**destructive** *a.* -**destructively** *adv.* -**destruc'tor** *n.* that which destroys, *esp.* a furnace for destroying refuse. -**destroyer** *n.* one who destroys; swift war vessel using guns and torpedoes. [L. *destruere,* 'unbuild']
des'uetude (-swi-) *n.* state of disuse. [F. *desuetude,* fr. L. *desuetude,* disuse]
des'ultory *a.* off and on, flitting from one thing to another, unmethodical. [L. *desultor,* circus rider, *lit.* leaper down]
detach' (-tsh) *v.t.* unfasten, disconnect, separate. -**detached'** *a.* standing apart, isolated. -**detach'ment** *n.* a detaching; part of a body of troops separated for a special duty. -**detach'able** *a.* [F. *détacher. See* **attach**]
de'tail *n.* item or particular; treatment of anything item by item; small or unimportant part; party or man told off for a duty in the army *etc.* **detail'** *v.t.* relate with full particulars; appoint for a duty. [F. *detail*]
detain' *v.t.* keep under restraint; keep from going; keep waiting. -**deten'tion** *n.* [L. *detinere,* hold back]
detect' *v.t.* find out or discover the exist ence or presence or nature or identity of. -**detect'or** *n.* device for detecting electrical waves. -**detec'tion** *n.* -**detect'ive** *a.* employed in or apt for detection. -*n.* policeman or other person employed in detecting criminals. [L. *detegere,* detect, uncover]
détente' (da-tongt') *n.* slackening of tension in international crises. [F.]
deter' *v.t.* make to abstain (from); discourage, frighten. -**deterr'ent** *a.* [L. *deterrere,* frighten off]
detergent *a.* cleansing. -*n.* cleansing substance (for wounds, *etc.*); chemical substance which, added to water, removes dirt from fabrics *etc.* [L. *detergere,* wipe off]
dete'riorate *v.i.* and *t.* become or make worse. -**deteriora'tion** *n.* [L. *deteriorate,* make worse]
deter'mine *v.t.* make up one's mind, decide; fix as known; bring to decision; be the deciding factor in; law, end. -*v.i.* come to an end; come to a decision. -**deter'inable** *a.* -**deter'minant** *a.* and *n.* -**deter'minate** *a.* fixed in scope or nature. -**determina'tion** *n.* a detering; resolve; firm or resolute conduct or purpose. -**deter'mined** *a.* resolute. -**deter'minism** *n.* theory that human ction is settled by forces independent of e will. -**deter'minist** *n.* -**deterministic** *a.* [L. *determinate*]
detest' *v.t.* hate, loathe. -**detest'able, detestably** *adv.* -**detesta'tion** *n.* [L. *testari,* execrate]
dethrone' *v.t.* remove from a throne. -**dethrone'ment** *n.* [*throne*]
det'inue *n.* action for recovery of goods. [*detain*]
det'onate *v.i.* and *t.* explode with a loud report; set off an explosive. -**detona'tion** *n.* -**detonator** *n. esp.* a detonating apparatus as the fuse of a bomb, *etc.* [L. *tonare,* thunder down]
de'tour *n.* course which leaves the main route to rejoin it later. [F. *detour,* a turning

aside]

detract′ *v.t.* and *i.* takeaway (apart) from; belittle. -**detrac′tion** *n.* -**detract′or** *n.* [L. *detrahere, detract-*, draw away]

detrain′ *v.i.* and *t.* alight or make alight from a train. (opposite of *entrain*]

det′riment *n.* harm done, loss, damage. -**detriment′al** *a.* **detriment′ally** *adv.* [L. *detrimentum*]

detri′tus *n.* gravel, debris, from wearing exposed surfaces. [L.]

deuce *n.* two at dice, cards, *etc.*; score of all at tennis. in exclamatory phrases, the devil. [F. *deux,* two]

deval′ue, devaluate *v.t.* reduce in value, *esp.* currency. -**devalua′tion** *n.* [*value*]

dev′astate *v.t.* lay waste. -**devasta′tion** *n.* [*devastaire*]

devel′op *v.t.* bring to maturity; bring, bring out; evolve. -*v.i.* grow to a maturer state. -**devel′oper** *n.* *esp.* photographic chemical; muscle exerciser. -**devel′opment** *n.* [F. *dovelopper*]

de′viate *v.i.* leave the way, turn aside, diverge. -**devia′tion** *n.* -**de′viator** *n.* [L. *viare*]

device′ *n.* contrivance, invention; fancy; scheme, plot; heraldic or semblematic or design. [F. *devis*]

dev′il *n.* personified spirit of evil; superhuman evil being, vice; fierceness in fighting; person of great wickedness, cruelty, *etc.*; one who devils for a lawyer or author; dish or devilled food. -*v.t.* do work that passes for the employer's, as for lawyer or author; grill with hot condiments. -**dev′ilish** *a.* -**dev′ilry** *n.* -**dev′ilment** *n.* -**dev′il-may-care** *a.* happy-go-lucky. -**dev′il's ad′vocate** *n.* one appointed to state the disqualifications of a person whom it is proposed to make a saint. [G. *diabolos,* slanderer]

de′vious *a.* roundabout; twisting; erring. (L. *devius,* out of the way]

devise′ (-z-) *v.t.* plan, frame, contrive; plot; leave by will. -**devi′sor** *n.* -**devisee′** *n.* [F. *deviser,* fr. L. *dividire,* divide]

devi′talize *v.t.* deprive of vitality, vigor. [*vital*]

devoid′ *a.* empty of, lacking, free from. [obs. *v. devoid,* empty out; cp. *avoid*]

devolve′ *v.i.* pass or fall (to, upon). -*v.t.* throw (a duty, *etc.*) on to another. -**devolu′tion** *n.* *esp.* modified self-government. [L. *devolvere,* roll down]

devote′ *v.t.* set apart, give up exclusively (to a person, purpose, *etc.*). **devotee′** *n.* one devoted, worshipper. -**devo′ted** *a.* *esp.* very loyal or loving. **devo′tion** *n.* a setting apart, application; dedication; religious earnestness; -*pl,* prayers, religious exercises. -**devo′tional** *a.* [L. *deuovere, devot-,* vow]

devour′ *v.t.* eat up, consume, destroy. -**devour′er** *n.* [L. *devorare,* swallow]

devout′ *a.* earnestly religious; reverent. -**devout′ly** *adv.* [F. *dovot*]

dew *n.* moisture from the air deposited as small drops on cool surfaces between nightfall and morning; any beaded moisture. -*v.t.* wet with, or as with, dew. -**dew′y** *a.* bedewed; fresh. -**dew′iness** *n.* [OE. *deaw*]

de′wan *n.* (India) finance or prime minister of state. [Pers. *diwan*]

dew′claw *n.* partly developed inner toe of some dogs. [*claw*]

dew′lap *n.* fold or loose skin hanging from the neck, *esp.* of cattle. [Lap, *i.e.*, fold, flap]

dexterity *n.* manual skill, neatness, adroitness. **dex′terous** *a.* neat-handed, skillful. -**dex′ter** *a.* on heraldry, on the bearer's righthand of a shield. [L. *dexter,* on the right hand]

dex′trose *n.* grape-sugar also made from starch; glucose. [L. *dexter*]

dey (da) *n.* dairymaid. [ME. *deye*]

dho′bi *n.* Hindu word for a laundryman.

dhow (dow) *n.* native sailing vessel in the East, often a slaver. [Arab.]

diabetes *n.* disease relating to an excess of sugar in the blood caused by the failure of the pancreas to produce insulin; urinary disease. **diabe′tic** *a.* [G. *diabaiein,* pass through]

diab′lerie *n.* magic, sorcery. [F., fr. *diable,* devil]

diabol′ic, diabolical *a.* devilish. -**diabol′ically** *adv.* -**diab′olism** *n.* devil worship. [*See* **devil**]

diac′onal *a.* relating to a deacon. -**diac′onate** *n.* office or rank of deacon; body of deacons. [*See* **deacon**]

di′adem *n.* crown. [G. *diadema,* fillet]

diaer′esis (di-c-r-) *n.* mark placed over a vowel to show that it is sounded separately from a preceding one (*e.g.*, in *aërate*). [G.]

diagnosis *n.* art or act of deciding from symptoms the nature of a disease; guess at the cause of anything. -**diagnose′** *v.t.* -**diagnos′tic** *a.* -**diagnosti′cian** *n.* [G.]

diag′onal *a.* from corner to corner; oblique. -*n.* line from corner to corner. -**diag′onally** *adv.* [G. *diagonios*]

di′agram *n.* drawing, figure in lines, to

illustrate something being expounded, as in a geometrical figure, weatherchart, *etc.* **-diagrammat'ic** *a.* **-diagrammat'ically** *adv.* [G. *diagramma*]

di'al *n.* plate marked with graduations on a circle or arc on which something may be recorded (*e.g.*, time on a sundial, dial of a clock, *etc.*); (*sl.*) face. -*v.t.* indicate on a dial; select a number on a telephone. [L. *dies*, day]

di'alect *n.* characteristic speech of a district; a local variety of a language. -**dialect'al** *a.* [G. *dialektos*, speech]

dialect'ic(s) *n.* art of arguing. **-dialect'ic** *a.* **-dialect'ically** *adv.* **-dia-lecti'cian** *n.* [G. *dialektikos*]

di'alogue, dialog *n.* conversation between two or more; literary work representing this; the conversational part of a novel, play, movie, *etc.* [G. *dialogos*, conversation]

dial'ysis *n.* (**dial'yses** *pl.*) (*chem.*) separation of substances by filtration. **-di'alyze** *v.t.* **-dialyt'ic** *a.* [G.]

diamanté' *n.* fabric covered with sparkling particles; imitation diamond jewelry. [F. *diamant*, diamond]

diam'eter *n.* straight line passing from side to side of a figure or body through its center; thickness; unit of magnifying power. **-diamet'rical** *a.* exact opposite. -**diamet'rically** *adv.* [G. *diametros*, measuring through]

di'amond *n.* very hard and brilliant precious stone; lozenge-shaped figure; card of the suit marked by (red) lozenges or diamonds. [F. *diamant*]

Dian'a (di-) *n.* Roman moon-goddess, huntress. [L.]

diapa'son (-zn) *n.* one of certain organ stops; compass of a voice or instrument; swelling chorus, burst of harmonious sounds. [G. *dia pasén*, through all]

di'aper *n.* fabric with a small woven pattern; pattern of that kind; towel, *etc.*, of the fabric; a baby's garment, made of cloth or another absorbent material, fitting between its legs and around its waist. -**di'apered** *a.* [OF. *diaspre*]

diaphanous *a.* transparent; showing through (a mist, *etc.*) [G. *diaphanes*]

diaphoret'ic *a.* causing perspiration; sudorific. -*n.* sudorific drug. [G. *diaphorein*, carry off]

diaphragm (-am) *n.* partition dividing the two cavities of the body, midriff, plate or disk wholly or partly closing an opening. [G. *diaphragms*]

di'archy *n.* government by two persons or bodies. [G. *di*, twice, *archein*, rule]

diarrhea *n.* excessive looseness of the bowels. [G. *diarrhoia*]

di'ary *n.* daily record of events or thoughts; book for such record. **di'arist** *n.* [L. *diarium*, daily allowance]

dias'pora *n.* dispersion of Jews from Palestine after Babylonian captivity; Jewish communities that arose after this; dispersion, as of people orig. of one nation. [G. *diaspeirein*, scatter]

di'astase *n.* organic ferment turning starch into sugar. [G. *diastases*, division]

dias'tole *n.* heart's dilating movement, opp. of systole, the contracting movement. [G.]

di'athermy *n.* curative treatment by heating parts of body by electric currents. [G. *dia*, through, *therme*, heat]

diaton'ic *a.* (*mus.*) of the natural major or minor scale. [G. *diatonikos*]

diatribe *n.* bitter speech of criticism, invective. [G. = a wearing away (of time)]

dibble *n.* implement for making holes in the ground for seeds or plants. -*v.t.* prepare (ground) or sow or plant with such implement. [*dab*]

dice. *See* **die.**

dichotomy *n.* division into two. -**dichot'omize,** *v.t.* and *i.* **-dichot'omous** *a.* [G. *dicha*, in two, *temnein*, cut]

dick'y *n.* detachable false shirt-front; seat for servants at the back of a carriage, *etc.* [prob. name *Dick*]

dicotyledon *n.* plant with two seed leaves or cotyledon. **dicotyle'donous** *a.* [G. *di-*, twice, *coty*, led on]

Dic'taphone *n.* machine which records human voice, used *esp.* to record letters for subsequent transcription by a typist. [Trademark]

dictate' *v.t.* and *i.* say or read for exact reproduction by another on paper; prescribe, lay down. **-dic'tate** *n.* bidding. **-dicta'tion** *n.* **dicta'tor** *n.* one with absolute authority, supreme ruler. -**dictator'ial** *a.* despotic; overbearing. -**dictator'ially** *adv.* **-dicta'torship** *n.* [L. *dictare*, say often]

dic'tion *n.* choice and use of words. -**dic'tum** *n.* (dic'ta) *a.* pronouncement, saying. [L. *dictio*, a speaking]

dic'tionary *n.* book setting forth, usually in alphabetical order, the words of a language with meanings, derivations, foreign equivalents, *etc.*; book of reference with items in alphabetical order. [Med. L. *dictionarium*, collection of sayings]

didac'tic *a.* instructive; meant, or meaning, to teach. **-didac'ticism** *n.* [G. *dieaktikos*]

die (di) *v.i.* cease to live; come to an end. **die'hard** *n.* one who resists (reform, *etc.*) to the end. [ON. *deyja*]

die (di) *n.* cube with sides marked one to six for games of chance; small cube of bread, *etc.*; (*pl.* **dice**); stamp for embossing, *etc.* (*pl.* **dies**). **-dice** *v.i.* to gamble with dice. **-di'cer** *n.* [F. *de*]

dielectric *a.* non-conducting. *-n.* substance transmitting electric force. [G. *dia*, through, and *electric*]

dies'el engine (dee-sl) *n.* oil-fueled internal combustion engine. [R. *Diesel*]

di'et *n.* kind of food lived on; regulated course of feeding, restricted choice of foods; food. *-v.i.* follow a prescribed diet. **-di'etary** *n.* allowance or character of food, *esp.* in an institution, *etc. -a.* relating to diet. **-diatet'ic** *a. -n. pl.* science of diet. [G. *diaita*, system of life]

di'et *n.* parliamentary assembly in certain European countries. [Med. L. diets]

diff'er *v.i.* be unlike; disagree. **-diff'erence** *n.* unlikeness; degree or point of unlikeness; disagreement; remainder left after subtraction. **-different** *a.* unlike. **-diff'erently** *adv.* **-differen'tial** *a.* varying with circumstances. differential gear *-n.* mechanism in an automobile which allows the back wheels to revolve at different speeds when rounding a corner. **differen'tially** *adv.* **-differen'tiate** *v.t.* make different; develop into unlikeness. *-v.i.* discriminate. **differentia'tion** *n.* [L. *differre*, carry apart]

difficulty *n.* hardness to be done or understood; hindrance, obstacle; an obscurity; embarrassment. difficult *a.* not easy, hard, obscure; captious, hard to please. [L. *difficultas*]

diff'ident *a.* timid, shy. **-diff'idently** *adv.* **-diff'idence** *n.* [L. *diffidere*, distrust]

diffract' *v.t.* break up, as ray of light. **diffirac'tion** *n.* **diffrac'tive** *a.* **-diffran'gible** *a.* [L. *diffringere, diffract*, break asunder]

diffuse' (-z) *v.t.* spread abroad. *-a.* (-s) loose, verbose. **-diffu'sion** *n.* **-diffu'sive** *a.* **-diffuse'ly** *adv.* **-diffu'sively** *adv.* [L. *diffundere, diffus-*, pour apart]

dig *v.i.* work with a spade. *-v.t.* turn up with a spade; hollow out, make a hole in; get by digging; thrust into; delve. **-digg'er** *n.* one who digs; gold-miner; Australian. [OF. *diguer*]

digest' *v.t.* prepare (*food*) in the stomach, *etc.*, for assimilation; bring into handy form by sorting, tabulating, summarizing; reflect on; absorb; endure. *-v.i.* of food, to undergo digestion. **di'gest** *n.* methodical summary, *esp.* of laws. **-digest'ible** *a.* **-digest'ive** *a.* **-diges'tion** *n.* [L. *digerere, digest-*]

dig'it (-j-) *n.* any of the numbers 0 to 9; finger or toe. **dig'ital** *a.* using digits, *esp.* in a display. **-dig'ital recording** *n.* a sound recording process that converts audio signals into a series of pulses that correspond to the voltage level, which then can be stored on tape or on any other memory system. **-digita'lis** *n.* drug made from foxglove. [L. *digitus*, finger]

dig'nity *n.* worthiness, excellence, claim to respect; honorable office or title; stateliness, gravity. **-dig'nify** *v.t.* give dignity to. **-dig'nified** *a.* stately, majestic. **-dig'nitary** *n.* holder of high office. [L. *dignitas -dignus*, worthy]

digress' *v.t.* go aside from the main course, *esp.* deviate from the subject. **-digres'sion** *n.* **digress'ive** *a.* [L. *digredi*, digress-step aside]

dik-dik *n.* small E. African antelope. [orig. uncertain]

dike, dyke *n.* ditch; low wall; embankment. *-v.t.* wall or ditch. [OE. *dic*]

dilapidated *a.* ruinous, falling into decay. **-dilapida'tion** *n.* [L. *dilapidarei*, scatter stones apart]

dilate' (di-) *v.t.* widen, expand. *-v.i.* expand; talk or write at large (on). **-dilatation, dila'tion** *n.* [L. *dilatare*]

dilatory *a.* delaying, slow. **-dil'atorily** *adv.* **-dil'atoriness** *n.* [Late L. *dilatorious*, putting off (time)]

dilem'ma *n.* position in fact or argument offering choice only between two or more unwelcome courses. [G.]

dilettante *n.* person with taste and knowledge of the fine arts as a pasttime; amateur, dabbler. *-a.* amateur, desultory. **-dilettantism** *n.* [It. *dilettare*, delight]

dil'igent *a.* unremitting in effort, industrious. **dil'igence** *n.* industry; French stage-coach. [L. *diligere*, delight in]

dill *n.* medicinal herb. [OE. *dile*]

dillydally *v.i.* (*colloq.*) loiter; vacillate. [*dally*]

dilute' *a.* reduce (a liquid) in strength by adding water or other matter. *-a.* weakened thus. **-dilu'tion** *n.* [L. *diluere, dilut-*, wash away]

dilu'vium *n.* flood; (*geol.*) flood-deposit of sand, gravel *etc.* **-dilu'vial, dilu'vian,** *a.* of a flood, *esp.* of the Great Deluge of

Noah's time. [L.]

dim *a.* indistinct, faint, not bright. *-v.t.* and *i.* make or grow dim. -**dim'ly** *adv.* -**dim'ness** *n.* [OE. *dimm,* dark]

dime *n.* U. S. 10 cent piece. [F. *disme*]

dimension *n.* measurement, size. -**dimen'sional** *a.* [L. *dimensio*]

dimin'ish *v.t.* and *i.* lessen. **diminution** *n.* **dimin'utive** *a.* very small. *-n.* derivative word implying smallness. [L. *diminuere,* make less]

diminuendo *a. -adv.* (*music*) of sound, dying away. [L. *diminuere,* lessen]

dim'ity *n.* cotton fabric with woven pattern. [G. *dimitos,* of double thread]

dim'ple *n.* small hollow in the surface of the skin, *esp.* of the cheek; any small hollow. *-v.t.* and *i.* mark with or break into dimples. [orig. uncertain]

din *n.* continuous roar of confused noises. *-v.t.* repeat to weariness, ram (opinion, *etc.*) into. [OE, *dyne*]

dine *v.i.* take dinner. *-v.t.* give dinner to. -**di'ning-room** *n.* room used for meals. -**di'ner** *n.* one who dines; railroad restaurant-car; inexpensive restaurant. [F. *diner*]

ding *v.t./i.* ring, resound, beat, knock; (Scot.) defeat; surpass. [ME. *dingen*]

dinghy (ding'gi) *n.* small boat; ship's tender. [Hind. *dingi*]

ding'le (ding'-gl) *n.* small wooded valley, dell. [orig. uncertain]

ding'o *n.* Australian wild dog [fr. native name]

din'gy (-j-) *a.* dirty-looking, dull. -**din'giness** *n.* [orig. uncertain]

din'ic *a.* of dizziness. *-n.* remedy for this. [G. *dinoz,* whirling]

dink'y *a.* (*colloq.*) trim, dainty. [orig. unknown]

dinn'er *n.* chief meal of the day. [F. *diner*]

dinor'nis *n.* extinct giant bird. [G. *deinos,* terrible, *ornis,* bird]

di'nosaur *n.* extinct giant reptile. [G. *deinos,* terrible, *sauros,* lizard]

dint *n.* dent. -**by dint of,** by force of [OE. *dynt,* blow of weapon]

di'ocese *n.* district or jurisdiction ofa bishop. **dioc'esan** *a. -n.* bishop, or clergyman, or the people of a diocese. [F. *diocese*]

diop'trics *n. pl.* science of light refraction. -**diop'tric** *a.* [G. *dia,* through, *opsis,* sight]

diora'ma *n.* illuminated pictures seen through opening; exhibition of these. **dioram'ic** *a.* [G. *dia,* through, *moraein,* see]

diox'ide *n.* oxide with two parts of oxygen to one of a metal. [*oxide*]

dip *v.t.* put partly or for a moment into a liquid; immerse, involve; lower and raise again; take up in a ladle, bucket, *etc. -v.i.* plunge partially or temporarily; go down, sink; slope downwards. *-n.* act of dipping; downward slope; hollow. -**dipp'er** *n.* [OE. *dyppan*]

diphtheria *n.* infectious disease of the throat with membranous growth. **diphtherit'ic** *a.* [G. *diphthera,* skin]

diphthong *n.* union of two vowel sounds in a single compound sound. [G. *diphthongos,* having two sounds]

diplod'ocus *n.* extinct giant dinosaur. [G. *diploos,* double, *dokos,* beam]

diplo'ma *n.* document vouching for a person's title to some degree, honor, *etc.,* -**diplo'macy** *n.* management of international relations; skill in negotiation; tactful or adroit dealing. **dip'lomat** *n.* one engaged in official diplomacy. -**diplo'matist** *n.* diplomat; tactful or crafty person. -**diplomat'ic** *a.* **diplomat'-ically** *adv.* [G. -folded paper]

diplo'pia *n.* double vision. [G. *diploos,* double, *opsis,* sight]

dipp'er *n.* diving bird, water-ouzel; ladle; constellation, the Great Bear, the Little Bear. [*dip*]

dipsomania *n.* inability to keep from alcohol. -**dipsoma'niac** *n.* one suffering from dipsomania. [G. *dipsa,* thirst]

dip'tych (-tik) *n.* picture on two boards hinged to close like a book. (G. *diptychos,* double folded]

dire *a.* dread, terrible. [L. *dirus*]

direct' *v.t.* put in the straight way; address (a letter, *etc.*); aim, point, turn; control, manage, order. *-a.* straight; going straight to the point; lineal; immediate; frank, straightforward. -**direc'tion** *n.* a directing; body of directors; address, instruction; aim, course of movement. -**direc'tion finder,** (wireless) device for taking bearings from incoming waves. -**direct'ive** *a.* **direct'ly** *adv.* -**direct'ness** *n.* -**direct'or** *n.* one who directs; member of a board managing a company. -**direct'ress** *fem.* -**direct'orate** *n.* -**direct'orship** *n.* -**direct'ory** *n.* book of names and addresses, streets, *etc.* [L. *dirigere, direct-,* make straight]

dirge *n.* song of mourning. [L. *dirige,* in antiphon in Office for the Dead; *Dirige, Domine . . . viam meam,* Direct, O Lord. . . my way]

dirig'ible *a.* that may be steered. *n.* balloon or airship that can be steered. [L. *dirigere*, direct]

dirk *n.* short dagger orig. carried by Scottish clansmen. [orig. uncertain]

dirt'y *a.* unclean; soiled; mean. **-dirt** *n.* filth; mud, earth. **dirt' far'mer** *n.* farmer who farms his own land, usu. without the help of hired hands. **-dirt'ily** *adv.* **dirt'iness** *n.* [ON. *drit*, excrement]

dis- *prefix*, indicates negation, opposition, deprivation; in many verbs, it indicates the undoing of the action of the simple verb, *e.g.*, **-disembark'**, come out from what one embarked in; many verbs, nouns and adjectives in *dis-* mean the exact opposite of the simple word, *e.g.* **-disarrange', disorders, -disloy'al;** some verbs in **dis-** mean to deprive of the thing indicated by the simple word, *e.g.*, **-disembowel.** All such words are omitted, and the meaning should be sought under the simple word to which *dis-* is prefixed. [L.]

disa'ble *v.t.* incapacitate; disqualify; cripple. **disabil'ity** *n.* [*able*]

disabuse' (-z) *v.t.* undeceive. [fr. old sense of *abuse*, *i.e.*, deceive]

disaffected *a.* ill-disposed, inclined to sedition, **disaffec'tion** *n.* [*affect*]

disallow' *v.t.* reject the validity of (evidence *etc.*). [*allow*]

disappoint' *v.t.* fail to fulfill (hope) **-disappointment** *n.* [*appoint*]

disarm' *v.t.* take away weapons; reduce armaments; conciliate. **-disarm'ament** *n.* [*arm*]

disarray' *v.t.* throw into disorder; derange. *-n.* undress. [*array*]

disas'ter (-a-) *n.* calamity, a sudden or great misfortune. **-disas'trous** *a.* [orig. evil star. L. *astrum*]

disavow' *v.t.* disown; disclaim. **-disavowal** *n.* [OF. *desavouer*]

disband' *v.t.* and *i.* disperse. [*band*]

disburse' *v.t.* pay out money. **-disbursement** *n.* [F. *bourse*, purse]

disc. *See* **disk.**

discard' *v.t.* and *i.* reject, or play as worthless (a card); give up; cast off. [OF. *descarter*, scatter]

discern' *v.t.* make out; distinguish. **-discern'ment** *n.* insight. **-discern'ible** *a.* [L. *discernere*, separate, sift]

discharge' *v.t.* unload; fire off; release; dismiss; let go, pay; emit. *-n.* a discharging; a being discharged; matter emitted; document certifying release, payment, *etc.* [OF. *descharger*, unload]

disci'ple *n.* follower, one who takes another as teacher and model. **-discipleship** *n.* **-dis'cipline** (-in) *n.* training that produces orderliness, obedience, self-control; result of such training in order, conduct, *etc.*; system of rules; maintenance of subordination in an army, school, *etc.* *-v.t.* train; chastise. **disciplin'arian** *n.* **-dis'ciplinary** *a.* [L. *discipulus*, pupil]

disclaim' *v.t.* disavow. **disclaim'er** *n.* act of disavowal. [L. *disclamare*]

disclose' *v.t.* reveal, bring to light. **-disclo'sure** *n.* [*close*]

discob'olus *n.* Greek statue of a discus thrower. [G.]

dis'color *v.t.* and *i.* to change in color or hue. discoloration *n.* [*color*]

dis'combobulate *v.t.* upset, confuse. **-dis'combobulation** *n.* [orig. uncertain]

discom'fit (-um-) *v.t.* defeat, baffle. **-discom'fiture** *n.* [OF. *desconfit*, undone]

disconcert' *v.t.* derange, ruffle, confuse. [opposite of *concert*]

discon'solate *a.* unhappy, downcast; unconsoled. [*console*]

dis'cord *n.* absence of concord; difference, dissension; disagreement of sounds. **-discordant** *a.* **-discord'antly** *adv.* **-discord'ance** *n.* [L. *discordia*]

discount' *v.t.* give present value of (a bill of exchange, *etc.*); detract from; allow for exaggeration in. **-dis'count** *n.* deduction made on discounting a bill, receiving payment for an account, *etc.* [OF. *desconter*, count off]

discourage (-kur-) *v.t.* reduce the confidence of; deter from; show disapproval of. **-discour'agement** *n.* [*courage*]

discourse *n.* speech, treatise, sermon; conversation. **-discourse'** *v.i.* speak, converse. *-v.t.* utter. [L. *discursus*, running to and fro]

discov'er (-kuv-) *v.t.* find out, light upon; make known. **-discov'ery** *n.* **-discov'erer** *n.* **-discov'erable** *a.* [*cover*]

discredit *v.t.* refuse to believe; disgrace, damage reputation. *-n.* -discreditable *a.* shameful, disgraceful. [*credit*]

discreet' *a.* prudent, knowing when to be silent. **-discreet'ly** *adv.* **-discre'tion** (-eshén) *n.* [*discrete*]

discrepant *a.* not tallying; showing an inconsistency. **-discrep'ancy** *n.* [L. *discrepare*, jar, sound ill]

discrete' *a.* separate; disjoined. **-discreteness** *n.* **-discret'ive** *a.* [L. *discretus*, separated]

discrim'inate *v.t.* and *i.* detect or draw distinctions, distinguish from or between. **-discrimina'tion** *n.* [L. *discriminare,* divide, discern]

discursive *a.* passing from subject to subject, not keeping to the main thread. [L. *discursus,* running to and fro]

disc'us *n.* a disk which is thrown to perform a track-and-field sport of that name. [G. *diskos*]

discuss' *v.t.* exchange opinions on; debate; consume (food or drink). **-discus'sion** *n.* [L. *discutere, discuss-,* agitate]

disdain' *n.* scorn, contempt. *-v.t.* scorn. **-disdain'ful** *a.* **disdain'fully** *adv.* [OF. *desdain*; cp. *deign*]

disease' *n.* illness; disorder of health. [OF. *desaise,* discomfort]

disembody *v.t.* remove from body, *esp.* of spirits; disband. **-disembod'ied** *a.* [*embody*]

dis'favor *n.* disapproval; being out of favor-*v.t.* disapprove look upon without favor. [*favor*]

disfig'ure (-get) *v.t.* mar the appearance of, deface. **-disfig'urement** *n.* **-disfiguration** *n.* [*figure*]

disgorge' *v.t.* eject; restore what has been seized. [opposite of *gorge*]

disgrace' *n.* ignominy; cause of shame; loss of favor-*v.t.* bring shame or discredit upon. **-disgrace'ful** *a.* **-disgrace'fully** *adv.* [*grace*]

disgruntled *a.* dissatisfied; ill-humored. **disgrun'tle** *v.t.* [*grunt*]

disguise' (-giz) *v.t.* change the appearance of, make unrecognizable; conceal, cloak; misrepresent. *-n.* false appearance; dress or device to conceal identity. [OF. *desguiser,* change costume]

disgust' *n.* violent distaste, loathing. *v.t.* affect with loathing. [OF. *desgoust,* now *dogo* (It, distaste)]

dish *n.* shallow vessel for food; portion or variety of food; contents of a dish. *-v.t.* put in a dish; serve up. [OE. *disc,* platter]

disheveled *a.* with disordered hair; ruffled, untidy, disorderly. [OF. *deschevele,* fr. *chevel,* hair]

dishonor *n.* disgrace; loss of honor *-v.t.* disgrace; to insult; refuse payment on. [*honor*]

disillusion *n.* freeing from illusion. *v.t.* undeceive. illusion **-disinfect'** *v.t.* free from infection or germs; purify. **-disinfect'ant** *a.* /*n.* germ destroying (agent). [*infect*]

disinformation *n.* false information intended to deceive or mislead. [*inform*]

disintegrate *v.t.* break up, crumble, fall to pieces. **-disintegra'tion** *n.* [*integrate*]

disinterested *a.* unbiased, impartial. [*interest*]

disinvestment *n.* a process by which the capital stock of an economy or enterprise is reduced, as by not replacing obsolete plant and machinery; the act of withdrawing investment from an enterprise or country. [*invest*]

disk, disc *n.* thin circular plate; anything disk-like. **-disk jock'ey** *n.* (*sl.*) announcer on a radio program who introduces and plays recorded music. disk drive *n.* in computer technology the unit that controls the mechanism for handling a diskette. **-disk'ette** *n.* floppy disk, used for storing information from a computer. [G. *diskos,* a round plate]

dislocate *v.t.* put out of place, *esp.* of a bone; put into disorder. **-disloca'tion** *n.* [*locate*]

dislodge' *v.t.* eject from a position, lodgement. [*lodge*]

dis'mal (-z-) *a.* depressing, or depressed; cheerless, dreary. **-dis'mally** *adv.* [ME. in the dismal, L. *dies mali,* evil days]

dismantle *v.t.* deprive of defenses, furniture, *etc.*; remove equipment. [OF. *desmanteier,* strip]

dismay' *v.t.* dishearten, daunt. *-n.* consternation, horrified amazement. [OF. *desmayer,* deprive of power]

dismember *v.t.* tear or cut limb from limb; divide, partition. **-dismem'berment** *n.* [*member*]

dismiss' *v.t.* send away, disperse, disband; put away from employment, or from the mind. **-dismiss'al** *n.* [L. *mittere, miss-,* send]

disparage *v.t.* speak slightingly of; bring into disrepute. **-dispar'agement** *n.* [OF. *desparagier,* orig. marry unequally]

disparate *a.* essentially different, not related. **-dispar'ity** *n.* inequality. [*parity*]

dispassionate *a.* cool; unbiased. [*passion*]

dispatch, despatch' *v.t.* send off, send to a destination or on an errand; kill; eat up; finish off, get done with speed. *-n.* a sending off-, efficient speed; an official written message. *-pl.* state papers. [Sp. *despachar,* expedite]

dispel' *v.t.* clear away; banish. [L. *dispellere,* drive apart]

dispense' *v.t.* deal out; make up (a

medicine), relax, not insist on; do without; administer. *-v.i.* make up medicines. -**dispens′er** *n.* -**dispens′ary** *n.* place where medicine is made up. -**dispensation** *n.* license or exemption; provision of nature or providence; act of dispensing. -**dispens′able** *a.* [L. *dispen sare*, distribute by weight]

disperse′ *v.t.* scatter. -**dispersed′** *a.* scattered; placed here and there. -**disper′sion** *n.* [F. *disperser*]

dispir′it *v.t.* dishearten; cast down. -**dispir′ited** *a.* in low spirits; discouraged. [*spirit*]

display′ *v.t.* spread out for show; show, expose to view. *-n.* a displaying; show, exhibition; show, ostentation. [OF. *despleier*, L. *displicare*, unfold]

disport′ *v. refl.* gambol, move about for enjoyment, *esp.* in water, sunshine. [OF. *desporter*, carry away]

dispose′ (-z) *v.t.* arrange; make inclined (to). *-v.i.* ordain, appoint. -**dispose of**, sell, get rid of; have authority over. -**dispo′sal** *n.* -**disposi′tion** *n.* arrangement; plan; inclination; east of mind or temper. [F. *disposer*]

dispute′ *v.i.* debate, discuss. *-v.t.* call in question; debate, argue; oppose, contest; try to debar from. **dis′putable** *a.* -**dis′putant** *n.* -**disputa′tion** *n.* -**disputa′tious** *a.* [L. *disputare*, discuss]

disqui′et *n.* anxiety, uneasiness, restlessness. *-v.t.* make uneasy, restless. -**disqui′etude** *n.* [*quiet*]

disquisition *n.* learned or elaborate treatise or discourse. [L. *disquisition*]

disrupt′ *v.t.* shatter, break in pieces, split. -**disrup′tion** *n.* -**disrup′tive** *a.* [L. *disrumpere*, disrupt-, break asunder]

dissect′ *v.t.* cut up (a body, organism) for detailed examination; examine or criticize in detail. -**dissec′tion** *n.* -**dissec′tor** *n.* [L. *dissecare*, cut up]

dissemble *v.t.* and *i.* conceal or disguise (opinions, feelings, *etc.*); talk or act hypocritically. -**dissem′bler** *n.* [for earlier *dissimule*, fr. L. *dissimulate*]

disseminate *v.t.* spread abroad. -**dissemina′tion** *n.* -**dissem′inator** *n.* [L. *disseminate*, scatter seed]

dissent′ *v.i.* differ in opinion; express such difference; disagree with the doctrine, *etc.*, of an established church. *n.* such disagreement. -**dissent′er** *n.* -**dissentient** *a.* and *n.* -**dissen′sion** *n.* [L. *dissentire*, differ in feeling]

dissertation *n.* formal discourse; treatise. [L. *dissertation*]

dissident *a.* not in agreement. -**diss′idence** *n.* [L. *dissidere*, sit apart]

dissimulate *v.t.* and *i.* pretend not to have; practice deceit. -**dissimula′tion** *n.* [L. *dissimulate*]

dissipate *v.t.* scatter, clear away; waste, squander. *-v.i.* disappear, clear away. -**dissipa′tion** *n.* scattering; frivolous or dissolute way of life. **diss′ipated** *a.* corrupted, dissolute. [L. *dissipate*, scatter]

dissociate *v.t.* separate, sever. -**dissociation** *n.* [L. *socius*, companion]

dissolve′ *v.t.* absorb or melt in a fluid; break up, put an end to, annul. *-v.i.* melt in a fluid; disappear, vanish; break up, scatter. -**dissol′uble** *a.* -**dissolu′tion** *n.* [L. *dissolvers*, loosen]

dissolute *a.* lax in morals, profligate. -**diss′oluteness** *n.* [L. *dissolvers*, *dissolut-*, loosen]

dissonant *a.* jarring, discordant in sound. -**diss′onance** *n.* [L. *dissonare*, sound diversely]

dissuade′ (-sw-) *v.t.* advise to refrain, persuade not to. -**dissua′sion** *n.* -**dissua′sive** *a.* [L. *dissuadere-suadere*, advise]

dissyll′able *n.* word or foot having two syllables -**dissyllab′ic** *a.* [for *disyllable*, G. *di-*, twice, and *syllable*]

dis′taff *n.* cleft stick to hold wool, *etc.*, for hand-spinning. -**dis′taff side,** female line of family. [OE. *distoef*]

dis′tance *n.* amount of space between two things; remoteness; excessive dignity. *-v.t.* leave behind, *esp.* in a race. -**dis′tant** *a.* -**dis′tantly** *adv.* [L. *distans, distantis*, fr. *distare*, stand apart]

distaste′ *n.* dislike, aversion; disgust. -**distaste′ful** *a.* offensive to one's taste; unpleasant. [*taste*]

distemper *n.* disordered state of mind or body; disease of dogs; method of painting on plaster without oil; the paint used for this. *-v.t.* paint in distemper. [L. *temperate*, mix, temper]

distend′ *v.t.* and *i.* swell out by pressure from within. -**disten′sible** *a.* -**disten′sion** *n.* [L. *tendere*, stretch]

dis′tich (-tik) *n.* couplet. [G. *distichon*]

distill′ *v.i.* pass over or condense from a still; trickle down. *-v.t.* obtain (a substance or part of it) in a purified state by evaporating and then condensing it. -**distilla′tion** *n.* -**distill′er** *n.* one who distills, *esp.* a manufacturer of alcoholic spirits. -**distill′ery** *n.* place where these are distilled. [L. *distillate*, trickle down]

distinct′ *a.* clear, easily seen, sharp of outline; definite; separate, different. -**distinct′ly** *adv.* -**distinct′ness** *n.* distinction *n.* point of difference; act of distinguishing; eminence, high honor, high quality. -**distinct′ive** *a.* characteristic. -**disting′uish** *v.t.* class; make a difference in; recognize, make out; honor; make prominent or honored (*usu. refl.*). -*v.i.* draw a distinction, grasp a difference. -**disting′uishable** *a.* [L. *distinguere, -distinct-*, prick off]

distort′ *v.t.* put out of shape; misrepresent, garble. -**distor′tion** *n.* [L. *distorquere, distort-*, twist apart]

distract′ *v.t.* turn aside, divert; bewilder, drive mad. **distrac′tion** *n.* [L. *distrahere, distract-*, pull apart]

distraint′ *n.* legal seizure of goods to enforce payment. **distrain′** *v.i.* [L. *distringere*, pull asunder]

distrait′ *a.* absent-minded, abstracted. [F.]

distraught′ (-awt) *a.* bewildered, crazy. [fr. F. *distrait*, absentminded]

distress′ *n.* severe trouble, mental pain; pressure of hunger or fatigue or want; (*law*) -**distraint.** -*v.t.* afflict, give mental pain to. -**distress′ful** *a.* [OF. *destresse*, fr. L. *distringere*, pull asunder]

distribute *v.t.* deal out; spread, dispose at intervals; classify. -**distrib′utive** *a.* -**distribu′tion** *n.* -**distrib′utor** *n.* [L. *distribuereé* cp. *tribute*]

dis′trict *n.* portion of territory; region. [F. = control, region controlled]

disturb′ *v.t.* trouble, agitate; unsettle, derange. -**distur′bance** *n.* -**distur′ber** *n.* [L. *disturbare*, disorder]

ditch *n.* long narrow hollow dug in the ground, usually for drainage. -*v.t.* and *i.* make or repair ditches; discard. [OE. *die*]

dith′er *v.i.* shake, tremble, hesitate. [*imit.*]

dith′yramb (-amb) *n.* Greek hymn to Bacchus. -**dithyram′bic** *a.* wildly enthusiastic; rhapsodic. [G. *dithyrtambos*]

dittany *n.* aromatic plant. [OF. *dictame*]

dit′to (part of speech) same, aforesaid; (used to avoid repetition in lists, *etc.*). [It., fr. L. *dictus*, the said]

ditt′y *n.* simple song. [OF. *dite*, poem]

ditt′y-bag, ditt′y-box *n.* sailor's bag, box, for sewing materials, *etc.* [orig. uncertain]

diuret′ic (di-fir-) *a.* exciting discharge of urine. -*n.* substance with this property. [G. *diouretikos*]

diur′nal *a.* daily; in, or of, daytime; taking a day. [L. *diurnalis*, fr. *dies*, day]

di′va *n.* distinguished female singer; prima-donna. [L. = *divine*]

divagation (di-) *n.* wandering, digression. -**di′vagate** *v.i.* [L. *divagatio*]

di′van *n.* low seat by a wall; smokingroom; oriental council. [Turk.]

divar′icate *v.i.* brand, fork, diverge. -**divarica′tion** *n.* [L. *dis*, apart, *varus*, crooked]

dive *v.i.* plunge under the surface of water; descend suddenly; disappear; go deep down into. -*n.* an act of diving; (*sl.*) disreputable place of entertainment. -**di′ver** *n.* [OE. *dufan*, sink, and *dyfan*, dip]

diverge′ *v.i.* get further apart, separate. -**diver′gent** *a.* -**diver′gence** *n.* [L. *di-*, apart, and *uergere*, turn]

di′vers (-z) *a.* sundry. -**diverse′** *a.* different, varied. **divers′ify** *v.t.* -**diverse′ly** *adv.* -**diversifica′tion** *n.* -**diversity** *n.* [*divert*]

divert′ *v.t.* turn aside, ward off, cause to turn; amuse, entertain. -**diver′sion** *n.* a turning aside; that which diverts; amusement; entertainment. [L. *divertere*, turn aside]

divertissement *n.* theatrical interlude; ballet. [F.]

Di′ves *n.* rich man. [L.]

divest′ *v.t.* unclothe, strip, dispossess. [L. *devestire*, undress]

divide′ *v.t.* make into two or more parts, split up, separate; classify; cut off; deal out; take or have a share; part into two groups for voting; -**divide** a number by another, find out how many times the former contains the latter. -*v.i.* become divided. -**div′idend** *n.* number to be divided by another; share of profits, of money divided among creditors, *etc.* -**divi′ders** *n. pl.* measuring compasses. -**divis′ible** *a.* -**divis′ion** *n.* (-vizh-n). -**divis′ional** *a.* -**divi′sor** *n.* [L. *dividere, divis-*, to force asunder]

div′idivi *n.* pods of a W. Indian tree, used in tanning. [Carib.]

divine′ *a.* of, pertaining to, proceeding from, God; sacred; godlike, heavenly. -*n.* theologian; clergyman. -*v.t.* and *i.* guess; predict, tell by inspiration or magic. -**divine′ly** *adv.* -**divin′ity** *n.* quality of being divine; god; theology [L. *divinus*, of the gods]

divination *n.* divining. -**divi′ner** *n.* -**divi′ning-rod** *n.* switch for detecting underground water or minerals. [*divine*]

divorce′ *n.* legal dissolution of marriage; complete separation, disunion. -*v.t.* dissolve a marriage; put away; separate. -**divorcee'** *n.* divorced person. [F.]

div'ot *n.* patch of turf, *esp.* as dislodged accidentally in the game of golf. [Scot.]

divulge' *v.t.* reveal, let out (a secret). -**devul'gate** *v.t.* publish. [L. *divulgare*, spread among the people, *vulgus*]

divul'sive *a.* tearing apart. -**divul'sion** *n.* [L. *vellere*, pluck]

Dix'ie *n.* the Southern states of the U. S. [orig. uncertain]

dizz'y *a.* feeling dazed, unsteady; causing, or fit to cause, dizziness, as of speed, *etc.* *v.t.* to make dizzy. -**dizz'iness** *n.* -**dizz'ily** *adv.* [OE. *dysig*, foolish]

do *v.t.* perform, effect, transact, bring about, finish, prepare, cook; cheat. *v.i.* act, manage, work, fare, serve, suffice. -*v. aux.* makes negative and interrogative sentences and expresses emphasis. [OE. *don*]

dobb'in *n.* cart-horse. [F., dim. of *Robert*]

do'cile *a.* willing to obey; easily taught. -**docil'ity** *n.* [L. *docilis-, docere,* teach]

dock *n.* coarse weed. [OE. *docce*]

dock *n.* solid part of a tail; cut end, stump. -*v.t.* cut short, *esp.* a tail; curtail, deprive of. [orig. uncertain]

dock *n.* basin with flood-gates for loading or repairing ships. -*v.t.* put in a dock. *v.i.* go into dock. -**dock'yard** *n.* enclosure with docks, for building or repairing ships. -**dock'er** *n.* dock-worker or docklaborer. [O. Du. *dokke*]

dock *n.* enclosure in a criminal court in which the prisoner is placed. [Flem, *dok*, hutch, pen]

dock'et *n.* endorsement showing the contents of a document; memorandum; certificate of payment of customs. -*v.t.* make a memorandum, endorse with a summary. [earlier *dogget*, orig. uncertain]

doc'tor *n.* one holding a University's highest degree in any faculty; medical practitioner. -*v.t.* treat medically; adulterate, garble. -**doc'torate** *n.* -**doc'toral** *a.* [L. *doctrina*, fr. *docere*, teach]

doc'trine *n.* what is taught; teaching of a church, school, or person; belief, opinion, dogma; statement of official government policy. -**doctri'nal** *a.* -**doctrinaire'** *n.* person who seeks to apply principles or theory without regard for circumstances. [L. fr. *docere*, teach]

doc'ument *n.* something written furnishing evidence or information. -*v.t.* furnish with proofs, illustrations, certificates. -**document'ary** *a.* -**documenta'tion** *n.* [L. *documentum*, example]

dodd'er *n.* leafless parasitic plant. [OE.]

doddering *a.* trembling with ague or frailty; useless; pottering. [cp. *dither*]

dodec'agon *n.* twelve-sided, twelve-angled plane figure, [G. *dodeka*, twelve, *gonia*, angle]

dodge *v.i.* swerve, make zig-zag movement, *esp.* to avoid a pursuer or gain an advantage; shuffle. play fast and loose. *v.t.* elude by **dodging**. -*n.* an act of dodging; trick, artifice; shift, ingenious method. -**dodg'er** *n.* [orig. unknown]

do'do *n.* extinct bird. [Port.]

doe *n.* female of deer, hare, rabbit, antelope *etc.* [OE. *do*]

doff *v.t.* take off (hat, clothing). [do off]

dog *n.* familiar domestic quadruped; person (in contempt, abuse, or playfully). -*v.t.* follow steadily or closely. -**dogg'ed** *a.* persistent, resolute, tenacious. -**dogg'y** *a.* -**dogg'y bag** *n.* a bag into which leftovers from a meal may be put and taken away for the diner's dog. -**dog'like** *a.* -**dog'cart** *n.* open vehicle with crosswise back-to-back seats. -**dog'days** *n.* hot season of the rising of the dogstar. -dog-rose *n.* wild rose. -**dog's-ear** *n.* turned-down corner of a page in a book. -*v.t.* turn down corners of pages. -**dog'-leg** *n.* sharp bend or angle in a course, route, or object, resembling the bend of a dog's hind leg. -**dog'star** *n.* star Sirius. **dog'-watch** *n.* in ships, a short half-watch, 4-6, 6-8 P. M. -**dog wood** *n.* variety of shrub with white flowers and purple berries; cornel. [OE, *docga*]

do'ge (do-je) *n.* chief magistrate of Venetian Republic. [It., *for duce*, - L. *dux*, leader]

dogg'er *n.* two-masted Dutch fishingboat. [Du.]

dogg'erel *n.* slipshod, unpoetic or trivial verse. [orig. uncertain]

dogg'o *a.* (*sl.*) hidden; unobtrusively still, quiet (to lie doggo). [orig. uncertain]

dog'ma *n.* article of belief, *esp.* one laid down authoritatively by a church; body of beliefs. -**dogmat'ic** *a.* relating to dogma or dogmas; asserting opinions with arrogance. -**dogmat'ically** *adv.* -**dog'matism** *n.* arrogant assertion of opinion. **dog'matist** *n.* -**dog'matize** *v.i.* [G. *dokeiro*, to seem]

doi'ly *n.* small cloth, paper, piece of lace to place under a cake, finger-bowl, *etc.* [fr. *Doily*, 17th c. shopkeeper]

dol'drums *n.pl.* region of light winds and calms near the equator; state of depression, dumps. [*dull*]

dole *n.* charitable gift; (*sl.*) a payment from government funds to the unemployed. -*v.t.* (usually dole out) deal out, *esp.* in niggardly quantities. [OE. *dal*]

dole *n.* woe. -**dole'ful** *a.* full of grief; dismal. -**dole'fully** *adv.* [OF. *duel*]

doll, dolly *n.* child's toy image of a human being. [short for *Dorothy*]

doll'ar *n.* coin of Canada, U.S., and other countries. [Ger. *thater*]

dol'man *n.* cloak; hussar jacket, [F.]

dol'men *n.* prehistoric monument, standing stones capped by large stone slab. [Breton, *tol*, table, men, stone]

dol'or (-er) *n.* grief, sadness. -**dol'orous** *a.* -**dol'orously** *adv.* [L. *dolor*]

dol'phin *a.* sea mammal like a porpoise; figure of a curved, large-headed fish common in decoration and heraldry; buoy for mooring. -**dolphinar'ium** *n.* a pool or aquarium for dolphins, *esp.* one in which they give public displays. [OF. *dalfin*, fr. L. *delphinus*]

dolt *n.* stupid fellow. [*dull*]

domain' *n.* lands held or ruled over; sphere, field of influence, province. [F. *domaine*, fr. L. *dorninium*]

dome *n.* rounded vault forming a roof, large cupola. -**domed** *a.* [F. *dome*]

domes'day (doomz'-) *a.* in Domesday Book, the record of the survey of the land of England made in 1086. [ME. spelling of doomsday]

domes'tic *a.* of or in the home; of the home country, not foreign; home-keeping; of animals, tamed, kept by man. -**domes'ticate** *v.t.* -**domestica'tion** *n.* -**domesti'city** *n.* [L. *domesticus*]

dom'icile *n.* person's regular place of living (usually legal). -**domicil'iary** *a.* pert. to the domicile. [F.]

dom'inate *v.t.* rule, control, sway; of heights, to overlook. -*v.i.* control, be the most powerful or influential member or part of something. -**dom'inant** *a.* -**domina'tion** *n.* -**domineer'** *v.i.* to act imperiously, tyrannize. [L. *dominus*, lord]

domin'ical *a.* pert. to the Lord, or The Lord's Day. [L. *dominus*, Lord]

Domin'ican *a.* pert. to order of monks of St. Dominic. -*n.* Dominican monk. [*St. Dominic*]

dominion *n.* sovereignty, rule; territory of a government. [L. *dominio*]

dom'ino *n.* cloak with a half-mask for masquerading. -*pl.* game played with small flat pieces, marked on one side with 0 to 6 spots on each half of the face. -*sing.* one of these pieces. -**domino effect** *n.* the effect of one initial event setting off a series of similar or related events. [It.]

don *v.t.* put on (clothes). [*do on*]

don *n.* (**don'na** *fem.*) Spanish (courtesy) title = English air; fellow of a college; (*sl.*) expert. [Sp., fr. L. *dominus*]

donate' *v.t.* give. -**dona'tion** *n.* donor *n.* [L. *donare*, give]

don'gle *n.* in computer technology, an electronic device that accompanies a software item to prevent the unauthorized copying of programs. [orig. uncertain]

don'jon. *See* **dungeon.**

donk'ey *n.* ass. -**donk'ey-engine** *n.* small hauling or hoisting engine on a ship. [orig. uncertain]

doo'dle *v.i.* (*sl.*) scribble or draw absently. [orig. uncertain]

doo'dle-bug (*sl.*) *n.* flying bomb. [orig. uncertain]

doom *n.* fate, destiny; ruin; judicial sentence, condemnation; Last Judgment. -*v.t.* sentence, condemn; destine to destruction or suffering. -**dooms'day** *n.* day of the Last Judgment. -**doom'watch** *n.* surveillance of the environment to warn of and prevent harm to it from human factors such as pollution or overpopulation; a watching for or prediction of impending disaster. -**doom'watcher** *n.* [OE. *dom*]

door *n.* hinged, sliding, or revolving barrier to close the entrance to a room, carriage, *etc.* -**door'way** *n.* entrance provided, or capable of being provided, with a door. -**door-to-door** *a.* going from one building or destination to the next, *usu.* selling. [OE. *dor, duru*]

dopamine *n.* amine ($C_8H_{11}NO_2$) formed in the brain that is an essential neurotransmitter in the central nervous system's regulation of movement and emotions.

dope *v.t.* drug; stupefy with drugs. -*n.* narcotic drugs; stupid person. -**dope'y** *a.* dull-witted. [Du. *doop*, sauce]

dope *n.* any thick liquid, as axle-grease. [Du. *doopen*, dip]

dor'ic *n.* a Greek dialect. -*a.* simplest order of Greek architecture. [G. *dorikos*]

dor'mant *a.* not acting, in a state of suspension. -**dor'mancy** *n.* -**dorm'er** *n.* upright window set in a sloping roof -**dor'mitory** *n.* sleeping-room with a number of beds; building containing sleeping quarters. [L. *dormire*, sleep]

dor'mouse *n.* small hibernating rodent [F. *dormir*, sleep]

dor'my *a.* in golf as many holes up as there are holes to play. [orig. uncertain]
dorp *n.* village. [Du., cp. O. E. *thorp*]
dor'sal *a.* of or on the back. -**dor'sally** *adv.* [L. *dorsum*, back]
do'ry *n.* a flat-bottomed boat. [Miskito, *dori*, dugout]
DOS *n* (*compute.*) operating system for a computer. [*D*isk *O*perating *S*ystem]
dose *n.* amount (of a drug, *etc.*) administered at one time. -*v.t.* give doses to . -**dos'age** *n.* [F.]
doss *v.i.* sleep. -**doss'-house** *n.* common lodging-house. [obs. *doss*, back]
dossier (dos-ya) *n.* set of documents; record *esp.* of individual; brief. [F.]
dot *n.* small spot or mark. -*v.t.* mark with a dot or dots; place here and there. **dot ma'trix prin'ter** *n.* in computer technology, a printer in which each character is produced by a subset of an array of needles at the printhead. [OE. *dott*, speck]
dot (dot) *n.* dowry. [F.]
dote *v.i.* be silly or weak-minded; be passionately fond of. -**do'tage** *n.* feeble minded old age. -**do'tard** *n.* [AF. *doter*]
dott'erel *n.* kind of plover. [*dote*]
dou'ble (dub-) *a.* of two parts, layers *etc.*; folded; twice as much or many; of two kinds; ambiguous; deceitful. -*adv.* twice; to twice the amount or extent; in a pair. *n.* person or thing exactly like, or mistakable for, another; quantity twice as much as another; sharp turn; evasion or shift. *v.t.* and *i.* make or become double; increase twofold; fold in two; turn sharply; get round, sail round. -**doub'ly** *adv.* -**doub'let** *n.* close-fitting body-garment formerly worn by men. -**doubloon'** *n.* Spanish gold coin. -**double-cheating** *n.* cheating, duplicity. -**double-cross** *v.t.* deceive, betray by working for two sides simultaneously. -**double-dyed** *a.* villainous. -**double-team** *v.t.* (*sports*) guard, defend against, or block an opposing player with two players. [F. *double*, fr. L. *duplus*]
doubt (dowt) *v.t.* hesitate to believe, call in question; suspect. -*v.i.* be wavering or uncertain in belief or opinion. -*n.* state of uncertainty, wavering in belief; state of affairs giving cause for uncertainty. -**doubt'er** *n.* -**doubt'ful** *a.* -**doubt'fully** *adv.* **doubt'lessly** *adv.* [L. *dubitare*]
douceur' *n.* bribe; tip. [F. *sweetener*]
douche *n.* jet or spray of water applied to the body or some part of it; shower. -*v.t.* give a douche to. [F.]
dough *n.* flour or meal kneaded with water. -**dough'y** *a.* [OE. *dag*]
dought'y (dowt'i) *a.* valiant. **dought'ily** *adv.* -**dought'iness** *n.* [OE. *dyhtig*]
dour *a.* grim, stubborn. [F. *dur*]
douse, dowse *v.t.* plunge into water; souse; strike; extinguish. -*v.i.* fall into water. [O. Du. *doesen*, beat]
dove (duv) *n.* bird of the pigeon family. -**dove'cot**(e) *n.* house or hutch for doves. -**dove'tail** *n.* joint made with a tenon shaped as a spread **dove's tail**. -*v.t.* and *i.* fit together by dove-tails; unite or combine neatly or exactly. [cp. Du. *duif*]
dowager (-j-) *n.* woman with title or property derived from her late husband. [OF. *douagere*, fr. L. *dotare*, endow]
dow'dy *a.* lacking smartness; unattractively or shabbily dressed. -*n.* woman so dressed. [ME. *dowd*]
dow'er *n.* widow's share for life of her husband's estate; dowry. -*v.t.* give dowry to; endow. -**dow'ry** *n.* property which a wife brings to her husband; talent. [F. *douaire*, -L. *dotare*, endow]
down *n.* open expanse of high land, *esp.* in England, *e.g.*, the Sussex Downs. [OE. *dun*, hill]
down *adv.* to, or in, or towards, a lower position; with a current or wind; of paying, on the spot. -prep. from higher to lower part of; at a lower part of; along with. -**down'cast** *a.* looking down; dejected. -**down'pour** *n.* heavy fall of rain. -**down'right** *a.* plain, straightforward. *adv.* quite, thoroughly. -**down'size** *v.t.* to make a smaller version. -**down time** *n.* time during which a machine or plant is not working because it is incapable of production, as when under repair. -**down'town** *a.* towards the center of a town or city. -**down'trodden** *a.* trampled, oppressed. -**down'ward** *adv.* and *a.* -**down'wards** *adv.* [for *adown*, OE. of *dune*, off hill]
down *n.* fluff or fine hair of young birds; anything like this, soft and fluffy. -**down'y** *a.* [OE. *dunn*]
down'link *n.* communications path for transmission of information or signals from a spacecraft or satellite to earth.
dow'ry. *See* **dower.**
dowse *v.i.* seek for water, minerals, with aid of divining-rod or -**dows'ing-rod** *n.* -**dows'er** *n.* water-diviner. [earlier *dense*, perh. conn. with Ger. *deuter*, indicate]
doxol'ogy *n.* short formula of praise to God [G. *doxologia*, speak praise]
doy'en (dwa-yong) *n.* senior member of a body; ambassador, professor *etc.* [F.]

doy'ley *See* **doily.**
doze *v.i.* sleep drowsily, be half asleep. *n.* nap. [orig. uncertain]
doz'en *n./a.* twelve, a set of twelve. [F. *douzaine*, fr. L. *duo*, two, *decem*, ten]
drab *a.* of dull light brown; dull, monotonous. *-n.* drab color. [F. *drop*, cloth]
drab *n.* slut; prostitute. [Gael. *drabqg*]
drachm (dram) *n.* unit of weight, 1/8 of apoth. ounce, 1/16 of avoir. ounce. [G. *drachme*, handful]
draff *n.* brewery refuse (*esp.* dregs of malt), fed to cattle. [ON. *draf*, offal]
draft *n.* detachment of men, *esp.* troops, reinforcements; selection for compulsory military service; design, sketch; rough copy of a document; order for money; act of drinking, quantity drunk at once; one drawing of, or fish taken in, a net; dose; an inhaling; depth of water needed to float a ship; current of air between apertures in a room, *etc.* *-a.* constituting a preliminary version. *-v.t.* make an outline sketch or design of, make a preliminary version of something, *esp.* a piece of writing; to conscript for military service. **-drafts'man** *n.* one who draws plans and designs for buildings, ships, *etc.*, one skilled in drawing. **-drafts'manship** *n.* **-draft'y** *a.* disagreeable currents of air in an enclosed space. [*draw*]
drag *v.t.* pull along with difficulty or friction; trail, go heavily; sweep with a net; protract. *-v.i.* lag, trail; be tediously protracted. *-n.* check on progress; checked motion, iron shoe to check a wheel; vehicle; lure for hounds to hunt; kinds of harrow, sledge, net, grapnel, rake; (*fig.*) a tedious person or thing; (*sl.*) transvestite clothing. **-drag'gle** *v.t.* make limp, wet or dirty by trailing. [var. of *draw*]
dragoman *n.* guide, interpreter, in the East. [F., fr. Arab. *tarjuman*, interpreter]
drag'on *n.* mythical fire-breathing monster, like a winged crocodile. **-drag'onfly** *n.* long-bodied insect with large gauzy wings. **-dragoon'** *n.* cavalryman, usually of heavy cavalry. *v.t.* subject to military oppression; domineer over, persecute. [F.]
drain *v.t.* draw off (liquid) by pipes, ditches, *etc.*; dry; drink to the dregs; empty, exhaust. *-v.i.* flow off or away; become rid of liquid. *-n.* channel for removing liquid; constant outlet, expenditure, strain. **drain'age** *n.* [OE. *dreahnian*, strain a liquid]
drake *n.* male duck. [orig. uncertain]
dram *n.* small draught of strong drink; a drachm. [var of *drachm, q.v.*]
dr'a'ma (dra-) stage-play; art of literature of plays; play-like series of events. **-dramat'ic** *a.* of drama; vivid, arresting. **-dramatiza'tion** *n.* **-dram'atis perso'nae** *n.* characters of a play. [G. = *action*]
dramaturgy *n.* art, principles of dramatic writing. [G. *dramatourgia*, playwright]
drape *v.t.* cover, adorn with cloth; arrange in graceful folds. *-n.* **curtain dra'per** *n.* dealer in cloth, linen, *etc.* **-dra'pery** *n.* [F. *drop*, cloth]
dras'tic *a.* strongly effective. [G. *drastikos*, active]
droughts. *See* **draft.**
draw *v.t.* pull, pull along, haul; bend (a bow); inhale; entice, attract; bring (upon, out, *etc.*); get by lot; of a ship, require (depth of water); take from (a well, barrel, *etc.*); receive (money); delineate, portray with a pencil, *etc.*; frame, compose, droughts write. *-v.i.* pull; shrink; attract; make or admit a current of air; make pictures with pencil, *etc.*; write orders for money; come, approach (near). *-n.* act of drawing; casting of lots; unfinished game, a tie. **-draw'back** *n.* charge paid back; anything that takes away from satisfaction. **-draw'bridge** *n* . hinged bridge to pull up. **-draw'er** *n.* one who or that which draws; sliding box in a table or chest. *-pl.* two-legged undergarment. **-draw'ing** *n..* action of the verb; art of depicting in line; sketch so done. **-draw'ing-room** *n.* reception-room; orig. room to which ladies retire after dinner; court reception. [OE. *dragon*; *drawn game*, for *withdrawn*, the stakes being 'withdrawn' for lack of a decision; *drawing-room* for earlier *withdrawing room*]
drawl *v.t.* and *i.* speak slowly in indolence or affectation. *-n.* such speech. [Du. *dralen*]
dray *n.* low cart without sides. [OE. *drege*, see drag, draw]
dread (dred) *v.t.* fear greatly. *-n.* awe, terror. *-a.* feared, awful, revered. **-dread'ful** *a.* **-dreadlocks** *n. pl.* hair worn in the Rastafarian style of long matted or tightly curled strands. **-dread'nought** *n.* all-big-gun battleship; thick heavy coat; woolen cloth for such coats. [OE. *adrcovdan*]
dream *n.* vision during sleep; fancy, reverie, vision of something ideal. *v.i.* have dreams. *-v.t.* see or imagine in dreams; think of as possible. **-dream'er** *n.* **-dream'y** *a.* given to day-dreams, unpractical, vague. **-dream'less** *a.* [ME.]

drear'y *a.* dismal, dull; cheerless. **-drear** *a.* **-drear'ily** *adv.* **-drear'iness** *n.* fOE. *dreorig*, gory]

dredge *n.* machinery, appliance for bringing up mud, objects, *etc.*, from the bottom of sea or river. -*v.t.* bring up, clean, deepen, with such appliance. **-dredg'er** *n.* ship for dredging. [cp. *drag*]

dredge *v.t.* sprinkle with flour. **-dredg'er** *n.* box with holes in the lid for dredging. [F. *dragée*, sweetmeat]

dree *v.t.* endure, bear. [OE. *dreogan*, suffer]

dregs *n. pl.* sediment, grounds, worthless part. [ON. *dregg*]

drench *v.t.* wet thoroughly, soak; make (an animal) take a dose of medicine. -*n.* dose for an animal; soaking. [OE. *drencan*, make drink]

dress *v.t.* clothe; array for show; trim, smooth, prepare surface of. draw up (troops) in proper line; prepare (food) for the table; put dressing on. -*v.i.* put on one's clothes; form in proper line. -*n.* clothing, clothing for ceremonial evening wear; frock. **-dress'er** *n.* one who dresses; surgeon's assistant; kitchen sideboard; chest of drawers, bureau with a mirror. **-dress'ing** *n. esp.* something applied to something else, as ointment to a wound, manure to land, stiffening to linen, sauce to food, *etc.* **-dress'y** *a.* stylish:fond of dress. **dress-cir'cle** *n.* first galley in a theater. [F. *dresser*]

drib'ble *v.i.* flow in drops, trickle, run at the mouth; work a ball forward with small touches of the feet. -*v.t.* let trickle: work (ball) forward. -*n.* trickle, drop. **-dribblet** *n.* small installment. [*drip*]

drift *n.* being driven by a current; slow current or course; deviation from a course; (also **drift'age**); tendency; speaker's meaning; wind-heaped mass of snow, sand, *etc.*; material driven or carried by water; (in S. Africa) ford. -*v.i.* be carried as by current of air, water; move aimlessly or passively. **-drift'net** *n.* kind of net for sea-fishing. **-drift'er** *n.* one who drifts; fishing-vessel which uses a drift-net. [*drive*]

drill *n.* boring tool or machine; exercise of soldiers or others in handling of arms and maneuvers; routine teaching. -*v.t.* bore; exercise in military movements or other routine. -*v.i.* practice a routine. [Du. *dril*]

drill *n.* small furrow for seed; machine for sowing in drills. -*v.t.* sow in drills. [obs. *drill*, rivulet]

drill *n.* coarse twilled fabric. [L. *trilix*, three thread]

drink *v.t.* and *i.* swallow liquid; absorb; take intoxicating liquor, *esp.* to excess. *n.* liquid for drinking; portion of this; act of drinking; intoxicating liquor; excessive use of it. **-drink'er** *n.* **-drink'able** *a.* [OE. *drincan*]

drip *v.t.* and *i.* or let fall in drops. -*n.* process of dripping; that which falls by dripping. **drip'stone** *n.* projection over round window or door to stop dripping of water. **dripp'ing** *n.* act of dripping; melted fat that drips from roasting meat. [Scand.]

drive *v.t.* force to move in some direction; make move and steer (a vehicle, animal, *etc.*); chase; convey in a vehicle, fix by blows, as a nail; urge, impel. -*v.i.* keep a machine, animal, going, steer it; be conveyed in a vehicle; rush, dash, drift fast. -*n.* act or action of driving; journey in a carriage: carriage-road, *esp.* leading to a house; a driving of game (by beaters) towards shooting-party; organized (selling, *etc.*) campaign. **dri'ver** *n.* [OE. *drifan*]

drivel *v.i.* run at the mouth or nose; talk nonsense. -*n.* silly nonsense. **driv'eller** *n.* [OE. *dreflian*, slobber]

drive train *n.* system in a vehicle which delivers power from the transmission to the wheel axles, via the universal joint, drive shaft, and clutch.

driz'zle *v.i.* rain in fine drops -*n.* fine rain. [OE. *dreosan*, fall in drops]

drogue *n.* drag or brake fixed to harpoon-line of whaler; funnel-shaped device on the end of a feed-hose to facilitate mid-air refuelling of airplanes; small parachute which, when deployed, causes a larger parachute to open, or which is used as a brake. [*drag*]

droll *a.* funny, odd, queer. -*n.* funny fellow. **-drol'ly** *adv.* **-droll'ery** *n.* [F. *drole*, amusing rascal]

dromedary *n.* fast camel. [G. *dromas*, *dromados*, running]

drone *n.* male of the honey-bee; lazy idler; deep humming; bass pipe of bagpipe, or its note. -*v.t.* and *i.* hum; talk in a monotone. [OE. *dran*, bee]

droop *v.i.* hang down as in weariness, languish, flag. -*v.t.* let hang down. -*n.* drooping condition. [ON. *drupa*]

drop *n.* globule of liquid; very small quantity; fall, descent; thing that falls, as a gallows platform; distance through which a thing falls. -*v.t.* let fall; let fall in drops; utter casually; discontinue. -*v.i.* fall; fall in drops; lapse; come or go casually. [OE. *dropa*]

drop'sy *n.* disease with watery fluid collecting in the body. -**drop'sical** *a.* [G. *hydrops*, fr. *hydor*, water]

dross *n.* scum of molten metal, impurity, refuse; small coal. [OE. *dros*]

drought (-owt) *n.* long-continued dry weather; thirst. [OE. *drugoth*]

drove *n.* a herd, flock, crowd, *esp.* in motion. -**dro'ver** *n.* a driver of, or dealer in, cattle. [OE. *draft]*

drown *v.t.* suffocate in water; of sound, *etc.*, to overpower. -*v.i.* be suffocated in water. [OE. *druncnian*, to be drunk, get drowned]

drow'sy (-z-) *a.* half-asleep; lulling; dull, lacking life. -**drow'sily** *adv.* -**drow'siness** *n.* -**drowse** *v.i.* [obs. Du. *droosen*, become sleepy]

drub *v.t.* thrash, beat. (orig. bastinado). -**drubb'ing** *n.* [Arab. *daraba*, beat]

drudge *v.i.* work hard at mean or distasteful tasks. -*n.* one who drudges. -**drudg'ery** *n.* [orig. obscure]

drug *n.* medicinal substance; commodity not wanted (usually within the market). *v.t.* mix drugs with; administer a drug to, *esp.* one inducing sleep or unconsciousness. -**drug'store** *n.* retail store which sells medicines and a variety of other articles, such as food, film, household utensils, cosmetics. **drugg'ist** *n.* dealer in drugs, chemist. [F. *drogue*]

drugg'et *n.* coarse woolen stuff, crumb cloth, protecting carpet. [F. droguet]

dru'id *n.* ancient Celtic priest; an Eisteddfod official. -**druid'ic, druidical** *a.* -**dru'idism** *n.* [L. *druides*, (*pl.*)]

drum *n.* musical instrument, made of skin stretched over a round hollow frame or hemisphere, and played by beating with sticks; various things shaped like a drum; part of the ear. -*v.t.* and *i.* play a drum; tap or thump continuously. -**drum out**, expel from a regiment. -**drum'fire** *n.* heavy continuous rapid artillery fire. -**drum'stick** *n.* stick for beating a drum: lower joint of cooked fowl's leg. -**drumm'er** *n.* one who drums. [imit. orig.]

drunk *a.* overcome by strong drink; fig. under the influence of strong emotion. -**drunk'en** *a.* drunk; often drunk; caused by or showing intoxication. -**drunk'ard** *n.* one given to excessive drinking. -**drunk'enness** *n.* [*drink*]

drupe *n.* fleshy stone-fruit-plum, peach, *etc.* [G. *dryppa*, over-ripe olive]

dry *a.* without moisture; rainless; not yielding milk, or other liquid; not in or under water; cold, unfriendly; caustically witty; having prohibition of alcoholic drink; uninteresting, needing effort to study; lacking sweetness. -*v.t.* remove water, moisture. -*v.i.* become dry, evaporate. -**dri'ly** *adv.* -**dry'ness** *n.* -**dry-batt'ery** *n.* battery with non-liquid electrolyte. -**dry-fly** *a.* (angling) with the fly not submerged. -**dry'goods** *n. pl.* drapery, textiles. -**dry'point** *n.* needle for engraving without acid; an engraving so made. -**dry rot'** *n.* decay in wood not exposed to air. -**dry'shod** *a.* without wetting one's shoes. -**dry'stone** *a.* built of stone without mortar. [OE. *dryge*]

dry'ad *n.* wood-nymph. [G. *Dryas*]

du'al *a.* twofold; of two, forming a pair. -**dual'ity** *n.* -**du'alism** *n.* recognition of two independent powers or principles, as good and evil, mind and matter. -**dualis'tic** *a.* [L. *dualis*]

du'alin *n.* high-explosive. [L. *duo*, two]

dub *v.t.* confer knighthood on; give a title to; give fresh sound-track to (film); smear with grease, dubbin. -**dubb'in, dubbing** *n.* grease for making leather supple. [late OE. *dubbian*]

du'bious *a.* causing doubt, not clear or decided; of suspected character; hesitating. **dubi'ety** *n.* [L. *dubiosus*]

du'cal *a.* of, or relating to, a duke. [*See* **duke**]

due'at (duk-) *n.* former gold coin of Italy and other countries. [first coined for a *ducato* (It.) *duchy*]

duch'ess *n.* the wife or widow of a duke. -**duch'y** *n.* territory of a duke. [F. *duchesse, ducho*]

duck *n.* familiar swimming bird; amphibious motor vehicle. -**drake** *n. masc.* -**duck'ling** *n.* duck *v.i.* plunge under water; bend or bob down. -*v.t.* plunge someone under water. **duck'weed** *n.* common water-weed. -**duck' ing pond** *n.* pond in which scolds were ducked, tied to the -**duck'ing-stool** *n.* [OE. *duce*, diver]

duck *n.* strong linen or cotton fabric. -*pl.* trousers of it. [Du. *doek*, linen]

duck'bill, duck'-billed plat'ypus *See* **platypus.**

duct *n.* channel or tube. -**duct'less** *a.* (of glands) secreting directly certain substances essential to health. [L. *ductus*]

ductile *a.* capable of being drawn into wire; flexible and tough; docile. -**ductil'ity** *n.* [L. *ducere*, lead]

dud *n.* (*sl.*) shell that fails to explode; futile person or project or thing. *a.* [orig. uncertain]

dude *n.* someone from the city, *esp.* an Easterner in the West; dandy; guy. [orig. uncertain]

du'deen *n.* short clay tobacco-pipe. [Ir.]
dudg'eon (-jn) *n.* anger, indignation, resentment. [orig. uncertain]
due *a.* that is owing; proper to be given, inflicted, *etc.*; adequate, fitting; usual, ascribable; under engagement to arrive, be present. *-adv.* (with points of the compass), exactly. *-n.* person's fair share; charge fee, *etc.* (*usu.* in *pl.*)-**du'ly** *adv.* [F. *du*, fr. *devoir*, L. *debere*, owe]
du'el *n.* fight with deadly weapons between two persons; keen two-sided contest. *-v.i.* fight in a dual or duels. **-du'ellist** *n.* [F.]
duenn'a *n.* Spanish lady-in-waiting; governess, chaperon. [Sp. *dueña*]
duet' *n.* piece of music for two performers. [It. *duetto*, fr. L. *duo*, two]
duff *n.* dough; pudding boiled in a cloth, *e.g.,* plumduff. [*dough*]
duff'el, duf'fle *n.* coarse woolen cloth; coat of this. [*Duffel*, in Brabant]
duff'er (dufer) *n.* stupid or inefficient person; something faked; the faker. [Sc. *douf*, deaf, stupid]
dug'out *n.* shelter for troops, civilians, in trenches, *etc.*, at any depth underground; hollowed-out tree canoe. [*dig*]
du'gong *n.* marine mammal allied to seals; sea-cow. (Malay. *duyong*]
dui'ker (di-) *n.* small S. African antelope. [Du.]
du jour *a.* available or served on that particular day; of the day. [F]
duke *n.* peer of rank next below a prince; sovereign of a small state called a duchy. **-duke'dom** *n.* [L. *dux*, leader]
dul'cet (-set) *a.* (of sounds) sweet, harmonious, melodious. [L. *dulcis*]
dul'cimer (-sim-) *n.* stringed instrument played with hammers, an ancestor of the piano. [L. *dulce melos*, sweet tune]
dull *a.* stupid; sluggish; tedious; not keen or clear or bright or sharp or defined; lacking liveliness or variety; gloomy, overcast. *-v.t.* and *i.* make or become dull. —**dul'ly** *adv.* **-dull'ard** *n.* **-dull'ness** *n.* [OE. *dol*, foolish]
dulse *n.* kind of edible seaweed. [Gael. *duileasg*, water-leaf]
du'ly. *See* **due.**
dumb *a.* incapable of speech; silent; (*sl.*) stupid. **-dumb'bell** *n.* weight for exercises. **-dumbfound', dumbfound'er** *v.t.* confound into silence. **-dumb'show** *n.* acting without words. **-dumb'ly** adv. **-dumb'ness** *n.* [OE.]
dumm'y *n.* imaginary card-player; tailor's model; baby's teat; imitation object. (OE.]
dum'dum *n.* soft-nosed bullet which expands on impact causing severe wounding. [*Dumdum*, near Calcutta]
du'mose *a.* thorny. [L. *dumus*, thornbush]
dump *v.t.* throw down in a mass; send low-priced goods for sale abroad. *-n.* rubbish-heap; temporary depot of stores or munitions. **-dump'ling** *n.* round pudding of dough, often with fruit inside. **-dum'py** *a.* short and stout. **-dumps** *n.pl.* low spirits, dejection. **-dump** *n.* dumpy object. [orig. uncertain]
dun *a.* of a dull grayish brown. *-n.* this color; horse of dun color. [OE. *dunn*]
dun *v.t.* to make persistent demands, *esp.* for payment of debts. *-n.* one who duns. [orig. uncertain]
dunce *n.* a dullard, slow learner, blockhead. [earlier *dunsman*, fr. *Duns* Scotus (d. 1308) whose followers were regarded as dull pedants, foes of enlightenment]
dun'derhead *n.* blockhead. **-dun'der headed** *a.* [orig. uncertain]
dundrear'y *n.* side-whiskered dandy. **-dundrear'y whis'koo.** [char. in play]
dune *n.* mound of dry shifting sand on a coast or desert. **-dune buggy** *n.* lightweight vehicle with oversize, low-pressure tires used mainly for driving on sand dunes and beaches. [F.]
dung *n.* excrement of animals; manure. *v.t.* to manure. **-dung'hill** *n.* manure heap. [OE.]
dungaree (-ng-g-) *n.* coarse calico. *-pl.* trousers or overalls of this. [Hind. *dungri*]
dung'eon (dunjn) *n.* underground cell or vault for prisoners; formerly a tower or keep of a castle. [F. *donion*]
dunk shot *n.* (*sports*) basketball shot in which the player jumps high enough to slam the ball down through the basket with one or both hands. Also **slam dunk.**
dun'lin *n.* red-backed sandpiper. [*dun.*]
dunnage *n.* (*naut.*) loose wood to keep cargo out of bilge-water. [orig. unknown]
duode'cimo (-des-) *n.* size of a book in which each sheet is folded into twelve leaves; book of this size. *a.* of this size. [L.]
duode'nums *n.* upper part of small intestine, 12 in. long. **-duode'nal** *a.* **-duode'nal ul'cer,** lesion in wall of duodenum. [L. *duodeni*, twelve]
du'ologue *n.* dialogue between two persons. [L. *duo,* two; G. *logos*, discourse]
dupe *n.* victim of delusion or sharp prac-

tice. -*v.t.* deceive for an advantage. [F.]

du'plex *a.* two-fold -*n.* apartment having rooms on two floors; a house consisting of two family units. duplicate *v.t.* make an exact copy of; double. *a.* double; twofold. -*n.* exact copy. **-duplica'tion** *n.* - **du'plicator** *n.* copying machine. - **dupli'city** (-is'-) *n.* deceitfulness, double-dealing. [L.]

dupp'y *n.* spirit, ghost. [W. Ind.]

du'rable *a.* lasting, resisting wear. - **durabil'ity** *a.* **-dura'tion** *n.* time a thing lasts. **-du'rably** *adv.* [L. *durare*, last]

dural'umen *n.* an aluminum alloy. [Trademark. L. *durus*. hard, and aluminum]

du'rance *n.* continuance; imprisonment. [earlier *duress, q.v.*]

dur'bar *n.* levee of an Indian prince; a court. [Pers. *darbar*, court]

du'ress *n.* restraint, coercion, imprisonment; (*law*) illegal compulsion. [L. *durus*, hard]

du'ring *prep.* throughout, in the time of. [L. *durare*, last]

dur'ra *n.* Indian millet. [Arab.]

dusk *n.* darker stage of twilight; partial darkness. **-dusk'y** *a.* dark; dark colored. **-dusk'ily** *adv.* [OE. *dor*]

dust *n.* fine particles, powder, of earth or other matter, lying on a surface or blown along by the wind. -*v.t.* sprinkle with powder; rid of dust. **-dust'-cov'er** *n.* book-jacket. **-dust'er** *n.* cloth for removing dust. **dust'y** *a.* [OE.]

du'ty *n.* what one ought to do, moral or legal obligation; office, function, being occupied in these; tax on goods for the public revenue; respect. **-du'tiful** *a.* **-du'teous** *a.* **-du'tiable** *a.* liable to customs duty. - **du'ty-free** *a.* (of goods) free from duty. [AF. *duet*, what is due]

duvet' *n.* down-quilt. [F.]

dwarf *n.* very undersized person. -*a.* unusually small, stunted. -*v.t.* make stunted; make seem small by contrast. **-dwarf'ish** *a.* [OE. *dweorg*]

dwell *v.i.* live, make one's abode (in); fix one's attention, write or speak at length (on). **-dwell'ing** *n.* house. **-dwell'er** *n.* [OE. *dwellan*, linger]

dwindle *v.i.* grow less, waste away, to grow feeble. [OE. *dwinan*]

dy'archy *n.* form of government in which two (persons, *etc.*) share supreme power. [G. *di*, two, *archein*, rule]

dye (di) *v.t.* impregnate (cloth, *etc.*) with coloring matter; color thus. -*n.* coloring matter in solution which may be dissolved for dyeing; tinge, color. **-dy'er** *n.* [OE. *deagian*, v.; *deag*, *n.*]

dyke. *See* **dike.**

dynam'ics (di) *n. pl.* branch of physics dealing with force as producing or affecting motion; physical or moral forces. - **dynam'ic** *a.* of or relating to motive force, force in operation. **-dynam'ical** *a.* - **dynam'ically** *adv.* **-dy'namite** *n.* high explosive of nitroglycerin. -*v.t.* blow up with this. **-dy'namiter** *n.* **-dy'namo** *n.* machine to convert mechanical into electrical energy, generator of electricity. **-dyne** *n.* unit of force. **-dynamom'eter** *n.* instrument to measure energy expended. [G. *dynamis*, power]

dynasty (din-) *n.* line or family of hereditary rulers. **-dyn'ast** *n.* **-dynast'ic** *a.* [G. *dynastes*, prince]

dysentery (dis-) *n.* inflammatory disease of the bowels. [G. *dusenteria*]

dysgen'ic *a.* adversely affecting the race; opp. of **eugenic.** [G. *dys-*, ill, *genesis*, birth]

dyspepsia *n.* indigestion. **-dyspep'tic** *a.* and *n.* [G. *dyspepsia*]

dyspnoe'a *n.* difficulty in breathing. [G. *dys-*, ill, *pnoe*, breathing]

dysprax'ia *n.* an impairment in the control of the motor system. [G. *dys-*, ill, *praktikos*, concerned with action]

dystoc'ia *n.* abnormal, slow, or difficult childbirth, usually because of disordered or ineffective contractions of the uterus. [G. *dys-*, ill, *tokos*, childbirth]

dysprosium *n.* rare metallic element. [G. *dysprositos*, hard to get at]

E

each *a.* and *pron.* every one taken separately. [OE. *ælc*]

ea'ger (eg -) *a.* full of keen desire; keen, impatient. **-eag'erly** *adv.* **-eag'erness** *n.* [F. *aigre*, sour, keen]

ea'gle (eegl) *n.* large bird of prey with keen sight and strong flight; (golf) hole played in two under par. **-ea'glet** *n.* young eagle. [F. *aigle*]

ear *n.* organ of hearing, *esp.* external part, sensitiveness to musical sounds; attention. **-ear'drum** *n.* tympanum. **-ear'mark** *n.* owner's mark on ear of sheep, *etc.* -*v.t.* mark thus; assign or reserve for a definite purpose. **-ear' piercing** *a.* shrill. **-ear'shot** *n.* hearing distance. **-ear'wig** *n.* insect formerly thought to enter the head through the ear. [OE. *eare*]

ear *n.* spike or head of corn. [OE.]

earl (erl) *n.* peer of rank next below a marquis. -**earl′dom** *n.* [OE. *eorl,* nobleman, warrior]

earl′y (erl -) *a.* and *adv.* in the first part, or near or nearer the beginning, of some portion of time. [OE. *ærlice*]

earn (ern) *v.t.* get for labor, merit, *etc.* -**earn′ings** *n.pl.* what has been earned. [OE. *earnian*]

earnest (ern -) *a.* serious, ardent, sincere. -**earn′estness** *n.* -**earn′estly** *adv.* [OE. *eornost,* eagerness]

earnest (ern -) *n.* money paid over to bind a bargain; foretaste; token, pledge. [ME. *ernes,* corrupt. of *erles,* fr. F. *arrhes*]

earth (er-) *n.* ground, soil: dry land; planet or world we live on; mold, soil, mineral; fox's hole. -*v.t.* cover with earth; connect electrically with the earth. -**earth′en** (-th-) *a.* -**earth′ly** *a.* -**earth′y** *a.* -**earth′enware** (-th-) *n.* vessels of baked clay. -**earth′quake** *n.* volcanic convulsion of the surface of the earth. -**earth′work** *n.* bank of earth in fortification. [OE. *eorthe*]

ease (ez) *n.* comfort; freedom from constraint or annoyance or awkwardness or pain or trouble; idleness; informal position or step; relief, alleviation. -*v.t.* and *i.* to relieve of pain; reduce burden; give bodily or mental ease to; slacken, relax. -**ease′ful** *a.* -**ease′ment** *n.* (*law*) right over another's property, as right of way. -**eas′y** *a.* not difficult; free from bodily or mental pain, complaint; not in much demand; fitting loosely. -**eas′ily** *adv.* -**eas′y -go′ing** *a.* not fussy, content with things as they are. -**Easy Street** *n.* (*sl.*) a state of financial security. [F. *aise*]

eas′el (ez-) *n.* frame to support a picture, blackboard, *etc.* [Du. *ezel,* ass]

east *n.* part of the horizon where the sun-rises; regions towards that. -*a.* on or in or near the east; coming from the east. -*adv.* from, or to, the east. -**east′erly** *a.* and *adv.* from or to the east. -**east′ern** *a.* of or dwelling in the east. -**east′erner** *n.* **east′ward** *a.* and *n.* -**east′ward(s)** *adv.* [OE. *easte*]

East′er *n.* Christian festival of the resurrection of Christ. [OE. *Eastre,* goddess of spring festival]

eas′y. *See* **ease.**

eat *v.t.* and *i.* chew and swallow; swallow; consume, destroy; gnaw; wear away. -*n. pl.* (*sl.*) food ready for consumption, *usu.* of small quantity. -**eat′able** *a.* [OE. *etan*]

eaves (evz) *n. pl.* overhanging edges of a roof. -**eaves′dropper** *n.* one who stands under eaves or elsewhere to overhear. -**eaves′dropping** *n.* [OE. *efes*]

ebb *n.* flowing back of the tide; decline. -*v.i.* flow back; decline. [OE. *ebba*]

EBDIC *n.* (*compute.*) computer coding system that can represent 256 different characters [*Ex*tended *B*inary *C*oded *D*ecimal *I*nterchange *C*ode]

eb′ony *n.* hard black wood. -*a.* made of or black as ebony. -**eb′onite** *n.* vulcanite. [L. *ebenus*]

ebullient *a.* boiling; exuberant. -**ebull′ience** *n.* -**ebulli′tion** *n.* boiling; effervescence; outburst. [L. *ebullire,* boil out]

ebur′nine *a.* of, like, ivory. [L. *ebur*]

écar′té (a-kar-ta) *n.* card game for two. [F. *pp.* of *décarter,* discard]

ecau′date *a.* tailless. [L. *cauda,* tail]

ec′bole *n.* (*rhet.*) digression. [G.]

eccentric (-its-) *a.* not placed, or nothaving the axis placed, centrally; not circular (in orbit); irregular; odd, whimsical. -*n.* mechanical contrivance to change circular into to-and-fro movement, whimsical person -**eccen′trically** *adv.* -**eccentri′city** *n.* [G. *ekkentros,* out of center]

ecchymo′sis (ek-ki-) *n.* discoloration due to subcutaneous bleeding. [G. *ek,* out of, *chymos,* juice]

ecclesiastic (-klez-) *a.* of or belonging to the church- clergyman. -**ecclesias′tical** *a.* -**ecclesiol′ogy** *n.* science of church-building and decoration. [G. *ekklesiastikos, ekkiesia,* church]

ech′elon (ash -e -long) *n.* formation of troops or warships in parallel divisions each with its front clear of the one in front. [F. *echelon,* rung of ladder]

echid′na (ek -) *n.* Australian spiny anteater. [G. = viper]

echi′nus (ek -in -) *n.* sea urchin. [G. *echinos,* hedgehog]

ech′o (ek -) *n.* repetition of sounds by reflection; close imitation. -*v.i.* resound or be repeated by echo. -*v.t.* repeat as an echo; imitate opinions. [G.]

éclair *n.* cake finger filled with cream and iced. [F.]

eclat′ *n.* social distinction; brilliancy; ''sunburst' effect. [F.]

eclec′tic *a.* borrowing one's philosophy from various sources; catholic in views or taste. -*n.* eclectic person. -**eclec′ticism** *n.* [G. *eklektikos,* selective]

eclipse′ *n.* blotting out of the sun, moon, *etc.*, by another body coming between it and the eye or between it and the source of its light; loss of light or brilliance;

obscurity. -*v.t.* cause to suffer eclipse; outshine, surpass. -**eclip'tic** *a.* of an eclipse. -*n.* apparent path of the sun. [G. *ekleipsis*, leave out]

ec'logue (-og) *n.* short poem, *esp.* apastoral dialogue. [G. *ekloge*, selection]

ecol'ogy *n.* the science devoted to the system of interrelationships between organisms and their environments; the totality of these interrelationships; activity undertaken to maintain or restore the balance of nature. -**e'cological** *a.* relating to ecology; benefiting the balance of nature. -**ecol'ogist** *n.* one who studies ecology; an activist in ecological matters. [G. *oikos*, house]

econ'omy *n.* management, administration; thrift, frugal use, structure, organization. -**econom'ic** *a.* on business lines. **econom'ics** *n. pl.* political economy, the science of the production and distribution of wealth. **econom'ical** *a.* saving, frugal; of economics. **econom'ically** *adv.* -**econ'omist** *n.* -**econ'omize** *v.t.* and *i.* [G. *oikonomia*, house -law]

ecru' *n.* and *a.* color of unbleached linen. [F.]

ec'stasy *n.* exalted state of feeling, rapture; trance; frenzy. -**ecstat'ic** *a.* -**ecstat'ically** *adv.* [G. *ekstasis*]

ectoplasm *n.* in spiritualism, a semi-luminous plastic substance which exudes from the body of the medium. [G. *ektos*, outside, and *plasma*, mold]

ecumen'ic(al) *a.* pert. to the universe of the Christian world or church. -**ecumeni'city** *n.* [G. *oiken*, inhabit]

ec'zema *n.* skin disease. [G. *ekzema*]

Ed'das *n. pl.* **Eld'er Ed'da** (pre-12th *c.*), **Young'er Ed'da** (13th *c.*), old Norse mythology in poetry, prose. [Ice. = great-grandmother]

edd'y *n.* small whirl in water, smoke, *etc.* -*v.i.* move in whirls. [orig. uncertain]

ed'elweiss (a-del-vis) *n.* Alpine plant with white flower. [Ger. = noble white]

Ed'en *n.* garden of Adam and Eve; ideal spot. [Heb.]

eden'tate *a.* toothless. [L. *edentatus*]

edge *n.* cutting side of a blade; sharpness; border, boundary. -*v.t.* sharpen give an edge or border to; move gradually. -*v.i.* advance sideways or gradually. -**edge'ways, edge'wise** *adv.* -**ed'gy** *a.* irritable. -**on edge**, nervous, excited. [OE. *ecg*]

ed'ible *a.* eatable. -**edibil'ity** *n.* [L. *edibilis*, *edere*, eat]

e'dict *n.* order proclaimed by authority, adecree. [L. *edictum*]

ed'ifice (-fis) building, *esp.* a big one. -**ed'ify** *v.t.* improve morally. -**edifica'tion** *n.* [L. *edificare*, build]

ed'it *v.t.* prepare for publication. -**ed'ition** *n.* form in which a book is published; number of copies of a book, newspaper, *etc.*; printed at one time, issue. -**ed'itor** *n.* -**ed'itress** *fem.* -**edit-or'ial** *a.* of an editor. -*n.* newspaper article written or sanctioned by the editor. (L. *edere*, give out]

ed'ucate *v.t.* bring up; train mentally and morally; provide schooling for; train. **educa'tion** *n.* -**educa'tional** *a.* -**educationally** *adv.* **ed'ucable** *a.* -**educabil'ity** *n.* **edu'cator** *n.* -**educationalist** *n.* -**ed'ucative** *a.* [L. *educare, educat* -]

educe' *v.t.* bring out, develop; infer. -**edu'cible** deduction *n.* -**educ'tor** *n.* [L. *educere*, lead out]

eel *n.* snakelike fish. [OE. *sæl*]

ee'rie, ee'ry *a.* weird; superstitiously timid. [OE. *earg*, cowardly]

efface' *v.t.* wipe or rub out. -**effacement** *n.* [F. *effacer*]

effect' *n.* result, consequence; impression. -*pl.* property. -*v.t.* bring about, accomplish. -**effect'ive** *a.* -**effect'ively***adv.* -**effect'ual** *a.* -**effect'ually** *adv.* -**effect'uate** *v.t.* [L. *efficere, effect* -, bringabout]

effem'inate *a.* womanish, unmanly. -**effem'inacy** *n.* [L. *effeminate*, fr. *femina*, woman]

effen'di *n.* formerly in Turkey, title of respect; sir. [G. *authentes*, autocrat]

ef'ferent *a.* bearing outward, away. [L. *efferre*, fr. *ferre*, carry]

effervesce' (-es) *v.i* give off bubbles; issue in bubbles. -**efferves'cent** *a.* -**efferves'cence** *n.* [L. *effervescere*]

effete' *a.* worn -out, feeble. [L. *effetus*, exhausted by breeding]

efficacious *a.* producing or sure to produce a desired result. -**efficacy** *n.* [L. *efficere*, effect]

effi'cient *a.* capable, competent; producing effect. **effi'ciently** *adv.* -**effi'ciency** *n.* [L. *eflicere*, effect]

eff'igy *n.* image, likeness. [L. *effigies*, fr. *fingere*, form]

effloresce' (-es) *v.i.* burst into flower. -**efflores'cent** *a.* -**efflores'cence** *n.* [L. *efflorescere*, blossom]

eff'luent *n.* flowing out. -*n.* streamflowing from a larger stream, lake, *etc.* -**eff'luence** *n.* -**efflu'vium** *n.* (*pl.* -**ia**) invisible vapors, *esp.* those affecting lungs or sense of smell. -**eff'lux** *n.* -**efflux'ion** *n.* [L. *effluere*, flow out]

eff'ort *n.* exertion, endeavor. -**eff'ort-less** *a.* [F., fr. L. *fortis*, strong]

effrontery (-un-) *n.* brazen impudence. [F. *effronto a. lit.* without brow (for blushing)]

efful'gent *a.* radiant, shining brightly. -**efful'gence** *n.* [L. *fulgere*, shine]

effu'sion *n.* a pouring out; literary composition. -**effu'sive** *a.* gushing, demonstrative. -**effu'sively** *adv.* -**effu'siveness** *n.* -**effuse'** *v.t.* to pour out. [L. *effundere, effus* -, pour out]

eft *n.* newt. [OE. *efete*, cp. *newt*]

egg *n.* oval body produced by the female of birds, *etc., esp.* of domestic fowl, and containing the germ of their young. -**egg-flip** *n.* drink composed of wine and beaten egg. -**egg'-plant** *n.* plant with an edible, purpleskinned fruit of pearshaped form; the fruit of this plant, aubergine. [ON.]

egg *v.t.* egg on, encourage, urge. [ON. *eggia*, fr. *egg*, edge]

eglantine *n.* sweet briar. [F.]

eg'o *n.* the self, the conscious thinkingsubject. -**egocen'tric** *a.* self-centered. -**eg'oism** *n.* systematic selfishness; theory that bases morality on self-interest. -**eg'oist** *n.* -**egois'tic, egois'tical** *a.* -**eg'otism** *n.* talking habitually about oneself, self -conceit. -**eg'otist** *n.* -**egotis'tic, egotistical** *a.* [L. = I]

egregious (-jus) *a.* gross, notable *esp.* absurdly, as egregious as, blunder, *etc.* [L. *egregius*, out of the flock]

e'gress *n.* way out. [L. *egressus*]

e'gret *n.* lesser white heron. [F. *aigrette*]

ei'der (-i-) *n.* Arctic duck. -**ei'derdown** *n.* breast feathers of the eider; quilt stuffed with eider down. [ON. *æthr*]

eight (at) *a.* and *n.* cardinal number, one above seven. -**eighth** (at -th) *a.* ordinal number. -**eighth'ly** *adv.* -**eighteen'** *a.* and *n.* eight more than ten. -**eighteenth** *a.* -**eighteenth'ly** *adv.* -**eight'y** *a.* and *n.* ten times eight. -**eight'ieth** *a.* -**eight'fold** *a.* -**eighteen-fold** *a.* -**eight'yfold** *a.* -**eight** *n.* an eight-oared boat; its crew. -**fig'ure-of-eight** *n.* skating figure; any figure shaped as 8. [OE. *eahta*]

eistedd'fod (as-teTH'vod) *n.* congress of Welsh bards. [W. = session]

eith'er (-TH-) *a.* and *pron.* one or the other; one of two; each. -*adv.* or *conj.* bringing in first of alternatives or strengthening an added negation. [OE. *æther*]

ejaculate *v.t.* and *i.* exclaim, utter suddenly. -**ejacula'tion** *n.* -**ejac'ulatory** *a.* [L. *ejaculari*, shoot forth]

eject' *v.t.* throw out; expel, drive out. -**ejec'tion** *n.* -**eject'or** *n.* -**eject'ment** *n.* [L. *ejicere, eject-*, throw out]

eke *v.t.* eke out, supply deficiencies of, make with difficulty (a living, *etc.*). [OE. *ecan*, increase]

elaborate *v.t.* work out in detail; produce by labor. -*a.* worked out in detail; highly finished; complicated. -**elaboration** *n.* [L. *elaborate*]

élan' (a-long) *n.* verve, dash. [F.]

e'land *n.* S. African antelope. [Du.]

elapse' *v.i.* of time, to pass by. [L. *elabi, elaps-*, slip away]

elas'tic *a.* resuming normal shape after distortion; springy; not unalterable or inflexible. -*n.* cord, fabric, made elastic with interwoven rubber. -**elasti'city** *n.* [G. *elastikos*]

ela'tion *n.* high spirits; pride. -**elate'** *v.t.* [L. *elatus, pp.* of *efferre*, bring out]

el'bow *n,* outer part of the joint between the upper arm and the forearm. -*v.t.* thrust, jostle with the elbows. [OE. *elnboga*]

eld *n.* antiquity; old age. [OE. *eald*, old]

el'der *n.* a white -flowered tree with muchpitb. [OE. *ellern*]

el'der *a.* older. -*n.* person of greater age; old person; official of certain churches. -**el'derly** *a.* growing old. -**elédest** *a.* oldest. [*old*]

El Dora'do *n.* fictitious country rich in gold. [Sp. = the golden]

elect *v.t.* choose; choose by vote. -*a.* chosen; select, choice. -**elec'tion** *n.* choosing, *esp.* by voting -**electioneer'** to busy oneself in political elections. -**elect'ive** *a.* appointed, filled, chosen by election. -**elect'or** *n.* -**elect'oral** *a.* -**elect'orate** *n.* body of electors. [L. *eligere, elect-*, fr. *legere*, choose]

electricity (-is'-) *n.* active condition ofthe molecules of a body or of the etherround it, produced by friction, magnetism, *etc.*; force which shows itself in lightning, *etc.*; study of this. -**elec'tric** *a.* of, charged with, worked by, producing, electricity. -**elec'trical** *a.* -**elec'trically** *adv.* **elec'-trify** *v.t.* -**electrifica'tion** *n.* **electri'cian** *n.* [G. *elektron*, amber (the first substance observed to develop frictional electricity)]

elec'tro- *prefix* makes compounds meaning of, by, caused by, electricity, as. **elec'trobiol'ogy** *n.* science of electrical phenomena in living creatures. -

electrodynam'ics *n.* dynamics of electricity. **-elec'tro-mag'net** *n.* - **electrol'ysis** *n.* electrical decomposition of a chemical compound. **-elec'troscope** *n.* instrument to show the presence or kind of electricity. **-elec'trocute** *v.t.* cause deathby electric shock; execute (criminals) by electricity. - **elec'tromo'bile** *n.* vehicle run on self-generated electrical power. - **electrother'apy** *n.* treatment of disease. -and many other compound words. [G. *electron*, amber]

elec'trode *n.* terminal of electric circuit; conductor leading current into, out of, water or gas. [G. *hodos*, way]

elec'tron *n.* one of fundamental particles of matter identified with unit of charge of negative electricity and essential component of the atom. **-electron'ic** *a.* of electrons or electronics; using devices, such as semiconductors, transistors or valves, dependent on action of electrons. - **electron'ics** *pl. n.* technology concerned with development of electronic devices and circuits; science of behavior and control of electrons. **electron'ic brain** *n.* (*sl.*) electronic computer. **-electron'ic da'ta processing** *n.* data processing largely performed by electronic equipment. - **electron'ic mu'sic** *n.* music consisting of sounds produced by electric currents prerecorded on magnetic tape. - **electron'ic or'gan** *n.* keyboard instrument in which sounds are produced by electronic or electrical means. **-elec'tron microscope** *n.* microscope that uses electrons and electron lenses to produce magnified image. **-elec'tron tube** *n.* electrical device, such as valve, in which flow of electrons between electrodes takes place. **-elec'tron volt** unit of energy used in nuclear physics. [G. *electron*, amber]

eleemosynary *a.* charitable. [G. *eleemosyne*, charity]

el'egant *a.* graceful, tasteful; refined. - **el'egance** *n.* [L. *elegans*]

el'egy *n.* lament for the dead; sad poem. **-elegi'ac** *a.* plaintive. *-n.pl.* elegiac verses. [G. *elegeia*]

el'ement *n.* component part; substance which cannot be chemically analyzed; proper abode or sphere; resistance wire of electric heater. *-pl.* powers of the atmosphere; rudiments, first principles. - **elemental** *a.* of the powers of nature; tremendous; not compounded. - **element'ary** *a.* rudimentary, simple; primary. [L. *elementum*]

el'emi *n.* fragrant resin used in varnishes, *etc.* [Sp., It., orig. uncertain]

elench'us (e-lengk-) *n.* (logic) refutation of an argument. [G. *elengchos*]

el'ephant *n.* very big four-footed, thick-skinned animal with ivory tusks and a long trunk. **-elephant'ine** *a.* unwieldy, clumsy, heavily big. **-elephanti'asis** *n.* a skin disease. **-ele'phant seal** *n.* largest of the seals. [L. *elephas*]

el'evate *v.t.* raise, lift up. **-eleva'tion** *n.* raising; angle above the horizon, as of a gun; drawing of one side of a building, *etc.* **-el'evator** *n.* lift or hoist. [L. *elevare*]

elev'en *a.* and *n.* number next above ten, one added to ten; team of eleven persons. **-elev'enth** *a.* the ordinal number. - **elev'enthly** *adv.* **elev'enfold** *a.* and *adv.* [OE. *endleofan*]

elf *n.* fairy; small elemental being. **-elf'in, elf'ish, elv'ish** *a.* [OE. *ælf*]

elic'it (-a-) *v.t.* draw out. [L. *elicere*]

elide' *v.t.* omit in pronunciation (a vowel, syllable). **-elis'ion** *n.* [L. *elidere*, strike out]

el'igible *a.* fit or qualified to be chosen; suitable, desirable. **eligibil'ity** *n.* [L. *eligibilis -eligere*, fr. *legere*, choose]

eliminate *v.t.* remove, get rid of, set aside. **-elimina'tion** *n.* [E. *oliminare*, put out of doors]

eli'sion. *See* **elide.**

elite' *n.* pick of (society, *etc.*).

elix'ir *n.* preparation sought by the alchemists to change base metals into gold, or to prolong life; sovereign remedy. [Arab. *al-iksiri*]

elk *n.* large deer. [OE. *eoth*]

ell *n.* measure of length. [OE. *eln*]

ellipse' *n.* an oval; figure made by a plane cutting a cone at a smaller angle with the side than the base makes; *gram.* omission of words needed to complete the grammatical construction or full sense. - **ellip'sis** *n. gram.* ellipse. **-ellip'tic, ellip'tical** *a.* **-ellip'tically** *adv.* [L. *ellipsis*]

elm *n.* familiar tall tree with doubly-serrated leaves; its wood. [OE.]

elocution *n.* art of public speaking, recitation, voice, management. **-elocu'tionist** *n.* [L. *eloqui*, speak out]

e'longate *v.t.* lengthen. **-elonga'tion** *n.* [L. *e*, out, *longus*, long]

elope' *v.i.* run away with a lover; escape. **-elope'ment** *n.* [AF. *aloper*]

eloquence *n.* fluent and powerful use of language. **-el'oquent** *a.* **el'oquently** *adv.* [L. *eloqui*, speak out]

else *adv.* besides; otherwise. *-pron.* other.

-**elsewhere** *adv.* in or to someother place. [OE. *elles,* otherwise]

elu'cidate *v.t.* throw light upon, explain. -**elucida'tion** *n.* -**elu'cidatory** *a.* [L. *lucidus,* bright]

elude' (z) *v.t.* escape, slip away from, dodge. -**elu'sion** *n.* -**elu'sive** *a.* **elusory** *a.* **elusively** *adv.* [L. *eludere,* play off]

elv'ish. *See* **elf.**

Elys'ium *n.* (Greek myth.) abode of the happy dead. -**Elys'ian** *a.* [G. *elysion*]

em *n.* (*printing*) the square of any size of-type. [m.]

ema'ciate (shi-) *v.t.* to make lean. -**emacia'tion** *n.* [L. *emaciare,* emaciate, fr. *macies,* leanness]

em'anate *v.i.* issue from, originate. -**emana'tion** *n.* [L. *emanare,* flow out]

emancipate *v.t.* set free. -**emancipa'-tion** *n.* -**eman'cipator** *n.* -**eman'cipatory** *a.* [L. *emancipate,* emancipate]

emasculate *v.t.* castrate; enfeeble, weaken. -**emascula'tion** *n.* -**emas'cu-lative** *a.* [L. *emasculate*]

embalm' (-bam) *v.t.* preserve (dead body) from decay with spices, *etc.*; perfume; reverently preserve (*e.g.*, a memory). [*balm*]

embankment *n.* mound to carry road, railway, prevent overflow of river, *etc.* -**embank'** *v.t.* [*bank*]

embar'go *n.* order stopping the movement of ships; suspension of commerce; ban. -*v.t.* put under an embargo. [Sp.]

embark' *v.t.* and *i.* put, go, on board ship; engage, involve (in). **embarka'tion** *n.* [F. *embarquer,* cp. bark]

embarrass *v.t.* perplex, put into difficulty; encumber. -**embarr'assment** *n.* [F. *embarrasser,* orig. put within 'bars']

em'bassy *n.* office or work or residence of an ambassador; deputation. [*ambassador*]

embatt'le *v.t.* provide with battlements. -**embatt'led** *a.* [*See* **battlement**]

embed', imbed' *v.t.* fix fast in something solid. [*bed*]

embellish *v.t.* adorn. -**embell'ishment** *n.* [F. *embellir*]

em'ber *n.* glowing cinder. [OE. *æmerge*]

em'ber *a.* Ember-days, days appointed by the Church for fasting, recurring in each of the four seasons. [OE. *ymbryne,* revolution, period]

embez'zle *v.t.* divert fraudulently, misappropriate (money in trust, *etc.*). -**embez'zler** *n.* -**embez'zlement** *n.* [AF. *embesiler,* damage, steal]

embitter *v.t.* make bitter. [*bitter*]

emblazon *v.t.* depict in a coat -of -arms; deck in bright colors; praise widely. [F. *blason,* coat-of-arms]

em'blem *n.* symbol; heraldic device -**emblemat'ic** *a.* **emblemat'icall y** *adv.* [G. *emblems,* inlaid work]

embod'y *v.t.* give body, concrete expression, to; represent, be an expression of. **embod'iment** *n.* [*body*]

embold'en *v.t.* encourage. [*bold*]

em'bolism *n.* obstruction of artery by blood clot. [G. *embolismos,* what is thrown in]

embonpoint' *n.* plumpness. *a.* (F.]

emboss' *v.t.* mold, stamp or carve in relief. [OF. *embosser,* cp. *boss*]

embour'geoisement (-zhwa) *n.* the process of becoming middle class; the assimilation into the middle class of traditionally working-class people. [Fr. *bourgeois,* middle-class]

embrace' *v.t.* clasp in the arms; seize, avail oneself of, accept. -*n.* clasping in the arms. [F. *embrasser*]

embrasure (-zher) *n.* opening in a wall for a cannon; bevelling of a wall at the sides of a window. [F.]

embroca'tion *n.* lotion for rubbing limbs, *etc.* [G. *embroche,* lotion]

embroider *v.t.* ornament with needlework; embellish, exaggerate (a story). -**embroi'dery** *n.* [F. *broder*]

embroil *v.t.* bring into confusion; involve in hostility. -**embroil'ment** *n.* [F. *embrouiller,* entangle]

em'bryo *n.* unborn or undeveloped offspring, germ; undeveloped thing. -**embryon'ic** *a.* -**embryol'ogy** *n.* -**embryol'ogist** *n.* [G. *embryon*]

emend' *v.t.* remove errors from, correct. -**emenda'tion** *n.* -**e'mendator** *n.* [L. *emendare, emendat-,* fr. *menda,* fault]

em'erald *n.* green precious stone. *a.* of the color of emerald. [F. *emeraude*]

emerge' *v.i.* come up, out; rise to notice; come out on inquiry. -**emer'gence** *n.* -**emer'gent** *a.* -**emer'gency** *n.* sudden unforeseen thing or event needing prompt action. [L. *emergere*]

emer'itus *a.* retired, honorably discharged, *esp.* of a professor. [L.]

em'ery *n.* hard mineral used for polishing. [F. *émeri*]

emet'ic *a.* causing vomiting. -*n.* medicine doing this. [G. *emetikos*]

em'igrate *v.t.* go and settle in another country. -**emigra'tion** *n.* **em'igrant** *n.* [L.

emigrare]

em'inent *a.* distinguished, notable. -**em'inently** *adv.* -**em'inence** *n.* distinction; rising ground. -**Em'inence**, title of cardinal. [L. *eminere*, stand out]

emir' title given to Arab chief and to descendants of Mohammad. [Arab. *amir*, ruler]

emit' *v.t.* give out, put forth. -**emitt'er** *n.* -**emis'sion** *a.* -**em'issary** *n.* one sen tout on a mission. -**emissiv'ity** *n.* power of emitting. [L. *emittere*]

emm'et *n.* ant. [OE. *aemete*]

emollient *a.* softening. -*n.* ointment or other softening application. [L. *emollire*, soften]

emolument *n.* pay, profit. [L. *emolumentum*, fr. *moliri*, toil]

emo'tion *n.* mental agitation, excited state of feeling. -**emo'tional** *a.* given to emotion; appealing to the emotions. [L. *emotio*, fr. *emovere*, stir]

em'pathy *n.* ability to enter fully into another's feelings, experience. [G. *en*, in, *pathos*, feeling]

em'peror *n.* sovereign of an empire. -**em'press** *fem.* [L. *imperator*, fr. *imperare*, command]

em'phasis *n.* stress on words; vigor of speech, expression; importance attached. *n.* -**em'phasize** *v.t.* **emphat'ic** *a.* forcible; stressed. -**emphat'ically** *adv.* tG.]

em'pire *n.* large territory, *esp.* an aggregate of states under one supreme control. [F. fr. L. *imperium*]

empiric *a.* relying on experiment or experience, not on theory. -*n.* empiric scientist, physician. -**empir'ically** *adv.* -**empir'icism** *n.* [G. *ernpeirikos*, experienced]

emplacement *n.* platform or other prepared position for guns. [*place*]

emplane' *v.i.* board aircraft. [*airplane*]

employ' *n.* use; keep occupied; use theservices of, keep in one's service. -**employ'er** *n.* -**employee'** *n.* -**employ'ment** *n.* [F. *employer*]

emporium *n.* center of commerce; (in affected language) store. [L. *mart*]

empow'er *v.t.* enable, authorize [*power*]

em'press. *See* **emperor.**

empresse'ment (ong-pres-mong) *n.* cordiality. [F.]

emp'ty *a.* containing nothing; unoccupied; senseless; vain, foolish. -*v.t.* and *i.* make or become empty. -*n.* empty box, basket, *etc.* -**emp'tiness** *n.* [OE. *æmettig*]

empy'ma *n.* collection of pus in the pleura. [G. *em*, in, *pyon*, pus]

empyre'an *n.* sky. *a.* -**empyre'al** *a.* of the heavens; sublime. [G. *empyros*, fiery]

e'mu *n.* large Australian bird like an ostrich. [Port. *ema*, ostrich]

em'ulate *v.t.* strive to equal or excel; imitate. -**em'utator** *n.* **emula'tion** *n.* competition, rivalry. -**em'ulative** *a.* -**em'ulous** *a.* [L. *æmulari*, rival]

emul'sion *n.* milky liquid mixture withoily or resinous particles in suspension. -**emul'sifier** *n.* an agent that forms or preserves an emulsion, *esp.* any food additive that prevents separation of sauces or other processed foods. -**emul'sive** *a.* -**emul'sify** *v.t.* [L. *mulgere*, milk]

en- *prefix* forms verbs with sense of putin, into, on; as: **engulf'** *v.t.* swallow up. -**enrage'** *v.t.* to put into a rage. Many such words are omitted and the meaning and derivation should be sought under the simple word. [F. *en*, L. *in*]

en (*typography*) half of an **em** (*q.v.*)

ena'ble *v.t.* make able, authorize; give power or strength. [*able*]

enact' *v.t.* make law; play, act. [act]

enam'el *n.* glasslike coating applied to metal, *etc.* to preserve the surface; coating of the teeth; any hard outer coating. -*v.t.* cover with enamel; adorn with colors. [*en-*, and obs. *amel*, F. *émail*, enamel]

enam'or (-er) *v.t.* inspire with love. [F. *enamourer*]

encamp' *v.t.* and *i* settle in a camp. -**encamp'ment** *n.* [*camp*]

encaustic *a.* burnt in. -*n.* art of burning colored designs into tiles, *etc.* [G. *enkaustikos*, burnt in]

enceinte' *a.* (of a woman) pregnant. -*n.* (in fortification) an enclosure. [F.]

encephalitis *n.* inflammation of the brain. -**encephali'tis lethar'gica**, sleeping sickness. [G. *Kephale*, head]

enchant' (-a-) *v.t.* bewitch, delight. -**enchant'ment** *n.* -**enchant'er** *n.* -**enchantress** *fem.* [F. *enchanter*]

encir'cle *v.t.* surround; embrace; go round. [*circle*]

enclave' *n.* portion of territory entirely surrounded by foreign land. [F.]

enclit'ic *a.* inclined; (*gram.*) pronounced as part of (another word). -*a.* enclitic word. [G. *enklitikus*]

enclose' *v.t.* shut; place in with something else (in a letter, *etc.*); fence, *esp.* common land. -**enclo'sure** (zher) *n.* [*close*]

enco'mium *n.* formal praise; eulogy. -**enco'miast** *n.* -**encomias'tic** *a.* [L.]

encom'pass (-kum-) *v.t.* surround; include. [*compass*]
en'core *interj.* again, once more. -*n.* call for the repetition of a song, *etc.*; the repetition. -*v.t.* call for repetition. [F.]
encounter *v.t.* meet in hostility; meet with. -*n.* hostile or casual meeting. [OF. *encontrer*]
encourage (-kur-) *v.t.* hearten, inspirit. -**encouragement** *n.* [*courage*]
en'craty *n.* self-control. [G. *en*, in, *kratos*, strength]
en'crinite *n.* fossil crinoid, stone-lily. [G. *en*, in, *krinon*, lily]
encroach' *v.i* intrude (on) as a usurper. -**encroach'ment** *n.* [F. *accrocher*, hook on]
encrust' *v.i.* cover with hard coating crust. [L. *incrustare*]
encrypt' *v.t.* put (a message) into code; to put (computer data) into a coded form; to distort (a television or other signal) so that it cannot be understood without the appropriate decryption equipment. -**encrypted** *a.* -**en'cryption** *n.* [G. *kryptein*, hide]
encum'ber *v.t.* hamper; burden. -**encum'brance** *n.* [OF. *encombrer*]
encyc'lical *n.* circular letter from pope to bishops, on public affairs, *etc.* (G. *kyklos*, circle]
encyclope'dia, encyclopae'dia *n.* book of information on all subjects, or on every branch of a subject, usually arranged alphabetically. -**encyclope'dic, encyclopae'dic** *a.* -**encyclope'dist, encyclopae'dist** *n.* (fr. G. *enkyklios paideia*, all-round education]
end *n.* limit; extremity; conclusion; fragment; latter part; death; event, issue; purpose, aim. -*v.t.* put an end to. -*v.i.* come to an end. -**end'ing** *n.* -**end'less** *a.* -**endpapers** *n.pl.* blank pages at beginning and end of book. **end'ways** *adv.* [OE. *ende*]
endang'er *v.t.* expose to danger. -**endangered** *a.* in danger; used *esp.* of animals in danger of extinction. [F. fr. L. *dominium*, rule]
endeav'or (-dev-er) *v.i* try, attempt. -*n.* attempt, effort. [F. *devoir*, duty]
endec'agon. *See* **hendecagon.**
endem'ic *a.* regularly existing or found in a country or district. -*n.* -**endemic disease.** [G. *en*, in, *demos*, people]
en'dive *n.* curly-leaved chicory. (F.]
en'docarp *n.* inner shell, coat, of fruit. [G. *endon*, within, *karpos*, fruit]
en'docrine *n.* substance absorbed from the ductless glands into the bloodstream. *a.* -**endocrinol'ogy** *n.* [fr. G. *endon*, within, *krinein*, to separate]
en'dogen (-j-) *n.* plant growing from within. **endog'enous** *a.* [G. *endon*, within, *gener*, barn]
endorse' *v.t.* write (*esp.* sign one's name) on the back of, ratify; confirm. -**endorse'ment** *n.* [F. *endosser*, fr. *dos*, back]
endow' *v.t.* provide a permanent income for; furnish. -**endow'ment** *n.* [OF. *endouer*]
endue' *v.t.* invest, furnish (with aquality, *etc.*). [OF. *enduire*]
endure' *v.i* last. -*v.t.* undergo; tolerate, put up with. -**endu'rance** *n.* power of enduring. -**endu'rable** *a.* [L. *indurate*, fr. *durus*, hard]
ene'ma, en'ema *n.* rectal injection; instrument for this. [G. *enienai*, send in]
en'emy *n.* hostile person, opponent; armed foe; hostile force or ship. (F. *ennemi*, fr. L. *inimicus*]
en'ergy *n.* vigor, force, activity. -**energet'ic** *a.* -**energet'ically** *adv.* -**en'ergize** *v.t.* give vigor to. [F. *Onergie*]
en'ervate *v.t.* weaken, deprive of vigor. -**enerva'tion** *n.* [L. *enervare*, deprive of sinew]
enfee'ble *v.t.* weaken. -**enfee'blement** *n.* [*feeble*]
enfeoff' (-fef) *v.t.* give fief to, surrender. -**enfeoff'ment** *n.* [*fief*]
en'filade *n.* fire from artillery, *etc.*, sweeping a line from end to end. -*v.t.* subject to enfilade; a vista. [F. *enfiler*, string on a thread]
enfold' *v.t.* enwrap; encompass. [*fold*]
enforce' *v.t.* compel obedience to; impose (action) upon; drive home. -**enforce'ment** *n.* -**enforce'able** *a.* [OF. *enforcier*, strengthen]
enfran'chise *v.t.* give the right of voting for members of parliament; give parliamentary representation to; set free. -**enfran'chisement** *n.* [*franchise*]
engage' *v.t.* bind by contract or promise; hire; order; pledge oneself, undertake; attract, occupy; bring into conflict; interlock. -*v.i.* begin to fight; employ oneself (in); promise. -**engage'ment** *n.* [F. *engager-gage*, pledge]
engen'der *v.t.* give rise to, beget; sow the seeds of. [F. *engendrer*]
en'gine *n.* complex mechanical contrivance; machine; instrument of war. -**engineer'** *n.* one who constructs or is in charge of engines, military works, or

works of public utility (*e.g.* bridges, roads). -*v.t.* construct as an engineer; contrive. [F. *engin*, fr. L. *ingenium*, skill]

English (ing'gl-) *a.* of England. -*n.* language or people of England and of all peoples who have adopted this language. [OE. *Englise*]

engraft' (-a-) *v.t.* graft in [*graft*]

engrain' *v.t.* dye deep; implant firmly. [*grain*, cochineal dye]

engrave' *v.t.* and *i.* cut in lines on metal for printing; carve, incise; impress deeply. -**engra'ving** *n.* copy of a picture printed from an engraved plate. -**engra'ver** *n.* [*grave*]

engross' *v.t.* write out in large letters or in legal form; absorb (attention). -**engross'ment** *n.* [AF. *engrosser*, fr. *grosse*, large (letter)]

enhance' *v.t.* heighten, intensify, raise in price. -**enhance'ment** *n.* -**enhanc' ive** *a.* [F. *hausser*, rasie]

enig'ma *n.* riddle; puzzling thing or person. -**enigmat'ic, enigmatical** *a.* -**enigmat'ically** *adv.* [G. *ainigma*]

enja'mbment (in-ja'm-ment) *n.* inverse, continuation of sense beyond end of line. [F. *enjamber*, stride, encroach]

enjoin' *v.t.* command, impose, prescribe. [F. *enjoindre*]

enjoy' *v.t.* take pleasure in; have the use or benefit of. -*v. refl.* be happy. -**enjoy'ment** *n.* -**enjoy'able** *a.* [*joy*]

enlarge' *v.t.* make bigger; set free. -*v.i.* grow bigger; talk at large (with on) -**enlarge'ment** *n.* [*large*]

enlighten (-lit-) *v.t.* instruct, inform. -**enlight'ened** *a.* factually well-informed, tolerant of alternative opinions, and guided by rational thought; privy to or claiming a sense of spiritual or religious revelation of truth. -**enlight'enment** *n.* [*light*]

enlist' *v.t.* and *i.* engage as a soldier or helper; gain (sympathies, *etc.*). -**enlistment** *n.* [*list*]

enli'ven *v.t.* brighten, make more lively or cheerful. [*life*]

enmesh' *v.t.* entangle; take in a net (*lit.* or *fig*). [*mesh*]

en'mity *n.* ill -will; hostility. [AF. *enimitg*]

enno'ble (-n-n-) *v.t.* make noble; raise to the peerage. [*noble*]

ennui' *n.* boredom. [F.]

enor'mous *a.* very big, vast. -**enor'mity** *n.* gross offense; great wickedness. [L. *enormis*, abnormal]

enough' (e-nuf) *a.* as much or as manyas need be, sufficient. -*n.* sufficient quantity. *adv.* sufficiently. -**enow'** *a.*, *n.*, and *adv.* enough. [OE. *genog*]

enounce' *v.t.* enunciate. (F. *énoneer*]

enquire'. *See* **inquire.**

enrich' *v.t.* make rich; add to. -**enrich'ment** *n.* [*rich*]

enroll', enrol' *v.t.* write the name on a roll or list; engage, enlist, take in as a member; enter, record. -**enroll'ment** *n.* [F. *enrôler*]

ensconce' *v.t.* place snugly, comfortably in safety. [*sconce*]

ensem'ble *n.* effect of any combination regarded as a whole; woman's matching dress; (*mus.*) concerted piece, passage. [F.]

en'sign (-sin) *n.* naval or military flag; badge, emblem; a commissioned officer of the lowest rank. [F. *enseigne*]

en'silage *n.* storing of fodder in a silo; fodder so stored. [F.]

enslave' *v.t.* make into a slave. -**enslave'ment** *n.* -**ensla'ver** *n.* [*slave*]

ensue' *v.i* follow, happen, after; result from. -*v.t.* strive for. [F. *ensuiure,* fr. L. *insequi*, follow up]

ensure' *v.t.* make safe, certain to happen. [F. *assurer*, cp. *assure*]

entab'lature *n.* in architecture, part resting on capital of column. [L. *tabula*, table]

entail' *v.t.* settle (land, *etc.*) on persons in succession, none of whom can then dispose of it; involve as result. -*n.* such settlement. [F. *entailler*, cut into]

entang'le (-ng-gi) *v.t.* entwine; involve; ensnare. -**entang'lement** *n.* [tangle]

entel'echy (-k-) *n.* (*philos.*) life-principle realizing itself in the organism. [G. *teleos,* complete]

entente' (ong-tongt) *n.* a friendly understanding between nations. [F.]

ent'er *v.t.* go or come into; join (a society, *etc.*); write in, register. -*v.i.* go or come in; join; begin; engage. -**en'trance** *n.* going or coming in; right to enter; fee paid for this; door or passage to enter. -**en'trant** *n.* one who enters, *esp.* a contest. -**en'try** *n.* entrance; an entering; item entered, *e.g.*, in an account, list. -**en'tryism** *n.* the policy or practice of members of a particular political group joining an existing political party with the intentionof changing its principles and policies, instead of forming a new party. -**en'tryist** *n.*, *a.* [F. *entrer*]

enter'ic *n.* typhoid fever. *a.* typhoid; of the intestines. [G. *enterikos*]

en'terprise *n.* design, undertaking, usually a bold or difficult one; -**enterprising** *a.* bold and active in spirit. [F.]

entertain′ *v.t.* receive as guest; amuse; maintain; consider favorably, cherish. -**entertain′er** *n.* -**entertaining** *a.* amusing. -**entertain′ment** *n.* hospitality; amusement; public performance. [F. *entretenir*]

enthral′ (-awl) *v.t.* make a slave of, entrance; absorb. [*thrall*]

enthu′siasm *n.* ardent eagerness, zeal. -**enthu′siast** *n.* **enthusias′tic** *a.* -**enthusias′tically** *adv.* **enthuse′** *v.i* (colloq.) show enthusiasm. [G. *enthousiasmos*, inspiration]

entice′ *v.t.* allure; attract or entrap adroitly. -**entice′ment** *n.* (OF. *enticier,* provoke]

entire′ *a.* whole, complete, not broken. -**entire′ly** *adv.* -**entire′ty** *n.* [F. *entier,* fr. L. *integer*, whole]

enti′tle *v.t.* give a title or claim to. [*title*]

en′tity *n.* thing's being or existences; thing having real existence. [Late L. *entitas*, fr. *esse,* be]

entomology *n.* study of insects, -**entomol′ogist** *n.* -**entomological** (-**oj′** -) *a.* [G. *entomon*, insect]

entourage′ *n.* retinue, suite; surroundings. [F.]

entr′acte′ (ong-trakt) *n.* interval between acts of a play; (*mus.*) interval piece. [F.]

en′trails *n. pl.* bowels, intestines; inner parts. [F. *entrailles*]

entrain′ *v.t.* and *i.* put, go, aboard a train. [*train*]

entrance. *See* **enter.**

entrap′ *v.t.* catch in a trap; lure into atrap; lure into a position which compromises the victim. -**entrap′ment** *n.* the luring into a trap; *esp.* the luring, by a police officer, of a person into committinga crime so that he may be prosecuted for it. [*trap*]

entreat′ *v.t.* ask earnestly, beg, implore. entreat′y *n.* [*treat*]

entrée′ *n.* freedom of access; side dish served between courses; the main course itself. [F.]

en′trepot *n.* warehouse; port for overseas trade. [F.]

entrust′ *v.t.* confide (to); commit, put incharge. [*trust*]

entry. *See* **enter.**

entwine′ *v.t.* plait, interweave; wreathe (with). [*twine*]

enumerate *v.* count. -**enumera′tion** *n.* -**enumerator** *n.* one who enumerates. [L. *enumerate*, number of]

enunciate *v.t.* state clearly; pronounce. **enuncia′tion** *n* - **enunciator** *n.* **enun′ciative** *a.* [L. *eauntiare*]

envel′op *v.t.* wrap up, enclose. -**envel′opment** *n.* **en′velope** *n.* folded, gummed cover of a letter; covering, wrapper. [F. *envelopper*]

enven′om *v.t.* put poison in. [*venom*]

envi′ron *v.t.* surround. -**envi′ronment** *n.* surroundings; conditions of life or growth. -**envi′rons** *n. pl.* districts round (a town, *etc.*). [F. *adv.*]

envisage *v.t.* view; look at. [*visage*]

en′voy *n.* messenger; diplomatic minister of rank below an ambassador. (F. *envoyé,* one sent]

en′voy *n.* short concluding stanza of a poem. [F. *envoi*]

en′vy *n.* bitter or longing considerationof another's better fortune or success or qualities; object of this feeling. -*v.t.* feel envy of. -**en′vious** *a.* -**en′viable** *a.* [F. *envie*, L. *invidia*]

en′zyme *n.* digestive ferment; leaven. [G. *zyme,* leaven]

eo′an *a.* of dawn. -**e′ocene** *a.* (*geol*). of earliest tertiary rocks. [G. *eos,* dawn, *anthranos,* man]

e′olith *n.* prehistoric flint implement. [G. *eos*, dawn, *lithos*, stone]

epanalep′sis *n.* the repetition, after a more or less lengthy passage of subordinate or parenthetic text, of a word or clause that was used before. [G. *lepsis,* taking]

epanorthos′is *n.* the almost immediatete placement of a preceding, word or phrase by a more correct or more emphatic one. [G. *orthos*, straight]

epaulette *n.* ornamental shoulder-piece of a uniform. [F. *Epaulette*]

epergne′ (-pern) *n.* ornament for the middle of a dining-table. [orig. uncertain]

ephemeral *a.* short-lived, lasting only for a day, or few days. -**ephem′eron, ephem′era** *n.* ephemeral insect or thing. [G. *ephemeros*]

e′phod *n.* Jewish priestly vestment. [*heb.*]

ep′ic *a.* telling in continuous story the achievements of a hero or heroes. -*n.* **epic poem**. [G. *epikos*]

ep′icene *a.* denoting either sex; for, or having the characteristics of both sexes. [G. *epikoinos*]

ep′icure *n.* one dainty in eating and drinking. -**epicure′an** *a.* of -**Epicurus,** who taught that pleasure, in the shape of practice of virtue, was the highest good; given to refined sensuous enjoyment. -*n.* such a person or philosopher. -**epicure′anism** *n.*

[*Epicurus*, of Athens (300 B.C.)]

ep'icycle *n.* circle whose center moves round circumference of greater circle. -**ep'icyc'lic** *a.* [G. *epi*, upon, *kyklos*, circle]

epidemic *a.* prevalent for a time among a community. -*n.* -**epidemic disease.** [fr. G. *epi*, upon, *demos*, people]

epidermis *n.* outer skin. -**epidermic** *a.* [G.]

epiglott'is *n.* cartilage at root of tongue, closing larynx in swallowing. [G. *epi*, upon, *glotta*, tongue]

epigram *n.* short poem with a witty or-satirical ending; pointed saying. -**epigrammatic** *a.* **epigrammat'ically***adv.* -**epigram'matist** *n.* [G. *epigramma*, inscription]

epigraph *n.* inscription. [G. *epigrapheepi*, upon, *graphein*, write]

epilepsy *n.* disease in which the sufferer-falls down in a fit, with foaming and spasms. **epilep'tic** *a.* subject to epilepsy. -*n.* person who suffers from epilepsy. [G. *epilepsia*, seizure]

epilim'nion *n. pl.* (-**nia**) warm, upper layer of a lake above the thermocline.

ep'ilogue (-og) *n.* short speech or poem at the end of a play; the concluding part of a book. [G. *epilogos*, peroration]

epimey'sium *n.* external sheath of connective tissue around a muscle.

Epiph'any *n.* festival of the appearance of Christ to the Magi. [G. *epiphania*, manifestation]

episcopal *a.* of a bishop; ruled by bishops. -**epis'capacy** *n.* government by bishops; body of bisbops. -**episcopa'lian** *a.* of an episcopal system or churchman. member or adherent of an episcopal church. -**epis'copate***n.* bishop's office, see, or duration of office; the body ofbishops. [*See* **bishop**]

episeot'omy *n.* incision of the perineum to facilitate childbirth.

ep'isode *n.* incident; incidental narrativeor series of events; part of a Greek tragedy between choric songs. -**episod'ic, episod'ical** *a.* [G. *epeisodion*, coming in-besides]

emistem'ic *a.* of or pertaining to knowledge; cognitive. -**epistemol'ogy** *n.* study of the source, nature and limitations of knowledge. -**epist'emological** *a.* [G. *episteme*, knowledge]

epis'tie (-sl) *n.* letter, *esp.* of the apostles; poem in the form of a letter. -**epis'tolary** *a.* [G. *epistole*]

ep'itaph *n.* inscription on a tomb. [G. *epitaphion*, fr. *taphos*, tomb]

epithala'mium *n.* marriage-song. [G. *epithalamion*]

ep'ithet *n.* adjective expressing a quality or attribute; name full of meaning. -**epithet'ic** *a.* [G. *epitheton*]

epit'ome (-me) *n.* summary, abridgment. -**epitomize** *v.t.* **epit'omist** *n.* [G., fr. *epitemnein*, cut into]

epiton'ic *a.* overstrained. [G.]

epizo'ic *a.* living or attached to the surface of an animal.

e'poch (-ok) *n.* beginning of a period; period, era, *esp.* one marked by notable events. -**e'pochal** *a.* [G. *epoche*, stoppage]

ep'ode *n.* type of lyric poem; last part of lyric ode. **epod'ic** *a.* [G. *epi*, upon, *ōidé*, ode]

epon'ymous *a.* commemorated by the adoption of the name. [G. *eponymos*, giving name to]

eq'uable *a.* uniform, even-tempered, not easily disturbed. -**eq'uably** *adv.*, -**equability** *n.* [L. *aequabilis*]

e'qual *a.* same in number, size, merit, *etc.* ; fit or qualified; evenly balanced. -*n.* one equal to another. *v.t.* be equal to. -**equal'ity** *n.* -**e'qually** *adv.* -**e'qualize** *v.t.* and *i.* -**equaliza'tion** *n.* [L. *æqualis*, fr. *æquus*, level]

e'qual opportun'ity *n.* theory and practice of employment opportunity unbiased because of race, color, religion, gender, age, national origin, or mental or physical handicap.

equanimity *n.* calmness, evenness of mind or temper. [L. æquanimitas]

equate' *v.t.* state or assume the quality of -**equa'tion** *n.* statement of equality between two mathematical expressions; balancing; compensation for inaccuracy. -**equa'tor** *n.* great circle of the earth equidistant from the poles. -**equator'ial** *a.* [L. *æquare, equat-*, make equal]

eq'uerry *n.* king's officer in charge of horses; officer in attendance on an English sovereign. [F. *curie*, stable]

equestrian *a.* of, skilled in, horseriding; mounted on a horse. -*n.* rider or performer on a horse. [L. *equestris*]

equi- *prefix*, equal, at equal. [L. *æqui-*] -**equiangular** (-ng-g-) *a.* having equal angles. [*angular*] -**equidis'tant** *a.* at equal distances. [*distant*] . -**equilat'eral** *a.* having equal sides. [*lateral*]

equilib'rium *n.* state of balance; balanced mind. -**equili'brate** *v.t.* and *i.* -**equil'ibrist** *n.* -**equil'ibrator** *n.* stabilizing plane, fin,

of airplane; acrobat, rope-walker. [L. -*equilibrium*, fr. *libra*, scales]
eq'uine *a.* of a horse. [L. *equinus*, fr. *equus*, horse]
e'quinox *n.* time at which the sun crosses the equator and day and night are equal. -*pl.* points at which the sun crosses the equator. -**equinoc'tial** *a.* [L. *æquinoctium*, fr. *nox*, night]
equip' *v.t.* supply, fit out, array. -**equip'ment** *n.* -**eq'uipage** *n.* carriage, horses and attendants; retinue; outfit. [F. *équiper*]
eq'uity *n.* fairness; use of the principles of justice to supplement the law; system of law so made. **eq'uitable** *a.* fair, reasonable, just. -**eq'uitably** *adv.* [L. *æquitas*, fr. *æquus*, equal]
equitation *n.* art of riding. [L. *equ itare*]
equivalent *a.* equal in value; having the same meaning or result; corresponding. -*n.* equivalent thing, amount, *etc.* -**equiv'alence, equivalency** *n.* [F. *equivalent*, L. *valens, ualentis*, worth]
equivocal *a.* ambiguous, of double or doubtful meaning; questionable, liable to suspicion. -**equiv'ocate** *v.i* use equivocal words to hide the truth. -**equivoca'tion** *n.* -**equiv'ocater** *n.* -**eq'uivoque, eq'uivoke** *n.* pun. [Late L. *quivocare*, call alike]
e'ra *n.* system of time in which years are numbered from a particular event; time of the event; memorable date; period. [L. *æra*, brasses (as counters)]
eradicate *v.t.* root out. -**eradica'tion** *n.* **eradicator** *n.* (L. *eradicate*]
erase' *v.t.* rub out; efface. -**eraser** *n.* -**era'sure** *n.* [L. *eradere, eras-*, scrape out]
Eras'tian *a. pert.* to doctrine of physician Erastus subjecting church to state. [*Erastus*]
Er'ato *n.* muse of amatory poetry. [G.]
erbéium *n.* rare metal found in gadolinite. [*Yatterby*, Sweden]
ere *prep.* and *conj.* before. [OE. *mr*]
Er'ebus *n.* Hades, hell. [G. *Erebos*]
erect' *a.* upright. -*v.t.* set up; build. -**erect'ile** *a.* -**erec'tion** *n.* **erect'or** *n.* [L. *erectus*, upright]
er'emite *n.* hermit. (G. *eremos*, desert]
erg *n.* unit of work. [G. *ergon*, work]
er'go *adv.* therefore. [L.]
er'gonomics *n.* applied science, concerned with the nature and characteristics of people as they relate to design and activities with the intention of producing more effective results and greater safety. -**er'gonomic** *a.* -**ergon'omist** *n.* **er'got** *n.* disease of rye and other plants; diseased seed used as a drug. -**er'gotism** *n.* ergot poisoning. [F.]
ering'o *n.* genus of plants including the sea-holly. [G. *eryngos*]
er'mine *n.* animal like a weasel with fur brown in summer and white, except for black tail-tip, in winter; its fur *usu.* white. [OF.]
erne *n.* eagle, *esp.* sea-eagle. [OE. *earn*]
erode' *v.t.* wear out, eat away. -**ero'sion** *n.* -**ero'sive** *a.* [L. *erodere, eros-*]
erot'ic *a.* relating to sexual love. [G. *erotikos*, fr. *Eros*, god of love]
err *v.i* make mistakes; be wrong; sin. -**errat'ic** *a.* irregular in movement, conduct, *etc.* **erra'tum** (-a-) *n.* **erra'ta** *pl.* mistake noted for correction. -**erroneous** *a.* mistaken, wrong. -**err'or** *n.* mistake; wrong opinion; sin. -**err'ant** *a.* wandering in search of adventure; erring. -**err'ancy** *n.* erring state orconduct. -**err'antry** *n.* state or conduct of a knight errant. [F. *errer*, wander]
err'and *n.* short journey for a simple business; the business; purpose. -**err'and boy** *n.* [OE. *ærende*, message]
erratic *a.* odd, eccentric; following an irregular course. [*err*]
ersatz' (-zats) *a.* substitute. [Ger.]
Erse *n.* the ancient Celtic language of the Highlands of Scotland and Ireland. [var. of *Irish*]
erst, erstwhile *adv.* of old. [OE. *rest*]
erubesc'ent *a.* blushing, red. -**erubesc'ence** *n.* [L. *ruber*, red]
eructation *n.* belching. [L. *eructare*]
er'udite *a.* learned. -**erudi'tion** *n.* knowledge got by study. [L. *eruditas*]
erupt' *v.i* burst out. -**erup'tion** *n.* bursting out, *esp.* a volcanic outbreak; rash. -**erupt'ive** *a.* [L. *erurnpere, erupt-*]
erysip'elas *n.* disease causing a deep red coloring of the skin, [G. *erysipelas*]
erythro'mycin *n.* antibiotic ($C_{37}H_{67}NO_{13}$) obtained from an actinomycete used in treating bacterial infections.
escalade' *n.* a scaling of walls with ladders. -**es'calator** *n.* moving staircase. [F.]
escallo'nia *n.* S. American shrub with aromatic flowers. [*Escallon*, finder]
escall'op. *See* **scallop.**
escape' *v.i* get free; get off safely; go unpunished; find a way out. -*v.t.* elude; come out unawares from. -*n.* an escaping; leakage. -**escape'ment** *n.* mechanism connecting the motive power to the regulator

of a clock or watch. -**escapade'** *n.* flighty exploit. -**escap'ist** *n.* one who tries to escape from reality. [ONF. *escaper*, fr. L. *ex*, out of, *cappa*, cloak]

escarp' *n.* steep bank under a rampart. -*v.t.* cut into a steep slope. -**escarp'ment** *n.* [F. *escarpe*]

eschatol'ogy (-k-) *n.* doctrine of death, judgment, last things. [G. *eschatos*, last, *logos*, a discourse]

escheat' *n.* lapse of a property to the state on the death of the tenant without proper heirs; estate so lapsing. -*v.t.* make an escheat of, confiscate. -*v.i.* become an escheat. [OF. *escheoir*, fall due]

eschew' *v.t.* avoid, abstain from. [OF. *eschuer*]

eschsekolt'zia (e-sholt-sia) *n.* genus of plants including the Californian poppy. [J. F. von *Eschschatz*]

es'cort *n.* armed guard for a traveler, criminal, ships, *etc.* ; person or persons accompanying another for protection or courtesy. -**escort'** *v.t.* act as escort to. [F. *escorte*]

es'critoire (-twar) *n.* writing desk with drawers. [OF.]

es'culent *a.* eatable. [L. *esculentus*]

escutcheon (-chun) *n.* shield with a coat of arms. [L. *scutum*, shield]

Es'kimo *n.* inhabitant of Arctic Amer., Greenland, *etc.* ; Inuit; the language. -*a. pert.* to Eskimos and their language. [orig. uncertain]

ESL *abbr.* English as a Second Language.

esoteric *a.* secret; for the initiated. [G. *esoterikos*, fr. *eso*, within]

espalier *n.* lattice on which fruit-trees are trained; tree so trained. [F.]

espart'o *n.* grass grown in Spain, *etc.* and used in paper -making, cordage *etc.* [Sp.]

espe'cial (-esh'l) *a.* preeminent, more than ordinary. -**espe'cially** *adv.* [OF, *especiet*, fr. L. *species*, kind]

Esperan'to *n.* artificial language meant to be universal. -**Esperan'tist** *n.* user of Esperanto. [L. *sperare*, hope]

espionage *n.* spying; the use of spies [F. *espionnage*]

esplanade' *n.* level space, *esp.* one used as a public promenade. [F.]

espouse' (-z) *v.t.* marry; support, attach oneself to (a cause, *etc.*). -**espous'al** *n.* [OF. *espouser*]

espy' *v.t.* catch sight of. -**espi'al** *n.* [OF. *espier. See* **spy**]

esquire' *n.* title of respect added to a gentleman's name, *esp.* on the address of a letter; formerly, a squire. [OF. *escuyer*, fr. L. *scutarius*, shield-bearer]

essay' *v.t.* try, attempt; test. -**ess'ay** *n.* literary composition, usually short and inprose; attempt. -**ess'ayist** *n.* writer of essays. [F. *essayer*]

ess'ence *n.* existence, being; absolute being, reality; all that makes a thing what it is; extract got by distillation; perfume, scent. -**essen'tial** *a.* of, or constituting, the essence of a thing. -*n.* indispensable element; chief point. -**essential'ity** *n.* -**essen'tially** *adv.* [F.]

establish *v.t.* set up; settle; found; prove. -**estab'lishment** *n.* establishing; church system established by law; permanent organized body; full number of a regiment, *etc.*; household; house of business; public institution. (L. *stabilire*, fr. *stare*, stand]

estam'inet *n.* cafe. [F.]

estan'cia *n.* Spanish American cattle ranch. [Sp.]

estate' *n.* landed property; person's property; a class as part of a nation; rank, state, condition. [OF. *estat*]

esteem' *v.t.* think highly of, consider; -*n.* favorable opinion, regard -**esteemed'** *a.* highly respected. [L. *œtimare*]

es'thete. *See* **aesthetic.**

esthetic. *See* **aesthetic.**

es'timate *v.t.* form an approximate idea of (amounts, measurements, *etc.*); form an opinion of, quote a probable price for. -*n.* approximate judgment of amounts, *etc.* ; the amount, *etc.*, arrived at; opinion; price quoted by a contractor. -**es'timable** *a.* worthy of regard. -**estima'tion** *n.* opinion, judgment, esteem. [L. *stimare*]

es'tival *a.* of or in the summer. -**es'tivate** *v.i.* to remain dormant in summer, opposite to hibernate. -**es'tivation** *n.* [L. *aestas*, summer]

estrange' *v.t.* make unfriendly, put a stop to affection. -**estrange'ment** *n.* [OF. *estrangier*, make strange]

es'tuary *n.* tidal mouth of a river. [L. *æstuarium*, tidal]

esu'rient *a.* hungry; in need. -**esu'rience** *n.* [L. *esurire*, be hungry]

et cet'era (abbrev. *etc.*), 'and the rest'. -*n. pl.* accessories, trimmings. [L.]

etch *v.t.* make an engraving by eating away the surface of a metal plate with acids, *etc.* -*v.i.* practice this art -**etch'ing** *n.* **etch'er** *n.* [Du. *etsen*]

eter'nal *a.* without beginning or end; everlasting; changeless. -**eter'nally** *adv.* **eter'nity** *n.* [L. *mternus*]

eth'ane *n.* gas without color or smell, burning with pale flame. [*ether*]

e'ther (-th-) *n.* substance or fluid supposed to fill all space; the clear sky, region above the clouds; colorless volatile liquid used as an anesthetic. -**ethe'real** *a.* light, airy; heavenlv. -**ethereal'ity** *n.* [L. *ether*, upper air]

eth'ic, ethical *a.* relating to, or treating of, morals. -**eth'ically** *adv.* -**eth'ics** *n. pl.* science of morals; moral principles, rules of conduct. [G. *ethikos*, fr. *ethos*, character]

eth'nic *a.* of race. -**ethnog'raphy** *n.* description of races of men. -**ethnograph'ic** *a.* -**ethnol'ogy** *n.* science of races. **ethnolo'gical** *a.* [G. *ethnikos*, fr. *ethnos*, nation]

ethno'botony *n.* branch of botany concerned with the use of plants in the customs and folklore of a people.

e'thos *n.* distinctive character, genius, ethical make-up of an age, race, *etc.* [G.]

eth'yl *n.* base of alcohol, ether, *etc.*; type of petrol. [*ether*]

e'tiolate *v.t.* make pale by shutting out-light. -**etiola'tion** *n.* [F. *étioler*]

etiol'ogy *n.* study of causes, *esp.* inquiry into the origin of disease. -**etiol'ogical** *a.* [G. *aitia*, cause]

etiquette *n.* conventional rules of manners; court ceremonial; code of conduct for a profession. [F. *Otiquette*]

etymology *n.* tracing, or an account of, a word's formation, origin, development; science of this. -**etymolo'gical** *a.* -**etymolo'gically** *adv.* -**etymol'ogist** *n.* -**et'ymon** *n.* primitive word from which a derivative comes. [G, *etymologia*, fr. *etymos*, true]

euca'ine, eucaine' *n.* local anesthetic. [G. *eu*, well, and *cocaine*]

eucalyptus *n.* Australian gum-tree and allied plants. -**eucalypt'us-oil'** *n.* disinfectant. [fr. G. *eu*, well, and *kalyptos*, covered]

Eu'charist (-k-) *n.* sacrament of the Lord's Supper; consecrated elements. -**eucharis'tic** *a.* [G. *eucharistia*, thanksgiving]

Euclid'ian geom'etry *n.* theory based on the postulates of Euclid, including that only one line may be drawn through a given point parallel to a given line.

eugenic *a.* relating to, or tending towards, the production of fine offspring. -*n. pl.* science of this. -**eugen'ist** *n.* [G. *eu-*, well, and *root gen-*, bring forth]

eu'logy *n.* speech or writing in praise of aperson; praise. -**eu'logize** *v.t.* -**eu'logist** *n.* **eologistic** *a.* -**eulogis'tically** *adv.* [G. *eulogia*, praise]

eu'nuch (-k) *n.* castrated man, *esp.* one employed in a harem. [G *eunouchos*, bedguard]

eupep'sy *n.* good digestion. -**eupep'tic** *a.* [G. *eu*, well, *peptos*, digested]

euphemism *n.* substitution of a mild word or expression for a blunt one; instance of this. -**euphemis'tic** *a.* -**euphemis'tically** *adv.* -**eu'phemist** *n.* [G. *euphemismos*, speaking fair]

eu'phony *n.* pleasantness of sound -**euphon'ic** *a.* -**eupho'nious** *a.* -**eupho'nium** *n.* bass saxhorn. [G. *euphonia*, fr. *phone*, voice]

eu'phuism *n.* affected or high flown manner of writing, *esp.* in imitation of Lyly's *Euphues* (1580). -**eu'phuist** *n.* -**euphuis'tic** *a.* [Lyly's *Euphues*; G. *euphues*, of good nature]

Eura'sian *a.* of mixed European and Asiatic descent; of Europe and Asia as a single continent. -*n.* Eurasian person. [*European-Asian*]

eure'ka *interj.* 'I've found it' (to announce discovery, *etc.*). [G. *heureka*]

eurhyth'mics *n. pl.* art of rhythmical free movement to music, of expression indance movement. -**eurhyth'mic** *a.* [*rhythmic*] [Jaques -Dalcroze, 1865 -1950]

Europe'an *a./n.* (native) of continent of Europe. [G. *Europe]*

eu'sol *n.* antiseptic. [*E*dinburgh *U*niversity *sol*ution]

Euter'pe (-pe) *n.* muse of music. -**Euter'pean** *a.* of music. [G]

euthanasia *n.* gentle, easy death; theory that incurables, *etc.* should be painlessly removed. [G.]

euthen'ics *n.* science of relation of environment to human beings. [G. *eutheneein*, flourish]

evac'uate *v.t.* empty; discharge; withdraw from; remove (people) from area. -**evacua'tion** *n.* -**evacuee'** *n.* evacuated person. [L. *vacuus*, empty]

evade' *v.t.* avoid, escape from; elude; frustrate. -**eva'sion** *n.* -**eva'sive** *a.* -**eva'sively** *adv.* [L. *euadere*, eva]

eval'uate *v.t.* find or state the value or number of. -**evalua'tion** *n.* [*value]*

evanesce' (-es) *v.i.* fade away. -**evanes'cent** *a.* -**evanes'cence** *n.* [L. *evanescere*, vanish]

evan'gel *n.* gospel. -**evangel'ical** *a.* of or according to the gospel teaching; of the

Protestant school which maintains salvation by faith. -**evangel'icalism, evangelism** *n.* -**evan'gelist** *n.* writer of one of the four Gospels; preacher of the gospel; revivalist. -**evan'gelize** *v.t.* preach to; convert. -**evangeliza'tion** *n.* [G. *evangelion*, good tidings]

evap'orate *v.i* turn into vapor; pass off in vapor. -*v.t.* turn into vapor. -**evapora'tion** *n.* -**evap'orator** *n.* -**evap'orative** *a.* [L. *eva'porare*, fr. *vapor,* vapour]

evasions *See* **evade.**

eve *n.* evening before (a festival, *etc.*); time just before (an event, *etc.*); evening. [*even*]

e'ven *n.* evening. -**e'vensong** *n.* evening prayer. [OE. *æfen*]

e'ven *a.* flat, smooth; uniform in quality; equal in amount, balanced; divisable by two; impartial. -*v.t.* make even. *adv.* invites comparison with something les sstrong included by implication in the statement - *e.g.*, 'the dog eats even the bones' (not just the meat); or introduces an extreme case: *e.g.*, 'even a worm will turn'; archaic, quote. [OE. *efen*]

e'vening *n.* close of day; of one's life, old age. [OE. *zefnung*]

event' *n.* occurrence of a thing; notable occurrence; issue; result. -**event'ful** *a.* full of exciting events. -**event'ual** *a.* that will happen under certain conditions; resulting in the end. -**event'ually** *adv.* -**eventual'ity** *n.* possible event. -**event'uate** *v.i.* turn out; end. (L. *evenire, event* -, come out]

ev'er *adv.* always; constantly; at any time; by any chance. **ev'erglade** *n.* swamp. - **ev'ergreen** *n.* non-deciduous plant, shrub. -*a.* [OE. *æfre*]

everlasting *a.* eternal. -*n.* eternity; plant with lasting flowers, immortal. [*ever* and *lasting*]

evert' *v.t.* turn outside in. -**ever'sion** *n.* [L. *evertere*]

ev'ery (-vr-) *a.* each of all; all possible. -**ev'erybody** *n.* -**ev'eryday** *a.* usual, ordinary. **ev'eryone** *n.* -**ev'erything** *n.* **ev'erywhere** *adv.* in all places. [OE. *æfre lis*, ever each]

evict *v.t.* expel by legal process, turnout. -**evic'tion** *n.* -**evict'or** *n.* [L. *evincere, evict* -, prove]

ev'ident *a.* plain, obvious -**ev'idently** *adv.* -**ev'idence** *n.* sign, indications ground for belief, testimony; in evidence, conspicuous. -*v.t.* indicate, prove. -**evidential** *a.* [L. *videre*, see]

e'vil *a.* bad, harmful. -*n.* what is bad or harmful; sin. -**e'villy** *adv.* [OE. *yfel*]

evince' *v.t.* show, indicate. -**evinc'ible** *a.* -**evinc'ive** *a.* [L. *evincere*, prove]

eviscerate (-vis-er-) *v.t.* disembowel. - **eviscera'tion** *n.* [L. *eviscerate*]

evoke' *v.t.* call up. -**evoca'tion** *n.* - **evoc'ative** *a.* [L. *evocare]*

evolve' *v.t.* develop; unfold, open out; produce. -*v.i.* develop, *esp.* by natural process; open out. -**evolu'tion** *n.* an evolving; development of species fromearlier forms; movement of troops or ships; movement in dancing, *etc.* -**evolu'tional, evolutionary** *a.* -**evolu'tionist** *n.* [L. *evolvere, evolut* -, to roll out]

evulse' *v.t.* pluck out forcibly. -**evul'sion** *n.* [L. *é,* out, *vellere*, pluck]

ewe (fi) *n.* female sheep. [OE. *eowu*]

ew'er (fi'-) *n.* pitcher, water-jug. [OF. *euwier,* fr. *eau*, water]

ex'- formerly, as in *ex-king, etc.* [G.]

exacerbate *v.t.* aggravate, embitter. - **exacerba'tion** *n.* [L. *exacerbare*, cp. *acerbity*]

exact' (-gz-) *a.* precise, accurate, strictly correct. -*v.t.* demand, extort; insist upon; enforce. -**exact'ly** *adv.* -**exac'tion** *n.* - **exact'ness** *n.* -**exact'itude** *n.* **exact'or** *n.* [L. *exigere, exact* -, to weigh, *prove*, forceout]

exaggerate *v.t.* magnify beyond truth, overstate. -**exaggera'tion** *n,* **exagg'erator** *n.* -**exagg'erative** *a.* [L. *exaggerate*, heap up]

exalt' (egz-awlt') *v.t.* raise up; praise; make noble. -**exalta'tion** *n.* an exalting; rapture. [L. *exaltare*, fr. *altos*, high]

exam'ine (-gz-) *v.t.* investigate; ask questions of, test the knowledge or proficiency of by oral or written questions; inquire into. **examina'tion** *n.* -**exam'iner** *n.* - **examinee'** *n.* [L. *examinare*, weigh accurately]

exam'ple (-ga-a-) *n.* thing illustrating a general rule; specimen; model, pattern; warning, precedent. [L. *exemplum*, sample]

exasperate (-gz-) *v.t.* irritate, enrage; intensify, make worse. -**exaspera'tion** *n.* [L. *exasperate*, fr. *asper*, rough]

ex'cavate *v.t.* hollow out; make a hole by digging; unearth. -**excava'tion** *n.* act of excavating; resulting cavity. -**ex'cavator** *n.* [L. *excavare*, fr. *cavus*, hollow]

exceed' *v.t.* be greater than; do more than authorized, go beyond; surpass. - **exceed'ingly** *adv.* very. -**excess'** *n.* an exceeding; amount by which a thing exceeds; too great an amount; intemperance or immoderate conduct. -**excess'ive** *a.* -

excess'ively *adv.* [L. *excedere, excess* -, to go beyond]
excel' *v.t.* be very good, pre-eminent. -*v.t.* surpass, be better than. -**ex'cellent** *a.* very good. -**ex'cellence** *n.* -**ex'cellency** *n.* title of ambassadors, *etc.* [L. *excellere*, rise above]
excelsior *interj.* higher. [L. comp. of *excelsis*, high, lofty]
except' *v.t.* leave or take out; exclude. -*v.i.* raise objection. -*prep.* not including; but. *conj.* unless. -**except'ing** *prep.* not including. -**excep'tion** *n.* an excepting; thing excepted, not included in a rule; objection. -**excep'tional** *a.* unusual. -**excep'tionally** *adv.* -**excep'tionable** *a.* open to objection. [L. *exceptus*, taken out]
excerpt (ek'serpt) *n.* quotation; selected passage; extract. -*v.t.* take out; quote from, *carpere*, to pick]
excess' *See* **exceed.**
exchange' *v.t.* give (something) in return for something else. -*v.i.* of an officer, change posts with another. -*n.* giving one thing and receiving another; giving or receiving coin, bills. *etc.* of one country for those of another; thing given for another; building where merchants meet for business. -**exchange'able** *a.* -**exchangeabil'ity** *n.* [*change*]
exchequer (-ker) *n.* public treasury; in Britain, government department in charge of the revenue. [OF. *eschequier*, chess-board (royal revenue accounts were orig. kept by means of counters on a table marked out in squares)]
excise' (-z) *n.* duty charged on homegoods during manufacture or before sale. -**exci'sable** *a.* liable to excise. [Du. *accijns*]
excise' *v.t.* cut out, cut away. -**excis'ion** *n.* [L. *excidere, ercis-]*
excite' *v.t.* rouse up, set in motion; stimulate, move to strong emotion. -**exci'table** *a.* -**exci'tably** *adv.* -**excitabil'ity** *n.* -**excite'ment** *n.* [L. *excitare*]
exclaim *v.i* and *t.* cry out. -**exclamation** *n.* -**exclama'tion point** *or* **mark,** *n.* punctuation mark (!) used to indicate an interjection or an element of surprise or stress in an utterance. -**exclam'atory** *a.* expressing exclamation. [L. *exclamare*, shout out]
ex'clave *n.* disjoined portion of a country, *etc.*, enclosed by foreign territory. [L. *ex*, out, *clavis*, key]
exclude' *v.t.* shut out; debar from. -**exclu'sion** *n.* -**exclu'sive** *a.* excluding; inclined to keep out (from society, *etc.*); sole, only; different from all others. -**exclu'sively** *adv.* [L. *excludere*]
excog'itate (-koj-) *v.t.* think out. -**excogita'tion** *n.* [L. *excogitare*]
excommunicate *v.t.* shut off from the sacraments of the church. -**excommunica'tion** *n.* -**excommu'nicative, excommu'nicatory** *a.* [Church L. *excommunicare*, expel from communion]
excoriate *v.t.* remove skin from; attack bitterly. -**excoria'tion** *n.* [L. *excoriate*, flay]
excorti'cate *v.t.* strip the bark from. [L. *cortex, cortices*, bark]
excrement *n.* waste matter discharged from the bowels, dung. -**excrement'al** *a.* -**excrete'** *v.t.* discharge from the system. -**excre'tion** *n.* -**excre'tory** *a.* [L. *excernere, excret* -, sift out]
excrescent *a.* growing out of something abnormally; redundant. -**excres'cence** *n.* [L. *excrescere*, grow out]
excruciate *v.t.* pain acutely, torture, in body or mind. -**excrucia'tion** *n.* [L. *excruciate*, fr. *crux*, cross]
exculpate *v.t.* free from blame, clear from a charge. -**exculpa'tion** *n.* -**exculpatory** *a.* [L. *ex*-, from, *culpa*, fault]
excursion *n.* journey, ramble, trip, for pleasure; deviation from planned route. -**excur'sus** *n.* discussion of a special point, usually at the end of a book. [L. *excursiona*, running out]
excuse' (-z) *v.t.* try to clear from blame; overlook, forgive, gain exemption; set free, remit. -**excuse'** *n.* that which serves to excuse; apology. -**excu'sable** (-z-) *a.* [L. *excusare*, fr. *causa*, cause]
ex'eat *n.* formal leave of absence, *esp.* for a college student. [L. = 'let him go out']
ex'ecrate *v.t.* feel or express abhorrence, hatred for; curse. -**execra'tion** *n.* -**ex'ecrable** *a.* abominable, hatefully bad. [L. *exsecrari*, curse]
ex'ecute *v.t.* carry out, perform; sign (adocument); kill (criminals). **execu'tion** *n.* **execu'tioner** *n.* one employed to kill those sentenced to death by law. -**exec'utant** *n.* performer, *esp.* of music. -**exec'utive** *a.* carrying into effect, *esp.* of branch of a government enforcing laws. -*n.* committee carrying on the business of a society, *etc.*; the administrative branchof government; a person with administrative or managerial control, *esp.* in business. **exec'utor** *n.* person appointed by one making a will to carry out the provisions of the will. **exec'utrix** *fem.* **exec'utive priv'ilege** *n.* the right of the president to

refuse to give confidential information requested by a legislative or judiciary body if the disclosure would adversely affect government functions of processes. [L. *exsequi, exsecut-*, follow out]

exege'ses (-j-) *n.* literary interpretation, *esp.* of Scripture. -**exeget'ic, exeget'ical** *a.* [G.]

exem'plar *n.* model type. -**exemp'lary** *a.* fit to be imitated, serving as an example. -**exemp'larily** *adv.* -**exemp'lify** *v.t.* serve as example of, make an attested copy of -**exemplifica'tion** *n.* [L. *exemplum*, sample]

exempt' (-gz-) *a.* freed from, not liable. -*v.t.* free from. **exemp'tion** *n.* [L. *exemptus*, taken out]

ex'equies (-kwiz) *n. pl.* funeral rites. [L. *exequiæ*, funeral procession]

ex'ercise (-z) *n.* employment, use (of limbs, faculty, *etc.*); use of limbs for health; practice for the sake of training; task set for training. -*v.t.* use, employ; give (training, health) exercise to; carryout, discharge; trouble, harass. -*v.i.* take exercise. [L. *exercere*, keep at work]

exert' (-gz -) *v.t.* bring into activeoperation. -**exer'tion** *n.* [L. *exserere, exsert -*, put forth]

exhale' *v.t.* breathe out; give off as vapor. -*v.i.* breathe out; pass of as vapor. -**exhala'tion** *n.* [L. *exhalare*, breathe out]

exhaust' (igz -awst') *v.t.* draw off; use up; empty, treat, discuss, thoroughly; tire out. -*n.* used steam, fluid or gas from an engine; passage for, or coming out of, this. -**exhaust'-valve** *n.* **exhaus'tion** *n.* -**exhaust'ive** *a.* -**exhaust'ible** *a.* -**exhaustibil'ity** *n.* [L. *exhaurire, exhaust-, drain out]*

exhibit (-gz-) *v.t.* show, display; manifest; show publicly in competition. -*n.* thing shown, *esp.* in competition or as evidence in a court. -**exhibi'tion** *n.* display; act of displaying; public show (of works of art, *etc.*); allowance made to a student, scholarship. -**exhibi'tionism** *n.* excessive tendency to display one's personality, show off. '**exhib'itor** *n.* one who exhibits *esp.* in a show. [L. *exhibere*, hold forth]

exhilarate (-gz-) *v.t.* enliven, gladden. -**exhilara'tion** *n.* [L. *exhilarate*, fr. *hilaris*, happy, merry]

exhorté (-gz-) *v.t.* urge, admonish earnestly. -**exhorta'tion** *n.* -**exhort'er** *n.* [L. *hortari*, encourage]

exhume' *v.t.* unearth; take out again what has been buried. -**exhuma'tion** *n.* [L. *ex*, out of, *humus*, ground]

exigent (-j-) *a.* exacting; urgent. -**ex'igence, exigency** *n.* pressing need; emergency. -**ex'igible** *a.* that may be exacted. [L. *exigere*, force out]

exig'uous *a.* scanty, small. **exigu'ity** *n.* [L. *exiguus*, scanty]

ex'ile *n.* banishment, expulsion from one's own country; long absence abroad; one banished. -*v.t.* banish. [F. *exil*]

exil'ity *n.* slenderness; delicacy; subtlety, [L. *exilist*, for *exigilis*, slender]

exist' (-gz-) *v.i* be, have being, continue to be. -**exist'ence** *n.* -**exist'ent** a. -**existen'tialism** *n.* theory of the fortuitous nature of the universe, in which we create our own values. [F. *exister*, fr. L. *ex(s)istere*, make to stand out]

ex'it *n.* actor's departure from the stage; a going out; way out; death. -**ex'it** *v.i sing.* 'goes out'. **ex'eunt** (-i unt) *pl.* 'go out' *n.* stage directions, to indicate the going off of a player or players. (L. *exire*, go out]

ex-libris *n.* book-plate. [L. = 'from the books of']

ex'odus *n.* departure, *esp.* of a crowd. -**Ex'odus**, second book of Old Testament, relating the departure of the Israelites from Egypt. [G. *exodus*, way out]

exog'amy *n.* marriage outside of the tribe only. -**exog'amous** *a.* [G. *exo*, out, *gamos*, marriage]

ex'ogen (-jen) *a.* dicotyledon, opposite of endogen. [G. *exo*, outside, gen root of *gignesthai*, be produced]

exonerate *v.t.* free, declare free, from blame; exculpate; acquit. -**exonera'tion** *n.* **exon'erative** *a.* [L. *exonerate*, un burden]

exophthal'mia, exophthal'mus *n.* protrusion of the eyeball. -**exophthal'mic** *a.* [G. *ex*, out, *ophthalmos*, eye]

exorbitant *a.* very excessive, immoderate. -**exorb'itantly** *adv.* **exorbitance** *n.* [L. *exorbitare*, go out of one's orbit]

ex'orcize, exorcise (-z) *v.t.* cast out (evil spirits) by invocation; free a person of evil spirits. -**ex'orcism** *n.* -**ex'orcist** *n.* [G. *exorkizein*, from ex, out, *horkos*, oath]

exord'ium *n.* introductory part of a speech or treatise. [L.]

exoskeleton *n.* bony outer structure of, *e.g.*, crab, turtle; any hard or horny outercasing. [G. *exo*, outside, and *skeleton*]

exosmo'sis *n.* percolation of body fluids outwards through membranous walls. [L.]

exoter'ic *a.* understandable by the many; ordinary, popular (opposite of esoteric). [G. *exoterikos*]

exot'ic *a.* brought in from abroad, not native. -*n.* exotic plant, *etc.* [G. ex*otikos*, fr. *exo*, outside]
expand' *v.t.* and *i.* spread out; enlarge, increase in bulk, develop. -**expan'sion** *n.* -**expan'sive** *a.* wide-spreading; effusive. -**expan'sible** *a.* -**expansibil'ity***n.* **expanse'** *n.* wide space; open stretch of land. [L. *expanders*]
expatiate (-shi-) *v.i* speak or write at great length (on). [L. *ex(s)patiari*, walk about, fr. *spatium*, space]
expatriate *v.t.* banish. **expatria'tion** *n.* [L. *patria*, country]
expect' *v.t.* look on as likely to happen; look for as due, -**expect'ant** *a.* -**expect'ancy** *n.* -**expect'antly** *adv.* -**expecta'tion** *n.* (L. *exspectare*, look out for]
expectorate *v.t.* and *i.* spit out (phlegm, *etc.*) -**expectora'tion** *n.* [L. *expectorate*, fr. *pectus*, breast]
expedient *a.* fitting, advisable; politic. -*n.* device, contrivance. -**expe'diently** *adv.* -**expe'diency** *n.* [*expedite*]
ex'pedite (-lt) *v.t.* help on, hasten. -**expedi'tion** *n.* promptness; journey for a definite purpose; warlike enterprise; body of men sent on such enterprise. -**expedi'tionary** *a.* -**expedi'tious** *a.* prompt, speedy. [L. *expedite*, free the foot, help on]
expel' *v.t.* drive, cast out. -**expul'sion** *n.* **expulsive** *a.* [L. *expellere, expuls -]*
expend' *v.t.* spend, pay out; use up. -**expend'iture** *n.* -**expense'** *n.* spending; cost. -*pl.* charges, outlay incurred. -**expens'ive** *a.* costly. [L. *expendere*, fr. *pendere, pens* -, weigh]
experience *n.* observation of facts as a source of knowledge; a being affected consciously by an event; the event; knowledge, skill, gained by contact with factsand events. -*v.t.* undergo, suffer, meet with. -**experien'tial** *a.* [L. *experiential* fr. *experire*, test thoroughly]
experiment *n.* test, trial; something done in the hope that it may succeed, or to test a theory. -*v.i.* make an experiment. -**experiment'al** *a.* -**experiment'ally** *adv.* [L. *experiri*, test]
ex'pert *a.* practiced, skillful. -*n.* one expert in something; an authority. [L. *experiri*, test]
ex'piate *v.t.* pay the penalty for; make amends for. **expia'tion** *n.* -**ex'piator** *n.* -**ex'piatory** *a.* [L. *expiare*, make amends for]
expire' *v.t.* breathe out. -*v.i.* give out breath; die; die away; come to an end. -**expira'tion** *n.* -**expi'ratory** *a.* -**expi'ry** *n.* end. [L. *ex(s)pirare*]
expis'cate *v.t.* fish out; extract skillfully, discover by examination. -**expis'cation** *n.* -**expis'catory** *a.* [L. *ex*, out, *piscis*, fish]
explain' *v.t.* make clear, intelligible; give details of, account for. -**explana'tion** *n.* **explan'atory** *a.* [L. *explanare*, make smooth]
expletive *a.* serving only to fill out a sentence, *etc.* -*n.* expletive word, *esp.* oath. [L. *expletivus*, filling out]
explicable *a.* explainable. -**ex'plicate** *v.t.* develop, explain. -**ex'plicative** *a.* -**ex'plicatory** *a.* (L. *explicate*, unfold]
explic'it (-a-) *a.* stated in detail; stated, not merely implied; outspoken. [L. *explicare*, unfold]
explode' *v.i* go off with a bang; burst violently. -*v.t.* made explode; discredit, expose (a theory, *etc.*). -**explo'sion** *n.* -**explo'sive** *a.* and *n.* [L. *explodere, explos* -, clap out (of theater)]
ex'ploit *n.* brilliant feat, deed. -*v.t.* turn to advantage; make use of for one's own ends. -**exploita'tion** *n.* [F.]
explore' *v.t.* examine (a country, *etc.*) by going through it; investigate. -**explora'tion** *n.* -**explor'atory** *a.* -**explor'er** *n.* [L. *explorare*, announce discovery]
explosion. *See* **explode.**
exponents *See* **expound.**
ex'port *v.t.* send (goods) out of the country. -*n.* exported article. -**exporta'tion** *n.* -**export'er** *n.* [L. *exportare*, carry out]
expose' (-z) *v.t.* leave unprotected; lay open (to); exhibit, put up for sale; unmask; disclose. -**expo'sure** *n.* act of exposing, being exposed; (*photo.*) the exposing of the sensitive plate to light; duration of this. [F. *exposer*]
exposition. *See* **expound.**
expostulate *v.i* make (*esp.* friendly) remonstrances. -**expostula'tion** *n.* -**expostulatory** *a.* [L. *expostulate*, demand urgently]
expound' *v.t.* explain, interpret. -**expo'nent** *n.* one who expounds; executant; maths. index, symbol showing the power of a factor. -**exponen'tial** *a.* -**exposi'tion** *n.* explanation, description; exhibition of goods, *etc.* -**expos'itory** *a.* -**expos'itor** *n.* [L. *exponere*, put forth]
express' *v.t.* put into words; make known or understood by words; conduct, *etc.*;

squeeze out; send by express. -*a.* definitely stated, specially designed; of a messenger, specially sent off, of a train, fast and making few stops. -*n.* express train or messenger. -*adv.* specially, on purpose; with speed. -**express'ly** *adv.* -**express'ible** *a.* -**expres'sion** *n.* a pressing out; phrase, saying; what the features convey of thought, feeling, *etc.* -**expres'sionism** *n.* theory that art, literature, should be primarily an expression of the artist's personality. -**express'ive** *a.* -**express'way** *n.* highway designed with several lanes and intersections so as to allow traffic to travel at high speed. [L. *expressus*, squeezed out, clearly stated]

expromis'sion *n.* transfer of a debt from one person to another, whereby the first is discharged. [*promise*]

expropriate *v.t.* dispossess; take out of the owner's hands. -**expropria'tion** *n.* -**expro'priator** *n.* [L. *expropriate*, deprive of one's own. cp. *proper*]

expulsion. *See* **expel.**

expunge' *v.t.* strike out, erase. [L. *expungere*, mark for deletion by dots; fr. *pungere*, prick]

expurgate *v.t.* remove objectionable parts (from a book, *etc.*). -**expurga'tion** *n.* -**ex'purgator** *n.* -**expurg'atory** *a.* [L. *expurgate*, make pure]

exquisite (-iz-it) *a.* of extreme beauty or delicacy; keen, acute; keenly sensitive. -*n.* dandy. -**ex'quisitely** *adv.* [L. *exquisitus*, sought out]

exscind' (-sind) *v.t.* cut out. [L. *ex*, out, *scindere*, cleave]

extant' *a.* of a document, *etc.*, still existing. [L. *exstare*, stand forth]

extempore (-ri) *a.* and *adj.* without preparation, off-hand. -**extempora'neous** *a.* -**extemp'orary** *a.* -**extemp'orize** *v.t.* speak without preparation; devise for the occasion. -**extemporiza'tion.** [L. *ex tempore*, out of thetime]

extend' *v.t.* stretch out, lengthen; prolong in duration; widen in area, scope; accord, grant. -*v.i.* reach; cover an area; have arange or scope; become larger or wider. -**exten'sible** *a.* -**extensibil'ity** *n.* -**extension** *n.* -**extens'ive** *a.* wide, large, comprehensive. -**extent'** *n.* size, scope; space, area; degree. -**exten'sile** *a.* that can be extended. -**exten'sor** *n.* muscle that straightens a joint. [L. *extenders, extens -*, stretch out]

extend'ed fam'ily *n.* nuclear family and close relatives, often living under one roof.

extenuate *v.t.* make less blameworthy. **extenua'tion** *n.* [L. *extenuate*, make thin, fr. *tenuis*, thin]

exte'rior *a.* outer, outward. -*n.* outside; outward appearance. [L.]

exterminate *v.t.* root out, destroy utterly. -**extermina'tion** *n.* [L. *exterminare*, drive over the boundary]

extern'al *a.* outside. **extern'ally** *adv.* [L. *externus*]

exterritor'ial *a.* free from the jurisdiction of the territory one lives in. -**exterritorial'ity** *n.* [*territory*]

exter'sion *n.* act of erasing, rubbing out. [L. *ex*, out, *tergere, ters -*, rub, wipe]

extinct' *a.* quenched, no longer burning; having died out or come to an end. -**extinc'tion** *n.* -**exting'uish** *v.t.* put out, quench; wipe out. -**exting' uishable** *a.* -**exting'uisher** *n.* that which extinguishes; cap to put out a candle; apparatus for putting out a fire. [L. *extinguere, extinct -*, quench]

extirpate *v.t.* root out, destroy utterly. -**extirpa'tion** *n.* -**ex'tirpator** *n.* [L. *ex(s)tirpare*, fr. *stirps*, stem]

extol *v.t.* praise highly; exalt. [L. *extollere*, lift up]

extort' *v.t.* get by force or threats; extract illegally. -**extor'tion** *n.* -**extor'tionate** *a.* -**extor'tioner** *n.* [L. *extorquere*, extort -, wrench away]

ex'tra *a.* additional; larger, better than usual. -*adv.* additionally; more than usually. -*n.* extra thing; something charged as additional. -**extrajudi'cial** *a.* outside court or normal legal practice. [for *extraordinary*]

extract' *v.t.* take out, *esp.* by force; obtain against a person's will; get by pressure, distillation, *etc.*; deduce, derive; copy out, quote. -**ex'tract** *n.* matter got by distilation; concentrated juice; passage from a book. -**extrac'tion** *n.* extracting; ancestry. -**extract'or** *n.* [L. *extrahere*, extract -, draw out]

extradi'tion *n.* delivery, under a treaty, of a foreign fugitive from justice to the authorities concerned. **ex'tradite** *v.t.* give or obtain such delivery. **extradi'table** *a.* [L. *extradition*, handing over]

extramur'al *a.* outside the walls, boundaries; (of a university lecturer) one not of the faculty. [*mural*]

extra'neous *a.* added from without, not naturally belonging. [L. *extraneus*]

extraord'inary *a.* out of the usual course; additional; unusual, surprising, exceptional. -**extraord'inarily** *adv.* [L. *extraordinarius*, fr. *extraordinem*, outside the order]

extraterrest'rial *a.* of, or from outside the earth's atmosphere. [L. *extra*, outside, *terra*, earth]

extraterritor'ial *See* **exterritorial.**

extrav'agant *a.* wild, absurd; wasteful; exorbitant. **extrav'agantly** *adv.* **extrav'agance** *n.* -**extravagan'za** *n.* fantastic composition (in music, literature, *etc.*). [L. *extrauagari*, wander outside the bounds]

extrav'asate *v.t.* force out (blood, *etc.*) from its vessel. -*v.i.* flow out. -**extravasa'tion** *n.* [L. *uas*, vessel]

extreme' *a.* at the end, outermost; of a high or the highest degree; severe; going beyond moderation. -*n.* thing at one end or the other, first and last of a series; utmost degree. -**extreme'ly** *adv.* -**extre'mist** *n.* advocate of extreme measures. **extrem'ity** *n.* end. -*pl.* hands and feet; utmost distress; extreme measures. [*extremus*]

ex'tricate *v.t.* disentangle, set free. -**ex'tricable** *a.* -**extrica'tion** *n.* [L. *extricare*, extricate]

extrin'sic *a.* accessory, not belonging, not intrinsic. -**extrin'sically** *adv.* [F. *extrinseque*, L. *extrinsecus*]

extrorse' *a.* (of an antler) turned outward. [L. *extrorsus*]

extrovert *n.* (*psych.*) one whose mind is turned outward away from himself. *usu.* a cheerful and uninhibited person. [L. *extra*, outside, *vertere*, turn]

extrude' *v.t.* thrust out. -**extru'sion** *n.* [L. extruders]

exu'berant *a.* prolific, abundant, luxuriant; effusive, high-flown. -**exu'berance** *n.* -**exu'berantly** *adv.* [L. *uber*, fertile]

exude' *v.i* ooze out. -*v.t.* give off (moisture). -**exuda'tion** *n.* [L. *exsudare*, sweat out]

exult' *v.i* rejoice, triumph. -**exulta'tion** *n.* **exult'ant** *a.* [L. *ex(s)ultare* leap for joy]

exu'viae *n.pl.* skins, shells, *etc.*, cast by animals. -**exu'vial** *a.* -**exu'viate** *v.t.* shed, cast (skin). -**exuvia'tion** *n.* [L. *exuire*, draw off]

eye *n.* organ of sight; look, glance; attention; various things resembling an eye. -*v.t.* look at; observe. -**eye-ball** *n.* pupil. -**eye'bright** *n.* small flowering plant once used as eye remedy. -**eye'brow** *n.* fringe of hair above the eye. -**eye'lash** *n.* hair fringing the eyelid. -**eye'less** *a.* -**eye'let** *n.* small hole for a rope, *etc.* to pass through. -**eye'lid** *n.* lid or cover of the eye. -**eye-salve** *n.* ointment for eye infections. -**eye-service** *n.* work done only under the overseer's eye. -**eye'sore** *n.* ugly mark, thing that annoys one to see. **eye'tooth** *n.* canine tooth. -**eye'wash** *n.* humbug, dissimulation. -**eye'-witness** *n.* one who saw something for himself. [OE. *eager*]

eyot *n.* small island, *esp.* in a river. [OE. *igath*]

ey're (air) *n.* circuit, court, of visiting justices. [OF. *eire*, L. *iter*, journey]

eyr'ie. *See* **aerie.**

F

fable *n.* tale; legend; short story with a moral, *esp.* one with talking animals as characters. -*v.t.* invent, tell fables about. -**fab'ulist** *n.* writer of fables. -**fab'ulous** *a.* told of in fables; unhistorical; absurd, unbelievable. [L. *fabula*, fr. *fari*, speak]

fab'liau (fab-le-o) *n.* early French metrical tales. [F.]

fab'ric *n.* thing put together; building, frame, structure; woven stuff, texture. -**fabricate** *v.t.* invent (a lie, *etc.*); forge (a document). -**fab'ricator** *n.* -**fabrica'tion** *n.* [L. *fabrica*, fr. *faber*, smith]

façade' *n.* front of a building. [F.]

face *n.* front of the head; front, surface, chief side of anything; outward appearance: look; coolness, impudence. *v.t.* meet boldly; look or front towards; give a covering surface. -*v.i.* turn. -**fa'cer** *n.* blow in the face; sudden difficulty. [F.]

fac'et (fas'-) *n.* one side of a many-sided body, *esp.* of a cut gem. -**fa'cial** (fa'shl) *a.* [F. *facette*, dim. of face]

facetious (fas-e-shus) *a.* waggish, jocose, given to jesting. -**face'tiae** (-se, 'shi) *n. pl.* pleasantries, witticisms. [L. *facetus*, graceful]

fac'ile *a.* easy; working easily; easygoing. -**facil'itate** (-sit-) *v.t.* make easy, help. -**facil'ity** *n.* easiness; dexterity. -*pl.* opportunities, good conditions. -**facilita'tion** *n.* -**facil'itator** *n.* [F.]

facsim'ile (fak-sim'li) *n.* exact copy. -**facsim'ile machine'** *n.* (**FAX**) device that scans a page of text or graphics and converts it into electronic pulses for transmission to other locations via telephone lines. [L. *fac simile*, make like]

fact *n.* thing known to be true or to have occurred. [L. *factum*, thing done]

fac'tion *n.* political or other party (used alwavs in a bad sense); misguided party spirit. -**fac'tious** *a.* [L. *factio*]

fac'tion *n.* a television program, film, or

literary work comprising a dramatized presentation of actual events. [fr. *fact* and *fiction*]

facti'tious *a.* artificial, specially got up. [L. *factitius*, made by art]

fac'tor *n.* something contributing to a result; one of numbers that multiplied together give a given number; agent, one who buvs and sells for another. -**fac'tory** *n.* building where things are manufactured; trading station in a foreign country. [L. *facere*, to do]

facto'tum *n.* servant managing affairs, man-of-all-work. [L. fr. *facere*, do, make, *totum*, all]

fac'ula *n.* (**fac'ulae** *pl.*) spot of more intense brightness on the surface of the sun. [L. dim. of fax, torch]

fac'ulty *n.* ability, aptitude; inherent power; a power of the mind; department of a university; members of a profession; authorization. -**fac'ultative** *a.* optional. [L. *facultas*, power]

fad *n.* pet idea, craze. -**fadd'y** *a.* -**fadd'ist** *n.* [orig. uncertain]

fade *v.i.* wither; lose color; grow dim; disappear gradually. -**fade in'**, -**out'**, gradual appearance, disappearance, of a cinema scene; similar effect with sounds in radio. -**fade'less** *a.* [OF. *fader*]

fae'ces. *See* **feces.**

fag *n.* toil, tedious task. (*Brit. sl.*) cigarette. -*v.t.* weary; make act as fag. -*v.i.* toil; act as fag. -**fag'end'** *n.* last part, inferior remnant. [orig. uncertain]

fagg'ot, fag'ot *n.* bundle of sticks bound together; bundle of steel rods. -*v.t.* bind in a faggot. [F. *fagot*]

Fah'renheit *a.* of the thermometric scale on which the freezing point of water is 32° and the boiling point, 212° [*Fahrenheit*, Ger. inventor (d. 1736)]

fai'ence (fi-ong-s) *n.* glazed earthenware or china. [*Faenza*, in Italy]

fail *v.i.* be insufficient; run short; lose power; die away; be wanting at need; be unsuccessful; become bankrupt. -*v.t.* disappoint, give no help to. -**fail'-safe** *a.* designed to return to safe condition in the event of a failure or malfunction; (of a nuclear weapon) capable of being deactivated in the event of a failure or accident; unlikely to fail; foolproof. -**fail'ure** *n.* [L. *falterer*, to deceive]

fain *a.* glad, willing; inclined; constrained. -*adv.* gladly. [OE. *fævgen*, glad]

faine'ant (fen-a-ong) *n.* idler; one content to be a puppet, figurehead, idle, inactive. [F.]

faint *a.* feeble; dim; pale; weak; inclined to swoon. -*v.i.* swoon: to fade or decay; lose courage. -*n.* swoon. -**faint'ly** *adv.* [OF. *feint*, sluggish]

fair (far) *n.* periodical gathering for trade, often with amusements added of shows and roundabouts. -**fair'ing** *n.* present from a fair; streamlining of an aircraft. [L. *feria*, holiday]

fair (far) *a.* beautiful; ample; blond; unblemished; of moderate quality or amount; just, honest; of weather, favorable. -*adv.* honestly. -**fair'ish** *a.* -**fair'ly** *adv.* -**fair'ness** *n.* [OE. *foeger*]

fair'way *n.* navigable channel in river; roadstead, *etc.*; (*golf*) main track from green to green, with 'rough' on either side. [*fair*]

fairy *n.* small elemental being with powers of magic. *a.* of fairies; like a fairy, beautiful and delicate. -**fair'lamp; fair'y-light** *n.* small colored light for outdoor illuminations. -**fair'yland** *n.* -**fair'y-ring** *n.* circle of darker color in grass. -**fair'y-tale** *n*- [OF. *faierie*, land of fays]

faith *n.* trust; belief; belief without proof, religion; promise; loyalty. -**faith'ful** *a.* -**faith'less** *a.* -**faith'fully** *adv.* [OF. *feid* fr. L. *fides*; cp. fidelity]

fake *v.t.* counterfeit; falsify; adulterate. -*n.* sham; counterfeit; dodge or trick. -*a.* [earlier *feak, feague*; Ger. *fegen*, furbish]

fakir' (-er) *a.* Hindu, religious mendicant, often gifted with strange powers. [Arab, *faqir*, poor]

Falash'a *n.* member of the tribe of black Ethiopian Jews. [fr. Amharic, *falasi*, stranger]

fal'chion *n.* broad curved sword. [OF. *faucon*, fr. L. *falx*, sickle]

fal'con *n.* small bird of prey, *esp.* trained in hawking for sport. -**fal'coner** *n.* one who keeps, trains, or hunts with falcons. -**fal'conry** *n.* flow [L. *falcon-*, fr. *falx*, sickle (shape of wings, beak, claws)]

faidett'a *n.* Maltese hooded cloak. [It.]

fal'deral *n.* flimsy ornament; gewgaw; meaningless refrain. [fr. *fol-de-rol*, a song refrain]

fall (-aw-) *v.i.* drop, come down freely; hang down; become lower; come to the ground, cease to stand; perish; collapse; be captured; pass into a condition; become; happen. -*n.* a falling; amount that falls; amount of descent; yielding to temptation; autumn; rope of hoisting tackle. -**fall'ing-sick'ness** *n.* epilepsy. -**fall'ing- star',** meteor. [OE. *feallan*]

fall'acy (fal'-a-si) *n.* misleading argument; flaw in logic; mistaken belief. -**falla'cious** *a.* [L. *allere*, deceive]

fal'lal *n.* piece of finery, or frippery. [orig. uncertain]

fall'ible *a.* liable to error. -**fall'ibly** *adv.* -**fallibil'ity** *n.* [F. fr. *Low.* L. *fallibilis*]

fallow *a.* plowed and harrowed but left without crop; uncultivated. -*n.* fallow land. -*v.t.* break up (land). [OE. *fealg*, harrow]

fallow *a.* pale brown or reddish yellow. -**fall'ow-deer** *n.* [OE. *fealo*]

false (-aw-) *a.* wrong, erroneous; deceptive; faithless; sham; artificial; untrue. -**false'ly** *adv.* -**false'hood** *n.* lie. -**false'ness**. -**fal'sity** *n.* -**fal'sify** *v.t.* to alter fraudulently; misrepresent; disappoint (hopes, *etc.*). -**falsification** *n.* [L. *falsus*, mistaken, fr. *fallere, fals-*, deceive]

falset'to *n.* forced voice above the natural range. [It. dim. of *falso*, false]

fal'ter- *v.i.* stumble; speak hesitatingly; waver. -*v.t.* say hesitatingly. [orig. uncertain]

fame *n.* reputation; renown; rumor. -**famed** *a.* -**fa'mous** *a.* -**fa'mously** *adv.* [L. *fama*, report]

familiar *a.* intimate; closely acquainted; well-known, common; unceremonious. -*n.* familiar friend or demon. -**famil'iarly** *adv.* -**familiar'ity** *n.* -**famil'iarize** *v.t.* -**familiariza'tion** *n.* [L. *familiaris*, fr. *familia* household]

fam'ily *n.* household of parents and their children; group of parents and children, or near relatives; person's children; all descendants of a common ancestor; class, group of allied objects. -**fam'ily-tree'** *n.* lineage of a person, family, in graphic form. [L. *familia*, household, fr. *famulus*, servant]

fam'ine (-in) *n.* extreme scarcity of food; starvation. -**fam'ish** *v.t.* starve. -*v.i.* be very hungry. [F. , fr. L. *fames*, hunger]

fa'mous. *See* **fame.**

fan *n.* instrument for producing a current of air, *esp.* for cooling the face; winnowing machine; propeller blade; thing spread out as a bird's tail; ventilating machine. -*v.t.* winnow, blow, or cool with a fan. -**fan'light** *n.* fanshaped window over a door. -**fan'-tail** *n.* kind of pigeon with fanshaped tail. [OE. *fann*, fr. L. *vannus*]

fan *n.* enthusiastic follower (of a game, *etc.*), devotee (of a person). -**fan'mail** *n.* letters from one's fans. [for *fanatic*]

fanat'ic *a.* filled with mistaken enthusiasm, *esp.* in religion. -*n.* fanatic person; zealot. -**fanat'ical** *a.* -**fanat'ically** *adv.* -**fanaticism** *n.* [L. *fanaticus*]

fan'cy *n.* power of imagination; mental image; notion, whim, caprice; liking, inclination; followers of a hobby. *a.* ornamental, not plain; of whimsical or arbitrary kind. -*v.t.* imagine; be inclined to believe; have or take a liking for. -**fan'cier** *n.* one with liking and expert knowledge (respecting some specified thing). -**fan'ciful** *a.* -**fan'cifully** *adv.* [shortened fr. *fantasy*]

fandan'go *n.* lively Spanish dance; music for it. [Sp.]

fane *n.* temple. [L. *fanum*]

fan'fare *n.* flourish of trumpets. [F.]

fang *n.* long pointed tooth; snake's poison tooth; root of a tooth. [OE. *fang*, booty, fr. *fon*, seize]

fank *n.* sheep-fold. [Gael. *fang*]

fan'tasy *n.* power of imagination, *esp.* extravagant; mental image; fanciful invention or design. -**fanta'sia** (-z-) *n.* fanciful musical composition. -**fantas'tic** *a.* quaint, grotesque, extremely fanciful. -**fantas'tically** *adv.* [G. *phantasia*]

far *adv.* at or to a great distance or advanced point; by very much. *a.* distant. -*n.* great distance or amount. -**far'-fetched** *a.* forced, not natural. -**far'sighted** *a.* able to see the future effects of present action; able to see objects clearly only when they are far from the eyes. [OE. *feorr*]

far'ad *n.* unit of electrical capacity. [Michael *Faraday*, 1791-1867]

farce *n.* play meant only to excite laughter; absurd and futile proceeding. -**far'cical** *a.* -**far'cically** *adv.* [F.]

fare (fer) *n.* money paid by a passenger for conveyance; passenger; food -*v.i.* happen; get on; travel. -**farewell'** *interj.* goodbye. -*n.* leave-taking. [OE. *faran*, travel]

fari'na *n.* meal; powder; starch; pollen. -**farina'ceous** *a.* mealy; starchy. [L.]

farm *n.* tract of cultivated land. -*v.t.* pay or take a fixed sum for the proceeds of (a tax, *etc.*); cultivate. -**farm'stead** (-sted) *n.* -**farm'house** *n.* -**farm'yard** *n.* -**farm'er** *n.* [F. *ferme*]

fa'ro *n.* a card-game not dependent on skill. [*Pharoah*]

farouche' *a.* sullen, lowering. [F. fr. L. *ferox*, fierce]

farra'go *n.* a medley, hotchpotch. [L. mixed fodder]

farrier *n.* shoeing smith; one who treats diseases of horses. -**farr'iery** *n.* [L. *ferrarius*, fr. *ferrum*, iron]

farr'ow *n.* litter of pigs. -*v.t.* and *i.* produce this. [OE. *fearth*, young pig]

far'ther (-TH-) *a.* more distant. -*adv.* to, at, greater distance. -**far'thest** *a.* most far. *adv.* to, at, greatest distance. [*far*]

far'thing (-TH-) *n.* formerly, quarter of a penny. [OE. *feorthung*, fourti part]

far'thingale (-TH-) *n.* hooped petticoat. [Sp. *verdugado*, fr. *verdugo*, green switch (used for hoop)]

fas'cia *n.* long flat surface of wood or stone in a building; part of shop-front bearing the merchant's name. [L.]

fascinate *v.t.* make powerless by look or presence; charm, attract. -**fascina'tion** *n.* -**fas'cinator** *n.* charmer; headscarf for evening wear. [L. *fascinate*, enchant]

fas'cis *n.pl.* bundle of rods bound together round axe, as Roman badge of office; emblem of Italian Fascists. [L. = bundles]

Fas'cist *n.* member of Italian or similar political party aiming at the overthrow of communists, radicals, *etc.*, by violence, and of strong rule by a dictator. [It. fascistic members of a *fascio*, union]

fash'ion (-shun) *n.* make, style; manner; custom, esp. in dress. -*v.t.* shape, make. -**fash'ionable** *a.* in the prevailing mode. -**fash'ionably** *adv.* [F. *faqon*]

fast (-a-) *v.t.* go without food or some kinds of food *esp.* as a religious exercise. -*n.* act or appointed time, of fasting. -**fast'day** *n.* [OE. *fæstan*]

fast (-a-) *a.* firm, fixed, steady, permanent; rapid; ahead of true time; dissipated. -*adv.* firmly, tightly; rapidly; in a dissipated way. -**fast'ness** *n.* fast state; fortress. [OE. *fæst*, firm]

fast'en (-sen) *v.t.* attach, fix, secure. -*v.i.* seize (upon) [*fast*]

fastidious *a.* hard to please; easily disgusted. [F. *fastidieux*, L. *fastidiosus*]

fastig'iate (-j-) *a.* pointed, sloping to a peak or edge. [L. *fastigium*, summit]

fat *a.* plump, thick, solid; containing much fat; fertile. -*n.* oily substance of animal bodies; fat part. -*v.t.* feed (animals) for slaughter. -**fatt'en** *v.t.* and *i.* -**fat'ness** *n.* -**fatt'y** *a.* [OE. *fætt*]

fate *n.* power supposed to predetermine events; goddess of destiny; destiny; person's appointed lot or condition; death or destruction. -*v.t.* preordain. -**fate'ful** *a.* prophetic, fraught with destiny. -**fa'tal** *a.* deadly, ending in death; destructive; very ill-advised, disastrous; inevitable. -**fa'tally** adj. -**fatal'ity** n. rule of fate; calamity; death by accident. -**fa'talism** *n.* belief that everything is predetermined; submission to fate. -**fa'talist** *n.* -**fatalist'ic** *a.* -**fatalis'tically** *adv.* [L. *fatum*, decree of the gods]

fa'ther *n.* male parent; forefather, ancestor; originator, early leader; priest, confessor; oldest member of a society. -*v.t.* beget; originate; pass as father or author of, act as father to; fix the paternity of - **fa'therhood** *n.* -**fa'ther-in-law** *n.* father of one's husband or wife. -**fa'therly** *a.* - **fa'therless** *a.* -**fa'therland** *n.* one's country. -**Fa'ther's Day** *n.* day in which the father is honored by the family, *usu.* the third Sunday in June. [OE. *fæder*]

fath'om (-ia'TH-) *n.* (*naut.*) measure of six feet. -*v.t.* sound (water); get to the bottom of, understand. -**fath'omless** *a.* too deep to fathom. -**fath'omable** *a.* [OE. *fæthm*, two arms outstretched]

fatigue' *v.t.* weary. -*n.* weariness of body or mind; toil; soldier's non-military duty- *n. pl.* informal army clothes. [F. *fatiquer*, L. *fatigare*].

fat'uous *a.* silly, foolish. -**fatu'ity** *n.* - **fat'uousness** *n.* [L. *fatuus*]

fau'ces *n.pl.* upper part of throat. -**fau'cal** *a.* (of sound) guttural. [L.]

fau'cet (-set) *n.* apparatus for controlling the flow of liquid from a pipe, *esp.* in a kitchen or bathroom; tap [F. *fausseti]*

faugh *interj.* exclamation of disgust. [imit. orig.]

fault *n.* defect; misdeed; blame, culpability; (*tennis*) ball wrongly served; (*hunting*) failure of scent; (*geol.*) a break in strata. -**fault'y** *a.* -**fault'less** *a.* -**fault'ily** *adv.* -**fault'lessly** *adv.* [F. *faute*]

faun *n.* Roman countryside god with tail and horns. [L. *Faunus*]

faun'a *n.* animals of a region or period. [L. *Fauna*, sister of *Faunus*; *v.s.*]

fauteu'il *n.* arm-chair; seat of one of the 40 members of the French Academy; theater-stall. [F.]

faux' pas (fo-pa) awkward blunder. [F. = false step]

fave'olate (-va) *a.* honeycombed. [L. *faveolus*, fr. *favus*, honeycomb]

favo'nian *a.* of the west wind; favorable. [L. *favonius*, west wind]

favor (-ver) *n.* goodwill; approval; partiality; especial kindness; badge or knot of ribbons. -*v.t.* regard or treat with favor; oblige; treat with partiality; aid support. -**favorably** *adv.* -**fa'vorite** (-it) *n.* favored person or thing; horse, *etc.*, expected to win race. *a.* chosen, preferred. - **fa'voritism** *n.* practice of showing undue preference. [L. *favor*]

fawn *n.* young fallow-deer. *a.* of a light

yellowish-brown. [F. *faon*]

fawn *v.i.* of a dog, *etc.*, show affection by wagging the tail and grovelling; of a person, cringe, court favor in a servile manner. [OE. *fahnian*]

fay *n.* fairy. [F. *fée*]

faze *v.t.* (*sl.*) discomfit. [OE. *fesiani*]

fe'alty *n.* fidelity of a vassal to his lord. [OF. fr. L. *fidelis*, faithful]

fear *n.* dread, alarm; unpleasant emotion caused by coming evil or danger. *-v.i.* regard with fear; revere; hesitate, shrink from (doing something). **-fear'ful** *a.* **-fear'fully** adv. **-fear'some** *a.* **-fear'less** *a.* **-fear'lessly** *adv.* [OE. *fær*, sudden peril]

feas'ible (-z-) *a.* practicable, that can be done. **-feas'ibly** *adv.* **-feasibil'ity** *n.* [F. *faisable*, fr. *faire*, do]

feast *n.* banquet, lavish meal; religious anniversary to be kept with joy; annual village festival. *-v.i.* partake ofa banquet, fare sumptuously. *-v.t.* regale with a feast. [L. *festa*]

feat *n.* notable deed; surprising trick. [F. *fait*, fr. L. *factum*, deed]

feath'er (feTH'-) *n.* one of the barbed shafts which form the covering of birds. *-v.t.* provide with feathers; turn (an oar) edgeways. *-v.i.* grow feathers; turn an oar. **-feath'ery** *a.* **-feath'er-weight** *n.* very light person or thing. [OE. *fether*]

feat'ure *n.* part of the face (*usu. pl.*); characteristic or notable part of anything. *-v.t.* portray; give prominence to. **-feat'ureless** *a.* flat, undistinguished [OF. *faiture*, shape]

febrifuge (-j-) *n.* medicine to reduce fever. **-feb'rile** *a.* of fever. [L. *febris*, fever, and *fugare*, put to flight]

Feb'ruary *n.* second month of the year. [L. *Februarius*]

fe'ces *n.pl.* excrement, bodily waste matter. **-fe'cal** *a.* [L. *faex*, dregs]

feckless *a.* inefficient, weak, spiritless. [Scot. = effectless]

fec'ulent *a.* full of sediment, turbid. **-fec'ulence** *n.* [L. *fæculentus*]

fec'und *a.* fertile. **-fecund'ity** *n.* **-fec'undate** *v.t.* fertilize, impregnate. **-fecunda'tion** *n.* [L. *fecundus*, fruitful]

fed' up (*sl.*) bored, sated, disgruntled. [*feed*]

fed'eral *a.* of, or like, the government of states which are united but retain more or less independence within themselves; *pert.* to the Union in the Civil War. **-fed'eralism** *n.* **-fed'eralist** *n.* **-fed'erate** *v.i.* enter into a league, a federal union. **-federation** *n.* act of federating; federated society. [L. *fædus, foeder-*, alliance]

fee *n.* payment for services, *esp.* one due to a public official or a professional man; entrance-money. *-v.t.* pay a fee to. [OE. *feoh*, cattle, money]

fee'ble *a.* weak; ineffective; insipid. **-fee'bly** *adv.* [F. *faible*]

feed *v.t.* give food to; supply, support. *-v.i.* take food. *-n.* a feeding; fodder, pasturage; allowance of fodder; material supplied to a machine; part of a machine taking in material. **-feed'er** *n.* **-feed stock** *n.* the main raw material used in the manufacture of a product. [OE. fedan]

feel *v.t.* examine, search, by touch; perceive, have knowledge of, by touch or in emotions. *-v.i.* use the sense of touch; grope; be conscious; have, be affected by (a sentiment); sympathize. *-n.* sense of touch; impression on it. **-feel'er** *n.* special organ of touch in some animals; proposal put forward to test others' opinion; that which feels. **-feel'ing** *n.* sense of touch; physical sensation; emotion; sympathy, tenderness; conviction or opinion not solely based on reason. *-pl.* susceptibilities. *a.* sensitive, sympathetic. [OE. *felan*]

feet. *See* **foot.**

feign (fan) *v.t.* pretend, simulate. *-v.i.* pretend. [F. *feindre*, fr. L. *fingere*, invent]

feint (fant) *n.* sham attack or blow meant to deceive an opponent. *-v.i.* make such move. (F. *feinte*]

feld'spar, fel'spar *n.* crystalline mineral forming granite and other rocks. [Ger. *feld*, field, and *spar*]

feli'city (-is'-) *n.* great happiness, bliss; appropriateness of wording. **-feli'citous** *a.* apt, well-chosen; happy. **-feli'citate** *v.t.* congratulate. **-felicita'tion** *n.* (*usu.* in *pl.*), congratulations. [L. *felix, felic-*, happy]

fe'line *a.* of cats; catlike. **-felin'ity** *n.* [L. *felinus*, fr. *felis*, cat]

fell *n.* skin or hide with hair; thick matted hair. [OE.]

fell *n.* mountain, stretch of moorland, *esp.* in north of England. [ON. *fjall*]

fell *v.t.* knock down; cut down (a tree). [OE. *fellan*]

fell *a.* fierce, terrible. [F. *felon*]

fell'ah *n.* Egyptian peasant. *-pl.* **fell'-ahs, fellahin**. [Arab. *fallah*]

fell'ic *a.* of or obtained from bile. [L. *fel*, gall]

fell'oe, fell'y *n.* outer part of a wheel; section of this. [OE, *felge*]

fell'ow *n.* comrade, associate; counterpart, like thing; member (of certain learned societies, *etc*); person. *-a.* of the same class, associated. **-fell'owship** *n.* [ON. *felagi*, partner]

felo de se *n.* suicide. [Anglo -L. = *felon* of himself]

fel'on *n.* one who has committed a felony. *a.* cruel, fierce. **-fel'ony** *n.* crime more serious than a misdemeanor. **-felo'nious** *a.* [F. *folon*]

felt *n.* cloth made by rolling and pressing wool with size; thing made of this. *-v.t.* make into, or cover with, felt. [OE.]

feluc'ca *n.* two-masted vessel with lateen sails used in Mediterranean. [It. *feluca*]

fe'male *a.* of the sex which bears offspring; relating to this sex or to women. *-n.* one of this sex. **-fe'male screw'**, screw cut on the inside surface of a screw-hole. [F. *femelle*]

fem'inine (-in) *a.* of women; womanly; (*gram.*) of the gender proper to women's names. **-feminin'ity** *n.* **-fem'inism** *n.* influence of women; advocacy of this, of women's political rights, *etc.* **-fem'inist** *n.* [L. *femininus*]

fem'oral *a.* of the thigh. [Late L. *femoralis*, fr. *femur*, thigh]

fen *n.* tract of marshy land; bog, morass. **-fenn'y** *a.* [OE. *fenn*]

fence *n.* art of using a sword; hedge or railing; (*sl.*) receiver of stolen goods. *-v.t.* put a hedge round, enclose. *-v.i.* practice sword-play. **-fen'cing** *n.* [*defence*]

fend *v.t.* ward off, repel. *-v.i.* provide (for oneself, *etc*).. **-fend'er** *n.* bundle of rope, *etc.*, hung over a ship's side to prevent chafing; frame round a hearth; guard of the wheel of an automobile. [*defend*]

fenestra'tion *n.* (*archit.*) arrangement of windows in a building. [L. *fenestra*, window]

Fe'nian *n.* member of Irish nationalist association founded in New York in 1857 to overthrow the English Govt. in Ireland. (Ir. *fene*, ancient people of Ireland]

fen'nee *n.* African desert fox. [*Moorish*]

fenn'el *n.* yellow-flowered fragrant herb. [OE. *finol*, fr. L. *feniculum*]

feoff (fef) *n.* fief. *-v.t.* grant possession of. **-feoff'ee** *n.* one granted fief. **-feoff'er, feoffor**, *n.* -feoffment *n.* [*fee*]

fe'ral, fe'rine (fe-) *a.* of or like a wild beast. [L. *fera*, wild beast]

fe'rial (fe-) *a.* of holidays; of days neither feast-days nor fast-days. [L. *feria*, holiday]

fer'ment *n.* leaven, substance causing a thing to ferment; excitement, tumult. - **ferment'** *v.i.* undergo a chemical change with effervescence, liberation of heat and alteration of properties, *e.g.* process set up in dough by yeast. *-v.t.* subject to this process; stir up, excite. **-fermenta'tion** *n.* [L. *fermentum*]

fern *n.* plant with feathery fronds. **-fern'y** *a.* full of ferns. **-fern'ery** *n.* place for growing ferns. [OE. fearn]

ferocious (-ō-shus) *a.* fierce, savage, cruel. **-feroc'ity** (-os'-) *n.* savage cruelty. [L. *ferax, feroc-*]

ferr'et *n.* half-tamed animal like a weasel used to catch rabbits, rats, *etc.*; *-v.t.* take or clear with ferrets; search out. *-v.i.* search about, rummage. [F. *furet*]

ferr'ic *a.* **ferr'ous** *a.* containing iron. - **ferrif'erous** *a.* yielding iron. - **ferru'ginous** *a.* of iron-rust; reddish-brown. **-ferr'ocon'crete** *n.* concrete strengthened or reinforced by a framework of steel or iron. [L. *ferrum*, iron]

ferr'ule *n.* metal band or cap to strengthen the end of a stick. [F. *virole*]

ferry *v.t.* and *i.* carry, pass, by boat across a river, strait, *etc.* *-n.* place or a boat for ferrying. **-ferr'yman** *n.* [OE. *ferian*, carry]

fer'tile *a.* fruitful, producing abundantly. **-fertil'ity** *n.* **-fer'tilize** *v.t.* make fertile. - **fer'titizer** *n.* **-fertiliza'tion** *n.* [L. *fertilis*, fr. *ferre*, bear]

fer'ule *n.* flat stick, ruler, used for punishment. [L. *ferula*, giant fennel rod]

fer'vent *a.* hot, glowing; ardent, intense. **-fer'vently** adv, **-fer'vency** *n.* **-fer'vor** (-er) *n.* **-fer'vid** *a.* ardent, impassioned; zealous. **-fer'vidly** *adv.* [L. *fervere*, boil]

frescue *n.* kinds of grass useful for pasture; small pointer. (L. *festuca*, straw]

fes'tal *a.* of a feast; keeping holiday; gay. **-fes'tive** *a.* of a feast; joyous, gay; jovial. **-fes'tival** *n.* festal days; merrymaking; periodical musical celebration. **-festiv'ity** *n.* gaiety, mirth; occasion for rejoicing. *-pl.* festive proceedings. [L. *festum*, feast]

fes'ter *n.* suppurating condition, sore. *-v.i.* ulcerate, produce matter (in wound); rankle. *-v.t.* cause to fester. [OF. *festre*]

festoon *n.* chain of flowers, ribbons, *etc.*, hung in a curve between two points. *-v.t.* make into, or adorn with, festoons. [F. *feston*]

fetch *v.t.* go for and bring; draw forth; be sold for; charm. *-n.* trick. **-fetch'ing** *a.* attractive. [OE. *fetian*]

fetch *n.* wraith, double, of a living person, portending his death. [perh. fr. *fetch v.s.*]

fête (feht) *n.* festival; saint's day. *-v.t.* hold

festivities in honer of. [F.]

fet'id *a.* stinking. **-fe'tor** *n.* evil smell. [L. *fetidus* from *fetere*, to stink]

fet'ish *n.* inanimate object worshipped by savages; as enshrining a spirit; anything which is the object of irrational reverence. [F. *fetiche*]

fet'lock *n.* part of a horse's leg where a tuft of hair grows behind the pastern joint; the tuft. [ME. *fetiak*]

falter *n.* chain or shackle for the feet; check, restraint. *-pl.* captivity. *-v.t.* chain up; restrain, hamper. [OE. *feter*, fr. *fet*, feet]

fet'tle *n.* condition, trim. [perh. fr. OE. *fetel*, belt, in sense of girding onself]

fe'tus *n.* fully-developed young in womb or egg. **-fe'tal** *a.* [L. = offspring]

feu (fu) *n.* fief; (Scot.) perpetual possession of land at stipulated rent. *-v.t.* grant, let in feu. **-feu'ar** *n.* **-feu'-duty** *n.* [*fee*]

feud (fud) *n.* bitter and lasting mutual hostility, *esp.* between two families or tribes. [OF. *faide*]

feud (fiad) *n.* fief. **-feud'al** *a.* of a fief. **-feud'al system**, medieval political system based on the holding of land from a superior in return for service. **-feud'alism** *n.* [Med. L. *feudum*]

fe'ver *n.* condition of illness with high temperature and waste of tissue; nervous excitement. *-v.t.* throw into fever. **-fe'verish** *a.* **-fe'verishly** *adv.* **-fe'ver few** *n.* herb formerly used as a febrifuge. [OE. *fefer*, fr. L. *febris*]

few *a.* not many. *-n.* small number. **-few'ness** *n.* [OE. *feawe*]

fey *a.* fated to early death; excessively gay, elated; the supposed mark of one so doomed. [OE. *foege*, doomed]

fez *n.* tarboosh, Turkish cap with a tassel. [*Fez*, in Morocco]

fiancé (fe-ong-sa,) *n.* **fiancee'** *fem.* one betrothed. *a.* betrothed, engaged. [F.]

fias'co *n.* breakdown, ignominious failure. [It. = bottle]

fi'at *n.* decree; authorization; command. [L. = let it be done]

fib *n.* trivial lie. *-v.i.* tell a fib. **-fibb'er** *n.* [orig. uncertain]

fi'ber *n.* filament forming part of animal or plant tissue; substance that can be spun. **-fi'brous** *a.* **-fi'berglass** *n.* material made from glass fibers. **-fi'ber op'tics** *n.* cable consisting of glass or plastic fibers able to transmit data in the form of light. [L. *fibre*]

fibro'sis *n.* overgrowth of fibrous tissue. **-fibrosi'tis** (-i-) *n.* inflammation of fibrous tissue, kind of rheumatism. [*fibre*]

fib'ula *n.* outer leg-bone from knee to ankle; buckle; brooch, or clasp. [L.]

fich'u (fish-oo) *n.* triangular lace shawl for a woman's shoulders and neck. [F.]

fic'kle *a.* changeable, inconstant. **-fic'kleness** *n.* [OE. *ficol*, tricky]

fic'tile *a.* plastic; molded, as pottery. [L *fictilis*]

fic'tion *n.* invented statement or narrative; novels, stories collectively; conventionally accepted falsehood. **-ficti'tious** *a.* not genuine, imaginary; assumed. [L. *fictio*, fr. *fingere*, shape]

fid *n.* (*naut.*) wooden pin used in splicing rope. [orig. uncertain]

fid'dle *n.* violin; in a ship, a frame to stop things rolling off a table. *-v.i.* play the fiddle; make idle movements, trifle. **-fid'dlestick** *n.* bow. *-pl.* nonsense. **-fid'dler** *n.* [OE. *fithele*]

fidelity *n.* faithfulness. [L. *fidelitas*]

fidg'et *v.i.* move restlessly; be uneasy. *-n.* restless condition with aimless movements; restless mood; one who fidgets. **-fidg'ety** *a.* [orig. obscure]

fidu'ciary (-sh-) *a.* held or given in trust; relating to a trustee. *-n.* trustee. [L. *fiduciarius*, fr. *fides*, faith]

fie *interj.* exclamation of reproach, disgust 'for shame.' [ON. *fy*]

fief (fef) *n.* estate in land held of a superior in return for service. [F.]

field *n.* piece of land tilled or used as pasture; enclosed piece of land; battleground; tract of land rich in a specified product (*e.g.* gold field); all the players in a game or sport; all competitors but the favorite; surface of a shield, coin, *etc.*; range, area of operation or study. *-v.i.* and *t.* in certain sports, stop and return a ball. *n.* (*compute.*) group of related characters (bytes) treated as a unit. **-field'-day** *n.* day of maneuvers; day of athletic contests; important occasion. **-field'glass** *n.* binoculars for outdoor use. **-field'er** *n.* one who fields at baseball, cricket, *etc.* [OE. *feld*]

field'fare *n.* bird related to the thrush. [orig. uncertain]

fiend *n.* devil. **-fiend'ish** *a.* fiend-like, devilish. [OE. *feond*, enemy]

fierce *a.* savage, wild, raging. **-fierce'ness** *n.* **-fierce'ly** *adv.* [L. *ferus*, wild]

fi'ery (fi-) *a.* consisting of fire; blazing, glowing; flashing; irritable; spirited; ardent, eager. **-fi'ery cross'**, ancient Scottish signal for a rising. *n.* harred wooden cross dipped in blood and sent through the country. **-fi'erily** *adv.* [*fire*]

fife *n.* shrill flute played with drums in military music. -*v.i.* and *t.* play on a fife. -**fi'fer** *n.* [Ger. *pfeife*]

fifteen, fifty *See* **five.**

fifth *See* **five.**

fifth col'umn *n.* body of potential collaborators, working secretly in enemy interest. [fr. 'fifth column' of General Franco's army].

fifty-fif'ty *n.* (*sl.*) equal shares, chances. *a.* [*fifty* per cent.]

fig *n.* familiar soft round many-seeded fruit; tree bearing it. [F. *figue*, L. *ficus*]

fight (fit) *v.i.* contend in battle or in single combat. -*v.t.* contend with; maintain against an opponent; settle by combat; maneuver (ships, troops) in battle. -*n.* act of fighting, combat, battle; strife. -**fight'er** *n.* [OE. *feohtan*]

fig'ment *n.* invented statement purely imaginary thing. [L. *figmentum*]

fig'ure (-er) *n.* form, shape; bodily shape; appearance, *esp.* conspicuous appearance; space enclosed by lines or surfaces; diagram, illustration; likeness, image; pattern; movement in dancing, skating, *etc.*; numerical symbol; amount, number; abnormal form of expression for effect in speech, *e.g.*, a metaphor. -*v.i.* use numbers; show, be conspicuous; be estimated; consider. -*v.t.* to calculate, estimate; represent by picture or diagram; to ornament. -**fig'urative** *a.* metaphorical; full of figures of speech. -**fig'uratively** *adv.* [F.]

figurehead *n.* carved figure at ship's prow; one in nominal authority. [*figure* and *head*]

fila'ceous (-a-shus) *a.* made up of threads. -**fi'lar** *a.* of, like, a thread. -**fila'ria** *n.* threadlike organism causing disease. [L. *filum*, thread]

fil'ament *n.* thread-like body; (*elec.*) wire in lamp. [Late L. *filamentum*]

fil'bert *n.* cultivated hazel; its fruit or nut. [ripe about *St. Philibert's* day]

filch *v.t.* steal. [orig. uncertain]

file *n.* tool, usually of roughened steel, for smoothing or rubbing down metal or other material. -*v.t.* apply a file to, smooth, rub down, polish. -**fi'ling** *n.* action of using a file; scrap of metal removed by a file. (OE. *feol*]

file *n.* stiff wire on which papers are threaded; device for holding papers for reference; papers so arranged. -*v.t.* place in a file. [F. *fit*, thread]

file *n.* in formation of soldiers, a front-rank man and the man or men immediately behind him. -**in file**, arranged in two lines facing to one end of the rank.- **single file,** formation of a single line of men one behind the other. -*v.i.* march in file. [F. *file*, fr. *filer*, spin out]

fil'ial *a.* of, or befitting, a son or daughter. -**fil'ially** *adv.* [L. *filius*, son]

fil'ibeg *n.* kilt. [Gael. *feileadlbeag*, little fold]

filibuster *n.* one who deliberately obstructs the passage of legislation, *esp.* by making long speeches; adventurer in irregular warfare, privateer; pirate. -*v.i.* act as a filibuster. [F. *flibustier*]

fili'form *a.* thread-like, in form of fine thread. [L. *filum*, thread]

fil'igree *n.* fine tracery or open-work of metal, usually gold or silver wire. [F. *filigrane*, fr. L. *filum*, thread, *granum*, bead]

fill *v.t.* make full; occupy completely, hold, discharge duties of; stop up; satisfy; fulfill. -*v.i.* become full. -*n.* full supply; as much as desired. -**fill'er** *n.* -**fill'ing** *n.* what is used to pad, complete, stop a hole, *etc.* -**fill'ing station** *n.* roadside depot for oil and gasoline. [OE. *fyllan*]

fill'et, fil'et *n.* head-band; strip of meat; piece of meat or fish boned, rolled and tied. -*v.t.* encircle with a fillet; make into fillets. [F. *filet*]

fill'ip *n.* the sudden release of a finger bent against the thumb; flip so given; stimulus. -*v.t.* give a fillip to, flip; stimulate. [imit. orig.]

fill'y *n.* female foal. [ON. *fylja*]

film *n.* very thin skin or layer; thin sensitized sheet used in photography; sensitized celluloid roll used in cinema photography; cinematographic picture; dimness on the eyes; slight haze; thread. *v.t.* photograph or represent by moving pictures; cover with a film. -*v.i.* become covered with a film. -**film'y** *a.* -**film'star** *n.* popular actor or actress for films. [OE. *filmen*]

fil'ter *n.* cloth or other apparatus for straining liquids. -*v.t.* and *i.* pass through a filter. -*v.i.* make a way through. -**filtra'tion** *n.* (F. *filtre*]

filth (-th) *n.* loathsome dirt; garbage; vileness. -**filth'y** *a.* -**filth'ily** *adv.* -*filthiness n.* (OE. *fylth*]

fin *n.* propelling or steering organ of a fish; erection on tail of an airplane. [OE. *finn*]

fi'nal *a.* coming at the end; conclusive. -*n.* game, heat, examination, *etc.* , coming at the end of a series. -**fi'nally** *adv.* -**final'ity** *n.* -**finalize** *v.t.* -**fina'le** (-d-li) *n.* closing part of a musical composition, opera, *etc.* [L. *finis*, end]

finance′ *n.* management of money. *-pl.* money resources. *-v.t.* find capital for. *-v.i.* deal with money. -**finan′cial** *a.* -**finan′cially** *adv.* -**finan′cier** *n.* [F.]

finch *n.* one of a family of small singing birds. [OE. *fine*]

find (fi-) *v.t.* come across, light upon, obtain; recognize; experience, discover; discover by searching; ascertain; declare on inquiry; supply. *-n.* a finding; something found. -**find′er** *n.* [OE. *findan*]

fine *n.* sum fixed as a penalty; sum paid in consideration of a low rent. -**in fine**, to sum up. *-v.t.* punish by a fine. [Low L. *finis*, fine]

fine *a.* choice, pure, of high quality, delicate, subtle; in small particles; slender; excellent; handsome; showy; free from rain; fastidious. *-n.* fine weather. *-adv.* in fine manner. *-v.t.* make clear or pure; thin; refine. *-v.i.* become clear or pure or thinned. -**fine′ly** *adv.* -**fine′ness** *n.* -**fi′nery** *n.* showy dress. -**finesse′** (fin-) *n.* artfulness; subtle management; at cards, the attempt to take a trick with the lower of two cards not having the intermediate one. *-v.t.* and *i.* to use finesse. [F. *fin*]

fin′ger (-ng-g-) *n.* one of the jointed branches of the hand; various things like this. *-v.t.* touch or handle with the fingers. -**fing′erprint** *n.* impression of the tip of a finger, *esp.* as used for identifying criminals. -**fing′er-and-toe′** *n.* disease of turnips. [OE.]

fingering (-ng-g-) *n.* wool for stockings, for knitting. [earlier *fingram*, F. *fin grain*, fine grain]

fin′ial *n.* (*Gothic architecture*) ornament in shape of bunch of foliage at top of pinnacles, gables, spires *etc.* [L. *finis*, end]

finicking, fin′ical, fin′iken *a.* fastidious, overnice; too delicately wrought. [orig. uncertain]

fi′nis (fi-) *n.* the end, conclusion. [L.]

fin′ish *v.t.* bring to an end, complete, perfect: kill. *-v.i.* come to an end. *-n.* end, last stage; decisive result: completed state; anything serving to complete or perfect -**fin′isher** *n.* [L. *finire*]

fi′nite (fi-nit) *a.* bounded, limited, conditioned. [L. *finitus*, fr. *finire*]

finn′an, finn′an hadd′ock *n.* haddock cured with smoke of green wood, turf, or peat. [*Findon*, Scotland]

fiord′, fjord (fyord′) *n.* narrow inlet of the sea between cliffs. [*Norwegian*]

fir *n.* coniferious tree; its wood. [ON. *fyra*, cp. Dan. *fyr*, Ger. *föhre*]

fire *n.* state of burning, combustion, flame, glow; mass of burning fuel; destructive burning, conflagration; ardor, keenness, spirit; shooting of firearms. *-v.t.* make burn; supply with fuel; bake; inspire; explode; discharge (a firearm); propel from a firearm. *-v.i.* begin to burn; become excited; discharge a firearm; dismiss from employment. -**fire′arm** *n.* weapon shooting by explosion, a gun, pistol, cannon. -**fire′brand** *n.* burning piece of wood; one who stirs up strife. -**fire′-brigade, fire department** *n.* organized body of men with appliances to put out fires and rescue those in danger from fire. -**fire-bug** *n.* incendiary, pyromaniac. -**fire′damp** *n.* in mines, carburetted hydrogen; explosive mixture of this with air. -**fire door** *n.* door made of noncombustible material, the purpose of which is to prevent a fire from spreading within a building. -**fire′-eater** *n.* fire-eating juggler; combative braggart. -**fire′-engine** *n.* engine with apparatus for extinguishing fires. -**fire′-escape** *n.* apparatus for escaping from a burning house. -**fire′fly** *n.* insect giving out a glow of phosphorescent light. -**fire′irons** *n.pl.* tongs, poke, and shovel. -**fire′lock** *n.* musket fired with a spark. -**fire′man** *n.* member of a fire-brigade: stoker, assistant to a locomotive driver. -**fire′-new** *a.* as if fresh from the furnace. -**fire′place** *n.* hearth in a room. -**fire′-plug** *n.* connection in a water main for a hose. -**fire′-proof** *a.* resistant to fire, incombustible. -**fire′-ship** *n.* burning vessel sent drifting against enemy ships. -**fire′-step** *n.* step in a trench on which a soldier stands to fire. -**fire′water** *n.* strong spirits, *esp.* as supplied to Amer. Indians. -**fire′work** *n.* device giving spectacular effects by explosions and colored flames. [OE. *fyr*]

fir′kin *n.* small cask; quarter-barrel. [Du. *vierde*, fourth]

firm *a.* solid, fixed, stable; steadfast; resolute; settled. *-v.t.* make firm; solidify. *-n.* commercial house. partners carrying on a business. [L. *firrnus*]

firmament *n.* vault of heaven. [L. *firmamentum*, fr. *firmare*, make firm]

fir′man *n.* decree *esp.* one issued by eastern ruler. [Pers. *ferman*]

firn *n.* accumulated snow on mountain-tops forming source of glaciers. [Ger. *firn*, of last year]

first *a.* earliest in time or order; foremost in rank or position. *-adv.* before others in time, order, *etc.* -**first′-aid** *n.* help given to an injured person before the arrival of a doctor. -**first'ling** *n.* first fruits, first product, offspring. -**first'ly** *adv.* -**first' strike** *a.* (of a nuclear missile) intended for use in an opening attack calculated to destroy the enemy's nuclear weapons. [OE. *fyrest*, fr. *ftore*]

firth, frith *n.* arm of the sea, estuary. [ON. *fjorthr*]

fis'cal *a.* of a state treasury; of public revenue, taxation. [L. *fiscus*, purse]

fish *n.* vertebrate cold-blooded animal with gills, living in water; flesh of fish.- *v.i.* try to catch fish; search for; try in a roundabout way to elicit information. -*v.t.* try to catch fish in; draw (up); produce. -**fish'er** *n.* -**fish'erman** *n.* one who lives by fishing. -**fish'-hawk** *n.* osprey -**fish'-hook** *n.* -**fish'wife** *n.* woman who sells fish. -**fish'ery** *n.* business of fishing; fishing-ground. -**fishing frog** *n.* angler-fish. -**fish'ing-rod** *n.* rod used in angling. -**fish'y** *a.* of, or like, fish; abounding in fish; dubious, open to suspicion. [OE. *fisc*]

fish *n.* piece of wood for strengthening a mast; metal plate for strengthening a beam. -*v.t.* mend or join with a fish. -**fish'-plate** *n.* piece of metal for holding rails together. [orig. uncertain]

fis'sure (-sh-) *n.* cleft, split. -**fis'sile** *a.* capable of splitting; tending to split. -**fis'sion** *n.* splitting; division of living cells into more cells. -**fissip'arous** *a.* reproducing by fission. [L. fissura]

fist *n.* clenched hand; handwriting. -*v.t.* strike with the clenched hand. -**fisticuffs** *n. pl.* fighting with fists. [OE. *fyst*]

fist'ula *n.* pipelike ulcer. [L. = pipe]

fit *n.* sudden passing attack of illness; seizure with convulsions, spasms, loss of consciousness, *etc.*, as of epilepsy, hysteria, *etc.*; sudden and passing state, mood. -**fit'ful** *a.* spasmodic capricious. -**fit'fully** *adv.* [OE. *fitt*, conflict]

fit *a.* well-suited, worthy; proper, becoming; ready; in good condition. -*v.t.* be suited to; be properly adjusted to; arrange, adjust, apply, insert; supply, furnish. -*v.i.* be correctly adjusted or adapted, be of the right size. -*n.* way a garment fits; its style; adjustment. -**fit'ly** -*adv.* -**fit'ness** *n.* -**fitt'er** *n.* -**fit'ment** *n.* piece of furniture. -**fitt'ing** *n.* action of fitting; apparatus; fixture. *a.* that fits; becoming, proper. [orig. uncertain]

fitch *n.* polecat; its fur. [Du. *visse*]

five *a.* and *n.* cardinal number next after four. -**fifth** *a.* ordinal number. -**fifth'genera'tion** *a.* denoting developments in computer design to produce machines with artifical intelligence. -**five'fold** *a.* and *adv.* -**fifteen'** *a. and n.* ten and five. -**fifteen'th** *a.* -**fifth'ly** *adv.* -**fifteenth'ly** *adv.* -**fif'ty** *a.* and *n.* five tens. -**fif'tieth** *a.* -**fives** *n.* ball-game played with the hand or a bat in a court. [OE. *fif*]

fix *v.t.* fasten, make firm or stable; set, establish; appoint, assign, determine; make fast, permanent. -*v.i.* become firm or solidified; determine. -*n.* difficult situation. -**fix'ity** *n.* -**fix'edly** *adv.* -**fixa'tion** *n.* fixing. (*psychoanalysis*) arrest in development. -**fix'ative** *a.* -**fix'ture** *n.* thing fixed in position; thing annexed to a house; date for a sporting event; the event. [L. *ligere*, *fix-*]

fizz *v.i.* hiss, splutter. -*n.* hissing noise. -**fiz'zle** *v.i.* splutter weakly. -*n.* fizzling noise; fiasco. [limit. orig.]

flabbergast *v.t.* overwhelm with astonishment. [*aghast*]

flabb'y *a.* hanging loose, limp; feeble. -**flabb'ily** adv. -**flabb'iness** *n.* [*flap*]

flac'cid (-ks-) flabby. -**flaccid'ity** *n.* [L. *flaccidus*, fr. *flaccus*, flabby]

flac'on (-kong-) *n.* flask for perfume, *etc.* [F. = flagon]

flag *n.* water plant with sword-sbaped leaves, *esp.* the iris. -**flagg'y** *a.* [ME. *flagge*, *flegge*]

flag *n.* flat slab of stone. -*pl.* pavement of flags. -*v.t.* pave with flags. -**flag'-stone** *n.* [ON. *flaga*]

flag *n.* banner, piece of bunting attached to a staff or halyard as a standard or signal. -*v.t.* inform by flag-signals. -*v.i.* droop, languish. -**flag'-day** *n.* day on which small flags or emblems are sold in the streets for charity. -**flag'-off'icer** *n.* admiral entitled to show a flag as an indication of his rank; commander of a fleet or squadron. -**flag'ship** *n.* ship with an admiral on board. -**flag'staff** *n.* pole on which flag is hoisted. [orig. uncertain]

flag *v.i.* droop, fade; lose vigor. [orig. uncertain]

flagellate (-j-) *v.t.* scourge, flag. -**flagella'tion** *n.* -**flag'ellant** *n.* one who scourges himself in penance. [L. *flagellate*, fr. *flagrum*, scourge]

flag'eolet (-j-) small wind-instrument with mouthpiece at the end, six holes, and sometimes keys. [F.]

flagitious (-jish'us) *a.* deeply criminal or wicked. [L. *flagitium*, crime]

flag'on *n.* vessel, usually with handle, spout and lid, to hold liquor for the table; large oval bottle. [F. *flacon*]

fla'grant *a.* glaring, scandalous; enormous. -**fla'grantly** *adv.* -**fla'grancy** *n.* [L. *flagrare*, burn]

flail *n.* instrument for threshing corn by hand, long handle with a short thick stick swinging at the end. -*v.t.* [OF. *flaiel*, fr. L. *flagellum*, scourge]

flair *n.* intuitive feeling or special aptitude (with for). (F. = scent]

flak *n.* opposition put up by anti-aircraft defences. [*abbrev.* of Ger. *fliegerabwehrkanone*]

flake *n.* light fleecy piece, *esp.* of snow; thin broad piece, *esp.* split or peeled off, layer. -*v.t.* break flakes from. -*v.i.* come off in flakes. -**fla'ky** *a.* [orig. uncertain]

flam'beau (-bo) *n.* flaming torch. [F.]

flamboyant *a.* marked by wavy lines; florid, gorgeous; showy. [F.]

flame *n.* burning gas; portion of burning gas, *esp.* above a fire; visible burning; passion, *esp.* love; sweetheart. -*v.i.* give out flames, blaze; burst out in anger, *etc.* **flame'-thrower** *n.* device for throwing jets of flame in battle. -**flam'mable** *a.* capable of being easily ignited and of burning quickly. [L. *flamma*]

flamin'go (-ng-g-) *n.* large, bright pink bird with very long neck and legs. [Port. *flainengo*, Fleming]

flan *n.* uncovered tart. [F.]

flaneur' *n.* stroller; idler. -**flan'erie** *n.* idling [F.]

flange (-anj) *n.* projecting flat rim collar, or rib. -*v.t.* provide with a flange. [orig. uncertain]

flank *n.* fleshy part of the side between the hips and ribs; side of a building or body of troops. -*v.t.* guard or strengthen on the flank; attack or take in flank; be at, or move along, either side of. [F. *flanc*]

flann'el *n.* soft woolen cloth. -*pl.* garments of this, *esp.* trousers. *a.* made of flannel. -**flannelette'** *n.* cotton fabric imitating flannel. [Welsh *gwlanen*, fr. *gulan*, wool]

flap *v.t.* strike with something broad, flat and flexible; move (wings) up and down. -*v.i.* sway, swing, flutter. -*n.* act of flapping; broad piece of anything hanging from a hinge or loosely from one side. -**flapp'er** *n.* one who, that which, flaps; flighty young woman. -**flapdoo'dle** *n.* nonsense. [imit. orig.]

flap'jack *n.* kind of pancake; small case for face-powder, mirror. [*flap* and *jack*]

flare (-ar) *v.i.* blaze with bright unsteady flame. -*n.* act of flaring; bright unsteady flame; signal light used at sea. [orig. uncertain]

flash *v.i.* break into sudden flame; gleam; burst into view; appear suddenly. -*v.t.* cause to gleam; emit (light, *etc.*) suddenly. -*n.* sudden burst of light or flame; sudden short access; ribbon or badge; display. *a.* showy; sham. -**flash'y** *a.* -**flash-back** *n.* break in book, play, film, to insert what has previously taken place. -**flash'light** *n.* small battery-operated portable light; apparatus for taking flash photographs. -**flash'point** *n.* temperature at which oil vapor ignites; point at which trouble starts. [earlier meaning *dash*, *splash*; of imit. orig.]

flask (-a-) *n.* pocket-bottle; case for gunpowder; Italian bottle covered with wicker; long-necked bottle, *esp.* for scientific use. [F. *flasque*]

flat *a.* level; spread out; at full length; smooth; downright; dull, lifeless; below true pitch. -*n.* what is flat; simpleton; note half a tone below the natural pitch; punctured tire. -**flat'car** *n.* railroad freight vehicle with no raised sides and no roof. -**flat'fish** *n.* any flat-bodied fish, as sole, plaice. -**flat'ly** *adv.* -**flat'ness** *n.* -**flatt'en** *v.t.* and *i.* [ON. *flatr*]

flatt'er *v.t.* court, fawn on; praise insincerely; inspire a belief, *esp.* an unfounded one; gratify (senses); represent too favorably. -**flatt'erer** *n.* -**flatt'ery** *n.* [F. *flatter*, 'smooth']

flat'ulent *a.* generating gases in the intestines; caused by or attended by or troubled with such gases; vain, pretentious, turgid. -**flat'ulence** *n.* -**flat'ulency** *n.* [L. *flat-*, *flare*, blow]

flaunt *v.t.* and *i.* wave proudly; show off. [orig. uncertain]

flautist *n.* flute-player, flutist. [It. *flautista*]

flaves'cent *a.* yellowish; yellowing. [fr. L. *flavus*, yellow]

fla'vine *n.* yellow dye obtained from the bark of a N. American tree, the dyer's oak. [L. *flavus*, yellow]

fla'vor *n.* mixed sensation of smell and taste; distinctive taste; undefinable characteristic quality of anything. -*v.t.* give a flavor to; season. -**flavoring** *n.* [OF. *floor*, smell]

flaw *n.* crack; defect, blemish. -*v.t.* make a flaw in. -*v.i.* crack. -**flaw'less** *a.* [orig. uncertain]

flax *n.* plant grown for its textile fiber and seeds; its fibers; cloth of this, linen. -**flax'seed** *n.* linseed. -**flax'en** *a.* of flax;

pale brown; blond. [OE. *fleax*]

flay *v.t.* strip off skin or hide; criticize severely. [OE. *flean*]

flea (-e) *n.* small wingless jumping insect which feeds on human and other blood. **-flea'bane** *n.* wild plant. **-flea'-bite** *n.* the insect's bite; trifling injury; trifle; small red spot on a horse. **-flea'bitten** *a.* of a horse, with fleabites on a lighter ground. [OE.]

fleck *n.* spot on the skin, freckle; patch of color; speck. *-v.t.* mark with flecks, dapple, [ON. *flekkr*, spot]

fledge *v.t.* provide with feathers of down. **-fledge'ling** *n.* young bird just fledged [OE. *flycge*, fledged]

flee *v.i.* run away. *-v.t.* run away from; shun. [OE. *fleon*]

fleece *n.* sheep's wool. *-v.t.* rob. **-flee'cy** *a.* [OE. *fleos*]

fleer *v.i.* laugh mockingly, jeer; deride. *-n.* mocking laugh or look. [orig. uncertain]

fleet *n.* naval force under an admiral; number of ships, *etc.*, sailing in company; number of automobiles, aircraft, *etc.*, owned by one company. [OE. *fleet*, ship]

fleet *a.* swift, nimble. [ON. *fljotr*]

fleet *v.i.* glide away; pass quickly; flit, fly. **-fleet'ing** *a.* transient. [OE. *fleotan*, to drift]

Flem'ish *a.* of, pert. to Flanders or its people [Du. *Vlaamsch*]

flense *v.t.* strip the blubber from (a whale). [Dan. *flense*]

flesh *n.* soft part, muscular substance, between skin and bone; this as food; of plants, the pulp; fat; sensual appetites. **-flesh'ings** *n. pl.* close-fitting flesh-colored theatrical garments. **-flesh-pots** *n. pl.* high living. **-flesh'ly** *a.* carnal, material. **-flesh'y** *a.* plump, pulpy. **-flesh'ily** *adv.* [OE. *flæsc*]

fleur-de-lis (flur-di-le') *n.* iris; heraldic lily; royal arms of France. [F.]

flex'ible *a.* that may be bent without breaking, pliable; manageable; supple. **-flexibil'ity** *n.* **-flex'ibly** *adv.* **-flex'ion, flec'tion** *n.* bending, bent state.**-flex'time, flex'itime** *n.* system permitting variation in starting and finishing times of work, providing an agreed number of hours is worked over a specified period.**-flexure** *n.* bend. [L. *flexibilis*]

flibbertigibbet *n.* flighty or gossiping person. [orig. unknown]

flick *n.* light blow; jerk. *-v.t.* strike or move with a flick. [imit. orig.]

flick'er *v.i.* burn or shine unsteadily; quiver. *-n.* flickering light or movement. [OE. *flicerian*]

flight (-it) *n.* act or manner of flying through the air; swift movement or passage; sally; distance flown; airplane journeys; stairs between two landings; number flying together, as birds. arrows. **-flight'y** *a.* light-headed, thoughtless, capricious. [*fly*]

flight *n.* a running away. [*floe*]

flim'sy (-zi) *a.* very thin; unsubstantial; fragile. *-n.* very thin paper. **-flim'sily** *adv.* [Welsh *Ilymsi*]

flinch *v.i.* shrink, draw back. [earlier *flench*, ME. *fleechen*]

fling *v.t.* throw. *-v.i.* rush, go hastily; kick, plunge. *-n.* throw; hasty attempt; spell of indulgence; vigorous dance. [orig. uncertain]

flint *n.* hard stone found in gray lumps with a white crust; piece of this. **-flint'lock** *n.* gun or its lock discharged by a spark struck from flint. **-flint'y** *a.* of or like flint; hard, unrelenting. **-flint'ily** *adv.* [OE.]

flip *n.* flick or fillip, very light blow. *-v.t.* strike or move with a flick; turn over. *-v.i.* move in jerks; turn over; lose one's mind or composure. **-flip'per** *n.* limb or fin for swimming. [imit. orig.]

flip *n.* sweet drink of spirits, *etc.* ; as egg flip. [orig. uncertain]

flip'pant *a.* treating serious things with unbecoming lightness. **-flip'pantly** *adv.* **-flip'pancy** *n.* [*flip*]

flirt *v.t.* throw with a jerk, give a brisk motion to. *-v.i.* play at courtship. *-n.* jerk, sudden throw; one who plays at courtship. **-flirta'tion** *n.* [imit. orig.]

flit *v.i.* go away; change dwelling; pass lightly and rapidly; make short flights. [ON. *flytja*]

flitch *n.* side of bacon. [OE. *fliece*]

flitt'er *v.i.* move lightly, uncertainly. **-flitt'er-mouse** *n.* bat. [*flutter*]

float *v.i.* rest or drift on the surface of a liquid; be suspended freely (in a liquid). *-v.t.* of a liquid, support, bear along; commerce, get (a company) started. *-n.* anything small that floats (*esp.* to support something else, *e.g.*, a fishing net); low-bodied cart; footlight. **-flota'tion** *n.* act of floating, *esp.* floating of a company. [OE. *flotian*]

flock *n.* lock or tuft of wool, *etc.* *-pl.* wool refuse for stuffing. **-flocc'ulent** (-k-) *a.* like flocks, woolly. [L. *floecu*]

flock *n.* number of animals of one kind together; body of people, religious congregation. *-v.i.* gather in a crowd. [OE.

flocc, herd]

floe *n*. sheet of floating ice. [orig. uncertain]

flog *v.t.* beat with a whip, stick, *etc*. [orig, uncertain]

flong *n*. prepared paper for stereotyping. [F. *flan*]

flood (flud) *n*. flowing in of the tide; flowing water; overflow of water, inundation. -*v.t.* inundate; cover or fill with water. -**The Flood**, great deluge of Noah's time. -**flood'-gate** *n*. gate for letting water in or out. -**flood'-lighting** *n*. illumination of, *e.g.*, exterior of a building, by distant projectors. -**flood'lit** *a*. -**flood-tide** *n*. rising tide. [OE. *flod*]

floor (flor) *n*. lower surface of a room; set of rooms on one level; flat space. -*v.t.* supply with a floor; knock down; confound. [OE. *flor*]

flop *v.i.* sway about heavily; move clumsily; sit or fall with a thump. -*v.t.* throw down with a thud. -*n*. flopping movement or sound. *adv*. with a flop. -**flop'py** *a*. -**flop'py disk** *n*. flexible magnetic disk that stores information and can be used to store data for use in a microprocessor. -**flop'piness** *n*. -**flopp' ily** *adv*. -flop'house *n*. cheap rooming house or hotel. [imit. orig.]

flop *n*. (*sl*.) failure; something that falls flat. [*flop v. s*.]

flo'ra (**flaw'-**) *n*. plants of a region; a list of them. -**flo'ral** *a*. of flowers. -**flor'iculture** *n*. cultivation of flowers. -**floricul'tural** *a*. -**floricul'turist** *n*. -**flores'cence** *n*. state or time of flowering. -**flor'et** *n*. small flower forming part of a composite flower. -**flor'ist** *n*. one who deals in, grows, or studies, flowers. [L. *flos, flor-*, flower]

flor'id *a*. flowery, ornate; ruddy, high-colored. -**florid'ity** *n*. [L. *flos*, flower]

flor'in *n*. formerly British silver coin worth two shillings; a coin of various countries. [*Florence*, in Italy]

flo'ruit *n*. (*abbrev*. fl.) period in which a person lived, flourished, or date indicating that period. [L. = 'he flourished']

floss *n*. rough silk on a cocoon; silk for embroidery; fluff. -**floss'y** *a*. light and downy. [OF. *flosche*, down]

flota'tion. *See* **float.**

flotill'a *n*. fleet of small vessels, *esp*. group of destroyers *etc*., fleet. [Sp. dim of *flota*, fleet]

flot'sam *n*. floating wreckage. [F. *flottaison*, fr. *flotter*, float]

flounce *v.i.* go or move abruptly and impatiently. -*n*. fling, jerk of the body or a limb. [orig. uncertain]

flounce *n*. ornamental strip of material on a woman's garment, attached by one edge, and put on full or gathered. -*v.t.* adorn with a flounce. [earlier *frounce*, pleat. OF. *fronce*]

flound'er *n*. flat-fish. [OF. *flondre*]

flound'er *v.i.* plunge and struggle, *esp*. in water or mud; proceed in bungling or hesitating manner. -*n*. act of floundering. [orig. uncertain]

flour *n*. sifted finer part of meal; wheat meal; fine soft powder. -*v.t.* sprinkle with flour. -**flour'y** *a*. -**flour'iness** *n*. [flower of wheat]

flour'ish (flur-) *v.i.* thrive; be in the prime. -*v.t.* brandish, display; wave about. -*n*. ornamental curve in writing; florid expression; waving of hard, weapon, *etc*.; fanfare (of trumpets). [OF. *florir*, to bloom]

flout *v.t.* show contempt for by act or word. -*n*. jeer. [orig. uncertain]

flow (flo) *v.i.* glide along as a stream; hang loose; move easily; move in waves; be ample in form; run full; abound. -*n*. act or fact of flowing; quantity that flows; rise of tide; ample supply; outpouring. [OE. *flowan*]

flow'er (flow-) *n*. colored (not green) part of a plant from which the fruit is developed, bloom, blossom; ornamentation; choicest part, pick. -*v.i.* bloom, or blossom. -*v.t.* ornament with worked flowers. -**flow'eret** *n*. small flower. -**flow'ery** *a*. abounding in flowers; full of fine words, ornamented with figures of speech. -**flow'er-de-luce** *n*. **fleur-de-lis**, *q.v.* [F. *fleur*, fr. L. *flos, flor-*]

flown *a*. inflated; puffed up. [*flow*]

flu *abbrev*. of influenza, *q.v.* **fluc'tuate** *v.i.* vary irregularly, rise and fall; waver, be unstable. -**fluctua'tion** *n*. [L. *fluctuare*, fr. *fluctus*, wave]

flue *n*. passage for smoke or hot air, chimney. [orig. unknown]

flue *n*. soft light down, fur. [cp. *fluff*]

flu'ent *a*. flowing, copious and ready (in words); graceful (in movement). -**flu'ency** *adv*. -**flu'ency** *n*. [L. *fluere*, flow]

fluff *n*. soft feathery stuff; down. -*v.t.* make into fluff. [orig. uncertain]

flu'id *a*. flowing easily, not solid. -*n*. fluid substance, gas or liquid. -**fluid'ity** *n*. [L. *fluidus*, fr. *fluere*, flow]

fluke *n*. flat-fish, flounder. [OE. *floc*]

fluke *n*. flat triangular point of an anchor.

[orig. uncertain]

fluke *n.* lucky stroke. *-v.i.* make a fluke. **-flu'ky** *a.* [orig. uncertain]

flume *n.* artificial water-course; steep narrow gorge. [L. *flumen*, river]

flumm'ery *n.* dish of milk, flour, eggs, *etc.*; nonsense. [Welsh *llymru*, boiled jellied sour oatmeal]

flumm'ox *v.t.* (*sl.*) baffle, confound. [orig. uncertain]

flump *v.t.* and *i.* plump down. [imit.]

flunk *v.t.* fail someone in an examination or course. *-v.i.* fail in an examination or course. [orig. uncertain]

flunk'y, flunk'ey *n.* footman in livery; toady, snob. [orig. uncertain]

flu'or *n.* mineral containing fluorine. **-fluores'cence** *n.* luminous state produced in a transparent body by direct action of light, *esp.* violet and ultra-violet rays; power of rendering ultra-violet rays visible. **-fluores'cent** *a.* **-fluores'cent lighting**, lighting by electric discharge acting on fluorescent coating of tube, lamp. **-fluoresce'** *v.i.* **-flu'orine** *n.* nonmetallic element of the chlorine group. [L. fr. *fluere*, flow]

flurry *n.* squall, gust; nervous haste; death-agony of whale. *-v.t.* agitate, bewilder. [imit. orig.]

flush *v.i.* take wing and fly away. *-v.t.* cause to do this. *-n.* number of birds flushed at once. [orig. uncertain]

flush *n.* set of cards all of one suit. [L. *fluxus*, flow]

flush *v.i.* become suffused with blood; turn suddenly red in the face; blush. *-v.t.* cleanse by rush of water; cause to glow or redden; inflame with pride, *etc.* *-n.* rush of water; excitement; elation; glow of color; reddening; freshness, vigor. *a.* full, in flood; well supplied, *esp.* with money; level with a surrounding surface. [orig. uncertain]

flus'ter *v.t.* flurry, bustle; confuse with drink. *-v.i.* be in a flurry. *-n.* flurry. [orig. uncertain]

flute *n.* musical wind instrument, wooden pipe with holes stopped by the fingers or keys and a blow-hole in the side; flute player in a band; groove or channel. *-v.i.* play on a flute. *-v.t.* make grooves in. **-flut'ist, flautist** *n.* one who plays the flute. [F. *flute*]

flutt'er *v.i.* flap wings rapidly without flight or in short flights; move, come down, quiveringly; be excited, agitated. *-v.t.* flap quickly; agitate, *-n.* fluttering, occasional bet, speculation. [OE. *floterian*]

flu'vial *a.* of rivers. [L. *fluvius*, river]

flux *n.* morbid discharge, as of blood; a flowing; flow of the tide; constant succession of changes; substance mixed with metal to help melting. [L. *fluxus*]

fly *n.* two-winged insect; artificial fly of silk, *etc.*, used in angling. **-fly'-blown** *a.* tainted. **-fly'-catcher** *n.* bird; trap for flies. **-fly'screen** *n.* a wire-mesh screen over a window to prevent flies from entering a room. [OE. *fleoge*]

fly *v.i.* move through the air on wings or in aircraft; pass quickly through the air; float loosely, wave; spring, rush; flee, run away. *-v.t.* cause to fly; set flying; run from. *-n.* a flying; one-horse vehicle for hire; flap on a garment or tent; speedregulator in a machine. **-fly'-book** *n.* case for fishing flies. **-fly'-leaf** *n.* blank leaf at the beginning or end of a book. **-fly'posting** *n.* the posting of advertising or political bills, posters, *etc.* in unauthorized places. **-fly'-wheel** *n.* heavy wheel regulating a machine. **-fly'ing-boat** *n.* airplane fitted with floats instead of landing wheels. **-fly'ing-bomb** *n.* long-range jet projectile. **-fly'ing butt'ress** *n.* buttress to a wall at a slope with a space between its lower part and the wall. **-fly'ing-fish** *n.* fish which rises in the air by wing-like fins. **-flying fortress** *n.* large high-altitude 4-engined monoplane precision bomber developed by U.S.A.. during World War II. **-fly'ing-fox** *n.* large fruit-eating bat. [OE. *fleogan*]

foal *n.* young of the horse, ass, or other equine animal. *-v.t.* bear (a foal). *-v.i.* bear a foal. [OE. *fola*]

foam *n.* collection of small bubbles in a liquid; froth; froth of saliva or perspiration. *-v.i.* give out, or form into, foam. **-foam'y** *a.* [OE. *fam*]

fob *n.* small pocket in the waistband; watchchain with seals. [Ger. *fuppe*]

fo'c'sle *abbrev.* of *forecastle*. [*See* **fore**]

fo'cus *n.* point at which rays meet after being reflected or refracted; point of convergence; principal seat or centre. *-v.t.* bring to a focus. *-v.i.* come to a focus. **-fo'cal** *a.* [L. = hearth]

fodd'er *n.* dried food for horses, cattle, *etc.* *-v.t.* feed with fodder. [OE. *fodor*]

foe *n.* enemy. [OE. *fah*]

foetid. *See* **fetid.**

foe'tus. *See* **fetus.**

fog *n.* aftermath; mossy growth. [orig. unknown]

fog *n.* thick mist; unusually dark atmosphere. *-v.t.* cover in fog; puzzle. **-fogg'y** *a.* **-fog'horn** *n.* instrument to warn ships in

fog. [orig. uncertain]
fo'gey, fo'gy *n.* (usually **old fogey**), old-fashioned fellow. [orig. uncertain]
föhn (fen) *n.* hot dry Alpine wind. [Ger.]
foi'ble *n.* weak point in character; quality a person prides himself on mistakenly. [OF. = weak]
foil *n.* small arc or space in the tracery of a window; thin layer; metal in a thin sheet; leaf of metal set under a gem; anything which sets off another thing to advantage; light blunt sword for fencing. [L. *folium*, leaf]
foil *v.t.* baffle, defeat; frustrate. [F. *fouler*, trample]
foist *v.t.* bring in secretly or unwarrantably; palm (a thing off on a person). [Du. *vuist*, fist]
fold (-ō-) *n.* enclosure for sheep, a pen; body of believers, a church. -*v.t.* shut up in a fold. [OE. *falod*]
fold (-o-) *v.t.* double up; bend part of; clasp (in the arms); interlace (the arms); wrap up. -*v.i.* become folded; be or admit of being folded. -*n.* a folding; space between two thicknesses; coil; winding; line, made by folding, a crease. -**fold'er** *n.* [OE. *fealdan*]
folia'ceous *a.* of or made up of leaves. or thin layers or strata. [L. *foliaceus*, fr. *folium*, leaf]
fo'liage *n.* leaves collectively. [F. *feuillage*, fr. *feuille*, (L. *fola*), leaf]
fo'lio *n.* piece of paper numbered only on the front; two pages, or a page, with the opposite side of an account in a ledger; number of words as a unit of length; sheet of printing paper folded once into two leaves or four pages; book of such sheets. **in folio**, made of folios. *a.* made thus. [L. *folirim*, leaf]
folk (fōk) *n.* race of people; people in general. -**folk'-song** *n.* music originating among a people. -**folk'-lore** *n.* traditions, beliefs popularly held; study of these. -**folk'-dance** *n.* traditional dance among the people. [OE. *foic*]
foll'icle *n.* small sac; gland. -**follic'ular** *a.* [L. *folliculus*, dim. *offollis*, bag]
foll'ow *v.t.* go or come after; keep to (a path, *etc.*); accompany, attend on; take as a guide, conform to; engage in; be consequent on; grasp the meaning of. -*v.i.* go or come after; come next; result. -**foll'ower** *n.* -**foll'ow through** *n.* in ball games continuation of stroke after ball is struck. -**foll'ow up** *n.* deepening of impression, pursuing of advantage gained. [OE. *folgian*]
foll'y *n.* foolishness; foolish action, idea, enterprise, *etc.* [F. *folie*]
foment' *v.t.* bathe with hot lotions; encourage, instigate. -**fomenta'tion** *n.* [F. *fomenter*]
fond *a.* tender, loving; credulous; foolish. -fond of, having love or liking for. -**fond'ly** *adv.* -**fond'ness** *n.* -**fon'dle** *v.t.* caress. [ME. *fonnen*, be foolish]
fon'dant *n.* soft-sugar mixture used in making sweets. [F. = melting]
font *n.* bowl for baptismal water. [L. *fons, font-*, fountain]
fontanelle' *n.* gap between parietal bones of young child, animal. [F.]
food ('-ōō-) *n.* that which is eaten or meant to be; nourishment. [OE. *foda*]
fool (-ōō-) *n.* silly or empty-headed person; simpleton; jester, clown; dupe. -*v.i.* act as a fool. -*v.t.* delude; dupe; make a fool of, mock. *a.* foolish. -**fool'ish** *a.* -**fool'ishly** *adv.* -**fool'ery** *n.* -**fool'hardy** *a.* foolishly venturesome. -**foolhard'iness** *n.* -**foolproof** *a.* able to withstand careless or inexpert handling. -**fools'cap, fool'scap** *n.* jester's or dunce's cap; this as a watermark; size of paper which formerly had this mark. -**fool's'** paradises, happiness based on ignorance or misreading of true conditions. -**fool's'-pars'ley** *n.* poisonous wild plant resembling parsley. [F. *fol* (*fou*)]
fool *n.* dish of fruit stewed, crushed, and mixed with milk, *etc.* [orig. uncertain]
foot (-oo-) *n.* lowest part of the leg, from the ankle down; lowest part of anything, base, stand; end of a bed, *etc.*; infantry: measure of length of twelve inches; division of a verse. -*v.t.* set foot to; put a foot on (a stocking, *etc.*). -*v.i.* step, tread, dance. -**foot'ball** *n.* game played by two teams of eleven players in which the ball is passed from one player to another in an attempt to carry the ball over the opponent's goal line; elongated leather ball, filled with air, used in this game; spherical ball used in soccer. -**foot'gear** *n.* shoes and stockings. -**foot'hill** *n.* small hill at mountain foot. -**foot'ing** *n.* firm standing; relations, conditions. -**foot'lights** *n. pl.* row of lights at outer edge of stage. -**foot'man** *n.* liveried servant. -**foot'note** *n.* note at foot of page. -**foot'pad** *n.* unmounted highwayman. -**foot'print** *n.* mark left by a foot in the ground. [OE. *fot*]
foot'ling *a.* trivial, pottering; inefficient. -**foot'le** *v.i.* potter. (F. *foutre*]
fooz'le *v.t.* bungle, *esp.* a stroke at golf. [orig. uncertain]
fop *n.* dandy. -**fop'pish** *a.* -**fopp'ishly** **adv.**

-**fop'pery** *n.* [orig. uncertain]

for *prep.* because of, instead of; toward; on account of, , to prevent or heal; in favor of, respecting; during, in search of, in payment of; in the character of. -*conj.* because. -**forasmuch'** as *conj.* since. [OE.]

for'age *n.* food for cattle and horses, *esp.* of an army. -*v.i.* collect forage, make a roving search. -**for'age cap** *n.* undress cap in army. [F. *fourrage*]

for'ay *n.* raid. -*v.i.* make a raid. [OF. *forreor,* forager]

forbear' (-bar) *v.i.* refrain; be patient. *v.t.* refrain from; cease. -**forbear'ance** *n.* [OE. *forberan*]

forbid' *v.t.* order not to; refuse to allow. -**forbidden** *p.p.* prohibited, unlawful. -**forbidd'ing** *a.* uninviting. [OE. *forbeodan*]

force *n.* strength, power; body of troops; body of police; compulsion; mental or moral strength; measurable influence inclining a body to motion. -*v.t.* constrain, compel; break open; urge, strain; drive; produce by effort; hasten the maturity of. -**for'cible** *a.* -**for'cibly** *adv.* -**force'-ful** *a.* -**force'-pump** *n.* pump driving up water beyond the limit of atmospheric pressure. -**forced'-lan'ding** *n.* emergency landing of airplane due to mishap or defect. [F.]

force, foss *n.* waterfall. [ON. *fors*]

force'-meat *n.* meat chopped for stuffing. [obs. *force,* stuff, fr. *farce*]

for'ceps *n.* surgical pincers. [L.]

forelose'. *See* **foreclose.**

ford. *n.* place where a river may be crossed by wading. -**ford'able** *a.* [OE.]

fore- *prefix* meaning previous, before, front. [OE.]

fore *a.* in front. -*n.* front part. -**fore-and-aft** *a.* placed in the line from bow to stern of a ship. -**fore'arm** *n.* arm from wrist to elbow. -**forearm'** *v.t.* arm beforehand. -**fore'bear, for'bear** *n.* ancestor. -**forebode'** *v.t.* betoken. foreboding *n.* presentiment. -**forecast'** *v.t.* estimate beforehand, prophesy. -**fore-cast** *n.* conjecture, guess at a future event. -**fore'castle** (*abbrev.* **fo'c'sle**) (fo'ksl) *n.* forward raised part of a ship; sailors' quarter. -**foredoom'** *v.t.* doom beforehand. -**fore'father** *n.* ancestor. -**fore'finger** *n.* finger next the thumb. -**fore'front** *n.* the very front, foremost part. -**fore'ground** *n.* part of a view, *esp.* in a picture, nearest the spectator. -**fore' hand** *n.* part of a horse before the rider. -*a.* of a stroke in a game, made with the inner side of the wrist leading. -**fore'head** (for'hed) *n.* part of the face above the eyebrows and between the temples. -**forejudge'** *v.t.* judge before evidence is heard. -**foreknow'** *v.t.* know beforehand. -**fore'lock** *n.* lock of hair over forehead. -**fore'man** *n.* one in charge of work; leader of a jury. -**fore'mast** *n.* mast nearest the bow. -**foremen'tioned** *a.* mentioned before, *e.g.* in document, *etc.* -**fore'noon** *n.* morning. -**fore-ordain'** *v.t.* predestinate, pre-determine. -**fore'reach** *v.i.* (naut.) get ahead. -*v.t.* get ahead of; sail beyond. -**fore'runner** *n.* one who goes before, a precursor. -**fore'sail** *n.* principal sail on a foremast. -**forsee'** *v.t.* see beforehand. -**foreshad'ow** *v.t.* figure beforehand, be a type of. -**fore'-shore** *n.* part of the shore between high and low tide marks, -**foreshort'en** *v.t.* draw (an object) so that it appears shortened. -**foreshow'** *v.t.* show before, foretell, predict. -**fore'sight** *n.* foreseeing; care for the future; front sight of a gun. -**forestall'** *v.t.* be beforehand with. -**fore-tell'** *v.t.* prophesy. -**foreto'ken** *v.t.* give signal beforehand, portend. -*n.* omen. -**fore'top** *n.* 'top' of the foremast. -**forewarn'** *v.t.* warn beforehand. -**fore'word** *n.* preface. [*fore-*]

foreclose' *v.t.* take away the power of redeeming (a mortgage); shut out, bar. -**foreclo'sure** *n.* [F. *forclore*]

foregath'er. *See* **forgather.**

forego'. *See* **forgo.**

forego'ing *a.* preceding. -**foregone'** *a.* inevitable; predetermined, as in foregone conclusion. [*go*]

for'ein *a.* not of or in one's own country; introduced from outside; irrelevant; relating to, or connected with other countries [F. *forain*]

fore'land *n.* headland, promontory. [*land*]

fore'most *a.* most advanced, chief *adv.* in the first place. [OE. *formest*]

foren'sic *a.* of courts of law. [L. *forensis,* fr. *forum,* market-place]

foren'sics *n.* study and practice of debate and formal argument.

for'est *n.* large wood; the trees in it; tract of land mainly occupied by trees; region kept waste for hunting. -**for'ester** *n.* one who lives in a forest or is employed in charge of one. -**for'estry** *n.* management of forests. [Med. L. *forestis,* unfenced]

forev'er *adv.* constantly; eternally. [*for* and *ever*]

for'feit (-fit) *n.* thing lost by crime or fault; penalty, fine. -*pl.* game. *a.* lost by crime or fault. -*v.t.* lose, have to pay or give up. -**for'feiture** *n.* [F. *forfait,* crime, wrong]

forfend' *v.t.* avert, turn aside. [*fend*]
forgath'er, foregather (-TH-) *v.i.* meet, assemble, associate. [*gather*]
forge *v.t.* shape (metal) by heating in a fire and hammering; invent; make in fraudulent imitation of a thing, to counterfeit. *-n.* smithy; smith's hearth; workshop for melting or refining metal **for'ger** *n.* **-for'gery** *n.* forged document; the making of it. [F. *forger*, fr. L. *fabricate*]
forge *v.i.* advance, make headway, *esp.* of a boat, usually slowly or with effort. **forge ahead.** [corrupt. of *force*]
forget' *v.t.* lose memory of, not to remember. **-forget'ful** *a.* **-forget'fully** *adv.* **-forget'-me-not** *n.* plant with a small blue flower. [OE. *forgietan*]
forgive' (giv) *v.t.* pardon, remit. **-forgive'ness** *n.* [OE. *forgiefan*]
forgo', forego' *v.t.* go without; give up. [OE. *forgan*, pass over]
fork *n.* pronged farm tool for digging or lifting; pronged instrument for holding food in eating or cooking; division into branches; point of this division; one of the branches. *-v.i.* branch. *-v.t.* make fork shaped; dig, lift, or throw with a fork. forked *a.* [L. *urca*]
forlorn' *a.* forsaken; desperate. **-forlorn hope** *n.* a desperate enterprise; the party trying it. [obs. Du. *verloren hoop*, lost heap, troop (OE. *forleosan*, lose utterly)]
form *n.* shape, visible appearance; visible person or animal; structure; nature; species, kind; class in a school; customary way of doing a thing; set order of words; regularly drawn up document, *esp.* a printed one with blanks for particulars; behavior according to rule; condition, good condition; long seat without a back, a bench; hare's nest; frame for type (more often *forme*). *-v.t.* put into shape, mold, arrange, organize; train; shape in the mind, conceive; go to make up, make part of. *-v.i.* come into existence or shape. **-for'mal** *a.* ceremonial, according to rule; explicit; of outward form or routine; according to a rule that does not matter; precise; stiff. **-for'mally** *adv.* **-formal'-ity** *n.* **-for'malism** *n.* **-for'matist** *n.* **-for'mation** *n.* a forming; thing formed; structure, shape, arrangement. **-for'ma tive** *a.* serving or tending to form; used in forming. [L. *forma*, shape]
formaldehyde *n.* colorless pungent gas used in solution in water or absorbed into porous materials as antiseptic and disinfectant. [L. *formica,* ant]
for'malin *n.* antiseptic, preservative substance derived from a formic aldehyde. [*form*ic and *al*dehyde]
form'at (-ma) *n.* size and shape of a book. [F.]
for'mer *a.* earlier in time; of past times; first-named. *-pron.* first-named thing or person or fact. **-for'merly** *adv.* [fr. OE. *superl. formest*, foremost]
for'mic *a.* of or derived from ants. **-for'mic a'cid,** acid originally from ants. **-for'micant** *a.* with ant-like motion. **-for'micary** *n.* anthill. **-formica'tion** *n.* feeling of ants crawling on one's skin. [L. *formica*, ant]
formidable' *a.* to be feared; likely to cause difficulty serious. **-for'midably** *adv.* [L. *formido:r,* dread]
for'mula (-a-) *n.* set form of words setting forth a principle, or prescribed for an occasion; recipe; in science, a rule or fact expressed in symbols and figures. **-for'mulary** *n.* collection of formulas. **-for'mulate** *v.t.* express in a formula, or systematically. **-formula'tion** *n.* **-for'mulator** *n.* *-pl.* **form'ulae, form'ulas.** [L. , dim. of *forma*, form]
fornica'tion *n.* sexual intercourse between man and woman. **-for'nicate** *v.i.* [L. *fornix*, brothel]
forsake' *v.t.* abandon, desert; give up. *v.t.* forsook. **-forsaken** *a.* [OE. *forsacan*]
forsooth' (-th) *adv.* in truth (only in ironic use). [OE. *forsoth*, cp. *sooth*]
forswear' *v.t.* renounce. *-v. refl.* perjure. [OE. *forswerian*, renounce an oath]
forsyth'ia *n.* shrub with jasmine-like yellow flowers. [W. *Forsyth*]
fort *n.* fortified place. [L. *fortis*, strong]
fort'alice *n.* small fort or fortification. [L. *fortis*, strong]
forte *n.* one's strong point. [F. *fort,* upper half of sword-blade]
forte (-ti) *adv.* in music, loudly. **-fortiss'imo** adv. very loud. [It.]
forth (-th) *adv.* onwards, into view; onwards in time. **-forthcom'ing** *a.* about to come; ready when wanted. **-forth'right** *n.* straightforward; straightway. **-forthwith'** adv. at once, immediately. [OE.]
FORT'RAN *n.* high-level computer programming language for mathematical and scientific purposes. [fr. *For*mula *Tran*slation]
forthright *a.* candid, straightforward, blunt. [*forth* and *right*]
for'tieth. *See* **four.**
for'tify *v.t.* strengthen; provide with defensive works. **-fortifica'tion** *n.* [L. *for-*

tis, strong]

for'titude *n.* courage in adversity or pain. [L. *fortitude*, fr. *fortis*, strong]

fortnight (-nit) *n.* two weeks. -**fortnight'ly** *adv.* [*fourteen nights*]

fort'ress *n.* fortified place, military stronghold. [F. *forteresse*]

fortuitous *a.* accidental, due to chance. -**fortu'itously** *adv.* [L. *fortuitus*]

for'tune *n.* chance; luck, good luck, prosperity; wealth, stock of wealth. -**for'tunate** *a.* lucky, favorable. -**for'tunately** *adv.* -**for'tune-teller** *n.* one who predicts a person's future, usually for money. [L. *fortune*]

for'ty. *See* **four.**

fo'rum *n.* market-place, *esp.* of ancient Rome; law-courts; tribunal; any place of judicature. [L.]

for'ward *a.* lying in front of one, onward; prompt; precocious; pert. -*n.* in football, a player in the first line. -*adv.* towards the future; towards the front; to the front, into view; at or in the fore part of a ship; onward, so as to make progress. -*v.t.* help forward; send, dispatch. -**for'wards** *adv.* forward. -**for'wardly** *adv.* pertly. -**forwardness** *n.* [OE. *foreweard*]

foss, fosse *n.* (fort.) ditch; moat. [L. *fossa*]

foss'ick *v.i.* glean for gold, in wasteheaps, old diggings or creek-beds; (*fig.*) hunt about for pickings, gleanings. **foss'iker** *n.* [orig. uncertain]

foss'il *a.* petrified in the earth and recog nizable as the remains of animals or plants, *esp.* prehistoric ones; (of persons) antiquated. -*n.* fossilized thing. -**foss'ilize** *v.t.* and *i.* turn into a fossil. [L. *fossilis*, fr. *fodere*, *foss-*, to dig]

foster *v.t.* encourage; be favorable to; formerly, to tend, cherish. -**fos'ter-brother** *n.* one related by upbringing not by blood; thus, **fos'ter-father, foster-child** *n.* , *etc.* [OE. *fostor*, feeding, food]

foudroy'ant *a.* lightning-like, quick, dramatic. [F.]

fougasse' *n.* small undergound mine. [F.]

foul *a.* loathsome, offensive; dirty; charged with harmful matter; clogged, choked; unfair; wet, rough; obscene, disgustingly abusive. -*n.* collision; (in games) act of unfair play. -*adv.* unfairly. -*v.i.* become foul. -*v.t.* make foul; jam; collide with. -**foul'ly** *adv.* [OE. *ful*]

foulard' (foo-) *n.* thin soft fabric (originally silk) for blouses, ties, *etc.* [F.]

found *v.t.* establish, institute; lay the base of; base, ground. -**founda'tion** *n.* a founding; base, lowest part of a building; endowed institution. -**found'er** *n.* -**found'ress** *fem.* -**Founding Fathers** *n. pl.* American leaders who were members of the American Constitutional Convention of 1787. [F. *fonder*, fr. L. *fundus*, bottom]

found *v.t.* (of metals), melt and run into a mold. -**found'er** *n.* -**found'ry** *n.* workshop for founding. [F. *fondre*, fr. L. *fundare*, pour]

found'er *v.i.* of a horse, to fall lame, collapse. -*v.t.* cause to do this. [F. *effondrer*, knock out the bottom]

found'er *v.i.* of a ship, to sink. [OF. *enfondrir*, engulf]

foundling *n.* deserted infant. [*find*]

fount *n.* fountain. [L. *fons, font-*]

fount *n.* set of printer's type. [F.]

fount'ain (-in) *n.* spring; source; jet of water, *esp.* an ornamental one. [F. *fontaine*, fr. L. *fons, fontis*, spring]

four *n.* and *a.* cardinal number next after three. -**fourth** *a.* ordinal number. -**fourth'ly** *adv.* -**Fourth of July** *n.* U.S. public holiday celebrating the Declaration of Independence; Independence Day. -**four'teen'** *n.* and *a.* four and ten. -**fourteenth** *a.* -**for'ty** *n.* and *a.* four tens. -**for'tieth** *adv.* -**fourteen'fold** *adv.* -**for'tyfold** *adv.* -**four'-in-hand** *n.* vehicle with four horses all driven by a driver on the vehicle. -**four-post'er** *n.* bed with four posts for curtains, *etc.* -**four'some** *n.* (*golf*) game for four players, two against two. -**four'some reel'**, Scottish reel for four dancers. -**foursquare** *a.* firm, steady. -**four star** *a.* of the highest military rank; highest quality. -**fourth class** *a.* lowest rate and method of parcel post mailing. [OE. *feower*]

fowl *n.* domestic cock or hen; bird. -*v.i.* hunt wild birds. -**fowl'er** *n.* -**fowl'ing-piece** *n.* light gun. [OE. *fugol*]

fox *n.* red bushy-tailed animal, in many places preserved for hunting; cunning person. -*v.t.* discolor (paper) with brown spots. -*v.i.* act craftily; sham. -**foxy** *a.* **fox'glove** *n.* tall flowering plant yielding digitalis. -**fox'grape** *n.* N. American wild grape. -**fox-hole** *n.* (*sl.*) orig. in World War II small trench for one or two giving protection against snipers or divebombers. -**fox'hound** *n.* dog bred for hunting foxes. -**fox terr'ier** *n.* small dog now mainly kept as a pet. -**fox'trot** *n.* dance. [OE.]

foy'er *n.* hall of a theater. [F.]

fracas' *n.* noisy quarrel. [F.]

frac'tion *n.* numerical quantity not an integer; fragment, piece, small part. -

frac'tional *a.* [*fracture*]

frac'tious *a.* unruly, cross, fretful. [mixture of *factious* and *refractory*]

frac'ture *n.* breakage. -*v.t.* and *i.* break. [L. *frangere, fract-*, break]

fraga'ria *n.* plant genus including the strawberry plant. [L. *fragum*, strawberry]

frag'ile (-j-) *a.* breakable. -**fragility** *n.* [L. *fragilis*, fr. *frangere*, break]

frag'ment *n.* piece broken off, small portion; incomplete part. -**frag'mentary** *a.* [L. *fragmentum*]

fra'gor *n.* crash. [L.]

fra'grant (-ag-) *a.* sweet-smelling. -**fra'grance** *n.* -**fra'grantly** *adv.* [L. *fragrans, fragrant-* fr. *fragrare*, smell]

frail *a.* easily broken, delicate; morally weak, unchaste. -**frail'ty** *n.* -**frail'ly** *adv.* [F. *fraiel*, fr. L. *fragilis*]

frail *n.* rush basket. [F. *fraiel*]

frame *v.t.* put together, make; adapt; put into words; put into a frame; trump-up a charge against. -*n.* that in which a thing is set or inserted, as a square of wood round a picture, *etc.*; structure; constitution; mood. -**frame'-up** *n.* plot, manufactured evidence. -**frame'work** *n.* light wooden or other structure; structure into which completing parts can be fitted. [OE. *ramian*, avail]

franc *n.* French coin. [first struck bearing the words *Francorum Rex*, King of the Francs. cp. *frank*]

fran'chise *n.* person or company granted a license to operate a store, hotel, *etc.*, using the name of the parent company, but operating in an independent manner. -**franchisee'** *n.* person or company granted a franchise. *n.* right of voting; citizenship. [F. = *freedom*]

Francis'can *a.* of order of monks founded by St. Francis. [L. *Franciscus*, Francis]

frangible (-j-) *a.* breakable; easily broken. [L. *frangere*, break]

frank *a.* candid, outspoken, sincere. -*n.* signature on a letter of a person entitled to send it free of postage charges; letter with this. -*v.t.* mark a letter thus. -**frank'ly** *adv.* -**frank'ness** *n.* [F. *franc*, Frank, conqueror, 'free man.' (conquest of Gaul)]

frankincense *n.* aromatic gum resin. [F. = pure incense]

Frank'enstein *n.* (properly **Frank'enstein's mon'ster**) creation which threatens the safety or peace of its maker. [char. in fiction]

frank'lin *n.* in feudal England, a freeholder. [Low L. *Francus*, Frank, freeman]

fran'tic *a.* mad with rage, grief, joy, *etc.* **fran'tically** *adv.* [F. *frénétique*]

frappé' (-pa) *a.* iced, cooled. [F.]

fraternal *a.* of a brother; brotherly. -**frater'nally** *adv.* -**frater'nity** *n.* brotherliness; a brotherhood; club of male students *usu.* living in the same house. -**frat'ernize** *v.i.* associate, make friends. -**frat'ricide** *n.* killing of a brother or sister; the killer. -**frat'ricidal** *a.* [L. *frater*, brother]

fraud *n.* criminal deception; dishonest trick-**fraud'ulence** *n.* -**fraud'ulent** *a.* [L. *fraus, fraud-*]

fraught (-awt) *p.p.* and *a.* -fraught with, laden with, full of. [Du. *vracht*, freight]

fray *n.* fight. [for *affray*]

fray *v.t.* and *i.* wear through by rubbing, make or become ragged at the edge. [F. *frover*, fr. L. *fricare*, rub]

frazz'le *v.t.* fray. -*n.* frayed, exhausted, condition. *v.t.* and *i.* fray; tatter. [*fray* and obs. *fasel*]

freak *n.* caprice; prank; monstrosity. -**freak'ish** *a.* [orig. uncertain]

freck'le *n.* light brown spot on the skin. -*v.t.* and *i.* mark or become marked with such spots. [ON. *freknur*]

free *a.* having liberty; not in bondage; not restricted or impeded; released from strict law, literality, tax, obligation, *etc.*; disengaged; spontaneous; liberal; frank; familiar. -*v.t.* set at liberty, disengage. -**free'ly** *adv.* -**free'board** *n.* side of ship between deck and waterline. -**free'dom** *n.* -**free fall** *n.* unchecked motion of a body in flight. -**free'hand** *a.* of drawing, done without guiding instruments. -**free'hold** *n.* tenure of land without obligation of service or rent; land so held. -**free'lance** *n.* medieval mercenary; unattached journalist, artist, *etc.*; politician independent of party. -**free'load** *v.i.* live off money and gifts provided by others without giving anything in return. -**free'man** *n.* person not a slave; one with civil rights, admitted a citizen. -**free market** *n.* market in which prices are not government regulated but are based on supply and demand. -**free'mason** (-a-) *n.* member of a fraternity, originally of masons, now a fraternity of lodges united for social and other purposes. -**free'masonry** *n.* -**free'stone** *n.* kind of sandstone, limestone. -**free'thinker** *n.* one who rejects authority in re ligion. -**free'-trade** *n.* unrestricted trade, trade without tariffs. -**free'wheel** *n.* mechanism enabling bicycle wheel to revolve while pedals are at rest- *v.i.* -**free'-will** *n.* spontaneity; freedom of choice. *a.* unrestrained, voluntary. [OE. *freo*, not in bondage]

freebooter *n.* pirate; pillaging adventurer. [Du. *Lrijbuiter.* p. *booty*]

free'sia (-zh-) *n.* S. African flower of iris family. [E. M. *Fries*, Sw. botanist]

freeze *v.i.* become ice; become rigid with cold; feel very cold. -*v.t.* turn solid by cold; chill; affect with frost. -*v.t.* and *i.* stop *esp.* if then held in a static position. -**freez'ing-point** *n.* temperature at which water becomes solid. -**freeze'-frame** *n.* single frame of a film repeated to give an effect like a still photograph; single frame of a video recording viewed as a still by stopping the tape. [OE. *freosan*]

freight (-at) *n.* hire of a ship; cargo; a load which is being transported; charge for the conveyance of goods. -*v.t.* hire or load (a ship). -**freighter** *n.* -**freight'age** *n.* [earlier *fraught, q.v.*]

French *a.* of France. -**french-bean** *n.* kidney or haricot bean, eaten with pod. **French fries** *n. pl.* long thin pieces of potato which have been deep-fried in oil or fat. -**french-polish** *n.* shellac varnish for furniture. -**french doors** *n. pl.* doors mostly of glass, opening from a room to the outdoors, and serving also as a window. [OE. *Frencise*]

fren'zy *n.* fury, delirious excitement. -**fren'zied** *a.* [F. *frénésie*]

fre'quent *a.* happening often; common, habitual; numerous. -**fre'quently** *adv.* -**fre'quency** *n.* -**frequent'** *v.t.* go often or habitually to. -**frequent'ative** *a.* expressing repetition. [L. *frequens*]

fres'co *n.* method of painting in water color on the plaster of a wall before it dries; painting done thus. -*v.t.* -**fres'coed** *a.*. [It.]

fresh *a.* new; additional; different; recent; inexperienced; pure; not pickled, salted, *etc.*; not stale; not faded or dimmed; not tired; of wind, strong. -**fresh'ly** *adv.* -**fresh'ness** *n.* -**fresh'en** *v.t.* and *i.* -**fresh'et** *n.* rush of water at a river mouth; flood of river water. -**fresh'man** *n.* member of a college in his first year. [OE. *fersc*, not salt]

fret *v.t.* and *i.* chafe, worry. -*n.* irritation. -**fret'ful** *a.* irritable, easily vexed. fOE. *fretan*, gnaw]

fret *n.* pattern of straight lines intersecting; bar to aid the fingering of a stringed instrument. -*v.t.* ornament with carved pattern. -**fret'-saw** *n.* narrowbladed saw for fretwork. -**fret'-work** *n.* thin board with cut out pattern. [orig. uncertain]

fri'able *a.* easily crumbled. -**friabil'ity** *n.* [F., L. *friabilis*, fr. *friare*, crumble]

fri'ar *n.* member of a mendicant religious order. -**fri'ary** *n.* convent of friars. [F. *frère*, brother]

fricassee' *n.* fowl, game, *etc.*, jointed or cut up small and cooked in sauce. [F.]

fric'tion *n.* rubbing; resistance met with by a body moving over another; unpleasantness, ill-feeling. -**fric'tional** *a.* [L. *fricare, frict-*, rub]

Fri'day *n.* sixth day of the week. -**Good Friday**, Friday before Easter. [OE. *frigedæg*, day of *Freyja*, Norse goddess of love]

friend (frend) *n.* one attached to another by affection and esteem; intimate associate; supporter; Quaker. -**friend'less** *a.* -**friend'ly** *a.* -**friend'ship** *n.* -**friendliness** *n.* [OE. *freond*]

frieze (frez) n, coarse woolen cloth. [OF. *drop de Frise*, cloth of Friesland]

frieze (frcz) *n.* band of decoration on wall of building. [F. *frise*]

frig'ate *n.* warship formerly next in size to a ship of the line; now smaller than a destroyer. [F. , formerly *frégate*]

fright *n.* sudden fear, grotesque person or thing. -*v.t.* terrify. -**fright'en** *v.t.* terrify. -**fright'ful** *a.* -**fright'fulness** *n.* [OE. *fyrhto*]

fri'gid *a.* cold; formal; dull. -**fri'gidly** *adv.* -**fridid'ity** *n.* [L. *frigidus*]

frilt *n.* ruff; fluted strip of fabric gathered at one edge; similar paper ornament; fringe. -*v.t.* make into, or decorate with a frill. [orig. uncertain]

fringe *n.* ornamental border of threads, tassels, anything resembling this; border, outskirts. -*v.t.* adorn with, serve as, a fringe. [F. *frange*]

fripp'ery *n.* finery, *esp.* cheap or tawdry finery. [OE. *freperie*, old clothes]

frisk *v.i.* frolic. -*n.* frolic. -**frisk'y** *a.* -**frisk'ily** *adv.* [OF. *frisque*, lively]

frit'-fly *n.* small fly destructive to wheat. [orig. uncertain]

frith. *See* **firth.**

frit'illary *n.* plant with delicately speckled flowers; butterfly with spotted wings. [L. *fritillus*, dice-box]

fritt'er *n.* fruit, *etc.*, dipped in batter and fried. [F. *friture*, fr. *frire*, to fry]

fritt'er *v.t.* fritter away, throw away, waste. [OE. *freture*, fragment]

frivolous *a.* silly, trifling; given to trifling. -**frivol'ity** *n.* [L. *frivolus*]

frizz *v.i.* sputter in frying. -**frizzle** *v.t.* and

i. fry, toast or broil with sputtering noise, [imit. extension of fry]

frizz *v.t.* crisp, curl up into small curls. -**frizz'le** *v.t.* and *i.* frizz. -**frizz'y** *a.* [F. *friser*, curl]

fro *adv.* away, from; (only in *to* and *fro*). [ON. *fra*, from]

frock *n.* woman's dress; monk's gown. -*v.t.* invest with the office of priest. -**frock coat** *n.* man's long coat not cut away in front. [F. *froc*]

frog *n.* tailless amphibious animal developed from a tadpole. [OE. *frogga*]

frog *n.* horny growth in the sole of horse's hoof. [orig. uncertain]

frog *n.* attachment to a belt to carry a sword; military coat-fastening of button and loop. -**frog'-man** *n.* diver equipped with rubber suit with finned feet. [orig. uncertain]

frog'-bit *n.* small aquatic plant with floating leaves. [*frog*]

frog'mouth *n.* Australian nightjar. [*frog*]

frol'ic *a.* sportive. -*v.i.* gambol, play pranks. -*n.* prank, merry-making. -**frolicsome** *a.* [Du. *vroolijk*]

from *prep.* expressing departure, moving away, source, distance, cause, change of state, *etc.* [OE. *from*]

frond *n.* plant organ consisting of stem and foliage, usually with fruit forms, *esp.* in ferns. -**frondesc'ence** *n.* opening out of leaves. -**frondesc'ent** *a.* [L. *frons, frond-*, leaf]

front (-unt) *n.* fore part: forehead. -*v.i.* look, face. -*v.t.* face; oppose. *a.* of or at the front. -**front'age** *n.* -**front'al** *a.* -**front'let** *n.* band for the forehead. [L. *frons, front-*, forehead]

front'ier *n.* part of a country which borders on another. [F. *frontiers*]

frontispiece *n.* illustration facing the title-page of a book; principal face of a building. [F. *frontispice*]

frost *n.* act or state of freezing; weather in which the temperature falls below the point at which water turns to ice; frozen dew or mist. -*v.t.* injure by frost; cover with rime; powder with sugar, *etc.*; give a slightly roughened surface; turn (hair) white. -**frost'y** *a.* -**frost'ily** *adv.* -**frost'bite** *n.* inflammation of the skin due to cold. [OE.]

froth (-th) *n.* collection of small bubbles, foam; scum; idle talk. -*v.i.* and *t.* throw up, or cause to throw up, froth. -**froth'y** *a.* foamy; empty, light. -**froth'ily** adv. [ON. *frotha*]

fro'ward *a.* (*arch.*) perverse, ungovernable. [*fro* and *-ward.* cp. *wayward*]

frown *v.i.* knit the brows, *esp.* in anger or deep thought. -*n.* a knitting of the brows. [OF. *froignier*]

frow'sty *a.* fusty; close and ill-smelling. [cp. *frowzy*]

frow'zy *a.* ill-smelling; dirty, slatternly; unwashed; unkempt. [orig. obscure]

fructesc'ence *n.* time when fruit ripens. [L. *fructescere*, bear fruit]

fruc'tify *v.i.* bear fruit. -*v.t.* make fruitful. -**fructifica'tion** *n.* [L. *fructificare*]

fru'gal *a.* sparing, economical, *esp.* in use of food. -**fru'gally** *adv.* -**frugal'ity** *n.* [L. *frugalis*, fr. *frux, frug-*, fruit]

frugiferous *a.* fruit bearing. [L. *fructus*, fruit]

frugiv'orous (-jiv-) *a.* fruit-eating. [L. *frux, frug-*, fruit]

fruit *n.* seed and its envelope, *esp.* an eatable one; vegetable products (*usu.* in *pl.*); produce; result, benefit. -*v.i.* bear fruit. -**fruit'ful** *a.* -**fruit'less** *a.* - **frui'tion** *n.* enjoyment; realization of hopes. -**fruit'y** *a.* [L. *fructus*, fr. *frui, fruct-*, enjoy]

frum'enty, fur'menty *n.* hulled wheat boiled in milk and sweetened. [F. *froment*, wheat]

frump *n.* dowdy woman. -**frump'ish** *a.* dowdy, plain. [orig. uncertain]

frustrate' *v.t.* baffle, disappoint. -**frustration** *n.* [L. *frustrari*]

frust'um *n.* piece cut off solid body; part cone, pyramid, *etc.* left after top is cut [L. *frustum*, bit]

frutesc'ent, fru'ticose *a.* like a shrub. [L. *frutex*, shrub]

fry *n.* young fishes. -**small fry,** young or insignificant beings. [F. *frai*]

fry *v.t.* cook with fat in a shallow pan. internal parts of animals usually eaten fried. -**fry'ing pan** *n.* [F. *frire*]

fub'sy *a.* chubby; dumpy. [orig. uncertain]

fu'chsia *n.* ornamental shrub. [*Fuchs*, Ger. botanist]

fud'dle *v.t.* intoxicate, confuse. -*v.i.* pple. [orig. unknown]

fudge *v.t.* bungle; fake. -*n.* makeshift kind of candy. [orig. uncertain]

fudge *interj.* nonsense, rubbish. -*n.* [cp. Ger. *futsch*, no good]

fuel *n.* material for burning. -*v.t.* provide fuel for; take in fuel; provide a source of energy for. [ME. *fewel*, fr. L. *cus*, hearth]

fug *n.* stuffiness; fusty atmosphere; frowsiness. -*v.i.* sit in a stuffy atmosphere. [orig. uncertain]

fuga'cious *a.* fleeting, transient. -**fugac'ity** *n.* [L. *fugere*, flee]
fu'gitive *a.* that runs, or has run away; fleeting, transient. -*n.* one who flees; exile, refugee. [L. *fugitivus*, fr. *fugere, fugit-*, flee]
fug'leman *n.* soldier who by standing at of company demonstrates drill, *etc.*; ringleader. -**fu'gle** *v.i.* act as fugleman. [Ger. *flugel*, wing]
fugue *n.* musical piece in which the emes seem to answer each other; loss of memory. [F.]
Führer (fur-) *n.* leader, title of German dictator, *esp.* Hitler. [Ger. *leader*]
fulcrum *n.* (**ful'cra** *pl.*) point on which lever is placed for support. [L.]
fulfill' (fool-) *v.t.* satisfy; carry out; obey; satisfy the requirements of. -**fulfill'ment** *n.* [OE. *fullfyllan*]
ful'gent (-j-) *a.* shining. -**ful'gency** *n.* [L. *fulgere, fulgent-*, shine]
ful'gurate *v.i.* flash like lighting. -**ful'gurant** *a.* [L. *fulgar*, lightning]
fuli'ginous (-ij-) *a.* sooty. -**fuliginos'ity** *n.* [L. *fuligos, fuligin-*, soot]
full (fool) *a.* holding all it can; containing abundance; ample; complete; plump. -*adv.* very; quite; exactly. -**full'y** *adv.* -**ful'ness, full'ness** *n.* -**full-blown** *a.* of flowers, completely open. -**full-face(d)** *a.* with broad face; seen from directly in front. -**full-orbed** *a.* completely round, as full moon. [OE.]
full'er (fool-) *n.* one who cleans and thickens cloth. -**fuller's earth** *n.* clay used for this. -**full** *v.t.* [fr. L. *fullo*]
ful'mar *n.* sea-bird, one of the petrels, [ON. *ful*, foul, *mar*, mew]
fulminate *v.i.* explode. -*v.t.* and *i.* thunder out (blame, *etc.*). -*n.* chemical compound exploding readily. -**fulmina'tion** *n.* [L. *fulmen*, thunderbolt]
ful'some *a.* offending by excess, cloying; fawning. [OE.]
ful'vous *a.* tawny; of a deep yellow color. [L. *fulvus*, tawny]
fum'arole *n.* smoke-outlet of a volcano. [F. *furnerole*]
fum'ble *v.i.* and *t.* handle awkwardly, grope about.[lorig, uncertain]
fume *n.* smoke; vapor; exhalation. -*v.i.* emit fumes: give way to anger, chafe. -**fuma'cious** *a.* smoky. [L. *lumare*, smoke]
fum'et *n.* strong-flavored liquid made from cooking fish, meat, or game, used to flavor sauces, [F. *aroma*]
fu'migate *v.t.* apply fumes or smoke to, *esp.* to disinfect. -**fumiga'tion** *n.* [*fume*]
fun *n.* sport, amusement, jest, diversion. -*v.i.* joke. -**funn'y** *a.* -**funn'y bone**, ulnar nerve at point of elbow. -**funn'ily, funn'y** *adv.* [ME, *fonnen*, be foolish]
funambula'tion *n.* rope-walking. -**funam'bulist** *n.* rope-walker. [L. *funis*, rope, *ambulare*, walk]
func'tion *n.* work a thing is designed to do; official duty; profession; public occasion or ceremony. -*v.i.* operate, work. -**func'tional** *a.* -**func'tionary** *n.* official. [L. *functio*]
fund *n.* permanent stock; stock or sum of money. -*pl.* money resources. -*v.t.* convert (debt) into permanent form; invest money permanently. -**fund'ament** *n.* buttocks. -**fundament'al** *a.* essential, primary; of, affecting, or serving as, the base. -*n.* one laying stress on belief in literal and verbal inspiration of the Bible or other traditional creeds. -**funda-ment'alism** *n.* [L. *fundus*, bottom]
fu'neral *a.* of, or relating to, the burial of the dead. -*n.* ceremonies at a burial. -**fune'real** *a.* fit for a funeral, dismal. [L. *funus, funer-*, burial]
fun'gus (-ng-g-) *n.* **fun'gi** (-ji) **fun'-guses** *pl.* mushroom or allied plant; spongy morbid growth. -**fun'gous** *a.* -**fun'gicide** *n.* substance used to destroy fungus. [L.]
funic'utar *a.* of or worked by a rope. -**funic'ular** railways mountain or other cable-railway. [L. *funiculus*, dim. of *funis*, rope]
funk *n.* fear, panic; coward. -*v.i.* show fear. -*v.t.* be afraid of. -**funk'y** *a.* [Flem. *fonck*]
funn'el *n.* cone-shaped vessel or tube; chimney of locomotive or ship; ventilating shaft. [L. *fundere*, pour]
funn'y. *See* **fun.**
fur *n.* short soft hair of certain animals; lining or trimming or garment of dressed skins with such hair; crust or coating resembling this. -*v.t.* provide with fur. -**furr'ier** *n.* one who deals in furs. -**furr'y** *a.* [F. *v. fourrer*, fr. OF. *fourre*, sheath, cover]
fur'below *n.* flounce, trimming. [earlier *falbala* (F.)]
fur'bish *v.t.* clean-up. [F. fourbir]
fur'cate *a.* forked, branched, [L. *furca*, fork]
furl *v.t.* roll up and bind (a sail, an umbrella. *etc.*). [F. *ferier*]
fur'long *n.* eighth of a mile. [OE. *furlang*, length of a furrow, *furh*]
fur'lough *n.* leave of absence, *esp.* of sol-

dier. [Du. *verlol*]

fur'nace *n.* apparatus for applying great heat to metals; hot place; closed fireplace for heating a boiler, *etc.* [F. *fournaise*]

fur'nish *v.t.* supply, fit up with; fit up a house with furniture: yield. -**fur'niture** *n.* movable contents of a house or room. [F. *fournir*]

furor' *n.* burst of enthusiastic popular admiration. [It.]

furr'ow (-a) *n.* trench made bv a plow ship's track; rut, groove. -*v.t.* make furrows in. [OE. *furh*]

furry. *See* **fur.**

fur'ther (-TH-) *adv.* more; in addition; at or to a greater extent. *a.* additional; -*v.t.* help forward. -**fur'therance** *n.* -**fur'therer** *n.* -**fur'thermore** *adv.* besides. -**fur'thest** *a.* and *adv.* (*superl.*). -**fur'thermost** *a.* [OE. *furthra a.; furthor adv.*]

fur'tive *a.* stealthy, sly. -**fur'tively** *adv.* [L. *furtivus*, fr. *fur,* thief]

fu'ry *n.* wild anger, rage; fierce passion; violence of storm, *etc.*; snake-haired avenging deity (*usu. pl.*). -**fu'rious** *a.* -**fu'riously** *adv.* [L. *furia*]

furze *n.* yellow-flowered prickly shrub growing wild on heaths. [OE. *fyrs*]

fusc, fusc'ous *a.* dark-brown; dingy; somber-hued. [L. *fuscus*]

fuse *n.* tube containing material for setting light to a bomb, firework, *etc.*; device used as a safety measure which interrupts an electric circuit. [L. *fusus*, spindle]

fuse *v.t.* and *i.* melt with heat; blend by melting. -**fu'sible** *a.* -**fu'sion** *n.* [L. *fundere, fus-*, pour]

fusee' *n.* conical wheel or pulley in a watch or clock; large-headed match. [*fuse*]

fu'selage *n.* spindle-shaped body of an airplane. [L. *fusus*, spindle]

fu'sel oil *n.* mixture of crude alcohols. [Ger. = bad brandy]

fu'sil *n.* light musket. -**fusilier'** *n.* soldier of certain regiments formerly armed with a fusil. -**fusillade'** *n.* continuous discharge of firearms. [F.]

fuss *n.* needless bustle or concern. -*v.*iI make a fuss. -*v.t.* hustle. -**fuss'y** *a.* **fuss'ily** *adv.* -**fuss'iness** *n.* [orig. uncertain]

fustic *n.* W. Indian tree; its wood used for dyeing. [F. *fustoc*, yellow]

fus'tian *n.* thick cotton cloth, moleskin; inflated language. [OF. *fustaigne*]

fus'tigate *v.t.* beat with a cudgel. -**fustiga'tion** *n.* [L. *fustis,* cudgel]

fusty *a.* moldy; smelling of damp. -**fus'tily** *adv.* -**fus'tiness** *n.* [OF. *fusté*, tasting of the cask, *fust*]

fu'tile *a.* useless, ineffectual, frivolous. -**futil'ity** *n.* [L. *futilis*, leaky]

fu'ture *a.* that will be; of, or relating to, time to come. -*n.* time to come; what will happen; tense of a verb indicating this. -**futu'rity** *n.* -**fu'turism** *n.* movement in art marked by complete abandonment of tradition. -**fu'turist** *n.* and *a.* [L. *futurus,* about to be]

fuzz *n.* fluff. -**fuzz'y** *a.* -**fuzz box** *n.* an electronic device that breaks up the sound passing through it, used *esp.* by guitarists. [imit. of blowing away light particles]

fyrd' *n.* English militia in Anglo-Saxon times. [OE. *fyrd,* army]

G

gab *n.* talk, chatter; gift of the gab, eloquence. -**gab'ble** *v.i.* and *t.* talk, utter inarticulately or too fast. -*n.* such talk. [imit. orig.]

gab'bro *n.* granite-like rock containing feldspar. [It.]

gaberdine *n.* fine hard-laid cloth; raincoat of this; loose upper garment, as of Jews. [orig. uncertain]

gab'ion (ga-) *n.* earth-filled cylinder of wicker used as defense against enemy fire. -**ga'bionade** *n.* line of gabions. [It. *gabbia,* cafe]

ga'ble *n.* triangular upper part of the wall at the end of a ridged roof. [OF.]

ga'by *n.* simpleton. [orig. uncertain]

gad *v.i.* go about idly. -**gad'about** *n.* gadding person. [fr. obs. *gadling*-OE. *gædeling*, comrade]

gad'fly *n.* cattle-biting fly. [obs. *gad,* spike, fr. ON. *gaddr*]

gadg'et *n.* small fitting or contrivance. [orig. uncertain]

Gael (gal) *n.* Scottish Highlander, Celt. **Gael'ic** *a.* of Gael or his language. [Gael, *Gaidheal*]

gaff *n.* barbed fishing spear; stick with an iron hook for landing fish; spar for the top of a fore-and-aft sail. -*v.t.* seize (a fish) with a gaff. [F. *gaffe*]

gaff *n.* formerly, public fair; low-class theatrical entertainment. [orig. unknown]

gaffe *n.* tactless or embarrassing blunder. [F.]

gaff'er *n.* aged rustic; foreman. [grandfather]

gag *n.* thing thrust into the mouth to prevent speech or hold it open for operation; closure in a debate. -*v.t.* apply a gag to; silence. [orig. *v.* strangle; imit. of victim's noises]

gag *n.* words inserted by an actor in his part. *-v.i.* of an actor, to put in words not in his part. [orig. uncertain]

ga'ga *a.* fatuous, gibbering. [F.]

gage *n.* pledge, thing given as security; challenge, or something symbolizing one. *-v.t.* pledge, stake. *See also* **gauge.** [F.]

gag'gle *n.* string of geese; cackle of geese. **-gagg'ling** *a.* garrulous. [imit.]

gaiety. *See* **gain**

gay. *v.t.* obtain, secure; obtain as profit; win; earn; persuade; reach. *-v.i.* increase, improve. *-n.* profit, increase, improvement. [F. *gagner*]

gainsay' *v.t.* deny, contradict. [OE. prefix gean-, against, and say]

gait *n.* manner of walking. [same as gate, street, way]

gait'er *n.* covering of leather, cloth, *etc.*, for the lower leg. [F. *guotre*]

gala *n.* festive occasion. [It.]

gala'go *n.* African tree; lemur. [Mod. L.]

gal'antine *n.* boned spiced white meat served cold. [F.]

gal'axy *n.* Milky Way; any other of the stellar universes; brilliant company. **-galac'tic** *a.* [G. *gala*, *galakt-*, milk]

gale *n.* strong wind. [orig. uncertain]

gale, sweet-'gale *n.* low-growing marsh shrub, the bog-myrtle. [orig. uncertain]

gale'na *n.* lead ore. [L.]

Galen'ic *a.* of Galen, 2nd c. Greek physician; of his theories.

gal'ingale *n.* aromatic E. Indian root [OF. *galingal*]

gall (gawl) *n.* bile of animals; bitterness, rancour. [OE. *gealla*]

gall (gawl) *n.* painful swelling, *esp.* on a horse; sore caused by chafing. *-v.t.* make sore by rubbing; vex, irritate. **-gall'ing** *a.* irritating. [OE. *gealla*]

gall (gawl) *n.* growth caused by insects on trees; oak-apple. [L. *galla*]

gall'ant *a.* fine, stately, brave; chivalrous; very attentive to women, amatory. *n.* man of fashion; lover, paramour. **-gall'antly** *adv.* (also **gallant'ly**). **-gall' antry** *n.* [F. *galant*]

gall'eon *n.* large high-built Spanish sailing ship of war. [Sp. *galeon*]

gall'ery *n.* raised floor over part of the area of a building, *esp.* a church; top floor of seats in a theatre; its occupants; long narrow platform on the outside of a building; passage in a wall, open to the interior of a building; covered walk with side openings, a colonnade; room or rooms for showing works of art; horizontal passage in mining. [F. *galerie*]

gall'ey *n.* one-decked vessel with sails and oars, usually rowed by slaves or criminals; large rowing-boat, *esp.* that used by the captain of a warship; ship's kitchen; printer's tray for set-up type. **-gall'ey-proof** *n.* printer's proof in long slip form. (OF. *galee*]

gall'iard (gal-yard) *n.* sprightly dance in triple time; gay fellow. [OF. *galliard*]

Gall'ic *a.* of, pert. to, Gaul, French. **-gall'icism** *n.* French idiom or word. [L. *Gallia, Gaul*]

gall'igaskins *n. pl.* breeches, leggings. [orig. uncertain]

gallina'ceous *a.* of order of domestic birds, *etc.* fowls, pheasants. [L. *gallina*, hen]

gall'ipot *n.* small earthenware pot. [galley pot; first imported in galleys]

gall'ist *n.* small galley; old type of Dutch cargo-boat. [L. L. *galea*, galley]

gall'ium *n.* lustrous grayish-white metal. [L. *gallus*, cock (fr. discoverer, *Lecoq de Boisbaudron*)]

gallivant' *v.i.* sally out in search of pleasure, *esp.* flirtation. [fr. *gallant*]

gall'on *n.* liquid measure of eight pints or four quarts. [ONF. *galon*]

galloon' *n.* variety of lace or braid for trimming. [F. *galon*]

gall'op *v.i.* go at a gallop. *-v.t.* cause to move at a gallop. *-n.* horse's, or other quadruped's, fastest pace, with all four feet off the ground together in each stride; ride at this pace. **-gall'oper** *n.* [F. *galoper*]

Gall'oway *n.* breed of small horse, breed of large cattle. [*Galloway* in Scotland]

gall'ows *n.* structure, usually of two upright beams and a cross-bar, *esp.* for hanging criminals on. [OE. gealga]

gal'on (-on) *n.* trimming of narrow silk braid; gold lace. [F.]

gal'op *n.* lively round dance. *-v.i.* dance the galop. [F. = *gallop*]

galore' *adv.* in plenty; in profusion. [Ir. *go leor*, in sufficiency]

galosh', golosh' *n.* overshoe, usually of rubber. [F. *galoche*]

galvanism *n.* electricity produced by chemical action. **-galvan'ic** *a.* **-galvan'ic batt'ery** *n.* **-gal'vanize** *v.t.* apply galvanism to; stimulate thus; rouse by shock; coat with metal by galvanism. **-galvaniza'tion** *n.* **-galvanom'eter** *n.* instrument for measuring galvanism. [*Gal-*

vani, It. physicist, (d. 1798)]

gam'bit *n.* chess opening involving the sacrifice of a piece. [It. *gambetto*, wrestler's trip, fr. *gamba*, leg]

gam'ble *v.i.* play games of chance for money stakes; speculate wildly; risk much for great gain. *-n.* risky undertaking. **-gam'bler** *n.* [fr. *game n.*]

gamboge' (zh) *n.* gum-resin used as yellow pigment. [Cambodia, in Annam, the source of it]

gam'bol *n.* caper, playful leap. *-v.i.* caper, leap about. [F. *gambade*]

game *n.* diversion, pastime, jest; contest for amusement; scheme, plan of action; animals or birds hunted; their flesh, *a.* plucky, spirited. *-v.i.* gamble. **-game'ly** *a.* **-game'ster** *n.* gambler. **-game'cock** *n.* fowl bred for fighting. **-game'keeper** *n.* man employed to breed game, prevent poaching, *etc.* **-gam'y** *a.* having the flavor of hung game; spirited. [OE. gamen]

game, gamm'y *a.* of arm or leg, crippled. [OF. *gambi*, bent]

gamete' *n.* sexual reproductive cell. [G. gamos, marriage]

gam'in *n.* city urchin, street arab. [F.]

gamm'a-rays *n. pl.* rays given off by radio-active substances, *e.g.*, radium. [G. letter *gamma*]

gamm'er *n.* old woman. [grandmother]

gamm'on *n.* humbug, nonsense. *-v.t.* humbug, deceive. [ME. *gamen*, game]

gamm'on *n.* the bottom piece of a flitch of bacon. [ONF. *gambon*, ham]

gamp *n.* (*sl.*) umbrella, [Sarah *Gamp*, Dickens character]

gam'ut *n.* whole series of musical notes; scale; compass of a voice. [Med, L. *gamma*, and *ut*, names of notes]

gan'der *n.* male goose. [OE. gandra]

gang *n.* company, band. **-gang'er** *n.* foreman over a gang of workmen. **gang'way** *n.* bridge from a ship to the shore; anything similar; passage between rows of seats. [OE. = going, way]

gang'lion (-ng-gl-) *n.* knot on a nerve from which nerve fibers spread out; nerve nucleus. [G. *ganglion*]

gang'rel *n.* vagrant, vagabond. *n.* [OE. *gangan*, walk]

gang'rene (-ng-gr-) *n.* mortification, decomposition of a part of the body. *-v.t.* affect with this. *-v.i.* be affected with this. **-gang'renous** *a.* [L. *gangraena*, G. *gangraina*]

gang'ster *n.* member of a gang of criminals, toughs. [gang]

gann'et *n.* solan goose, a sea-bird. [OE. *ganot*]

gan'try, gaun'try *n.* structure to support a crane, railway signals, *etc.* ; stand for barrels. [L. *cantherius*, rafter, pack-horse]

gaol *See* **jail.**

gap *n.* breach, opening; empty space. (ON. = chasm]

gape *v.i.* open the mouth wide; stare; yawn. *-n.* yawn; wide opening of the mouth. [ON, *gapa*]

gar *n.* fish with slender body and pointed head, kind of pike. [OF. = dart]

gar'age *n.* building to house automobiles. **-gar'age sale** *n.* sale of personal belongings or household effects held at a person's home, usually in the garage. **-garag'ing** *n.* accommodation for housing automobiles. *-v.t.* put into a garage. [F., fr. *garer*, make safe]

garb *n.* dress, fashion of dress. *-v.t.* dress, clothe. [OF. *garbe*, contour]

garb'age (-ij) *n.* offal; refuse; anything worthless; originally, giblets. [orig. uncertain]

gar'ble *v.t.* make selections from unfairly, so as to misrepresent. **-gar'bled** *a.* [arab. *ghirbal*, sieve]

gar'den *n.* ground for growing flowers, fruit, or vegetables. *-v.i.* cultivate a garden. **-gar'dener** *n.* **-gar'den ci'ty,** planned town with parks and planted areas. **-gar'dening** *n.* the planning and cultivation of a garden. [ONF. *gardin*]

garde'nia (-d-) *n.* tropical, subtropical shrub with fragrant white flowers. [Dr. A. *Garden* (d. 1791)]

gare'fowl *n.* great auk. [ON. *geirfugl*]

gar'fish. *See* **gargantuan**

gar *a.* huge, prodigious. [*Gargantua*, character of Rabelais]

gar'gle *v.i.* and *i.* wash the throat with liquid kept moving by the breath. *-n.* liquid used for this. [F. *gargouiller*]

gar'goyle *n.* grotesque water-spout. [F. *gargouille*, fr. L. *gargulio*, throat]

garibal'di *n.* loose blouse; fruit biscuit. [*Garibaldi*, It. patriot]

gar'ish *a.* showy; glaring; tawdry. [orig. uncertain]

gar'land *n.* wreath of flowers worn or hung as a decoration. *-v.t.* decorate with garlands. [OF. *garlandle*]

gar'lic *n.* plant with a strong smell and taste, used in cooking. [OE. *garleac*, spear leek]

gar'ment *n.* article of dress. *-pl.* clothes. [F. *garniment*, equipment]

garn'er *n.* a granary. *-v.t.* store up. [F. *grenier*, fr. L. *granarium*]
gar'net *n.* precious stone. [F. grenat]
gar'nish *v.t.* adorn, decorate (*esp.* food or literary matter). *-n.* material for this. **gar'niture** *n.* furniture, ornaments, trimming. [F. *garnir*]
garr'et *n.* room on the top floor, an attic. [orig. turret, OF. *garite*, refuge]
garrison *n.* troops stationed in a town, fort, *etc.* *-v.t.* furnish, or occupy, with a garrison; defend by this means. [OF. *garison*, fr. *garir*, protect]
garrotte' *n.* Spanish capital punishment by strangling; apparatus for this; robbery by throttling the victim. *-v.t.* execute, or rob, thus. [Sp. *garrote*, tourniquet]
garr'ulous *a.* talkative. **-garrul'ity** *n.* [L. *garrulus -garrire*, chatter]
gar'ter *n.* band worn near the knee to keep a stocking up. [ONF. *gartier*, fr. *garet*, bend of the knee]
garth *n.* paddock. [ON. *garthr*]
gas *n.* elastic fluid such as air, *esp.* one not liquid or solid at ordinary temperature; such fluid, *esp.* coal-gas used for heating or lighting; such fluid or a mixture used as poison in warfare, or found as an explosive in mines, or employed as an anesthetic, *etc.*; gasoline. *-v.t.* project gas over; poison with gas. **-gas'-bag** *n.* vacuous talker. **-gas'mask** *n.* mask to protect against poison gases. **-gas'-me'ter** *n.* device for measuring consumption of gas. **-gas'eous** *a.* **-gaselier'** *n.* lamp of several burners for gas. **-gasom'eter** *n.* apparatus for measuring or storing gas. **-gass'y** *a.* of, or like, or full of, gas. [coined by Du. chemist, *Van Helmont* (d. 1664)]
gasconade' *n.* boastful talk. [F., fr. *Gascon*, native of Gascony]
gash *a.* long deep cut, slash. *-v.t.* make a gash in. [earlier *garshe*, F. *gercer*, chap]
gas'oline, gas'olene *n.* liquid from petroleum, used as fuel. [gas]
gasp *v.i.* catch the breath with open mouth, as in exhaustion or surprise. *-n.* convulsive catching of the breath. [ON, *geispa*, yawn]
gas'tric *a.* of the stomach. **-gastron'omy** *n.* art of good eating. **-gastronom'ical** *a.* **-gastron'omer, gas'tronome** *n.* judge of cooking. **-gas'teropod** *n.* mollusk, *e.g.* a snail, with organ of locomotion placed ventrally. [G. *gaster*, belly]
gate *n.* opening in a wall which may be closed by a barrier; barrier for closing it; device for regulating the flow of water; any entrance or way out; entrance-money at, *e.g.*, a football-game **-gate'crasher** *n.* one who attends a party, *etc.* without being invited. [OE. *geat*]
gate *n.* (*compute.*) electronic circuit which performs logical or mathematical calculations or operations.
gath'er (-TH-) *v.t.* bring together; collect; draw together, pucker; deduce. *-v.i.* come together; collect; form a swelling full of pus. **-gathers** *n. pl.* puckered part of a dress. [OE. *gadrian*]
gat'ling *n.* type of machine-gun. [R. J. Gatling, inventor]
gauche (gosh) *a.* awkward, clumsy. [F. left-handed]
gau'cho (gow-cho) *n.* S. American cowboy. [Sp.]
gaud (gawd) *n.* showy ornament. **-gaud'y** *a.* showy without taste. **-gaud'ily** *adv.* **-gaud'iness** *n.* [orig. uncertain]
gauge, gage *n.* standard measure, as of diameter of wire, *etc.* ; distance between rails of a railway; capacity, extent; instruments for measuring such things as size of wire, rainfall, height of water in a boiler, *etc.* *-v.t.* measure, test, estimate. [ONF.]
gaunt (gaw-) *a.* lean, haggard, starved-looking. [orig. uncertain]
gaunt'let (gaw-) *n.* armored glove; glove covering part of the arm. [F. *gantelet*, dim. of gant, glove]
gaunt'let (gaw-) *n.* run the gauntlet, punishment in which the victim had to run between two lines of men who struck at him with sticks, *etc.* to brave criticism. [Se. *gatlopp*, 'gate run']
gauze (gawz) *n.* thin transparent fabric of silk, wire, *etc.* **-gauz'y** *a.* [F. *gaze*]
gav'el *n.* a mallet; chairman's or auctioneer's hammer. [orig. unknown]
ga'vial *n.* crocodile of the R. Ganges. [F., fr. Hindu. *ghariyal*]
gavotte' *n.* lively dance; music written for it. [F.]
gawk *n.* awkward or bashful person **-gawk'y** *a.* [orig, uncertain]
gay *a.* light-hearted; showy; dissolute; homosexual. **-gai'ly** *adv.* **-gai'ety** *n.* [F. *gai*]
gaze *v.i.* look fixedly. *-n.* long intent look. [orig. uncertain]
gaze'bo *n.* outlook turret on roof or wall; summer-house with wide prospect; belvedere. [orig. unknown]
gazelle' *n.* small soft-eyed antelope. [Arab. *ghazal*, wild goat]
gazette' *n.* official newspaper for announcements of government appoint-

ments, bankruptcies, *etc.* ; title for a newspaper. -*v.t.* publish in the official gazette. -**gazetteer'** *n.* geographical dictionary. [It. *gazzetta*]

gaz'ogene, gas'ogene *n.* apparatus for making aerated water. [F. *gaz*, gas]

gean (e) *n.* wild cherry. [OF, *guigne*]

gear *n.* apparatus, tackle, tools; set of wheels working together, *esp.* by engaging cogs; rigging; harness; equipment; clothing; goods, utensils. -*v.t.* provide with gear; put in gear. -**gear'-box, -case** *n.* box, case protecting gearing of bicycle, car. -**gear'-wheel** *n.* wheel with cogs, *etc.* for transmitting motion in cycle. -**in gear**, connected and in working order. -**out of gear**, disconnected, out of sorts. [ME. *gere*, fr. ON.]

geck'o *n.* small lizard. [Malay *gekoq*]

Gei'ger counter (gi) *n.* instrument for measuring density of radio-active field. [Geiger, German physicist]

gei'sha *n.* Japanese dancing-girl. [Chin. *iche*, artistic ones]

gelatin, gel'atine *n.* transparent substance made by stewing skin, tendons, *etc.* -**gelat'inize** *v.t.* -**gelat'inous** *a.* [It. *gelatins*, fr. *gelata*, jelly]

geld (g-) *v.t.* castrate. -**geld'ing** *n.* castrated horse. [ON. *geldr*, barren]

gel'id (jel) *a.* very cold. [L. *gelidus*]

gel'ignite (jel'-ig-nit) *n.* high explosive. [*gelatin* and *ignite*]

gem *n.* precious stone; thing of great beauty or worth. -*v.t.* adorn with gems. [L. *gemma*, bud, gem]

gem'ini (jem'-i-ni) *n.* constellation containing Castor and Pollux; third sign of the zodiac (the twins) which sun enters c. May 21st. [L. *pl.* of *geminus*, twin]

gen *n.* (*sl.*) information [general information]

gen'der *n.* sex, male or female; classification of nouns, corresponding roughly to sexes and sexlessness (in English). [F, *genre*, fr. L. *genus*, gener-, kind]

gene (jen) *n.* one of the biological factors determining heredity. [G. *genos*, race]

genealogy (je) *n.* account of descent from an ancestor or ancestors; pedigree; study of pedigrees. -**genealog'ical** *a.* -**geneal'ogize** *v.i.* -**geneal'ogist** *n.* [G. *geneaolgia*, fr. *genea*, race]

gen'eral *a.* not particular or partial; including or affecting or applicable to all or most; not restricted to one department; usual, prevalent; miscellaneous; dealing with main elements only. -*n.* officer in the armed forces of rank above lieutenant general. -**generaliss'imo** *n.* supreme commander. -**general'ity** *n.* -**gen'eralize** *v.t.* reduce to general laws. -*v.i.* draw general conclusions. -**generaliza'tion** *n.* -**gen'erally** *adv.* -**gen'eralship** *n.* military skill; management. [L. *generalis*, fr. *genus*, gener-, kind]

gen'erate *v.t.* bring into being; produce. -**genera'tion** *n.* bringing into being; step in a pedigree; all persons born about the same time; average time in which children are ready to replace their parents (about 30 years). -**gen'erative** *a.* -**gen'erator** *n.* a begetter; apparatus for producing (steam, *etc.*). -**gen'erating-sta'tion** *n.* place where electricity is generated. [L. *generare*, procreate]

generic *a.* belonging to, characteristic of, a class or genus. -**gener'ically** *adv.* [L. *genus, gener-*, race]

gen'erous *a.* noble-minded; liberal, free in giving; copious; of wine, rich. -**gen'erously** *adv.* -**generos'ity** *n.* [L. *generosus*, of noble birth]

gen'esis *n.* origin; mode of formation. -**Genesis** *n.* first book of the Old Testament. [G.]

genetics *n.* science dealing with heredity, variation, reproduction. -**genet'ic** *a.* [G. *genesis*]

gene'va *n.* gin, *q.v.*

ge'nial *a.* kindly, jovial; sympathetic; mild, conducive to growth. -**ge'nially** *adv.* -**genial'ity** *n.* [L. *genialis*]

ge'nie *n.* (ge'nii *pl.*) a demon. [F. *genie*, used for Arab. *jinni*]

gen'ital *a.* of generation. -*n. pl.* external generative organs. [L. *gignere*, *genit-*, beget]

gen'itive *n.* (gram.) possessive case. -**geniti'val** *a.* [L. *genitivus*]

ge'nius *n.* with high power of mind; person with this; tutelary spirit; prevalent feeling, taste; character, spirit. [L. = a spirit watching over a person from birth, fr. *gignere*, gen-, beget]

genre' (zhong'r) *n.* kind, variety; style of painting homely scenes. [F.]

genteel' *a.* elegant (usually ironical). -**genteel'ly** *adv.* [F. *gentil*, gentle]

gen'tian *n.* plant, usually with blue flowers. [L. *gentiana*]

gen'tile *a.* of race other than Jewish; -*n.* gentile person. [L. *gens*, *gent-*, race, translating G. *ta ethne*, the nations]

gen'tle *a.* mild, quiet, not rough or severe; courteous; noble; well-born. -**gentil'ity** *n.*

social superiority. **-gen'tleman** *n.* chivalrous well-bred man; man of good social position; man of noble birth; man (used as a mark of politeness). **-gen'tlemanly, -gen'tleman-like** *a.* **-gen'tlewoman** *n.* **-gen'tleness** *n.* **-gent'ly** *adv.* **-gent'ry** *n.* people next below the nobility. [F. *gentil*]

gen'uflect *v.i.* bend the knee, *esp.* in worship. **-genuflec'tion, genuflex'ion** *n.* [fr. L. *genu*, knee, and *flectere*, flex, bend]

gen'uine *a.* real, true, not sham, properly so called. [L. *genuinus*, native]

ge'nus *n.* **(gen'era** *pl.*) race, tribe, kind, class. [L.]

geode' *n.* rock cavity lined with crystals; stone containing this. [G. *geodes*, earth]

geod'esy *n.* science of earth measurement. [G. *ge*, earth, *daisis*, division]

geography *n.* science of the earth's form, physical features, climate, popu lation, *etc.*; book on this. **-geog'rapher** *n.* **-geograph'ical** *a.* **-geograph'ically** *adv.* [G. *ge*, earth, *graphein*, write]

geol'ogy *n.* science of the earth's crust, the rocks, their strata, *etc.* **-geol'ogist** *n.* **-geolog'ical** *a.* **-geolog'ically** *adv.* **-geol'ogize** *v.i.* practice geology. [G. *ge*, earth, *logia*, discourse]

geom'etry *n.* science of the properties and relations of magnitudes in space, as lines, surfaces, *etc.* **-geometri'cian** *n.* **-geomet'rical** *a.* **-geomet'rically** *adv.* [G. *ge*, earth, *metron*, measure]

georgette' (jor-jet) *n.* fine semi-transparent fabric. [F. name *Georgette*]

geor'gic *a.* of farming. *-n.* poem of husbandry. [G. *georgia*, fr. *ge*, earth, *ergon*, work]

gera'nium *n.* genus of plants with fruit resembling a crane's bill. [L., G. *geranos*, crane]

ge'rent (je-) *n.* ruler, governor. [L. *gerere*, manage]

gerfal'con *n.* large kind of falcon. [OF. *gerfaucon*]

germ *n.* rudiment of a new organism, of an animal or plant; microbe; elementary thing. **-germ'icide** *n.* substance for destroying disease-germs. **-germici'dal** *a.* **-germ'inate** *v.i.* sprout. *-v.t.* cause to sprout. **-germina'tion** *n.* **-germ warfare** *n.* warring method in which the weapons are germs release to produce disease among the enemy. [L. *gerrnen*, seed]

germane' *a.* relevant, belonging to a subject. [L. *germanus*, *v.s.*]

gerontoc'racy *n.* government by old men. [G. *geron*, old man, *kratos*, power]

gerrymander *v.t.* arrange matters for an election, manipulate an electoral district, so as to give undue influence to one side. [fr. Governor *Gerry* of Mass. and salamander]

gest *n.* exploit. mediaeval romance. [L. *gesta*, doings]

Gesta'po *n.* secret state police of Nazi Germany. [*Ge*heime *Sto*ats *Pol*izei]

gestation *n.* carrying of young in the womb between conception and birth; period of gestation. [L. *gestatio*]

gesticulate *v.i.* use expressive or lively movements accompanying, or instead of, speech. **-gesticula'tion** *n.* [L. *gestus*, action]

ges'ture *n.* movement to convey some meaning. [Low L. *gestura*]

get (g-) *v.t.* obtain, procure, earn; cause to go or come; bring into a position or state; induce; (in *perf. tense*) be in possession of, have (to do). *-v.i.* reach, attain; become. **get'-away** *n.* escape. [ON. *geta*]

ge'um *n.* kind of herb, avens. [L.]

gew'gaw (g-) *n.* gaudy toy, plaything, trifle. [orig. uncertain]

gey'ser (giz-, gez-) *n.* hot spring spouting at intervals; apparatus for heating water and delivering it from a tap. [Ice. *geysir*]

ghast'ly (ga-) *a.* horrible, shocking; death-like, pallid; grim. *-adv.* horribly. [obs. *gast*, terrify cp. *aghast*]

ghat *n.* mountain pass; place of cremation, *esp.* Benares. [Hind. = river stairs]

ghee *n.* clarified butter from buffalo-milk. [Hind. *ghi*]

gher'kin (g-) *n.* kind of small cucumber. [Old Du. dim. of *gurk*, for *agurk*, cucumber]

ghett'o *n.* part of a city where members of a particular national or racial group predominate, or are restricted. [It.]

ghost *n.* spirit, dead person appearing again, specter; semblance. **ghost'ly** *a.* [OE. *gast*, spirit]

ghoul *n.* in Eastern tales, a spirit preying on corpses. **-ghoul'ish** *a.* revelling in the gruesome. [Arab. *ghul*]

gi'ant *n.* human being of superhuman size; very tall person, plant, *etc.* -a. huge. **-gigant'ic** *a.* enormous, huge [F. *goant*, fr. L. *gigas*, *gigant*]

gibb'er *v.i.* make meaningless sounds with the mouth, jabber, chatter like an ape. [imit. orig.]

gibberish *n.* meaningless speech. [orig. uncertain]

gibb'et *n.* post with an arm on which an

executed criminal was hung; death by hanging. *-v.t.* hang on a gibbet. hold up to contempt. [F. *gibet*]

gibb'on (g-) *n.* long-armed ape. [F.]

gibb'ous (g-) *a.* convex; of moon, with bright part greater than a semicircle. **gibbos'ity** *n.* [L. *gibbus*, hump]

gibe, jibe *v.i.* utter taunts. *-v.t.* taunt. *n.* jeer. [orig. uncertain]

gib'let *n.* (in *pl.*) edible internal portion of a fowl, goose, *etc.*, removed before cooking. [orig. unknown]

gi'bus *n.* man's opera hat. [inventor]

gidd'y (g-) *a.* dizzy, feeling a swimming in the head; liable to cause this feeling; flighty, frivolous. **-gidd'ily** *adv.* **-gidd'iness** *n.* [OE. *gydig*, insane]

gift (g-) thing given, present; faculty, power. *-v.t.* endow or present (with). **gift'ed** *a.* talented. [give]

gift wrap *v.t.* to wrap a present in decorative paper and trimmings. **-gift wrap** *n.* **-gift wrapping** *n.* **-gift wrapper** *n.*

gig (g-) *n.* light two-wheeled carriage; light ship's boat; rowing boat; performance of modern popular music. [orig. uncertain]

gigabit *n.* (*comp.*) unit of information equal to one billion bits or binary digits.

gigahertz *n. pl.* **-gigahertz** unit of frequency equal to one billion hertz; formerly **gigacycle** [*abbr.* **GHz**]

gigantic. *See* **giant.**

gig'gle *v.i.* laugh in a half-suppressed way, foolishly or uncontrollably. *-n.* such a laugh. [limit. orig.]

GIGO (*compute.*) term used to stress the fact that computer results are dependant upon the quality of the computer input. [*G*arbage *I*n/*G*arbage *O*ut]

gig'olo *n.* male professional dancing partner. [F.]

gig'ot *n.* leg of mutton. [F.]

gi'la mon'ster, *n.* black-and-yellow poisonous lizard of Arizona. [Gila River]

gild (g-) *v t.* put a thin layer of gold on. **-gilt** *a.* **gilded** *-n.* layer of gold put on. [OE. *gyldan*, fr. gold]

gild. *See* **guild.**

gill *n.* measure, the fourth of a pint. [orig. uncertain]

gill (g-) *n.* breathing organ in fishes; flesh below a person's jaws and ears. [orig. unknown. cp, Sw. *gill*, Dan. *giaelle*]

gill (g-) *n.* glen, ravine. [ON. *gil*]

gill'yflower *n.* clove-scented pink; other similar scented flowers, *e.g.* the wall flower. [F. *giroflee*, fr. G. *karyophyllon*, nut leaf]

gilt. *See* **gild.**

gim'bals *n. pl.* contrivance of rings, *etc.*, for keeping a thing horizontal at sea. [L. *gemellus*, twin]

gim'crack *a.* flimsy, fanciful. *-n.* showy but worthless article. [orig. uncertain]

gim'let *n.* boring tool, usually with a screw point. [OF. *guimbelet*]

gimp *n.* kind of trimming, of silk covered cord. [F. *guimpe*]

gin *n.* snare, trap; kind of crane; machine for separating cotton from seeds. *-v.t.* snare; treat (cotton) in a gin. [F. *engin*, L. *ingenium*, skill]

gin *n.* spirit flavored with juniper. [short for *geneva*, F. *genievre*, fr. L. *juniperus*, juniper]

gin'ger *n.* plant with a hot-tasting spicy root used in cooking, *etc.* ; the root; spirit, mettle; light reddish yellow color. -- **gin'ger-bread** *n.* cake flavored with ginger. **-gin'gery** *a.* [Late L. *gingiber*, of Eastern orig.]

gin'gerly *a.* such as to avoid noise or injury; cautious. *-adv.* in a gingerly manner. [orig. uncertain]

gingham (-am) *n.* cotton woven in stripes or checks. [F. *guingan*, fr. Malay *ginggan*, striped]

gip'sy. See **gypsy.**

giraffe' *n.* African ruminant animal, with spotted coat and very long neck and legs. [F. *girafe*, fr. Arab.]

gird (g-) *v.t.* put a belt round; fasten clothes thus; equip with or belt on a sword; encircle. **-gird'er** *n.* beam supporting joists; iron or steel beam. **-gir'dle** *n.* belt. *-v.t.* surround. **-gird** *v.i.* gibe. *-n.* gibe. [OE. *gyrdan*]

girl *n.* female child; young unmarried woman; woman. **-Girl Scouts,** girls' organization corresponding to the Boy Scouts. [ME. *gurie*; of unknown orig.]

girth (g-) *n.* band put round a horse to hold the saddle, *etc.*; measurement round a thing. *-v.t.* surround, secure, with a girth. [ON. *gjdrth*]

gis'mo, giz'mo *n.* device, gadget. [orig. uncertain]

gist *n.* substance, essential point (of remarks, *etc.*). [OF. *gist* 'it lies']

gita'na O-) *n.* Spanish gypsy woman. [Sp. *gitano*]

give (g-) *v.t.* bestow, confer ownership of, make a present of, deliver, impart; assign; yield, supply; make over, cause to have. *v.i.* yield, give way. *-n.* yielding, elasticity.

(**-gave** p.t. **-given** p.p.)**-giv'er** *n.* [OE. *giefan*]

gizz'ard (g-) *n.* bird's second stomach for grinding food. [F. *gésier*]

glabrous (gla-) *a.* hairless, smooth. [L. *glaber*, smooth]

glac'é- (glass) *a.* of cakes, fruit; smoothly iced, sugared. [F.]

gla'cier (-a-, -a-) *n.* river of ice, a slow-moving mass of ice formed by accumulated snow in mountain valleys. **-gla'cial** (-shal) *a.* of ice, or of glaciers; crystalized. **-glacia'tion** *n.* **-gla'cis** (-se) *n.* outer sloping bank of a fortification. [F., fr. *glace*, ice]

glad *a.* pleased; happy, joyous; giving joy. -*v.t.* make glad. **-gladd'en** *v.t.* **-glad'ly** *adv.* **-glad'ness** *n.* **-glad'some** *a.* **-glad'someness** *n.* [OE. glæd]

glade *n.* clear space in a wood or forest. [orig. uncertain]

gladiator *n.* trained fighter in ancient Roman shows. [L. fr. *gladius*, sword]

gladiolus *n.* flowering plant of the iris family, with sword-shaped leaves. [L., dim. of *gladius*, sword]

glair *n.* white of egg. [F. *glaire*]

glaive *n.* sword, type of halberd. [OF.]

glam'or *n.* magic, enchantment. **-glam'orous** *a.* **-glamorize** *n.* make seem glamorous, *esp.* deceptively. [corrupt. of *grammar, gramarye*, magic]

glance *v.i.* glide off something struck; pass quickly; allude, touch; look rapidly. *v.t.* direct (the eyes) rapidly. -*n.* brief look; flash; sudden oblique movement or blow. [F. *glacer*, (formerly) slide]

gland *n.* organ separating constituents of the blood, for use or ejection. **-gland'ular** *a.* [L. *glans, gland-*, acorn]

gland'ers *n.* contagious disease of horses. [gland]

glandif'erous *a.* acorn-bearing. **-gland'iform** *a.* acorn or gland-shaped. [L. *glans*, gland]

glare *v.t.* shine with oppressive brightness; look fiercely. -*n.* dazzling brightness; fierce look. [ME. *glareni*]

glass *n.* hard transparent substance made by fusing sand with; a potash, *etc.*; things made of it collectively; glass drinking vessel; contents of this; lens; telescope, barometer, or other instrument. *pl.* spectacles. **-glass'y** *a.* **-glass'ily** *adv.* **-glassiness** *n.* **-glass'paper** *n.* strong paper coated with powdered glass or other abrasive material for smoothing and polishing. **-glaze** *v.t.* furnish with glass; cover with glassy substance or glaze. -*v.i.* become glassy. -*n.* transparent coating; substance used to give this; glossy surface. **-gla'zier** *n.* one whose trade is to glaze windows. [OE. *glæs*]

glauco'ma *n.* eye disease. [G.]

glau'cous *a.* sea-green. [G. *glaukos*]

gleam *n.* slight or passing beam of light; faint or momentary show. -*v.i.* give out gleams. [OE. *glaees*]

glean *v.t.* and *i.* gather, pick up, after reapers in a cornfield; pick up (facts, *etc.*). **-glean'er** *n.* [F. *glaner*]

glebe *n.* land forming part of a clergyman's benefice; soil. [L. *gleba*, clod]

glee *n.* mirth, merriment; musical composition for three or more voices, a catch. **glee'ful** *a.* **-glee'fully** *adv.* **-glee'man** *n.* minstrel. [OE. *gliw*, minstrelsy]

glen *n.* narrow valley, usually wooded and with a stream. [Gael. *gleann*]

glib *a.* fluent; more voluble than sincere. **-glib'ly** *adv.* **-glib'ness** *n.* [orig. uncertain. cp. Du. *glibberig*, slippery]

glide *v.i.* pass smoothly and continuously; go stealthily or gradually; of an airplane, move with engines shut off. -*n.* smooth, silent movement; in music, sounds made in passing from tone to tone. **-glid'er** *n.* one or that which glides; airplane for flying without mechanical power. [OE. *glidani*]

glimm'er *v.i.* shine faintly or with flickering. -*n.* such light. [ME. *glimeren*]

glimpse *n.* momentary view; passing flash or appearance. -*v.t.* catch a glimpse of-*v.i.* glimmer. [gleam]

glint *v.i.* and *t.* flash, glitter; reflect. -*n.* glitter; glancing reflection. [ME. *glent*]

glissade' *n.* slide, usually on the feet, down a slope of ice. -*v.i.* slide thus. [F.]

glis'ten (-is'n) *v.i.* glitter, sparkle, shine. [OE. *glisnian*, shine]

glitt'er *v.i.* shine with bright quivering light, sparkle. -*n.* [ON. *glitra*]

glitz *n.* (*sl.*) showy or flashy appearance or display; ostentatious glamor; gaudiness *v.t.* **-glitzy** *a.*

gloam'ing *n.* evening twilight. [OE. *glomung*, fr. *glom*, twilight]

gloat *v.i.* feast the eyes, *usu.* with unholy joy. [orig. uncertain]

globe *n.* round body, sphere; heavenly sphere, *esp.* the earth; sphere with a map of the earth or the stars; anything of about this shape, as a lampshade, fish-bowl, *etc.* **-glob'al** *a.* **-glob'al village** *n.* the whole world considered as being closely connected by modern telecommunications and as being interdependent economically, socially, and politically. -**globe' flower** *n.* plant with pale-yellow globe-shaped flowers. -**globe'-trotter** *n.* hasty, sight-seeing traveller. -**glob'ule** *n.* small round body; drop. -**glob'ular** *a.* globe-shaped. [L. *globus*, round mass]

gloom *n.* darkness; melancholy, depression. -*v.i.* look sullen, or dark. -*v.t.* make dark or dismal. -**gloom'y** *a.* -**gloom'ily** *adv.* -**gloom'iness** *n.* [cp. *glum*]

glor'y *n.* renown, honorable fame; splendor; heavenly bliss; exalted or prosperous state. -*v.i.* take pride (in). **glor'ify** *v.t.* make glorious, invest with glory. -**glorifica'tion** *n.* -**glor'ious** *a.* **glor'iously** *adv.* [fL. *gloria*]

gloss *n.* surface shine. -*v.t.* put a gloss on. -**gloss'y** *a.* smooth and shining **gloss'iness** *n.* [orig. uncertain]

gloss *n.* marginal interpretation of a word; comment, explanation. -*v.t.* interpret; comment; explain away. -**gloss'ary** *n.* collection of glosses; dictionary or vocabulary of special words. [F. *glose*, fr. G. *glossa*, tongue]

glottis *n.* opening at the top of the larynx (windpipe). [G.]

glove (-uv) *n.* covering for the hand. -*v.t.* provide with, or put on, gloves. -**glo'ver** *n.* dealer in gloves. [OE. *glof*]

glow (-o) *v.i.* give out light and heat without flames; shine; be, or look, very hot, burn with emotion. -*n.* shining heat; feeling of bodily heat; warmth of color; ardor. -**glow'worm** *n.* small luminous insect. [OE. *glowan*]

glower *v.i.* scowl. [orig. uncertain]

gloxin'ia *n.* plant with bell-like flowers. [B. P. *Gloxin*]

gloze *v.t.* explain away. -*v.i.* use fair words. [F. *gloser*, ep. gloss]

glu'cose *n.* grape-sugar, dextrose. [G. *glykys*, sweet]

glue (-oo) *n.* hard substance made from horns, hoofs, *etc.*, and used warm as a cement. -*v.t.* fasten with glue. -**glu'ey** *a.* [F. *glu*, bird-lime]

glum *a.* sullen, frowning, dejected. [orig. uncertain] [*gloom*]

glume *n.* husk, bract of grasses. **gluma'ceous, glumose'** *a.* like glume. [L. *gluma*, husk]

glut *v.t.* feed, gratify to the full or to excess; overstock. -*n.* excessive supply. [OF. *gloutir*, swallow]

glu'ten *n.* nitrogenous part of wheat flour, *etc.*; any viscid substance. [L.]

glutinous *a.* sticky; tenacious. [*gluten*]

glutt'on *n.* one who eats too much, a greedy person; one eagerly devouring (books, work, *etc.*). -**glutt'onous** *a.* **glutt'ony** *n.* [F. *glouton*]

glutt'on *n.* carnivorous animal, the wolverine.

glycerine, glycerine (glis'er-in) *n.* colorless, sweet liquid obtained from oils and used in medicine and the making of explosives. [G. *glykeros*, sweet]

gnarled (narld) *a.* of a tree, knobby, rugged, twisted. [*var.* of *knurled*]

gnash (n-) *v.t.* and *i.* grind (the teeth) together. [imit. orig.]

gnat (n-) *n.* small two-winged fly; mosquito. [OE. *gnæt*]

gnaw (n-) *v.t.* bite steadily, wear away by biting; corrode. [O. E. *gnagan*]

gneiss (nis) *n.* (*geol.*) rock made up of quartz, mica and feldspar. [Ger.]

gnome (n-) *n.* goblin, a fairy living underground. [Mod. L. *gnomus*]

gno'mic (no) *a.* sententious, pithy. [G. *gnome*, thought, judgment]

gno'mon *n.* pin or rod which casts the shadow on a sundial; an indicator. [G. = *inspector*, indicator]

gnos'tic (n-) *a.* of knowledge; having mystical knowledge; pert. to the Gnostics. [G. *gnostikos*]

gnu (nu-) *n.* S. African antelope somewhat like an ox. [*Kaffir nqu*]

go *v.i.* move along, make way; be moving; depart; elapse; be kept, put, be able to be put; result; contribute to a result; tend to; become. -*n.* energy, vigor. -**go'er** *n.* **go'gett'er** *n.* pushful, assertive person. [OE. *gan*]

goad *n.* spiked stick for driving cattle. *v.t.* drive with a goad; urge on: irritate. [OE. *gad*]

goal *n.* end of a race; object of effort; posts through which the ball or disk is to be driven in football, soccer, hockey, *etc.*; act of doing this. [orig. uncertain]

goat *n.* four-footed animal with long hair and horns, and a beard. -**goat'herd** *n.* one who tends goats. -**goat'ee** *n.* beard like a goat's. [OE. *gat*]

gob *n.* lump, mouthful. -**gobb'et** *n.* lump of food. -**gob'ble** *v.t.* eat hastily and noisily. [orig. uncertain]

gob'ble *v.i.* of a turkey, to make a gurgling noise in the throat. [imit.]

gob'let *n.* drinking cup. [F. *gobelet*]

gob'lin *n.* mischievous and ugly demon.

[F. *gobelin*]

go'by *n.* small sea-fish. [L. *gobius*]

god *n.* superhuman being worshipped as having supernatural power; object of worship, idol. **-God** *n.* Supreme Being. **godd'ess** *fem.* **-god'father** *n.* **-god'-mother** *fem.* sponsor at baptism. **god'child** *n.* one considered in relation to a godparent *n.* **-god'head** *n.* divine nature. **-god'fearing** *a.* religious, good. **-god'less** *a.* **-god'like** *a.* **-god'ly** *a.* religious. **-god'liness** *n.* **-god'-forsaken** *a.* devoid of merit, dismal. **god'send** *n.* unexpected or opportune benefit. **-God'speed,** may God speed (you) and bring (you) success. [OE.

gode'tia *n.* plant allied to evening primrose. [C. H. *Godet*, botanist]

god'wit *n.* long-legged, long-billed bird allied to the plover. [orig, uncertain]

goffer, gauffer *v.t.* make wavy, crimp with hot irons. [F. *gaufrer*, stamp with honeycomb pattern]

gog'gle *v.i.* roll the eyes. *-v.t.* roll about (the eyes), -a. rolling, sticking out (only of eyes). *-n.* in *pl.* large spectacles to protect the eyes from glare, dust, *etc.* [orig. uncertain]

go'iter *n.* enlargement of the thyroid gland. **-goi'tered** *a.* **-goi'trous** *a.* [F.]

gold *n.* yellow precious metal; coins of this, wealth; fig. beautiful or precious material or thing; color of gold. *-a.* of like, or having the color of, gold. **-gold'en** *a.* **-gold-digger** *n.* girl skilled in obtaining money from men. **-gold'finch** *n.* bird with lovely feathers. **-gold'fish** *n.* red Chinese carp. **-gold'-rush** *n.* rush to new gold fields. **-gold'smith** *n.* worker in gold. **-gold-standard** *n.* financial arrangement whereby currencies are expressed in fixed terms of gold. [OE.]

golf *n.* game in which a small hard ball is struck with clubs. *-v.i.* play this game. **golf'er** *n.* **-golf course** *n.*, place where golf is played, consisting of tees, greens and fairway. [Du. *kilf*, club]

golosh. *See* **galosh.**

go'nad *n.* sex gland. [G. *gone*, generation]

gon'dola *n.* Venetian canal-boat; car suspended from an airsbip. **-gondolier'** *n.* [It.]

gon'falcon *n.* banner or ensign with streamers. **-gonfalonier'** *n.* bearer of one. [F.]

gong *n.* metal disk with turned rim which resounds as a bell when struck with a soft mallet; anything used in the same way. [Malay]

gonorrhea *n.* venereal disease. [G. *gonorroia*]

gonopore *n.* reproductive opening of certain worms and insects through which the egg or sperm is released.

good *a.* right; proper; excellent; virtuous; kind; safe; adequate; sound; valid. *-n.* that which is good; well-being; profit. *-pl.* property, wares. **-good'-breeding** *n.* politeness. **-good-day,** a greeting. **-good fellowship** *n.* sociability, merry company. **Good Friday,** Friday before Easter commemorating Christ's crucifixion. **good-humor** *n.* pleasant disposition, cheerfulness. **-good'ly** *a.* handsome; of considerable size. **-good-nature** *n.* mild disposition, good-humor. **-good'ness** *n.* **good-night,** parting salutation. **-good'-will'** *n.* kindly feeling; heartiness; right of trading as a recognized successor. **-goody** *n.* candy. *-a.* obtrusively or weakly virtuous (also **goody-goody**). [OE. *god*]

good-bye' *interj.* farewell. [earlier *godbwye*, for God be with you]

goon *n.* (*sl.*) stupid person; hired ruffian. [fr. *gooney*, simpleton]

goosan'der *n.* arctic bird, kind of duck. [orig. uncertain]

goose *n.* large web-footed bird; its flesh; simpleton; tailor's smoothing iron. **goose'flesh** *n.* bristling state of the skin due to cold or fright. **-goose'-quill** *n.* pen. **-goose'-step** *n.* recruit's balancing drill; formal parade step. [OE. *gosi*]

gooseberry (-z-) *n.* thorny shrub; its eatable berry; chaperon to lovers. [orig. uncertain]

gore *n.* clotted shed blood. **-gor'y** *a.* **gor'ily** *adv.* [OE. *gor*, blood, filth]

gore *n.* triangular piece of cloth inserted to shape a garment. *-v.t.* shape with one. [OE. *gara*]

gore *v.t.* pierce with horns, tusks, spear, *etc.* [orig. uncertain]

gorge *n.* inside of the throat; surfeit; narrow opening between hills. *-v.i.* feed greedily. *-v.t.* stuff with food; devour greedily. **-gorg'et** *n.* piece of armor for the throat. [F.]

gorge'ous (-jus) *a.* splendid, showy, dazzling. [OF. *gorgias*, swaggering)

gor'gio *n.* Romany name for anyone not a gypsy. [orig. unknown]

gor'gon *n.* hideous mythical female creature, believed to turn beholder to stone; ugly woman. **-gorgo'nian** *a.* [G. *gorgo*]

Gorgonzo'la *n.* rich cheese. [It. town]

gorill'a *n.* anthropoid ape of the largest

kind. [orig. unknown]

gor'mandize *v.t.* eat like a glutton. [fr. *gormand*, old form of gourmand]

gorse *n.* prickly shrub with fragrant yellow flowers, furze, whin. [OE. *gorst*]

gory. *See* **gore.**

gos'hawk *n.* large short-winged hawk. [OE. *goshafoc*, goose hawk]

gos'ling (-z-) *n.* young goose. [dim. of goose]

gos'pel *n.* tidings preached by Jesus; record of his life; any of the four books by the evangelists. [OE. *godspel, god spel*, good tidings]

goss'amer *n.* filmy substance of spiders' web floating in calm air or spread on grass; filmy thing; delicate gauze. light, flimsy. [goose summer]

goss'ip *n.* idle talk about other persons, *esp.* regardless of fact; idle talk or writing; one who talks thus; formerly, a familiar friend. -*v.i.* talk gossip. [OE. *godsibb*, God *akin*, sponsor]

Goth'ic *a.* of Goths; barbarous; in architecture, of the pointed arch style common in Europe 12th-16th c.; a printing type. [L. *Gothi*, Goths]

gouge *n.* chisel with a curved cutting edge. -*v.i.* cut with a gouge, hollow (out). [F.]

gou'lash *n.* well-seasoned stew of beef and vegetables. [Hung. *gulyas*]

gourd (gord, goord) *n.* trailing or climbing plant; its large fleshy fruit; rind of this as a vessel. [F. *gourde*]

gour'mand *a.* greedy. -*n.* love of good fare. **-gourmandize'** *n.* greediness for food. [F.]

gour'met *n.* connoisseur of wine or food. [F.]

gout (gowt) *n.* disease with inflammation, *esp.* of the smaller joints; drop, splash. **gout'y** *a.* [F. *goutte*, drop]

govern (guv-) *v.t.* rule, direct, guide, control; serve as a precedent for; be followed by (a grammatical case, *etc.*). **gov'ernable** *a.* **-gov'ernance** *n.* **-gov'ernor** *n.* **-gov'erness** *n.* woman teacher esp. in a private household. **gov'ernment** *n.* rule; control; ruling body of a state; the state. **-gov'ernmental** *a.* [F. *gouverner*, fr. L. *gubernare*, steer]

gown *n.* loose flowing upper garment; woman's frock; official robe, as in a university, *etc.* [OF. *gonne*]

grab *v.t.* grasp suddenly, snatch. -*n.* sudden clutch; greedy proceedings. **grab'bing** *a.* greedy. [orig. uncertain]

grace *n.* charm, attractiveness; easy and refined motion, manners, *etc.* ; ornament, accomplishment; favor; divine favor; short thanksgiving before or after a meal; title of a duke or archbishop. -*v.t.* add grace to honor. **-grace'ful** *a.* **-grace'less** *a.* shameless, depraved. **-gra'cious** *a.* indulgent, beneficent, condescending. **grace'fully** *adv.* **-gra'ciously** *adv.* [F. *grace*, fr. L. *gratia*, pleasing quality, favor]

grack'le *n.* N. Amer. blackbird, myna. [L. *graculus*, jackdaw]

grade *n.* step or stage; degree of rank, *etc.* ; class; slope; gradient. -*v.t.* arrange in classes. **-grada'tion** *n.* series of degrees or steps; each of them; arrangement in steps; insensible passing from one shade, *etc.*, to another. **-grade school** *n.* elementary school. **-gra'dient** *n.* degree of slope. **-grad'ual** *a.* taking place by es; moving step by step; slow and steady; not steep. **-grad'ually** *adv.* **grad'uate** *v.i.* receive a university degree diploma; one who has received a university degree or diploma. **-gradua'tion** *n.* [L. *gradus*, step]

graft *n.* shoot of a plant set in a stock of another plant; the process; (*sl.*) work. *v.t.* insert (a shoot) in another stock; transplant (living tissue in surgery). [earlier *graffe*, F. *greefe*]

graft *n.* bribery, corruption; profit or advancement obtained by corrupt means. [orig. uncertain]

grail *n.* Holy Grail, platter or cup used by Christ at the Last Supper. [OF. *graal*]

grain *n.* seed or fruit of a cereal plant; wheat and allied plants; small hard particle; unit of weight, 1-7000th of the pound; texture; arrangement of fibers; formerly cochineal, scarlet dye, dye in general. -*v.t.* paint in imitation of wood grain. **-grainy** *a.* [F., cp. granary]

grall'och *v.t.* disembowel (deer). -*n.* [Gael. *grealach*]

gram, gramme *n.* unit of weight in the metric system. [F., fr. G. *gramma* letter, small weight]

gram'arye *n.* magic. [*grammar*]

graminiv'orous *a.* grass-eating. [L. *gramen*, grass]

gramm'ar *n.* science of the structure and usages of a language; book on this; correct use of words. **grammar'ian** (-ar-) *n.* **grammat'ical** *a.* **-grammat'ically** *adv.* **-gramm'ar school** *n.* elementary school. [G. *gramma*, letter]

gram'ophone *n.* an instrument for recording and reproducing sounds; phonograph. [phonogram reversed; (a trade name)]

gram'pus *n.* blowing and spouting sea creature of the whale family; person who breathes heavily. [earlier *graunde-pose*, ME. *grapeys*, OF. *graspeis*, fr. L. *crassus piscis*, fat fish]

granadifl'a *n.* passion-flower, its edible fruit. [Sp.]

gran'ary *n.* storehouse for grain. [L. *granarium*, fr. *granum*, grain]

grand *a.* chief, of chief importance; splendid, magnificent; lofty; imposing; final. -**grand'child** *n.* child of children. **grand'daughter** *fem.*, child of children. **grandee'** *n.* Spanish or Portuguese nobleman. -**grand'eur** *n.* nobility; magnificence; dignity. -**grand'father** *n.* parent of parents. -**grandil'oquence** *n.* -**grandil'oquent** *a.* pompous in speech. -**grandil'oquently** *adu.* -**grand'iose** *a.* imposing; planned on a great scale. -**grand'ly** *adv.* -**grand-master** *n.* head of order of knights or freemasons. -**grand'mother** *fem.* parent of parents. -**grand-slam'** *n.* (cards) taking of every trick in bridge. -**grand'son** *n.* child of children. -**grand'stand** *n.* raised seats for spectators at races, *etc.* [L. *grandis*, great]

grange *n.* granary; country-house with farm buildings. [F.]

granite (-it) *n.* hard crystalline rock, used for building. [It. *granito*]

grant *v.t.* consent to fulfill (a request); permit; bestow, give formally; admit. -*n.* a granting; thing granted. -**grant'or** *n.* **grant'ee** *n.* [AF. *graanter*]

gran'ule *n.* small grain. -**granular** *a.* of, or like, grains. -**gran'ulate** *v.t.* form into grains. -*v.i.* take the form of grains; of a wound, to begin to grow in small prominences like grains. -**granula'tion** *n.* [L. *granum*, grain]

grape *n.* fruit of the vine. -**grape'fruit** *n.* large citrus fruit, kind of shaddock. **grape'shot** *n.* bullets as scattering charge for a cannon. -**grape'-sugar** *n.* dext rose. -**grape'-vine** *n.* circulation of news, *etc.*, *esp.* among natives, without obvious means of communication. [F. *grappe* (*de raisin*), bunch (of grapes)]

grapheme *n.* smallest unit of a writing system or language; letter or combination of letters that represent a speech sound or phoneme; a letter of an alphabet.

graphic *a.* of, in, or relating to writing, drawing, painting, *etc.* ; vividly descriptive. -**graph** *n.* graphic formula, diagram showing symbolically a series of connections. -**graph'ically** *adv.* -**graph'ite** *n.* form of carbon (used in pencils).

graphol'ogy *n.* study of handwriting. [G. *graphein*, write]

grap'nel *n.* iron instrument of hooks for seizing, as an enemy ship; small anchor with several flukes. [dim. fr. F. *grappin*, dim. of OF. *grappe*, hook]

grap'ple *n.* grapnel; grip; contest at close quarters. -*v.t.* seize with a grapnel; seize firmly. -*v.i.* contend (with), come to grips. [*See* **grapnel**]

grasp *v.t.* seize firmly, clutch; understand. -*v.i.* clutch (at). -*n.* firm hold; mastery. (ME. *graspen*]

grass *n.* herbage, plants grown for cattle to eat, to cover lawns, *etc.* ; plant of this kind. -*v.t.* cover with turf, put down on grass. -**grass'hopper** *n.* jumping, chirping insect. -**grass'-snake** *n.* harmless British snake. -**grass'widow** *n.* wife whose husband is away from her. **grass'y** *a.* [OE. *gærs*]

grate *n.* fireplace, frame of bars for holding fuel; framework of crossed bars (also grating *n.*). -**graticula'tion** *n.* division (of a photograph, *etc.*) into squares for reproduction. [L. *cratis*, hurdle]

grate *v.t.* rub into small bits with something rough. -*v.i.* rub with harsh noise; have an irritating effect. -**gra'ter** *n.* [F. *gratter*, scratch]

grate'ful *a.* thankful; pleasing. -**grate'fully** *adv.* -**grat'itude** *n.* sense of being thankful for something received. [L. *gratus*, pleasing]

grat'ify *v.t.* do a favor to; indulge. **gratifica'tion** *n.* [L. *gratificare*, fr. *gratus*, pleasing]

gra'tis *adv.* and *a.* free, for nothing. [L. *gratiis-gratia*, favor]

gratu'ity *n.* gift of money. -**gratu'itous** *a.* given free, done for nothing; uncalled for. -**gratu'itously** *adv.* [Low L. *gratuitat-*, fr. *gratus*, pleasing]

grava'men *n.* heaviest part (of an accusation); grievance. [Med. L.]

grave *n.* hole dug for a dead body; monument on this; death. [OE. *graf*]

grave *v.t.* carve, engrave. -**gra'ven** *a.* [OE. *grafan*, dig]

grave *a.* serious, weighty; dignified, solemn; plain, dark in color, deep in note. -**grave'ly** *adv.* [L. *gravis*, heavy]

grave *v.t.* clean (a ship's bottom) by burning and tarring. -**gra'ving-dock** *n.* place for this. [F. *grève*, beach]

grav'el *n.* small stones, coarse sand; aggregation of urinary crystals; disease due to this. -*v.t.* cover with gravel; puzzle. -

grav'elly *a.* [F. *gravelle*]

grav'ity *n.* importance; seriousness, heaviness; force of attraction of one body for another, *esp.* of objects to the earth. **grav'itate** *v.i.* move -by gravity; sink, settle. **-gravita'tion** *n.* [L. *gravitate*, fr. *gravis*, heavy]

gra'vy *n.* juices from meat in cooking; dressing or sauce for food made from these juices. [orig. uncertain]

gray, grey *a.* between black and white in color, as ashes or lead; clouded; dismal; turning white; aged. *-n.* gray color; gray horse. **-gray'ling** *n.* gray fish. [OE. *græg*]

graze *v.i.* and *t.* feed on grass. **-gra'zier** *n.* one who feeds cattle for market. [OE. *grasiani*]

graze *v.t.* touch lightly in passing; abrade the skin thus. *-v.i.* move so as to touch lightly. *-n.* [orig. uncertain]

grease *n.* soft melted fat of animals; thick oil as a lubricant-*v.t.* apply grease to. **-greas'y** *a.* **-greas'ily** *adv.* **-greas'- iness** *n.* **-greas'er** *n.* [F. *graisse*]

great (-at) *a.* large, big; important; preeminent, distinguished. as *prefix*, indicates a degree further removed in relationship, *e.g.* **great-grand'father** *n.* father of a grandfather or grandmother. **great'uncle** *n.* uncle of a parent. **great'ly** *adv.* **-great'ness** *n.* **-great'-coat** *n.* overcoat, *esp.* military. [OE.]

greave *n.* armor for the leg below the knee. [OF. *greve,* shin]

grebe *n.* diving bird. [F. *grebe*]

Gre'cian *a.* Greek. [Greece]

greed'y *a.* gluttonous, over-eager for food, wealth, *etc.* **-greed** *n.* **-greed'ily** *adv.* **-greed'iness** *n.* [OE. *graedig*]

Greek *n.* native of Greece. *-a.* of Greece. [G. *Graikoi*, Greeks]

green *a.* of color between blue and yellow, colored like growing grass; emerald, *etc.*; unripe; inexperienced; easily deceived. *n.* the color; piece of grass-covered land. (golf) **putting-green**, ground about each hole. *-pl.* green vegetables. **-green'ery** *n.* vegetation. **-green'back** *n.* Amer. paper money printed in green. **-green'-finch** *n.* small bird, a greenish-colored finch. **-green'fly** *n.* aphis. **-green'gage** *n.* a kind of plum. **-green'-heart** *n.* W. Indian hardwood. **-green'born** *n.* novice, learner; recently arrived immigrant. **-green'house** *n.* glasshouse for rearing plants. **-green'room** *n.* room for actors when not on the stage. **green'sand** *n.* sandstone with (green) iron particles. **-green'sward** *n.* turf. **-greenwood** *n.* woodlands in summer. **-green'ish** *a.* [OE. *grene*]

Green'wich time (grin-ich), British standard time; basis for calculating time throughout the world. [reckoned from the sun's passage over Greenwich meridian]

greet *v.t.* accost or salute; receive; meet. **greet'ing** *n.* [OE. *gretan*]

greff'ier *n.* registrar [F.]

gregarious (-ar-) *a.* living or gathering in flocks; fond of company. [L. *gregarius*, fr. *grex, greg-*, herd]

Grego'rian *a.* of, pert. to Pope Gregory; Gregorian-calendar *n.* calendar now in use, established in 1582 by Gregory XIII.

grem'lin *n.* sportive pixie which is alleged to cause faults in airplanes; troublemaker. [orig. uncertain]

grenade' *n.* explosive shell or bomb, thrown by hand or shot from a rifle. **grenadier'** *n.* soldier of the Grenadier Guards; formerly, a soldier who threw grenades. [F. = *pomegranate*]

grey. *See* **gray.**

greyhound *n.* swift slender dog used in racing. [OE. *grighund*]

greyweth'er *n.* large sandstone block. [grey and wether, ram]

grice (-i-) *n.* small pig. [ON. *griss*]

grid *n.* frame of bars; grating; grid-iron. [gridiron]

grid *n.* (*elec.*) system of power transmission lines; (radio) perforated screen as part of amplifying mechanism. [gridiron]

grid'elin *a.* violet-gray. [F. *gris de lin*, flax-gray]

grid'iron *n.* cooking utensil of metal bars for broiling; football field. **-gridd'le** *n.* flat round iron plate for cooking. [AF. *gridil*]

grief *n.* deep sorrow. **-griev'ance** *n.* real or imaginary ground of complaint. **grieve** *v.i.* feel grief. *-v.t.* cause grief to. **griev'ous** *a.* painful, oppressive. [F. *grever*, afflict]

griff'in, griff'on, gryph'on *n.* mythical monster with eagle's head and wings and lion's body. [G. *gryps*]

grig *n.* cricket; small eel; lively creature. [orig. uncertain]

grill *n.* gridiron; food cooked on one. *-v.t.* and *i.* broil on a gridiron. [F. *gril*]

grille *n.* lattice; grating; openwork metal screen. [*grill*]

grilse *n.* young salmon that has only been once to the sea. [orig. uncertain]

grim *a.* stem; of stern or harsh aspect; joyless. **-grimly** *adv.* [OE. grimm, fierce]

grimace' *n.* wry face. *-v.i.* make one. [F. orig. uncertain]

grimal'kin *n.* (old) cat. (Grey, Malkin,

Maud]

grime *n.* soot, dirt. -*v.t.* soil; befoul. **gri'my** *a.* -**gri'miness** *n.* [orig. uncertain]

grin *v.i.* show the teeth. -*n.* act of grinning; impish smile. [OE. *grennian*]

grind *v.t.* crush to powder between hard surfaces; oppress; make sharp or smooth; grate. -*v.i.* perform the action of grinding; work (*esp.* study) hard; -*n.* action of grinding; hard work. -**grind'stone** *n.* revolving disk of stone for grinding, *etc.* -**grind'er** *n.* [OE. *grindan*]

grin'go *n.* in Spanish-America, contemptuous word for a foreigner, *esp.* American or English-speaking. [Sp.]

grip *n.* firm hold, grasp; grasping power; mastery; handle; bag. -*v.t.* grasp or hold tightly. [OE. *gripa*]

gripe *v.t.* grip; oppress; afflict with pains of colic. -*n.* grip. -*pl.* colic pains. **gri'ping** *a.* [OE. *gripan*]

grippe *n.* influenza. [F. *seizure*]

gris'ly (-z) *a.* grim, horrible, causing terror. [OE, *grislic*, terrible]

grist *n.* corn to be ground. [OE.]

gris'tle (grist) *n.* cartilage, tough flexible tissue. -**gris'tly** *a.* [OE.]

grit *n.* particles of sand; coarse sandstone; courage. -*v.i.* make a grinding sound. *v.t.* grind (teeth). -**gritt'y** *a.* -**gritt'iness** *n.* [OE. *greot*, sand]

grizz'ly *a.* gray-haired, gray. -**grizz'ly bear** *n.* large N. Amer. bear. -**griz'zled** *a.* grizzly. [F. *gris*, gray; the bear's name is perhaps from *grisly*]

groan *v.i.* make a low deep sound of grief, pain or displeasure; be in pain or overburdened. -*n.* the sound. [OE. *granian*]

groat *n.* in England, silver fourpenny piece; formerly, various European coins. [Du. *groot*, great, thick]

groats *n. pl.* hulled grain, *esp.* oats. [OE. *grot*, particle]

gro'cer *n.* dealer in, tea, spices, domestic stores; storekeeper. -**gro'cery** *n.* his trade, or, *pl.* wares. [OF. *grossier*, wholesaler]

grog *n.* spirit (*esp.* rum) and water. **grogg'y** *a.* unsteady, shaky, weak. [Old Grog, nickname, fr. *grogram cloak* of Admiral Vernon, who first ordered watering of sailors' rum (1740)]

grog'ram *n.* coarse fabric of silk, mohair, *etc.* [Fr. *gros grain,* coarse grain]

groin *n.* depression between belly and thigh; edge made by intersection of two vaults; structure of timber, *etc.* to stop shifting of sand on sea beach. -*v.t.* build with groins. [orig. uncertain]

groom *n.* servant in charge of horses; bridegroom; officer in a royal household. *v.t.* tend, curry (a horse); neaten, smarten. -**groomsman** *n.* friend attending a bridegroom. [orig. obscure]

groove *n.* channel, hollow, *esp.* cut by a tool as a guide, or to receive a ridge; rut, routine. -*v.t.* cut a groove in. [Du. *groef*, trench]

grope *v.i.* feel about, search blindly. **gro'pingly** *adv.* [OE. *grapian*]

gros'beak *n.* small bird of finch family with strong beak. [F. *gros*, thick, *bec*, beak]

gross *a.* rank; overfed; flagrant; total, not net; thick, solid; coarse; indecent. -*n.* twelve dozen. -**gross'ly** *adv.* -**gross out** *v.t.* (*sl.*) to cause (a person) to feel distaste or strong dislike for (something). -**gross-out** *n.* a person or thing regarded as disgusting or objectionable. [F. *gros*, fr. L. *grossus*, thick]

grot *n.* grotto. [F. *grotte*]

grotesque' (-esk) *n.* fantastic decorative painting; comically distorted figure. -*a.* in grotesque style; distorted; absurd. -**grotesquely** *adv.* [F.]

grott'o *n.* cave; *esp.* artificial cave as garden retreat. [It. *grotta*]

grouch *n.* complaining person, grumbler. -*v.i.* [grudge]

ground (-ow-) *n.* bottom of the sea; surface of the earth; position, area, on this; soil; special area; reason, motive; surface or coating to work on with paint. -*pl.* dregs; enclosed land round a house. -*v.t.* establish; instruct (in elementary principles); place on the ground. -*v.i.* run ashore. -**ground'-hog** *n.* woodchuck. **groundless** *a.* without reason. -**ground'-nut** *n.* peanut, monkey-nut. -**ground' plan** *n.* plan, section of ground floor of building. -**ground'-rent** *n.* rent paid for ground on which building stands. **ground'-swell** *n.* large unbroken motion of the sea, caused by far-off-storm. **ground'work** *n.* foundation; basis. [OE. *grund*]

ground'sel (-ow-) *n.* weed used as a food for cage-birds. (OE. *grundeswelge*]

group *n.* number of persons or things near together, or placed or classified together; class; two or more figures forming one artistic design. -*v.t.* arrange in a group. -*v.i.* fall into a group. [P. *groppo*, bunch]

group therapy *n.* (*psych.*) therapeutic technique in which patients are treated as a group, includes supervised, interactive discussion in an attempt to find solutions for problems.

grouse (-ows) *n.* game-bird, the moor

fowl; its flesh. [orig. uncertain]

grouse *v.i.* (*mil. sl.*) grumble. *-n.* grumble. **-grous'er** *n.* [origin unknown]

grout (-owt) *n.* thin fluid mortar. *-v.t.* fill with this. [OE. *grut,* coarse meal]

grove *n.* small wood. [OE. *graf*]

grov'el *v.i.* lie face down; abase oneself. [ON. *grufa*]

grow *v.i.* develop naturally; increase in size, height, *etc.*; be produced; become by degrees. *-v.t.* produce by cultivation. **-growth** *n.* growing; increase; what has grown or is growing. [OE, *growan*]

growl *v.i.* make a low guttural sound of anger, as of dog; murmur, complain. *-n.* such sound. **-growl'er** *n.* one who growls. [imit. orig.]

grub *v.t.* dig superficially; root up. *-v.i.* dig, rummage; plod. *-n.* larva of an insect; *(sl.)* food. **-grubb'y** *a.* dirty. [ME. *grobben,* dig]

grudge *v.t.* be unwilling to give or allow. *-n.* feeling of ill-will; earlier *grutch,* grumble. [OF. *groucier*]

gru'el *n.* food of oatmeal, *etc.*, boiled in milk or water. **-gru'eling** *a.* exhausting. [OF. = crushed grain]

grue'some *a.* fearful, horrible, disgusting. [ME. *grue,* shudder]

gruff *a.* surly, rough in manner or voice. **-gruff'ly** *adv.* [Du. *grof*]

grum'ble *v.i.* make growling sounds; murmur, complain. *-n.* low growl; complaint. **-grum'bler** *n.* limit. orig.]

grume *n.* blood-clot; thick liquid. **grum'ous** *a.* [L. L. *grumus,* small heap]

grump'y *a.* ill-tempered, surly. **-grump'ily** *adv.* **-grump'iness** *n.* [imit. orig.]

grunt *v.i.* of a hog, to make its characteristic sound; utter a sound like this, grumble. *-n.* hog's sound; noise like this. [OE. *grunnettan*]

Gruyère *n.* Swiss whole-milk cheese. [name of town]

guai'acum (gwi-) W. Indian tree, lignum vitae; its resin. (Sp. *guayaco*]

guana'co *n.* S. American llama. [Sp., fr. native word]

gua'no (gwa-) *n.* sea-fowl manure. [Sp.]

guarantee' (ga-) *n.* giver of guaranty of security; guaranty. *-v.t.* answer for the fulfillment, or genuineness or permanence of. secure (to) a person; secure (against risk, *etc.*). **-guar'anty** *n.* written or other undertaking to answer for performance of obligation; ground or basis of security. **guar'antor** *n.* [F. *garantir,* protect]

guard (ga-) *n.* posture of defense; watch; protector; sentry; soldiers protecting anything; official in charge of a train; protection; defense. *-v.t.* protect, defend. *-v.i.* be careful. **-guard'ian** *n.* keeper, protector; person having custody of an infant, *etc.* **-guard'ianship** *n.* **-guard'room** *n.* room for a guard, or for prisoners. **-Guards** *n. pl.* certain British regiments. **guardsman** *n.* soldier in the Guards. (F. *garde*]

gua'va (gwa-) *n.* tropical tree; its acid fruit used to make jelly. [Sp. *guayaba,* Fr. *Braz.* word]

gudge'on *n.* small fresh-water fish resembling the carp. [F. *goujion*]

guel'der-rose (gel') *n.* tree with white ball-shaped flowers, the snowball-tree. [*Guelders,* town]

guer'don (g-) *n.* reward. [OF.]

guerill'a (g-) *n.* irregular war; one engaged in it. [Sp. *guerrilla,* dim. of *guerra,* war]

guess (ges) *v.t.* estimate without calculation or measurement; conjecture, think likely. *-v.i.* form conjectures. *-n.* rough estimate. [ME. *gessen*]

guest (gest) *n.* one entertained at another's house; one living in a hotel. **pay'ing guest',** *n.* boarder. [ON. *gestr*]

guffaw' *n.* burst of laughter. *-v.i.* laugh loudly. [imit. orig.]

guich'et *n.* small aperture, as 'window' of ticket-office. [F.]

guide *n.* one who shows the way; adviser; book of instruction or infor. mation; contrivance for directing motion. *-v.t.* lead, act as guide to; arrange. **guid'ance** *n.* **-guide'-book** *n.* manual for travellers. **-guide'-post** *n.* signpost. **-guid'ed missile** *n.* projectile, rocket *etc.* directed by remote control. [F.]

guild, gild (g-) *n.* society for mutual help, or with common object. [OE. *gield,* payment]

guile *n.* cunning, treachery, deceit. **guile'ful** *a.* **-guile'less** *a.* [OF.]

guill'emot (gil'i-) *n.* sea-bird. [F.]

guillotine *n.* machine for beheading; machine for cutting paper; drastic curtailment of parliamentary debate. *-v.t.* use a guillotine upon. [F., Dr. *Guillotin* suggested its use (1789)]

guilt (gilt) *n.* fact or state of having offended; culpability. **-guilt'y** *a.* having committed an offence. **-guilt'ily** *adv-* **guilt'less** *a.* **-guilt'iness** *n.* [OE. *gylt*]

guin'ea *n.* in Britain, formerly, sum of 21 shillings; a gold coin of this value. -

guin'ea-fowl *n.* fowl allied to the pheasant. [Guinea, in W. Africa]

guin'ea-pig *n.* S. American rodent brought home by the *Guineamen*, slavers.

guipure' *n.* bold-patterned lace with no mesh ground. [F.]

guise *n.* external appearance, *esp.* one assumed. [F. *guise*, manner]

guitar' (git-) *n.* musical instrument with six strings. [F. *guitare*, L. *cithara*]

gulch *n.* gully. [orig. uncertain]

gules *n.* and *a.* in heraldry, red. [F. *guetule*, throat]

gulf *n.* partly enclosed portion of the sea; chasm, abyss. -**gulf stream** *n.* current of warm water moving from Gulf of Mexico to *n.* Atlantic and Europe. [F. *golfer*]

gull *n.* long-winged web-footed seabird. [Celtic orig.]

gull *n.* dupe, fool. -*v.t.* dupe, cheat. **gull'ible** *a.* easily deceived. -**gullibi'lity** *n.* [orig. uncertain]

gull'et *n.* food-passage from throat to stomach. [F. *goulet*, *gueule*, throat]

gull'y *n.* channel or ravine worn by water; a groove. [F. *goulet*]

gulp *v.t.* swallow. -*v.i.* gasp, choke. -*n.* act of gulping; effort to swallow; large mouthful. [imit.]

gum *n.* firm flesh in which the teeth are set. -**gum'boil** *n.* abscess in the gum. [OE. *goma*]

gum *n.* sticky substance issuing from certain trees; this prepared for use to stick papers, *etc.*, together. -*v.t.* stick with gum. -**chew'ing gum** *n.* sticky substance for chewing. [F. *gomme*]

gum'bo *n.* okra plant, pods; dishes made from these. [Creole]

g'ump'tion *n.* good sense; tact; shrewdness. [orig. uncertain]

gun *n.* weapon consisting mainly of a metal tube from which missiles are thrown by explosion; cannon, pistol, *etc.* **gunn'er** *n.* -**gunn'ery** *n.* use of large guns. -**gun'boat** *n.* small warship. **gun'carriage** *n.* wheeled mount for cannon or gun. -**gun'-cotton** *n.* explosive of cotton steeped in nitric and sulfuric acids. -**gun'man** *n.* armed gangster. **gun'-metal** *n.* alloy of copper and tin or zinc, formerly used for guns. -**gun'powder** *n.* explosive mixture of saltpeter, sulfur, and -charcoal. -**gun'room** *n.* in a warship, the messroom of junior officers. **gun'shot** *n.* range of a gun. -*a.* caused by missile from a gun. -**gun'wale, gunn'el** *n.* upper edge of the side of a boat or ship. [short for *Gunhilda*, name of a medieval war-engine]

gunn'y *n.* jute-cloth used for seeking. **gunn'y-sack** *n.* (Hind. *gon*, sacking]

gur'gle *n.* bubbling noise. -*v.i.* to make a gurgle. [imit.]

gurn'ard *n.* spiny sea-fish. [OF. *gornard*, fr. *groaner*, grunt]

gu'ru (goo-roo) *n.* spiritual teacher, *esp.* in India; a venerable person. [Hind.]

gush *v.i.* flow out suddenly and copiously. -*n.* sudden copious flow; effusiveness. -**gush'er** *n.* gushing person or oil-well. [orig. uncertain]

guss'et *n.* triangle of material let into a garment. -**guss'etted** *a.* [F. *gousset*]

gust *n.* sudden blast of wind; burst of rain, anger, *etc.* -**gust'y** *a.* -**gust'ily** *adv.* [ON. *gustr*, blast]

gust'o *n.* enjoyment in doing a thing, zest. [It. = taste]

gut *n.* in *pl.* entrails, intestines; (*sl.*) courage, spirit. -*sing.* material made from guts of animals, as for violin strings, *etc.*; narrow passage, strait. -*v.t.* remove the guts from (fish); remove or destroy the contents of (a house). [OE. *guttas* (pl.)]

gutta-percha *n.* horny flexible substance, the hardened juice of a Malayan tree. (Malay *getah* gum, and *percha*, tree giving it]

gutt'er *n.* channel for carrying off water from a roof, from the side of a street. -*v.t.* make channels in. -*v.i.* flow in streams; of a candle, melt away by the wax forming channels and running down. -**gutt'er press** *n.* sensational newspapers. **gutt'er-snipe** *n.* child homeless or living mainly in the streets. [F. *gouttiere*, fr. *goutte*, drop]

gutt'ural *a.* of, relating to, or produced in, the throat. -*n.* guttural sound or letter. [L. *guttur*, throat]

guy *n.* rope or chain to steady or secure something. -*v.t.* to secure with a guy. -**guy'-rope** *n.* [OF. *guier*, guide]

guy *n.* effigy of Guy Fawkes to be burnt on Nov. 5th; ridiculously dressed person. -(*sl.*) fellow. -*v.t.* exhibit in effigy; ridicule. [*Guy* Fawkes (d. 1606)]

guz'zle *v.t.* and *i.* eat or drink greedily. **guzz'ler** *n.* [imit.]

gybe. *See* **jibe.**

gymkha'na *n.* athletic display; place for one. [Urdu *gendkhana*, racquet-court, *lit.* ball-house]

gymna'sium *n.* place fitted up for muscular exercises, athletic training. **gymnast'ic** *a.* of exercise. -*n.* (in *pl*). muscular exercises, with or without apparatus such as parallel bars. **gym'nast** *n.* expert in gymnastics. [G. *gymnasion*, fr. *gymnos*, naked]

gymno'tus *n.* electric eel. [G. *gymnos*, naked, *notos*, back]

gynecology (gin-, jin-) *n.* part of medicine dealing with functions and diseases of women. [G. *gyne*, woman]

gypsoph'ila *n.* small-flowered plant allied to pinks, gypsy grass. [G. *gypsos*, chalk, *phileein*, love]

gyp'sum (jip-) *n.* mineral, source of plaster of Paris. [G. *gypsos*, chalk]

gypsy *n.* one of a wandering race of people, orig. from India, *usu.* maintaining a migratory way of life; one who lives in a way that resembles the life of a gypsy. [fr. Egyptian]

gy'rate *v.i.* move in a circle, revolve. **gyra'tion** *n.* **-gy'ratory** *a.* **-gy'roscope** *n.* wheel spinning at great speed to preserve equilibrium. [G. *gyros*, ring]

gyro *n. pl.* **gyros** a gyroscope. *n.* (*sl.*) Greek sandwich of roasted lamb or beef stuffed in pita bread with vegetables.

gyve *n.* (*usu.* in *pl.*) fetter, *esp.* for the leg. *-v.t.* shackle. [AF. give]

H

ha *interj.* exclamation of surprise, pleasure, *etc.* [imit.]

haar' *n.* sea-mist, fog. [ON. *hárr*, hoary]

hab'eas cor'pus *n.* writ issued to produce prisoner in court. [L. = have the body]

haberdasher *n.* dealer in men's clothing. **-hab'erdashery** *n.* [orig. uncertain]

hab'ergeon (-ji-on) *n.* armor in form of sleeveless coat. [F. *haubergeon*]

habil'iments *n.pl.* dress. [F. *habillement*, fr. L. *habilis*, ready]

hab'it *n.* settled tendency or practice; constitution; dress (*esp.* riding-habit). *v.t.* dress. **-habit'ual** *a.* that is a habit, customary. **-habit'ually** *adv.* **-habit'uate,** *v.t.* accustom. **-habitua'tion** *n.* **habit'ué** *n.* constant visitor; resident. **-hab'itude** *n.* customary manner of action. [F.]

hab'itable *a.* fit to live in **-habitation-** *n.* dwelling. **-hab'itat** *n.* natural home of an animal. [L. *habitare*, dwell]

hach'ure (-sh-) *n.* shading on a map to show hills. *-v.t.* mark with this. [F.]

hacienda (as-) *n.* Spanish-American ranch, estate. [Sp.]

hack *v.t.* cut, mangle, gash. *-n.* notch; bruise. **-hack'er** *n.* person that hacks; (*sl.*) a computer fanatic, *esp.* one who through a personal computer breaks into the computer system of a company, government, *etc.* [OE. *haccian*]

hack *n.* hired horse; horse for ordinary riding; literary drudge. *-v.t.* **hackney.** [short for *hackney*]

hack'le *n.* *comb* for flax; neck feathers of a cock. [cp. Ger. *hechel]*

hack'ney *n.* horse for ordinary riding; carriage kept for hire. *-v.t.* make trite or common. [*Hackney*, Middlesex]

hadd'ock *n.* fish like a cod. [OF. *hadot*]

Ha'des *n.* abode of the dead; lower world, hell. [G.]

haft *n.* handle (or knife). [OE. *hæft*]

hag *n.* ugly old woman; witch. **-hag-ridden** *a.* troubled with nightmares. [OE. *hoegtesse*, witch]

hagg'ard *a.* lean; wild-looking. *-n.* untamed hawk. [F. *hagard*]

hagg'is *n.* Scottish dish of chopped liver, onions, oatmeal, *etc.* boiled in sheep's stomach-bag. [orig. uncertain]

hag'gle *v.i.* dispute terms, chaffer. *-n.* chaffering. [ON. *hoggva,* chop]

hagiol'ogy (-hag-) *n.* literature of the lives of saints. **-hagiog'rapher** *n.* sacred writer. [G. *hagios*, holy]

ha'ha *n.* sunk fence. [F. *haha*]

hail *n.* frozen vapor falling in pellets. *v.i.* **it hails, hail falls.** *-v.t.* pour down. **hailstone** *n.* [OE. *hagol*]

hail *interj.* greeting. *-v.t.* greet; call. *-v.i.* **hail from,** be arrived from. *-n.* call, shout. [obs. *n.* hail health; ON. *heill*]

hair *n.* filament growing from the skin of an animal, as the covering of a man's head; such filaments collectively. **hair'y** *a.* **-hair'iness** *n.* **-hair'breadth** *n.* breadth of a hair; infinitesimal breadth. **-hair'pin** *n.* pin to secure hair in place. **-hair'pin curve** *n.* v-shaped bend on road. **-hair'-splitting** *a.* drawing over-fine distinctions. **-hair'spring** *n.* fine spring in a watch. **-hair'-stroke** *n.* fine upward line in handwriting. **-hair'trigger** *n.* secondary trigger releasing the main one. [OE. *hær*]

hake *n.* cod-like fish. [orig. uncertain]

hal'berd *n.* combined spear and battle-ax. **-halberdier'** *n.* [F. *hallebarde*]

hal'cyon *n.* bird fabled to calm the sea to breed on a floating nest. **-halcyon days,** calm, happy days. [L. = *kingfisher*]

hale *a.* robust, healthy, *esp.* in old age. [OE. *hal,* whole]

hale *v.t.* drag. [F. *haler,* pull]

half (haf) *n.* **halves** (havz) *pl.* either of two equal parts of a thing. *-a.* forming a half

-*adv*. the extent of half **-half'-blood** *n*. relationship of persons with one common parent. **-half'breed** *n*. one of mixed parentage. **-half'-brother, -sister** *n*. brother (sister) by one parent only. **half'caste** *n*. half-breed *esp*. of European and Asiatic parents. **-half'-pay,** (*esp*. in army) reduced salary to one not on active service. **-halfpenny** *n*. British bronze coin worth half a penny. **-half'-title** *n*. (shortened) title of book printed on page before title page. **-half'-tone** *n*. illustration with light and shade represented by varying size of dots. **-half'-voll'ey** *n*. ball struck the instant it bounces; the striking. -*v.t.* strike thus. **half'-way** *a*. at equal distance from two points. **-half'-witted** *a*. imbecile, mentally defective. **-half'-yearly** *a*. happening twice a year. **-halve** (häv) *v.t.* divide into halves. [OE. *healf*]

hal'ibut *n*. large flat edible fish. [ME *haly*, holy, and *butt*, flatfish]

hatic'ore *n*. dugong, sea-cow. [G. *hals*, sea, *kore*, maid]

halio'tis *n*. ear-shell, yielding mother-of-pearl. [G. *hals*, sea, *ous, ot-*, ear]

halitosis *n*. bad breath. **-hal'itous** *a*. [L. *halitus*, breath]

hall (hawl) *n*. large room; house of a landed proprietor; building belonging to a guild; entrance passage. **-hall'mark** *n*. mark used to indicate standard of tested gold and silver. -*v.t.* stamp with this. [OE. *heall*]

hallelujah *n*. and *interj*. 'Praise ye Jehovah'; hymn, song of praise. Also **alleluia.** [Heb. *halelu*, praise ye, *Jah*, Jehovah]

halo', halloa' *interj*. shout to call attention, hail. [OE. *eala*]

halloo' *n*. hunting cry. -*v.i.* cry halloo. *v.t.* chase, encourage, with this cry. [perh. fr. OF. *ha lou*. (F. *loup*, wolf)]

hall'ow *v.t.* make, or honor as, holy. [OE. *halgian*, fr. *halig*, holy]

Hallowe'en' *n*. All Hallows Eve, (Oct. 31) [OE. *halgian*. hallow]

Hall'owmas *n*. All Saints day (lst. Nov.) [O. E. *halgian*, hallow]

hallucinate *v.t.* produce illusion in the mind of. **-hallucina'tion** *n*. illusion; see, hear, something that is not present. [L. *hallucinari*, wander in mind]

ha'lo *n*. circle of light round the moon, sun, *etc*.; disk of light round a saint's head in a picture; ideal glory attaching to a person. -*v.t.* surround with a halo. [G. *halos*, threshing-floor, disk]

halt (hawlt) *a*. lame. -*v.i.* limp; proceed hesitatingly. **-halt'ing** *a*. [OE. *healt*]

halt (hawlt) *n*. stoppage on a march or journey. -*v.i.* make a halt. -*v.t.* bring to a halt. [Ger.]

halt'er *n*. rope or strap with headstall to fasten horses or cattle; noose for hanging criminals. -*v.t.* fasten with a halter. [OE. *hælfter*]

halyard, hall'iard *n*. rope for raising a sail, *etc*. [corrupt. of *halier*, fr. *hale*]

ham *n*. hollow of the knee; back of the thigh; hog's thigh salted and dried. **ham'string** *n*. tendon at the back of the knee. -*v.t.* cripple by cutting this. [OE. *hamm*]

hamadry'ad *n*. nymph living and dying with the tree she inhabited; Indian snake. [G. *hamadryas*; *See* **dryad**]

hamar'tiology *n*. doctrine of sin in Christian theology. [G. *harmatia*, sin]

hamburger *n*. ground beef formed into cakes, fried or broiled and *usu*. served in a bun. [Hamburg, Germany]

ham'let *n*. small village. [OF. *hamelet*]

hamm'er *n*. tool, usually with a heavy head at the end of a handle, for beating, driving nails, *etc*.; machine for the same purposes; contrivance for exploding the charge of a gun; auctioneer's mallet. -*v.t.* and *i*. beat with, or as with, a hammer. [OE. *hamor*]

hammerhead *n*. kind of shark. [fr. shape of head]

hamm'ock *n*. bed of canvas, *etc*., hung on ropes. [F. *hamac* (Carib. word)]

hamp'er *n*. large covered basket. [OF. *hanapier*, case for *hanaps*, goblets]

hamp'er *v.t.* impede, obstruct the movements of. -*n*. in a ship, cumbrous equipment. [orig. uncertain]

ham'ster *n*. rodent mammal with large cheek-pouches. [Ger.]

hamstring. *See* **ham.**

hand *n*. extremity of the arm beyond the wrist; side, quarter, direction; style of writing; cards dealt to a player; measure of four inches; manual worker; person as a source. -*v.t.* lead or help with the hand; deliver; pass; hold out. **-hand'-barrow** *n*. one without wheels, carried by handles. **hand'bag** *n*. bag for carrying in the hand. **-hand'bill** *n*. small printed notice for distribution by hand. **-hand'book** *n*. short treatise. **-hand(s)'breadth** *n*. breadth of hand, about 4 inches. **-hand' cart** *n*. hand-drawn cart. **-hand'cuff** *n*. fetter for the wrist, usually joined in a pair. -*v.t.* secure with these. **hand'ful** *n*. small quantity. -

hand' glass *n.* lens, mirror with handle. **hand'icraft** *n.* manual occupation or skill. **-hand'ily** *adv.* **-hand'iwork** *n.* thing done by any one in person. **hand'kerchief** *n.* small square of fabric carried in the pocket for wiping the nose, *etc.*, or worn round the neck. **-hand'maiden** *n.* female servant. **-hand -rail** *n.* rail as support *esp.* on stair. **-hand'-on** *a.* involving practical experience of equipment, *etc.* **hand'spike** *n.* levering bar. **-hand'-writing** *n.* way a person writes. **-hand'y** *a.* convenient; clever with the hands. [OE.]

handicap *n.* race or contest in which the competitors' chances are equalized by starts, weights carried, *etc.*; condition so imposed; disability. *-v.t.* impose such conditions. **-handicapper** *n.* [*hand* in *cap;* orig. lottery game]

han'dle *n.* part of a thing made to hold it by; fact that may be taken advantage of *-v.t.* touch, feel, with the hands; manage, deal with; deal in. [OE. *handle* n. *handlian* v.t.]

hand'sel (-ns-) *n.* gift on beginning something; earnest money; first use. *-v.t.* give a handsel to; be the first to use. [ON. *handsal*, hand sale]

hand'some (-ns-) *a.* of fine appearance; generous. **-hand'somely** *adv.* [*hand*; orig. pleasant to handle]

hang *v.t.* fasten to an object above, suspend; kill by suspending from gallows; attach or set up (wallpaper, doors, *etc.*). *v.i.* be suspended; cling. **-hangdog** *a.* of sneaking aspect. **-hangman** *n.* executioner. [OE. *hangian*]

hang'ar (-ng-) *n.* shed for aircraft. [F.]

hang'er *n.* short sword. [Du.]

hang'er *n.* that by which a thing is suspended, *e.g.* **coat-hanger.** [*hang*]

hank *n.* coil, *esp.* as a measure of yarn. [ON. *hönk*, skein]

hank'er *v.i.* crave. [orig. uncertain]

hanky-panky *n.* trickery, sleight of hand. [orig. uncertain]

han'som *n.* two-wheeled cab for two to ride inside with the driver mounted up behind. [*Hansom*, inventor, 1834]

Han'ukkah, Chan'ukah *n.* eight-day Jewish festival of lights beginning on the 25th of Kislev and commemorating the rededication of the temple by Judas Maccabeus in 165 B. C. [fr. Heb. literally: a dedication]

hanuman' *n.* E. Indian sacred monkey. [Hind.]

hap *n.* chance. *-v.i.* happen. **-hap'less** *a.* unlucky. **-haphaz'ard** *a.* random, without design. *-adv.* by chance. **-hap'ly** *adv.* perhaps. **-happ'en** *v.i.* come about, occur. **-happ'enstance** *n.* circumstances ascribed to chance. [ON. *happ*, luck]

happ'y *a.* glad, content; lucky, fortunate; apt. **-happ'ily** *adv.* **-happ'iness** *n.* **happ'y-go-lucky** *a.* casual. *[hap]*

ha'ra-ki'ri *n.* ceremonial suicide by disembowelment. [Jap.]

harangue' (-ang) *n.* vehement speech. *v.i.* make one. *-v.t.* speak vehemently to, [F.]

har'ass *v.t.* worry, trouble; attack repeatedly. **-har'assed** *a.* [F. *harasser*]

harbinger (-j-) *n.* one who announces another's approach; forerunner. [ME. *herbegeur*, one sent on to get lodgings]

har'bor (-ber) *n.* place of shelter for ships; shelter, *-v.t.* give shelter to. *-v.i.* take shelter. [ME. *herberwe*]

hard *a.* firm, resisting pressure, solid; difficult to understand; harsh, unfeeling; difficult to bear; stingy; heavy; strenuous; of water, not making lather well with soap. *-adv.* vigorously; with difficulty; close. **-hard-bitt'en** *a.* tough in a fight. **hard'-boiled** *a.* (*sl.*) tough thick-skinned. **-hard'en** *v.t.* and *i.* **-hard-head'ed** *a.* wise, sensible, shrewd. **-hard'-hearted** *a.* unsympathetic, unkind. **-hard'ly** *adv.* **-hard'-mouthed** *a.* (of horse) not controlled by bit. **-hardness** *n.* **hard'ship** *n.* ill-luck; severe toil or suffering; instance of this. **-hard up'**, short of cash. **-hard'ware** *n.* small ware of metal. **-hard'ware** *n.* (*compute.*) computer equipment used to process data; physical equipment, *e.g.*, printer, disk drive, *etc.* [OE. *heard*]

hard copy *n.* (*compute.*) paper printout of data from computer; physical form of data originating from the computer, originally viewed on the monitor.

hard'y *a.* robust, vigorous; able to endure hardship; bold; of plants, able to grow in the open all the year round. **-hard'ily** *adv.* **-hard'iness** *n.* **-hard'ihood** *n.* extreme boldness. [F. *hardi*, bold]

hare *n.* rodent with long ears, short tail, and divided upper lip, noted for its speed. **-hare'bell** *n.* plant with delicate blue bell-shaped flowers. **-hare'brained** *a.* rash, wild. **-hare'lip** *n.* fissure of the upper lip. [OE. *hara*]

ha'rem *n.* women's part of a Muslim dwelling; a group of wives or concubines. [Arab. *haram*]

har'icot *n.* French bean; ragout, of mutton, vegetables, *etc.* [F.]

hark *v.i.* listen. [ME. *herkien*]

harlequin *n.* in pantomime, a mute character supposed to be invisible to the clown and pantaloon. **-harlequinade'** *n.* harlequin's part. **-har'lequin duck'** marine duck with variegated plumage. [It. *arlecchino*]

har'lot *n.* prostitute. **-har'lotry** *n.* [OF. = *vagabond*]

harm *n.* damage, hurt. **-harm'ful** *a.* **harm'less** *a.* **-harm'fully** *adv.* **-harmlessly** *adv.* [OE. *hearm*]

harmatt'an *n.* hot landwind blowing from African desert to the Atlantic coast. [Twi, *haramata*]

har'mony *n.* agreement; combination of musical notes to make chords; melodious sound. **-harmo'nious** *a.* **-harmo'niously** *adv.* **-harmon'ic** *a.* of harmony. *-n.* tone got by vibration of an aliquot part of a string, *etc.* **-harmo'nium** *n.* small organ. **-harmon'ica** *n.* various musical intruments. **-har'monize** *v.t.* bring into harmony. *-v.i.* be in harmony. **-har' monist** *n.* **-harmoniza'tion** *n.* [G. *harmonia*]

har'ness *n.* gear of a draught horse; armor. *-v.t.* put harness on. **-in har' ness,** at work. [F. *harnais*]

harp *n.* musical instrument of strings played by the hand. *-v.i.* play on a harp; dwell on continuously. **-harp'er** *n.* **harp'ist** *n.* **-harp'sichord** *n.* stringed instrument with keyboard, an ancestor of the piano. [OE. *hearpe*]

harpoon' *n.* barbed dart with a line attached for catching whales, *etc.* *-v.t.* strike with a harpoon. **-harpoon'er** *n.* **-harpoon'-gun** *n.* [F. *harpon*]

harp'y *n.* monster with body of woman and wings and claws of bird of prey; rapacious monster. [G. *harpuia*]

harquebus. *See* **arquebus.**

harridan *n.* haggard old woman; shrewish woman. [corrupt. of F. *haridelle*, worn out horse]

harrier *n.* hound used in hunting hares; cross-country runner. [*harry*]

harr'ow *n.* frame with iron teeth for breaking up clods. *-v.t.* draw a harrow over; distress greatly. **-harr'owing** *a.* [ME. *harwe*]

harr'y *v.t.* ravage; plunder; harass. [OE. *hergian*, make war]

harsh *a.* rough, bitter, unpleasing to the touch or taste: severe; unfeeling. **-harshly** *adv.* [ME. *harsk*]

hart *n.* male deer. **-harts'horn** *n.* material made from harts' horns, formerly the chief source of ammonia. **-hart's'-tongue** *n.* fern with long tongue-like fronds. [OE. *heort*]

har'tal *n.* political strike. [Hind.]

hartebeest *n.* S. African antelope. [S. African Du.]

ha'rum-sca'rum *a.* reckless, wild. [obs. *hare, harass*, and *scare*]

har'vest *n.* season for gathering in grain; the gathering; the crop; product of an action. *-v.t.* gather in. **-har'vester** *n.* **har'vest home** *n.* festival at end of harvest. **-harvest-queen** *n.* image of Ceres. [OE. *hærfest*]

hash *v.t.* cut up small. *-n.* dish of hashed meat. [F. *hacher*, chop]

hashish *n.* narcotic drug prepared from Indian hemp. [Arab.]

Ha'sid *n.*, **Ha'sidim** *n. pl.* sect of Jewish mystics characterized by religious zeal and a spirit of prayer, joy, and charity; Jewish sect of the 2nd century B. C., formed to combat Hellenistic influences. **-Ha'sidic** *a.* **-Ha'sidism** *n.* [Heb.]

hasp *n.* clasp passing over a staple for fastening a door, *-v.t.* fasten with a hasp. [OE. *hasp*]

has'sle *v.t.* and *i.* annoy persistently; insist repeatedly; argue *-n.* troublesome concern; argument. [fr. *harass* and hustler]

hass'ock *n.* kneeling-cushion; tuft of grass. [OE. *hassuc*, coarse grass]

has'tate *a.* spear-like or -shaped. [L. *hasta*, spear]

haste *n.* speed, quickness; hurry. *v.i.* hasten. **-hast'en** (-sen) *v.i.* come or go quickly or hurriedly. *-v.t.* hurry; accelerate. **-ha'sty** *a.* quick; impetuous. **ha'stily** *adv.* [OF.]

hat *n.* covering for the head, usually with a brim. **-hatt'er** *n.* dealer in, or maker of, hats. [OE. *hætt*]

hatch *n.* lower half of a divided door; hatchway; trapdoor over it. **-hatch'way** *n.* opening in the deck of a ship for cargo, *etc.* [OE. hæc]

hatch *v.t.* bring forth young birds from the shell; incubate. *-v.i.* come forth from the shell. *-n.* a hatching; the brood hatched. **-hatch'ery** *n.* hatching place for fish. [ME. *hacchen*]

hatch *v.t.* engrave or draw lines on for shading; shade thus. [F. *hacher*]

hatch'et *n.* small ax. [F. *hachette*, dim. of *hache*, axe]

hatch'ment *n.* armorial bearings of a deceased person, set in a black lozenge-shaped frame and affixed to his house or tomb. [OF. *hachement*]

hate *v.t.* dislike strongly; bear malice to. *-n.* **hatred. -hate'ful** *a.* **-hate'fully** *adv.* **-ha'tred** *n.* emotion of extreme dislike. active ill-will. [OE. *hatian*, hate]

hatter. *See* **hat.**

hau'berk *n.* tunic of chainmail. [OF. *haubere*]

haughty (hawt'i) *a.* proud, arrogant. **haught'ily** *adv.* [F. *haut*, high]

haul *v.t.* pull, drag. *-v.i.* of wind, to shift. *-n.* a hauling; draught of fishes; acquisition. **-haul'age** *n.* carrying of loads; charge of this. [*hale*]

haulm, halm (hawm) *n.* stalks of beans, *etc.*; thatch of this. [OE. *healm*]

haunch (hawnsh) *n.* part of the body between ribs and thighs; leg and loin of venison, *etc.* [F. *hanche*]

haunt *v.t.* resort to habitually; of ghosts, visit regularly. *-n.* place of frequent resort. [F. *hanter*, frequent]

hautboy *n.* oboe. [F. *hautbois*, lit. high wood]

hauteur' *n.* haughtiness. [F.]

have (hav) *v.t.* hold or possess; be possessed or affected with; be obliged (to do); engage in, carry on; obtain; (as auxiliary forms perfect and other tenses). [OE. *habban*]

ha'ven *n.* harbor; refuge. [OE. *hæfn*]

haver *v.i.* to talk foolishly. [*sl.*]

haversack *n.* soldier's canvas ration bag; similar bag for travellers or hikers. [F. *havresac*]

hav'oc *n.* pillage, devastation, ruin. [orig. to cry *havoc*, gave the signal for pillage; OF. *havo*]

haw *n.* red berry of the hawthorn. **haw'thorn** *n.* thorny flowering shrub used for hedges; the may. **-haw'finch** *n.* small bird. [OE. *haga*, hedge]

hawk *n.* bird of prey *-v.t.* and *i.* hunt with hawks. [OE. *hafoc*]

hawk *v.i.* clear throat noisily. [imit.]

hawk'er *n.* one who carries wares for sale. **-hawk** *v.t.* [Du. *heuker*, huckster]

hawks'bill *n.* hawk-beaked turtle. [fr. shape of mouth]

hawse (-z) *n.* part of a ship's bows with holes for cables. [OE. *heals*, prow]

haw'ser (-z-) *n.* large rope or small cable, often of steel. [orig. uncertain]

hay *n.* grass mown and dried. **-hay'box** *n.* box filled with hay in which heated food is left to finish cooking. **-hay'cock** *n.* conical heap of hay. **-hay'seed** *n.* grass seed. **-hay'stack, hay'rick** *n.* large pile of hay with ridged or pointed top. **hay'wire** *a.* (*sl.*) disordered, crazy. [OE. *hieg*]

hay *n.* hedge or fence. [OE. *hege*]

haz'ard *n.* game at dice; chance, a chance; risk, danger; (*golf*) bunker or other hindrance. *-v.t.* expose to risk; run the risk of. **-haz'ardous** *a.* risky, perilous. [F. *hasard*]

haze *n.* misty appearance in the air, often due to heat; mental obscurity. **-ha'zy** *a.* misty. [orig. uncertain]

haze *v.t.* bully; tease with practical jokes, rag. [OF, *haser*, annoy]

hazer *n.* bush bearing nuts; reddish-brown color of the nuts. *-v.* of this color. [OE. *hæsel*]

he *pron.* male person or animal already referred to. *-n.* a male. [OE.]

head (hed) *n.* upper part of a man's or animal's body, containing mouth, sense organs and brain; upper part of anything; chief part; leader; progress; title, heading; headland. *-v.t.* provide with a head; get the lead of. *-v.i.* face, front. **-head'ache** (-ak) *n.* continuous pain in the head. **head'dress** *n.* covering, often ornamental, for head. **-head'er** *n.* that or who heads; plunge head foremost; brick laid with end in face of wall. **-head'-gear** *n.* hat, head covering. **-head'ing** *n.* a title. **-head'-land** *n.* promontory. **headlight** *n.* front light of automobile or other vehicle. **-head'lines** *n. pl.* headings in newspaper. **-head'long** *adv.* head foremost, in a rush. **-head'most** *a.* foremost. **-head'piece** *n.* head, hat, helmet. **-headquar'ters** *n. pl.* residence of commander-in-chief, center of operations. **-head'ship** *n.* office of chief. **head'stall** *n.* part of bridle fitting round horse's head. **-head'stone** *n.* tombstone. **-head'strong** *a.* self-willed. **head'way** *n.* progress. **-head'wing** *n.* one blowing directly against. **-head'y** *a.* impetuous; apt to intoxicate. [OE. *heafod*]

heal *v.t.* restore to health, make well, cure. *-v.t.* become sound. -**health** *n.* soundness of body; condition of body; toast drunk in a person's honor. **health'ful** *a.* health-giving. **-health'y** *a.* having, or tending to give, health. **health'ily** *adv.* [OE. *hælan*]

heap *n.* number of things lying one on another; great quantity. *-v.t.* pile up; load (with gifts, *etc.*). [OE.]

hear *v.t.* perceive with the ear; listen to; try (a case); get to know. *-v.i.* perceive sound; learn. **-hear'er** *n.* **-hear'say** *n.* rumor. *a.* not based on personal knowledge. [OE. *hieran*]

heark'en *v.i.* listen; hear with attention. [OE. *heorcnian*]

hearse *n.* carriage for a coffin. [F. *herse,* harrow; orig. a frame for candles over coffin]

heart (hart) *n.* hollow organ which makes the blood circulate; seat of the emotions and affections; mind, soul; courage; middle of anything; playing card marked with a figure of a heart, one of these marks. **-heartache** *n.* grief, anguish. **heart'broken** *a.* crushed by grief. **heart'burn** *n.* sharp, burning feeling at heart, caused by gastric acidity. **-heart'-burning** *n.* discontent, secret grudge. **heart'en** *v.t.* gladden, inspire **-heart'felt** *a.* very sincere. **-heart'less** *a.* unfeeling. **-heart'rending** *a.* extremely sad, agonizing. **-hearts'ease** *n.* pansy. **heart'y** *a.* friendly; vigorous; in good health; satisfying the appetite. **-heart'ily** *adj* . [OE. *heorth*]

hearth (harth) *n.* place where a fire is made in a house. **-hearth'stone** *n.* stone forming fireplace; soft whitening stone for hearths. [OE. *heorth*]

heat *n.* hotness; sensation of this; hot weather or climate; warmth of feeling, anger, *etc.*; sexual excitement in animals; race (one of several) to decide the persons to compete in a deciding course. *-v.t.* make hot. *-v.i.* become hot. **-heat'edly** *adv.* [OE. *hæte*]

heath *n.* tract of waste land; shrubs (genus Erica) found on this. [OE. *hæth*]

heathen (-TH-) *n.* one who is an adherent of a lower form of religion, or who has no religion; a pagan. **-hea'thenish** *a.* **hea'thenism** *n.* **-hea'thendom** *n.* [OE, *hæthen*]

heath'er (heTH'er) *n.* shrub growing on heaths and mountains; heath. [orig. uncertain]

heave *v.t.* lift with effort; throw something heavy), utter (a sigh). *-v.i.* swell, rise. *-n.* a heaving. **-heave to'** (of a ship) come to a stop. [OE. *hebban]*

heav'en *n.* sky; abode of God: God; place of bliss. **-heav'enly** *a.* of, like heaven; divine. [OE. *hæfon*]

Heav'iside lay'er *n.* layer of upper atmosphere deflecting radio waves. [O. *Heaviside,* 1850-1925]

heav'y (hev-) *a.* of great weight; striking or failing with force; sluggish; difficult; severe; sorrowful; serious; dull; over compact. **-heav'ily** *adv.* **-heav'iness** *n.* **heav'y wat'er,** water in which hydrogen is replaced by deuterium. [OE. *hefig*]

hebdom'adal *a.* weekly. [G. *hebdoinas,* seven]

He'brew *n.* Jew, Jewish language. **hebra'ic** *a.* [I., *Hebraeus*]

hec'atomb *n.* great public sacrifice. [G. *hekatombe-hekaton.* hundred, *bous.* ox]

heck'le *n.* hackle. *-v.t.* comb with a hackle; question severely, tease with questions. [*See* **hackle**]

hec'tic *a.* constitutional; (*sl.*) exciting. **hec'tic flush',** feverish, consumptive, flush. [G. *hektikos,* habitual]

hectograph *n.* apparatus for multiplying copies of writing. **-hec'togram** *n.* one hundred grams. **-hec'tometer** *n.* **hec'toliter** *n.* [G. *hekaton,* hundred]

hec'tor *v t.* and *i.* bully, bluster. [G. *Hector,* in Homeric epic]

hedge *n.* fence of bushes. *-v.t.* surround with a hedge. *-v.i.* make or trim hedges; bet on both sides; secure against loss; shift, shuffle. **-hedge'hog** *n.* small animal covered with spines. **-hedge'row** *n.* bushes forming a hedge. **-hedge' sparrow** *n.* small bird. [OE. *hœg*]

hed'onism *n.* doctrine that pleasure is the chief good. **-hed'onist** *n.* **-hedonist'ic** *a.* [G. *hedone,* pleasure]

heed *v.t.* take notice of, care for. **heed'ful** *a.* **-heed'less** *a.* [OE. *hedani]*

heel *n.* hinder part of the foot; part of a shoe supporting this; (*colloq*) unpleasant person. *-v.t.* supply with a heel; touch ground or a ball, with the heel. **-heel'ball** *a.* cobbler's wax. **-heel'-tap** *n.* drop of liquor left in glass. [OE. *hela*]

heel *v.i.* of a ship, to lean to one side. *v.t.* cause to do this. *-n.* a heeling. [OE. *hieldan,* incline]

heft'y *a.* brawny; sturdy; muscular, strong. [*heft* obs. p.p. of *heave*]

hegem'ony *n.* leadership. political domination. **-hegemon'ic** *a.* [G. *hegemon,* leader]

heg'ira, hej'ira *n.* flight of Mohammed from Niecca, 622 A.D., marking the beginning of the Islamic era; any flight. [Arab. *hijirah,* departure]

heif'er *n.* young cow that has not had a calf. [OE. *heahfore*]

height *n.* measure from base to top: quality of being high; high position, highest degree; hill-top. **-height'en** *v.t.* make higher; intensity. [OE. *hiehthu*]

hei'nous *a.* atrocious, very bad. [F. *hanieux.* fr. *hair,* hate]

heir *n.* person legally entitled to succeed to property or rank. **-heir'ess** *fem.* **-heir'loom** *n.* chattel that goes with real estate; thing that has been in a family for generations. [L. *heres*]

hel'ical *a.* spiral. **-helicop'ter** *n.* aircraft made to rise vertically by the pull of an air-screw or screws, revolving horizontally. **-heli'port, heli'pad** *n.* a place for helicopters to land and take off. [G. *helix*, spiral; *pteron*, wing]

heliograph *n.* apparatus to signal by reflecting the sun's rays. **-heliom'eter** *n.* instrument for measuring sun's diameter. **-he'lioscope** *n.* instrument for looking at sun without injury to eyes. **heliother'apy** *n.* medical treatment by exposure to sun's rays. **-he'liotrope** *n.* plant with purple flowers; the color of the flowers. **-heliotrop'ic** *a.* (of plants) turning under the influence of light. [C. *helios*, sun, and graph]

he'lium *n.* gaseous element, first discovered in the sun's atmosphere by Lockyer in 1868. [G. *helios*, sun]

he'lix *n.* coil, spiral; snail; outer rim of ear. [G. *helix*, spiral]

hell *n.* abode of the damned; place or state of wickedness, or misery, or torture; abode of the dead generally; gambling resort. **hell'ish** *a.* [OE.]

hell'ebore *n.* plant formerly thought to cure madness. (G. *helleboros*]

Hellen'ic *a.* relating to the Hellenes or Greeks, period 776-323 B.C. -Grecian; **Hellenism** *n.* [G. *Hellenes*, the Greeks]

helm *n.* tiller or wheel for turning the rudder of a ship. [OE. *helma*]

helm *n.* helmet. **-helm'et** *n.* defensive covering for the head. [OE.]

hel'ot *n.* serf. [G. Heilotes (*pl.*)]

help *v.t.* aid, assist; serve (food, with food); remedy, prevent. *-n.* aid, assistance; an aid, support. **-help'er** *n.* **-help'ful** *a.* **help'less** *a.* **-help'lessly** *adv.* **-help'mate, help'meet** *n.* helpful companion, a husband or wife. [OE. *helpan*]

helter-skelter *adv.* in confused flight. *-n.* medley. *-a.* confused. [imit.]

helve *n.* handle of weapon, tool *esp.* of ax. [OE. *hielf*]

Helvet'ic, Helve'tian *a.* Swiss. [L. *Helvetia*, Switzerland]

hem *n.* border of a piece of cloth, esp. one made by turning over the edge and sewing it down. *-v.t.* sew thus; confine, shut in. **hem'stitch** *n.* ornamental stitch. *-v.t.* sew with this. [OE.]

he'matite *n.* iron-ore, often reddish. [G. *haematilés*, blood-like]

hemisphere *n.* half sphere; half of the celestial sphere; half of the earth. **-hemispher'ical** *a.* [G. *hemi-*, half]

hem'istich (-ik) *n.* half a line of verse. [G. *hemi-*, half]

hem'lock *n.* poisonous plant; coniferous tree. [OE. *hymlice*]

hemoglobin *n.* red coloring matter of the blood. [G. *haima*, blood, *globus*, ball]

hemophilia *n.* tendency to excessive bleeding from slight injuries. **hemophil'iac** *n.* [G. *haima*, blood]

hemorrhage *n.* bleeding. [G. *haumorragia*, fr. *haima*, blood]

hemorrhoids *n.* piles. [G. *haimorrois, haimorroid-*, v.s.]

hemp *n.* Indian plant of which the fiber is used to make rope; the fiber. **-hemp'en** *a.* [OE. *henep*]

hen *n.* female of the domestic fowl and other birds. **-hen'bane** *n.* poisonous plant allied to nightshade. **-hen'pecked** *a.* domineered over by a wife. [OE. *henn*]

hence *adv.* from this point; for this reason. **-hencefor'ward** *adv.* **-hence'forth** *adv.* [ME. *hennes*]

hench'man *n.* squire; servant; supporter. [ME. *henxt-man*, groom]

hendec'agon *n.* plane figure of eleven sides and angles. **-hendecag'onal** *a.* [G. *hendeka*, eleven, *gonia*, angle]

henn'a *n.* Egyptian privet; dye made from it. [Arab. *hinna*]

henot'ic *a.* unifying. [G. *henotikos*]

hen'ry *n.* **hen'ries** *pl.* (*elec.*) unit of inductance. [J. *Henry*, 1797-1878]

hepar'ica *n.* variety of anemone with liver-like leaves. [L. *hepar*, liver]

hepat'ic *a. pert.* to the liver. **-hepatit'is** *n.* disease or condition relating to inflammation of the liver. [L. *hepar*, liver]

hep'tagon *n.* plane figure with seven sides, angles. **-heptag'onal** *a.* **-hep'tarchy** (-ki) *n.* rule by seven. **-hep'tateuch** (-tuk) *n.* first seven books of the Old Testament. [G. *hepta*, seven]

her *pron.* obj., *possess.*, of *she*. **-herself'**, emphatic, reflex, of *she, her;* in her proper character. [OE. *hire*, fr. *heo* she]

her'ald *n.* officer who makes royal proclamations, arranges ceremonies, keeps records of genealogies and those entitled to armorial bearings, *etc.*; messenger, envoy. *-v.t.* announce; proclaim the approach of. **-heral'dic** *a.* **-her'aldry** *n.* science of heraldic bearings. [OF. *heralt*]

herb *n.* plant with a soft stem which dies down after flowering; plant of which parts are used for medicine, food or scent. **herba'ceous** (-shus) *a.* of or like a herb.

herb'age *n.* herbs; grass, pasture. **herb'al** *a.* of herbs. -*n.* book on herbs. **herb'alist** *n.* writer on herbs; dealer in medicinal herbs. -**herbar'ium** *n.* collection of dried plants. -**herb'y** *a.* of herbs. [L. *herba*, grass]

Hercu'lean *a.* very strong; very difficult. [*Hercules*, Greek hero; his twelve labors]

herd *n.* number of animals feeding or traveling together; large number of people (*in contempt*); herdsman. -*v.i.* go to a herd. -*v.t.* tend (a herd); crowd together. **herds'man** *n.* [OE. *heord*]

here *adv.* in this place; at or to this point. [OE. *her*]

hered'ity *n.* tendency of an organism to transmit its nature to its descendants. -**hered'itary** *a.* descending by inheritance; holding office by inheritance; that can be transmitted from one generation to another. -**hered'itarily** *adv.* -**heredit'ament** *n.* something that can be inherited. -**heritable** *a.* that can be inherited. -**her'itage** *n.* that which may be or is inherited; portion or lot. [L. *heres, hered-*, heir]

her'esy *n.* opinion contrary to the orthodox opinion. -**here'siarch** originator or leader of a heresy. -**her'etic** *n.* holder of a heresy. -**heret'ical** *a.* **heret'ically** *adv.* [G. *hairesis*, sect, school of thought]

hermaph'rodite *n.* person or animal with the characteristics of both sexes. [G. *Hermaphroditos*, in G. myth.]

hermet'ic *a.* of alchemy; sealed. — **hermet'ic sea'ling,** airtight closing of a vessel by melting the edges together, *etc.*; **hermet'ically** *adv.* [G. *Hermes*, Mercury, regarded as the patron of alchemy]

her'mit *n.* person living in solitude, *esp.* from religious motives. -**her'mitage** *n.* his abode. -**her'mit-crab'** *n.* kind of crab living in discarded mollusk shells. [G. *eremites*, fr. *eremia*, desert]

hern'ia *n.* protrusion of an internal organ through the wall of tissue that encloses it; rupture. [L.]

he'ro *n.* illustrious warrior; one greatly regarded for achievements or qualities chief man in a poem, play, or story; demigod. -**hero'ic** *a.* -**hero'ically** *adv,* **her'oism** *n.* -**he'ro-worshipper** *n.*[G. *heros*, demigod, hero]

her'oin *n.* strongly addictive narcotic drug derived from morphine. [Ger. trade-name]

her'on *n.* long-legged, long-necked wading bird. -**her'onry** *n.* place where herons breed. [F. *héron*]

her'pes *n.* any of several skin diseases, including shingles (*herpeszoster*) and cold sores (*herpes simplex*). [G. *herpein*, creep.]

herr'ing *n.* familiar sea-fish. -**herr'ing-bone** *n.* stitch or pattern of zigzag lines. [OE. *hæring*]

hertz *n.* (*radio*) unit of frequency. [H. *Hertz*, 1857-94]

hes'itate *v.i.* hold back, feel, show, indecision; be reluctant. -**hes'itant** *a.* **hes'itantly** *adv.* -**hes'itancy** *n.* indecision, doubt. -**hesita'tion** *n.*[L. *hæsitare*, fr. *hærere, hæs-*, stick fast]

hess'ian *n.* coarse jute cloth. [*Hesse*, Germany]

het'erodox *a.* not orthodox. • **het'erodoxy** *n.* [G. *heteros*, other]

heterody'ning *n.* (*radio*) superimposing of a wave on another of different length to produce a beat of audible frequency. [G. *heteros*, other, *dynamis*, strength]

heteroge'neous *a.* composed of diverse elements. -**heterogene'ity** *n.* [G. *heteros*, other, *genos*, kind]

hew *v.t.* and *i.* chop or cut with ax or sword. -**hew'er** *n.* [OE. *heawan*]

hex'agon *n.* figure with six sides, angles. -**hexag'onal** *a.* -**hexam'eter** *n.* verse line of six feet. [G. *hex*, six]

hey'day *n.* bloom, prime, height of one's vigor, success. [orig. uncertain]

hia'tus *n.* gap in a series; break between two vowels, *esp.* in consecutive words. [L. fr. *hiare, hiat-*, gape]

Hiber'nian *a.* of, pert. to Ireland, Irish (person). -**hibernianism, Hiber'nicism** *n.* Irish idiom. [L. *Hibernia*, Ireland]

hibernate *v.i.* pass the winter, *esp.* in torpor. -**hiberna'tion** *n.* [L. *hibernare* hibernat, fr. *heims* winter]

hibis'cus *n.* tropical plant of the mallow family. [G. *hibiskos*]

hiccup *n.* spasm of the breathing organs with an abrupt sound. -*v.i.* have this. [imit.]

hick *n.* farmer; unsophisticated country person. -a. [fr. *Richard*]

hick'ory *n.* N. Amer. tree like walnut with tough wood and edible nuts. [*pohickery*, native name]

hidal'go *n.* lesser Spanish nobleman. [Sp. *hijo de algo]*

hide *n.* skin, raw or dressed. -**hide' bound** *a.* with skin tight to body as cattle. (*sl.*) prejudiced, narrow-minded. [OE. *hyd*]

hide *n.* old measure of land. [OE. *hid*]

hide *v.t.* put or keep out of sight; conceal, keep secret. -*v.i.* conceal oneself. **hid'den**

a. [OE. *hydan*]

hid'eous *a.* repulsive, revolting. **hideously** *adv.* [F. *hideux*]

hie *v.i.* and *refl.* go quickly; betake (oneself, . [OE. *higian*, strive]

hierarch (-k) *n.* chief priest. **-hi'erarchy** *n.* graded priesthood or other organization. **-hierarch'ical** *a.* **-hierat'ic** *a.* of the priests (*esp.* of old Egyptian writing). **-hi'eroglyph** *n.* figure of an object standing for a word or sound as in ancient Egyptian writing. **-hieroglyph'ic** *a.* **-hieroglyph'ics** *n. pl.* **hi'erograph** *n.* sacred writing. **-hi'erophant** *n.* expounder of sacred mysteries. [C *hieros*, holy]

hig'gle dispute about terms; carry wares for sale. **-hig'gler** *n.* [*haggle*]

higgledy-piggledy *adv.* and *a.* in confusion. [earlier *higly-pigly*, probably 'huddled together like pigs']

high *a.* of great or specified extent upwards; far up; of great rank, quality or importance; of roads, main; of meat, tainted; of a season, well advanced; of sound, acute in pitch. *-adv.* far up; strongly, to a great extent; at or to a high pitch; at a high rate. **-high-born** *a.* of noble birth. **-high-breed** *a.* of noble breed or family. **-high'brow** *a.* intellectual-*n.* **-high'-explosive** *n.* powerful explosive as lyddite, T.N.T. *-a.* **-high'falutin**, *a.* pompous, pretentious. **high'-flown** *a.* turgid, affectedly sublime. **-high'-handed** *a.* overbearing. **High'lander** *n.* **-high'lands** *n. pl.* mountainous country. **-high'ly** *adv.* **-high'-minded** *a.* **-high'ness** *n.* quality of being high; title of princes. **-high-principled** *a.* of upright, noble character. **-high'road** *n.* chief, main road, highway. **-high seas** *n.* ocean. **-high-souled** *a.* of lofty spirit. **high-spirited** *a.* courageous, daring. **high'strung** *a.* super-sensitive. **-high-water** *n.* high tide. **-high'way** *n.* main road; ordinary route. **-high'way code** *n.* rules of the road. **-high'wayman** *n.* robber on the road, esp. a mounted one. [OE. *heah*]

hi'jack *-v.t.* divert criminally, *esp.* means of transport and for purposes of extortion. *-n.* **-hi'jacker** *n.* one who carries out a hijack. [orig. uncertain]

hike *v.t.* hoist, shoulder. *-v.i.* tramp, camp out, *esp.* carrying one's equipment. *-n.* ramble, walking-tour. **-hi'ker** *n.* [orig. uncertain]

hilar'ity *n.* cheerfulness, boisterous joy. **-hilar'ious** *a.* [G. *hilaros*, cheerful]

hill *n.* natural elevation, small mountain; mound. **-hill'ock** *n.* little hillbilly *a.* **-hill'iness** *n.* [OE. *hyll*]

hillbilly *n.* backwoodsman. *-a.* [*hill*]

hilt *n.* handle of a sword, *etc.* [OE.]

him *pron., obj.* of *he*. **-himself'**, emphatic and reflex. of *he*, *him*; in his proper character, sane. **-his**, *possess.* of *he*. [OE.]

hind (hind) *n.* female deer. [OE.]

hind *n.* farm workman, bailiff. [ME. *hine*, peasant]

hind, hind'er *a.* at the back. **hind'most, hind'ermost** *a.* farthest behind. [OE. *hinder*, backwards]

hind'er *v.t.* obstruct, bamper. **-hind'rance** *n.* obstacle. [OE. *hinder*, behind]

Hindu' *n.* Indian, devotee of Hinduism. **Hindu'ism** *n.* religion and philosophy of Hindus. [Hind. *Hind*, India]

hinge (-j) *n.* movable joint, as that on which a door bangs. *-v.t.* attach with, or as with, a hinge. *-v.i.* turn on, depend on. [ME. *heng*]

hint *n.* slight indication, covert suggestion. *-v.t.* give a hint of. *-v.i.* make a hint. [OE. *hentan*, pursue]

hint'erland *n.* outlying district behind the coast, riverbank, *etc.* [Ger.]

hio'pid *a.* (botany) rough and hairy, bristly. **-hiopid'ity** *n.* [L. *hiopidus*]

hip *n.* projecting part of thigh; the hip joint. [OE. *hype*]

hip *n.* fruit of the wild rose. [OE. *heope]*

hip'pie, hip'py *n.* young person whose behavior, dress *etc.* implies rejection of conventional values, *usu.* favoring communal living *etc.* [orig. uncertain]

hip'-hop *n.* pop culture movement of the 1980s comprising rap music, graffiti, and break dancing. [imit.]

hipped *a.* depressed. [*hypochondria*]

hipp'ocampus *n.* genus of small fishes including the sea-horse. [G. *hippos*, horse, *kampos*, sea-monster]

hippo'drome *n.* race-course; circus. [G. *hippos*, horse]

hippo'potamus *n.* large African animal living in rivers. [G. *hippos*, horse, *potamus*, river]

hipp'ogriff, hipp'ogryph *n.* griffin-like creature with horse's body. [G. *hippos*, horse]

hire *n.* payment for the use of a thing; wages; a hiring or being hired. *-v.t.* take or give on hire. **-hire'ling** n, one who serves for wages (usually in contempt). **hi'rer** *n.* [OE. *hyr*, wages]

hir'cine *a.* of or like a goat. **hircos'ity** *n.* [F., L. *hircinus*]

hir'sute *a.* hairy. [L. *hirsutus*, shaggy]

his *See* **him.**

hiss *v.i.* make a sharp sound of the letter S, *esp.* in disapproval. *-v.t.* express disapproval of, with hissing. *-n.* the sound. [imit.]

hist *interj.* hark! silence! [imit.]

histology *n.* science dealing with minute structure of organic tissues. **histol'ogist** *n.* [G. *histos*, web]

his'tory *n.* study of past events; record of these; past events; train of events, public or private; course of life or existence; systematic account of phenomena. **histor'ian** *n.* writer of history. **-histor'ic** *a.* noted in history. **-histor'ical** *a.* of, or based on history; belonging to the past. **histor'ically** *adv.* **-histori'city** *n.* being historical, not legendary. **-historiog'rapher** *n.* writer of history, *esp.* as official historian. [G. *historia* narrative]

histrionic *a.* of acting, affected. *-n. pl.* theatricals. [L. *histrio*, actor]

hit *v.t.* strike with a blow or missile; affect injuriously; find; suit. *-v.i.* strike; light (upon). *-n.* blow; success, *esp.* relating to music, theater *etc.* **-hitt'er** *n.* **-hit list** *n.* list of people to be murdered; list of targets to be eliminated in some way. [ON. *hitta*, meet with]

hitch *v.t.* raise or move with a jerk; fasten with a loop, *etc.* *-v.i.* be caught or fastened. *-n.* jerk; fastening, loop or knot; difficulty, obstruction. **-hitch'hike** *v.i.* progress by hiking and by getting free rides from vehicles. (hitch and hike). [orig. uncertain]

hithe *n.* small haven. [OE. *hyth*]

hith'er (-TH-) *adv.* to or towards this place. *-a.* situated on this side. **-hither- to'** *adv.* up to now. [OE. *hider*]

Hit'lerite *a.* of, *pert.* to Hitler and his National Socialist Party in Germany. [Adolph *Hitler*, 1889-1945]

hive *n.* box in which bees are housed. *v.t.* gather or place (bees) in a hive. *-v.i.* enter a hive. [OE. *kvf*]

hives *n. pl.* skin disease, *e.g.*, nettle rash; laryngitis. [unknown]

hoar, hoary *a.* gray with age; grayish-white. **-hoar'frost** *n.* white frost, frozen dew. [OE. *har*]

hoard *n.* stock, store, *esp.* hidden away. *-v.t.* amass and hide away; store. [OE, *hord*, treasure]

hoard'ing *n.* temporary board fence round a building or piece of ground, *esp.* when used for posting bills. [F. *hourd*, palisade]

hoarse *a.* rough and harsh sounding, husky; having a hoarse voice. **hoarsely** *adv.* **-hoarse'ness** *n.* [OE. *has*]

hoary. *See* **hoar.**

hoax *v.t.* deceive by an amusing or mischievous story. *-n.* such deception. [contr. of *hocus*]

hob *n.* flat-topped casing of fireplace; peg used as a mark in some games. **-hob'nail** *n.* large-headed nail for boot-soles. [orig. uncertain]

hob *n.* rustic; clown. **-hob-gob'lin** *n.* mischievous imp. [*Hob*, for Robert]

hobble *v.i.* walk lamely. *-v.t.* tie the legs together of (horse, *etc.*). *-n.* limping gait; rope for hobbling. [orig. uncertain]

hob'bledehoy *n.* clumsy youth. [orig. uncertain]

hobb'y *n.* formerly a small horse; favorite occupation as a pastime. **hobb'yhorse** *n.* wicker horse fastened round a dancer's waist; stick with a horse's head as a toy; rocking-horse; roundabout horse. [*Hob*, for Robert]

hob'nob *v.i.* drink together; be familiar (with). [orig. uncertain]

ho'bo *n.* tramp. [orig. unknown]

hock *n.* joint of a quadruped's hind leg between knee and fetlock. *-v.t.* disable by cutting the tendons of the hock. [OE. *hoh*, heel]

hock *n.* German white wine. [Ger. *hochheimer*, fr. *Hochheim*]

hock'ey *n.* game played with a ball or disk and curved sticks. **-field hock'ey** *n.* **-ice hock'ey** *n.* [OF. *hoquet*, crook]

hocus-pocus *n.* jugglery, trickery; conjuring formula. *-v.t.* play tricks on. **ho'cus** *v.t.* play tricks on; stupefy with drugs. [*sham* L. formula]

hod *n.* small trough on a staff for carrying mortar. [F. *hotte*, basket]

hodge *n.* countryman. [Hodge, Roger]

hodier'nal *a.* of the present-day. [L. *hodiernus-hodie*, today]

hoe *n.* tool for scraping up weeds, breaking ground, etc.—*v.t.* break up or weed with a hoe. [F. *houe*]

hoe *n.* promontory [OE. *hoh*]

hog *n.* pig, *esp.* one required for fattening; greedy or dirty person. **-hogs'head** *n.* large cask; liquid measure of 52½ gallons. [OE. *hogg*]

Hogmanay' *n.* in Scotland, last day of year; festivities held then; gift presented on that day. [unknown]

hoi polloi' *n.* common people. [G.]

hoist *v.t.* raise aloft, raise with tackle, *etc.* *-n.* a hoisting; lift, elevator. [earlier *hysse*,

Du. *hijschen*]

hold *v.t.* keep fast, grasp; support in or with the hands, *etc.*; maintain in a position; have capacity for: own, occupy; carry on; detain; celebrate; keep back; believe. *-v.i.* cling; not give way; abide (by), keep (to); last, proceed, be in force; occur. *-n.* grasp; fortress. **-hold'er** *n.* **hold'-all** *n.* portable wrapping as baggage. **-hold'fast** *n.* clamp. **-hold'ing** *n.* thing held, *e.g.* stocks, land, *etc.* **hold'up** *n.* armed robbery. [OE. *healdan*]

hold *n.* space below deck of a ship for cargo. [earlier *hole*]

hole *n.* hollow place, cavity; perforation, opening. *-v.t.* perforate, make a hole in. [OE. *hol*, *a.* hollow]

Hol'erith card *n.* (*compute.*) card containing data represented by 12 rows and 80 columns of punch positions; punch cards.

holiday *n.* day or period of rest from work, or of recreation; originally a religious festival. [*holy day*]

holl'and *n.* linen fabric. **-Holl'ands** *n.* spirit, gin. [Holland]

holl'ow *n.* cavity, hole, valley. *-a.* having a cavity, not solid; empty; false; not full-toned. *-v.t.* make a hollow in; bend hollow. [OE *holh*]

holl'y *n.* evergreen shrub with prickly leaves and red berries. [OE. *holegn*]

hollyhock *n.* tall plant bearing many flowers along the stem. [*holy hock*, OE. *hocc*, mallow]

holm *n.* islet, *esp.* in a river; flat ground by a river. [ON. *holmr*]

holm, holm-oak *n.* evergreen oak, ilex. [dialect *holm*, holly]

holocaust *n.* burnt sacrifice; great slaughter or sacrifice. [G. *holos*, whole]

holograph *n.* document wholly written by the signer. **-holog'raphy** *n.* science of using lasers to produce a photographic record. **-hol'ogram** *n.* photographic record produced by illuminating the object with light (as from a laser), *esp.* in order to produce a three-dimensional image. [G. *holos*, whole]

hol'ster *n.* leather case for a pistol fixed to a saddle or belt. [Du.]

holt *n.* wood, copse, [OE.]

ho'ly *a.* belonging to, or devoted to, God; free from sin, divine. **-ho'lily** *adv.*- **ho'liness** *n.* quality of being holy; title of the Pope. **-ho'ly orders** *n. pl.* ordination as clergyman. **-Ho'ly Writ** *n.* the Bible. **Holy Week** *n.* that before Easter. [OE. *halig*]

ho'lystone *n.* soft sandstone for scouring a ship's deck. *-v.t.* scour with this. [origin uncertain]

hom'age *n.* formal acknowledgment of allegiance; tribute, respect paid. [F. *hommage*, fr. *homme*, man]

home *n.* dwelling-place; fixed residence; native place; institution for the infirm, *etc.* *-a.* of or connected with home; not foreign. *-adv.* to or at one's home: to the point aimed at. **-home'less** *a.* **-home'ly** *a.* plain. **-hom'er** *n.* carrier-pigeon, trained to fly home. **-Home Rule** *n.* self-government. **-home'-sick** *a.* depressed by absence from home. **-home'spun** *a.* spun or made at home. *-n.* cloth made of home-spun yarn: anything plain or homely. **home'stead** *n.* house with outbuildings, farm. **-home'ward** *a.* and *adv.* **-home'wards** *adv.* [OE. *ham*]

homeopathy *n.* treatment of disease by small doses of what would produce the symptoms in a healthy person. **-homeopath'ic** *a.* **-homeopath'ically** *adv.* **-ho'meopath** *n.* **homeop'athist** *n.* [fr. G. *homoios*, of the same kind, and *pathos*, suffering]

Homer'ic *a.* of Homer, Greek poet, or his poems.

homicide *n.* killing of a human being; the killer. **-hom'icidal** *a.* [L. *homicide*, man slayer]

hom'ily *n.* sermon. **-homilet'ic** *a.* of sermons. *-n. pl.* art of preaching. [G. *homilia*, converse]

hom'iny *n.* maize porridge. [Algonkin *rockahomonie*]

homogeneous *a.* of the same nature: formed of uniform parts. **-homogene'ity** *n.* **-homog'enize** *v.t.* make uniform, blend. [G. *homos*, same, *genos*, kind]

homologous *a.* having the same relation, relative position, *etc.* **-hom'ologue** *n.* homologous thing. [G. *homos*, same, *logos*, ratio]

hom'onym *n.* word of the same form as another but of different sense. [G. *homos*, same, *onoma*, name]

homosexuality *n.* sexuality between members of same sex. [G. *homos*, same]

hone *n.* whetstone. *-v.t.* sharpen on one. [OE. *han*. stone]

hon'est (on-) *a.* upright, just; free from fraud; unadulterated. **-hon'estly** *adv.*- **hon'esty** *n.* uprightness; plant with semi-transparent pods. [L. *honestus*]

hon'ey *n.* sweet fluid collected by bees. **-hon'eycomb** *n.* structure of wax in hexagonal cells in which bees place honey, eggs, *etc.* *-v.t.* fill with cells of perforations. **-hon'eydew** *n.* sweet sticky substance found on plants. **-hon'eymoon** *n.* month after marriage; holiday taken by a newly-wedded pair. **-hon'eysuckle** *n.* climbing plant, woodbine. [OE. *hunig*]

Hon'iton *a.* name of superior type of lace. [*Honiton*, Devon, England]

honk *n.* cry of wild geese; any sound resembling this. *-v.i.* [imit.]

hon'or (on-er) *n.* high respect; renown; reputation; sense of what is right or due; chastity; high rank or position; source or cause of honor; court-card. *-pl.* mark of respect; distinction in examination. *-v.t.* respect highly; confer honor on; accept or pay (a bill, *etc.*) when due. **-hon'orable** *a.* **-hon'orably** *adv.* **-hon'orary** *a.* conferred for the sake of honor only; holding a position without pay or usual requirements; giving services without pay. - **honorif'ic** *a.* conferring honor. **honorarium** *n.* fee. [F. *honneur*, fr. L. *honos*, honor-]

hooch *n.* strong drink; bootlegger whisky. [Ind. *hoochinoo*]

hood (hood) *n.* cover for the head and neck, often part of a cloak; cover for the engine of an automobile. *-v.t.* put a hood on. **-hood'wink** *v.t.* deceive. [OE. *hod*]

hoodlum *n.* ruffian, hooligan. [orig. uncertain]

hoo'doo *n.* bad luck; unlucky object; foreboding of bad luck; rocky pinnacle. *v.t.* to bring bad luck; to bewitch. [*voodoo*]

hoof *n.* horny casing of the foot of a horse, *etc.* [OE. *hof*]

hook (hook) *n.* bent piece of metal, *etc.* for catching hold, hanging up, *etc.*; curved cutting tool. *-v.t.* catch or secure with a hook. [OE. *hoe*]

hook'ah *n.* pipe in which the smoke is drawn through water and a long tube. [Arab. *huqqah*, vessel]

hook'er *n.* small sailing ship; fishing smack. [Du. *hoker*]

hooligan *n.* street rough, rowdy. [*name*]

hoop *n.* band of metal, *etc.* for binding a cask; circle of wood or metal for trundling as a toy; circle of flexible material for expanding a woman's skirt. *v.t.* bind with a hoop. [OE. *hop*]

hoop'ing-cough *n. See* **whoop.**

hoop'oe *n.* crested bird with variegated plumage. [L. *upupa]*

hoot *n.* cry of an owl; cry of disapproval. *-v.t.* assail with hoots. *-v.i.* utter hoots. - **hoot'er** *n.* siren. [imit.]

hop *n.* climbing plant with bitter cones used to flavor beer, *etc.* *-pl.* the cones. **hopping** *n.* gathering hops. **-hop'garden** *n.* field of hops. [Du.]

hop *v.i.* spring (of person on one foot; of animals, on all feet at once). *-n.* act or the action of hopping. -(*sl.*) dance. **-hopp'er** *n.* one who hops; device for feeding material into a mill or machine; boat which takes away dredged matter. **hop'scotch** *n.* game played by hopping in an arrangement of squares. [OE. *hopian*]

hope *n.* expectation of something desired; thing that gives, or an object of, this feeling. *-v.i.* feel hope. *-v.t.* expect and desire. **-hope'ful** *a.* optimistic. **-hope'fully** *adv.* **-hope'less** *a.* [OE. *hopian*]

ho'ral *a.* of hours; occurring once an hour, hourly. [L. *hora*, hour]

horde *n.* troop of nomads; gang, rabble. [Turk. *orda, urdu*, camp]

horehound *n.* plant with bitter juice used for coughs, *etc.* [OE. *harehune*]

horizon *n.* boundary of the part of the earth seen from any given point; line where earth (or sea) and sky seem to meet; boundary of mental outlook. **-horizon'tal** *a.* parallel with the horizon, level. **horizon'tally** *adv.* [G. = *bounding*]

hor'mone *n.* internal glandular secretion stimulating growth, action of organs, *etc.* [G *hormaein*, stir up]

horn *n.* hard projection on the heads of certain animals, *e.g.*, cows; substance of it; various things made of it, or resembling a horn; wind instrument originally made of a horn. **-horn'ed** (-nd) *a.* having horns. **horn'y** *a.* **-horn'beam** *n.* tree like a beech. **-horn'-book** *n.* old primer in frame and covered with thin layer of horn. - **horn'pipe** *n.* lively dance, *esp.* with sailors. [OE.]

horn'blende *n.* mineral composed of silica, magnesia, lime or iron. [Ger.]

horn'et *n.* large insect of the wasp family. [OE. *hyrnet]*

horog'raphy *n.* science of reckoning time, *esp.* by sundials; art of making sundials. [G. *hora*, hour, *graphein*, describe]

hor'ologe *n.* timepiece. **-horol'ogy** *n.* science of measuring time; clock-making. [G. *horologion*, hour-telling]

horoscope *n.* observation of, or a scheme showing the disposition of the planets, *etc.*, at a given moment; prediction of the events in a person's life made by this means. [G. *horoskopos*, fr. *hora*, time]

horr'or *n.* terror; intense dislike or fear; something causing this. **-horr'ible** *a.* exciting horror, hideous, shocking. **horr'ibly** *adv.* **-horr'id** *a.* horrible. **horr'idly** *adv.*

-horr'ify *v.t.* move to horror. **-horrif'ic** *a.* [L. *horrere*, bristle]
hors-d'oeuvres' *n. pl.* dish served at the start of a meal as appetizer. [F.]
horse *n.* familiar four-footed animal used for riding and draught; cavalry; vaulting-block; frame for support. *-v.t.* provide with a horse or horses; carry or support on the back. **-horse-breaker** *n.* one who breaks in horses. **-horse'-chestnut** *n.* tree with conical clusters of white or pink flowers and large nuts. **-horse'-hair** *n.* horse's hair; haircloth. **-horse'-lat'itudes** *n. pl.* regions of calm in the Atlantic Ocean. **-horse laugh** *n.* rough boisterous laugh. **-horse'man** *n.* (skilled) rider. **-horse'manship** *n.* art of riding. **horse'mill'iner** *n.* maker of ornaments, *etc.*, for horses. **-horse'-play** *n.* rough play. **-horse'-power** *n.* unit of rate of work of an engine, *etc.*; 550 foot-pounds per second. **-horse'radish** *n.* plant with a pungent root. **-horse'shoe** *n.* iron shoe for a horse; thing so shaped. **-horse-tail** *n.* variety of plant resembling horse's tail. **-horse'man** *n.*; **horse-woman** *fem.* rider on a horse. **-horse tra'ding** *n.* hard bargaining to obtain equal concessions by both sides in a dispute. [OE. *hors*]
hortatory, hortative *a.* serving to exhort. [L. *hortari, hortat-*, exhort]
horticulture *n.* gardening. **-horticult'ural** *a.* **-horticult'urist** *n.* [L. *hortus*, garden *cultura-colere*, cultivate]
hosann'a *n.* cry of praise, adoration to God. [Heb. *hoshi'-ahnna*, save, we pray]
hose *n.* stockings; flexible tube for conveying water. *-v.t.* water with a hose. **-ho'sier** *n.* dealer in stockings, *etc.* **-ho'siery** *n.* his goods. [OE. *hosa*]
hos'pice *n.* travellers' house of rest kept by a religious order; hospital for the terminally ill. [*host*]
hos'pital *n.* institution for the care of the sick; charitable institution. [OF.]
hospitality *n.* friendly and liberal reception of strangers or guests. **hospitable** *a.* **-hos'pitably** *adv.* **-hos'pitaller** *n.* one of charitable religious order. **-hospitalize** *v.t.* place in a hospital as a patient. [*host*]
host *n.* one who entertains another; the keeper of an inn. **-hostess** *fem.* [L. *hospes, hospit-*, host, guest]
host *n.* army; large crowd. **hostil'ity** *n.* [*host*]
host *n.* bread consecrated in the Eucharist. [L. *hostia*, victim]
hos'tage *n.* person taken or given as a pledge; person seized for the purposes of extortion. [OE. *ostage*]
hos'tel *n.* a house of residence for students; an inn. **-hos'telry** *n.* an inn. [host]
hos'tile *a.* of an enemy; opposed. [L. *hostis, hostil-*, enemy]
hot *a.* of high temperature, very warm, giving or feeling heat; pungent; angry; severe. **-hot air** *n.* (*sl.*) nonsense. empty talk. **-hot'-bed** *n.* glass-covered bed for forcing plants; atmosphere favorable to growth. **-hot'-blooded** *a.* ardent, passionate; irritable. **-hot'-dog** *n.* hot sausage in a long roll. **-hot'-head** *n.* a hasty person. **-hot-headed** *a.* rash, impetuous. **hot'house** *n.* glass-house for rearing of delicate palnts. **-hotly'** *adv.* **-hot'ness** *n.* **-hot'-pot** *n.* stew of mutton and potatoes. [OE. *hat*]
hotch'potch *n.* dish of many ingredients: medley. [F. *hochepot*, fr. *hocher*, shake]
hotel' *n.* large or superior inn. **hotel'-keeper** *n.* **-hotel'ier** *n.* [F. *hotel]*
hound *n.* hunting dog; runner following scent in a paperchase; despicable man. *v.t.* chase (as) with hounds. [OE. *hund*]
hour (owr) *n.* twenty-fourth part of a day; time of day; appointed time *-pl.* fixed times for prayer; the prayers; book of them. **-hour'ly** *adv.* every hour; frequently. *-a.* frequent; happening every hour. **-hour'-glass** *n.* sand-glass running an hour. [F, *heure*. fr. L. *hora*]
houri *n.* nymph of the Muslim paradise; beautiful woman. [Pers. *huri*]
house *n.* building for human habitation; building for other specified purpose; inn; legislative or other assembly; family: business firm; school boarding-house. *-v.t.* receive, store in a house; furnish with houses. *-v.i.* dwell, take shelter. **-house'boat** *n.* boat fitted for living in on a river, *etc.* **-house'breaker** *n.* burglar; man employed to demolish old houses. **house'hold** *n.* inmates of a house collectively. **-house'holder** *n.* one who occupies a house as his dwelling; head of a household. **-house'keeper** *n.* woman managing the affairs of a household. **house'maid** *n.* maidservant who cleans rooms, *etc.* **-house'-party** *n.* company of guests staying at a country house. **house'warming** *n.* party to celebrate the entry into a new house. **-house'wife** *n.* mistress of a household; case for needles, thread, *etc.* [OE. *hus*]
housing *n.* horse-cloth (*usu. pl.*). [F. *housse*]
hov'el *n.* mean dwelling; open shed. [orig. uncertain]

hov'er *v.i.* hang in the air (or bird, *etc.*); be undecided. [orig. uncertain]

how *adv.* in what way; by what means; in what condition; to what degree; (in direct or dependent question). **-how-be'it** *adv.* nevertheless. **-howev'er** *adv.* in whatever manner, to whatever extent; all the same. [OE. *hu*]

how'dah *n.* seat or pavillion on an elephant's back. [Arab. haudaj]

how'itzer *n.* short gun firing shells at high elevation. [Bohemian *houfnice*, engine for hurling stones]

howl *v.i.* utter long, loud cry. *-n.* such cry. **-how'ler** *n.* loud-voiced S. Amer. monkey; (*sl.*) comical error. **-howl'round** *n.* the condition, resulting in a howling noise, when sound from a loudspeaker is fed back into the microphone of a public address or recording system. *-also* **howl'back.** [imit.]

hoy *n.* small coasting vessel. [obs. Du. *hooi*]

hoy'den *n.* boisterous girl. [Du. *heiden*, heathen]

hub *n.* middle part of a wheel, from which the spokes radiate; central point of activity. [orig. uncertain]

hub'bub *n.* uproar; confused din. [Ir.]

huck'aback *n.* rough linen for towels. [orig. uncertain]

huckleberry *n.* N. Amer. shrub; its fruit, a blueberry. [orig. uncertain]

huck'ster *n.* hawker; mercenary person. *-v.i.* haggle. *-v.t.* deal in a small scale. [obs. Du. *hoekster*]

hud'dle *v.t.* and *i.* heap, crowd together confusedly. *-n.* confused heap. [orig. uncertain]

hue *n.* color, complexion. [OE. *hiw*]

hue *n.* hue and cry, outcry after a criminal. [F. *huer*, hoot]

huff *v.t.* bully; offend. *-v.i.* take offence. *n.* fit of petulance. **-huff'y** *a.* **-huff'ily** *adv.* [imit.]

hug *v.t.* clasp tightly in the arms; cling; keep close to. *-n.* strong clasp. [orig. uncertain]

huge *a.* very big. **-huge'ly** *adv.* very much. [OF. *ahuge*]

Hu'guenot *n.* French Protestant. [F. fr. G. *eidgenoss*]

hugg'er-mugg'er *n.* confusion; secrecy. *-a.* secret; confused. *-adv.* in confusion or secrecy. [orig. uncertain]

hu'la (hoo'-) *n.* woman's dance of Hawaii. [Hawaiian]

hulk *n.* hull; dismantled ship; this used as a prison; big person or mass. **-hulk'ing** *a.* big, unwieldy; ungainly, bulky. [OE. *hule*, ship]

hull *n.* shell, husk; body of a ship. *-v.t.* remove shell or husk; send a shot into the hull of (a ship). [OE. *hulu*, husk]

hullabaloo' *n.* uproar. [imit.]

hum *v.i.* make a low continuous sound as a bee or top. *-v.t.* sing with closed lips. *n.* humming sound. **-humm'ing bird** *n.* very small bird whose wings hum. [imit.]

hu'man *a.* of man, relating to, or characteristic of the nature of man. **-hu'manly** *adv.* **-humane'** *a.* benevolent, kind; tending to refine. **-hu'manize** *v.t.* make human; civilize. **-hu'manism** *n.* literary culture; devotion to human interests. **hu'manist** *n.* classical scholar. **-humanitar'ian** *n.* philanthropist. *-a.* of, or holding the views of a humanitarian. **human'ity** *n.* human nature; human race. **-human'ities** *n. pl.* polite learning *esp.* Latin and Greek. [L. *humanus*]

hum'ble *a.* not proud, lowly, modest. *v.t.* bring low, abase. **-hum'bly** *adv.* [L. *humilis*, fr. *humus*, ground]

hum'ble-pie *n.* pie of *umbles* (liver, *etc.* of deer). **-eat hum'ble-pie,** submit to humiliation. [for *umble-pie*]

hum'bug *n.* sham, nonsense, deception: impostor. *v.t.* delude. [orig. unknown]

hum'drum *a.* commonplace. [*redupl.* of *hum*, imit. of *monotony*]

hu'merus *n.* bone of upper arm. [L.]

hu'mid *a.* moist, damp. **-humid'ity** *n.* [L. *humidus*, fr. *humere*. be moist]

humiliate *v.t.* lower the dignity of, abase, mortify. **-humilia'tion** *n.* [L. *humiliare*, *humiliat-*]

humil'ity *n.* state of being humble, meekness. [L. *humilis*, low. cp. humble]

humm'ock *n.* low knoll, hillock. **humm'ocky** *a.* [orig. uncertain]

hu'mor *n.* state of mind, mood; temperment; faculty of saying, or perceiving what excites amusement; transparent fluid of an animal or plant. *-v.t.* gratify, indulge. - **humoresque'** (-esk) *n.* musical caprice. - **hu'morist** *n.* **-hu'morous** *a.* witty; facetious. **-hu'morously** *adv.* [L. *humor*, moisture]

hump *n.* normal or deforming lump, *esp.* on the back. *-v.t.* make humpshaped. **hump'back** *n.* person with a hump. **hump'backed** *a.* having a hump. [orig. uncertain]

hu'mus *n.* decomposed vegetable matter, garden mold. [L. *humus*, ground]

Hun *n.* one of savage nomadic race which

overran Europe in 4th and 5th cents.; barbarian. [OE.]

hunch *v.t.* thrust or bend into a hump. *n.* hump, lump; (*sl.*) idea. **-hunch'back** *n.* humpback. [orig. uncertain]

hun'dred *n.* and *a.* cardinal number, ten times ten; subdivision of a county. **hun'dredth** *a.* ordinal number. - **hun'dredfold** *a.* and *adv.* - **hun'dredweight** *n.* weight of 112 lbs., twentieth part of a ton. [OE.]

hun'ger *n.* discomfort or exhaustion caused by lack of food; strong desire. -*v.i.* feel hunger. **-hung'ry** *a.* **hung'rily** *adv.* [OE. *hungor*]

hunk *n.* thick piece. [orig. uncertain]

hun'ker *v.i.* squat, crouch. [perh. ON. *huka*, squat]

hunks *n.* miser. [Dan. hundsk, stingy]

hunt *v.i.* go in pursuit of wild animals or game. -*v.t.* pursue (game, *etc.*); do this over (a district); use (dogs, horses) in hunting; search for. -*n.* hunting; hunting district or society. **-hunts'man** *n.* man in charge of a pack of hounds. **-hunt'er** *n.* **hunt'ress** *fem.* [OE. *huntian*]

hur'dle *n.* portable frame of bars to make temporary fences or as obstacles in a hurdle-race *n.* **-hurd'ler** *n.* -one who makes, or races over, hurdles. [OE. *hurdel*]

hur'dy-gur'dy *n.* portable hand-organ, barrel-organ. [imit.]

hurl *v.t.* throw with violence. -*n.* violent throw. **-hur'ly-bur'ly** *n.* tumult, [orig. uncertain]

hurrah' *interj.* of acclamation, joy, *etc.* [fr. earlier *huzza*]

hurricane *n.* violent storm, tempest. **hurr'icane-lamp** *n.* lamp made to be carried in wind. [Sp. *huracan*]

hurr'y *n.* undue haste; eagerness. -*v.t.* move or act in great haste. -*v.t.* cause to act with haste; urge to haste. **-hurr'iedly** *adv.* [orig. uncertain]

hurst *n.* wood; woody hill. [OE. *hyrst*]

hurt *v.t.* injure, damage, give pain to, wound-*n.* wound, injury, harm. **hurt'ful** *a.* [F. *heurter*, dash against]

hur'tle *v.i.* move quickly with rushing sound. [*hurt*]

hus'band (-z-) *n.* man married to a woman. -*v.t.* economize. **-hus'bandman** *n.* farmer. **-hus'bandry** *n.* farming. [OE. *husbonda*, master of the house]

hush *v.t.* silence. -*v.i.* be silent. -*n.* silence. -also *interj.* [imit.]

husk *n.* dry covering of certain seeds and fruits; worthless outside part. -*v.t.* remove the husk from. [orig. uncertain]

husk'y *a.* of, or full of, husks; dry as a husk, dry in the throat; hefty, powerful, vigorous. -*n.* Eskimo dog. [orig. uncertain]

hussar' (-z-) *n.* light cavalry soldier. [Hung. *huszar*, freebooter]

huss'y *n.* pert girl; woman of bad behavior. [for *housewife*]

hust'ings *n.* platform from which parliamentary candidates were nominated; any such platform; electoral activity. [OE. justing, 'house thing', assembly]

hustle *v.t.* push about, jostle. -*v.i.* push one's way, bustle. -*n.* bustle. [Du. *hutselen*, shake up]

hut *n.* small mean dwelling; temporary wooden house. **-hut'ment** *n.* camp of huts. [F. *huttle*]

hutch *n.* pen for rabbits; coal wagon used in pits, *etc.* [F. *huche*, coffer]

huzza' *interj.* expressing joy, hurrah. [prob. mere exclamation]

hy'acinth *n.* bulbous plant with bell-shaped flowers, *esp.* blue; this blue; orange precious stone. [G. *hyakinthos*]

hy'aline *a.* of or like glass, crystal-clear. [G. *hyalos*, glass]

hy'brid *n.* offspring of two plants or animals of different species; mongrel. -*a.* cross-bred. **-hy'bridize** *v.t.* and *i.* **-hy'bridism** *n.* [L. *hybrida*]

hy'dra (hi-) *n.* mythical, many-headed water serpent; fresh-water polyp. **-hydra-headed** *a.* many headed, difficult to root out. [G. *hudra*]

hydrangea (-je-a) *n.* shrub with large heads of showy flowers. [G. *hydor*, water, *angos*, vessel fr. shape of seed-vessel]

hydro- *prefix.* [G. *hydor*, water] in **hydrant** *n.* water-pipe with a nozzle for a hose. **-hydraul'ic** *a.* relating to the conveyance of water; worked by water power. -*n.* (in *pl.*) science of water conveyance or water-power. **-hydrocar'bon** *n.* compound of hydrogen and carbon. **hydrochlor'ic** *a.* of acid containing hydrogen and carbon. **-hydrodynam'ics** *n.* science of the force of fluids, at rest (*hydrostatics*) and in motion (*hydro kinetics*). **-hydroelec'tric** *a.* of electricity obtained from water power or steam. **hy'drogen** *n.* colorless gas which combines with oxygen to form water. **hydrog'raphy** *n.* description of the waters of the earth. **-hydrog'rapher** *n.* **-hydrograph'ic** *a.* **-hydrol'ysis** *n.* (chem.) changing of compounds into other compounds by taking up the elements of water. **-hydrom'eter** *n.* instrument for measuring specific gravity of liquids. **hydrop'athy** *n.* treatment of disease by water. —**hydropath'ic** *a.* -**hy'drophone** *n.* instrument for detecting sound through water. -**hy'droplane** *n.* light skimming motor-boat. -**hydropho'bia** *n.* aversion to water, *esp.* as symptom of rabies in man. -**hydropon'ics** *n. pl.* science of cultivating plants in water without using soil. -**hydrostat'ic** *a.* of hydrostatics. **hydrostat'ics** *n. pl.* science of fluids at rest. Also many other compounds.

hy'ena *n.* wild animal related to the dog. [G. *hyaina*, swine]

hy'giene *n.* principles of health; sanitary science. -**hygien'ic** *a.* -**hygien'ically** *adv.* -**hy'gienist** *n.* [G. *hygies*, healthy]

hygrometer *n.* instrument for measuring the amount of moisture in air. [G. *hygros*, fluid]

hymene'al *a.* of marriage. [G. *hymen*, god of marriage]

hymenop'tera *n.* order of insects with four membranous wings. [G. *hymen*, membrane, *pteron*, wing]

hymn (him) *n.* song of praise, *esp.* to God. -*v.t.* praise in song. -**hym'nal** *a.* of hymns. -*n.* book of hymns. -**hym'nody** *n.* singing or composition of hymns. **hymn'odist** *n.* -**hymnol'ogy** *n.* study of hymns. [G. *hymnos*]

hyperbola *n.* curve produced when a cone is cut by a plane making a larger angle with the base than the side makes. [G. *hyperbole*, hyper, beyond, *ballein*, throw]

hyperbole *n.* rhetorical exaggeration. -**hyperbol'ical** *a.* [*hyperbola*]

hyperbor'ean *a.* of the extreme north. -*n.* dweller in such region. [Fr. G. *hyper.* over, and *Boreas*]

hypercritical *a.* too critical. [G. *hyper*, over. and *critical*]

hyperesthe'sia *n.* morbid sensitivity. [G. *hyper*, beyond, *aristhanesthai.*, perceive]

hyper'trophy *n.* over-nourishment: overgrowth of an organ, *etc.*, caused by this. [G. *hyper*, above, *trophe*, nourishment]

hy'phen *n.* a short stroke joining two words or syllables. **hyphenate** *v.t.* to connect by a hyphen. [G. *hypo-*, under, *hen*, one]

hypno'sis (hip-) *n.* state like deep sleep in which the subject acts on external suggestion. -**hypnot'ic** *a.* of hypnosis. *n.* person under hypnosis; thing producing it. -**hyp'notism** *n.* production of hypnosis. -**hyp'notist** *n.* -**hyp'notize** *v.t.* [G. *hypnos*, sleep]

hypochon'dria *n.* morbid depression. -**hypochon'driac** *a.* affected by this. -*n.* sufferer from it. -**hypochrondri'acal** *a.* [G. *hypochondria*, parts below the costal cartilages (as the seat of melancholy)]

hypoc'risy *n.* assuming of a false appearance of virtue; insincerity **hypocrite** *n.* -**hypocrit'ical** *a.* -**hypocrit'ically** *adv.* [G. *hypokrisis*, acting a part]

hypoderm'ic *a.* introduced beneath the skin. [G. *hypo*, under, *derma*, skin]

hypot'enuse *n.* side of a right-angled triangle opposite the right angle. [G. *hypoteinousa*, 'subtending']

hypoth'ecate *v.t.* pledge, mortgage. -**hypotheca'tion** *n.* [G. *hypotheke*]

hypoth'esis *n.* supposition as a basis for reasoning; assumption. -**hypothet'ical** *a.* -**hypothet'ically** *adv.* [fr. G. *hypo*, under, and *tithenai*, place]

hyss'op *n.* aromatic herb. [G. *hyssopos*]

hy'rax *n.* marmot-like mammal of Africa, Asia, Biblical 'cony'. [G.]

hyste'ria (his-) *n.* disturbance of (a woman's) nervous system with convulsions, disturbance of mental faculties, *etc.*; morbid excitement. -**hyster'ical** *a.* -**hyster'ically** *adv.* -**hyster'ics** *n. pl.* fits of hysteria. [G. *hystera*, womb]

I

I *pron.* pronoun of the first person singular. [OE. *ic*]

iamb'us, i'amb *n.* metrical foot of a short followed by a long syllable. -**iamb'ic** *a.* [G. *iambos*]

Ibe'rian *a.* of Spain and Portugal. [*Iberia*]

i'bex *n.* wild goat with large horns. [L.]

i'bis *n.* stork-like wading bird. [G.]

ice *n.* frozen water; frozen confection. -*v.t.* cover with ice; cool with ice: cover with sugar. -**ice'-age** *n.* glacial period. -**ice'ax** *n.* climber's ax for ice. -**ice'berg** *n.* large floating mass of ice. -**ice'-blink** *n.* reflection in air of distant ice. -**ice'-bound** *a.* bound, surrounded by ice. -**icecap** *n.* frozen region at N., S. Pole. -**ice'-cream** *a.* frozen flavored cream or similar substance. -**ice'field** *n.* large expanse of ice. -**ice'-floc** *n.* floating ice field. -**ice'-rink** *n.*, sheet of ice for skating. -**ice'-yacht** *n.* ship on runners for sailing on ice. -**i'cicle** *n.* tapering spike of ice hanging where water has dripped. -**i'cy** *a.* -**i'cily** *adv.* [OE. *is*]

ichneu'mon (ik-nu-) *n.* mongoose-like animal living on crocodile's eggs; kind of parasitic fly. (G. *ichneuein*, track]

ich'nite, ich'nolite (ik-) *n.* fossil footprint. [G. *ichnos*, footprint]

i'chor *n.* in mythology, the blood of the god; watery fluid from wound, *etc.* [G.]

ichthyol'ogy (ikth-) *n.* branch of zoology treating of fishes. -**ichthyosaur'us** *n.* prehistoric marine animal. [G. *ichthys*, fish, *sauros*, lizard]

icicle. *See* **ice.**

i'con, ikon *n.* image; sacred picture. -**icon'oclast** *n.* breaker of images. -**iconoclas'tic** *a.* [G, *eikon*, likeness]

id *n.* (*psych.*) instinctive impulses of the individual. [L. = it]

ide'a *n.* notion in the mind; way of thinking; vague belief, plan, aim. -**ide'al** *a.* existing only in idea; visionary; perfect. -*n.* perfect type. -**ide'ally** *adv.* **ide'alism** *n.* imaginative treatment; philosophy that the object of external perception consists of ideas. -**ide'alist** *n.* -**ide'alize** *v.t.* represent or look upon as ideal. -**idealization** *n.* [G. = *look*; semblance]

ident'ity *n.* absolute sameness; individuality. -**ident'ical** *a.* the very same. -**ident'ically** *adv.* -**ident'ify** *v.t.* establish the identity of; associate (oneself) within separably; treat as identical. -**identifica'tion** *n.* [L. *idem*, same]

Ides *n. pl.* in Ancient Roman Calendar 15th March, May, July and Oct. and 13th of other months. [L. *idus*]

idiocy. *See* **idiot.**

ideol'ogy *n.* science of ideas; system of ideas; abstract speculation. -**ideol'ogist** *n.* [*idea* and G. *logia*, discourse]

id'iom *n.* one's language; way of expression natural to a language; expression peculiar to it. -**idiomat'ic** *a.* characteristic of a language; marked by the use of idioms, colloquial. -**idiomat'ically** *adv.* [*See* **idiot**]

idiosyn'crasy *n.* feeling or view peculiar to a person. [G. *idios*, one's own, *synkrasis*, mixture]

id'iot *n.* mentally deficient person. -**id'iocy** *n.* state of being an idiot. -**idiot'ic** *a.* -**idiot'ically** *adv.* [G. *idios*, own, peculiar]

i'dle *a.* doing nothing; lazy; useless, vain, groundless. -*v.i.* be idle. -*v.t.* pass time in idleness. -**i'dleness** *n.* -**i'dly** *adv.* -**i'dler** *n.* [OE. *idel*, useless]

i'dol *n.* image of a deity as an object of worship; false god; object of excessive devotion. -**idol'ator** *n.* worshipper of idols. -**idol'atress** *fem.* -**idol'atry** *n.* -**idol'atrous** *a.* -**i'dolize** *v.i.* make an idol of; love or venerate to excess. [G. *eidolon*, image]

i'dyll *n.* short description, usually in verse, of a picturesque scene or incident, *esp.* of rustic life. -**idyll'ic** *a.* [G. *eidyllion*, dim. of *eidos*, picture]

if *conj.* on the condition or supposition that; whether. [OE. *gif*]

ig'loo *n.* Eskimo snow-hut. [Eskimo]

ig'neous *a.* fiery; resulting from fire. -**ignite'** *v.t.* set on fire. -*v.t.* take fire. -**igni'tion** *n.* device for igniting explosive mixture in internal-combustion engine. -**ig'nis fat'uus** *n.* phosphorescent light flitting over marshes, will-o'-the-wisp. [L. *ignis*, fire]

igno'ble *a.* mean, base. low-born. -**igno'bly** *adv.* [L. *ignobilis*]

ig'nominy *n.* dishonor, disgrace; infamous conduct. -**ignomin'ious** *a.* -**ignomin'iously** *adv.* [L. *ignominia*]

ignore' *v.t.* disregard, leave out of account. -**ignora'mus** *n.* ignorant person. -**ig'norance** *n.* lack of knowledge. -**ig'norant** *a.* -**ig'norantly** *adv.* [L. *ignorare*, not to know]

igua'na (igwä-) *n.* large tree lizard of tropical America; S. African monitor lizard. -**igua'nodon** *n.* extinct giant lizard. [Sp. fr. Carib.]

i'lex *n.* holm-oak. [L.]

il'iac *a.* of the loins. [L. *ilia*, loins]

Il'iad *n.* epic poem by Homer on siege of Troy. [G. *Ilias*, Troy]

il- *prefix*, for in- before '*l*', negatives the idea of the simple word: *e.g.* **ille'gal** *a.* not legal. -**illeg'ible** *a.* not legible; *etc.* Such words are not given where the meaning and derivation are clear from the simple word.

ill *a.* out of health; bad, evil; faulty. -*n.* evil, harm; *adv.* not well; faultily, unfavorably. -**ill'-bred'** *a.* bad-mannered. -**ill'favored** *a.* ugly. -**ill'-feeling** *a.* resentment, unpleasantness. -**ill-natured** *a.* bad-tempered. -**ill'ness** *n.* -**ill-omened** *a.* having unfavorable omens, unfortunate. -**ill-starred'** *a.* unlucky. -**ill-tempered** *a.* cross, morose. -**ill-timed** *a.* inopportune. -**ill-will** *n.* enmity. [ON. *illr*]

illegit'imate *a.* illegal; born out of wedlock. -*n.* bastard. -**illegit'imacy** *n.* [L. *illegitirnus*]

illic'it *a.* unlawful; forbidden. [L. *il*, (*in*), not-*licere*, to be lawful]

illim'itable *a.* infinite, boundless. [L. *il-*, not-*limes*, -*itis*, boundary]

illit'erate *a.* unable to read or write. -**illit'eracy** *n.* [L. *il-*, not, -*litteratus*]

illude' *v.t.* deceive, trick. [L. *il*, upon,

ludere, play]

illu'minate *v.t.* light up; decorate with lights; decorate with gold and colors. -**illumina'tion** *n.* -**illu'minative** *a.* -**ill'minant** *n.* agent of lighting. -**illu'mine, illume'** *v.t.* light up. [L. *illuminare*, throw into light, *lumen*]

illu'sion *n.* deceptive appearance, belief, or statement. -**illu'sionist** *n.* conjuror. -**illu'sive** *a.* -**illu'sory** *a.* [L. *illudere, illus-*, mock]

ill'ustrate *v.t.* make clear, *esp.* by examples or drawings; adorn with pictures. -**illustra'tion** *n.* -**illus'trative** *a.* -**ill'us trator** *n.* -**illus'trious** *a.* famous. [L. *illustrare*, throw into brightness]

im'age *n.* statue; semblance; type; simile, metaphor; counterpart; optical counterpart, as in a mirror. -*v.t.* make an image of, reflect. -**im'agery** *n.* images; use of rhetorical figures. [L. *imago, imagin-*, image]

imag'ine (-j-) *v.t.* picture to oneself; conjecture; think. -**imag'inable** *a.* -**imag'inary** *a.* existing only in fancy. -**imagina'tion** *n.* faculty of making mental images; fancy. -**imag'inative** *a.* -**imag'inatively** *adv.* [image]

ima'go *n.* latest, perfect state of an insect. [L.]

im'becile *a.* mentally weak. -*n.* person of weak mind. -**imbecil'ity** *n.* [L. *imbecillus*, weak in body or mind]

imbibe' *v.t.* drink in. [L. *imbibere*]

imbrica'tion *n.* an overlapping, as of tiles. -**im'bricate** *v.t.* and *i.* [L. *imbricare*, fr. *imbrex*, tile]

imbroglio *n.* complicated situation. [It. = confusion]

imbrue' *v.t.* soak; wet or moisten; dye or stain. [OF. *embrouer*]

imbue' *v.t.* saturate, dye, inspire. [L. *imbuere*, make drink in]

im'itate *v.t.* take as model; mimic, copy. -**im'itable** *a.* -**imita'tion** *n.* -**im'itative** *a.* -**im'itator** *n.* [L. *imitari*]

im- *prefix*, for *in-* before '*m*', negatives the idea of the simple word: *e.g.*, **imm'ature** *a.* not mature. -**immo'bile** *a.* not mobile, *etc.* Such words are not given where the meaning and derivation are clear from the simple word.

immac'ulate *a.* spotless; pure. -**immac'ulately** *adv.* [L. *macula*, spot]

imm'anent *a.* abiding in, inherent. -**imm'anence** *n.* [L. *manere*, dwell]

immate'rial *a.* not composed of matter; unimportant. [L. *im-* and *materialis*]

imme'diate *a.* occurring at once; direct, not separated by others. -**imme'diately** *adv.* -**imme'diacy** *n.* [Med. L. *immediatus*]

immemor'ial *a.* beyond memory. -**immemor'ially** *adv.* [*memory*]

immense' *a.* huge, vast, immeasurable. -**immen'sity** *n.* -**immense'ly** *adv.* [L. *immensus*, unmeasured]

immerse' *v.t.* dip, plunge, into a liquid. -**immer'sion** *n.* -**immer'sion heat'er, immer'ser** *n.* electric water-heater immersed in the water. [L. *immergere, immers-*]

imm'igrate *v.i.* come into a country as a settler. -**immigra'tion** *n.* -**imm'igrant** *n.* -*a.* [L. *immigrate, iminigrat-*]

imm'inent *a.* close at hand. -**imminently** *adv.* -**imm'inence** *n.* [L. *imminere, imminent-*, overhang]

immob'ilize *v.t.* put out of action; deprive of mobility. [*mobile*]

imm'olate *v.t.* sacrifice. -**immola'tion** *n.* [L. *immolare, immolate-*]

immor'tal *a.* not mortal, undying, everlasting. -**immor'talize** *v.t.* render immortal; make famous for ever. [L. *immortalis*]

immortelle' *n.* everlasting (flower). [F.]

immune' *a.* secure, exempt; proof (against a disease, *etc.*). -**immunize'** *v.t.* -**immu'nity** *n.* [L. *immunis*, exempt, orig, from public service, *munus*]

immure' *v.t.* imprison. [L. *murus*, wall]

im- *prefix*, for *in-* before '*p*', negatives the idea of the simple word: *e.g.*, **impal'pable** *a.* not palpable, untouchable. -**impar'tial** *a.* not partial, fair; *etc.* Such words are not given where the meaning and derivation are clear from the simple word.

imp *n.* little devil; mischievous child; graft. -*v.t.* graft. -**imp'ish** *a.* mischievous. [OE. *impa*, shoot, graft]

im'pact *n.* collision, or the impulse resulting therefrom. [L. *impingere, impact-*, dash against]

impair' *v.t.* weaken, damage. -**impair'ment** *n.* [F. *empirer*, make worse]

impale' *v.t.* transfix, *esp.* on a stake, to put to death; combine (two coats of arms) by placing them side by side with a line between. -**impale'ment** *n.* [F. *empaler*, fr. *pal*, stake]

impart' *v.t.* give a share of; communicate. [L. *impartire*, fr. *pars*, part]

impar'tial *a.* unbiased. [L. *im-*, and *pars, partis*]

im'passe *n.* position, situation from which there is no escape; deadlock. [F.]

impass'ible *a.* not liable to pain or suffering. -**impassibil'ity** *n.* -**impass'ive** *a.* without feeling or emotion; calm. -**impassiv'ity** *n.* [L. *pati, pass-*, suffer]

impas'sioned *a.* deeply moved; showing deep feeling. [*passion*]

impeach' *v.t.* call in question; accuse; accuse of treason. -**impeach'able** *a.* -**impeach'ment** *n.* [orig. *hinder*, F. *empecher*, prevent]

impecc'able *a.* incapable of sin or error. [L. *impeccabilis*, fr. *peccare*, sin]

impecu'nious *a.* having no money. -**impecunios'ity** *n.* [L. *pecuniosus*, rich]

impede' *v.t.* hinder. -**imped'iment** *n.* -**impediment'a** *n. pl.* baggage, *esp.* of an army. [L. *impedire*, shackle]

impel' *v.t.* drive, force. [L. *pellere*]

impend' *v.i.* be imminent; threaten. [L. *impendere*, hang over]

imper'ative *a.* expressing command; obligatory. -*n.* imperative mood. -**imper'atively** *adv.* [L. *imperare*, command]

imper'fect *a.* not perfect, having flaws; (*gram.*) of tense denoting continuous action in the past [L *imperfectus*]

impe'rial *a.* of an empire; of an emperor; majestic. -*n.* small part of the beard left growing below the lower lip (after Napoleon III). -**impe'rialism** *n.* extension of empire; belief in colonial empire. -**impe'rialist** *n.* -**imperialis'tic** *a.* -**impe'rious** *a.* domineering. [L. *imperium*, rule, empire]

imper'il *v.t.* bring into peril. [*peril*]

imper'sonate *v.t.* play the part of. -**impersona'tion** *n* -**imper'sonator** *n.* one who impersonates another, *esp.* on the stage. [*person*]

impert'inent *a.* insolent, saucy, irrelevant. -**impert'inence** *n.* -**impert'inently** *adv.* [*pertinent*]

imper'vious *a.* unable to be penetrated or affected. [L. *imperuius*]

impeti'go *n.* acute infectious disease of the skin. [L. = attack]

im'petus *n.* force with which a body moves; impulse. -**impet'uous** *a.* ardent, vehement; acting or moving with a rush. -**impet'uously** *adv.* -**impetuos'-ity** *n.* ardor; rashness [L. = attack]

impinge' *v.i.* dash, strike; touch (with, on, upon). [L. *impingere*]

im'pious *a.* irreligious, profane. [L. *impius*]

implac'able *a.* not to be appeased, inexorable. [L. *implacabilis*]

implant' *v.t.* insert, fix. [*plant*]

im'plement *n.* tool, instrument, utensil. -*v.t.* (im-ple-ment') carry (a contract, *etc.*) into effect. [L. *implore*, fill up]

im'plicate *v.t.* involve, include; entangle; imply. -**implica'tion** *n.* -**implic'it** (-s-) *a.* implied but not expressed; involved in a general principle, exclusive of individual judgment. -**implic'itly** (-s-) *adv.* -**imply'** *v.t.* involve the truth of, mean. [L. *implicare*, entangle]

implore' *v.t.* entreat earnestly. [L. *implo rare*, fr. *plorare*, weep]

imply. *See* **implicate.**

impon'derable *a.* without perceptible weight, as electricity, light. -*n.* [L. *pondus, ponder-*, weight]

import' *v.t.* bring in, introduce (*esp.* goods from a foreign country); imply, mean; express; be of consequence to. -**im'port** *n.* thing imported; meaning; importance. -**importa'tion** *n.* -**import'er** *n.* -**import'able** *a.* -**import'ant** *a.* of consequence; momentous; pompous. -**import'antly** *adv.* -**import'ance** *n.* [L. *importare*, fr. *portare*, carry]

importune' *v.t.* solicit pressingly. -**impor'tunate** *a.* persistent in soliciting. -**importu'nity** *n.* -**impor'tunately** *adj.* [L. *importunus*, troublesome]

impose' *v.t.* lay (a tax, duty, *etc.*) upon. *v.i.* be impressive take advantage, practice deceit (on). -**imposi'tion** *n.* -**impos'ter** *n.* deceiver, one who assumes a false character. -**impos'ture** *n.* - **im'post** *n.* duty, tax; upper course of a pillar. [F. *imposer*]

impos'thume *n.* abscess. [for *apostume*, G. *apostema*, separation]

im'potent *a.* powerless, ineffective. **im'potence** *n.* -**im'potently** *adj.* [*potent*]

impound' *v.t.* shut up (cattle, *etc.*) in a pound; confiscate. [*pound*]

impov'erish *v.t.* make poor or weak. -**impov'erishment** *n.* [OF. *enipourir*]

impreca'tion *n.* an invoking of (evil) curse. -**im'precate** *v.t.* [L. *imprecari*, invoke by prayer]

impreg'nable *a.* proof against attack. -**impregnabil'ity** *n.* -**impreg'nably** *adv.* [F. *imprenable*, fr. *prendre*, take]

impreg'nate *v.t.* make pregnant; saturate. -**impregna'tion** *n.* [*pregnant*]

impresa'rio *n.* organizer of a public entertainment; operatic manager. [It.]

impress' *v.t.* imprint, stamp; fix; affect deeply. -**im'press** *n.* act of impressing; mark impressed. -**impress'ible** *a.* -**impressibil'ity** *n.* -**impres'sion** *n.* impress; printed copy; total of copies printed at once; effect produced, *esp.* on mind or feelings; notion, belief. -**impres'sionable** *a.* -**impressionabil'ity** *n.* -**impres'sionism** *n.* method of painting or writing to give general effect without detail. **impres'sionist** *n.* -**impressionis'tic** *a.* -**impress'ive** *a.* making a deep impression. [L. *imprimere, impress-*, fr. *premere*, press]

impress' *v.t.* press into service. **impress'ment** *n.* [*press*]

im'prest *n.* money advanced; earnest money. [OF. *prest*, loan]

imprima'tur *n.* licence to print books; official approval. [L. = let it be printed, from *imprimere*, to impress]

impri'mis *adv.* in the first place. [L.]

imprint' *v.t.* impress; stamp; publisher's name on the title page of a book. -**im'print** *n.* impression, stamp. [*print*]

impris'on (-z-) *v.t.* put in prison. -**impris'onment** *n.* [*prison*]

impromp'tu *adv.* and *a.* extempore. -*n.* something composed or said extempore. [F., fr. L. *promptus*, readiness]

impro'priate *v.t.* place (tithes, *etc.*) in hands of a layman. -**impropria'tion** *n.* [Med. L. *impropriare, impropriat-*]

improve' *v.t.* make better; make good use of. -*v.i.* become better. -**improve'ment** *n.* -**improv'er** *n.* [A.F. *emprower*, turn to profit, OF. *prou*, profit]

im'provise *v.t.* compose or utter extempore; get up, arrange, extempore. -**improvisa'tion** *n.* [F. *improviser*]

im'pudent *a.* pert, insolent, saucy. -**im'pudently** *adv.* -**im'pudence** *n.* [L. *impudens, impudent-*, shameless]

impugn' *v.t.* call in question, challenge. [L. *impugnare*, assail]

im'pulse *n.* sudden application of force; motion caused by it; sudden inclination to act; incitement. -**impul'sion** *n.* impulse, usually in the first sense. -**impul'sive** *a.* given to acting without reflection. -**impul'sively** *adv.* [L. *impellere, impuls-*, cp. *impel*]

impu'nity *n.* freedom from injurious consequences. (L. *impunitas*]

impute' *v.t.* set to the account of, ascribe. -**imputabil'ity** *n.* -**imputa'tion** *n.* [L. *imputare*, fr. *putare*, reckon]

in *prep.* expresses inclusion within limits of space. time, circumstances, *etc.* -*adv.* in or into some state, place, *etc.* [OE.]

in- *prefix* negatives the idea of the simple word; *e.g.*, **inact'ive** *a.* not active; incapable *a.* not capable, *etc.* Such words are omitted where the meaning and derivation may easily be inferred from the simple word. [L. *in-*, not]

inadvert'ent *a.* failing to pay attention; unintentional. -**inadvert'ence, inadvert'ency** *n.* -**inadvert'ently** *adv.* [obs. *advertent*; L. *advertere*, turn to]

inane' *a.* empty, void; foolish, silly. -**inan'ity** *n.* -**inani'tion** *n.* being empty, exhaustion. [L. *inanis*, empty]

in'asmuch *adv.* seeing that; (only in inasmuch as). [*in as much*]

inaug'urate *v.t.* admit to office; begin, initiate, *esp.* with ceremony. -**inaug'ural** *a.* -**inaug'urally** *adv.* -**inaugura'tion** *n.* -**inaug'urator** *n.* [L. *inaugurate*, take auguries before action]

in'born *a.* born with. [*born*]

inbred' *a.* inherent, innate. [*bred*]

incandes'cent *a.* glowing with heat, shining; of artificial light; produced by glowing filament. -**incandes'cence** *n.* -**incandesce'** *v.i.* and *t.* [L. *candescere*, begin to glow, *candere*]

incanta'tion *n.* magic spell, charm. [L. *incantare*, sing spells; cp. *enchant*]

incapac'itate (-as-) *v.t.* make unable; disqualify. -**incapac'ity** *n.* inability; disability. [L. *capere*, hold]

incarcerate *v.t.* imprison, shut up. -**incarcera'tion** *n.* -**incar'cerator** *n.* [L. *in*, in, *carcer*, prison]

incarn'adine *v.t.* dye crimson. -*a.* crimson. [orig. flesh-colored; *v.s.*]

incarn'ate *v.t.* embody in flesh, *esp.* in human form. -*a.* embodied thus. -**incarna'tion** *n.* [L. *incarnare, caro, carn-*, flesh]

incen'diary *a.* of the malicious setting on fire of property; guilty of this; inflammatory. -*n.* one guilty of arson, incendiary person. -**incen'diarism** *n.* [L. *incendere*, set on fire]

incense' *v.t.* enrage; incite, urge. [L. *incendere, incens-*]

in'cense *n.* gum or spice giving a sweet smell when burned; its smoke; flattery. *v.t.* burn incense to; perfume with incense. [L. *incendere, incens-*, kindle]

incen'tive *a.* arousing. -*n.* something that arouses to feeling or action. [L. *incentivus*, setting the tune]

incep'tion *n.* beginning. -**incep'tive** *a.* initial. [L. *incipere, incept-*, begin]

incess'ant *a.* unceasing; continual; without intermission. -**incessantly** *adv.* [L. *cessare*, cease]

in'cest *n.* sexual intercourse of kindred

within forbidden degrees. -**incest'uous** *a.* [L. *incestus*, impure, unchaste]

inch (-sh) *n.* one-twelfth of a foot. [OE. *ynce*, L. *uncia*, twelfth part]

inch (-sh) *n.* island. [Gael. *innis*]

in'choate (in-ko-) *a.* just begun; unformed. [L. *inchoare, inchoate-*, begin]

in'cident *n.* event, occurrence. *-a.* naturally attaching to; striking, falling (upon). -**in'cidence** *n.* failing on, or affecting. -**incident'al** *a.* casual, not essential. -**incident'ally** *adv.* [L. *incidere*, fall in]

incin'erate *v.t.* consume by fire. -**incin'erator** *n.* -**incinera'tion** *n.* [Med. L. *incinerare*, reduce to ashes]

incip'ient *a.* beginning. -**incip'ience** *n.* -**incip'iently** *a.* [L. *incipere*, begin]

incise' *v.t.* cut into; engrave. -**inci'sion** (-sizh-) *n.* -**inci'sive** *a.* sharp; pointed, trenchant. -**inci'sor** *n.* cutting tooth. [L. *incidere, incis-*, cut into]

incite' *v.t.* urge, stir up. -**incite'ment** *n.* [L. *incitare*, rouse]

inclem'ent *a.* of weather, stormy, severe, cold. -**inclem'ency** *n.* [*clement*]

incline' *v.t.* bend, turn from the vertical; dispose. *-v.i.* slope; be disposed. -**in'cline** *n.* slope. -**inclina'tion** *n.* [F. *incliner*, cp. *decline*]

include' *v.t.* reckon in; comprise. -**inclu'sion** *n.* -**inclu'sive** *a.* -**inclu'sively** *adv.* [L. *includere*, shut in]

incog'nito *adv.* with identity concealed or not avowed. *-a.* concealing or not avowing identity. *-n.* this condition. [It., fr. L. *incognitus*, unknown]

incohe'rent *a.* unable to be understood. [*in-* and L. *cohaerere*]

in'come *n.* receipts, *esp.* annual, from work, investments, *etc.* -**in'come-tax** *n.* direct tax on income. [*in* and *come*]

incong'ruous (-ng-g-) *a.* not accordant, absurd. -**incongru'ity** *n.* -**incong'ruously** *adv.* [*See* **congruent**]

incor'porate *n.* form legally into a corporation; include. -**incorpora'tion** *n.* -**incorpo'real** *a.* bodiless; intangible. [L. *corpus, corpor-*, body]

increase' *v.i.* become greater in size, number, *etc.* *-v.t.* make greater. -**in'crease** *n.* growth, enlargement, multiplication. -**in'crement** *n.* increase; profit. [L. *increscere*, fr. *crescere*, grow]

incrim'inate *v.t.* charge with crime; involve in an accusation. -**incrim'inatory** *a.* [L. *crimen*, crime]

incrust. *See* **encrust.**

in'cubate *v.t.* hatch (eggs). *-v.i.* sit on eggs; of disease germs, pass through the stage between infection and appearance of symptoms. -**incuba'tion** *n.* -**in'cubator** *n.* apparatus for artificially hatching eggs. [L. *incubare*)

in'cubus *n.* nightmare; oppressive person or thing. [Late L., for *incubo*, nightmare-*in*, on, *cubere*, lie]

in'culcate *v.t.* impress on the mind by frequent repetition, *etc.* -**inculca'tion** *n.* [L. *inculcare*, stamp in]

incumb'ent *a.* lying, resting on, *-n.* present holder of an office. -**incumb'ency** *n.* office or tenure of an incumbent. [L. *incumbere*, lie upon]

incunab'ula *n.pl.* early printed books, as from the cradle of printing. [L. *in*, in, *cunabula*, cradle]

incur' *v.t.* fall into, bring upon oneself [L. *incurrere*, run into]

incur'sion *n.* invasion, inroad. [*incur*]

indebt'ed *a.* owing; under an obligation. -**indebt'edness** *n.* [*debt*]

indeed' *adv.* in truth, really. [*in deed*]

indefat'igable *v.* untiring. -**indefat'igably** *adv.* [L. *defatigare*, tire out]

indefeas'ible *a.* that cannot be lost or annulled. [OF. *desfaire*, undo]

indel'ible *a.* that cannot be blotted out, or effaced; permanent. -**indel'ibly** *adv.* -**indelibil'ity** *n.* [L. *delere*, wipe out]

indem'nity *n.* security against loss; compensation, *esp.* exacted by a victorious country after war. -**indem'nify** *v.t.* compensate. -**indemnifica'tion** *n.* [L. *indemnis*, unharmed]

indent' *v.t.* make notches or holes in; draw up a document in duplicate; make an order (upon some one *for*); requisition, order by indent; (*print.*) give relatively wider margin to (line, passage). -**in'dent** *n.* notch; an order, requisition. -**indenta'tion** *n.* -**indent'ure** *n.* indented document 'sealed agreement, *esp.* one binding apprentice to master. *v.t.* bind by indenture. [Med. L. *iridetitare*, give a serrated edge, *esp.* in cutting a document in two, so that the fitting of the halves proved them genuine]

indepen'dent *a.* not subject to others; self-reliant; free; valid in itself; politically of no party. -**inde'pen'dence** *or* **indepen'dency** *n.* being independent; self-reliance; self-support. -**Indepen'dence Day** *n.* holiday to celebrate the beginning of national independence, in U.S. July 4 (date of the adoption of the Declaration of Independence, 1776). [L. *depinigere*, depend]

in'dex *n.* (**in'dexes**, **in'dices** *pl.)*

forefinger; anything that points out. an indicator; alphabetical list of references, usually at the end of a book. *-v.t.* provide a book with an index; insert in an index. **-in'dex num'ber,** number to indicate cost of living at a given time. **-in'dicate** *v.t.* point out, state briefly. **-indica'tion** *n.* -**indic'ative** *a.* that indicates; *gram.* stating as a fact. **-in'dicator** *n.* [L. *indicare,* fr. *dicare,* make known]

In'dian *a.* of India, the Indies; or the aborigines of America. **-In'diaman** *n.* large sailing ship trading with India. -**in'dia-rub'ber** *n.* natural rubber made from latex. **-In'dian corn',** maize. -**In'dian cress',** nasturtium. **-In'dian file,** single file. **-In'dian hemp',** kind of hemp source of various narcotic drugs, *e.g.,* hashish. **-In'dian sum'mer,** period of summer weather in late autumn. [L. *India* - *Indus,* the Indus]

in'dicate. *See* **index.**

indict' *v.t.* accuse, *esp.* by legal process. **-indict'ment** *n.* **-indict'able** *a.* [OF. *enditer,* fr. L. *dictare,* proclaim]

indiff'erent *a.* impartial; careless; unimportant neither good nor bad, tolerable; having no inclination for or against. -**indiff'erently** *adv.* **-indiff'erence** *n.* [*different*]

indi'genous *a.* born in or natural to a country. [L. *indigena,* native]

in'digent (-j-) *a.* poor, needy. **-in'digence** *n.* [L. *indigere,* lack]

indig'nant *a.* moved bv anger and scorn; angered by injury. **-indig'nantly** *adv.* -**indigna'tion** *n.* contemptuous resentment. **-indig'nity** *n.* unworthy treatment; insult. [L. *indignari,* be angry at something unworthy, *indignus*]

in'digo *n.* blue dye obtained from a plant; the plant. [earlier *indico,* fr. L. *Indicus,* of India]

indite' *v.t.* write, put into words. [ME. *enditen,* OF. *enditer,* cp. *indict*]

individ'ual *a.* single; characteristic of a single person or thing. *-n.* single person. **-individ'ually** *adv.* **-individual'ity** *n.* individual existence or character. -**individ'ualism** *n.* social theory of free action of individuals. **-individ'ualist** *n.* **-individualis'tic** *a.* **-individua'tion** *n.* the development of separate but mutually interdependent units [L. *iridividuus.* undivided, single]

in'dolent *a.* lazy. **-in'dolence** *n.* -**in'dolently** *adv.* [F.]

indom'itable *a.* unsubduable. -**indom'itably** *adv.* [L. *domare, domit-,* tame]

in'door *a.* within, used within, *etc.,* a house. **-indoors'** *adv.* [*door*]

indorse. *See* **endorse.**

indu'bitable *a.* beyond doubt, indisputable. [L. *dubitare,* doubt]

induce' *v.t.* persuade; bring about; infer; produce (electricity) by induction. -**induce'ment** *n.* incentive, attraction.

induct' *v.t.* instal in office. **-induc'tion** *n.* inducting; general inference from particular instances; production of electric or magnetic state in a body by its being near (not touching) an electrified or magnetized body. **-induc'tive** *a.* **-induc'tively** *adv.* -**induc'tor** *n.* [L. *inducere, induct-,* lead in]

indulge *v.t.* gratify; give free course to; take pleasure in freely. **-indul'gent** *a.* -**indul'gence** *n.* **-indul'gently** *adv.* [L. *indulgere,* be courteous]

indum'entum *n.* outer covering, such as hairs or down on a plant or leaf, feathers, fur, *etc.* [L. *garment*]

in'durate *v.t.* harden. [L. *durus,* hard]

in'dustry *n.* diligence; habitual hard work; branch of manufacture or trade. -**indus'trious** *a.* diligent. **-indus'trial** *a.* of industries, trades. **-indus'trialism** *n.* factory system. **-indus'trialize** *v.t.* [L. *industria*]

ine'briate *v.t.* make drunk. *-a.* drunken. *-n.* drunkard. **-inebria'tion** *n.* **-inebri'ety** *n.* [L. *ebrius,* drunk]

ineff'able *a.* unspeakable, too great for words. **-ineff'ably** *adv..* [L. *ineffabilis,* fr. *effari,* utter]

ineluct'able *a.* inescapable, inevitable. [L. *eluctari,* struggle out]

inept' *a.* absurd, out of place, irrelevant; fatuous. **-inept'itude** *n.* [L. *ineptus,* fr. *aptus,* cp. *apt*]

inert' *a.* without power of action or resistance; slow, sluggish. **-iner'tia** (-shya) *n.* property by which matter continues in its existing state of rest or motion in a straight line unless that state is changed by external force; inability to exert oneself. **-inert'ly** *adv.* **-inert'ness** *n.* [L. *iners, inert-,* sluggish]

inev'itable *a.* unavoidable, not to be escaped. **-inev'itably** *adv.* **-inevitabil'ity** *n.* [L. *inevitabilis,* fr. *euitare,* avoid]

inex'orable *a.* unrelenting. **-inex'orably** *adv.* [L. *exorare,* entreat]

inexpug'nable *a.* impregnable; of argument, unanswerable. [L. *inexpugnabilis,* fr. *expugnare,* take by attack]

infall'ible *a.* never wrong, certain, unfailing. [*in-*, and Low L. *fallibilis*]

in'famous *a.* of ill fame, shameless, bad. -**in'famy** *n.* ill repute; vileness. -**in'famously** *adv.* [*fame*]

in'fant *n.* small child; person under one year old, a minor. -**in'fancy** *n.* -**infant'icide** *n.* murder of new-born child; person guilty of this. -**in'fantile** *a.* childish. -**in'fantile paralysis**, inflammation of the spinal cord, poliomyelitis. [L. *infans, infant-*, unable to speak]

infan'te *n.* title of son of Spanish or Portuguese Kings except eldest. -**infan'ta** *n. fem.* [Sp., Port., fr. L. *infans, infantis*, child]

in'fantry *n.* foot soldier. [It. *infanteria*]

infat'uate *v.t.* affect to folly or foolish passion. -**infatua'tion** *n.* [L. *infatuare*, fr. *fatuus*, foolish]

infect' *v.t.* make noxious; affect (with disease). -**infec'tion** *n.* -**infec'tious** *a.* catching. [L. *inficere, infect-*, dip in]

infer' *v.t.* deduce by reasoning, conclude. -**inference** *n.* -**inferen'tial** *a.* -**infer'able** *a.* [L. *inferre*, bring in]

infe'rior *a.* lower; of poor quality. -*n.* one lower (in rank, *etc.*). -**inferior'ity** *n.* -**inferior'ity complex** (*psych.*) suppressed sense of inferiority. resulting in undue self-assertion; (*colloq.*) sense of inferiority. [L. comp. of *inferus*, low]

infern'al *a.* of the lower world; hellish. -**intern'ally** *adv.* [L. *infernalis*, fr. *infernus*, lower]

infest' *v.t.* haunt, warmin. [L. *infestore*, fr. *infestus*, unsafe]

in'fidel *n.* unbeliever. -*a.* unbelieving. -**infidel'ity** *n.* disbelief (in religion); disloyalty. [L. *infidelis*, fr. *fides*, faith]

infilt'rate *v.i.* percolate, trickle through. -*v.t.* cause to pass through pores. -**infiltra'tion** *n.* [*See* **filter**]

in'finite (-it) *a.* boundless. -**infinites'imal** *a.* extremely or infinitely small. -**in'finitely** *adv.* -**infin'ity** *n.* -**infin'itive** *a. gram.* in the mood expressing the notion of the verb without limitation bv any particular subject. -*n.* verb in this mood; the mood, [L. *infinitus*, unbounded]

infirm' *a.* physically, mentally, weak, irresolute. -**infirm'ity** *n.* -**infirm'ary** *n.* hospital. [L. *infirm us*, cp. *firm*]

inflame' *v.t.* set alight, raise to heat or excitement. -*v.i.* catch fire; become excited. -**inflamm'able** *a.* easily set on fire; excitable; flammable. -**inflammabil'ity** *n.* -**inflamma'tion** *n.* morbid process affecting part of the body with heat, swelling and redness. -**inflamm'atory** *a.* [L. *inflammare*, set on fire]

inflate' *v.t.* blow up with air or gas; raise (price) artificially; increase (currency of a state) abnormally. -**infla'tion** *n.* [L, *flare, flat-*, blow]

inflect' *v.t.* bend; modify (words) to show grammatical relationships. -**inflec'tion, inflex'ion** *n.* [L. *inflectere*]

inflex'ible *a.* unbending, unyielding; stern. [L. *in-, flexibilis*, yielding]

inflict' *v.t.* impose, deliver forcibly, cause to be borne. -**inflic'tion** *n.* inflicting; boring experience. [L. *infligere, inflict-*.]

in'fluence *n.* agent or action working invisibly (upon); moral power (over, with); thing or person exercising this. -*v.t.* exert influence upon. -**influen'tial** *a.* -**influen'tially** *adv.* [L. *fluere*, flow]

influen'za *n.* contagious feverish illness; severe catarrh. [It.]

in'flux *n.* a flowing in. [L. *influxus*]

inform' *v.t.* tell; inspire. -*v.i.* bring a charge against. -**inform'ant** *n.* one who tells. -**informa'tion** *n.* telling; what is told, knowledge. -**informa'tion techno'logy** *n.* the technology of the production, storage, and communication of information using computers and microelectronics. -**inform'ative** *a.* -**inform'er** *n.* one who brings a charge. [L. *informare*, give form to]

infraction. *See* **infringe.**

in'fra-red *a.* beyond the red end of the spectrum, as in infra-red rays. [L. *infra*, below, and *red*]

infringe' *v.t.* transgress, break. -**infringe'ment** *n.* -**infrac'tion** *n.* (L. *infringere*, fr., *frangere, fract-*, break]

infundib'ular *a.* funnel-shaped. [L. *infundibulum*, funnel]

infuriate *v.t.* fill with fury. [*fury*]

infuse' *v.t.* pour in, instill; steep in order to extract soluble properties. -**infu'sion** *n.* infusing; liquid extracts obtained. [L, *fundere, fus-*, pour]

infuso'ria *n. pl.* microscopic organisms present in stagnant water *etc.* [L.]

infem'inate (-jem-) *v.t.* repeat. -**infemina'tion** *n.* [L. *ingeminare*, fr. *geminus*, twin]

inge'nious *a.* clever at contriving; cleverly contrived. -**ingenu'ity** *n.* skill in planning, invention. -**inge'niously** *adv.* [L. *ingenium*, natural ability]

in'génue *n.* artless young girl, *esp.* as a stage type. [F.]

ingen'uous *a.* frank, artless, innocent. -**ingen'uously** *adv.* -**ingen'uousness** *n.* [L.

ingenuus, free-born, frank]

ingesʹtion *n.* taking into the body. [L. *in*, in, and *gerere*, carry]

ingʹle (ingʹgl) *n.* fire on a hearth. -**ingʹle-nook** *n.* chimney-corner. [Gael. *aingeal*, fire]

inʹgot (ing-g-) *n.* brick or cast metal, *esp.* gold or silver. [OE. *geotan*, pour]

ingraʹtiate *v. refl.* work oneself into a position of favor. [L. *in gratiam*, into favor]

ingreʹdient *n.* component part of a mixture. [L. *ingredi*, step in]

inʹgress *n.* entry; right, means, of entry. [L. *ingressus*]

inguiʹnal (ing-gwi-) *a.* of the groin. [L. *inguinus*, groin]

inhabʹit *v.t.* dwell in. -**inhabʹitable** *a.* -**inhabʹitant** *n.* [L. *habitare*, dwell]

inhaleʹ *v.t.* breathe in. -*v.i.* breathe in air. -**inhalaʹtion** *n.* [L. *inhalare*]

inhereʹ*v. v.i.* of qualities, to exist (in); of rights, to be vested (in person). -**inheʹrent** *a.* innate, natural. -**inheʹrently** *adv.* -**inheʹrence** *n.* [L. *inhærere*]

inherʹit *v.t.* take as heir; derive from parents. -*v.i.* succeed as heir. -**inherʹitance** *n.* -**inherʹitor** *n.* -**inherʹitress, inheritrix** *fem.* [L. *heres*, heir]

inhibʹit *v.t.* forbid; forbid to exercise clerical functions; hinder (action). -**inhibition** *n.* (*psych.*) restraint imposed by one's own subconscious mind. **inhibited, inhibitory** *a.* [L. *inhibere, inhibit-*, hold in]

inhumeʹ *v.t.* bury. -**inhumaʹtion** *n.* [L. *inhumare-, humus,* earth]

inimʹical *a.* hostile, hurtful. [L. *inimicus-in*, not, *amicus,* friend]

inimʹitable *a.* defying imitation. -**inimʹitably** *adv.* [*imitate*]

iniqʹuity *n.* wickedness; gross injustice. -**iniquitous** *a.* -**iniqʹuitously** *adv.* [L. *iniquitas, æquus,* fair, even]

iniʹtial (-ish-) *a.* of the beginning, occurring at the beginning. -*n.* initial letter. *v.t.* mark, sign, with one's initials. -**iniʹtiate** *v.t.* set on foot, begin; admit, *esp.* into a secret society. -*n.* initiated person. -**initiaʹtion** *n.* -**iniʹtiative** *n.* first step, lead; power of acting independently. -*a.* originating. -**iniʹtiatory** *a.* [L. *initialis,* fr. *initium*, beginning]

inject *v.t.* force in (fluid, medicine, *etc.*), as with a syringe; fill thus. -**injecʹtion** *n.* [L. *injicere, inject-*, throw in]

injuncʹtion *n.* judicial order to restrain; authoritative order; exhortation. [Late L. *injunctio*, cp. *enjoin*]

inʹjury *n.* wrong, damage, harm. -**inʹjure** *v.t.* do wrong to, damage. -**injurious** *a.* harmful. -**injuʹriously** *adv.* [L. *injuria*, fr. *jus, jur-*, law]

ink *a.* fluid used for writing; paste used for printing. -*v.t.* mark with ink; cover or smear with it. -**inkʹbottle** *n.* -**inkʹer** *n.* instrument marking, or recording with ink. -**inkʹ-pot** *n.* -**inkʹstand** *n.* -**inkʹ-well** *n.* vessel for ink. -**inkʹy** *a.* of or like ink; black. [ME. *enke*. G. *enkhaustos,* burnt in]

inkʹling *n.* hint, slight knowledge or suspicion. [ME. *inklen*, whisper]

inʹland *n.* interior of a country. -*a.* in this; away from the sea; within a country. *adv.* in or towards the inland. -**inʹland revenues** revenue drawn from within the country, department controlling this. [*in* and *land*]

in-law *n.* relative by marriage as mother in-law. [*in* and *law*]

inʹlay *v.t.* embed; decorate thus. -*n.* inlaid work. [*in* and *lay*]

inʹlet *n.* entrance; creek; piece inserted. [*in* and *let*]

inʹly *adv.* in the heart, inwardly. [*in*]

inʹmate *n.* occupant, inhabitant *esp.* in institution. [*in* and *mate*]

inʹmost *a.* most inward. [*in* and *most*]

inn *n.* public house for the lodging or refreshment of travelers. -**innʹkeeper** *n.* [OE.]

innateʹ *a.* inborn. [L. *innatus*]

innʹer *a.* lying within. [compar. of *in*]

innʹings *n. pl.* in games, batsman's turn of play, side's turn of batting. [*in*]

innʹocent *a.* free from guilt; guileless; harmless. -*n.* innocent person, *esp.* a young child; idiot. -**innʹocence** *n.* -**innʹocently** *adv.* [L. *nocere*, harm]

innocʹuous *a.* harmless. -**innocʹuousness** *n.* [*See* **innocent**]

innʹovate *v.t.* bring in changes, new things. -**innʹovator** *n.* -**innovaʹtion** *n.* [L. *innocare*, fr. *novus*, new]

innuenʹdo *n.* allusive remark, hint (usually depreciatory). [L. = by nodding to, fr. *nuere*, nod]

inocʹulate *v.t.* treat with disease germs, *esp.* as a protection; implant (disease germs). -**inoculaʹtion** *n.* [orig. graft, L. *inoculate*, fr. *oculus*, eye, bud]

inordʹinate *a.* excessive. [L. *inordinatus*, unordered, cp. *order*]

inorganʹic *a.* not organic or organized; of substance without carbon. [*in-*, and L. *organcus*]

inʹput *n.* power or information supplied to machine; work or money put into an enterprise. [*in* and *put*]

in'quest *n.* legal or judicial inquiry, *esp.* into cause of sudden, violent, death. [OF. *enqueste*, inquiry]

in'quiline *a.* (*zool.*) living in (another's) abode, as, *e.g.*, the hermit crab. *-n.* -**inquili'nous** *a.* [L. *inquiliitus*, fr. *incolere*, inhabit]

inquire', enquire' *v.t.* seek information. *-v.t.* ask to be told. -**inqui'rer, enqui'r-er** *n.* -**inqui'ry, enqui'ry** *n.* -**inquisi'tion** *n.* investigation, official inquiry. **Inquisition** *n.* tribunal for the suppression of heresy. -**inquis'itor** *n.* -**inquisitor'ial** *a.* -**inquis'itive** *a.* given to inquiring, curious; prying. -**inquis'itively** *adv.* [L. *inquirere, inquis-]*

in'road *n.* incursion; encroachment. [*road* in sense of riding]

insane' *a.* mad. -**insan'ity** *n.* [L. *insanus*]

inscribe' *v.t.* write (in or on something); mark; trace (figure) within another; dedicate. -**inscrip'tion** *n.* inscribing, words inscribed on a monument, coin, *etc.* [L. *inscribere, inscript-*]

inscru'table *a.* mysterious, impenetrable. -**inscru'tably** *adv.* -**inscrutabil'ity** *n.* [*See* **scrutiny**]

in'sect *n.* small invertebrate animal with six legs, body divided into segments and two or four wings. --**insect'icide** *n.* preparation for killing insects. -**insectiv'orous** *a.* insect-eating. [L. *insectum*, cut into (from the segments)]

insem'inate *v.t.* sow; impregnate. -**insemina'tion** *n.* [*in-*, and L. *seminare*, to sow]

insen'sate *a.* without sense, sensibility; stupid, foolish. [L. *sensatus*, gifted with sense, feeling]

insert' *v.t.* place or put (in, into, between); introduce (into written matter, *etc.*). -**inser'tion** *n.* [L. *inserere*, fr. *serere, sert-*, join]

insesso'rial *a.* (of birds) adapted for perching, climbing. [L. *incessor*, fr. *insidere, insess-*, sit on]

in'set *n.* something extra inserted; picture set into a larger one. [*in* and *set*]

in'shore *a.* at sea, near the shore. *-adv.* towards the shore. [*shore*]

in'side *n.* inner side, surface, or part. *-a.* of, in, or on, the inside. *-adv.* in or into the inside. *-prep.* within, on the inner side. [*in* and *side*]

in'sidious *a.* stealthy, treacherous. -**insid'iously** *adv.* [L. *insidiosus*, fr. *insidere*, lie in wait]

in'sight *n.* mental penetration. [*sight*]

insig'nia *n. pl.* badges or emblems of an honor or office. [L. = distinguished things; fr. *signurn*, sign]

insin'uate *v.t.* bring or get (something into something) gradually or subtly; hint. -**insinua'tion** *n.* [L. *insinuate*, introduce tortuously. cp. *sinuous*]

insip'id *a.* dull, tasteless. -**insipid'ity** *n.* [L. *insipidus*, fr. *sapidus*, tasty]

insist' *v.i.* dwell on, maintain, demand persistently. -**insist'ent** *a.* -**insist'ently** *adv.* -**insist'ence** *n.* pertinacity. [L. *insistere*, fr. *sistere*, stand]

in'solent *a.* insulting, offensively contemptuous. -**in'solently** *adv.* -**in'solence** *n.* [L. *insolens*; orig. unaccustomed]

insom'nia *n.* sleeplessness. [L.]

insou'ciant (ang-soos-i-ong) *n.* careless, unconcerned. [F.]

in'span *v.t.* yoke (animals) to wagon, *etc.* [Du. *inspannen*]

inspect' *v.t.* examine closely or officially. -**inspec'tion** *n.* -**inspec'tor** *n.* [L. *inspicere, inspect-*, look into]

inspire' *v.t.* breathe in; infuse thought or feeling into; arouse, to create. -**inspira'tion** *n.* breath; influence, *esp.* divine influence. [L. *inspirare*]

inspir'it *v.t.* animate, put spirit or courage, into. [*spirit*]

inspiss'ate *v.t.* thicken (a liquid) by evaporation. -**inspissa'tion** *n.* [L. *spissare-spissus*, dense]

install' *v.t.* place (person in an office, *etc.*) with ceremony; establish, have put in. **installa'tion** *n.* [F. *installer*, put in a stall]

install'ment (-awl-) *n.* payment of part of a debt; any of parts of a whole delivered in succession; installation. [earlier *estallment*, fr. OF, *estaler*, fix]

in'stance *n.* example; particular case; request; place in a series. *-v.t.* cite. -**in'stant** *a.* urgent; belonging to the current month; immediate. *-n.* moment, point of time. -**in'stantly** *adv.* at once. -**instanta'neous** *a.* happening in an instant. -**instanta'neously** *adv.* -**instant'er** *adv.* at once. [L. *instantia*, fr. *instare*, be present, urge]

instead' (-ed) *adv.* in place (of). [*stead*]

in'step *n.* top of the foot between toes and ankle. [orig. uncertain]

in'stigate *v.t.* incite. -**instiga'tion** *n.* -**in'stigator** *n.* [L. *instigate*]

instill' *v.t.* put in by drops; drop slowly (into the mind). -**instilla'tion** *n.* instillment *n.* [L. *stillare*, drop]

in'stinct *n.* inborn impulse or propensity;

unconscious skill; intuition; involuntary impulse. -**instinct'** *a.* charged, full. -**instinct'ive** *a.* -**instinct'ively** *adv.* [L. *instinctus*, fr. *instinguere*, urge]

in'stitute *v.t.* establish, found; appoint; set going. -*n.* society for promoting some public object, *esp.* scientific; its building. -**institu'tion** *n.* instituting; established custom or law; institute. -**institu'tional** *a.* -**in'stitutor** *n.* [L. *instituere, institute*, set up]

instruct' *v.t.* teach, inform, give directions to. -**instruc'tion** *n.* -**instruc'tive** *a.* -**instruc'tively** *adv.* -**instruc'tor** *n.* [L. *instruere, instruct-*, build]

in'strument *n.* tool or implement, *esp.* for scientific purposes; person or thing made use of; contrivance for producing music; legal document. -**instrument'al** *a.* -**instrument'alist** *n.* player of musical instrument. -**instrument'ally** *adv.* -**instrumentality** *n.* -**instrumenta'tion** *n.* arrangement of music for instruments. [L. *instrumentum*, fr. *instruere*, build]

insubo'rdinate *a.* disobedient. -**insubor'dination** *n.* [*in-*, and Med. L. *subordinatus*]

in'sufflate *v.t.* blow, breath on, in. -**insuffla'tion** *n.* -**insuffla'tor** *n.* [L. *insufflare*, blow on]

in'sular *a.* of an island; of islanders. -**insular'ity** *n.* -**in'sulate** *v.t.* make into an island; isolate, *esp.* by materials not conducting electricity or beat. **insulation** *n.* -**in'sulator** *n.* [L. *insula*, island]

in'sulin *n.* extract used in the treatment of diabetes and mental diseases, derived from cell-islets in the pancreas of animals. [L. *insula*, island]

insult' *v.t.* assail with abuse in act or word. -**in'sult** *n.* scornful abuse, affront. [L. *insultare*, jump at]

insu'perable *a.* not to be got over. -**insu'perably** *adv.* -**insuperabil'ity** *n.* [L. *superare*, overcome, fr. *super*, over]

insure' *v.t.* secure the payment of a sum in event of loss, death, *etc.*, by a contract and payment of sums called premiums; make such contract about; make safe (against); make certain. -**insu'rance** *n.* -**insur'able** *a.* -**insu'rer** *n.* -**insu'rance-policy** *n.* contract of insurance, [var. of *ensure*]

insur'gent *a.* in revolt. -*n.* one in revolt. -**insurrec'tion** *n.* revolt. [L. *insurgere, insurrect-*, rise upon]

intact' *a.* untouched; whole, uninjured. [L. *tangere, tact-*, touch]

inta'glio (-tal-) *n.* incised design; gem so cut. [It., fr. *tagliare*, cut]

in'take *n.* inlet; narrower point of tube or stocking; reclaimed land. [*in* and *take*]

intang'ible *a.* not perceptible to touch, elusive. -**intangibil'ity** *n.* [*in-*, and L. *tangibilis*]

in'teger (-j-) *n.* whole number. -**in'tegral** (-g-) *a.* -**in'tegrate** *v.t.* combine into a whole. -**integra'tion** *n.* -**integ'rity** *n.* original perfect state; honesty, uprightness. [L. = untouched]

integ'ument *n.* covering, skin, rind. [L. *integunientum*, fr. *tegere*, cover]

in'tellect *n.* faculty of thinking and reasoning. -**intellec'tual** *a.* of, or appealing to, the intellect; having good intellect. -*n.* intellectual person, high-brow. -**intellectuality** *n.* [L. *intellegere*, intellect, understand]

intell'igent *a.* having or showing good intellect; quick at understanding. -**intelligently** *adv.* -**intell'igence** *n.* intellect; quickness of understanding; information. news. -**intell'igible** *a.* that can be understood. -**intell'igibly** *adv.* -**intelligibil'ity** *n.* -**intell'igence quo'tient** (-shent'),ratio indicated in percentages) of one's mental age to one's actual age (*abbrev.* IQ). -**intell'igence test' questionnaire,** *etc.*, to arrive at this. [L. *intelligens, intelligent-*]

intelligent'sia *n.* part of a nation claiming power of independent thought. [Russ.]

intem'perate *a.* not temperate, immoderate in drinking; passionate. [L. *intemperatus*]

intempes'tive *a.* unseasonable. [L. *intempestivus*]

intend' *v.t.* design, purpose, mean. [L. *intenders, intens-, intent-*, bend the mind on, fr. *tendere*, stretch]

intense' *a.* very strong or acute -**intens'ify** *v.t.* -**intensifica'tion** *n.* -**intens'ity** *n.* -**intens'ive** *a.* giving emphasis; aiming at increased productiveness. -**intens'ively** *adv.* [*See* **intend**]

intent' *n.* purpose. -a. eager; resolved, bent. -**intent'ly** *adv.* -**inten'tion** *n.* purpose, aim. -**inten'tional** *a.* -**intent'ness** *n.* [*See* **intend**]

inter' *v.t.* bury. -**inter'ment** *n.* [F. *enterrer*, fr. *terre*, earth]

inter' *prefix* meaning between, among, mutually; forms compounds, *e.g.*, **intercolo'nial** *a.* between colonies. -**interrela'tion** *n.* mutual relation, *etc.* Such words are not given where the meaning and derivation may easily be inferred from the simple word. [L. *inter*, between]

interac'tive lang'uage *n.* (*compute.*) means or method by which programmers communicate while executing a program.

inter′calary, inter′calar *a.* inserted, as days, months, to adjust calendar to solar year. **-inter′calcate** *v.t.* insert thus. **-intercala′tion** . **-inter′calative** *a.* [L. *intercalate, intercalate,* fr. *calare*, call, proclaim]

intercede′ *v.i.* plead. **-intercession** *n.* **-intercess′or** *n.* [L. *cedere, cess-,* go]

intercept′ *v.t.* cut off, seize in transit. **-intercep′tion** *n.* [L. *capere, capt-,* take]

intercil′ium *n.* space between the eyebrows. [L. *cilia,* eyelids, eyelashes]

in′tercourse *n.* mutual dealings; communication; connection. [OF. *entrecours,* fr. *entrecourre,* run between]

in′terdict *n.* prohibition; prohibitory decree. **-interdict′** *v.t.* prohibit; restrain. **-interdiction** *n.* **-interdict′ory** *a.* [L. *interdicere, interdict-,* decree]

in′terest *n.* concern, curiosity; thing exciting this; money paid for use of borrowed money; legal concern; right; advantage; personal influence. *-v.t.* excite interest; cause to feel interest. **-interesting** *a.* **-in′terestingly** *adv.* [L. *interesse,* be a concern to]

interfere′ *v.i.* meddle; clash; of rays, *etc.*, strike together. **-interfe′rence** *n.* in telecommunications, spoiling of reception by other signals on similar wave-lengths, or by atmospheric conditions. **-interfe′ringly** *adv.* [L. *ferire,* strike]

in′terim *n.* meantime. *-a.* temporary, intervening. [L. = meanwhile]

inte′rior *a.* situated within; inland. *-n.* inside, inland. [L. comp. of *interns,* fr. L. *intra,* within]

interja′cent *a.* intervening. [L. *jacere,* lie]

interjec′tion *n.* word thrown in, or uttered abruptly. **-interject′** *v.t.* [L. *interjectio,* fr. *jicere, ject-,* throw]

interloc′utor *n.* one who takes part in a conversation or in dialogue. **-interlocu′tion** *n.* dialogue, **-interloc′utory** *a.* [L. *loqui, locut-,* speak]

in′terloper *n.* one intruding in another's affairs. [Du. *enterlooper,* smuggling ship, fr. *loosen,* run]

in′terlude *n.* intermission in a play; something filling it, as music, intermezzo; interval. [L. *ludus,* play]

interlu′nar *a.* (period) between old moon and new. [*lunar]*

interme′diate *a.* coming between two; interposed. **-interme′diary** *n.* one acting between two parties, go-between. [L. *medius,* middle]

intermezz′o (-dz-) *n.* short performance between acts of a play or opera; short musical interlude. [It.]

interm′inable *a.* endless. **-interm′inably** *adv.* [*terminable*]

intermit′ *v.t.* and *i.* stop for a time. **-intermis′sion** *n.* **-intermitt′ent** *a.* ceasing at intervals. [L. *mittere,* put, send]

intern′ *v.t.* oblige to live within prescribed limits. *-n.* resident assistant surgeon, physician, in hospital. also **interne′** **-intern′ment** *n.* [F. *interner,* fr. *interne,* resident within)

inter′nal *a.* in, of, the interior; of home (as opposed to foreign) affairs. **-inter′nal-combus′tion en′gine,** engine driven by explosions of gas within its cylinder. [L. *internus*]

interna′tional (-nash-) *a.* between nations. *-n.* international (games, *etc.*) contest; one taking part in such. **-internationale′** *n.* socialist hymn. **-interna′tionally** *adv* . *nationa]*

interne′cine *a.* mutually destructive; formerly, deadly. [L. *necare,* kill, and *inter-,* with intensive force]

inter′pellate *v.t.* to interrupt the business of the day in an assembly in order to demand an explanation. **-interpella′tion** *n.* [L. *interpellere,* interrupt]

inter′polate *v.t.* put in new (*esp.* misleading) matter (in book, *etc.*). **-interpola′tion** *n.* **-inter′polative** *a.* [L. *interpolale,* furbish up]

interpose′ *v.t.* insert; say as interruption; put in the way. *-v.i.* intervene; obstruct, mediate. **-interposi′tion** *n.* [F. *interposer]*

inter′pret *v.t.* explain; explain to oneself; translate for another's benefit; in art, render, represent. **-inter′preter** *n.* **- interpretation** *n.* [L. *interpretari*]

inter′preter *n.* (*compute.*) computer program which converts information from programming language into machine language.

interreg′num *n.* interval between reigns. **-in′terrex** *n.* regent. [L.]

interr′ogate *v.t.* question *esp.* closely or officially. **-interroga′tion** *n.* **-interrog′tive** *a.* questioning; used in asking a question. **-interr′ogator** *n.* **-interrog′atory** *a.* of enquiry. *-n.* question. set of questions. [L. *rogare*, ask]

interrupt′ *v.t.* break in upon; stop the course of. **-interrup′tion** *n.* [L. *rumpere, rapt-,* break]

intersect′ *v.t.* cut into or through; divide;

cross (each other). -**intersec'tion** *n.* -**intersec'tional** *a.* [L. *secare, sect-*, cut]

intersperse' *v.t.* scatter; diversify. -**intersper'sion** *n.* [L. *spargere, spars-*, scatter]

inter'stice *n.* chink, gap. -**intersti'tial** *a.* [fr. L. *intersistere*, stand between]

in'terval *n.* pause, break, intervening time or space; difference of pitch between any two musical tones. [L. *intervallum*, orig. space between ramparts]

intervene' *v.i.* happen in the meantime; be placed, come in, between others; interfere. -**interven'tion** *n.* interference; mediation. [L. *venire*, come]

in'terview *n.* meeting, *esp.* formally arranged; meeting of a journalist and person whose views he wishes to publish.-*v.t.* have an interview with. -**in'terviewer** *n.* [F. *entrevue*, fr. *voir*, see]

intest'ate *a.* not having made a will. -*n.* intestate person. -**intes'tacy** *n.* [L. *testari, testat-*, make a will]

intest'ine *a.* internal. civil. -*n.* (usu. *pl.*) lower part of the alimentary canal. -**intest'inal** *a.* [L. *intestines*)

in'timate *a.* familiar, closely acquainted; close. -*n.* intimate friend. -**in'timacy** *n.* -**in'timate** *v.t.* make known; announce. -**intima'tion** *v.i.* [L. *intimatus*]

in'timidate *v.t.* force or deter by threats. -**intimida'tion** *n.* -**intim'idator** *n.* [Late L. *intimidate*, fr. *timidus*, timid]

in'to *prep.* expresses motion to a point within. [*in to*]

intone' *v.t.* recite in monotone or singing voice. -**intona'tion** *n.* modulation of voice; intoning. [Church L. *intoniare*, fr. *tonus*, tone]

intox'icate *v.t.* make drunk; excite beyond self-control. -**intox'icant** *a.* **intoxicating.** -*n.* intoxicating liquor. -**intoxication** *n.* [G. *toxicon*, arrow poison]

intran'sigent *a.* refusing to come to terms. -*n.* politically irreconcilable. -**intran'-sigence, -intran'sigency** *n.* [F. *intransigeant*, fr. Sp. *in transigentes*, extreme Republican party]

intrep'id *a.* fearless. -**intrepid'ity** *n.* [L. *trepidus*, alarmed]

in'tricate *a.* involved, puzzlingly entangled. -**in'tricately** *adj.* -**in'tricacy** *n.* [L. *intricatus*, entangled]

intrigue' *n.* underhand plotting or plot; secret love affair. -*v.i.* carry on an intrigue. -*v.t.* whet the interest of, fascinate. -**intri'guer** *n.* [F., fr. L. *intricare*, entangle, *v.s.*]

intrin'sic *a.* inherent, essential. -**intrin'sically** *adv.* -**intrinsical'ity** *n.* [L. *intrinsecus, adv.* inwardly]

introduce' *v.t.* bring in, forward; make known formally; bring to notice; insert. -**introduc'tion** *n.* preface to a book. -**introduc'tory** *a.* [L. *introducere*, lead in]

in'troit *n.* in R.C. church, anthem sung at beginning of service as priest approaches altar. [L. *intro*, inwards, *ire*, go]

introrse' *a.* turned, facing, inwards. [L. *introrsus*, towards the middle]

introspec'tion *n.* examination of one's own thoughts. -**introspec'tive** *a.* -**introspect'ively** *adv.* [L. *introspicere, introspect-*, look within]

introvert' *v.t.* turn inwards. -*n.* (in'-) (*psych.*) introspective person, one whose mind is turned within. -**introversion** *n.* [L. *vertere*, turn]

intrude' *v.i.* thrust in without invitation or right. -*v.t.* force in. -**intru'sion** *n.* -**intru'sive** *a.* [L. *intruders, intrus-*, thrust in]

intui'tion (-ish-) *n.* immediate or direct apprehension by the mind without reasoning; immediate insight. -**intu'itive** *a.* -**intu'itively** *adv.* [Med. L. *intuitio*, fr. *inteuri, intuit-*, look upon]

intussuscep'tion *n.* withdrawal of part of a tube (*e.g.*, the bowel) into an adjacent part. (L. *intus*, within, *suscipere, suscept-*, take]

in'undate *v.t.* flood. -**inunda'tion** *n.* [L. *inundate*, fr. *unda*, wave]

inure' *v.t.* accustom [*in-*, into and obs. *ure*, work fr. F. *oeuvre*, work]

invade' *v.t.* enter with hostile intent; assail; encroach on. -**inva'der** *n.* -**inva'sion** *n.* [L. *invadere, invas-*, go in]

inval'id *a.* not valid, of no legal force. -**inval'idate** *v.t.* -**invalid'ity** *n.* -**in'valid** *a.* ill, enfeebled by sickness or injury. -*n.* person so disabled. [L, *invalidus* fr. *validus*, strong]

inval'uable *a.* above price. [*valuable]*

in'var *n.* alloy of steel and nickel used for making scientific instruments. [For invariability] [Trademark]

inva'sion. *See* **invade.**

inveigh' *v.i.* speak violently (against). -**invective** *n.* abusive speech or oratory. [L. *invehere, inuect-*, carry into; E. sense fr. the passive, 'to be carried away against (in words)']

invei'gle *v.t.* entice, seduce. -**invei'glement** *n.* [F. *aveugler*, blind]

invent' *v.t.* devise, originate. -**inven'tion**

n. **-invent'ive** *a.* **-invent'ively** *adv.* - **invent'or** *n.* [L. *invenire, invent-*, come upon, discover]

in'ventory *n.* list of goods, *etc.* -*v.t.* enter in an inventory. [L. *inventarium*]

invert' *v.t.* turn upside down; reverse the position or relations of. **-in'verse** *a.* inverted. -*n.* opposite. **-in'versely** *adv.* - **inver'sion** *n.* **-inverse ratio**, the ratio of reciprocals. [L. *invertere, invers-*,]

inver'tebrate *a/n.* (animal) with no backbone; spineless, weak. [L. *in-*, and *vertebra*]

invest' *v.t.* lay out (money); clothe; endue; cover as a garment; lay siege to. - **invest'iture** *n.* formal installation of person in office or rank. **-invest'ment** *n.* investing; money invested; stocks and shares bought. **-invest'or** *n.* [L. *inuestire*, clothe]

invest'igate *v.t.* inquire into. - **investiga'tion** *n.* **-invest'igator** *n.* [L. *investgare*, fr. *vestigare*, track]

invet'erate *a.* deep-rooted, long established. **-invet'eracy** *n.* [L. *inveterate*, make old, *vetus, veter-*]

invid'ious *a.* likely to arouse ill-will, envy, or resentment. **-invid'iously** *adv.* [L. *invidiosus*, fr. *invidia*, envy]

invig'ilate *v.t.* supervise at examinations. **-invigilation** *n.* **-invigilator** *n.* [L. *in*, on, and *vigilare*, watch]

invigorate *v.t.* give vigor to. - **invig'orating** *a.* strengthening. [*See* **vigorous**]

invin'cible *a.* unconquerable. - **invincibil'ity** *n.* [L. *vincere*, conquer]

invite' *v.t.* request courteously; attract, tend to call forth. **-invita'tion** *n.* **-invi'ting** *a.* enticing, attractive. invitingly *adv.* [L. *invitare*]

in'voice *n.* list of goods sent, with prices. -*v.t.* make an invoice of. [*pl.* of obs, *invoy*, F. *envoi*, sending]

invoke' *v.t.* call on; appeal to; ask earnestly for. **-invoca'tion** *n.* [L. *invocare*, fr. *vocare*, call]

invol'untary *a.* without power of will or choice; unintentional. [L. *involuntarius*]

involve' *v.t.* wrap up, entangle, implicate; imply, entail. **-in'volute** *a.* intricate; rolled spirally. **-involu'tion** *n.* [L. *involvere*, fr. *volvere, volut-*, roll]

in'ward *adv.* towards the inside, centre. -*a.* internal; in the heart, mind. **-in'wardly** *adv.* **-in'wardness** *n.* inner meaning. [OE. *innanweard*]

I/O *n.* equipment or data used to communicate with a computer [*I*nput/*O*utput]

i'odine *n.* non-metallic element of the chlorine group, used in medicine. **-i'odize** *v.t.* treat with iodine. **-io'doform** *n.* antiseptic. [G. *iodes*, violet-colored, fr. color of its vapor]

i'on *n.* electrically charged atom or group of atoms. **-io'nium** *n.* radioactive element. **-i'onize** *v.t.* divide into ions. **-ioniza'tion** *n.* [G. = going]

ion'ic *a.* of Iona in Greece, pert. to style of architecture characterized by column with ramshorn volute at top. [Ionia]

io'ta *n.* Greek letter *i;* an atom, jot, insignificant particle. [G.]

ipecacuan'ha *n.* root of a S. Amer. plant used as an emetic; the plant. (Port. fr. native name]

ire *n.* anger, wrath. **-irate** *a.* angry. - **iras'cible** *a.* hot-tempered. **-irascibil'ity** *n.* **-iras'cibly** *adv.* [L. *ira*]

ire'nic *a.* making for peace; pacific. [G. *eirene*, peace]

irid'ium *n.* white heavy metal allied to platinum. [*iris*]

i'ris *n.* genus of plants with sword-shaped leaves and showy flowers: circular membrane of the eye containing the pupil; formerly, rainbow. **-irides'cent** *a.* showing colors like a rainbow; changing color with change of position. **-irides'cence** *n.* [G. = *rainbow*]

I'rish *a.* of Ireland. **-I'rish bull'**, laughable contradiction in speech. **-I'rish moss'**, carrageen. **-I'rish stew'**, stew of mutton, onions, potatoes. [OE. *Irise*]

irk *v.t.* weary, trouble. **-irk'some** *a.* [ME. irken, weary, disgust]

i'ron *n.* metal, much used for tools, utensils, *etc.*, and the raw material of steel: tool, *etc.*, of this metal; smoothing iron; (*golf*) iron-headed club. -*pl.* fetters- *a.* of, or like, iron; inflexible, unyielding; robust. -*v.t.* smooth, cover, bind, *etc.*, with iron or an iron. **-i'ron-clad** *a.* protected with iron. -*n.* ship so protected. **-i'ron lung'**, external apparatus for inflation, deflating, of lung (in paralysis). **-i'ronmaster** *n.* manufacturer of iron. **-i'ronmonger** *n.* dealer in hardware. [OE. *iren*]

i'rony *n.* speech in which the meaning is the opposite of that actually expressed; words used with an inner meaning. - **iron'ical** *a.* **-iron'ically** *adv.* [G. *eironeia*, dissimulation, affected ignorance]

ir- *prefix* for *in* - before '*r*'. Many words are omitted in which the prefix simply negatives the idea of the simple word, as in *irregular a.* not regular, *etc.* **irra'diate** *v.t.* shine upon, throw light upon. -

irradia'tion *n.* [L. *radius*, ray]
irref'ragable *a.* that cannot be refuted. [L. *refragari*, oppose]
irrespec'tive *a.* without taking account (of), without regard (to). [*respect*]
irr'igate *v.t.* water by channels or streams. **-irriga'tion** *n.* **-irr'igator** *n.* [L. *irrigare*, irrigate, fr. *rigare*, moisten]
irri'tate *v.t.* excite to anger; excite, inflame, stimulate. **-irrita'tion** *n.* **-irritant** *a.* causing irritation. *-n.* thing doing this. **-irr'itable** *a.* easily annoyed. **-irr'itably** *adv.* [L. *irritare, irritat*]
irrup'tion *n.* invasion; bursting in. [L. *irruption* fr. *rumpere, rupt-*, break]
is *v.* 3rd. pers. sing. pres. of *be.* [OE.]
i'singlass (-iz'ing-glas) *n.* gelatin obtained from fish, *esp.* sturgeon, lobster. [Du. *huysenblas*, lit. sturgeon bladder]
Is'lam, Is'lamism *n.* the Muslim religion; the entire Muslim world. **-Islamic** *a.* [Ar., *slam -salama*, to submit to God]
i'sland (-il-) piece of land surrounded by water; anything like this, *e.g.*, a street refuge. **-i'slander** *n.* dweller on an island. [earlier *iland*, OE. *iegland*]
isle (-il) *n.* island, little island. [OF. *isle*, L. *insula*]
ism *n.* doctrine, theory, practice, *esp.* of a faddy or extravagant nature. [Suffix *-ism*, G. *-ismos*]
i'so *pref.* equal. [G. *isos*]
i'sobar *n.* line (on chart *etc.*) connecting places of equal barometric pressure. [G. *baros*, weight]
isocli'nal *n.* line connecting places where dip, inclination of magnetic needle is the same. *-a.* [G. *klinein*, bend]
i'solate *v.t.* place apart or alone. **-isola'tion** *n.* **-isola'tionism** *n.* political doctrine of (national) isolation. [L. *insula*, island]
isom'erism *n.* relation between substances with same elements in same proportions but with different chemical properties. **-i'somer** *n.* **-isomer'ic** *a.* [G. *meros*, part]
isos'celes *a.* of a triangle, having two of its sides equal. [G. *isosceles*, fr. *isos*, equal, and *skelos*, leg]
i'sotherm *n.* a line passing through points of equal mean temperature. [fr. G. *isos*, equal, and *therme*, heat]
i'sotope *n.* element chemically identical with others, but having a different nuclear mass, hence atomic weight. [G. *topos*, place]
iss'ue *n.* going or passing out; outlet; offspring, children; outcome, result; question, dispute; a sending or giving out officially or publicly; number or amount so given out. *-v.i.* go out; result in; arise (from). *-v.t.* emit, give out, send out. [OF. *issir*, go out, L. *exire*]
isth'mus *n.* a narrow neck of land connecting two larger areas. [G. *isthmos*]
it *pron.* neuter pronoun of the third person. **-itself** *pron.* reflex and emphatic of it. [OE. *hit*]
ital'ic *a.* of type, sloping. **-ital'ics** *n. pl.* this type, now used for emphasis, foreign words, *etc.* **-ital'icize** *v.t.* put in italics. [L. *Italicus*, Italian]
itch *v.i.* feel an irritation in the skin; be anxious or keen to. *-n.* irritation in the skin; impatient desire. **-itch'y** *a.* [OE. *giccan*]
i'tem *n.* any of a list of things; detail; entry in an account or list. *-adv.* **-itemize** *v.t.* list item by item; give particulars. [L. *adv* = in like manner; formerly used in inventories to introduce entries]
it'erate *v.t.* repeat. **-itera'tion** *n.* **-it'erative** *a.* [L. *iterare-iterum*, again]
itin'erant *a.* travelling from place to place; travelling on circuit. **-itin'eracy** *n.* **-itin'erary** *n.* record of travel; route, line of travel; guide-book. [L. *iter, itiner-*, journey]
i'vory *n.* hard white substance of the tusks of elephants, *etc.* **-ivory black** *n.* black pigment from burnt ivory. [F. *iuoire*]
i'vy *n.* climbing evergreen plant. **-i'vied** *a.* overgrown with ivy. [OE. *ifig*]

J

jab *v.t.* poke roughly, thrust abruptly.*-n.* poke.[var.of job]
jabb'er *v.i.* chatter rapidly. *-v.t.* utter thus. *-n.* gabble. [imit.]
jab'ot *n.* frill on bodice, *etc.* [F,]
jacaran'da *n.* S. American hardwood tree. [Braz.]
jac'inth *n.* reddish-orange precious stone. [L. *hyacinthus*]
jack *n.* sailor; boy, servant; knave in a pack of cards; various mechanical appliances, *esp.* for raising heavy weights; flag or ensign; various small things; added to names of animals, indicates male, as in **jack'ass**, or small, as in **-jack-snipe**. [F., *Jacques*, James, but in E. a pet form of John]
jack *n.* leather coat; leather bottle for liquor. [F. *Jacque*]
jack'al *n.* wild animal closely allied to the dog. [Pers. *shagal*]

jack'anapes *n.* pert child; impertinent fellow.

Jack o' Naples *n.* pet monkey

jackaroo' *n.* (Austr. *sl.*) greenhorn, novice. [*Jack* and *kangaroo*]

jack'ass *n.* male donkey; stupid fellow [Jack = the *male,* and *ass*]

jack'boot *n.* large boot coming above the knee. [orig. uncertain]

jack'daw *n.* small crow, daw. [Jack, *daw*]

jack'et *n.* sleeved outer garment, a short coat; outer casing. [F. *jaquette*]

Jacobe'an *a.* of the reign of James I. of England (1603-25). **Jac'obin** *n.* Dominican friar; member of a democratic club set up in 1789 in Paris in a Jacobin convent; extreme radical. **Jac'obite** *n.* adherent of the Stuarts after the abdication of James II. **Jacob's ladder** *n.* plant; rope-ladder with wooden rungs. [L. *Jacobus,* James]

jacta'tion *n.* act of throwing; boasting. [L. *jactare,* throw about]

jactita'tion *n.* false representation of being married to another; (*med.*) restlessness. [Med. L. *jactitatio*]

jacu'zzi *n.* system of underwater jets that keep the water in a bath or pool constantly agitated; a bath or pool equipped with this. [Trademark]

jade *n.* sorry nag, worn-out horse; in contempt, a woman. *-v.t.* tire out; weary. [orig. uncertain]

jade *n.* ornamental stone, usually green. **-jade'ite** *n.* a green or white complex silicate, translucent stone; true jad. [Sp. (*piedra de) ijada, colie* (stone), as supposed to cure pain]

jae'ger *n.* German rifleman; a kind of skua. [Ger. *huntsman*]

jag *n.* sharp projection, *e.g.,* point of rock. **-jagg'ed** *a.* [orig. unknown]

jag'uar *n.* large spotted, wild animal of the cat tribe. [Braz. *jaguara*]

jail *n.* building for confinement of criminals or suspects; *-v.t.* send to, confine in prison. **-jail'er, jail'or** *n.* **-jail'bird** *n.* hardened criminal. [OF. *gaole,* prison]

jal'ap *n.* purgative. [*Jalapa* or *Xalapa,* in Mexico]

jalousie' *n.* outside slatted shutters. [F. = *jealousy*]

jam *v.t.* squeeze; cause to stick and become unworkable; pack together; interfere with. *-v.i.* stick and become unworkable. *-n.* fruit preserved by boiling with sugar; blockage, *esp.* traffic; musical improvisation by a group of musicians. [orig. uncertain]

jamb (jam) *n.* door-post. [F. *jambe,* leg]

jamai'ca-pepp'er *n.* allspice. (. Jamaica, W. I.]

jamboree' *n.* spree, celebration. [orig. uncertain]

jang'le (-ng-gl) *v.i.* sound harshly, as a bell. *-v.t.* make do this. *-n.* harsh metallic sound; wrangle. [OF. *jangler*]

jan'issary, jan'izary *n.* formerly, soldier of the bodyguard of the Turkish Sultan. [Turk. *yeni cheri,* new soldiery]

jan'itor *n.* caretaker, doorkeeper. [L.]

Jan'uary *n.* first month of the year. [L. *januarius,* of Janus]

japan' *n.* very hard varnish. *-v.t.* cover with this. [Japan]

jape *n.* joke. *-v.i.* joke. [OF. *japer*]

japon'ica *n.* Japanese quince. [Med. L. *Pyrus japonica*]

jar *n.* vessel of glass, earthenware, *etc.* [Arab., *iarrah,* earthen vessel]

jar *v.i.* make a grating noise; vibrate gratingly, wrangle. *v.t.* cause to vibrate. *-n.* jarring sound; shock, *etc.* [imit.]

jar'gon *n.* barbarous or distorted language; gibberish; excessively technical language. [F.]

jargonelle' *n.* early pear. [F,]

jarr'ah *n.* Western Australian mahogany gum-tree. [native]

jas'mine, jas'min, jessamine *n.* flowering shrub. [Arab. *yasmin*]

jas'per *n.* red, yellow, or brown stone, kind of quartz. [G. *iaspis*]

jaundice (-dis) *n.* disease marked by yellowness of the skin. **-jaun'diced** *a.* jealous, of soured outlook. [F. *jaunisse,* fr. *jaune,* yellow]

jaunt *n.* short pleasure excursion. *-v.i.* make one. **-jaunt'ing-car** *n.* two-wheeled vehicle common in Ireland. [orig. uncertain]

jaunt'y *a.* sprightly; briskly pleased with life. **-jaunt'ily** *adv.* [F. *gentil*]

jav'elin *n.* light spear for throwing. [F. *javelins*]

jaw *n.* one of the bones in which the teeth are set. *-pl.* mouth; gripping part of vice, *etc.* [F. *joue,* cheek]

jay *n.* noisy bird of brilliant plumage; chatterer. **-jay'walk'er,** careless pedestrian, *esp.* one who ignores traffic rules. [F. *geai*]

jazz *n.* syncopated music and dance. *-v.i.* indulge in jazz. *-a.* discordant or bizarre in color, *etc.* **-jazz up'** (*sl.*) liven. [orig. unknown]

jeal'ous *a.* suspiciously watchful; distrustful of the faithfulness (of); envious; anxiously solicitous (for). **-jeal'ousy** *n.* **jeal'ously** *adv.* [F. *jaloux*]

jean *n.* twilled cotton cloth. *-n. pl.* overalls; trousers. [Genoa]

jeep' *n.* small high-powered open car first used in U.S. army. [G.P., for 'general purposes']

jeer *v.t.* and *i.* scoff, deride. *-n.* scoff, mocking taunt. [orig. uncertain]

Jeho'vah *n.* Hebrew name for God. [Heb. *Yahweh*]

jejune' *a.* poor, uninteresting, unsatisfying. [L. *jejunus*, fasting]

jell'y *n.* semi-transparent food made with gelatin, becoming stiff as it cools; anything of the consistency of this. **-jel'lify** *v.t., v.i.* transform into a gelatinous substance or food. **-jell'y-fish** *n.* jelly-like small sea-animal. [F. *gelée*, fr. *geler*, freeze]

jenn'et *n.* small Spanish horse. [Sp. *ginete*, fr. Moorish]

jeop'ardy *n.* danger. **-jeop'ardize** *v.t.* endanger. [F. *jeu parti*, even game]

jerbo'a *n.* small, jumping desert rodent. (Arab. *yarbu*]

jeremi'ad *n.* doleful complaint, tale of woe. [*Jeremiah*]

jerk *n.* sharp, abruptly stopped movement, twitch, start, sharp pull. *-v.t.* and *i.* move, or throw, with a jerk; sneer. **-jerk'y** *a.* spasmodic. **-jerk'ily** *adv.* **jerk'iness** *n.* [orig. unknown]

jerk' *v.t.* cut (beef) in strips and dry. **jerked'beef** *n.* beef so treated. [Peruv. *echarqui*]

jer'kin *n.* close-fitting jacket, *esp.* of leather. [Du. *jurk*, frock]

jerry-built *a.* of flimsy construction with bad materials. **-jer'ry-builder** *n.* [orig. uncertain]

jer'sey (-z-) *n.* close-fitted knitted jacket. [*Jersey*, in Channel Islands]

jest *n.* joke. *-v.i.* joke. **-jest'er** *n.* joker, *esp.* professional fool of a court. [F. *geste*, exploit]

Jes'uit *n.* member of the Society of Jesus, an Order founded by Ignatius Loyola in 1533. **-Jesuit'ical** *a.* [Jesus]

jet *n.* hard black mineral capable of a brilliant polish. [G. *gagates*]

jet *n.* stream of liquid, gas, *etc.*, *esp.* shot from a small hole; the small hole; spout, nozzle; aircraft driven by jet propulsion. *-v.t.* and *i.* spurt out in jets. **-jet lag** *n.* fatigue caused by crossing time zones in jet aircraft. **-jet'-propul'sion** *n.* mode of propulsion with jet (of air, gas, fluid) as motive power. **-jet set** *n.* rich, fashionable social set, members of which travel widely for pleasure. [F., fr. *jeter*, to throw]

jet'sam *n.* goods thrown out to lighten a ship and later washed ashore. **-jett'ison** *v.t.* throw overboard thus. [OF. *jetaison*, fr. *jeter*, throw]

jett'y *n.* small pier or landing-place. [F. *jetge*, fr. *jeter*, throw]

jew'el *n.* precious stone; personal ornament containing one; precious thing. **jew'eler,** *n.* dealer in jewels. **-jew'elry** *n.* [OF. *goiel*]

jib *n.* ship's triangular staysail. *-v.t.* pull over (a sail) to the other side; of a horse or person, to stop and refuse to go on, object to precede. **-jibboom'** *n.* spar from the end of the bowsprit. **-jibb'er** *n.* a jibbing horse. [var. of *gybe*]

jibe *v.i.* of the boom of a for-and-aft sail, to swing over to the other side with following wind. *-v.t.* cause this; change course thus. [Du. *gijpen*]

jiffy *n.* (*colloq.*) instant. [orig. unknown]

jig *n.* lively dance; music for it; various mechanisms or fittings. *-v.i.* dance a jig; make jerky up-and-down movements. **-jig'saw** *n.* machine fretsaw. **-jig'saw puzzle** picture cut into irregular pieces to be fitted together again. **-jigg'er** *n.* **-jigg'ered** *a.* (*sl.*) confounded. exhausted. [orig. uncertain]

jilt *v.t.* cast off (over) after encouraging. *-n.* one who does this. [earlier *jillet*, dim. of Jill]

jimm'y *n.* burglar's crowbar. [James]

jing'le *n.* metallic noise. as of shaken chain; repetition of same sounds in words. *-v.i.* make the sound. *-v.t.* cause to make it. [imit.]

jing'o (-ng-g-) warmonger. **-jingo'ism** *n.* **-by Jingo,** a form of asseveration. [orig. uncertain; political sense due to use of *by Jingo* in music-hall song (1878)]

jinx' *n.* unlucky thing, person; hoodoo. [L. *iynx*]

jit'ney *n.* motor bus running on set routes at low fare. *-a.* cheap, shoddy. [perh. F. *eton*, a counter]

jitt'ers *n. pl.* state of nerves, trepidation. **-jitt'ery** *a.* **-jitt'erbug** *n.* jazz dance, dancer; alarmist. [prob, imit.]

jiu-jit'su. *See* **ju-jitsu.**

jive *n.* spectacular swing music. [orig. unknown]

job *n.* piece of work; employment; unscrupulous transaction. *-v.i.* do odd jobs:

deal in stocks. -**jobb'er** *n*.- **Jobbery** *n*. - **job'master** *n*. one who hires horses. [orig. uncertain]

job *n*. prod, jab. [imit.]

jock'ey *a*. professional rider in horse-races. -*v.t*. cheat; maneuver. [dim. of *Jock*, var. of Jack]

jocose' *a*. waggish, humorous. **jocosity** *n*. -**joc'ular** *a*. joking, given to joking. - **jocular'ity** *n*. [L. *jocus*. game]

joc'und *a*. merry. -**jocund'ity** *n*. [L. *jucundus*, pleasant]

jodh'purs *n*. *pl*. riding breeches, tight from knee to ankle. [*Jodhpur*, India]

jog *v.t*. move or push with a jerk. -*v.i*. walk or ride with jolting pace; take exercise. -*n*. a jogging. -**jog'ger** *n*. person who runs at a jog trot over some distance for exercise, usually regularly. -**jog'ging** *n*. running at a slow regular pace usually over a long distance as part of an exercise routine. - **jog'trot** *n*. slow regular trot. -**jog'gle** *v.t*. and *i*. move to and fro in jerks. -*n*. slight jog. -**jogg'le** *v.t*. and *i*. shake slightly. [orig. uncertain]

join *v.t*. put together. fasten, unite. -*v.i*. become united or connected. -*n*. a joining; place of joining. -**join'er** *n*. one who joins; maker of furniture and light woodwork. -**join'ery** *n*. his work. -**joint** *n*. arrangement by which two things fit or are joined together, rigidly or loosely: bone with meat on, as food, low-class public house.-*a*. common: share of or by two or more. -*v.t*. connect by joints: divide at the joints. - **joint'ly** *adv*. -**joint'-stock** *n*. common stock, share, capital. -**join'ture** *n*. property settled on a wife for her use after the husband's death. [F. *joindre*, fr. L. . *jungere, junct-*, join]

joist *n*. parallel beam stretched from wall to wall on which to fix floor or ceiling. [OF. *giste*, fr. L. *jacere*, lie]

jojob'a (hohoba) *n*. a shrub or small tree of SW North America that has edible seeds containing a valuable oil. [Mex. Sp.]

joke *n*. thing said or done to cause laughter, something not in earnest. *v.i*. make jokes. *v.t*. banter. -**jo'ker** *n*. [L. *jocus*, jest]

joll'y *a*. festive, merry. -**joll'ity** *n*. - **jollifica'tion** *n*. merrymaking. [F. *joli]*

joll'y-boat *n*. small ship's boat. [orig. uncertain]

Jolly Roger *n*. pirate's flag: black with white skull and cross-bones. [*jolly* and *Roger*, name]

jolt *n*. jerk; throwing up or forwards. as from a seat -*v.t*. and *i*. move or shake with jolts. [orig. uncertain]

jon'quil *n*. rush-leaved, narcissus. [L. *juncus, rush*. fr. its rush-like leaves]

jor'um *n*. large drinking-bowl; its contents. [fr. name *Joram*]

josh' *v.t*. tease, ridicule. -*n*. hoax, jape. - **josh'er** *n*. [orig. uncertain]

joss' *n*. Chinese idol. -**joss-stick** *n*. incense-stick. [port. *deos*, god]

jos'tle *v.t*. and *i*. knock or push against. -*n*. a jostling. -**joust** *n*. encounter with lances between two mounted knights. -*v.i*. take part in a joust. [OF, jouster]

jot *n*. small amount. -*v.t*. write (down) briefly. -**jott'er** *n*. book for rough notes; one who jots. -**jott'ing** *n*. a rough note. [G. *iota*]

joule *n*. unit of electrical energy; unit of heat. [J. P. *Joule*, 1818-1891]

jour'nal *n*. daily record; logbook; daily newspaper or other periodical; part of an axle or shaft resting on the bearings. - **journalese'** *n*. jargon of journalists. - **jour'nalism** *n*. editing, or writing in, periodicals. -**jour'nalist** *n*. **journalis'tic** *a*. [F. *journal*, fr. L. *diurnalis*]

jour'ney *n*. a going to a place; distance traveled. *v.t*. travel. -**jour'neyman** *n*. one who has learned a trade and works as an artisan paid by the day, hireling. [*See* **journal**]

joust. *See* **jostle.**

jo'vial *a*. jolly, convivial. [*Jove*]

jowl *n*. cheek, jaw; outside of the throat when prominent. [orig. obscure]

joy *n*. gladness, pleasure; cause of this. -**joy'ful** *a*. -**joy'less** *a*. -**joy'fully** *adv*. - **joy'ous** *a*. -**joy'-ride** *n*. *(sl.)* pleasurable, reckless (and often unlawful) drive in a vehicle. -**joy'stick** *n*. control-lever, *esp*. of an airplane. [F. *joie*]

ju'bate *a*. maned. [L. *juba*, mane]

ju'bilate *v.i*. rejoice. -**ju'bilant** *a*. - **ju'bilantly** *adv*. -**jubila'tion** *n*. [L. *jubilare*, shout]

ju'bilee *n*. fiftieth anniversary; time of rejoicing. [Heb. *joebl*, horn, trumpet]

Juda'ic(al) *a*. of Jews. -**Ju'daize** *v.t*. /*i*. make, become Jewish in belief. **Ju'daism** *n*. doctrine of Jews. [G, *Joudaios*, Jew]

judge (juj) *n*. officer appointed to try and decide cases in law court; one who decides a dispute, question. contest; one fit to decide on the merits of a question or thing; umpire; in Jewish history, a ruler. -*v.i*. act as judge. -*v.t*. act as a judge of; try, estimate; decide. -**judg'ment** *n*. sentence of a court; opinion; faculty of judging: misfortune regarded as a sign of divine displeasure.

-**ju'dicature** *n.* administration of justice; body of judges. **judicial** (-ish-) *a.* of, or by, a court, or judge; proper to a judge; impartial; critical. -**judi'cially** *adv.* -**judi'cious** *a.* sensible, prudent. -**judi'ciously** *adv.* -**judi'ciary** *n.* courts of law, system of courts and judges. [L. *judex, n. judicare,* v., fr. *jus,* law]

ju'do *n.* variation on *ju-jitsu.* [Jap.]

jug *n.* deep vessel for liquids; contents of one. -*v.t.* stew (*esp.* a hare) in a jug or jar **jugged** *p.t./p.p.* **jugg'ing** *pres. p.; (sl.)* imprison. [orig. uncertain]

Jugg'ernaut (-nawt) *n.* symbolic image of Hindu God Krishna, dragged yearly in great car under wheels of which devotees are wrongly believed to have thrown themselves; belief to which person devotes himself. [Sans. *Jagannatha,* lord of world]

jugg'ins *n.* simpleton, sap. [orig. uncertain]

jug'gle *v.i.* play conjuring tricks, amuse by sleight of hand; practice deceit. -*v.t.* trick or cheat (out of). -*n.* a juggling. **jug'gler** *n.* -**jug'gler** *n.* -**jug'glery** *n.* [OF. *joglere,* L. *joculari,* jest]

jug'ular *a.* of or in the neck or throat. [L. *jugulum,* collar-bone]

juice *n.* liquid part of vegetable, fruit, meat; (coll.) gasoline or other source of power. -**juic'y** *a.* [L. *jus,* broth]

ju-jit'su, ju'jutsu *n.* Japanese art of wrestling and self-defense. [Jap. fr. Chin. *jou-shu,* 'gentle art']

ju'-ju *n.* West African fetish, charm. [F. *jou-jou,* toy]

ju'jube *n.* lozenge of gelatin, sugar, *etc.*, a fruit; shrub producing it. [G. *zizyphon,* jujube-tree]

juke-box *n.* automatic slot-machine playing records. [orig. unknown]

ju'lep *n.* sweet drink; medicated drink. [Pers. *gul-ab,* rose-water]

Ju'lian *a.* of Julius Caesar. -**Julian calendar**, calendar as established by Julius Caesar in 46 B. C. with year consisting of 365 days, 6 hours, instead of 365 days.

July' *n.* seventh month of the year. [L. birth-month of Julius *Caesar*]

jum'ble *v.t.* mingle, mix in confusion. -*v.i.* move about in disorder. -*n.* a confused heap, muddle. [imit. orig.]

jump *v.i.* spring from the ground. -*v.t.* pass by jumping. -*n.* leap, sudden upward movement. -**jump'er** *n.* -**jump'y** *a.* nervous. [of It. orig.]

jum'per *n.* sailor's loose jacket; woman's loose outer garment slipped over the head and reaching to the hips. [earlier *jump* fr. F. *jupe,* petticoat]

jun'co *n.* Amer. finch or show-bird. [L. *juncus.* rush]

junc'tion *n.* joining; place of joining; railway station where lines join. -**junc'ture** *n.* state of affairs; critical point. [L. *jungere, junct-,* join]

June *n.* sixth month of the year. [L. *Junius*]

jung'le (-ng-gl) *n.* tangled vegetation; land covered with it, *esp.* in India and the tropics; tangled mass. -**jung'ly** *a.* [Hind. *jangal,* Sans. *jangala,* desert]

jun'ior *a.* young person. -**junior'ity** *n.* [L., comp, of *juenis,* young]

juniper *n.* evergreen shrub with berries yielding oil of juniper, used for medicine and gin. [L. *juniperus*]

junk *n.* old rope; salt meat; old odds and ends. -**jun'k food** *n.* food that is low in nutritional value, often highly processed or ready-prepared, and eaten instead of or in addition to well-balanced meals. [orig. unknown]

junk *n.* sailing vessel of the Chinese seas. [Port. *junco*]

junk'et *n.* curdled milk flavored and sweetened. -*v.i.* feast, picnic. [orig. a basket, fr. L. *juncus,* reed]

junt'a *n.* council in Spain, Italy; group of persons, *esp.* military, holding power after a revolution. [Sp.]

Ju'piter *n.* Roman chief of gods; largest of the planets. [L.]

jurid'ical *a.* relating to the administration of law, legal. -**jurisconsult'** *n.* one learned in law. -**jurisdic'tion** *n.* administration of justice; authority; territory covered by a court or authority. **jurispru'dence** *n.* science of, and skill in, law. -**jurist** *n.* one skilled in law. **juris'tic** *a.* [L. *jus, jur-,* law]

jur'y *n.* body of persons sworn to render a verdict in a court of law; body of judges in a competition. -**jur'or** *n.* one who serves on a jury. [L. *jurare,* swear, fr. *jus,* law]

jur'y-mast *n.* temporary mast rigged in place of a broken one. [orig. obscure]

jus'sive *a.* expressing a command or order in grammar [L. *jussus*]

just *a.* upright, fair; proper, right, equitable. -*adv.* exactly, barely. -**just'ly** *adv.* -**justice** (-is) *n.* quality of being just, fairness; judicial proceedings; judge, magistrate. -**just'ify** *v.t.* show to be right or true or innocent; be sufficient grounds for. -**justifi'able** *a.* -**justifi'ably** *adv.* **justifica'tion** *n.* [L. *justus,* fr. *jus,* law, right]

jut *v.i.* project. *-n.* projection. [*jet*]
jute *n.* fiber of certain plants, used for rope, canvas, *etc.* [Bengali *jhoto*]
ju'venile *a.* young; of, or for, the youthful. *-n.* young person, child. **juvenil'ia** *n. pl.* early, youthful, writings. **-juvenility** *n.* **-juvenes'cent** *a.* becoming young. **-juvenes'cence** *n.* [L. *juvenilis-juvenis*, young]
juxtapose' (-z) *v.t.* put side by side. **juxtaposi'tion** *n.* [L. *juxta*, beside]

K

Kai'ser *n.* emperor, *esp.* of Germany. [L. *Caesar*]
kale, kail *n.* cabbage, cole; (Scot.) broth. **-kail'yard** *n.* kitchen garden. [L. *caulis*]
kaleid'oscope *n.* tube in which patterns are produced by reflection of pieces of colored glass as tube is rotated. **-kaleidoscop'ic** *a.* swiftly changing. [G. *kalos*, beautiful, *eidos*, shape]
kalol'ogy *n.* science of abstract beauty. [G. *kalos*, beautiful]
kalong' *n.* large Malay fruit-bat, the flying fox. [Malay]
kampong' *n.* village, enclosure. [Malay]
kangaroo' *n.* Australian pouched mammal with very strong hind legs for jumping. [orig. uncertain]
ka'olin *n.* fine white China clay. [Chin. *kaoting*, high hill, mountain where first found]
ka'pok *n.* fiber for cushions, *etc.*; a tree-cotton. [Malay *kapoq*]
kar'ma *n.* physical action; the law of cause and effect or ethical causation; self-created destiny. [Sans. = *action*]
katab'olism *n.* disruptive metabolism. [G. *katabollein*, throw down]
ka'tydid *n.* American insect resembling grasshopper. [imit.]
kau'ri *n.* New Zealand pine. **kau'ri-gum** *n.* its resin, used in varnish. [Maori]
kay'ak (ki-) *n.* skin-covered Eskimo canoe. [Eskimo]
kedge *n.* small anchor. *-v.t.* move (a ship) by a cable attached to a kedge. [ME. *caggen*, fasten]
kedg'eree *n.* dish of rice, fish, eggs, *etc.* [Hind. *khichri*]
keel *n.* lowest longitudinal timber, or steel substitute, on which a ship is built up. *-v.t.* turn keel up. capsize. **-keel'less** *a.* **-keel'son** *n.* line of timbers or plates bolted to the keel. [ON. *kjölr*]
keen *a.* sharp, vivid, acute, eager, strong. **-keenly** *adv.* [OE. *cene*]
keen *n.* funeral lament. *-v.i.* wail over the dead. [Ir. *caoine*]
keep *v.t.* observe, carry out; retain possession of, not lose; maintain; detain; cause to continue; reserve; manage. *-v.i.* remain good; remain; continue. *-n.* maintenance, food; central tower of a castle, a stronghold. **-keep'er** *n.* **-keep'ing** *n.* care, charge. possession; harmony, agreement. **-keep'sake** *n.* thing treasured for giver's sake. [OE. *cepan*]
keg *n.* small cask. [ON. *kaggi*, cask]
kelp *n.* large seaweed; ashes of it for extraction of iodine. [ME. *culp*]
kel'pie, kel'py *n.* water spirit in the form of a horse. [Sc.]
kelt *n.* newly-spawned salmon. [orig. unknown]
ken *v.t.* know. *-n.* range of knowledge. [OE. *cenrian*]
kenn'el *n.* house of shelter for dogs; place where dogs are bred or lodged; hovel. *-v.t.* put into a kennel. [F. *chenit*, fr. L. *canis*, dog]
kenn'el *n.* gutter. [AF. *canel.*]
ker'atin *n.* essential substance of horns, nails, *etc.* **-ker'atinize** *v.t.* and *i.* to make or become horny. **-ker'atose** *a.* horny. [G. *keras.* horn]
kerb. *See* **curb.**
ker'chief (-if) *n.* headcloth. [F. *couvrechef*, cover-head]
kerm'es *n.* cochineal insect used for red dyestuff. [Arab. *qirmiz* worm]
kern'el *n.* inner soft part of a nut or fruitstone; central or essential part. [OE. *kyrnel* dim. of corn]
ker'osene *n.* lamp-oil or burning oil from petroleum or coal and shale. [G. *keros*, wax]
kers'ey (-zi) *n.* coarse woolen cloth. [*Kersey*, Suffolk, England]
kers'eymere *n.* twilled cloth of fine wool. [corrupt. of cashmere]
kes'trel *n.* small hawk. [F. *crécerelle*]
ketch *n.* two-masted or cutter-rigged sailing vessel. [earlier catch, of uncertain orig.]
ketch'up. *See* **catsup.**
ket'tle *n.* metal vessel with spout and handle, for boiling liquids. **-ket'tledrum** *n.* drum of parchment stretched over a metal hemisphere. [ON. ketill]
key *n.* instrument for moving the bolt of a lock; *fig.* anything that 'unlocks'; music, a set of related notes, lever to play a note of piano, organ, *etc.* **-key'board** *n.* set of

keys on a piano, *etc*. **-key'grip** *n*. person in charge of moving and setting up camera tracks and scenery in a film or television studio. **-key'-hole** *n*. hole into which key is inserted. **-key'light** *n*. in photography, *etc*. the main stage or studio light that gives the required overall intensity of illumination. **-key'note** *n*. note on which a musical key is based; dominant idea. **-key'pad** *n*. small keyboard with push buttons, as on a pocket calculator, remote control unit for a television, *etc*.; a data input device consisting of a limited number of keys, each with nominated functions. **-key'stone** *n*. central stone of an arch which locks all in position. [OE. *caeg*]

key *See* **cay.**

kha'ki *a*. dull yellowish-brown. *-n*. khaki cloth, military uniform, [Pers. *khak*, dust]

kham'sin *n*. hot S. E. wind blowing in Egypt for about 50 days from mid-March. [Arab. *khamin*, fifty]

khedive' *n*. former title of viceroy of Egypt. [Pers. *khidiv*; prince]

ki'ao'ra *interj*. in N. Z., your health! [Maori]

kiang' *n*. Tibetan wild ass. [Tibet. *kyang*]

ki'bosh *n*. (*sl*.) nonsense. *-v.t*. put an end to, scotch. [orig. unknown]

kick *v.i*. strike out with the foot; be recalcitrant; recoil. *-v.t*. strike with the feet. *-n*. blow with the foot; recoil. [ME. *kiken*, of unknown orig.]

kick'shaws *n. pl*. toys, trifles; unidentified dainties at table. [F. *quelque* somethings]

kid *n*. young goat; leather of its skin; (*sl*.) child. *v.t*. (*sl*.) to hoax. [ON. *kith*]

kid'nap' *v.t*. steal (a child), abduct (a person). **-kid'naper** *n*. [*kid*, child, *nap*, nab]

kid'ney *n*. either of the pair of organs which secretes the urine; nature, kind. [orig. uncertain]

kil'derkin *n*. malt barrel; liquid measure (18 gals.). [Du. *kindeken*, dim. of *kind*, child]

kill *v.t*. deprive of life, slay. [ME. *kellen]*

kiln *n*. furnace, oven. [OE. *cylen*, L. *culina*, kitchen]

kil'ogram *n*. weight of 1,000 grams. **-kil'ometer** *n*. **-kil'oliter** *n*. **-kil'owatt** *n*. electrical power of 1,000 watts. [G. *chilioi*, thousand]

kilt *v.t*. gather in vertical pleats; tuck up. *-n*. short skirt-like garment, *esp*. tartan, worn by Scottish Highlanders. [Dan. *kilte*]

kil'ter *n*. proper or orderly arrangement; good dispostion: *usu*. preceded by *in* or *out of*.

kimo'no *n*. loose outer robe. [Jap.]

kin *n*. family, relatives. *-a*. related by blood. **-kin'dred** *n*. relatives. *-a*. related. **-kin'ship** *n*. **-kins'man** *n*.; **kins'woman** *fem*.; **kins'folk** *n*. [OE. *cynn*]

kind *n*. genus, sort, variety, class. *-a*. having a sympathetic nature, considerate, good, benevolent. **-kind'ly** *a*. kind, genial. **-kind'liness** *n*. **-kind'ly** *adj*. [OE. *gecynd*, nature]

kin'dergarten *n*. school for teaching young children by games, *etc*. [Ger. = children's garden; (coined by Froebel)]

kin'dle *v.t*. set on fire. *-v.i*. catch fire. **-kind'ling** *n*. act of lighting; small wood to kindle fires. [ON. *kynda*]

kine *n*. cows. [OE. *cu*, cow, double *pl*. *yen*]

kinemat'ic (ki-) *a*. relating to pure motion. *-n. pl*. science of this. **-kinemat'ograph** (*See* **cinematograph.**) **-kinet'ic** *a*. of motion in relation to force. *-n. pl*. science of this, [G. *kinein*, move]

king *n*. male sovereign ruler of an independent state; piece in the game of chess; card in each suit with a picture of a king. **-king'dom** *n*. state ruled by a king. realm, sphere. **-king'cup** *n*. marsh marigold. **-king'fisher** *n*. small bird of bright plumage which dives for fish. **-king's evil** *n*. scrofula, thought to be curable by a king's touch. **-king'ly** *a*. **king'ship** *n*. [OE. *ying*]

kink *n*. short twist of a rope, wire, *etc*. *-v.i*. and *t*. form a kink. [Scand.]

kin'kajou *n*. raccoon-like animal of South America. [Amer. Ind.]

kiosk *n*. small open pavilion; covered stall. [Turk. *kioshk*]

kip *n*. skin of young beast. **-kipskin** *n*. leather made from skin of young cattle between calf-skin and cow-hide. [orig. unknown]

kipp'er *v.t*. cure (fish) by splitting open, rubbing with salt, and drying or smoking. *-n*. kippered fish; salmon in spawning time. [OE. *cyperia*]

kirk *n*. in Scotland, church. [Scand.]

kir'tle *n*. mantle, gown, outer petticoat. **kir'tled** *a*. [OE. *cyrtl*]

kis'met *n*. fate, destiny. [Turk. *qismat*]

kiss *n*. caress with the lips. *-v.t., v.i*. exchange kisses. [OE. *cyssan*]

kit *n*. wooden tub; outfit; personal effects, *esp*. of traveller. **-kit'-bag** *n*. bag for soldier's or traveler's kit. [orig. uncertain]

kitch'en *n*. room used for cooking. **-kitch'en-garden** *n*. garden for vegetables, fruit. **-kitch'enmaid** *n*. **kitch'ener** *n*. cooking-range. **kitchenette** *n.* small compact kitchen. [OE. *cycene*]

kite *n.* bird of prey; light frame flown in wind. [OE. *cyta*]

kith *n.* acquaintances (only in *kith* and *kin*). [OE. *cyththu*]

kitt'en *n.* young cat. [var. of F. *chaton,* dim. of *chat,* cat]

kitt'iwake *n.* species of gull. [imit.]

ki'wi *n.* New Zealand wingless bird, the Apteryx. [Maori]

kleptoma'nia *n.* morbid tendency to steal for the sake of theft. **-kleptomaniac** *n.* [G. *kleptes,* thief]

klip'springer *n.* small S. African antelope. [Du. = *rock-springer*]

kloof' *n.* ravine. [Du. = *cleft*]

knack (n) *n.* toy, trifle; acquired faculty for doing something adroitly; trick. [orig. uncertain]

knack'er (n-) *n.* one who buys worn-out horses for slaughtering. [orig. uncertain]

knag (nag) *n.* knot in wood, peg. **-knag'gy** *a.* [cp. Ger. *knagge*]

knap (nap) *v.t.* break off with snapping sound; hammer to pieces; rap. [Du. *knappen,* crack]

knap'sack (n-) *n.* soldier's, traveler's, bag to strap to back. [Du. knapzak]

knave (na-) *n.* rogue; at cards, lowest court card, jack. **-kna'very** *n.* **-kna'vish** *a.* [orig. boy, OE. *cnafa*]

knead *v.t.* work up into dough; work, massage. [OE. *enedan*]

knee (n-) *n.* joint between the thigh and lower leg; corresponding joint in animals; part of a garment covering the knee. **-knee'cap** *n.* (also **kneepan** *n.*) knee, protective covering for a bone in the front of the knee. [OE. *cneow*]

kneel (n-) *v.i.* fall or rest on the knees. [OE. *cneowlian.* cp. knee]

knell (-n-) *n.* sound of a bell, *esp.* **at a** funeral or after a death. [OE. *cynll*]

knick'erbockers (n-) *n. pl.* loose-fitting breeches gathered in at the knee (also **knick'ers** *n. pl.*) [Cruikshank's illustrations to *Knickerbocker's* (Washington Irving's) History of New York]

knickknack (n-, n-) *n.* light dainty article, trinket. [*knack*]

knife (n-) *n.* (knives *pl.*) cutting blade in a handle. *-v.t.* cut or stab with a knife. **knife'board** *n.* board for cleaning knives [OE. *cnif*]

knight (nit) *n.* person of a rank below baronet, given the right to prefix Sir to his name; military follower, a champion; piece in the game of chess. *-v.t.* make (person) a knight. **-knight er'rant** *n.* knight wandering in search of adventure. **-knighthood** *n.* **-knight'age** *n.* the knights; list of them. **-knight'ly** *a.* **-knight-service** *n.* holding of land by knight in return for military service. [OE. *cniht,* youth]

knit (n-) *v.t.* form a fabric by putting together a series of loops in wool, or other yarn; make close or compact. *-v.i.* unite. [OE *cynttan*]

knit'tle *n.* purse string that gathers the top of the purse; draws in the top of the purse; a ship's line used to sling hammocks.

knob (n-) *n.* rounded lump, *esp.* at the end or on the surface of anything. **-knobb'y** *a.* [of Teutonic origin; cp. Ger. *knopf,* button]

knock (n-) *v.t.* strike, hit. *-n.* blow, rap. **-knock'er** *n.* who or what knocks; metal appliance for knocking on a door. **-knock'-kneed** *a.* having incurved legs. **-knock-'out** *n.* boxer's finishing blow. [OE. *cnocian*]

knoll *n.* small rounded hill, hillock. [OE. *cnoll*]

knop (nop) *n.* knob; bud. [M. E.]

knot (n-) *n.* twisting together of parts of two or more strings, ropes, *etc.*, to fasten them together; cockade, cluster; hard lump, *esp.* of wood where a branch joins or has joined in; measure of speed of ships, *e.g.*, ten knots means ten nautical miles per hour; difficulty. *-v.t.* tie with or in knots. **-knott'y** *a.* full of knots; puzzling, difficult. [OE. *enotta*]

knout (n-) *n.* whip once used in Russia. *-v.t.* flog with this. [Russ. *knut*]

know *v.t.* be aware of, have information about, be acquainted with, recognize, have experience, understand. *-v.i.* have information or understanding. **-know'able** *a.* **-know'ing** *a.* that knows; cunning, shrewd. **-know'ingly** *adv.* **-knowledge** (nol-) *n.* knowing; what one knows; all that is or may be known, **-knowl'edgeable** (nolij-) *a.* intelligent, well-informed. [OE. *cnawan*]

knowe (now) *n.* hillock, knoll. [Northern form of *knoll, q.v.*]

knuc'kle (nuc-kl) *n.* bone at a finger joint. *-v.i.* knuckle down, to put the knuckles on the ground in playing marbles; yield *-v.t.* strike with the knuckles. [ME. *knokel*]

knur (n-) *n.* knot on a tree-trunk; hard lump; wooden ball, [ME. *knurre*]

knurl (n-) *n.* knob or ridge. **-knurled'** (-ld) *a.* knotty, gnarled. [dim. of *knur*]

koa'la *n.* Australian 'native bear', a small marsupial. [native]

ko'bold *n.* spirit, goblin, of the mines. [Ger.]

kohl *n.* powdered antimony for darkening the eyelids. [Arab. *kuhl*]

ko'la *n.* African tree; its nuts, used as a stimulant. [native]

kook'aburr'a *n.* Australian bird, the laughing jackass. [native]

kop'je *n.* in S. Africa, a hill. [Du.]

Koran (kor'an, koran') *n.* sacred book of Islam. [Arab. *qur'an*, reading]

ko'sher *a.* of food, *etc.* . fulfilling the Jewish law. *-n.* kosher food or shop. [Heb. *kosher*, right]

kotow, kowtow' *a.* in China, touching the ground with the head in respect or submission. *-v.t.* salute thus; act obsequiously in order to curry favor. [Chin. *ho'-t'ou*, knock head]

kou'miss *n.* intoxicating drink made from mare's milk. [Tartar *kumiz*]

kraal (kral) *n.* S. African native village within a fence. [Du.]

krait, karait *n.* deadly Indian rock snake. [Hind.]

Krem'lin *n.* citadel *esp.* in Moscow; government of Russia. [Russ. *kreml*]

ku'dos *n.* credit, prestige. [G.]

ku'du, koo'doo *n.* spiral-horned African antelope. [native]

kuk'ri (koo-) *n.* heavy curved Gurkha knife. [Hind.]

küm'mel *n.* cumin and caraway seed flavored liqueur. [Ger. *kummel*]

Kur'dish *n.* Iranian language of the nomadic Moslem people; language of the Kurds.

kym'ograph *n.* instrument for recording fluid pressures, *esp.* blood, oscillations, sound-waves. [G. *kyma*, wave, *graphein*, write]

kyr'ie (kir-ie, kir'i) *n.* form of Greek prayer; part of Mass in R. C. church. [G. *kyrie, eleison*, Lord, have pity]

L

laa'ger *n.* S. African camp protected by circle of ox-wagons; encampment, [S. Afr. Du.]

la'bel *n.* slip of paper, metal, *etc.*, fixed to an object to give some information about it. *-v.t.* affix a label to; (fig.) a descriptive phrase associated with a person. [OF. narrow strip]

la'bial *a.* of the lips; pronounced with the lips. *-n.* sound so pronounced: letter representing it. **-la'biate** *a.* like, with lips; of flowers, with corolla divided into two. **-labioden'tal** *a.* of sound produced by both lips and teeth. [L. *labium*, lip]

la'bile *a.* likely to slip, err, lapse; unstable [L. *labilis, labi*]

la'bor (-her) *n.* exertion of the body or mind; task; pains of childbirth workmen collectively. *-v.i.* work hard; strive; maintain normal motion with difficulty; *esp.* of a ship, be tossed heavily. *-v.t.* elaborate; stress to excess. **-La'bor Day** *n.* (in the U.S. and Canada) a public holiday in honor of labor, held on the first Monday in September. **-la'borer** *n.* one who labors, *esp.* a man doing manual work for wages. **-laborious** *a.* hard-working: toilsome. **labor'iously** *adv;* **-lab'oratory** *n.* place set apart for scientific investigations or for manufacture of chemicals. [L. *labor*, toil]

Lab'rador *n.* breed of large, smooth-coated retriever dog. also **Lab'rador retrie'ver** *n.* [Labrador]

labur'num *n.* tree or shrub with yellow hanging flowers. [L.]

labyrinth *v.i.* network of passages in which it is hard to find the way, a maze. **labyrin'thine** *a.* [G. *labyrinthos*]

lac *n.* dark resin. [*hind.* lak]

lac, lakh *n.* one hundred thousand (usually of rupees). [Hind.]

lace *n.* cord to draw edges together, *e.g.*, to tighten shoes, stays, *etc.*; ornamental braid; fine open work fabric, often of elaborate pattern. *-v.t.* fasten with laces: intertwine; flavor with spirit. [L. *laqueus*, noose]

la'cerate (las-) *v.t.* tear,, mangle; distress. **-lacera'tion** *n.* [L. *lacerate*]

lachrymal *a.* of tears. **-lach'rymatory** *n.* tear bottle. *-a.* causing tears or inflammation of the eyes, **lach'rimato t** *n.* tear gas, **-lach'rymose** *a.* tearful. [L. *lacrima*, tear]

lack *n.* deficiency, want. *-v.t.* be without, or poorly supplied with [Teut.]

lackadaisical *a.* languid, avoiding enthusiasm. [*alack-a-day*]

lack'ey *n.* footman; menial attendant; obsequious person. *-v.t.* be, or play the, lackey to. [F. *laquais*]

laconic *a.* using, or expressed in, few words. **-lacon'ically** *adv.* **-lacon'icism** *n.* [G. *Lakonikos*, Spartan]

lac'quer *n.* hard varnish made from lac. *-v.t.* coat with lacquer. [Port. *lacre*, sealing-wax, fr. *lac*, *q.v.*]

lacrosse' *n.* ball-game played with long-handled rackets. [F. *(jeu de) la crosse*, the crook]

lac'tic *a.* of milk. **-lacta'tion** *n.* secreting of milk. **-lac'teal** *a.* of milk. **-lac'tose** *n.* milk sugar. **-lac'tic a'cid,** acid from sour milk, [L. *lac, lact-*, milk]

lacu'na *n.* gap, missing portion in a document or series. [L. = *pit*]

lacus'trine *a.* of, dwelling in, lakes. [L. *lacus*, lake]

lad *n.* boy, young fellow; stripling. **-lad's love,** (*prov.*) southernwood. [ME., *servant*]

ladd'er *n.* appliance consisting of two poles connected by cross-bars (rungs) used as means of ascent. [OE. *hlaeder*]

lade *v.t.* load; ship; burden. **-la'ding** *n.* cargo, freight. [OE. *hladan*]

la'dle *n.* spoon with a long handle and large bowl. *-v.t.* lift out with a ladle. **la'dleful** *n.* [OE. *hladan*]

la'dy *n.* woman of good breeding or social position; title of woman of rank; formerly, mistress, wife, love; polite term for any woman. **-our Lady,** Virgin Mary. **la'dylike** *a.* **-la'dyship** *n.* **-la'dybird** *n.* small beetle usually red with black spots. **-La'dyday** *n.* the Feast of the Annunciation, 25th March. **-la'dy's-slipp'er** *n.* orchidaceous wildflower. **la'dy's-smock** *n.* cuckoo flower. [OE. *hloefdige*, loaf-kneader]

lag *v.i.* go too slow, fall, behind. *-n.* (*sl.*) convict. **-lagg'ard** *n.* one who lags. *-a.* loitering, slow. [orig. obscure]

lag'an *n.* wreckage, *etc.*, lying on sea floor; nets laid in the sea. [OF.]

la'ger *n.* kind of light beer. [Ger. *lager bier*, fr. *lager*, storehouse]

lagoon' *n.* salt-water lake, often one enclosed by a reef or an atoll. [F. *lagune*, fr. L. *locus*. lake]

la'ic, la'icise *See* **lay.**

lair (lar) *n.* resting-place of a wild animal. **-lair'age** *n.* accommodation for farm animals, *esp.* at docks or markets. [OE. *leger*, couch]

laird *n.* Scottish landed proprietor; a landlord. [Sc. form of *lord*]

laissez-faire (les-a-fer) *n.* leaving alone; principle of non-intervention. [F.]

la'ity. *See* **lay.**

lake *n.* large body of water surrounded by land. **-lake'let** *n.* small lake. **-lake'-dwelling,** *n.* prehistoric dwelling built on piles in a lake. [OE. *lac*, L. *locus*]

lake *n.* red pigment, [var. of *lac, q.v.*]

lam *v.t.* (*sl.*) beat, lame. **-lam'ming** *n.* beating. [ME. *lam*, of imit. origin]

la'ma (la-) *n.* Tibetan buddhist priest or monk. **-la'maism** *n.* his religion, founded on Buddhism. [Tibet]

lamb (lam) *n.* young of the sheep; its meat; innocent or helpless creature. *-v.i.* of a sheep, to give birth to a lamb. **lambing** *n.* birth of lambs; shepherd's work tending the ewes and newborn lambs at this time. **-lamb'like** *a.* meek. [OE.]

lambaste' *v.t.* thrash; criticize, scold severely. [*lanz* and *baste*]

lam'bent *a.* playing on a surface; softly shining; flickering. **-lam'bency** *n.* [L. *lambere*, lick]

lamé *n.* fabric woven with gold or silver thread. [F.]

lame *a.* crippled in a limb, *esp.* leg or foot; limping; of an excuse, *etc.*, unconvincing. *v.t.* make lame. **-lame duck** *n.* disabled person; useless political official. [OE. *lama*]

lament' *n.* passionate expression of grief, song of grief. *-v.t.* and *i.* feel or express sorrow (for). **-lamenta'tion** *n.* **-lam'entable** *a.* deplorable. [L. *lamentum*, cry of mourning]

la'mia *n.* in classical mythology, female vampire of E. Europe, [G.]

lam'ina *n.* thin plate, scale, flake. **lam'inate** v.*t.* beat into, cover with, plates or layers. *-v.i.* split into layers. **laminated** *a.* composed of thin sheets (of plastic, wood, *etc.*) superimposed and bonded together by synthetic resins, usually under heat and pressure, covered with a thin protective layer of plastic or synthetic resin. **-lamina'tion** *n.* [L.]

Lamm'as *n.* 1st August, formerly a harvest festival. [OE. *hlafmoesse*, loaf mass]

lamp *n.* vessel holding oil to be burnt at a wick for lighting; various other appliances as sources of light. **lamp'black** *n.* pigment made from soot. **lamp'ion** *n.* fairy lamp. [G. *lampas*]

lampoon' *n.* venomous satire on an individual, *-v.t.* write lampoons against. [F. *lampon*, fr. *lampons*, 'let us guzzle' refrain to scurrilous songs]

lamp'rey *n.* fish like an eel with a sucker mouth. [F. *lamproie*]

la'nate (la-) *a.* woolly. **-la'nary** *n.* wool store. **-lanif'erous** *a.* wool-bearing. [L. *lana*, wool]

lance (-a-) *n.* horseman's spear. *-v.t.* pierce with a lance or lancet. **-lan'cet** *n.* pointed two-edged surgical knife. **lan'cer** *n.* cavalry soldier armed with a lance. **-lan'ceolate** *a.* lance-shaped [F.]

land *n.* solid part of the earth's surface; ground, soil; country; property consisting of land. *-pl.* estates. *-v.i-* come to land, disembark. *-v.t.* bring to land. **-land'-breeze** *n.* one blowing from land to sea. **-land'ed** *a.* possessing, or consisting of, lands. - **land'fall** *n.* ship's approach to land at the end of a voyage. **-land-force** *n.* soldiers serving on land. **-land'holder** *n.* possessor of land. **-land'ing** *n.* act of landing; platform between flights of stairs. **-land'ing-carriage** *n.* wheeled under-structure of a plane. **-land'ing-stage** *n.* platform for embarkation and disembarkation. - **land'locked** *a.* enclosed by land. - **land'lord** *n.* **-land'lady** *fem.* person who lets land or houses, *etc.*; master or mistress of an inn, boardinghouse, *etc.* - **land'lubber** *n.* person ignorant of the sea and ships. **-land'-mark** *n.* boundary-mark, a conspicuous object as a guide for direction, *etc.* **-land'-mine** *n.* mine hidden under surface of earth exploding when stepped upon; large bomb dropped by parachute. **-land'owner** *n.* one who owns land. **-land'rail** *n.* corncrake. **-land'slide** *n.* fall of earth from a cliff-, notable collapse of apolitical party. **land'slip** *n.* - **lands'man** *n.* one not a sailor. **-land'-steward** *n.* estate manager. **-land'-tax** *n.* tax upon land. **land'ward** *a.* and *adv.* - **land'wards** *adv.* **-land'wind** *n.* wind blowing off the land. [OE.]

land'grave *n.* German count. (**land'gravine** *n. fem.*). [Ger. *land,* land]

landscape *n.* piece of inland scenery; picture of it. **-land'scape-painter** *n.* - **land'scape-gard'ening** *n.* laying out of grounds picturesquely. [Du. *landschap*]

lan'dau *n.* four-wheeled carriage with a top which can be opened or closed. [*Landau,* in Bavaria]

lane *n.* narrow road or street; passage in a crowd of people. [OE.]

lang'oustine *n.* large prawn or small lobster. [F.]

lang'uage (-ng-gw-) *n.* speech; words used by a people; words used in a branch of learning; style of speech. [F. *langage,* fr. L. *lingua,* tongue]

lang'uish (ng-gw-) *v.i.* be or become weak or faint; be in depressing or painful conditions; droop, pine. **-lang'uid** *a.* weak, faint, spiritless, dull. **-lang'uidly** *adv.* - **lang'uor** (-gur) *n.* faintness; want of energy or interest; tender mood; softness of atmosphere. **-lang'uorous** *a.* [F. *languir*]

lan'iary *a.* tearing. *-n.* slaughter-house. [L. *lanius,* butcher]

lanif'erous *a.* wool bearing. [L. *lana,* wool]

lank *a.* lean and tall; long and limp. **lank'y** *a.* awkwardly tall and lean. [OE. *hlanc,* slender]

lan'olin *n.* oily substance obtained from wool. [fr. L. *lana,* wool, *oleum,* oil]

lant'ern *n.* transparent case for a lamp or candle; erection on a dome or roof to admit light. **-lant'horn** *n.* lantern. **lant'ern-jaws** *n. pl.* long thin jaws, giving concave effect. [L. *lanterns*]

lan'thanum *n.* rare metallic element discovered 1839. [G. *lanthanein,* lurk]

lanug'inous *a.* downy. [L. *lanugo, lanugin,* down]

lan'yard *n.* (*naut.*) short rope for fastening; short cord, as for securing a knife or whistle. [F. *lanière,* thong]

lap *n.* fold, flap; front of a woman's skirt as used to hold anything; seat or receptacle made by a sitting person's thighs; single turn of wound thread, *etc.*; round of a racecourse. *-v.t.* enfold, wrapa round. **lap'dog** *n.* small pet dog. [OE. *lappa*]

lap *v.t.* drink by scooping up with the tongue; of waves, *etc.*, to make a sound like an animal lapping. [OE. *lapian*]

lapa'roscope *n.* medical instrument consisting of a tube that is inserted through the abdominal wall and illuminated to enable a doctor to view the internal organs. - **lapa'roscopy** *n.* [G. *lapara,* flank]

lapel' *n.* part of the front of a coat folded back toward the shoulders. [*lap*]

lapp'et *n.* flap or fold. [*lap*]

lapidary *a.* of stones; engraved on stone. *-n.* cutter, engraver, of stones, *esp.* jewels. [L. *lapis, rapid-,* stone]

lap'is laz'uli *n.* bright blue stone, pigment. [Med. L. = *azure stone*]

lapse *n.* slip; mistake; fall from virtue; passing (of time, *etc.*). *-v.i.* fall away; come to an end, *esp.* through some failure. [L. *lapsus,* slip]

lap'wing *n.* plover. [OE. *hleapewince*]

lar'board *n.* and *a.* formerly, port (side of ship). [ME. *ladeborde*]

lar'ceny *n.* theft. [F. *larcin*]

larch *n.* coniferous tree. [Ger. *lärche*]

lard *n.* prepared pig's fat. *-v.t.* insert strips of bacon; intersperse or decorate (speech with strange words, *etc.*) **-lard'y** *a.* [F. = *bacon*]

lard'er *n.* store-room for meat and other food. [OF. *lardier,* bacon-tub]

large *a.* broad in range or area; great in size, number, *etc.*; liberal; generous. **large'ly** *adv.* [L. *largus,* copious]

largess', largesse' *n.* formerly, money

or gifts scattered on an occasion of rejoicing. -**largi'tion** *n.* [*large*]

lar'go *a.* (*mus.*) in broad and dignified style. -*adv.* -*n.* movement played thus. [It.]

lar'iat *n.* picketing-rope; lasso. [Sp. (*la*), *reata*, (the) tethering-rope]

lark *n.* familiar singing-bird. -**lark'spur** *n.* showy border plant, the delphinium. [earlier *laverock*, OE. *lawerce*]

lark *n.* frolic, spree. -*v.i.* indulge in one. **lark'y** *a.* [ME. *laik*, sport; ON. *leikr*]

larr'up *v.t.* (colloq.) thrash, flog. [perh. fr. Du. *larpen*, thresh (corn)]

lar'va *n.* (**lar'vae** *pl.*) insect in the stage between grub and caterpillar. -**lar'val** *a.* [L. = *ghost, mask*]

lar'ynx *n.* part of the throat containing the vocal chords. -**laryngi'tis** *n.* inflammation of this. [G.]

lascivious *a.* lustful, lewd. [L. *lascivus*, sportive, wanton]

la'ser *n.* device for concentrating electromagnetic radiation or light of mixed frequencies into an intense, narrow concentrated beam. [fr. *L*ight *A*mplication by *S*timulayed *E*mission of *R*adiation]

lash *n.* stroke with a whip; flexible part of a whip. -*v.t.* strike with a whip thong, *etc.*, *v.i.* aim a violent blow of a whip, *etc.* [orig. uncertain]

lash *v.t.* fasten or bind with cord, *etc.* [OF. *lachier*, lace]

lass *n.* girl. [orig. unknown]

lassitude *n.* weariness. [L. *lassitude*]

lass'o *n.* rope with a noose for catching cattle, *etc.*, by throwing the noose over the head. -*v.t.* catch with a lasso. [Sp. *lazo*, fr. L. *laqueus*, noose]

last *n.* model of foot on which shoemaker shapes boots, *etc.* [OE. *loeste*]

last *n.* large measure of quantity (*usu.* 4000 lbs.) [OE. *hloest*, load]

last *a.* and *adv.* last person or thing. **last'ly** *adv.* -**last'post'** (*mil.*) bugle call at retiring hour, sounded also at military funerals. [OE. *latost*, fr. late]

last *v.i.* continue, hold out, remain alive or unexhausted. [OE. *loestan*, follow, continue]

lataki'a *n.* superior Turkish tobacco. [Latakia, Syria]

latch *v.t.* fasten with a latch. -*n.* fastening for a door, consisting of a bar, a catch for it. and a lever to lift it, small lock with spring action. -**latch'key** *n.* [OE. *loeccan*, catch]

latchet *n.* shoe-lace. [OF. *lachet*]

late *a.* after the proper time, backward; far on in a period of time; that was recently but now is not; recently dead; recent in date; of a late stage of development. -*adv.* after the proper time; recently; at or till a late hour. -**late'ly** *adv.* not long since. [OE. *læt*, tardy]

lateen' *a.* lateen sail, triangular sail on a long yard at an angle of 45 degrees to the mast. [F. (*voile*) *latine*, Latin (sail)]

la'tent *a.* existing but not developed. [L. *latere*, lie hidden]

lat'eral *a.* of or at the side. -**lat'erally** *adv.* [L. *laterals*, fr. *latus*, later-, side]

lateric'eous (-ish-) *a.* of brick. [L. *latericius* -*later*, brick]

lat'erite *n.* brick-colored Indian sandstone. [L. *later*, brick]

la'tex (la-) *n.* milky plant-juice. [L.]

lath (lath) *n.* strip of wood. -**lath'y** *a.* like a lath; tall and thin. [OE. *loett*]

lathe *n.* machine for spinning an object while it is being cut or shaped. [orig. uncertain]

lath'er (-TH-) *n.* froth of soap and water; frothy sweat. -*v.t.* cover (chin) with lather. -*v.i.* form a lather. [OE. leather, foam, washing-soda]

lath'yrism *n.* neurological disease often resulting in weakness and paralysis of the legs, caused by eating the pealike seeds of the leguminous plant Lathyrus sativus. [fr. *plant*]

lat'i *prefix* broad, as **latifo'liate** *a.* broad-leaved; **latipenn'ate** *a.* broad-winged; **latiros'tral** *a.* broad-billed.

Lat'in *a.* of the ancient Romans; of or in their language; speaking a language descended from theirs; of such people. -*n.* language of the ancient Romans. **latin'ity** *n.* manner of writing Latin; Latin style. -**lat'inism** *n.* word of idiom imitating Latin. [L. *Latinus*, of Latium (the part of Italy which included Rome)]

lat'itude *n.* freedom from restriction; scope. (*geog.*) angular distance on a meridian reckoned North or South from the equator. -*pl.* regions, climes. **latitudinarian** *a.* claiming or showing latitude of thought, *esp.* in religion. -*n.* person with such views. **latitudinar'ianism** *n.* [L. *latus*, wide]

latrine' (-en) *n.* camp or barracks substitute for a toilet; any such toilet. [L. *latrina*, for *lavatrina*, lavatory]

latt'en *n.* type of brass or similar alloy; tin-plate. [OE. laton]

latt'er *a.* later; recent; second of two. **latt'erly** *adv.* lately. [OE. *laetra*, later]

latt'ice *n.* structure of laths crossing with spaces between; window so made. **latt'iced** *a.* [F. *lattis-latte*, lath]

laud *n.* praise, song of praise. *-v.t.* - **laud'able** *a.* **-laud'ably** *adv.* **-lauda'tion** *n.* [L. *laus*, laud-]

laud'anum *n.* tincture of opium. [coined by Paracelsus for an elixir]

laugh *v.i.* make the sounds instinctively expressing amusement or merriment or scorn. *-n.* sound or act of laughing. - **laugh'able** *a.* funny. **-laugh'ably** *adv.* - **laugh'ing-stock** *n.* object of general derision. **-laugh'ing-gas** *n.* nitrous oxide as an anesthetic. **laugh'ter** *n.* laughing. [OE. *hliehhan*]

launch *v.t.* hurl; set going; set afloat. *v.i.* enter on a course. *-n.* the setting afloat of a vessel. [F. *lancer*]

launch *n.* largest boat carried by a warship; large power-driven boat. [Sp. *lancha*]

laundress *n.* washerwoman. **-laun'dry** *n.* place for washing clothes, *esp.* as a business. **-laun'der** *v.t.* wash and iron, *etc.* - **launderette, laundromat** *n.* self-service laundry. [ME. *lavander*, L. *lavare*, wash]

lau'rel *n.* glossy-leaved shrub, the bay tree. *-pl.* wreath of bay-leaves, emblem of victory or merit. **-lau'reate** *a.* crowned with laurels. **-poet laureate,** *n.* poet appointed, *esp.* as by the British sovereign, nominally to write court odes. - **lau'reatship** *n.* [L. *Taurus*]

laurusti'nus (-tin-) *n.* evergreen flowering shrub. [L. *laurus*, laurel, and *tinus* (name of this shrub)]

lau'wine (law-vin) *n.* avalanche. [Ger.]

la'va (la-) *n.* matter thrown out by volcanoes in fluid form and solidifying as it cools. [It., fr. L. *lavare*, wash]

lave *v.t.* wash, bathe. **-lav'atory** *n.* vessel for washing, basin; room for washing; place for water-closets, *etc.* [L. *lavare*, wash]

lav'ender *n.* shrub with fragrant flowers; color of the flowers, a pale blue tinged with lilac. [Med. L. *livendula*]

laverock. *See* **lark.**

lav'ish *a.* giving or spending profusely; very or too abundant. *-v.t.* spend, give, profusely. [OE. *lavasse*, deluge of rain]

law *n.* rule binding on a community; system of such rules; branch of this system; knowledge of it, administration of it; general principle deduced from facts; invariable sequence of events in nature. **law'ful** *a.* allowed by the law. **-law'giver** *n.* one who makes laws. **-law'less** *a.* regardless of the laws. **-law'fully** *adv.* **law'lessly** *adv.* **-law'yer** *n.* professional expert in law. **-law'-abiding** *a.* obedient to the laws. **-law'suit** *n.* carrying on of a claim in a court. [OE. *lagu*]

lawn *n.* fine linen. [*laon*, in France]

lawn *n.* stretch of carefully tended turf in a garden, *etc.* **-lawn' mower** *n.* machine for cutting grass. **-lawn' tennis** *n.* game played on a flat ground with a net across the middle. [earlier, *launde*, glade, fr. F. *lande*, moor]

lawyer. *See* **law.**

lax *a.* loose, slack, negligent; not strict. **lax'ative** *a.* loosening the bowels. *-n.* laxative drug. **-lax'ity** *n.* **-lax'ly** *adv.* [L. *laxus*, slack]

lay *v.t.* deposit on a surface, cause to lie; produce eggs. **-lay'er** *n.* one who lays; thickness of matter spread on a surface; one of several such; shoot fastened down to take root. *-v.t.* propagate plants by making layers. **-lay off,** cease; discontinue or suspend. **-lay-out** *v.t.* display, plan; knock down; prepare for burial. **-lay waste** *v.t.* destroy, ravage. [OE. *lecgan*]

lay *n.* minstrel's song, ballad. [F. *lai*]

lay *a.* not clerical; of or done by persons not clergymen; non-professional. **-lay'man** *n.* [G. *laikos*, of the people]

layette' (-et) *n.* clothes needed for a newborn child. [F. dim. of *laie*, box]

lay'-figure *n.* jointed figure of the body used by artists. [earlier *layman*, Du. *leeman*, jointed man]

laz'ar *n.* leper. **-lazarett'o** *n.* leper hospital. [*Lazarus* (Luke xvi. 20)]

la'zy *a.* averse to work, indolent. **-la'zily** *adv.* **-la'ziness** *n.* -laze *v.i.* indulge in laziness. [orig. uncertain]

lea *n.* piece of meadow or open ground. [OE. *leah*, track of ground]

leach *v.t.* and *i.* remove or be removed from substance by percolating liquid; lose soluble substances by action of percolating liquid. *-n.* act or process of leaching; substance that is leached or constituents removed by leaching; porous vessel for leaching. **-leachate** *n.* water that carries salts dissolved out of materials through which it has percolated, *esp.* polluted water from a refuse tip. [perh. *retch*, muddy ditch]

lead (led) *n.* soft, heavy grey metal; plummet or lump of this used for sounding depths of water; graphite in a pencil. *-pl.* piece of roof covered with the metal; strips of it used to widen spaces in printing, *etc.*

-*v.t.* cover, weight or space with lead. -**leads'man** *n.* sailor who heaves the lead. -**lead'en** *a.* of or resembling lead. -**lead'-pencil** *n.* drawing, writing, implement of graphite enclosed in wood. [OE.]

lead (led) *v.t.* guide, conduct; persuade; serve as a way, conduct people. -*v.i.* be or go or play the first. -*n.* leading; example; front place. -**lead'er** *n.* one who leads; article in a newspaper expressing editorial views. -also reading artéicle. -**lead'er-ship** *n.* -**lead'ing case** *n.* legal decision used as a precedent. -**lead'ing question** *n.* question worded to prompt the answer desired; question which demands exploration of considerations not yet taken into account. [OE. *Icedan*]

leaf *n.* (**leaves** *pl.*) part of a plant's foliage consisting usually of a green blade on a stem; two pages of a book, *etc.*; thin sheet; flap or movable part of a table, *etc.* -**leaf'let** *n.* small leaf; single sheet, often folded, of printed matter for distribution, a hand-bill. -**leaf'y** *a.* -**leaf'less** *a.* -**leaf'-mold** *n.* soil or humus from decayed leaves, *etc.* [OE.]

league *n.* measure ofroad distance, about three miles. [OF. *legue*]

league (leg) *n.* agreement for mutual help; parties to it; federation of clubs, *etc.* -*v.t.* and *i.* combine in a league. **leag'uer** *n.* member of a league.

League' of Na'tions *n.* international organization founded 1920 in an effort to establish law and order in the world at large. [F. *ligue*]

leag'uer (-ger) *n.* siege; besieging camp. -*v.t.* to beleaguer. [Du. *leger*]

leak *n.* hole or break through which a liquid undesirably passes in or out. -*v.i.* let liquid in or out of; of a liquid, to find its way through a leak. -**leak'age** *n.* a leaking; gradual escape or loss. -**leak'y** *a.* [cp. Ger. *lech*]

lean *a.* not fat; thin. -*n.* lean part of meat, mainly muscular tissue. -**lean'ness** *n.* [OE. *hloene*]

lean *v.i.* bend or incline; tend (toward). *v.t.* cause to lean, prop (against). [OE. *hlinian*]

leap *v.i.* spring from the ground. -*v.t.* spring over. -*n.* jump. -**leap'-frog** *n.* game in which a player vaults over another bending down. -**leap'-year** *n.* year with February 29th as an extra day. [OE. *hleapan*]

learn *v.t.* gain skill or knowledge by study, practice or being taught. -*v.i.* gain knowledge; be taught; find out. **learn'ed** *a.* showing or requiring learning. -**learned'ly** *adv.* -**learn'er** *n.* -**learn'ing** *n.* knowledge got by study. [OE. *leornian*]

lease *n.* a contract by which land or property is given for a stated time by an owner to a tenant, usually for a rent. -*v.t.* take or give the use of by a lease. -**lease'hold** *n.* -**less'or** *n.* granter of a lease. -**less'ee** *n.* one to whom a lease is granted. [OF. *lais*, fr. *laisser*, leave]

leash *n.* thong for holding dogs; set of three animals. [F. *laisse*]

least *a.* smallest. -*n.* smallest one. -*adv.* in smallest degree. [OE. *læst]*

leath'er (leTH'-) *n.* skin of an animal prepared for use. -**leath'ern** *a.* of leather. -**leath'ery** *a.* tough. [OE. *lether*]

leave *v.t.* go away from; deposit; allow to remain; depart without taking; bequeath. -*v.i.* go away, set out. (left, p.t./p.p. - leaving, press). [OE. *loefan*]

leave *n.* permission; permission to be absent from duty. [OE. *leaf*]

leav'en (lev-) *n.* fermenting dough: yeast. -*v.t.* treat with it. [L. *levarnen]*

leben'sraum *n.* space for country's expanding population. [Ger. = *living space*]

lech'er *n.* lewd man. -*v.i.* practice lewdness. -**lecherous** *a.* lewd, lustful. -**lecherously** *adv.* -**lecherousness** *n.* [OF, *lecher*, lick]

lec'tion *n.* difference in copies of manuscript of book; reading. -**lec'tionary** *n.* book, list of, scripture for particular days. -**lector** *n.* (**lec'tress** *n. fem.*) reader. [L. *legere*, read]

lec'tern *n.* reading-desk in church. [OF. *letrin*, fr. L. *legere*, to read]

lect'ure *n.* discourse for the instruction of an audience; speech of reproof. -*v.t.* reprove. -*v.i.* deliver a discourse. **lect'urer** *n.* -**lect'ureship** *n.* appointment as lecturer. [L. *lecture*, reading]

ledge *n.* narrow flat surface projecting from a wall, cliff, *etc.*; ridge or rock below the surface of the sea. [ME. *legge*]

ledg'er *n.* book of debit and credit accounts, chief account book of a firm. **led'ger-line** *n.* in music, a short line, added above or below the stave. -also **le'ger-line.** [orig. a (church) book lying permanently in one place, fr. ME. *liggen*, lie]

lee *n.* shelter; side of anything, *esp.* a ship, away from the wind. -**lee'-shore** *n.* shore on lee-side of ship. -**lee-side** *n.* sheltered side (of ships, *etc.*). [OE. *hleo*]

leech *n.* blood-sucking worm; (formerly) physician. [OE. *loece*]

leech *n.* edge of a sail. [cp. ON. *lik*]

leek *n.* herb like an onion with long bulb

and thick stem. [OE. *leac*]

leer *v.i.* glance with malign, sly, or immodest expression. -*n.* such glance. [orig. uncertain]

lees *n. pl.* sediment of wine, *etc.* [F. *lie*]

left *a.* denotes the side, limb, *etc.*, opposite to the right; (see right). -*n.* left hand or part. -(pol.) Socialist, democratic, party; their more extreme sections. **-left'ist** *n. adj.* on or towards the left. **-left'-handed** *a.* having more power, skill, in the left hand. [OE. *lyft*, weak]

leg *n.* one of the limbs on which a person or animal walks, runs, or stands; support resembling this; part of a garment covering a leg. **-legg'ing** *n.* (*usu.* in *pl.*) covering of leather or other material for the leg. **-leg'gy** *a.* long-legged, lanky. **leg'less** *a.* **-leg'-iron** *n.* fetter. **-leg'-pull** *n.* (*sl.*) hoax. [ON. *leggr*]

leg'acy *n.* anything left by a will; thing handed down to a successor. [L. *legare*, bequeath, fr. *lex, leg-*, law]

le'gal *a.* of, appointed or permitted by, or based on, law. **-le'gally** *adv.* **-legal'ity** *n.* **-le'galize** *v.t.* to make legal. **legalization** *n.* **-le'gal ten'der,** money which can legally be used in paying a debt. [L. *legalis*, fr. *lex*, law]

leg'ate *n.* ambassador, *esp.* of the Pope. **lega'tion** *n.* diplomatic minister and his suite; their mission or residence. **leg'ateship** *n.* [L. *legatus*]

legatee' *n.* one who receives a legacy. [irregularly fr. *legacy*]

lega'to *a.* (*mus.*) smooth. -*adv.* smoothly. -*n.* passage played thus. [It.]

leg'end *n.* traditional story or myth; traditional literature; inscription. **-legendary** *a.* [L. *legenda*, be read]

legerdemain (lei-) *n.* juggling, conjuring. [F. *léger de main*, light of hand]

leg'horn *n.* kind of fine straw for hats; breed of domestic fowl. [*Livorno*, earlier Legorno, in Italy]

leg'ible (-j-) *a.* easily read. **-legibil'ity** *n.* **-leg'ibly** *adv.* [L. *legere*, read]

le'gion *n.* body of infantry in the Roman army; various modern military bodies; association of veterans; large number. **-le'gionary** *a.* and *n.* [L. *legio*, fr. *legere*, levy]

legis'lator (-j-) *n.* maker of laws. **leg'islate** *v.i.* **-legisla'tion** *n.* **-leg'islative** *a.* **-leg'islature** *n* body that makes laws. [L. *legislator* proposer of laws]

legit'imate (-j-) *a.* lawful, proper, regular; born in wedlock. **-legit'imacy** *n.* -*v.t.* (also legitimize) make legitimate. **-legitima'tion** *n.* **-legit'imism** *n.* **-legit'imist** *n.* supporter of an hereditary title to a monarchy. [L. *legitimus*, fr. *lex, leg-*, law]

legum'inous *a.* of plants, bearing fruit in valved pods, as peas and beans. [F. *légume*, vegetable]

lei'sure *n.* freedom from occupation, spare time. **-leis'urely** *a.* deliberate. **-leis'urely** *adv.* **-leis'ured** *a.* having plenty of spare time. [F. *loisir*, fr. L. *licere*, be lawful]

leitmotiv' *n.* (*mus.*) recurrent theme identified with a particular character or idea. [Ger.]

lem'an *n.* sweetheart, (unlawful) lover. [OE. *leof*, fief, *mann*, man]

lemm'a *n.* premise, proposition, to be taken for granted, as already proved. [G.]

lemm'ing *n.* small Arctic rodent, noted for its supposed self-destruction in large numbers during migration. [Dan.]

lem'on *n.* pale-yellow fruit with acid juice; tree bearing it; its color. **lemonade'** *n.* drink made from lemon juice. **-lem'ony** *a.* [F. *limon*, lime]

lem'on sole *n.* kind of plaice resembling sole. [F. *limanole*, flat-fish]

lem'ur *n.* nocturnal animal like a monkey. [L. = *ghost]*

lend *v.t.* give the temporary use of, let out for hire or interest; give, bestow. **-lends itself to,** is adapted to. **-lend'er** *n.* [OE. *laenan*]

lend'-lease *n.* agreement by which America exchanged, sold and gave goods to enemies of Axis in World War II. [*lend* and *lease*]

length (-th) *n.* quality of being long; measurement from end to end; long stretch; piece of a certain length. **length'en** *v.t.* and *i.* **-length'wise** *a.* and *adv.* **-length'y** *a.* **-length'ily** *adv.* -at length, at last. [OE. *lengthu*]

le'nient *a.* mild, being without severity. **-le'nience, le'niency** *n.* **leniently** *adj.* **-len'ity** *n.* **-len'itive** *n.* a soothing or mildly laxative drug. [L. *lenis*, mild]

len'is *a.* weakly articulated, as pertaining to phonetics.

lens (-z) *n.* **len'ses** *pl.* piece of glass with one or both sides curved, used for concentrating or dispersing light in cameras, spectacles, telescopes, *etc.*; combination of such glasses in an instrument. **-lentic'ula** *n.* small lens; freckle. **-lentic'ular** *a.* like a lens; double-convex. -also **len'tiform** *a.* **-len'toid** *a.* lens-shaped. [L. *lentil* (fr. its shape)]

Lent *n.* period of fasting from Ash Wednesday to Easter-Eve (40 days). **-lent'en** *a.* of, in, or suitable to, Lent; fleshless. **Lent'-li'ly** *n.* daffodil [OE. *lencten,* Spring]

lent'il *n.* eatable seed of a leguminous plant. **-lentic'ular** *a.* like lentil. [F. *lentille,* dim. fr. L. *lens,* lentil]

lent'isk *n.* mastic-tree. [L. *lentiscus*]

len'to *a.* (*mus.*) slow. *adv.* slowly. **lentamen'te** *adv.* in slow time. [It.]

len'tous *a.* viscous, sticky. **-len'titude** *n.* [L. *tentus,* slow]

Le'o *n.* the lion, 5th sign of Zodiac, which sun enters c. 22nd July; constellation. **le'onine** *a.* like a lion. [L. *leo,* lion]

leop'ard (lep') *n.* large carnivorous animal with spotted coat. **-leop'ardess** *fem.* [G. *leopardos,* lionpard]

lep'er *n.* one suffering from leprosy; outcast. **-lep'rosy** *n.* disease forming silvery scales on the skin and eating away parts affected. **-lep'rous** *a.* [G. *lepis,* scale]

lepidop'tera *n.pl.* order of insects having four wings covered with tiny scales, *e.g.,* butterflies, moths. **-lepidop'iterous** *a.* [G. *lepis,* scale, *pteron,* wing]

lep'orine *a.* of or like a hare. [L. *lepus, leper-,* hare]

leprechaun (-re-CHawn) *n.* Irish fairy brownie. [Ir. *luchorpan,* small person]

leprosy. *See* **leper.**

les'bian *a.* homosexual (of women). **lesbianism** *n.* [island of *Lesbos*]

le'sion *n.* wound, injury. [L. *laedere,* hurt]

less *a.* comp. of little; not so much. *-adv.* to smaller extent or degree. *-pron.* less amount or number. *-prep.* after deductions, minus. **-less'en** *v.t.* make less, diminish. **-less'er** *a.* [OE. *laessa,* less]

lese-maj'esty (lez-) *n.* treason. [F. *lèse majesté,* violated majesty]

lessee, lessor *See* **lease.**

less'on *n.* portion of Scripture read in church; something to be learnt by a pupil; part of a course of teacbing; experience that teaches. *-v.t.* teach, discipline. [F. *lecon,* L. *lectio,* reading]

lest *conj.* in order that . . . not, for fear that. [ME. *les* the]

let *v.t.* allow, enable, cause to; allow to escape; grant use of for rent, lease. *-v.i.* be leased. [OE. *loetan*]

let *v.t.* hinder. *-n.* hindrance; in games, an obstruction of a ball or player cancelling the stroke. **-let alone',** not to mention; not interfere with. **-let down',** disappoint, desert, fail. **-let go',** cease to hold. **-let off,** withhold punishment. **-let on'** (*sl.*) pretend; disclose (secret, *etc.*; let out', make a way of escape for. [OE. *lettan*]

le'thal *a.* deadly, fatal. [L. *lethalis*]

leth'argy *n.* drowsiness, apathy, want of energy or interest. **-lethar'gic** *a.* **-lethargically** *adv.* [G. *lethargia*]

Le'the *n.* river of Hades the waters of which produced forgetfulness in those who drank them. [G. *myth*]

lett'er *n.* one of the symbols with which words are written; a written message. *-pl.* literature, knowledge of books. *v.t.* mark with letters. **-lett'ered** *a.* learned. **lett'erpress** *n.* matter printed from type [F. *lettre,* fr. L. *littera*]

lett'uce (-tis) *n.* salad plant with milky juice. [L. *lactuca,* fr. *lac,* milk]

leu'cocyte *n.* white corpuscle of blood or lymph. [G. l*eukos,* whiter]

leukemia, leukaem'ia *n.* a progressive blood disease characterized by an excessive number of white corpuscles. [G. *leukos,* white]

Levant' *n.* eastern part of the Mediterranean and the adjoining countries; wind of those regions. **-Levant'ine** *n.* [F. *levant,* rising, east]

levant' *v.i.* abscond. **-levant'er** *n.* [Sp. *levantar,* move]

lev'ee *n.* sovereign's reception for men only; formerly, a great person's reception on rising; a pier or embankment. [F. *lever,* rise]

lev'el *n.* instrument for showing or testing a horizontal line or surface; horizontal passage in a mine; social or moral standard. *-a.* horizontal; even in surface; even in style, quality, *etc.* *-v.t.* make level, bring to the same level; lay low; aim (a gun). **-level-head'ed** *a.* not apt to be carried away by emotion or excitement. [L. *libella,* dim. of *libra,* balance]

le'ver *n.* bar used to apply force at one end by pressure exerted at the other, a point in between resting against a fixed support. **-le'verage** *n.* action or power of a lever. [L. *levare,* raise]

lev'eret *n.* young hare. [L. *lepus,* hare]

leviathan *n.* sea-monster; huge ship; anything very large of its kind. [Heb. *livyathan*]

levitation *n.* power of raising a solid body into the air by annulling gravitational pull. **-lev'itate** *v.t.* and *i.* to make lighter. [L. *levis,* light]

Le'vite *n.* member of tribe of Levi, son of

Jacob, whose descendants formed class of assistant priests. **lev'ity** *n.* inclination to make a joke of serious matters, frivolity. [L. *levis*, light]

lev'ulose *n.* fruit-sugar. [L. *laevus*, left]

lev'y *n.* act of collecting taxes or enrolling troops; amount or number levied. *-v.t.* raise or impose by compulsion. [F. *lever*, raise]

lewd *a.* indecent. **-lewd'ly** *adv.* **-lewd'ness** *n.* [OE. *loewede*, lay, layman]

lew'isite *n.* blistering liquid used in chemical warfare. [W. L. *Lewis*]

lex'icon *n.* dictionary. **-lexicog'raphy** *n.* compiling of dictionaries. **-lexicog'rapher** *n.* [G. *lexikon* (*biblion*), word (book)]

li'able *a.* subject (to), exposed (to), answerable. **-liabil'ity** *n.* state of being liable. *-pl.* debts. [F. *lier*, bind]

liai'son *n.* connecting link; illicit love. **-liai'son off'icer,** officer linking two commands, *etc.* [F.]

lian'a *n.* any tropical climbing or twining plants. [F. *liane*]

liar. *See* **lie.**

liba'tion *n.* drink poured out as an offering to the gods. [L. *libatio*]

li'bel *n.* written, published, statement damaging to a person's reputation. *-v.t.* write, publish, a libel against. **-li'belous** *a.* **-li'belously** *adv.* [L. *libellus*, dim. of *liber*, book]

lib'eral *a.* generous; open-minded; of a political party, favoring changes making towards democracy. *-n.* one of such a party. **-lib'eralism** *n.* **-liberal'ity** *n.* munificence. **-lib'eralize** *v.t.* **-lib'erally** *adv.* [L. *liber*, free]

libertine *n.* a dissolute man. *-a.* dissolute. **-lib'ertinism** *n.* [F. libertin]

lib'erty *n.* freedom. **-lib'erate** *v.t.* set free. **-libera'tion** *n.* **-lib'erator** *n.* **- lib'erty-man** *n.* sailor, with shore leave. **-lib'erty-boat** *n.* boat for such. [L. *liber*]

libidinous *a.* lustful. **-libi'do** *n.* (*psych.*) emotional urge behind human activities, *e.g.*, sex. [L. *libido*, lust]

Li'bra *n.* the Balance 7th. sign of zodiac, which sun enters c. Sept. 22nd, zodiacal constellation; pound weight. [L.]

li'brary *n.* collection of books; place where the books are kept; reading or writing room in a house. **-librar'ian** *n.* keeper of a library. **-librar'ianship** *n.* [L. *liber*, book]

li'brate *v.t.* balance, poise. *-v.i.* be poised; sway slightly, as when evenly balanced; vibrate. **-libra'tion** *n.* [L. *libra*, balance]

librett'o *n.* book of words of an opera. **librett'ist** *n.* [It. = little book]

li'cense *n.* leave, permission; formal permission; document giving it; excessive liberty; dissoluteness; writer's or artist's transgression of the rules of his art (often poetic license). **-li'cense** *v.t.* grant a license to. **-licen'tiate** *n.* one licensed to practice an art or profession. **-licen'tious** *a.* sexually immoral. **-licen'tiously** *adv.* **-licensee'** *n.* holder of a license. [L. *licentia*, fr. *licere*, be allowed]

lice. *See* **louse.**

li'chen (li'-ken, lich'en) *n.* small flowerless plant forming a crust on rocks, trees, *etc.* **-li'chened** *a.* [L.]

lich'-gate, lych'-gate *n.* roofed gate of a churchyard, under which a corpse is placed to await the clergyman at a funeral. [OE. *lic*, body, *geat*,, gate]

lic'it (lis-) *a.* lawful, allowed. [L.]

lick *v.t.* pass the tongue over; (*sl.*) beat. *n.* act of licking. [OE. *liccian*]

lic'orice. *See* **liquorice**

lic'tor *n.* officer bearing fasces, who attends Roman magistrate. [L.]

lid *n.* movable cover; cover of the eye, the eyelid. **-lidd'ed** *a.* [OE. *hlid*]

li'do *n.* bathing beach. [L. *litus*, shore]

lie *v.i.* be horizontal or at rest; be situated; recline. *-n.* direction; state (of affairs, *etc.*). [OE. *licgan*]

lie *v.i.* make a false statement. *-n.* untrue statement. **-li'ar** *n.* [OE, *leogan*]

lied' *n.* lieder *pl.* German song, ballad. [Ger.]

lief *adv.* gladly, willingly. *-a.* (arch.) dear. [OE. *leof*, dear]

liege (lej) *a.* bound to render feudal service; privileged to receive it. *-n.* vassal; lord; loyal subject. [F. *lige*]

lien *n.* right to hold property until a claim is met. [F. = *bond*]

lieu *n.* in lieu of, instead of. **lieuten'ant** *n.* substitute; junior army or navy officer. [F. fr. L. *locus*, place]

life *n.* lives *pl.* active principle of the existence of animals and plants, animate existence; time of its lasting; history of such an existence; manner of living; vigor, vivacity. **-life'-belt** *n.* **-life'-jacket** *n.* **life'-preserv'er** *n.* devices to keep one afloat in water. **-life-blood** *n.* blood on which life depends. **-life'boat** *n.* boat for rescuing shipwrecked persons. **-life'buoy** *n.* buoy to support a person in water. **-life'-class** *n.* art class with living models. **-life'-cycle** *n.* successive stages of an organism through a complete generation. **-life-guard** *n.* body-guard. rescuer of bathers in difficulties. **life'less** *a.* **-life-long** *a.* lasting lifetime. **-life'time,** duration of one's life. [OE. *lif*]

lift *v.t.* raise to a higher position. -*v.i.* rise. -*n.* act of lifting; journey as a pass enger in someone else's vehicle, given free of charge; in Britain, elevator. [ON. *lypta*]

lig'ament *n.* band of tissue joining bones. **-lig'ature** *n.* thread for tying up an artery. [L. *ligare*, bind]

li'gan *n.* goods sunk at sea with buoy attached. [L. ligare, bind]

light *a.* of, or bearing, little weight; gentle; easy, requiring little effort; trivial. -*adv.* in a light manner. **-light'** *v.i.* get down from a horse or vehicle; come by chance (upon). **-light'en** *v.t.* reduce or remove a load, *etc.* **-light'-fing'ered** *a.* thievish. **-light'-hand'ed** *a.* having a light touch. **-light'-headed** *a.* delirious, giddy. **-light-infantry** *n.* light-armed soldiers. **-light'ly** *adv.* **-light'ness** *n.* **light'ning-conductor, light'ning-rod** *n.* rod attached to buildings to protect them from lightning. **-lights** *n. pl* lungs of animals. **-lightship** *n.* anchored ship with beacon acting as light-house. **light'weight** *a.* and *n.* boxing weight (135 lb) **-light'-year** *n.* (*astron.*) distance which light travels in a year. [OE. *leoht*]

light *n.* natural agent by which things are visible; source of this; window; mental vision; light part of anything. -*a.* bright; pale, not dark-*v.t.* set burning; give light to. -*v.i.* take fire; brighten. **light'en** *v.t.* give light to. **-light'ning** *n.* visible discharge of electricity in the atmosphere. **-light'house** *n.* tower with a light to guide ships. **-light'some** *a.* radiant. [OE. *leoht*]

lighter *n.* large boat used for loading and unloading ships. [*light*]

lign-al'oes (lin-) *n.* aloes-wood. [L. *lignum*, wood, and aloes]

lig'neous *a.* of, or of the nature of, wood. **-lig'nite** *n.* brown coal. **-lig'num vi'tae,** S. American hardwood tree. [L. *lignum*, wood]

lig'uloid *a.* that which may resemble a small tongue, strap or ligule.

like *a.* similar, resembling. -*adv.* in the manner of. -*pron.* similar thing. **-like'ly** *a.* probably true; hopeful, promising. *adv.* probably. **-like'lihood** *n.* **-liken** *v.t.* compare. **-like'ness** *n.* quality of being like; portrait. **-like'wise** *adv.* in like manner. [OE. *gelic*, similar]

like *v.t.* to find agreeable. -*v.i.* to be pleasing. **-like'able** *a.* [OE. lician, please]

li'lac *n.* shrub bearing pale violet flowers; their color. -*a.* of this color. [OF. Pers. *lilak*, blue]

Lillipu'tian *a.* very small, dwarf-like. *n.* [Lilliput, "Gulliver's Travels"]

lilt *v.t.* and *i.* sing merrily. -*n.* rhythmical effect in music. [ME. *lulten*, strike up loudly]

lil'y *n.* bulbous flowering plant. **lilia'ceous** *a.* **-li'ly of the valley,** plant with fragrant small white bells. [L. *liliurn*]

lima'ceous *a.* of or like a slug. [L. *limax*, slug]

lima'tion (li-) *n.* filing or polishing. [L. *lima*, file]

limb (lim) *n.* arm or leg; branch of a tree. [OE. *tim*]

limb (lim) *n.* edge of the sun or moon. [L. *limbus*, edge]

lim'ber *n.* detachable front part of a gun-carriage. -*v.t.* attach the limber to (a gun). [orig. uncertain]

limber *a.* lithe, supple. [orig. uncertain]

lim'bo *n.* a supposed region on the borders of Hell for unbaptized persons, *etc.*; prison. [L. *limbus*, edge]

lime *n.* sticky substance used for catching birds; alkaline earth from which mortar is made. -*v.t.* smear, or catch, with lime; treat (land) with lime. **-lime'light** *n.* bright light got by heating quicklime; publicity. **-lime'stone** *n.* rock which yields lime when burnt. [OE. *liin*]

lime *n.* acid fruit like a lemon. [F.]

lime *n.* ornamental tree with sweet-scented blossoms, the linden. [OE. *lind*]

lim'erick *n.* popular five-line nonsense-verse form. [orig. uncertain]

limit *n.* boundary; utmost extent or duration. -*v.t.* restrict, bound. **-limita'tion** *n.* **-lim'itable** *a.* [L. *limes, limit-*, boundary]

limn *v.t.* paint, depict. [OF. *luminer*, illuminate]

limnol'ogy *n.* study of lakes, ponds. [G. *limne*, lake]

limousine' (-zen) *n.* closed type of automobile with the top projecting over the driver's seat. [F. fr. hood worn by natives of province of *Limousin*]

limp *a.* without firmness or stiffness. **limp'ly** *adv.* [orig. uncertain]

limp *v.i.* walk lamely. -*n.* limping gait. [orig. uncertain]

limp'et *n.* shellfish which adheres firmly to rocks. [OE. *lempeclu*]

limp'id *a.* clear. **-limpid'ity** *n.* **-limp'idly** *adv.* [L. l*impidus*]

linch'pin *n.* pin to hold a wheel on its axle.

[OE. *lynis*, axle-tree]

lind'en *n.* lime tree. *See* **lime.**

line *n.* linen thread; any cord or string; wire; stroke made with a pen, *etc.*; long narrow mark; continuous length without breadth; row; series; course; province of activity; trade or business. -*v.t.* cover inside; mark with a line or lines; bring into line. **-li'ning** *n.* covering for the inside of a garment, *etc.* **-lin'eage** *n.* descent from, or the descendants of an ancestor. **-lin'eal** *a.* of lines; in direct line of descent. -**lin'eament** *n.* feature. **lin'ear** *a.* of or in lines. [OE.]

lin'en *a.* made of flax. -*n.* cloth made of flax; linen articles collectively. [L. *linum*, flax]

li'ner *n.* large passenger ship or airplane. [*line*]

ling *n.* slender fish. [ME. *lenge*]

ling *n.* kind of heather. [ON. *lyng*]

ling'er (-ng-g) *v.i.* tarry, loiter; remain long. [OE. *lengan*, prolong]

linge'rie (lang-zb'-re) *n.* linen goods, *esp.* women's underwear. [F.]

ling'o (ng-g-) *n.* language, dialect; jargon. [L. *lingua*, language]

ling'ual (-ng-gw-) *a.* of the tongue or language. -*n.* lingual sound. **-ling'uist** *n.* one skilled in languages. **-linguist'ic** *n.* of languages. -*n.* in *pl.* science of languages. [L. *lingua*, tongue]

lin'hay *n.* open-fronted shed. [OE. *hlinian*, lean; obs. hay, fence]

liniment *n.* embrocation. [L. *linimentum*, fr. *linere*, smear]

link *n.* ring of a chain; connection. -*v.t*, join with, or as with, a link. -*v.i.* be so joined. **-link'up** *n.* establishing of a connection or union between objects, groups, organizations, *etc.*; connection or union established. [of ON. orig.]

link *n.* torch. [orig. uncertain]

links *n. pl.* undulating ground near sea; golfcourse. [OE. *hlinc*]

linn *n.* waterfall, cascade, part formed by this. [Gael. *linne*, pool]

Linnae'an *a.* pert. to botanist *Linnaeus* and his system of classification.

linn'et *n.* familiar song-bird, kind of finch. [F. *linotte*]

lino'leum *n.* floorcloth surfaced with hardened linseed oil. **-linocut** *n.* engraving on linoleum instead of wood; print from this. [L. *linum*, flax, *oleum*, oil]

li'notype *n.* machine for producing lines of words cast in one piece; line of type so cast. [line-of-type]

lin'seed *n.* flax seed. [L. *linum*, flax]

lin'sey *n.* linen-and-wood fabric. **-lin'sey-wool'sey** *a.* of this stuff, mean, shoddy. [*linen* and *wool*]

lin'stock *n.* formerly, staff with match for firing cannon. [Du. *lont*, match, *stok*, stick]

lint *n.* soft material of fluffed-up linen; fluff, scraps of thread. [ME. *linnet*]

lint'el *n.* top piece of a door or window. [OF.]

li'on *n.* large animal of the cat tribe; person of importance. **-li'oness** *fem.* **li'onize** *v.t.* treat as a celebrity. **-li'onet** *n.* young lion. [F., fr. L. *leo, leon-*]

lip *n.* either edge of the mouth; edge or margin; (*sl.*) insolence. **-lipp'ed** *a.* **-lip'-service** *n.* insincere devotion. **-lip'stick** *n.* cosmetic in stick form for coloring lips. [OE. *lippa*]

lipo- *prefix* fat, as in **lipoid'** *a.* fat-like. [G. *lipos*, fat]

liqu'ate *v.t.* melt *esp.* metals- **liqua'tion** *n.* [L. *liquare*, liquefy]

liq'uid *a.* fluid, not solid or gaseous, bright, clear. -*n.* a liquid substance. **liq'uefy** *v.t.* and *i.* **-liquefac'tion** *n.* **liques'cent** *a.* tending to become liquid. **liques'cence** *n.* [L. *liquere*, be clear]

liquidate *v.t.* pay (debt); arrange the affairs of, and dissolve (a company *sl.*) put out of action, wipe out. **-liquida'tion** *n.* **-liq'uidator** *n.* [L. *liquere*, be clear]

liq'uor (lik'er) *n.* liquid, *esp.* alcoholic one for drinking. **-liqueur'** (li. kur) *n.* alcoholic liquor flavored and sweetened. [L. *liquere*, be clear]

liq'uorice, licorice (-kur-is) *n.* black substance used in medicine and as a sweetmeat; plant or its root, from which the substance is obtained. [fr. G. *glykus*, sweet, and *rhiza*, root]

lisle' *a.* of Lille, as in lisle thread. [Lille (formerly *l'isle*), France]

lisp *v.t.* and *i.* speak with faulty pronunciation of the sibilants; speak falteringly. *n.* a lisping. [OE. *awlyspian*]

liss'om *a.* supple, agile. [for *lithesorae*]

list *n.* border or edge of cloth; strips of cloth, *esp.* used as material for slippers. *pl.* space for tilting. [OE. *lislè*]

list *n.* roll or catalogue. -*v.t.* write down in a list. [list, *v.s.*]

list *v.i.* desire; of a ship, incline, lean to one side. -*n.* desire; inclination of a ship. -**list'less** *a.* indifferent, languid. **list'lessly** *adv.* (OE. *lystan*, please]

list *v.t.* and *i.* listen. **-list'en** (lis'en) *v.i.* try to hear, give attention in order to hear. **-lis-**

ten in *v.i.* listen to a radio broadcast. -**list'ener** *n.* (OE. *hlystan*]

lit'any *n.* form of prayer. [G. *litaneia*]

lit'er *n.* measure of capacity in the French decimal system, equal to 2.11 pints. [F.]

lit'eral *a.* of letters; exact as to words; according to the sense of actual words, not figurative or metaphorical. -**lit'erally** *adv.* [L. *litera*, letter]

lit'erary *a.* of, or learned in, literature. **li'terate** *a.* educated. -**lit'eracy** *n.* -**litera'tim** *adv.* letter for letter. -**lit'erature** *n.* books and writings of artistic value; production of these; profession of writers. [L. *litera*, letter]

lithe *a.* supple. -**lithe'some** *a.* [OE.]

lith'ic *a.* of, obtained from, stone. **lith'oid** *a.* resembling stone. [G. *lithos*, stone]

lith'ium *n.* very light metallic element. [G. lithos, stone]

lith'o- *prefix* pertaining to stone, as in **lith'ocarp** *n.* fossil fruit. -**lith'oglyph** *n.* engraving on stone, *esp.* on a gem. -**lith'ophyl** *n.* fossil leaf -**lith'ophyte** *n.* coral polyp. -**lith'osphere** *n.* earth's solid crust. -**lithot'omy** *n.* (surg.) operating of cutting for stone in bladder. -**lith'otrity** *n.* operation of crushing such stone. [G. *lithos*, stone]

lithog'raphy *n.* the making of drawings on stone for printing. -**lith'ograph** *n.* print so produced. -*v.t.* print thus. **lithog'rapher** *n.* -**lithograph'ic** *a.* [G. *lithos*, stone, *graphein*, write]

lit'igate *v.i.* go to law. -**lit'igant** *a.* and *n.* -**litiga'tion** *n.* -**litig'ious** (-j-) *a.* fond of going to law. -**litig'iousness** *n.* [L. *litigare*, fr. *lis, lit-*, lawsuit]

lit'mus *n.* blue coloring-matter turned red by acids. -**lit'mus-paper** *n.* (ON. *litmose*, lichen (used in dyeing)]

litt'er *n.* portable couch; kind of stretcher for the wounded; straw, *etc.*, as bedding for animals; fragments lying about, untidy refuse of paper, *etc.*; young of an animal produced at a birth. -*v.t.* strew (a place) with litter; bring forth. [F. *litiere*, fr. *lit*, bed]

lit'tle *a.* small, not much. -*n.* small quantity. -*adv.* slightlv. [OE. *lytel*]

litt'oral *a.* of, or on, the sea shore. -*n.* littoral district. [L. *litus, litor-*, shore]

lit'urgy *n.* form of public worship. **litur'gical** *a.* -**lit'urgist** *n.* state. [G. *leitourgia*, public worship]

live *v.i.* have life; pass one's life, continue in life; dwell; feed. -**liv'ing** *n.* state of being in life; means of earning livelihood; church benefice. [OE. *lifian*]

live *a.* living; flaming. -**live-stock** domestic animals *esp.* horses, cattle, pigs. -**live'-wire** *n.* wire carrying an electric current; (*sl.*) energetic person. (from alive) **livelihood** *n.* means of living. [OE. *liflad*, life-course]

live'ly *a.* brisk, active, vivid. -**live'liness** *n.* [OE. *liflic*, like life]

liv'er *n.* organ which secretes bile. *a.* liver-colored, reddish-brown. -**liv'erish** *a.* of liver; irritable. [OE. *lifer*]

liv'ery *n.* allowance of food for horses; distinctive dress of a person's servants. **liv'ery-stable** *n.* stable where horses are kept at a charge, or hired out. [F. *livrée*, handed over (orig. of any allowance)]

liv'id *a.* black-and-blue, as a bruise. [L. *lividus*, lead-colored]

liz'ard *n.* four-footed, five-toed reptile with scaly body; saurian. [L. *lacertus*]

lla'ma *n.* Peruvian animal used as a beast of burden; its wool. [Peruv.]

lla'no *n.* level, treeless plain in northern S. America. (Sp.]

lo *interj.* took 'behold' [OE. la]

loach *n.* small fresh-water fish of carp family. [F. *loche*]

load *n.* burden; amount usually carried at once. -*v.i.* put a load on or into; charge (a gun); weigh down. -**load'stone, lode'stone** *n.* magnetic iron ore; magnet. **load'star, lode'star** *n.* Pole Star. [OE. *lad*, way, journey]

loaf *n.* loaves *pl.* mass of bread as baked; cone of sugar. [OE. *hlaf*]

loaf *v.i.* idle. -**loaf'er** *n.* [orig. uncertain loam *n.* fertile soil. [OE. *lam*]

loam *n.* rich, dark soil, often a result of the mixture of sand and clay, used *usu.* for platering, foundry molds, *etc.* [AS. *lam*]

loan *n.* thing lent; an act of lending. -*v.t.* lend. [ON. *lan*]

loath, loth (-th) *a.* unwilling. -**loath'ly** *a.* -**loath'some** *a.* disgusting. -**loathe** (-TH) *v.t.* abhor. [OE. *lath*, repulsive]

lobb'y *n.* corridor into which rooms open; pressure group, *esp.* one seeking influence on government. -*v.t.* and *i.* exert pressure in this way. [med. L. *lobium*]

lobe *n.* soft hanging part of the ear; any similar flap. [G. *lobos*, lobe of ear]

lobe'lia *n.* small garden plant with bright-blue flowers. [Lobel, botanist]

lob'ster *n.* shellfish with long tail and claws, which turns scarlet when boiled. [OE. *loppestre*]

lo'cal *a.* relating to place; of or existing in

a particular place. **-local'ity** *n.* place, situation; district. **-lo'cally** *adv.* **-lo'calize** *v.t.* **-locate'** *v.t.* attribute to a place; find the place of. **-loca'tion** *n.* a placing; situation. **-loc'ative** *a.* and *n.* grammatical case denoting 'place where'. **-lo'cal col'or** (in writing, *etc.*), careful detail producing a true-to-life effect. [L. *locus*. place]

loch *n.* lake *esp.* in Scotland; arm of the sea. [Gael.]

lock *n.* tress of hair. [OE. *loc*]

lock *n.* appliance for fastening a door, lid, *etc.*; mechanism for discharging a firearm; enclosure in a river or canal for moving boats from one level to another; close crowd of vehicles. *-v.t.* fasten with a lock; join firmly; embrace closely-*v.i.* become fixed or united. **-lock'er** *n.* small cupboard with a lock. **-lock'jaw** *n.* tetanus. **-lookout** *n.* exclusion of workmen by employers as a means of coercion. **-lock'smith** *n.* one who makes and mends locks. **-lock'et** *n.* small pendant of precious metal for a portrait, *etc.* **-lock-up** *n.* place for housing prisoners, cars, *etc.* [OE. *loc*]

locomo'tive *a.* having the power of moving from place to place. *-n.* engine moving from place to place by its own power; railway engine. **-locomo'tion** *n.* action or power of moving from place to place. **-lo'comotor atax'y** *n.* nervous disorder causing unsteadiness of limbs. [fr. L. *loco*, from a place, and *moveri*, be moved]

lo'cum-tenens (ten) *n.* deputy, *esp.* for a doctor. **-lo'cumten'ency** *n.* [L. *locus*, place, *tenere*, hold]

lo'cust *n.* destructive winged insect; carob-tree; its fruit, resembling a bean in shape. [L. *locusta*, lobster]

locu'tion *n.* style of speech; form of expression. [L. *locutio*]

lode *n.* vein of ore. [*See* **load**]

lodge *n.* house for a shooting or hunting party; house at the gate of an estate; meeting-place of a branch of freemasons, *etc.*; the branch. *-v.t.* house; deposit. *-v.i.* live in another's house at a fixed charge; become fixed after being thrown. **lodg'er** *n.* - **lodge'ment** *n.* lodging or being lodged. [F. *loge*]

lo'ess *n.* fertile soil deposit in certain river valleys. [Ger.]

loft *n.* attic; room over a stable; gallery in a church. *-v.t.* send (a golf-ball) high. **loft'y** *a.* of great height; elevated. **loft'ily** *adv.* [ON. *lopt*, sky]

log *n.* unhewn portion of a felled tree; apparatus for measuring the speed of a ship; journal kept on board ship, *etc.*, **-log'-book** *n.* *-v.t.* record, *usu.* as written data on a regular basis. **-log'ger** *n.* a lumberjack. - **log'wood** *n.* Central American tree; its wood. [orig. uncertain]

lo'ganberry *n.* cross between raspberry and blackberry. [Judge J. H. *Logan*]

log'arithm *n.* one of a series of arithmetical functions tabulated for use in calculation. **-logarith'mic** *a.* [G. *logos*, word, ratio, *arithmos*, number]

loggerhead *n.* blockhead. **-at loggerheads**, quarrelling. [*log*]

logg'ia *n.* open-fronted arcade, gallery; open balcony. [It.]

log'ic *n.* art of reasoning. **-log'ical** *a.* relating to logic; according to reason; able to reason well. **-log'ically** *adv.* **log'ician** *n.* [G. *logos*, word]

loin *n.* part of the body on either side between ribs and hip. [OF. *loigne*, fr. L. *lumlus*]

loi'ter *v.i.* waste time on the way, hang about. **-loi'terer** *n.* [Du. *leuteren*]

loll *v.i.* sit or lie lazily; of the tongue, hang out. *-v.t.* hang out (the tongue). [imit. orig.]

lollipop *n.* a sweet. [child language]

lone *a.* solitary. **-lone'ly** *a.* alone; feeling sad because alone. **-lone'liness** *n.* **lone'some** *a.* [for *alone*]

long *a.* having length, *esp.* great length. *adv.* for a long time. **-long-headed** *a.* shrewd, intelligent. **-long-run** *n.* outcome, result. **-longshoreman** *n.* dock laborer. - **long-sighted** *a.* able to see far, shrewd. **-long-suffering** *a.* enduring patiently. [OE. *long*]

long *v.i.* have a keen desire. **-long'ing** *n.* [OE. *langian*, grow long]

longevity (-j-) *n.* long existence of life. **longe'vial** *a.* [L. *longaevus-aevum*, age]

longitude *n.* distance of a place east or west from a standard meridian. **longitu'dinal** *a.* of length or longitude. [L. *longus*, long]

loo'fah *n.* pod of a plant used as a sponge; the plant. [Arab, *lufah*]

look *v.i.* direct or use the eyes; face; take care; seem; hope. *-n.* a looking; expression; aspect. **-look'alike** *n.* a person, *esp.* a celebrity, or thing that is the double of another. **-look'ing** glass *n.* mirror. **-look af'ter**, take care of. **-look alive'**, hasten. **-look'-out** *n.* watch; place for watching; watchman. [OE. *locian*]

loom *n.* machine for weaving. [OE. *geloma*, tool]

loom *v.i.* appear dimly, *esp.* with vague or enlarged appearance, or (fig.) out of the future. [orig. unknown]

loon′ *n.* diving sea-bird. [Ice. *lomr*]

loop *n.* figure made by a curved line crossing itself; similar rounded shape in a cord or rope, *etc.*, crossed on itself. *v.t.* form into a loop. -*v.i.* form a loop. **-loop′line** *n.* part of a railway line which leaves the main line and joins it again. **-loop′hole** *n.* slit in a wall, *esp.* for shooting through; means of escape, of evading a rule without infringing it. **-loop the loop**, complete upward and backward circle, *esp.* of aircraft. [orig. uncertain]

loose *a.* not tight or fastened or fixed or exact or tense; slack; vague; dissolute. *v.t.* set free; unfasten; make slack. -*v.i.* shoot, let fly. **-loose′ly** *adv.* **-loos′en** *v.t.* make loose. **-loose′ness** *n.* [ON. *lauss*]

loose′strife *n.* marsh or wood plant with yellow or purple flowers. [E. trans. of G. proper name *Lysimachos*]

loot *n.* and *v.t.* plunder. [Hind. *lut*]

lop *v.t.* cut away twigs and branches; chop off. [OE. *loppian*]

lop *v.i.* hang; imply. **-lop′-ear** *n.* drooping ear; rabbit with such ears. **lopsi′ded** *a.* with one side lower than the other, badly balanced. [orig. uncertain]

lope′ *v.i.* run with long, easy strides. [ON. *hlaupa*]

loquacious (-kwa-) *a.* talkative. **loquac′ity** *n.* [L. *loquax, loquac-*]

lo′quat *n.* eastern tree; its fruit. [Chin. *lou kwet*, rush orange]

lord *n.* feudal superior; one ruling others; owner; God; title of peers of the realm. *v.i.* domineer. **-lord′ling** *n.* petty lord. **lord′ly** *a.* **-lord′liness** *n.* **-lord′ship** *n.* rule, ownership; domain; title of peers, *e.g.*, your lordship, *etc.* [OE. *hlafweard*, loaf-ward]

lore *n.* learning; body of facts and traditions. [OE. *lar*]

lorgnette′ (lorn-yet′) *n.* pair of eyeglasses with a long handle. [F.]

lor′imer, lor′iner *n.* harness-maker. [F. *lormier*]

lo′ris *n.* 'Ceylon sloth' a lemur. [F.]

lorn *a.* abandoned. [obs. v. *lesse*, lose]

lorr′y *n.* four-wheeled wagon without sides; in Britain, truck. [orig. unknown]

lo′ry *n.* kind of parrot found, in E. Asia and Australia. [Malay *luri*]

lose *v.t.* be deprived of, fail to retain; let slip; fail to get; be late for; be defeated in. -*v.i.* suffer loss. **-loss** *n.* a losing; what is lost; harm or damage resulting from losing. **-los′er** *n.* **-lost** *a.* [OE. *losian*, be lost]

lot *n.* one of a set of objects used to decide something by chance (to cast lots); fate, destiny; item at an auction; collection; large quantity. [OE. *hlot*]

lo′tion *n.* liquid for washing wounds, improving the skin, *etc.* [L. *lotio*]

lott′ery *n.* gamble in which part of the money paid for tickets is distributed to some owners of tickets selected by chance. [*lot*]

lott′o *n.* game of chance. [*lot*]

lo′tus *n.* legendary plant supposed to yield a fruit causing forgetfulness when eaten; Egyptian water-lily. [G. *lotos*]

loud *a.* strongly audible; noisy; obtrusive. **-loud′ly** *adv.* **-loud′speak′er** *n.* device for magnifying sound. [OE. *hlud*]

lough′ (loh) *n.* Irish loch, lake. [Ir.]

lounge *v.i.* loll; move lazily. -*n.* place for, or a spell of, lounging; deep chair or sofa. [orig. uncertain]

lour. *See* **lower.**

louse *n.* lice *pl.* parasitic insect. **-lous′y** *a.* infested with lice; (fig.) bad, mean. [OE. *lus*]

lout *n.* awkward fellow lacking manners. [orig. uncertain]

lou′ver, lou′vre *n.* set of boards or slats set parallel and slanting to admit air without rain; ventilating structure of these. [OF. *lover*]

lov′age (luv′-) *n.* salad plant; drink made from it. [OF. *luvesche*]

love (luv) *n.* warm affection; sexual passion; sweetheart; score of nothing. -*v.t.* have love for. -*v.i.* be in love. **-lov′able** *a.* **-love′less** *a.* **-love′lorn** *a.* forsaken by, or pining for, a lover. **-love′ly** *a.* beautiful, delightful. **-lov′er** *n.* **-love′-apple** *n.* tomato. **-love′-bird** *n.* small green parrot. **-love′-child** *n.* illegitimate. **-lov′ing-cup** *n.* bowl passed round at a banquet. **-love′-in-a-mist** *n.* blue-flowered garden plant. **-love′-lies-bleeding** *n.* red-flowered garden plant. [OE. *lufu*]

low *a.* not tall or high or elevated; humble; commonplace; vulgar; dejected; not loud. **-low′er** *v.t.* cause or allow to descend; diminish; degrade. **-low′land** *n.* low-lying country. **-low′ly** *a.* modest, humble. **-low′liness** *n.* **-low′brow** *n.* person not an intellectual. -*a.* **-low′ down** *a.* mean, despicable. -*n.* inside information. [OE. *lah*]

low *v.i.* of cattle, to utter their cry. *n.* the cry. [OE. *hlowan*]

lower, lour *v.i.* scowl. -*n.* scowl. **low′ering** *a.* sullen; (of sky) threatening rain, storm. [orig. uncertain]

loy'al *a.* faithful; true to allegiance. **loy'ally** *adv.* -**loy'alty** *n.* -**loy'alist** *n.* [F., fr. L. *legalis*, legal]

loz'enge *n.* diamond figure; small sweetmeat or tablet of medicine, formerly of this shape. [F. *losange*]

lubb'er *n.* clumsy fellow. -**lubb'erly** *a.* awkward. [orig. uncertain]

lub'ricate *v.t.* oil or grease; make slippery. -**lu'bricant** *n.* substance used for this. -**lubrica'tion** *n.* -**lu'bricator** *n.* -**lubri'city** *n.* slipperiness; lewdness. [L. *lubricate*, fr. *lubricus*, slippery]

lu'cent *a.* bright. [L. *lucidus*, fr. *lux*, light]

lucerne' *n.* purple-flowered fodder plant like clover. [F. *luzerne*]

lu'cid *a.* clear; easily understood. **lucid'ity** *n.* -**lu'cidly** *adv.* -**lu'cifer** *n.* morning star; Satan; match. [L. *lucidus*, fr. *lux*, light]

luck *n.* fortune, good or ill; chance. **luck'y** *a.* having good luck. -**luck'less** *a.* -**luck'ily** *adv.* fortunately. [Du. *luk*]

lu'cre *n.* gain or profit as a motive; money. -**lu'crative** *a.* yielding profit. [F. fr. L. *lucrum*, gain]

lu'cubration *n.* labored composition, 'smelling of the lamp.' -**lu'cubrate** *v.i.* [L. *lucubrare*, work by lamplight]

lu'culent *a.* bright, clear; apparent. [L. *luculentus-lux*, light]

lu'dicrous *a.* absurd, laughable. [L. *ludicrus*, fr. *ludere*, play]

luff *n.* part of a fore-and-aft sail nearest the mast. -*v.t.* and *i.* bring (head of a ship) nearer the wind. [OF. of some contrivance for altering course]

luft'waffe *n.* German air force. [Ger. =*air arm*]

lug *v.t.* drag with effort. -*v.i.* pull hard. *n.* act of lugging. [orig. uncertain]

luge *n.* light Alpine sleigh for one. -*v.i.* [F.]

lugg'age *n.* traveler's baggage. [orig. uncertain]

lug'sail *n.* oblong sail fixed on a yard which hangs slanting on a mast. -**lugg'er** *n.* vessel with such sails. [orig. uncertain]

lugubrious *a.* mournful. [L. *lugere*, mourn]

luke'warm *a.* moderately warm, tepid; lacking enthusiasm, indifferent, [obs. *luke*, tepid]

lull *v.t.* soothe with sounds, sing to sleep; make quiet. -*v.i.* become quiet. -*n.* brief time of quiet in storm or pain. -**lull'aby** (-bi) *n.* lulling song or sounds. [imit. origin]

lum'bar *a.* relating to the loins. **lumba'go** *n.* rheumatism in the loins. [L. *lumbus*, loin]

lum'ber *v.i.* move heavily; obstruct. -*n.* disused articles, useless rubbish; timber, *esp.* in planks. [orig. obscure]

lu'minous *a.* bright, shedding light. -**lu'minary** *n.* heavenly body giving light; person noted for learning. **luminos'ity** *n.* [L. *lumen, lumin-*, light]

lump *n.* shapeless piece, mass; swelling; sum covering various items. -*v.t.* throw together in one mass or sum. -*v.i.* move heavily. -**lump'ish** *a.* clumsy; stupid. **lump'y** *a.* [orig. uncertain]

lu'nar *a.* of the moon. -**lunar caustic,** nitrate of silver. [L. *luna*, moon]

lu'natic *a.* insane. -*n.* insane person. **lu'nacy** *n.* [L. *luna*, moon]

lunch *n.* meal taken in the middle of the day. -**lunch'eon** (-shn) *n.* lunch; midday banquet. [orig. uncertain]

lung *n.* light, spongy air-breathing organ. [OE. *lungen*]

lunge *v.i.* thrust with a sword, *etc.* -*n.* such thrust, or thrusting movement. [F. *allonger*, lengthen, stretch out]

lu'pin *n.* border plant with tall showy flower-spikes. [orig. uncertain]

lu'pine *a.* of, like, a wolf. [L. *lupinus*, *lupus*, wolf]

lu'pus *n.* chronic tubercular skin disease. [L. = *wolf*]

lurch *n.* leave in the lurch, leave in difficulties, abandon (a comrade) [obs. card game of lurch]

lurch *n.* sudden roll to one side. -*v.i.* make a lurch. [orig. uncertain]

lurch'er *n.* poacher's mongrel dog. [obs. *lurch*, prowl about, lurk]

lure *n.* falconer's apparatus for recalling a hawk; something which entices, a bait. -*v.i.* recall (a hawk); entice. [F. *leurre*]

lu'rid *a.* ghastly, pale, glaring. -**lu'ridly** *adv.* [L. *luridus*, yellowish]

lurk *v.i.* lie hidden; be latent. -**lurk'er** *n.* -**lurk'ing** *a.* [orig. uncertain]

lus'cious (-shus) *a.* sweet; sickly sweet; over-rich. [delicious and lush]

lush *a.* of grass, *etc.*, luxuriant and juicy. -*n.* (*sl.*) habitually drunken person. [orig. uncertain]

lust *n.* sensual desire; passionate desire. *v.i.* have passionate desire. -**lust'ful** *a.* **lust'y** *a.* healthy, vigorous. -**lust'ily** *adv.* [OE. = *pleasure*]

lus'ter *n.* gloss, shine; splendid reputation, glory; glossy material. -**lus'trous** *a*

[L. *lustrare*, shine]
lus'trum *n.* period of five years. **lustra'tion** *n.* purification by sacrifice. **lus'trate** *v.t.* **-tus'tral** *a.* [L. *lustrum*, five-yearly sacrifice for purification]
lu'sus *n.* variation from type; freak. [L.]
lute *n.* stringed musical instrument played with the fingers. **-lu'tanist** *n.* lute-player. [Arab. *al-'ud.* (aloe) wood]
Lu'theran *a.* pert. to Luther, Protestant reformer, and his doctrines.
lux'ury *n.* possession and use of costly and choice things for enjoyment; enjoyable but not necessary thing; comfortable surroundings. **-luxu'rious** *a.* **-luxu'riously** *adv.* **-luxu'riate** *v.i.* indulge in luxury; grow rank; take delight (in). **-luxu'riant** *a.* growing profusely; abundant. **-luxu'riantly** *adv.* **-luxu'riance** *n.* [L. *luxuria*]
lycan'thropy *n.* supposed power to change into a wolf, delusion of such. **lycan'thrope** *n.* were-wolf [G. *lykos*, wolf, *anthropos*, man]
lyce'um *n.* college, building in which lectures are given. [G. *Lukeion*, place where Aristotle taught]
lychgate. *See* **lichgate.**
lydd'ite *n.* powerful explosive used in shells. [first tested at *Lydd*, in Kent]
lye *n.* water made alkali with wood ashes, *etc.*, for washing. [OE. *leag*]
lymph *n.* colorless animal fluid; matter from cowpox used in vaccination. **-lymphat'ic** *a.* of lymph; flabby, sluggish. *-n.* vessel in the body conveying lymph. [L. *lympha*, water]
lynch *n.* lynch law, procedure of a self appointed court trying and executing an accused person. *-v.t.* put to death without proper trial. [orig. uncertain]
lynx *n.* animal of cat tribe noted for keen sight. **-lynx-eyed** *a.* quick-sighted. [G.]
lyre *n.* instrument like a harp. **-lyr'ic, lyr'ical** *a.* relating to the lyre; meant to be sung; of short poems, expressing the poet's own thoughts and feelings; describing a poet who writes such poems. **-lyr'ic** *n.* lyric poem. **-lyricist** *n.* lyric poet. [G. *Tyra*]

M

maca'bre (-a-ber) *a.* gruesomely imaginative. [F.]
macadam *n.* road surface of small broken stone. [J. L. *McAdam* (d. 1836)]
macaro'ni *n.* Italian paste of wheat in long tubes. [It. *maccheroni*]
macaroon' *n.* small cake containing ground almonds. [It. *maccherone*]
macaw' *n.* parrot. [Port. *macao*]
mace *n.* staff of office carried before officials. [F. *masse*]
mace *n.* spice made of the husk of the nutmeg. [L. *macis*]
mac'erate *v.t.* soften by steeping; cause to waste away. **-macera'tion** *n.* [L. *macerare, macerat-*]
Mach number (maCH) *n.* ratio between speed of airflow and speed of sound, used instead of miles-per-hour ratio to calculate speed of fast aircraft. [*Mach*, German scientist]
mach'air *n.* flat, shorewise pasture. [Gael.]
mache'te (-cha-ta) *n.* W. Indian cutlass. [Sp.]
Machiavell'ian (mak-i-a-vell'-yan) *a.* crafty, unprincipled, in politics; dictated by expediency. [*Machiavelli*, It. statesman (d. 1527)]
machination (-kin-) *n.* plotting, intrigue. **-mac'hinate** *v.i.* lay plots.
machine' (-shen) *n.* apparatus combining the action of several parts, to apply mechanical force for some purpose; person like a machine from regulation or sensibility; controlling organization; bicycle, vehicle, automobile. *-v.t.* sew, print with a machine. **-machi'nery** *n.* parts of a machine collectively; machines. **-machi'nist** *n.* one who makes or works machines. **-machine'-gun** *n.* gun firing repeatedly and continuously by means of a loading and firing mechanisms [G. *mechane*]
mach'o (-ch-) *a.* denoting or exhibiting pride in characteristics believed to be typically masculine, as physical strength, sexual appetite, *etc.* *-n.* man who displays such characteristics. [Sp. = *male*]
mack'erel *n.* sea-fish with blue and silver barred skin. **-mack'erel-sky** *n.* sky barred or dappled with thin white cloud. (F. *maquereau*]
mackintosh *n.* (*abbrev.* **mack**) cloth waterproofed with rubber; coat made of this or of similar waterproof substance; coat made of such material. [Charles *Mackintosh* (1823 patent)]
macro- *prefix* great, long, as in **macrobiot'ic** *a.* long-lived. **-macrop'terous** *a.* long-winged. **-macru'rous** *a.* long-tailed. [G. *makros*, long, large]
mac'rocosm *n.* universe. [fr. G. *makros*, great, and *kosmos*, world]

macroscop'ic *a.* visible to the naked eye, *opp.* to microscopic. [G. *makros,* large, *skopeein,* to look at]

mac'ulate *v.t.* stain, spot. **-macula'tion** *n.* [L. *macula,* spot]

mad *a.* suffering from mental disease, insane; wildly foolish; excited; angry. **-mad'ly** *adv.* **-mad'man** *n.* **-mad'ness** *a.* **-mad'den** *v.t.* make mad. **-mad'cap** *n.* reckless person. [OE.]

mad'am *n.* polite form of address to a woman. [F. *madame,* my lady]

madd'er *n.* climbing plant; its root; dyestuff made from this. [OE. *mædere*]

Madeir'a *n.* white wine. **-Madeir'a-cake** *n.* kind of sponge-cake. [*Madeira* Islands]

mademoiselle *n.* a young unmarried woman; Miss. [F.]

madonn'a *n.* Virgin Mary; picture or statue of the Virgin Mary. [It.]

mad'rigal *n.* short love poem or song; part song for three or more voices. [F.]

maelstrom (mal-) *n.* great whirlpool; (*fig.*) turmoil. [Du. *maalstroom*]

mae'nad *n.* Bacchante; frenzied female. [G. *mainas, mainad-,* raving]

mae'stro (mi-) *n.* master, *esp.* of music. [It.]

Maf'ia *n.* international secret criminal organization. [It.]

magazine' *n.* storehouse for explosives and the military stores; a periodical with stories and articles by different writers; an appliance for supplying cartridges automatically to a gun. [F. *magasn,* store, shop]

magent'a (-j-) *n.* bluish crimson alkaline dye. *-a.* of this color. [named fr. Battle of *Magenta,* 1859]

magg'ot *n.* grub, larva; crazy notion. **magg'oty** *a.* [OE. *matha,* worm]

magi *n. pl.* priests of ancient Persia; the wise men from the East. [L. fr. O. Pers. *magus*]

mag'ic (-j-) *n.* art of influencing events by controlling nature or spirits, any mysterious agency of power; witchcraft, conjuring. **-magic-lant'ern** *n.* apparatus by which pictures are projected on a white screen in a darkened room. **-mag'ical** *a.* **mag'ically** *adv.* **-magi'cian** *n.* [G. *magos*]

magilp, megilp' *n.* artist's vehicle for oil-colors. [orig. uncertain]

magistrate (-j-) *n.* civil officer administering the law. **-magiste'rial** *a.* at or referring to a magistrate or master; dictatorial. **-mag'istracy** *n.* office of a magistrate; magistrates collectively. [L. *magister,* master]

magnanimous *a.* great souled, above resentment, *etc.* **-magnanim'ity** *n.* [fr. L. *magnus,* great, *animus,* soul]

mag'nate *n.* person of influence by wealth or position. [L. *magnus,* great]

magne'sium *n.* metallic chemical element. **-magne'sia** *n.* white powder compound of this used in medicine. [*Magnesia,* in Greece]

mag'net *n.* piece of iron having the properties of attracting iron and pointing north and south when suspended; lodestone. **-magnet'ic** *a.* **-magnet'ically** *adv.* **-mag'netism** *n.* magnetic phenomena; the science of this; personal charm or power of attracting others. **-an'imal magnetism,** hypnotism. **-mag'netize** *v.t.* make into a magnet. **-magnetiza'tion** *n.* **-mag'netite** *n.* apparatus for ignition in an internal combustion engine. **-magnet'ic mine,** mine set off by magnetic needle on ship's approach. [G. *magnes,* Magnesian stone. v.s.]

Magnif'icat *n.* Virgin Mary's song in Luke i. 46-55, first word of Vulgate. [L. *magnificare,* magnify]

magnificent *a.* splendid, stately, imposing, excellent. **-magnif'icently** *a.* **-magnificence** *n.* [*magnify*]

mag'nify *v.t.* exaggerate; make greater; increase the apparent size, as with a lens; praise. [L. *magnus,* great, *facere,* make]

magniloquent *a.* speaking loftily. **-magnil'oquence** *n.* [L. *magniloquus*]

magnitude *n.* size; extent, amount; importance. [L. *magnitudae*]

magno'lia *n.* flowering tree, [*Magnol,* French botanist (d. 1715)]

mag'num *n.* wine bottle holding two quarts. [L. *magnus,* great]

mag'pie *n.* black and white chattering bird. [*pie,* with name prefixed mag]

Mag'yar *n.* member of ruling class of Hungary. [*native*]

maharajah *n.* Indian princely title. [Sans. *maha,* great, *raja,* prince]

mahat'ma *n.* master, adept. [Sans. = *great-souled*]

Mahidi *n.* Islamic looked-for leader, deliverer. [Arab. *Mahdiy,* led]

mah'jong *n.* old Chinese table game. [Chin. *ma-ch'iao*]

mahl'stick. *See* **maulstick.**

mahog'any *n.* tropical American tree; its reddish-brown wood. [W. Ind.]

ma'hout *n.* elephant driver. [Hind. *mahawat*]

maid'en *n.* young unmarried woman. *-a.* unmarried; of, or suited to, a maiden;

having a blank record. -**maid** *n.* young unmarried woman; woman servant. **maid'enhair** *n.* fern with delicate stalks and fronds. -**maid'enhead** *n.* virginity. -**maid'enhood** *n.* -**maid'enly** *a.* [OE. *mægden*, girl]

mail *n.* armor made of interlaced rings or overlapping plates. -**mail'ed** *a.* covered with mail. [L. *macula*, mesh]

mail *n.* bag of letters; letters conveyed at one time; official despatch of letters. -*v.t.* send by mail. -**mail'box** *n.* public box for depositing mail that is being sent out; box at a house or business to which mail is delivered for the occupier. -**mail'man** *n.* one who delivers mail. [OF. *male*, leather bag]

maim *v.t.* cripple, mutilate. [OF. *mahaignier*, mutilate]

main *n.* open sea, chief matter; strength, power. -*a.* chief, principal, leading. -**main-deck** *n.* ship's chief deck. -**main'land** *n.* stretch of land which forms the main part of the country. -**main'ly** *adv.* -**main'mast** *n.* chief mast in a ship. -**main'sail** *n.* lowest sail of a mainmast. -**main'spring** *n.* chief spring of a watch or clock. -**main'stay** *n.* rope from top of mainmast to deck; chief support. -**main'-yard** *n.* lower yard on main-mast. [OE. *mægen*, strength]

main'frame *n.* in a large computer, the central processing unit.

maintain' *v.t.* carry on; preserve; support, sustain, keep up; keep supplied; affirm. -**maintain'able** *a.* -**main'tenance** *n.* [L. *manu tenere*, hold with the hand]

maisonnette' (mez-on-et') *n.* small modern house, flat. [F.]

maize *n.* Indian corn, a cereal. [Sp. *maiz*, fr. Cuban]

maj'esty *n.* stateliness; kingship or queenship. -**majes'tic** *a.* -**majes'tically** *adv.* [L. *majestas*]

majol'ica *n.* fine glazed Italian pottery. [It., early name of *Majorca*]

major *a.* greater; out of minority. -*n.* one out of minority; officer in the army, ranking below lieutenant-colonel. -**major'ity** *n.* state of having reached the full legal age; the greater number; the larger party voting together; excess of the vote on one side. -**major'-do'mo** *n.* head-servant of large household. [L. = *greater*]

make *v.t.* construct; produce; bring into being, establish; appoint; amount to; cause to do something; accomplish; reach; earn. -*v.i.* tend; contribute, of the title, to raise. -*n.* style of construction, form, manufacture. -**ma'ker** *n.* -**make-do'** *a.* makeshift. –**make'shift** *n.* method, tool, *etc.* used for want of something better. **make-up** *n.* constituents; style; cosmetics. -**make'-weight** *n.* trifle added to make something seem stronger or better. **make'-believe** *v.i.* pretend. -*n.* -*a.* [OE. *macian*]

mal- *prefix* ill, badly, miss; not (L. *male*, ill) -**maladjust'ment** *n.* faulty adjustment. -**maladministra'tion** *n.* faulty administration. -**maladroit'** *a.* clumsy, not dexterous. -**mal'content** *a.* actively discontented. -*n.* malcontent person. -**malediction** *n.* curse. -**male'factor** *n.* criminal. -**malef'icient** *a.* hurtful. -**maleficence** *n.* -**malev'olent** *a.* full of ill-will. -**malev'olence** *n.* -**malforma'tion** *n.* faulty information. -**malnutri'tion** *n.* faulty, inadequate. nutrition. -**malo'dorous** *a.* evil-smelling. -**malprac'tice** *n.* wrong-doing. -**mal'treat** *v.t.* treat ill, handle roughly. -**maltreat'ment** *a.* -**malversa'tion** *n.* corrupt handling of trust money.

malacc'a *n.* brown cane, used for walking sticks, *etc.* [*Malacca*, Malava]

malachite *n.* green mineral. [G. *malache*, mallow]

mal'ady *n.* disease. [F. *maladie*]

malaise' *n.* vague discomfort, uneasiness. as in fever. [OF.]

mal'apert *a.* impudent, bold. [OF.]

mal'apropism *n.* laughable misuse of words. (Mrs. *Malaprop*, char. in play]

malar'ia (-Ar-) *n.* fever due to mosquito bites. -**malar'ial** *n.* -**malar'ious** *n.* [It. *maléaria*, bad air]

male *a.* of the begetting sex; of man or male animals. -*n.* male person or animal. [F. *mâle*, fr. L. *masculus*]

ma'lic *a.* derived from fruit-juice, *esp.* apple-juice. [L. *malum*, apple]

mal'ice *n.* action of ill-will. -**malic'ious** *a.* -**malic'iously** *adv.* [L. *malitia*]

malign (-lin) *a.* hurtful. -*v.t.* slander, misrepresent. -**malig'nant** *a.* feeling extreme ill-will; of a disease, very virulent. -**malig'nantly** *adv.* -**malig'nancy** *n.* -**malig'nity** *n.* malignant disposition. [L. *malignus*]

mating'erer *n.* one who pretends illness to escape duty. -**maling'er** *v.i.* [OF. *malingreux*, beggar with artificial sores]

mal'ison *n.* curse. [OF. *maleison*]

mall (mawl, mal) *n.* level shaded walk or avenue; urban shopping area with a variety of shops facing onto spaces reserved for pedestrian traffic only; old game pall-mall; hammer used; alley for this game. [L. *mal-*

leus, hammer]

mall'ard *n.* wild duck, drake; flesh of these. [F. *malart*]

mall'eable *a.* capable of being hammered into shape. -**malleabil'ity** *n.* [L. *malleus*, hammer]

mall'et *n.* hammer, usually of wood. [F. *maillet, malleus*, hammer]

mall'ow *n.* wild plant with purple flowers. [L. *malva*]

malm'sey (mam-) *n.* strong sweet wine. [G. *Monembasia*, in the Morea]

malt *n.* grain used for brewing. -*v.t.* make into malt. -**malt' extract** *n.* medicinal substance prepared from malt. **malt'ster** *n.* [OE. *mealt*]

malthu'sian *a.* of teaching of Malthus. -*n.* advocate of birth control. [Thomas *Malthus*]

mam'ba *n.* large deadly African snake. [*Kaffir*]

mamm'al *a.* animal of the type feeding their young with their milk. -**mamma'lian** *a.* [L. *mamma*, breast]

mammee' *n.* edible fruit of tropical *mammea* tree. [Haitian]

mamm'oin *n.* wealth as an object of pursuit or of evil influence; devil of covetousness. [Aram. *mamon*, riches]

mamm'oth *n.* extinct animal like an elephant. [Russ. *mamont*]

man *n.* **men** *pl.* human being; person: human race; adult human male; man- servant; piece used in a game, *e.g.*, chess. -*v.t.* supply (a ship, *etc.*), with necessary men. -**man'ful** *a.* brave, resolute. -**man'fully** *adv.* -**man'hole** *n.* opening through which a man may pass. -**man'hood** *n.* -**man'ikin** *n.* little man; model of the human body. -**mankind'** *n.* human beings in general. -**man'like** *a.* **man'ly** *a.* -**man'liness** *n.* - **mann'ish** *a.* manlike. -**man'hand'le** *v.t.* move by man-power; (*sl.*) knock about. -**man'-pow'er** *n.* man's work, energy; human resources available for work, etc. -**man'slaughter** *n.* killing of a human being unintentionally or in provocation. [OE. *mann*]

man'acle *n.* fetter for the hand. -*v.t.* handcuff. [L. *manicula*, small sleeve]

man'age *v.t.* carry on, conduct; succeed in doing; handle; persuade. -*v.i.* conduct affairs. -**man'ageable** *a.* -**man'agement** *n.* -**man'ager** *n.* -**man'ageress** *fem.* - **manage'rial** *a.* [It. *maneggiare*, train horses]

manana *n.* (putting off till) tomorrow, dilatoriness. -*adv.* [Sp.]

manatee' *n.* dugong, sea-cow. [Carib.]

mandarin *n.* Chinese official; small sweet orange. [Port. *mandarim*]

man'date *a.* command of, or commission to act for another; commission from the League of Nations to govern a people not qualified for independence; instruction from an electorate to a representative. **man'datary** *n.* holder of a mandate. **man'datory** *a.* [L. *mandatum*]

man'dible *n.* lower jaw bone;, either part of a bird's beak. -**mandib'ular** *a.* **mandib'ulated** *a.* [OF. fr. L. *mandere*, chew]

man'dolin(e) *n.* stringed musical instrument like a lute. [F.]

man'drake, mandrag'ora *n.* narcotic plant. [G. *mandragoras*]

man'drel *n.* axis on which material revolves in a lathe; rod round which metal is cast or forged. [orig. uncertain]

man'drill *n.* large, ferocious W. African baboon. [orig. uncertain]

mane *n.* long hair at the back of the neck of a horse, lion, *etc.* [OE. *manu*]

manège' (-ezh') *n.* riding-school; management and training of horses. [F.]

maneuv'er *n.* movement of troops or ships in war, stratagem. -*v.t.* cause to perform maneuvers. -*v.i.* perform maneuvers; employ stratagems, to work adroitly. [F.]

manganese (-ng-g-) *n.* metallic element; black oxide of this, used in glass making, *etc.* [F. *manganese*]

mange *n.* skin disease of dogs, *etc.* - **ma'ngy** *a.* [OF. *manjue*, itch]

mang'el-wurz'el (-g-) **mang'old-wurz'el** *n.* variety of beet, used as cattle food. [Ger. *mangold-wurzel*]

man'ger (j) *n.* eating trough in a stable or byre. [F. *mangeoire*]

mang'le (mang'gl) *n.* machine for rolling washed linen, *etc.* -*v.t.* put through a mangle. [Du. *mangelstok*, smoothing roll]

mang'le (mang'gl) *v.t.* hack, mutilate, spoil. (AF. *mahangler*]

mang'o *n.* East Indian fruit; the tree bearing it. [Port. *manga*]

mang'osteen *n.* E. Indian edible fruit; tree bearing it. [*Malay*]

man'grove *n.* swamp-growing tropical tree whose drooping shoots take root. [orig. uncertain]

ma'nia *n.* madness; prevailing craze. - **ma'niac** *a.* affected by mania. -*n.* mad person. -**mani'acal** a, [G.]

man'icure *n.* treatment of the nails and hands; person doing this professionally.

-*v.t.* apply such treatment to. -**man'icurist** *n.* [L. *manus* hand, *cura,* care]

man'ifest *a.* clearly revealed, visible, undoubted. -*v.t.* make manifest. -*n.* list of cargo for the Customs. -**manifesta'tion** *n.* -**manifes'to** *n.* declaration of policy by a sovereign or commander or body of persons; any formal declaration of overall political intent. [L. *manifestos*]

man'ifold *a.* numerous, varied. -*n.* pipe with several outlets. -*v.t.* make copies of (a document). [*many* and *fold*]

manikin. *See* **man.**

manil'a *n.* fiber used for ropes; cheroot. [*Manila,* Philippines]

man'iple *n.* Roman infantry company (60-120 men); priest's scarf worn on left arm at Mass. [L. *manus,* hand]

manipulate *v.t.* handle; deal with skillfully; manage craftily. -**manip'ulator** *n.* -**manipula'tion** *n.* -**manip'ulative** *a.* [L. *manipulus,* handful]

mann'a *n.* food of the Israelites in the wilderness; sweet tree-juice used in medicine. [Heb. *man*]

mann'equin, mann'ekin *n.* live model employed by dressmakers, *etc.* [F.]

mann'er *n.* way a thing happens or is done; sort or kind; custom; style. -*pl.* social behavior. -**mann'erism** *n.* addiction to a literary or artistic manner; habitual trick of style or behavior. -**mann'erly** *a.* having good manners. [F. *manière*]

manom'eter *n.* instrument for measuring density of gases or vapors. [G. *manos,* rare]

man'or *n.* unit of land in the feudal period. -**man'or-house** *n.* residence of the lord of the manor. -**manor'ial** *a.* [F. *manoir,* L. *manere,* dwell]

manse *n.* minister's house. [fr. L. *manere, mans-,* to dwell, remain]

man'sion *n.* large dwelling-house. [L. *mansio*]

man'suetude *n.* mild temper. [L. *mansuetudo,* gentleness]

man'tel *n.* structure enclosing a fireplace. -**man'tel-shelf** *n.* shelf at the top of the mantel. -**man'telpiece** *n.* mantel or mantel-shelf. [var. of *mantle*]

man'tic *a.* of divination. -**mantol'ogy** *n.* [G. *mantis,* prophet]

man'ticore *n.* fabulous beast, lion with human head. [G. *mantichoras*]

mantill'a *n.* scarf, worn as a headdress. [Sp. dim. of *manta,* mantle]

man'tis *n.* locustlike insect. -**praying man'tis** *n.* mantis that crosses its forelegs as if in prayer. [G.]

man'tle *n.* loose cloak; covering; hood fixed round a gas jet for incandescent light. -*v.t.* cover; conceal. -*v.i.* become covered with scum; of the blood, rush to the checks; of the face, blush. -**mant'let** *n.* short mantle; moveable bullet-proof screen. [L. *mantellum,* cloak]

man'tua *n.* woman's loose mantle in 18th c. [F. *manteau,* mantle]

man'ual *a.* of or done with the hands. -*n.* handbook, text book; organ keyboard. [L. *manualis-manus,* hand]

manufac'ture *n.* making of articles or materials, *esp.* in large quantities for sale. -*v.t.* produce (articles), work up (materials) into finished articles. **manufac'tory** *n.* factory or workshop. -**manufac'turer** *n.* owner of a factory. [F. fr. L. *manu facere,* make by hand]

manumit' *v.t.* give freedom to (a slave). -**manumis'sion** *n.* [L. *manumittere,* send from one's hand]

manure' *v.t.* enrich land. -*n.* dung or other substances used for fertilizing land. [F. *manceuvrer*]

man'uscript *a.* written by hand. -*n.* book, document, *etc.,* written by hand; copy of matter to be printed. [Med. L. *manuscriptum*]

Manx *a.* of the Isle of Man. -*n.* Manx language. [fr. *Man*]

man'y (men'i) *a.* numerous. -*n.* large number. [OE. *manig*]

Mao'ri (mow'-ri) *n.* native of N.Z.; this race, language. [*native*]

map *n.* flat representation of the earth or some part of it, or of the heavens. -*v.t.* make a map of. [L. *mappa,* cloth]

ma'ple *n.* tree of the sycamore family, one kind yielding sugar. [OE. *mapel*]

ma'quis *n.* in Corsica, thick scrub giving cover to brigands, hence any guerilla band. [F.]

mar *v.t.* spoil, impair. -**mar'plot** *n.* one who frustrates plans. [OE. *mierran*]

mar'abou(t) *n.* African adjutant stork; its down. [F.]

mar'athon *n.* long-distance race. [*Marathon,* Greece]

maraud' *v.t.* and *i.* make a raid for plunder. -**maraud'er** *n.* [F. *marauder*]

mar'ble *n.* kind of lime stone capable of taking a polish; slab of this; small ball used in a game called **marbles.** -*v.t.* color so as to resemble veined marble. [L. *marmor*]

marc' *n.* refuse of crushed grapes; liquor distilled from this. [F.]

mar'casite *n.* iron pyrites. [F.]

marcel′ *v.t.* wave (hair) with hot irons. -**marcel-wave** *n.* [*Marcel*, inventor]
March *n.* third month of the year. [L. *martius* (*mensis*), (month) of Mars]
march *n.* border or frontier. -*v.i.* border. [F. *marche*]
march *v.i.* walk with a military step; start on a march; go. -*v.t.* cause to march or go. -*n.* action of marching; distance marched in a day; tune to accompany marching. [F. *marcher*, walk]
marchioness (-shon-) *n.* wife or widow of a marquis. [Med. L. *marchionissa*]
marco′nigram *n.* wireless telegram. [*Marconi*, inventor, 1874-1937]
mare *n.* female of the horse or other equine animal. -**mare's nest** *n.* fancied discovery. [OE. *mere*]
margarine (-j-) *n.* vegetable substance imitating butter, and containing vegetable and animal oils. [F.]
mar′gin (-j-) *n.* border or edge; amount allowed beyond what is absolutely necessary; blank space round a printed page. -**marge** *n.* margin. -**mar′ginal** *a.* -**mar′ginalize** *v.t.* relegate to the fringes, out of the mainstream; make seem unimportant. -**mar′ginali′zation** *n.* [L. *margo, margin-*]
mar′grave *n.* formerly German nobleman (**margravine** *n. fem.*) [Du. *markgrave*, border count]
Marguerite *n.* ox-eye daisy. [F.]
marigold *n.* plant with yellow flowers; Calendula. [Virgin *Mary* and *gold*]
mar′igraph *n.* self-recording tide gauge. -**mar′igram** *n.* [L. *mare*, sea]
marim′ba *n.* native African xylophone [native orig.]
marinade′ *v.t.* soak (meat, fish) in wine spices, *etc.*, before cooking. -*n.* the marinading liquor. [F.]
marine′ *a.* of the sea or shipping; used at sea. -*n.* shipping collectively; soldier serving on board a ship. -**mar′iner** *n.* sailor. [L. *mare*, sea]
Mariol′atry *n.* worship of Virgin Mary. [G. *Maria*, Mary, *latreia*, worship]
marionette′ *n.* puppet worked with strings. [F.]
mar′ital *a.* relating to a husband or marriage. [L. *maritus*, husband]
mar′itime *a.* bordering on the sea; connected with seafaring or navigation. [L. *maritimus*, fr. *mare*, sea]
mar′joram *n.* aromatic herb of the mint family. [orig. uncertain]
mark *n.* something set up to be aimed at; sign or token; inscription; line, dot, scar, or any visible trace or impression. -*v.t.* make a mark on; indicate, be a distinguishing mark of, watch. -*v.i.* take notice. **marks′man** *n.* one skilled in shooting. -**mark′er** *n.* [OE. *mearc*]
mark *n.* German coin; various old coins. [orig. uncertain]
mark′et *n.* place or assembly for buying and selling; demand for goods; place or center for trade. -*v.t.* bring to or sell in a market. -**mark′etable** *a.* [L. *mercari, mercat*, trade]
mar′khor *n.* Asian wild goat. [Pers.]
marl *n.* clayey soil used as a fertilizer. -*v.t.* fertilize with it. [OF. *marle*]
marl′ine (-in) *n.* two-strand cord. -**marl′ine spike** *n.* pointed hook for unravelling rope to be spliced. [Du. *marlijn*, fr. *marren*, bind]
marmalade *n.* orange preserve. [F. *marmalade*]
marmo′real *a.* of, like, marble. [L. *marmor*, *marble*]
mar′moset *n.* small S. American bush-tailed monkey. [F. *marmouset*]
mar′mot *n.* rodent allied to the squirrel. [F. *marmotte*]
mar′ocain (*n.* dress fabric with grained surface. [F.]
maroon′ *n.* brownish crimson color; kind of firework. -*a.* of the color. [F. *marron*, chestnut]
maroon′ *n.* fugitive slave in the West Indies; marooned person. -*v.t.* leave on a desert island. [Sp, *cimarron*, wild]
marque (-k) *n.* letters of marque, license to act as a privateer. [F.]
marquee′ (-ke) *n.* roof-like structure or awning, *usu.* at the entrance of a building; large tent. [F. *marquise*, lit. *marchioness*]
marquetry (-ket-) *n.* inlaid work of wood, ivory, *etc.* [F. *marqueterie*]
marquise, mar′quess *n.* nobleman of rank next below a duke. -**mar′quisate** *n.* [OF. *marchis*, L. *marca*, boundary]
mar′ram *n.* Bent-grass. [ON. *marr*, sea, *halmr*, haulm]
ma′rrow *n.* fatty substance inside bones. -**vegetable marrow**, gourd cooked as a table vegetable. -**mar′rowfat** *n.* large pea. -**mar′rowy** *a.* [OE. *merg*]
ma′rry *v.t.* join as husband and wife; take as husband or wife. -*v.i.* take a husband or wife. -**mar′riage** (-rij) *n.* state of being married: act of marrying. -**mar′riageable** *a.* [F. *marier*, L. *maritare*]
Mars′ *n.* Roman god of war; 2nd nearest

planet to earth. -**Martian** *a.* of Mars. -*n.* supposed dweller in Mars. [L. *Mars, Mart-*]

Marseillaise′ *n.* French national anthem. [*Marseilles*]

marsh *n.* low-lying wet land. -**marshmall′ow** *n.* herb growing near marshes; soft candy orig. made from this. -**marshmar′igold** *n.* plant with yellow flowers growing in wet places. -**marsh′y** *a.* [OE. *mersc*]

marsh′al *n.* high officer of state; military rank; chief officer of a district. -*v.t.* arrange in due order; conduct with ceremony. [F. *maréchal*, orig. a horse-servant]

marsupial *n.* animal that carries its young in a pouch, *e.g.* the kangaroo. [G. *marsupion*, small bag]

mart *n.* market place or market hall; auction room. [Du. *markt*, market]

martell′o *n.* round tower for coast defense. [Cape *Mortella*, Corsica]

mart′en *n.* weasellike animal yielding a valuable fur. [OF. *martrine*, fr. *martre*, marten]

mar′tial (-shal) *a.* relating to war; warlike. [L. *Mars*, god of war]

mar′tin *n.* species of swallow. [fr. name *Martin*]

martinet′ *n.* strict disciplinarian. [orig. uncertain]

martingale *n.* strap to keep horse from throwing up its head; system of doubling stakes at gambling. [F.]

Mar′tinmas *n.* feast of St. Martin, 11th November.

mart′let *n.* (*her.*) martin; swift. [dim. of *martin*]

mar′tyr (-ter) *n.* one put to death for refusing to give up a belief or cause, *esp.* the Christian faith; one who suffers in some cause; one in constant suffering. -*v.t.* make a martyr of. -**mar′tyrdom** *n.* -**martyrol′ogy** *n.* list or history of martyrs. [G. = *witness*]

mar′vel *n.* wonderful thing. -*v.i.* wonder. -**mar′velous** *a.* [F. *merueille*]

Marx′ist (-ks-) *a.* of Karl *Marx*, Socialist (d. 1883) of his works or doctrine. -**Marxism** *n.* Marx's doctrine of materialist conception of history.

ma′rybud. *See* **marigold.**

marzipan′ *n.* paste of sugar and ground almonds. [Ger.]

masca′ra *n.* eyelash cosmetic. [Sp.]

mas′cot *n.* thing supposed to bring good luck. [F. *mascotte*]

masculine (-lin) *a.* of males; manly, vigorous; (*gram.*) of the gender to which names of males belong. [L. *masculinus*]

mash *n.* meal mixed with warm water; warm food for horses, *etc.* -*v.t.* make into a mash; crush into a soft mass. [OE. *masc*]

mash′er *n.* (*sl.*) dandy, lady-killer. [orig. unknown]

mash′ie *n.* (*golf*) iron club for lofting. [orig. uncertain]

mask *n.* covering for the face; disguise or pretense. -*v.t.* cover with mask; hide, disguise. -**masque** *n.* form of amateur theatrical performance; masquerade. -**masquerade** *n.* masked ball. -*v.i.* go about in disguise. [F. *masque*]

masochism *n.* form of sexual perversion which delights in endurance of pain. -**mas′ochist** *n.* [*Sacher-Masoch*, novelist]

ma′son *n.* worker in stone; freemason. —**mason′ic** *a.* of freemasonry. -**ma′sonry** *n.* stonework. [F. *macon*]

mass *n.* service of the Eucharist. [L. *missa*, fr. *mittere*, send]

mass *n.* quantity of matter; dense collection of this; large quantity. -**the mass′es,** the populace. -*v.t.* and *i.* form into a mass. -**mass′y** *a.* solid, weighty. -**mass′ive** *a.* having great size and weight. -**mass′ production**, large-scale production. [G. *maza*, barley cake]

mass′acre (-ker) *n.* general slaughter; indiscriminate killing, *esp.* of unresisting people. -*v.t.* make a massacre of. [F.]

mass′age *a.* rubbing and kneading the muscles, *etc.*, as curative treatment. *v.t.* apply this treatment to. -**mass′eur** *n.* -**mass′euse** *fem.*, one who practices massage. [F. fr. G. *massein*, knead]

massif′ *n.* mountain-group. [F.]

mast *n.* (*naut.*) of timber, steel, *etc.*, pole for supporting sails, derricks, *etc.* [OE. *mcest*]

mast *n.* fruit of beech, oak, *etc.*, used as food for pigs. [OE. *mæst*]

mast′er *n.* one who employs another; head of a household; owner; one in control; captain of a merchant ship; teacher; artist of great reputation. -*v.t.* overcome; acquire knowledge of, or skill in. -**mast′erful** *a.* imperious, self- willed. -**mast′erly** *a.* skillfully done. -**mast′ery** *n.* victory, authority. -**mast′erpiece** *n.* finest work of artist or craftsman. -**mast′ership** *n.* position of master. [L. *magister*]

mas′tic *n.* a gum-resin got from certain trees and used in varnish, *etc.* [F.]

mas′ticate *v.t.* chew. -**mastica′tion** *n.* [L. *masticate*, chew gum]

mas'tiff *n.* large dog used as watch-dog. [OF. *mastin* (*a.*), domestic]

mast'odon *n.* extinct elephant. [G. *mastos*, breast, *odous, odon-*, tooth]

mast'oid *a.* breast-shaped, *esp.* of the bone behind the ear. *-n.* this bone; sinusitis of the mastoid. [G. *mastos*, breast]

mat *n.* small carpet or strip of plaited rushes, *etc.*; thick tangled mass. *-v.t.* and *i.* form into such a mass. **-matt'ing** *n.* fabric of mats. [L. *matta*]

mat, matt, matte *a.* dull, unpolished. [F.]

mat'ador *n.* man who kills the bull in a bull fight. [Sp. fr. L. *mactare*, to kill]

match *n.* person or thing exactly corresponding to another; one able to contend equally with another; trial of skill; marriage; person regarded as eligible for marriage. *-v.t.* join in marriage; meet equally in contest; place in contest with; get something corresponding to (a color, pattern, *etc.*). *-v.i.* correspond. **-match'less** *a.* unequalled. **-match'board** *n.* thin boards fitted into each other by tongue and groove. **-match'maker** *n.* woman fond of arranging marriages. [OE. *gernæcca*]

match *n.* small stick with a head of combustible material, which bursts into flame when rubbed; fuse. **-match'lock** *n.* old musket fired by a fuse. **-match'wood** *n.* small splinters. [F. *meche*, wick]

mate *n.* checkmate. *-v.t.* [*See* **check**]

mate *n.* comrade, husband or wife; officer in a merchant ship immediately below the captain. *-v.t.* marry. *-v.i.* keep company. [Du. *maat*]

mate'ria med'ica *n.* science of the substances used in medicine. [Med. L. trans. of G. *hyle iatrike*, physician's material]

mate'rial *a.* of matter or body; unspiritual; essential, important. *-n.* stuff from which anything is made; stuff or fabric. **-materialism** *n.* opinion that nothing exists except matter **-mate'rialist** *a.* and *n.* **-materialis'tic** *a.* **-mate'rialize** *v.t.* make material. *-v.i.* come into existence. **-materially** *adv.* [L. *materia*, matter]

mater'nal *a.* of or related through a mother. **-matern'ity** *n.* motherhood. [L. *mater*, mother]

mathematics *n. pl.* science of space and number. **-mathemat'ical** *a.* **mathematically** *adv.* **-mathemati'cian** *n.* [*mathernatike*, fr. G. *manthanein*, learn]

mat'inee *n.* morning and afternoon performance. **-mat'ins** *n. pl.* morning prayers; one of the canonical hours, a midnight or daybreak office. [F. *matins*, morning]

matriarch *n.* mother as ruler of family. **-matriarchy** *n.* government by mothers or in which descent is through female line. [L. *mater*, mother]

matricide *n.* killing of one's own mother; the killer. [L. *mater*, mother]

matriculate *v.t.* enter on a college or university register. *-v.i.* enter one's name on such register; pass an examination entitling one to do this. **-matricula'tion** *n.* [Med. L. *matricula*, register of numbers]

matrimony *n.* marriage. **-matrimo'nial** *a.* [L. *matrimoniurn, mater*, mother]

mat'rix *n.* mold for casting. [L.]

ma'tron *n.* married woman; woman superintendent of a hospital, school, *etc.* **ma'tronly** *a.* [L. *matrona*]

matt, matte *See* **mat.**

matt'er *n.* substance of which a thing is made up; physical or bodily substance in general; pus; substance of a book, *etc.*; affair; reason, cause of trouble. *-v.i.* be of importance. **-matter-of-fact** *a.* prosaic. [F. *matiere* fr. L. *materia*]

matt'ock *n.* tool for breaking up hard ground. [OE. *mattuc*]

matt'ress *n.* stuffed flat case used as or under a bed; a frame with stretched wires for supporting a bed. [OF. *materas*]

mature' *a.* ripe, completely developed, grown. *-v.t.* bring to maturity. *- v.i.* come to maturity; of a bill, become due. **matu'rity** *n.* [L. *maturus*, ripe]

matuti'nal *a. pert.* to the morning. [Late L. *matutinalis*]

maud'lin *a.* weakly sentimental. [L. *magdalena*, Mary *Magdalen*, fr. pictures showing her weeping]

maul, mawl *n.* heavy wooden hammer, **-maul** *v.t.* beat or bruise; handle roughly. [L. *mialleus*, hammer]

maul'stick, mahl'-stick *n.* tapered stick, painter's rest for right hand. [Du. *maalé stok*, paint-stick]

maund'er *v.i.* mutter, grumble; whine; wander in talking. [orig. uncertain]

maun'dy *n.* foot-washing ceremony on Thursday before Easter (*cp.* John xiii, 14); royal alms given on that day. [OF. *mandé*, mandate]

mausole'um *n.* stately building as a tomb. [L. fr. *Mausolus*, King of Caria]

mauve *n.* bright purple aniline dye; color of this dye. *-a.* this color. [F., fr. L. *malva*, mallow]

mav'erick *n.* unbranded steer, stray cow; independent, unorthodox person. [perh. Samuel *Maverick*, Texas rancher]

ma'vis *n.* song-thrush. [F. *mauvis*]

maw *n.* stomach. [OE. *tnaga*]

mawk'ish *a.* having a sickly flavor; weakly sentimental. [orig. 'nauseating', fr. dial. *mawk*, maggot]

maxill'a *n.* jawbone. -**maxill'ary** *a.* of the jaw or jawbone. [L.]

max'im *n.* short pithy saying; axiom; rule of conduct. [F. *maxime*]

max'im *n.* a machine-gun. [Sir H. *Maxim*, inventor]

max'imum *n.* greatest possible size or number. -*a.* greatest. -**maximize** *v.t.* [L. = *greatest*]

May *n.* fifth month of the year; hawthorn; its flowers. -*v.i.* take part in May-day festivities. -**may'fly** *n.* short-lived fly of May. -**may'pole** *n.* pole for dancing round on May-day (1st May). [L. *Maius*, fr. *Maia*, goddess of growth]

may *v. aux.* express possibility, permission, opportunity, *etc.* -**may'be** *adv.* possibly, perhaps. [OE. *mæg*]

may'hem *n.* crime of maiming (a person); severe disruption, willful damage or violence. [ME. *mahaym*, maim]

mayonnaise' *n.* sauce of egg-yolk, olive-oil, lemon-juice, *etc.* [F.]

may'or *n.* head of a municipality. -**may'oral** *a.* -**may'oralty** *n.* office or time of office, of a mayor. -**may'oress** *n.* mayor's wife; lady mayor. [L. *major*, greater]

maze *n.* labyrinth; network of paths or lines. -*v.t.* stupefy. [cp. *amaze*]

mazour'ka, mazur'ka *n.* lively Polish dance; music for it.

me *pron.* objective case singular of the 1st personal pronoun I. [OE.]

mead *n.* alcoholic drink made from honey. [OE. *meodu*]

mead *n.* meadow. -**mead'ow** *n.* piece of grassland. -**mead'ow-saff'ron** *n.* autumn crocus. -**mead'ow-sweet** *n.* sweet-smelling flowering plant. [OE. *maed*]

mea'ger *a.* lean, thin, scanty. [F. *maigre*, thin]

meal *n.* grain ground to powder. -**meal'y** *a.* -**meal'y-mouthed** *a.* soft-spoken; prim in choice of words. [OE. melo]

meal *n.* occasion of taking food; food taken. [OE. *mael*, time fixed]

mean *a.* inferior; shabby; small-minded; niggardly, miserly; bad-tempered. **mean'ly** *adv.* -**mean'ness.** [OE. *gemaene*]

mean *a.* intermediate in time; quality, *etc.* -*n.* anything which is intermediate. *pl.* that by which something is done; money resources. -**mean'time** *n.* **meanwhile** *n.* time between one happening and another. -*adv.* during this time. [OF. *meien*]

mean *v.t.* intend, design; signify; import. -**mean'ing** *n.* sense, significance. -*a.* expressive. -**mean'ingly** *adv.* -**mean'ingless** *a.* IOE. *mænan*]

meand'er *v.i.* flow windingly; wander aimlessly . -**meandering** *n.* (*usu. pl.*) winding; roundabout way. [G. *Maiandros*, winding river of Phrygia]

meas'les (mez'ls) *n.pl.* infectious disease with red spots. -**meas'ly** *a.* of measles; poor, wretched. [ME. *maseles*]

meas'ure (mezh-er) *n.* size or quantity; vessel, rod, line, *etc.*, for ascertaining size or quantity; unit of size or quantity; poetical rhythm; order or tune; musical time; slow dance; course or plan of action; law. -*v.t.* ascertain size or quantity of-, estimate; bring into competition (with). *v.i.* be (so much) in size or quantity. -**meas'urable** *a.* -**meas'ured** *a.* carefully considered. -**meas'urement** *n.* [F. *mesure*]

meat *n.* food; flesh of animals used as food. -**meat'y** *a.* [OE. *mete*]

Mecc'a *n.* place of pilgrimage. [*Mecca*, birthplace of Mohammad]

mechan'ic (-k-) *a.* relating to a machine. -*n.* one employed in working with machinery; skilled workman. -*pl.* branch of science dealing with motion and tendency of motion. -**mechan'ical** *a.* concerned with machines or manual operation; worked or produced by, or as though by, a machine; like a machine; relating to mechanics. -**mechan'ically** *adv.* -**mechani'cian** *n.* -**mech'anize** *v.t.* substitute mechanical power for manpower (horse-power, *etc.*) -**mech'anism** *n.* structure of a machine; piece of machinery. [G. *mechane*, machine]

Mech'lin *n.* lace made at *Mechlin* (Malines).

med'al *n.* piece of metal usually round or star-shaped with an inscription, *etc.*, and used as a reward or memento. -**medall'ion** *n.* large medal; various things like this in decorative work. -**med'alist** *n.* winner of a medal; maker of medals. [L. *metallum*, metal]

med'dle *v.i.* interfere, busy one's self with unnecessarily. -**meddlesome** *a.* [AF. *medlar*, OF. *mesler* (mod. *méler*) mix]

me'dial *a.* middle; average. -**me'dian** *a.* [L. *medius*, middle]

me'diate *v.i.* go between in order to reconcile. -*v.t.* bring about by mediation. -*a.* not immediate, depending on something intermediate. **-media'tion** *a.* **me'diator** *a.* [Late L. *mediare*]

med'ic(k) *n.* purple-flowered fodder plant, alfalfa, lucerne. [L. *medica*]

medicine *n.* art of healing by remedies and the regulation of diet: remedy or mixture of drugs. **-med'ical** *a.* **-med'ically** *adv.* **-med'icament** *n.* remedy. **med'icate** *v.t.* impregnate with medicinal substances. **-medica'tion** *n.* **-med'icative** *a.* healing. **-medic'inal** *a.* having healing properties, curative. [L. *medicinal* fr. *medicus*, physician]

Medieval *a.* relating to the Middle Ages. **-medie'valism** *n.* **-medie'valist** *n.* one who studies the Middle Ages. [fr. L. *medius*, middle, and *ævum*, age]

me'diocre *a.* neither bad nor good, ordinary. **-medioc'rity** *n.* [L. *mediocris*]

meditate *v.t.* think about; plan. *-v.i.* be occupied in thought. **-medita'tion** *n.* **-med'itative** *a.* reflective. **-med'itatively** *adv.* [L. *meditari*]

Meditera'nean *n.* the sea between Europe and Africa. [L. *medius*, middle, *terra*, earth]

me'dium *n.* (**me'diums, me'dia** *pl.*) middle quality or degree; intermediate substance conveying force; surroundings; environment; means, agency; (*spirit.*) person as medium for spirit manifestations. *-a.* between two qualities, degrees, moderate, *etc.* [L.]

med'lar *n.* tree with a fruit like a small apple, eaten when decayed; the fruit. [G. *mespilon*]

med'ley *n.* miscellaneous mixture; jumble. [OF. *mesler*, mix]

medull'a *n.* pith, marrow, inner tissue. **-medull'ary** *a.* [L. *medulla*, marrow]

Medusa *n.* one of the three Gorgons, she had snakes for hair and a stare which turned beholders to stone. [L.]

meed *n.* a reward. [OE. *med*]

meek *a.* submissive, humble. **-meek'ly** *adv.* **-meek'ness** *n.* [ON. *miukr*, soft]

meerschaum (-shum) *n.* white substance resembling clay used for bowls of tobacco pipes. [Ger. = *sea foam*]

meet *a.* fit, suitable. **-meet'ly** *adv.* **meet'ness** *n.* IOE. *gemæte*]

meet *v.t.* come face to face with; encounter; satisfy, pay. *-v.i.* come face to face; assemble; come into contact. *-n.* meeting for a hunt. **-meet'ing** *n.* assembly. [OE. *metan*]

meg'a- *prefix* great. (G. *mesas, mesa*, great) **-megabyte** *n.* (*compute.*) about 1 million bytes, 1,024 kilobytes. **-meg'afog** *n.* fog-signal fitted withmegaphones. **-megalith'ic** *a.* consisting of great stones. **-megaloma'nia** *n.* a passion for great things. **-megaloma'niac** *a.* and *n.* **-megalosaur'us** *n.* giant extinct reptile. • **meg'aphone** *n.* an instrument for carrying the sound of the voice to a distance. **-meg'astar** *n.* a very well-known personality in the entertainment business. **-megathe'rium** *n.* giant extinct quadruped. **me'grim** *n.* severe headache generally affecting only one side of head. [F. *méigraine*]

meio'sis (mi-c-) *n.* rhetorical understatement opposite of hyperbole. [G. *meiosiss*, diminution]

meistersinger *n.* one of the German burgher poets and musicians of the 14th-16th c. [Ger.]

melancholy (-k-) *n.* sadness, dejection, gloom. *-a.* gloomy, dejected. **-melancho'lia** *n.* mental disease accompanied by depression. **-melanchol'ic** *a.* [G. *melangcholia*, black bile]

melange (ma-longzh') *n.* a mixture; medley [F.]

melan'ic *a.* black. **-mel'anism** *n.* abnormal pigmentation of the skin, *etc.* [G. *melas, melar-*, black]

mêlée (mel'a) *n.* mixed fight. [F.]

mel'inite *n.* high explosive. [F.]

me'liorate *v.t.* and *i.* improve, better. **-meliora'tion** *n.* **-me'liorism** *n.* doctrine that the world may be improved by human effort. [L. *melior*, better]

mellifluous *a.* sweet as honey. **-mellif'luence** *n.* [L. *mellifluus*, flowing with honey]

mell'ow *a.* ripe; juicy; (*colloq.*) partly drunk. *-v.t.* and *i.* make or become mellow. [ME. *melwe*, ripe]

melodrama *n.* play full of sensational happenings and ending happily. **melodramatic** *a.* [F. *mélodrame*]

mel'ody *n.* sweet sound; series of musical notes arranged to make a tune. **-melo'dious** *a.* **-mel'odist** *n.* singer; composer of melodies, [G. *melos*, song]

mel'on *n.* various gourds eaten as fruit, *esp.* watermelon. [G. *melon*, apple]

Melpom'ene *n.* muse of tragedy. [G.]

melt *v.i.* become liquid by heat; be dissolved; become softened; waste away. *-v.t.* cause to soften or dissolve or become liquid by heat. **-melt'down** *n.* (in nuclear reactor) the melting of the fuel rods as a result of a defect in the cooling system, with the possible escape of radiation into the environment. [OE. *meltan*]

mem'ber *n.* limb; any part of a complicated structure; any of the individuals making up a body or society. -**mem'bership** *n.* [L. *membrum*, limb]

mem'brane *n.* thin flexible tissue in a plant or animal body. [L. *membrane*]

mement'o *n.* thing serving to remind; a souvenir. [L. = *remember*]

mem'oir *a.* record of events; autobiography or biography. [F. *mémoire*, memory]

mem'ory *n.* faculty of recollecting or recalling to mind; recollection; length of time one can remember. -**memor'ial** *a.* of or preserving memory. -*n.* something which serves to keep in memory; statement in a petition. -**memor'ialize** *v.t.* commemorate; petition. -**memor'ialist** *n.* -**mem'orize** *v.t.* commit to memory. **mem'orable** *a.* worthy of being remembered. -**mem'orably** *adv.* -**memoran'dum, mem'o** *n.* note to help the memory; note of a contract; informal letter. [L. *memor*, mindful]

men'ace *n.* threat. -*v.t.* threaten. [F., fr. L. *minari*, threaten]

ménage' *n.* household; management of a household. [F.]

menagerie (-j-) *n.* collection of wild animals kept for show. [F. *menagerie*]

mend *v.t.* repair, correct, put right. -*v.i.* improve, *esp.* in health. -*n.* [*amend*]

mendacious *a.* untruthful. -**mendac'ity** *n.* [L. *mendax, mendac-*]

mendicant *a.* begging. -*n.* beggar. -**mend'icancy** *n.* [L. *mendicus*, beggar]

men'hir *n.* prehistoric standing stone. [W. *maen hir*, long stone]

menial *a.* retating to a servant in a house; servile. -*n.* household servant. [ME. *meinie*, household]

meningi'tis *n.* inflammation of membranes of brain. [G. *méninx*, membrane]

menis'cus *n.* convex or concave shape of the apex of a column of liquid. [G. *meniskos*, crescent]

menopause *n.* cessation of menstruation. [G. *men*, month, *pausis*, cessation]

men'sal *a.* monthly. -**men'ses** *n. pl.* monthly discharge from uterus. -**men'strual** *a.* -**menstrua'tion** *n.* approximately monthly discharge of blood and cellular debris from womb of nonpregnant woman. -**men'struate** *v.i.* [L. *mensis*, month]

Menshevik *n.* Russian minority socialist. [Russ. = *the lesser*]

menstruation. *See* **mensal.**

mensuration *n.* measuring, *esp.* of areas. [Late L. *mensurare*, measurer]

ment'al *a.* relating to or done by the mind. -**ment'ally** *adv.* -**mental'ity** *n.* quality of mind. [L. *mens, ment-*, mind]

menta'tion *n.* activities of the mind; thinking.

men'thol *n.* kind of camphor extracted from peppermint. [L. *mentha*, mint]

men'tion (-shun) *n.* reference to or remark about (person or thing). -*v.t.* refer to, speak of. -**men'tionable** *a.* fit to be mentioned. [L. *mentio*]

men'tor *n.* wise and trusted adviser. [G. *Mentor*, counselor of the son of Ulysses]

men'u *n.* bill of fare. [F. = *detailed*]

mep'acrine *n.* synthetic drug, substitute for quinine. [compound fr. L. *mephitis*, malaria]

mephi'tis (-fi-) *n.* poisonous exhalation (from the ground, *etc.*) -**mephitéic** *a.* [L.]

mercantile (-k-) *a.* of trade; engaged in trade. [It. *mercante*, merchant]

mercenary (-s-) *a.* hired; working simply for reward. -*n.* hired soldier in foreign service. [L. *merces*, reward]

mer'cer *n.* dealer in fabrics, *esp.* silks. [L. *merx, merc-*, merchandise -**mer'chant** *n.* wholesale trader. **mer'chandise** *n.* things in which he deals. -**mer'chantman** *n.* trading ship. [F. *Marchand*]

mer'cury *n.* liquid white metal, quicksilver. -**Mercury**, Roman god of eloquence, messenger of the gods; planet nearest to the sun. -**mercu'rial** *a.* lively, sprightly of, or containing mercury. [L. *Mercurius*, orig. god of merchandiser]

mer'cy *n.* quality of compassion, clemency; a refraining from the infliction of suffering by one who has the right or power to inflict it. -**mer'ciful** *a.* **mer'ciless** *a.* [L. *merces*, reward]

mere *n.* lake, pool. [OE.]

mere *a.* only; not of more value or size, *etc.*, than name implies. -**mere'ly** *adv.* [L. *merus*, unmixed]

meretricious *a.* cheap and tawdry, superficial. [L. *meretrix*, prostitute]

merganser *n.* marine duck. [L. *mergus*, diver, *anser*, goose]

merge *v.i.* lose identity, mix in. -*v.t.* cause to lose identity or to be absorbed. -**mer'ger** (-j-) *n.* a being absorbed into something greater; a combining of business firms. [L. *mergere*, dip]

merid'ian *a.* relating to noon, or the position of the sun at noon. -*n.* noon; highest point reached by a star, *etc.*; period of greatest splendor; imaginary circle in the sky passing through the celestial pole; circle of the earth passing through the poles and a place stated. [L. *meridies*, mid-day]

meringue′ *n.* cake, sweet; of sugar and white of egg. [F.]

merin′o *n.* variety of sheep; fine fabric of merino wool. [Sp.]

mer′it *n.* excellence, worth; quality of deserving well. -*pl.* excellences or defects. -*v.t.* deserve. -**meritor′ious** *a.* deserving well. [L. *meritum*]

merle *n.* blackbird. [F.]

mer′lin *n.* small hawk. [F. *emerillon*]

mer′maid *n.* imaginary sea creature having the upper part of a woman and the tail of a fish. [obs. *mere*, sea]

mer′ry *a.* joyous, cheerful. -**merr′ily** *adv.* -**merr′iment** *n.* -**merr′ythought** *n.* forked bone between the head and breast of a bird. -**merr′y-go-round** *n.* revolving machine with wooden horses, model automobiles, *etc.* [OE. *myrge*]

me′sa *n.* flat-topped hill. [Sp.]

meseems *v.i.* it seems to me. [*me* and *seem*]

mesh *n.* one of the open spaces of a net. -*v.t.* catch in meshes. [OE. *masc*]

mesmerism *n.* system of inducing a hypnotic state by influence on a patient. **mesmer′ic** *a.* -**mes′merist** *n.* -**mes′merize** *v.t.* [*Mesmer,* Austrian physician (1733-1815)]

mess *n.* portion of food; state of untidy confusion; company of people who regularly eat together; place where they do this. -*v.i.* take one's meals thus; busy one's self untidily. -*v.t.* make a mess of, to muddle. -**mess′mate** *n.* companion at meals; member of a mess. [OF. *mes*, fr. *mettre*, put]

message *n.* communication from one person to another. -**mess′enger** *n.* message-bearer. [F. fr. L. *mittere, miss-*, send]

Messi′ah *n.* promised deliverer of the Jews; Christ. -**Messian′ic** *a.* [Heb. *mashiah*, anointed

Messieurs (written **Mess′rs.** *pron.* **mes′ers**) *n., pl.* of Mister [*q.v.*]

mess′uage *n.* house with outbuildings and land. [AF. *mesuage*]

meta- *prefix* over, beyond; also expressing change. [G.]

metabolism *n.* process of chemical change in a living organism. -**metabol′ic** *a.* [G. *metabole*, change]

metachro′sis *n.* color-change, as in chameleon. [G. *meta-*, *chrosis*, coloring]

met′al *n.* any of a number of chemical elements usually bright and easy to melt, *e.g.*, gold, iron, *etc.*, broken stone used for macadam roads. -**metall′ic** *a.* -**met′allurgy** *n.* art of refining metals. -**met′allurgist** *n.* [G. *metallon*, mine]

met′amer *n.* (*chem.*) compound that has the same molecular weight and same elements in the same proportion as another compound, but differs in structure.

metamorphosis *n.* change of shape, substance, character, *etc.* -**metamor′phose** *v.t.* transform. [G. *morphe*, form]

metaphor *n.* (*rhet.*) transference of a term to something it does not literally apply to; substance of this. -**metaphor′ical** *a.* [G. *pherein*, carry]

met′aphrase *n.* a word for word translation as distinct from a paraphrase. [G. *metaphrasis*]

metaphysics *n.pl.* theory of being and knowing. -**metaphys′ical** *a.* -**metaphysician** *n.* [fr. books of Aristotle, called in G. *tametataphysika*, 'the (works) after the physics,' referring to position but later mistaken for 'Works beyond or above physics']

metath′esis *n.* transposition, *esp.* of letters in a word, *e.g.*, movement of *r* in *bird.* [OE. *bridd.*] [G.]

mete (met) *v.t.* measure. -**me′ter** *n.* instrument for measuring. [OE. *metan*]

metempsycho′sis *n.* transmigration of the soul after death. [G. *en*, in, *psyche*, soul]

me′teor *n.* shining body appearing temporarily in the sky; shooting star. -- **meteor′ic** *a.* -**me′teorite** *n.* fallen meteor. -**meteorol′ogy** *n.* science of weather. -**meteorolog′ical** *a.* -**meteorol′ogist** *n.* [G. *meteorosa*, lofty]

me′ter *n.* instrument for measuring, *esp.* gas or electricity consumption; verse, rhythm; unit of length in the French decimal system, 39.37 inches. -**met′ric** *a.* of this system. -**met′rical** *a.* of measurement or of poetic meter. [G. *metron*, measurer]

methane *n.* a light colorless gas, marsh-gas. [G. *methan*]

methinks′ *v. impers.* it seems to me. [OE. *thyncan*, seem]

meth′od *n.* a way of doing something; orderliness, system. -**method′ical** *a.* -**Meth′odist** *n.* member of any of the churches originated by John Wesley and G. Whitefield. -**Meth′odism** *n.* -**meth′od-ize**

v.t. reduce to order. [G. *methodos*, investigation]

meth'yl *n.* base of wood spirit; many other organic compounds. **-meth'ylate** *v.t.* mix with methyl. [fr. G. *methy*, wine, *hyle*, wood]

meth'ylated spirit *n.* alcohol made unpalatable with wood spirit *etc.* [G. *meta*, after, with, *hyle*, wood]

meticulous *a.* (over) particular about details. [L. *meticulosus*, timid]

mé'tier *n.* one's proper calling; forte. [F.]

metonymy *n.* (*rhet.*) use of one term for another related, as 'the stage' for dramatic art. [G. *metoonymia*]

met'ric. *See* **meter.**

metronome *n.* (*music*) device for beating time at the required tempo. [F. *metronome*]

metropolis *n.* (**metropolises**) *pl.* chief city of a state. **-metropol'itan** *a.* of the metropolis. *-n.* archbishop or other bishop with authority over bishops of a province. [G. *meter*, mother, *polis*, city]

met'tle *n.* courage, spirit. **-met'tlesome** *a.* [var. of *metal*]

mew *n.* kind of sea-gull. [OE. *mæw*]

mew *v.i.* of a hawk, to molt. *-v.t.* put (hawk) into a cage for moving; imprison, shut up. *-n.* cage for molting hawks. **-mews** *n. pl.* (*usu.* treated as *sing.*) set of stables round an open space. [F. *muer*, L. *mutare*, change]

mew *n.* cry of a cat. *-v.i.* utter this cry. [imit. orig.]

mezzanine *n.* (*archit.*) in a building, low story between two higher ones. [It. mezzanine]

mezzo-soprano (met'so-) *n.* singer, voice, part, between soprano and contralto. [It. *mezzo*, middle]

mez'zotint *n.* method of engraving in which lights and half lights are made by scraping a roughened surface; print so produced. [It. *mezzo*, middle]

mias'ma *n.* harmful exhalations from marshes, *etc.* **-Mias'mal** *a.* [G.]

mi'ca *n.* mineral found in glittering scales or plates. [L. = *crumb*]

Mich'aelmas (mik'el-) *n.* feast of St. Michael the Archangel, 29th September. **-Mich'aelmas-dais'y** *n.* kind of aster with pale-purple flowers. [*Michael*; mass]

micro- *prefix* small. (G. *mikros*) **-mi'crochip** *n.* a small piece of semiconductor material carrying many integrated circuits. **-mi'crocomputer** *n.* a small computer in which the central processing unit is contained in one or more silicon chips. **-mi'crocosm** *n.* world of man; man as an epitome of the universe. **-microcos'mic** *a.* **-mi'crofilm** *n.* minute film of book or manuscript. **-mi'crolight** *n.* small private aircraft carrying no more than two people, with an empty weight of not more than 150 kg and a wing area not less than 10 square meters. **-micro'meter** *n.* instrument for making very small measurements. **-mi'crophone** *n.* instrument for recording or making sounds louder, *e.g.*, as part of a telephone or of broadcasting apparatus. **micropro'cessor** *n.* integrated circuit acting as central processing unit in a small computer. **-mi'croscope** *n.* instrument by which a very small body is magnified and made, visible. **-microscop'ic** *a.* relating to a microscope; so small as to be only visible through a microscope. **-micros'copy** *n.* use of the miscroscope. **-mi'crosurgery** *n.* intricate surgery performed on cells, tissues, *etc.*, using a specially designed operating microscope and miniature precision instruments. **-microwrit'er** *n.* a small device with six keys for creating text that can be printed or displayed on a visual display unit. **-mi'crobe** *n.* minute plant or animal, *esp.* one causing disease or fermentation. [F., fr. G. *mikros*, small *bios*, life]

mid- *prefix* intermediate, that is in the middle. **-mid'day** *n.* noon or about then. **-midd'ling** *a.* medium, mediocre, fair. **-mid'land** *n.* middle part of a country. **-mid'night** *n.* twelve o'clock at night. **-mid'rib** *n.* rib along center of leaf. **-midsection** *n.* middle part of something, *esp.* the body; midriff. **-mid'ship** *n.* middle part of ship. **-mid'shipman** *n.* junior naval officer attending service academy. **-mid'summer** *n.* summer solstice; middle part of the summer. **-Mid'summer Day** *n.* June 24th. **-mid'way** *a.* and *adv.* half-way. [OE. *midd*]

mid'den *n.* dunghill: refuse heap. [Scand. orig.]

mid'dle *a.* equal distance from, or between. two extremes; medium, intermediate. *-n.* middle point or part. **-mid'dleman** *n.* trader handling goods between producer and consumer. **-mid'dlings** *n. pl.* coarser part of ground wheat. **-Mid'dle A'ges**, roughly, period from 5th to 15th c. **-mid'dle weight** *n.* and *a.* (jockey, boxer) between light and heavy weight. [OE. *middel*]

midge *n.* gnat or similar insect. **-mid'get** *n.* a very small person or thing; dwarf. [OE. *mycg*]

mid'riff *n.* diaphragm. [OE. *mid*, mid, *hrif*, belly]

midst *n.* in the midst of, surrounded by, among. *-prep.* among. [ME. *middes*]
mid'wife *n.* woman who assists others in childbirth. **-mid'wifery** (-wif-ri) art or practise of doing this. [OE. *mid,* with, *wif,* woman]
mien *n.* bearing or look. [F. *mine*]
might *n.* power, strength. **-might'y** *a.* - **might'ily** *adv.* [OE. *miht*]
mignonette' (min-yon-) *n.* plant with sweet-smelling flowers. [F.]
mi'graine *n.* severe sick headache, often affecting one side of head. [F., fr. G. *hemi,* half, *kranion,* skull]
mi'grate *v.i.* move from one place to another. **-mi'grant** *a.* and *n.* **-migra'tion** *n.* **-mi'gratory***a.* [L. *migrare*]
mika'do *n.* Emperor of Japan. [Jap.]
mike. *See* **microphone.**
milch *a.* giving milk. [OE. *milce*]
mild (-i-) *a.* gentle, merciful, indulgent; not strongly flavored. **-mild'ly** *a.* - **mild'ness** *n.* [OE. *milde*]
mil'dew *n.* destructive fungus on plants or things exposed to damp. *-v.i.* become tainted with mildew. *-v.t.* affect with mildew. [OE. *meledeaw,* honey dew]
mile *n.* measure of length, 1,760 yards. - **mi'leage** *n.* distance in miles. **-mile'stone** *n.* stone at mile intervals to mark distances. [L. *mille* (*passuum*) thousand (paces)]
mil'foil *n.* herb, the yarrow. [L. *millefolium,* thousand leaf]
mil'iary *a.* like millet-seed; of fever characterized by eruption like millet-seed. [L. *milium,* millet]
milieu' *n.* environment, surroundings. [F.]
mil'itary *a.* of, or for, soldiers or armies or warfare. *-n.* soldiers. **-mil'itant** *a.* engaged in warfare; combative. *-n.* militant person. **-mil'itancy** *n.* - **mil'itarism** *n.* enthusiasm for military force and methods. **-mil'itarist** *n.* - **mil'itate** *v.i.* to have weight, to tell (against). **-mili'tia** (-ish-a) *n.* force of citizens, not professional soldiers, which may be called on at need for military service. [L. *miles, milit-,* soldier]
milk *n.* white fluid with which animals feed their young. *-v.t.* draw milk from. **milk'sop** *n.* effeminate man or youth. - **milk'maid** *n.* woman working with cows or in a dairy. **-milk'-teeth** *n.* first set of animal teeth. **-milk'weed, milk'wort** *n.* plants producing milky juice. **-milk'y** *a.* containing or like milk. **-Milk'y Way,** the galaxy. [OE. *meolc*]
mill *n.* machinery for grinding corn, *etc.*; building containing this; various manufacturing machines; factory. *-v.t.* put through a mill; pound. **-mill'er** *n.* **-mill'race** *n.* stream of water driving a mill wheel. - **mill'stone** *n.* one of a pair of flat circular stones used for grinding. **-mill'wright** *n.* builder and repairer of mills. [OE. *myln*]
millefior'i *n.* decorative glassware in which colored glass rods are fused and cut to create flower patterns. [It. = *a thousand flowers*]
millennium *n.* period of a thousand years; period of Christ's reign on earth at his Second Coming. **-millenn'ial** *a.* [L. *mille,* thousand]
mill'epede, millipede *n.* many-legged wormlike insect. [L. *mille,* thousand, *ped,* foot]
milles'imal *a.* thousandth. - **milles'imally** *adv.* [L. *mille,* thousand]
mill'et *n.* small grain of an Indian cereal plant; the plant. [F.]
mill'iard *n.* thousand millions. [L. *mille,* thousand]
milligram *n.* thousandth part of a gram. **-mill'imeter** *n.* **-mill'iliter** *n.* [L. *mille,* thousand]
mill'iner *n.* one who makes up or deals in women's hats, ribbons, *etc.* **-mill'inery** *n.* [for *Milaner,* orig. a dealer in articles of *Milan* (Italy)]
mill'ion *n.* thousand thousands. **-millionaire** *n.* owner of a million of money, extremely rich person. [L. *mille,* thousand]
milt *n.* spawn of male fish. [OE. *milte*]
mime *n.* jester; old form of dramatic representation, *esp.* one not using words. - **mim'eograph** *n.* form of duplicating machine. **-mim'ic** *a.* imitated, feigned, *esp.* to amuse. *-n.* one skilled in amusing imitation. *-v.t.* imitate, ludicrously or closely. **-mim'icry** *n.* [G. *mimos,* buffoon]
mimo'sa *n.* shrub with feathery clusters of yellow flowers; sensitive plant. [G. *mimos,* mimic]
mim'ulus *n.* low-growing garden plant, kind of figwort. [G. *mimos*]
minaret' *n.* tall slender tower by a mosque. [Arab. *manarat,* lighthouse]
mi'natory *a.* threatening; menacing. [L. *minari,* threaten]
mince *v.t.* cut or chop small; utter with affected carefulness. *-v.i.* walk in an affected manner. *-n.* minced-meat. **-mince'-meat** *n.* mixture of chopped currants, spices, suet, *etc.* **-mince'pie** *n.* pie containing mince-meat. [OF. *mincier,* small]

mind *n.* thinking faculties as distinguished from the body, intellectual faculties; memory; attention; intentions taste. *-v.t.* attend to; care for; keep in memory. **-mind'ed** *a.* disposed. **-mind' ful** *a.* taking thought; keeping in memory. **-mind set** *n.* frame of mind or fixed mental attitude of an individual or group. [OE. *gemynd*]

mine *pron.* that belonging to me. [OE. *min*, gen. of *I, me*]

mine *n.* deep hole for digging out coal, metals, *etc.*; underground gallery with a charge of explosive; large shell or canister of explosive placed in the sea to destroy ships. *-v.t.* dig from a mine; make a mine in or under. *-v.i.* make or work in a mine. **-mine'-field** *n.* area of sea sown with mines. **-mine'-layer** *n.* ship used for laying mines. **-mine'-sweeper** *n.* ship used to clear away mines. [F.]

min'eral *a.* got by mining; inorganic. *-n.* mineral substance. **-mineral'ogy** *n.* science of minerals. **-mineral'ist** *n.* **-mineralog'ical** (-j-) *a.* **-min'eral-jell'y** *n.* soft substance derived from petroleum. **-min'eral-water** *n.* water containing some mineral, *etc.*, natural or artificial kinds used for drinking. [F.]

Miner'va *n.* Roman goddess of wisdom, counterpart of Greek Athene. [L.]

Ming *n.* Chinese dynasty (1368-1643); fine porcelain of this period. **-min'gle** *v.t.* and *i.* mix; unite. [OE. *mengan*]

min'iature *n.* small painted portrait; book or model on a small scale. *-a.* small scale. **-min'iaturist** *n.* painter of miniatures. [It. *miniatura*, fr. *miniare*, paint in red lead]

min'ify *v.t.* make to appear less; depreciate, *opp.* of **magnify.** [*minor*]

min'im *n.* in music, note half the length of a semibreve; smallest fluid measure, one-sixtieth of a fluid dram. **-min'imize** *v.t.* bring to, estimate at, the smallest possible amount. **-min'imum** *n.* lowest size, quantity. *-a.* smallest in size, quantity. [L. *minimus*, smallest]

min'ion *n.* favorite; creature, servile dependent. [F. *mignon*, darling]

min'ister *n.* person in charge of a department of the State; diplomatic representative; clergyman. *-v.t.* supply. *-v.i.* serve; contribute; be serviceable or helpful. **-ministe'rial** *a.* **-min'istry** *n.* office of clergymen; body of ministers forming a government; agency; action of ministering. **-ministe'rialist** *n.* supporter of the government. **-min'istrant** *a.* ministering. *-n.* officiating clergyman. **-ministra'tion** *n.* rendering a help, *esp.* to the sick or needy. [L. = *servant*]

min'iver *n.* white fur, winter ermine. [OF. *menu vair*, little fur]

mink (-ngk) *n.* weasel-like animal; its valuable fur. [cp. Low Ger. *mink*, otter]

minn'ow *n.* small freshwater fish. [F. *menuise*, small fish]

mi'nor *a.* lesser; smaller; underage. *-n.* person under the legal age. **-Mi'norite** *n.* Franciscan friar. **-minor'ity** *n.* state of being a minor; lesser number; smaller party voting together. [L.]

minor'ca *n.* breed of domestic fowl. [island of *Minorca*]

Min'otaur *n.* mythical monster, half bull, half-man. [G. *Minos*, in Crete, and *tauros*. bull]

minister *n.* monastery church; cathedral. [OE. *mynster*]

min'stret *n.* medieval singer or musician. **-min'strelsy** *n.* art or poetry of minstrels. [OF. *menestrel*]

mint *n.* place where money is coined. *-v.t.* to coin money. [L. *moneta*]

mint *n.* aromatic plant used in cooking. [G. *mintha*]

min'uend *n.* number from which another is to be subtracted. [L. *minure*, lessen]

minuet' *n.* stately dance; music for it. [F. *menuet*]

mi'nus *prep.* less, with the deduction of. *-a.* quantities, negative. [L.]

minute' *a.* very small; very precise. **-minute'ly** *adv.* **- minu'tiae** *n. pl.* trifles, precise details. [L. *minutus*, small]

min'ute *n.* 60th part of an hour or of a degree or angle; moment; memorandum. *-pl.* record of the proceedings of a meeting, *etc.* *-v.t.* make a minute of, record in minutes. **-min'ute book** *n.* book of minutes or notes. **-min'ute-gun** *n.* gun fired every minute, *esp.* to signify distress or mourning. **-min'ute-hand** *n.* on clock, *etc.*, hand indicating minutes. [*minute* (v.s.)]

minx *n.* pert girl, hussy. [Low Ger. *minsk*, wench]

miracle *n.* supernatural event; marvel. **-miraculous** *a.* **-mirac'ulously** *adv.* **mir'acle-play** *n.* drama (*esp.* medieval) based on the life of Christ or ofsome saint. [F., fr. L. *mirus*, wonderful]

mirage' *n.* deceptive image in the atmosphere, *e.g.*, of a lake in the desert. [F. fr. *se mirer*, be reflected]

mire *n.* bog, deep mud—*v.t.* stick in, dirty with mud. **-mi'ry** *a.* [ON. *myrr*]

mirif'ic *a.* miraculous, wonder-working. [L. *mirus*, wonderful]
mirk. *See* **murk.**
mirr'or *n.* polished surface for reflecting images. -*v.t.* reflect an image of [OF. *mireor*, L. *mirari*, contemplate]
mirth *n.* merriment. -**mirth'ful** *a.* [OE. *myrgth-merg*, merry]
mis- *prefix* meaning amiss, wrongly; makes compounds, *e.g.*, **misapply'** *v.t.* apply wrongly. -**misman'agement** *n.* bad management. Such words are not given where the meaning and derivation may easily be found from the simple word.
misadventure *n.* mishap, accident, bad luck. [OF. *mesaventure*]
misalliance *n.* improper or degrading marriage. [*alliance*]
misanthrope *n.* hater of mankind. -**misanthrop'ic** *a.* -**misan'thropy** *n.* **misan'thropist** *n.* [G. *misein*, hate, *anthropos*, man]
misappropriate *v.t.* embezzle, put to wrong use. [*mis-* and Low L. *appropriare*]
mis'beggoten *a.* illegitimate (often used as a vague term of reproach). [*mis-* and *beget*]
misbehave *v.i.* to behave improperly. -**misbehavior** *n.* [*mis-* and *behave*]
mis'call *v.t.* call wrongly; abuse. [*mis* and ON. *kalla*]
miscegenation *n.* interbreeding of races; marriage or sexual relations between two people of different race. [L. *miscue*, mix, *genus*, race]
miscar'ry *v.i.* go wrong, fail to come off; bring forth young prematurely. **miscarriage** *n.* [*carry*]
miscellaneous *a.* mixed, assorted. -**miscell'any** *n.* collection of assorted writings in one book, literary medley. [L. *miscellaneous*, fr. *miscere*, mix]
mischance' *n.* ill-luck. [*chance*]
mis'chief (-chif) *n.* source of harm or annoyance; annoying conduct. -**mis'chievous** *a.* having harmful effect; disposed to or full of mischief. [OF. *meschief*, fr. *meschever*, come to grief]
mis'cible *a.* that may be mixed. -**mis'cibility** *n.* [F., fr. L. *miscere*, to mix]
misconceive' *v.t.* and *v.i.* to conceive or understand wrongly. -**mis'conception** *n.* a mistaken idea. [*mis-* and *conceive*]
misconduct *n.* bad behavior; wrong management. [*mis-* and *conduct*]
misconstrue' *v.t.* to interpret wrongly. -**misconstruction** *n.* [*mis-* and *construe*]
miscreant *n.* wicked person. [OF. *mescreant*, unbelieving]
mis'deed *n.* evil deed; crime. [OE. *misdaed*]
misdemeanor *n.* (law) offense less than a felony. [*demeanor*]
mi'ser (-z-) *n.* one who hoards instead of using money; stingy person. -**mi'serly** *a.* [L. = *wretched*]
miserable *a.* very unhappy, wretched; mean; disappointing. -**mis'ery** *n.* great unhappiness; distress, poverty. [L. *miser*]
Misere're *n.* 50th psalm of the Vulgate (51st in A.V.); musical setting for this. [L. *miser*, wretched]
misfire' *v.i.* to fail to explode; (*fig.*) to produce no effect. [*mis-* and *fire*]
mis'fit *n.* a bad fit; a person unable to adapt himself to his surroundings. [*mis* and *fit*]
misfortune *n.* bad luck; calamity. [*mis* and *fortune*)]
misgiving *n.* doubt, mistrust. -**misgive'** *v.t.* [ME. give = suggest]
mis'hap *n.* accident, calamity. [*hap*]
mislay' *v.t.* to place badly; to lay in a place not remembered, to lose. -*p.p.* **mislaid'.** [*mis-* and *lay*]
mislead' *v.t.* to lead astray; to deceive -*p.p.* **misled'**, -**mislead'ing** *a.* deceptive, [*mis-* and *lead*]
misno'mer *n.* wrong name; use of one. [OF. *mesnorner*, fr. L. *norninare*, name]
misog'amy *n.* hatred of marriage. -**misog'amist** *n.* [G. *misein, gamos*, marriage]
misog'yny (-j-) *n.* hatred of women. -**misog'ynist** *n.* [G. *misein, gyne*, woman]
mis'print *n.* printing error. [*mis-* and OF. *preinte*]
misquote' *v.t.* to quote wrongly. -**misquota'tion** *n.* an incorrect quotation. [*mis-* and *quotation*]
misrepresent' *v.t.* to give a false description on account of -**misrepresenta'tion** *n.* [*mis-* and *represent*]
Miss *n.* title of an unmarried woman or girl; girl. [short for *mistress*]
miss *v.t.* fail to hit, reach, find, catch, notice; not be in time for; omit, notice, regret absence of. -*n.* fact of missing. -**miss'ing** *a.* lost, absent, [OE. *missan*]
miss'al *n.* mass-book. [Church L. *missale*, fr. *missa*, mass]
miss'el-thrush *n.* large European thrush which feeds on mistletoe berries. [obs. *missel*, mistletoe]
miss'ile (-il), *n.* that which may be thrown or shot to do damage. -**guid'ed miss'ile** *n.* air rocket or other explosive weapon which

is guided to the target either from the ground, or by its own internal mechanism. [L. *missiles*, fr. *mittere miss-*, send]

mis'sion (mish'un) *n.* sending or being sent on some service; party of persons sent; person's calling in life. **missionary** *n.* of religious missions. *-n.* one who goes on religious missions. [L. *mission*]

miss'ive *n.* a letter or message; legal document. *-a.* sent or for sending. [L. *mission*]

mist *n.* water vapor in fine drops. **mist'y** *a.* **-mist'ily** *adj*. [OE. = *darkness*]

mistake' *v.t.* not to understand; form a wrong opinion about; take (a person or thing) for another. *-v.i.* be in error. *-n.* error in thought or action. [*take*]

mis'ter *n.* courteous form of address to a man (written *Mr.*). [*master*]

mistletoe (-sl-) *n.* parasitic plant with white berries which grows on various trees. [OE. *misteltan*]

mis'tral *n.* cold N.W. wind on the Mediterranean coasts. [F.]

mis'tress *n.* woman who employs other persons; woman with mastery or control; woman teacher; object of a man's illicit love; mode of address to a woman (written *Mrs.*, pron. *mis'iz*). [OF. *maistresse*, fem. of *maistre*, master]

mistrust *v.t.* to feel no confidence in; to look on with suspicion. *-n.* want of trust. [*mis-* and *trust*]

misunderstand' *v.t.* to take a wrong meaning from. **-misunderstood'** *p.p.* **-misunderstand'ing** *n.* mistake as to meaning; disagreement or quarrel. [*mis* and *understand*]

mite *n.* very small insect; very small coin; small but well-meant contribution; very small child or person. [OE.]

mi'ter *n.* bishop's headdress; joint between two pieces of wood, *etc.* meeting at right angles with the line of their joining bisecting the right angle. *-v.t.* put a miter on; join with or shape for a miter-joint. [G. *mitra*, headband]

mit'igate *v.t.* make less severe. **-mitiga'tion** *n.* [L. *mitigare-mitis*, mild]

mitrailleuse' *n.* rapid firing machine-gun. [F.]

mitt'en *n.* glove without separate fingers. [F. *mitaine*]

mix *v.t.* put together or combine or blend, mingle. *-v.i.* be mixed; associate. **-mix'er** *n.* one that mixes; person at ease in any society. **-mix'ture** *n.* [L. *mixtus*, mixed, fr. *miscere*, mix]

miz'mate *n.* labyrinth; perplexity. [*maze*]

mizz'en, miz'en *n.* lowest fore and aft sail on the aftermost mast of a ship. **-miz(z)enmast** *n.* aftermost mast on a full-rigged ship. [F. *misaine*]

mizz'le *n.* fine rain. *-v.t.* drizzle. [cp. LG. *miseln*, mist]

mnemon'ic (n-) *a.* helping the memory. *-n.* something intended to help the memory. *-pl.* art of improving the memory. [G. *mnemon*, mindful]

mo'a *n.* extinct ostrich-like bird of New Zealand. [*Maori*]

moan *n.* low murmur, usually indicating pain. *-v.t.* bewail. *-v.i.* utter a moan. [OE. *muan*]

moat *n.* deep wide ditch round a town or building. *-v.t.* surround with a moat. [ME. *mote*, mound]

mob *n.* disorderly crowd of people; mixed assembly. *-v.t.* attack in a mob, hustle or ill-treat. [*abbrev.* fr. L. *mobile* (*vulgus*), fickle (crowd)]

mob'cap *n.* indoor cap formerly worn by women. [orig. uncertain]

mo'bile (-bil) *a.* capable of movement; easily moved or changed. **-mobil'ity** *n.* **mo'bilize** *v.t.* prepare (forces) for active service. *-v.i.* an army, prepare for active service. **-mobiliza'tion** *n.* [L. *mobilis*]

mocc'asin *n.* Native Amer. soft shoe, usually of deerskin; shoe or slipper of similar shape; poisonous water snake. [*Native American*]

mocha *n.* a fine coffee, orig. from Mocha on the Red Sea.

mock *v.t.* make fun of, hold up to ridicule; disappoint. *-v.i.* scoff. *-n.* act of mocking; laughing stock. *-a.* sham, imitation. **mock'er** *n.* **-mock'ery** *n.* **-mock sun,** bright light, *usu.* near sun caused by refraction of light by atmospheric ice. **-mock moon,** bright disk in moon's halo. **-mock'ing bird** *n.* N. Amer. bird which mimics other birds' notes. [F. *moquer*]

mod' *n.* musical and bardic contest in Scottish Highlands. [Gael., cp. *moot*]

mode *n.* method, manner, fashion. **-mo'dish** *a.* in the fashion. [F.]

mod'el *n.* representation of an object made to scale; pattern; person or thing worthy of imitation; person employed by an artist to pose, or by a dressmaker to show off clothes. *-v.t.* work into shape; make according to a model. [F. *modèle*]

mo'dem *n.* (*compute.*) device used to connect computer terminals to telephone transmission lines [*mo*dulator/*dem*odulator]

mod'erate (-it) *a.* not going to extremes, not excessive. medium. *-n.* person of moderate views. *-v.t.* and *i.* make or become less violent or excessive, -**modera'tion** *n.* -**mod'erator** *n.* go-between or mediator; president of a Presbyterian body. [L. *moderatus*]

mod'ern *a.* of present or recent times; new fashioned. *-n.* person living in modern times. -**mod'ernism** *n.* of modern character or views. -**mod'ernist** *n.* -**modern'ity** *n.* -**mod'ernize** *v.t.* adapt to modern ways or views. -**moderniza'tion** *n.* [F. *moderne*, Late L. *modernus*]

mod'est *a.* unassuming, retiring, not overrating one's qualities or achievements. -**mod'esty** *n.* [L. *modestus*]

mod'icum *n.* small quantity. [L.]

mod'ify (fi) *v.t.* make small changes in, tone down. -**modifica'tion** *n.* [L. *modificare*, limit]

mod'ulate *v.t.* regulate; vary in tone. *-v.i.* change the key of music. -**modulation** *n.* [L. *modulari* , measure]

mo'hair *n.* fine cloth of goat's hair. [Arab. *mukhayyar*]

Mohamm'edan, Muhammadan *a.* of Mohammed or his religion; Muslim; Islamic. *-n.* believer in Mohammed. [*Mohammed*]

moi'der *v.i.* drudge; wander in mind. *-v.t.* confuse. -**moi'dered** *a.* bemused, bewildered. [orig. uncertain]

moi'ety *n.* half; share. [F. *moitié*]

moil *v.i.* drudge. [early var. of *mule*]

moir'e *a.* watered. *-n.* watered fabric, usually of silk. [F.]

moist *a.* damp, slightly wet. -**moist'en** *v.t.* -**mois'ture** *n.* liquid, *esp.* diffused or in drops. [OF. *moiste*]

moke' *n.* (*sl.*) donkey. [orig. uncertain]

mo'lar *a.* of teeth, serving to grind. *-n.* molar tooth. [L. *molaris*, fr. *mola*, millstone]

molass'es (-ez) *n.* drainings of raw sugar, treacle. [L. *mel*, honey]

mold (mold) *n.* rich soil. -**mold'er** *v.i.* decay into dust. [OE. *molde*]

mold (mold) *n.* pattern for shaping; hollow object in which metal is cast; character, form. *-v.t.* shape or pattern. -**mold'er** *v.i.* crumble, decay, rot. -**mold'ing** *n.* molded object; decoration, *esp.* a long strip of ornamental section. [F. *moule*]

mold *n.* growth caused by dampness. -**mold'y** *a.* [ME. *moulen*, become mildewed]

mole *n.* small dark growth on the skin. [OE. *mal*, spot]

mole *n.* small burrowing animal. -**mole'skin** *n.* its fur; kind of fustian. [earlier *mouldwarp*, 'earth-thrower']

mole *n.* breakwater. [L. *moles*, heap]

mol'ecule *n.* one of the uniform small particles, composed of atoms, of which a homogeneous substance is made up. -**molec'ular** *a.* [F., fr. L. *moles*, mass]

molest' *v.t.* interfere with, meddle with so as to annoy or injure. -**molesta'tion** *n.* [L. *molestare*]

moll'ient *a.* softening. [L. *mollire*, soften]

mortify *v.t.* calm down. -**mollifica'tion** *a.* [L. *mollificare*, make soft]

mollusks, moll'usc *n.* soft-bodied and usually hard-shelled animal. [L. *molluscus-mollis, soft]*

molt *v.i.* change feathers. *-v.t.* shed (feathers). *-n.* action of molting. [OE. *mutian*, fr. L. *mutare*, change]

molt'en *a.* melted. [old *pp.* of *melt*]

molybdenum *n.* rare silvery metal. [G., fr. *molybdos*, lead]

moment *n.* very short space of time. -**mo'mentary** *a.* lasting a moment. -**mo'mentarily** *adv.* -**moment'ous** *a.* important. -**moment'um** *n.* force of moving body. [L. *momentum*, movement]

mon'ad *n.* ray from the one universal Absolute; simplest element of matter; chemical element with valency one; smallest kind of animalcule. [G. *monas*, *monad*-from *monos*, sole]

mon'arch (-k) *n.* sovereign ruler of a state. -**mon'archy** *n.* state ruled by a sovereigns his rule. -**monarch'ic** *a.* -**mon'archist** *n.* supporter of monarchy. [G. *monos*, alone, *archein*, ruler]

monastery *n.* house occupied by a religious order. -**monast'ic** *a.* relating to monks, nuns, or monasteries. -**monast'icism** *n.* [Late G. *monasterion*, fr. *monazein*, live alone]

Mon'day (mun'da) *n.* second day of the week. [OE. *monandæg*, moon day]

mon'ey (mun'-) *n.* current coin; medium of exchange. -**mon'etary** *a.* -**mon'etarism** *n.* theory that inflation is caused by an excess quantity of money in an economy; economic policy based on this theory and on a belief in the efficiency of free market forces. -**mon'etarist** *n.* and *a.* -**mon'etize** *v.t.* make into or recognize as money. -**monetiza'tion** *n.* -**money changer** *n.* one who changes money from one currency to another. -**money-market** *n.* financial system for the trade of low-risk, short-term securities. [F. *monnaie. See* **mint**]

mon'ger *n.* dealer or trader. [OE. *mangian*, trade]

Mongoose *n.* small Indian animal noted for killing snakes. [*Mahratti mangus*]

mon'grel *n.* animal, *esp.* a dog. of mixed breed. *-a.* that is a mongrel. [obs. *mong*, mix]

mon'itor *n.* one who gives warning or advice; senior pupil in a school charged with special duties and authority; small warship with heavy guns; kind of lizard. **-mon'itress** *fem.* **-mon'itory** *a.* **-moni'tion** *n.* a warning. [L. fr. *monere, monit-*, admonish]

monk (monk) *n.* one of a religious community of men living apart under vows. **-monk'ish** *a.* **-monk's-hood** *n.* poisonous plant, the aconite. [OE. *munic*, Late G. *monachos*, solitary]

monk'ey (munk'i) *n.* animal closely allied to man; imitative or mischievous child. *-v.i.* play tricks. **-monk'ey nut** *n.* peanut. **-monkey-puzzle** *n.* kind of pricklv tree. **-monk'ey-wrench** *n.* wrench with movable jaw. [G. *Moneke*, son of Martin the Ape, in 15th c. version of Reynard the Fox]

mono- *prefix.* [G. *monos*, alone, single] **-monochrome** *n.* representation in one color. *-a.* of only one color. **-monochromatic** *a.* **-mon'ochord** *n.* one stringed musical instrument. **-mon'ocle** *n.* single eyeglass. **-monoclonal** *a.* of, or pertaining to, cells cloned from one cell; derived from a single clone. **-mon'ody** *n.* lament. **-monog'amy** *n.* custom of being married to only one person at a time. **-mon'ogram** *n.* two or more letters interwoven. **-mon'ograph** *n.* short book on a single subject. **-mon'olith** *n.* prehistoric monument, a single large stone. **-mon'ologue, mon'olog** *n.* dramatic composition with only one speaker. **-monoma'nia** *n.* madness on one subject. **-monoma'niac** *n.* **-Mon'omark** *v.i.* (trade name) combination of letters and numbers used instead of owner's name to identify property. **-mon'oplane** *n.* airplane with single wings. **-monop'oly** *n.* exclusive possession of a trade, privilege, *etc.* **-monop'olize** *v.t.* **-monop'olist** *n.*- **mon'orail** *n.* railway having cars running on or suspended from a single rail. **-mon'ostich** *n.* one-line poem. **-monos'tichous** *n.* [G. *stich, os*, line]. **-mon'osyllable** *n.* word of one syllable. **-monosyllab'ic** *a.* **-mon'otheism** *n.* belief that there is only one God. **mon'otheist** *n.* **-mon'otone** *n.* continuing on one note. **-monot'onous** *a.* lacking in variety, wearisome. **-monot'ony** *n.* **-mon'otype** *n.* machine for casting and setting printing type in individual letters.

monsoon' *n.* seasonal wind of the Indian Ocean; other periodical winds. [Arab. *mausim*, lit. season]

mon'ster *n.* misshapen animal or plant; person of great wickedness huge animal or thing. *-a.* huge. **-mon'strous** *a.* **-mon'strously** *adv.* **-monstros'ity** *n.* monstrous being; monster. [L. *monstrum*, marvel]

montage' *n.* art of assembling 'shots' to make a film; picture made up of a variety of elements from different sources. [F.]

montbre'tia *n.* garden plant with spikes of orange flowers. [C. de *Montbret*, (1780-1801)]

Montesso'ri system *n.* system of education for very young and for defective children. [Dr. Maria *Montessori*, (1870-1952)]

month (munth) *n.* one of the twelve periods into which a year is divided; period of the revolution of the moon. **-month'ly** *a.* happening, payable, *etc.* **once a month.** *-adv.* once a month. *-n.* **monthly magazine.** [OE. *monath*; fr. *moon*]

mon'ument *n.* anything that commemorates; written record. **-monument'al** *a.* of or serving as a monument; vast, stupendous. [L. *monumentum*]

mooch', mouch' *v.i.* [*colloq.*) loaf, slink; sponge. [OF. *muchier*, skulk]

mood *n.* state of mind and feelings. **-mood'y** *a.* changeable in mood; gloomy. **-mood'ily** *adv.* **-mood'iness** *n.* [OE. *mod*]

mood *n.* (*gram.*) group of forms indicating function of verb. [var. of *mode*]

moon *n.* satellite revolving round the earth; satellite of a planet. *-v.i.* go about dreamily. **-moon'light** *n.* **-moon'shine** *n.* nonsense; smuggled liquor. **-moon'stone** *n.* precious stone. **-moon'-struck** *a.* lunatic. [OE. *mona*]

moor *n.* tract of waste land, often hilly and heath-clad; land preserved for grouse shooting. **-moor'cock** *n.* male of the red grouse. **-moor'hen** *n.* water-hen. [OE. *mor*]

moor *v.t.* fasten (a ship) with chains, ropes or cable and anchor. *-v.i.* secure a ship thus. **-moorings** *n.* [orig. uncertain]

moose *n.* Amer. elk. [Algonkin, *mus*]

moot *v.t.* bring for discussion. *-a.* open to argument. *-n.* (*hist.*) meeting, as **town-moot, folk-moot.** [OE. *mot*]

mop *n.* bundle of yarn, cloth, *etc.* fastened to the end of a stick and used for cleaning. *-v.t.* clean or wipe with a mop or with any absorbent stuff. [OF. *mappe*, L. *mappa*, napkin]

mope *v.i.* be depressed, dull or dispirited. [Du. *moppen*, sulk]

moquette (-ket') *n.* strong fabric for carpets, upholstery. [F.]

moraine' *n.* mass of débris edging a glacier. **-morainic** *a.* [F.]

mor'al *a.* concerned with right and wrong conduct; of good conduct. **-moral victory** *n.* failure or defeat that inspirits instead of crushing the loser. **-moral certainty** *n.* thing that can hardly fail. *-n.* practical lesson, *e.g.* of a fable. *-pl.* habits with respect to right and wrong, *esp.* in matters of sex. **-morale'** *n.* discipline and spirit of an army or other body of persons. **-mor'alist** *n.* teacher of morals. **-moral'ity** *n.* good moral conduct; moral goodness or badness; kind of medieval drama, containing a moral lesson. **-mor'alize** *v.t.* interpret morally. *-v.i.* write or think on moral aspects of things. **-mor'ally** *adv.* [L. *moralis]*

morass' *n.* marsh, bog. [Du. *moeras*]

moratorium *n.* government's authority to delay payment of debts during national emergency; suspension of activity, *esp.* during a period of reconsideration. [L. *mora*, delay]

mor'bid *a.* unwholesome, sickly. **-mor'bidly** *adv.* **-morbid'ity** *n.* [L. *morbidus*, from *morbus*, disease]

mord'ant *a.* biting. [L. *mordax*]

more *a.* greater in quantity or number. *-adv.* to a greater extent; in addition. *-pron.* greater or additional amount or number. **-moreo'ver** *adv.* besides. [OE. *mora*]

morganatic *a.* **morganatic marriage,** marriage of a king or prince in which the wife does not share her husband's rank or possessions and the children do not inherit from their father. [cp. Ger. *morgengabe*, morning gift]

morgue' (morg) *n.* mortuary in which dead bodies are placed for identification, *etc.* [F.]

moribund *a.* dying. [L. *moribundus*]

mor'ion *n.* helmet with no visor or beaver. [F.]

Mor'mon *n.* member of the Church of Jesus Christ of Latter-Day Saints, founded in U.S. by Joseph Smith (1805-1844) in 1830. **-Mormonism** *n.* [fr. *Mormon*, alleged author of *The Book of Mormon*]

morn *n.* morning. **-morn'ing** *n.* early part of the day. **-morn'ing glo'ry** *n.* convolvulus. [OE. *morgen*]

morocc'o *n.* fine kind of goatskin leather. [orig. made in *Morocco*]

mo'ron *n.* adult with mental capacity of a child. [G. *moros*, foolish]

morose' *a.* sullen, unsociable. [L. *morosus*, moody]

morph'ia, morph'ine *n.* narcotic part of opium. [G. *Morpheus*, god of sleep]

morphology *n.* science of the forms of living organisms. **-morpholog'ic** *a.* **-morphol'ogist** *n.* [G. *morphe*, form]

morr'is *n.* dance by persons in fancy dress representing characters of the Robin Hood stories. [for *Moorish*]

morr'ow *n.* next day [ME. *morwe*]

Morse *a.* **Morse-code** *n.* system of signalling in which the letters of the alphabet are represented by various combinations of dots and dashes, short and long flashes, *etc.* [*Morse*, inventor (d. 1872)]

mor'sel *n.* mouthful; fragment. [L. *morsus*, bite]

mort'al *a.* subject to death; fatal. *-n.* mortal creature. **-mortal'ity** *n.* being mortal; great loss of life; death rate. **-mort'ally** *adv.* [L. *mors, mort-*, death]

mort'ar *n.* vessel in which substances are pounded; short gun throwing at high angles; mixture of lime, sand, and water for holding bricks and stones together. [L. *mortarium*]

mort'gage (morg-aj) *n.* conveyance of property as security for debt with provision that the property be reconveyed at payment within an agreed time. *-v.t.* convey by mortgage. **-mortgagor** (morg'a-jer) *n.* **mortgagee'** *n.* [OF. = *dead pledger*]

morti'cian (-ish-) *n.* funeral undertaker. [L. *mors, mort-*, death]

mort'ify *v.i.* subdue by self-denial; humiliate. *-v.i.* be affected with gangrene. **-mortifica'tion** *n.* [L. *mortificare*, make dead]

mort'ise (-is) *n.* hole made in a piece of wood, *etc.*, to receive the tongue at the end of another piece called a tenon. *-v.t.* make a mortise in; fasten by mortise and tenon. [F. *mortaise*]

mort'main *n.* land granted to corporation, so called as ownership is perpetual and it thus yields no feudal dues on transfer. [F. *mort*, dead, *main*, hand]

mort'uary *a.* of or for burial. *-n.* building where dead bodies are kept for a time. [L. *mortuarius-mors*, death]

mosa'ic *n.* picture or pattern made by fixing side by side small bits of colored stone, glass, *etc.*; this process of decoration. [F. *mosaique*]

moschatel' (-ka-tel) *n.* variety of plant with pate-green flowers and musky scent. [F. *moscatelle*, musk]

Moselle' *n.* light white wine from Moselle district of France. [F.]

Mos'lem. *See* **Mus'lim.**

mosque (mosk) *n.* Islamic place of worship. [Arab. *masjid*]

mosqui'to (-ke-to) *n.* various kinds of gnat. [Sp., fr. L. *musca*, fly]

moss *n.* swamp; small plant growing in masses on a surface. -*v.t.* cover with moss. -**moss'-rose** *n.* variety of rose with mossy calyx. -**moss'y** *a.* [OE. *mos*]

most *a.* greatest in size, number, degree. -*n.* greatest amount, degree. -*adv.* in the greatest degree. -**most'ly** *adv.* for the most part. [OE. *moest*]

mot' (mo) *n.* pithy or witty saying. -**mot juste**, right word. [F.]

mote *n.* speck of dust. [OE. *mot*]

motet' *n.* short sacred choral work, anthem. [F. *mot*, word]

moth' *n.* nocturnal insect of butterfly family. -**moth'eaten** *a.* [OE. *moththe*]

moth'er (muTH-) *n.* female parent; head of a religious community of women. -*a.* inborn. -*v.t.* act as a mother to. -**moth'erhood** *n.* -**moth'erly** *a.* -**moth'er-in-law** *n.* mother of one's wife or husband. -**moth'erboard** *n.* (in an electronic system) a printed circuit board through which signals between all other boards are routed. -**mother-of-millions** *n.* ivy-leaved toadflax. -**moth'er of pearl'** *n.* iridescent substance forming the lining of certain shells. -**Moth'er's Day** *n.* day in which the mother is honored by the family, *usu.* the second Sunday in May. [OE. *moder*]

motif' *n.* theme, *esp.* in music. [F.]

mo'tion *n.* process or action or way of moving; proposal in a meeting; application to a judge. -*v.t.* direct by a sign. -**mo'tionless** *a.* -**mo'tile** *a.* capable of motion. -**mo'tive** *a.* causing motion. -*n.* that which makes a person act in a particular way; chief idea in a work of art. [L. *motio*, fr. *movere, mot-*, move]

mot'ley *a.* checkered. -*n.* motley color; jester's dress. [orig. uncertain]

mot'tle *n.* blotch on a surface; arrangement of blotches. -*v.t.* mark with blotches. -**mott'led** *a.* blotchy. [prob. from *motley*, (*v.s.*)]

mo'tor *n.* that which imparts movement; machine to supply motive power. **mo'torize** *v.t.* mechanize. -**mo'torboat** (-**bus**, -**launch**, *etc.*) *n.* one moved by an engine carried inside it. -**mo'torcade** *n.* formal procession of motor vehicles. -**mo'torist** *n.* user of an automobile. [*motion*]

mott'o *n.* (**mott'oes** *pl.*) saying adopted as a rule of conduct; short inscribed sentence; word or sentence accompanying a heraldic crest. [It.]

moue' *n.* pout. [F.]

mouff'lon *n.* wild mountain sheep. [F.]

mou'jik *n.* Russian peasant. [Russ. *muzhik*]

mould. *See* **mold.**

moult. *See* **molt.**

mound *n.* heap of earth or stones; small hill. [orig. uncertain]

mount *n.* hill; that on which anything is supported or fitted; horse. -*v.i.* go up; get on horseback; rise. -*v.t.* go up; get on the back of, set on a mount; furnish with a horse. -**mount'ain** *n.* hill of great size. -**mountaineer'** *n.* one who lives among or climbs mountains. -**mount'ainous** *a.* -**mountain sickness** *n.* sickness caused by rarefied air at high altitudes. -**mount'ing** *n.* act of mounting (horse); setting, framing of picture. [L. *mons, mont-*, hill]

mountebank *n.* quack; market-place entertainer; impostor. [It. *montambanco*, mount on bench]

mourn -*v.i.* feel or show sorrow. -*v.t.* grieve for. -**mourn'er** *n.* -**mourn'ful** *a.* -**mourn'fully** *adv.* -**mourn'ing** *n.* act of mourning; conventional signs of grief for a death; clothes of a mourner. [OE. *murnan*]

mouse *n.* (**mice** *pl.*) small rodent animal. -*v.i.* catch mice. -**mous'er** *n.* cat good at catching mice. -**mouse' deer** *n.* small Asian deer. [OE. *mus*]

mouse *n.* (*compute.*) input device that is moved about on a tabletop or pad and directs a pointer (cursor) on a video screen.

mousse' *n.* dish of frozen whipped cream; similar cold dishes. [F.]

mouth (-th; *pl.* -THz) *n.* opening in the head, used for eating, speaking, *etc.*; opening into anything hollow; outfall of a river, entrance to harbor, *etc.* -(-TH) *v.t.* take into the mouth; declaim. -*v.i.* declaim. -**mouth' organ** *n.* small musical instrument played by the mouth, the harmonica. -**mouth'piece** *n.* end of anything intended to be put between the lips; one who speaks for others. [OE. *muth*]

move -*v.t.* change the position of-, stir; propose. -*v.i.* change places; take action. -*n.* a moving; motion making towards some goal. -**mov'able** *a.* and *n.*- **move'ment** *n.* process or action of moving; moving parts of a machine; main division of a piece of music. -**mov'ie** *n.* (*sl.*) motion picture, film. [L. *movere*]

mow *v.t.* cut (grass, *etc.*); cut down, kill. -*v.i.* cut grass. -**mow'ing-machine** *n.* [OE. *mawan*]

much *a.* in quantity. -*n.* large amount; important matter. -*adv.* in a great degree, nearly. [ME. *muche*]

mu'cilage *n.* gum. [F.]

muck *n.* cattle dung; unclean refuse. - **muck'y** *a.* [orig. uncertain]

mu'cus *n.* viscous secretion of the mucous membrane. -**mu'cous** *a.* -**mu'cous membrane**, lining of body cavities, canals. [L.]

mud *a.* wet and soft earth. -**mud'dle** *v.t.* confuse; bewilder; mismanage. -*v.i.* be busy in a fumbling way. -*n.* confusion. - **mudd'y** *a.* [Teut. orig.]

mud'ra *n.* any of the numerous, intricate symbolic finger and hand gestures incorporated into the dances and religious ceremonies of India.

muezzin *n.* official of Islam who, at certain hours, calls the faithful to prayer. [Arab.]

muff *n.* covering, *usu.* of fur, to keep the hands warm. [Du. *mof*]

muff *n.* one with no practical skill or sense. -*v.t.* fumble, spoil, bungle, miss. [orig. uncertain]

muff'in *n.* light round flat cake, toasted and buttered. [orig. uncertain]

muffle *v.t.* wrap up; of sound, deaden. - **muff'ler** *n.* scarf to cover neck and throat; device which deadens sound, *esp.* as attached to the exhaust system of an automobile, *etc.* [F. *emmoufler*, swathe]

muf'ti *n.* Muslim priest; plain clothes as distinct from uniform. [*Arab.*]

mug *n.* drinking cup. -(*sl.*) face; fool. -*v.i.* study hard; to attack or threaten with the intention of robbing, *usu.* in the street. - **mugg'er** *n.* one who robs in this way. [fr. *mugan*]

mugg'er *n.* broad-nosed Indian crocodile. [Hind. *magar*]

mugg'y *a.* damp and stifling. [dial. *mug*, mist, fr. ON. *mugga*]

mug'wump *n.* big chief; one who holds independent political views. [Algonkin *mugquomp*]

Muhammadan. *See* **Mohammedan.**

mulatt'o *n.* person with one white and one black parent. [Sp. *mulato*, hybrid]

mul'berry *n.* tree whose leaves are used to feed silkworms; its fruit. [F. *mure*, mulberry and E. *berry*]

mulch *n.* straw, leaves, *etc.*, spread as a protection for the roots of plants. -*v.t.* protect in this way. [orig. uncertain]

mulct *n.* fine. -*v.t.* fine. [L. *mulctare*]

mule *n.* cross between horse and ass; obstinate person. -**muleteer'** *n.* mule driver. -**mu'lish** *a.* [L. *mulus*]

mule *n.* heelless slipper. [F.]

mull *v.t.* heat (wine or ale) with sugar and spices. [orig. uncertain]

mull *n.* promontory. [prob. Gael. *maol*]

mull *v.t.* blunder, bungle, muddle. [orig. uncertain]

mull'ein (-in) *n.* yellow-flowered plant with woolly leaves. [OF. *moleine*]

mull'et *n.* sea fish found near coasts and sought after as food. [F. *mulet*]

mulligataw'ny *n.* soup made with curry. [Tamil *milagu- tannir*, pepper-water]

mullion *n.* upright dividing bar in a window or screen. [orig. uncertain]

mult-, multi- *prefix* much, many. [L. *multus*, much] -**multian'gular** (-ng-g-) *a.* many-angled. -**multicult'ural** *a.* consisting of, relating to, or designed for the cultures of several different races. - **multidisc'iplinary** *n.* of, or relating to, or involving, many disciplines or branches of learning. **multieth'nic** *a.* consisting of, relating to, or designed for various different races. -**multifa'rious** *a.* manifold, varied. -**mul'tiform** *a.* many forms. - **multilat'eral** *a.* many-sided. -**multilinear** *a.* having many lines. -**mul'tiped** *n.* many footed animal. -**mul'tiple** *a.* having many parts. -*n.* quantity which contains another an exact number of times. -**mul'tiple shop'**, shop with widespread branches, chain store. -**mul'tiplex** *a.* manifold. - **mul'tiplicand** *n.* number to be multiplied by another. -**multiplica'tion** *n.* -**multiplicity**, variety, greatness in number. - **mul'tiply** *v.t.* make many; find the sum of a given number taken a stated number of times. -*v.i.* increase in number or amount. -**mul'titude** *n.* great number; great crowd. -**multitu'dinous** *a.* very numerous.

mum' *a.* silent. [imit.]

mum'ble *v.i.* and *t.* speak indistinctly. [ME. *momelen*]

mum'bo-jum'bo *n.* African idol; anything senselessly reverenced, feared;

malignant spirit. [native]

mumm'er *n.* one who acts in a dumb-show. -**mumm'ery** *n.* [OF. *momeur*]

mumm'y *n.* embalmed body. -**mumm'ify** *v.t.* [Arab. *mumiyah*]

mump *v.i.* gloom, sulk. [*mum*]

mumps *n. pl.* contagious disease marked by swelling in the glands of the neck. [obs. *mump*, grimace]

munch *v.t.* chew. [imit. orig.]

mundane *a.* worldly; ordinary. [L. *mundanus*]

municipal (-is'-) *a.* belonging to the affairs of a city or town. -**municipal'ity** *n.* city or town with local self-government; its governing body. [L. *municipium*, town with rights of Roman citizenship]

munificent *a.* magnificently generous. -**munif'icence** *n.* [L. *munificus*]

mu'niment *n.* defense. -*pl.* charters, title-deeds. [L. *munimentum*]

muni'tion (-ish'-) *n.* (*usu. pt.*) military stores. [L. *munitio*]

mu'ral *a.* of or on a wall. -*n.* wall painting. [L. *murus*, wall]

mur'der *n.* the unlawful and deliberate killing of a human being. -*v.t.* to kill thus. -**mur'derer** *n.* -**mur'deress** *fem.* -**murderous** *a.* [OE. *morthor*]

murk *n.* thick darkness. -**murk'y** *a.* [ON. *myrkr*, darkness]

mur'mur *v.i.* make a low continuous sound; complain. -*v.t.* utter in a low voice. -*n.* sound or act of murmuring. [L. *murmurare*]

murr'ain *n.* infectious cattle plague. [OF. *moraine*, pestilence]

mus'cat *n.* musk-flavored grape; strong wine made from it. -**muscatel'** *n.* muscat. [F.]

mus'cle (mus'l) *n.* part of the body which produces movement by contracting; part of the body made up of muscles. -**mus'cular** *a.* [F.]

Muse (-z) *n.* one of the nine goddesses inspiring learning and the arts. [L. *musa*]

muse (-z) *v.i.* be lost in thought. -*n.* state of musing. [F. *muser*]

muse'um *n.* place to show objects illustrating the arts, history, *etc.* [L.]

mush *n.* pulp; boiled corn meal; (fig.) sentimentality. [*mash*]

mush'room *n.* kind of edible fungus. -*a.* of rapid growth. [F. mousseron]

mu'sic (-z-) *n.* art of expressing or causing an emotion by melodious and harmonious combination of notes; the laws of this; composition in this art; such composition represented on paper. -**mu'sical** *a.* -**mu'sically** *adv.* -**musi'cian** *n.* -**mu'sical** *n.* colorful light drama with songs, music. [G. *mousike* (*techne*), (art of the) muses]

musk *n.* a scent obtained from a gland of the musk-deer; various plants with a similar scent. -**musk'y** *a.* -**musk' deer** *n.* Asian hornless deer. -**musk' ox** *n.* ox with musky odor. -**muskrat** *n.* musquash. [F. *musc*]

mus'keg *n.* swamp. [Native Amer]

musk'et *n.* infantryman's gun, *esp.* unrifled. -**musketeer'** *n.* -**musk'etry** *n.* use of firearms. [F. *mousquet*]

Mus'lim, Mos'lem *n.* follower of Mohammed. -*a.* of the Islamic religion. [Arab. *salama*, submit to God]

mus'lin (-z-) *n.* fine cotton fabric. [orig. fr. *Mosul*, in Mesopotamia]

mus'quash *n.* muskrat; its fur. [Native Amer]

muss'el *n.* bivalve shellfish. [L. *musculus*, little mouse]

Muss'ulman *n.* Mohammedan. [Pers. *musulman*]

must *n.* unfermented wine. [L. *mustum*]

must *v. aux.* be obliged to, or certain to. [OE. *moste*]

mustache (mus-tash) *n.* hair on the upper lip. [F.]

mus'tang *n.* wild horse of American prairies. [Sp. *mestengo*]

mustard *n.* powdered seeds of a plant used in paste as a condiment; the plant. -**must'ard gas**, blistering gas used in warfare. [OF. *moustarde*]

must'er *v.t.* and *i.* assemble. -*n.* assembly, *esp.* for exercise, inspection. **must'er-roll** *n.* [L. *monstrare*, show]

must'y *a.* moldy. [orig. uncertain]

mu'table *a.* liable to change. -**muta'tion** *n.* [L. *mutabilis-mutare*, change]

mute *a.* dumb; silent. -*n.* dumb person; hired mourner; clip, *etc.* to deaden sound of musical instruments. -**mute'ly** *a.* -**mute'ness** *n.* [L. *mutus*]

mu'tilate *v.t.* deprive of a limb or other part; damage. -**mutila'tion** *n.* -**mu'tilator** *n.* [L. *mutilare*]

mu'tiny *n.* rebellion against authority, *esp.* against the officers of a disciplined body. -*v.i.* commit mutiny. -**mu'tinous** *a.* -**mutineer'** *n.* [F. *mutiner*]

mutt'er *v.i.* speak with the mouth nearly closed, indistinctly. -*v.t.* utter in such tones. -*n.* act of muttering. [imit.]

mutt'on *n.* flesh of sheep used as food. [F. *mouton*, sheep]

mu'tual *a.* done, possessed, *etc.*, by each of two with respect to the other. **mu'tually** *adv.* common to both. [L. *mutuus*]

muz'zle *n.* projecting mouth and nose of an animal; thing put over these to prevent biting; end of a firearm bv which the projectile leaves. *-v.t.* put a muzzle on. [OF. *musel*, snout]

my *poss. a.* belonging to me. **-myself** *pron.* emphatic and reflex, of I, me. [for *mine*]

mycol'ogy *n.* science of fungi. [G. *mykes*, mushroom]

myco'toxin *n.* toxic substance produced from a fungus.

myeli'tis *n.* inflammation of the spinal cord. [G. *myelos*. marrow]

myop'athy *n.* any disease of the muscles or their tissues.

myo'pia *n.* short-sightedness. **-my'opic** *a.* [G. *myein*, close, ops, eye]

myeso'tis *n.* various small flowering plants including the forget-me-not. (*myosote*). [G. *mys.*, mouse, *ous, ot-*, ear]

myr'iad (mir-) *n.* ten thousand; endless number. *-a.* innumerable. [G. *myrias, myriad-*]

myr'iapod *n.* animal with many legs. [G. *myriopons, -podos*, many-footed]

myr'midon *n.* servile follower. *pl.* retinue, following. [G. *kfyrmidones*. Greek tribe; followers of Achilles]

myrrh (mer) *n.* aromatic gum of the balsamodendron. [G. *myrrha*]

myrtle *n.* evergreen shrub. [OF. *myrtille*, myrtle-berry]

mys'tery (mis-) *n.* obscure or secret thing; state of being obscure; religious rite; miracle-play. **-myste'rious** *a.* **-myste'riously** *adv.* **-myst'ic** *a.* of hidden meaning, *esp.* in a religious sense. *-n.* one who seeks direct communication with God by self-surrender or contemplation. **-myst'ical** *a.* **-myst'icism** *n.* **-myst'ify** *v.t.* bewilder. **-mystifica'tion** *n.* [G. *mysterion*, secret]

myth (mith) *n.* tale with supernatural characters or events; imaginary person or object. **-myth'ical** *a.* **-mythol'ogy** *n.* myths collectively; study of these. **mytholog'ical** (-j-) *a.* **-mythologist** *n.* [G. *mythos*, fable]

myxomato'sis *n.* contagious and highly fatal, filterable virus disease of rabbits. [G. *myxa*, mucus]

N

nab *v.t.* (*sl.*) seize, catch, [orig. uncertain. cp. *nap*]

na'bob *n.* (formerly) Indian governor: rich retired Anglo-Indian. [Arab. *nawwāb*]

nacelle' (-sel') *n.* streamlined part of an aircraft that houses engine, crew, passengers, and cargo. [L. *navicella*, little ship]

na'cre (na-ker) *n.* mother-of-pearl. [F.]

na'dir *n.* point opposite the zenith. [Arab. *niazir*, opposite]

naeve, naevus *n.* birth-mark, pigmentation of skin. [L.]

nag *n.* small horse for riding; horse. [orig. uncertain]

nag *v.t.* and *i.* worry, be worrying, by constant fault-finding. [Sw. *nagga*, peck]

nai'ad (ni-) *n.* river nymph. [G. *naias. naiad;* fr. *naein*. flow]

nail *n.* horny shield of the ends of the fingers; claw; small metal spike for fixing wood, *etc.* *-v.t.* fix with a nail. [OE. *nægel*]

nain'sook *n.* type of muslin. [Hind. *nain*, eye, *sukh*, pleasure]

naive' *a.* simple, unaffected. [F.]

na'ked *a.* bare, unclothed. **-na'kedness** *n.* **-na'kedly** *adv.* [OE. *nacod*]

namby-pamby *a.* insipid, silly, weakly sentimental. [Arnbrose *Philips*, poet (d. 1749)]

name *n.* word by which a person, thing, *etc.* is denoted; reputation. *-v.t.* give a name to; call by a name; appoint: mention. **-name'less** *a.* **-name'ly** *adj*, . that is to say. **-name'sake** *n.* person having the same name as another. [OE. *nama*]

na'nism *n.* stunted growth. **-na'noid** *a.* **-naniza'tion** *n.* dwarfing of trees. [G. *nanos*, dwarf]

nankeen *n.* yellow cotton cloth. [*Nankin*, in China]

nann'y *n.* female goat (also **nann'ygoat**); children's nurse. [*name*]

nano'second *n.* one billionth of a second.

nap *n.* roughish surface cloth made by projecting fibers. [Du. *nop*]

nap *v.i.* take a short sleep. *-n.* short sleep. [OE. *knappian*]

nap *n.* card game. [*Napoleon*]

na'palm *n.* jellied gasoline, used *esp.* in certain kinds of incendiary bombs. [fr. *napthene* and *palmitate*]

nape *n.* back of the neck; hollow there. [OE. *hnoepp*, bowl]

na'pery *n.* table linen. [OF. *naperie*]

naph'tha *n.* flammable oil distilled from coal, *etc.* **-naph'thalene** *n.* disinfectant. [G.]

nap'kin *n.* square piece of linen for wiping fingers or lips at table; similar such pieces of cloth or absorbent material. [F. *nappe*, cloth]

napo'leon *n.* gold coin worth 20 francs issued by *Napoleon.*

narcissus *n.* bulbous plant with a white scented flower; (*psycho.*) one who loves himself. [G. *narkissos*]

narcotic *n.* drug causing sleep, insensibility or hallucination. -*a.* **-narco'sis** *n.* stupefying effect of narcotic. [G. *narkotikos*]

nard *n.* spikenard, variety of aromatic plant; ointment made from this. [G. *nardos*]

nark' *n.* police spy; informer; spoilsport *v.i.* **-nark'y** *a.* [Rom. *nak*, nose]

narrate' *v.t.* relate, tell (story). **-narration** *n.* **-narr'ative** *n.* account or story. -*a.* **-narra'tor** *n.* [L. *narrare*]

narr'ow *a.* of little breadth. -*n. pl.* narrow part of a strait. -*v.t.* and *i.* make, become, narrow. **-narr'owly** *adv.* **-narr'ow-minded** *a.* bigoted. **-narr'owness** *n.* [OE. *nearu*]

nar'whal *n.* dolphin, *usu.* with a single tusk, sea-unicorn. [Dan. *narhval*]

na'sal (-z-) *a.* of the nose. -*n.* sound uttered through the nose. **-na'salize** *v.t.* make nasal in sound. [L. *nasus*, nose]

nas'cent *a.* just coming into existence. [L. *nascens, nascent-*, fr. *nasci*, be born]

nasturtium (-shum) *n.* watercress; Indian cress, a garden plant with red or orange flowers. [L. = *nose-twist*]

nas'ty *a.* foul, disagreeable. **-nast'ily** *adv.* **-nas'tiness** *n.* [orig. uncertain]

na'tal *a.* relating to birth. [L. *natalis*]

nata'tion *n.* swimming. [L. *natatio*]

na'tion (-shun) *n.* people or race organized as a state. **-na'tional** (nash-) *a.* **nationally** *adv.* **-national'ity** *n.* national quality or feeling; facts of belonging to a particular nation. **-nat'ionalist** *n.* one who supports national rights. **-nat'ionalize** *v.t.* convert into the property of a nation. - **nat'ional park'**, large tract preserved by the state for its beauty or interest. [L. *natio*]

na'tive (-tiv) *a.* born in a particular place; originating from that country; found in a pure state; of one's birth. -*n.* one born in a place; oyster reared in an artificial bed. **-nativ'ity** *n.* **-Nativ'ity** *n.* birth of Christ; Christmas. [L. *natiuus- nasci*, be born]

na'tron *n.* crude carbonate of soda. [G. *nitron*]

natt'y *a.* neat and smart. **-natt'ily** *adv.* - **natt'iness** *n.* [orig. unknown]

na'ture *n.* innate or essential qualities of a thing; class, sort; life force; disposition; power underlying all phenomena in the material world; material world as a whole. **-nat'ural** *a.* of, according to, occurring in, provided by, nature. -*n.* half-witted person; (*mus.*) sign restoring sharp or flat note to its natural pitch. **nat'urally** *adv.* - **nat'uralist** *n.* one who studies plants and animals. **-nat'uralize** *v.t.* admit to citizenship; accustom to a new climate. - **naturaliza'tion** *n.* [L. *aatura*, fr. *nasci*, *not-*, to be born]

naught (nawt) *n.* nothing, zero. *a.* bad, useless. **-naught'y** *a.* wayward, not behaving well. **-naught'ily** *adv.* - **naughtiness** *n.* [OE. *nawiht*, no whit]

nau'sea *n.* sickness. **-nau'seate** *v.t.* affect with sickness; reject with loathing. - **nau'seous** *a.* [L. = *seasickness*]

nautch (nawch) *n.* Indian dancing performance by girl. [Hind. *nãch*, dance]

nautical *a.* of seamen or ships. [G. *nautes*, sailor]

nautilus *n.* shellfish with a membrane which acts as a sail. [G. *nautilos*, sailor]

naval. *See* **navy.**

nave *n.* hub of a wheel. [OE. *nafu*]

nave *n.* main body of a church building. [L. *nauis*, ship]

na'vel *n.* small pit on the abdomen. [OE. *nafela*, dim. of *nafu*, nave, hub]

nav'icert *n.* certificate given to a neutral ship that she carries no contraband of war. [*navi*gational *cert*ificate]

navigate *v.i.* sail. -*v.t.* sail over; direct the steering of a ship. **-nav'igator** *n.* one who navigates; worker digging a canal. - **nav'igable** *a.* **-naviga'tion** *n.* **-navv'y** *n.* laborer (navigator in second sense). [L. *navigare*, fr. *nauis*, ship]

na'vy *n.* fleet; warships of a country with their crews and organization. **-na'val** *a.* [OF. *navie- navis*, ship]

nay *adv.* no. [ON. *nei*, never]

Naz'arite *n.* Jewish abstainer *esp.* from strong drink. [Heb. *nazar*, consecrate]

naze *n.* headland, cape. (= ness]

Nazi *n.* German National Socialist Party; member of this; one holding views similar to this. *a.* [contr. of Ger. *Na*tional so*zi*alist]

Nean'derthal man (ne-an'-der-tal), primitive type of prehistoric man. [fr. skull found in the *Neanderthal*, valley near Dusseldorf]

neap *a.* neap tide, low tide at moon's first and third quarters. [OE. *nep*]

near *adv.* at or to a short distance. *-prep.* close to. *-a.* close at hand, close; closely related; stingy; of horses, vehicles, *etc.*, left. *-v.t.* and *i.* approach. **-near'ly** *adv.* closely; almost. **-near'ness** *n.* - **near'sighted** *a.* able to see objects clearly only if they are near to the eyes.

neat *n.* ox, cow; cattle. **-neat'herd** *n.* cowherd. [OE.]

neat *a.* pure, undiluted; simple and elegant; cleverly worded; deft. **-neat'ly** *adv.* **-neat'ness** *n.* [F. *net*, clean]

neb'ula *n.* star-cluster. **-neb'ular** *a.* - **neb'ulous** *a.* cloudy; vague. [L. = *mist*]

necessary (nes'-) *a.* needful, requisite, that must be done. *-n.* needful thing. **nec'essarily** *adv.* **-necess'ity** *n.* compel, give power or state of affairs; a being needful; needful thing; poverty. **necessitate** *v.t.* make necessary. **-necessitous** *a.* poor, needy; destitute. [L. *aecessarius*]

neck *n.* part of the body joining the head to the shoulders; narrower part of a bottle, *etc.*; narrow piece of anything between wider parts. **-neck'erchief** (chif) *n.* kerchief for the neck. **-neck'lace** *n.* ornament round the neck. **-neck'let** *n.* ornament, piece of fur, *etc.*, to go round the neck. **-neck'tie** *n.* narrow strip of tailored material worn about the neck and tied at the front. [OE. *hnecca*, nape of neck]

necrol'ogy *n.* list of deaths, obituaries. [G. *nekros*, dead body]

necroman'cy *n.* magic, *esp.* by communication with the dead. **-nec'romancer** *n.* [G. *nekros*, corpse]

necrop'olis *n.* cemetery. [G. *nekros* and *polis*, city]

necro'sis *n.* mortification of bone. [G. *nekros*, dead]

nec'tar *n.* drink of the gods; the honey of flowers. **-nect'arine** *a.* *-n.* variety of peach. [G. *nektar*]

née *a.* born, preceding maiden surname of a married woman. [F.]

need *n.* want, requirement; necessity; poverty. *-v.t.* want, require. **-need'ful** *a.* **-need'less** *a.* **-needs** *adv.* of necessity (only in **needs must** or **must needs**). **- need'y** *a.* poor. [OE. *nied*]

need'le *n.* pointed pin with an eye and no head, for passing thread through cloth, *etc.*; knitting pin; magnetized bar of a compass; obelisk. [OE. ntdl]

nefarious *a.* wicked, abominable. [L. *nefarius*]

neg'ative *a.* expressing denial or refusal; wanting in positive qualities; not positive. *-n.* negative word or statement; in photography, a picture made by the action of light on chemicals in which the lights and shades are reversed. *-v.t.* disprove, reject. **-negate'** *v.t.* deny. **-nega'tion** *n.* [L. *negativus, negare*, deny]

neglect' *v.t.* disregard, take no care of; fail to do; omit through carelessness. *-n.* fact of neglecting or being neglected. **neglect'ful** *a.* **-neg'ligence** *n.* **-neg'ligent** *a.* **-neg'ligently** *adv.* [L. *neglegere, neglect-*, not to pick up]

neg'ligée (-zhi) *n.* informal attire; loose robe. [F.]

negotiate *v.i.* discuss with a view to finding terms of agreement. *-v.t.* arrange by conference; transfer (bill, *etc.*); get over (an obstacle), **-nego'tiable** *a.* - **negotia'tion** *n.* **-nego'tiator** *n.* [L. *negotiari, negotium*, business]

Ne'gro *n.* member of the black African race. **-Ne'gress** *fem.* **-ne'groid** *a.* [Sp., fr. L. *niger, negr-*, black]

ne'gus *n.* hot mixture of wine and water, flavored. [Colonel *Negus* (d. 1732)]

neigh *v.i.* of a horse, to utter its cry. *-n.* the cry. [OE. *hnægan*]

neigh'bor *n.* one who lives, stands, *etc.* near another. **-neigh'boring** *a.* situated near by. **-neigh'borhood** *n.* district; people of a district; region round about. - **neigh'borly** *a.* as or fitting a good or friendly neighbor. [OE. *neahgebur*, 'nigh boor', near by farmer]

nei'ther *a.* and *pron.* not either. *-adv.* not on the one hand; not either. *-conj.* nor yet. [OE. *nahwæther*, not whether]

nek'ton *n.* collective term for various marine organisms. [G. = *swimming*]

nem'atoid *a.* thread-like. *-n.* threadworm. [G. *nema*, thread]

Nem'esis *n.* retribution; goddess of retribution. [G.]

nem'oral *a.* of a wood. [L. *nemus*, grove]

neo- new. [G. *neos*, new]

neolith'ic *a.* of the later stone age. - **neol'ogism** *n.* new coined word or phrase. **-neontol'ogy** *n.* study of still-existing races of animals. **-neoter'ic** *a.* modern. - **ne'ophyte** *n.* new convert; beginner.

ne'on *n.* rare atmospheric gas. **-ne'on lighting**, produced by passing an electric current through a tube containing neon. [G. *neos*, new]

nepen'thes *n.* pain-killing drug. - **nepen'the** *n.* pitcher-plant. [G.]

neph'ew *n.* brother's or sister's son, [F. *neveu*, fr. L. *nepos*]

ne'potism *n.* favoritism. [It. *nepotismo,* fr. *nepote,* nephew. (orig. because of favors bestowed by a pope on his nephews)]

Nep'tune *n.* Roman god of the sea; one of the outermost planets of the Solar system. -**Neptu'nian** *a.* of the sea or its action on rocks. [G. *Neptunus*]

ne'reid *n.* sea-nymph. [G.]

nerve *n.* sinew, tendon; fiber or bundle of fibers conveying feeling, impulses to motion, *etc.* between the brain and other parts of the body; assurance, coolness in danger. (*sl.*) impudence. -*pl.* irritability, unusual sensitiveness to fear, annoyance, *etc.* -*v.t.* give courage or strength to. -**nerve'less** *a.* -**nerv'ous** *a.* of the nerves; vigorous; excitable, timid. -**nerv'ously** *adv.* -**nerv'ousness** *n.* -**nerv'y** *a.* brash; courageous. [L. *nervus,* sinew]

nes'cient (nesh'yent) *a.* ignorant. **nes'cience** *n.* [L. *nescire,* not to know]

ness *n.* headland. [OE. *næss*]

nest *n.* place in which a bird lays and hatches its eggs; animal's breeding place; any snug retreat. -*v.i.* make or have a nest. -**nes'tle** (-sl) *v.i.* settle comfortably, usually pressing in or close to something. -**nest'ling** *n.* bird too young to leave the nest. [OE.]

net *n.* open-work fabric of meshes of cord, *etc.*; piece of it used to catch fish, *etc.* -*v.t.* to cover with, or catch in, a net. -*v.i.* make net. -**net'ting** *n.* string or wire net. -**net'work** *n.* intricate system-*e.g.*, of transport systems. -**net'working** *n.* interconnection of two or more networks in different places, *esp.* as in working at home with a link to a central computer in an office; forming business connections and contacts through informal social meetings. [OE. *nett*]

net, nett *a.* left after all deductions; clear profit. -*v.t.* gain as clear profit. [F. *clean*]

neth'er (-TH-) *a.* lower. [OE. *neothera*]

nett'le *n.* plant with stinging hairs on the leaves. -*v.t.* irritate, provoke. -**nett'le rash** *n.* disorder of the skin like nettle stings. [OE. *netele*]

neuralgia *n.* pain in the nerves, *esp.* of face and head. -**neural'gic** *a.* -**neurasthe'nia** *n.* nervous debility. -**neurasthen'ic** *a.* -**neuri'tis** *n.* inflammation of nerves. -**neuro'sis** *n.* nervous disorder. -**neurot'ic** *a.* suffering from neurosis; abnormally sensitive. -*n.* neurotic person. [G. *neuron,* nerve]

neut'er *a.* neither masculine nor feminine. -*n.* neuter word; neuter gender. [L. = *neither*]

neut'ral *a.* taking neither side in a war; dispute, *etc.*; without marked qualities; belonging to neither of two classes. -*n.* neutral state, or a subject of one. **neutral'ity** *n.* impartiality. -**neut'ralize** *v.t.* make ineffective; counterbalance. [L. = *neither*]

neut'ron *n.* electrically uncharged particle of the atom. -**neut'ron bomb** *n.* nuclear bomb designed to destroy people but not buildings. [L. *neuter,* neither]

neve' *n.* glacier snow. [F.]

nev'er *adv.* at no time. -**nevertheless'** *adv.* for all that. [OE. *næfre]*

new *a.* not existing before, fresh; lately come into some state or existence. *adv.* (usu. new-) recently, fresh. -**newfang'led** (-ng-gid) *a.* of new fashion. **new'ly** *adv.* -**new'ness** *n.* -**news** *n.* report of recent happenings, fresh information. -**news'-dealer** *n.* one who deals in newspaper, magazines, *etc.* -**news' flash** *n.* brief item of important news, often interrupting a radio or television program. -**news'-monger** *n.* a gossip. **news'paper** *n.* periodical publication containing news. -**news'room** *n.* reading-room with newspapers; department for news or newspapers. -**news' vendor** *n.* one who sells newspapers. [OE. *niave,* new; cp. F. *nouvelles*]

newel *n.* central pillar of a winding staircase; post at the top or bottom of a staircase rail. [OF. *noiel,* kernel]

newt *n.* small tailed amphibious creature. [for an *ewt; ewt* for *evet, eft,* OE. *efete*; cp. *nickname*]

next *a.* nearest; immediately following. -*adv.* on the first future occasion. [OE. *niehst,* superl. of *neah,* high]

nex'us *n.* connecting link. [L.]

nib *n.* pen-point. -*pl.* crushed cocoa beans. [earlier *neb,* beak, OE. *nebb*]

nib'ble *v.t.* take little bites of. -*v.i.* take little bites. -*n.* little bite. -**nib'bler** *n.* person, animal, or thing that nibbles; a tool that cuts sheet material by a series of small rapidly reciprocating cuts. [fr. *nip*]

nib'lick *n.* heavy-headed golf club for lofting. [orig. unknown]

nice *a.* hard to please; careful, exact; difficult to decide; minute; subtle, fine; (*sl.*) pleasant, friendly, kind, agreeable, *etc.* -**nice'ly** *adv.* -**ni'cety** *n.* precision; minute distinction or detail. [OF. *nice,* foolish]

Ni'cene *a. pert.* to Nice in Bithynia, Asia Minor, where ecumenical council in 325 discussed Arian controversy. it promulgated the **Nicene Creed.**

niche (-tsh) *n.* recess in a wall. [F.]

nick *v.t.* make a notch in, indent; just catch in time. -*n.* notch; exact point of time. [orig. uncertain]

nick'el *n.* silver-white metal much used in alloys and plating; five cent piece. [Sw. abbrev. fr. Ger. *kupfernickel*, copper nickel (ore)]

nick'name *n.* name added to or replacing an ordinary name. -*v.t.* give a nickname to. [earlier, a *nickname* was an *eke-name*; fr. *eke*, also, [OE. *ecan*, cp. *newt*]

nic'otine *n.* poisonous oily liquid in tobacco. **-nic'otinism** *n.* tobacco poisoning. [F. fr. J. *Nicot*, who sent tobacco plants to France (1560)]

nidifica'tion *n.* nest-building. **-nid'ify** *v.t.* [L. *nidus*, nest]

niece *n.* brother's or sister's daughter. [F. *niece*, fr. L. *neptis*]

nigg'ard *n.* stingy person. **-nigg'ardly** *a.* and *adv.* [orig. uncertain]

nigg'le *v.i.* fiddle, waste time on trifles. **-nigg'ling** *a.* fussy finicking; cramped (of writing). [orig. uncertain]

nigh *a., adv., prep.* near. [OE. *neah*]

night *n.* time of darkness between day and day; end of daylight; dark. **night'-blind'ness** *n.* inability to see in a dim light. **-night'-club** *n.* club open at night for dancing, entertainment. **-night'fall** *n.* end of day. **-night'ingale** *n.* small bird which sings usually at night. **-night'jar** *n.* bird, the goal sucker. **-night'ly** *a.* happening or done every night; of the night. **-night'ly** *adj.* every night, by night. **-night'mare** *n.* feeling of distress during sleep; bad dream. **-night'shade** *n.* various plants of the potato family, some of them with very poisonous berries. **-night'-shift** *n.* night duty; relay of workmen on night duty. **-night'stick** *n.* policeman's club. **-night' walker** *n.* sleepwalker; one who walks about streets at night *esp.* for no good purpose. **-night'watch** *n.* watch or watcher by night. [OE. *niht*]

ni'hilism *n.* denial of all reality; rejection of all religious and moral principles: opposition to all constituted authority or government. **-ni'hilist** *n.* [L. *nihil*, nothing]

nil *n.* nothing, zero. [contr. of L. *nihil*]

nim'ble *a.* active, quick. **-nim'bly** *adv.* [OE. *niman*, take, capture]

nim'bus *n.* cloud of glory, halo; raincloud or stormcloud. [L. = *cloud*]

nincompoop *n.* feeble character, fool. [orig. uncertain]

nine *a.* and *n.* cardinal number next above eight. **-ninth (-i-)** *a.* **-ninth'ly** *adv.* **-nine'teen** *a.* and *n.* nine and ten. **-nine'teenth** *a.* **-nine'ty** *a.* and *n.* nine tens. **-nine'tieth** *a.* **-nine'pins** *n. pl.* game in which nine wooden 'pins' are set up to be knocked down by a ball rolled at them, skittles. [OE. *nigon*]

nin'ja *n.* member of secret Japanese feudal organization.

ninn'y *n.* simpleton; fool. [It. *ninno, a* child]

nip *v.t.* pinch sharply; detach by pinching; check growth (of plants) thus. -*n.* pinch; check to growth; sharp coldness of weather. **-nipp'er** *n.* small boy. -*pl.* pincers. [orig. uncertain]

nipp'le *n.* point of a breast, teat. [orig. uncertain]

Nirva'na *n.* in Buddhism, attainment of union with the divine by the conquest of personal desires and passions. [Sanskrit = *extinction*]

Niss'en hut *n.* hut roughly constructed of corrugated iron *usu.* semicircular in shape, for temporary use in war time. [Col. P. N. *Nissen*, designer]

nit *n.* egg of a louse. [OE. *hnitu*]

ni'ter *n.* potassium nitrate, saltpeter. **-ni'trate** *n.* compound of nitric acid and an alkali. **-ni'tric** *a.* **-ni'trious** *a.* [G. *nitron*]

nit'ia *a.* shining, lustrous. [L. *nitere*. shine]

ni'trogen *n.* colorless, tasteless gaseous element forming four-fifths of the atmosphere. **-nitrog'enous** (-j-) *a.* of or containing nitrogen. [G. *nitron*]

nitroglyc'erin *n.* high explosive produced by interaction of glycerin and nitric or sulfuric acids. [G. *nitron*]

ni'val *a.* snowy. **-niv'eous** *a.* [L. *nix, niu*, snow]

nix' *n.* tricky water-sprite. [Ger.]

nix' *n.* (*sl.*) nothing. [Ger. *nichts*]

no *a.* not any. -*adv.* expresses a negative reply to question or request. **-no'body** *n.* no person; person of no importance. **-noth'ing** (nuth'-) *n.* not anything. [*a.* for earlier **none**; *adv.* OE. *na*]

no'ble *a.* distinguished by deeds, character, rank or birth; of lofty characters impressive; excellent. -*n.* member of the nobility. **-nobil'ity** *n.* class holding special rank, *usu.* hereditary, in a state; a noble being. **-no'bly** *adv.* **no'bleman** *n.* [L. *nobilis*]

noctur'nal *a.* of, in, or by night; active by night. **-noc'tule** *n.* night-flying list. **-noc'turne** *n.* dreamy piece of music; night scene. [L. *nocturnus*, fr. *nox, noct-*, night]

nod *v.i.* bow the head slightly and quickly in assent, command, *etc.* let the head droop with sleep, err through carelessness or inattention. -*v.t.* incline (the head) thus. -*n.* an act of nodding. [orig. uncertain]

nod'dle *n.* head. [orig. uncertain]

node *n.* knot or knob; point at which a curve crosses itself. -*n.* (*compute.*) central point around which are clustered a group of local computer terminals or work stations in a telecommunications network. -**no'dal** *a.* -**nod'ule** *n.* small lump, knot. [L. *nodus*, knot]

Noël' *n.* Christmas; Christmas carol. [F.]

no-fault *a.* of, or pertaining to, automobile insurance which guarantees that an accident victim is compensated for damages by their insurance company without determination of blame.

no-frills *a.* (*sl.*) basic; plain; reduced to the essentials; without extras or special features.

nogg'in *n.* small wooden mug; liquid measure = 1 gill. [Gael. *noigean*]

noise *n.* clamor, din; any sound. -*v.t.* rumor. -**noise'less** *a.* -**nois'y** *a.* -**nois'ily** *adv.* (F.]

nois'ome *a.* disgusting; noxious; pestilential. [obs. *noy*, for annoy]

nom'ad *a.* roaming from pasture to pasture; not having a fixed place of dwelling. -*n.* member of a nomad tribe; wanderer. -**nomad'ic** *a.* [G. *nomas, nomad-*]

no'man's-land *n.* ground separating trenches of hostile armies.

nom'-de-plume (nong) *n.* pseudonym. [F., lit. pen-name; an E. const. based on F. *nom-de-guerre*, war-name]

nomen'clature *n.* system of names or naming. [L. *nomen*, name]

nom'inal *a.* of a name or names; existing only in name. -**nom'inally** *adv.* **nom'inate** *v.t.* propose as a candidate appoint to an office. -**nom'inator** *n.* **nomina'tion** *n.* -**nominee'** *n.* [L. *nominalis*, fr. *nomen*, name]

non- *prefix* makes compounds that negative the idea of the simple word, *e.g.*, -**noncom'batant** *n.* one who does not fight; noncommissioned *a.* not commissioned. The meaning and derivation of those not given should be sought by reference to the simple word. -**non'age** *n.* minority.

nonagenar'ian *a.* between ninety and a hundred years old. -*n.* person of such age. [L. *nonagenarius*, fr. *nonageni*, ninety each]

non'agon *n.* nine-sided, nine-angled plane figure. [L. *nonus*, ninth]

nonce *n.* for the nonce, for the occasion only. [earlier the(n) ones, the once]

nonchalant' (-sh-) *a.* unconcerned. **non'chalantly** *adv.* -**non'chalance** *n.* [F.]

noncommitt'al *a.* not committing or pledging oneself to opinion, *etc.* [*non-*, and L. *committere*]

nonconform'ist *n.* one who does not conform to the established church. **nonconform'ity** *n.* [*conform*]

non'descript *a.* not easily described. indeterminate. [*describe*]

none (nun) *pron.* no one. -*a.* no. -*adv.* in no way. -**none'-so-prett'y** *n.* garden plant, London pride. -**none'-the-less'** *adv.* nevertheless. [OE. *nan* for *ne an*, not one]

nonent'ity *n.* non-existence; non existent thing; person of no importance [*entity*]

none'such *a.* unique apart, unrivalled. [*none such*]

non'invasive *a.* not entering the body by penetration, *esp.* surgery and diagnostic procedures.

nonpareil' (-rel') *a.* unequalled. -*n.* something unequalled [F.]

nonplus' *n.* state of perplexity, deadlock. -*v.t.* bring to a nonplus. [L. *non plus*, not more]

non'sense *n.* words or actions that are foolish or meaningless -**nonsen'sical** *a.* [*non-* and *sense*]

non'violence *n.* belief or practice of peaceful methods in pursuit of any goal; lack or absence of violence.

noo'dle *n.* simpleton. [orig. unknown]

nood'le *n.* (*cookery*) hardened paste of flour and eggs, used in soup. [Ger. *nudel*]

nook *n.* sheltered corner. [cp. Gael. *niue*]

noon *n.* midday. -**noon'time** *n.* time about noon. [L. *nona* (*hora*), ninth (hour)]

noose *n.* running loop; snare. -*v.t.* to catch in a noose. [L. *nodus*, knot]

nor *conj.* and not. [ME. *nother*]

norm *n.* rule; pattern; type. -**nor'mal** *a.* perpendicular; conforming to type, ordinary. -**normal'ity** *n.* -**nor'mally** *adv.* -**normal'ize** *v.t.* to render normal; bring into conformity with standard; heat (steel) above critical temperature and allow it to cool in air to relieve internal stresses. -**normal'ization** *n.* [L. *norma*, carpenter's square]

Nor'man *n.* of, *pert.* to Normandy in France.

Norse *a.* of Norway. -*n.* Norwegian people or language.

north (-th) *n.* region or cardinal point opposite to the midday sun; part of the world, of a country, *etc.*, towards this point. *-adv.* towards or in the north. *-a.* to, from, or in the north. **-nor′therly** (-TH-) *a.* - **nor′thern** *a.* **-nor′therner** *n.* - **northwards** *adv.* [OE.]

Norwe′gian *a.* of, *pert.* to Norway. *-n.* [OE. *Northweg*]

nose *n.* organ of smell, used also in breathing. *-v.t.* detect by smell. *-v.i.* smell. - **nose′gay** *n.* bunch of sweet-smelling flowers. [OE. *nosu*]

nosol′ogy *n.* science of diseases. - **nosol′ogist** *n.* [G. *nosos,* disease]

nostal′gia *n.* home-sickness. [G. *nostos,* return home, *algos*, pain]

nos′tril *n.* one of the openings of the nose. [OE. nosthvri, nose-hole]

nostrums *n.* quack medicine; pet scheme. [L. = *our* (panacea, *etc.*)]

not *adv.* expressing negation. [*nought*]

no′table *a.* worthy of note, remarkable. **-no′tably** *adv.* **-notabil′ity** *n.* eminent person. [*note*]

no′talry *n.* person authorized to draw up deeds, *etc.* [L. *notarius*]

nota′tion *n.* representing of numbers, quantities, *etc.*, by symbols; set of such symbols. [L. *notare, notat-*, note]

notch *n.* small V-shaped cut or indention. - *v.t.* make a notch in; score. [F. *oche*]

note *n.* symbol standing for a musical sound; single tone; mark, sign; brief written message, memorandum, letter; fame, regard. *-v.t.* observe; set down. **-no′ted** *a.* well known. **-note′worthy** *a.* worth noting, remarkable. [L. *nota,* mark; *notare,* note]

nothing (nuth′-) *n.* no thing; not anything. *adv.* not at all. [no thing]

no′tice (-tis) *n.* warning, intimation, announcement; bill, *etc.*, with an announcement. *-v.t.* mention; observe; give attention to. **-no′ticeable** *a.* [L. *notus,* known]

no′tify *v.t.* report, give notice of or to. - **notifica′tion** *n.* [L. *notilicare*]

no′tion *n.* idea, opinion, belief, fancy. (*colloq.*) desire, whim. [F. fr. L. *notio*]

notorious *a.* known for something bad; well known. **-notori′ety** *n.* [Low L. *notorius*]

notwithstanding *prep.* in spite of. *-adv.* all the same. *-conj.* although. [*withstand,* oppose]

nougat *n.* soft confection usually containing nuts. [F.]

nought (nawt) *n.* nothing; cipher (0) [OE. *nowiht*]

noun (nown) *n.* word used as a name of person, or thing. [L. *nomen*, name]

nourish (nur′-) *v.t.* supply with food; keep up. **-nour′ishment** *n.* [F. *nourrir,* fr. L. *nutrire*, feed]

nous′ (news) *n.* intellect; (colloq.) common-sense, intelligence. [G.]

no′va *n.* (**novae** *pl.*) new star. [L.]

nov′el *a.* new, strange. *-n.* fictitious tale published as a book. **-nov′elist** *n.* writer of novels. **-nov′elty** *n.* **-novelette′** *n.* short novel. [L. *novus,* new]

November *n.* eleventh month of the year. [L. *novem,* nine]

nov′ice *n.* candidate for admission to a religious order; one new to anything. - **novi′tiate, novi′ciate** (-vish-) [L. *novitius,* fr. *novus*, new]

now *adv.* at the present time. **now′adays** *adv.* in these times. [OE. *nu*]

no′where *adv.* not anywhere; (*sl.*) far behind; defeated. [*no* and *where]*

nox′ious (-ksh) *a.* hurtful, harmful, dangerous. [L. *noxa,* harm]

noz′zle *n.* pointed spout, *esp.* at the end of a hose. [dim. of *nose*]

nu′ance (-ong-s) shade of difference. [F.]

nu′bile *a.* marriageable. [L. *nubere,* marry]

nu′cleus *n.* center, kernel; beginning meant to receive additions; head of a comet; central part of an atom. **-nu′clear** *a.* of, pert. to atomic nucleus. **nucleonics** *n. pl.* (with *sing. v.*) branch of physics dealing with applications of nuclear energy. **-nu′clear bomb** *n.* bomb whose force is due to uncontrolled nuclear fusion or nuclear fission. **-nu′clear disarmament** *n.* elimination of nuclear weapons from country's armament. **-nu′clear en′ergy** *n.* energy released by nuclear fission. - **nu′clear fam′ily** *n.* primary social unit consisting of parents and their offspring. **-nu′clear fis′sion** *n.* disintegration of the atom. **-nu′clear fu′sion** *n.* reaction in which two nuclei combine to form nucleus with release of energy (also **fu′sion**). - **nu′clear phy′sics** *n.* branch of physics concerned with structure of nucleus and particles of which it consists. **-nu′clear reac′tion** *n.* change in structure and energy content of atomic nucleus by interaction with another nucleus, particle. **-nu′clear threshold** *n.* point in war at which a combatant brings nuclear weapons into use. **-nu′clear win′ter** *n.* period of extremely low temperatures and little light that has been suggested would occur as a result of a nuclear war. -**nucle'ic a'cid** *n.* any of group of complex compounds with high molecular weight that are vital constituents of all living cells. [L. = *kernel*]

nude *a.* naked. -**nu'dity** *n.* [L. *nudus*]

nudge *v.t.* touch with the elbow. -*n.* such touch. [orig. uncertain]

nu'gatory *a.* trifling. [L. *nugatorius*, fr. *nugce*, rubbish, trifles]

nugg'et *n.* rough lump of native gold. [orig. uncertain]

nuisance *n.* something offensive or annoying. [F. *noire, nuis-*, harm]

null *a.* of no effect, void. -**null'ity** *n.* -**null'ify** *v.t.* [L. *nullus*, none]

null'ah *n.* dried-up watercourse. [Hind. *nala*]

numb (num) *a.* deprived of feeling, *esp.* by cold. -*v.t.* [OE. *numen*]

num'ber *n.* sum or aggregate; word or symbol saying how many; single issue of a paper, *etc.*, issued in regular series; classification as to singular or plural; rhythm; metrical feet or verses; company or collection. -*v.t.* count; class, reckon; give a number to; amount to. **num'berless** *a.* that cannot be counted. -**nu'meral** *a.* of or expressing number. -*n.* sign or word denoting a number. -**nu'merate** *v.t.* count. -*a.* able to count. -**numera'tion** *n.* -**nu'merator** *n.* top part of a fraction, figure showing how many of the fractional units are taken. -**numer'ical** *a.* of, or in respect of, number, or numbers. -**nu'merous** *a.* many. [L. *numerus*]

numismatic *a.* of coins. -*n.* in *pl.* study of coins. -**numis'matist** *n.* [L. *numisma*, current coin]

num'skull *n.* dolt. [*numb skull*]

nun *n.* woman living in a convent under religious vows. -**nunn'ery** *n.* convent of nuns. [Church L. *nonna, fem.* of *nonnus*, monk]

nun'cio (-shi-) *n.* representative of the Pope at a foreign court. [It.]

nup'tial *a.* of or relating to marriage or a marriage. -*n.* in *pl.* marriage. [L. *nupti-*, wedding]

nurse *n.* person trained for the care of the sick or injured; woman tending another's child. -*v.t.* act as a nurse to. -**nurs'ery** *n.* room for children; rearing place for plants. -**nurs'eryman** *n.* owner of a nursery garden. -**nurs'ling** *n.* infant. -**nurs'ing home** *n.* private hospital. [L. *nutrix*, foster-mother]

nur'ture *n.* bringing-up. -*v.t.* bring up. [F. *nourriture*, nourishment]

nut *n.* fruit consisting of a hard shell and kernel; small block with a hole to be screwed on a bolt. -*v.i.* gather nuts. [OE. *hnutu*]

nutate' *v.i.* nod, droop. -**nu'tant** *a.* -**nuta'tion** *n.* [L. *nutare*, nod]

nut'hatch *n.* small bird, a tree-creeper. [ME. *notehach*, nuthacker]

nut'meg *n.* aromatic flavoring spice. [ME. *notemugge*]

nu'tria *n.* fur of the coypu, resembling beaver. [Sp.]

nutriment *n.* food. -**nutri'tion** (-trish'n) *n.* the receiving or supply of food; food. -**nutri'tious** *a.* good in effects as food. -**nu'tritive** *a.* [L. *nutrire*, nourish]

nux vom'ica *n.* seed of an Eastern tree which yields strychnine. [Med. L.]

nuz'zle *v.i.* burrow or press with the nose; nestle. [*nose*]

ny'lon *n.* synthetic filament of great strength and fineness, made into fabrics, *etc.* -*pl.* nylon stockings. (*N*ew *Y*ork, *Lon*don]

nymph *n.* legendary semi-divine maiden living in the sea, woods, mountains, *etc.* [G. *nymphe*, bride]

O

oaf *n.* changeling; dolt. [ON. *alfr*, elf]

oak *n.* familiar forest tree. -**oak'en** *a.* -**oak-apple** *n.* insect-gall on the oak. [OE. *ac*]

oak'um *n.* loose fiber produced by picking old rope. [OE. *acumbe*, off-combings]

oar *n.* wooden lever with a broad blade worked by the hands to propel a boat. **oars'man** *n.* -**oars'manship** *n.* [OE. *ar*]

oa'sis *n.* fertile spot in the desert. [G. of Egypt, orig.]

oast *n.* kiln for drying hops. [OE. *ast*]

oat *n.* grain of a common cereal plant (*usu. pl.*); the plant. -**oat'en** *n.* -**oat'cake** *n.* -**oat'meal** *n.* [OE. *ate*]

oath *n.* confirmation of the truth of a statement by the naming of something sacred; act of swearing. [OE. *ath*]

obblig'ato *n.* (*music*) accompaniment, *e.g.*, of a flute, as an essential part of the piece. [It.]

ob'durate *a.* stubborn. -**ob'duracy** *n.* [L. *obduratus-durare, durat-*, harden]

obedient. *See* **obey.**

obeis'ance *n.* bow, curtsy. [F. *obéissance*, obedience]

ob'elisk *n.* tapering stone shaft of rectangular section. [G. *obeliskos*]

obese′ *a.* very fat. -**obe′sity** *n.* corpulence. [L. *obesus]*
obey *v.t.* do the bidding of, be moved by. -**obe′dience** *n.* -**obe′dient** *a.* -**obe′diently** *adv.* [L. *oboedire*]
ob′fuscate *v.t.* confuse; make dark or obscure. [L. *obfuscare*, darken]
o′bi *n.* African magic, fetishism. [W. Afr.]
ob′iter *adv.* incidentally, in passing. -**ob′iter dictum** incidental opinion, *esp.* of judge. [L. *ob iter*, by the way]
obit′uary *n.* notice or record of a death or deaths. [Med. L. *obituarius*, fr. *obitus*, departure]
ob′ject *n.* material thing; that to which feeling or action is directed; end or aim; word dependent on a verb or preposition. -**object′** *v.t.* state in opposition. -*v.i.* feel dislike or reluctance to something. -**objec′tion** *n.* -**objec′tionable** *a.* -**objective** *a.* external to the mind. -*n.* thing or place aimed at. -**objectiv′ity** *n.* -**objec′tor** *n.* [Med, L. *objectum*, thrown in the way]
ob′jurgate *v.t.* scold, reprove. -**objurga′tion** *n.* [L. *objurgare*]
oblate′ *a.* of a sphere, flattened at the poles. [Med. L. *oblatus*]
obla′tion *n.* ritual offering, sacrifice. -**ob′late** *n.* person dedicated to religious work. [L. *oblatio*]
oblige′ *v.t.* bind morally or legally to do a service to; compel. -**obliga′tion** *n.* binding promise; debt of gratitude; indebtedness for a favor; duty. -**oblig′atory** *a.* required, binding. -**ob′ligate** *v.t.* -**obli′ging** *a.* ready to serve others. [L. *obligare*, fr. *ligare*, bind]
oblique′ *a.* slanting; indirect. -**obliq′uity** *n.* -**oblique′ly** *adv.* [F., fr. L *obliquus-liquis*, slanting]
oblit′erate *v.t.* blot out. -**oblitera′tion** *n.* [L. *obliterare*, fr. *literà*, letter]
obliv′ion *n.* forgetting or being forgotten. -**obliv′ious** *a.* [L. *oblivio]*
ob′long *a.* rectangular with adjacent sides unequal. -*n.* oblong figure. [L. *oblongus*]
ob′loquy *n.* abuse; disgrace. [Late L. *obloquium*, speaking against]
obnox′ious (-okshus) *a.* offensive, disliked. [L. *obnoxius*, exposed to harm]
o′boe *n.* wood wind instrument. **o′boist** *n.* [F. *hautbois*, hautboy]
ob′ol *n.* ancient Greek coin. -**ob′olus** *n.* obol, in Middle Ages, various coins of low value. [fr. G. *obolos*]
ob′secrate *v.t.* beseech, implore. -**obsecra′tion** *n.* [L. *obsecrare*, entreat]
obscene′ *a.* indecent; offensive. -**obscen′ity** *n.* [L. *obscœnus*]
obscure′ *a.* dark, dim; indistinct; unexplained; humble. -*v.t.* dim; conceal; make unintelligible. -**obscu′rant** *n.* one who opposes enlightenment or reform. -**obscu′rantism** *n.* -**obscu′rantist** *n.* -**obscu′rity** *n.* [L. *obscurus*]
ob′sequies (-iz) *n. pl.* funeral rites. -**obse′quial** *a.* [Med. L. *obsequiæ*]
obse′quious *a.* servile, fawning. [L. *obsequiosus*, compliant]
observe′ (-z-) *v.t.* keep, follow; watch; note systematically; notice; remark. *v.i.* make a remark. -**observ′able** *a.* -**observ′ably** *adv.* -**observ′ant** *a.* quick to notice. -**observ′ance** *n.* paying attention; keeping. -**observa′tion** *n.* action or habit of observing; noticing; remark. -**observ′atory** *n.* a building scientifically equipped for the observation of stars, *etc.* -**observ′er** *n.* one who observes; flying officer engaged in reconnaissance, *etc.* [L. *observare*, fr. *servare*, guard]
obsess′ *v.t.* haunt, fill the mind.-**obses′sion** *n.* -**obsess′ional** *a.* [L. *obsidere, obsess*, besiege]
obsid′ian *n.* volcanic rock forming dark hard natural glass. [stone found in Ethiopia by *Obsius* (wrongly *Obsidius*)]
ob′solete *a.* no longer in use, out of date. -**obsoles′cent** *a.* going out of use. [L. *obsolescere*, grow out of use]
ob′stacle *n.* thing in the way; hindrance to progress. [L. *obstaculum*]
obstet′ric *a.* of midwifery. -*n.* in *pl.* midwifery. [L. *obstetrix*, midwife]
ob′stinate *a.* stubborn. -**ob′stinacy** *n.* -**ob′stinately** *adv.* [L. *obstinatus*]
obstrep′erous *a.* clamorous; obtrusive; unruly. [L. *obstreperus*]
obstruct′ *v.t.* hinder; block up. -**obstruc′tion** *n.* -**obstruc′tionist** *n.*-**obstructive** *a.* [L. *obstruere, obstruct-*, build up against]
obtain *v.t.* get. -*v.i.* be customary. -**obtain′able** *a.* [L. *obtinere*]
obtrude′ *v.t.* thrust forward unduly. -**obtru′sion** *n.* -**obtru′sive** *a.* **obtru′sively** *adv.* [L. *obtrudere*]
obtuse′ *a.* not sharp or pointed; greater than a right angle; stupid. -**obtuse′ly** *adv.* [L. *obtusus*, blunt]
ob′verse *n.* side of a coin or medal with the chief design. -*a.* turned towards one. [L. *obversus*, turned towards]
ob′viate *v.t.* prevent. [Late L. *obviare*]
ob′vious *a.* clear, evident. [L. *obvius*, what meets one in the way]

ocari'na *n.* egg-shaped musical instrument played by the mouth. [It.]

occa'sion *n.* opportunity; reason, need; immediate but subsidiary cause; time when a thing happens. *-v.t.* cause. -**occa'sional** *a.* happening or found now and then. -**occa'sionally** *adv.* sometimes, now and then. [L. *occasio*]

oc'cident (-ks-) *n.* the West, Occidental *a.* [L. *occidere*, set]

occult' *a.* secret, mysterious. *-v.t.* hide from view. -**occulta'tion** *n.* -**occult'ism** *n.* study of philosophy, esoteric religion *etc.* -**occult'ist** *n.* [L. *occultus*, fr. *occulere*, hide]

occ'upy *v.t.* take possession of; inhabit; fill; employ. -**occ'upancy** *n.* fact of occupying; residing. -**occ'upant** *n.* -**occupa'tion** *n.* seizure; possession; employment. -**occ'upier** *n.* [L. *occupare*, take possession of]

occur' *v.i.* happen; come to mind. -**occurr'ence** *n.* [L. *occurrere*, run against]

o'cean *n.* great body of water surrounding the land of the globe; large division of this; sea. -**ocean'ic** *a.* [G. *okeanos*, stream encircling the world]

o'celot *n.* S. American tiger-cat. [Mex. *ocelotl*, jaguar]

o'cher *n.* various earths used as yellow or brown pigments. [G. *ochra*]

OCR *n.* (*compute.*) ability of certain light sensitive machines to recognize printed letters, numbers, and special characters, and translate them into computer terms. [*O*ptical *C*haracter *R*ecognition]

oct-', oc'ta-, oc'to- *prefix* eight. -**oc'tagon** *n.* figure with eight angles. -**octag'onal** *a.* -**octang'ular** *a.* having eight angles. -**oct'ant** *n.* eighth part of circle; instrument for measuring angles; having arc of 45°. -**oc'tave** *n.* group of eight days; eight lines of verse; note eight degrees above or below a given note; this space. -**octa'vo** *n.* size of book in which each sheet is folded into eight leaves. -**Octo'ber** *n.* tenth month of the year. (Roman eighth.) - **octodec'imo** *a.* and *n.* (book) having 18 leaves to the sheet. -**octogena'rian** *a.* of an age between eighty and ninety. *-n.* a person of such age. -**oc'topus** *n.* a mollusk with eight arms covered with suckers. -**octosyll'able** *n.* word of eight syllables. -**octet** *n.* group of eight. [G. and L. *okto*, eight]

oc'ular *a.* of the eye or sight. -**oc'ularly** *adv.* -**oc'ulate** *a.* -**oc'ulist** *n.* eye surgeon. [L. *oculus*, eye]

odd *a.* that is one in addition when the rest have been divided into two equal groups; not even; not part of a set; strange, queer. -**odd'ity** *n.* quality of being odd; odd person or thing. -**odd'ments** *n. pl.* odd things. -**odds** *n. pl.* difference, balance; advantage to one of two competitors; advantage conceded in betting; likelihood. -**odds and ends** odd fragments or left-over things. [ON. *odda(tala)*, odd (number)]

ode *n.* lyric poem of lofty style. [G.]

o'dium *n.* hatred, widespread dislike; blame. -**o'dious** *a.* hateful. [L.]

odontol'ogy *n.* science, study, of the teeth. [G. *odous, odont-*, tooth]

o'dor *n.* smell. -**o'dorize** *v.t.* fill with scent. -**o'dorous** *a.* -**odorif'erous** *a.* spreading an odor. [L. *odor*]

oen'ophile *n.* lover or connoisseur of wines. [G. *oinos*, wine, *philos*, loving]

oesoph'agus, esophagus *n.* upper part of the alimentary canal, the gullet. -**oesophag'eal, esophag'eal** *a.* [G. *oisophagos*]

of *prep.* denotes removal, separation, ownership, attribute, material, quality, *etc.* [OE.]

off *adv.* away. *-prep.* away from. *-a.* distant; of horses, vehicles, *etc.*, right. **off'chance** *n.* remote possibility. -**off'col'or**, indisposed, not at one's best. **off-hand'** *a.* and *adv.* without previous thought or preparation. -**off-scourings** *n. pl.* worst part, dregs. -**off'set** *n.* side branch. -**off'shoot** *n.* branch from main stem. **off'spring** *n.* children, issue. -**off'ing** *n.* more distant part of the sea visible to an observer. [var. of *of*]

off'al *n.* parts cut out in preparing a carcase for food; refuse. [= *off-fall*]

offend' *v.t.* displease. *-v.i.* do wrong. -**offense'** *n.* -**offend'er** *n.* -**offen'sive** *a.* causing displeasure. *-n.* position or movement of attack. [L. *offendere*, strike against]

off'er *v.t.* present for acceptance or refusal; propose; attempt. *-v.i.* present itself-*n.* offering, bid. -**off'erer** *n.* -**off'ertory** *n.* collection in a church service. [L. *offerre*]

off'ice *n.* service; duty; official position; form of worship; place for doing business; corporation carrying on business. -**off'icer** *n.* one in command in an army, navy, air force, *etc.* *-v.t.* supply with officers. -**offi'cial (fish'-)** *a.* having or by authority. *-n.* one holding an office, *esp.* in a public body. -**offi'cialism** *n.* undue official authority or routine. -**offi'cialdom** *n.* officials collectively; their work, usually in a contemptuous sense. -**offi'ciate** *v.i.* to perform the duties of an office; perform a service. -**offi'cious** (-ish'us) *a.* meddlesome, importunate in offering service. -**offi'ciousness** *n.* [L. *officium*, duty]

off'ing, off'shoot *See* **off.**

oft, of'ten (of'n) *adv.* many times, frequently. [OE.]

o'gee *n.* molding of two members, one concave, the other convex, like an S. [F. *ogive*]

ogive' *n.* pointed arch. [F.]

o'gle *v.i.* make eyes. -*v.t.* make eyes at. *n.* amorous glance. [Low Ger. *oegeln*, eye]

o'gre *n.* fabled man-eating giant. -**o'gress** *fem.* [F.]

ohm *n.* unit of electrical resistance. [*Ohm*, Ger. physicist (d. 1854)]

oil *n.* light flammable viscous liquid, obtained from various plants, animal substances, and minerals. -*v.t.* apply oil to. -*v.i.* of a ship *etc.*, take in oil fuel. **oil'cake** *n.* cattle food made from linseed *etc.* -**oil'cloth** *n.* oil-coated canvas, linoleum. -**oil'skin** *n.* material made waterproof with oil. -**oil'y** *a.* [L. *oleum*]

oint'ment *n.* greasy preparation for healing the skin. [OF. *oignement*]

oka'pi *n.* giraffe-like animal of Central Africa. [native]

okay', OK *adv.* and *a.* all right. -*v.t.* pass as correct. [perh. abbrev. for *orl korrect*]

old *a.* advanced in age, having lived or existed long; belonging to an earlier period. -**old'en** *a.* old. -**old-fash'ioned** *a.* in the style of an earlier period, out of date; fond of old ways. -**old-maid'** *n.* spinster unlikely to marry. -**old'-ti'mer** *n.* one who has long occupied a place, position. -**old'-world** *a.* quaint, old-fashioned. [OE. *eald*]

oleag'inous *a.* oily, producing oil; unctuous. -**oleag'inousness** *n.* [L. *oleaginus*]

olean'der *n.* poisonous evergreen flowering shrub. [Med. L.]

olea'ster *n.* wild olive. [L. *oleaster*, olive tree]

o'leograph *n.* picture printed in oils, to imitate a painting. [L. *oleum*]

oleom'eter *n.* instrument for ascertaining the weight and purity of oils. [L. *oleum*, oil, and *meter*, measure]

olfac'tory *a.* of smell. -**olfac'tion** *n.* [L. *olfacere*, cause to smell]

ol'igarchy (-ki) *n.* government by a few. -**ol'igarch** *n.* -**oligarch'ic** *a.* [G. *oligarchia*, fr. *oligos*, few]

ol'ive (-iv) *n.* evergreen tree; its oil-yielding fruit. -*a.* gray-green in color. [L. *oliva*]

Olym'pic *a.* of Olympus. -**Olym'pic Games'**, great athletic festival of ancient Greece; (*mod.*) international sports meeting held every four years. [G.]

olym'piad *n.* four-year period between Olympic Games. [G. *Olympus*, home of Greek gods]

o'mega *n.* last letter of Greek alphabet; end. [G.]

om'elet, om'elette *n.* dish of fried eggs with seasoning, *etc.* [F. *omelette*]

o'men *n.* prophetic object or happening. -**om'inous** *a.* portending evil. [L.]

omit' *v.t.* leave out, neglect. -**omis'sion** *n.* [L. *omittere*]

omni- *prefix.* all. [L. *omnis*, all] -**om'nibus** *n.* road vehicle travelling on a fixed route and taking passengers at any stage; several books bound in one volume. -*a.* serving or containing several objects. -**omnip'otent** *a.* all powerful. -**omnip'otence** *n.* -**omnipres'ent** *a.* everywhere at the same time. -**omnipres'cence** *n.* -**omnis'cient** (shient) *a.* knowing everything. -**omnis'cience** *n.* -**omniv'orous** *a.* devouring all foods. [L. *ominis*, all]

on *prep*, above and touching, at, near, towards, *etc.* -*adv*. so as to be on, forwards, continuously, *etc.* -**on'ward** *a.* and *adv.* -**on'wards** *adv.* [OE.]

once (wuns) *adv.* one time; ever; formerly. [ME. *ones*, fr. *one*]

on'cost *n.* overhead expenses. -*a*, causing oncost; paid by time. -**on'costman** *n.* miner paid by the day. [*on, cost*]

one (wun) *a.* lowest cardinal number; single; united; only, without others; identical. -*n.* number or figure 1; unity; single specimen. -*pron.* particular but not stated person; any person. -**oneself'** *pron.* -**one'-sided** *a.* lop-sided; biased. -**one-sidedness** *n.* -**one'ness** *n.* [OE. *an*]

on'erous *a.* burdensome. [L. *onerosus*]

on'ion (un'yun) *n.* plant with a bulb of pungent flavor. [L. *unio*]

on'ly *a.* that is the one specimen. *adv.* solely, merely, exclusively. *conj.* but, excepting that. [OE. *anlic*, one like]

onomatopoe'ia *n.* formation of a word by using sounds that resemble or suggest the object or action to be named. -**onomatopoe'ic, onomatopoet'ic** *a.* [G. *onomatopoiia*]

on'set *n.* assault, attack; start. [*on. set*]

on'slaught (-awt) *n.* attack. [Du. *aanslag*]

ontol'ogy *n.* science of being, of the real

nature of things. **-ontolog'ical** *a.* - **ontol'ogist** *n.* [G. *on*, being]

o'nus *n.* responsibility. [L. = *burden*]

on'yx *n.* variety of quartz. [G. = *nail*]

oo'dles *n.pl.* (*sl.*) abundance. [orig. uncertain]

o'olite *n.* roe-stone, limestone with loose grain like fish roe. **oolit'ic** *a.* [G. *oion*, egg, *lithos*, stone]

ool'ogy *n.* study of eggs and of nesting birds. [G. *oion*, egg, *logos*, discourse]

ooze *n.* wet mud, slime; sluggish flow. *v.i.* pass slowly through, exude. [OE. *was*, juice; *wase*, mud]

o'pal *n.* white or bluish stone with iridescent reflections. **-opales'cent** *a.* showing changing colors. [G. *oppallios*]

opaque' *a.* not transparent. **-opa'city** *n.* [L. *opacus*]

o'pen *a.* not shut or blocked up; without lid or door; bare; undisguised; not enclosed or covered or limited or exclusive; frank; free. *-v.t.* set open, uncover, give access to; disclose, lay bare; begin; make a hole in. *-v.i.* become open. *-n.* clear space, unenclosed country. **-o'pen-eyed** *a.* watchful. **-o'pen-handed** *a.* generous. **-o'pen-hearted** *a.* generous, frank. **o'pening** *n.* hole, gap; beginning. **-o'penly** *adv.* without concealment. **open-minded** *a.* unprejudiced. **-o'pen-mouthed** *a.* agape; greedy, over-talkative. [OE.]

op'era *n.* musical drama. **-operat'ic** *a.* - **op'era-glass** *n.* binoculars for viewing stage performance. [It. L. = *work*]

op'erating sys'tem *n.* (*compute.*) software that controls the execution of computer programs.

opera'tion *n.* working, way a thing works; scope; act of surgery. **-op'erate** *v.i.* **-op'erative** *a.* workingman. *n.* mechanic. **-op'erator** *n.* **-operating theater** *n.* specially equipped room in hospital, *etc.* in which surgical operations are performed. [L. *operation* fr. *opus*, work]

ophid'ian *a.* of or like a serpent. [G. *ophidion*]

ophthal'mia *n.* inflammation of the eye. **-ophthal'mic** *n.* **-ophthalmol'ogist** *n.* specialist in eye infections. [G.]

opiate. *See* **opium.**

opin'ion *n.* what one thinks about some thing; belief, judgment. **-opine'** *v.t.* think; utter an opinion. **-opin'ionated, opinionative** *a.* stubborn in holding an opinion. [L. *opinio*]

o'pium *n.* sedative and narcotic drug made from the poppy. **-o'piate** *v.t.* mix with opium. *-n.* opiated drug. [L.]

oposs'um *n.* small American marsupial animal. [N. Amer. Ind.]

oppo'nent *n.* adversary. *a..* opposed, adverse. [L. *opponere*, place against]

opportune *a.* seasonable, well timed. - **opportu'nity** *n.* favorable time or condition. **-opp'ortunism** *n.* policy of doing what is expedient at the time regardless of principle. **-opp'ortunistic** *a.* of or characterized by opportunism. [L. *opportunus*]

oppose' (-z) *v.t.* set against; contrast; resist, withstand. *-p.p.* adverse. **-oppo'ser** *n.* **-opp'osite** (-zit) *a.* contrary facing, diametrically different. **-opposi'tion** (-ish) *n.* a being opposite; resistance; party opposed to that in power. [F. *opposer*]

oppress' *v.t.* govern with tyranny; weigh down. **-oppress'ive** *a.* **-oppress'ively** *adv.* **-oppres'sion** *n.* **-oppress'or** *n.* [L. *opprimere, oppress-*, press down]

oppro'brium *n.* disgrace; contemptuous reproach. **-oppro'brious** *a.* [L.]

oppugn' *v.t.* fight, *esp.* with argument; oppose. **-oppug'nancy** (opug-) *n.* - **oppug'nant** *a.* [L. *oppugnare*, attack]

op'tative *n.* mood of verb expressing wish. [L. *optare*, choose]

op'tic *a.* of the eye or sight. *-n.* eye; in *pl.* science of sight or light. **-op'tical** *a.* **opti'cian** (-ish-) *n.* maker of, dealer in, optical instruments. [G. *optikos*]

op'timism *n.* belief that the world is the best possible world; doctrine that good must prevail in the end; disposition to look on the bright side. **-op'timist** *n.* - **optimis'tic** *a.* **-optimis'tically** *adv.* [L. *optimus*, best]

op'tion *n.* choice. **-op'tional** *a.* [L. *optio*, fr. *optare*, choose]

op'ulent *a.* rich; profuse. **-op'ulence** *n.* [L. *opulentus*, wealthy]

o'pus *n.* (**op'era** *pl.*) musical composition of a particular composer, usually numbered in sequence. [L.]

or *conj.* introduces alternatives; if not. [ME. *other* (mod. *either*)]

or'acle *n.* place where divine utterances were supposed to be given; answer there given, often ambiguous; wise or mysterious adviser. **-orac'ular** *a.* of an oracle; of dogmatic or doubtful meaning. [L. *oraculum*, orate, speak]

or'al *a.* by mouth; spoken. **-or'ally** *adv.* [L. *os, or-*, mouth]

or'ange (-inj) *n.* familiar bright reddish-yellow round fruit; tree bearing it; color of the fruit. *-a.* of the color of an orange. -

or'ange-stick' *n.* orange-wood stick used in manicure. [Pers. *narang*]

Or'angeman *n.* member of Irish Protestant sect. [William of *Orange*]

orang'-outang', orang-utan' *n.* large ape. [Malay = *man of the woods*]

or'ator *n.* maker of a speech, skillful speaker. **-ora'tion** *n.* formal speech. - **orator'ical** *a.* of an orator or oration. - **or'atory** *n.* speeches; eloquent language; small chapel. **-orator'io** *n.* semidramatic composition of sacred music. [L. *orare*, speak]

orb *n.* globe, sphere. **orbed', orbic'ular, orbic'ulate(d)** *a.* spherical. **-orb'it** *n.* cavity holding the eye; track of a heavenly body. **-or'bital** *a.* pert. to orbit. [L. *orbis*, circle]

Orca'dian *n.* pert. to Orkney. *-n.* native of Orkney. [L. *orcades*, Orkney]

orch'ard *n.* enclosure containing fruit trees. [OE. *ortgeard]*

or'chestra *n.* band of musicians; place occupied by such band in a theater, *etc.*; the forward section of seats on the main floor of a theater. **-orchest'ral** *a.* **-or'chestrate,** *v.t.* compose or arrange music for an orchestra. **-orchestra'tion** *n.* [G. = *dancing* space for chorus]

or'chid (-k-) *n.* various flowering plants. [Med. L. *orchideæ]*

ordain' *v.t.* admit to Christian ministry; confer holy orders upon; decree, destine. **-ordina'tion** *n.* [OF. *ordener*, fr. L. *ordo*, order]

ord'inance *n.* decree, rule, municipal regulation; ceremony. [L. *ordinare*]

or'deal *n.* method of trial by requiring the accused to undergo a dangerous physical test; trying experience. [OE. *ordal*, judicial test]

or'der *n.* rank, class, group; monastic society; sequence, succession, arrangement; command, pass, instruction. *-v.t.* arrange; command; require. **-or'derly** *a.* methodical. *-n.* soldier following an officer to carry orders; soldier in a military hospital acting as attendant. **-or'derliness** *n.* [F. *ordre*-L. *ordo, ordin*]

or'dinal *a.* showing number or position in a series, as first, second, *etc.* [*order*]

or'dinary *a.* usually commonplace. *-n.* bishop in his province; public meal supplied at a fixed time and price. [L. *ordo, ordin-*, order]

ord'nance *n.* guns, cannon; military stores. [var. of *ordinance. See* **ordain**]

or'dure *n.* filth; dung. [L. *horridus*, rough]

ore *n.* native mineral from which metal is extracted. [OE. *ora*]

oreg'ano *n.* herb, variety of marjoram. [G. *origanon*, wild marjoram]

or'gan *n.* musical instrument of pipes worked by bellows and played by keys; member of an animal or plant carrying out a particular function; means of action; newspaper. **-organ'ic** *a.* of the bodily organs; affecting bodily organs; having vital organs; organized, systematic. - **organ'ically** *adv.* **-or'ganism** *n.* organized body or system. **-or'ganist** *n.* one who plays an organ. **-or'ganize** *v.t.* furnish with news; give a definite structure; get up, arrange, put into working order. - **organiza'tion** *n.* **-or'ganizer** *n.* [G. *organon*, instrument]

or'gandie *n.* thin, fine transparent muslin. [F. *organdi*]

or'gasm *n.* paroxysm of emotion, *esp.* sexual; climax of sexual arousal. [G. *orgasmos*, swelling]

or'gone *n.* a substance postulated by Wilhelm Reich, who thought it was present everywhere and needed to be incorporated in people for sexual activity and mental health. [fr. *orgasm* and *hormone*]

or'gy (-ji) *n.* drunken or licentious revel. **-orgias'tic** *a.* [G. *orgia, pl.*, secret rites]

or'iel *n.* projecting part of an upper room with a window. [OF. *oriol*]

or'ient *n.* the East; luster of the best pearls. *-a.* rising; Eastern; of pearls, from the Indian seas. *-v.t.* place so as to face the east; find one's bearings. **-orien'tal** *a.* and *n.* **-orienta'tion** *n.* **-orien'talist** *n.* expert in Eastern languages and history. **-or'ientate** *v.t.* relate to the points of the compass; take bearings of. [L. *oriens, orient-*, rising]

or'ifice *n.* opening, mouth of a cavity. [Late L. *orifium*]

or'iflamme *n.* ancient French small red silk banner split into many points, carried on a gilt staff. [L. *aurum*, gold, *flamma*, a flame]

or'igin *n.* beginning, source, parentage. - **original** (-ij-) *a.* primitive, earliest; new, not copied or derived; thinking or acting for oneself, eccentric. *-n.* pattern, thing from which another is copied; eccentric person. **-ori'ginally** *adv.* **-original'ity** *n.* **-ori'ginate** *v.t.* bring into existence. - **origina'tion** *n.* **-ori'ginator** n [L. *origo, origin-*, fr. *oriri*, rise]

or'iole *n.* golden thrush. [OF. *oriol* fr. L. *aureolus-aurum*, gold]

Ori'on *n.* constellation containing seven

very bright stars, three of which form Orion's belt. [*Orion*, a hunter placed among the stars at his death]

or'ison *n.* prayer. [L. *orare*, speak]

or'lop *n.* lowest deck in ship with three or more decks. [Du. *overloop*, covering]

or'molu *n.* gilded bronze; yellow alloy. [F. *or moulu*, 'ground gold']

or'nament *n.* decoration. -*v.t.* adorn. -**ornament'al** *a.* -**ornamenta'tion** *n.* **ornate'** *a.* highly decorated, elaborate. [L. *orna mentum*]

ornithol'ogy *n.* science of birds. -**ornitholo'gical** *a.* -**ornithol'ogist** *n.* [G *ornis, ornith-*, bird]

orog'raphy *n.* geography of mountains -**orograph'ical** *a.* [G. *oros*, mountain]

o'rotund *a.* round, full, musical; pompous, grandiloquent. [L. *ore rotundo*, with round mouth]

or'phan *n.* child bereaved of one or both of its parents. -**or'phanage** *n.* institution for the care of orphans. -**or'phanhood** *n.* [G. *orphanos*, bereaved]

or'piment *n.* yellow compound of arsenic used as coloring matter. [L. *aurum*, gold, *pigmentum*, paint]

orr'ery *n.* mechanical working model of the solar system. [Earl of *Orrery*]

orr'is *n.* kind of iris with violet-scented root. [var. of *iris*]

ortho- *prefix* right. [G. *orthos*, right] -**or'thodox** *a.* holding accepted views or doctrine; conventional. -**or'tbodoxy** *n.* -**orthog'raphy** *n.* correct spelling. -**orthopedic, -orthopaed'ic** *a.* for curing deformity.

ort'olan *n.* small bird, a bunting, *esp.* as a table delicacy, [F.]

orts *n.pl.* fragments; leftovers. [Low Ger. *ort*]

or'yx *n.* kind of straight-horned antelope. [G. = *pickax*]

os'cillate *v.i.* swing to and fro; vary between extremes; set up wave motion in wireless apparatus. -**oscilla'tion** *n.* -**os'cillator** *n.* one that oscillates, *esp.* a person setting up unauthorized wireless waves from a radio receiving set. [L. *oscillare*, swing]

os'culate *v.t.* and *i.* kiss. -**oscula'tion** *n.* -**oscula'tory** *a.* [L. *osculari*, fr. *as*, mouth]

o'sier (-z-) *n.* kind of willow. [F.]

os'mium *n.* hard, heavy metallic substance. [G. *osme*, smell]

osmo'sis *n.* intermixing of fluids by percolation through a dividing membrane. [G. *osmos*, impulse]

os'prey *n.* fishing eagle; egret plume. [L. *ossifraga*, 'bone-breaker']

oss'eous *n.* of or like bone. [L. *os*, bone]

os'sifrage *n.* osprey; sea-eagle. [L. *os*, bone, *frangere*, break]

osten'sible *n.* professed, used as a blind. -**osten'sibly** *adv.* -**ostenta'tion** *n.* show, display. -**ostenta'tious** *a.* -**ostenta'tiously** *adv.* [L. *ostendere*, show]

osteop'athy *n.* art of treating diseases by removing structural derangement by manipulation, *esp.* of spine. -**os'teopath** *n.* one skilled in this art. [G. *osteon*, bone, and *patheia*, suffering]

os'tler (-sl-) *n.* man who attends to horses at an inn. [*hostler*, orig. an innkeeper, fr. *hostel*]

os'tracize *v.t.* exclude from society, exile. -**os'tracism** *n.* [G. *ostrakizein*]

os'trich *n.* large swift-running flightless African bird. [OF. *austruche*]

oth'er (uTH'-) *a.* not this, not the same; alternative, different. -*pron.* other person or thing. -**oth'erwise** (-iz) *adv.* differently, [OE.]

otiose' *a.* lazy, futile; at leisure. [L. *otiosus*]

ott'er *n.* furry aquatic fish-eating animal. [OE. *otor*]

ott'oman *n.* cushioned seat without back or arms. [*Othman*, founder of a Turk. dynasty]

oubliette' *n.* dungeon with opening only in roof. [F. *oublier*, forget]

ouch, nouch *n.* (setting of) jewel; clasp. [OF. *nouch*]

ought (awt) *v. aux.* expressing duty or obligation or advisability. [*owe*]

ounce *n.* weight, twelfth of the Troy pound, sixteenth of the avoirdupois pound. [L. *uncia*]

ounce *n.* snow-leopard. [F. once]

our *pron.* belonging to us. [OE. *ure*]

ou'sel, ou'zel *n.* blackbird. [OE. *osle*]

oust *v.t.* put out. [OF. *oster*]

out *adv.* from within, from among, away, not in the usual or right state. -**out'ing** *n.* pleasure excursion. -**out'side** *n.* outer side, exterior. *n*, exterior; external. *adv.* on the outer side. -*prep.* beyond. -**out'ward** *a.* and *adv.* -**out'wards** *adv.* -**out'wardly** *adv.* [OE. *ut*]

out- as *prefix* makes many compounds with the sense of beyond, in excess, *etc.*, *e.g.*, **outflank'** *v.t.* get beyond the flank. -**out'put** *n.* quantity put out, *etc.* These are not given where the meaning and derivation may easily be found from the simple word.

out'age *n.* quantity of something lost during storage or transportation; failure, interruption, *esp.* in the supply of electric current; period or time during such a failure. [*out*]

out'back *n.* (Australia) remote open country. [*out* and *back*]

out'break *n.* breaking, bursting out. [*out* and *break*]

out'cast *n.* homeless person; vagabond, pariah. [ME.]

outclass' *v.t.* excel, surpass. [*out* and *class*]

out'come *n.* result, consequence. [ME.]

out'crop *n.* in geology appearance of stratum on surface. -*v.i.* come out to surface. [*out* and *crop*]

out'land *n.* foreign country. -**outland'ish** *a.* queer, extravagantly strange. [OE. *utland*]

out'law *n.* one placed beyond the protection of the law, an exile. -**out'lawry** *n.* [ON. *utlagi*]

out'post *n.* post, station beyond main company. [*out* and *post*]

out'rage *n.* violation of others' rights; gross or violent offense or indignity. -*v.t.* injure, violate, ravish, insult. [F.]

ou'tré *a.* extravagant, odd, bizarre. [F.]

out'rigger *n.* frame outside a ship's gunwale; frame on the side of a rowing boat with a rowlock at the outer edge; boat with one; boat, *usu.* a sailboat, with a hull and separate floats to the side for stability. [earlier *outlegger*, Du. *uitlegger,* 'outlyer']

out'right *a.* complete, unreserved. -*adv.* completely, [*out* and *right]*

outskirts *n. pl.* environs; parts farthest from the center. [*out* and *skirts*]

out'set *n.* beginning, start. [*out* and *set*]

outstrip' *v.t.* outrun, surpass. [*out* and *strip*]

out'take *n.* unreleased take from a recording session, film, or television program. [*out* and *take*]

out'work *n.* outer fortification. [*out* and *work*]

o'val *a.* egg-shaped, elliptical. -*n.* oval figure or thing. -**o'vary** *n.* egg-producing organ. -**ovariec'tomy** *n.* surgical removal of one or both ovaries. [L. *ovum,* egg]

ova'tion *n.* enthusiastic burst of applause. [L. *ovatio*]

ov'en (uv-) *n.* heated iron box or other receptacle for baking in. [OE. *ofn*]

o'ver *adv.* above, above and beyond, going beyond in excess, too much, past, finished, in repetition, across, *etc.* -*prep.* above, on, upon, more than, in excess of, along, across, *etc. a.* upper, outer. [OE. *ofer*]

o'ver- as *prefix* makes compounds with meaning of too, too much, in excess, above, *e.g.*, -**o'verdo** *v.t.* do too much. -**overdraw'** *v.t.* draw in excess of what is in credit, *etc.* These words are not given where the meaning and derivation may be found from the simple word.

overbear' *v.t.* bear down, dominate, overwhelm. -**overbear'ing** *a.* domineering, haughty. [*over* and *bear*]

overboard' *adv.* over ship's side into water. [*over* and *board*]

overcast' *a.* dull and heavy, (of sky) clouded. [*over* and *cast*]

overhaul' *v.t.* come up with in pursuit; examine and set in order. -*n.* thorough examination, *esp.* for repairs. [*haul*]

o'verhead *a.* over one's head, above. *adv.* above. -**o'verhead charg'es,** costs, business expenses apart from cost of production. [*over* and *head*]

o'verland *a.* made, performed by land. *adv.* by land. [*over* and *land*]

over'leaf *adv.* on the reverse side of a page or sheet of paper.

o'verpass *n.* elevated level to allow free flow of traffic over traffic moving in another direction.

overreach' *v.t.* and *i.* extend beyond; outwit. [ME.]

oversee' *v.t.* look, see over. -**overseer'** *n.* supervisor of work. [OE. *oferseon*]

o'versight *n.* error, *esp.* of omission. [ME.]

o'vert *a.* open, unconcealed. -**o'vertly** *adv.* [OF. = *opened*]

overtake' *v.t.* come up with in pursuit; catch up. [*take]*

overthrow' *v.t./i.* vanquish; overturn; remove from office; throw too far. -*n.* ruin, disaster; defeat.

overtime *adv./n.* (work) done after regular hours. [*over* and *time*]

o'vertone *n.* harmonic. [*over* and *tone*]

o'verture *n.* opening of negotiations; proposal; introduction of an opera, *etc.* [OF. = *opening*]

overween'ing *a.* thinking too much of oneself. [OE. *oferwenian,* become insolent]

overwhelm' *v.t.* flow over, submerge, overbear. -**overwhelm'ing** *a.* resistless. [*over* and *whelm*]

o'vine *a.* sheep-like. [L. *ovis,* sheep]

ovip'arous *a.* egg-laying. [L. *ovum,*

parere, bring forth]

ovi'ferous *a.* egg-carrying. [L. *ovum*, egg, *forma*, form]

o'void *a.* egg-shaped. [L. *ovum*, egg, G. *cidos*, form]

owe *v.t.* be bound to repay, be indebted for. **-ow'ing** *a.* owed, due. **-owing to,** caused by. [OE. *agan*, own]

owl *n.* night bird of prey. **-owl'et** *n.* young owl. **-owl'ish** *a.* solemn and dull. [OE. *ule*]

own *a.* emphasizes possession. *-v.t.* possess; acknowledge. *-v.i.* confess. **own'er** *n.* **-own'ership** *n.* [OE. *agen*, a., one's own, *agnian*, v.]

ox *n.* **ox'en** *pl.* large cloven-footed and usually horned animal used for draft, milk, and meat, a bull or cow. **-ox'eye** *n.* large daisy—**ox'lip** *n.* hybrid between cowslip and primrose. [OE. *oxa*]

oxal'ic *a.* of wood-sorrel. **-ox'alis** *n.* wood-sorrel. [G. *oxys*, sour]

ox'ygen *n.* gas in the atmosphere which is essential to life, burning, *etc.* **-ox'ide** *n.* compound of oxygen. **-ox'idize** *v.t.* cause to combine with oxygen; cover with oxide, make rusty. *-v.i.* combine with oxygen, rust. **-ox'yacet'ylene** *a.* involving, using mixture of oxygen and acetylene. [G. *oxys*, sour]

oxymoron *n.* (*rhet.*) figure of speech combining incongruous terms. [G. *oxys*, sharp, *moros*, foolish]

oyez' *n.* call, usually uttered three times, by a public crier or court official to attract attention. [OF., imperative. of *oir*, L. *audire*, heart]

oy'ster *n.* bivalve mollusk or shellfish, *usu.* eaten alive. [G. *ostreon*]

o'zone *n.* condensed form of oxygen with a pungent odor; refreshing influence. [G. *ozein*, smell]

P

pab'ulum *n.* food, nourishment. [L.]

pace *n.* step; length of a step; walk or speed of stepping; speed. *-v.i.* step. *-v.t.* cross or measure with steps; set the speed for. **-pa'cer** *n.* **-pace'maker** *n.* one that sets the pace at which something happens or should happen; electronic device surgically implanted in those with heart disease. [L. *passus*]

pach'yderm (-k-) *n.* thick-skinned animal, *e.g.*, an elephant. **-pachyderm'atous** *a.* [G. *pachydermos*]

pacif'ic *a.* quiet; tending to peace. **-pac'ify** (-s-) *v.t.* calm; establish peace. **pacification** *n.* **-pacif'icatory** *a.* **-pacif'icist, pa'cifist** *n.* advocate of the abolition of war; one who refuses to help in war. **-pac'ificism** *n.* (L. *pacifus*, peacemaking, fr. *pax, pac-*, peace]

pack *n.* bundle; company of animals, large set of people or things; set of playing cards; packet; mass of floating ice. *-v.t.* make into a bundle; put together in a box, *etc.*; arrange one's luggage for traveling; fill with things; order off. **-pack'age** *n.* parcel. **-pack'ager** *n.* someone or something that packages; independent firm specializing in design and production, as of illustrated books or television programs, which are sold to publishers or television companies as finished product. **-pack'er** *n.* **-pack'et** *n.* small parcel. **-pack'-horse** *n.* horse for carrying bundles of goods. **-pack' saddle** *n.* saddle to carry goods. **-pack'-thread** *n.* stout thread for packing. [Du. *pak*]

pact *n.* covenant of agreement. -also **pac'tion.** [L. *pactus*, contract]

pad *v.i.* travel on foot. *-n.* easy paced horse. [Du. = path. *cp. footpath*]

pad *n.* piece of soft stuff used as a cushion; shin-guard; sheets of paper fastened together in a block; foot or sole of various animals. *-v.t.* make soft, fill in, protect, *etc.*, with a pad or padding. **-padd'ing** *n.* stuffing; literary matter put in simply to increase quantity. [orig. uncertain]

pad'ang *n.* field. [Malay.]

pad'dle *n.* short oar with a broad blade at one or each end; blade of a paddle wheel. *-v.i.* move by paddles; roll gently. *-v.t.* propel by paddles. **-pad'dle-wheel** *n.* wheel with crosswise blades which strike the water successively to propel a ship. **-pad'dle-box** *n.* upper casing of a paddle-wheel. [orig. unknown]

pad'dle *v.i.* walk with bare feet in shallow water. [orig. uncertain]

padd'ock *n.* small grass field. [earlier *parrock*, OE. *pearroc*. cp. *park*]

padd'y *n.* growing rice. **-padd'y-field** *n.* [Malay., *padi*]

pad'lock *n.* detachable lock with a hinged hoop to go through a staple or ring. *-v.t.* fasten with padlock. [orig. uncertain]

pa'dre *n.* parson; priest; chaplain to the forces. [Port. =*father*]

paean *n.* shout or song of triumph. [G. *paian*, hymn, chant]

paedophil'ia. *See* **pedophilia.**

pa'gan *a.* heathen. *-n.* heathen. **-pa'ganism** *n.* [L. *paganus*, rustic]

page *n.* boy servant, attendant. [F.]

page *n.* one side of a leaf of a book. -*v.t.* number the pages of-**pa'ginate** *v.t.* number the pages of. -**pagina'tion** *n.* [L. *pagina-pangere*, fasten]

pa'geant (paj'-ent) *n.* procession, dramatic show, of persons in costume, *usu.* illustrating history, brilliant show. -**pa'geantry** *n.* [orig. uncertain]

pago'da *n.* temple or sacred tower of Chinese or Indian type. [Port. *pagode*]

pail *n.* large round open vessel for carrying liquids, *etc.*; bucket. -**pail'ful** *n.* [orig. uncertain]

pain *n.* bodily or mental suffering; penalty. -*v.t.* inflict pain upon. -**pain'ful** *a.* -**pain'fully** *adv.* -**pain'less** *a.* -**pain'lessly** *adv.* -**pains'taking** *a.* diligent, careful. [L. *poena*, penalty]

paint *n.* coloring matter prepared for putting on a surface with brushes. -*v.t.* portray, color, coat, or make a picture of, with paint; describe. -**paint'er** *n.* -**paint'ing** *n.* picture in paint. [F. *peint*, p.p- of *peindre*]

paint'er *n.* rope for fastening bow of a boat to a ship, *etc.* [L. *pendere*, hang]

pair *n.* set of two, *esp.* existing or generally used together. -*v.t.* arrange in a pair or pairs. -*v.i.* come together in pair or pairs. [L. *par*, equal]

paja'mas *n. pl.* sleeping suit of loose trousers and jacket. [Pers. *pae, jamah*, leg garment]

pal'ace *n.* official residence of a king, bishop, *etc.*; stately mansion. -**pala'tial** *a.* -**pal'atine** *a.* having or exercising royal privileges. [L. *palatium*]

pal'adin *n.* chivalrous person (originally one of the twelve peers of Charlemagne). [F.]

palan'quin, palankeen' *n.* light covered litter for one person used in eastern countries, carried by poles, resting on men's shoulders. [Hind. *palang*, a bed]

pal'ate *n.* roof of the mouth; sense of taste. -**pal'atable** *a.* agreeable to eat. -**pal'atal** *a.* of the palate; made by placing the tongue against the palate. -*n.* **palatal sound.** [L. *palatum*]

pala'tial, pal'atine. *See* **palace.**

pala'ver *n.* conference; empty talk. -*v.i.* use of many words. -*v.t.* to talk over. [Port. *palavra*, word]

pale *a.* faint in color, dim, whitish. -*v.i.* grow white. [L. *pallidus*]

pale *n.* stake, boundary. -**pa'ling** *n.* (*usu.* in *pl.*) fence. [L. *palus*]

paleo- *prefix* ancient. [G. *palaios*). **paleobot'any** *n.* a study of fossil plants. -**paleo'graphy** *n.* ancient writing. -**paleolith'ic** *a.* of the early part of the Stone Age. -**paleontol'ogy** *n.* study of ancient life (through fossils, *etc.*). **paleozool'ogy** *n.* study of fossil animals.

pal'ette *n.* artist's flat board for mixing colors on. -**palette-knife** *n.* [F.]

pal'frey *n.* small saddle-horse, suitable for a lady. [F. *palefroi*]

pal'impsest *n.* superimposed writing, drawing, through which the original can still be seen. [G. *palimpseston*]

palisade' *n.* fence of pointed stakes. *esp.* for defense. -*v.t.* enclose with one. [F. *palissade*, fr. *pal*, stake]

pall (pawl) *n.* cloth spread over a coffin. [L. *pallium*, cloak]

pall (pawl) *i.* become tasteless or tiresome. -*v.t.* to cloy, dull. [for *appal*]

pall'et *n.* straw bed, small bed, portable platform for storing or moving goods. [A. F. *paillette*, fr. *paille*, straw]

palliasse (pal'yas) **pall'aisse** *n.* straw mattress. [F., fr. *paille*, straw]

pall'iate *v.t.* relieve without curing; excuse. -**pallia'tion** *n.* -**pall'iative** *a.* giving temporary or partial relief-*n.* thing doing this. [L. *pallium*, cloak]

pall'id *a.* pale. -**pall'or** *n.* paleness. [L. *pallidus*, pale]

palm (pim) *n.* flat of the hand: tropical tree; leaf of the tree as a symbol of victory. -*v.t.* conceal in the palm of the hand; pass off by trickery. -**palm'istry** *n.* fortune-telling from the lines on the palm of the hand. -**palm'ist** *n.* -**palm'ary** *a.* worthy of a palm of victory, distinguished. -**palm'er** *n.* pilgrim returned from the Holy Land. -**Palm Sunday** *n.* Sunday before Easter. -**palm'y** *a.* flourishing. [L. *palma*]

pal'pable *a.* that may be touched or felt; certain, obvious. -**pal'pably** *adv.* [F., fr. L. *palpare*, feel]

pal'pitate *v.t.* throb. -**palpita'tion** *n.* [L. *palpare, palpitarè*, freq. of feel]

pal'sy (pawl-) *n.* paralysis. -**pal'sied** *a*, affected with palsy. [OF. *paralysis*, fr. paralysis]

pal'ter (pawl-) *v.t.* shuffle, deal evasively. -**pal'try** *a.* worthless, contemptible. [orig. uncertain]

palu'dal *a.* of marshes, marshy, malarial. [L. *palus*, marsh]

pam'pas *n. pl.* vast grassy plains of S. America. -**pam'pas grass** *n.* tall feathery grass of the pampas. [Sp.]

pam'per *v.t.* over-indulge. [orig. uncertain]

pamph'let *n.* thin paper cover book, stitched but not bound. -**pamphleteer'** *n.* writer of pamphlets. [OF. *Pamphilet*, title of a medieval poem (taken as type of a small book)]

pan *n.* broad, shallow vessel. -**pan'cake** *n.* thin cake of fried batter. -**pan'cake** landing, awkward flat landing of aircraft. -**pan'handle** *v.i.* beg for food or money in the street. [OE. *panne*]

panace'a *n.* universal remedy. [G. *panakeia*, all-healing]

panache' (-ash') *n.* dashing style; swagger. [F.]

pan'ada *n.* kind of batter. [Sp.]

pan'ama *n.* hat made of fine straw-like material. [made in S. Amer., but not in Panama]

pan'creas *n.* large gland secreting a digestive fluid, sweetbread. -**pancreat'ic** *a.* -**pan'creatin** *n.* pancreatic secretion. [G. *pan*. all, *kreas*, flesh]

pan'da *n.* raccoon-like Himalayan animal allied to the bears. [native]

Pande'an *a.* of the Greek god Pan. -**Pan's pipes** *n. pl.* musical instrument, the syrinx. [Pan]

pandem'ic *a.* universal. -*n.* widespread epidemic disease. [G. *pas, pan*, all, *demos*, people]

pandemo'nium *n.* scene of din and commotion. [coined by Milton]

pan'der *n.* go-between in illicit love affair; procurer. *v.t.* minister basely. [fr. *Pandarus*, prince who acted as agent between Troilus and Cressida]

pane *n.* piece of glass in a window. [F *pan*. flat section]

panegyr'ic (-i-jir-) *n.* speech of praise: encomium. -**panegyr'ical** *n.* -**pan'egyrist** *n.* [G. *panegyrikos*]

pan'el *n.* compartment of a surface, usually raised or sunk, *e.g.*, in a door; strip of different material in a dress; thin board with a picture on it; list of jurors, doctors, *etc.* -*v.t.* decorate with panels. -**pan'eling** *n.* paneled work. [OF. = *small pane*]

pang *n.* sudden pain. [orig. uncertain]

pango'lin *n.* scaly ant-eater. [Malay.]

pan'ic *n.* sudden and infectious fear. -*a.* of such fear; due to uncontrollable general impulse. [G. *panikos*, of Pan]

pann'ier *n.* basket of the type carried by a beast of burden or on a person's shoulders; part of a skirt looped up round the hips. [L. *panarium*, bread basket, fr. *panis*, bread]

pann'ikin *n.* small metal drinking cup; small saucepan. [dim. of *pan*]

pan'oply *n.* full suit of armor; complete, magnificent array. [G. *panoplia-pan-*, all, *hoplon*, weapon]

panoram'a *n.* picture arranged round a spectator or unrolled before him; wide or complete view. -**panoram'ic** *a.* (G. *pan-*, all, *horama*, view]

pan'sy (-zi) *n.* flowering plant; a species of violet. [F. *pensèe*, thought]

pant *v.i.* gasp for breath. -*n.* gasp. -**pant'ing** *adv.* [orig. uncertain]

pantaloon' *n.* in pantomime, foolish old man who is the butt of the clown. -*pl.* wide trousers. [It. *pantalone*, name of a character in old Italian stock comedy]

pantech'nicon (-k-) *n.* storehouse; van, for transporting furniture. [G. *pan-*, all, *teknikos*, of the arts]

pan'theism *n.* identification of God with the universe. -**pan'theist** *n.* -**pan'theon** *n.* temple of all the gods; building for memorials of a nation's great dead. [G. *pan-*, all, *theos*, a god]

pan'ther *n.* variety of leopard; cougar; jaguar. [G.]

pan'tile *n.* curved roofing tile. [*pan* and *ile*]

pan'tograph *n.* instrument for copying diagrams, maps, *etc.*, to any scale. [G. *pan-*, all, *graphein*, write]

pantom'eter *n.* instrument for measuring angles or perpendiculars. [G. *pan*, all, *metron*, measure]

pan'tomime *n.* dramatic entertainment in dumb show; Christmas-time dramatic entertainment. -**pantomim'ic** *a.* [G. *pantomimes*, all mimic]

pan'try *n.* room for storing food or utensils. [F. *paneterie-* L. *panis*, bread]

pants *n. pl.* trousers. [*pantaloons*]

pan'zer *a.* armored. -**panzer division** *n.* German mechanized division of all arms including tanks and airplanes. [Ger.]

pap *n.* soft food for infants, *etc.* [imit.]

pa'pacy *n.* office of the Pope; papal system. -**pa'pist** *a.* of, or relating to, the Pope. -**pa'pist** *n.* -**papist'ic** *a.* [Med. L. *papatia*, see pope]

papav'erous *a.* poppy-like. [L. *popover*, poppy]

pa'per *n.* material made by pressing pulp of rags, straw, wood, *etc.*, into thin flat sheets; sheet of paper written or printed on; newspaper; article or essay. -*pl.* documents, *etc.* -*v.t.* cover with paper. **pa'perless** *a.* of, relating to, or denoting a means of communication, record keeping, *etc.*, *esp.* electronic, that does not use paper. -**pap′ier mâ′ché** *n.* paper pulp shaped by molding and dried hard. [G. *papyros*, Nile rush from which paper was made]

papoose′ *n.* N. Amer. Indian child. [native]

pap′rika *n.* Hungarian red pepper. [Hung.]

papy′rus *n.* reed from which paper was made by the ancient Egyptians; this paper; a manuscript on papyrus. [L. *papyrus*-, G. *papyros*; prob. Egyptian]

par *n.* equality of value or standing; equality between market and nominal value. -**par′ity** *n.* equality. [L. = *equal*]

par′able *n.* allegory, story pointing a moral. [G. *parabole*, comparison]

parab′ola *n.* curve formed by cutting cone with plane parallel to its slope. [G. *para*, beside, *ballein*, throw]

parab′ole *n.* parable, sustained simile. [*See* **parabola**]

parachute′ (-sh-) *n.* apparatus extending like an umbrella to enable a person to come safely to earth from a great height. [L. *parare*, ward off, and *chute*]

parade′ *n.* display; muster of troops; parade ground. -*v.t.* muster; display. -*v.i.* march with display. [F.]

par′adigm (-dim) *n.* model, example. -**paradigmot′ic** *a.* [G. *paradeigma*]

par′adise *n.* garden of Eden; Heaven; state of bliss. [G. *paradeisos*, pleasureground]

par′adox *n.* statement that seems absurd but may be true. -**paradox′ical** *a.* [G. *paradoxos*, contrary to opinion]

par′affin *n.* wax or oil distilled from shale, wood, *etc.* [fr. L. *parum*, little, and affinis, related (because of its lack of affinity with other bodies)]

paraglid′ing *n.* sport of cross-country gliding using a specially designed parachute shaped like flexible wings. [L. *parare*, ward off, and glide]

par′agon *n.* pattern or model. [OF.]

par′agram *n.* pun; play upon words. [G. *para*, beside, *gamma*, writing]

par′agraph *n.* section of a chapter or book; short record. -*v.t.* arrange in para graphs. [G. *paragraphos*, written beside (orig. of the sign indicating the new section)]

para′keet, par′oquet *n.* small parrot. [F. *perroquet*]

paraleip′sis (-lip′-) *n.* (*rhet.*) figure in which emphasis is laid on something by pretending to ignore it. [G. *para*, beside, *leipein*, leave]

par′allel *a.* continuously at equal distances; precisely corresponding. -*n.* line of latitude; thing exactly like another; comparison. -*v.t.* represent as similar, compare. -**par′allelism** *n.* [G. *parallelos*, beside one another]

parallel′ogram *n.* four-sided plane figure with opposite sides equal and parallel. [L.]

parallel′ out′put *n.* (*compute.*) form of computer output in which all characters on a line are transmitted at the same instant.

paral′ysis *n.* incapacity to move or feel, due to damage to the nerve system. -**par′alyze** *v.t.* [G. *paralysis*, cp. *palsy*]

paramed′ical *a.* of persons working in various capacities in support of medical profession. [G. *para*, beside, L. *medicus*, physician]

par′amount *a.* supreme. [F. *par amont*, upwards]

par′amour *n.* illicit lover. [F. *par amour*, by love]

par′anoia (-a-noi′-A) *n.* kind of mental disease. -**parano′ic** *n.* [G. *para*, beside, *noein*, to think]

par′apet *n.* low wall; breast-high defense: mound along the front of a trench. [F.]

paraphema′lia *n. pl.* personal belongings, trappings, odds and ends of equipment. [Med. L.]

paraphrase *n.* expression of a meaning of a passage in other words. -*v.t.* put the meaning of in other words. [G. *paraphrases*, beside phrase]

par′asail′ing *n.* sport in which a waterskier wearing a parachute is towed by a speedboat, becomes airborne and sails along in the air. [L. *parare*, ward off, and sail]

parascend′ing *n.* sport in which a participant wears a parachute and becomes airborne by being towed by a vehicle into the wind and then descends by parachute. [L. *parare*, ward off, and ascend]

par′asite *n.* self-interested hanger-on; animal or plant living in or on another. -**parasit′ic** *a.* -**parasit′ically** *adv.* -**par′asitism** *n.* -**parasitol′ogy** *n.* [G. *parasitos*]

parasol′ *n.* light umbrella for protection against the sun. [It. *parasols*]

par′atroops *n. pl.* airborne troops to be dropped by parachute. -**par′atrooper** *n.* [*parachute* and *troops*]

par'avane *n.* anti-mine device towed by ships at sea. [G. *para*, against and vane]

par'boil *v.i.* scald the surface in boiling water, boil partly; scorch. [OF. *parboillir*, boil thoroughly]

par'buckle *n.* rope for raising or lowering round objects, the middle being secured at the higher level and the ends passed under and round the object. *-v.t.* raise or lower in this way. [orig. uncertain]

par'cel *n.* packet of goods, specially one enclosed in paper; quantity dealt with at one time; piece of land. *-v.t.* divide into parts; make up in a parcel, [F. *parcelle*, small part]

parch *v.t.* and *i.* dry by exposure to heat, roast slightly, make or become hot and dry. [ME. *perche*, contr. of perish]

parch'ment *n.* skin prepared for writing; manuscript of this. [*pergamum*, in Asia Minor (where first used)]

pard *n.* leopard. [G. *pardos*]

pard *n.* (*sl.*) partner. [*partner*]

par'don *v.t.* forgive. *-n.* forgiveness. -**par'donable** *a.* -**par'donably** *adv.* -**par'doner** *n.* [F. *pardonner*]

pare *v.t.* trim by cutting away the edge or surface of -**par'ing** *n.* piece pared off. [F. *parer*, make ready]

paregor'ic *a.* soothing. *-n.* soothing medicine; tincture of opium. [G. *paregorikos*, comforting]

par'ent (pAr-) *n.* father or mother. -**parent'al** *a.* -**par'enthood** *n.* -**par'entage** *n.* descent, [L. *parere*, bring forth]

paren'thesis *n.* **paren'theses** *pl. n.* word, phrase, or sentence inserted in a passage independently of the grammatical sequence and usually marked off by brackets, dashes, or commas. *-pl.* round brackets, (), used for this. -**parenthet'ic** *a.* [G.]

par'iah *n.* Indian of no caste; social outcast. -**pariah dog**, yellow roaming dog in India. [Tamil, *parairyar*]

pari'etal *a.* of, pert. to wall *esp.* body walls. [L. *paries*, wall]

par'ish *n.* district under a priest; subdivision of a county. -**parish'ioner** *n.* inhabitant of a parish. [F. *paroisse*]

par'ity. *See* **par.**

par'ity check *n.* (*compute.*) system for detecting errors during transmission between computers, checking whether the number of bits (0s or 1s) is odd or even.

park *n.* large enclosed piece of ground, *usu.* with grass or woodland, attached to a country house or set aside for public use; recreation ground in a town; artillery of a military force; its space in a camp; place set aside for storing automobiles, aircraft, *etc. -v.t.* arrange or leave in a park. [F. *parc*]

par'kin *n.* ginger bread biscuit made from oatmeal and treacle. [orig. uncertain]

parl'ance *n.* way of speaking. -**parl'ey** *n.* meeting between leaders or representatives of opposing forces to discuss terms. *v.i.* hold a discussion about terms. [F. *parler*, speak]

parl'iament *n.* legislature of the United Kingdom; any legislative assembly. **parliament'ary** *a.* -**parliamenta'rian** *n.* [F. *parlement-parler,* speak]

parl'or *n.* sitting-room or room for receiving company in a small house; private room in an inn; store selling some special service or goods. [F. *parloir* fr. *parler,* speak]

parl'ous *a.* hard to escape from; perilous; shrewd, unsatisfactory. [var. of *perilous*]

Parmesan' (-z-) *a.* of Parma. -**Parmesan' cheese**.

paro'chial (-k-) *a.* of a parish; narrow, provincial. -**paro'chialism** *n.* concentration on the local interests. (Late L. *parochial* parish]

par'ody *n.* composition in which author's characteristics are made fun of by imitation; burlesque; feeble imitation. *-v.t.* write a parody of. -**par'odist** *n.* [G. *parodia*]

parole' *n.* early freeing of prisoner on condition he is of good behavior; word of honor. *-v.t.* place on parole. [F.]

par'onym *n.* word with same derivation; word with same sound but differing spelling and meaning, *e.g.*, moat, mote. -**paron'ymous** *a.* [G. *para*, beside, *onoma*, name]

par'oquet. *See* **parakeet.**

par'oxysm *n.* sudden violent attack of pain, rage, laughter, *etc.* [G. *paroxysmos para*, beyond, *oxys*, sharp]

par'quet (-ka) *n.* flooring of wooden blocks. *-v.t.* lay a parquet. -**par'quetry** *n.* parquet work. [F.]

parr *n.* young salmon. [orig. unknown]

parr'icide *n.* murder or murderer of one's own parent. [L. *parricida*]

parr'ot *n.* bird with short hooked beak, some varieties of which can be taught to imitate speech; unintelligent imitator. [dim. of F. *Pierre*, Peter]

parr'y *v.t.* ward off. *-n.* act of parrying, *esp.*in fencing. [F. *parer]*

parse (-z) *v.t.* describe (a word) or analyze (a sentence) in terms of grammar. [fr. school question, L. *quæ pars orationis?*

What part of speech?]

par'simony *n.* stingyness; undue economy. -**parsimo'nious** *a.* [L. *parsimonia,* fr. *parcere*, spare]

par'sley *n.* herb used for seasoning, *etc.* [G. *petroselinon*, rock parsley]

par'snip *n.* plant with a yellow root cooked as a vegetable. [L. *pastinaca,* fr. *pastinare*, dig up]

par'son *n.* clergyman of a parish or church; clergyman. -**par'sonage** *n.* parson's house. [*person*]

part *n.* portion, section, share; duty; character given to an actor to play; interest. -*v.t.* divide; separate; distribute. -*v.i.* separate from. -**parta'ker** *n.* one taking a share. -**partake'** *v.t.* have a share in. -*v.i.* take or have a share. -**part'ly** *adv.* [L. *pars, part-*, part]

parterre' *n.* tract of lawn, gravel, laid out with flower-beds. [F.]

par'tial *a.* prejudiced; fond of; being only in part. -**partial'ity** *n.* -**par'tially** *adv.* [L. *partials*]

partic'ipate (-is-) *v.t.* and *i.* share in. -**partic'ipant** *n.* -**partic'ipator** *n.* -**participa'tion** *n.* -**part'iciple** *n.* adjective made by inflection from a verb and keeping the verb's relation to dependent words. -**particip'ial** *a.* [L. *participate*, fr. *pars*, part, and *capere*, take]

part'icle *n.* minute portion of matter; least possible amount; minor part of speech. [L. *particular* dim. of *pars*, part]

partic'ular *a.* relating to one, not general; considered apart from others; minute; exact, fastidious. -*n.* detail or item. -*pl.* details. -**particular'ity** *n.* -**partic'ularly** *adv.* -**partic'ularize** *v.t.* mention in detail. [L. *particularist*]

partisan' (-z-) *n.* adherent of a party. -*a.* adherent to a faction. [F.]

parti'tion *n.* division; dividing wall. -*v.t.* divide. [L. *partition*]

part'ner *n.* member of a partnership; one that dances with another; husband or wife. -**part'nership** *n.* association of persons for business, *etc.* [OF. *parconier*]

part'ridge *n.* small game bird of the grouse family. [G. *perdix*]

parturi'tion *n.* bring forth young, childbirth. [L. *parere,* bring forth]

part'y *n.* number of persons united in opinion; side; social assembly. -*a.* of, or belonging to, a faction. -**part'y col'ored** *a.* differently colored in different parts, variegated. [F. *parti*]

par'venue *n.* newly rich person, upstart. [F. *parvenire*, arrive]

pas'chal (-sk-) *a.* of the Passover or Easter. [Heb. *pasakh*, pass over]

pash'a *n.* title of high Turkish or Egyptian official. [Turk. *bash*, chief]

pasquinade' *n.* lampoon, satire. [It. *Parquino*]

pass (-ki-) *v.t.* go by, beyond, through, *etc.*; exceed; be accepted by. -*v.i.* go; be transferred from one state to another; elapse; undergo examination successfully. -*n.* way, *esp.* a narrow and difficult way; passport; condition; successful result from a test. -**pass'able** *a.* -**past** *a.* ended. -*n.* bygone times. -*adv.* by; along. -*prep.* beyond; after. [L. *passus*, step]

pass'age *n.* journey; voyage; fare; part of a book, *etc.*; encounter. -**pass'enger** *n.* traveler, *etc.* by some conveyance. -**pass'port** *n.* document granting permission to pass. -**pass'word** *n.* in warfare, secret word to distinguish friend from foe. [F.]

passié *n.* (**passée** *fem.*) out of date; faded. [F.]

passe-partout' *n.* master-key, light frame for picture. [F.]

pass'erine *a.* denoting order of perching birds. [L. *passer*, sparrow]

pas'sion *n.* suffering; strong feeling; wrath; object of ardent desire. **passionate** *a.* easily moved to anger; moved by strong emotions. -**passion flower** *n.* flower resembling Crown of Thorns, the emblem of Christ's passion. -**passion fruit** *n.* small hard shelled fruit. -**Passion play** *n.* religious play representing Christ's passion. -**Passion Week** *n.* week preceeding Easter. [L. *passio*]

pass'ive *a.* suffering; submissive; denoting the grammatical mood of a verb in which the action is suffered by the subject. [L. *pati, pass-*, suffer]

Pass'over *n.* feast of the Jews to commemorate the time when God, smiting the first-born of the Egyptians, passed over the houses of Israel. (*fig.*) Christ the paschal lamb. [*pass over*]

paste *n.* soft composition, as of flour and water; fine glass to imitate gems. -*v.t.* fasten with paste. -**past'y** *n.* pie enclosed in paste. -*a.* like paste. -**pa'stry** *n.* articles of food made chiefly of paste. **paste'board** *n.* stiff, thick paper. [G. *barley* porridge]

pas'tel *n.* crayon; art of crayon-drawing; a drawing in this medium. -**pas'tellist** *n.* -**pas'tel-shades** *n. pl.* delicate colors. [F.]

pas'tern *n.* part of horse's foot between hoof and fetlock. [OF. *pasturon*]

pas'teurize *v.t.* sterilize (milk, *etc.*) by heating. [Louis *Pasteur* d. 1895]

pastiche' *n.* work of art, literary, musical, *etc.* composed of parts borrowed from other works; potpouri [F.]

pas'tille, pas'til (pastcl) *n.* lozenge; aromatic substance burnt as a fumigator. [L. *pastillus*, little loaf, fr. *pastas*, food]

pas'time (-ã-) *n.* that which serves to make time pass agreeably, recreation. [*pass* and *time*]

pas'tor (-a-) *n.* minister of the gospel. -**past'oral** *a.* relating to shepherds or rural life; relating to the office of pastor. -*n.* poem describing rural life. -**past'orate** *n.* office or jurisdiction of a spiritual pastor. [L. = *shepherd*]

past'ure *n.* grass for food of cattle; ground on which cattle graze. -*v.t.* feed on grass. -*v.i.* graze. -**past'urage** *n.* business of grazing cattle; pasture. [L. *pascere, past-*, feed]

pat *n.* light, quick blow; small mass as of butternut, tap. [imit. orig.]

patch *n.* piece of cloth sewed on a garment; spot or plot; plot of ground. -*v.t.* mend; repair clumsily. -**patch'y** *a.* full of patches. [OF. *pieche*, piece]

pate *n.* head; crown of head. [orig. uncertain]

pâté *n.* paste; cold dish of baked minced meats. -**pâté' de foie gras,** (-fwa gra) goose-liver paste. [F.]

pat'en *n.* plate for bread in the Eucharist. [L. *patina*, plate]

pa'tent *a.* open; evident; manifest; open to public perusal, as letters patent. -*n.* deed securing to a person the exclusive right to an invention. -*v.t.* secure a patent. -**patentee** *n.* one that has a patent. [L. *patens, patent-*, fr. *patere*, lie open]

pater'nal *a.* of a father; fatherly. -**patern'ity** *n.* relation of a father to his offspring. [L. *pater*, father]

paternos'ter *n.* Lord's Prayer; R. C. rosary used in devotion. [L. *Pater noster*, Our Father]

path *n.* way or track; course of action. [OE. *pæth*]

pathol'ogy *n.* science of the causes and nature of diseases. -**patholog'ical** *a.* pert. to science of disease; due to disease, morbid, unhealthy, diseased. -**pathol'ogist** *n.* [G. = *suffering*]

pa'thos *n.* power of exciting tender emotions. -**pathet'ic, pathet'ical** *a.* affecting or moving such emotions. (G. = *feeling*]

pa'tient (-shent) *a.* bearing trials without murmuring. -*n.* person under medical treatment. -**pa'tience** *n.* quality of enduring. [L. *pati*, suffer]

pat'ina *n.* sheen, luster on polished surface. [L. *patina*, dish]

patois' (-wa') *n.* vulgar or provincial dialect. [F.]

pa'triarch (-k) *n.* father and ruler of a family, *esp.* in Biblical history; venerable old man. -**patriarch'al** *a.* [G. *patriarches*, head of a family]

patri'cian (-shan) *n.* noble of ancient Rome; person of noble birth. -*a.* of noble birth. (cp. *plebeian*). [fr. L. *patricius*, one sprung from the *patres conscripti*, or senators]

pat'ricide. *See* **parricide.**

pat'rimony *n.* right or estate inherited from ancestors. [L. *patrimonium*]

pat'riot *n.* one that loves and serves his country. -*a.* patriotic. -**patriot'ic** *a.* inspired by love of one's country. -**pat'riotism** *n.* love of, desire to, serve, one's country. [G. *patriotes*, fellow-countryman]

patris'tic(al) *a.* pert. to Fathers of the Church. [L. *pater*, father]

patrol' *n.* marching round as a guard; small body patroling. -*v.i.* go round on guard, or reconnoitering. [F. *patrouiller*]

pa'tron *n.* man under whose protection another has placed himself, guardian saint; one that has the disposition of a church-living, *etc.* -**pat'ronage** *n.* special countenance or support; right of presentation to a church-living, *etc.* -**pat'ronize** *v.t.* assume the air of a superior towards; frequent as a customer. [L. *patronus*]

patronym'ic *n.* name derived from that of one's father or ancestor. [G. *pater*, a father, *onyma* (*onoma*), a name]

patt'en *n.* wood-soled shoe, clog. [F. *patin*]

patt'er *v.i.* tap in quick succession; make a noise, as the sound of quick, short steps; pray or talk rapidly. -*n.* quick succession of small sounds. [*pat*]

patt'ern *n.* model for imitation; specimen. [L. *patronus*]

patt'y *n.* small pie, pasty. (F. *paté*]

pau'city *n.* scarcity; smallness of quantity. [L. *paucitas*]

paunch *n.* belly. [F. *panse*]

pau'per *n.* poor person, *esp.* one supported by the public. -**pau'perism** *n.* state of being destitute of the means of support. -**pau'perize** *v.t.* reduce to pauperism. [L. = *poor*]

pause *n.* stop or rest. -*v.i.* cease for a time.

[G. *pausis*]

pave *v.t.* form a surface with stone or brick. -**pave'ment** *n.* paved floor or footpath; material for paving. [L. *pavire*, ram down]

pavil'ion *n.* tent raised on posts; any similar building, as a summerhouse or a club-house on a playing field, *etc.* [F. *pavillon*]

pav'onine (-in) *a.* of, like, the peacock. [L. *pavo, pavon-*, peacock]

paw *n.* foot of an animal with claws. -*v.i.* scrape with the fore foot. [OF. *poe*]

paw'ky *a.* (Scotland) shrewd; arch, cunning; dry (of humor). [orig. unknown]

pawn *n.* goods deposited as security for money borrowed. -*v.t.* pledge. -**pawn'-broker** *n.* one that lends money on goods pledged. [OF. *pan*]

pawn *n.* piece in a game, *esp.*chess. [OF. *paon*, fr. L. *pedo, pedon-*, footsoldier]

pay *v.t.* give money, *etc.*, for goods received or services rendered; compensate. -*v.i.* be remunerative. -*n.* wages. -**pay'able** *a.* justly due. -**pay'ment** *n.* discharge of a debt. [F. *payer*]

pea *n.* fruit, growing in pods, of a leguminous plant; the plant. -**pea'nut** *n.* groundnut. [G. *pison*]

peace *n.* calm; repose; freedom from war; quietness of mind. -**peace'able** *a.* disposed to peace. -**peace'ful** *a.* -**peace'fully** *adv.* -**peace'keeping** *n.* a maintenance of peace, *esp.* the prevention of further fighting between hostile forces in an area. -**peace'keeper** *n.* [L. *pax, pac-*]

peach *a.* stone-fruit of delicate flavor; tree which bears this. [F. *pêche*]

pea'cock *n.* bird, remarkable for the beauty of its plumage and fan-like spotted tail. [L. *pavo* and *cock*]

pea'-jacket *n.* seaman's thick woolen jacket. [Du. *pij*, rough coat]

peak *n.* pointed end of anything, *esp.* the sharp top of a hill; maximum point in a curve or record. [var. of *pike*]

peal *n.* loud sound, or succession of loud sounds; chime; set of bells. -*v.i.* sound loudly. [for *appeal*]

peal *n.* square tower or keep. [L. *palus*, stake]

pear *n.* tree yielding sweet, juicy fruit; the fruit. [L. *pirum*]

perl *n.* hard, smooth, lustrous substance, found in several mollusks, particularly the pearl oyster; jewel. -**pear'ly** *a.* clear; pure. [F. *perie*]

peas'ant (pez'-) *n.* rural laborer; rustic. -*a.* rural. -**peas'antry** *n.* peasants collectively. [F. *paysan-pays*, country]

pease *n.* peas. -**pease-pudding** *n.* porridge of boiled peas. [ME. *pese* pl.]

peat *n.* decomposed vegetable substance, dried and used for fuel. [Celt. orig.]

peb'ble *n.* small, roundish stone; transparent and colorless rock-crystal. [OE. *popelstan*]

pecan' *n.* N. American tree; its nut-also **pecan'-nut**. [Chin.]

pecc'able *a.* prone to sin. -**peccabil'ity, peccancy** *n.* sinfulness. -**pecc'ant** *a.* [L. *peccare*, sin]

peccadill'o *n.* trivial sin, fault. [Sp. *pecadillo*]

pec'cary *n.* S. American animal resembling the pig. [fr. Carib.]

peck *n.* fourth part of a bushel; great deal. [AF. *pek*]

peck *v.t.* and *i.* pick or strike with the beak; eat with beak. [var. of *pick*]

pec'tin *n.* jellying element in unripe fruit. -**pec'tose** *n.* substance yielding it. -**pec'tic** *a.* [G. *pektikos*, congealing]

pec'toral *a.* of the chest. -*n.* medicine for chest ailments; breast-plate; cross worn over chest. [L. *pectoralis*]

pec'ulate *v.t.* and *i.* embezzle. -**pecula'tion** *n.* -**pec'ulator** *n.* [L. *peculari*, fr. *peculium*, private property]

pecu'liar *a.* one's own; particular; strange. -**peculiar'ity** *n.* something that belongs to, or is found in, one person or thing only. [L. *peculiaris*]

pecu'niary *a.* relating to, or consisting of, money. [L. *pecunia*, money]

ped'agogue (-gog) *n.* schoolmaster; pedantic or narrow-minded teacher. [G. *paidogogos*, 'boy-leader']

ped'al *a.* of a foot. -*n.* something to transmit motion from the foot. -*v.i.* use a pedal. [L. *pedalis*, fr. *pes*, foot]

ped'ant *n.* one who overvalues, or insists unreasonably on, petty details of book-learning, grammatical rules, *etc.* -**pedant'ic** *a.* [F. *pédant*]

ped'estal *n.* base of a column, pillar, *etc.* [F. *pédestal*; L. *pes, pedis*, foot]

pedes'trian *a.* going on foot. -*n.* one that walks on foot. -**pedes'trianism** *n.* the practice of walking. [L. *pedester, pedestr-*, fr. *pes*, foot]

pediat'rics *n.* treatment of children's diseases. -**pedia'trician** *n.* [G. *paidos*, child]

ped'icel, ped'icle *n.* small stalk *e.g.*, of flower. [L. *pes*, foot]

ped'icure *n.* treatment of corns, bunions, *etc.* [L. *pes, pedis*, foot]

ped'igree *n.* register of ancestors; genealogy. [AF. *pe de gru*, crane's foot]
ped'iment *n.* triangular space over a Greek portico, *etc.* [earlier *periment* for *pyramid*]
ped'lar, pedd'ler *n.* one who travels about hawking small commodities. -**ped'dle** *v.t.* and *i.* [OE. *ped*, basket]
pedom'eter *n.* instrument which records the distance walked by a person. [L. *pes, pedis*, a foot, G. *metron*, a measure]
pe'dophilia *n.* sexual perversion of which children are the object of desire. -**pe'dophile** *n.* one who practices this. [G. *paidos*, child, *philos*, loving]
pedun'cle *n.* flower-stalk, stem. -**pedun'cular, pedun'culate** *a.* [L. pes, foot]
peel *v.t.* strip off the skin, bark or rind. -*v.i.* come off, as the skin or rind. -*n.* rind, skin. [F. *peler*]
peep *v.i.* cry, as a chick; chirp. -*n.* cry of a young chicken. [imit. orig.]
peep *v.i.* look slyly or momentarily. -*n.* such look. -**peep'show** *n.* show seen through a small hole fitted with lens. [orig. uncertain]
peer *n.* one of the same rank; nobleman. -**peer'less** *a.* unequaled; matchless. -**peer'age** *n.* rank of a peer; body of peers. [L. *par*, equal]
peer *v.i.* peep; look narrowly, as with shortsighted eyes. [Teut. orig.]
peev'ish *a.* fretful; querulous. -**peev'ishly** *adv.* -**peev'ishness** *n.* -**peeve** *v.t.* put out of temper. [orig. uncertain]
pee'wit *n.* lapwing. [imit. of *cry*]
peg *n.* wooden nail or pin. -*v.t.* fasten with pegs. -*v.i.* (colloq.) persevere. [orig. uncertain]
pe'kinese *n.* Chinese pug-dog. -also **peke**. [*Pekin*]
pe'koe *n.* choice black tea. [Chin. *pek*, white, *ho*, down]
pelag'ic (pe-laj'-) *a.* oceanic; deep sea. **pelag'ian** *a.* of or inhabiting the open seas. [G. *pelagos*, sea]
pelargo'nium *n.* low-growing garden plant with large brilliant flowers. [G. *pelargos*, stork]
pelf *n.* money (in contempt). [OF. *pelfre*, plunder]
pel'ican *n.* large water-fowl, remarkable for the enormous pouch beneath its bill. [G. *pelekan*]
pelisse' *n.* woman's long-sleeved cloak; child's loose coat; hussar's jacket. (F.]
pellag'ra *n.* deficiency disease of the skin, *etc.* [orig. uncertain]
pell'et *n.* little ball. [F. *pelote*]
pell'itory *n.* wall plant, the feverfew. [fr. L. *parietaria*]
pell-mell' *adv.* in utter confusion. [F. *pêle-mêle*, fr. *mêler*, mix]
pellu'cid *a.* translucent; clear. [L. *pellucidus-lucidus*, fr. *lucere*, shine]
pel'met *n.* decorative frill, *etc.*, for window-top. [F. *palmette*, palm leaf]
pelo'ta *n.* Basque game using hard ball and wicker racket. [Sp. = *ball*]
pelt *v.t.* strike with missiles. -*v.i.* throw missiles; fall persistently, as rain. [orig. uncertain]
pelt *n.* hide or skin. [L. *pellis*]
pel'vis *n.* bony cavity at lower end of the body. [L. = *basin*]
pemm'ican *n.* dried meat pounded and pressed into a cake. [Cree Ind. *pimecan*]
pen *n.* instrument for writing. -*v.t.* compose and commit to paper; write. **pen-knife** *n.* pocket-knife. -**pen'name** *n.* one skilled in hand-writing, author. **pen'manship** *n.* [L. *penna*, feather]
pen *n.* small enclosure, as for sheep. -*v.t.* shut up. -**pent** *a.* closely confined; shut up. [OE. *penn*]
pe'nal *a.* relating to, incurring, or inflicting, punishment. -**pen'alty** *n.* punishment for a crime or offense. -**pe'nalize** *v.t.* lay under penalty. [L. *penalis, poena*, punishment]
pen'ance *n.* suffering submitted to as an expression of penitence. [OF. *peneance*, L. *pœnitentia*]
pence. *See* **penny.**
pen'chant (pong-shong) *n.* bias, inclination, [F.]
pen'cil *n.* small brush used by painters; instrument, as of graphite, for writing, *etc.* -*v.t.* paint or draw; mark with a pencil. [L. *penicillum*, little tail]
pend'ant *n.* hanging ornament. -*a.* suspended; hanging; projecting. -**pend'ing** *prep.* during. -*a.* awaiting decision. [L. *pendere*, hang]
pen'dent *a.* pendant, hanging. [L. *pendere*, hang]
pend'ulum *n.* suspended weight swinging to and fro, *esp.* as a regulator for a clock. -**pend'ulous** *a.* hanging loosely; swinging. [L. *pendulus*, hanging]
pen'etrate *v.t.* enter into; pierce; arrive at the meaning of. -**pen'etrable** *a.* capable of being pierced. -**penetrabil'ity** *n.* quality of being penetrable. -**penetra'tion** *n.* insight; acuteness. -**pen'etrative** *a.* piercing; dis-

cerning. -**penetra'tor** *n.* [L. *penetrare*]

pen'guin *n.* swimming bird, unable to fly. [Welsh *pen gwyn*, white head]

penicill'in *n.* extract of the mold *penicillium notatum*, used to prevent growth of bacteria. [L. *penicillus*, little tail]

penin'sula *n.* land nearly surrounded by water. [L. *paene*, almost, *insula*, island]

pe'nis *n.* male organ of generation. [L.]

pen'itent *a.* affected by a sense of guilt. -*n.* one that repents of sin. -**pen'itence** *n.* sorrow for sin; repentance. -**peniten'tial** *a.* of, or expressing, penitence. -**peniten'tiary** *a.* relating to penance, or to the rules of penance. -*n.* prison. [L. *pænitere*, repent]

penn'ant *n.* narrow piece of bunting, *esp* . a long narrow flag, on a lance, *etc.* -also **pennon.** [L. *penna*, plume]

penn'on *n.* small pointed flag or streamer borne as ensign of regiment of lancers. [OF. *penon*, streamer]

penn'y *n.* **penn'ies** *pl.* (denoting the number of coins). -**pence** *pl.* (amount of pennies in value), copper coin; cent; 100th part of a pound. -**penn'iless** *a.* having no money. -**penny'weight** *n.* troy weight of 24 grains. -**penn'ysworth** *n.* what may be obtained for one penny. [OE. *pennig*]

pennyroy'al *n.* aromatic herb, once used in medicine. [orig. uncertain]

pen'sile *a.* hanging, suspended. [L. *pendere*, hang]

pen'sion *n.* allowance for past services; annuity paid to retired public officers, soldiers, *etc.* -*v.t.* grant a pension to. -**pen'sioner** *n.* [L. *pensio-pendere, pens*, weigh]

pen'sion (pong'syong) *n.* French boarding-bouse or school. [F.]

pen'sive *a.* thoughtful with sadness, wistful. [F. *pensif*, L. *pensare*, weigh]

pent'agon *n.* plane figure having five sides and five angles. -**Pent'agon** *n.* headquarters of the Department of Defense; the U.S. military leadership. -**pentag'onal** *a.* -**pent'ateuch** (-k) *n.* the first five books of the Old Testament. [G. *pente*, five]

pentam'eter, pentap'ody *n.* verse of five feet. [G. *pente*, five]

Pent'ateuch *n.* first five books of Old Testament. [G. *pentatenchos*, five volumed]

Pent'ecost *n.* Jewish festival on the fiftieth day after the Passover; Whitsuntide. [G. *pentekoste*, fiftieth]

pent'house *n.* shed standing with its roof sloping against a higher wall; structure or dwelling built on the roof of a building. [F. *appentis*, L. *appendicium*, appendage]

pentste'mon *n.* perennial garden plant with handsome flowers. [G. *pente*, five, *stemen*, stamen]

penulti'mate *n.* second last. [L. *paene*, almost, *ultimus*, last]

penum'bra *n.* imperfect shadow; partial shade between shadow and full light. -**penum'bral** *a.* [L. *paene*, almost, *umbra*, shadow]

pen'ury *n.* want; extreme poverty. **penu'rious** *a.* niggardly. [L. *penuria*]

pe'ony *n.* plant with showy flowers. [AS. *peonie*, G. *paionia*]

peo'ple *n.* body of persons that compose a community, nation; persons generally. -*v.t.* stock with inhabitants. [F. *peuple*, nation; L. *populus*]

pep' *n.* (*sl.*) energy, vigor. [*pepper*]

pepp'er *n.* fruit of a climbing plant, which yields a pungent aromatic spice. -*v.t.* sprinkle with pepper; pelt with shot. -**pepp'ery** *a.* having the qualities of pepper; irritable. -**pepp'ermint** *n.* aromatic plant. [G. *peperi*]

pep'sin *n.* digestive enzyme of the gastric juices. [G. *pepsis*, digestion]

peradven'ture *adv.* perhaps; by chance. [OF. *par aventure*]

peram'bulate *v.t.* walk through or over, traverse. -*v.i.* walk about. -**peram'bulator** *n.* small carriage for a child. [L. *perambulare, per*, through, *ambulare*, walk]

perceive' *v.t.* obtain knowledge of through the senses; observe; understand. -**perceiv'able** *a.* -**percep'tible** *a.* discernible. -**perceptibil'ity** *n.* -**percep'tion** *n.* faculty of perceiving. [L. *percipere*]

percent'age *n.* proportion or rate per hundred. -**percent**, in each hundred. [L. *per centum*, by the hundred]

percen'tile *n.* one of 99 actual or notional values of a variable dividing its distribution into 100 groups with equal frequencies; centile. [L. *per centum*, by the hundred]

perch *n.* fresh-water fish. [G. *perke*]

perch *n.* pole or rod; measure of five yards and a half; roost. -*v.t.* place, as on a perch. -*v.i.* light or settle on a fixed body; roost. [F. *perche*, pole]

perchance' *adv.* perhaps. [*chance*]

percip'ient *a.* with faculty of perception, perceiving. -*n.* one who perceives. -**percip'ience** *n.* [L. *percipere*, perceive]

per'colate *v.t.* and *i.* pass through small interstices, as a liquor; filter. -**percola'tion**

n. [L. *percolate*]

percus'sion *n.* collision; vibratory shock. -**percus'sion instrument,** musical instrument played by striking, *e.g.*, drum or cymbal. [L. *percussio*]

perdi'tion (-ish-) *n.* ruin; future misery; hell. [L. *perditio*]

per'egrinate *v.i.* travel from place to place. -**peregrina'tion** *n.* journey travel. [L. *peregrinus*, foreigner]

perempt'ory *a.* authoritative; forbidding debate; final; absolute. [L. *peremptorius*, destructive]

perenn'ial *a.* lasting through the years; perpetual; (*bot.*) continuing more than two years. [L. *perennis*]

per'fect *a.* complete; finished. -*n.* tense denoting a complete act. -*v.t.* finish; make skillful. -**perfect'able** *a.* capable of becoming perfect. -**perfec'tion** *n.* state of being perfect. [L. *perfectus*, done thoroughly]

perfer'vid *a.* intensely fervid. [L. *prae*, before, *fervidus*, fervid]

per'fidy *n.* treachery. -**perfid'ious** *a.* [L. *perfidia*, faithlessness]

per'forate *v.t.* pierce. -**perfora'tion** *n.* hole bored through anything. [L. *perforare-per*, through, *forare*, bore]

perforce' *adv.* of necessity. [F. *par force*]

perform' *v.t.* bring to completion; fulfill; represent on the stage. -*v.i.* act a part; play, as on a musical instrument. **perform'ance** *n.* -**perform'er** *n.* one who performs, *esp.* actor or other entertainer. [OF. *par-fournir*, furnish through]

per'fume *n.* agreeable scent; fragrance. -*v.t.* scent. -**perfu'mer** *n.* -**perfu'mery** *n.* perfumes in general. [L. *perfumare*, perfume]

perfunct'ory *a.* done indifferently, careless. -**perfunct'orily** *adv.* [L. *perfungi, perfunct-*, get done with]

per'gola *n.* arbor; walk covered in with trellised roses, *etc.* [L. *pergula*, projecting roof]

perhaps' *adv.* it may be; possibly. [E. *hap*, chance]

pe'ri (pe'-) *n.* Eastern fairy. [Pers. *pari*]

pericard'ium *n.* membrane, enclosing heart. -**pericard'iac, pericard'ial** *a.* **pericardi'tis** *n.* inflammation of pericardium. [G. *peri*, around, *kardia*, heart]

per'icarp *n.* fruit seed-vessel. -**pericarp'ial** *a.* [G. *peri*, around, *karops*, fruit]

pericra'nium *n.* membrane enclosing skull. [G. *peri*, around, *kranion*, cranium]

perigee *n.* point on moon or planet's orbit, at which it is nearest earth. -**perige'al, perige'an** *a.* [G. *peri*, around, *ge*, earth]

perihelion *n.* nearest the sun, point in the orbit of a planet or comet. [G.]

per'il *n.* danger; exposure to injury. -**per'ilous** *a.* full of peril. [L. *periculum*]

perim'eter *n.* outer boundary of a plane figure. [G. *perimetros*]

pe'riod *n.* time in which a heavenly body makes a revolution; particular portion of time; complete sentence, punctuation mark at the end of a sentence (.). -**period'ic** *a.* recurring at regular intervals. -**period'ical** *a.* relating to a period; periodic. -*n.* publication issued at regular intervals. [G. *periodos*, circuit]

peripatet'ic *a.* walking about. -**peripatet'ic philos'ophy**, philosophy of Aristotle, who walked about while teaching. [G. *peripatetikos*]

periph'ery *n.* circumference; surface; outside. [G. *peri*, around, *pherein*, carry]

periph'erals *n. pl.* (*compute.*) any hardware device separate and distinct from the main computer. also **periph'eral equpment.**

periph'rasis *n.* circumlocution; wordiness. -**periphras'tic** *a.* -**periphras'tically** *adv.* [G.]

per'iscrope *n.* an instrument, used *esp.* in submarines, for giving a view of objects that are on a different level. [G. *peri-*, round, and *skopein*, to look]

per'ish *v.i.* die, waste away. **per'ishable** *a.* [L. *perire*]

peri'style *n.* row or pillars surrounding square or court. [G. *peri*, around, *stulos*, pillar]

peritone'um *n.* membrane enclosing the abdominal viscera. [G. *peritoneion*]

peritoni'tis *n.* inflammation of the peritoneum. [G. *peritoneion*]

per'iwig *n.* small wig, peruke. [Du. *peruyk*]

peri'winkle *n.* flowering plant. [OE. *perwince*, F. *pervenche*]

peri'winkle *n.* common mollusk. [OE, *pinewincle*]

per'jure (-jer) *v.t.* forswear. -*v.i.* bear false witness. -**per'jury** *n.* false swearing; crime of false testimony on oath. [L. *perjurare*]

perk *v.t.* and *i.* smarten; become cheerful; toss head. -**perky** *a.* smart, cheeky. [orig. uncertain]

per'manent *a.* continuing in the same state; lasting. -**per'manence, per'manency** *n.* fixed. -**per'manent wave,** lasting artificial hairwave. [L. *permanere*]

per'meate *v.t.* pass through the pores of, saturate. -**per'meable** *a.* admitting of the passage of fluids. [L. *permeate, permeate*, pass through]

permit' *v.t.* allow; give leave to; give leave. *n.* written permission. -**permis'sion** *n.* leave; liberty. -**permiss'ible** *a.* allowable. -**permiss'ive** *a.* allowing. [L. *permittere, permiss-*]

permute' *v.t.* interchange. -**permuta'tion** *n.* mutual transference; (*alg.*) change in the arrangement of a number of quantities. [L. *permutare*, change thoroughly]

perni'cious (-nish'-) *a.* having the quality of destroying or injuring; hurtful. [L. *perniciosus*]

perora'tion *n.* concluding part of an oration. [L. *peroratio*]

perox'ide *n.* oxide with largest proportion of oxygen. -**perox'ide of hy'drogen,** liquid used to bleach the hair, *etc.* [L. *per*, intens., and *oxide*]

perpendic'ular *a.* exactly upright; at right angles to the plane of the horizon; at right angles to a given line or surface. -*n.* line at right angles to the plane of the horizon; line falling at right angles on another line or plane. [L. *perpendicularis*]

per'petrate *v.t.* commit (something bad). -**perpetra'tion** *n.* -**per'petrator** *n.* [L. *perpetrare*, accomplish]

perpet'ual *a.* continuous, lasting for ever. -**perpet'ually** *adv.* -**perpet'uate** *v.t.* make perpetual; not to allow to be forgotten. -**perpetua'tion** *n.* -**perpetu'ity** *n.* [L. *perpetualis*]

perplex' *v.t.* puzzle; complicate. **perplex'ity** *n.* puzzled or tangled state. [L. *perplexus*, entangled]

per'quisite (-it) *n.* casual payment in addition to salary belonging to an employment; thing that after serving its purpose is customarily taken possession of by servant, *etc.* [L. *perquisitum*, thing eagerly sought]

perr'y *n.* a fermented drink made from pears. [OF. *pere*]

per'secute *v.t.* oppress for the holding of an opinion; subject to persistent ill treatment. -**persecu'tion** *n.* -**per'secutor** *n.* [L. *persequi*, persecute, pursue]

persevere' *v.i.* persist, maintain an effort. -**perseve'rance** *n.* [L. *perseverare*]

per'siflage *n.* airy banter. [F.]

persimm'on *n.* N. American tree bearing edible plum-like fruit; the fruit. [Algonkin]

persist' *v.i.* continue in a state or action in spite of obstacles or objections. **persist'ent** *a.* -**persist'ence** *n.* [L. *persistere*, fr. *sistere*, stand]

per'son *n.* individual human being; individual divine being; character in a play, *etc.*; in grammar a classification, or one of the classes, of pronouns, and verb-forms according to the person speaking, spoken to, or spoken of. -**per'sonable** *a.* good-looking. -**per'sonage** *n.* notable person. -**per'sonal** *a.* individual, private, of one's own; of or relating to grammatical person. -**per'sonal property** or **estate'**, all property except land and interests in land that pass to an heir. -**personal'ity** *n.* distinctive character. -**per'sonally** *adv.* in person. -**per'sonalty** *n.* personal property. -**per'sonate** *v.t.* pass oneself off as. -**persona'tion** *n.* -**person'ify** *v.t.* represent as a person; typify. **personifica'tion** *n.* -**personnel'** *n.* staff employed in a service or institution. [L. *persona*, char. in a play]

perspec'tive (-iv) *n.* art of drawing on a flat surface to give the effect of solidity and relative distances and sizes; drawing in perspective; mental view. -**in perspective**, in due proportion. [L. *perspicere, perspect-*, look through]

perspic'uous *a.* clearly expressed. -**perspicu'ity** *n.* -**perspica'cious** *a.* having quick mental insight. -**perspicacity** (-kas'-) *n.* [L. *perspicere*, see through]

perspire' *v.i.* sweat. -**perspira'tion** *n.* [L. *perspirare*, breathe through]

persuade' (-sw-) *v.t.* convince; bring (any one to do something) by argument, *etc.* -**persuasion** *n.* -**persua'sive** *a.* [L. *persuadere, persuas-*]

pert *a.* forward, saucy. [L. *apertus*, open (ready, skilled)]

pertain' *v.i.* belong, relate. -**pert'inent** *a.* to the point. -**pert'inence** *n.* [L. *pertinere*, belong]

pertinacity (-as'-) *n.* -**pertina'cious** *a.* obstinate, persistent. [L. *pertinax*]

perturb' *v.t.* disturb gradually; alarm. -**perturb'able** *a.* -**perturba'tion** *n.* [L. *perturbare*]

peruke' *n.* wig. [F. *perruque*]

peruse' *v.t.* read, *esp.* in a slow or careful manner. -**peru'sal** *n.* [orig. uncertain]

Peru'vian *a.* of Peru. -**Peru'vian bark,** cinchona from which quinine is obtained. [*Peru*]

pervade' *v.t.* spread through. -**perva'sion** *n.* -**perva'sive** *a.* [L. *pervadere, pervas*, go through]

pervert′ *v.t.* turn to a wrong use; lead astray. -**per′vert** *a.* one who has turned to error, *esp.* in religion, morals, *etc.*; abnormal person in matters of sex. **perver′sion** *n.* -**perver′sive** *a.* -**perverse′** *a.* obstinately or unreasonably wrong, wayward, *etc.* -**perver′sity** *n.* [L. *pervertere, perverse,* turn away]

per′vious *a.* able to be penetrated, permeable, giving passage. [L. *per,* through, *via,* way]

pess′imism *n.* theory that everything turns to evil; tendency to see the worst side of things. -**pess′imist** *n.* -**pessimist′ic** *a.* [L. *pessimus,* worst]

pest *n.* troublesome or harmful thing or person; plague. -**pestif′erous** *a.* bringing plague; harmful, deadly. -**pest′ilent** *a.* troublesome; deadly. -**pest′ilence** *n.* deadly plague. -**pestilen′tial** *a.* -**pestol′ogy** *n.* science of pests and their treatment. [L. *pestis*]

pest′er *v.t.* annoy, trouble or vex persistently. [OF. *empestrer*]

pes′tle (-l) *n.* instrument with which things are pounded in a mortar. [L. *pistillum,* fr. *pinsere,* pound]

pet *n.* animal or person kept or regarded with affection. -*v.t.* make a pet of [orig. uncertain]

pet *n.* fit of ill-temper or sulking. -**pett′ish** *a.* [orig. uncertain]

pet′al *n.* colored flower leaf. [G. *petalon,* thin plate]

petard′ *n.* explosive device formerly used in war for bursting gates, *etc.* open. [F. *petard*]

pet′iole *n.* leaf-stalk. -*petiolar a.* of, like, petiole. -**petiolate** *a.* having petiole. [L. *petiolus,* little foot]

petit′ *a.* **petité,** *fem.,* small, dainty. [F.]

peti′tion (-ish′-) *n.* request, *esp.* one presented to a sovereign or government. *v.t.* present a petition to. -**peti′tionary** *a.* -**peti′tioner** *n.* [L. *petitio*]

pet′rel *n.* small sea-bird. [*St. Peter*]

pet′rify *v.t.* turn into stone; paralyze with fear, *etc.* -**petrifac′tion** *n.* [L. *petra,* rock]

petro′leum *n.* mineral oil. -**pet′rol** *n.* refined petroleum; gasoline. -**petro′leum jelly,** soft paraffin, vaseline. -**petrochem′ical** *n.* any substance, such as acetone or ethanol, obtained from petroleum. *a.* of petrochemicals; related to petrochemistry. -**petrochem′istry** *n.* -**petrocur′rency** *n.* currency oil-producing countries acquire as profit from oil sales to other countries. [fr. L. *petra,* rock, and *oleum,* oil]

petti′coat *n.* woman's underskirt. [orig. *petty coat,* small coat]

petti′fogger *n.* low class lawyer; one given to mean dealing in small matters. **pett′ifog** *v.i.* be or act like a pettifogger. [orig. uncertain]

pett′y *a.* unimportant, trivial; on a small scale. -**pett′y off′icer** *n.* non-commissioned naval officer. [F. *petit,* small]

pet′ulant *a.* given to small fits of temper. -**pet′ulance.** [L. *petulans, petulant-, pert,* wanton]

petu′nia *n.* plant with funnel-shaped flowers allied to tobacco. -*a.* purplish pink. [Amer. Ind. *petun,* tobacco]

pew *n.* fixed seat in a church. [OF. *puie,* fr. G. *podium,* pedestal]

pe′wee *n.* flycatcher. [imit.]

pe′wit. *See* **peewit.**

pew′ter *n.* alloy of tin and lead; ware made of this. [OF. *peutre*]

phae′ton (fa-) *n.* light four-wheeled open carriage. [G. *Phcethon,* son of Helios, the sun (who tried to drive his father's chariot)]

phag′ocyte (fag′o-sit) *n.* white blood corpuscle, leucocyte, devouring microbes. [G. *phagein,* eat, *kytos,* cell]

phal′anger *n.* small Australian marsupial. [F., G. *phalangion,* spider's web-fr. its webbed feet]

phalanx *n.* square of infantry in close formation; compact body of troops. *esp.* Macedonian. [G.]

phan′tasm *n.* illusion; vision of an absent person. -**phantas′mal** *a.* **phantasmagoria** *n.* exhibition of illusions, crowd of dirn or unreal figures. **phan′tasy** *n.* **phan′tom** *n.* apparition or ghost. *See* **fantasy.** [G. *phantasma*]

pharisaic, pharisaical *a.* hypo-critical; self-righteous. [*Pharisee,* one of a strict Jewish sect]

pharmaceut′ic *a.* relating to pharmacy. -*n.* in *pl.* science of pharmacy. -**pharmaceut′ical** *a.* -**pharmacopoe′ia** *n.* official book with a list and directions for the use of drugs. -**phar′macy** *n.* preparation and dispensing of drugs; drugstore. -**phar′macist** *n.* [G. *pharmakon,* poison, drug]

pha′ros (fa-) *n.* lighthouse, beacon. [light-house on island of *pharos*]

phar′ynx (far′ingks) *n.* tube or cavity that connects the mouth with the gullet. [E. *pharynx. -yngos*]

phase (-z) *n.* aspect of the moon or a planet; stage of levelopment. -**pha'sic** *a.* [G. *phasis*]

phase. *See* **faze**

pheas'ant (fez') *n.* game-bird. [G. *Phasis*, river in Colchis (where the bird first came from)]

phenomenon , **phenomena** *pl.* anything appearing r observed; remarkable person or thing. -**henom'enal** *a.* (*colloq.*) exceptional. [G.*hainein*, show]

phi'al. *See* **vial.**

phil- *prefix* lovi. -**philan'der** *v.i.* amuse oneself with lovmaking. -**philan'thropy** *n.* love of manki; practice of doing good to one's fellow en. -**philanthrop'ic** *a.* -**philan'thropis**. -**philat'ely** *n.* stamp collecting. -**phi'elist** *n.* -**philatel'ic** *a.* -**phil'harmon'i** musical (only for titles of societies). -**pol'ogy** *n.* science of the structure and ddopment of languages. -**philological** -**philol'ogist** *n.* **philos'ophy** *n.* suit of wisdom; study of realities and eral principles; system of theories on nature of things or on conduct; calmnof mind expected of a philosopher. -**ps'opher** *n.* one who studies, or pcsses, or originates, philosophy. -**phoph'ic, philosophical** *a.* -**philosophiz**. [G. *philein*, love]

philip'pic *n.* sp, discourse full of invective, diatri [from speeches of Demosthenes agt *Philip*]

phil'omel *n.* nigale. [Myth.]

phil'ter *n.* loveon. [G. *philtron*, fr. *philos*, loving]

phlebitis *n.* inflnation of a vein. [G. *phleps, phlep-*,

phlebotomy *n*ding, blood-letting. -**phlebot'omist** *phleps*, vein]

phlegm (flem) scid secretion of the mucus membrajected by coughing, *etc.*; calmness, shness. -**phlegmatic** (-eg-) *a.* not easitated. [G. *phlegma*, inflammation]

phlox *n.* floweiant. [G. = *flame*]

pho'bia *n.* mc fear, dislike. [G. *Phobos*, fear]

phoenix *n.* fabbird supposed to be only one of itsand after living for centuries to bu) and rise renewed from the ashes; thing. [G. *Phoiinix*, purple red.]

phone *n.*, *a.*, ar*bbrev.* of telephone. [G. *phone*, voiod]

pho'ney *a.* note. [orig. uncertain]

phon'ic(al) *a.* nd, phonetic. [G. *phone*, voice, s

phono- *prefix.* [G. *phone*, voice]. **phonet'ic** *a.* of, or relating to, vocal sounds. -*n.* in *pl.* the science of vocal sounds. -**phoneti'cian** *n.* -**pho'nograph** *n.* instrument recording and reproducing sounds. -**phonograph'ic** *a.* **phonol'ogy** *n.* study of speech-sounds and their development. -**phon'otype** *n.* printing type of phonetic alphabet. **phonotyp'ic(al)** *a.* **phosphorus** *n.* non-metallic element which appears luminous in the dark. **phos'phate** *n.* -**phos'phide** *n.* -**phos'phite** *n.* compounds of phosphorus. -**phosphores'cence** *n.* faint glow in the dark. [G. *phos*, light]

pho'to- *prefix* light. -**pho'toelectri'city** *n.* electricity produced or affected by the action of light. -**pho'tograph** *n.* picture made by the chemical action of light on a sensitive film. -*v.t.* take a photograph of. -**photog'rapher** *n.* -**photograph'ic** *a.* -**photog'raphy** *a.* -**photogravure'** *n.* process of etching a product of photography. -*n.* picture so produced. -**photom'eter** *n.* instrument for measuring the intensity of light. -**photom'etry** *n.* -**photomontage'** *n.* technique of producing composite pictures by combining several photographs; composite picture so produced. -**photopho'bia** *n.* fear of light. -**pho'toplay** *n.* film drama. -**photoreal'ism** *n.* style of painting and sculpture that depicts *esp.* commonplace urban images with meticulously accurate detail. -**pho'tosphere** *n.* sun's luminous envelope. -**pho'tostat** *n.* photographic apparatus for obtaining exact copies of manuscript, drawing, *etc.* **photosyn'thesis** *n.* (*bot.*) formation of complex compounds by the action of light on chlorophyll. **photogenic** *a.* able to photograph well and attractively. [G. *phos. phot-*, light, and *gignesthai*]

phrase (-z) *n.* mode of expression; small group of words; pithy expression. -*v.t.* express in words. -**phraseology** (-i-ol'-) *n.* manner of expression, choice of words. [G. *phrasis*]

phrenol'ogy *n.* study of the shape of the skull; theory that mental powers are indicated by the shape of the skull. -**phrenol'ogist** *n.* [G. *phren*, mind]

phthi'sis (th-) *n.* consumption of the lungs. -**phthi'sical** (tiz-) *a.* -**phthisiol'ogy** (tiz-) *n.* [G. = *wasting away*]

phylactery *n.* amulet. -**phylac'teric** *a.* [G. *phylakterion*, guard]

phys'ics (-iz'–) *n.* medicine. -*pl.* science of the properties of matter and energy. -*v.t.*

dose with medicine. -**phys'ical** *a.* relating to physic, or physics, or the body. -**physically** *adv.* -**physi'cian** *n.* qualified medical practitioner. -**phys'icist** *n.* student of physics. -**physiog'nomy** *n.* judging character by face; the face. -**physiog'raphy** *n.* science of the earth's surface. -**physiog'rapher** *n.* -**physiol'ogy** *n.* science of the normal function of living things. -**physiol'ogist** *n.* -**physique'** *n.* bodily structure and development. [G. *physis*, nature]

phy'toid *a.* (of animals) plant-like. [G. *phyton*, plant, *eidos*, form]

phy'tochemistry *n.* branch of chemistry concerned with plants, their chemical composition and processes. **phytochem'ist** *n.* [G. *phyton*, plant, and *chemistry*]

phytol'ogy *n.* botany. [G. *phyton*, plant]

pian'o *a.* and *adv.* in a low tone or voice. -*n.* **pianoforte.** -**pian'oforte** (-ta) *n.* musical instrument with strings which are struck by hammers worked by a keyboard. -**pi'anist** *n.* performer on the pianoforte. -**piano'la** *n.* mechanical device for playing on the piano. [It. *piano*, soft, *forte*, loud]

piazz'a *n.* public square; arcade. [It.]

pi'broch *n.* martial music for the bagpipes. [Gael. *piobaireachd*, pipe music]

pic'ador *n.* mounted bull-fighter armed with a lance, who excites the bull. [Sp. *pica*, a pike]

picaresque' (-esk) *a.* of fiction, dealing with the adventures of rogues. [F.]

pic'ayune *n.* small Sp. coin; (*sl.*) person, thing of slight value or significance, trifle. -*a.* paltry, mean. [orig. unknown)

picc'olo *n.* small flute. [It. = *little*]

pick *n.* tool consisting of a curved iron crossbar and a wooden shaft for breaking up hard ground or masonry. -**pick'ax** *n.* pick. -**pick'lock** *n.* instrument for opening locks. -**pick'pocket** *n.* one who thieves from pockets. [orig. *piker*]

pick *v.t.* break the surface of, skin with something pointed; gather; choose, select carefully; find an occasion for. -*n.* act of picking; choicest part. -**pick'ings** *n. pl.* odds and ends of profit. [OE. *pycan*]

pick'-a-back *adv.* carried on the back or shoulders. [earlier a *pick pack*]

pick'et *n.* prong or pointed stake: small body of soldiers on police duty; party of trade unionists posted to deter would-be workers during a strike. -*v.t.* tether to a peg; post as a picket; beset with pickets. [F. *piquet*]

pic'kie (pik'l) *n.* brine or other liquid for preserving food; sorry plight; troublesome child. -*pl.* pickled vegetalles. -*v.t.* preserve in pickle. [Du. *pekel*]

pic'nic *n.* pleasure excusion including a meal out of doors. -*v.i.* tak part in a picnic. [F. *pique-nique*]

picotee' *n.* kind of arnation with variegated edges. [F. *picter*, prick]

pic'ric acid, bitter acid ued as dye and in explosives. [G. *pikros*, bter]

pic'ture *n.* drawing painting or photograph; representaon; image. -*v.t.* represent in, or as in, a pture. -**pictor'ial** *a.* of, in, with, painting orctures; graphic. -*n.* newspaper with my pictures. -**pictor'ially** *adv.* -**pictusque'** (-esk) *a.* such as would be effece in a picture; striking, vivid. [L. *pictu-pingere, pict-*, paint]

pid'gin *n.* broken Englideveloped as a common trading languain various parts of the world. [perh. corrion of business English by Chinese trad

pie *n.* a magpie, wooecker; dish of meat, fruit, *etc.*, coveredh pastry; mass of printer's type in confun, *etc.* [L. *pica*]

pie'bald *a.* irregularly ked with black and white; motley. -*n.*:bald horse or other animal. -**pied** *a.* pld; as magpie. [*pie* and *bald*]

piece *n.* separate part agment; single object; literary or mus composition, *etc.* -*v.t.* mend, put togr. -**piece'meal** *adv.* by, in, or into pieceork done thus. -**piece'work** *n.* work pa amount done regardless of time take *piece*]

pier *n.* piece of solid up masonry, *esp.* supporting a bridge oreen two windows; structure runnino the sea as a landing stage, *etc.* -**piess** *n.* tall mirror. [Med. L. *pera*]

pierce *v.t.* make a hol make a way through. [F. *percer*]

pier'rot *n.* French parne character; member of a troupe of einers, *usu.* in white costume trimmeh black pompoms. -**pier'rette** *fem.*

pi'ety *n.* godliness, dess; dutifulness. -**pi'etism** *n.* affec exaggerated piety. [L. *pietas*]

pig *n.* swine; oblong of smelted metal. -*v.i.* of a sow, duce a litter; herded together in a ntidy way. -**pigg'ery** *n.* place foing pigs. -**pigg'ish** *a.* -**pig'tail** *n.* hair hanging from the back of the hf Teut. orig.]

pi'geon (pij'en) *n.* biny wild and domesticated varietien trained to carry messages, *etc.* -**phole** *n.* compartment for papers. [F.]

pig'ment *n.* coloring matter, paint or dye. [L. *pigmentum*]

pig'my. *See* **pygmy.**

pike *n.* spear formerly used by infantry; peaked hill; large freshwater fish; turnpike or tollgate. -**piked** *a.* -**pike-man** *n.* soldier with pike. [OE. *pic*]

pike'staff *n.* plain as a pikestaff, easy to see or understand. [orig. *packstaff,* pole for carrying a pack]

pilas'ter *n.* square column often set in wall. [L. *pila,* pillar]

pil'chard *n.* small sea fish resembling the herring. [orig. unknown]

pile *n.* beam driven into the ground, *esp.* as a foundation for building in water or wet ground. [L. *pilum,* dart]

pile *n.* heap; mass of building; electric battery. *v.t.* heaped up. [L. *pila,* pillar]

pile *n.* nap of cloth, *esp.* of velvet, carpet. [L. *pilus,* hair]

piles *n.* (in *pl.*) tumors of veins of rectum; hemorrhoids. [L. *pila,* ball]

pil'fer *v.t.* steal in small quantities. -**pil'ferage** *n.* [OF. *pelfrer*]

pil'grim *n.* one who walks to sacred place; wanderer. -**pil'grimage** *n.* [L. *peregrinus*]

pill *n.* pellet of medicine. [L. *pila,* ball]

pill'age *n.* seizing goods by force; *esp.* in war; plunder. -*v.t.* and *i.* plunder. [F.]

pill'ar *n.* slender upright structure, column. [L. *pila,* pile]

pill'box *n.* (*mil. sl.*) small concrete fort or blockhouse. [*pill* and *box*]

pill'ion (-yun) *n.* cushion or seat for a person to ride behind a man on a horse, motorcycle, *etc.* [Gael. *pillean,* packsaddle]

pill'ory *n.* frame with holes for head and hands in which an offender was confined and exposed to pelting and ridicule. -*v.t.* set in pillory; expose to ridicule and abuse. [F. *pilori*]

pill'ow *n.* cushion for the head, especially in bed. -*v.t.* lay on a pillow. -**pill'owy** *a.* soft, resilient. -**pill'ow-case, pill'ow-slip** *n.* covering for pillow. [L. *pulvinus*]

pi'lot *n.* person qualified to take charge of a ship entering or leaving a harbor, or where knowledge of local waters is needed; steersman; navigator of an airplane; guide. -*v.t.* act as pilot to. -**pi'lotage** *n.* work or payment of a pilot. -**pi'lot boat** *n.* boat from which pilot guides ship into harbor. -**pi'lot cloth** *n.* thick blue cloth for overcoats. -**pi'lot engine** *n.* engine sent in front to ensure railway line is clear. -**pi'lot fish** *n.* small fish of mackerel family. -**pi'lot jet** *n.* in motoring, carburetor jet for starting and slow running. -**pi'lot** *a.* experimental and preliminary. -**pi'lot plant** *n.* a small scale industrial plant in which problems can be identified and solved before the full-scale plant is built. -**pi'lot stud'y** *n.* a small-scale experiment or set of observations undertaken to decide how and whether to launch a full-scale project. [F. *pilote*]

pil'ule *n.* small pill. [F.]

pimen'to *n.* Jamaica pepper, allspice. [Port. *pimenta*]

pimp *n.* procurer; pander. -*v.i.* pander. [orig. unknown]

pimpernel *n.* plant with small scarlet or blue or white flowers closing in dull weather. [F. *pirnprenelle*]

pim'ple *n.* small pustular spot on the skin. -**pim'ply** *a.* [orig. uncertain]

pin *n.* short thin piece of stiff wire with a point and head for fastening soft materials together; wooden or metal peg or rivet. -*v.t.* fasten with a pin or pins; seize and hold fast. -**pin'-cushion** *n.* pad into which pins are stuck. -**pin'-money** *n.* allowance made to a woman for her private expenditure. -**pin'point** *v.t.* single out with exactitude. [OE. *pinn,* peg]

pin'afore *n.* washing apron or overall. [because pinned afore the dress]

piñata *n.* papier-maché or clay form filled with candy or toys, hung at parties and festivities to be broken with a stick.

pince'-nez *n.* eye-glasses held on the nose by a spring catch. [F.]

pincers *n.pl.* tool for gripping, composed of two limbs crossed and pivoted. [F. *pincer*]

pinch *v.t.* nip, squeeze. -*n.* nip; stress: as much as can be taken up between finger and thumb. [ONF. *pinchier*]

pinchbeck *n.* zinc and copper alloy; cheap jewelry. -*a.* counterfeit, flashy. [invented by C. *Pinchbeck,* a London watchmaker (d. 1732)]

pine *n.* evergreen coniferous tree. -**pine'apple** *n.* tropical fruit. [L. *pinus*]

pine *v.i.* waste away with grief, want, *etc.* -**pi'nory** *n.* pine-wood. [OE. *pinian,* fr. *pin,* pain]

pin'fold *n.* place for confining cattle, pound. [*pound, fold*]

ping'-pong *n.* table-tennis. [imit.]

pin'ion *n.* wing. -*v.t.* disable by binding wings, arms. [L. *penna,* feather]

pin'ion *n.* small cog-wheel. (F. *pignon*]

pink *n.* garden plant of carnation family;

height of excellence. -*a.* pale red in color. -*v.t.* pierce; ornament with perforations. [Teut. orig.]

pink' *v.i.* (of a motor engine) detonate, make a knocking sound. [imit.]

pinnace *n.* warship's eight-oared boat; formerly, a small ship attending on a larger one. [orig. uncertain]

pinn'acle *n.* pointed turret on a buttress or roof; mountain peak; highest pitch or point. [L. *pinna,* point]

pinn'ate *a.* feather-shaped; with leaflets on both sides of stem; winged. [L. *pinna,* feather]

pint (pint) *n.* liquid and dry measure, half a quart. [F. *pinte*]

pioneer' *n.* one of an advanced body preparing a road for troops; explorer; one who first originates. -*v.i.* act as pioneer or leader. [F. *pionier,* fr. *pion,* foot soldier]

pi'ous *n.* devout. [L. *pius*]

pip *n.* contagious disease of fowls, *etc.* (*sl.*) fit of depression. [Du.]

pip *n.* spot on playing cards, dice, or dominoes. [orig. *peep*]

pip *n.* seed in a fruit. [short for *pippin*]

pipe *n.* tube of metal or other material; musical instrument, a whistle; shrill voice, or bird's note; tube with a small bowl at the end for smoking tobacco; wine cask. -*v.i.* and *t.* play on a pipe. **-pipe'clay** *n.* clay used for tobacco pipes and for whitening military equipment, *etc.* -*v.t.* whiten with pipeclay. **-pipe'line** *n.* long line of pipes to carry water, oil, *etc.* **-pi'per** *n.* player on a pipe or bagpipes. [OE.]

pip'it *n.* bird like lark. [prob. imit.]

pipistrelle' *n.* small kind of bat. [F.]

pip'kin *n.* small earthenware jar or pan. [orig. uncertain]

pipp'in *n.* various sorts of apples. [F. *pepin,* seed]

pi'quant *a.* pungent; stimulating. **-pi'quancy** *n.* **-pi'quantly** *adv.* [F. *piquer,* string, prick]

pique *v.t.* irritate; hurt the pride of; stimulate. -*n.* feeling of injury or baffled curiosity. [F.]

pi'qué *n.* stiff ribbed cotton fabric. [F.]

piquet' (-ket') *n.* card game. [F.]

pi'rate *n.* sea-robber; publisher, *etc.,* who infringes copyright. -*v.t.* publish or reproduce regardless of copyright. **-pi'racy** *n.* **-pirat'ical** *a.* **-pirat'ically** *adv.* [G. *peirates,* fr. *peiran,* attack]

pirouette' *n.* spinning round on the toe. -*v.i.* do this. [F.]

Pisc'es *n. pl.* the Fishes, 12th sign of the zodiac, which the sun enters c. Feb. 19. **-pis'cine** *a.* of or like a fish. **-piscatol'ogy** *n.* study of fishes. **-piscato'rial** *a.* of fish or fishing. **-piscicul'ture** *n.* breeding of fish. [L. *piscis,* fish]

pis'mire *n.* ant. [*piss,* from smell of ant-hill, ME. *mire,* ant]

pist'il *n.* female organ of a flower consisting of ovary, style, stigma. [L. *pistillum,* pestle]

pist'ol *n.* small gun used with one hand. -*v.t.* shoot with a pistol. [F. *pistolet*]

pist'on *n.* plug fitting a cylinder and working up and down, *e.g.,* as in a steam engine, *etc.* **-piston-rod** *n.* rod connecting piston with other parts of machinery. [F.]

pit *n.* deep hole in the ground; coal mine or its shaft; depression in any surface; in a theater, section for musicians in front of the stage; enclosure in which animals were set to fight. -*v.t.* set to fight; mark with small scars. **-pit'fall** *n.* covered pit for catching animals or men; concealed danger. **-pit'man** *n.* miner. [L. *puteus,* well]

pit *n.* stone of a fruit. [OE. *pitha*]

pit-a-pat *adv.* quickly and lightly *e.g.,* of heart beats or footsteps. [imit.]

pitch *n.* dark sticky substance obtained from tar or turpentine. -*v.t.* coat with this. **-pitch'-blende** *n.* an oxide of uranium. **-pitch'pine** *n.* resinous kind of pine. **-pitch'y** *a.* covered with pitch; black as pitch. [L. *pix, pic-*]

pitch *v.t.* set up; cast or throw. -*v.i.* fix upon; fall headlong; of a ship to plunge lengthwise. -*n.* act of pitching; degree height, station; slope; degree of acuteness of sounds. **-pitch'er** *n.* **-pitch'fork** *n.* fork for lifting and pitching hay, *etc.* -*v.t.* throw with, or as with, a pitchfork. [orig. uncertain]

pitch'er *n.* large jug. [OF. *pichier*]

pith *n.* tissue in the stems and branches of certain plants; essential substance, most important part. **-pith'less** *a.* lacking in energy, spirit. **-pith'y** *a.* consisting of pith; terse, concise. **-pith'ily** *adv.* [OE. *pitha*]

pithecanthrop'us *n.* fossil apeman. [G. *pithekos,* ape, *anthropos,* man]

pitt'ance *n.* small allowance; inadequate wages. [F. *pitance,* orig. = *pity*]

pituitary *a.* mucous. **-pitu'itary gland,** small ductless gland situated beneath the brain. [L. *pituitarius*]

pit'y *n.* sympathy or sorrow for others' suffering; regrettable fact. -*v.t.* feel pity for. **-pit'eous** *a.* deserving pity. **-pit'iable** *a.* **-pit'iably** *adv.* **-pit'iful** *a.* full of pity; contemptible. **-pit'iless** *a.* [F. *pitie* fr. L. *pietas*, piety]

piv'ot *n.* shaft or pin on which something turns; central fact; important factor. *-v.t.* furnish with a pivot. *-v.i.* to turn on one. [F.]

pix'el *n.* any of a number of very small picture elements that make up a picture, as on a visual display unit. [fr. *pix* (pictures) and *elements*]

pix'y, pix'ie *n.* fairy. **-pix'y ring'**, fairy ring, ring of greener grass in a meadow. [orig. uncertain]

pizzica'to *a.* and *n.* (music) note, passage played by plucking instrument string with finger. [It.]

plac'ard *n.* paper with a notice for posting up. *-v.t.* post placards on; advertise or display on placards. [F.]

placate' *v.t.* conciliate, pacify. **-plac'able** *a.* [L. *placare*]

place *n.* particular part of space, spot; position; town, village, residence, buildings; office or employment. *-v.t.* put in a particular place. **-place'man** *n.* one who holds office. [F.]

placenta (pla-sen'ta) *n.* organ connecting the parent with the unborn mammal; that portion of a plant to which the seeds are attached. [L. *placenta*, a flat cake]

pla'cer *n.* deposit yielding gold after washing. [Sp.]

pla'cid (-as'-) *a.* calm; not easily agitated. **-placid'ity** *n.* [L. *placidus]*

pla'giary *n.* one who publishes borrowed or copied literary work as original; act of so doing. **-pla'giarism** *n.* **-pla'giarist** *n.* **-pla'giarize** *v.t.* and *i.* [L. *plagiarius*, kidnapper]

plague *n.* pestilence; affliction. *-v.t.* trouble or annoy. **-pla'guy** *a.* **-pla'guily** *adv.* [L. *plaga*, stroke]

plaice *n.* flat fish. [G. *platys, flat*]

plaid *n.* long Scottish-Highland shawl. [Gael. *plaide*, blanket, fr. *peallaid*, sheepskin]

plain *a.* flat, level; unobstructed, not intricate; easily understood; simple, ordinary; unadorned; not beautiful. *-n.* tract of level country. *adv.* clearly. **-plain'ly** *adv.* **-plain'-dealing** *n.* honesty, candidness. **-plain'-speaking** *n.* outspokenness, frankness. [L. planus, smooth]

plaint *n.* statement of complaint in a law court; lament. **-plaint'iff** *n.* one who sues in a law court. **-plaint'ive** *a.* sad. [F. *plaindre*]

plait (plat) *n.* fold; braid of hair, straw, *etc.* *-v.t.* form into plaits. [OF. *pleit*]

plan *n.* drawing representing a thing's horizontal section; diagram, map; project, design; way of proceeding. *-v.t.* make a plan of; make a design; arrange beforehand. [F. fr. L. *planus*, level]

plane *n.* broad-leaved tree. [G. *platanos*]

plane *n.* carpenter's tool for smoothing wood. *-v.t.* make smooth with one. [L. *planus*, level]

plane *a.* perfect, flat, or level; smooth surface. [var. of *plain*]

plane *n.* *abbrev.* of airplane; wing of an airplane or glider. *-v.t.* glide in an airplane. [F. *planer*, hover]

plan'et *n.* heavenly body revolving round the sun. **-plan'etary** *a.* [G. *planetes*, wanderer]

planeta'rian *n.* apparatus showing movement of sun, moon, stars and planets by projecting lights on inside of dome; building in which the apparatus is housed. [G. *planetes*, wanderer]

plank *n.* long flat piece of sawn timber. [Late L. *planca*]

plank'ton *n.* general term for free-floating organisms in sea or lake, *etc.* [G. *plangktos*, wandering]

plant *n.* member of the vegetable kingdom, living organism feeding on inorganic substances and without power of locomotion; equipment or machinery needed for a manufacture. *-v.t.* set in the ground, to grow; fix firmly; support or establish; stock with plants. **-planta'tion** *n.* wood of planted trees; estate for cultivation of tea, tobacco, *etc.*; formerly, a colony. **-plant'er** *n.* one who plants; grower of tropical produce. [L. *planta*]

plant'ain *n.* low-growing herb with broad leaves. [L. *plants*, sole of foot (referring to shape of leaves)]

plant'ain *n.* tropical tree like a banana; its fruit. [Sp. *plantano*]

plaque' (plak) *n.* ornamental plate or tablet; plate of clasp or brooch. [F.]

plash *n.* puddle, splash. [imit]

plast'er *n.* mixture of lime, sand, *etc.*, to spread on walls, *etc.*; piece of fabric spread with a medicinal or adhesive substance for application to the body. *-v.t.* apply plaster to. **-plast'erer** *n.* [G. *plassein*, mold]

plast'ic *a.* produced by molding; easily molded; molding shapeless matter. **Plast'icine** plastic modelling material (Trademark). **-plasti'city** *n.* aptness to be molded. [G. *plastikos-plassein*, mold]

plas'tics *n. pl.* name for various synthetic

or natural substances capable of being molded into shape, *e.g.*, casein, bitumen, resins. [*plastic*]

plat *n.* plot of ground. [=*plot*]

plat *v.t.* plait. (**plattéed** *p.t.* and *pp.* **platt'ing** *pres. p.*) -*n.* straw-plait. [=*plait*]

plate *n.* flat thin sheet of metal, glass, *etc.*; utensils of gold or silver; shallow round dish from which food is eaten. -*v.t.* cover with a thin coating of gold, silver, or other metal. -**plate'ful** *n.* -**plate-layer** *n.* workman on and repairer of railroad tracks. [G. *platus*, broad, flat]

plat'eau *n.* level high land. [F.]

plat'en *n.* plate by which paper is pressed against type in a printing press; roller in a typewriter. [G. *platus*, broad, flat]

plat'form *n.* raised level surface or floor. [F. *plate-forme*, flat form]

platitude *n.* commonplace remark. -**platitu'dinous** *a.* [F. -*plat*, flat]

platinum *n.* white heavy malleable metal. -**plat'inotype** *n.* photographic process or print in which platinum is used. [Sp. *platina*, dim. of plate, silver]

Platon'ic *a.* of, pert. to Plato and his philosophy; (of love) spiritual, friendly. [*Plato*]

platoon' *n.* small body of soldiers employed as a unit; sub-division of an infantry company. [F. *peloton*]

platt'er *n.* a flat dish. [AF. *plater*]

plaud'it *n.* act of applause. [L. *plaudere*, clap the hands]

plausible *a.* something fair or reasonable; fair-spoken. -**plausibil'ity** *n.* [L. *plausibilis*]

play *v.i.* move with light or irregular motion, flicker, *etc.*; amuse oneself; take part in a game; perform on a musical instrument. -*v.t.* use or work (an instrument); take part in (a game); contend with in a game; perform (*mus.*), perform on (an instrument); act; act the part of -*n.* brisk or free movement; activity; sport; amusement; gambling; dramatic piece or performance. -**play'er** *n.* -**play'fellow, play'mate** *n.* friend, companion in play. **play'group** *n.* regular meeting of small children arranged by their parents or a welfare agency to give them an opportunity of supervised creative play. **play'house** *n.* theater. -**play'ful** *n.* **play'thing** *n.* toy. -**play'wright** *n.* author of plays. [OE. *plegian*]

plea *n.* that is pleaded; excuse; statement of a prisoner or defendant. -**plead** *v.i.* address a court of law; make an earnest appeal. -*v.t.* bring forward as an excuse or plea. [F. *plaid*]

pleach' *v.t.* interweave the branches of (a hedge, *etc.*). [OF. *presser*]

please *v.t.* be agreeable to. -*v.i.* like; be willing. -**pleas'ance** (plez'-) *n.* delight; pleasure-ground. -**pleas'ure** *n.* enjoyment; satisfaction; will, choice. -**pleas'urable** *a.* giving pleasure. -**pleas'ant** *a.* pleasing, agreeable. -**pleas'antly** *adv.* -**pleasantry** *n.* joke. [F. *plaire, plais-* fr. L. *placere*]

pleat *n.* three-fold band on a garment, *etc.*, made by folding the material on itself. *v.i.* make a pleat in. [*plait*]

plebeian *a.* belonging to the common people; low or rough. -*n.* one of the common people. [L. *plebs*, common people]

plebiscite *n*. a decision by direct voting of a whole people. [F.]

pledge *n.* thing given as security; toast; promise. -*v.t.* give over as security; engage; drink the health of. [OF. *plege*]

Plei'ades (pli-) *n. pl.* group of seven stars in the constellation Taurus. [G.]

Plei'stocene *a.* of Glacial period or formation. [G. *pleistos*, most, *kainos*, new]

ple'nary *a.* complete, without limitations. -**plen'itude** *n.* completeness, abundance. [L. *plenus*, full]

plenipotentiary *a.* having full powers. -*n.* envoy or ambassador with full powers. [Low L. *plenipotentiarius*]

plenitude *n.* completeness, abundance. [L. *plenus*, full]

plent'y *n.* quite enough; abundance. -**plent'eous** *a.* -**plent'iful** *a.* abundant. [OF. *plente*-L. *plenus*, full]

ple'onasm *n.* use of more words than are needed for the sense; redundancy. -**pleonast'ic** *a.* [G. *plenomasmos*]

pleth'ora *n.* excess of red corpuscles in the blood; oversupply. -**plethor'ic** *a.* [G. *plethein*, become full]

pleu'ra *n.* membrane enclosing lung. -**pleu'ral** *a.* [G. *pleura*, side]

pleur'isy *n.* inflammation of membrane round the lungs. -**pleuro-pneumonia** *n.* inflammation of pleura and lungs. [G. *pleura*, side]

plex'us *n.* network of nerves, blood vessels *etc.* [L. *plectere*, plait]

pli'able *a.* easily bent or influenced. -**pliabil'ity** *n.* -**pli'ant** *a.* pliable. -**pli'ancy** *n.* [F.]

pli'ers *n. pl.* small pincers with a flat grip. [L. *plicare*, bend]

plight *n.* promise. -*v.t.* promise, engage oneself to. [OE. *pliht*, risk]

plight *n.* state (usually of a distressing kind); predicament. [OE. *plit*, fold or plait]

Plim'soll mark indicating load-line of a ship. [S. *Plimsoll*, d. 1898]

plim'solis *n.pl.* canvas shoes with rubber soles. [orig. uncertain]

plinth *n.* square slab as the base of a column, *etc.* [G. *plinthos*, brick]

plod *v.i.* walk or work doggedly. -**plod'der** *n.* -**plod'ding** *a.* [imit. orig.]

plot *n.* small piece of land; plan or essential facts of a story, play, *etc.*; secret design, conspiracy. -*v.t.* make a map of; devise secretly. -*v.i.* take part in conspiracy. [OE.]

plough. *See* **plow.**

plo'ver (pluv-) *n.* various birds, including the lapwing. [F. *pluvier*]

plow *n.* implement for turning up the soil. -*v.t.* turn up with a plow, furrow. -**plow'share** *n.* cutting blade of plow. -**plow'man** *n.* man who steers plow. [ON. *plogr*]

pluck *v.i.* pull or pick off, strip the feathers from; reject in an examination. -*n.* plucking; beast's heart, lungs, *etc.*; courage. -**pluck'y** *a.* -**pluck'ily** *adv.* [OE. *pluecian*]

plug *n.* something fitting into and filling a hole; tobacco pressed hard; piece of this for chewing. -*v.t.* stop with a plug. -(*sl.*) push; advertise persistently. [Du. = *bung*]

plum *n.* stone fruit; tree bearing it. **plum-cake, plum-pudding** *n.* rich cake, pudding full of raisins, other fruits and spices. [OE. *plume*, L. *prune*]

plumb (-m) *n.* ball of lead attached to a string and used for sounding, finding the perpendicular, *etc.* -*a.* perpendicular. -*adv.* perpendicularly; exactly. -*v.t.* find the depth of, set exactly upright. -**plumb'er** (-mer) *n.* one who works in lead, *etc.* and repairs water pipes, *etc.* -**plumm'et** *n.* plumb. -**plumb'-line** *n.* cord with a plumb attached. [L. *plumbuimi*, lead]

plumba'go *n.* black lead, graphite. [L. *plumbum*, lead]

plume *n.* feather; ornament consisting of feathers or horse-hair. -*v.t.* furnish with plumes; strip of feathers; boast. -**plu'mage** *n.* feathers of a bird. [L. *pluma*, feather]

plump *a.* of rounded form, moderately fat. [Du. *plomp*, blunt]

plump *v.i.* sit or fall abruptly; vote only for. -*v.t.* drop or throw abruptly. -*adv.* abruptly, bluntly. -**plump'er** *n.* unsplit vote. [imit. orig.]

plun'der *v.t.* rob systematically; take by open force. -*v.i.* rob. -*n.* violent robbery; property so obtained, spoils. [Ger. *plundern*, pillage]

plunge *v.t.* put forcibly (into). -*v.i.* throw oneself (into); enter or move forward with violence. -*n.* plunge, dive. -**plun'ger** *n.* [F. *plonger*]

pluperfect *a.* of a tense, expressing action completed before a past point of time. [L. *plus quam perfectum*, more than perfect]

plus *prep.* with addition of (usually indicated by the sign +). -*a.* to be added; positive. -**plus-fours** *n.pl.* long baggy knickers for golf, *etc.* [L. *plus*, more]

plur'al *a.* more than one; denoting more than one person or thing. -*n.* word in its plural form. -**plu'ralism** *n.* holding more than one appointment, vote, *etc.* -**plu'ralist** *n.* -**plural'ity** *n.* [L. *plus, plur-*, more]

plush *n.* fabric like velvet, but with a long soft nap. [F. *peluche*]

Plu'to *n.* outermost of the planets so far discovered. -**Pluto'nian** *a.* pert. to Pluto; dark subterranean; igneous. [G. *Plouton*, god of the underworld]

plutocracy *n.* government by the rich, wealthy class. -**plu'tocrat** *n.* wealthy person. -**plutocrat'ic** *a.* [G. *ploutokratia*, power by wealth]

plutonium *n.* element produced by radioactive decay of neptunium. [*Pluto*]

plu'vial *a.* of, caused by rain's action. **plu'vious** *a.* rainy. [L. *pluvia*, rain]

ply *n.* fold, thickness. [L. *plicare*, fold]

ply *v.t.* wield, work at; supply pressingly. -*v.i.* go to and fro. [*apply*]

pneumatic *a.* of, or coated by, or inflated with, wind or air. -**pneumo'nia** *n.* inflammation of the lungs. [G. *pneuma*, breath]

poach *v.i.* cook (an egg) by dropping without the shell into boiling water. [F. *pocher*, pocket]

poach *v.t.* hunt (game) illegally. -*v.i.* trespass for this purpose. -**poach'er** *n.* [orig. uncertain]

pock *n.* pustule as in smallpox, *etc.* **pock-marks, pock'pit** *n.* mark or small hole left on skin after smallpox, *etc.* [OE. *poc*]

pock'et *n.* small bag inserted in a garment; cavity filled with ore, *etc.*; mass of water or air differing in some way from that surrounding it. -*v.t.* put into one's pocket; appropriate. -**pock'etbook** *n.* small bag or case for holding money, papers, *etc.* [F. *poche*, cp. *poke*]

pod *n.* long seed-vessel, as of peas, beans, *etc.* -*v.i.* form pods. -*v.t.* shell. [orig. uncertain]

po'em *n.* imaginative composition in verse. -**po'et** *n.* writer of poems. -**po'etess** *fem.* -**po'etry** *n.* art or work of a poet. -**po'esy** *n.* poetry. -**poet'ic, poet'ical** *a.* -**poet'ically** *adv.* -**po'etaster** *n.* inferior or paltry verse-writer. [G. *poiein*, make]

pog'ram *n.* concerted rising (against, *e.g.*, the Jews), with massacre and pillage. [Russ.]

poign'ant (poin'-) *a.* pungent, stinging, moving, vivid. -**poign'ancy** *n.* [F. *poindre, poign-*, fr. L. *pungere*, prick]

poilu' *n.* (*sl.*) French private soldier. [F. = *hairy*]

point *n.* dot or mark; punctuation mark; item, detail; unit of value; position, degree, stage; moment; essential object or thing; sharp end; headland; movable rail, changing a train to other rails; one of the direction marks of a compass; striking or effective part or quality; act of pointing. -*v.t.* sharpen; give value to (words, *etc.*); fill up joints with mortar; aim or direct. -*v.i.* show direction or position by extending a finger, stick, *etc.*; direct attention; of a dog, to indicate the position of game by standing facing it. -**point'ed** *a.* -**pointedly** *adv.* -**point'er** *n.* index, indicating rod, *etc.*, used for pointing; dog trained to point. -**point'less** *a.* -**point'-blank'** *a.* aimed horizontally; at short range. *adv.* with level aim (there being no necessity to elevate for distances), at short range. -**point-to-point** *n.* steeple chase. -**points'man** *n.* one working on rail points; man on point duty. [L. *puncture*, fr. *pungere*, prick]

poise *v.t.* place or hold in a balanced or steady position. -*v.i.* be so held; hover. -*n.* balance, equilibrium, carriage (of body, *etc.*). [OF. *pois*, weight]

poi'son (-z-) *n.* substance which kills or injures when introduced into living organism. -*v.t.* give poison to; infect; pervert, spoil. -**poi'soner** *n.* -**poi'sonous** *a.* [F.]

poke *v.t.* push or thrust with a finger, stick, *etc.*; thrust forward. -*v.i.* make thrusts; to pry. -*n.* act of poking. -**po'ker** *n.* metal rod for poking a fire. -**po'ky** *n.* bag; pouch. [ONF. *paque*; F. *poche*, of Teut. orig.]

po'ker *n.* card game. [orig. uncertain]

Pol'aroid *n.* type of plastic which polarizes light; camera that develops print very quickly inside itself. [Trademark]

pole *n.* long rounded piece of wood; measure of length, 5½ yards; measure of are, 30¼ square yards. -*v.t.* propel with a pole. [OE. *pal*, fr. L. *palus*]

pole *n.* each of the two points about which the stars appear to revolve; each of the ends of the axis of the earth; each of the opposite ends of a magnet, electric cell, *etc.* -**po'lar** *a.* -**polar'ity** *n.* -**po'larize** *v.t.* give magnetic polarity to; affect light so that its vibrations are kept to one plane. -**polariza'tion** *n.* -**pole'-star** *n.* north star; guide, lodestar. [G. *polos*, pivot]

pole'-ax *n.* long-handled battle-ax; butcher's ax. [ME. *pollax*]

pole'cat *n.* small animal of the weasel family; skunk. [F. *poule*, hen (fr. its preying on *poultry*)]

polem'ic *a.* controversial. -*n. pl.* war of words; art of controversy; branch of theology dealing with differences in doctrines. -**polem'ical** *a.* [G. *polemos*, war]

police' *n.* public order; civil force which maintains public order. -*v.t.* keep in order. -**police'man** *n.* -**police'woman** *fem.* member of the police. [G. *polis*, city]

pol'icy *n.* a contract of insurance. [It. *polizza*, invoice]

pol'icy *n.* political wisdom; course of action adopted, *esp.* in state affairs; prudent procedure. [OF. *policie* fr. G. *politeia*, government]

poliomyelitis, polio *n.* inflammation of the spinal cord; infantile paralysis. [G. *polios*, gray, *myelos*, marrow]

pol'ish *v.t.* make smooth and glossy; refine. -*n.* act of polishing; gloss; refinement of manners; substance used in polishing. [L. *polire*, make to shine]

polite' *a.* refined; having refined manners, courteous. -**polite'ly** *adv.* -**polite'ness** *n.* [L. *politus*]

pol'itic (pol'-it-ic) *a.* wise, shrewd, expedient, cunning. -*n.* in *pl.* art of government; political affairs or life. -**polit'ical** *a.* of the state or its affairs. -**politi'cian** n, one engaged in politics. -**pol'ity** *n.* civil government; form of government; state. [fr. G. *polites*, a citizen]

pol'itics *n.* science and art of civil government; political principles or opinions; political methods. -**pol'itic** *a.* prudent; crafty, scheming. -**political** *a.* [*v.s.*]

pol'ka *n.* quick, round dance; music for it. -*v.i.* dance a polka. [Polish]

poll *n.* head or top of the head, counting of voters; voting; number of votes recorded. -*v.t.* cut off the top of; take the votes of, receive (votes). *v.i.* to vote. -**poll' tax** *n.* tax on each head, or person. [of Teut. orig.]

poll'ack *n.* fish of cod family [orig. uncertain]

poll'ard *n.* tree on which a close head of young branches has been made by polling: hornless animal of a normally horned variety. -*v.t.* make a pollard of (a tree). [*poll*]

poll'en *n.* fertilizing dust of a flower. -**pollina'tion** *n.* transferring of pollen to stigma by insects, *etc.* [L. =*fine dust*]

pollute *v.t.* make foul: desecrate. -**pollu'tion** *n.* [L. *polluere, pollut-*]

po'lo *n.* game like hockey played by men on ponies, four-a-side. -**wa'ter po'lo,** ballgame played in water. [Balti = *ball*]

polonaise' *n.* Polish dance; music for it; gown looped up over hooped petticoat, [F. = Polish]

polo'nium *n.* radio-active element discovered by Mme. Curie (a Pole). [L. *Pilonia*, Poland]

polo'ny *n.* kind of meat sausage. [*Bologna*]

polter'geist *n.* (*psych. research*) spirit, ghost, throwing things about and causing unexplained noises. [Ger.]

poltroon' *n.* coward, despicable fellow. -**poltroon'ery** *n.* [F. *poltron*]

poly- *prefix* many. [G. *polus,* many] -**polyan'dry** *n.* polygamy in which one woman has more than one husband. -**polyan'thus** *n.* cultivated, primrose. -**pol'ychrome** *a.* many colors. -*n.* work of art in many colors. -**polychromat'ic** *a.* -**polyeth'ylene** *n.* tough thermoplastic material. -**polyg'amy** *n.* custom of being married to several persons at a time. -**polyg'amist** *n.* -**pol'yglot** *a.* speaking, writing, or written in several languages. -**pol'ygon** *n.* figure with many angles or sides. -**polyg'onal** *a.* -**polygyny** *n.* polygamy in which one man has more than one wife. -**polyhe'dron** *n.* solid figure contained by many faces. -**Polyhymnia** *n.* muse of the hymn. -**pol'yp** *n.* coral insect or other creature of low organization. -**pol'ypod** *a.* and *n.* (animal) with many feet. **polysyll'able** *n.* word of many syllables. -**polysyllab'ic** *a.* -**polytech'nic** *a.* dealing with various arts and crafts. -*n.* school doing this. -**pol'ytheism** *n.* belief in many gods. -**pol'ytheist** *n.* -**polytheist'ic** *a.*

pomade' *n.* scented ointment for the head or hair. -**poma'tum** *n.* pomade. [F. *pomuiade*]

pom'egranate *n.* large fruit with thick rind containing many seeds in a red pulp; the tree. [OF. *pome grenade*]

Pomera'nian, pom *n.* breed of small dogs with pointed muzzle and thick soft coat. [*Pomerania*]

pomm'el *n.* knob of a sword hilt; front of a saddle. -*v.t.* strike repeatedly; strike with a sword-pommel, [OF. *pomel,* small apple]

pomp *n.* splendid display or ceremony. -**pomp'ous** *a.* self-important; puffed up; of language, inflated. -**pompos'ity** *n.* [G. *pompe*, solemn procession]

pom-pom *n.* automatic quick-firing gun. [imit. of its noise]

pom'-pon *n.* tuft or ball of ribbon, wool, *etc.*, decorating a hat, shoe, *etc.* - also **pom-pom**.[F.]

pon'cho *n.* blanket worn orig. by S. American Indians. [Sp.]

pond *n.* small body of still water, *esp.* for watering cattle, *etc.* [same as *pound*]

pon'der *v.t.* and *i.* meditate, think over; -**pond'erable** *a.* capable of being weighed. -**pond'erous** *a.* heavy, unwieldy. [L. *pondus, ponder-*, weight]

pone' *n.* corn pone, maize bread; a maize cake. [Amer. Ind.]

pongee' *n.* soft Chinese silk made from the cocoons of wild silkworms. [Chin.]

poniard *n.* dagger. -*v.t.* stab with one. [F. *poignard*]

pon'tiff *n.* Pope; high priest. **pontif'ical** *a.* pompous and dogmatic. -**pontif'icate** *v.i.* . [L. *pontifex*, high priest]

pontoon' flat bottomed boat or metal rum for use in supporting a temporary bridge. [L. *ponto*, punt]

pontoon' *n.* card game of chance. [fr. F. *vingt-et-un*, twenty-one]

po'ny *n.* horse of a small breed. [Gael. *poniadh*]

poo'dle *n.* variety of pet dog with long curly hair often clipped fancifully. [Ger. *pudel*, orig. water dog]

pool *n.* small body of still water (*esp.* of natural formation); deep place in a river. [OE. *pol*]

pool *n.* collective stakes in various games; variety of billiards; combination of capitalists to fix prices and divide business; common fund. -*v.t.* throw into a common fund. [F. *poule*, hen]

poop *n.* stern of a ship; a high deck there. -*v.t.* break over the poop of. [L. *puppis*, stern]

poor *a.* having little money; unproductive, inadequate, insignificant, unfortunate. -**poor'ly** *a.* not in good health. -**poor'ness** *v.* -**poor-house** *n.* work-house; institution for upkeep of poor. -**poor rate** *n.* rate for relief of poor. -**poor-spirited** *a.* cowardly. [L. *pauper*]

pop *n.* abrupt small explosive sound. *v.i.* make such sound; go or come unexpectedly or suddenly. -*v.t.* put or place suddenly.

pop-corn *n.* Indian corn puffed up through exposure to heat. [imit. orig.]

pop *n.* music of general appeal, *esp.* to young people. -*a.* popular. [fr. *popular*]

Pope *n.* bishop of Rome as head of the Roman Catholic Church. -**po'pery** *a.* (*usu.* in hostile sense) the papal system. -**po'pish** *a.* [G. *pappas*, father]

pop'injay *n.* fop; target in shape of a parrot. [orig. parrot; OF. *papegai*]

pop'lar *n.* tree noted for slender tallness and tremulous leaves. [L. *populus*]

pop'lin *n.* corded fabric of silk and worsted. [It. *papalina* (*fem.*), papal, because made at Avignon (seat of the Pope, 1309-1408)]

popp'y *n.* bright flowered plant which yields opium. [OE. *popig*, L. *papaver*]

poppycock *n.* nonsense, rubbish, balderdash. [orig. unknown]

pop'ulace *n.* common people. -**pop'ular** *a.* of or by the people; finding general favor. -**popular'ity** *n.* being generally liked. -**pop'ularize** *v.t.* make popular. -**populariza'tion** *n.* -**pop'ularly** *adv.* -**populate** *v.t.* fill with inhabitants. -**population** *n.* inhabitants; the number of them. -**pop'ulous** *a.* thickly populated. [L. *populus*]

porcelain *n.* fine earthenware, china. [F. *porcelaine*]

porch *n.* covered approach to the entrance of a building; a veranda. [F. *porche*, fr. L. *porticos*, colonnade]

por'cine *a.* of or like a pig or pigs. [L. *porcinus*]

porcupine *n.* rodent animal covered with long pointed quills. [OF. *porc esp.* in "Spiny pig"]

pore *n.* minute opening, *esp.* in the skin. -**por'ous** *a.* full of pores; allowing a liquid to soak through. -**poros'ity, porousness** *n.* [G. *poros*]

pore *v.i.* fix the eyes or mind upon; study attentively. [ME. *pouren*]

pork *n.* pig's flesh as food. -**pork'er** *n.* pig raised for food. -**pork'y** *a.* fleshy; fat. [L. *porcus*, pig]

pornography *n.* indecent art, literature. [G. *porne*, whore, *graphein*, write, draw]

porph'yry *n.* reddish stone with embedded crystals. [G. *porphyreos*, purple]

por'poise (-pus) *n.* blunt-nosed sea animal about five feet long. [OF. *porpeis*, pig-fish]

porridge *n.* soft food of oatmeal or other meal boiled in water. -**porr'inger** *n.* small basin. [var. of *pottage*]

port *n.* harbor or haven; town with a harbor. [L. *portus*]

port *n.* city gate; opening in the side of a ship. [L. *porta*, a gate]

port *n.* strong red wine. [*Oporto*]

port *n.* bearing. -*v.t.* carry (a rifle) slanting upwards in front of the body. -**port'able** *a.* easily carried. -**port'age** *n.* carrying or transporting. -**port'ly** *a.* large and dignified in appearance. [L. *portare*, carry]

port'al *n.* large door or gate. [OF.]

portcullis *n.* grating to raise or lower in front of a gateway. [F. *porte-coulisse*, sliding door]

portend' *v.t.* foretell; be an omen of. **port'ent** *n.* omen, marvel. -**portent'ous** *a.* [L. *portendere*, foretell]

port'er *n.* door keeper. [L. *porta*, gate]

port'er *n.* person employed to carry burdens, *esp.* at airports *etc.*; railway sleeping-car attendant; a dark beer. [L. *portare*, carry]

port'erhouse *n.* place where porter (beer) was served. -**port'erhouse steak** *n.* choice cut of beef from the thick end of the short loin. [L. *portare*, carry]

portfol'io *n.* case for papers, *etc.*; office of a minister of state. [corrupt. of It. *portafogli*, carry leaves]

port'hole *n.* small opening in the side or superstructure of a ship for light and air. [L. *porta*, a gate]

port'ico *n.* colonnade, covered walk. [It.]

por'tion *n.* part or share; destiny, lot; dowry. -*v.t.* divide into shares; give dowry to. -**por'tionless** *a.* [L. *portio*]

port'manteau *n.* traveling bag. [F. = *carry cloak*]

portray' *v.t.* make a picture of, describe. -**port'rait** *n.* likeness. -**port'raiture** *n.* -**portray'al** *n.* [L. *protrahere*, draw forth]

posa'da *n.* inn. [Sp.]

pose *v.t.* lay down; place in an attitude. -*v.i.* assume an attitude, give oneself out as. -*n.* attitude, *esp.* one assumed for effect. -**poseur'** (-ur) *n.* one who poses for effect. [F. *poser*]

pose *v.t.* puzzle. -**po'ser** *n.* puzzling question. [for oppose]

posh *a.* (*sl.*) stylish, smart. -*v.t.* spruce up. [perh. *p*ort *o*ut, *s*tarboard *h*ome, the fashionable sides of the ship to travel to India during the British Raj]

position *n.* way a thing is placed; situation, attitude; state of affairs; office for employment; strategic point. [L. *ponere*, *posit-*, lay down]

positive *a.* firmly laid down; definite; absolute, unquestionable; confident; over-confident; not negative; greater than zero. -*n.* positive degree; in photography, print in which the lights and shadows are not reversed. —**pos'itively** *adv.* -**pos'itivism** *n.* philosophy recognising only matters of fact and experience. -**positivist** *n.* [L. *positivus, posit-*]

poss'e *n.* a force, body (of police or others with legal authority). [L. *posse*, be able]

possess' (-zes') *v.t.* own; of an evil spirit, have the mastery of. -**posses'sion** *n.* -**possess'ive** *a.* of or indicating possession *n.* possessive case in grammar. -**possessor** *n.* [L. *possidere, possess-*]

poss'et *n.* warm spiced drink of milk curdled with ale or wine. [ME. *possyt*]

possible *a.* that can or may be, exist, happen, be done. -**possibil'ity** *n.* - **poss'ibly** *adv.* [L. *possibilis*]

post *n.* upright pole of timber or metal fixed firmly, usually as a support for something. -*v.t.* display; stick up (on a post, notice board, *etc.*). -**post'er** *n.* placard; advertising bill. [L. *postis*]

post *n.* official carrying of letters or parcels; collection or delivery of these; point, station or place of duty; place where a soldier is stationed; place held by a body of troops, fort; office or situation. -*v.t.* put into the official box for carriage by post; transfer (entries) to a ledger; supply with latest information; station (soldiers, *etc.*) in a particular spot. *v.i.* travel with post horses. -*adv.* in haste. -**post'age** *n.* charge for carrying a letter, *etc.* -**post'al** *a.* -**post'card** *n.* card with message sent by post. -**post'-chaise** *n.* traveling carriage hired and drawn from stage to stage by post-horses. -**post'haste** *adv.* with all speed. -**post'-horse** *n.* horse (formerly) kept for hire at intervals on main roads for use in relays. -**post'man** *n.* man who collects or delivers the post. **post'mark** *n.* official mark with the name of the office, *etc.*, stamped on letters. -**post'master** *n.* official in charge of a post office. -**post'master general** *n.* minister in charge of post-office department. **post office** *n.* office which receives and transmits mail; government department in charge of conveying of mail. -**post' production** *n.* editing of a film or recording that takes place after the artists' taping is complete. [L. *ponere, posit-*, place]

post-, later, after. [L. *post*, after]. -**postdate'** *v.t.* give a date later than the actual date. -post-grad'uate *a.* carried on after graduation. -**post-prand'ial** *a.* after-dinner. -**poste'rior** (post-) *a.* later; hinder. -**poster'ity** *n.* descendants; later generations. -**post'ern** *n.* back or private door. -**post'humous** *a.* born after the father's death; published after the author's death; occurring, conferred, *etc.*, after death. -**postmortem** *a.* taking place after death. -*n.* medical examination of a dead body. -**postpone'** *v.t.* put off to a later time. -**postpone'ment** *n.* -**post'script** *n.* addition to a letter or book.

pos'til *n.* marginal note *esp.* in Scriptures. [L. L. *postilla*, note]

postil'ion *n.* man who rides one of the horses drawing a carriage; postboy. [F. *postillon*]

post'lude *n.* music played at the end of a church service; concluding movement. [*post-* and L. *ludus*, play]

postmerid'ian *a.* of the afternoon. -*n.* afternoon, *cont.* P.M. [L. *post*, after]

post o'bit *a.* taking effect after death. -*n.* bond given by borrower securing repayment on death of one from whom he has expectations. [L. *post*, after, *obitus*, death]

postulate *v.t.* claim, demand, take for granted. -*n.* something taken for granted. [L. *postulare*, demand]

pos'ture *n.* attitude, position. [L. *positura*, fr. *ponere*, place]

po'sy *n.* bunch of flowers; verse accompanying it. [shortened fr. *poesy*]

pot *n.* round vessel; cooking vessel. -*v.t.* put into or preserve in a pot. -**pot'herb** *n.* flavoring vegetable, *e.g.* parsley. -**pot'hook** *n.* hook above fire, on which pots are hung. -**pot'-house** *n.* low inn. -**pot'luck** *n.* whatever happens to be in the pot. [OE. *pott*]

po'table *a.* drinkable. -**pota'tion** *n.* drink or drinking. [L. *potare*, drink]

pot'ash *n.* alkali used in soap, *etc.*; crude potassium carbonate. -**potass'ium** *n.* white metal. [orig. *pot ashes*]

pota'to *n.* plant with tubers grown for food. -(*pl.*) potatoes. -**pota'to-bug** *n.* Colorado beetle. [Sp. *patata*]

po'tent *a.* powerful. -**po'tency** *n.* -**po'tentate** *a.* ruler. -**poten'tial** *a.* latent, may or might but does not now exist or act. -*n.* amount of potential energy or work. -**potential'ity** *n.* -**po'tently** *adv.* -**poten'tiary** *n.* person with influence. [L. *potens*, pres. p. of *posse*, be able]

poth'er (-th-) *n.* disturbance, fuss. [orig. uncertain]

po'tion *n.* a draught; dose of medicine or poison. [L. *potio-potare*, drink]

potpourri' *n.*mixture of rose petals,

spices, *etc.*; musical or literary medley. [F.]

pot'sherd *n.* broken fragment of pottery. [*pot, shard*]

pottage *n.* soup or stew. [F. *potage*]

pott'er *n.* maker of earthenware vessels. -**pott'ery** *n.* place where earthenware is made; earthenware; art of making it. [*pot*]

pott'le *n.* small fruit-basket. [*pot*]

pouch *n.* small bag. -*v.t.* put into one. [F. *poche*, pocket]

pouffe' *n.* deep round cushion or hassock. [F.]

poult *n.* chicken. -**poult'erer** *n.* dealer in poultry. -**poult'ry** *n.* domestic fowls. [F. *poulet*, dim. of *poule*, hen]

poult'ice (polt'is) *n.* mass of bread, linseed, or other substance mixed with hot water, spread on a cloth, and applied to the skin for the treatment of sores, lesions, *etc.* -*v.t.* put on a poultice. [L. *puls, pult-*, porridge]

pounce *v.i.* spring upon suddenly, swoop. -*n.* swoop or sudden descent upon something. [orig. uncertain]

pounce *n.* fine powder used to prevent ink from spreading on unsized paper, *etc.* [F. *ponce*, fr. L. *pumex, pumic-*, pumice]

pound *n.* weight, 12 oz. troy, 16 oz. avoirdupois; unit of money, 100 pence. **pound'age** *n.* payment or commission of so much per pound (money); charge of so much per pound (weight). [OE. *pund*, L. *pondus*, weight]

pound *n.* enclosure for stray cattle. -*v.t.* shut up in one. [OE. *pund*]

pound *v.t.* crush to pieces or powder; thump; cannonade. [OE. *punian*]

pour (pawr) *v.i.* come out in a stream, crowd, *etc.* -*v.t.* give out thus; cause to run out. [orig. unknown]

pour'boire' *n.* tip. [F. *pour*, for, *boire*, drink]

pout *v.i.* thrust out the lips. -*v.t.* thrust out (the lips). -*n.* act of pouting. -**pout'er** *n.* pigeon with the power of inflating its crop. [orig. uncertain]

pov'erty *n.* the condition of being poor; poorness, lack. [F. *pauvreté*]

pow'der *n.* solid matter in fine dry particles; medicine in this form; gunpowder. -*v.t.* apply powder to, reduce to powder. -**pow'dery** *a.* [F. *poudre*]

pow'er *n.* ability to do or act; authority; person or thing having authority. -**pow'erful** *a.* -**pow'erless** *a.* -**pow'erhouse; power station** *n.* building where electrical power is generated. [OF. *poeir*]

pow'-wow *n.* N. Amer. Indian conference before an expedition, *etc.*; discussion, talk. [Amer. Ind.]

pox *n.* one of several diseases marked by pustular eruptions of skin, *e.g.*, chickenpox, smallpox. [pl. of *pock*]

prac'tice *v.t.* do habitually; put into action; work at; exercise oneself in. -*v.i.* exercise oneself, exercise a profession. -*n.* habitual doing; action as distinguished from theory; habit; exercise in an art or profession. -**prac'tical** *a.* relating to action or real existence; given to action rather than theory; that is (something) in effect though not in name. -**prac'tically** *adv.* virtually, almost; in actuality, rather than in theory. -**prac'ticable** *a.* that can be done or used or followed. **practicability** *n.* -**practi'tioner** *n.* one engaged in a profession. [G. *praktikos*, concerned with action]

prac'ticum *n.* educational course based on the practical application of theory through field work or research; course offering supervised practical experience.

prae'tor *n.* ancient Roman magistrate beneath consul in rank. **praeto'rian** *a.* [L.]

pragmatic *a.* of the affairs of a state; concerned with practical consequences; officious, dogmatic. -**pragmat'ical** *a.* -**prag'matism** *n.* -**prag'matist** *n.* [G. *pragmatikos*, skilled in business]

prair'ie *n.* large tract of grass-land without trees. [F. = *meadow*]

praise *v.t.* express approval or admiration of, glorify. -*n.* commendation; fact or state of being praised. -**praise'worthy** *a.* [OF. *preisier*]

pral'ine *n.* sweet composed of nuts and sugar. [F.]

pram *n.* *abbrev.* of perambulator.

prance *v.i.* walk with bounds; strut about. -*n.* a prancing. [orig. uncertain]

prank *n.* frolicsome trick or escapade. [orig. uncertain]

prank *v.t.* adorn, rig out showily. -*v.i.* make a great display. [orig. uncertain]

prate *v.i.* talk idly, chatter; give away a secret. -*n.* chatter. -**prat'tle** *v.i.* and *v.t.* utter childishly. -*n.* childish chatter. -**pratt'ler** *n.* [Du. *praten*]

prawn *n.* edible sea crustacean like a shrimp. [orig. unknown]

pray *v.t.* ask earnestly. -*v.i.* offer prayers, especially to God. -**pray'er** *n.* earnest entreaty; action or practice of praying to God. -**pray'erful** *a.* [OF. *preier* fr. L. *precari*]

pre- *prefix*, makes compounds with the

meaning of before, or beforehand; *e.g.*, **predeter'mine** *v.t.* determine beforehand. **pre-war** *a.* before the war. These are not given where the meaning and derivation can easily be found from the simple word. [L. *prae-, pre-*, before]

preach *v.i.* deliver a sermon. -*v.t.* set forth in religious discourse. -**preach'er** *n.* [F. *precher*, fr. L. *praedicare*, fr. *dicare*, to proclaim]

pream'ble *n.* introductory part; preface. [L. *proeambulus*, going before]

preb'end *n.* stipend of a canon or member of a cathedral chapter. -**preb'endary** *n.* holder of a prebend. [Med. L. *praebenda*, pittance]

precarious *a.* insecure, unstable, perilous. [L. *precarius*, uncertainly possessed]

precaution *n.* preventive measure; cautious foresight. -**precautionary** *a.*

precede' *v.t.* go or come before in rank, order, time, *etc.* -*v.i.* go or come before. -**pre'cedence** *n.* higher or more honorable place; right to this. -**prec'edent** (pres'-) *n.* previous case or occurrence taken as a rule. [L. *praecedere*, go before]

precent'or *n.* leader of singing in church. [Late L. *praecentor*]

pre'cept *n.* rule for conduct; maxim. -**precept'or** *n.* teacher. -**precept'ress** *fem.* -**preceptor'ial** *a.* [L. *praecipere, praecept-*, take before, order]

pre'cinct *n.* ground attached to a sacred or official building; limit or boundary; division of a city as relates to policing, voting, *etc.* [Med. L. *præcinctum*, enclosure]

prec'ious (presh'us) *a.* of great value, highly valued; affected, overrefined. **prec'iously** *adv.* -**prec'iousness** *n.* **precios'ity** *n.* over-refinement in art or literature. [L. *pretiosus*, valuable]

precipice (pres'-) *n.* very steep cliff or rockface. -**precip'itous** *a.* [L. *præcipitium*, fr. *praeceps*, head first]

precipitate *v.t.* throw headlong; hasten the happening of; in chemistry, cause to be deposited in solid form from a solution. -*a.* over-sudden, rash. -*n.* substance chemically precipitated. -**precip'itately** *adv.* -**precipita'tion** *n.* -**precip'itance, precipitancy** *n.* rashness, speed, hastiness. [L. *praecipitare*]

pré'cis (press) *n.* abstract or summary. [F.]

precise' *a.* exact, strictly; worded; particular; careful in observance. -**precisely** *adv.* -**preci'sian** *n.* punctilious or formal person. -**preci'sion** *n.* accuracy. [L. *praecisus*, cut off in front]

preclude' *v.t.* prevent. [L. *praecludere*]

precocious *a.* developed too soon, *esp.* mentally. -**preco'city** (-os-) *n.* [L. *praecox, precoc-*, early ripe]

precognition *n.* knowledge beforehand. [*pre-*, and L. *cognoscere, cognit-*, know]

preconceive' *v.t.* conceive opinion or idea without previous knowledge. **preconcep'tion** *n.* [*pre-*, and F. *concevoir*]

preconcert' *v.t.* agree upon, settle before. [*pre-* and F. *concerter*]

precursor *n.* forerunner. [L.]

predatory *a.* relating to plunder; given to plundering; rapacious. -**preda'cious** *a.* of animals, living by capturing prey. [L. *praeda*, booty]

predecessor *n.* one who precedes another in an office, *etc.* [Late L. *praedecessor*, fr. *decessor*, one who withdraws]

predestine *v.t.* destine, ordain beforehand. -**predes'tinate** *v.t.* foreordain by unchangeable purpose. -**predes'tined** *a.* -**predestina'tion** *n.* doctrine that man's fate is unalterably fixed. [*pre-*, and L. *destinare*, make fast]

predicate *v.t.* affirm or assert. -*n.* that which is predicated; in grammar, a statement made about a subject. -**pred'icable** *a.* -**predica'tion** *n.* -**predic'ative** *a.* -**predic'ament** *n.* state or situation, usually an unpleasant one. [L. *praedicare*, proclaim]

predict' *v.t.* foretell. -**predic'tion** *n.* [L. *praedicere, predict-*, say before]

predilection *n.* preference or liking; predisposition in favor of. [F. *predilection*]

predominate *v.i.* be the main or controlling element. -**predom'inance** *n.* -**predom'inant** *a.* [*dominate*]

pre-eminent *a.* excelling all others. -**pre-em'inently** *adv.* outstandingly. **pre'em'inence** *n.* [*eminent*]

pre-emption *n.* buying, or the right to buy, before opportunity is given to others; acting before another event or others to gain a more advantageous position. -**preemp'tive** *a.* -**pre-emp'tor** *n.* [L. *emptio*, a buying]

preen *v.t.* trim (feathers) with a beak; smarten oneself. [var. of *prune*]

prefabricate *v.t.* make beforehand parts (of a house, *etc.*) to be assembled at a chosen site. -**prefab** *n.* (*sl.*) prefabricated house. [L. *fabricari*, fabricate, construct]

pref'ace *n.* introduction to a book, *etc.* -*v.t.* introduce. -**prefatory** *a.* [L. *prae fatio*, speaking beforehand]

pre'fect *n.* person put in authority; Roman official; head of a department; schoolboy with responsibility for maintaining discipline. -**pre'fecture** *n.* office, residence, district of a prefect. [L. *praefectus*]

prefer *v.t.* like better; promote. **preferable** *a.* -**pref'erably** *adv.* -**preference** *n.* -**preferen'tial** *a.* giving or receiving a preference. -**prefer'ment** *n.* promotion. [L. *praeferre*, bear before]

pre'fix *n.* preposition or particle put at the beginning of a word or title. -**prefix'** *v.t.* put as introduction; put before a word to make a compound. [*fix*]

preg'nant *a.* with child; full of meaning. -**preg'nancy** *n.* [L. *praegnans*]

prehen'sile *a.* capable of grasping. [L. *prehendre, prehens-*, seize]

prejudice (is) *n.* judgment or bias decided beforehand; harm likely to happen to a person or his rights as a result of others' action or judgment; prepossession (*usu.* unfavorable). -*v.t.* influence unfairly; injure. -**prejudi'cial** *a.* harmful; detrimental. [L. *praejudicium*]

prel'ate *n.* bishop or other church dignitary of equal or higher rank. -**prel'acy** *n.* -**prelat'ical** *a.* [L. *praelatus*, pp. of *praeferre*, put before]

prelim'inary *a.* preparatory, introductory. -*n.* introductory or preparatory statement or action. [F. *préliminaire*, fr. L. *limen*, threshold]

prel'ude *n.* performance, event, *etc.*, serving as an introduction; in music, introductory movement. -*v.i.* and *t.* serve as prelude. [L. *ludere*, play]

premature *a.* happening or done before the proper time. [*mature*]

premeditate *v.t.* think out beforehand. [*meditate*]

premens'trual *a.* of or occurring before a menstrual period. -**pre'menstrual ten'sion** or **syn'drome** *n.* any of various symptoms, including, *esp.*nervous tension, that may be experienced as a result of hormonal changes in the days before a menstrual period starts. [*pre-*, and L. *menstruus*, monthly]

prem'ier *a.* chief, foremost. -*n.* prime minister. -**prem'iership** *n.* [F. =*first*]

première' (-yer) *n.* first performance of a play or film. [F.]

prem'ise (prem'is) *n.* in logic, a proposition from which an inference is drawn. -*pl.* in law, beginning of a deed; house or buildings with its belongings. -**premise'** (-iz) *v.t.* state by way of introduction. -**prem'iss** *n.* (logical) premise. [L. *praemittere, prerni*, send in front]

premium *n.* reward; sum paid for insurance; bonus; excess over nominal value. [L. *praemium*, booty, reward]

preoccupy (-pi) *v.t.* occupy to the exclusion of other things. -**preoccupa'tion** *n.* mental concentration with the appearance of absentmindedness. [*occupy*]

prep *n.* (schoolboy *sl.*) preparation (of lessons). -**prep school,** *contr.* for preparatory school.

prepare' *v.t.* make ready; make. -*v.i.* get ready. -**prepara'tion** *n.* -**prepar'atory** *a.* [L. *praeparare*, make ready before]

prepense' *a.* deliberate, premeditated. [OF. *purpense*]

preponderate *v.i.* be of greater weight, numbers, or power. -**prepond'erance** *n.* [L. *pondus*, weight]

preposition *n.* part of speech; a word marking the relation between two other words. -**preposi'tional** *a.* [L. *praeponere, praeposit-*, put before]

prepossess' *v.t.* impress, *esp.*favorably, beforehand. -**prepossess'ing** *a.* **prepossess'ion** *n.* [*possess*]

preposterous *a.* utterly absurd. [L. *praeposterus*, lit. 'before behind']

prep'py *a.* characteristic of or denoting a fashion style of neat, understated, and often expensive clothes, suggesting that the wearer is well off, upper class, and conservative. -*n.* a person exhibiting such style. [fr. preparatory school]

pre'quel *n.* book, film, play, or other work that is based on another but describes a time that preceded those in the original work, or the characters at an earlier stage.

Pre-Raphaelite *a.* and *n.* (member) of school of artists advocating return to style of Italian art practiced before *Raphael.*

prerogative *n.* peculiar power or right, *esp.* as vested in a sovereign. [L. *praerogative*, right to vote first]

pres'age *n.* omen, indication of something to come. -**presage'** *v.t.* foretell. [L. *praesagium*]

pres'byter (-z-) *n.* elder in a church; priest. -**pres'bytery** *n.* priest's house (in the Roman Catholic Church); eastern part of the chancel; in certain churches, a court composed of ministers and elders. -**presbyte'rian** *a.* -**presbyte'rianism** *n.* [G. *presbyteros*, comp. of *presbys*, old]

pres'cience (pre'-shi-ens) *n.* foreknowledge. -**pres'cient** (pre'-shi-ent) *a.* [L. *pre scientia*, knowledge]

prescribe' *v.t.* and *i.* order, appoint; order

the use of (a medicine). -**prescription** *n.* prescribing; thing prescribed; written statement of it; in law, uninterrupted use as the basis of a right or title; such title. -**prescrip'tive** *a.* [L. *praescribere, praescript-*, write before]

pre'sell *v.t.* to promote (a product, entertainment, *etc.*) with publicity in advance of its appearance; to prepare (the public) for a product, entertainment, *etc.*, with advance publicity; to agree to a sale of (a product) before it is available; to sell (a book) before its publication date. [L. *prae-, pre-*, before, OE. *sellan*, sell]

pres'ent *a.* that is here, now existing or happening. -*n.* present time. -**pres'ently** *adv.* soon. -**pres'ence** *n.* a being present; personal appearance. [L. *praesens*, pres.p. of *prae-esse*, be before]

present' *v.t.* introduce formally; show; point or aim; give, offer. -**pres'ent** *n.* gift. -**present'able** *a.* fit to be seen. -**presenta'tion** *n.* -**present'ment** *n.* [L. *praesentare*, place before]

present'iment (-z-) *n.* foreboding. [L. *praesentire*, feel before]

preserve' (-z-) *v.t.* keep from harm or injury or decay. -*n.* jam; place where game is kept for shooting. -**preserva'tion** *n.* -**preserv'ative** *a.* and *n.* [L. *servare*, protect]

preside' (-z-) *v.i.* be chairman; superintend. -**pres'ident** *n.* head of a society, company, republic. -**pres'idency** *n.* -**presiden'tial** *a.* [L. *præsidere*, fr. *sedere*, sit]

press *v.t.* subject to push or squeeze; urge steadily or earnestly. -*v.i.* bring weight to bear. -*n.* crowd; machine for pressing, *esp.* a printing machine; printing house; its work or art; newspapers collectively; large cupboard. -**press'ing** *a.* urgent. -**pres'sure** *n.* and *v.t.* -**press'urize** *v.t.* apply pressure to; maintain normal atmospheric pressure inside the cabin during high-altitude flying, *etc.* -**press'urized** *a.* [L. *pressare*, frequent, of *premere*]

press *v.t.* force to serve in the navy or army; take for royal or public use. **press'gang** *n.* body of men employed in pressing men for the navy. [earlier *prest* fr. L. *praestare*, furnish]

prestidig'itator (-j-) *n.* conjurer. -**prestidigita'tion** *n.* [F. *prestidigitateur]*

prestige' *n.* reputation, or influence depending on it. [F. = *magic*]

pres'to *adv.* quick; immediately; (*mus.*) quickly. [It.]

presume' (-z-) *v.t.* take for granted. -*v.i.* take liberties. -**presu'mable** *a.* -**presumably** *adv.* -**presump'tion** *n.* -**presump'tive** *a.* that may be assumed as true or valid until the contrary is proved. -**presump'tuous** *a.* forward, taking liberties. -**presump'tuously** *adv.* [L. *praesumere, praesumpt-*, take before]

pretend' *v.t.* feign, make believe. -*v.i.* lay claim, feign. -**pretense'** *n.* -**pretend'er** *n.* -**preten'tion** *n.* -**preten'tious** *a.* making claim to special (and *usu.* unjustified) merit or importance. [L. *praetendere*, hold before, put forward]

pret'erite (-it) *a.* past; expressing past state or action. [L. *praeteritus*, gone by]

preternat'ural (pre-) *a.* out of the ordinary way of nature, extraordinary. [L. *praeter*, beyond]

pre'text *n.* excuse; ostensible motive. [L. *praetexere*, weave in front]

prett'y (prit'-i) *a.* having beauty that is attractive rather than imposing; charming, *etc. adv.* fairly, moderately. -**prett'ily** *adv.* [OE. *praettig*, tricky]

prevail' *v.i.* gain the mastery; be in fashion or generally established. -**prevalence** *n.* -**prev'alent** *a.* [L. *praevalere-valere*, be powerful]

prevar'icate *v.i.* make evasive or misleading statements. -**prevarica'tion** *n.* -**prevar'icator** *n.* [L. *praevaricare*, walk crookedly]

prevent' *v.t.* stop from happening. -**preven'tion** *n.* -**prevent'ive** *a.* and *n.* -**prevent'able** *a.* [L. *praevenire, praevent-*, come before]

pre'vious *a.* preceding; happening before. -**pre'viously** *adv.* [L. *praevius*, fr. *via*, way]

prey *n.* that is hunted and killed by carnivorous animals; victim. -*v.i.* prey upon; treat as prey, afflict. [OF. *preie*, fr. L. *praeda*, booty]

pri'apic *a.* overly concerned with masculinity or virility. [Greek god, *Priapus*, god of procreation]

price *n.* that for which a thing is bought or sold. -*v.t.* fix or ask a price of. -**price'less** *a.* invaluable. [F. *prix*, fr. L. *pretium*, reward, value]

prick *n.* slight hole made by pricking; a pricking or being pricked. -*v.t.* pierce slightly with a sharp point; mark by a prick; erect (the ears). -**pric'kle** *n.* thorn or spike. -*v.i.* feel a tingling or prickling sensation. -**prick'ly** *a.* [OE. *prica*, point]

prick'et *n.* buck in its second year. [*prick*]

pride *n.* too high an opinion of oneself, haughtiness; feeling of elation or great satisfaction; something causing this. *-v. refl.* take pride. [OE. *pryto*]

pride *n.* company (of lions). [*pride*]

priest *n.* official minister of a religion; clergyman. **-priest'ess** *fem.* **-priest'hood** *n.* **-priest'ly** *a.* [OE. *preost*]

prig *n.* self-righteous person who professes superior culture, morality, *etc.* **-prigg'ish** *a.* [orig. uncertain]

prim *a.* very restrained, formally prudish. [orig. uncertain]

pri'ma don'na *n.* leading woman singer in opera; (*fig.*) woman, *usu.* of some standing, who demands special treatment. [It.]

pri'mal *a.* of the earliest age; first, original. **-pri'mal ther'apy** *n.* form of psychotherapy in which patients are encouraged to scream abusively about their parents and agonizingly about their own suffering in infancy. **-pri'mary** *a.* chief, of the first stage, decision, *etc.* **-primarily** *adv.* [L. *primus*, first]

pri'mate *n.* archbishop. **-pri'macy** *n.* **preeminence**; office of archbishop. **-prima'tial** *a.* [*prime*]

pri'mates *n. pl.* first order of mammals, including man and the higher apes. [L. *primus*, first]

prime *a.* first in time, quality, *etc.* **Prime Min'ister,** the leader of a government. *-n.* office for the first canonical hour of the day; first or best part of anything. [L. *primus*, first]

prime *v.t.* fill up, *e.g.*, with information; prepare (a gun, explosive charge, *etc.*), for being let off by laying a trail of powder; prepare canvas for paint with preliminary coating of oil, *etc.* [orig. uncertain]

prim'er *n.* elementary school book. [*prime*]

prime'val *a.* of the earliest age of the world. [L. *primaevus*]

primitive *a.* of an early, undeveloped kind. [L. *primitivus*]

primogeniture *n.* rule by which real estate passes to the firstborn. [L. *primogenitus*, first-born]

primordial *a.* existing at or from the beginning. [L. *primus*, first, *ordo*, order]

prim'rose *n.* plant bearing pale yellow flowers in spring; color of the flowers. *a.* of this color. [altered fr. ME, *primerole*, fr. Med. L. *primula*]

prim'ula *n.* genus of plants, including primrose. [Med. L. fr. L. *primus*, first]

prince *n.* ruler or chief; son of a king or queen. **-prin'cess** *fem.* **-prince'ly** *a.* **-prince'ling** *n.* young prince; petty ruler. [L. *princess, princip-*, first, chief]

principal *a.* chief in importance. *-n.* head of certain institutes, *esp.* schools or colleges, person for whom another is agent or second; sum of money lent and yielding interest; chief actor. **-principal'ity** *n.* territory or dignity of a prince. [L. *principalis*]

principle *n.* fundamental truth or element; moral rule or settled reason of action; uprightness. [L. *principium*]

prink *v.t.* dress ostentatiously; smarten. *-v.i.* strut. [*prank*]

print *v.t.* impress; reproduce (words, pictures, *etc.*), by pressing inked types on blocks to paper, *etc.*, produce in this way; stamp (a fabric) with a colored design. *-n.* impression mark left on a surface by something that has pressed against it; printed cotton fabric, printed lettering; photograph; written imitation of printed type. **-print'er** *n.* one engaged in printing. [OF. *preinte* fr. L. *premere*, press]

pri'or *a.* earlier. *-adv.* prior to, before. *-n.* chief of a religious house or order. **-pri'oress** *fem.* **-prior'ity** *n.* precedence in time or importance. **-prior'itize** *v.t.* arrange (items to be attended to) in order of their relative importance; give priority to or establish as a priority. **-pri'ory** *n.* monastery or nunnery under a prior or prioress. [L. = *superior*, former]

prise. *See* **prize.**

prism *n.* solid whose two ends are similar, equal, of parallel rectilinear figures and whose sides are parallelograms; transparent body of this form usually with triangular ends by which light can be reflected **-prismat'ic** *a.* of prism shape; of color, such as is produced by refraction through a prism, rainbow-like. [G. *prisma*, piece sawn off]

pris'on (-z-) *n.* jail. **-pris'oner** *n.* one kept in prison; one captured in war. [F. fr. *prehendere, prehens-*, seize]

prist'ine *a.* original, primitive, unspoiled. [L. *pristinus*]

prith'ee *interj.* corruption of I pray thee.

pri'vate *a.* not public, reserved for or belonging to or concerning an individual only; of a soldier, not holding any rank. *-n.* private soldier. **-pri'vacy** *n.* **privately** *adv.* **-privateer'** *n.* privately owned armed vessel authorized by a government to take part in a war; captain of such a ship. **-privateer'ing** *n.* use of privateers. **-priva'tion** *n.* act of depriving; want of comforts or necessaries, hardship. **-priv'ative** *a.* denoting privation or nega-

tion. [L. *privatus*, set apart]
priv'et *n.* bushy evergreen shrub used for hedges. [orig. uncertain]
privilege *n.* right or advantage belonging to a person or class; an advantage or favor that only a few obtain. -*v.t.* give an advantage to. [L. *privilegium*, private law, fr. *lex*, law]
priv'y *a.* private, confidential. -*n.* latrine. -**Privy Council,** a body of persons appointed by the sovereign, *esp.* in recognition of great public services. -**priv'ily** *adv.* -**privy seal** *n.* seal used for state documents of lesser importance. [F. *priue*, fr. L. *privatus*, private]
prize *n.* reward for success in competition; thing striven for; thing that is won, *e.g.*, in a lottery, *etc.* -**prize'-fight** *n.* boxing match with money prize. -**prize'-money** *n.* money from the sale of prizes. -**prize'-ring** *n.* arena in which prize fight takes place. -*v.t.* value highly. [OF. *pris*, fr. L. *pretium*]
prize *n.* ship or property captured in naval warfare. -**prize-court** *n.* court dealing with prizes gained at sea. [F. *prise*, capture]
prize, prise *v.t.* force by leverage. [F. *prise*, leverage]
prob'able *a.* likely. -**probabil'ity** *n.* **prob'ably** *adv.* [L. *probabilis-probare*, prove]
pro'bate *n.* a proving of a will; certificate of this. [L. *probare, probat-*, prove]
probation *n.* testing of a candidate before admission to full membership of some body; system of releasing offenders, *esp.* juvenile ones, or first offenders, so that their punishment may be canceled by a period of good behavior. -**proba'tioner** *n.* candidate on trial. [F.]
probe *n.* blunt rod for examining a wound. -*v.t.* explore with a probe; examine into. (L. *probare*, prove]
pro'bity *n.* honesty, uprightness. [L. *probitas-probus*, good]
problems *n.* question or difficulty set for or needing a solution. -**problemat'ic, problematical** *a.* -**problemat'ically** *adv.* [G. *problema*, thing thrown before]
proboscis (-sis) *n.* trunk or long snout, *e.g.*, of an elephant. [G. *proboskis*, 'food instrument']
proceed' *v.i.* go forward; be carried on; go to law. -**proce'dure** *n.* act or manner of proceeding; method of conducting business proceedings; conduct. -**pro'ceeds** *n.pl.* price or profit. -**pro'cess** *n.* state of going on, series of actions or changes; method of operation; action of law; outgrowth. -**proces'sion** *n.* body of persons going along in a fixed or formal order. **processional** *a.* [L. *procedere, process-*, to go forward]
proclaim' *v.t.* announce, make public. **proclama'tion** *n.* [L. *proclamare*]
proclivity *n.* inclination; tendency. [L. *proclivitas*, downward slope]
proconsul *n.* Roman officer discharging consul's duties; governor of province. [L.]
procrastinate *v.i.* put off, delay. -**procrastina'tion** *n.* -**procrast'inator** *n.* [L. *procrastinate*, fr. *cras*, tomorrow]
procreate *v.t.* beget; bring into being. -**procrea'tion** *n.* [L. *procreare*]
proc'tor *n.* university official with disciplinary powers; attorney in an ecclesiastical court. [for *procurator*]
procum'bent *a.* lying face down, prone; (*bot.*) trailing on ground. [L. *procumbere*, fall forward]
procure' *v.t.* obtain; bring about. -**procu'rable** *a.* -**procura'tor** *n.* Roman official in a province; one who manages another's affairs. -**procura'tion** *n.* appointment or hority of a procurator. -**procure'ment** *n.* act or an instance of procuring; act of buying. [L. *procurare*, bring about, get as agent]
prod *v.t.* poke with something pointed. -*n.* a prodding. [orig. uncertain]
prod'igal *a.* wasteful. -*n.* spendthrift. -**prodigal'ity** *n.* -**prod'igally** *adv.* [L. *prodigere*, squander]
prod'igy (-ji) *n.* marvel; person with some marvellous gift. -**prodi'gious** *a.* -**prodi'giously** *adv.* [L. *prodigium*]
produce' *v.t.* bring forward; bring into existence, make; stage, or prepare to stage (a play, *etc.*); extend in length. -**prod'uce** *n.* that which is yielded or made.-**produ'cer** *n.* one who grows or makes produce; one who produces plays, *etc.* -**produ'cer goods,** raw materials, *etc.* used in production. -**prod'uct** *n.* result of a process of manufacture; number resulting from a multiplication. -**produc'tion** *n.* producing; things produced. -**produc'tive** *a.* -**productiv'ity** *n.* [L. *producere, product-*, bring forth]
pro'em *n.* preface, introduction. [G. *pro*, before, *oimé*, song]
profane' *a.* not sacred; blasphemous, irreverent. -*v.t.* pollute, desecrate. **profanation** *n.* -**profan'ity** *n.* profane talk or behavior. [L. *profanus*]
profess' *v.t.* assert; lay claim to; have as one's profession or business; teach as a professor. -**profess'edly** *adv.* avowedly. -

profession *n.* a professing, vow of religious faith, entering a religious order; calling or occupation, *esp.* learned or scientific or artistic. -**profes'sional** *a.* of a profession. -*n.* paid player. -**profess'or** *n.* teacher of the highest rank in a university. -**professo'rial** *adv.* - **professorship** *n.* - **profess'orate** *n.* professorship. - **professor'iate** *n.* body of professors of a university. [L. *profiteri, profess-*, own or acknowledge]

proff'er *v.t.* offer. -*n.* [OF. *poroffrir*]

proficient (ish'-) *a.* skilled. -*n.* one who is skilled. -**profi'ciency** *n.* [L. *proficere*, be useful]

pro'file (-fil) *n.* outline of anything as seen from the side. [It. *proffilo*]

profit *n.* benefit obtained; money gains. -*v.t.* and *i.* benefit. -**profitable** *a.* yielding profit. -**profitless** *a.* [F. fr. L. *profectus*, progress, profit]

prof'ligate *a.* dissolute; reckless; abandoned. -*n.* dissolute man. -**prof'ligacy** *n.* [L. *pro-fligatus*, ruined, fr. *fligare*, strike down]

profound' *a.* deep; very learned. - **profun'dity** *n.* [L. *profundus*]

profuse' *a.* abundant, prodigal. - **profusion** *n.* [L. *profusus*, poured out]

pro'geny *n.* descendants. -**progenitor** *n.* ancestor. [L. *progenies]*

prognath'ous *a.* having projecting jaws. -**progna'thic** *a.* -**prog'nathism** *n.* [G. *pro*, forward, *gnathos*, jaw]

progno'sis *n.* forecast, *esp.* of the course of a disease from observation of its symptoms. -**prognost'ic** *n.* prediction. -*a.* foretelling. -**prognost'icate** *v.t.* foretell. - **prognostica'tion** *n.* [G.]

pro'grams *n.* plan, detailed notes of intended proceedings; broadcast on radio or television; syllabus or curriculum; detailed instructions for computer. -*v.t.* feed program into (computer); arrange detailed instructions for (computer) **pro'grammer** *n.* [G. *programma*, public written notice]

pro'gress *n.* onward movement; development; state journey. -**progress'** *v.i.* go forward —**progres'sion** *n.* -**progress'ive** *a.* [L. *progressus*]

prohib'it *v.t.* forbid. -**prohibi'tion** *n.* forbidding by law of the sale of intoxicants. -**prohibi'tionist** *n.* -**prohib'itive** *a.* tending to forbid. -**prohib'itory** *a.* [L. *prohibere*, prohibit]

proj'ect *n.* plan. -**project'** *v.t.* throw; plan; cause to appear on a distant background. -*v.i.* stick out. -**project'ile** *a.* capable of being thrown. -*n.* heavy missile, *esp.* shell from big gun. -**projec'tion** *n.* -**project'or** *n.* machine which throws pictures on the cinema screen and reproduces sound from the sound-track. [L. *projectum*, thrown forward]

prolegom'enon *n.* preliminary matter, introductory remarks prefixed to book, preface. (-**ena** *n. pl.*) [G.]

prolep'sis *n.* dating an event before its time; (*rhet.*) figure raising and disposing of anticipated objections . -**prolep'tic** *a.* [G. *pro*, before, *lambanein*, take]

proletar'iat, proletar'iats *n.* lowest class of a community, common people. - **proletar'ian** *a.* [L. *proles*, offspring with which Roman proletarius served the state]

prolif'erate *v.i.* and *t.* reproduce by process of budding or cell division; increase in numbers in a similar way. - **prolif'eration** *n.* [L. *proles*, progeny, *ferre*, bear]

prolif'ic *a.* fruitful; producing much, [L. *proles*, offspring, *ferre*, bear]

pro'lix *a.* wordy, long-winded. **prolixity** *n.* [L. *prolixus*, flowing forth]

pro'logue, prolog *n.* preface, *esp.* to a lay. [G. *prologos*, 'fore-speech']

prolong' *v.t.* lengthen out. - **prolonga'tion** *n.* [L. *longus*, long]

promenade' *n.* leisurely walk; lace made or used for this. -*v.i.* take a leisurely walk; go up and down. [F.]

prom'inent *a.* sticking out; distinguished; eminent. -**prom'inence** *n.* [L. *prominere*, jut out]

promis'cuous *a.* mixing without distinction, indiscriminate; having a number of sexual partners without formal attachment. -**promiscu'ity** *n.* [L. *propiscuus*, fr. *miscere*, mix]

prom'ise (-is) *n.* undertaking to do or not do something. -*v.t.* make a promise -*v.i.* make a promise. -**prom'issory** *a.* containing a promise. [L. *promittere, promiss-*, send forth]

prom'ontory *n.* point of high land jutting out into the sea; headland. [Med. *promontoriurn*]

promote' *v.t.* move up to a higher rank or sition; help forward; begin the process of forming or making. -**promo'ter** *n.* - **promo'tion** *n.* [L. *promovere, promot-*, move forward]

prompt *a.* done at once; ready. -*v.t.* and *i.* suggest, help out (an actor or speaker) by reading his next words or suggesting words. -**prompt'er** *n.* -**prompt'itude** *n.* - **prompt'ly** *adv.* -**prompt box** *n.*

prompter's place in the theater. [L. *promptus*, pp. of *promere*, put forth]

prom'ulgate *v.t.* proclaim or publish. -**promulga'tion** *n.* [L. *promulgate*]

prone *a.* lying face or front downward; inclined to. [OF. fr. L. *pronus*]

prong *n.* one spike of a fork or similar instrument. [orig. uncertain]

pro'noun *n.* word used to represent a noun. -**pronom'inal** *a.* [L. *pronomen*]

pronounce' *v.t.* utter formally; form with the organs of speech. -*v.i.* give an opinion or decision. -**pronounce'able** *a.* -**pronounced'** *a.* strongly marked, decided. -**pronounce'ment** *n.* declaration. -**pronuncia'tion** *n.* way a word, *etc.*, is pronounced. [F. *prononcer*, L. *pronuntiare*, proclaim]

pron'to *adv.* quickly, at once. [Sp.]

proof *n.* something which proves; test or demonstration; standard of strength of spirits; trial impression from type or an engraved plate. -*a.* of proved strength; giving impenetrable defense against. -**proof'mark** *n.* mark on a proved, or tested, gun. -**proof'-reader** *n.* reader and corrector of printer's proofs. [F. *preuve*. *See* **prove**]

prop *n.* pole, beam, *etc.*, used as a support. -*v.t.* support, hold up. [Du.]

propaganda *n.* association or scheme for propagating a doctrine; attempt, or material used, to propagate a doctrine. -**propagand'ist** *n.* [L. *propagandus*]

propagate *v.t.* reproduce or breed; spread by sowing, breeding, example, instruction, persuasion, *etc.* -*v.i.* breed or multiply. -**propaga'tion** *n.* [L. *propagare*, propagate, fr. *propago*, slip for transplanting]

propel' *v.t.* cause to move forward. -**propell'er** *n.* revolving shaft with blades for driving a ship or airplane. **propulsion** *n.* [L. *propellers, propuls-*]

propensity *n.* inclination or bent. [L. propensus, leaning forward]

prop'er *a.* own, peculiar, individual; of a noun, denoting an individual person or place; fit, suitable; strict; conforming to etiquette, decorous. -**prop'erly** *adv.* [L. *proprius*, own]

prop'erty *n.* owning; being owned; that is owned; quality or attribute belonging to something; article used on the stage in a play, *etc.* [F. *propriété*]

proph'et *n.* inspired teacher or revealer of the Divine Will; one who foretells future events. -**proph'etess** *fem.* -**proph'ecy** (-si) *n.* prediction or prophetic utterance. -**proph'esy** (-si) *v.i.* utter predictions. -*v.t.* foretell. -**prophet'ic** *a.* -**prophet'ically** *adv.* [G. *prophetes*, fore-speaker]

prophylactic (pro-) *a.* done or used to ward off disease. -*n.* prophylactic medicine or measure. [G. *prophylaktikos*, guarding, before]

propinquity *n.* nearness; affinity. [L. *propinquitas*]

propitiate (-ish-) *v.t.* appease, gain the favor of. -**propitia'tion** *n.* -**propi'tiatory** *a.* -**propi'tious** *a.* favorable. [L. *propitiare, propitiat-*, make favorable]

prop'olis *n.* reddish waxy resin used by bees to repair cells, *etc.* [G. *pro*, before, *polis*, city]

proportion *n.* share; relation; comparison; relative size or number; due relation between connected things or parts. -*v.t.* arrange proportions of. **proportional** *a.* -**propor'tionable** *a.* in due proportion. -**propor'tionally** *adv.* [L. *proportio-portio*, share]

propose' *v.t.* put forward for consideration; present (someone) for office, membership, *etc.*; propose a toast to be drunk. -*v.i.* offer marriage. -**propo'sal** *n.* -**propo'ser** *n.* [L. *proporere, proposit-*]

proposition *n.* statement or assertion; suggestion of terms. [L. *propositio*]

propound' *v.i.* put forward for consideration or solution. (L. *proponere*, to put forward]

proprietor *n.* owner. -**propri'etress** *fem.* -**propri'etary** *a.* holding or held as property. [F. *propriété*]

propriety *n.* fitness; properness; correct conduct. [L. *proprietarius*, fr. *proprietas*, property]

propulsion. *See* **propel.**

pro-ra'ta in proportion (to one's share). -**prorate'** *v.t.* rate thus. [L.]

prorogue' *v.t.* dismiss at the end of a session without dissolution. -**pro'rogate** *v.t.* -**proroga'tion** *n.* [L. *prorogare*, extend term of officer]

prosce'nium *n.* front of the stage. [G. *skene*, stage]

proscribe' *v.t.* outlaw, condemn. -**proscrip'tion** *n.* [L. *proscribere*]

prose *n.* speech or writing not verse. -*v.t.* talk or write prosily. -**prosa'ic** *a.* commonplace. -**pro'sy** *a.* tedious, dull. -**pro'sily** *adv.* -**pro'siness** *n.* [L. *prosus*, straightforward]

prosecute *v.t.* carry on, bring legal proceedings against. -**prosecu'tion** *n.* -**pros'ecutor** *n.* -**pros'ecutrix** *fem.* [L. *prosequi*, fr. *sequi, secut-*, to follow]

pros'elyte *n.* convert. -**proselytize'** *v.t.* [G. *proselytos,* having come]

pros'ody *n.* science of versification. -**pros'odist** *n.* [G. *prosodia-ode,* song]

prosopope'ia *n.* (*rhet.*) figure personifying inanimate objects. [G. *prosopopoiia*]

pros'pect *n.* view; mental view; that is to be expected. -*v.t.* and *i.* explore, *esp.* for gold. -**prospect'ive** *a.* future. -**prospect'ively** *adv.* -**prospect'or** *n.* -**prospect'us** *n.* circular describing a company, school, *etc.* [L. *prospicere, prospect-,* look forward]

pros'per *v.i.* do well. -*v.t.* cause to do well. -**prosper'ity** *n.* good fortune, well-being. -**pros'perous** *a.* flourishing; rich. -**pros'perously** *adv.* [L.]

prostitute *n.* woman who hires herself for sexual intercourse. -*v.t.* make a prostitute of; sell basely, put to an infamous use. -**prostitu'tion** *n.* [L. *prostituere, prostitut-,* offer for sale]

prostrate *a.* lying full length; overcome; exhausted. -*v.t.* throw down; overthrow; exhaust; lay flat; bow (oneself) to the ground. -**prostra'tion** *n.* [L. *pro,* forward, *sternere, strat-,* strew]

protagonist *n.* leading actor in a play; leading figure in a cause, debate, *etc.* [G. *protos,* first, *agonistes,* combatant]

pro'tea *n.* S. African flowering shrub. [*See* **protean**]

pro'tean (ti-an) variable; versatile. [G. *Proteus,* sea-god with power of changing form]

protect' *v.i.* defend or guard. -**protec'tion** *n.* -**protect'ive** *a.* -**protec'tionist** *n.* one who advocates protecting industries by taxing competing imports. -**protector** *n.* one who protects; regent. -**protect'orate** *n.* office or period of a protector of a state; relation of a state to a territory that it protects and controls; such territory. [L. *protegere, protect-,* cover in front]

prot'égé *n.* -**pro'tégée** *fem.* person who is under the care and protection of another. (F.]

pro'tein *n.* kinds of organic compound, which form the most essential part of the food of living creatures. **protein'ic** *a.* [G. *protos,* first]

protest' *v.i.* assert formally; make a declaration against. -**pro'test** *n.* declar. ation of objection. -**Prot'estant** *a.* belonging to any branch of the Western Church outside the Roman communion. -*n.* member of such church. -**Prot'estantism** *n.* -**protesta'tion** *n.* [L. *protestari,* testify]

pro'tocol *n.* draft of terms signed by the parties as the basis of a formal treaty; rules of diplomatic etiquette. [G. *protokollon,* first leaf]

pro'ton *n.* electrically positive nucleus containing same quantity of electricity, but greater mass, than the electron, [G. *proton,* first]

pro'tophyte *n.* lowest order of plants. [G. *protos,* first, *phyton,* plant]

protoplasm *n.* physical basis of all living organisms, a colorless, formless substance resembling albumen. -**protoplas'mic** *a.* [G. *protos,* first, *plasma,* form]

prototype *n.* original type or model. [G. *protos,* first, and *type*]

protozo'a *n.* lowest class of animals. [G. *protos,* first, *zōon,* animal]

protract' *v.t.* lengthen; draw to scale. -**protrac'tion** *n.* -**protract'or** *n.* instrument for setting out angles on paper. [L. *protrahere, protract-,* draw forward]

protrude' *v.i.* and *t.* stick out. -**protru'sion** *n.* [L. *protudere]*

protuberant *a.* bulging out. -**protuberance** *n.* bulge or swelling. [L. *protuberare,* swell]

proud *a.* feeling or displaying pride, that is the cause of pride; stately. -**proud'ly** *adv.* [OE. *prud*]

prove *v.t.* demonstrate, test; establish the validity of (a will, *etc.*). -*v.i.* turn out (to be, *etc.*). [F. *prouver,* fr. L. *probare*]

provender *n.* fodder; food. [OF. *provendre*]

prov'erb *n.* short pithy saying in common use, *esp.* one with a moral. **proverb'ial** *a.* [L. *proverbium*]

provide' *v.i.* make preparation. -*v.t.* supply or equip, get in what will be required. -**provi'ded** (that) *conj.* on condition that. -**prov'ident** *a.* thrifty; showing foresight. -**prov'idence** *n.* foresight, economy; kindly care of God or nature. -**providen'tial** *a.* strikingly fortunate. -**providen'tially** *adv.* -**provi'sion** *n.* a providing; thing provided. -*pl.* food. -*v.t.* supply with food. -**provi'sional** *a.* temporary. -**provi'so** *n.* condition. [L. *providere, provis-,* foresee]

prov'ince *n.* division of a country; a sphere of action. -*pl.* any part of the country outside the capital. -**provin'cial** *n.* one belonging to a province. -*a.* narrow, lacking in polish. -**provin'cialism** *n.* [L. *provincia*]

provoke' *v.t.* bring about, irritate. -**provocation** *n.* -**provoc'ative** *a.* [L. *provocare,* call forth]

provolone' *n.* hard, light-colored Italian

cheese made of cow's milk.

prov'ost *n.* head of certain colleges, or administrative assistant to the president. -**provost-marshal** (prove) head of a body of military police. [OF. fr. Late L. *propositus*, placed before]

prow *n.* bow of a ship. [F. *proue*]

prow'ess *n.* bravery, fighting capacity. [F. *prouesse*, gallantry]

prowl *v.i.* roam stealthily, *esp.* in search of prey, *etc.* [ME. *prollen*]

prox'imate *a.* nearest, next, immediate. -**proxim'ity** *n.* -**prox'imo** *adv.* in the next month. [L. *proximus*, nearest]

prox'y *n.* authorized agent or substitute; writing authorizing a substitute. [fr. *procuracy. See* **procure**]

prude *n.* woman who affects excessive propriety with regard to relations of the sexes. -**pru'dish** *a.* -**pru'dery** *n.* [F.]

pru'dent *a.* careful, discreet, exercising forethought. -**pru'dence** *n.* -**pruden'- tial** *a.* [L. *prudens, prudent-*, far-seeing]

prune *n.* dried plum. [F.]

prune *v.t.* cut out dead parts, excessive branches, *etc.* [OF. *prooignier*]

pru'rient *a.* given to or springing from lewd thoughts. -**pru'rience** *n.* [L. *pruriens*, p.p. of *prurire*, itch]

prus'sian *a.* of Prussia. -**Prussian blue**, blue pigment. -**pruss'ic acid** *n.* hydrocyanic acid, a poison, originally got from Prussian blue. [*Prussia*]

pry *v.i.* look curiously; make furtive or inquisitive enquiries. [ME. *prien*]

psalm *n.* sacred song. -**psalm'ist** *n.* writer of psalms. -**psalm'ody** *n.* art or practice of singing sacred music. -**psal'ter** *n.* book of psalms; copy of the psalms as a separate book. -**psal'tery** *n.* obsolete stringed instrument. [G. *psalmos*, twanging of strings]

pseudo- *prefix*, sham. -**pseu'donym** *n.* false name. -**pseudon'ymous** *a.* -**pseudoesthe'sia** *n.* imaginary feeling. -**pseudoblep'sis** *n.* illusory vision. -**pseudomor'phous** *a.* of deceptive form. [G. *pseudes*, false]

psittaco'sis (sit-) *n.* parrot disease communicable to man. [G. *psittakos*, parrot]

psy'chic (si'kik) *a.* of the soul or mind; that appears to be outside the region of physical law. -**psychi'atrist** *n.* one who treats mental diseases. -**psy'chical** *a.* psychic. -**psy'cho-anal'ysis** *n.* theory that the mind can be divided into conscious and unconscious elements; medical practice based on this. -**psy'choan'alyst** *n.* -**psychol'ogy** *n.* study of the mind. -**psycholo'gical** *a.* -**psychol'ogist** *n.* -**psychosomat'ic** *a. pert.* to mind and body as one unit, of physical disease having emotion as origin. -**psy'chother'apy** *n.* treatment of disease by mental influence. [G. *psyche*, breath, soul]

psycho'babble *n.* jargon of pscyhotherapy, pschology, or psychiatry, employed in speech or writing, *esp.* in a superficial or inaccurate way.

ptarmigan (t-) *n.* grouse whose plumage turns white in winter. [Gael. *tarmachan*]

ptero- (ter-) *prefix.* winged. (G. *pteron*, wing] **pterocar'pous** *a.* having winged seeds. -**pterodac'tyl** *n.* prehistoric large flying reptile with bat-like wings. -**pter'omys** *n.* kinds of flying squirrel. -**pter'ope** *n.* flying-fox, fruit-bat.

pto'maine (t-) *n.* poisonous alkaloid found in putrefying animal or vegetable matter. [G. *ptoma*, dead body]

pto'sis *n.* droop of upper eyelid, due to disease. [G.]

pu'berty *n.* sexual maturity. -**pubescent** *a.* -**pu'bic** *a.* [L. *pubertas*]

pub'lic *a.* of or concerning the public as a whole; not private; open to general observation or knowledge. -*n.* community or its members. -**publica'tion** *n.* -**pub'licist** *n.* writer on public concerns. -**publi'city** *n.* being generally known; notoriety. -**pub'licly** *adv.* [L. *publicus*, fr. *populus*, people]

pub'lish *v.t.* make generally known; prepare and issue for sale (books, music, *etc.*). -**pub'lisher** *n.* [*public*]

puce *n.* flea color, purplish brown. -*a.* of this color. [F. =*flea*]

puck' *n.* mischievous fairy. [OE. *puca*]

puc'ker *v.t.* and *i.* gather into wrinkles. -*n.* wrinkle. [fr. *poke*, bag]

pud'ding (pood-) *n.* form of cooked food usually in a soft mass. [F. *boudin*, black pudding]

pud'dle *n.* small muddy pool; rough cement for lining ponds, *etc.* -*v.t.* line with puddle; produce wrought iron. [OE. *pudd*, ditch]

pu'erile *a.* childish. [L. *puer*, boy]

puer'peral *a.* of, caused by childbirth. **puerper'ium** *n.* state of a woman during and immediately after childbirth. [L. *puer*, child, *parere*, bear]

puff *n.* short blast of breath of wind, *etc.*; its sound; piece of pastry; laudatory notice, piece of advertisement. -*v.i.* blow abruptly; breathe hard. -*v.t.* send out in a puff, blow up; advertise; smoke hard. -**puff'y** *a.* -**puff add'er** *n.* poisonous African snake. -**puff ball** *n.* spherical dried fungus filled with dust. [imit. orig.]

puff'in *n.* sea bird with a large parrot-like beak. [ME. *pofin*]

pug *n.* small snub-nosed dog. -**pug'-nose** *n.* snub nose. [orig. uncertain]

pugg'aree *n.* scarf round hat to keep the sun off. [Hind. *pagri*, turban]

pu'gilist *n.* boxer. -**pu'gilism** *n.* **pugilist'ic** *a.* [L. *pugil*, boxer]

pugna'cious *a.* given to fighting. **pugna'city** *n.* (L. *pugnax, pugnac-*,]

puis'ne *a.* young, inferior in rank; later. -*n.* junior judge. [OF.]

puke *v.t.* vomit. -*n.* [orig. unknown]

pukk'a *a.* genuine, sound. [Hind. *pakka*, ripe]

pulchritude *n.* beauty. [L. *pulchritude*]

pule *v.i.* fret, complain whiningly. [imit.]

pull (pool) *v.t.* pluck or tug at; draw or haul; propel by rowing. -*n.* an act of pulling; force exerted by it; draught of liquor. [OE. *pullian*, snatch]

pull'et (pool-) *n.* young hen. [F. *poulette*, dim. of *poule*, hen]

pull'ey (poo-) *n.* wheel with a groove in the rim for a cord, used to raise weights by a downward pull. [F. *poulie*]

Pull'man car *n.* railway sleeping car. [*designer*]

pul'monalry *a.* of, or affecting the lungs. [L. *pulmo*, lung]

pulp *n.* soft moist vegetable or animal matter. -*v.t.* reduce to Pulp. -**Pul'py** *a.* -**pulpiness** *n.* [L. *pulpa]*

pul'pit (poo-) *n.* erection or platform for a preacher. (L. *pulpitum*, a stage]

pulse *n.* throbbing of the arteries, *esp.* in the wrist; vibration. -**pulsate'** *v.i.* throb, quiver. -**pulsa'tion** *n.* [L. *pulsus*]

pulse *n.* edible seeds of such plants as beans, lentils, *etc.* [L. *puls*]

pulverize *v.t.* reduce to powder. -**pulveriza'tion** *n.* [L. *pulvis, pulver-*, powder]

pu'ma *n.* large American carnivorous animal of the cat family. [*Peruv.*]

pum'ice (-is) *n.* light porous variety of lava. [L. *pumex*]

pumm'el *v.t.* pommel, *q.v.*

pump *n.* appliance in which the piston and handle are used for raising water, or putting in or taking out air or liquid, *etc.* -*v.t.* raise, put in, take out, *etc.*, with a pump. -*v.i.* work a pump. [orig. uncertain]

pump *n.* light shoe. [Du. *pampoesje*]

pump'kin *n.* large gourd used as food. [OF. *pompon*]

pun *n.* play on words. -*v.i.* make one. -**pun'ster** *n.* [orig. uncertain]

punch *n.* tool for perforating or stamping; blow with the fist; (*sl.*) energy, drive. -*v.t.* stamp or perforate with a punch; strike with the fist; drive (of cattle). [F. *poincon*, awl, fr. *pungere*, pierce]

punch *n.* drink made of spirit, or wine with water or milk, lemon, spice, *etc.* -**punch bowl** *n.* [Hindu *panch*, five (ingredients)]

Punch, *dim.* of **Punchinell'o** *n.* puppet hero of Punch and Judy show. [It. *Pulcinella*]

punch'eon (-shun) *n.* cask; liquid measure (72, 84 or 120 gal.). [OF. *poincon*]

punctilio *n.* minute detail of conduct; mere form. -**punctil'ious** *a.* making much of punctilios. [Sp. *puntillo*]

punc'tual *a.* in good time, not late. -**punctual'ity** *n.* -**punc'tually** *adv.* [L. *punctus*, point]

punctuate *v.t.* to put in punctuation marks. -**punctua'tion** *n.* putting in marks, *e.g.*, commas, colons, *etc.*, in writing or printing to assist in making the sense clear. [L. *punctus*, point]

punc'ture *n.* an act of pricking; a hole made by pricking. -*v.t.* to prick a hole in. [L. *punctura*]

pun'dit *n.* one learned in Hindu philosophy; any learned person. [Hind. *pandit*]

pungent *a.* biting; irritant. -**pun'gency** *n.* -**pun'gently** *adv.* [L. *pungens, pungent-*, fr. *pungere*, prick]

Pu'nic *a.* pert. to Carthaginians; faithless, treacherous, disloyal. [L. *Punicus*]

pun'ish *v.t.* cause to suffer for an offense, inflict a penalty on. -(*sl.*) treat roughly. -**pun'ishable** *a.* -**pun'ishment** *n.* -**pu'nitive** *a.* inflicting or intending to inflict punishment. [L. *punire*]

punk *a.* crumbling, decayed; worthless. -*n.* young, inexperienced person; petty gangster; style of rock music characterized by a savage rejection of convention; one who follows such a style. [orig. uncertain]

punn'et *n.* small chip-basket for fruit. [orig. uncertain]

punt *n.* flat-bottomed, square-ended boat, propelled by pushing with a pole. -*v.t.* propel with a pole. [L. *ponto*]

punt' *v.i.* (*sl.*) back horses. -**puntéer** *n.*, habitual gambler. [F. *ponter*]

pu'ny *a.* small and feeble. [OF. *puisne*, fr.

L. *post natus*, younger]

pup *See* **puppy.**

pu'pa *n.* **pu'pae** *pl.* chrysalis. [L. = *doll*]

pu'pil *n.* person being taught; opening in the middle of the eye. **-pu'pillary** *a.* [L. *pupillus*, child]

pupp'et *n.* figure of a human being often with jointed limbs controlled by wire, a marionette. **-pupp'et-show** *n.* show with puppets, worked by a hidden showman. [OF. *poupette*, doll]

pupp'y *n.* young dog; conceited young man. **-pup** *n.* puppy. [F. *poupée*, doll]

pur'blind *n.* dim sighted. [orig. uncertain]

pur'chase *v.t.* buy. *-n.* buying; what is bought; leverage, grip, good position for applying force. [F. *pourchasser*, to obtain by pursuit]

pur'dah *n.* (India and Pakistan) curtain screening women's quarters; mark of caste. [Urdu and Pers. *pardah*]

pure *a.* unmixed, untainted; simple; spotless; faultless; innocent. **-pure'ly** *adv.* **pu'rify** *v.t.* and *i.* **-purifica'tion** *n* **purifica'tory** *a.* **-pu'rism** *n.* excessive insistence on correctness of language. - **pu'rist** *n.* **-pu'rity** *n.* state of being pure. **-Pu'ritan** *n.* member of the extreme Protestant party, who desired further *purification* of the church after the Elizabethan reformation; person of extreme strictness in morals or religion. - **puritan'ical** *a.* [L. *purus*, clean, pure]

purée' *n.* fruit, vegetables, boiled to a pulp and sieved or blended. [F.]

purge *v.t.* make clean, clear out. *-n.* aperient. **-purga'tion** *n.* **-purg'ative** *a.* and *n.* **-purg'atory** *n.* place for spiritual purging; state of pain or distress. **-purgator'ial** *a.* [L. *purgare*]

purl *n.* edging of gold or silver wire or of small loops; stitch that forms a rib in knitting. *-v.t.* ornament with purls. *-v.i.* knit in purl. [It. *pirlare*, twirl]

purl *v.i.* flow with a burbling sound, as a shallow brook. [imit. orig.]

pur'lieu *n.* formerly tract of land on the edge of a royal forest; ground bordering on something, outskirts (*usu. pl.*) [OF. *pourallee*, survey]

purloin *v.t.* steal. [OF. *porloignier*, remove, fr. *loin*, far]

pur'ple *n.* color between crimson and violet. *a.* of this color. *-v.t.* make purple. [G. *Porphyra*, shell-fish that gave Tyrian purple]

purport' *v.t.* mean; be intended to seem. **-pur'port** *n.* meaning, apparent meaning. [OF. *porporter*, embody]

pur'pose (-pos) *n.* intention, design, aim. *-v.t.* intend. **-pur'posely** *adv.* [OF. *porpos*, fr. *porposer*, propose]

purr *n.* noise a cat makes when pleased. *-v.i.* make this sound. [imit.]

purse *n.* small bag for money. *-v.t.* contract in wrinkles. *-v.i.* become wrinkled and drawn in. **-pur'ser** *n.* officer who keeps accounts, *etc.*, on a ship. [G. *pyrsa*, hide, leather]

purs'lane *n.* salad plant. [F. *porcelaine*]

pursue' *v.t.* run after; aim at; engage in. *-v.i.* go in pursuit; continue. **pursu'ance** *n.* carrying out. **-pursu'ant** *adv.* accordingly. **-pursu'er** *n.* **-pursuit'** *n.* running after, attempt to catch; occupation. [F. *poursuivre*, fr. L. *prosequi*, follow]

pur'suivant *n.* officer of the College of Arms ranking below a herald. [OF. *poursivant*]

purs'y *a.* short-winded, fat. [OF. *polsif*, fr. L. *pulsate*, blow or pant]

pur'ulent. *See* **pus.**

purvey' *v.t.* to supply. **-purvey'or** *n.* [F. *pourvoir*, fr. L. *providere*, to provide]

pur'view *n.* scope or range. [AF. *purveu est*, it is provided (words used to introduce new enactment in a law)]

pus *n.* matter formed or discharged in a sore or inflammation. **-pu'rulent** *a.* forming pus. **-pu'rulence** *n.* [L.]

push (poosh) *v.t.* move or try to move away by pressure. *-v.i.* make one's way. *-n.* an act of pushing; persevering self assertion. **-push'ful** *a.* given to pushing oneself. [F. *pousser*]

pusillanimous *a.* cowardly. **pusillanim'ity** *n.* [fr. L. *pusillus*, very small, and *animus*, spirit]

puss (poos) *n.* cat; hare. **-puss'y** *n.* [orig. name to call a cat]

pus'tule *n.* small pimple containing pus. [L. *pustula*]

put (poot) *v.t.* place or set; express; **put on,** don (clothes); assume (airs) **-put out,** annoy; disconcert; eject. **-put-up** *a.* concocted. **-put up with,** tolerate. [Late OE. *putian*]

pu'tative *a.* supposed, reputed. **putatively** *adv.* [L. *putare*, think]

putsch' *n.* sudden sharp revolt. [Ger.]

pu'trid *a.* rotten. **-pu'trefy** *v.t.* and *i.* make or become rotten. **-putrefac'tion** *n.* - **putres'cent** *a.* becoming rotten. - **putres'cence** *n.* **-putrid'ity** *n.* [L. *putrid us*]

putt (put) *v.t.* throw (a weight or shot) from

the shoulder; strike (a gold ball) along the ground in the direction of the hole. -**putt′er** *n.* golf club for putting. [var. of *put*]

puttee′ *n.* strip of cloth wound round the leg like a bandage, serving as a gaiter. [Hind. *patti,* bandage]

putt′er *v.i.* work or act in a feeble, unsystematic way. [OE. *potian,* poker]

putt′y *n.* paste of whiting and oil used by glaziers; polishing powder of calcined tin used by jewelers. -*v.t.* fix or fill with putty. [F. *potée*]

puz′zle *n.* bewildering or perplexing question, problem, or toy. -*v.t.* perplex. -*v.i.* think in perplexity. [fr. ME. *opposal,* question, interrogation]

pye′-dog *n.* pariah dog. [Hind. *pahi,* outsider; and *dog*]

pyg′my, pig′my *n.* dwarfed. dwarf. [G. *pygmaios,* fr. *pygme,* measure of length, 13½ inches]

pyja′mas. *See* **pajamas.**

py′lon *n.* gateway to Egyptian temple; steel erection to mark out an airfield or carry power cables, *etc.* [G. = *gateway*]

pyorrhoe′a *n.* infection of the gums. [G. *pyon,* pus]

pyr′amid *n.* solid figure with sloping sides meeting at an apex; solid structure of this shape, *esp.* the ancient Egyptian monuments (*usu.* with a square base); group of persons or things highest in the middle. -**pyram′idal** *a.* [G. *pyramis, pyramid-,*]

pyre *n.* pile of wood for burning a dead body. -**pyrol′ogy** *n.* science of heat. [G. *pyr,* fire]

pyreth′rum *n.* kinds of garden plant including golden feather (feverfew). [L.]

Py′rex *n.* glassware resistant to heat. [Trademark]

pyri′tes *n.* term for sulfides of various metals (*e.g.,* iron) in gold-colored crystals. [L.]

pyromania *n.* uncontrollable impulse and practice of setting things on fire. **pyroman′iac** *n.* [G. *pyr,* fire, and *mania*]

pyrotechnics (-k-) *n.* art of making or using fireworks; firework display. [G. *pyr* and *technikos,* skilled]

pyrrhic *n.* in verse, foot of 2 short syllables. —**pyrr′hic vic′tory** *n.* one achieved at high cost. [G.]

Pythagore′an *a.* of, pert. to *Pythagores* or his doctrine of transmigration of souls.

Pyth′ian *a.* pert. to (oracle at) Delphi. The Pythian Appollo. [G. *Putho,* Delphi]

py′thon (-th-) *n.* large nonpoisonous snake that crushes its prey. -**py′thoness** *n.* Apollo's priestess at Delphi; witch. [G. *Python,* name of a serpent killed by Apollo]

pyx (piks) *n.* vessel in which the Host is reserved; box in which specimen coins are placed to be tested at the Mint. [G. *pyxis,* box]

Q

qua (qua) *conj.* as, in capacity of [L.]

quack *n.* harsh cry of the duck; pretender to medical or other skill. -*v.i.* of a duck, to utter its cry. [imit.]

quadr-, *prefix.* four. [L. *quattuor*]. -**Quadrages′ima** (Sunday) *n.* first Sunday in Lent, 40 days of fast preceding Easter. **Quadrages′imal** *a.* -**quad′rangle** *n.* four-sided figure; four sided court in a building. *contr.* quad. -**quadrang′ular** *a.* -**quad′rant** *n.* quarter of a circle; instrument for taking angular measurements. -**quadrate′** *v.t.* make square. -**quad′rate** *a.* square. -**quadrat′ic** *a.* of an equation, involving the square of an unknown quantity. -**quadrem′tial** *a.* lasting, happening every four years. **quadri′ga** *n.* four-horsed chariot. -**quadrilat′eral** *a.* four-sided. -*n.* four-sided figure. -**quadrille′** *n.* square dance. **quadroon′** *n.* offspring of mulatto and white; quarter-blooded person. -**quad′ruped** *n.* four-footed animal. -**quad′ruple** *a.* fourfold. -*v.t.* and *i.* make or become four times as much. -**quad′ruplet** *n.* one of four children born at same time. -**quadru′plicate** *v.t.* increase by four times, make four copies.

quae′stor *n.* Ancient Roman magistrate. [L.]

quaff *v.i.* drink deeply. -*v.t.* drink, drain. [orig. uncertain]

quag, quag′mire *n.* marshy tract with quaking surface. [*quake*]

quail *n.* small bird of the partridge family. [OF. *quaille*]

quail *v.i.* flinch. [F. *cailler,* curdle]

quaint *a.* interestingly old-fashioned or odd. -**quaint′ly** *adv.* [OF. *cointe*]

quake *v.i.* shake or tremble (from fear, apprehension). -**Qua′ker** *n.* member of the Society of Friends, a Christian religious sect. -**Qua′keress** *fem.* - **qua′ky** *a.* [OE. *cwacian*]

qual′ify (kwol′-) *v.t.* ascribe a quality to, describe; make competent; moderate. -*v.i.* make oneself competent, *esp.* by passing an examination. -**qualific′ation** *n.* qualifying, thing that qualifies. -**qual′ity** *n.* attribute, characteristic, property; degree of excellence; rank. -**qual'itative** *a.* relating to quality. [L. *qualis*, of what kind]

qualm (kwam) *n.* sudden feeling of sickness; misgiving; scruple. [Du.]

quandary state of perplexity, puzzling situation. [orig. uncertain]

quan'tity (kwon'-) *n.* size, number, amount; specified or considerable amount. **quan'titative** *a.* -**quan'tum** *n.* desired or required amount. **quan'tum the'ory** *n.* theory that in radiation, energy of electrons is discharged not continuously but in discrete units or quanta. -**quan'tum leap** *n.* sudden highly significant advance, breakthrough.[L. *quantus*, how much]

quan'tum. *See* **quantity.**

quarantine *n.* isolation to prevent infection. -*v.t.* put in quarantine. [L. *quadriginta*, forty (ref to days of isolation)]

quark *n.* in physics, any of several hypothetical particles thought to be fundamental units of matter. [word coined by Murray Gell-Mann, physicist]

quarr'el (kwor'-) *n.* angry dispute; breakup of friendship. -*v.i.* fall out with; find fault with. -**quarr'elsome** -*a.*[F. *querelle* fr. L. *queri*, complain]

quarr'el *n.* crossbow arrow; diamond-shaped pane of glass. [L. *quadrus*, squarer]

quarr'y *n.* object of a hunt. [F. *curée*]

quarr'y *n.* place where stone is got from the ground for building, *etc.* -*v.t.* and *i.* get from a quarry. [L. *quadrare*, square (stones)]

quart (kwort) *n.* quarter of a gallon, or two pints. [*quarter*]

quar'tan *a.* and *n.* (fever, *etc.*) occurring every third or fourth day. [L. *quartos*, fourth]

quar'ter *n.* fourth part; region, district; mercy. -*pl.* lodgings. -*v.t.* divide into quarters. -**quart'erdeck** *n.* part of upper deck used by officers. -**quart'erday** *n.* any or four days in the year when certain payments become due. -**quart'ermaster** *n.* officer responsible for stores; in navy, petty officer with particular responsibility for navigational duties. -**quart'erstaff** *n.* long staff for fighting. -**quart'erly** *a.* happening, due, *etc.*, each quarter of the year *n.* quarterly periodical. -**quartet'** *n.* music for four performers; group of four musicians. -**quart'o** *n.* size of book in which each sheet is folded into four leaves. *a.* of this size. [L. *quartus*, fourth]

quaternary *a.* of the number four, having four parts; (*geology*) of most recent period after Tertiary. -**quater'nion** *n.* number four, set of four. [L.]

quartz (kworts) *n.* stone of silica, often containing gold. [Ger. *quarz*]

quasar *n.* extremely distant starlike object emitting powerful radio waves. [Fr. *quasi*, stellar]

quash (kwosh) *v.t.* annul, *esp.* by legal procedure. [F. *casser*, break]

qua'si *conj.* and *adv.* almost; in a sense; in appearance. [L. *quam si*, as if]

qua'ssia (-a-shi-a) *n.* S. American tree; its bark with tonic properties; drug obtained from this. [*Quassi*, discoverer]

quat'rain *n.* four-lined stanza, with alternate rhymes. [F.]

qua'ver *v.i.* tremble, shake, say or sing in quavering tones. -*n.* trill; musical note half the length of a crotchet. [orig. uncertain]

quay (kc) *n.* fixed landing stage for shipping. [F. *quai*]

quean *n.* hussy; girl. [OE. *cwene*, woman]

queas'y *a.* inclined to, or causing, sickness. [orig. uncertain]

queen *n.* wife of a king; female sovereign; piece of the game of chess; perfect female bee, wasp, *etc.*; court card. -**queen'ly** *a.* [OE. *cwen*]

queer *a.* odd, strange. -**queer'ly** *adv.* [Ger. quer, athwart, across]

quell *v.t.* crush, put down, suppress; allay. [OE. *cwellan*, kill]

quench *v.t.* extinguish, put out; slake. [OE. *cwencan*, quench]

quenelle' *n.* forcemeat ball. [F.]

quern *n.* handmill for grain, *etc.* [OE. *cweorn*]

querulous *a.* full of complaints, bad-tempered. [L. *queri*, complain]

que'ry *n.* question; mark of interrogation. -*v.t.* question, ask; mark with a query. [L. *quaere*, seek]

quest *n.* search. -*v.i.* search. [L. *qusit-*, to seek]

ques'tion (-chn) *n.* sentence seeking for an answer; problem; debate, strife. -*v.t.* ask questions of, interrogate; dispute. **ques'tionable** *a.* doubtful, *esp.* -**question' master** *n.* chairman of a quiz game. [F.]

quet'zal *n.* Cent. American bird of gorgeous plumage. [Aztec, *quelzalli*]

queue *n.* plait of hair; in Britain, line of waiting persons, vehicles, *etc.* -*v.i.* wait thus. [F. = *tail*]

quib'ble *n.* play on words; evasion, merely verbal point in argument. -*v.i.* evade a point by a quibble. **quibb'ler** *n.* [dim. of obs. *quib*]

quick *a.* rapid, swift, keen, brisk; living.

-*n.* sensitive flesh. -*adv*, . rapidly. -**quick'ly** *adv.* -**quick'en** *v.t.* give life to; make speedier, stir up. -*v.t.*, *i.* become living; become faster. -**quick'lime** *n.* unslaked lime. -**quick'sand** *n.* loose wet sand which swallows up animals, ships, *etc.* -**quick'set** *a.* of a hedge, made of living plants. -**quick'silver** *n.* mercury. -**quick'step** *n.* foxtrot in quick time; quick march, music for it. [OE. *cwic*, living]

quid *n.* lump of tobacco for chewing; *(sl.)* a pound sterling. [var. of *cud*]

quidd'ity *n.* thing's true nature or character; quibble. [L. *quid*, whet]

quid'nunc *n.* curious person, one who pretends to know everything. [L. = *what now*]

qui'et *a.* undisturbed; with little or no motion or noise. -*n.* state of peacefulness, absence of noise or disturbance. -*v.t.* and *i.* make or become quiet. -**qui'etly** *adv.* -**quies'cent** *a.* at rest. -**quies'cence** *n.* -**qui'etude** *n.* -**qui'etism** *n.* passive attitude to life, *esp.* as a matter of religion. -**qui'estist** *n.* -**quie'tus** *n.* death; being got rid of; formerly, a receipt for a bill. [L. *quies*, quiet-, n. quiet]

quiff *n.* plastered-down curl on forehead formerly much affected by soldiers. [orig. unknown]

quill *n.* hollow stem of a large feather; spine of a porcupine; pen, fishing-float, *etc.*, made of a feather-quill. -**quill'ing** *n.* decorative craft-work in which a material such as glass, fabric, or paper is formed into small bands or rolls that form the basis of a design. [orig. uncertain]

quill'et *n.* verbal nicety, quibble. [orig. uncertain]

quilt *n.* padded coverlet. -*v.t.* stitch (two pieces of cloth) with padding between. [L. *culcita*, cushion]

qui'nary *a.* of number five, composed of five parts. [L. *quinque*, five]

quince *n.* acid pear-shaped fruit; tree bearing it. [F. *coing*]

quinine' *n.* bitter drug made from the bark of a tree and used to cure fever, *etc.* [Peruv. *kina*, bark]

Quinquages'ima *n.* Sunday 50 days before Easter, Sunday preceding Lent, *a.* fiftieth. [L. *quinquaginta*, fifty]

quinquenn'ial *a.* lasting five years, occurring every five years. [L. *quinque*, five]

quin'quereme *n.* galley with five banks of oars. [L. *quinque*, five]

quin'sy (-zi) *n.* inflammation of the throat or tonsils. [OF. *quinansie*, fr. G. *kynangche*, 'dog-throttling']

quintain' *n.* post for tilting practice. [OF. *quintaine*]

quintes'sence *n.* purest form or essential feature. -**quintessen'tial** *a.* [Med. L. *quinta essentia*, substance of the heavenly bodies; (outside the 'four elements')]

quintet', quintette' *n.* musical piece for five singers, players; the singers, players. [It. *quintetto*]

quintuple *a.* multiplied by five, greater by five times, composed of five parts. [L. *quintus*, fifth]

quip *n.* smart saying, epigram. [L. *quippe*, forsooth (ironical)]

qui'pu *n.* 'language' of colored knotted cords of the ancient Incas. [Peruv.]

quire *n.* twenty-four sheets of writing paper. [F. *cahier*]

quirk *n.* fanciful turn; quibble; evasion. -**quirk'y** *a.* full of twists; peculiar. (orig. unknown]

quis'ling *n.* collaborator; traitor to his own (occupied) country. [V. *Quisling*, Norwegian traitor]

quit *a.* free, rid. -*v.t.* leave, go away on equal or even terms by repayment, *etc.* **quitt'ance** *n.* receipt, discharge. **quitt'er** *n.* shirker; deserter. -**quit' claim** *v.t.* relinquish or give up a claim to a right or property. -**quit'rent** *n.* rent reserved in grants of land, by payment of which tenant is quit of all other service. -**quits** *a.* being on even terms by repayment. [L. *quietus*, discharge]

quite *a.* wholly, completely. [*quit*]

quiv'er *n.* a carrying-case for arrows. [OF. *cuivre*, ult. of Teut. orig.]

quiv'er *v.i.* shake or tremble. -*n.* an act of quivering. [*quaver*]

quixot'ic *a.* showing enthusiasm for visionary ideals, generous, helpful, against one's own interests. [Don *Quixote*, hero of novel of Cervantes (d. 1616)]

quiz *v.t.* make fun of, look at curiously or critically. -*n.* entertainment in which general or specific knowledge of players is tested by questions; examination, interrogation. -**quizz'ical** *a.* questioning; mocking. [orig. uncertain]

quoin *n.* external corner-stone of wall or wedge-shaped piece of metal, *etc.*, building. -**quoin post** *n.* the vertical post at the side of a lock gate, about which the gate swings. [*conj*]

quoit (k-) *n.* ring for throwing at a mark as a game. [orig. uncertain]

quon'dam *a.* former, formerly. [L.]

quor'um *n.* number that must be present

in a meeting to make its transactions valid. [L. = *of whom*]

quo'ta *n.* share to be contributed or received. [L. *quot*, how many]

quote *v.t.* copy or repeat passages from; refer to, *esp.* to confirm a view; state a price for. **-quota'tion** *n.* **-quota'tion mark** *n.* marks of punctuation ("-") indicating the beginning and end of quotation. **-quo'table** *a.* **-quo'tably** *adv.* [Med. L. *quotare*, distinguish by numbers]

quoth *v.t.* said. [past tense of ME. *quethen*, OE. *cwethan*]

quotidian *a.* daily; everyday, commonplace. [L. *quotidie*, every day]

quo'tient (-shent) *n.* number resulting from dividing one number by another. [L. *quotiens*, how many times]

R

rabb'et *n.* groove cut in edge of plank allowing another to fit into it. *-v.t.* cut rabbet in. [OF. *rabat*, abatement]

rabb'i *n.* Jewish teacher, doctor of law; pastor of congregation. **-rabbin'ic, rabbinical** *a.* **-rabbin'ics** *n.* the study of rabbinic literature of the post-Talmudic period]

rabb'it *n.* small rodent animal which resembles the hare. *-v.i.* hunt rabbits. [orig. uncertain]

rab'ble *n.* crowd of vulgar, noisy people; mob. [orig. unknown]

rab'id *a.* raging; mad. **-rab'idly** *adv.* **rab'idness** *n.* **-ra'bies** *n.* canine madness. [L. *rabere*, to be mad]

rac(c)oon' *n.* climbing American animal of the bear family; its fur. [Algonkin]

race *n.* descendants of a common ancestor; one of the distinct varieties of the human species; peculiar breed, as of horses, *etc.* **-ra'cial** *a.* of race or lineage. **-rac'ialism, rac'ism** *n.* belief in innate superiority of particular race, antagonism towards members of different race based on this belief-**rac'ialist, rac'ist** *a./n.* **-race relations** (with *pl. v.*) relations between members of two or more human races, *esp.* within single community; (with *sing. v.*) branch of sociology concerned with such relations. [F.]

race *n.* running; act of running in competition for a prize; strong current of water, *esp.* leading to a water-wheel. *-pl.* meeting for the sport of horse-racing. *-v.t.* contend with in a race. *-v.i.* run swiftly. **ra'cer** *n.* **-race'course** *n.* ground on which horse races are run. **-race'horse** *n.* horse bred for racing only. [ON. *ras*]

raceme' *n.* flower-cluster, as of laburnum. [L. *racemus*, bunch of grapes]

rachi'tis *n.* rickets. **-rachi'tic** *a.* [G. *rhachis*, spine]

rack *v.t.* stretch or strain; stretch on the rack or wheel; torture. *-n.* instrument for stretching anything. hence, torture; wooden frame in which hay is laid; framework on which earthenware, bottles, or other articles are arranged; in mechanics. a straight bar with teeth on its edge, to work with a pinion. **-rack'rent** *n.* highest rent that can be exacted. [Du. *rak; n.* fr. *rekken*, stretch]

rack *n.* thin, flying clouds. [orig. uncertain. cogn. with *wrack*, wreck]

rack'et *n.* bat used in tennis, badminton, *etc.* *-pl.* ball game played in a paved court surrounded by four walls. **-rack'et court** *n.* [F. *raquette*]

rack'et *n.* loud noise, uproar; (*sl.*) dishonest enterprise; organized fraud or roguery. **-rack'eteer** *n.* gangster, swindler. *-v.i.* make a noise. [Gael. *racaid*]

ra'cy *a.* having a strong flavor; spicy; spirited; piquant. **-ra'cily** *adv.* **-ra'ciness** *n.* [F. *race*]

ra'dar (ra'-) *n.* device for finding range and direction by ultrahigh frequency point-to-point radio waves, which reflect back to their source and reveal position and nature of objects sought **-ra'dar trap** *n.* device using radar to detect drivers exceeding speed limit. [*ra*dio *a*ngle *d*etection *a*nd *r*anging]

ra'diate *v.t.* emit rays. *-v.t.* emit in rays. **-radia'tion** *n.* transmission of heat, light *etc.* from one body to another; particles, rays emitted in nuclear decay; act of radiating. **-ra'diance** *n.* brightness. **-ra'diant** *a.* **-ra'diator** *n.* that which radiates, *esp.* heating apparatus for a room, or a part of an engine for cooling it. [L. *radius*, ray, wheel-spoke]

radical *a.* of a root; fundamental; thorough. *-n.* politician desiring thorough reforms. **-rad'icalism** *n.* [L. *radix, radic-*, root]

radicch'io *n.* Italian variety of chicory, having purple leaves streaked with white that are eaten raw in salads. [It.]

ra'dio *n.* use of electromagnetic waves for broadcasting, communication *etc.*; device for receiving, amplifying radio signals; broadcasting, content of radio program. *v.t.* transmit (message, *etc.*) by radio. **radioac'tive** *a.* emitting invisible rays that penetrate matter. **-radioactiv'ity** *n.* **-ra'dio**

astronomy *n.* astronomy in which radio telescope is used to detect and analyze radio signals received on earth from radio sources in space. **radiocarbon da'ting,** technique for determining age of organic materials based on their content of radioisotope ^{14}C acquired from atmosphere when they formed part of living plant. **radiochem'ical** *a.* **-radiochem'ist** *n.* **radiochem'istry** *n.* chemistry of radioactive elements and their compounds. **ra'dio frequency** any frequency that lies in range 10 kilohertz to 300, 000 megahertz and can be used for broadcasting; frequency transmitted by particular radio station. **-ra'diograph** *n.* image produced on sensitized film or plate by radiation. **-radiographer** *n.* **radiography** *n.* production of image on film or plate by radiation. **-radiois'otope** *n.* radioactive isotope. **-radiol'ogist** *n.* **radiol'ogy** *n.* science of use of rays in medicine **-ra'dio microphone** *n.* microphone incorporating a radio transmitter so that the user can move around freely. **ra'diosonde** *n.* airborne instrument to send meteorological information back to earth by radio. **-radiotel'egraph** *v.* /*n.* **- radioteleg'raphy** *n.* telegraphy in which messages (*usu.* in Morse code) are transmitted by radio waves. **-radiotel'ephone** *n.* device for communications by means of radio waves; -*v.* telephone (person) by radiotelephone **-radioteleph'ony** *n.* **ra'dio telescope** instrument used in radio astronomy to pick up and analyze radio waves from space and to transmit radio waves. **-radio'ther'apy** *n.* diagnosis and treatment of disease by x-rays.

rad'ish *n.* pungent root. [L. *radix*]

ra'dium *n.* rare metal named from its radioactive power. [*radiate*]

ra'dius *n.* straight line from center to circumference of a circle or sphere. **ra'dial** *a.* of a ray or rays; of a radius; of radium. [*radiate*]

rad'ix *n.* root, source, origin. [L. *radix*, root]

ra'don (rA-) *n.* rare gas, an emanation from radium. [*radium*]

raff'ia *n.* prepared palm fiber used for making mats, *etc.* [Malagasy]

raff'ish *a.* disreputable. [obs. *raff*, rabble; *See* **riff-raff**]

raf'fle *n.* lottery in which an article is assigned by lot to one of those buying tickets. -*v.t.* dispose of by raffle. [orig. dicing game, F. *rafle*]

raft *n.* number of logs or planks, *etc.*, of wood tied together and floating. [ON. *raptr*, beam]

raft'er *n.* one of the main beams of a roof. [OE. *roefter*]

rag *n.* fragment of cloth; torn piece. **ragg'ed** *a.* shaggy; torn; clothed in frayed or torn clothes; wanting smoothness. **rag'time** *n.* music with strong syncopation. **-rag'wort** *n.* wild, yellow-flowered plant with ragged leaves. [OE. *ragg*]

rag *v.t.* tease; torment. [contr. of *bullyrag*]

rag'amuffin *n.* ragged person or boy; disreputable fellow. [orig. uncertain]

rage *n.* violent anger or passion; fury. *v.i.* speak or act with fury; be widely and violently prevalent. **-the rage,** the fashion. [F. fr. L. *rabies*, madness]

rag'lan *n.* straight-cut, loose-fitting overcoat with wide sleeves. [Lord *Raglan*]

ragout' *n.* stew of meat and vegetables with herbs, spices, *etc.* (F.]

raid *n.* rush, attack; foray. -*v.t.* make a raid on. **-raid'er** *n.* [var. of *road*, cp. inroad]

rail *n.* horizontal bar, *esp.* as part of a fence, railway line, *etc.* -*v.t.* enclose with rails. **-rail'ing** *n.* fence of rails. -rail *n.* road with lines of iron rails on which trains run. **-rail** *n.* [OF. *reille* fr. L. *regula*, ruler]

rail *n.* kinds of bird including corncrake and the water-rails. [F. *râile-râler*, rattle]

rail *v.i.* utter abuse. **-raill'ery** *n.* light-hearted banter. [F. *railler*]

rai'ment *n.* clothing. [for *arrayment*]

rain *n.* moisture falling in drops from the clouds; fall of such drops. -*v.i.* fall as rain. -*v.t.* pour down like rain. **-rain'y** *a.* **- rain'bow** *n.* arch of prismatic colors formed in the sky by the sun's rays. **-rain check** *n.* ticket for a future performance, game, *etc.* when one has been postponed by rain; agreement that one may claim later something that is being offered now. **rain'coat** *n.* light rainproof overcoat. **rain'fall** *n.* quantity of rain falling in given area. **-rain gauge** *n.* instrument for measuring rainfall. [OE. *regn*]

raise *v.t.* set up, rear; lift up; breed, bring into existence; levy, collect; end (a siege). -*n.* rise, *esp.* in salary. [ON. *reisa*]

rai'sin *n.* dried grape. [F. = *grape*]

raj *n.* rule, sovereignty esp, in India. [Hind.]

ra'jah *n.* king or ruler in India, Java, Borneo *etc.* [Hind. *raja*]

rake *n.* tool consisting of a long handle with a cross-piece armed with teeth for drawing together hay, *etc.*, or breaking the ground. -*v.t.* draw or break with a rake;

sweep or search over; sweep with shot. **rake'-off** *n.* illegal or unofficial commission. [OE. *raca*]

rake *n.* (*naut.*) projection of stem and stern beyond limits of keel; degree of inclination of masts, funnels, *etc.* **-ra'kish** *a.* [Sw. *raka*, reach]

rake *n.* dissolute man. **-ra'kish** *a.* [for obs. *rake*-hell]

rall'y *v.t.* bring together, *esp.* what has been scattered, as a routed army or dispersed troops. *-v.i.* come together; regain health or strength *n.* act of rallying. [F. *rallier*]

rall'y *v.t.* tease. [*See* **rail**]

ram *n.* male sheep; swinging beam with metal head for battering hydraulic machine; beak projecting from bow of a warship. *-v.t.* beat down; stuff, strike with a ram. **-ram'rod** *n.* rod for pressing down charge of a muzzle-loading gun. [OE. *ramm*]

Ram'adan *n.* ninth month of the Islamic (lunar) year during which fasting is observed from dawn until dusk. [Arab.]

ram'ble *v.i.* walk without definite route, wander; talk incoherently. *-n.* rambling walk. **-ram'bler** *n.* one who rambles; climbing rose. **-ram'bling** *a.* [ME. *ramen*, roam]

ram'ify *v.t.* and *i.* spread in branches. - **ramifica'tion** *n.* branching; consequence. **-ram'ose** *a.* having many branches. [L. *ramus*, branch]

ramp *v.i.* stand on the hind legs. *-n.* slope. **-ramp'ant** *a.* rearing; violent. **-rampa'geous** *a.* boisterous, violent, obstreperous. **-rampage'** *v.i.* [F. *ramper* clamber]

ramp *n.* (*sl.*) swindle; widespread fraudulent operations. [orig. uncertain]

ramp'art *n.* mound for defence, *esp.* of a fortification. [F. *rempart*]

ramshackle *a.* tumbledown, rickety. formerly ransackle. [*See* **ransack**]

ranch *n.* very large farm, *esp.* one where sheep, cattle or horses are produced. *-v.i.* conduct such a form. *-v.i.* conduct one. **ranch'er** *n.* [Sp. *rancho*, row (of huts, *etc.*)]

ran'cid *a.* smelling or tasting like stale fat. **-rancid'ity** *n.* [L. *rancidus*]

ran'cor *n.* bitter and inveterate illfeeling. **-ran'corous** *a.* [L. *rancor*]

ran'dom *n.* **at random**, haphazard. *a.* made or done at random. [OF. *randon*, headlong rush]

ran'ee *n.* Indian princess, wife of rajah. [Hind.]

range *n.* rank; area, scope, sphere; distance a gun can reach; distance of a mark shot at; place for practicing shooting; kitchen stove. *-v.t.* set in a row; roam. *-v.i.* extend; roam. **-ran'ger** *n.* **range' finder** *n.* instrument to determine distance of object. **-range'land** *n.* land that naturally produces forage plants suitable for grazing but where rainfall is too low or erratic for growing crops. [F. *rang*]

ran'ger *n.* one who guards a tract of forest; armed patrol man. [fr. *range*, v.]

rank *n.* row or line; order; social position; high social position; relative place or position. *-v.t.* draw up in a rank, classify. *-v.i.* have rank or place. (F. *rang*]

rank *a.* growing too thickly or coarsely; offensively strong; vile; flagrant. **rank'ly** *adv.* [OE. *ranc*, insolent]

rank'le *v.i.* fester, continue to cause anger. [OF. *raoncle*, sore]

ransack *v.t.* search thoroughly. [ON. *rann*, house, *soekaj*, seek]

ran'som *n.* release from captivity by payment; amount paid. *-v.t.* pay ransom for. **-ran'somer** *n.* [F. *rancon* fr. L. *redemptio*, buying back]

rant' *v.i.* talk, preach, in a loud, bombastic way. *-n.* bombast. **-rant'er** *n.* [O. Du. *ranten*, rave]

ranun'culus *n.* variety of plants *e.g.*, buttercup. [L.]

rap *n.* smart slight blow. *-v.t.* give a rap to. *-v.i.* [imit. orig.]- **rap** *n.* talk, conversation. *-v.i.* [orig. uncertain]

rapa'cious *a.* greedy, grasping. **rapa'city** (-pas'-) *n.* [L. *rapax, rapac-*]

rape *n.* plant with oil-yielding seeds; plant fed to sheep. [L. *rapum*, turnip]

rape *v.t.* violate; force a person to submit unwillingly to sexual intercourse. *-n.* act of raping. **-ra'pist** *n.* [ME. *rappen*, seize. L. *rapere*, seize]

rap'id *a.* quick, swift; speedy. **-rapid'ity** *n.* **-rap'idly** *adv.* [L. *rapidus*]

ra'pier *n.* light, pointed sword for thrusting only. [F. *rapière*]

rap'ine *n.* plunder. [L. *rapina*]

rapparee' *n.* Irish freebooter. [Ir. *rapaire*, pike]

rappee' *n.* strong, coarse snuff. [F. *râpé*, grated]

rapport' *n.* rotation; harmony, sympathy. [F.]

rapproche'ment (-prozh-mong) *n.* (re-)establishment or renewal of friendly relations. [F.]

rapscall'ion *n.* scamp, rogue, rascal. [*rascal*]
rapt *a.* snatched away; lost in thought; intent. **-rap'ture** *n.* ecstasy. **-rap'turous** *a.* [L. *rapere*, snatch]
rare *a.* uncommon; of uncommon quality. **-rare'bit** *n.* Welsh rabbit, cheese sauce on toast. **-rar'efy** *v.t.* lessen the density of. **-rarefac'tion** *n.* **-rare'ly** *adv.* **-rar'ity** *n.* anything rare. [L. *rarus*, thinly sown]
rare *a.* raw, underdone. [OE. *hrér*, half-cooked]
ras'cal *n.* rogue, knave. **-ras'cally** *a.* **rascal'ity** *n.* [OF. *rascaille*, rabble]
rase. *See* **raze.**
rash *n.* skin eruption. [OF. *rasche*]
rash *a.* hasty, reckless, without due caution. **-rash'ly** *adv.* [Du. *rasch*, quick]
rash'er *n.* thin slice of bacon or ham. [orig. uncertain]
rasp *n.* coarse file. *-v.t.* scrape with one. *-v.i.* scrape; make a scraping noise, [OF. *raspe*]
raspberry *n.* familiar soft fruit; the plant. [orig. uncertain]
Rastafar'ian *n.* member of a Jamaican cult that regards Ras Tafari, former emperor of Ethiopia, Haile Selassie, as God. *-a.* of Rastafarians.
rat *n.* small rodent animal; one who deserts his party. **-ratt'y** *a.* (*sl.*) riled. *v.i.* hunt rats; desert one's party. **-rat's bane** *n.* poison for rats. [OE. *rcet*]
ratafi'a *n.* almond-flavored biscuit or liqueur. [F.]
rat'chet *n.* set of teeth on a bar wheel allowing motion in one direction only. [F. *rochet*]
rate *n.* proportion between two things; charge; degree of speed, *etc.* *-v.t.* estimate the value of. **-rat'able** *a.* that can be rated; liable to pay rates. [Med. L. *rata*, fr. *reri*, *rat-*, think, judge]
rate *v.t.* scold. [OF. *reter*, accuse]
ra'ther *adv.* some extent; in preference. [OE. *hrathe*, quickly]
rat'ify *v.t.* confirm, make valid. **ratifica'tion** *n.* [F. *ratifier*]
ra'ting *n.* (*naut.*) grading of a seaman on ship's books; tonnage-class of racing yacht; amount fixed as a rate. [*rate*]
ra'tio *n.* relative magnitude; proportion. [L. = *reason*]
ratiocinate *v.i.* reason. **-ratiocina'tion** *n.* [L. *ratiocinari, ratiocinat*]
ra'tion (rash'un) *n.* fixed daily allowance. *-v.t.* supply with, or limit to, rations. [L. *ratio*]
ra'tional *a.* reasonable. **-ra'tionalism** *n.* philosophy which regards reason as the only guide or authority. **-ra'tionalist** *n.* **-ra'tionalize** *v.t.* explain away by reasoning. **-rational'ity** *n.* **-ra'tionally** *adv.* [L., fr. *veri, rat-*, think, judge]
rat'lines (-inz) *n. pl.* cords fixed across a ship's shrouds. [orig. uncertain]
rattan' *n.* palm with long thin jointed stems; cane of this. [Malay *rotan*]
rat'tle *v.i.* give out a succession of short sharp sounds, as of shaking small stones in a box. *-v.t.* cause to sound thus; (*sl.*) irritate, make angry. *-n.* the sound; instrument for making it; set of horny rings in a rattlesnake's tail. **-rat'tle-snake** *n.* poisonous snake that makes a rattling noise with its tail. [imit. orig.]
rauc'ous *a.* hoarse; harsh-sounding. [L. *raucus*]
rav'age *v.t.* lay waste. *-n.* destruction and pillage; devastation. [F.]
rave *v.i.* talk in delirium or with great enthusiasm. [F. *rêver*, dream]
rav'el *v.t.* entangle or disentangle, fray out. [Du *rafelen*]
rave'lin *n.* detached work with two faces meeting in salient angle at front and open at rear. [F.]
ra'ven *n.* black bird of the crow family. [OE. *hroefn*]
rav'en *v.i.* and *t.* seek prey or plunder. **rav'enous** *a.* very hungry. [OF. *ravine* -L. *rapina*, plunder]
ravine' *n.* narrow gorge worn by running water. [F. fr. L. *rapina*]
rav'ish *v.t.* carry off, sweep away; commit rape upon (a woman); enrapture. **rav'ishment** *n.* [F. *ravir* fr. L. *rapere*, snatch]
raw *a.* uncooked; not manufactured; crude, inexperienced, uncultivated; stripped of skin; sensitive; chilly. [OE. *hreaw*]
ray *n.* single line or narrow beam of light, heat, *etc.*; any of a set of radiating lines. *v.i.* radiate. (OF. *rai*, fr. L. *radius*]
ray *n.* any of a number of fishes related to the sharks. [L. *raia*]
ray'on *n.* artificial silk, wool, cotton, *etc.* [Trademark, F. = *ray]*
raze *v.t.* destroy completely; level to the ground; wipe out, delete. [F. *raser*, fr. L. *radere, ras-*, scrape]
raz'or *n.* an instrument for shaving. **-razor-bill** *n.* bird, a kind of auk. [F. *raser*, fr. L. *radere, ras-*, scrape]
re, in re *prep.* in the matter of. [L.]

re- *prefix* makes compounds with meaning of, again, *e.g.*, **readdress'** *v.t.* address afresh. **-recap'ture** *v.t.* capture again. These are not given where the meaning and derivation may easily be found from the simple word. [L.]

reach *v.t.* succeed in touching; arrive at. *-v.i.* stretch out the hand; extend. *-n.* act of reaching; grasp, scope; stretch of river between two bends, (OE. *roecan*, stretch out]

react' *v.i.* act in return or opposition or towards a former state. **-reac'tion** *n.* **reac'tionary** *n.* one advocating backward movement, in politics, *etc.* *-a.* of or inclined to such reaction. **-rea'gent** *n.* chemical substance that reacts with another and is used to detect the presence of the other. [*act*]

read *v.t.* look at and understand written or printed matter; interpret mentally; learn by reading; read and utter. *-v.i.* be occupied in reading; find mentioned in reading. **-read'able** *a.* that can be read with pleasure. **-readabil'ity** *n.* **-read'er** *n.* [OE. *roedan*, make out]

read'y (red'i) *a.* prepared, prompt. **read'iness** *n.* **-read'ily** *adv.* [OE. *gerode*]

re'al *a.* existing in fact; happening; actual; of property, consisting of land and houses. **-re'alism** *n.* regarding things as they are; artistic treatment with this outlook. **-re'alist** *n.* **-realist'ic** *a.* **real'ity** *n.* real existence. **-re'alize** *v.t.* make real; convert into money. **realiza'tion** *n.* **-re'ally** *adv.* **-real estate'** *n.* immovable property, as houses, *etc.* **-real'tor** *n.* real estate agent. **re'alty** *n.* real estate. [F. *reel*, fr. L. *res*, thing]

realm (relm) *n.* kingdom, province, sphere. [OF. *reame*, fr. L. *regimen*]

ream *n.* twenty quires of paper, *usu.* 500 sheets. [Arab. *rizmah*, bundle]

reap *v.i.* cut grain. *-v.t.* cut (grain). **reap'er** *n.* [OE. *repan*]

rear *n.* back part. **-rear'-guard** *n.* troops protecting rear of an army. [arrear]

rear *v.t.* set on end; build up; breed, bring up. *-v.i.* rise on the hind feet. [OE. *roeran*, raise]

reas'on (-z-) *n.* ground or motive; faculty of thinking; sensible or logical view. *-v.i.* think logically in forming conclusions. *v.t.* persuade by logical argument (into doing, *etc.*). **-reas'onable** *a.* sensible, not excessive, suitable; marked by logic. [F. *raison*, fr. L. *ratio*]

reassure' *v.t.* calm, give confidence to. **-reassu'rance** *n.* [*assure*]

reast *v.i.* become rancid, *a.* bacon. **-reast'y** *a.* [OF. *rests*, left over]

reave, reive, *v.t.* and *i.* plunder. **reav'er, reiver**, *n.* [OE. *reafian*]

re'bate *n.* discount. *-v.t.* diminish; allow as discount. [F. *rabattre]*

re'bec (re'-) *n.* ancient stringed instrument. [Arab. *rebab*]

rebel' *v.i.* revolt, take arms against the ruling power. **-reb'el** *n.* one who rebels; one resisting authority. *-a.* in rebellion. **-rebell'ion** *n.* organized open resistance to authority. **-rebell'ious** *a.* **-rebell'iously** *adv.* [L. *rebellare*]

rebound' *v.t.* drive back. *-v.i.* spring back; re-echo; recoil. *-n.* [*bound*]

rebuke' *v.t.* reprove, reprimand, find fault with. *-n.* act of rebuking. [OF. *rebuchier*, repulse]

re'bus *n.* riddle in which words are represented by pictures standing for the syllables, *etc.* [L. = '*by things*']

rebut' *v.t.* force back, refute evidence, *etc.* **-rebutt'al** [F. *rebouter]*

recalcitrant *a.* refractory. [L. *recalcitrare, recalcitrant-*, kick out]

recant' *v.t.* withdraw a statement, opinion, *etc.* **-recanta'tion** *n.* [L. *recantare*, fr. *cantare* sing]

recapitulate *v.t.* state again briefly. **-recapitula'tion** *n.* (L. *recapitulare-capitulum*, chapter]

recast' *v.i.* remold; reshape. [cast]

recede' *v.t.* go back. **-rece'ding** *a.* going, sloping, backward. [L. *recedere*]

receipt' *n.* written acknowledgment of money received; fact of receiving or being received; recipe. **-receive'** *v.t.* take, accept, get; experience. **receiv'er** *n.* **-receivable** *a.* [L. *recipere recept-*, fr. *capere*, take]

re'cent *a.* that has lately happened, new, fresh. **-re'cently** *adv.* [L. *recens*]

receptacle *n.* containing vessel, place or space. **-recep'tion** *n.* receiving; manner of receiving; formal receiving of guests. **-recep'tionist** *n.* one who receives (hotel) guests or clients. **receptive** *a.* able or quick to receive, *esp.* impressions. **-receptiv'ity** *n.* [L. *recipere*, receive]

re'cess *n.* vacation or holiday; niche or alcove; secret hidden place. [*recede*]

recessional *n.* hymn sung while the clergy are retiring. **-recess'ive** *a.* receding. [L. *recedere, recess-*, withdraw]

recherché (re-sher-sha) *a.* choice, select, elegant. [F.]

recid'ivist *n.* one who relapses into crime. [L. *recidere*, fall back]

re'cipe (res'i-pe) *n.* directions for cooking a dish, prescription. [L. *recipere,* receive]
recipient *a.* that can or does receive. *n.* that which receives. [L. *recipere,* receive]
reciprocal *a.* in return, mutual. **recip'rocally** *adv.* **-recip'rocate** *v.i.* move backwards and forwards. *-v.t.* give in return, give and receive mutually. **reciproca'tion** *n.* **-recipro'city** *n.* [L. *reciprocus*]
recite' *v.t.* repeat aloud, *esp.* to an audience. **-reci'tal** *n.* narrative; musical performance by one person. **-recita'tion** *n.* **-recitative'** *n.* musical declamation. - **reci'ter** *n.* [L. *recitare*]
reck *v.i.* care, heed. **-reck'less** *a.* rash; heedless; careless. [OE. *reccan*]
reck'on *v.t.* count; include; consider. *-v.i.* make calculations, cast accounts. **reck'oner** *n.* [OE. *gerecenian*]
reclaim' *v.t.* bring back (from wrong); make fit for cultivation. **-reclaim'able** *a.* **-reclama'tion** *n.* reformation; regaining, as of land from the sea. [L. *reclamare,* call back]
recline' *v.i.* sit or lie with back supported on a slope; repose. [L. *reclinare*]
recluse' *a.* living in complete retirement. *-n.* hermit. [L. *reclusus*]
recognize *v.t.* know again; treat as valid; notice. **-recogni'tion** *n.* **-recogni'zable** *a.* **-recog'nizance** *n.* legal bond by which a person undertakes before a court to observe some condition. [L. *recognoscere*]
recoil' *n.* rebound, *esp.* of a gun when fired; act of recoiling. *-v.i.* draw or spring back. [F. *reculer*]
recollect' *v.t.* call back to mind, remember. **-recollec'tion** *n.* [L. *recolligere, recollect-,* collect again]
recommend' *v.t.* entrust; present as worthy of favor or trial; make acceptable. - **recommenda'tion** *n.* [F. *recommander.* cp. command, commend]
recompense *v.t.* reward, punish; requite. *-n.* reward. [F. *recompenser*]
reconcile *v.t.* bring back into friendship; adjust, settle, harmonize. **-reconcilia'tion** *n.* **-reconcile'ment** *n.* **-reconci'lable** *a.* [L. *reconciliare*]
recondite *a.* obscure, abstruse. [L. *reconditus,* hidden away]
recondition *v.t.* refit; make over; restore to working order. [*condition*]
reconnoiter (-ter) *v.t.* survey the position of an enemy, strange district, *etc.* *-v.i.* make a reconnaissance. **reconnaissance** *n.* such survey. [OF. *reconnoitre* (F. *reconnoitre*) recognize]
reconstruct' *v.t.* rebuild. **-reconstruc'tion** *n.* a rebuilding; rebuilding of a country, its trade, *etc.*, after war. [*construct*]
record' *v.t.* put down in writing. **rec'ord** *n.* a being recorded; document or other thing that records, *e.g.*, gramophone record; best recorded achievement. **record'er** *n.* a person or thing that records; type of flute. **record'ing** *n.* art of registering sounds for reproduction. [L. *recordari,* get by heart]
recount' *v.t.* tell in detail. *-n.* second count (of votes, *etc.*) [OF, *reconter*]
recoup' *v.t.* recompense; indemnify. [F. *recouper,* cut back]
recourse' *n.* resorting to for help. [L, *recurrere, recurs-,* run back]
recov'er (-kuv) *v.t.* get back. *-v.i.* get back health. **-recov'erable** *a.* **-recov'ery** *n.* [F. *recouvrir,* fr. L. *recuperare*]
rec'reant *a.* craven, cowardly; apostate. *-n.* recreant person. [OF. *recreire,* take back one's pledge]
rec'reate *v.t.* restore. *-v.i.* take recreation. **-recrea'tion** *n.* agreeable or refreshing occupation. **-rec'reative** *a.* [L. *recreare,* make again]
recriminate *v.i.* make a counter charge or mutual accusation. **-recrimina'tion** *n.* - **recrim'inatory** *a.* [L. *crimen,* charge, crime]
recrudesce' (-es) *v.i.* break out again. **recrudes'cence** *n.* [L. *recrudescere,* become raw again]
recruit' (-oot) *n.* newly-enlisted soldier; one newly joining a society. *-v.i.* enlist, *v.t.* enlist fresh soldiers, *etc.*; recover health. **-recruit'ment** *n.* [OF. *recrue,* reinforcement]
rectangle *n.* four-sided figure with four right-angles. **-rectang'ular** *a.* [L. *rectus,* right, straight]
rect'ify (-fi) *v.t.* put right, purify; (*elec.*) change from alternate to direct current. **rectifica'tion** *n.* **-rectifi'er** *n.* [L. *rectus,* right]
rectilin'eal, rectilinear *a.* in a straight line, of or characterized by straight lines. [L. *rectus*]
rectitude *n.* moral uprightness; honesty. [L. *rectus*]
rec'to *n.* right hand page, front of a leaf. [L. *rectus*]
rec'tor *n.* clergyman of the Protestant Episcopal Church in charge of a parish; head of certain schools and colleges.

recto'rial *a.* of a rector. **-rec'tory** *n.* house or province of a rector. [L. *regere, rect-*, rule]

rect'um *n.* the final section of the large intestine. [L. *rectus*]

recumbent *a.* lying down; reclining. [L. *recumbere*, to lie down]

recuperate *v.t.* and *i.* to restore, be restored from illness. losses, *etc.* **recuperation** *n.* **-recup'erative** *a.* [L. *recuperate*, to recover]

recur' *v.i.* go or come back in mind; happen again. **-recurr'ent** *a.* **-recurr'ence** *n.* [L. *recurrere*, run back]

rec'usant *a.* stubborn in refusal *esp.* to conform to doctrine of Established Church. *-n.* [L. *causa*, cause]

red *a.* of a color varying from crimson to orange and seen in blood, rubies, glowing fire, *etc.*; (politics) communist. *-n.* the color. **-red ad'miral,** kind of butterfly. **red bidd'y,** mixture of wine and methylated spirits. **-red'breast** *n.* robin. **-Red Cross',** international society for the care of the sick and wounded **-redd'en** *v.t.* and *i.* **-redd'ish** *a.* **-red-handed** *a.* in the act. **-red-hot** *a.* heated to point of redness; fiery; very angry. **-red lead** *n.* oxide of lead. **-red-lett'er day** auspicious, as a saint's day, *etc.*, shown in old calendars in red. **-red light',** danger signal. **-red'start** *n.* songbird. **-red tape',** excessive or irksome officialism. [OE. *read*]

redact' *v.t.* edit. **-redac'tion** *n.* [L. *redigere*, bring back]

redan' *n.* fieldwork of two-faces forming salient. [L. re, back, *dens*, both]

redeem' *v.t.* ransom, atone for; save: fulfill (a promise); make good use of (time). **-redeem'er** *n.* **-the Redeem'er** Jesus Christ **-redemp'tive** *a.* **-redemp'tion** *n.* [L. *redimere, redempt-*]

red'olent *a.* scented with, diffusing the fragrance, odor of. **-red'olence** *n.* [F.]

redoub'le (-dub-) *v.t.* and *i.* to increase, multiply. [*doubler*]

redoubt' (-dowt) *n.* detached outwork in fortifications, [F. *redoute*]

redoubtable (-dowt-) *a.* valiant, formidable. **-redoubt'ed** *a.* [F. *redoubtable*]

redound' *v.i.* contribute or turn to. [L. *redundare*, overflow]

redress *v.t.* set right. *-n.* compensation. [F. *redresser*, put right again]

red'start. *See* **red.**

reduce *v.t.* bring down, lower, lessen; bring by force or necessity to some state or action. *-v.i.* slim. **-redu'cible** *a.* - **reduc'tion** *n.* [L. *reducere, reduct-*, lead back]

redundant *a.* superfluous, unnecesary; become deprived of a job. **-redundancy** *n.* [L. *redundare*, overflow]

reduplicate *v.t.* double again. **reduplication** *n.* **-redup'licative** *a.* [*duplicate*]

reed *n.* various marsh or water plants; tall straight stem of one; vibrating part of certain musical instruments. **-reed'y** *a.* full of reeds; like a reed instrument in tone. [OE. *hreod*]

reef *n.* part of a sail which can be rolled up to reduce the area; ridge of rock near the surface of the sea; lodge of auriferous quartz. *-v.t.* take in a reef of. [ON. *rif*, reef, rib]

reek *n.* strong smell or smoke. *-v.i.* smoke, emit fumes. **-reek'y** *a.* smoky. [OE. *reocan*, to smoke]

reel *n.* winding apparatus; cylinder for winding cotton, *etc.*, on; act of staggering. *-v.t.* wind on a reel. *-v.i.* stagger away. [OE. *hreol*]

reel *n.* lively dance; music for it, [Gael. *righil*]

reeve *v.t.* pass (a rope) through a hole, in a block, *etc.* [It. *refare*]

refectory *n.* dining-hall in a monastery, convent or school, *etc.* **-refec'tion** *n.* meal. [L. *reficere. refect-*, remake]

refer' *v.t.* trace or ascribe to; submit for decision; send to for information. *-v.i.* have relation, allude. **-ref'erable** *a.* **-referee'** *n.* umpire; arbitrator. **-ref'erence** *n.* - **referen'dum** *n.* submitting of a question to a whole body of voters. [L. *referre*, carry back]

refine' *v.t.* purify. **-refine'ment** *n.* **refi'ner** *n.* **-refi'nery** *n.* place where sugar, *etc.*, is refined. [F. *raffiner*]

reflect' *v.t.* throw back, *esp.* rays of light; cast (discredit, fame, etc.), upon. *-v.i.* meditate. **-reflec'tion, reflex'ion** *n.* **reflect'ive** *a.* **-reflect'or** *n.* a polished surface for reflecting light, *etc.* **-re'flex** *a.* reflected, bent back; of muscular action, involuntary. **-reflex'ive** *a.* in grammar, describes a verb denoting the agent's action on himself. **-reflex'ology** *n.* form of therapy practiced as a treatment in alternative medicine in which the soles of the feet are massaged; belief that behavior can be understood in terms of combinations of reflexes. [L. *reflectere*, bend back]

re'flux *n.* a flowing back. **-ref'luent** *a.* flowing back, ebbing. [L. *fluxus*, flow]

reform' *v.t.* and *i.* amend, improve. *-n.*

amendment, improvement. **-reforma′tion** *n.* **-reform′atory, reform′ school** *n.* institution for reforming juvenile offenders. *-a.* reforming. **reform′er** *n.* [L. *reformare*, reshape]

refract′ *v.t.* break the course of (light, *etc.*). **-refract′ive** *a.* **-refrac′tion** *n.* **refract′ory** *a.* unmanageable, difficult to treat or work. [L. *refringere*, break back]

refrain′ *n.* chorus of a song. [F.]

refrain′ *v.i.* abstain from. *-v.t.* check. [L. *refrenare*, bridle]

refrangible *a.* capable of being refracted, such as rays of light. **refrangibility** *n.* property (or amount) of refraction. [L. *re-*, back; *frangere*, to break]

refresh′ *v.t.* give freshness to. **-refresher** *n.* **-refresh′ment** *n.* that which refreshes, *esp.* food or drink. [F. *rafraichir-frais*, fresh]

refrig′erate *v.t.* freeze, cool. **-refrigera′tion** *n.* **-refrig′erator** *n.* apparatus for cooling or freezing. [L. *frigus, frigerare, frigerat-*, cold]

ref′uge *n.* shelter, protection. **-refugee′** *n.* one who seeks refuge, *esp.* in a foreign country. [L. *refugium*, fr. *fugere*, flee]

refulgent (-j-) *a.* shining **-reful′gence** *n.* **-reful′gency** *n.* [L. *fulgere*, shine]

refund′ *v.t.* pay back; restore. *-n.* **refunder** *n.* [L. *refundere*, pour back]

refuse′ (-z) *v.t.* and *i.* decline. **-ref′use** (-s) *a.* discarded. *-n.* rubbish, useless matter. **-refu′sal** *n.* [L. *refusare*]

refute′ *v.t.* disprove. **-refu′table** *a.* **refuta′tion** *n.* (L. *refutare*, repel]

re′gal *a.* of, or like, a king. **-rega′lia** *n. pl.* insignia of royalty, as used at a coronation, *etc.* **-re′gally** *adv.* **-regal′ity** *n.* [L. *regales*, fr. *rex, reg-*, king]

regale′ *v. v.t.* and *i.* feast. [F. *régaler*]

regard′ *v.t.* look at; consider (as); heed; relate to. *-n.* look; particular respect; esteem. *-pl.* expression of goodwill. **regard′ful** *a.* **-regard′ing** *prep.* concerning. **-regard′less** *a.* [F. *regarder*]

regatt′a *n.* meeting for yacht or boat races. [It.]

regen′erate *v.t.* and *i.* cause spiritual rebirth, reform morally; reproduce, recreate, reorganize. **-regenera′tion** *n.* **regen′erative** *a.* **-regen′erator** *n.* device on furnace to conserve fuel by heating incoming air. [*generate*]

re′gent *a.* ruling. *-n.* one who rules a kingdom during the absence, minority, *etc.*, of its king. **-re′gency** *n.* [L. *regere*, rule]

reg′gae *n.* style of popular West Indian music with accent on the off beat. [orig. uncertain]

re′gicide *n.* one who kills a king; his crime. [L. *rex, reg-*, king]

régime′ *n.* system of government. [F.]

reg′imen (-j-) *n.* prescribed system of diet. (L.]

regiment *n.* an organized body of troops as a unit of an army. **-regiment′al** *a.* of a regiment. *-n.* in *pl.* uniform. [F. *régiment*]

re′gion (-jun) *n.* area, district. [L. *regio, region-*, fr. *regere*, rule]

reg′ister (-j-) *n.* written record; compass of a voice; device for registering. *-v.t.* set down in writing; enter in a register; express. *-v.i.* make a visible impress. - **registrar′** *n.* keeper of a register. - **registra′tion** *n.* **-reg′istry** *n.* registering; place where registers are kept. [F. *registre*]

reg′ius *a.* royal, as in *regius professor*, holding chair appointed by crown. [L. *rex*, king]

reg′nant *a.* reigning. **-reg′nal** *a.* **reg′nancy** *n.* [L. *regnans, regnant*]

regress *n.* passage back; ability to pass back. **-regress′ive** *a.* passing back, salon *n.* returning, retrogression. [L. *re*, back, *gradi*, step]

regret′ *v.t.* grieve for the loss of, or on account of *-n.* grief for something done or left undone or lost. **-regret′ful** *a.* - **regrett′able** *a.* (F. *regretter*]

reg′ular *a.* done according to rule; habitual; living under rule; belonging to the standing army. *-n.* regular soldier. **regular′ity** *n.* **-reg′ulate** *v.t.* adjust; put under rule. **-regula′tion** *n.* rule; law; ordinance. **-reg′ulator** *n.* [L. *regularis*, fr. *regula*, rule]

regurg′itate *v.t.* throw, pour back, bring again into the mouth after swallowing. **regurgita′tion** *n.* [L. *re*, back, *gurges*, gulf]

rehabil′itate *v.t.* restore to reputation or former physical state. **-rehabilita′tion** *n.* (L. *habilitare*, make fit]

rehearse′ (-hers) *v.t.* repeat aloud; say over again; practice (a play, *etc.*). **rehears′al** *n.* [OF. *rehercier*, repeat (lit. rake over again)]

Reich′stag *n.* German parliament. [Ger.]

reign *n.* royal power; dominion; supremacy; period of a sovereign's rule. *-v.i.* be sovereign. [L. *regnum*]

reimburse′ *v.t.* pay back, refund (expenses, *etc.*). **-reimburse′ment** *n.* [F. *rembourser*, fr. *bourse*, purse]

rein *n.* narrow strap attached to the bit to check or guide a horse. -*v.t.* check or manage with reins. [OF. *reine*, fr. L. *retinere*, hold back]

rein'deer *n.* deer of cold regions. [ON. *hreindyri*]

reinforce' *v.t.* strengthen, *esp.* by sending fresh men. -**reinforce'ment** *n.* -**reinforced' con'crete,** concrete strengthened with steel. [F. *reinforcer*]

reinstate' *v.t.* replace, restore. -**reinstate'ment** *n.* [obs. *insate*]

reiterate *v.t.* repeat over and over again. -**reitera'tion** *n.* [*iterate*]

reject' *v.t.* refuse, put aside; decline. **rejec'tion** *n.* [L. *rejacere, reject-*, throw back]

rejoice' *v.t.* and *i.* make or be joyful. [F. *rejouir, rejouiss-*,]

rejoin' *v.t.* say in answer. -**rejoin'der** *n.* answer; response. [F. *réjoindre*]

rejuvenate *v.t.* restore to youth. **rejuvena'tion** *n.* -**rejuvenes'cence** *n.* **rejuvenes'cent** *a.* [L. *juvenis*, young]

relapse' *v.i.* fall back, into evil, illness, *etc.* -*n.* [L. *relabi, relaps-*, slip back]

relate' *v.t.* narrate, recount; establish relation between; have reference or relation to. -**rela'tion** *n.* narration, narrative; correspondence, connection; connection by blood or marriage. -**rel'ative** *a.* dependent on relation to something else not absolute; have reference or relation to. -*n.* relative word or thing; one connected by blood or marriage. -**rel'atively** *adv.* -**rela'tionship** *n.* -**relativ'ity** *n.* Einstein's theory in physics that motion or velocity is relative, not absolute, and that time is a correlate of space. [F. *relater*]

relax' *v.t.* make loose or slack. -*v.i.* become loosened or slack; become more friendly. -**relaxa'tion** *n.* relaxing; recreation. [L. *laxus*, loose]

re'lay *n.* set of fresh horses to replace tired ones; gang of men, supply of material, *etc.*, used similarly; (radio) broadcast relayed from another station. *v.t.* pass on broadcast thus. -**re'lay-race** *n.* race between teams of which each runner does part of the distance. [F. *relais*]

release' *v.t.* give up, surrender, set free. -*n.* a releasing; written discharge. [OF. *relaissier*]

rel'egate *v.t.* banish, consign. -**relegation** *n.* [L. *relegare, relegat-*]

relent' *v.i.* give up harsh intention, become less severe. -**relent'less** *a.* -**relent'lessly** *adv.* [L. *lentus*, slow]

rel'evant *a.* having to do with the matter in hand; pertinent. -**rel'evance** *n.* [L. *relevare*, raise up]

reli'able. *See* **rely.**

rel'ic *n.* something remaining as a memorial of a saint, *etc.*; a thing kept as a memento. -*pl.* dead body; remains, surviving traces. -**rel'ict** *n.* a widow. [L. *relinquere, relict-*, to leave]

relief' *n.* alleviation or end of pain, distress, *etc.*; money or food given to victims of a disaster, poverty, *etc.*; release from duty; one who relieves another; projection of a carved design from a surface; distinctness, prominence. [OF. *relief* fr. *relever*]

relieve' *v.t.* bring or give relief to; set free; free (a person or duty) by taking his place. [F. *relever,* raise up]

relie'vo *n.* in painting, sculpture, *etc.* work in relief-*pl.* -**vos.** [It. *relievo*]

reli'gion (-ijun) *n.* system of faith and worship. -**reli'gious** *a.* -**reli'giously** *adv.* -**religiousness** *n.* [L. *religio*]

relinquish (-inkw-) *v.t.* give up. **relin'quishment** *n.* [L. *relinquere*]

reliquary (-kwer-i) *n.* case or shrine for relics. [F. *reliquaire*]

rel'ish *n.* taste or flavor; savory taste; liking. -*v.t.* enjoy, like. [OF. *relaissier*, leave behind, (after-taste)]

reluctant *a.* unwilling. -**reluct'ance** *n.* [L. *reluctari*, struggle against]

rely' *v.i.* depend (on). -**reli'able** *a.* trustworthy. -**reliabil'ity** *n.* -**reli'ance** *n.* [L. *religare*, bind together]

remain' *v.i.* stay or be left behind; continue. -**remaind'er** *n.* rest, what is left after substraction. [L. *remanere*]

remand' *v.t.* send back, *esp.* into custody. [L. *remandare*, order back]

remark' *v.t.* take notice of; say. -*v.i.* make a remark (on). -*n.* observation, comment. -**remark'able** *a.* noteworthy, unusual. -**remark'ably** *adv.* -**remark'ableness** *n.* [F. *remarquer*]

rem'edy *n.* means of curing, counteracting or relieving a disease, trouble, *etc.* -*v.t.* put right. -**reme'dial** *a.* **reme'diable** *a.* [L. *remedium*]

remem'ber *v.t.* retain in or recall to the memory. -*v.i.* have in mind. -**remem'brance** *n.* -**remem'brancer** *n.* one who or that which reminds, *esp,* as a title of an official. [L. *memor*, mindful]

remind' (-mind) *v.t.* put in mind (of). **remind'er** *n.* [mind]

reminisc'ence *n.* remembering; thing recollected. -**reminis'cent** *a.* reminding.

[L. *reminisce*, remember]

remiss' *a.* negligent. **-remiss'ly** *adv.*

remit' *v.t.* forgive, not to exact, give up; slacken. *-v.i.* slacken, give up. **remissible** *a.* **-remis'sion** *n.* **-remit'tance** *n.* a sending of money; money sent. [L. *remittere, remiss-*, send back, slacken]

rem'nant *n.* fragment or small piece remaining. [OF. *remanant*, remaining]

remon'strate *v.i.* protest, expostulate, argue. **-remon'strance** *n.* [Med. *remonstrare*, point out]

remorse' *a.* regret and repentance. **-remorse'ful** *a.* **-remorse'fully** *adv.* **remorse'less** *a.* pitiless. [L. *remordere, remors-*, bite again]

remote' *a.* far away; distant in time or place. **-remote'ly** *adv.* [L. *removere, remot-*]

remove' *v.t.* take away or off. *v.i.* go away; change residence. **-remo'val** *n.* removable *a.* [L.]

remunerate *v.t.* reward, pay. **remuneration** *n.* **-remu'nerative** *a.* **remu'nerable** *a.* [L. *remunerare*]

renaissance *n.* revival, rebirth, *esp.* revival or learning in the 14th-16th c. [F. *renaissance*, fr. L. *nasci*, be born]

re'nal *a.* of the kidneys. [L. *renalis*]

renascent *a.* springing up again. **renas'cence** *n.* renaissance. [F. *renaissance*, fr. L. *nasci*, be born]

rencoun'ter (-kown'-) **rencon'tre** (rong-kongtr') *n.* casual encounter; duel. [F. *rencontre*]

rend *v.t.* and *i.* tear. [OE. *rendan*]

rend'er *v.t.* give in return, deliver up; submit, present; portray, represent; melt down. **-rendi'tion** *n.* surrender; translation. [F. *rendre*]

rend'ezvous *n.* meeting; meeting place. *-v.i.* meet, come together. [F.]

ren'egade *n.* deserter; outlaw; rebel. [L. *negare*, deny]

renege' *v.i.* revoke at cards; back out; renounce. [L. *negare*, deny]

renn'et *n.* preparation for curdling milk. [fr. *renne*, old form of run]

renounce' *v.t.* give up, cast off. *-v.i.* in cards, fail to follow suit. **-renuncia'tion** *n.* [F. *renoncer*, fr. L. *renuntiare*, protest against]

ren'ovate *v.t.* restore, repair. **renovation** *n.* (L. *renovare-novus*, new]

renown' *n.* fame. [OF. renon]

rent *n.* payment for the use of land or buildings. *-v.t.* hold as a tenant; lease; hire **-rent'al** *n.* sum payable as rent. **rent-roll** *n.* list, register of total rents of estate. [F. *rente*, income]

rent *n.* tear. [obs. *rent = rend*]

renuncia'tion *See* **renounce.**

rep *n.* fabric of wool, silk, cotton *etc.* with corded surface. [orig. uncertain]

repair' *v.i.* resort, betake oneself (to). [OF. *repairier*, fr. Late L. *repatriare*, go home, return to one's country]

repair' *v.t.* mend. *-n.* mend. **-repair'able** *a.* **-repara'tion** *n.* a repairing; amends, compensation. [L. *reparare*, fr. *parare*, prepare]

repartee' *n.* witty retort; gift of making them. [F. *repartie*; orig. an answering thrust in fencing]

repast' *n.* a meal; food. [F. repast]

repa'triate *v.t.* restore to one's own country. [Late L. *repatriate*]

repay' *v.t.* pay back; make return for. **repay'ment** *n.* **-repay'able** *a.* [pay]

repeal' *v.t.* annul, cancel. *-n.* act of repealing, [appeal]

repeat' *v.t.* say or do again, reproduce. **repeat'edly** *adv.* **-repeat'er** *n.* **-repeti'tion** *n.* [L. *repetere, repetit-*, try again]

repel' *v.t.* drive back, ward off, refuse. **repell'ent** *a.* [L. *repellere*]

repent' *v.i.* feel penitence; feel regret for a deed or omission. *-v.t.* feel regret for. **repent'ant** *a.* **-repent'ance** *n.* [F. *se repentir*]

repercussion *n.* recoil; echo; indirect effect. [*percussion*]

repertoire (-twar) *n.* stock of plays, songs, *etc.*, that a player or company is prepared to give. [F.]

repertory *n.* store; repertoire. **repertory the'ater,** theater with a permanent company and a stock of plays. [L. *repertorium*]

repine' *v.i.* fret. [pine]

replace' *v.t.* put back; fill up with a substitute for. **-replace'ment** *n.* [*place*]

replenish *v.t.* fill up again. **replenishment** *n.* [OF. *replenir*]

replete' *a.* filled; abounding in. **-reple'tion** *n.* superabundant, fullness **-replete'ness** *n.* [L. *repletus*]

rep'lica *n.* copy of a work of art made by the artist; reproduction. [It.]

reply' *v.i.* and *t.* answer. *-n.* answer. (F. *replier*, fold back]

report' *v.i.* relate; take down in writing; make or give an account of, name as an offender. *-v.i.* make a report. *-n.* rumor; account or statement; repute; bang. **report'er** *n.* one who reports, *esp.* for a newspaper. [L. *reportare*, bring back]

repose′ *v.i.* take rest. -*v.t.* give rest to; put (trust, etc). -*n.* rest. **-repos′itory** *n.* store or shop. [F. *reposer*]

repoussé′ *a.* of metal-work, hammered into relief from reverse side. [F.]

reprehend′ *v.t.* find fault with. reprehen′sible *a.* deserving censure. **reprehen′sion** *n.* [L. *reprehendere, reprehens-*, lit. take hold again]

represent′ *v.t.* call up by description or portrait; make out to be; act, play, symbolize; act as deputy for; stand for. **representa′tion** *n.* **-represent′ative** *n.* and *a.* [F. *reprosenter*]

repress′ *v.t.* keep down or under. **-repress′ive** *a.* **-repres′sion** *n.* [L. *reprimere, repress-*, press back]

reprieve′ *v.t.* suspend the execution of (condemned person); a reprieving or warrant for it. [for earlier *repry*, fr. F. *repris*, taken back]

rep′rimand *n.* sharp, rebuke. -*v.t.* rebuke sharply. [F. *reprimande*, fr. *réprimer*, repress]

reprint′ *v.t.* print again. -*n.* book, publication reprinted. [print]

reproach′ *v.t.* scold, rebuke. -*n.* scolding or upbraiding; expression of this; thing bringing discredit. **-reproach′ful** *a.* [F. *reprocher*]

rep′robate *v.t.* disapprove of, reject. -*a.* depraved, cast off by God. -*n.* reprobate person. **-reproba′tion** *n.* [L. *reprobare, reprobat-*, reprove, reject]

reproduce′ *v.t.* produce anew; produce a copy of-, bring new individuals into existence. **-reproduct′ive** *a.* [*produce*]

reprove′ *v.t.* blame, rebuke. **reproof′** *n.* [L. *reprobare*]

rep′tile *n.* cold-blooded air-breathing vertebrate with horny scales or plates, such as a snake, lizard, tortoise, *etc.* **reptil′ian** *a.* [L. *reptiles- repere*, creep]

repub′lic *n.* state in which the supremacy of the people or its elected representatives is formally acknowledged. **-repub′lican** *a.* and *n.* **-repub′licanism** *n.* [L. *res publica*, common weal]

repudiate *v.t.* cast off, disown; disclaim. **-repudia′tion** *n.* [L. *repudiare*, fr. *repudium*, divorce]

repugnant *a.* contrary; distasteful; refractory. **-repug′nance** *n.* **-repug′nancy** *n.* [L. *repugnare*, fight back]

repulse′ *v.t.* drive back; rebuff. **-repul′sion** *n.* repulsing; distaste, aversion. **-repul′sive** *a.* loathsome, disgusting. [L. *repellere, repuls-*,]

repute′ *v.t.* reckon, consider. -*n.* reputation, credit. **-reputa′tion** *n.* what is generally believed about a character; good fame. **-rep′utable** *a.* of good repute. [L. *reputare*, consider, weigh]

request′ *n.* asking; thing asked for. -*v.t.* ask. [OF. requester]

req′uiem *n.* mass for the dead. [L. = *rest* (the first word of *Introit* in the Mass for the Dead)]

require′ *v.t.* demand; want, need. **require′ment** *n.* **-req′uisite** (-zit) *a.* needed. -*n.* something necessary. **-requisition** *n.* formal demand, usually for military supplies, *etc.* -*v.t.* demand by an order of requisition; press into service. [L. *requirere*, requisite,]

requite′ *v.t.* repay; make return for; retaliate on. **-requi′tal** *n.* [quit]

rere′dos *n.* ornamental screen on wall behind altar. [AF. *areredos*]

rescind′ (-s-) *v.t.* cancel, annul. **rescission** *n.* [L. *rescindere*, cut off]

res′cue *v.t.* save, deliver. -*n.* rescuing. **res′cuer** *n.* [OF. *resourre*]

research′ *n.* investigation, *esp.* scientific study to try to discover facts. **-research′er** *n.* [*search*]

rese′da *n.* kinds of plant including the mignonette; grayish-green color. (F. *réséda*]

resem′ble (-z-) *v.t.* be like. **-resem′blance** *n.* [F. *ressembler*]

resent′ *v.t.* show or feel indignation at, retain bitterness about. **-resent′ment** *n.* **-resent′ful** *a.* [F. *ressentir*]

reserve′ *v.t.* hold back, set apart, keep for future use. -*n.* something reserved; part of an army only called out in emergency; reticence, concealment of feelings or friendliness. -*pl.* troops in support. **-reserva′tion** *n.* reserving or thing reserved; exception or limitation; land reserved for some public use. **reserved′** *a.* not showing feelings, lacking cordiality. **-reserv′ist** *n.* one serving in the reserve. [L. *reseruare*, keep back]

reservoir *n.* receptacle for liquid, *esp.* a large one built for storing water. [F. *reservoir*]

reset′ *v.t.* set again as jewels, bones, type *etc.* [*re-*, and *set*]

reside′ (-z-) *v.i.* dwell. **-res′idence** *n.* dwelling; house. **-res′idency** *n.* act or time of dwelling in a place. **-res′ident** *a.* and *n.* **-residen′tial** *a.* (L. *residere*, fr. *sedere*, sit]

res′idue (-z-) *n.* what is left. **-resid′ual** *a.* **-resid′uary** *a.* [L. *residuum*]

resign′ (-zin) *v.t.* give up—*v.i.* give up an office, employment, *etc.* **-resigned′** *a.* content to endure. **-resigna′tion** *n.* resigning; being resigned. [L. *resignare*, unseal]
resilient (-z-) *a.* rebounding. **-resil′ience** *n.* [L. *resilire*, jump back]
res′in (-z-) sticky substance formed in and oozing from plants, *esp.* firs and pines. -**res′inous** *a.* **-res′iny** *a.* **-res′inoid** *a.* **ros′in** *n.* resin. [L. resina]
resipisc′ence *n.* regret; wisdom after event. [L. *re*, again, *sapere*, be wiser]
resist′(-z-) *v.t.* withstand. -*v.i.* oppose. **resist′ance** *n.* **-resist′ant** *a.* **-resist′ible** *a.* **-resist′less** *a.* [L. *resistere*]
res′olute *a.* resolved; fixed in purpose. **res′olutely** *adv.* **-resolu′tion** *n.* a resolving; fixed determination; firmness; formal proposal put before a meeting; (*mus.*) resolving of a discord. [resolve]
resolve′ *v.t.* break up into parts, disintegrate; dissolve, disperse; solve (a problem); decide, determine; (*mus.*) follow a discord by a concord. **-resol′vable** *a.* -**resolvent** *n.* **-resolved′** *a.* firm; set on a course of action. -[F., L. *resolvers, resolut-*, loose]
res′onant (-z-) *a.* echoing, resounding. **res′onance** *n.* [L. *resonare*, resound]
resort′ (-z-) *v.i.* have recourse; frequent. -*n.* recourse; frequented place. [F. *ressortir*, rebound, go back]
resound′ (-z-) *v.i.* echo, ring, go on sounding. [sound]
resource′ *n.* skill in devising means. -*pl.* means of supplying a want; stock that can be drawn on, means of support. -**resource′ful** *a.* **-resource′-** fully *adv.* [F. *resource*]
respect′ *v.t.* defer to, treat with esteem. esteem; point or aspect. **-respect′able** *a.* worthy of respect. **-respectabil′ity** *n.* **respect′ful** *a.* **-respect′ive** *a.* several, separate. **-respect′ively** *adv.* [L. *respicere, respect-*, look back at]
respire′ *v.i.* breathe. **-respi′rable** *a.* **respira′tion** *n.* **-res′pirator** *n.* apparatus worn over the mouth and breathed through as a protection against dust, poison-gas, *etc.*, or to provide artificial respiration. -**res′piratory** *a.* [L. *respir- are*]
res′pite *n.* delay; breathing space; suspension of capital sentence; reprieve; suspension of labor. -*v.t.* grant respite to; reprieve; relieve by resting. [L. *respectus*, respect]
resplendent *a.* brilliant, shining. **resplend′ence** *n.* [L. *resplendere*, shine]
respond′ *v.i.* answer; act in answer. **respond′ent** *a.* replying. -*n.* one who answers; defendant. **-response′** *n.* answer. **-responsible** *a.* liable to answer for something; of good credit or position. **responsibil′ity** *n.* **-respon′sive** *a.* [L. *responders*, response,]
rest *n.* repose; freedom from exertion or activity; pause; supporting appliance; *v.i.* take rest; be supported. -*v.t.* give rest to; place on a support. **-rest′ful** *a.* **rest′less** *a.* [OE. *roest*]
rest *n.* remainder. -*v.i.* be left over. [F. *reste-* L. *restare*, remain]
rest *n.* appliance holding the butt of a lance when charging. [*arrest*]
restaurant *n.* eating-house. **restauranteur′** *n.* keeper of one. [F.]
restitution *n.* giving back or making up; indemnification. [L. *restitutio*]
rest′ive *a.* stubborn, resisting control; refractory. **-restiveness** *n.* [OF. *restif*]
restore′ *v.t.* build up again, repair, renew; re-establish; give back. **restoration** *n.* -**restor′ative** *a.* **restoring.** -*n.* medicine to strengthen, *etc.* [L, *restaurare, restaurat-*, repair]
restrain′ *v.t.* check, hold back. **-restraint′** *a.* restraining or means of restraining. [L. *restringere*, restrict]
restrict′ *v.t.* limit, bound. **-restric′tion** *n.* **-restrict′ive** *a.* [L. *restringere*, restrict]
result′ (-z-) *v.i.* follow as a consequence, end. -*n.* effect, outcome. **-result′ant** *a.* [L. *resultare*, leap back]
resume′ *v.t.* begin again; summarize. -**ré′sumé** *n.* summary. **-resump′tion** *n.* a resuming. **-resump′tive** *a.* [L. *resumere, resumpt-*, take back]
resurge′ *v.i.* rise again. **-resur′gent** *a.* [L. *resurgere*]
resurrect′ *v.t.* restore to life. **ressurec′tion** *n.* rising again; revival. [L. *resurrec, resurgere*, resurrect]
resuscitate *v.t.* revive, bring back from being nearly dead. **-resuscita′tion** *n.* [L. *resuscitare*, raise up again]
re′tail *n.* sale in small quantities. -*v.t.* sell in small quantities; recount. -*adv.* by retail. **-re′tailer** *n.* [OF. *retailler*, cut up]
retain′ *v.t.* keep; engage services of **retain′er** *n.* fee to retain a lawyer, or other professional person; follower of a nobleman, *etc* **-reten′tion** *n.* **-retent′ive** *a.* [L. *retinere*, hold back]
retaliate *v.t.* and *i.* repay in kind. **retalia′tion** *n.* **-retal′iatory** *a.* [L. *retaliare, retaliate*, fr. *talis*, like, such]
retard′ *v.t.* make slow or late.

retarda'tion *n.* [L. *retardate, tardus,* slow]

retch *v.i.* try to vomit. [OE. *hrcecan*]

ret'icent *a.* reserved in speech, not communicative. **-ret'icence** *n.* [L. *reticere,* fr. *tacere,* be silent]

reticulate, reticulated *a.* made or arranged like a net. **-retic'ulate** *v.t.* and *i.* make or be like a net. **-reticula'tion** *n.* **-ret'icule** *n.* small bag. [L. *reticule,* dim. of *rete,* net]

ret'ina *n.* sensitive layer at the back of the eye. [Med. L.]

ret'inue *n.* band of followers; group of attendants. [F. *retenir,* retain]

retire' *v.i.* withdraw; give up office or work: go away; go to bed. *-v.t.* cause to retire. **-retired'** *a.* that has retired from office, *etc.* **-retire'ment** *n.* **-reti'ring** *a.* unobtrusive, shy. [F. *retirer,* pull back]

retort' *v.t.* repay in kind; reply; hurl back (a charge, *etc.*). *-n.* thing done or said as vigorous reply or repartee; vessel with a bent neck used for distilling. [L. *retorquere, retort,* twist back]

retract' *v.t.* draw back; recant. *-v.i.* recant. **-retracta'tion** *n.* [L. *retrahere, retract,* draw back]

retral *a.* at or near the back; end; posterior.

retreat' *n.* act of, or military signal for, retiring; sunset call on a bugle, *etc;* place of seclusion. *-v.i.* retire. [F. *retraite,* fr. *retraire,* draw back]

retrench' *v.t.* cut down, reduce amount of (expense, *etc.*). **-retrench'ment** *n.* [F. *retrancher,* to cut off]

retribution *n.* recompense, *esp.* for evil deed; vengeance. **-retrib'utive** *a.* [L. *retributio* payment]

retrieve' *v.t.* bring in; regain; restore; rescue from a bad state. **-retriev'al** *n.* **retriev'er** *n.* dog trained to find and bring in shot game. **-retriev'able** *a.* **-retriev'ably** *adv.* [F. *retrouver,* find again]

retro- *prefix.* backward. [L.] **-ret'rograde** *a.* going backwards, reverting reactionary. **-retrogres'sion** *n.* **-retrogress'ive** *a.* **-ret'rospect** *n.* a looking back, survey of the past. **-retrospect'ive** *a.* **retrospection** *n.* **-retroces'sion** *n.* ceding back again. **-re'trovert** *n.* one who returns to his former creed.

retro'virus *n. pl.* **retro'viruses** any of a group of viruses that use RNA and reverse transcriptase to encode information and which cause cancers, AIDS, leukemia, etc.

retsin'a *n.* strong Greek wine flavored with pine resin.

return *v.i.* go or come back. *-v.t.* give or send back report officially; report as being elected; elect. *-n.* returning; being returned; profit; official report. [F. *retourner.* -L. *tornare,* turn]

rev *n.* (*sl.*) *abbrev.* of revolution (of engine)-**rev up** *v.t.* and *i.* cause (engine) to quicken speed; speed up.

reveal' *v.t.* make known; disclose. **revela'tion** *n.* what is revealed. *esp.* by divine inspiration. [L. *revelare,* draw back the veil, *velum*]

reveill'e *n.* morning bugle-call, *etc.*, to waken soldiers. [F. *rèveillez-vous,* wake up]

rev'el *v.i.* make merry. *-n.* merrymaking. **-rev'eler** *n.* **-rev'elry** *n.* [OF. *reveler,* make tumult]

revenant' *n.* ghost; one returning after long exile. [F.]

revenge' *v. refl.* avenge oneself-*v.t.* make retaliation for; avenge. *-n.* a revenging, desire for vengeance; act that satisfies this. **-revenge'ful** *a.* [OF. *revengier,* fr. L. *revindicare*]

rev'enue *n.* income, *esp.* of a state or institution; receipts; profits. [L. *revenière,* come back]

reverberate *v.t.* and *i.* echo or throw back. **-reverbera'tion** *n.* [L. *reverberare,* beat back]

revere' *v.t.* hold in great regard or religious respect. **-rev'erence** *n.* **revering;** veneration; capacity for revering. **rev'erend** *a.* worthy of reverence, *esp.* as a prefix to a clergyman's name. **rev'erent** *a.* showing reverence. **reverential** *a.* marked by reverence. [L. *revereri,* fr. *vereri,* fear]

rev'erie *n.* daydream, fit of musing. [F. *réverie,* dream]

revers' *n.* part of garment turned back *e.g.* lapels. [F.]

reverse' *v.t.* turn upside down or the other way round; change completely. *-n.* opposite or contrary; side opposite the obverse; defeat. *a.* opposite, contrary, **revers'al** *n.* **-revers'ible** *a.* **-rever'sion** *n.* return of an estate at the expiry of a grant to the person granting it; right to succeed to an estate, *etc.*, on a death or other condition; a returning to a state or condition. **-rever'sionary** *a.* **-rever'sioner** *n.* one holding a reversionary right. **-revert'** *v.i.* return to a former state; come back to a subject. [L. *vertere, vers-,* turn]

revet' *v.t.* face a wall with masonry, sandbags, *etc.* **-revet'ment** *n.* retaining wall. [F. *revétir,* clothe]

review′ *n.* revision; survey, inspection, *esp.* of massed military forces; critical notice of a book, *etc.*; periodical with critical articles, discussion of current events, *etc.* -*v.t.* hold, make, or write, a review of **-review′er** *n.* writer of reviews. [F. *revue*, fr. *revoir*, see again, revise]

revile′ *v.t.* abuse, reproach. [OF. *reviler*]

revise′ *v.t.* look over and correct. **-revi′ser** *n.* **-revi′sion** *n.* [L. *revisere*]

revive′ *v.i.* come back to life, vigor, *etc.* -*v.t.* bring back to life, vigor, use, *etc.* **revi′val** *n.* a reviving, *esp.* of religious fervor. **revivalist** *n.* organizer of religious revival. [L. *viuere*, live]

revoke′ *v.t.* annul. -*v.i.* at cards, to fail to follow suit though able to. -*n.* at cards, an act of revoking. **-rev′ocable** *a.* **revoca′tion** *n.* [L. *revocare*, call back]

revolt′ *v.i.* rise in rebellion; feel disgust. -*v.t.* affect with disgust. -*n.* rebellion. - **revolt′ing** *a.* disgusting, horrible. [F. *révolter*]

revolve′ *v.i.* turn round, rotate. -*v.t.* rotate; meditate upon. **-revolu′tion** *n.* rotation or turning round; turning or spinning round; great change; the violent overthrow of a system of government. **revolu′tionary** *a.* and *n.* **-revolu′tionize** *v.t.* **-revol′ver** *n.* repeating pistol with a revolving cartridge-magazine. [L. *revoluere, revolut-*]

revue′ *n.* bright and topical variety show with songs and dancing. [F.]

revulsion *n.* sudden violent change of feeling; strong distaste. [L. *revulsio*]

reward′ (-word) *v.t.* pay, or make return, for service, conduct, *etc.* -*n.* recompense or return. [ONF. *rewarder*]

rey′nard *n.* fox. [fr. German tale of *Reynard* the Fox]

rhab′domancy *n.* divination by means of rods, *esp.* water-finding (dowsing). **rhab′domantist** *n.* dowser. [G. *rhabdes*, rod, *manteia*, divination]

rhadaman′thine *a.* strict, severely just. [*Rhadamanthus*, judge of lower world]

rhap′sody *n.* enthusiastic or highflown composition. **-rhapsod′ic** *a.* **-rhap′sodist** *n.* (G. *rhapsodia*, piece of epic verse for one recital]

Rhe′nish *a.* and *n.* pert. to the river Rhine; Rhine wine. [L. *Rhenus*, Rhine]

rhe′ostat *n.* instrument for regulating electric current to constant degree of power. [G. *rheos*, stream]

rhe′sus *n.* sacred monkey of India, the bandar. **-rhe′sus fac′tor** *n.* feature distinguishing different types of human blood. [G. *myth.*]

rhetoric *n.* art of effective speaking or writing; artificial or exaggerated language. **-rhetor′ical** *a.* **-rhetori′cian** *n.* [G. *rhetor*, orator]

rheum *n.* watery catarrhal discharge from eyes and nose. **rheumatism** *n.* painful inflammation of joints. **-rheumat′ic** *a.* [G. *rheuma*, flow]

rhinoceros *n.* large thick-skinned animal with one or two horns on its nose. [G. *rhinokeros*, 'nosehorn']

rhino′virus *n. pl.* **-rhino′viruses** any of a large group of picornaviruses which are the cause of the common cold and other respiratory diseases.

rhizo′sphere *n.* the region of soil immediately surrounding and influenced by the roots of the plant. **-rhizo′spheric** *a.*

Rhode′island red *n.* breed of domestic fowl. [Rhode Island]

rhododendron *n.* flowering shrub. [G. = 'rose-tree']

rhom′bus, rhomb *n.* equilateral but not right-angled parallelogram, diamond or lozenge. [G. *rhombus*, thing that can be twirled]

rhu′barb *n.* plant of which the fleshy stalks are cooked and used as fruit; purgative from the root of a Chinese plant. [L. *rhabarbarum*, foreign 'rha,' G. *rha*, rhubarb]

rhumb (rum) *n.* any of the points on the compass, [*rhombus*]

rhyme *n.* identity of sounds at ends of lines of verse, or in words, word or syllable identical in sound to another; verse marked by rhyme; *v.t.* use (word) to make rhymes. **-rhymester, rhym′er** *n.* poet, *esp.* one considered mediocre; poetaster, versifier. **-rhyme scheme** *n.* pattern of rhymes used in piece of verse, *usu.* indicated by letters. **-rhym′ing slang** *n.* slang in which word is replaced by word or phrase that rhymes with it. [F. *rime*, fr. G. *rhythmos*, rhythm]

rhythm (riTHm) *n.* measured beat or flow, *esp*, of words, music, *etc.* **-rhyth′mic** *a.* **-rhyth′mical** *a.* **-rhyth′mically** *adv.* [G. *rhythmos*]

rib *n.* one of the curved bones springing from the spine and making the framework of the upper part of the body; curved timber of the framework of a boat. -*v.t.* furnish or mark with ribs. **-ribcage** *n.* cagelike enclosure of the chest fomred by the ribs and their connecting bones. [OE. *ribb*]

rib′ald *a.* irreverent, scurrilous, indecent. -*n.* ribald person. **-rib′aldry** *n.* ribald talk. [F. *ribaud*]

ribb'on, rib'and *n.* narrow band of fine fabric. [OF. *riban*]

ribo'somal RNA *n.* type of ribonucleic acid that is a basic, permanent component of the ribosomes and plays a major part in protein synthesis. [abbr. *rRNA*]

rice *n.* white seeds of an Eastern plant, used as food; the plant. **-rice'-paper** *n.* fine Chinese paper. [F. *riz*]

rich *a.* wealthy; fertile; abounding in some product or material; valuable; of food, containing much fat or sugar; mellow; amusing. **-rich'es** *n. pl.* wealth. **-rich'ly** *adv.* [OE. *rice*, powerful, rich]

rick *n.* stack of hay, *etc.* [OE. *hreac*]

rick'ets *n.* disease of children marked by softening of bones, bowlegs, *etc.* **-rick'ety** *a.* suffering from rickets; shaky, insecure. [orig. uncertain]

rick'shaw *n.* light two-wheeled vehicle drawn by man. [Jap. abbrev. of *jiurick* show, *jin*, man, *riki*, power, *sha* carriage]

ric'ochet *n.* skipping on water or ground of a bullet or other projectile; hit made after it. *-v.i.* skip thus. *-v.t.* hit or aim with a ricochet. [F.]

rocott'a *n.* soft Italian cheese made from whey, whole milk, or both.

rid *v.t.* clear, relieve of **-ridd'ance** *n.* [ON. *rythja,* to clear (land)]

rid'dle *n.* question made puzzling to test the ingenuity of the hearer, enigma; puzzling fact, thing, or person. *-v.i.* speak in or make riddles. [OE. roedels]

rid'dle *n.* coarse sieve. *-v.t.* pass through a sieve; pierce with many holes like those of a sieve. [OE. *hrider*]

ride *v.i.* go on horseback or in a vehicle; lie at anchor; float lightly. *-n.* journey on a horse or other animal or in any vehicle; road for riding on horseback. **-ri'der** *n.* one who rides; supplementary clause; mathematical problem on a given proposition. **-ri'derless** *n.* [OE. *ridan*]

ridge *n.* line of meeting of two sloping surfaces; long narrow hill; long narrow elevation on a surface. *-v.t.* form into ridges. [OE. *hyrcg*, spine, back]

ridiculous *a.* deserving to be laughed at, absurd, foolish. **-rid'icule** *v.t.* laugh at, hold up as ridiculous. *-n.* treatment of a person or thing as ridiculous. [L. *ridiculus-ridere,* laugh]

rife *a.* prevalent; plentiful. [OE.]

riff'-raff *n.* rabble, disreputable people. (earlier *riff* and *raff.* OF. *rif et raf]*

ri'fle *v.t.* search and rob; make spiral grooves in (gun-barrel, *etc.*). *-n.* firearm with a long barrel. **-ri'fling** *n.* arrangement of grooves in a gun barrel. [F. *rifler*]

rift *n.* a crack, split. **-rift'-vall'ey** *n.* (*geol.*) subsistence between two faults. [ON. *ript*]

rig *v.t.* provide (a ship) with spars, ropes, *etc.*; equip; set up, *esp.* as a makeshift. *-n.* way a ship's masts and sails are arranged; costume; style of dress; apparatus for drilling oil and gas. **-rigg'ing** *n.* spars and ropes of a ship. [orig. uncertain]

rigaton'i *n.* pasta in the form of short, curved, thick tubes with grooved sides.

right (rit) *a.* straight; just; proper; true; correct; genuine. -right side, side of a person which is to the east when he faces north, opposite of left. *-v.t.* bring back to a vertical position; do justice to. *-v.i.* come back to a vertical position-*n.* what is right, just, or due. *-adv.* straight; properly; very; on or to the right side. **-righteous** (ri-chus) *a.* just, upright. **righteousness** *n.* **-right'ful** *a.* **-right'ly** *adv.* **-right'-hand man**, subordinate chiefly relied on. [OE. *riht*]

ri'gid *a.* stiff; harsh; unyielding. **rigid'ity** *n.* **-ri'gidly** *adv.* [L. *rigidus]*

rig'marole *n.* meaningless string of words. [earlier *ragman-roll*, catalog]

rig'or *n.* harshness, severity, strictness; sense of chill and shivering. **-rig'orous** *a.* [L. *rigor*]

rijs'ttafel *n.* Indonesian food consisting of a selection of rice dishes to which are added small pieces of a variety of other foods, such as meat, fish, fruit, pickles, and curry. [Du. *rijst,* rice, *tafei*, table]

rile *v.t.* make angry. [earlier *roil,* disturb, fr. OF. *rouil*, mud]

rill *n.* small stream. [of Teut. orig.]

rim *n.* outer ring of a wheel; edge, border. **-rim'less** *a.* [OE. *rima*]

rime. *See* **rhyme.**

rime *n.* hoar-frost. [OE. *hrim*]

rind *n.* outer coating of trees, fruits, *etc.* [OE]

rin'derpest *n.* a contagious cattle disease. [Ger. cattle plague]

ring *n.* small circle of gold, *etc.*, *esp.* as worn on the finger; any circular appliance, band, coil, rim, *etc.*; circle of persons. *-v.t.* put a ring round. **-ring'let** *n.* curly lock of hair. **-ring'leader** *n.* instigator of a mutiny, riot, *etc.* **-ring'-dove** *n.* woodpigeon. **-ring'ou'zel** *n.* kind of thrush. **-ring'worm** *n.* skin disease in circular patches. [OE. *hring*]

ring *v.i.* give out a clear resonant sound, as a bell; resound. *-v.t.* cause (a bell) to sound.

-*n.* a ringing. [OE. *hringan*]

rink *n.* sheet of ice for skating; floor for roller-skating. [Sc.]

rinse (-s) *v.t.* clean by putting in and emptying out water; wash lightly. -*n.* a rinsing. [F. *rincer*]

ri'ot *n.* tumult, disorder; loud revelry; unrestrained indulgence or display. -*v.i.* make or engage in a riot; brawl. **-ri'otous** *a.* **-ri'otously** *adv.* [F. *riotte*]

rip *v.t.* cut or tear away, slash, rend. -*n.* rent or tear, broken water, as in tide-rip. [of Teut. orig.]

rip *n.* worthless horse, man; dissolute man. [orig. uncertain.]

ripa'rian *a.* of or on the banks of a river. [L. *ripa,* river-bank]

ripe *a.* matured, ready to be reaped, eaten, *etc.* **-ri'pen** *v.i.* and *t.* [OE.]

riposte' *n.* (fencing) quick return thrust after parry; verbal counter-stroke, *repartee.* [F.]

rip'ple *v.i.* flow or form into little waves. -*v.t.* form ripples on. -*n.* slight wave or ruffling of surface. [*rip*]

rise *v.i.* get up; move upwards; reach a higher level; appear above the horizon; adjourn. -*n.* rising; upslope; increase; beginning. [OE. *risan*]

risible (-z-) *a.* laughable; inclined to laugh. **-risibil'ity** *n.* [L. *risibilis*]

ri'sing *n.* revolt. [rise]

risk *n.* danger. -*v.t.* venture. **-risk'y** *a.* **risk'ily** *adv.* (F. *risque]*

risot'to *n.* dish or rice cooked in stock with various other ingredients. [It.]

riss'ole *n.* cake of chopped meat, *etc.* fried. (F.]

rite *n.* a formal practice or custom, *esp.* religious. **-rit'ual** *a.* concerning rites. -*n.* prescribed order or book of rites. **-rit'ualism** *n.* practice of ritual. **-rit'ualist** *n.* [L. *ritus*]

ri'val *n.* one that competes with another for favor, success, *etc.* -*v.t.* vie with. *a.* in the position of a rival. **-ri'valry** *n.* emulation; competition. (L. rivalis]

rive *v.t.* and *i.* to split. [ON. *rifa*]

riv'er *n.* large stream of water. **riv'erbead** *n.* spring, source, of a river. **riv'er** basin *n.* land that is drained by a river and its tributaries. **-riv'er-horse** *n.* hippopotamus. [F. *rivière*]

riv'et *n.* bolt for fastening plates of metal together, the end being put through the holes and then beaten flat. -*v.t.* fasten with rivets; clinch; (*fig.*) fascinate, enthrall. [F.]

riv'ulet *n.* small stream. [It. *rivoletto*]

roach. *See* **cockroach.**

roach *n.* freshwater fish. [OF. *roche*]

road *n.* track or way prepared for passengers, vehicles, *etc.*; direction, way; roadstead. **-road' book** *n.* guide-book. **road'house** *n.* roadside refreshment house. **-road' metal** *n.* stones broken up for road-making. **-road'stead** *n.* piece of water near the shore where ships may lie at anchor. **-road'ster** *n.* horse, bicycle, *etc.*, suited for the road. **-road'way** *n.* main part of road used by vehicles. [OE. *rad,* riding]

roam *v.t.* and *i.* wander about, rove. [orig. uncertain]

roan *a.* having a coat in which the main color is thickly interspersed with another, *esp.* bay or sorrel or chestnut mixed with white or gray. -*n.* animal with such a coat. [F. rouan]

roan *n.* soft sheepskin leather. [orig. uncertain]

roar *n.* loud deep hoarse sound as of a lion, thunder, voice in anger, *etc.* -make such sound. -*v.t.* utter in roaring voice, shout out. [OE. *rarian*]

roast *v.t.* cook by exposure to an open fire, achieve a similar effect by cooking in an oven. -*v.i.* be roasted. -*n.* **roasted joint.** *a.* roasted. [OF. *rostir*]

rob *v.t.* plunder, steal from. **-robb'er** *n.* - **robb'ery** *n.* [OF. *rober*]

robe *n.* long outer garment. -*v.t.* dress. *v.i.* put on robes or vestments. (F.]

rob'in *n.* brown red-breasted bird of the thrush family. **-robin-red'-breast** *n.* [Robin]

ro'bot *n.* automated machine, *esp.* performing functions in a human manner; automaton, mechanical slave. **-ro'botics** *n.* science or technology of designing, building, and using robots; robot dancing. **-ro'botize** *v.t.* automate; cause (a person) to be or become mechanical and lifeless, like a robot. [Czech, fr. Karel Kapek's play, *R.U.R.* (Rossum's Universal Robots)]

robust' *a.* sturdy. [L. *robustus*]

roc *n.* giant fabulous bird. [Pers. *rukh*]

rock *n.* stone; large rugged mass of stone; hard toffee. **-rockery, rock garden** *n.* mound or grotto of stones or rocks for plants in a garden. **-rock'y** *a.* -also in compounds, as **rock badger, rock crab, rock pigeon, rock rose, rock serpent,** *etc.* [F. *roche*]

rock *v.i.* sway to and fro. -*v.t.* cause to do this. **-rock'er** *n.* curved piece of wood, *etc.*, on which a thing may rock; rocking chair. **-rock-and-roll, rock-'n'-roll** *n.* type of pop music of 1950s, blend of rhythm-and-blues and country-and-western; dancing performed to such music. **-rock mus'ic** *n.* pop music developing from the rock-and-roll idiom. [OE. *rocoian*]

rock'et *n.* self-propelling device powered by burning of explosive contents, used as firework, for display, signalling, line carrying, weapon, *etc.*; vehicle propelled by rocket engine, as weapon or carrying spacecraft. *-v.i.* move fast, *esp.* upwards, as **rocket, rock'etry** *n.* [It. *rocchetta*, dim. of *rocca*, distaff]

roco'co *a.* of furniture, architecture, *etc.*, having much conventional decoration, tastelessly florid; antiquated. *-n.* rococo style. [F.]

rod *n.* slender, straight round bar, wand, stick or switch; birch or cane; measure a pole. [OE. *rood*]

ro'dent *a.* gnawing. *-n.* gnawing animal, *e.g.*, rat, hare, *etc.* [L. *rodere*, gnaw]

ro'deo *n.* gathering of cattle to be branded or marked; exhibition of skill in steer wrestling, and bronco riding, *etc.* [Mex. -Sp.]

rodomontade' *n.* boastful talk. [F.]

roe *n.* small species of deer. [OE. *ra*]

roe *n.* mass of eggs in a fish. [of Teut orig.]

Roent'gen rays *See* **x-rays.**

roga'tion *n.* supplication; Rogation Days, the three days before Ascension Day. [L. *rogare*, to ask]

rogue *n.* rascal, knave; sturdy beggar; mischief-loving person or child wild beast of savage temper living apart from its herd. **-ro'guish** (-gish) *a.* **ro'guery** *n.* [orig. uncertain]

roi'ster *v.i.* swagger, bluster, revel noisily. **-roisterer** *n.* [OF. *rustre*, rough fellow]

role *n.* actor's part; part played in real life. [F]

roll *n.* piece of paper, *etc.*, rolled up; list or catalogue; small loaf-*v.t.* move by turning over and over; wind round; smooth out with a roller. *-v.i.* move by turning over and over; move or sweep along; of a ship, swing from side to side. **roll'-call** *n.* calling out of a list of names, *e.g.*, as in schools, army. **-roll'er** *n.* cylinder used for pressing or smoothing, supporting something to be moved, winding something on, *etc.* **-roll'er-bear'ing** *n.* **-roll'er mill** *n.* **-roll'er skate** *n.*, *etc.* **-roll'ing-stock** *n.* locomotives, carriages, *etc.* of railway. [F. *rouler*, fr. L. *rotula*, dim. of *rota*, wheel]

rollicking *a.* boisterously jovial. *-n.* jollity; frolic. [orig. unknown]

ro'ly-po'ly *n.* pudding of paste covered with jam and rolled up. *-a.* fat, podgy. [*redupl.* of roll]

Ro'man *a.* of Rome or the Church of Rome. **-Roman type,** plain upright letters, ordinary script of printing. **-Roman figures,** letters, V, X, L, C, D, M, used to represent numbers in the manner of the Romans. **-Roman'ic** *a.* evolved from Latin. **-Ro'manize** *v.t.* make Roman or Roman Catholic. [L. *Romanus*, fr. *Roma*, Rome]

Romance' *n.* vernacular language of certain countries, developed from Latin and developing into French, Spanish, *etc.* **-romance'** *n.* tale of chivalry; tale with scenes remote from ordinary life; literature like this; love-affair or event or atmosphere suggesting it; sympathetic imagination; exaggeration; picturesque falsehood. **-roman'cer** *n.* **-roman'tic** *a.* characterized by romance; of literature, *etc.*, preferring passion and imagination to proportion and finish. **-romant'icism** *n.* [OF. *romanz*]

Rom'any *n.* gypsy; gypsy languages. gypsy. [Romany *rom*, man]

romp *v.i.* frolic. *-n.* spell of romping; child given to romping. [earlier *ramp*]

ron'deau *n.* poem, usually of 13 iambic lines; rondo. **-ron'del** *n.* short, similar poem. **-ron'delet** *n.* poem of 7 lines, of which 2 are refrains. [F.]

ron'do *n.* piece of music with leading theme to which return is made; rondeau. [It.]

rood *n.* the Cross on which Christ died; crucifix; quarter of an acre. [OE. *rod*, gallows, measure of land]

roof *n.* outside upper covering of a building; (aircraft) flying height limit. *v.t.* put a roof on, be a roof over. **-roof-garden** *n.* garden on a flat roof. [OE. *hrol*]

rook (-oo) *n.* bird of the crow family. **rook'ery** *n.* colony of rooks; breeding-ground of seals. [OE. *hroc*]

rook *n.* piece at chess, also called a castle. [Pars. *rukh*]

rook'ie *n.* (*sl.*) raw recruit. [*recruit*]

room *n.* space; space enough; division of a house. **-room'ing house** *n.* building divided into separate rooms for rent. **-room'y** *a.* having plenty of space. [OE. *rum*]

roost *n.* perch for fowls; henhouse. *v.i.* perch. **-roost'er** *n.* barnyard cock. [OE. *hrost*]

root *n.* part of a plant that grows down into the earth and conveys nourishment to the plant; source, origin; original or vital part. *-v.t.* cause to take root; pull by the roots. -*v.i.* take root. [ON. *rot*]

root, root'le *v.t.* turn up with snout, as a pig; rummage. [OE. *wrotan*]

rope *n.* thick cord. -*v.t.* secure or mark off with a rope. **-ro'py** *a.* sticky and stringy. **-rope-dancer** *n.* tight-rope performer. **-rope' trick** *n.* Indian vanishing trick. **-rope' walk** *n.* long shed for rope-spinning. **-rope' walk'er** *n.* walker on the tight rope, an acrobat. [OE. *rap*]

ror'qual *n.* large variety of whale. [Norw. *rond*, red, *kval*, whale]

rose *n.* beautiful flower of many varieties rose bush; perforated flat nozzle for a hose, *etc.*; pink color -*a.* of this color. **-rosa'ceous** *a.* like a rose, of rose family. **ro'sary** *n.* string of beads for keeping count of prayers, form of prayer. **-ro'sery** *n.* **rose-garden. -ros'eate** *a.* rose-colored, rosy. **-rosette'** *n.* rose-shaped bunch of ribbon; rose-shaped architectural ornament. **-rose'wood** *n.* fragrant wood. **-ro'sy** *a.* rose-colored; flushed; hopeful. [L. *rose*]

rose'mary *n.* evergreen fragrant shrub. [L. *ros marinus*, 'sea-dew']

ros'in. *See* **resin.**

ros'ter *n.* list or plan showing turns of duty. [Du. *rooster,* list]

ros'trum *n.* platform for public speaking. [L. = *beak* (the platform in the Roman Forum being adorned with beaks of captured ships)]

rot *v.t.* and *i.* decompose naturally. -*n.* decay, putrefaction; disease of sheep; nonsense. **-rott'en** *a.* decomposed; corrupt. **-rott'er** *n.* (*sl.*) 'bad egg', waster. [OE, *rotian*]

ro'ta *n.* roll (of scholars, *etc.*) [L.]

ro'tary *a.* of movement, circular. **rotate'** *v.i.* move round a center or on a pivot. -*v.t.* cause to do this. **-rota'tion** *n.* **-ro'tatory** (ro'–ta-tory) *a.* **-Rotary Club,** one of an international group of business men's clubs for community service, *etc.* [L. *rota*, wheel]

rote *n.* by rote, by memory without understanding. [orig. uncertain]

ro'tor *n.* rotating part of machine or apparatus, *e.g.*, dynamo, turbine, *etc.* [L. *rota*, wheel]

rotund' *a.* round; plump; rich sounding. **-rotundity** *n.* [L. *rotuitdas* fr. *rota,* wheel]

rouge *n.* red powder used to color the cheeks or lips. -*v.t.* and *i.* color with rouge. [F. = *red*]

rough (ruf), *a.* not smooth, of irregular surface; violent, boisterous; lacking refinement; approximate; in a preliminary form. -*v.t.* make rough; plan out approximately. -*n.* disorderly ruffian; rough state; (*golf*) rough ground adjoining the fairway. **-rough'age** *n.* bulky, unassimilated portion of food promoting proper intestinal action. **-rough'en** *v.t.* **roughcast** *a.* coated with a mixture of lime and gravel. -*n.* such mixture. -*v.t.* coat with it. **-rough' hew** *v.t.* shape roughly. **-rough'ly** *adv.* **-rough'-house** *n.* indoor brawl. **-rough'neck** *n.* bad-tempered man; member of drilling team at an oil well. [OE. *ruh*]

roul'eau *n.* cylindrical packet of coins. [F.]

roulette' *n.* game of chance played with a ball on a table with a revolving center. [F.]

round (rownd) *a.* spherical or cylindrical or circular or nearly so; roughly correct; large; plain. -*adv.* with a circular or circuitous course. -*n.* something round in shape; rung; movement in a circle; recurrent duties; customary course, as of a postman or military patrol; cartridge for a firearm. -*prep.* about; on all sides of. *v.t.* make round; get round. -*v.i.* become round. **-round'about** *n.* merry-go-round; *a.* circuitous. **-round'ly** *adv.* **-round'ers** *n. pl.* ball game. **-round'-rob'in** *n.* petition signed with names in a circle so that it may not be known who signed first. **-round-trip** *n.* journey to a place and back again, *usu.* by the same route. **-round'-up** *n.* driving of cattle together; arresting of criminals. [F. *rond*]

round'el *n.* small disk, rondeau. [OF. *rondel*]

round'elay *n.* simple song with refrain. [OE.]

rouse (rowz) *v.t.* wake up, stir up, cause to rise. -*v.i.* waken. **-rous'ing** *a.* stirring. [orig. unknown]

rout (rowt) *n.* troop; disorderly crowd; large evening party; disorderly retreat. *v.t.* defeat decisively; throw into disarray. [L. *rupta*, broken]

route *n.* road, way. [F.]

routine' *n.* regular course; regularity of procedure. [F. fr. *route*]

rove *v.i.* wander without fixed destination. -*v.t.* wander over. **-ro'ver** *n.* one who roves; pirate. [orig. uncertain]

row *n.* number of things in a straight line. [OE. *raw*]

row *v.i.* propel a boat by oars. -*v.t.* propel by oars. -*n.* spell of rowing. [OE. *rowan*]

row *n.* uproar; dispute. [orig. uncertain]

row'an *n.* mountain ash. [Scand. orig.]

rowd'y *n.* rough. -*a.* disorderly.

row'diness *n*. -**row'dyism** *n*. [orig. uncertain]

row'el *n*. small wheel with points on a spur. [F. *roue*, wheel]

rowl'ock *n*. appliance serving as point of leverage for an oar. [earlier *oarlock*, OE. *arloc*, oar-fastening]

roy'al *a*. of, worthy of, befitting, patronzed by, a king or queen; splendid. -**roy'alist** *n*. supporter of monarchy. -**roy'alty** *n*. royal dignity or power; royal persons; payment to an owner of land for the right to work minerals, or to an inventor for use of his invention; payment to an author based on sales. [F. fr. L. *regalia*, fr. *rex. reg*, king]

rub *v.t.* subject to friction; pass the hand over; abrade, chafe; remove by friction. *v.i.* come into contact accompanied by friction, become frayed or worn with friction. -**rub'bing** *n*. [orig. obscure]

rubb'er *n*. coagulated sap of rough, elastic consistency, of certain tropical trees (also **In'dia rubb'er, gum elastic, ca'outchoue**); piece of rubber, *etc*. used for erasing. -*a*. made of rubber; -**rub'berize** *v.t.* coat, impregnate, treat with rubber. -**rub'bery** *a*. -**rub'berneck** (*sl.*) *n*. person who gapes inquisitively; sightseer, tourist. -*v.i.* stare in naive or foolish manner. -**rub'ber stamp** *n*. device for imprinting dates, *etc*.; automatic authorization. [orig. obscure]

rubb'er *n*. series of three games at various card games; series of an odd number of games or contests at various games; two out of three games won. [orig. uncertain]

rubb'ish *n*. refuse, waste material; trash, nonsense. -**rubb'ishy** *a*. valueless. [orig. uncertain]

rub'ble *n*. irregular pieces of stone, brick, *etc*.; masonry made of this. [orig. uncertain. c.f. rubbish]

rubesc'ent *a*. -pubescence *n*. reddening. [L. *rubens*, red]

ru'bicund *a*. ruddy; red-faced. [L. *rubicundus*]

ru'bric *n*. chapter heading; direction in a liturgy (properly one printed in red) -**ru'bric** *v.t.* mark, write, or print in red; supply with rubrics -**rubrica'tion** *n*. [L. *rubrica*, red earth]

ru'by *n*. red precious stone; its color. -*a*. of this color. [L. *ruber*, red]

ruche, rouche *n*. pleated frilling; ruffle. [F.]

ruck *n*. crowd; band. [of Scand. orig.]

ruck *n*. a crease. -*v.t.* and *i*. to make or become wrinkled. [ON. *hrukka*]

ruck'sack (rook'-) *n*. pack carried on the back by hikers, climbers. [Ger. *rüken*. back, sack, bag]

rudd *n*. freshwater fish, the red-eye. [obs. *rud*, red]

rudd'er *n*. flat piece hinged to the stern of a ship, boat, airplane, *etc*. to steer by. [OE. *rothor*, steering oar]

rudd'y *a*. of a fresh or healthy red; ruddy-faced. [OE. *rudig*]

rude *a*. primitive; roughly made; uneducated; uncivil. -**rude'ly** *adv*. [L. *rudis*, rough]

ru'diment *n*. beginning, germ. -*pl*. elements, first principles. -**rudimen'tary** *a*. [L. *rudis*, rough]

rue *n*. plant with strong-smelling bitter leaves. [OF. fr. L. *ruta*]

rue *v.t.* and *i*. regret; repent; lament; suffer for. -*n*. repentance. -**rue'ful** *a*. -**rue'fully** *adv*. (OE. *hreowan*]

ruff *n*. starched and frilled collar; bird with cuff of feathers. -(**reeve** *fem*.) -**ruf'fle** *n*. frilled cuff. -*v.t.* crumple, disorder; frill or pleat; annoy, put out. [orig. uncertain]

ruff *n*. at cards, act of trumping. -*v.t.* and *i*. trump. [orig. a game, F. *ronfle*]

ruff'ian *n*. rough lawless fellow, a desperado. -**ruff'ianism** *n*. -**ruff'ianly** *a*. [It. *ruffiana*, pander]

ru'fous *a*. reddish-brown in color. [L. *rufus*]

rug *n*. thick woolen wrap; floor-mat, of shaggy or thick-piled surface. -**rugg'ed** *a*. rough, broken; furrowed; unpolishable; harsh. [of Scand. orig.]

rug'by *n*. British football game, played with two teams of fifteen players each. -**rugg'er** *n*. (*sl.*) [Rugby school]

ru'gose *a*. wrinkled. -**rugos'ity** *n*. [L. *ruga*, wrinkle]

ru'in *n*. downfall; fallen or broken state; decay, destruction. -*pl*. ruined buildings, *etc*. -*v.t.* reduce to ruins; bring to decay or destruction, spoil; cause loss of fortune to. -**ruina'tion** *n*. -**ru'inous** *a*. -**ru'inously** *adv*. [L. *ruina*, fr. *ruere*, rush down]

rule *n*. a principle or precept; what is usual; government; strip of wood, *etc*., for measuring length. -*v.t.* govern, decide. -**ru'ler** *n*. one who governs; strip of wood, *etc*., for measuring or drawing straight lines. [OF. *reule*, fr. L. *reguila-regere*, govern]

rum *n*. spirit distilled from sugar cane. [orig. uncertain]

rum *a*. odd, strange. [Romany]

rum'ba *n*. Cuban dance. [Sp]

rum'ble *v.i.* make a noise as of distant thunder, a heavy cart moving along, *etc.* -*n.* such noise. [imit. orig.]

ru'minate *v.i.* chew and cud; meditate. **-ru'minant** *a.* cud-chewing. -*n.* cud-chewing animal. **-rumina'tion** *n.* -**rum'inative** *a.* reflective; considered. [L. *ruminari*, chew the cud]

rumm'age *v.t.* and *i.* search thoroughly. -*n.* a ransacking; odds and ends; upheaval. [orig. stowage of casks. OF. *arrumage*]

rumm'er *n.* large drinking-glass. [Du. *rœmer*]

rumm'y *n.* card game. [orig. uncertain]

ru'mor *n.* hearsay, common talk; current but unproved statement, usually rather vague. -*v.t.* put round as a rumor. [L. *rumor*, noise]

rump *n.* tail-end; buttocks. [ME. *rumpe*]

rum'ple *v.t.* crease or winkle. -*n.* crease. [of Teut. orig.]

rum'pus *n.* (*sl.*) uproar; disturbance, [orig. uncertain]

run *v.i.* move rapidly on the legs; go quickly; flow; flee; compete in a race, revolve; continue; have a certain meaning. -*v.t.* expose oneself, be exposed; cause to run, land and dispose of (smuggled goods). -*n.* act or spell of running, rush; tendency, course; space for keeping chickens. -**runn'er** *n.* **-runner-up** *n.* next after winner in a contest. **-run'way** *n.* pathway made by animals to and from feeding ground or water; level stretch of ground for aircraft landing and taking off. [OE. *rinnan*]

run'agate *n.* deserter, fugitive; vagabond. [var. of *renegade*]

rune *n.* character of the earliest Teutonic alphabet. **-ru'nic** *a.* [ON. *run*, mystery]

rung *n.* cross-bar or spoke, *esp.* in a ladder. [OE. *hrung*]

run'let *n.* small wine-cask. [OF. *rondelet*]

runn'el *n.* gutter; small stream or brook. [OE. *rinnelle*, brook]

runt *n.* dwarf, undersized animal; cabbage-stalk. [orig. unknown]

rupee' *n.* Indian unit of money. [Hind. *rupiyah*]

rup'ture *n.* breaking or breach; hernia. -*v.t.* and *i.* break or burst. [L. *rupture*, fr. *rumpere*, break]

ru'ral *a.* of the country; rustic. **-ru'rally** *adv.* [L. *ruralis*, fr. *rus*, *rur*, country]

ruse (-z-) *n.* stratagem, trick. [F.]

rush *n.* plant with a slender pithy stem growing in marshes, *etc.*; the stems as a material for baskets. **-rush-bottomed** *a.* of chair with seat made from rushes. -**rush'en** *a.* made of rushes. **-rush'light** *n.* candle, *etc.*, with rushpith wick. **-rush'y** *a.* full of rushes. [OE. *rysc*]

rush *v.t.* impel or carry along violently and rapidly; take by sudden assault. -*v.i.* move violently or rapidly. -*n.* a rushing; pressure of business affairs. [AF. *russher*, OF. *ruser*, drive back]

rusk *n.* piece of bread rebaked; various biscuits. [Sp. *rosca*, twist (of bread)]

russ'et *a.* of reddish-brown color. -*n.* the color; kind of apple. [F. *roux*, red]

rust *n.* reddish-brown coating formed on iron by oxidation and corrosion; disease of plants. -*v.i.* and *v.t.* contract or affect with rust. **-rust'y** *a.* **-rust'less** *a.* **-rust'proof** *a.* [OE.]

rust'ic *a.* of, or as of, country people; rural; of rude manufacture; made of untrimmed branches. -*n.* country-man, peasant. **-rusti'city** *n.* **-rust'icate** *v.t.* banish from a university. -*v.i.* live a country life. **-rustica'tion** *n.* [L. *rusticus*, fr. *rus*, country]

rus'tle (-sl-) *v.i.* make a sound as of brown dead leaves, *etc.*; steal, *esp.* cattle. -*n.* the sound. **-rus'tler** *n.* someone, something, that rustles; cattle thief. [imit. orig.]

rut *n.* periodical sexual excitement of the male deer and certain other animals. *v.i.* be under the influence of this. [F., fr. L. *rugire*, roar]

rut *n.* furrow made by a wheel; settled habit or way of living. **-rutt'y** *a.* [F. *rotate*, way, track, *etc.*]

ruth *n.* pity. **-ruth'less** *a.* pitiless. -**ruth'lessly** *adv.* [*rue*]

Ruth *n.* book of the Old Testament.

rye *n.* grain used as fodder or for bread; plant bearing it.; whiskey made from it **-rye bread** *n.* [OE. *ryge*]

rye-grass *n.* kinds of grass cultivated for fodder. [earlier *ray-grass*, fr. obs. *ray*, darnel]

S

Sabb'ath *n.* Jewish Sunday or seventh day, *i.e.*, Christian Saturday. -**Sabbata'rian** *n.* strict observer of Sunday. **-Sabbatar'ianism** *n.* **-Sabbat'ical** *a.* [Heb. *shabbath*]

sa'ber (-her) *n.* cavalry sword, slightly curved. -*v.t.* strike with one. [F.]

sa'ble *n.* small Arctic animal; its fur; black. -*a.* black. [OF.]

sab'ot *n.* wooden shoe worn by some European peasants. **-sab'otage** *n.* intentional damage done by workmen to their materials, *etc.* -**saboteur'** *n.* [F.]

sac *n.* cavity in an animal or vegetable body. [F. = *sack*]

sacc'ade *n.* movement of the eye when it makes a sudden change of fixation, as in reading; sudden check given to a horse. [F. = jerk on the reins of a horse]

sacc'harin(e) *a.* pertaining to sugar. -*n.* extremely sweet substance from coal tar. [F., fr. G. *sakcharon*, sugar]

sacerdotal (sas'-) *a.* of priests. -**sacerdo'talism** *n.* -**sacerdo'talist** *n.* [L. *sacerdos, sacerdot-*, priest]

sa'chet (sa'sha) *n.* small envelope or bag. [F.]

sack *n.* large bag, usually of some coarse textile material; (*sl.*) dismissal. -*v.t.* pillage (a captured town, *etc.*); (*sl.*) dismiss. -**sack'-cloth** *n.* coarse fabric used for sacks. -**sacking** *n.* material used for sacks. [Heb. *saq*]

sack *n.* dry wine; warmed and spiced drink. [F. *vin see*, dry wine]

sack'but *n.* old wind instrument resembling trombone. [F. *saquebute*]

sacrament *n.* one of certain ceremonies of the Christian Church, *esp.* the Eucharist. -**sacrament'al** *a.* [L. *sacramentum*]

sa'cred *a.* dedicated, regarded as holy. -**sa'credly** *adv.* [OF. *sacrer-*, L. *sacer*, sacred]

sac'rifice *n.* making of an offering to a god; thing offered; giving something up for the sake of something else; act of giving up; thing so given up as a sacrifice. -*v.t.* offer as sacrifice. -**sacrifi'cial** *a.* pert. to sacrifice. [OF.]

sacrilege *n.* violation of something sacred. -**sacrile'gious** *a.* [F. fr. L. *sacer*, holy]

sacristan *n.* an official in charge of the vestments and vessels of a church. -**sac'risty** *n.* vestry, room where sacred vestments, *etc.* are kept. [Low L. *sacristia*, vestry]

sac'rosanct *a.* secure by religious fear against desecration or violence. [L. *sacrosametus* fr. *sacer*, sacred]

sad *a.* sorrowful; deplorably bad; of color; dull, sober. -**sad'ly** *adv.* -**sadd'en** *v.t.* [OE. *sæd*, sated]

sad'dle *n.* rider's seat to fasten on a horse, or form part of a bicycle, *etc.*; part of a shaft; joint of mutton or venison; ridge of a hill. -*v.t.* put a saddle on-**sadd'le-back** *n.* hill with saddle-shaped depression on top. -**sadd'le-bag** *n.* bag hung from horse's or bicycle saddle. -**sadd'le-bow** *n.* arched front of saddle. -**sadd'le-cloth** *n.* cloth placed on horse's back under saddle. -**sadd'ler** *n.* maker of saddles, *etc.* -**sadd'lery** *n.* -**sad'dle-tree** *n.* saddle frame. [OE. *sadol*]

Sadd'ucee *n.* member of ancient Jewish sect which believed in immortality but denied resurrection. [G. *Suddoukaios*]

sa'dism (-a-) *n.* psychological perversion involving delight in cruelty; (*colloq.*) love of cruelty. [Marquis de *Sade*, 1740-1814]

safa'ri *n.* (party) making overland (hunting) trip, *esp.* in Africa. [*Swahili*]

safe *a.* uninjured, out of danger; not involving risk; cautious; trustworthy. -*n.* strong box; ventilated cupboard for meat, *etc.* -**safe'ly** *adv.* -**safe'ty** *n.* -**safecon'duct** *n.* passport or permit to pass somewhere. -**safe'-guard** *n.* protection. -*v.t.* protect. -**safety-curtain** *n.* in theater, fire-proof curtain. -**safe'ty-lamp** *n.* miner's lamp constructed to prevent its flame igniting flammable gases. -**safety-valve** *n.* valve allowing escape of excess steam, *etc.*; outlet for emotion. [F. *sauf*, fr. L *salvos*]

saff'ron *n.* orange-red coloring matter obtained from the crocus. -*a.* of this color.[F. *safran*]

sag *v.i.* sink in the middle, hang sideways or curve downwards under pressure. [of Teut. orig.]

sa'ga *n.* medieval tale of Norse heroes; any such long tale of events. [ON. cp. *saw*]

sagacious *a.* shrewd, mentally acute; judicious; wise. -**saga'ciously** *adv.* -**saga'city** *n.* [L. *sagax, sagac-*]

sage *n.* aromatic herb. [F. *sauge*, fr. L. *salvia*]

sage *a.* wise, discreet. -*n.* very wise man. -**sage'ly** *adv.* [F., fr. L. *sapere*, be wise]

Sagitta'rius *n.* (The Archer) 9th sign of Zodiac, operative Nov. 22-Dec. 20; southern constellation. [L. *Sagitta*, arrow]

sa'go *n.* a starch; foodstuff made from it, obtained from palms. [Malay *sagu*]

sah'ib *n.* Hindu term of respect for air, Mr. [Arab. = *friend*]

sail *n.* piece of canvas stretched to catch the wind for propelling a ship; windcatching appliance forming the arm of a windmill; ships collectively; act of sailing. -*v.i.* travel by water; begin a voyage. -*v.t.* navigate. -**sail'board** *n.* craft used for windsurfing, consisting of a molded board like a surfboard, to which a mast bearing a single sail is attached by a swivel joint. -**sail'or** *n.* [OE. *segl*]

sain'foin *n.* forage plant. [F. = *wholesome hay*]

saint *adj.* holy; title of a canonized person. -*n.* one who has been canonized. -**saint'ly** *adj.* -**saint'ed** *a.* canonized; sacred. -**saint'liness** *n.* -**St. Bernard** *n.* kind of large dog used to rescue travellers in the snow. *n.* -**St. Vitus's dance** *n.* chores. [F., fr. L. *sanctus*, consecrated]

sake *n.* for the sake of, on behalf of, to please or benefit, or get, or keep. [OE. *sacu*, dispute at law]

sake', saki' *n.* Japanese alcoholic drink made from fermented rice. [*Jap.*]

salaam' (-lam) *n.* salutation or mark of respect in the East (bow with right hand touching forehead). -*v.t.* salute. [*Arab.*]

sala'cious *a.* lustful. -**sala'city** *n.* [L. *salax, salac-*]

sal'ad *n.* uncooked vegetables as food; lettuce or other plant suitable for this use. [F. *salade*]

sala'mi, sala'me *n.* highly-spiced sausage. [It.]

sal'ary *n.* fixed payment of persons employed in non-manual or non-mechanical work. -**sal'aried** *a.* [L. *solarium*, soldiers' pay]

sale *n.* a selling; special disposal of stock at low prices; auction. -**sales'man** *n.* shop assistant or traveler. -**sales'manship** *n.* -**sale' price** *n.* special price at a sale. [OE. *sala*]

Sal'ic Law *n.* rule limiting succession a males. [fr. code of laws of the *Salian* ranks]

sa'lient *a.* jutting out. -*n.* salient angle, *esp.* in fortification. -**sa'lience** *n.* [L. *lire*, leap]

sa'line *n.* fruit salt. -*a.* salty. [L. *salinus*]

sali'va *n.* liquid which forms in the mouth. -**sali'vary** *a.* [L.]

sall'ow *n.* kind of willow. -**sall'owy** *n.* [OE. *sealh*]

sall'ow *a.* of a sickly yellow or pale in color. -**sall'owness** *n.* [OE. *sato]*

sall'y *v.i.* rush; set out. -*n.* a rushing out, *esp*. from a fort; an outburst; witty remark. [F. *saillir*, rush]

salm'on (sam'-) *n.* large silvery-scaled fish with orange-pink flesh valued as food; color of its flesh. -*a.* of this color. [OF. *aulmon*, fr. L. *salmon*]

sal'on (-ong) *n.* drawing-room; reception graced by celebrities. [F.]

saloon' *n.* large reception room; public dining-room; principal cabin or sitting-room in a passenger ship; Pullman car on a railway; public place where liquor is sold and consumed. [F. *salon*]

sal'sify *n.* plant with edible root, the oyster plant. [F.]

salt (solt) *n.* sodium chloride, a substance which gives sea-water its taste; chemical compound of an acid and a metal. -*a.* preserved with, or full of, or tasting like, salt. -*v.i.* preserved with salt; put salt on. -**salt'ern** *n.* salt works. -**salt'ing** *n.* area of low ground regularly inundated with salt water. -**sait'y** *a.* -**salt'ness** *n.* -**salt' cellar** *n.* small vessel for salt on the table. -**salt lake** *n.* inland lake of high salinity resulting from inland drainage in an and area of high evaporation. -**salt marsh** *n.* area of marshy ground that is intermittently inundated with salt water or that retains pools or rivulets of salt or brackish. -**salt' peter** *n.* potassium nitrate used in gunpowder. [OE. *sealt*]

sal'tant *a.* leaping, dancing. -**sal'tatory** *a.* -**salta'tion** *n.* [L. *salire*, leap]

sal'tire *n.* St. Andrew's Cross. [L. *saltare*, leap]

salu'brious *a.* favorable to health. -**salu'brity** *n.* [L. *salubris*, healthy]

sal'utary *n.* wholesome, resulting in good. [L. *salutaris*]

salute' *v.t.* greet with words or sign. -*v.i.* perform a military salute. -*n.* word or sign by which one greets another: prescribed motion of the arm as a mark of respect to a superior, *etc.*, in military usage. -**saluta'tion** *n.* [L. *salus, salut-*, health]

sal'vage *n.* payment for saving a ship from danger; act of saving a ship or other property from danger; property or materials so saved. [OF.]

salva'tion *n.* fact or state of being saved. -**salva'tionist** *n.* member of religious group, Salvation Army. -**salve** *v.* save from peril. [L. *salvus*, safe]

salve *n.* healing ointment. -*v.i.* anoint with such. [OE. *sealf*]

sal'ver *n.* tray for refreshments, visiting cards, *etc.* [Sp. *salva*]

salvo *n.* simultaneous discharge of guns as a salute, or in battle. [It. *salva*]

sal-volat'ile (-il-i) *n.* preparation of ammonia used to restore persons who faint, *etc.* [L. = volatile, salt]

same *a.* identical, not different, unchanged, unvarying. -**same'ness** *n.* monotony. [ON. *samr*]

sa'mite (sa-) *n.* medieval heavy silk stuff. [OF. *samit*]

samovar' *n.* Russian tea-urn, heated by charcoal pipes. [*Russ.*]

sam'pan *n.* Chinese boat, sculled from stern, *usu.* with a sail and a cabin made of mats. (Chin. *sam*, three, *pan*, board]

sam'phire *n*. herb found on rocky coasts; St. Peter's wort; sea-feud. [F. *Saint-Pierre*, St. Peter]

sam'ple *n*. specimen. *-v.i.* take or give a sample of. **-sam'pler** *a*. beginner's exercise in embroidery. [for ME. *essample*, *See* **example**]

san'abte *a*. curable; that can be healed. **-sanabil'ity** *n*. **-san'ative** *a*. healing. [L. *sanabilis-sanare*, heal]

sanatoriums *n*. establishment for the treatment of invalids, *esp*. by therapy and diet; health resort. [L.]

sanc'tify *v.t.* set apart as holy; free from sin. **-sanctifica'tion** *n*. **-sanctimo'nious** *a*. making a show of piety. **-sanc'timony, sanctimoniousness** *n*. assumed outward holiness. **-sanc'tity** *n*. saintliness, sacredness; inviolability. **-sanc'tuary** *n*. holy place; place where a fugitive was safe from arrest or violence. **-sanc'tum** *n*. sacred place or shrine; person's private room. [L. *sanctus*, holy]

sanc'tion *n*. penalty or reward following the breaking or observing of a law; treaty; permission with authority; countenance given by custom. *-n. pl.* boycott or other coercive measure, *esp*. by one state against another regarded as having violated a law, right, *etc*. *-v.i.* allow or authorize. [L. *sanctus*, holy]

sand *n*. powdery substance made by the wearing down of rock. *-pl.* stretches or banks of this, *usu*. forming a seashore. *-v.t.* cover or mix with sand. **-sand'stone** *n*. rock composed of sand. **-sand'bag** *n*. bag filled with sand or earth and used in fortification. **-sand'paper** *n*. paper with sand stuck on it for scraping or polishing wood, *etc*. **-sand'piper** *n*. longlegged wading bird, *etc*. **-sand'y** *a*. [OE.]

san'dal *n*. shoe consisting of a sole attached by straps. [G. *sandalon*]

sandalwood *n*. yellowish, fine-grained scented wood. [Arab. *sandal*]

sand'wich *n*. two slices of bread with meat or other substance between. *-v.t.* insert between two other different things. [Earl of *Sandwich* (d. 1792)]

sane *a*. of sound mind, sensible. **-san'ity** *n*. [L. *sanus*, healthy]

sang-froid' (song-frwa') *n*. coolness, nonchalance. [F.]

sanguinary *a*. bloodthirsty; accompanied by bloodshed; delighting in bloodshed. **-sanguin'eous** *a*. of blood; full-blooded; blood-colored. [L. *sanguis*, *sanguin-*, blood]

san'guine (sang-gwin) *a*. hopeful or confident; florid. [L. *sanguis*, *sanguin-*, blood]

Sanhe'drin (-drin) *n*. supreme Jewish Council and Court of justice in ancient Jerusalem. [G. *sun*, together, *hedra*, seat]

san'itary *a*. promoting health by protection against dirt, *etc*. **-sanitar'ium** *n*. sanatorium. **-sanita'tion** *n*. improving of sanitary conditions. [L. *Sanitas*]

sansculotte' (song-) *n*. violent low-class revolutionary. [F. *sans culotte*, without breeches]

Sans'krit *n*. ancient classical language of India. [Sans. *Sam*, together, *kr*. make]

San'ta Claus' *n*. in nursery folk lore, gift-bringer of Christmas Eve, riding over the roofs in a sled drawn by reindeer. [Du. *Sint Klaas*, St. Nicholas]

sap *n*. juice of plants. **-sap'less** *a*. **-sap'ling** *n*. young tree. [OE. *scep*]

sap *n*. covered trench approaching a besieged place or enemy trench. *-v.t.* construct such trenches. *-v.i.* undermine; destroy insidiously. **-sapp'er** *n*. one who saps; Royal Engineer. [It. *zappa*, spade]

sap'id *a*. flavorsome. [L. *sapidus*, taste]

sa'pient *a*. wise (*usu*. ironical). **-sa'pience** *n*. [L. *sapere*, know]

sapona'ceous *a*. of or containing soap. [L. *sapo, sapon-*, soap]

Sapph'ic *a*. of Sappho, Grecian poetess; verse of 3 lines of 5 feet each, followed by line of 2 feet. *-n.* sapphic verse. [*Sappho*]

sapph'ire (saf-) *n*. blue precious stone. [G. *sappheiros*]

sapsucker *n*. small N. Amer. black and white woodpecker.

sar'aband *n*. slow Spanish dance; music for it. [Sp. *zambanda*]

sarcasm *n*. bitter or wounding ironic remarks; such remarks; power of using them. **-sarcast'ic** *a*. **-sarcast'ically** *adv*. [G. *sarkasmos*]

Sar'acen *n*. Arabian; adherent of Islam in Syria and Palestine; infidel. **-Saracen'ic** *a*. [Late. L. *Saracenus*]

sar'cenet, sar'senet *n*. fine silk made by Saracens. [AF. *Sarzinett*]

sarcophagus *n*. stone coffin; stone used for it. [G. *sarkophagos*]

sard, sar'dius *n*. precious stone, variety of chalcedony. [*Sardis* in Lydia]

sardine' *n*. small fish of herring family, usually packed in oil. [F.]

sardon'ic *a*. of a smile or laughter, bitter, scornful. [L. *sardonius*]

sardon'yx *n*. onyx composed of alternating layers of sard and chalcedony. [G. *sardonyx*, fr. *onyx*, nail]

sa'ri *n.* Hindu woman's outer garment, a long straight piece of cotton, silk. [Hind.]

sarong' *n.* skirtlike garment worn in Asian and Pacific countries. [Malay, *sarung*]

sarsparill'a *n.* varieties of smilax of tropical Amer. with root which when dried yields medicinal decoction. [G. *zarzaparrilia*]

sartorial *a.* pertaining to a tailor. [L. *sartor*, tailor]

sash *n.* frame forming a window, usually sliding up or down. [F. *chdssis*]

sash *n.* scarf wound around the body. [Arab. *shash*]

Sa'tan *n.* the devil. [Low L.]

sat'chel *n.* small bag, or bag for school books. (L. *saccellus*, a small sack]

sate *v.t.* gratify to the full; glut. [earlier *sade*, make sad]

sateen' *See* **satin.**

sat'ellite *n.* in astronomy, planet revolving round another; man-made projectile orbiting a planet; person or country dependent on another. [L. *satellites*, *pl.*]

satiate *v.t.* satisfy to the full; surfeit. -**sa'tiable** *a.* -**satia'tion** *n.* -**sati'ety** *n.* feeling of having had too much. [L. *satiare*-*satis*, enough]

sat'in *n.* silk fabric with a glossy surface. -**sateen'** *n.* glossy cotton or woolen fabric. -**sat'inwood** *n.* ornamental wood of a tropical tree. -**sat'iny** *a.* [F., from It. *seta*, silk]

sat'ire *n.* composition in which vice or folly, or a foolish person, is held up to ridicule; use of ridicule or sarcasm to expose vice and folly. -**satir'ic, satirica** *a.* -**sat'irist** *n.* -**sat'irize** *v.t.* [L. *satura*, poetic medley]

sat'isfy *v.t.* content, meet the wishes of, pay, fulfill, supply adequately; convince; be sufficient. -**satisfac'tion** *n.* -**satisfac'tory** *a.* [L. *satisfacere*]

Satrap *n.* governor of Ancient Persian province, tyrant. [old Pers. *khsathra*, province, *pa*, protect]

saturate *v.t.* soak thoroughly; cause to dissolve a maximum amount. -**satura'tion** *n.* -**sat'uration point** *n.* point at which no more (people, things, ideas, *etc.*) can be absorbed, accommodated, used, *etc*; in chemistry, the point at which no more solute can be dissolved in a solution or gaseous material absorbed in a vapor. [L. *saturate*]

Sat'urday *n.* seventh day of the week. Jewish Sabbath. [*Saturn*]

Sat'urn *n.* Roman god; one of the major planets. -**sat'urnine** *a.* gloomy; sluggish in temperament. -**saturn'alia** *n.* ancient festival of Saturn; noisy orgy or revel. [L. *Saturnus*, god of agricultura]

sat'yr (-r) *n.* woodland god, part man and part goat. -**satyr'ic** *a.* [G. *satyros*]

sauce *n.* liquid added to food to give relish. -*v.t.* add sauce to. -**sauce'pan** *n.* cooking-pot. -**sau'cy** *a.* impudent, cheeky. -**sau'cily** *adv.* [F.]

sau'cer *n.* curved plate put under a cup, *etc.*, to catch spilt liquid. [OF. *saussiere*]

sauerkraut (sour-krout) *n.* German dish of chopped and pickled cabbage. [Ger.]

saunter *v.i.* walk in leisurely manner, stroll. -*n.* leisurely walk or stroll. [AF. *sauntrer*, adventure]

saurian *n.* scaly animal, reptile, as the lizard. [G. *sauros*, lizard]

sausage *n.* minced meat enclosed in a tube of thin membrane. -**saus'age meat** *n.* [F. *saucisse*]

sau'té *a.* fried lightly and quickly. [F.]

savage *a.* uncivilized, primitive; wild. -*n.* member of a savage tribe, barbarian. *v.t.* attack with trampling, biting. **sav'agery** *n.* -**sav'agely** *adv.* [F. *sauvage*, fr. L. *silva*, wood]

savan'nah, sava'nna *n.* prairies of tropical America. [Sp. *zavana*]

sav'ant *n.* learned man. [F.]

save *v.t.* rescue, preserve; keep for the future, lay by; prevent the need of. -*v.i.* lay by money. -*prep.* except. *conj.* but. -**sa'ving** *a.* frugal. -*n.pl.* what is saved, laid by. -**sa'vior** *n.* deliverer or redeemer; Christ. [F. *sauver*, fr. L. *saluare*]

sav'eloy *n.* highly-seasoned dried sausage. [earlier, *cervelas*, It. *cervellata*, fr. *cervello*, brain]

savoir-faire' *n.* tact; knowing what to do. -**savoir-vivre'** *n.* knowledge of polite usages; social adequacy; good breeding. [F.]

sa'vor *n.* characteristic taste. -*v.i.* smack of -**sa'vory** *a.* having an appetizing taste or smell. -*n.* savory dish at beginning or end of dinner; aromatic mint. [L. *sapor*]

savoy' *n.* variety of cabbage. [*Savoy*]

savv'y *v.t.* and *i.* know; understand. -*n.* good sense. [Sp. *sabe, saber*, know]

saw *n.* old saying, maxim. [OE. *sagu*]

saw *n.* tool for cutting wood, *etc.* toothed. -*v.t.* cut with a saw. -*v.i.* make the movements of sawing. -**saw'dust** *n.* fine wood dust made in sawing. -**saw'fish** *n.* fish armed with a toothed snout. -**saw'mill** *n.*

one for mechanical sawing of timber. -**saw'pit** *n.* pit in which one of wielders of two-handed saw stands. -**saw'yer** *n.* workman who saws timber. [OE. *saga*]

saxe *n.* shade of blue. [F. = *Saxony*]

sax'horn *n.* instrument of the trumpet class. -**sax'ophone** *n.* large instrument like a clarinet. [invented by C. J. *Sax*, a Belgian (d. 1865)]

sax'ifrage *n.* Alpine or rock plant. [L. *saxifraga*, stone breaker]

say *v.t.* utter or deliver with the speaking voice; state; express; take as an example or as near enough; deliver an opinion. -*n.* what one has to say; chance of saying it; share in a decision. -**say'ing** *n.* maxim, proverb. [OE. *secgan*]

scab' *n.* crust formed over a wound; skin disease; disease of plants; somebody who works while his colleagues are on strike. **scabb'y** *a.* -**scab'lands** *pl. n.* type of terrain consisting of bare rock surfaces deeply channelled by glacial floodwaters. [ON. *skabbi*]

scabb'ard *n.* sheath for sword or dagger. [OF. *escalberc*]

sca'bies *n.* the itch, caused by parasites below the skin. [L. *scabere*, to scratch]

scabrous *n.* blue or pink-flowered plant of the teasel family. [L. *scabiosa*]

sca'brous *a.* rough, scurfy; indecent. [L. *scaber*, rough]

scaff'old *n.* temporary platform for workmen; gallows. -**scaff'olding** *n.* framework of poles and platforms for workmen. [ONF. *escafaut*]

scal'awag *n.* undersized animal; rascal, scamp. [fr. small-sized cattle of *Scalloway*, Scotland]

scald (skold) *v.t.* injure with boiling liquid or steam; clean with boiling water. -*n.* injury by scalding. [ONF. *escaider*, fr. L. *calidus*, hot]

scald (skold) *n.* ancient Scandinavian poet. [ON. *skaid*]

scale *n.* pan of a balance; weighing instrument. -*v.t.* weigh in scales; have the weight of. [ON. *skal*, bowl]

scale *n.* one of the plates forming the outer covering of fishes and reptiles; thin flakes. -*v.t.* remove the scales from. -*v.i.* come off in scales. -**sca'ly** *a.* -**sca'liness** *n.* [OF. *escale*, husk]

scale *n.* series of musical notes, degrees, or graduations; steps of graduating measuring instrument; relative size, ratio of enlarging or reduction (*e.g.*, in a map, *etc.*). -*v.t.* climb; attack with ladders. [L. *scala*, ladder]

sca'lene *a.* of a triangle, having its three sides unequal. [G. *skalenos*]

scallion *n.* variety of shallot; green onion. [L. *cepa Ascalonia*, onion of Ascalon]

scall'op *n.* edible shellfish; edging in small curves imitating the edge of a scallop shell. -*v.t.* shape in this way; cook in a scallop shell or a dish resembling one. [OF. *escalope*, shell]

scalp *n.* skin and hair of the top of the head. -*v.t.* cut off the scalp of; reprimand severely. [contr. of *scallop*]

scalper *n.* small surgical knife. -**scal'per** *n.* engraver's gouge. [L. *scalpere*, cut]

scamp *n.* rascal; worthless fellow. [OF. *escamper*, decamp]

scamp *v.t.* do hastily or negligently. [orig. uncertain]

scamp'er *v.i.* run about; run hastily from place to place. -*n.* scampering. [fr. *scamp*, rascal]

scan *v.t.* look at carefully; measure or read (verse) by its metrical feet; examine, search by systematically varying the direction or a radar or sonar beam; glance over quickly. -*n.* -**scann'er** *n.* one that scans. *n.* (*compute.*) input devise that reads symbols or codes by passing a light or laser beam over them. -**scan'sion** *n.* analysis or metrical structure of verse. [L. *scandere*, climb]

scand'al *n.* malicious gossip; feeling that something is an outrage or cause of discussion; thing causing such feeling. **scan'dalize** *v.t.* shock. -**scan'dalous** *a.* outrageous; disgraceful. -**scan'dalmonger** *n.* one who spreads malicious rumors. [G. *skandalon*, cause of stumbling]

scant *a.* barely sufficient; not sufficient. -*v.t.* put on short allowance; supply grudgingly. -**scant'y** *a.* -**scant'ily** *adv.* -**scantiness** *n.* [ON. *skamt*, short]

scantling *n.* size to which stone or wood is to be cut; small beam, *esp.* one under five inches square. [ONF. *escantillon*, sampler]

scape *n.* and *v.t.* (*arch.*) escape. -**scape'goat** *n.* person unwillingly bearing blame due to others. -**scape'grace** *n.* incorrigible fellow. [*escape*]

scap'ula *n.* shoulder-blade. -**scap'ular** *a.* of the shoulder. -**scap'ulary** *n.* small shoulder-garment worn as badge of a religious order. [L.]

scar *n.* mark left by a healed wound, burn or sore. -*v.t.* mark with a scar. -*v.i.* heal with a scar. [ON. *scarth*, cleft]

scar *n.* rocky face of hillside. [ON. *sker*, skerry]

scar'ab *n.* sacred beetle of ancient Egypt; gem cut in the shape of this beetle. [L. *scarabceus*]

scar'amouch (-mowch) *n.* braggart, buffoon. [F. *scaramouche*]

scarce *a.* hard to find; existing or available in insufficient quantity. -**scarce'ly** *adv.* only just; not quite. **scarce'ness** *n.* -**scar'city** *n.* [OF. *escars*]

scare *v.t.* frighten. -*n.* fright or panic. -**sca'ry** *a.* timid. [ON. *skirra*]

scarf *n.* scarfs, scarves, *pl.* long narrow strip of material to put round neck, shoulders, *etc.* [OE. *scearfe*, piece]

scarf *v.t.* join two timbers. [Sw. *scarfa*]

scarify *v.t.* scratch or cut slightly all over; criticize mercilessly. -**scarifica'tion** *n.* [L. *scarificare*]

scar'let *n.* brilliant red color; cloth or clothing of this color, *esp.* military uniform. -*a.* of this color. -**scar'let fe'ver** *n.* infectious fever with a scarlet rash. -**scar'let runn'er** *n.* trailing bean with scarlet flowers. -**scariati'na** (-e'-) *n.* **scarlet fever.** [Pers. *saqirtat*, broadcloth]

scarp *n.* inside slope of a ditch in fortifications; any steep slope. -*v.t.* make steep. [It. *scarpa*]

scathe (-TH) *n.* injury. -*v.t.* injure, especially by withering up. -**scathe'less** *a.* unharmed. [ON. *skatha*]

scatter *v.t.* throw or put here and there; sprinkle. -*v.i.* disperse. -**scatt'er-brained** *a.* giddy, thoughtless. [orig. uncertain]

scaup *n.* marine duck which frequents mussel beds. [Ice. *scalp*]

scavenger *n.* one employed in cleaning streets, removing refuse, *etc.* -**scav'enge** *v.t.* clean (streets). -*v.i.* work as a scavenger; originally a kind of Customs Inspector. [OF. *escauuer*, inspect]

scene *n.* place of the action of a novel, play, *etc.*; place of any action; subdivision of a play; view; episode; stormy conversation, *esp.* with display of temper. -**sce'nery** *n.* stage scenes; natural features of a district. -**sce'nic** *a.* picturesque; of, or on, the stage. -**scenar'io** *n.* written version of a play to be produced by cinematograph. [L. *scena*]

scent (a-) *v.t.* track by smell; detect; give a perfume to. -*n.* smell; liquid perfume. [F. *sentir*, smell]

scep'ter (s-) *n.* ornamental staff as a symbol of royal power; royal or imperial dignity. [G. *skeptron*, staff]

sched'ule (sk-) *n.* plan or procedure of a project; list; timetable. -*v.t.* enter in a schedule; plan to occur at a certain time. [Late L. *scedula*, small scroll]

sche'ma *n.* image to aid the process of thought; synopsis; diagrammatic outline. -**schemat'ic** *a.* [*scheme*]

scheme (sk-) *n.* plan or design; project; list or table; outline or syllabus. -*v.i.* make plans, especially as a secret intrigue. -*v.t.* plan, bring about. -**sche'mer** *n.* -**sche'ming** *a.* plotting, intriguing. [G. *schema*, form]

scher'zo *n.* (*mus.*) quick playful passage, movement. -**scherzan'do** *a.* playful. [It.]

schis'm (sizm) *n.* division in a church or party. -**schismat'ic** *n.* and *a.* -**schis'mat'ical** *a.* [G. *schisma*, cleft]

schist (shist) *n.* crystalline rock which splits into layers. -**schist'ose** *a.* [G. *schiotos*, split stone]

schizophrenia *n.* split personality; dementia præcox, a mental disorder. -**schizophren'ic** *a.* [G. *schizein*, cleave, *phren*, mind]

schnap(p)s *n.* spirit distilled from potatoes; any strong liquor, *esp.* Holland gin. [Ger. = *snappen*, to swallow]

school *n.* institution for teaching or for giving instruction in any subject; buildings of such institution; time of lessons; group of thinkers, writers, artists, *etc.*, with principles or methods in common. -*v.t.* educate; bring under control, train. -**school'man** *n.* medieval philosopher. -**schol'ar** *n.* one taught in a school; one quick to learn; learned person; person holding a scholarship. -**schol'arly** *a.* -**schol'arship** *n.* learning; prize or grant to a student for payment of school or college fees. -**scholast'ic** *a.* relating to schools or schoolmen; pedantic. [G. *schole*, leisure; place for discussion]

school (sk-) *n.* shoal (of fish, whales, *etc.*). [Du. *school*, crowd]

schooner (sk-) *n.* ship having fore and aft sails or two or more masts. [orig. uncertain]

schottische' *n.* variety of polka; music for this. [Ger. = *Scottish*]

sciatica (si-) *n.* pain in the sciatic nerve. -**sciat'ic** *a.* of the hip. [Low L.]

science *n.* systematic knowledge; investigation of this; any branch of study concerned with a body of observed material facts. -**scientif'ic** *a.* -**scientif'ically** *adv.* -**sci'entist** *n.* [L. *scientia*, knowledge]

scill'a (sil'-a) *n.* kinds of flowering plant. [G. *skilla*]

scim'itar (a-) *n.* short, single-edged

curved sword. [F. *cimeterre*]

scintill'a (a-) *n.* spark. **-scin'tillate** *v.i.* sparkle. **-scintilla'tion** *n.* [L.]

sci'olism (si-) *n.* superficial knowledge or learning; conceit of this. [L. *scius*, knowing]

sci'on (a-) *n.* slip for grafting; descendant or heir. [F.]

scirr'hus (skir-) *n.* hard cancerous growth. **-scirr'hous** *a.* [G. *skirrhos*, hard tumour]

scissors (siz'-) *n.pl.* cutting instrument of two blades pivoted together so that the edges slip over each other. [OF. *cisoires*]

sclerosis *n.* hardening of bodily organs, tissues, *etc.* [G. *skleros*, hard (*See* **arteriosclerosis**)]

scoff (sk-) *n.* taunt; mocking words. *-v.i.* jeer, mock. **-scoff'er** *n.* **-scoffing'ly** *adv.* [of Teut. orig.]

scoff *n.* (*sl.*) food. *-v.t.* devour. [Du. *schoft*, meal]

scold (sk-) *n.* nagging woman. *-v.i.* find fault noisily. *-v.t.* rebuke. [ON. *skald*, poet, later lampooner]

sconce *n.* bracket candlestick on a wall. [orig. screened lantern. OF. *esconce*]

sconce *n.* head, pate. [orig. uncertain]

scone (skon) *n.* round griddle cake. [SC. fr. Du. *schoonbrot*, fine bread]

scoop *n.* article for ladling; kind of shovel; tool for hollowing out. *-v.t.* ladle out; hollow out or rake in with a scoop; exclusive news-story. [of Teut. orig.]

scoot *v.i.* (*sl.*) move off quickly. **-scoot'er** *n.* toy consisting of small platform with two wheels and a guiding handle, to carry one person. [Sw. *skjuta*, shoot (*v.*i.)]

scope *n.* range of activity or applications room, play. [It. *scopo*, target]

scopol'amine *n.* vegetable alkaloid used as anesthetic. [*Scopoli*, It. naturalist]

scorbutic *a.* affected with, or concerning, scurvy. [orig. uncertain]

scorch *v.t.* burn the surface of. *-v.i.* be burnt on the surface. **-scorched' earth' policy** (of a retreating army) of laying waste as it goes. [orig. uncertain]

score *n.* group or set of twenty; cut, notch, stroke, or mark; written or printed piece of orchestral music; tally; reason; sake; number of points made in a game, measure of weight, 20 lbs. *-v.i.* notch or mark; cross out; record; make (points) in a game. *-v.i.* achieve a success. **-scor'er** *n.* [ON. *skor*, notch]

sco'ria *n.* slag, dross (**-riae** *n.pl.*). [G. *skōr*, dung]

scorn *n.* contempt, derision. *-v.t.* despise **-scorn'er** *n.* **-scorn'fully** *adv.* **-scorn'ful** *a.* [OF. *escarnir*]

scorpion *n.* small lobster-shaped animal with a sting at the end of its jointed tail. **-Scorpio** *n.* 8th sign of the zodiac, which sun enters about 22nd October. [L. *scorpio*]

scot *n.* payment or a person's share of it. **-scot-free'** *a.* free from payment, punishment, *etc.* [ON. *skot*]

Scot *n.* native of Scotland. **-Scott'ish** *a.* (also **Scotch**, **Scots**). **-Scots'man** *n.* - **scott'icism** *n.* Scottish turn of speech. **Scotch** *n.* or Scotland; Scotch whiskey. **Scotch' terrier**, short-legged, long-bodied rough terrier. [OE. *Scottas* (*pl.*), Irishmen]

scotch *n.* notch preventing wheel from slipping. [orig. unknown]

scotch *v.t.* disable, wound, or maim mortally. [AF. *escocher*]

sco'ter *n.* large northern marine duck. [orig. uncertain]

scoun'drel *n.* villain. **-scound'relly** *a.* [orig. uncertain]

scour *v.t.* clear or polish by rubbing; clear out. [OF. *escurer*]

scour *v.t.* . run or move hastily. *-v.t.* move rapidly along or over in search of something. [OF. *escourre*]

scourge (skurj) *n.* whip or lash; an evil pest or plague. *-v.t.* flog. [OF. *escorgiee*]

scout *n.* man sent out to reconnoiter; ship used for reconnoitering; small fast airplane; Boy Scout or Girl Scout. *-v.i.* go out or act as a scout. [OF. *escoute*]

scout *v.t.* reject scornfully: dismiss as absurd. [orig. uncertain]

scow *n.* large flat-bottomed boat. [Du. *schouw*]

scowl *v.t.* frown gloomily or sullenly. *-n.* gloomy frown. [of Scand. orig.]

scrag *n.* lean person or animal; lean end of a neck or mutton. **-scragg'y** *a.* lean, thin; scraggly. [earlier *crag*]

scram *v.i.* to clear off, to depart hurriedly (when unwanted) [U.S. *slang*]

scram'ble *v.i.* move along or up by crawling, climbing, *etc.*, struggle with others for; cook (eggs) by stirring them, when broken, in the pan. *-n.* scrambling; disorderly proceeding. [orig. uncertain]

scrap *n.* small detached piece of fragment; fight, quarrel. **-scrapp'y** *a.* **-scrap'-book** *n.* book in which scraps, cuttings are pasted. (ON. *skrap*]

scrape *v.t.* rub with something sharp;

clean or smooth in this way; rub with harsh noise. -*v.i.* make an awkward bow. -*n.* act or sound of scraping; awkward situation, *esp.* one resulting from an escapade. -**scra'per** *n.* [OE. *scrapian*]

scrap'ie *n.* fatal virus disease of sheep and goats affecting the central nervous system, characterized by intense itching. [*scrape*]

scratch *v.t.* score or mark a narrow surface wound with claws, nails, or anything pointed; make marks on with pointed instruments; remove from a list. *v.i.* use claws or nails. -*n.* wound or mark or sound made by scratching; line or starting point. -*a.* got together at short notice; impromptu. -**scratch'ily** *a.* [mixture of earlier *scrat* and *crotch*, both of Teut. orig.]

scrawl *v.t.* write or draw untidily. -*n.* something scrawled; careless writing. [orig. uncertain]

scream *v.i.* utter a piercing cry; whistle or hoot shrilly. -*n.* shrill piercing cry; (*sl.*) something ludicrous. -**scream'er** *n.* [imit. orig.]

scree *n.* slope covered with loose stones. [ON. *skritha*, landslip]

screech *v.i.* and *n.* scream. -**screech owl** *n.* barn-owl. [earlier *scratch*, of imit. orig.]

screed *n.* long letter or passage; list of grievances, *etc.* [OE. *screade*, shred]

screen *n.* piece of furniture to shelter from heat, light, draught or observation; anything used for such purpose; sheet or board to display cinema pictures, *etc.*, wooden or stone partition in a church. -*v.t.* shelter or hide; protect from detection; sift, assort, as coal; examine a person's political antecedents. [OF. *escren*]

screw *n.* cylinder with a spiral ridge running round it, outside or inside; ship's propeller; turn of a screw; twist; miser; worn-out horse. -*v.t.* fasten with a screw; press or stretch with a screw; obtain by pressure, extort; work by turning, twist round. [OF. *escroue*]

scrib'ble *v.t.* wrote or draw carelessly. *v.i.* write or draw carelessly; make meaningless marks with a pen or pencil. -*n.* something scribbled. [*scribe*]

scribe *n.* writer; copyist; author. [L. *scribere*, write]

scrimmage *n.* scuffle. [*skirmish*]

scrimp *v.t.* and *i.* make short or scanty; limit; straiten. -**scrimp'y** *a.* scanty. [OE. *scrimpan*]

scrip *n.* small wallet. [OF. escrepe]

scrip *n.* certificate of holding stocks or shares. -**scrip'ophily** *n.* hobby of collecting bonds and share certificates, *esp.* those of historical interest. **scrip'ophile** *n.* [for *subscription* (receipt)]

script *n.* handwriting; written characters. -**script'ure** *n.* sacred writings; the Bible. -**script'ural** *adv.* [L. *scribere, script-*, write]

scrivener *n.* copyist or clerk. [L. *scrihere, script-*, write]

scrof'ula *n.* constitutional disease characterized by swelling of lymphatic glands, *esp.* those of neck; King's evil. -**scrof'ulous** *a.* [L. *scrofulae*]

scroll *n.* roll or parchment of paper; list; ornament shaped like a scroll of paper. [OF. *escrou*]

scrounge' (-ow-) *v.t.* and *i.* (*sl.*) pinch; cadge. -**scroung'er** *n.* [orig. unknown]

scrub *v.t.* clean with a hard brush and water. -*n.* a scrubbing. -**scrubb'ing brush** *n.* [obs. Du. *schrubben*]

scruff *n.* nape (of neck). [of Teut. orig.]

scrum'mage, scrum *n.* in Rugby football, close skirmish between opposing forwards. [var. of *scrimmage*]

scru'ple *n.* small weight; feeling of doubt about a proposed action; conscientious objection. -*v.i.* hesitate. -**scru'pulous** *a.* extremely conscientious, thorough; attentive to small points of conscience. -**scrupulos'ity** *n.* [L. *scrupulus*, small sharp stone]

scru'tiny *n.* investigation, official examination of votes; searching look. -**scrutineer'** *n.* examiner of votes. -**scrutinize** *v.t.* examine closely. **scru'table** *a.* [L. *scrutari*, examine closely]

scud *v.i.* run quickly; run before the wind. -*n.* act of scudding. [orig. uncertain]

scuf'fle *v.i.* struggle at close quarters. -*n.* confused struggle. [Sw. *skuffa*, push]

scull *n.* oar used for the stern of a boat; short oar used in pairs. -*v.t.* and *i.* propel or move by means of a scull or sculls. [orig. unknown]

scull'ery *n.* place for washing dishes, *etc.* [OF. *escuelerie*, from *escuele*, dish]

scullion *n.* (*arch.*) kitchen underservant. [OF. *escouvillon*, mop]

sculpture *n.* art of forming figures in relief or solid; product of this art. -*v.t.* represent, by sculpture. -**sculp'tural** *a.* -**sculp'tor** *n.* [L. *sculpere, sculpt-*, carve]

scum *n.* froth or other floating matter on a liquid; waste part of anything. [OF. *escume*]

scupp'er *n.* hole in the side of a ship level with the deck. [orig. uncertain]

scurf *n.* dried flakes detached from the

skin. -**scurf'y** *a.* [OE. *sceorf*]

scurr'ilous *a.* coarse or indecent language. -**scurril'ity** *n.* [L. *scurrilis*]

scurr'y *v.i.* run hastily. -*n.* bustling haste. [orig. uncertain]

scur'vy *n.* disease due to lack of fresh vegetable food. -*a.* afflicted with the disease; mean, low, contemptible. [*scurg*]

scut *n.* rabbit's, hare's tail. [ME. *short* (garment); hare]

scutch'eon. *See* **escutcheon.**

scu'tage *n.* money paid instead of military service by feudal landowner. [L. *scutum*, shield]

scut'tie *n.* vessel for coal; large open basket. [OE. *scutel*, fr. L. *scutella*]

scut'tle *v.i.* rush away. [freq. of *scud*]

scut'tle *n.* lidded opening in the side or deck of a ship. -*v.i.* make a hole in a ship, *esp.* to sink it, or to salve the cargo. [OF. *escoutile*, hatchway]

scythe (sith) *n.* mowing implement consisting of a long curved blade swung by a bent handle held in both hands. -*v.t.* cut with a scythe. [OE. *sithe*]

sea *n.* mass of solid water covering most of the earth; broad tract of this; waves; swell. -**sea'board** *n.* coast. -**sea'-cow** *n.* dugong. -**sea'-dog** *n.* old sailor. **seafaring** *a.* occupied in sea voyages. **seagull** *n.* gull. -**sea-horse** *n.* fabulous sea-monster; walrus; warm-water fish remarkable for its horse-like head. -**sea'man** *n.* sailor. -**sea'mew** *n.* gull. -**sea'weed** *n.* plant growing in the sea. -**sea'worthy** *a.* in a fit condition to put to sea. -**sea'plane** *n.* amphibious aircraft. -**sea'power,** nation's naval strength. -**sea ur'chin** *n.* marine annual with globular body enclosed in rigid, spine-covered shell. [OE. *sce*]

seal *n.* amphibious marine animal with flippers as limbs, of which some varieties have valuable fur. -*v.i.* hunt seals. **seal'skin** *n.* skin or fur of seals. -**seal'er** *n.* man or ship engaged in sealing. [OF. *seolh*]

seal *n.* piece of metal or stone engraved with a device for impression on wax, *etc.*, impression made by this (on letters, documents, *etc.*) -*v.t.* affix a seal to; ratify; mark with a stamp as evidence of some quality; keep close, or secret; settle, as doom. -**seal'ing wax** *n.* [OF. *seet,* fr. L. *sigillum*, seal]

seam *n.* line of junction of two edges, *e.g.*, of two pieces of cloth, or two planks; thin layer of stratum. -*v.t.* mark with furrows or wrinkles. -**seam'less** *a.* -**seam'stress, semp'stress** *n.* sewing woman. -**seam'y** *a.* marked with seams. -**seam'y-side,** worst side. [OE.]

sé'ance *n.* session of a public body; meeting of Spiritualists. [F.]

sear *v.t.* scorch or brand with a hot iron; deaden. [OE. *seartan*]

search *v.t.* look over or through in order to find something: probe into. -*v.i.* explore. look for something. -*n.* act of searching; quest. -**search'ing** *a.* keen thorough. -**search'light** *n.* electric arelight which sends a concentrated beam in any desired direction. -**search warrant** *n.* authorization enabling police to search house, *etc.*, [F. *chercher*]

seas'on *n.* one of the four divisions of the year associated with a type of weather and a stage of agriculture: proper time; period during which something happens, grows, is active, *etc.* -*v.t* . bring into sound condition; flavor with salt or condiments, *etc.* -**seas'onable** *a.* suitable for the season. -**seas'onal** *a.* depending on, or varying with seasons. -**seas'oning** *n.* flavoring materials. [F. *saison*, fr. L. *satio*, sowing]

seat *n.* thing made or used for sitting on: manner of sitting (of riding, *etc.*); right to sit (*e.g.*, in a council, *etc.*); sitting part of the body; locality of a disease, trouble, *etc.*, country house. -*v.t.* make to sit; provide sitting accommodation for. [ON. *salti*]

sebaceous (seba'shus) *a.* fatty, pertaining to, secreting, fat. [L. *sebaceus sebum*, tallow]

sec'ant *a.* cutting. -*n.* line that cuts another; (*trig.*) line from center of a circle through one end of an arc, cutting the tangent from the other end. [L. *secare*, cut]

se'cateur *n.* pruning shears. -also in *pl.* [F.]

secede' *v.i.* withdraw from a federation, *etc.* -**seces'sion** *n.* -**seces'sionist** *n.* [L. *secedere, secess-*, go apart]

seclude' *v.t.* guard from, remove from sight or resort, -**seclu'sion** *n.* [L. *secludere, seclus -*, shut away]

sec'ond *a.* next after the first. -*n.* person or thing coming second; one giving aid, *esp.* assisting a principal in a duel; sixtieth part of a minute. -*v.t* . support further; support (a motion in a meeting) so that discussion may be in order. -**sec'ondly** *adv.* -**sec'ondary** *a.* subsidiary, or of less importance; of education, coming between primary and university stages. -**sec'ondarily** *adv.* -**sec'onder** *n.* -**sec'cond-hand'** *a.* buy after use by a previous owner, not original. -**sec'ond-rate** *a.* inferior, mediocre. -**sec'ond sight',** faculty of prophetic vision. [L. *secundus*]

se'cret *a.* kept or meant to be kept from general knowledge; hidden. -*n.* something kept secret. -**se'cretly** *adv.* **se'crecy** *n.* keeping or being kept secret; ability to keep secrets. -**se'cretive** *a.* uncommunicative. -**se'cretiveness** *n.* [L. *secretus*, separated]

secretary *n.* one employed by another to deal with papers and correspondence, keep records, prepare business, *etc.*; official in charge of certain departments of government. -**secreta'rial** *a.* -**sec'retariat** *n.* body of officials led by a secretary; body of secretaries. -**sec'retaryship** *n.* [Med. L. *secretarius*]

secrete' *v.t.* hide; of a gland, *etc.*, collect and supply a particular substance in the body. -**secre'tion** *n.* -**secre'tory** *a.* -**secre'tive** *a.* [L. *secernere, secret-*, to put apart]

sect *n.* party within a church; religious denomination. -**sect'ary** *n.* -**secta'rian** *a.* [L. *sequi, sect-*, follow]

sec'tion *n.* cutting; part cut off, drawing of anything as if cut through. -**sec'tional** *a.* -**sec'tor** *n.* a part of a circle enclosed by two radii and the arc which they cut off, a sub-division of the front occupied by an army. [L. *secare, sect-*, cut]

sec'ular *a.* wordly; lay; not monastic; lasting for, or occurring once in, an age- **sec'ularist** *n.* one who would exclude religion from schools. -**sec'ularism** *n.* **sec'ularize** *v.t.* transfer from religious to lay possession or use. -**seculariza'tion** *n.* [L. *secularis*, fr. *seculurn*, age, century]

secure' *a.* safe; free from care; firmly fixed. -*v.t.* make safe; free (a creditor) from risk of loss; make firm; gain possession of. -**secure'ly** *adv.* -**secu'rity** *n.* [L. *secur-us*]

sedan' *n.* small covered vehicle for one, carried on poles by two men; enclosed automobile seating four to seven people, including, driver, and with two or four doors. -(also *sedan-chair*). [orig. uncert ain]

sedate' *a.* calm, collected, serious. **sedate'ly** *adv* . -**sed'ative** *a.* soothing. -*n.* soothing drug. -**sed'entary** *a.* sitting much; done in a chair. [L. *sedere*, sit]

sede'runt *n.* session meeting of court, *etc.* [L. *sedere*, sit]

sedge *n.* kind of coarse grass which grows in swampy ground. [OE. *secg*]

sed'iment *n.* matter which settles to the bottom of liquid. [L. *sedimentum-sedere*, sit]

sedi'tion *n.* talk or speech urging to rebellion. -**sedi'tious** *a.* [L. *seditio*, a going apart]

seduce *v.t.* lead astray, persuade to commit some sin or folly; induce (a woman) to surrender her chastity. -**seduc'tion** *n.* -**seduct'ive** *a.* alluring, winning. [L. *seducere, seduct-*, lead away]

sed'utous *a.* persevering; assiduous; persistent. -**sedu'lity** *n.* [L. *sedulus*]

see *v.t.* perceive with the eyes or mentally; find out, reflect; come to know; interview. -*v.i.* perceive; understand. -**seer** *n.* prophet. -**see'ing** *conj.* since. [OE. *seon*]

see *n.* diocese and work of a bishop. [OF. *sie*, fr. L. *sedere*, sit]

seed *n.* reproductive germs of flowering plants; one grain of this; such grains saved or used for sowing; offspring. -*v.i.* produce seed. -*v.t.* sow with seed. -**seed'ling** *n.* young plant raised from seed. -**seeds'man** *n.* one who sells seed. -**seed'y** *a.* run to seed; shabby; feeling ill. [OE. *soed*]

seek *v.t.* make search or enquiry for. -*v.i.* search. [OE. *secant*]

seem *v.i.* appear (to be or to do). -**seem'ingly** *adv.* -**seem'ly** *a.* becoming and proper. -**seem'liness** *n.* [ON. *soma*]

seep *v.i.* oak through; ooze. [OE. *sipean*]

seer. *See* **see.**

seersucker *n.* thin E. Indian fabric with colored stripes, some of which are ruffled in weaving. [Pers. *shir a shakkar*]

see'saw *n.* game in which children sit at opposite ends of a plank supported in the middle and swing up and down, plank used for this. -*v.i.* move up and down. [redupl. on *saw*]

seethe *v.t.* boil, cook or soak in hot liquid. -*v.i.* be agitated or in confused movement. [OE. *seothan*, boil]

seg'ment *n.* piece cut off, section; part of a circle cut off by a straight line. [L. *segmentum*]

segregate *v.t.* set apart from the rest. -**segrega'tion** *n.* [L. *segregate*, remove from the flock, *grex, greg-*]

segue *v.i.* proceed from one section or piece of music to another without a break; (imperative) play on without pause; a musical direction. *n.* practice or an instance of playing music in this way. [It. *seguire*, follow]

seign'eur (sen'-yer) *n.* feudal lord, lord of manor. -**seign(i)o'rial** *a.* [F.]

seine (son) *n.* large upright fishing net. [F.]

seis'm (sizm) *n.* earthquake. -**seis'mic** *a.* of earthquakes. -**seis'micity** *n.* seismic activity; the phenomenon of earthquake activity or the occurrence of artificially produced earth tremors. -**seis'mograph** *n.* instrument to record earthquakes. -**seismol'ogy** *n.* science of earthquakes. [G. *seismos,* earthquake]

seize *v.t.* grasp; lay hold of; perceive. -**seiz'able** *a.* -**seiz'ure** *n.* a seizing; sudden illness. [F. *saisir*]

se'lah (se-) *n.* word found in psalms supposed to be a musical or liturgical direction. [Heb.]

sel'dom *adv.* rarely. [OE. *seldan*]

select' *v.t.* pick out, choose. -*a.* choice, picked; exclusive. -**selec'tion** *n.* -**select'or** *n.* [L. *seligere, select-*]

self *pron.* **selves** *pl.* is used to express emphasis or a reflexive usage. -*a.* of a color, uniform, the same throughout. -*n.* one's own person or individuality. -**self-deceit,** -**deception** *n.* deceiving oneself, **self-denial** *n.* unselfishness, denying oneself pleasure. -**self-evident** *a.* explaining itself without proof. -**self'ish** *a.* concerned unduly over personal profit or pleasure, lacking consideration for others. -**self'ishly** *adv.* -**self'less** *a.* - **self'contained'** *a.* complete in itself, (of a person) reserved. -**self-possessed** *a.* calm, composed. -**self-posses'sion** *n.* -**self-righteous** *a.* smug, believing oneself better than others. -**self'-same** *a.* very same. -**self-seeking** *a.* striving for one's own advancement only. -**self-sufficient** *a.* independent of others, presumptuous. -**self-will** *n.* obstinacy. [OE.]

sell *v.t.* hand over for a price; betray or cheat; of an idea, *etc.* promote it with 'sales talk.' -*v.i.* find purchasers. -*n.* (*sl.*) disappointment. -**sell'er** *n.* [OE. *sellan*]

selt'zer *n.* alkaline mineral water. [*Selters,* Germany]

selvedges, sel'vage *n.* edge of cloth finished to prevent raveling out. **sel'vedged** *a.* -**sel'vaged** *a.* [for *selfedge*]

seman'tic *a.* concerned with the meanings of words. - *n.pl.* science of the meanings of words. [G. *seinantikos,* significant]

semaphore *n.* post with movable arm or arms used for signaling; system of signaling by human or mechanical arms. [G. *sema,* sign, *phoros,* bearing]

sem'blance *n.* appearance; image; likeness. [F. *sembler,* seem]

seme'ster *n.* university or college half-year course; one of the two, or three, divisions of the school year. [L. *semestris-* six months (course)]

semi- *prefix.* half as in **sem'ibreve** *n.* musical note half the length of a breve. -**sem'icircle** *n.* half a circle. -**semicir'cular** *a.* -**semico'lon** *n.* punctuation mark (;)-**semiconduc'tor** *n.* (*compute.*) solid-state electronic switching device that performs functions similar to an electron tube. **sem'iquaver** *n.* musical note half the length of a quaver. -**sem'itone** *n.* musical half note. -**sem'i-detach'ed** *a.* of a house, joined to another on one side only. -**sem'i-fi'nal** *a.* and *n.* last but one (match) of series. [L. *semi,* half]

seminal *a.* pert. to semen or seed; reproductive; capable of developing; influential. [L. *semen,* seed]

seminary *n.* school or college, *esp.* for priests. [L. *seminarium,* seed plot]

sem'iotics *n.* philosophical theory of signs and symbols. -**semiotic'ian** *n.* one who studies semiotics. [G. *semeion,* sign]

Semi'tic *a.* of Semites. (Jews, Arabs, *etc.*) of their languages; the languages. [G. *Sem,* Shem]

semolin'a *a.* hard grains left after the sifting of flour, used for puddings, *etc.* [L. *simila,* wheatmeal]

sempiter'nal *a.* everlasting, perpetual. [L. *semper,* always, *aeternus,* eternal]

semp'stress. *See* **seamstress.**

sen'ary *a.* of number 6, of 6 parts. [L. *sex,* six]

sen'ate *n.* upper council of a state, university, *etc.* -**sen'ator** *n.* -**senator'ial** *a.* [L. *senatus,* council of old men]

send *v.t.* cause to go or be conveyed; despatch; discharge. [OE. *setidan*]

sen'eschal *n.* steward or major domo of medieval castle. [OF.]

se'nile *a.* showing the weakness of old age. -**senil'ity** *n.* [L. *senex,* old]

se'nior *a.* older; superior in rank or standing. -*n.* an elder person; a superior. -**senior'ity** *n.* [L. compar. of *senex,* old]

senn'a *n.* kind of cassia; its leaves, pods, used in medicine. [F.]

sen'night *n.* week. [for *seven nights*]

sense *n.* any of the bodily functions of perception or feeling; sensitiveness ofany or all of these faculties; ability to perceive, mental alertness; consciousness; meaning; coherence, intelligible meaning. -**sensa'tion** *n.* operation of a sense, feeling; excited feeling or state of excitement; exciting event. -**sensa'tional** *a.* -**sensa'tionalism** *n.* -**sense'less** *a.* -**sense'lessly** *adv.* -**sen'sible** *a.* that can be perceived by the senses; aware, mindful; considerable; appreciable; reasonable, wise. -**sensibly** *adv.* -**sensibil'ity** *n.* delicacy of perception, feeling. -**sen'sitive**

a. open to or acutely affected by external impressions; easily affected or altered; responsive to slight changes. -**sen'sitively** *adv.* -**sen'sitiveness** *n.* **sensitize** *v.t.* make sensitive, *esp.* to make (photographic film, *etc.*) sensitive to light. -**senso'rial, sen'sory** *a. pert* to senses, sensation. -**sen'sual** *a.* depending on the senses only and not on the mind; given to the pursuit of pleasure of sense, self-indulgent; licentious. -**sensual'ity** *n.* -**sen'sualist** *n.* -**sen'sualism** *n.* -**sen'suous** *a.* stimulating or apprehended by the senses. [L. *sensus,* fr. *sentire,* feel]

sen'tence *n.* judgment passed on criminal by court or judge; combination of words which is complete as expressing thought. -*v.t.* condemn. -**senten'tial** *a.* of sentence. [L. *sentire,* feel]

sententious *a.* full of axioms and maxims; short and energetic; pithy; bombastic. -**senten'tiously** *adv.* -**senten'tioness** *n.* [L. *sentire,* feel]

sen'tient *a.* feeling or capable of feeling. [L. *sentire,* feel]

sentiment *n.* a mental feeling; emotion; tendency to be moved by feeling rather than reason; verbal expression of feeling. -**sentiment'al** *a.* -**sentiment'alist** *n.* -**sentimental'ity** *n.* [Fr., fr. L. *sentire,* feel]

sentinel *n.* sentry. [F. *sentinelle*]

sent'ry *n.* soldier on watch. [fr. *sanctuary,* place of safety, shelter for a watchman]

sep'al *n.* leaf of a fiower's calyx. [L. *separ,* separate]

sep'arate *v.t.* put apart; occupy a place between. -*v.i.* withdraw, become parted from. *a.* disconnected, apart. -**sep'arately** *adv.* -**sep'arable** *a.* -**separa'tion** *n.* -**sep'arator** *n.* that which separates, *esp.* an apparatus for separating cream from milk. [L. *separare*]

se'pia *n.* brown pigment made from a fluid secreted by the cuttle fish. -*a.* of this color. [G. = *cuttlefish*]

sept'-, *prefix.* [L. *septem,* seven] -**Septem'ber** *n.* ninth month (seventh in the Roman reckoning). -**septenn'ial** *a.* occurring every seven years. -**septent'rional** *a.* northern. -**septet(te)** *n.* music for seven instruments or voices. -**septuagena'rian** *n.* person in his seventies. -**sept'uagint** *n.* the Greek version of the Old Testament. [L. *septem,* seven]

sep'tic *a.* causing or caused by blood poisoning or putrefaction. -**sep'sis** *n.* septic state. [G. *septikos*]

Septuages'ima (-jes'-) *n.* third Sunday before Lent. [L. *septuaginta,* seventy]

sep'tuagilit *n.* Greek version of Old Testament. [L. *septuaginta,* seventy]

sepul'cher (-ker) *n.* tomb. -**sepul'chral** *a.* -**sep'ulture** *n.* burial. [L. *sepulcrum-sepelire, sepult-,* bury]

se'quel *n.* consequence or continuation. -**se'quent** *a.* following. -**se'quence** *n.* connected series, succession. [L. *sequelase-qui,* follow]

sequest'er *v.t.* seclude. -**sequest'rate** *v.t.* confiscate; divert to satisfy claims against its owner. -**sequestra'tion** *n.* [L. *sequestrate,* put in safe keeping]

se'quin *n.* ornamental metal disk on dresses, *etc.*; formerly, a Venetian gold coin. [It. *zecchino,* fr. *zecca,* mint]

sequoi'a *n.* kind of giant conifers of California. [Cherokee chief *Sequoiah*]

seraglio *n.* harem, Turkish Sultan's palace. [L. *sera,* lock]

ser'aph *n.* one belonging to the highest order of angels (*pl.* **ser'aphim**), **seraph'ic** *a.* [Heb. *saraph,* burn]

sere *a.* dried up, withered. [OE. *sear*]

serenade' *n.* music sung or played at night below a person's window, *esp.* by a lover. -*v.t.* entertain with a serenade. [It. *serenata,* fr. *sereno,* open air]

serene' *a.* calm, tranquil. -**serene'ly** *a.* -**seren'ity** *n.* [L. *serenus*]

serf *n.* one of a class of laborers bound to, and transferred with, land. -**serf'dom** *n.* [L. *servus,* slave]

serge *n.* twilled worsted fabric.[F.]

serg'eant (sarj-ant) *n.* non-commissioned officer; police officer; officer at a law court. -**serg'eant-at-arms** *n.* ceremonial official responsible for discipline. -**sergeant-ma'jor** *n.* highest non-commissioned officer. [F. *sergent,* fr. L. *serviens, servient-,* serving]

serial output *n.* (*compute.*) form of computer output in which characters are printed letter by letter *usu.* from left to right.

ser'ies *a.* sequence, succession, set. -**se'rial** *a.* of and forming a series; published in instalments. -**se'rialize** *v.t.* n. serial story or publication. -**seria'tim** *adv.* one after another. [L.]

ser'if *n.* fine cross-line finishing off stroke of letter, as for example at the top and base of H. [orig. uncertain]

serious *a.* earnest, sedate, thoughtful; not jesting; of importance. -**se'riously** *adv.* [L. *serius,* heavy]

ser'mon *n.* discourse of religious instruction or exhortation spoken or read from a pulpit; any similar discourse. -**ser'monize** *v.i.* talk like a preacher; compose sermons. [L. *sermo, sermon-*, discourse]

ser'ow *n.* Himalayan goat-antelope. [native name]

serp'ent *n.* snake; kind of firework; obsolete wind instrument. -**serp'entine** *a.* like or shaped like a serpent or snake; tortuous. [L. *serpere*, creep]

serra'ted *a.* notched like a saw. -**serra'tion** *n.* [L. *serra*, saw]

ser'ried *a.* in close order, press shoulder to shoulder. [F. *serrer*, lock]

ser'um (ser-) *n.* watery animal fluid, *esp.* a thin part of blood as used for inoculation. -**ser'ous** *a.* [L. = *whey*]

serve *v.i.* work under another; carry out duties; be a member of a military unit; be useful or suitable or enough; in tennis, start play by striking the ball. -*v.t.* work for, attend on, help to food; supply something; be useful to; contribute to; deliver formally; treat in a specified way. **ser'vant** *n.* personal or domestic attendant. -**ser'vice** *n.* state of being a servant; work done for and benefit conferred on another; military, naval, air-force duty; set of dishes, *etc.* -**ser'viceable** *a.* useful or profitable. -**serviette'** *n.* table napkin. -**ser'vile** *a.* slavish, without independence. -**servil'ity** *n.* -**ser'vitor** *n.* servant; student assisted out of college funds in certain colleges. -**ser'vitude** *n.* bondage or slavery. [L. *servire*]

ser'vice *n.* a tree like a mountain ash with a pear-shaped fruit. [L. *sorbus*]

se'same *n.* eastern plant whose seeds yield gingili-oil. **o'pen se'same,** magic formula to gain entrance. [G.]

sesquipeda'lian *a.* 1½ feet in length; (of word) pedantic, unwieldly. [L.]

ses'sion *n.* meeting of a court, *etc.*; continuous series of such meetings. -**ses'sional** *a.* [L. *sessio*, fr. *sedere, sess-*, sit]

set *v.t.* cause to sit, put in place; fix, point, put up; make ready; put to music; put in position, *etc.* -*v.i.* of the sun, to go down, become firm or fixed; have a directions. deliberate; formal, arranged beforehand; unvarying. -*n.* a setting; tendency; habit. [OE. *settan*]

set *n.* number of things or persons associated as being similar or complementary or used together, *etc.*; (tennis) series of games. [OF. *sette, sect*]

settee' *n.* couch. [var. of *settle*]

sett'er *n.* breed of dog which sets (crouches) on scenting game. (*e.g.*, Gordon, Irish, English)[*set*]

set'tle *n.* bench with a back and arms. [OE. *setl*]

set'tle *v.t.* put in order; establish, make firm or secure or quiet; decide upon; bring (a dispute, *etc.*), to an end; pay. -*v.i.* come to rest; subside; become clear; take up an abode; come to an agreement. -**set'tlement** *n.* -**sett'ler** *n.* [OE. *setlan*, fix]

sev'en *a.* and *n.* cardinal number, next after six. -**sev'enth** *a.* ordinal number. -**sev'enth heav'en,** state of supreme bliss. [OE. *soefon*]

sev'er *v.t.* separate, divide; cut off. -*v.i.* divide. -**sev'erance** *n.* -**sev'eral** *a.* separate; individual; some, a few. -*pron*. a few. -**sev'erally** *adv.* [F. *seurer*, wean, fr. L. *separate*]

severe' *a.* strict; rigorous; simple and austere; hard to do or undo. **severe'ly** *adv.* **sever'ity** *n.* [L. *severus*]

sew *v.t.* join with thread. -*v.i.* be occupied in sewing. [OE *seowian*]

sew'er (sia-) *n.* underground drain to remove waste water and refuse. -**sew'age** *n.* the refuse. [OE. *esseveur*]

sex *n.* state of being male or female; males or females collectively; sexual intercourse. -**sex'ism** *n.* discrimination on the basis of sex. -**sex'ist** *a.* and *n.* -**sex'ual** *a.* **sexually** *adv.* [L. *sexus*]

sext'ant *n.* instrument with a graduated arc of a sixth of a circle to measure angles, altitudes of a heavenly body, *etc.* [L. *sextans*, sixth part]

sextet' *n.* (*mus.*) composition for six voices, instruments; the singers, players. [L. *sex*, six]

sext'on *n.* official in charge of a church, often acting as gravedigger. [contr. of *sacristan*]

sextu'ple *a.* sixfold. [L. *sex*, six]

shabb'y *a.* poorly dressed; faded, worn; dishonorable. -**shabb'ily** *adv.* -**shabb'iness** *n.* [OE. *sceabb*, scab]

shack' n. hut, cabin. [*shake*]

shac'kle *n.* fetter; manacles; link to join two pieces of chain, *etc.*; anything that hampers. -*v.t.* fetter or hamper. [OE. *scacul*, bond]

shad *n.* fish of herring family. [OE. *sceadd*]

shade *n.* partial darkness; darker part of anything; depth of color; tinge; shelter or a place sheltered from light, heat, *etc.*; ghost. -*v.t.* screen from light, darken; represent shades in a drawing. -**shad'ow** *n.* patch of shade; dark figure projected by anything that intercepts rays of light. -*v.t.* cast a shadow over; follow and watch closely. -**shad'owy** *a.* -**sha'dy** *a.* [OE. *sceadu,* shadow]

shaft (-a-) *n.* straight rod, stem, or handle; one of the bars between which a horse is harnessed; entrance boring of a mine; revolving rod for transmitting power. [OE. *sceaft*, shaft of spear]

shag *n.* matted wool or hair; cloth with a long nap; fine cut tobacco. -**shagg'y** *a.* [OE. *sceacga*, head of hair]

shagreen' *n.* dressed sharkskin; rough untanned leather. [*See* **chagrin**]

Shah *n.* king of Persia. [Pers.]

shake *v.i.* tremble, totter, vibrate. -*v.t.* cause to shake. -*n.* act of shaking; vibration; jolt. -**sha'ky** *a.* -**sha'kily** *adv.* -**shake'-down** *n.* make-shift bed, as of hay or straw. [OE. *sceancan*]

shako' *n.* military cap with a peak. [Magyar *esako,* peaked cap]

shak *n.* clay rock like slate but softer. [OE. *scealu*, scale]

shall *v. aux.* makes compound tenses to express obligation, command, condition or intention. [OE. *sceal*]

shall'op *n.* light open boat, sometimes masted. [OF. *chalupe*]

shallot' *n.* small onion. [F. *échalotte*]

shall'ow (-b) *a.* not deep. -*n.* shallow place, shoal, sandbank. [ep. *shoal*]

sham *n.* imitation, counterfeit. -*a.* imitation. -*v.t.* and *i.* pretend; feign (sickness). [orig. uncertain]

sha'ma *n.* Indian song-bird. [Hind.]

sha'man *n.* priest of shamanism; medicine man of similar religion. -**sham'anism** *n.* religion of certain peoples of northern Asia, based on belief in good and evil spirits who can be controlled only by shamans. [Russ. fr. *Tungus*]

shamble *v.i.* walk with shuffling gait. [orig. uncertain]

shamb'les *n.pl.* messy, disorderly thing or place; slaughter-house [OE. *sceamel*, bench]

shame *n.* emotion caused by consciousness of something wrong or dishonoring in one's conduct or state; cause of disgrace. *v.t.* cause to feel shame; disgrace. **shame'faced** *a.* (earlier shame-fast) shy. -**shame'ful** *a.* -**shame'fully** *adv.* -**shame'less** *a.* bold, immodest. [OE. *sceamu*]

shampoo' *v.t.* wash (*esp.* hair) with something forming a lather in rubbing. *n* . any of various preparations of liquid soap for washing hair, carpets, *etc*. [Hind. *sharnpo*, kind of massager]

sham'rock *n.* trefoil plant taken as the emblem of Ireland. [Ir. *searnrog*]

shan'dy *n.* drink of beer and lemonade. [orig. unknown]

shanghai' *v.t.* drug (sailor) and convey on board ship for service; force or trick someone into doing something. [*Shanghai*, China]

shank *n.* the lower leg; the shinbone; a stem of a thing. [OE. *sceanca*, leg]

shantung' *n.* kind of Chinese silk [*Shantung*]

shant'y *n.* hut; ramshackle or temporary house. [F. *chantier*, workshop]

shant'y *n.* sailor's song with chorus sung by crew at work. [*See* **chanty**]

shape *n.* external form or appearance; mold or pattern. -*v.t.* give shape to; mold, fashion, make. -**shape'less** *a.* -**shape'ly** *a.* well-proportioned. [OE. *gesceap* n.; *sciep-pan* v.]

shard *n.* broken fragment, *esp.* of earthenware. [OE. *sceard*]

share *n.* blade of a plough [OE. *scear*]

share (sher) *n.* portion; dividend. -*v.t.* give or allot a share. -*v.i.* take a share. -**share'holder** *n.* holder of shares in a company, *etc.* [OE. *scearu*, cutting or division]

shark *n.* large, *usu.* predatory, sea fish; grasping person; sharper. [orig. unknown]

sharp *a.* having a keen edge or fine point; apt, keen; brisk; harsh; dealing cleverly but unfairly; shrill; strongly marked, *esp.* in outline. -*n.* in music, a note half a tone above the natural pitch. -**sharp'ly** *adv.* **sharp'en** *v.t.* -**sharp'er** *n.* swindler. -**sharp'ness** *n.* -**sharp'-shooter** *n.* marksman. -**sharp'-set** *a.* hungry, ravenous. [OE. *scearp*]

shatt'er *v.t.* break in pieces. -*v.i.* fly in pieces. [var. of *scatter*]

shave *v.t.* pare away; cut close, *esp.* the hair of the face or head; graze. -*v.i.* shave oneself. -*n.* shaving; narrow escape. -**sha'ver** *n.* (*sl.*) youngster. -**shave'ling** *n.* tonsured monk. -**shav'ing** *n.* act of shaving; splinter, thin slice of wood. [OE. *sceafan*, scrape]

shaw *n.* copse, thicket, wooded area. [OE. *sceaga*]

shawl *n.* square of fabric mainly used to cover the shoulders. [Pers. *shal*]

shawm *n.* musical instrument like an oboe, used in Middle Ages. [OF. *chalemel*, fr. L. *calamus*, reed]

she *pron.* third person singular feminine

pronoun. [OE. *seo*]

she'a-butt'er *n.* butter derived from W. African shea-tree. [native, *shea*]

sheaf *n.* bundle, *esp.* corn. [OE. *sceaf*]

shear *v.t.* cut through; clip or cut; clip the hair or wool from. -*n.* in *pl.* cutting implement like a large pair of scissors; scissor-shaped erection of beams used as a crane. -**shear'er** *n.* -**shear'water** *n.* sea bird of the petrel family. [OE. *scieran*]

sheath *n.* close-fitting cover, *esp.* for a knife or sword; scabbard. -**sheathe** *v.t.* put into a sheath. [OE. *scceth*]

sheave *n.* grooved wheel of pulley. [OE. *shine*]

shebeen' *n.* place for illegal sale of intoxicants. [Ir.]

shed *n.* roofed shelter used as a store or workshop. [var. of *shade*]

shed *v.t.* cast off, scatter, throw off, divide. -*n.* dividing ridge; hair-parting. [OE. *sceadan*, divider]

sheen *n.* gloss, brightness, luster. **sheen'y** *a.* [OE. *sciene*, beautiful]

sheep *n.* ruminant animal with a heavy coat of wool. -**sheep'ish** *a.* shy, awkwardly bashful. -**sheep'cot, sheep'cote** *n.* shelter for sheep. [OE. *sceap*]

sheer *a.* pure; perpendicular. [OE. *scir*, pure, bright]

sheer *v.i.* deviate from a course. -**sheer off'**, avoid, leave. [var. of *shear*, divide]

sheet *n.* large piece of linen, *etc.*, to cover a bed; broad piece of any thin material; large expanse. -*v.t.* cover with a sheet. [OE. *sciete*]

sheet *n.* rope fastened to the corner of a sail. -**sheet'-anchor** *n.* large anchor used only in an emergency. [OE. *sceata*]

sheikh *n.* Arab chief, head of village, *etc.* [Arab, *shaikh*, old man]

shek'el *n.* Jewish weight and coin. -*pl.* (*sl.*) money, wealth. [Heb. *shegel*]

shelf *n.* board fixed horizontally (on a wall, *etc.*), on which to put things; underwater ledge. -**shelve** *v.t.* put on a shelf: put off, slope. [LG. *schelf*]

shell *n.* hard outer case of an animal, fruit, *etc.*; explosive projectile; inner coffin; outer part of a structure left when the interior is removed. -*v.t.* take a shell from, or from a shell; fire at with shells. **shellfish** *n.* sea-animal covered in shell. -**shell'-shock** *n.* nervous or mental disorder caused by shock from bursting shells, bombs, *etc.* [OE. *sciell*]

shellac' *n.* refined lac use for making varnish. [for *shell lac*]

shelt'er *n.* place or structure giving protection; protection. -*v.t.* give protection to, screen. -*v.i.* take shelter. [orig. uncertain]

shep'herd (shep'-erd) *n.* man who tends sheep. -**shep'herdess** *fem.* [OE. *sceaphirde*, sheep herd]

sher'bet *n.* oriental drink of sugar, water and fruit juices. [Pers.]

sher'iff *n.* county or city officer; chief law-enforcement officer. -**sher'iffdom, sher'iffship** *n.* office, area of jurisdiction of sheriff. [OE. *scirgerefa*, shire reeve]

sherr'y *n.* Spanish wine. [wine of *Seres* (now *Jerez*)]

shew'bread *n.* unleavened bread used in ancient Jewish sabbatical ritual. [*sheiv*]

shibboleth *n.* test word; party catchword. [Heb. (Judges xii. 4)]

shield *n.* plate of armor carried on the left arm; protective covering. -*v.t.* cover, screen. [OE. *scield*]

shiel'ing *n.* a shepherd's hut or a small cottage, *esp.* in the Scottish Highlands. [orig. uncertain]

shift *v.t.* move, remove. -*v.i.* remove; change position. -*n.* evasion; expendient; relay of workmen; time of their working; removal; formerly, a woman's undergarment. -**shift'less** *a.* lacking in resource or character. -**shift'y** *a.* shuffling, full of evasions. -**shift'iness** *n.* [OE. *sciftan*, arrange]

shikar'ee, shikar'i *n.* hunter. -**shikar'** *n.* hunting. [Pers.]

shillelagh *n*. cudgel. [of wood from *Shillelagh* in Wicklow, Ireland]

shill'ing *n.* formerly, British silver coin = twelve pence. [OE. *scilling*]

shilly-shally *v.i.* waver. -*n.* wavering, indecision. [redupl. on *shall I*]

shimm'er *v.i.* shine with faint quivering light. -*n.* such light; glimmer. [OE. *seymrian*, shine]

shimm'y *v.i.* dance with wriggling motion. [corrupt. of *chemise*]

shin *n.* front of the lower leg. -*v.i.* climb with arms and legs. [OE. *scinu*]

shin'dy *n.* row. [orig. uncertain]

shine *v.i.* give out or reflect light. -*n.* brightness. -**shi'ny** *a.* [OE. *scinan*]

shin'gle *n.* flat piece of wood used as a tile. -*v.t.* cover with shingles; name board; cut (a woman's hair) close. [L. *scindula*, for *scandula*]

shin'gle (-ng-gl) *n.* pebbles on the shore, of river, sea. [fr. *chink*]

shin'gles (-ng-glz) *n.* disease with eruptions often forming a belt round the body; herpes. [L. *cingula*, belt]

Shin'to *n.* native religion of Japan. **Shin'toism** *n.* [Chin. *shen too*, way of the gods]

shin'ty *n.* game like hockey played by the Scots and Irish. [orig. uncertain]

ship *n.* large sea-going vessel. -*v.t.* put on or send in a ship. -*v.i.* embark; take service in a ship. -*v.i.* -**ship'ment** *n.* act of shipping; goods shipped. -**shipp'ing** *n.* ships collectively. -**ship'shape** *a.* orderly, trim. [OE. *scip*]

shire *n.* county. [OE. *scir*, district]

shirk *v.t.* evade, try to avoid (duty, *etc.*). -**shirk'er** *n.* [orig. uncertain]

shirt *n.* undergarment for the upper part of the body; blouse. [OE. *seyrte*]

shiv'er *n.* splinter. -*v.t.* shatter. -*v.i.* split into pieces. [ME. *scifre*]

shiv'er *v.i.* tremble, usually with cold or fear. -*n.* act or state of shivering. [orig. uncertain]

shoal *n.* sandbank or bar, shallow; school of fish. -*v.i.* become shallow; collect in a shoal. [OE. *sceald*]

shock *v.t.* horrify, scandalize. -*n.* violent or damaging blow; collision. -**shock'er** *n.* sensational novel. -**shock'ing** *a.* [F. *choquer*]

shock *n.* mass of hair. *a.* shaggy. (obs. *shock-dog*, fr. OE. *scucca*, demon]

shod'dy *n.* cloth made of mixed old and new wool. -*a.* worthless, second-rate, of poor material. [orig. unknown]

shoe *n.* covering for the foot, like a boot, but not enclosing the ankle; metal rim or curved bar put on a horse's hoof, various protective plates or undercoverings. -*v.t.* provide with shoes. -**shoe' black** *n.* one who polishes shoes. -**shoe'horn** *v.t* . implement to ease heel into shoe. [OE. *scoh*]

sho'gun *n.* hereditary commander-in-chief of Japanese army prior to 1867. [Jap. *shogun*]

shoot *v.i.* move swiftly and suddenly; let off a gun, bow, *etc.*; go after game with a gun; sprout. -*v.t.* pass quickly under or along; dump; discharge; kill or wound with a missile. -*n.* act of shooting; expedition to shoot; young branch or stem. -**shoot'ing** *n.* area where game is preserved. [OE. *sceotan*]

shop *n.* place where goods are made, or bought and sold. -*v.i.* visit shops. **shop'lifter** *n.* one who steals from a shop. -**shop' steward** *n.* trade union representative of factory workers, *etc.* in negotiating with employers. -**shop'walker** *n.* overseer who directs customers to various departments. [F. *schoppe*, booth]

shore *n*. edge of the sea, or large lake. [Du. *schor*]

shore *n* . *prop*, *esp.* for a ship on the slips. -*v.t.* prop. [orig. uncertain]

short *a.* having little length: brief, hasty: friable. -*n.* in *pl.* short trousers coming to. and open at, the knee; underpants of a similar style. -*adv.* abruptly. -**short'age** *a.* deficiency. -**short'en** *v.t.* and *i.* **short'bread** *n.* rich cookie made with butter. -**short'cake** *n.* cake topped with fruit and whipped cream. -**short-cir'cuit** *n.* (*elec.*) deviation of current by path of small resistance. -*v.t.* take a short-cut to. -**short'coming** *n.* failing, fault, defect. -**short'hand** *n.* method of rapid writing by signs or contractions. -**short'ly** *adv.* soon; briefly. -**short waves** *n.* (wireless) waves between 10 and 50 meters. [OE. *sceort*]

shot *n.* act of shooting, shooter; missile; lead in small pellets; bill at a tavern; film scene. -*a.* woven so that the color is different according to the angle of the light. [OE. *sceot*]

shoul'der *n.* part of a body to which an arm or foreleg is attached; support or bracket. -*v.t.* put on one's shoulder. -*v.t.* make a way by pushing. -**shoulder'blade** *n.* shoulder bone; clavicle. [OE. *sculdor*]

shout *n.* loud cry. -*v.i.* utter one. -*v.t.* utter with a very loud voice. [orig. uncertain]

shove *v.t.* and *n.* push. [OE. *scufan*]

shov'el (-uv-) *n.* broad spade with a long or short handle. -*v.t.* lift or move with a shovel. [OE. *scofl*]

show *v.t.* expose to view, point out; guide; accord (favor, *etc.*). -*v.i.* appear; be visible. -*n.* something shown; display, spectacle. -**show'y** *a.* -**show'ily** *adv.* -**show'down** *n.* disclosure of true state of things. -**show'man** *n.* -**show'off** -*v.* display. [OE. *sceau, ian*, look at]

show'er *n.* short fall of rain; anything coming down like rain. -*v.t.* and *i.* rain. -**show'ery** *a.* [OE. *scur*]

shrap'nel *n.* shell filled with bullets which are discharged by the explosion of the shell. [invented (about 1803) by General *Shrapnel*]

shred *n.* fragment, torn strip. -*v.t.* break or tear to shreds. [OE. *scread*]

shrew *n.* animal like a mouse; malicious person; scold. -**shrew'mouse** *n.* shrew. -**shrew'ish** *a.* -**shrewd** *a.* intelligent, crafty; coming near the truth. -**shrewd'ly** *adv* .

-shrewd'ness *n.* [OE. *screawa*, shrew-mouse]

shriek *v.t.* and *i.* and *n.* (to utter) a loud. piercing cry of alarm, pain, *etc.* [imit. orig.]

shrike *n.* butcher-bird. [imit. of *cry*]

shrill *a.* piercing, sharp in tone. **-shril'ly** *adv.* [imit. orig.]

shrimp *n.* small crustacean of lobster shape. *-v.i.* go catching shrimps. **shrimp'er** *n.* [orig. uncertain]

shrine *n.* case for relics; altar; chapel; temple. [L. *scrinium*, coffer]

shrink *v.i.* become smaller; retire, flinch. *-v.t.* make shrink. **-shrink'age** *n.* [OE. *scrincan*]

shrive *v.t.* give absolution to. **-shrift** *n.* [OE. *scrifan*, prescribe (penance)]

shriv'el *v.i.* shrink and wrinkle. *-v.t.* wither up; scorch. [orig. uncertain]

shroud *n.* sheet for a corpse; covering. *-pl.* set of ropes to a masthead. *-v.t.* put a shroud on; screen, wrap up (fig.) conceal. [OE. *scrud*, garment]

Shrove'tide *n.* days just before Lent. **Shrove Tues'day.** [fr. *shrive*]

shrub *n.* woody or bushy plant. **-shrubb'y** *a.* **-shrubb'ery** *n.* plantation of shrubs, part of a garden filled with them. [OE. *scrybb*]

shrub *n.* drink of fruit juice, rum, *etc.* [Arab. *sharab*]

shrug *v.i.* raise and narrow the shoulders. as a sign of disdain, *etc.* *-v.t.* move (the shoulders) thus. *-n.* shrugging. [orig. unknown]

shudd'er *v.i.* tremble violently, *esp.* with horror. *-n.* shuddering. **-shudd'ering** *a.* [of Teut. orig.]

shuf'fle *v.i.* move the feet without lifting them; act evasively. *-v.t.* mix (cards); (with off) evade, pass to another. Also *n.* [orig. uncertain]

shun *v.t.* avoid. [OE. *scrunian*]

shunt *v.t.* move (a train) from one line to another; push aside; switch over. [orig. uncertain]

shut *v.t.* and *i.* close. **-shutt'er** *n.* movable screen for a window usually hinged to the frame. [OE. *scyttan*]

shut'tle *n.* instrument which threads the wool between the threads of the warp in weaving; similar appliance in a sewing machine; airplane, bus, *etc.* traveling to and fro over a short distance. **-shuttlecock** *n.* cork with cup-shaped fan of feathers stuck in it for use with battledore or badminton racquet. [OE. *scytel*, missile]

shy *a.* timid, bashful, awkward in company; reluctant. *-v.i.* start back in sudden fear; show sudden reluctance. *-n.* sudden start of fear by a horse. **-shy'ly** *adv.* **-shy'ness** *n.* [OF. *eschif*]

shy *v.t.* and *n.* throw. [orig. uncertain]

si'al (at-) *n.* top layer of earth's crust. [*silica, alumina*]

si'amang (se-) *n.* large E. Indian ape, one of the gibbons. [Malay.]

sib'ilant *a.* having a hissing sound. *-n.* speech sound with a hissing effect. [L. *sibilare*, whistler]

sib'yl *n.* pagan prophetess, witch. **-sib'ylline** *a.* oracular. [G. *sibylla*]

sicc'ate *v.t.* dry. **-sicc'ative** *a.* drying. [L. *siccare, siccat-*, dry]

sick *a.* affected by disease or ill health; tired of; disgusted. **-sick'en** *v.t.* and *i.* **sick'ly** *a.* **-sick'ness** *n.* **-sick'bay** *n.* on a ship, *etc.*, place for treating the sick. [OE. *seoc*]

sic'kle *n.* reaping hook. [OE. *sicol*, fr. L. *secula-asecare*, cut]

side *n.* one of the surfaces of an object, *esp.* upright inner or outer surface; either surface of a thing having only two; part of the body that is to the right or left; region nearer or farther than, or right or left of, a dividing line, *etc.*; one of two parties or sets of opponents. *-v.i.* take up the cause of. **-side'arms** *n. pl.* weapons worn at the side. **-side'board** *n.* piece of furniture for holding dishes, *etc.*, in a dining room. **-side'kick** *n.* person closely associated with another, *usu.* as subordinate. **-side'long** *adv.* obliquely. **-side'walk** *n.* paved walkway for pedestrians at the side of a street. **-side'ways** *adv.* **-si'ding** *n.* track added at the side of a railway. **-si'die** *v.i.* edge along. **-side'show** *n.* (auxiliary) fairground show. **-side'track** *v.t.* shunt; divert. **-side'slip** *n.* skid. [OE.]

sider'eal *a.* relating to the stars. [L. *sidus, sider-*, constellation]

si'dle *v.i.* edge along, or sideways [*side*]

siege *n.* a besieging of a town or fortifield place. [F. *siege*, seat, siege]

sienn'a *n.* brown earth pigment. [It. *Tierra di Siena*, Sienna earth]

sierr'a *n.* mountain drawn with saw-like ridges. [Sp.]

siest'a *n.* rest or sleep in the afternoon. [Sp. = sixth (hour)]

sieve (siv) *n.* utensil with network or a perforated bottom for sifting. **-sift** *v.t.* separate coarser portion from finer; solid from liquid. [OE, *site*]

sigh (a!) *v.i.* utter a long audible breath. *-n.*

such a breath. [OE. *sican*]

sight (sit) *n.* faculty of seeing; a seeing; something seen; device (on a rifle, *etc.*) for guiding the eye; (*sl.*) large number. *-v.t.* catch sight of; adjust sights of. **-sight'less** *a.* **-sight'ly** *a.* good to look at. [OE. *sihth*, from *seon*, see]

sign (sin) *n.* movement, mark, or indication to convey some meaning; spoor, trail. *-v.t.* put one's signature to. *-v.i.* make a sign or gesture; affix a signature. **-sign'-manual** (sin-) *n.* autograph signature, *esp.* of a sovereign. **-sign' post** *n.* post supporting a signboard, *esp.* to show the way at cross roads. **-sign'board** (sin-) *n.* board with some device or inscription. [L. *signum*]

sig'nal *n.* sign to convey an order, *etc.*, semaphore, *esp.* on a railwav. *-v.t.* make signals to. *-v.i.* give orders, *etc.*, by signals. *-a.* remarkable, striking. **-sig'nally** *adv.* **-sig'nalize** *v.t.* make notable. [L. *signalis*]

signature *n.* person's name written by himself; act of writing it. **-sig'natory** *n.* one of those who sign a document. **sig'nature tune'**, tune announcing a particular performer, radio feature, *etc.* [L. *signore, signat-*]

sig'net *n.* small seal. **-sig'net ring** *n.* one with seal set in it. [OF.]

sig'nify *v.t.* mean; to intimate. *-v.i.* to be of importance. **-signif'icant** *a.* expressing the importance. **-signif'icantly** *adv.* **-significance** *n.* **-significa'tion** *n.* the meaning. [L. *signum*, sign]

Sikh (sek) *n.* member of an Indian religious sect from the Punjab. [Hind. *sikh*, disciple]

si'lence *n.* stillness, absence of noise; refraining from speech. *-v.t.* make silent. **-si'lent** *a.* **-si'lencer** *n.* expansion chamber in internal combustion engine, minimizing sound of exhaust; device to deaden report of firearm. [L. *silentium*]

silhouette' *n.* portrait or picture cut from black paper or done in solid black on white; outline of an object seen against the light. [E. *de Silhouette*, French politician (d. 1767)]

sil'icon *n.* non-metallic base of silica. sil'ica *n.* mineral found in rock-crystal, quartz, *etc.* **-sil'icon chip** *n.* tiny wafer of silicon forming an integrated circuit in a computer. **-silico'sis** *n.* stonemason's disease caused by inhaling silicia-dust. [L. *silex, sitic-*, flint]

silk *n.* fiber made by the larvae of certain moths; thread or fabric made from this. **-silk'en** *a.* **-silk'y** *a.* **-silk'iness** *adv.* **-silk'ily** *a.* [OE. *seole*]

sill *n.* slab of wood or stone at bottom of a door or window. [OE. *syll*]

sill'y *a.* foolish; weak in intellect. **-sill'iness** *n.* [OE. *gescelig*, happy]

si'lo *n.* pit or tower for storing fodder or grain; underground missile launching site. **-si'lage** *n* . the fodder, *etc* . [Sp.]

silt *n.* mud deposited by water. *-v.t.* and *i.* fill with silt. [orig. uncertain]

Silu'rian *a./n.* (of) division of Palaeozoic rocks before Devonian. [L. *Silurs*, ancient Welsh tribe]

sil'van *a.* wooded; rural. [L. *silua*, wood]

sil'ver *n.* white precious metal; things made of it; silver coins. *-v.t.* coat with silver. **-sil'very** *a.* **-sil'ver-fish** *n.* small wingless insect, the spring-tail. [OE. *siolfor*]

si'ma (si'-) *n.* second layer of earth's crust. [*silicon*, magnesium]

sim'ian *a.* of apes; apelike. *-n.* ape; any kind of monkey. [L. *simia*, ape]

sim'ilar *a.* resembling, like. **-sim'ilarly** *adv.* **-similar'ity** *n.* likeness. **-simile** (sim-i-li) *n.* (*rhet.*) comparison, *esp.* in poetry. **-simil'itude** *n.* outward appear ance; guise. [L. *similis*]

simm'er *v.t.* and *i.* keep or be just bubbling or just below boiling point; be in a state of suppressed anger or laughter. [imit. orig.]

sim'nel *n.* richly spiced cake made at Christmas, Easter, *etc.* - **sim'nelbread, sim'nelcake** *n.* [L. *simila*, fine flour]

si'mony *n.* buying or selling of church preferment. [fr. *Simon* Magus (Acts viii. 18)]

si'moom *n.* hot, dry wind that blows from the Arabian and African deserts. [Arab. *samum*]

sim'per *v.i.* smile in a silly or affected way. [orig. uncertain]

sim'ple *a.* plain; straightforward; ordinary, mere. **-sim'ply** *adv.* **-sim'pleton** *n.* foolish person. **-simpli'city** *n.* **simplify** *v.t.* **-simplifica'tion** *n.* [L. *simplus*]

sim'ulate *v.t.* pretend to be. **-simulac'rum** *n.* **-simulac'ra** *pl.* shadowy likeness; unreal thing. **-simula'tion** *n.* [L. *simulare*, make like]

simultaneous *a.* occurring at the same time. **-simulta'neously** *adv.* **-simul'taneity** *n.* [L. *simmul*, at the same time]

sin *n.* transgression against divine or moral law, *esp.* one committed consciously; conduct or state of mind of a habitual or unrepentant sinner. *-v.i.* commit sin. **-sin'ful** *a.* of the nature of sin; guilty of sin. -

sin'fully *a.* **-sinn'er** *n.* [OE. *synn*]

since *adv.* from then till now; subsequently; ago. *-prep.* at some time subsequent to. *-conj.* from the time that; seeing that. [earlier *sithens*, OE. *siththan*, after that]

sincere' *a.* not assumed or merely professed; actually moved by or feeling the apparent motives; straightforward. -**sincere'ly** *adv.* **-sincer'it y** *n.* honesty of purpose; frankness. [L. *sincerus*, pure]

sine *abbrev.* **sin** *n.* (trigonometry) in a right-angled triangle the sine of an acute angle is the ratio of its opposite side to the hypotenuse. [L. *sinus*, a bay]

si'necure *n.* office with pay, but no duties. [orig. a church benefice without cure of souls; L. *sine cure*]

sin'ew *n.* tendon. *-pl.* muscles, strength; mainstay or motive power. **-sin'ewy** *a.* [OE. *sinu*]

sing *v.i.* utter musical sounds. *-v.t.* utter (words) with musical modulation; celebrate in song or poetry. **-sing'er** *n.* one who, or that which, sings. [OE. *singan*]

singe (-nj) *v.t.* burn the surface of. *-n.* act or effect of singeing. [OE. *sengan*, make to hiss]

sin'gle (-ng-gl) *a.* one only; alone, separate; unmarried; formed of only one part, fold, *etc.* *-v.t.* pick (out). **-singlet** (-ng-gl-) *n.* undergarment. **-sin'gleton** *n.* single thing; only card of a suit in a hand. **-sin'gly** *adv.* **-sin'gle-stick** *n.* fencing with a basket-hilted stick; the stick. **-sin'gular** *a.* unique; remarkable; odd; denoting one person or thing. *-n.* word in singular. -**sin'gularly** *adv.* **-singular'ity** *n.* [L. *singuli*, one at a time]

Sinhalese, Singhalese *a.* of people living mainly in Sri Lanka. [Sans. *Sinhalam*, Ceylon]

sin'ister *a.* evil-looking; wicked; ill omened; in heraldry, on the left-hand side. [L. = on the left hand]

sink *v.i.* become submerged in water; drop, give way, decline. *-v.t.* cause to sink; make by digging out; invest. *-n.* receptacle for washing up with a pipe for carrying away waste water; ditch or tunnel for carrying off sewage; place where evil, corruption collects. **-sink'er** *n.* weight used to sink line. [OE. *sincan*]

Sinn Fein' *n.* Irish republican political movement. [Ir. = *we ourselves*]

sin'uous *a.* curving, winding **-sin'uously** *adv.* **-sinuos'ity** *n.* [L. *sinuosus*]

si'nus *n.* an opening; a hollow; a recess in the shore; a bay; (*surg.*) a cavity in a bone or other part; an abscess with a small orifice (**si'nuses, si'nusi** *pl.*) [L. *sinus*, a curve]

sip *v.t.* and *i.* drink in very small draughts. *-n.* portion of liquid sipped. **-sipp'er** *n.* [var. of *sup*]

si'phon *n.* bent tube for drawing off liquids; bottle with a tape at the top through which liquid is forced by pressure of gas inside. [G. = *tube*]

sir *n.* title of a knight or baronet (with Christian name and surname); public or respectful form of address. [*sire*]

sire *n.* term of address to a king, a father. [F. fr. L. *senior*, elder]

si'ren *n.* legendary female monster supposed to lure sailors to destruction; fog signal; air-raid or fire signal. [L.]

sir'loin *n.* upper part of a loin of beef. [OF. *surloigne*, over loin]

sirocco *n.* hot Mediterranean wind blowing from Africa. [Arab. *sharq*, east]

si'sal, si'sal-hemp *n.* fiber of the agave. [*Sisal*, Yucatan]

sis'ter *n.* daughter of the same parents or having a common parent. *a.* closely related, exactly similar. **-sis'terly** *a.* -**sis'terhood** *n.* relation of sister; order or band of women. **-sis'ter-in-law** *n.* sister of a husband or wife; wife of a brother. [ON. *systir*]

sit *v.i.* rest on the lower part of the body as on a chair, seat oneself; hold a session; incubate. *-v.t.* sit upon (horse). **-sitt'ing** *n.* act of sitting down or being seated; session, meeting; posing for artist; church seat. [OE. *sittan*]

site *n.* place, situation, plot of ground for, or with, a building. **-sit'uate, sit'uated** *a.* placed. **-situa'tion** *n.* place or position; employment or post; state of affairs. [L. *situs*, place]

six *a.* and *n.* cardinal number one more than five. **-sixth** *a.* ordinal number. *-n.* sixth part. **-six'pence** *n.* sum of six pence; silver coin of this value. **-six'penny** *a.* costing sixpence. [OE. *siex*]

size *n.* bigness, dimensions. *-v.t.* sort or estimate by size. [for *assize*]

size *n.* substance resembling glue. *-v.t.* coat or treat with size. [F. *assise*]

sizz'le *v.i.* hiss as when frying. *-n.* hissing sound; great heat. **-sizz'ling** *a.* [imit. orig.]

skald *n.* old Norse bard. [Ice.]

skate *n.* flat fish. [ON. *skata*]

skate *n.* steel blade with a framework to attach it to a boot, for gliding over ice. *-v.i.* glide on skates. [Du. *schaats*]

skean-dhu, skene-dhu *n.* a dagger worn in the stocking. [Gael. *sgian*, knife, *dhu*, black]
skedadd'le *v.i.* (*sl.*) run off. -*n.* disorderly flight.
skein *n.* yarn, wool, *etc.*, in a loose knot. [OF. *escagne*]
skel'eton *n.* bones of an animal. -**skel'eton key'**, key used for picking locks -**skel'eton in the closet**, hidden domestic secret. [G. = *dried up*]
skep *n.* type of basket, beehive. [ON. *skeppa*]
skerry *n.* rocky islet. [Ice. *sker*]
sketch *n.* rough drawing; brief account; essay, *etc.* -*v.t.* make a sketch of. -*v.i.* practice sketching. -**sketch'y** *a.* rough, unfinished. [Du. *schets*]
skew *v.i.* move obliquely. -*a.* slanting, oblique. [OF. *escuer*]
skew'bald *a.* bay and white in patches. [ME. skewed, of doubtful orig.]
skew'er *n.* pin to fasten meat together. *v.i.* pierce or fasten with a skewer. [orig. uncertain]
ski *n.* long runner fastened to the foot for sliding over snow. -*v.i.* slide on skis. [Norw.]
skid *n.* drag for a wheel; side-slip. -*v.t.* apply a skid to. -*v.i.* of a wheel, slip without revolving, slip sideways. [orig. uncertain]
skiff *n.* small boat. [F. *esquif*]
skill *n.* practical ability, cleverness. -**skill'ful** *a.* -**skill'fully** *adv.* [ON, *skil*, distinction]
skill'et *n.* pan with long handle; small cauldron. [ON. *skjola*, pail]
skim *v.t.* rid of floating matter; remove from the surface of a liquid; move over lightly and rapidly; read in this way. -*v.i.* move thus. [OF. *escumer*]
skin *n.* outer covering, *esp.* of an animal or fruit. -*v.t.* remove the skin of. -**skinn'y** *a.* thin. -**skin'flint** *n.* miser, niggard. [ON. *skinn*]
skip *v.i.* leap lightly; jump a rope as it is swung under one. -*v.t.* pass over. -*n.* act. of skipping. [orig. uncertain]
skipp'er *n.* captain of a ship. [Du. *scipper*, fr. *scip*, ship]
skirl *v.i.*/n. shriek, scream; of bagpipes, sound. [Scand.]
skirm'ish *n.* fight between small parties, small battle. -*v.i.* fight slightly or irregularly. [F. *escarmouche*]
skirt *n.* lower part of a woman's dress, coat, *etc.*, outlying part. -*v.t.* border; go round. [ON. *skyrta*]
skit *n.* satire or caricature. -**skitt'ish** *a.* frisky, frivolous. [orig. uncertain]
skit'tles *n.pl.* game of ninepins. [orig. uncertain]
ski'ver *n.* split sheepskin for bookbinding, *etc.* [ON. *skifa*, split]
sku'a *n.* large pirate gull. [ON. *skufr*]
skulk *v.i.* sneak out of the way; lurk; malinger. -**skulk'er** *n.* [Nor. *skulka*, to lurk]
skull *n.* bony case enclosing the brain. [orig. uncertain]
skunk *n.* small N. American animal like a weasel, which defends itself by emitting an evil-smelling fluid; mean fellow. [N. Amer. Ind. *segankw*]
sky *n.* apparent canopy of the heavens; heavenly regions. -**sky-lark** *n.* lark; prank. -**sky-light** *n.* window in roof; **sky-scraper** *n.* very tall building. -**sky'-writing** *n.* smoke writing executed in the sky by an airplane. [ON. = *cloud*]
Skye ter'rier *n.*, small long-haired terrier. [Isle of *Skye*, Scotland]
slab *n.* thick broad piece. [orig. uncertain]
slack *a.* loose, sluggish, not busy. -*n.* loose part. -*v.t.* mix (lime) with water. -*v.i.* be idle or lazy. -**slack'ly** *adv* . **slack'en** *v.t.* and *i.* [OE. *sloec*]
slack *n.* small coal. **slack'-water** *n.* ebb-tide. [Ger. *schlacke*, dross]
slacks *n. pl.* loose trousers for men or women. [fr. *slack* a. q.v.]
slag *n.* dross of melted metal; spongy volcanic lava. -*v.i.* to form into slag. [Ger. *schlacke*, dross]
slake *v.i.* moderate. -*v.t.* quench; slack (time). [OE. *slacian*]
slam *v.t.* shut noisily; dash down. -*v.i.* shut with a bang. -*n.* noisy shutting or other bang. [imit. orig.]
slander *n.* false or malicious statement about a person. -*v.t.* utter such statement. -**slan'derer** *n.* -**slan'derous** *a.* [F. *esclandre*, fr. L. *scandal*, scandal]
slang *n.* colloquial language. -*v.t.* scold violently. [orig. uncertain]
slant (-a-) *v.t.* and *i.* and *n.* slope; idea; viewpoint. *v.* in a slanting manner. - *a.* sloping, oblique. [orig. uncertain]
slap *n.* blow with the open hand or a flat instrument. -*v.t.* strike thus. -**slap'-dash** *a.* careless, rash, slipshod. *adv.* -**slap'stick** (comedy) *n.* rough knockabout comedy, farce. [imit. orig.]
slash *v.t.* gash; lash. -*n.* gash; cutting stroke. [orig. uncertain]
slat *n.* narrow strip of wood or metal; thin,

flat stone. [OF. *esclat*]

slate *n.* kind of stone which splits easily in flat sheets; piece of this for covering a roof or for writing on. *-v.t.* cover with slates. [var. of *slat*]

slate (-a-) *v.t.* to criticize savagely **-slating** *n.* severe criticism. [ON.]

slatt'ern *n.* severe criticism. [ON.]

slatt'ern *n.* slut. **-statt'ernly** *a.* [fr. dial. *slatter*, spill, slop things about]

slaughter *n.* killing *v.t.* kill. **-slaught'erous** *a.* **-slaught'er** *-n.* place for killing animals for food. [ON. *site*, butcher's meat]

slave *n.* captive, person without freedom or personal rights. *-v.i.* work like a slave. **-sla'very** *n.* **-sla'vish** *a.* **-sla'ver** *n.* person or ship engaged in slave traffic. [*slav*]

slav'er *v.i.* let saliva run from the mouth. *-n.* saliva running from mouth, gross flattery. [of Scand. orig.]

slay *v.t.* kill. **-slay'er** *n.* [OE. *stean*]

sledge, sledge-ham'mer *n.* heavy blacksmith's hammer. [OE. *sleog*]

sledge, sled *n.* carriage on runners for sliding on snow; toboggan. *-v.t.* and *i.* [Du. *slede*]

sleek *a.* glossy and smooth. [*stick*]

sleep *n.* unconscious state regularly occurring in men and animals. *-v.i.* take rest in sleep, slumber. **-sleep'er** *n.* one who sleeps; sleeping-car. **-sleep'less** *a.* **sleep'iness** *n.* **-sleep'y** *a.* **-sleep'ily** *adv.* **-sleep'ing sick'ness** *n.* tropical African disease spread by tsetse fly. **-steep'y-sick'ness** *n.* disease marked by pronounced lethargy of mind and body, encephalitis lethargica. **-sleepwalker** *n.* one who walks in sleep, somnambulist. [OE. *slcepan*]

sleet *n.* partly-thawed snow-flakes. *-v.i.* rain sleet. [orig. uncertain]

sleeve *n.* part of a garment covering the arm. **-sleeve'less** *a.* [OE. *slicfe*]

sleigh *n.* sledge. [Du. *sleet*]

sleight *n.* dexterity. **-sleight'-of-hand'** *n.* conjuring. [OE. *sleegth*]

slender *a.* slim, slight, small. [orig. uncertain]

sleuth *n.* track; bloodhound; relentless tracker; detective. [ON. *sloth*, track]

slew past tense of *slay* (*q.v.*) slew *v.t.* and *i.* swing round, as a ship; turn on a pivot. [orig. unknown]

slice *n.* thin flat piece cut off. *-v.t.* cut into slices. [OF. *esclice*]

slick *a.* smooth; smooth-tongued; smart. *-adv.* deftly. *-v.t.* make glossy. **-slick'er** *n.* waterproof [OE. *slycian*, sleek]

slide *v.i.* slip smoothly along. *-v.t.* cause to slide. *-n.* a sliding track on ice made for or by sliding; sliding part of mechanism. **-slide'-rule** *n.* ruler with sliding graduated scale to simplify calculations. **-sti'ding scale'**, scale of *e.g.*, wages, which varies in ratio to the variations of another factor. **-sli'der** *n.* sliding part of a machine, *etc.* [OE. *slidan*]

slight (-it) *a.* slim, slender; not substantial; trifling. *-v.t.* disregard; neglect. *-n.* indifference; act of discourtesy. **-slight'ly** *adv.* [ON. *slettr*]

slim *a.* thin, slight; crafty. *-v.i.* reduce, grow thinner. [Du. = *crafty*]

slime *n.* sticky mud. **-sli'my** *a.* **-sli'miness** *n.* [OE. *slim*]

sling *n.* pocket with a string attached at each end for hurling a stone; hanging bandage for a wounded limb; any rope, belt, *etc.*, for hoisting or carrying weights. *-v.t.* throw; hoist or swing by means of a rope. [ON. *slyngua*]

slink *v.i.* move stealthily (*p.t.* and *p.p.*, slunk, *pres. p.* **slinking**). [OE. *slincan*, creep]

slip *n.* twig cut for grafting or planting; long narrow strip; landing place; slope on which ships are built; leash; mistake; act of slipping. *-v.i.* lose one's foothold. *-v.t.* cause to slip; put on or off easily or gently; release (a dog). **-slipp'er** *n.* light shoe for indoor use. **-stipp'ery** *a.* so smooth as to cause slipping or to be difficult to hold or catch. **-slip'shod** *a.* slovenly, careless. **-slip'-way** *n.* sloping launching-way with one end under water. [OE. *slipor*, slippery]

slit *v.t.* cut open, sever. *-a.* cut, torn. *-n.* straight narrow cut. [OE. *slitan*]

slith'er *n.* slip or splinter of wood; long strip. *-v.t.* divide into long, thin or very small pieces. *-v.i.* split; become split off. [OE. *slifan*, split]

slobb'er *v.i.* slaver. *-v.t.* wet with saliva. *-n.* running saliva. **-slobb'ery** *a.* [*slop*]

sloe *n.* blackthorn; its blue-black fruit. **-sloe-gin** *n.* liqueur made from sloes. [OE. *slah*]

slog *v.i.* hit hard; work doggedly. **-slogg'er** *n.* [orig. uncertain]

slo'gan *n.* Scottish Highland war-cry; catchword, motto. [Gael. *sluagh-ghairm*, army cry]

sloop *n.* one-masted cutter-rigged vessel; small warship. [Du. *sloep*]

slop *n.* overall. *-pl.* ready-made clothing. **-slop'shop** *n.* [OE.]

slop *n.* dirty liquid; semi-liquid food. -*v.t.* spill or splash. -*v.i.* spill. -**slopp'y** *a.* (*sl.*) weakly sentimental. [OE. *sloppe*]

slope *n.* slant, upward or downward inclination. -*v.t.* move obliquely. -*v.t.* place slanting; (*sl.*) abscond; stroll off. [OE. *aslupan*, slip away]

slot *n.* narrow hole, depression; slit for coins in, *e.g.*, stamp machine. -*v.i.* make a slot or slots in. -**slotted** *a.* (OF. esclot]

slot *n.* trail of an animal, *esp.* of a deer. [ON. *sloth*, track]

sloth *n.* sluggishness; sluggish S. Amer. animal. -**sloth'fully** *a.* idle; unwilling to exert oneself. [fr. *slow*]

slouch *n.* stooping, or shambling walk. -*v.i.* walk in this way. -*v.t.* pull down (a hat). [orig. uncertain]

slough (-ow) *n.* bog. [OE. *sloh*]

slough (-uf) *n.* skin shed by a snake; dead tissue from a sore. -*v.i.* of such tissue to be shed. -*v.t.* shed (skin). [of Scand. orig.]

slov'en (-uv-) *n.* dirty, untidy person. -**slov'enly** *a.* [orig. uncertain]

slow *a.* moving at a low rate of speed; behindhand; dull. -*v.i.* slacken speed. -**slow'ly** *adv.* -**slow'ness** *n.* [OE. *slaw*, sluggish]

slow'-worm *n.* small lizard; blind worm. [OE. *slawyrm*, 'slay worm' wrongly considered dangerous]

sludge *n.* slush, sewage. [*slush*]

slug *n.* land snail with no shell; lazy fellow. -**slugg'ard** *n.* -**slugg'ish** *a.* slow moving; lazy. -**slugg'ishness** *n.* [of Scand. orig.]

slug *n.* oval or cylindrical bullet. [of Scand. orig.]

sluice *n.* sliding gate or door to control a flow of water. -*v.t.* pour water over; drench. [OF. *escluse*]

slum *n.* squalid street or neighborhood. -*v.i.* visit slums. [orig. unknown]

slum'ber *v.i.* sleep. -*n.* sleep. -**slumbrous** *a.* sleepy, inducing slumber. [OE. *sluma*]

slump *v.i.* of prices, *etc.*, to fall suddenly or heavily. -*n.* such fall. [imit.]

slur *v.t.* pass over lightly; depreciate. -*n.* slight. [orig. uncertain]

slut *n.* a dirty untidy woman. -**slutt'tish** *a.* [orig. uncertain]

sly *a.* cunning, wily; done with artful dexterity. -**sly'ly** *adv.* -**sly'ness** *n.* -**on the sly'**, surreptitiously. [ON. *slcegr*]

smack *n.* taste, flavor. -*v.i.* taste (of). [OE. *smcec*]

smack *v.t.* open (the lips) with a loud sound; slap. -*n.* smacking or slap; sound of a slap. [imit. orig.]

smack *n.* small sailing vessel, usually for fishing. [Du. *smak*]

small (-awl) *a.* little. -**small'ness** *n.* -**small'pox** *n.* contagious disease. -**small'talk** *n.* polite conversation. [OE. *smcel*]

smar'my *a.* unctuous. [fr. *smarm*, anoint, orig. unknown]

smart *a.* brisk; clever; trim, well dressed; fashionable. -*v.i.* be very painful; suffer acutely. -*n.* sharp pain. -**smart'en** *v.t.* -**smart'ly** *adv.* -**smart'ness** *n.* [OE. *smeortan*, to be painful]

smash *v.t.* shatter; dash. -*v.i* break. -*n.* heavy blow; wrecked state; accident wrecking vehicles. [fr. *mash*]

smattering *n.* superficial knowledge. -**smatt'er** *v.i.* have a smattering. -**smatt'er** *n.* [orig. unknown]

smear *v.t.* rub with grease, *etc.* -*n.* mark made thus. [OE. *smeoru*, fat]

smell *v.t.* perceive by the nose. -*v.i.* use the nose; give out an odor. -*n.* odor; faculty of perceiving odors by the nose. [orig. unknown]

smelt *n.* small flavorsome fish allied to the salmon. [OE.]

smelt *v.t.* extract metal from ore. -**smelt'ing-fur'nace** *n.* [obs. Du. *smelten*]

smi'lax *n.* climbing shrub. [G.]

smile *v.i.* assume a pleased or amused expression. -*n.* act of smiling. -**smi'ling** *a.* -**smi'tingly** *adv.* [orig. uncertain]

smirch *v.t.* make dirty; soil; dishonor. -*n.* mark, blot; stain. [orig. uncertain]

smirk *v.i.* smile affectedly. -*n.* such smile. [OE. *smearcian*]

smite *v.t.* strike; attack; affect, *esp.* with love. [OE. *smitan*, smear]

smith *n.* worker in iron, *etc.* -**smith'y** (-TH-) *n.* his workshop. [OE.]

smith'ereeris (-TH-) *n. pl.* small fragments. (Ir. *smidirin*]

smock *n.* loose garment with the upper part gathered. -*v.t.* gather by diagonal lines of sewing. -**smock'-frock** *n.* laborer's smock. [OE. *smoc*]

smog *n.* mixture of smoke and fog. [*smo*ke, *fog*]

smoke *n.* cloudy mass of suspended particles that rises from fire or anything burning; spell of tobacco smoking. -*v.i.* give off smoke; inhale and expel the smoke of burning tobacco. -*v.t.* expose to smoke (*esp.* in curing fish, *etc.*); consume (tobacco) by smoking. -**smo'ker** *n.* -**smo'ky** *a.* -*n.* smoked haddock. -**smo'kily** *adv.* -**smokestack** *n.* funnel, chimney, from a

steam boiler, *etc.* -**smoke-screen** *n.* in warfare, cloud of smoke to conceal activities of ships or troops. [OE. *smoca*]
smol'der *v.i.* burn slowly without flame. [orig. uncertain]
smolt *n.* young salmon. [Scot. *smout*]
smooth (-TH) *a.* not rough, even of surface; plausible. -*v.t.* make smooth, quieten. -**smooth'ly** *adv.* [OE. *smoth*]
smoth'er (-uTH-) *n.* dense smoke, spray, foam, *etc.* -*v.t.* suffocate, suppress. -*v.i.* be suffocated. [OE. *smorian*]
smudge *n.* smear, dirty mark. -*v.t.* make a dirty mark on. [orig. uncertain]
smug *a.* self-satisfied, complacent. -**smug'ly** *adv.* [Low Ger. *smuk*, neat]
smug'gle *v.t.* bring into a country without payment of legal customs duties. -**smugg'ler** *n.* [LG. *smuggeln*]
smut *n.* piece of soot, black particle of dirt; disease of grain; lewd or obscene talk. -*v.t.* blacken, smudge. -**smutt'y** *a.* [Low Ger.]
snack *n.* light meal. -**snack'-bar** *n.* bar, counter, for this. [dial. *snack*, bite]
snaf'fle *n.* light bit for a horse. -*v.t.* put one on. [orig. uncertain]
snaff'le *v.t.* (*sl.*) steal, purloin. [*o.s.*]
snag *n.* stump, *esp.* a tree-trunk in a river; any obstacle or impediment. [ON. *snagi*, point]
snail *n.* slow-moving mollusk with a shell, common in gardens. [OE. *sncegel*]
snake *n.* long slimy limbless reptile. -**sna'ky** *a.* [OE. *snaca*]
snap *v.i.* make a quick bite or snatch. -*v.t.* snatch or bite; break abruptly; photograph. -*n.* quick sharp sound; bite; break; photograph. -**snapp'y** *a.* -**snapp'ish** *a.* -**snap'dragon** *n.* plant with flowers resembling a mouth; game of snatching raisins from burning brandy. -**snap'shot** *n.* instantaneous photography; print of this; shot without deliberate aim. [Du. *snappen*]
snare *n.* noose used as a trap. -*v.t.* catch with one. [ON. snara]
snarl *n.* growling sound made by an angry dog. -*v.i.* make this sound; grumble. [imit. orig.]
snarl *n.* tangle. [fr. *snare*]
snatch *v.i.* make a quick grab or bite (at). -*v.t.* seize, catch. -*n.* grab; short spell. [cp. *snack*]
sneak *v.i.* slink. -*n.* mean or treacherous person. [OE. *snican*, creep]
sneer *v.i.* smile, speak or write scornfully. -*n.* a sneering. [orig. uncertain]
sneeze *v.i.* emit breath with a sudden convulsive spasm and noise. -*n.* sneezing. [OE. *fneosan*]
snick *v.t.* cut, nick. [Ice. *snikka*, nick]
snick'er *v.t.* snigger, giggle. [imit.]
sniff *v.i.* draw in breath through the nose with a sharp hiss; express disapproval, *etc.*, by sniffing. -*v.t.* take up through the nose, smell. -*n.* a sniffing. [imit. orig.]
snigg'er *v.i.* giggle furtively or in a suppressed way. [imit.]
snip *v.t.* cut, cut bits off. -*n.* bit cut off, small cut. -**snipp'et** *n.* shred, fragment. [Du. *snippen*]
snipe *n.* long-billed marsh-bird. -*v.i.* shoot at enemy individuals from cover. *v.t.* hit by so shooting. -**sni'per** *n.* [ON. *snipe*]
sniv'el *v.i.* sniff to show real or sham emotion, *esp.* sorrow. [OE. *snyflan*]
snob *n.* one who judges by social rank or wealth rather than merit. -**snobb'ery** *n.* -**snobb'ish** *a.* -**snobb'ishly** *adv.* [orig. uncertain]
snoek *n.* kinds of S. African fish. [Du. = *pike*]
snood *n.* a type of hair-covering for women, often mesh. [OE. *snod*, thread]
snook'er *n.* variety of game of pool played on billiard table. [orig, unknown]
snoop *v.i.* pry, sneak around. -**snoop'er** *n.* [Du. *snoepen*]
snooze *v.i.* take a short sleep, be half-asleep. -*n.* nap. [orig. unknown]
snore *v.i.* make noises with the breath when asleep. -*n.* act of snoring. [imit. orig.]
snort *v.i.* make a noise by driving breath through the nostrils; show defiance; contempt. -*n.* such noise. [imit. orig.]
snout *n.* nose of an animal. [OE. *snut*]
snow *n.* frozen vapor which falls in flakes. -(*sl.*) cocaine. -*v.i.* it snows, snow is falling. -*v.t.* let fall or throw down like snow; cover with snow. -**snow blink** *n.* reflection in sky of snow or ice. -**snow' bun'ting** *n.* a northern finch. -**snow' drop** *n.* bulbous plant with white flowers in early spring. -**snow line** *n.* elevation above which snow does not melt. -**snow'y** *a.* [OE. *snow*]
snub *v.t.* mortify or repress intentionally; rebuke. -*n.* snubbing. -**snub'nose** *n.* turned-up stumpy nose. [ON. *snubba*, rebuke]
snuff *n.* charred candle-wick; powdered tobacco for inhaling through the nose; act of snuffing. -*v.t.* free (a candle) from snuff; put out; draw up or through the nostrils. *v.i.* draw air or snuff into the nose. [cp. *sniff*]
snug *a.* cosy; trim. -**snug'ly** *adv.* -**snugg'ery** *n.* cosy room. -**snuggle** *v.i.* nestle. [orig. uncertain]

so *adv.* in such manner; very; the case being such. -*conj.* therefore; in case that. [OE. *swa*]

soak *v.i.* lie in a liquid. -*v.t.* steep, make throughly wet. -*n.* a soaking. [OE. *socian*]

soap *n.* compound of alkali and oil used in washing. -*v.t.* apply soap to. **-soap'stone** *n.* soft kind of rock, steatite. **-soap'y** *a.* [OE. *sape*]

soar *v.i.* to fly high.[F. *essorer*]

sob *v.i.* catch the breath, *esp.* in weeping. -*n.* sobbing. **-sob'-stuff** *n.* cheap pathos. [imit.]

so'ber *a.* temperate; subdued; not drunk. -*v.t.* and *i.* make or become sober. **-so'berly** *adv.* **-sobri'ety** *n.* [L. *sobrius*]

sobriquet (-ket) *n.* nickname. [F.]

socc'er *n.* association football, game between two teams of eleven players using a round ball which is kicked from one to another in order to score goals between goalposts. [fr. association football]

so'cial *a.* living in communities; relating to society; sociable. **-so'cially** *adv.* **-so'ciable** *a.* inclined to be friendly, of ready companionship. **-sociabil'ity** *n.* **-so'ciably** *adv.* **-soci'ety** *n.* compansionship; living associated with others; those so living; fashionable people collectively; association or club. **-sociol'ogy** *n.* social science. **-so'cialism** *n.* policy aiming at ownership of means of production and transport, *etc.*, by the community. **-so'cialist** *n.* **-socialis'tic** *a.* [L. *socius*, companion]

sock *n.* short stocking; inner sole, formerly, light shoe worn by actors in comedy; hence, comedy. [L. *soccus*]

sock *v.t.* (*sl.*) hit, punch. [orig. unknown]

sock'et *n.* hole for something to fit into. [AF. *soket*, spear-head]

sod *n.* flat piece of earth with grass; a turf. [orig. uncertain]

so'da *n.* alkali. **-so'da water** *n.* water charged with gas. [It. -L. *solids*, firm]

sodal'ity *n.* an association, society, fraternity. [L. *sodalis*, comrade]

sodd'en *a.* soaked; like dough; of ground, boggy. [orig. pp. of *seethe*]

so'dium *n.* a metallic element found in soda, salt and other compounds. [Latinized from *soda*]

sod'omy *n.* unnatural sexual intercourse, *esp.* between males; anal intercourse. [*Sodom* (Gen. xviii)]

so'fa *n.* long padded seat with a back and one or two ends. [F.]

soft *a.* yielding easily to pressure; not hard; not loud; mild; easy; subdued; over-sentimental. **-soft'ly** *adv.* **-soft'en** (sofn) *v.t.* and *i.* [OE. *softe*]

soft'ware *n.* (*compute.*) programs, procedures, rules, and documentation that direct or relate to the operation of a computer system.

sogg'y *a.* soaked, soden, marshly; damp and heavy. [orig. uncertain]

soi-di'sant *a.* self-styled; pretended. [F.]

soigné (swa-nya) **soignée**, *fem. a.* extremely well-groomed. (F.]

soil *n.* earth, ground. [L. *solum*]

soil *v.t.* and *i.* make or become dirty. -*n.* dirt; sewage. [F. *souiller*]

soirée (swa-ra) *n.* evening party; social or congregational meeting with tea, *etc.* [F.]

soj'ourn *v.i.* stay for a time. **-soj'ourner** *n.* [OF. *sojorner*]

so'lace *n.* and *v.t.* comfort; consolation in distress. [L. *solari*, comfort]

so'lan *n.* large sea-bird like a goose; gannet. [orig. uncertain]

so'lar *a.* of the sun. **-sola'rium** *n.* sunroom. **-so'lar hea'ting** *n.* heat radiation from the sun collected by heat-absorbing panels through which water is circulated. **-so'lar pan'el** *n.* a panel exposed to radiation of heat from the sun, used for heating water or, when mounted with solar cells, to produce electricity direct, *esp.* for powering instruments in satellites. **-so'lar pow'er** *n.* heat radiation from the sun converted to electrical energy by specially designed steam boilers and turbogenerators. **-so'lar sys'tem**, system of planets, *etc.* revolving round the sun. **-so'lar myth'**, myth personifying the sun. **-so'lar plex'us,** nerve network at pit of stomach. [L. *sol*, sun]

sola'tiurn *n.* money compensation. [L.]

sold'er (sod-) *n.* an easily melted alloy used for joining metal. -*v.t.* to join with it. **-sol'dering iron** *n.* [L. *solidare*, to make solid]

sol'dier *n.* one serving in an army. -*v.i.* serve in the army. **-sol'dierly** *a.* **-sol'diery** *n.* troops.[F. *solde*, pay]

sole *n.* flat of the foot; under part of a boot or shoe, *etc.* -*v.t.* supply with a sole. [F. fr. L. *solea*]

sole *n.* flat-fish. [F. fr. L. *solea*]

sole *a.* only, unique; single. **-sole'ly** *adv.* only; singly. [L. *solus*]

sole *n.* flat of the under part of a boot or shoe, *etc.* -*v.t.* supply with a sole. [F. fr. L. *solea*]

sole *n.* flat-fish. [F. fr. L. *solea*]

sole *a.* only, unique; single. **-sole'ly** *adv.*

only; singly. [L. *solus*]

sol'ecism *n.* breach of grammar or etiquette. (G. *soloikismos*]

sol'emn (-M) *a.* serious, grave; formal; impressive. **-sol'emnly** *adv.* **-solem'nity** *n.* **-sol'emnize** *v.t.* celebrate, perform; make solemn. **-solemniza'tion** *n.* [L. *sollemnis*, appointed]

sol'fa *n.* use of names for notes of musical scale. [fr. syllables *sol*, *fa* of scale]

soli'cit (-lis'-) *v.t.* urge; request; entice. **-solicita'tion** *n.* **-soli'citor** *n.* one who solicits; lawyer. **-soli'citous** *a.* anxious. **-solicitude** *n.* [L. *sollicitare*]

sol'id *a.* not hollow; compact; substantial; unanimous. *-n.* body of three dimensions. **-sol'idly** *adv.* **-solid'ity** *n.* **-solid'ify** *v.t.* and *i.* **-solidifica'tion** *n.* **-solidar'ity** *n.* united state. [L. *solidus*]

solid state *See* **semiconductor.**

soliloquy *n.* talking with oneself. **-solil'oquize** *v.i.* [Late L. *soliloquium*]

solitaire' *n.* single precious stone set by itself; game for one. [L. *solus*, alone]

solitary *a.* alone, single. *-n.* hermit. **-sol'itude** *n.* [L. *solitarius*]

so'lo *n.* music for one performer; a solo part; motor-bicycle without sidecar. **-so'loist** *n.* **-so'lo flight'**, flight by one person alone. [F.]

sol'stice *n.* period of the year when the sun is overhead at one of the tropics. **-solsti'tial** *a.* [L. *solstitium*]

solve *v.t.* work out, clear up, find the answer of. **-sol'uble** *a.* capable of solution. **-solubil'ity** *n.* **-solu'tion** *n.* answer to a problem; a dissolving; liquid with something dissolved in it. **-sol'vable** *a.* **-sol'vent** *a.* able to pay debts, having more assets than liabilities. *-n.* liquid with a power of dissolving. **-sol'vency** *n.* state of being able to pay one's debts. [L. *solvere, solut-*, loosen]

somatol'ogy *n.* science of bodies and material substance (physiology, physics). [G. *soma*, body]

som'ber *a.* dark or gloomy. **-som'berly** *adv.* **-somberness** *n.* (F.]

sombre'ro *n.* wide-brimmed felt hat worn in Mexico. [Sp.]

some (sum) *pron.* portion, quantity. *-a.* one or other; amount of; certain; approximately; **some'body** *n.* **-some'how** *adv.* **-some'thing** *n.* **-some'time** *a.* former. *-adv.* formerly; at some (past or future) time. **-some'times** *adv.* on occasion. **-some'what** *n.* something. *-adv.* to some extent, rather. **-some'where** *adv.* [OE. *sum*]

somersault (sum-) *n.* tumbling head over heels. [F. *soubresant*]

somnambulist *n.* sleep-walker. **-somnam'bulism** *n.* [fr. L. *somnus*, sleep, *ambulare*, ambulate, walk]

somnolent *a.* sleepy. **-som'nolence** *n.* [L. *somnus*, sleep]

son *n.* male child. **-son'-in-law** *n.* daughter's husband. [OE. *sunu*]

sona'ta (-d-) *n.* piece of music in several movements, mainly for a solo instrumental. **-sonati'na** *n.* short and simple sonata. [It.]

song *n.* singing; poem for singing; notes of certain birds. **-song'ster** *n.* **-song'stress** *fem.* [OE.]

so'nic *a.* of sound waves. [L. *sonus*, sound]

sonnet *n.* fourteen-line poem with a rhyme system. **-sonneteer'** *n.* [F.]

sonor'ous *a.* giving out deep sound, resonant. **-son'orously** *adv.* **-sonor'ity** *n.* [L. *sonorus-sonare*, sound]

soon *adv.* before long; early; without delay. [OE. *sona*, at once]

soot *n.* black substance formed from smoke. **-soot'y** *a.* [OE. *sot]*

sooth *n.* truth. **-sooth'sayer** *n.* person professing to foretell the future. **-sooth'saying** *n.* [OE. *soth*, true]

soothe *v.t.* calm, soften; please with soft words. **-sooth'ing** *a.* **-sooth'ingly** *adv.* [OE. *sothian*, show to be true]

sop *n.* piece of bread, *etc.*, soaked in liquid; bribe; something to quieten. *-v.t.* steep in water, *etc.* [OE. *sopp*]

soph'ist *n.* captious reasoner. **-soph'ism** *n.* specious argument. **-sophist'ical** *a.* **-soph'istry** *n.* **-sophisticate** *v.t.* make artificial, spoil, falsify. **-sophistic'ation** *n.* [G. *sophisma*] **-sophistication** *n.* [G. *sophisms*]

soporif'ic *a.* causing sleep. *-n.* drug, *etc.*, to cause sleep. [L. *sopor*, sleep]

sopran'o (-rd-) *n.* highest voice in women and boys; singer with this voice; musical part for it. [It.]

sor'cerer *n.* wizard. **-sor'ceress** *fem.* **-sor'cery** *n.* witchcraft.[F. *soreier*]

sor'did *a.* mean, squalid. **-sor'didly** *adv.* **-sor'didness** *n.* [L. *sordidus*]

sore *a.* painful; distressed. *adv.* grievously. *-n.* sore place, ulcer or boil, *etc.* **-sore'ness** *n.* **-sore'ly** *adv.* [OE. *sar*]

sorghums (-gum) *n.* various grasses cultivated for grain [Mod. L. fr. It. *sorgo*]

soror'ity *n.* club of women, *esp.* a

women's student organization formed chiefly for social purposes, *etc.* [L. *soror*, sister]

sorr'el *n.* reddish-brown; horse of this color. *-a.* of this color. [OF. *sorel*]

sorr'ow (-o) *n.* pain of mind, grief. *-v.i.* grieve. **-sorr'owful** *a.* **-sorr'owfully** *adv.* [OE. *sorh*]

sorr'y *a.* distressed; mean, poor. **-sorr'ily** *adv.* [OE. *sarig]*

sort *n.* kind or class. *-v.t.* classify. **-sort'er** *n.* [L. *sors, sort-*, share, lot]

sort'ie *n.* sally by besieged forces. [F.]

SOS *n.* letters of Morse Code sent as an appeal for help by ship at sea; a broadcast appeal for a relative of one dangerously ill; an urgent appeal.

sot *n.* drunkard. **-sott'ish** *a.* [F. =*fool*]

sou'fflé *n.* dish made with whisked white-of-egg. [F.]

sough (suf) *n.* sigh (of the wind); whisper, rumor. *-v.i.* [OE. *swogan*]

soul *n.* spiritual part of a human being; person. **-soul'ful** *a.* expressing elevated feeling. **-soul'less** *a.* mean, prosaic. **-soul food** *n.* food, as yams, *etc.*, traditionally eaten by southern black Americans. **-soul mate** *n.* person for whom one has deep affinity. **-soul music** *n.* type of Black music resulting from addition of jazz and gospel to urban blues style. [OE. *sawol*]

sound *n.* that which is heard; meaningless noise. *-v.i.* make a sound. *-v.t.* cause to sound. **-sound'ing** *n.* act of sounding; an ascertained depth. [L. *sonus*]

sound *a.* in good condition; solid; of good judgment. **-sound'ly** *adv.* thoroughly. [OE. *gesund*, healthy]

sound *n.* channel or strait. (ON. *sund*]

sound *v.t.* find the depth of *-v.i.* find the depth of water. [F. *sonder*]

soup *n.* liquid food made by boiling meat or vegetables. [F. *souse*]

sour *a.* acid; peevish. *-v.t.* and *i.* make or become sour. **-sour'ly** *adv.* **-sour'ness** *n.* **-sour'dough** *n.* leaven; old timer. [OE. *sur*]

source *n.* spring; origin. [F.]

souse *v.t.* pickle; soak. *-v.i.* soak; fall into water, *etc.* *-n.* an act of sousing. [OF. *souz*]

south *n.* cardinal point opposite the north; region, or part of a country, *etc.*, lying to that side. *a.* that is towards the south. *adv* . towards the south. **south'erly** (suTH-) *a.* **-south'ern** (suTH-) *a.* **-south'wards** *a.* and *adv.* **-south'wester, sou'wester** *n.* waterproof hat. [OE. *suth*]

souvenir' *n.* memory; keepsake. [F.]

sov'ereign (sov'rin) *n.* king or queen; ruler; formerly, gold coin *a.* supreme; efficacious. **-sov'ereignty** *n.* [OF. *soverain*]

soviet' *n.* council, *esp.* of soldiers and workmen, in Russia, forming basis of Russian national government. [Russ.]

sow *n.* female of the swine. [OE. *sugu*]

sow *v.i.* scatter seed. *-v.t.* scatter or deposit (seed); spread abroad. **-sow'er** *n.* [OE. *sawan*]

soy'a-bean *n.* Eastern edible bean. **-soy'a-flour** *n.* flour made from it. **-soy sauce** *n.* salty, dark brown sauce made from fermented soya beans, used *esp.* in Chinese cookery. [Jap. *shoyu*]

spa *n.* medicinal spring; place with one. [*Spa*, in Belgium]

space *n.* extent; period; area; expanse; expanse of the universe; empty place. *v.t.* place at intervals. **-spa'cious** *n.* roomy. [F. *espace*, fr. L. *spatium*]

spade *n.* tool for digging. [OE. *spadu*]

spades *n.pl.* suit at cards. *-sing.* card of this suit. [Sp. *espada*, sword]

spaghet'ti (-get'-) *n.* dried wheat-paste in long narrow tubes, thinner than macaroni. [It.]

span *n.* space from thumb to little finger as a measure; extent or space; the stretch of an arch, *etc.*; (airplane) distance between wingtips; team of oxen. *-v.t.* stretch over; measure with the hand; harness or yoke. **-spann'er** *n.* tool for gripping the nut of a screw. [OE. *spann*]

span'drel *n.* triangular space between the curves of an arch and the enclosing molding. [perch. from *expand*]

spang'le (-ng-gl) *n.* small piece of glittering metal as an ornament. [OE. *sprang*, buckle]

span'iel *n.* dog with long ears and hair. [OF. *espagneul*, 'Spanish']

spank *v.i.* move with vigor or spirit. **-spank'ing** *a.* brisk; fine, big. **-spank'er** *n.* fast-going horse, ship, *etc.* [Dan. *spanke*, strut]

spank *v.t.* slap with the flat of the hand, *esp.* in chastising children. [imit.]

spann'er. *See* **span.**

spar *n.* pole, *esp.* as part of a ship's rigging. [On. *sparri*]

spar *n.* crystalline mineral, as fluor-spar. [of Tent. orig.]

spar *v.i.* box; make boxing motions; dispute, *esp.* in fun. [orig. uncertain]

spare *a.* additional, in reserve, not in use. *-v.t.* leave unhurt; abstain from using; do without; give away. **spar'ing** using little;

economical. -**spar'ingly** *adv.* [OE. *sparian*]

spark *n.* small glowing or burning particle; trace; electric spark igniting explosive mixture in car cylinder. -*v.i.* emit sparks. -**spar'kie** *v.i.* glitter. [OE. *spearca*]

sparr'ow *n.* small brownish bird, common in towns. [OE. *spearswa*]

sparse *a.* thinly scattered. -**sparse'ly** *adv.* [L. *spargere, spars-*, scatter]

spar'tan *a.* hardy; frugal. [*Sparta*]

spas'm (-zm) *n.* convulsive muscular contraction. -**spasmod'ic** *a.* of the nature of a spasm; jerky; intermittent; disjointed. -**spa'stic** *a.* of, like spasms, spasmodic. [G. *spasmos*]

spat *n. usu. pl.* short gaiter. [short for *spatter-dash*, shield against splashes]

spate *n.* sudden flood in a river, following heavy rain. [Scot.]

spatt'er *v.t.* splash, cast drops over. -*v.i.* fall in drops. -*n.* slight splash. -**spatt'er-dash** *n.* protection against splashes. [Du. *spatten*, burst]

spat'ula *n.* broad blade, used for mixing paint, *etc.* [L.]

spav'in *n.* tumor on a horse's leg. -**spav'ined** *a.* [OF. e*spavian*]

spawn *n.* eggs of fish. -*v.i.* of fish, to cast eggs. [OF. *espandre*, shed]

speak *v.i.* utter words; converse; deliver a discourse. -*v.t.* utter; communicate with (a passing ship). -**speak'able** *a.* -**speak'er** *n.* [OE. *sprecan*]

spear *n.* long pointed weapon, pike. -*v.t.* pierce with a spear. -**spear'side** *n.* male side of family *pl*. distaff-side. [OE. *spere*]

spe'cial (spesh-) *a.* beyond the usual; particular, individual; distinct; limited. **spe'cially** *adv.* -**spe'cialist** *n.* one who devotes himself to a special subject or branch of a subject. -**spe'cialism** *n.* -**spe'cialize** *v.i.* be a specialist. -*v.t.* make special. -**special'ty** *n.* special product, characteristic, *etc.* [L. *species*, kind, appearance]

spe'cie *n.* coined money. [*special*]

spe'cies *n.* class; sub-division; sort or kind. [L.]

specific *a.* characteristic of a thing or kind; definite; specially efficacious for something. -**specif'ically** *adv.* -**spe'cify** (-fi) *v.t.* state definitely or in detait. -**specifica'tion** *n.* detailed description. [L. *species*, kind, appearance]

spe'cimen *n.* individual example; part used to typify a whole. [L. *specimen*]

spe'cious *a.* having a fair appearance; deceptively plausible. -**spe'ciously** *adv.* [L. *species*]

speck *n.* small spot, particle. -*v.t.* spot. -**spec'kle** *n.* and *v.* speck. -**spec'kled** *a.* -**speck'tess** *a.* spotless [OE. *specca*]

spectacle *n.* show; thing exhibited. -*pl.* arrangement of lenses to help defective sight. -**spectac'ular** *a.* -**specta'tor** *n.* one who looks on. [L. *specere, spect-*, look]

spec'ter *n.* ghost; threatening image. [L. *spec'trum*, vision]

spectrum *n.* -**spec'tra** *pl.* colored band into which a beam of light can be decomposed. -**spec'toscope** *n.* instrument for decomposing light and examining spectra. -**spectrohe'liograph** *n.* instrument for photographing the sun. [L.]

speculate *v.i.* make theories or guesses; engage in risky commercial transactions. -**spec'ulator** *n.* -**spec'ulative** *a.* -**specula'tion** *n.* [L. *speculatus*]

spec'ulum *n.* a mirror; a reflector of polished metal, *esp.* such as that used in reflecting telescopes. [L. *speculum*, a mirror-*specere*, to look at]

speech *n.* act or faculty of speaking words; language; conversation; discourse. -**speechify** *v.i.* make a speech. -**speech'less** *a.* [OE. *sprxc*]

speed *n.* swiftness; rate of progress. -*v.i.* move quickly; succeed. -*v.t.* further; expedite; bid farewell to. -**speedom'eter** *n.* instrument to show the speed of a moving vehicle. -**speed'y** *a.* -**speed'ily** *adv.* -**speed'way** *n.* track for racing. [OE. *spæd*]

speed'well *n.* plant with blue flowers. [*speed* and *well*]

spell *n.* magic formula; enchantment. -**spell'-bound** *a.* entranced. [OE.]

spell *n.* turn of work, *etc.*; bout. [OE. *spelian*, act for]

spell *v.t.* read letter by letter; give the letters of in order. [OF. *espeler*]

speller *n.* zinc. [orig. unknown]

spend *v.t.* lay out; disburse; employ. -**spend'thrift** *n.* wasteful person, prodigal. -**spend'er** *n.* [L. *expendere*, pay]

sperm *n.* animal seed; spawn of fishes, frogs. [G. *sperma*]

spermace'ti *n.* fatty substance obtained from the head of the spermwhale and used for making candles, ointment, *etc.* -**sperm'whale** *n.* large, toothed whale hunted for sperm oil, spermaceti and ambergris. [G. *sperma-speirein, sow, ketos*, whale]

spew *v.t.* vomit. [OE. *spiwan*]

sphag'num *n.* bog, peat moss. [G. *sphag-*

nos, name of various plants]

sphe'noid (sfe'-) *a.* wedge-shaped. [G. *sphen, sphenos*, wedge, *cidos*, form]

sphere *n.* globe; range, province. -**spher'ical** *a.* -**sphe'roid** *n.* body nearly a sphere in shape. [G. *sphaira*, ball]

sphinx *n.* statue, half woman, half lion; enigmatic person. [G. *Sphingx*]

spice *n.* aromatic or pungent vegetable substance; spices collectively; trace. -*v.t.* season with spices. -**spi'cy** *a.* piquant. -**spi'cily** *adv.* [OF. *espice*]

spick and span *a.* new and neat. [*spick, spike*, and ME. *span-new*, ON. *span-nyr*, chip-new]

spi'der *n.* animal which spins a web to catch its prey. -**spi'dery** *a.* [ME. *spithre*, fr. OE. *spinnam*, spin]

spig'ot *n.* peg for a hole in a cask. [orig. uncertain]

spike *n.* ear (of corn, *etc.*); sharp-pointed piece of metal, wood, nail. -*v.t.* drive a spike into, supply with spikes, fasten with spikes. [L. *spica*]

spike'nard *n.* aromatic substance got from an Eastern plant; the plant. [Late L. *spica nardi*]

spill *n.* splinter or twist of paper for use as a taper. [OE. *speld*, torch]

spiu *v.t.* shed (blood); pour out; throw off, scatter. -*v.i.* flow over. -*n.* fall. [OE. *spillan*, destroy]

spin *v.t.* twist into thread; revolve rapidly. -*v.i.* make thread; revolve rapidly. -*n.* rapid run or ride; spinning. -**spin'dle** *n.* rod or axis for spinning. -**spinn'er** *n.* -**spin'ster** *n.* one who spins. [OE. *spinnan*]

spin'ach *n.* edible green vegetable. [OF. *espinage*]

spin'drift *n.* spray blown along surface of sea, or dashed up from waves. [Scan. *speen*, drive before a strong wind, and *drift*]

spine *n.* thorn; various things like this; backbone. -**spi'nal** *a.* [L. *spina*]

spin'et *n.* instrument like a small harpsichord. [OF. *espiente*]

spinnaker *n.* large yacht sail spread by a boom. [orig. uncertain]

spin'ey *n.* small wood. [OF. *espinei*, fr. *espine*, thorn]

spin'ster *n.* unmarried woman. [*spin*]

spi'racle *n.* a vent; air-hole; the hole through which whales, *etc.*, breathe. [L. *spiraculum-spimre*, to breathe]

spirae'a *n.* low shrubby plant with feathery flowers. [L., G. *speimia*, meadowsweet]

spire *n.* pointed steeple on church or other building; peak, plant, *etc.*, of this form. -*v.t.* and *i.* shoot up; furnish into a spire. [OE. *spir*, sprout, shoot]

spire *n.* coil. -**spi'ral** *n.* continuous curve round a cylinder, like the thread of a screw. -*a.* of this form. -**spi'rally** *adv.* [G. *speira*, coil]

spir'it *n.* soul; ghost; essential character or meaning; courage, liveliness; frame of mind; liquid got by distillation, *esp.* an alcoholic one. -*v.t.* carry away mysteriously. -**spir'itual** *a.* hymn, *esp.* of Black Americans. -**spir'itually** *adv.* -**spir'itless** *a.* -**spir'ituality** *n.* -**spir'itualism, spir'itism** *n.* belief that the spirits of the dead can communicate with living people. -**spiritualist, spir'itist** *n.* -**spir'ituous** *a.* alcoholic. [L. *spiritus*, fr. *spirare*, breathe]

spirt *v.t.* and *i.* send or come out in a jet. -*n.* jet. [orig. uncertain]

spit *n.* sharp metal rod to put through meat for roasting; sandy point projecting into the sea. -*v.t.* thrust through; impale. [OE. *spitu*]

spit *v.i.* eject saliva. -*v.t.* eject from the mouth. -*n.* a spitting; saliva. -**spit'tle** *n.* saliva. -**spittoon'** *n.* vessel to spit into. [OE. *spittan*]

spit *n.* spadeful; depth of a spade blade as measure of depth for digging. [OE. *spittan*]

spite *n.* malice. -*v.t.* thwart. -**spite'ful** *a.* -**spite'fully** *adv.* [*despite*]

spiv *n.* (*sl.*) flashy idler who makes living by doubtful methods, as black market, currency transactions. [orig. uncertain]

splash *v.t.* spatter liquid over. -*v.i.* dash, scatter (of liquids). -*n.* sound or result of splashing. -**splash'board** *n.* mudguard. [imit. orig.]

splay *v.t.* spread out; make slanting. -*n.* slanting surface; spread. *a.* slanting. -**splay foot** *n.* flat foot turned outward. [for *display*]

spleen *n.* organ in the abdomen; irritable or morose temper. -**splenet'ic** *a.* melancholy, irritable. [G. *splen*]

splen'did *a.* magnificent, gorgeous; illus trious; excellent. -**splen'didly** *adv.* -**splen'dor** *n.* [L. *splendidus*]

splice *v.t.* join by interweaving strands; join (wood) by overlapping. -*n.* spliced joint. [Du. *splitsen*]

splint *n.* rigid strip of material for holding a broken limb in position. -**splin'ter** *n.* split-off fragment, chip. -*v.i.* break into fragments. [Du.]

split *v.t.* and *i.* break asunder; (*sl.*) give

away (a secret, *etc.*). -*n.* crack or fissure. [Du. *splitten*]

split screen *n.* (*compute.*) form of cathode ray tube display in which the screen is divided into sections for simultaneous display of different information.

splurge *n.* ostentatious display. -*v.i.* [orig. unknown]

splutt'er *v.t.* utter incoherently with spitting sounds. -*v.i.* emit such sounds. -*n.* the sounds. [imit. orig.]

spoil *v.t.* damage. or injure; pillage; damage the manners or behavior of by indulgence. -*v.i.* go bad. -*n.* booty. -**spolia'tion** *n.* [L. *spoliate*]

spoke *n.* radial bar of a wheel; rung of ladder. -**spoke'shave** *n.* tool for shaping wood. [OE. *spaca*]

spokesman *n.* one deputed to speak for others. [*speak*]

spon'dee *n.* in poetry, a measure of two long or accented syllables. [G. *sponde*, a drink offering]

sponge (-unj) *n.* marine growth used to absorb liquids. -*v.t.* wipe with a sponge. -*v.i.* live craftily at the expense of others. -**spon'gy** *a.* [L. *spongia*]

spon'sor *n.* guarantor; patron; one who provides financial backing for an enterprise, *usu.* in return for publicity; one who answers for an infant at baptism; surety. [L.]

spontaneous *a.* of one's own accord; involuntary; impulsive; self-produced; self motivated. -**spontane'ity** *n.* -**sponta'neously.** *adv.* [L. *spontaneous*]

spoof *n.* card game; hoax, trick. -*v.f.* [mod. *coinage*]

spook *n.* ghost; specter. [Du.]

spool *n.* reel. [Du. *spoel*]

spoon *n.* implement with a shallow bowl at the end of a handle for carrying food to the mouth, *etc.* -*v.t.* transfer with a spoon. [OE. *spon*, chip]

spoor *n.* trail of a wild beast. [Du.]

sporad'ic *a.* occurring at intervals or in small numbers. [G. *sporadikos-sporas, sporad-*, scattered]

spore *n.* tiny organ of reproduction in plants and protozoa. [G. *spora*, seed]

sporr'an *n.* a pouch worn in front of the kilt by Scottish Highlanders. [Gaet.]

sport *n.* pastime; merriment; (*sl.*) one prepared to take a risk, a sporting chance- *v.i.* amuse onself, take part in a game, *etc.* -**sport'ive** *a.* playful. -**sports'man** *n.* one who hunts, shoots, *etc.* -**sports'manship** *n.* [for *disport*]

spot *n.* small mark or stain; place. -*v.t.* mark with spots; detect. -**spot'less** *a.* -**spot'lessly** *adv.* -**spot'light** *n.* light thrown on one part of the stage. -**spott'ed dog** *n.* (*sl.*) plum-pudding. [ON. *spotti*]

spouse *n.* husband or wife. [OF. *espouse*, fr. L. *sponsus*, promised]

spout *v.t.* and *i.* pour out. -*n.* projecting tube for pouring a liquid; copious discharge. [orig. uncertain]

sprain *n.* and *v.t.* wrench or twist (of muscle, *etc.*). [OF. *espreindre*, press out]

sprat *n.* small sea fish. [OE. *sprott*]

sprawl *v.i.* lie or toss about awkwardly.-*n.* sprawling position. [OE. *spreawlian*]

spray *n.* twigs; graceful branch or twig; posy of flowers. [orig. uncertain]

spray *n.* water, *etc.*, flying in small, fine drops. -*v.t.* sprinkle with spray. [LG. *sprei*]

spread (-ed) *v.t.* stretch out; scatter. -*v.i.* become spread.-*n.* extent. -**spreader** *n.* -**spread'-eagle** *v.t.* tie up with outstretched arms and legs. [OE. *spraedan*]

spread'sheet *n.* (*compute.*) program that manipulates information and displays it in the form of an electronic ledger sheet and related graphs and charts.

spree *n.* frolic; carousal. [orig. Scot.]

sprig *n.* small twig; small headless nail. [orig. uncertain]

spright'ly *a.* lively, brisk. -**spright'liness** *n.* [fr. *sprite*]

spring *v.i.* leap; appear; crack. - *v.t.* produce unexpectedly. - *n.* flow of water from the earth; first season of the year; leap; recoil; piece of coiled or bent metal with much resilience. - **spring'bok** *n.* S. African antelope. -**spring'tide** *n.* high tide at new or full moon. -**spring'y** (-g-) *a.* having elasticity. [OE. *springan*]

sprin'kle (-ng-kl) *v.t.* scatter small drops on. - **sprink'ler** *n.* [OE *sprengan*]

sprint *v.i.* run a short distance at great speed. - *n.* such run or race. - **sprint'er** *n.* [of Scand. orig.]

sprit *n.* spar crossing sail of boat, extending and elevating. - **sprit' -sail** *n.* sail extended by sprit. [OE *spreot*, pole]

sprite *n.* fairy. [L. *spiritus*]

spritz'er *n.* a drink, *usu.* white wine with soda water added. [Ger. *spritzen*, splash]

sprout *v.i.* put forth shoots, spring up. - *n.* shoot. [OE. *spurtan*]

spruce *n.* variety of fir. - *a.* neat in dress. [earlier *pruce*, fr. *Pruce*, Prussia]

spry *a.* active; lively, gay. [orig. unknown]

spud *n.* small spade-like implement for cutting roots of weeds, *etc.*; (*sl.*) potato.

[orig. uncertain]

spume *n.* and *v.i.* foam. [L. *spuma*]

spunk *n.* woody tinder; courage; spark; spirit; match. - **spunky** *a.* [Scot.]

spur *n.* pricking instrument attached to a horseman's hell; projection on the leg of a cock; projecting mountain range; stimulus. - *v.t.* apply spurs to; urge. - *v.i.* ride hard. [OE. *sporu*]

spurious *a.* sham. [L. *spurius*]

spurn *v.t.* reject with scorn. - **spurn'ing** *n.* [OE. *spornan*, kick]

spurt *n.* a short sudden effort, *esp.* in a race. - *v.i.* gush. [var. of *spirt*]

sput'ter *v.t.* and *i.* and *n.* splutter. [imit. orig.]

spu'tum *n.* spittle. [L.}

spy *n.* one who enters hostile territory to observe and report. - *v.i.* act as a spy. - *v.t.* catch sight of. [OF. *espie*]

squab (-ob) *n.* unfledged bird; sofa cushion. - *a.* clumsy; squat. [imit. orig.]

squab'ble *n.* petty noisy quarrel. - *v.i.* engage in one. [imit. orig.]

squad (-od) *n.* small party, *esp.* of soldiers. - **squad'ron** *n.* division of a cavalry regiment or of a fleet, or of an air force. [F. *escouade*]

squal'id *a.* mean and dirty, as slums. - **squal'or** *n.* [L. *squalidus*]

squall (-awl) *n.* scream; sudden gust of wind. - *v.i.* scream. [imit. orig.]

squan'der (-on-) *v.t.* spend wastefully. [orig. uncertain]

square *n.* equilateral rectangle; area of this shape; product of a number multiplied by itself; instrument for drawing right angles. - *a.* square in form honest. - **square meal** *n.* a substantial meal consisting of enough food to satisfy. - *v.t.* make square; find the square of; pay; bribe. - *v.i.* fit, suit. - **square'ly** *adv.* - **square'-rigg'ed** *a.* having chief sails square on horizontal yards at right angles to keel. [OF. *esquarre*, fr. L. *ex-quadra*]

squash (-osh) *v.t.* crush flat or to pulp. - *n.* crowd; game (squash rackets) played with rackets and a rubber ball inside a specially constructed enclosed space. [OF. *esquasser*]

squash *n.* gourd-like vegetable [Amer. Ind. *asquash*]

squat (-ot) *v.i.* sit on the heels. - *a.* short and thick. - **squatt'er** *n.* one who settles on land without title. [OF. *esquati*, fr. *quatir*, press flat]

squaw *n.* N. American Indian wife or woman. [N. Amer. Ind. *squa*]

squeak *v.i.* make a short shrill sound. - *n.* such sound. - **squeak'er** *n.* one who betrays an accomplice. [imit. orig.]

squeal *n.* long squeak. - *v.i.* make one; turn informer. [imit. orig.]

squeam'ish *a.* easily made sick; over-scrupulous. [AF. *escoymos*]

squeeze *v.t.* press; subject to extortion. - *n.* a squeezing. [OE. *cwiesan*]

squib *n.* small firework; short satire. [orig. uncertain]

squid *n.* cuttle-fish. [var. of *squirt*]

squill *n.* plant of lily family, used medicinally. [L. *squilla*, sea-onion]

squint *v.i.* have the eyes turned in different directions. - *n.* this affection of the eyes; glance. [earlier *asquint*, of uncertain orig.]

squire *n.* country gentleman; lady's escort. -*v.t.* escort (a lady). [*esquire*]

squirm *v.i.* and *n.* wriggle. [imit. orig.]

squirr'el *n.* small graceful animal living in trees and having a large bushy tail. [OF. *escureul*]

squirt *v.t.* and *i.* eject, be ejected, in a jet. -*n.* instrument for squirting; small rapid stream. [orig. uncertain]

stab *v.i.* pierce with a pointed weapon. -*v.i.* strike with such weapon. -*n.* wound so inflicted. [Gael. *stob*, stake]

sta'ble *n.* building for horses. -*v.t.* put into one. [L. *stabulum*, stall]

sta'ble *a.* firmly fixed; resolute. -**sta'bly** *adv.* -**stabil'ity** *n.* -**sta'bilize** *v.t.* and *i.* [L. *stabilis*]

stacca'to *a.* (*mus.*) with disconnected, emphatic tones. [It.]

stack *n.* pile or heap, *esp.* of hay or straw; tall chimney. -*v.t.* pile in a stack. [ON. *stakkr*, haystack]

sta'dium *n.* (**sta'dia** *pl.*) sportsground; arena. [G. *stodion*]

staff *n.* (**staffs, staves** *pl.*), pole; body of officers or workers; five lines on which music is written. [OE. *stæf*]

stag *n.* male deer. [OE. *stagga*]

stage *n.* raised floor or platform; platform of a theater; dramatic art or literature, scene of action; point of development; stopping place on a road, distance between two of them. -*v.t.* put (a play) on the stage. -**sta'gy** *a.* theatrical. -**stage'coach** *n.* public passenger coach running between stages. -**stage'fright** *n.* nervousness before an audience. [OF. *estage*]

stagg'er *v.i.* walk or stand unsteadily. -*v.t.* shock; spread (*e.g.*, holidays) over a period to prevent overlapping. -*n.* act of staggering. [ON. *stakra*]

stag'nate *v.i.* to cease to flow, be motionless. -**stag'nant** *a.* -**stagna'tion** *n.* [L. *stagnum*, pool]

staid *a.* of sober and quiet character. -**staid'ness** *n.* -**staid'ly** *adv.* [for *stayed*]

stain *v.t.* and *i.* discolor, soil. -*n.* spot or mark; blemish. -**stain'less** *a.* -**stain'less steel**, rustless steel. [for *distain*, OF. *desteindre*]

stair *n.* set of steps, *esp.* as part of a house. -**stair'case** *n.* [OE. *stager*]

stake *n.* sharpened stick or post; money wagered or contended for; martyrdom. -*v.t.* secure or mark out with stakes; wager. [OE. *stoca*]

stalactite *n.* deposit of lime like an icicle on roof of a cave. -**stal'agmite** *n.* similar deposit on floor. [G. *stalaktos*, dropping; *stalagmos*, a dropping]

stale *a.* old, lacking freshness. -*n.* urine of horses. -*v.i.* of horses, make water. -**stale'mate** *n.* in chess, a draw through one player being unable to move. [OF. *estate*, spread out]

stalk (-awk) *n.* plant's stem. [OE. *stalu*]

stalk (-awk) *v.i.* steal up to game; walk in a stiff and stately manner. -*v.t.* steal up to. -*n.* a stalking. [OF. *stealcian*]

stall (-awl) *n.* compartment in a stable; erection for the display and sale of goods; seat in the chancel of a church; front seat in a theater, *etc.* -*v.t.* put in a stall. -*v.i.* stick fast; of an airplane, lose flying speed. [OE. *steall*, standing place, *esp.* for cattle]

stallion (stal'-yun) *n.* uncastrated male horse. [OF. *estalon*]

stal'wart *a.* strong, sturdy, brave. -*n.* stalwart person. -**stal'wartness** *n.* [OE. *stoelwierthe*, serviceable]

sta'men *n.* male organ of a flowering plant. [L. =*fibre*]

stamina *n. pl.* powers of endurance; vigor, vitality. [L. *stamen*, warp, thread]

stamm'er *v.t.* speak with repetitions of syllables, stutter. -*v.t.* utter thus. -*n.* habit of so speaking. -**stamm'erer** *n.* -**stamm'ering** *a.* [OE. *stamerian*]

stamp *v.i.* put down a foot with force. -*v.t.* impress a mark on; affix a postage stamp. -*n.* stamping with the foot; imprinted mark; appliance for marking; piece of gummed paper printed with a device as evidence of postage, *etc.*; character. [ME. cp. OE. *stempan*]

stampede' *n.* sudden frightened rush, *esp.* of a herd of cattle, crowd, *etc.* -*v.t.* and *i.* put into, take part in, a stampede. [Sp. *estampido*]

stance *n.* (golf, *etc.*) position, stand; site. [Scot.]

stanch. *See* **staunch.**

stanchion (-un) *n.* upright post or prop. [OF. *extanson*]

stand *v.i.* have an upright position; be situated; become or remain firm or stationary; be a symbol of, *etc.* -*v.t.* set upright; endure. -*n.* stoppage, a holding firm; something on which a thing may be placed; structure for spectators to stand on for better view. -**stand'ing** *n.* position (in society, *etc.*) -**stand'point** *n.* position from which things are viewed, judged. [OE. *standan*]

stand'ard *n.* flag; weight or measure to which others must conform; degree, quality; post, *e.g.* lamp-post. -**stand'ardize** *v.t.* [OF. *estendard*, royal banner]

stann'ary *a.* of a tin mine. -*n.* tin mine. [L. *stannum*, tin]

stan'za *n.* group of lines of verse. [It.]

sta'ple *n.* U-shaped piece of metal with pointed ends to drive into wood for use as a ring; main commodity; the fiber of wool. [OE. *stapol*, post]

star *n.* shining celestial body seen as a twinkling point of light; asterisk (*); celebrated player; medal or jewel, *etc.*, of the apparent shape of a star. -*v.t.* adorn with stars; to mark with an asterisk (*). -**stargazer** *n.* astrologer; astronomer. [OE. *steorra*]

starboard *n.* right-hand side of a ship looking forward. -*a.* of, or on, this side. -*v.t.* put (the helm) to starboard. [OE. *steorbord*, steer side (the steering oar being worked on this side)]

starch *n.* substance forming the main food element in bread, potatoes, *etc.*, and used, mixed with water, for stiffening linen, *etc.* -*v.t.* stiffen with it. [OE. *stearc*, rigid]

stare *v.i.* looked fixedly at; be prominent or obvious. -*v.t.* abash by staring at. -*n.* a staring. [OE. *starian*]

stark *a.* stiff, downright. *adv* . quite (*e.g.*, in stark-mad). [OE. *stearc*, hard, strong]

stark-naked *a.* quite naked. [for *startnaked*, fr. OE. *steart*, tail, rump]

starling *n.* speckled bird. [OE. *starling*, dim. of *steer*]

start *v.i.* make a sudden movement; begin, *esp.* a journey. -*v.t.* begin; set going. -*n.* abrupt movement; advantage of less distance to run in a race. [OE. *styrtan*]

star'tle *v.t.* give a fright to. -**start'ling** *a.* -**start'lingly** *adv.* [OE. *steartlian*]

starve *v.i.* suffer from cold, hunger; die of hunger. -*v.t.* kill or distress with lack of food, warmth, or other necessary thing. -**starve'ling** *n.* starving person. -**starvation** *n.* [OE. *steorfan*, di]

state *n.* condition; politically organized community; rank; pomp. -*v.t.* express in words; fix. -**state'ly** *a.* dignified. -**statement** *n.* expression in words; account. -**states'man** *n.* one able in managing the affairs of a state. -**states'manship** *n.* his art. -**state'room** *n.* separate cabin on a ship. [L. *status*, state, fr. *stare*, stand]

stat'ic *a.* motionless, at rest; dealing with forces in equilibrium. -*n.* in *pl.* the branch of physics studying such forces. [G. *statikos*, causing to stand]

sta'tion *n.* place where a thing stops or is placed; position in life; stopping place for trains. -*v.t.* put in a position. -**sta'tionary** *a.* not moving or not intended to be moved. [L. *statio-stare, stat-*, stand]

stationer *n.* one who deals in writing materials, *etc.* -**sta'tionery** *n.* his wares. [orig. tradesman with a *station*]

statistics *n. pl.* numerical facts collected systematically and arranged; study of them. -**statisti'cian,** *n.* one who deals with statistics. -**statist'ic** *a.* -**statist'ically** *adv.* [fr. obs. *statist*, politician]

status *n.* solid carved or cast image of a person, *etc.* -**stat'uary** *n.* statues collectively. -**statuesque'** *a.* like a statue. -**statuette'** *n.* small statue. [L. *status*]

sta'tus *n.* position, rank, 'standing'; position of affairs. [L.]

statute *n.* height (of a person). [F.]

stat'ute *n.* a written law. -**stat'utory** *a.* [L. *statuere, statut-*, set up]

staunch, stanch *v.t.* stop a flow (of blood) from. -*a.* trustworthy, loyal. [OF. *estancher*, stop a flow; *estanche*, watertight]

stave *n.* one of the pieces forming a cask; verse or stanza; (*mus.*) staff; snatch of song. -*v.t.* break a hole in; to ward (off). [new *sing.* fr. *pl.* of *staff*]

stay *v.t.* stop. -*v.i.* remain; sojourn; pause. -*n.* a remaining or sojourning. -**stay'-in-strike,** strike in which strikers stay in their place of work. [OF. *ester*, fr. L., *stare*, stand]

stay *n.* support, prop; rope supporting a mast, *etc.* -*pl.* corsets. -*v.t.* prop or support. [OE. *stay*]

stead (-ed) *n.* in stead, in place; in good stead, of service. -**stead'y** *a.* firm; regular; temperate. -**stead'ily** *adv.* -**stead'fast** *a.* firm, unyielding. -**stead'fastly** *adv.* -**steadiness** *n.* [OE. *stede*, position, place]

steadling (sted-) *n.* farm buildings, farmstead. [OE. *stede*, place]

steak *n.* slice of meat, fish for grilling, *etc.* [ON. *steik*, roast on a spit]

steal *v.i.* rob; move silently. -*v.t.* take without right or leave. -**stealth (stelth)** *n.* secrecy; slinking way. -**stealth'y** *a.* -**stealth'ily** *adv.* [OE. *stelan*]

steam *n.* vapor of boiling water. -*v.t.* cook or treat with steam. -*v.i.* give off steam; rise in vapor; move by steam power. -**steam'er** *n.* vessel for cooking or treating with steam; steam-propelled ship. -**steam' engine,** engine worked by steam power. [OE.]

steed *n.* (*poet.*) horse. [OE. *steda*, stallion]

steel *n.* hard and malleable metal made by mixing carbon in iron; tool or weapon of steel. -*v.t.* harden. -**steel'y** *a.* [OE. *stele*]

steelyard *n.* balance with unequal arms. [orig. uncertain]

steep *a.* having an abrupt or decided slope. -*n.* steep place. -**steep'ly** *adv.* [OE. *steep*, lofty]

steep *v.t.* soak. [orig. uncertain]

stee'ple *n.* church tower with a spire. **steeplechase** *n.* cross-country horserace over obstacles. [OE. *stepel*]

steer *v.t.* guide, direct the course of. -*v.i.* direct one's course. -**steer'age** *n.* effect of a helm; part of a ship allotted to the passengers paying lowest fare. -**steers'man** *n.* one who steers a ship. -**steer'ing-wheel** *n.* [OE. *stieran*]

steer *n.* young male ox, bullock. [OE. *steor*, bullock]

stein'bock (stin'-) *n.* Alpine ibex. [Ger. *stein*, stone, *bock*, buck]

ste'le *n.* (ste'lae *pl.*) ancient upright inscribed stone slab. [G.]

stem *n.* stalk; trunk; part of a word to which inflectional endings are added; foremost part of a ship. [OE. *stemm*]

stem *v.t.* check. [ON. *stemma*]

stench *n.* evil smell. [OE. *stenc*]

sten'cil *v.t.* paint with figures, *etc.*, by passing a brush over a pierced plate. -*n.* the plate; pattern made. [orig. uncertain]

sten' gun *n.* type of simple automatic rifle. [fr. designers, *S*heppard & *T*urpin & *En*field]

stenography *n.* shorthand writing. -**stenog'rapher** *n.* -**stenograph'ic** *a.* [G. *stenos*, narrow]

stentorian *a.* very loud. [*Stentor*, a G. warrior who had a very loud voice]

step *v.i.* move and set down a foot. -*v.t.*

measure in paces; set up (a mast). -*n*. act of stepping; mark made by the foot; measure, act, stage in a proceeding; board, rung, *etc*., to put the foot on; degree in a scale; mast socket. **-step' dance** *n*. solo dance with intricate steps. [OE. *stæeppan*]

step'child *n*. child of a husband or wife by a former marriage. thus **-step'father** *n*. **-step'mother** *n*. **-step'brother** *n*. **-step'sister** *n*. [OE. *steop-*, orphaned]

steppe *n*. one of the vast treeless plains of Russia, Asia. (Russ. *step'*]

stephano'tis (stef-) *n*. plant with fragrant flower. [G. *stephanos*, crown]

ster'eophonic *a*. (of sound reproduction) using two or more separate microphones to feed two or more loudspeakers through separate channels in order to give spatial effect to sound. **-ster'eo** *a./n*. (of, for) stereophonic sound system. [G. *stereos*, solid, *phone*, sound]

ster'eoscope *n*. instrument in which two pictures taken at different viewpoints are combined into one image with an effect of solidity. **-stereoscop'ic** *a*. [G. *stereos*, solid]

ster'eotype *n*. plate for printing cast from set-up type; something monotonously familiar, conventional, predictable. -*v.t*. make a stereotype from; make into an empty formula. [G. *stereos*, solid]

ster'ile *a*. barren; free from disease germs. **-ster'ilize** *v.t*. **-ster'ilizer** *n*. apparatus to destroy germs. [L. *sterilis*]

ster'ling *a*. of standard value or purity; of solid worth; in British coin. [AF. *esterling*]

stern *a*. severe, strict. **-stern'ly** *adv*. **-stern'ness** *n*. [OE. *stierne*]

stern *n*. after part of a ship; rump, tail, of an animal. [ON. *stjorn*, steering]

ster'ol *n*. solid alcohol such as ergosterol. [G. *stereos*, solid]

ster'torous *a*. snoring. **-ster'torousness** *n*. sound of this nature. [L. *stertere*, snore]

stet *v.t*. "let it stand," proofreader's direction to cancel previous alteration. [L.]

stethoscope *n*. instrument for listening to the action of the heart or lungs. [G. *stethos*, chest]

Stet'son *n*. broad-brimmed felt hat. [Trademark]

stevedore *n*. one who loads or unloads ships. [Sp. *estivador*, wool-packer]

stew *v.t*. and *i*. cook slowly in a closed vessel. -*n*. food so cooked. **-stew'pan** *n*. [OF. *estuve*, hot bath]

steward *n*. one who manages another's property; attendant on a ship's passengers; official managing a race-meeting assembly, *etc*. **-stew'ardess** *fem*. [OE. *stigweard*, majordomo]

stick *v.t*. jab, stab, fix, fasten. -*v.i*. adhere, project, come to a stop, *etc*. -*n*. rod. **-stick'y** *a*. adhesive, viscous. [OE. *stician*, pierce]

stic'kleback (-klb-) *n*. small fish with spines on its back. [OE. *sticel*, prick]

stickier *n*. one who insists on trifles of procedure, authority, *etc*. [OE. *stihtan*, control]

stiff *a*. rigid; awkward, difficult. **-stiff'ly** *adv*. **-stiff'en** *v.t*. and *i*. **-stiff'ness** *n*. **stiff'necked** *a*. obstinate, stubborn. [OE. *stil*]

sti'fle *v.t*. smother. [earlier *stuffle*; OF. *estouffer*]

stig'ma *n*. brand, mark. **-stig'matize** *v.t*. mark out, brand with disgrace. [G.]

stile *n*. arrangement of steps for climbing a fence. [OE. *stigel*]

stilett'o *n*. small dagger. [It.]

still *a*. motionless, noiseless. -*v.t*. quiet. -*adv*. to this time; yet; even. **-still'ness** *n*. **-still'y** *a*. quiet. **-still'born** *a*. born dead. **-still life** *n*. painting of inanimate objects. [OE. *stille*]

still *n*. apparatus for distilling, *esp*. spirits. **-still'-room** *n*. housekeeper's storeroom. [for *distil*]

stilt *n*. one of a pair of poles with footrests for walking raised from the ground. **stilt'ed** *a*. stiff in manner, pompous [Du. *stelt*]

Stil'ton *n*. kind of cheese. [made famous by an inn at *Stilton*, England]

stim'ulus *n*. something that rouses to activity. **-stim'ulate** *v.t*. rouse up, spur. **-stim'ulant** *a*. producing a temporary increase of energy. -*n*. drug, *etc*., doing this. **-stim'ulative** *a*. **-stimula'tion** *n*. [L. = *goad*]

sting *v.t*. thrust a sting into; cause sharp pain to. -*v.i*. be affected with sharp pain. -*n*. pointed weapon, often poisoned, of certain insects and animals; thrust, wound, or pain of one. **-stin'gy** (-ji) *a*. miserly. [OE. *stingan*, pierce]

stink *v.i*. give out a strongly offensive smell. -*n*. such smell. [OE. *stincan*]

stint *v.t*. keep on short allowance. -*n*. limitation of supply or effect. [OE. *styntan*, blunt]

stipend *n*. salary. **-stipend'iary** *a*. receiving a stipend. -*n*. stipendiary magistrate. [L. *stipendium*]

stip'ple *v.t*. engrave in dots. -*n*. this process. [Du. *stippelen*]

stipulate -*v.i.* insist on, mention in making a bargain. -**stipula'tion** *n.* -**stip'ulator** *n.* [L. *stipulari*, stipulate]

stir *v.t.* set or keep in motion. -*v.i.* begin to move, be out of bed. -*n.* commotion. -**stir'-cra'zy** *a.* (*sl.*) mentally disturbed as a result of being in prison or otherwise confined. [OE. *styrian*]

stirr'up *n.* metal loop hung from a strap, support to the foot of a horseman. -**stirr'up-cup** *n.* drink given to a departing rider. [OE. *stigrap*, mount rope]

stitch *n.* movement of the needle in sewing; its result in the work; sharp pain in the side *v.t.* and *i.* sew. -**stitch'ery** *n.* [OE. *stice*, puncture]

stoat *n.* ermine. [orig. unknown]

stock *n.* stump or post; stem; handle or piece to hold by; lineage; animals, materials, *etc.*, requisite for farming trade; supply; broth used as a foundation of soup; various sweet-smelling flowers; money invested in a concern. *pl.* frame of timber supporting a ship while building; frame with holes to confine the feet of offenders. -*v.t.* supply with, or keep, a stock. -**stock'ist** *n.* one who stocks (a particular brand of goods, *etc.*). -**stockbroker** *n.* agent for buying and selling shares in companies. -**stock exchange'** *n.* where stocks are bought and sold; association of stockbrokers. -**stock' jobber** *n.* dealer in stocks and shares. -**stock'piling** *n.* -**stock'still** *a.* motionless. [OE. *stoc*, trunk]

stockade' *n.* enclosure of stakes. -*v.t.* surround with a stockade. [F. *estocade*]

stock'ing *n.* close-fitting covering for leg and foot; anything resembling this. [for *nether stock*, lower hose]

stod'gy *a.* heavy, dull, indigestible. -**stodge** *n.* heavy food. [orig. uncertain]

stoep *n.* in S. Africa, an open veranda in front of a house. [Du.]

sto'ic *n.* philosopher holding virtue to be the highest good and teaching indifference to pleasure and pain; person of great selfcontrol. -**sto'ic, sto'ical** *a.* -**sto'ically** *adv.* -**sto'icism** *n.* [G. *stoa*, the Porch where Zeno taught this philosophy]

sto'ker *v.* one who tends a fire. -**stoke** *v.t.* and *i.* tend (a fire). [Du.]

stole *n.* priestly vestment; a long robe reaching to the feet; women's long scarf of fur or fabric. [G.]

stol'id *a.* hard to excite; phlegmatic; dull. -**stol'idly** *adv.* -**stolid'ity** *n.* [L. *stolidus*]

stom'ach (-u'-mak) *n.* bag forming the chief digestive organ; appetite; inclination. -*v.t.* put up with. -**stom'acher** *n.* chest-covering, often ornamented, worn by women of 15th-17th c. -**stomach'ic** *a.* [G. *stomachos*, gullet]

stone *n.* piece of rock; rock; gem; hard seed of a fruit; weight = 14 lbs. -*v.t.* throw stones at; free (fruit) from stones. -**stone'-blind'** *a.* quite blind. -**stone' crop** *n.* plant, the wall-pepper. -**stone' deaf'** *a.* -**stone pine** *n* . Mediterranean pine tree with branches forming an umbrella shape; umbrella pine. -**stone' ware** *n.* heavy common pottery. **sto'ny** *a.* -**sto'nily** *adv.* [OE. *stan*]

stonewall *v.i.* obstruct (government) business; play slow defensive game. [*stone* and *wall*]

stone'washed *a.* of new clothes, fabric, *etc.*, given a worn, faded look by being subjected to the abrasive action of many small pieces of pumice. [*stone* and *wash*]

stooge *n.* foil; butt; dupe; scapegoat. [orig. unknown]

stook *n.* set of sheaves in field. [ME. *stouk*]

stool *n.* chair with no back; place for evacuating the bowels; what is evacuated. [OE. *stol*, throne]

stoop *v.i.* lean forward or down. -*n.* stooping carriage of the body. [OE. *stupian*, bow]

stop *v.t.* fill up; check, bring to a halt. -*v.i.* cease, stay. -*n.* a stopping or being stopped; punctuation mark; set of organ pipes; lever for putting it in action. -**stopcock** *n.* tap turned by key. -**stop'gap** *n.* temporary expedient, substitute. -**stopp'age** *n.* -**stopp'er** *n.* a plug for closing a bottle. -**stop'over** *n.* stop at an intermediate point during a journey. -**stop-press'** *n.* news inserted at last possible minute before printing. -**stop'watch** *n.* watch with hands which can be stopped for exact timing of races. [OE. *stoppian*, to plug]

store *n.* abundance; stock; place for keeping goods. -*pl.* stocks of goods, provisions, *etc.* -*v.t.* stock, furnish, keep. -**stor'age** *n.* [OF. *estorer*, fr. L. *instaurare*, provide]

stor'ey *See* **story.**

stork *n.* wading bird. [OE. *store*]

storm *n.* violent wind or disturbance of the atmosphere; assault on a fortress. -*v.t.* take by storm. -*v.i.* rage. -**storm'y** *n.* [OE.]

stor'y *n.* tale; account; horizontal division of a building; plot of book or play; (*sl.*) lie. -**stor'ied** *a.* celebrated in tales. [L. *historia*]

stout *a.* sturdy; fat. -*n.* kind of beer. **stout'ly** *adv.* -**stout'ness** *n.* obesity. [OF. *estout*, proud, fierce]

stove *n.* apparatus for cooking, warming a room, *etc.* [Du.]

stow *v.t.* pack away. -**stow'age** *n.* -**stow'away** *n.* one who hides himself on a ship to obtain passage. [OE. = *place*]

strabismus (-iz'-) *n.* squint. -**strabis'mic** *a.* (G. *strabismos*]

strad'dle *v.i.* spread the legs wide. -*v.t.* bestride something in this way. [fr. OE. *straed-stridan,* stride]

strag'gle *v.i.* stray, get dispersed. -**strag'gler** *n.* [orig. uncertain]

straight [strat] *a.* without bend; honest; level; in order. -*n.* straight state or part. *adv.* direct. -**straight'en** *v.t.* and *i.* -**straightfor'ward** *a.* open, frank; simple. -**straightfor'wardly** *adv.* - **straightway** *adv.* at once. [ME. *streght,* p.p. of *stretch*]

strain *v.t.* stretch tightly; stretch to the full or to excess; filter. -*v.i.* make great effort. -*n.* stretching force; violent effort; injury from being strained; burst of music or poetry; tone of speaking or writing. -**strain'er** *n.* filter. [OF. *estreindre,* fr. L. *stringers*]

strain *n.* breed or race. [OE. *strean*]

strait *a.* narrow, strict. -*n.* channel of water connecting two larger areas. *pl.* position of difficulty or distress. **straitlaced** *a.* puritanical. -**straitjacket** *n.* jacket to confine the arms of maniacs, *etc.* [OF. *estreit,* fr. L. *strictus*]

strait'en *v.t.* make straight, narrow; distress *esp.* by poverty. [OE. *estreit*]

strand *n.* one of the strings or wires making up a rope. [OF. *estran,* rope]

strand *n.* shore of sea or lake. [OE.]

strange (-anj) *a.* unaccustomed, singular. -strangely *adv.* -**strange'ness** *n.* -**stra'nger** *n.* unknown person; a foreigner; one unaccustomed (to). [OF. *estrange,* fr. L. *extraneus,* -extra, beyond]

stran'gle (-ng-gl) *v.t.* kill by squeezing the windpipe. -**strangula'tion** *n.* [L. *strangulate, strangulat-*]

strap *n.* strip of leather or metal. -*v.t.* fasten with a strap; beat with one. **strapp'ing** *a.* tall and well-made. **strap'hanger** *n.* one who travels in crowded buses, trains, clinging to strap. [var. of *strop*]

stratagem *n.* artifice in war; a trick, device. -**strat'egy** *n.* art of handling troops, ships, *etc.*, to the best advantage. **strat'egist** *n.* -**strate'gic** *n.* [G. *stratagema,* piece of generalship]

strath *n.* wide valley. [Gael. *strath*]

stra'tum *n.* (**strata** *pl.*) layer. -**stra'tify** *v.t.* arrange things. -**stratifica'tion** *n.* -**stra'tosphere** *n.* high layer of atmosphere, with constant temperature. [L.]

straw *n.* dry cut stalks of corn. -**straw'berry** *n.* creeping plant producing a red fruit; the fruit. [OE. *streow*]

stray *v.i.* wander, get lost. -*a.* strayed; occasional. -*n.* stray animal, person (as in waifs and strays). [*astray*]

streak *n.* long line, band. -*v.t.* mark with streaks. -**streak'y** *a.* [OE. *strica*]

stream *n.* flowing body of water, or other liquid. -*v.i.* flow; run with liquid; float or wave in the air. -**stream'er** *n.* ribbon to stream in the air. -**stream'let** *n.* small stream. -**stream'lined** *a.* shaped to offer, when in motion, the minimum resistance to air or water. [OE.]

street *n.* road in a town or village with houses at the side. -**street'car** *n.* vehicle on rails for transporting passengers, *usu.* in a city. -**street'wise** *a.* attuned to and adept at surviving in an urban, poor and often criminal environment. also **street-smart** *a.* [Late L. *strata*]

strength *n.* power. -**strength'en** *v.t.* and *i.* [OE. *strengthu*]

stren'uous *a.* energetic, earnest. -**stren'uously** *adv.* [L. *strenuus*]

streptococc'us (-kok'-) *n.* **streptococ'ci** (-kok'-si) *pl.* bacterium causing pneumonia, diphtheria, *etc.* [G. *streptoe,* twisted, *koikos,* grain]

stress *n.* strain; impelling force; effort; emphasis. -*v.t.* emphasize; put mechanical stress on. [OF. *estrecier* and for *distress*]

stretch *v.t.* tighten, pull out; reach out; exert to the utmost. -*v.i.* reach; have elasticity. -*n.* stretching or being stretched; expanse; spell. -**stretch'er** *n.* person or thing that stretches; bar in a boat for a rower's feet; appliance on which an injured person can be carried. -**stretch'marks** *n.pl.* marks that remain visible on the abdomen after its distension in pregnancy. [OE. *streccan*]

strew *v.t.* scatter over a surface. [OE. *strewian*]

stri'a *n.* narrow groove or threadlike line in surface of shell, *etc.* (**stri'ae** *n. pl.*). **stri'ate** *a.* streaked. -**striate'** *v.t.* mark with streaks. -**stria'tion** *n.* [L. *stria,* furrow]

strict *a.* defined; without exception; stern, not lax or indulgent. -**strict'ly** *adv.* **strict'ness** *n.* -**stric'ture** *n.* critical remark; morbid contraction. [L. *stringers, strict-,* tighten]

stride *v.i.* walk with long steps. -*v.t.* pass over with one step. -*n.* step, or its length. [OE. *stridan*]

stri'dent *a.* harsh in tone. -**strid'ulous** *a.*

emitting a grating sound. **-stridor** *n.* harsh sound in breathing. [L. *stridere*, creak]

strife *n.* conflict; discord. [OF. *estrif*]

strike *v.t.* hit. *-v.i.* hit; cease work in order to enforce a demand. *-n.* such stoppage of work. **-stri'ker** *n.* **-stri'king** *a.* noteworthy. [OE. *strican*]

string *n.* fine cord; row or series; gut, *etc.* cord of a musical instrument. *-v.t.* tie with or thread on string. *-pl.* stringed instruments. **-string'y** *a.* fibrous. [OE. *streng*]

stringent *a.* strict. **-strin'gency** *n.* **string'gently** *adv.* [L. *stringers*, tighten]

strip *v.t.* lay bare, take the covering off. *-v.t.* take off one's clothes. *-n.* long narrow piece. **-strip'ling** *n.* youth **-com'ic strip**, in a newspaper, strip of small pictures telling a story. [OE. *stripan*, plunder]

stripe *n.* narrow mark or band; blow with a scourge. [of. LG. orig.]

strive *v.i.* try hard, struggle. [*strife*]

stroke *n.* blow, attack of paralysis, apoplexy; mark of a pen; completed movement in a series; rower sitting nearest the stern; act of stroking. *-v.t.* set the time in rowing; pass the hand lightly over. [OE. *stracian*]

stroll *v.i.* walk in a leisurely or idle or rambling manner. *-n.* leisurely walk. [orig. uncertain]

strong *a.* powerful, earnest; forceful; pronounced, *e.g.*, a strong flavor. **stron'gest** *a.* (superl.). **-strong'hold** *n.* fortress. **-strong'ly** *adv.* [OE. *strong*]

strop *n.* piece of leather for sharpening a razor. *-v.t.* sharpen on one. [L. *struppus*, garland, thong]

stro'phe *n.* stanza, song sung by Greek chorus moving from right to left of stage, answered by Antistrophe. [G. *strophi*, turn]

structure *n.* construction, building, something made of various pieces. **-struc'tural** *a.* **-struc'turally** *adv.* [L. *struere, struct-*, build]

strug'gle *v.i.* contend, fight; proceed or work with difficulty and effort. *-n.* contest, effort. [orig. uncertain]

strum *v.t.* and *i.* play piano, guitar, *etc.*, idly or inefficiently. [imit.]

strut *v.i.* walk affectedly or pompously. *-n.* such gait. **-strut'ting** *n.* and *a.* [OE. *strutian*, stick out stiffly]

strut *n.* rigid support, usually set obliquely. *-v.t.* stay with struts. [orig. uncertain]

strychnine *n.* poison got from nux vomica seeds, and used in medicine. [G. *strychnos*, nightshade]

stub *n.* tree-stump; end of a cigar, *etc.* *-v.t.* strike (one's toe) on an obstruction. **-stub'bed** *a.* [OE. *stubb*]

stub'ble *n.* stumps of cut grain. [L. *stipula*, dim. of *stipes*, stalk]

stubb'orn *a.* unyielding, obstinate. **-stubb'ornly** *adv.* **-stubb'orness** *n.* [*stub*]

stucc'o *n.* and *v.t.* plaster. (It.]

stud *n.* movable double button; nail with large head sticking out; boss. *-v.t.* set with studs. [OE. *studu*, post]

stud *n.* set of horses kept for breeding. **-stud'farm** *n.* [OE. *stod*]

stud'y *n.* effort to acquire knowledge; subject of this; room to study in; sketch. *-v.t.* make a study of; try constantly to do. *-v.i.* be engaged in learning. **-stu'dent** *n.* one who studies. **-stu'dio** *n.* workroom of an artist, photographer, *etc.*, building where film, television or radio shows are made, broadcast, *etc.* **-stu'dious** *a.* **stu'diously** *adv.* [L. *studere*, be zealous]

stuff *n.* material, fabric. *-v.t.* stop or fill up. *-v.i.* eat greedily. **-stuffy** *a.* lacking fresh air. [OE. *estoffe*, fr. L. *stuppa*, tow]

stult'ify *v.t.* make look ridiculous, make of no effect. **-stultifica'tion** *n.* **-stultifi'er** *n.* [L. *stultus*, foolish]

stum'ble *v.i.* trip and nearly fall; slip. *n.* **-stumbling** *a.* **-stum'bling block** *n.* obstacle. [ME. *stomelen*]

stu'mer *n.* (*sl.*) bad coin; counterfeit note; sham, anything worthless. [orig. unknown]

stump *n.* remnant of a tree, *etc.* when the main part has been cut away; one of the uprights of the wicket at cricket. *-v.i.* walk noisily. *-v.t.* walk heavily; confuse, puzzle; tour making speeches. **-stump'y** *a.* **-stump'orator** *n.* traveling speaker (as using tree-stumps for platforms). [of Teut. orig.]

stun *v.t.* knock senseless. [OF. *estoner*, astonish]

stunt *n.* spectacular effort or feat. [orig. uncertain]

stunt *v.t.* check the growth of. **-stunt'ed** *a.* dwarfed. [OE. *stunt*, dull]

stu'pefy *v.t.* make stupid, deprive of full consciousness. **-stupefac'tion** *n.* [L. *stupere*, be amazed]

stupendous *a.* amazing. [L. *stupendus*]

stu'pid *a.* slow-witted, dull. **-stupid'ity** *n.* **-stu'pidly** *adv.* [L. *stupidus*]

stu'por *n.* dazed state; torpor. [L. *stupor*]

stur'dy *a.* robust, strongly built. **-stur'dily** *adv.* **-stur'diness** *n.* [OF. *estordi*, reckless]

stur'geon *n.* large edible fish yielding caviar and isinglass. [F. *esturgeon*]
stutt'er *v.i.* and *t.* speak with difficulty, *esp.* with repetition of initial consonants; stammer. *-n.* act or habit of stuttering. [of obs. *stut*]
sty *n.* place to keep pigs in. [OE. *stig*]
sty, stye *n.* inflammation on the eyelid. [OE. *stigend*]
Styg'ian (-j-) *a.* of River Styx in Hades; dark, gloomy. [*Styx*]
style *n.* manner of writing, doing, etc,; designation; sort; superior manner or quality; pointed instrument for writing on waxed tablets. *-v.t.* designate. **-sty'lish** *a.* fashionable. **-sty'lishly** *adv.* **-sty'list** *n.* one cultivating style in literary or other execution. **-sty'listics** *n.* a branch of linguistics concerned with the study of characteristic choices in use of language, *esp.* literary language, as regards sound, form, or vocabulary. [L. *stilus*]
styp'tic *a.* stopping bleeding. [G. *styptikos-styphein*, contract]
suave *a.* smoothly polite. **-suave'ly** *adv.* **-sua'vity** *n.* [L. *suavis*, sweet]
sub- *prefix*, meaning under, in lower position, *etc.* Often used separated as *abbrev.* for the whole compound, *e.g.*, 'sub'= a subscription. [L.]
subalt'ern *a.* of inferior rank. [L. *subalternus*, succeeding in turn]
sub'committee *n.* section of a committee functioning separately. committee
subdivide' *v.t.* divide again. *-v.i.* separate. **-sudivis'ion** *n.* [*divide*]
subdue' *v.t.* overcome; tame; tone down. [OF. *souduire*, fr. L. *subducere*]
sub'ject *a.* liable to, owing allegiance. subject to, conditional upon. *-n.* one owing allegiance; that about which something is predicated; conscious self; topic, theme. **-subject'** *v.t.* make liable, or cause to undergo. **-subjec'tion** *n.* **subject'ive** *a.* relating to the self; displaying an artist's individuality. **-subjectiv'ity** *n.* [L. *subicere*, subject]
subjoin' *v.t.* add at the end; annex; append. [L. *jungere*, joint]
sub'jugate *v.t.* conquer. **-subjuga'tion** *n.* **-sub'jugator** *n.* [L. *jugum*, yoke]
subjunc'tive *n.* mood used mainly in conditional clauses. *-a.* in or of that mood. [L. *jungere, junct-*, join]
sublet' *v.t.* of a tenant, let to another the whole or part of what he himself has rented. [*let*]
sublime' *a* . inspiring awe. **-sub'limate** *v.t.* purify; heat into vapor and allow to solidify again. *-n.* sublimated substance. **-sublimation** *n.* purification of *e.g.*, an emotion. **-sublime'ly** *adv.* **-sublim'ity** *n.* [L. *sublimis*, lofty]
sublu'nary *a.* under the moon, earthly. [L. *luna*, moon]
sub'marine *a.* below the surface of the sea. *-n.* warship that can operate under water. [*marine*]
submerge' *v.t.* place under water. *-v.i.* go under. -also **submerse'** **-submersion** *n.* **-submers'ible** *a.* *-n.* submarine. [L. *mergere*, *mers-*, dip]
submit' *v.t.* put forward for consideration; surrender. *-v.i.* surrender; urge. **submiss'ive** *a.* **-submis'sion** *n.* [L. *mittere, miss-*, put]
subord'inate *a.* of lower rank or importance. *-n.* one under the orders of another. *-v.t.* make or treat as subordinate. **-subord'inately** *adv.* **-subordina'tion** *n.* [L. *ordinare*, set in order]
suborn' *v.t.* bribe to do evil. **-subornation** n. [L. *subornare*. equip secretly]
subpoena *n.* writ requiring attendance at a court of law. *-v.t.* summon by one. [L. *sub pœna*, under penalty (first words of the writ)]
subscribe' *v.t.* write one's name at the end of a document; assent; pay or promise to pay (a contribution). **-subscri'ber** *n.* **-subscription** *n.* [L. *scribere, script-*, write]
subsection *n.* division of a section (of a book, pamphlet, *etc.*). [*section*]
subsequent *a.* later; coming after. **-sub'sequence** *n.* **-sub'sequently** *adv.* [L. *sequi*, follow]
subserve' *v.t.* be useful to. **subservient** *a.* servile. **-subserv'iently** *adv.* **-subserv'ience** *n.* [L. *sert*, ire, serve]
subside' *v.i.* sink, settle; come to an end. **-sub'sidence** *n.* [L. *subsidere*, settle]
sub'sidy *n.* money granted, *e.g.*, by the state to an industry, or by one state to another. **-sub'sidize** *v.t.* pay a grant to. **-subsid'iary** *a.* supplementing. [*subsidium*, aid]
subsist' *v.i.* exist. **-subsist'ence** *n.* being; livelihood. **-subsist'ence allow'ance,** allowance for living expenses in special circumstances. [L. *sistere*, stand]
sub'soil *n.* soil beneath top soil. [*soil*]
sub'stance *n.* matter; particular kind of matter: chief part, essence; wealth. **-substan'tial** *a.* solid, big, important. **-substan'tially** *adv.* **-substantial'ity** *n.* **-sub'stantiate** *v.t.* bring evidence for.

-**substantia'tion** *n.* -**sub'stantive** *a.* having independent existence. -*n.* noun. [L. *substare*, stand under, be present]

sub'stitute *n.* thing or person put in place of another. -*v.t.* put in exchange for. -**substitu'tion** *n.* -**substitu'tional, substitutionary** *a.* [L. *statuere*, appoint]

subten'ant *n.* one to whom a tenant has sublet. [*tenant*]

subtend' *v.t.* be opposite to. [L. *tendere* stretch]

sub'terfuge *n.* evasion, lying excuse. [L. *fugere*, flee]

subterran'ean *a.* underground. -**subterra'neously** *adv.* [L. *terra*, earth]

sub'tile (sub'til, sut'-il) *a.* delicate, rare, tenuous; acute. -**sub'tilty** *n.* fineness; dialectic nicety; acuteness. [L. *subtilistela*, web]

subtle (sut'l) *a.* ingenious, clever; acute; crafty; tenuous. -**subt'ly** *adv.* -**subt'lety** *n.* [L. *subtilis*, fine woven]

subtract' *v.t.* take away a part. -**subtrac'tion** n. [L. *trahere, tract-*, draw]

sub'urb *n.* outlying part of a city. -**suburb'an** *a.* [L. *urbs*, city]

subven'tion *n.* act of aiding; subsidy. [L. subuenire, help]

subvert' *v.t.* overthrow; corrupt. -**subversive** *a.* -**subver'sion** *n.* [L. *vertere, vers*, turn]

sub'way *n.* underground passage, railway, roadway. [OE. *weg*]

succeed' (-ks-) *v.t.* follow, take the place of-*v.i.* follow; accomplish a purpose. **success'** *n.* accomplishment, attainment; issue, outcome. -**success'ful** *a.* -**success'fully** *adv.* -**succes'sion** *n.* a following; series; a succeeding. -**success'ive** *a.* -**success'ively** *adv.* -**success'or** *n.* [L. *succedere, success*]

succinct' *a.* terse, concise. -**succinct'ly** *adv.* -**succinct'ness** *n.* [L. *succingere, succinct-*, gird up]

succ'or *v.t.* and *n.* help. [L. *succurrere*]

succulent *a.* juicy. -**succ'ulence** *n.* [L. *succulentus-succus*, juice]

succumb' (-kum) *v.i.* yield; die. [L. *succumbere*, lie down under]

such *a.* of the kind, quality or degree mentioned; of the same kind. [OE. *swile*]

suck *v.t.* draw into the mouth; roll in the mouth. -*n.* a sucking. -**suck'er** *n.* person or thing that sucks; organ or appliance which adheres by suction; (*sl.*) mug, dupe. -**suc'kle** *v.t.* feed from the breast. -**suck'ling** *n.* unweaned child. -**suc'tion** *n.* drawing in or sucking, *esp.* of air. [OE. sucan]

sudd'en *a.* done or occurring unexpectedly, abrupt. -**sudd'enly** *adv.* -**sudd'enness** *n.* [F. *soudain*]

suds *n.pl.* froth of soap and water. [orig. Du. *sudde*, ooze]

sue *v.t.* seek justice from. -*v.i.* make application or entreaty. [F. *suivre*, follow]

suède *n.* soft kid leather with an unglazed surface. [F. = *Swedish*]

suet *n.* hard animal fat. [OF. *sicu*, fr. L. *sebum*, tallow]

suff'er *v.t.* undergo; permit. -*v.i.* undergo pain, hurt, *etc.* -**suff'erable** *a.* -**suff'erance** *n.* toleration. -**sufferer** *n.* -**suff'ering** *n.* trouble, distress. [F. *souffrir*]

suffice' *v.i.* be enough. -*v.t.* meet the needs of. -**suffi'cent** *a.* enough. -**suffi'ciency** *n.* [L. *sufficere*]

suffix *n.* letter or syllable added to the root word. [L. *suffigere*, suflix, fix under]

suff'ocate *v.t.* kill by stopping breathing. -*v.i.* feel suffocated. -**suffoca'tion** *n.* [L. *suffocate*, suffocate]

suff'ragan *n.* assistant bishop. *a* . assisting (a bishop). -**suffraganship** *n.* [med. L. *suffraganeus*]

suff'rage *n.* vote or right of voting. -**suff'ragist** *n.* one claiming a right of voting. -**suffragette'** *n.* militant woman suffragist. [L. *suffragium*]

suffuse' *v.t.* well up and spread over. -**suffu'sion** *n.* [L. *suffundere, suffus-*]

su'gar (shoog-) *n.* sweet crystalline vegetable substance. -*v.t.* sweeten with it. -**su'gary** *a.* [Arab. *sukkar*]

suggest' *v.t.* propose; call up the idea of. -**suggest'ible, suggestive** *a.* -**suggest'ively** *adv.* -**sugges'tion** *n.* [L. *suggerere, suggest-*]

suicide *n.* one who kills himself intentionally; self-murder. -**suici'dal** *a.* **suici'dally** *adv.* [Mod. L. *suicidium*, fr. *ccedere*, kill]

suit *n.* action at law; petition; courtship; set, *esp.* of outer clothes; one of the four sets in a pack of cards. -*v.t.* go with, be adapted to; meet the desires of, make fitting, *etc.* -*v.i.* be convenient. -**suit'able** *a.* fitting, convenient. -**suit'ably** *adv.* -**suitabil'ity** *n.* -**suite** *n.* set of things going or used together, *esp.* furniture; retinue. -**suit'or** *n.* one who sues; wooer. -**suit'case** *n.* portable traveling-case for clothes, *etc.* [F. *suite*]

sul'fate *n.* salt of sulfuric acid. [L.]

sulfon'amides *n. pl.* group of anti-bacterial drugs effective in the treatment of disease. [L. *sulphur*]

sul'fur *n.* pale-yellow non-metallic element. -**sul'furous** *a.* -**sulfu'ric** *a.* **sulfu'-reous** *a.* [L.]

sul'ky *a.* sullen; morose. -**sulks** *n. pl.* sulky mood. -**sulk** *v.i.* be sulky. -**sulk'ily** *adv.* [orig. unknown]

sull'en *a.* resentful, ill-humored; dismal. -**sull'enly** *adv.* [var. of *solemn*]

sull'y *v.t.* stain, tarnish. [F. *souiller*]

sul'tan *n.* Mohammedan sovereign. **sulta'na** *n.* mother, wife, daughter of a sultan; small kind of raisin. [Arab.]

sul'try *a.* hot and close. -**sul'triness** *n.* [obs. *v. sulter,* var. of *swelter*]

sum *n.* amount, total; arithmetical problem. -*v.t.* add up. -**summ'ary** *a.* done quickly. -*n.* abridgement or statement of the chief points of a longer document, speech, *etc.* -**summ'arily** *adv.* -**summ'arize** *v.t.* -**summa'tion** *n.* an adding up. -**sum up,** recapitulate. [F. *somme,* L. *summa*]

summ'er *n.* second season. -*v.i.* pass the summer. -**summ'ery** *a.* [OE. *sumor*]

summ'it *n.* top; peak. [F. *sommet*]

summ'on *v.t.* demand the attendance of, call on; gather up (energies, *etc.*). **summ'ons** *n.* call, authoritative demand. [L. *summonere*]

sump' *n.* lowest point of a mine; in a motor-car, space for overflow of lubricating oil. [LG.]

sump'tuary *a.* regulating expenditure, -**sumptuous** *a.* lavish, magnificent. -**sumptuously** *adv.* -**sump'tuousness** *n.* [L. *sumptus,* expense]

sun *n.* luminous body round which the earth revolves; its rays. -*v.t.* expose to the sun's rays. -**Sun'belt** *n.* the Southern states of the U. S. A. -**Sun'day** *n.* first day of the week. -**sun'down, sun'set** *n.* action of the sun dropping below the horizon at the end of the day; the time at which it does this-**sun'flower** *n.* plant with large golden flowers like pictures of the sun. -**sunn'y** *a.* -**sun'less** *a.* -**sun'bathing** *n.* exposure of the body to sun's rays. -**sun'rise, sun'up** *n.* action of the sun rising above the horizon at the beginning of the day, the time at which it does this. -**sun'rise in'dustry** *n.* any of the high-technology industries, such as electronics, that hold promise of future development. -**sun'stroke** *n.* collapse from excessive exposure to the sun. [OE. *sunne*]

sun'dae *n.* ice-cream with fruit, nuts, *etc.* [orig. uncertain]

sund'er *v.t.* separate. -**sund'ry** *a.* several, divers. -*n. pl.* odd items not mentioned in detail. [OE. *asyndrian*]

sup *v.t.* take by sips. -*v.i.* take supper. -*n.* sip of liquid. [OE. *supan*]

su'per- *prefix,* makes compounds with meaning of above, in excess, *e.g.*, superabundant *a.* excessively abundant, superhuman *a.* more than human, *etc*. These are not given where the meaning and derivation may easily be found from the simple word. [L. *super,* above]

su'perable *a.* that can be overcome. [L. *superabilis*]

superann'uate *v.t.* pension off, or discharge as too old. -**superannua'tion** *n.* [L. *annus,* year]

superb' *a.* splendid, grand, impressive. superb'ly *adv.* [L. *superbus,* haughty]

su'percargo *n.* one in charge of the commercial affairs of a ship. [*cargo*]

supercil'ious *a.* indifferent and haughty. -**superciliously** *adv.* -**supercil'iousness** *n.* [L. *supercilium,* eyebrow]

supereroga'tion *n.* a doing more than duty requires. -**supererog'atory** *a.* [L. *erogare,* pay out]

superfi'cies *n.* surface, area. -**superfi'cial** *a.* of or on a surface; without depth. -**superficial'ity** *n.* [L., fr. *facies,* face]

super'fluous *a.* extra, unnecessary. -**superflu'ity** *n.* -**super'flously** *adv.* [L. *superfluere,* overflow]

superintend' *v.t.* have charge of overlook. -**superintend'ent** *n.* -**superintend'ence** *n.* [L. *intenders,* attend to]

supe'rior *a.* upper, higher in position or rank or quality; showing a consciousness of being so. -**superior'ity** *n.* [L.]

superl'ative *a.* of or in the highest degree. -*n.* superlative degree of an adjective or adverb. [L. *superlativus*]

su'perman *n.* (ideal) man of an ideal and higher type; person of extraordinary powers. [trans. of Ger. *Ubermensch*]

supernat'ural *a.* above nature; occult; miraculous; spiritual. -**supernat'urally** *adv.* [*natural*]

supernum'erary *a.* in excess of the normal number. -*n.* supernumerary person or thing. [L. *numerus,* number]

supersede' *v.t.* set aside; supplant; take the place of -**superses'sion** *n.* [L. *supersedere, supersess* -, be superior to]

supersonic *a.* of waves of greater frequency than sound; faster than sound. [L. *sonus,* sound]

supersti'tion *n.* religion or opinion or practice based on a belief in luck or magic. -**supersti'tious** *a.* -**supersti'tiously** *adv.*

[L. *superstitio*]

su'pertax *n.* special tax on high incomes. [*tax*]

supervene' *v.i.* happen as an addition or change. -**superven'tion** *n.* [L. *venire*, come]

su'pervise *v.t.* superintend. -**supervi'sion** *n.* -**supervi'sor** *n.* [L. *videre*, *vis-*, see]

su'pine *a.* indolent; negligent; inactive. [L. *supinus*, lying on one's back]

supp'er *n.* last meal of the day when dinner is not the last. -**supp'erless** *a.* [F. *souper*, fr. LG. *supen*, sup]

supplant' *v.t.* take the place of, *esp.* unfairly. -**supplant'er** *n.* [L. *supplantare*, trip up]

sup'ple *a.* pliable; lithe; compliant. -*v.t.* sup'ply *adv.* -**sup'pleness** *n.* [L. *supplex*]

supp'lement *n.* something added to fill up, supply a deficiency. -*v.t.* add to. **supplement'al** *a.* -**supplement'ary** *a.* [L. *supplere*, fill up]

supp'licate *v.t.* and *i.* beg humbly. -**supplica'tion** *n.* -**supp'licatory** *a.* **supp'liant** *a.* petitioning. -*n.* petitioner. [L. *supplicate*, fr. *plicare*, bend]

supply' *v.t.* furnish; substitute for. -*n.* a supplying, substitute; stock, store. [L. *supplere*, fill up]

support' *v. t*. hold up; assist; sustain. -*n.* a supporting or being supported, or means of support. -**support'able** *a.* tolerable. -**support'er** *n.* adherent. [L. *supportare*, fr. *portare*, carry]

suppose' *v.t.* assume as a theory; take for granted; accept as likely. -**suppo'sable** *a*. -**supposi'tion** *n.* -**supposit'itious** *a.* sham. [F. *supposer*]

suppress' *v.t.* put down, restrain, keep or withdraw from publication. -**suppres'sion** *n.* [L. *supprimere*, *suppress-*]

supp'urate *v.i.* fester. -**suppura'tion** *n.* [L. *suppurate*, fr. *pus*, pur]

suprare'nal *a.* above the kidneys. **suprare'nal cap'sules,** adrenal glands. [L. *renes*, kidneys]

supreme' *a.* highest. -**supreme'ly** *adv.* -**suprem'acy** *n.* [L. *supremus*]

sur'charge *n.* excessive charge or load; additional charge. -*v.t.* exact such charge. [*charge*]

surd *a.* and *n.* (quality) unable to be expressed in rational numbers, as the square root of 2; radical; not sonant. [G. *surdus*, deaf]

sure *a.* certain; trustworthy; strong, secure. -*adv.* certaintly. -**sure'ly** *adv.* -**sure'ty** *n.* certainty; one who makes himself responsible for the obligations of another. [F. *sur*, fr. L. *securus*]

surf *n.* foam of breaking waves on a beach. -**surf'y** *a.* -**surfing** *n.* sport of riding the incoming waves on a surfboard. [orig. uncertain]

sur'face (-fis) *n.* outside face of a body; plane; top, visible side; lifting or controlling surface of an plane. [F.]

sur'feit (-fit) *n.* excess. -*v.t.* and *i.* feed to excess. [F. *surfaire*, overdo]

surge *v.i.* move in large waves. -*n.* a great wave. [L. *surgere*, rise]

sur'geon (-in) *n.* medical expert who performs operations. -**sur'gery** *n.* treatment by operation; doctor's consulting room. -**surg'ical** *a.* -**sur'gically** *adv.* [F. *chirurgien*, fr. G. *cheirourgos*, lit. hand worker]

sur'ly *a.* morose, ill-tempered. [fr. *sir-ly*, orig. like an arrogant master]

surmise' *v.t.* and *i.* and *n.* guess. [OF. fr. *surmettre*, accuse]

surmount' *v.t.* get over, overcome. **surmount'able** *a.* [F. *surmonter*]

sur'name *n.* family name. [*name*]

surpass' *v.t.* outdo. [F. *surpasser*]

sur'plice (-plis) *n.* loose white vestment worn by clergy and choristers. **sur'pliced** *a.* [OF. *surpeli* s]

sur'plus *n.* what remains over or in excess. *a*. excess. [F.]

surprise' *n.* what takes unawares; emotion roused by being taken unawares; a taking unawares. -*v.t.* cause surprise to. -**surprising** *a.* [OF., fr. *surprendre*, lit. overtaken]

surreal'ism *n.* movement in the creative arts, which endeavors to express the subjective and subconscious. -**surreal** *a.* of the world of the subconscious; dreamlike. -**surrealist** *n.* [*real*]

surren'der *v.t.* hand over. -*v.i.* yield. -*n.* act of surrendering. [OF. *surrendre*, hand over]

surrepti'tious *a.* done secretly or steathily. -**surrepti'tiously** *adv.* [L. *subripere*, snatch]

surr'ogate *n.* deputy, *esp.* of a bishop. -*a.* -**surr'ogate** motherhood or surrogacy *n.* role of a woman who bears a child on behalf of a couple unable to have a child, either by articial insemination from the man or implantation of an embryo from the woman. -**surr'ogate moth'er** *n.* [L. *surrogatus*]

sur'round *v.t.* be or come all round. -*n.* border. [OF. *suronder*, overflow]

sur'tax *n.* additional tax. -*v.t.* impose one on. [F. *surfaxe*]

surveill'ance *n.* close watching. [F. *veiller*, fr. L. *vigilare*, watch]

survey' *v.t.* view; measure or map (land). -**sur'vey** *n.* a surveying. -**survey'or** *n.* [OF. *veir*, fr. L. *videre*, see]

survive' *v.t.* outlive; come alive through. -*v.i.* continue to live or exist. **survi'val** *n.* -**surviv'alist** *n.* person who believes in ensuring personal survival of a catastrophic event by arming himself and often by living in the wild. **sur'viv'atism** *n.* -**survi'vor** *n.* [L. *supervivere*, overlive]

suscep'tible *a.* sensitive; impressionable. -**susceptibil'ity** *n.* [L. *suscipere, suscept-*, receive]

suspect' *v.t.* have an impression of the existence or presence of, be inclined to believe; doubt the innocence of. *a.* of suspected character. -*n.* (sus'-) suspected person. -**suspi'cion** *n.* a suspecting or being suspected. -**suspi'cious** *a.* **suspiciously** *adv.* [L. *suspicere, suspect-*, lit. look up at]

suspend' *v.t.* hang up; sustain in fluid; cause to cease for a time, keep inoperative. -**suspend'er** *n.* -**suspend'ers** *n. pl.* straps for supporting trousers, skirt *etc.* -**suspense'** *n.* state of uncertainty. -**suspen'sion** *n.* state of being hung up, or debarred. -**suspensory** *a.* [L. *suspendare*, suspense]

sus'tain *v.t.* keep or hold up; endure; confirm. -**sustain'able** *a.* -**sus'tenance** *n.* food. -**sustenta'tion** *n.* maintenance. [OF. *sostenir*, fr. L. *sustinere*, hold up]

sut'ler *n.* camp follower selling provisions. [Du. *zotelaar*]

sutt'ee *n.* immolition of widow on husband's funeral pyre; former Indian custom. [Sans. *sati*, virtuous woman]

su'ture *n.* act of joining together, as the exterior parts of a wound; the seam or joint that unites two bones, *esp.* of the skull. -*v.t.* to stitch up. [L. *sutura, -suere*, to sew]

su'zerain *n.* feudal lord; supreme or paramount ruler. -**su'zerainty** *n.* [F.]

svelte *a.* lithe, slender. [F.]

swab (-ob) *n.* mop; pad of surgical wool. -*v.t.* clean with a swab. -**swabb'er** *n.* [orig. uncertain]

swad'dle (-od-) *v.t.* swathe. -**swadd'ling bands** (-**clothes**) *n.pl.* clothes in which an infant is swathed. [fr. *swathe*]

swagg'er *v.i.* strut; talk boastfully. -*n.* strutting gait; boastful or overconfident manner. [orig. uncertain]

swain *n.* rustic lover. [ON. *sveinn*, boy]

swall'ow *n.* migratory bird with a skimming flight. [OE. *swealwe*]

swall'ow (-ol-o) *v.t.* cause or allow to pass down the gullet. -*n.* an act of swallowing. [OE. *swelgan*]

swamp (-omp) *n.* bog. -*v.t.* entangle in a swamp; overwhelm, flood. -**swamp'y** *a.* [of LG. orig. cp. *sump*]

swan (-on) *n.* large water bird with graceful curved neck. -**swan' song** *n.* fabled song of swan before its death; last work of poet, musician. [OE.]

swank *n.* (*sl.*) brag; display. -*v.i.* show off. -**swank'y** *a.* [Sc.]

swap, swop *v.t.* and *i.* and *n.* (*sl.*) exchange. (ME. *swappen*]

sward *n.* turf. [OE. *sweard*, skin]

swarm *n.* large cluster of insects; vast crowd. -*v.i.* of bees, to emigrate in a swarm; gather in larger numbers. [OE. *swearm*]

swarm *v.i.* climb grasping with hands and knees. [orig. uncertain]

swart *a.* dark in color. -**swar'thy** *a.* dark-complexioned. [OE. *sweart*]

swash'buckler *n.* swaggerer; blustering braggart. [obs. *swack*, strike]

swasti'ka *n.* form of cross with arms bent at right angles. [Sanskrit *swastika*, fortunate]

swathe *v.t.* cover with wraps or bandages. [OE. *swathian*]

swathe, swath *n.* band of mown grass or corn or track cut by scythe. [OE. *swceth*]

sway *v.i.* swing unsteadily. -*v.t.* make to do this; govern; wield. -*n.* swaying motion; government. [LG. *swajen*, swing in the wind]

swear *v.t.* promise on oath; cause to take an oath. -*v.i.* use profane oaths. [OE. *swerian*]

sweat (swet) *n.* moisture oozing from the skin. -*v.i.* exude sweat; toil. -*v.t.* cause to sweat; employ at wrongfully low wages. -**sweat'er** *n.* woolen jersey. [OE. *swcetan*]

swede *n.* variety of turnip. [for Swedish *turnip*]

sweep *v.i.* pass quickly or magnificently; extend in a continuous curve. -*v.t.* clean with a broom; carry impetuously. -*n.* sweeping motion; wide curve; range; act of cleaning with a broom; long oar; one who cleans chimneys. [OE. *swapan*]

sweep'stake *n.* gamble in which the winner takes the stakes contributed by all. [*sweep* and *stake*]

sweet *a.* tasting like sugar; agreeable; tuneful; in good condition. -*n.* sweet part;

sweetmeat. *-pl.* sweet dishes at table; delights. **-sweet'bread** *n.* animal's pancreas as food. **-sweet' brier** *n.* wild rose. **-sweetmeat** *n.* piece of confectionery. **-sweetheart** *n.* lover. **-sweetpea'** *n.* plant of the pea family with bright flowers. **-sweet' william** *n.* garden plant with flowers of many colours. **-sweet'en** *v.t.* and *i.* **-sweet'ly** *adv.* **-sweet'ish** *a.* [OE. *swete*]

swell *v.i.* expand. *-v.t.* cause to expand. *-n.* act of swelling or being swollen; heave of the sea after a storm; mechanism in an organ to vary the volume of sound. [OE. *swellan*]

swelt'er *v.i.* be oppressive, or oppressed, with heat. [OE. *sweltan*, die]

swerve *v.i.* swing round, change direction during motion; deviate. *-n.* a swerving. [OE. *sweorfan*]

swift *a.* rapid, quick, ready. *-n.* bird like a swallow. **-swift'ly** *adv.* [OE.]

swill *v.t.* pour water over or through; drink greedily. *-v.i.* drink greedily. *-n.* a rinsing; liquid food for pigs. [OE. *swillan*, wash]

swim *v.i.* support and move oneself in water; float; be flooded; have a feeling of dizziness. *-v.t.* cross by swimming. *-n.* spell of swimming. **-swimm'er** *n.* [OE. *swimman*]

swind'ler *n.* cheat. **-swin'dle** *v.t.* and *i.* and *n.* cheat. [Ger. *schwindler]*

swine *n.* pig. **-swine'herd** *n.* [OE. *swin*]

swing *v.i.* move to and fro, *esp.* as a suspended body; revolve; (*sl.*) be hanged. *-v.t.* cause to swing; suspend. *-n.* an act of swinging; a seat hung to swing on. **-swing' the lead'**, malinger. [OE. *swingan*]

swinge (-j) *v.t.* belabor, beat. [OE. *swengan*, shake]

swipe *n.* sweeping blow. *-v.t.* give a sweeping blow to; (*sl.*) steal. [var. of *sweep*]

swirl *v.i.* move with an eddying motion. *-v.t.* cause to do this. *-n.* such motion. [of Scand. orig.]

swish *v.i.* swing a rod, *etc.*, with an audible hissing sound; move with a similar sound. *-v.t.* swing cane thus. *-n.* the sound; stroke with a cane, *etc.* [imit.]

switch *n.* flexible stick or twig; mechanism to complete or interrupt an electric circuit, *etc.*; on railway, two movable rails for transferring locomotive or train from one set of tracks to another. *-v.t.* strike with a switch; affect (current, *etc.*) with a switch; swing round abruptly. **-switch'back** *n.* short railway in steep undulations as a fairground amusement. **-switch'blade** *n.* pocket-knife with a spring-operated blade which opens at the release of a button. **-switch'board** *n.* board with switches to connect telephones, *etc.* [orig. uncertain]

swiv'el *n.* mechanism of two parts which can resolve the one on the other. *-v.t.* and *i.* turn on a swivel. [OE. *swifan*, revolve]

swoon *v.i.* and *n.* faint. [ME. *swowenynge*]

swoop *v.i.* come down like a hawk. *-n.* an act of swooping. [OE. *swapan*, sweep]

swop *v.i.* barter, exchange. *-n.* (orig. strike hands in bargaining.) [imit.]

sword (sord) *n.* weapon, long blade for cutting or thrusting. **-sword'-fish** *n.* fish with a long sharp upper jaw. **-sword'play** *n.* fencing. [OE. *sweord*]

swot' *v.i.* study hard. [var. of *sweat*]

syb'arite *n.* luxurious person. [G. *Sybarites*, inhabitant of Sybaris (a city noted for luxury)]

syc'amore *n.* tree allied to maple and plane. [G. *sykomoros*]

syc'ophant *n.* flatterer. **-sycophant'ic.** *a.* **-syc'ophancy** *n.* obsequiousness. [G. *sykophantes*, informer]

syll'able *n.* division of a word as a unit for pronunication. **-syllab'ic** *a.* [G. *syllambanein*, take together]

syll'abub *n.* dish of cream curdled with wine. [orig. unknown]

syll'abus *n.* program; outline. [by a misunderstanding for G. *sittube*, label of a parchment]

syllo'gism (-j-) *n.* form of logical reasoning consisting of two premises and a conclusion. **-syllogist'ic** *a.* [G. *syllogismos*, reckoning together]

sylph *n.* sprite. [coined by *Paracelsus*]

syl'van. *See* **silvan.**

sym'bol *n.* sign; thing representing or typifying something. **-symbol'ic** *a.* **symbol'ically** *adv.* **-sym'bolize** *v.t.***sym'bolism** *n.* [G. *symbolon*, token]

symm'etry *n.* proportion between parts, balance of arrangement between two sides; regularity. **-symmet'rical** *a.* **symmet'rically** *adv.* [G. *symmetria*, fr. *metron*, measure]

sym'pathy *n.* feeling for another in pain, *etc.*; sharing of emotion, interest, desire, *etc.* **-sympathet'ic** *a.* **-sympathet'ically** *adv.* **-sym'pathize** *v.i.* [G. *sympatheia*, fr. *pathos*, feeling]

symph'ony *n.* (*mus.*) important composition, in several movements, for full orchestra. [G. *phone*, sound]

sympo'sium *n.* drinking party; friendly

discussion; set of magazine articles by various writers on the same subject. [G. *symposion*, fr. *posis*, drinking]

symp'tom *n.* sign, token; change in the body indicating its health or disease. **symptomat'ic** *a.* [G. *sympotoma*]

syn'agogue *n.* Jewish congregation; its meeting place. [G. *synagoge*, assembly]

synch'ronize *v.t.* make agree in time. -*v.i.* happen at the same time. **syn'chronism** *n.* -**synchroniza'tion** *n.* -**synchronous** *a.* [G. *synchronl-ein*]

synchro'tron *n.* device for acceleration of stream of electrons. [G. *sun*, together, *chronos*, time]

syn'cope (*pl.*) *n.* fainting; syncopated spelling, *etc.* -**syn'copate** *v.t.* shorten by the omission of an interior element (in words, music, *etc.*) -**syncopa'tion** *n.* [G. *synkope*, dashing together]

syn'dic, syndicate *n.* body of persons associated for some enterprise. [G. *syndikos*, one helping in a trial]

syn'drome *n.* symptoms occurring together in a disease. [G. *syn*, together, *dramein*, run]

synec'doche *n.* (*rhet.*) figure in which a part is put for the whole, or the whole for a part. [G.]

syn'od *n.* church council; group of presbyteries. [G. *syrzodos*, assembly]

synon'ym *n.* word with the same meaning as another. -**synon'ymous** *a.* -**synonym'ity** *n.* [G. *synonymso*]

synop'sis *n.* a summary. -**synop'tic** *a.* having the same viewpoint. [G. *synopsis*, seeing together]

syn'tax *n.* part of grammar treating of the arrangement of words. -**syntact'ic** *a.* -**syntact'ically** *adv.* [G. *syntaxis*, arrangement together]

syn'thesis *n.* a putting together, combination, *esp.* of ideas, theories, *etc.* -**syn'thesize** *v.t.* [G. *synthesis*]

synthet'ic *a.* (*colloq.*) artificial. -**synthetically** *adv.* [G. *sunthetikos*]

syph'ilis *n.* infectious venereal disease. -**syphilit'ic** *a.* [coined (1530) by a doctor of Verona]

syring'a (ng-ga) *n.* flowering shrub, the mock-orange. [G. *syri* = reed]

syringe' *n.* instrument for drawing in liquid by a piston and forcing it out in a fine stream or spray; squirt; (*med.*) injecting instrument. -*v.t.* spray with a syringe. [G. *syrinx*, shepherd's pipe, reed]

syr'up *n.* thick solution of sugar; treacle, *etc.* -**syr'upy** *a.* [Arab. *sharab*, fr. *shariba*, drink]

sys'tem *n.* complex whole; organization; method; classification. -**systemat'ic** *a.* methodical. -**systemat'ically** *adv.* -**sys'tematize** *v.t.* reduce to system. [G. *systems*, what stands together]

sys'tole *n.* shortening of long syllable; contraction of heart and arteries for expelling blood and carrying on circulation. -**systol'ic** *a.* contracting; of systole. [G. *syn*, together, *stellein*, place]

T

tab *n.* tag, label, short strap; bill, check; surveillance. [orig. uncertain]

tab'ard *n.* herald's coat; sleeveless tunic.

tabb'y *n.* brindled cat; she-cat. [F. *tabis*, striped taffeta]

tabernacle *n.* tent or booth; religious meeting-house. [L. *taberna*, hut]

ta'ble *n.* piece of furniture consisting mainly of a flat board supported by legs, brackets, *etc.*, about three feet from the ground; tablet; food; set of facts or figures arranged in lines or columns. -*v.t.* lay on a table. -**ta'ble cloth** *n.* cloth of linen, *etc.*, to cover table at mealtimes. -**ta'ble land** *n.* plateau. -**tab'let** *n.* small flat slab. -**tab'ular** *a.* shaped or arranged like a table. -**tab'ulate** *v.t.* arrange (figures, facts, *etc.*) in tables. -**tabula'tion** *n.* [L. *tabula*]

tab'leau *n.* -**tab'leaux** *pl.* dramatic situation. -**tableau vivant** *n.* group of persons, silent and motionless, arranged to represent some scene. [*table*]

tab'loid *n.* illustrated popular newspaper with brief sensational headlines. -concentrated, very short. [Trademark]

taboo' *n.* setting apart of a thing as sacred or accursed; ban or prohibition. *a.* put under a taboo. -*v.t.* to put under a taboo. [Polynesian]

ta'bor *n.* small drum. -**tab'ouret** *n.* low stool. [OF. *tabour*]

tac'it (tas'-) *a.* implied but not spoken. -**tac'itly** *adv.* -**tac'iturn** *a.* talking little, habitually silent. -**taciturn'ity** *n.* [L. *tacere*, be silent]

tack *n.* small nail; long loose stitch; rope at the corner of a sail; course of a ship obliquely to windward. -*v.t.* nail with tacks; stitch lightly; beat to windward with tacks; change from one tack to another. [ONF. *toque*, fastening]

tack *n.* food. -**hard tack** ship's biscuit. [for *tackle*]

tac'kle *n.* equipment, apparatus, *esp.* lifting appliances with ropes. -*v.t.* take in hand; grip. [LG. *takel*]

tack'y *a.* shabby, seedy, common; characterized by a lack of style. [orig. uncertain]

tact *n.* skill in dealing with people or situations. **-tact'ful** *a.* **-tact'less** *a.* **tact'fully** *adv.* **-tact'lessly** *adv.* **tact'ile** *a.* of or relating to the sense of touch. [L. *tactus-tangere, tact-*, touch]

tactics *n. pl.* art of handing troops or ships in battle; science of strategy. **tact'ical** *a.* **-tacti'cian** *n.* [G. *la taktika*, matters of arrangement]

tad'pole *n.* young frog in the tailed stage. [ME. *taddepol*, 'toad-head']

tafferel, taff'rail *n.* rail at the stern of a ship; flat ornamental part of the stern. [Du. *tafereel*, little picture]

taff'eta *n.* smooth, lustrous silk or silk and wool, fabric. [of Pers. orig.]

tag *n.* ragged end; pointed end of lace, *etc.*; trite quotation; address label; any appendage. *-v.t.* append. **-tag'rag** *n.* rabble. [of Scand. orig.]

t'ai chi ch'uan' *n.* Chinese system of physical exercises characterized by coordinated and rhythmic movements. [Chin. great art of boxing]

tail *n.* projecting continuation of the backbone at the hinder end of an animal; any tail-like appendage. **-tailed** *a.* **-tail'less** *a.* **-tail'spin** *n.* spiral dive of airplane. [OE. *taegel*]

tail'or *n.* maker of outer clothing. [F. *tailleur*, tailor, cutter]

taint *n.* stain; infection; moral infection. *v.t.* stain slightly; corrupt. *-v.i.* become corrupted. [for *attaint*]

take *v.t.* grasp, get hold of, get; receive, assume, adopt; accept; understand; consider; carry or conduct; captivate. *-v.i.* be effective. **-take'-off** *n.* of a plane, *etc.*, rise from the ground. [ON. *taka*]

talc *n.* white or green mineral of soapy feel; powder made from it. [Arab. *talq*]

tale *n.* story; number, count. [OE. *talu*, speech, number]

tal'ent *n.* natural ability or power; ancient weight or money. [L. *talenturn*, money of account]

tal'isman *n.* object supposed to have magic powers. **-talisman'ic** *a.* [G. *telesma*, payment, religious rite]

talk (tawk) *v.i.* speak or converse. *-v.t.* express in speech; use (a language); discuss. *-n.* speech; conversation; rumor. **-talkative** *a.* **-talk'ing head** *n.* (on television) a person, such as a news announcer, who is shown only from the shoulders up, and speaks without the use of any illustrative material. **-talk'er** *n.* [fr. *tale*]

tall *a.* high; of great stature; (*sl.*) of a story, to be taken with a pinch of salt. [OE. *getœl*, swift, prompt]

tall'low *n.* melted and clarified animal fat. *-v.t.* smear with tallow. *a.* made of tallow. [LG. *talg*]

tall'y *n.* notched rod for keeping accounts; account so kept; reckoning. *-v.t.* record by a tally. *-v.i.* agree, correspond. [F. *tailler*, cut]

tall'y-ho! *interj.* huntsman's cry on sighting the fox. [OF. *thialau*]

Tal'mud *n.* collection of volumes containing Jewish civil and canonical law. **-Talmud'ic** *a.* [Heb. *talmud*, instruction]

tal'on *n.* claw. [F. = *heel*]

tam'arind *n.* E. Indian tree; its pods, filled with a sweet pulp. [Arab. *tamrhindi*, Indian date]

tam'arisk *n.* evergreen flowering shrub. [Late L. *tamariscus*]

tam'bour *n.* large drum; round frame for embroidery. **-tambourine'** *n.* flat half-drum with jingling disks of metal attached. [F.]

tame *a.* not wild; domesticated: unexciting, uninteresting. *-v.t.* make tame. **tame'ly** *adv.* **-ta'mer** *n.* [OE. *tam*]

tam-o-shant'er *n.* broad flat bonnet. [char. in Burns's poem]

tamp'er *v.i.* interfere (with) improperly; meddle. [var. of *temper*]

tan *n.* crushed oak-bark; color of this. *v.t.* make into leather; make brown. **tann'in** *n.* astringent substance got from oak-bark, *etc.* [of Celt. orig.]

tan'dem *adv.* one behind the other. *-n.* vehicle with two horses one behind the other; bicycle for two riders one behind the other. [L. = *at length*]

tang *n.* pungent taste, odor; kind of seaweed. [ON. *tangi*, point]

tan'gent (-j-) *a.* touching, meeting without cutting. *-n.* line tangent to a curve. **-tangen'tial** *a.* **-tangen'tially** *adv.* [L. *tangere, tangent-*, touch]

tangent (tan'-jent) *abbrev.* **tan** *n.* (*trigonometry*) in a right-angled triangle, the tangent of an acute angle is the ratio of the perpendicular to the base. [fr. L. *tangere*, to touch]

tangerine' *n.* kind of small orange. [F. *Tanger*, Tangiers]

tan'gible *a.* that can be touched; definite. **-tangibil'ity** *n.* [L. *tangibilis*]

tan'gle *v.t.* twist together in a muddle. *-n.*

tangled mass, kind of edible seaweed. [orig. uncertain]

tang'o (-ng-go) *n.* S. American dance. [orig. uncertain]

tank *n.* storage vessel for liquids, *esp.* a large one; *(mil.)* heavily armed and armored tracked vehicle used in modern warfare. **-tank'er** *n.* vessel designed to carry petroleum in bulk. [Port, *tanque*]

tank'ard *n.* large drinking-cup of metal. [orig. uncertain]

tan'ner *n.* one who tans; *(sl.)* sixpence. **tannery** *n.* place where hides are tanned. [OE. *tannere*]

tan'noy *n.* sound-amplifying apparatus used as a public-address system *esp.* in a large building, such as a department store or airport. [Trademark]

tan'sy *n.* yellow-flowered aromatic herb. [G. *athanasia*, immortality]

tantalize *v.t.* torment by presenting and then taking away something desired. **-tan'talus** *n.* appliance for keeping decanters locked up. [fr. punishment of Tantalus, king of Phrygia]

tantamount *a.* equivalent in value or signification; equal. [L. *tantus*, so great, and E. *amount*]

tan'trum *n.* outburst of temper. [orig. unknown]

tap *n.* hollow plug for drawing off liquid; valve with a handle to regulate or stop the flow of a fluid in a pipe, *etc.* *-v.t.* put a tap in; draw off. **-tap'root** *n.* long tapering root growing directly downwards. **tap'ster** *n.* one who draws beer in an inn. [OE. *tæppa*]

tap *v.t.* strike lightly but with some noise. *-n.* slight blow or rap. [imit.]

tape *n.* narrow long strip of fabric, paper, *etc.* **-tape'worm** *n.* flat worm parasitic on animals. IOE. *teeppa*]

ta'per *n.* long wick covered with wax; thin candle. *-v.i.* become gradually thinner towards one end. *-v.t.* make thus. [OE. *tapur*]

tap'estry *n.* fabric decorated with woven designs in colors. [F. *tapisserie*]

tapio'ca *n.* granular food made from the cassava-root. [Sp. fr. Brazilian]

ta'pir (-er) *n.* American animal with flexible proboscis, allied to the pig. [Braz. *tapira*]

tar *n.* thick black liquid distilled from coal, resinous wood, *etc.* *-v.t.* coat with tar. **-tarr'y** *a.* [OE. *teru*]

tar'latan *n.* fine openwork muslin. [F. *tarlatane*]

tar'-macad'am, tar'mac *n.* road surface of broken up stones and tar. [*tar* and *Macadam* (inventor)]

tarantula *n.* large, poisonous spider of Southern Europe. [*Taranto*, in Italy]

tard'y *a.* slow, behindhand. **-tard'ily** *adv.* **-tard'iness** *n.* [L. *tardus*, late]

tare *n.* weed, the vetch. [orig. unknown]

tare *n.* allowance made for the weight of box, cart, *etc.*, when goods are weighed in such. [F. = *waste*]

targe *n.* shield. (ON. *targa*, shield]

tar'get *n.* mark to aim at in shooting; small shield. [ON. *targa*, shield]

tar'iff *n.* list of charges. [It. *tariffa*]

tarn *n.* small mountain lake. [ON. *törn*]

tar'nish *v.t.* discolor (*esp.* metal). *-v.i.* become stained, lose shine. *-n.* discoloration. [F. *ternir*, become dull, dingy]

tarpaulin *n.* canvas treated with tar or oil. [ME. *palyoun*, canopy]

tarr'y *v.i.* linger delay. [ME. *tarien*]

tart *n.* open pie of fruit, *etc.*; small covered fruit pie. [F. *tarte*]

tart *a.* sour. [OE. *teart*, severe]

tart'an *n.* woollen cloth woven in a pattern of stripes crossing at right angles; pattern used in this cloth. [OF. *tartarin*, rich fabric imported through Tartary]

Tar'tar *n.* Race of mixed origin now living in parts of Russia and central and western Persia; irascible person. [*Tatar*]

tar'tar *n.* crust deposited on the teeth; deposit on wine-casks, *etc.* **-tartar'ic** *a.* [F. *tartre*]

task *n.* piece of work set or undertaken. *-v.t.* put a task on, take to task, to reprove. **-task'master** *n.* [ONF. *tasque*, fr. L. *taxare*, appraise]

tass'el *n.* bunch of threads on a knob as an ornament. [OF. = 'little heap']

taste *v.t.* perceive or try the flavor of, eat or drink; experience. *-v.i.* have a flavor. *n.* small quantity; flavor; judgment in matters of beauty, style, *etc.* **-taste'ful** *a.* **-taste'fully** *adv.* **-taste'less** *a.* [OF. *taster*, touch, handle]

tatt'er *n.* rag-**tatterdema'lion** *n.* ragged fellow. [of Teut. orig.]

tat'tle *v.i.* gossip; talk idly; give away secrets. *-n.* [Flem. *tateln*. stammer]

tattoo' *n.* beat of drum and bugle-call; military spectacle, earlier *taptoo*: lights out, or closing time for taverns. [Du. *tap toe*, 'shut the tap to']

tattoo' *v.t.* mark the skin in patterns, *etc.*, by pricking and filling the punctures with coloring matter. *-n.* mark so made. [Polynesian]

taunt *n.* reproach, insulting words. *-v.t.* insult, reproach bitterly. [OF. *tanter*]

Taur'us *n.* the Bull, 2nd sign of the zodiac, which sun enters on 21st April. **taur'ian, taur'ine** *a.* of, like a bull. **taurom'achy** *n.* bull-fighting. [L.]

taut *a.* drawn tight. [orig. uncertain]

tautology *n.* repetition of the same thing in other words. **-tautolo'gical** *a.* [G. *tauto*, the same, *legein*, speak]

tav'ern *n.* inn or ale-house. [F. *taverner* fr. L. *taberna*, hut]

taw'dry *a.* showy but cheap and without taste. **-taw'drily** *adv.* [St. Audrey's fair (Oct. 17th) where trinkets were sold]

tawn'y *a.* yellowish-brown. *-n.* this color. [F. *tanné*, tanned]

tawse *n.pl.* leather strap fringed at the end for whipping children. [OE. *tawian*, prepare leather]

tax *v.t.* exact a contribution to the cost of government; examine accounts; put a burden or strain on. *-n.* charge imposed; a burden. **-taxa'tion** *n.* **-tax'able** *a.* **tax'-payer** *n.* [L. *taxare*, reckon]

tax'i- (cab) *n.* motor-cab for hire with driver. **-tax'i** *v.i.* go in a taxi; (of an airplane) run along the ground under its own power. *-pres. part.* **-tax'ying.** - **taxim'eter** *n.* instrument for measuring the time and distance to reckon the charge for a cab fitted with it. **-tax'i stand** *n.* place where taxis park while awaiting customers. [abbrev. of **taximeter.** *See* **tax**]

tax'idermy *n.* art of stuffing animals. **taxi'dermist** *n.* [fr. G. *taxis*, arrangement, and *derma*, skin]

tea *n.* dried leaves of a plant cultivated in China, India, *etc.*; infusion of it as a beverage; various herbal infusions; afternoon meal at which tea is served. [Du. *thee* (fr. Chin.)]

teach *v.t.* instruct; impart knowledge of, direct; discipline. *-v.i.* act as teacher. **teach'er** *n.* [OE. *toecan*]

teak *n.* East Indian tree; the very hard wood obtained from it. (Malayalam *tekka*]

teal *n.* small water-fowl allied to the duck. [orig. uncertain]

team *n.* set of animals, players of a game, *etc.*, associated in an activity. **-team'ster** *n.* one who drives a team of draught animals; driver of a truck, *esp.* as an occupation. [OE.]

tear *n.* drop of fluid in, or failing from, the eye. **-tear'ful** *a.* **-tear'less** *a.* **-tear'drop** *n.* **-tear'-stained** *a.* **-tear'-gas** *n.* irritant gas causing watering of the eyes. [OE.]

tear (tar) *v.t.* pull apart, rend. *-v.i.* become torn; rush. *-n.* rent. [OE. *teran*]

tease *v.t.* pull apart the fibers of, torment; irritate. *-n.* one who torments. **-teas'ing** *a.* [OE. *toesan*]

teaser *n.* plant with large burrs used to raise the nap on cloth; this burr. [OE. *toesel*]

teat *n.* nipple of a female breast; artificial substitute for this. [F. *tette*]

technical (tek-) *a.* of or used in an art, *esp.* an industrial art; belonging to a particular art. **-technical'ity** *n.* state of being technical; that which is technical. **-tech'nically** *adv.* **-technique'** *n.* method of performance. **techni'cian** *n.* **-technol'ogy** *n.* systematic knowledge of industrial arts. **technol'ogist** *n.* [G. *techne*, art, craft]

te'dium *n.* boredom or quality of boring. **-te'dious** *a.* wearisome. **-te'diously** *adv.* [L. *toedium*, fr. *toedere*, weary]

tee *n.* (*golf*) small peg or sand-heap from which the ball is played off at each hole. [orig. unknown]

teem *v.i.* abound with, swarm, be prolific. [OE. *tieman*]

teens *n.pl.* years of youth, between 12 and 20. **-teen'ager** *n.*

tee'pee. *See* **tepee.**

tee'ter *v.i.* make see-saw movements; hesitate. [var. of dial. *titter*, to *totter*]

teethe (-TH) *v.i.* cut teeth. [fr. *teeth*]

teeto'tal *a.* abstaining or pledged to abstain from intoxicating drink; relating to such abstinence or pledge. **-teeto'taler** *n.* [elaboration of *total*]

teeto'tum *n.* top, *esp.* one with marked sides for gambling, *etc.* [earlier *T-totum*, fr. the lucky side marked T]

teg'ument *n.* a covering; natural covering of an animal body. [L. *tegumentum* fr. tegere, cover]

tel- *prefix*, at a distance. [G. = *far off*] - **telecommunica'tions** *n.* transmission of data signals in digital, audio, or video form. **-tel'egraph** *n.* apparatus for sending messages mechanically to a distance, as by semaphore, electricity, *etc.* *-v.t.* and *i.* communicate by telegraph. **-teleg'raphist** *n.* one who works a telegraph. -telegraphic *a.* **-telegraph'ically** *adv.* **-teleg'raphy** *n.* - **tel'egram** *n.* message sent by telegraph. **-telekine'sis** *n.* motion caused by spirit or psychic force. **-telep'athy** *n.* action of one mind on another at a distance. **-telepath'ic** *a.* **-telepath'ically** *adv.* **-tel'ephone** *n.* apparatus for communicating sound to a distance. -*v.t.* and *i.* communicate or speak by telephone. **-telephon'ic** *a.* **teleph'ony** *n.* **-teleph'onist** *n.* **tel'ergy** *n.* supposed telepathic force. **tel'escope** *n.* instrument of lenses to see things more clearly at a distance. **telescop'ic** *a.* **-televi'sion** *n.* seeing at a distance by the use of wireless transmission.

tell *v.t.* narrate, make known; count. -*v.i.* give an account; be of weight or importance. **-tell'er** *n.* **-tell'ing** *a.* effective. **-tell'tale** *a.* indicating, betraying (secrets, *etc.*). -*n.* teller of secrets. **-tell'off** *v.t.* berate. [OE. *tellan*]

tellu'rian *a.* of the earth. -*n.* dweller on the earth. [L. *tellus, tellur-*, earth]

tel'pherage (-fer-) *n.* form of transport by electric monorail, the telpher-line. [G. *pherein*, carry]

temerity *n.* rashness. **-temera'rious** *a.* foolhardy. [F. *témérité*, fr. L. *temeritas*]

temp'er *v.t.* harden; bring to proper condition; restrain, moderate. -*n.* degree of hardness of steel, *etc.*; mental constitution, frame of mind; anger, *esp.* in noisy outburst. **-temp'erament** *n.* mental constitution. **-temperament'al** *a.* **-temperament'ally** *adv.* **-temp'erate** *a.* showing or practicing moderation. **-temp'erance** *n.* moderation, self-restraint **-temp'erately** *adv.* **-temp'erature** *n.* degree of heat or coldness. [L. *temperate*, proportion duly]

tempers *n.* distemper for frescoes. [L. *temperate*]

temp'est *n.* violent storm. **-tempest'uous** *a.* **-tempest'uously** *adv.* [L. *tempestas*, weather, storm]

tem'ple *n.* building for worship, or to house a deity. [L. *templum*]

tem'ple *n.* flat part on either side of the head above the cheekbone. [L. *temporal* pl.]

tem'po *n.* (*music*) time, rate; rhythm. [It.]

temp'oral *a.* relating to time, or to this life or world; secular. **-temporal'ity** *n.* **temp'orary** *a.* lasting or used only for a time. **-temp'orarily** *adv.* **-temp'orize** *v.t.* gain time by negotiation, *etc.*; conform to circumstances. **-temp'orizer** *n.* [L. *tempus, tempor-*, time]

tempt *v.t.* try; try to persuade, *esp.* to evil. **-tempt'er** *n.* **-temptress** *n.* *fem.* **tempta'tion** *n.* [OF. *tempter*, fr. L. *temptare*, test]

ten *n.* and *a.* cardinal number next after nine. **-tenth** *a.* ordinal number. **tenth'ly** *adv.* [OE. *tien*]

ten'able *a.* that may be held or defended. [F.]

tenacious *a.* holding fast. **-tenac'ity** *n.* [L. *tenax-tenere*, hold]

ten'ant *n.* one who holds lands or house, *etc.*, on a rent, or lease. **-ten'ancy** *n.* **ten'antry** *n.* body of tenants. **tenantable** *a.* fit for habitation. [F. fr. L. *tenere*, hold]

tench *n.* fresh-water fish. [OF. *tenche*]

tend *v.t.* take care of. **-tend'er** *n.* vessel attending a larger one; carriage for fuel and water attached to a locomotive. [for *attend*]

tend *v.i.* incline; make in direction of **tend'ency** *n.* **-tend'er** *v.t.* offer. -*n.* offer; what may legally be offered in payment. [L. *tendere*, stretch]

tend'er *a.* delicate, soft; fragile; gentle, loving, affectionate. **-tend'erly** *adv.* **tend'erness** *n.* **-tend'erfoot** *n.* new comer on plains; novice. **-tend'er loin** *n.* undercut of sirloin; (*sl.*) district of a city known for vice, corruption, *etc.* [F. *tendre*, fr. L. *tener*]

tend'on *n.* sinew attaching a muscle to a bone, *etc.* [G. *tenon*, sinew]

tend'ril *n.* slender curling stem by which a climbing plant attaches itself to anything. [F. *tendre*, stretch]

ten'ebrous *a.* dark; gloomy; obscure [L. *tenebrae*, darkness]

ten'ement *n.* piece of land or a house; part of a house forming a separate dwelling; block of flats. [L. *tenere*, hold]

ten'et *n.* doctrine. [L. = 'he holds']

ten'nis *n.* game in which a ball is struck between players on opposite sides of a net in a covered court; variation of this played on a grass or other court (also called lawn tennis). [F. *tenez*, take; (called by the server)]

ten'on *n.* tongue on the end of a piece of wood, *etc.*, to fit into a mortise. [F.]

ten'or *n.* meaning; trend; male voice between alto and bass, music for this; singer with this voice. [L.]

tense *n.* modification of a verb to show time of action, *etc.* **-ten'sity** *n.* [OF. *tens*, fr. L. *tempus*, time]

tense *a.* stretched tight. **-ten'sile** *a.* capable of being stretched. **-ten'sion** *n.* stretching or strain when stretched; mental strain. [L. *tendere, tens-*, tent-, stretch]

tent *n.* portable shelter of canvas. **-tent'pole** *n.* **-tent'-peg** *n.* [F. *tente*, fr. L. *tendere*, stretch]

tentacle *n.* feeler. **-tent'ative** *a.* done as a trial. -*n.* attempt. **-tent'atively** *adv.* [L. *tentare*, try]

tent'er *n.* frame for stretching cloth. **tenterhook** *n.* hook for holding the cloth.

on tenterhooks, in painful suspense. [F. *tentura, tapestry,* fr. L. *tendere,* stretch]

ten'uous *a.* thin. **-tenu'ity** *n.* [L. *tenuitas-tenuis,* slender]

ten'uire *n.* conditions or period of holding land, an office, *etc.* [OF.]

te'pee' *n.* American Indian skin-tent. [Sioux = *dwelling*]

tep'id *a.* moderately warm; lukewarm. [L. *tepidus*]

tequil'a *n.* strong Mexican liquor. [*Tequila,* district of Mexico]

tercenten'ary *n.* three-hundredth anniversary. *a.* pertaining to one. [L. *ter,* three times, *centum,* hundred]

tere'do *n.* boring worm, the ship-worm. [L.]

tergiversa'tion (-j-) *n.* shuffling; desertion of party. [L. *tergiversation* fr. *tergum,* back, *vertere, vers-,* turn]

term *n.* limit or end; fixed day for regular payment, *e.g.* rent; period during which courts sit, schools are open, *etc.* *-pl.* conditions, mutual relationship; word or expression. *-v.t.* name. **-term'inal** *a.* at or forming an end. *-n.* terminal part or structure. **-term'inate** *v.t.* bring to an ena. *-v.i.* come to an end. **-termina'tion** *n.* study of terms; set of technical terms or vocabulary. **-terminolo'gical** (-j-) *a.* **term'inus** *n.* finishing point; station at the end of a railway. [L. *terminus,* limit]

termagant *n.* brawling woman. [OF. *Tervagant,* supposed Saracen god]

ter'mite *n.* the so-called white ant. [L. *termes,* woodworm]

tern *n.* sea-bird allied to the gull. [Ice. *therna*]

tertiary *a.* in threes; proceeding in threes. [L. *terni,* three each]

Terpsich'ore *n.* Muse of dancing. [G.]

terrace *n.* raised level place, level cut out of a hill; row or street of uniform houses. *-v.t.* form into a terrace. [F. *terasse,* fr. *terre,* earth]

terra-cotta *n.* hard unglazed pottery, *-a.* brownish-red color. [It. = *cooked earth*]

terr'ain *n.* a region or tract of land; ground considered in relation to, *e.g.,* military operations. [F.]

terrest'rial *a.* of the earth; of land. [L. *terrestris,* fr. *terra,* earth]

terr'ible *a.* causing fear; excesive. **-terr'ibly** *adv.* **-terrif'ic** *a.* terrible, awesome. **-terrif'ically** *adv.* **terr'ify** *v.t.* frighten. **-terr'or** *n.* state of great fear. **-terr'orize** *v.t.* force or oppress by fear. **terrorism** *n.* **-terr'orist** *n.* [L. *terrere,* frighten]

terr'ier *n.* small dog of various breeds, orig. for following a quarry into a burrow. [F., fr. *terre,* earth]

territory *n.* region; land subject to a ruler. **-territo'rial** *a.* relating to a territory. [L. *territorium*]

ter'ror. *See* **terrible.**

terse *a.* pithy, concise. [L. *tersus*]

ter'tiary *a.* third. [L. *tertius,* third]

tess'ellated *a.* paved with small square tiles or with mosaic. [L. *tessella,* small square piece]

test *n.* means of trial. *-v.t.* try, put to the proof. **-test pa'per** *n.* paper impregnated with indicator for chemical tests; question sheet of test; paper completed by test candidate. **-test pi'lot** *n.* pilot who flies aircraft of new design to test performance in air. **-test tube** *n.* narrow cylindrical glass vessel used in scientific experiments. [OF. *test,* pot]

testament *n.* will; one of the two divisions of the Bible. **-testament'ary** *a.* **-test'ate** *a.* that has left a will. **test'acy** *n.* state of being testate. **testa'tor** *n.* **-testa'trix** *fem.* [L. *testamentum*]

test'icle *n.* male genital organ. [L. *testiculus*]

test'ify *v.i.* bear witness. *-v.t.* bear witness to. **-test'imony** *n.* evidence. **testimo'nial** *n.* certificate of character, ability, *etc.*; gift by a number of persons to express their regard for the recipient. [L. *testis,* witness]

test'y *a.* irritable, short-tempered. [OF. *testif,* heady, obstinate]

tet'anus *n.* lockjaw; rigidity of some or all muscles. [G. *tetanos,* muscular spasm]

tête-a-tête (tet'-a-tet') *a.* and *adv.* confidential. *-n.* private conversation. [F.]

teth'er *v.t.* tie up (a horse, *etc.*), with a rope. *-n.* rope or chain for fastening a grazing animal; limit of endurance (end of one's tether). [ON. *tjothr*]

tet'ragon *a.* figure with four angles and four sides. **-tetrag'onal** *a.* **-tetrahe'dron** *n.* solid contained by four plane faces. [G. *tetra,* four]

tet'rarch *n.* in Roman Empire, ruler of 4th part of a province. [G. *tetra,* four, *arches,* ruler]

Teuton'ic *a.* of, pert. to, Germanic race, *e.g.* Germans, Scandinavians, English. [L. *Teutonicus,* from the Teutones]

text *n.* actual words of a book, passage, *etc.*; main body of a literary work; letterpress; passage from the Scriptures, *etc.*, *esp.* as the subject of a discourse. -

text'book *n.* manual of instruction. -**text editing** *v.t.* (*compute.*) process of changing, adding, or deleting material on a computer. -**text'ual** *a.* of or in a text. [L. *textus-texere*, text-, weave]

text'ile *a.* woven; capable of being woven; relating to weaving. -*n.* a woven fabric. [L. *textilis*]

text'ure *n.* the character or structure of a textile fabric. [L. *texere, text-*, weave]

Thali'a *n.* Muse of pastoral and comic poetry. [G.]

than (TH-) *conj.* and *prep.* introduces second part of a comparison. [OE. *thanne*]

thane *n.* in feudal system, a lesser noble. [OE. *thegn*]

thank *v.t.* give thanks to, express gratitude to. -thanks *n. pl.* words of gratitude. -**thank'ful** *a.* feeling grateful. -**thankless** *a.* having or bringing no thanks. -**Thanks'giving Day** *n.* day appointed for giving thanks to God for blessings granted to the nation; in U.S., fourth Thursday in November; in Canada, second Monday in October. [OE *thanc*]

that (TH-) *a.* demonstrates or particularizes. *fem. pron.* particular thing meant. -*adv.* as. -*rel. pron.* which, who. -*conj.* introduces noun or adverbial clauses. [OE. *thcet*]

thatch *v.t.* roof (a house) with straw or similar material. -*n.* straw used in thatching. [OE. *thœc*, roof]

thau'maturge *n.* wonder-worker. **thau'maturgy** *n.* magic, miracle-working. [G. *thaumatourgos*, fr. *thauma*, wonder]

thaw *v.t.* and *i.* melt. -*n.* a melting (of frost, *etc.*). [OE. *thawian*]

the (TH-) is the definite article. [that]

the'ater (-ter) *n.* place where plays are performed; drama or dramatic works generally; surgical operating room. **theat'rical** *a.* of or for the theater; showy, spectacular. -**theat'rically** *adv.* -**theat'ricals** *n. pl.* amateur dramatic performances. [G. *theatron*]

theft *n.* stealing. [OF. *thiefth*]

their (THir) *a. -pron.* belonging to them. [ON. *theirra*]

the'ism *n.* belief in divine creation of the universe without denial of revelation. **the'ist** *n.* [G. *theos*, god]

them *pron.* objective case of they; those persons or things. [ON. *theim*]

theme *n.* subject of a composition; essay. [G. *theme*, proposition]

then (TH-) *adv.* at that time; next; that being so. [OE. *thanne*]

thence (TH-) *adv.* from that place, point of reasoning, *etc.* -**thence'forth,** thence forward *adv.* from that time on. [ME. *thannes*]

theodolite *n.* surveying instrument for measuring angles, *etc.* [orig. uncertain]

theol'ogy *n.* science treating of God. **theolo'gical** *a.* -**theolo'gically** *adv.* **theolo'gian** *n.* -**theoc'racy** *n.* government by God. -**theocrat'ic** *a.* [G. *theos*, god]

the'orem *n.* proposition which can be demonstrated by argument. -**the'ory** *n.* supposition to account for something; system of rules and principles; rules and reasoning, *etc.*, as distinguished from practice. -**theoret'ical** *a.* -**theoret'ically** *adv.* -**the'orist** *n.* -**the'orize** *v.i.* [G. *theorems*, proposition to be proved]

theosophy *n.* any of various ancient and modern systems of esoteric philosophy by which the soul may attain to knowledge of, and ultimate union with, the universal spirit. [G. *theosophos*, wise in the things of God]

therapeutic *a.* relating to healing. -*n.* in *pl.* art of healing. -**ther'apy** *n.* curative treatment. [G. *therapeutikos*]

there (TH-) *adv.* in that place, to that point. -**there'fore** *adv.* in consequence, that being so. [OE. *thcer*]

ther'mal *a.* of or pertaining to heat. **therm** *n.* unit of heat; unit of 1,000 calories. -**ther'mic** *a.* thermal. -**thermom'eter** *n.* instrument to measure temperature. -**thermomet'ric** *a.* **thermion'ic** valve *n.* apparatus for changing wireless waves into vibrations audible in telephony, and for amplifying and generating such waves. -**ther'mos bottle** *n.* flask keeping its contents hot or cold by a double wall with a vacuum between. (Trademark) [G. *therme*, heat]

thermodynam'ics *n. pl.* science dealing with conversion of heat into mechanical energy. [G. *thermos*, hot]

therm'ostat *n.* automatic regulator of temperature. -**thermostat'ic** *a.* [G. *thermos*, hot]

thesaur'us *n.* treasury; storehouse; *esp.* a collection of words and phrases; a lexicon or encyclopedia. [L. G. *thesauros*, *tithenae*, place]

the'sis *n.* proposition; dissertation. [G.]

thes'pian *a.* of the drama. [*Thespis*, founder of Greek drama]

thews *n. pl.* muscles, sinews; person's muscular strength. [OE. *theaw*, quality]

they *pron.* third person plural pronoun.

[ON. *their*]

thick *a.* having great thickness, not thin; dense, crowded; viscous; foggy. **-thick'ly** *adv.* **-thick'en** *v.t.* and *i.* **-thick'ness** *n.* dimension of anything measured through it, at right angles to the length and breadth. **-thick'et** *n.* thick growth of small trees. **-thick'set** *a.* set closely together; sturdy and solid in limbs and frame. [OE. *thicce*]

thief *n.* thieves *pl.* one who steals. **thieve** *v.t.* and *i.* steal. **-thieving, thiev'ish** *a.* **-thiev'ishness** *n.* [OE. *theof*]

thigh *n.* upper part of the leg above the knee. [OE. *theoh*]

thim'ble *n.* metal cover for the fingertip in sewing. [OE. *thymel,* fr. thumb]

thin *a.* not thick; of little density; loose, not closely packed. *-v.t.* and *i.* make or become thin. **-thin'ness** *n.* [OE. *thynne*]

thine (TH-in) *pron.* and *a.* belonging to thee. [OE. *thin,* thy]

thing *n.* material object; any possible object of thought. [OE. = assembly for deliberation; affairs; matters]

think *v.i.* have one's mind at work; reflect; hold an opinion. *-v.t.* conceive or consider in the mind. **-think'er** *n.* [OE. *thencan*]

third *a.* ordinal number corresponding to three. *-n.* third part. **-third degree',** drastic police methods to make a prisoner 'talk.' [ver. of *thrid,* fr. three]

thirst *n.* feeling caused by lack of drink. *v.i.* feel the lack of drink. **-thirst'y** *a.* **thirst'ily** *adv.* [OE. *thurst*]

thirteen' *a.* and *n.* number, three and ten. **-thirt'y** *n.* and *a.* number, three times ten. [OE. *threotyne; thritig*]

this, these *pl. -dem. a.* and *pron.* denotes a thing or person near, or just mentioned, *etc.* [OE.]

this'tle (*-sl*) *n.* prickly plant with a purple flower. [OE. *thistel*]

thith'er (THiTH'-) *adv.* to or toward that place. **-thith'erward** *adv.* [OE. *thider*]

thole *v.t.* endure, bear. [OE. *tholian,* cognate with L. *tolerate*]

thole-pin *n.* one of two pegs between which an oar works. [OE. *thol*]

thong *n.* narrow strip ofleather. *-v.t.* sew with thongs. [OE. *thwang,* strap]

thor'ax *n.* part of the body between neck and belly. [G. = *breastplate*]

thorn *n.* prickle on a plant; bush noted for its thorns. **-thorn'y** *a.* [OE.]

thor'ough *a.* complete, painstaking. **-thor'oughly** *adv.* **-thor'oughbred** *a.* of pure breed. *-n.* purebred animal, *esp.* horse. **-thor'oughfare** *n.* road or passage open at both ends; right of way. [var. of *through*]

those *a.* and *pron. pl.* of that. [OE. *thas*]

thou *pron.* (*arch.*) second person singular pronoun. [OE. *thu*]

though *conj.* in spite of the fact that. *-adv.* for all that. [OE. *theah*]

thought (thawt) *n.* process of thinking; what one thinks; a product of thinking; meditation. **-thought'ful** *a.* engaged in meditation; considerate. **-thought'less** *a.* careless, heedless, inconsiderate. [OE. *thoht*]

thou'sand (-z-) *a.* and *n.* cardinal number, ten hundreds. [OE. *thusend*]

thrall (-awl) *n.* slave; slavery. *-v.t.* enslave. **-thral'dom** *n.* [ON. *thraell*]

thrash, thresh *v.t.* of corn, *etc.*, beat out the grains of. **-thrash** *v.t.* beat, whip. [OE. *threscan*]

thread (-ed) *n.* fine cord; yarn; ridge cut spirally on a screw. *-v.t.* put a thread into; put on a thread; pick (one's way, *etc.*). **thread'bare** *a.* worn, with the nap rubbed off. [OE. *thrced*]

threat (-et) *n.* announcement of what the speaker intends to do if his orders or wishes are not complied with. **-threat'en** *v.t.* and *i.* utter threats against. **threat'ening** *a.* menacing. [OE. *pressure*]

three *n.* and *a.* cardinal number, one more than two. [OE. *threo*]

thren'ody *n.* dirge, lament. [G. *threnos,* lament, ode, song]

threshold (-old) *n.* the bar of stone or wood forming the bottom of the framework of a door. [OE. *therscold,* fr. *therscask,* tread]

thrice *adv.* three times. [fr. *three*]

thrift *n.* saving, economy. **-thrift'y** *a.* **thrift'ily** *adv.* **-thrift'less** *a.* [fr. *thrive*]

thrill *v.t.* send -a nervous tremor of emotion through. *-v.i.* feel one. *-n.* such emotional tremor. **-thrill'er** *n.* (*sl.*) sensational story. **-thrill'ing** *a.* exciting. [OE. *thyrlian,* pierce]

thrive *v.i.* grow well; flourish, prosper. [ON. *thrifa,* grasp]

throat *n.* front of the neck; either or both of the passages through it. **-throat'y** *a.* of voice, hoarse. [OE. *throte*]

throb *v.i.* beat or quiver strongly. *-n.* a throbbing. [orig. uncertain]

throe *n.* spasm or pang; acute pain; agony. [OE. *throwian,* suffer]

thrombosis *n.* formation of a bloodclot in artery or vein. (G. *thrombos,* clot]

throne *n.* seat of state, *esp.* of a king. *v.t.*

place on a throne. [G. *thronos*]

throng *n.* *v.t.*, and *i.* crowd. [OE. *gethrana*, fr. *thringan*, press]

thros'tle *n.* thrush. [OE.]

throt'tle *v.t.* and *i.* strangle. [fr. *throat]*

through *prep.* from end to end of. *adv.* from end to end; to the end. **throughout'** *adv.* in every part. *-prep.* in every part of [OE. *thurh*]

throw *v.t.* fling; bring down. *-n.* an act or distance of throwing. **-throw'back** *n.* reversion to an ancestral type. [OE. *thrawan*, to twist]

thrum *n.* the end of a weaver's thread or yarn; any loose thread; fringe-*v.t.* to weave with thrums. [OE.]

thrum *v.t.* to strum; to drum with the fingers. *-n.* the sound made by thrumming a stringed instrument, *etc.* [imit.]

thrush *n.* song-bird. [OE. *thrysce*]

thrush *n.* throat and mouth disease of children; foot disease of horses. [orig. uncertain]

thrust *v.t.* push, stab, drive. *-v.i.* lunge, stab; push one's way. *-n.* lunge or stab with sword, *etc.* [ON. *thrysta*]

thud *n.* dull heavy sound, as of a brick falling on earth. *-v.i.* make a thud. [imit. orig.]

thug *n.* one of a body of Indian assassins in early 19th c.; cutthroat; ruffian. [Hind.]

thumb *n.* short thick finger, the one which can be opposed to the others. *-v.t.* handle or dirty with the thumb. **thumb'tack** *n.* tack with a large flat head for pressing into a surface with the thumb. [OE. *thuma*]

thump *v.t.* strike heavily. *-n.* dull heavy blow; sound of one. [imit.]

thunder *n.* loud noise accompanying lightning. *-v.i.* of thunder, to sound. *-v.t.* utter loudly. **-thun'derbolt** *n.* lightning flash as agent of destruction. **-thun'dery** *a.* **-thun'derous** *a.* [OE. *thunor*]

Thurs'day *n.* fifth day of the week. [OE. *thunresdaeg*, day of Thor or thunder]

thus *adv.* in this way; therefore. [OE.]

thwack *v.t.* and *n.* whack. [imit.]

thwart *v.t.* foil, frustrate. *adv.* across. [ON. *thuert*, across]

thwart *n.* seat for a rower across a boat. [OE. *thofte*, rower's bench]

thy *pron.* or *a.* (*poss.* of *thou*) belonging to thee. [var. of *thine*]

thyme (tim) *n.* low-growing aromatic herb. **-thy'mol** *n.* antiseptic got from oil of thyme. [G. *thumon*]

thy'roid (gland) *n.* ductless gland at front of neck; chief cartilage of larynx. [G. *thyreos*, shield, *eidos*, form]

tiar'a *n.* jeweled head-ornmanent. [G.]

tib'ia *n.* shin-bone; flute. [L.]

tic *n.* spasmodic twitch in the muscles of the face; tic doloureux. [F.]

tick *n.* mite in hair or fur. [Teut. orig.]

tick *n.* mattress case. [G. *theke*, case]

tick *n.* slight sound as of a watch-movement; *-v.i.* make the sound; small mark *-v.t.* mark with a tick. **tick'er** *n.* something that ticks; telegraphic receiving apparatus which prints off information on a paper ribbon. **tick'er tape** *n.* paper ribbon used in a ticker machine; any such strips of paper thrown at a celebrating procession. [imit.]

tick *n.* (*sl.*) credit. **-give tick,** sell on credit. [ticket]

tick'et *n.* card or paper entitling to admission, travel, *etc.*; label. *-v.t.* attach a label to. [F. *étiquette*, label]

tickle *v.i.* itch. *-v.t.* make itch with light touches, *etc.* **-tick'lish** *a.* sensitive to tickling; requiring care or tact in handling. [orig. uncertain]

tide *n.* season or time; rise and fall of the sea happening twice each lunar day; stream. *-v.i.* tide over, get over or surmount. *-v.t.* enable someone to do this. - **ti'dal** *a.* of or resembling a tide. **ti'dal pow'er** *n.* the use of the rise and fall of tides involving very large volumes of water at low heads to generate electric power. [OE. *tid*, time]

ti'dings *n.* news; happenings; a report. [fr. *betide*]

ti'dy *a.* orderly, neat. *-v.t.* put in order. [orig.]

timely. *See* **tide**

tie *v.t.* fasten, bind; restrict. *-n.* that with which anything is bound; cravat; bond; drawn game with equal points; match. [OE. *teag* n.; *tigan* v.]

tier *n.* row, rank, *esp.* rising in a series. [F. *tirer*, draw]

tiff *n.* slight quarrel, huff. [imit.]

tiff'in *n.* slight quarrel, huff. [imit.]

tiff'in *n.* light refreshments in the East, *esp.* of curried dishes and fruit; lunch. [Anglo-Ind.]

ti'ger *n.* large carnivorous animal with striped coat. **-ti'gress** *fem.* [G. *tigris*]

tight *a.* firm; tense, taut; fitting close; not allowing the passage of water, *etc.*; (*colloq.*) drunk. **-tights** *n. pl.* tight-fitting elastic garments. **-tight'en** *v.t.* and *i.* **tight'ly** *adv.* [ON. *thettr*, watertight]

tile *n.* slab of baked clay, porcelain, *etc.* *v.t.*

cover with tiles. [L. *tegula*]

fill *n.* drawer for money in a shop. [orig. uncertain]

tilt *v.t.* cultivate. **-till'er** *n.* lever to move a rudder of a boat. [OF. *telier,* weaver's beam]

tilt *n.* canvas cover or hood for a wagon; stern-sheets of boat, *etc.* [orig. uncertain]

tilt *v.t.* and *i.* slope, slant. *-n.* inclination from the vertical. [OE. *tealt,* unsteady]

tilt *v.i.* take part in a medieval combat with lances, joust. *-n.* combat for mounted men with lances. [orig. uncertain]

tim'ber *n.* wood for building, *etc.* **tim'bered** *a.* made or partly made of wood. [OE. = house or material suitable to make one]

timbre n. distinctive quality of musical sound. [F.]

tim'brel *n.* ancient musical instrument, kind of tambourine. [OF. *timbre*]

time *n.* existence as a succession of states; hour; duration; period; point in duration. *-v.t.* choose or note the time of. **-time'ly** *a.* seasonable. **-time'ous** *a.* opportune, seasonable. **-time'piece** *n.* watch or clock. **-time'-honored** *a.* respected because old. **-time'scale** *n.* span of time within which certain events occur or are scheduled to occur considered in relation to any broader period of time. **time-ser'ver** *n.* opportunist. **-timeswitch** *n.* electric switch that can be set to operate an appliance, such as a light or an oven, at a particular time. **-time warp** *n.* imagined distortion of the progress of time so that it is not governed by its usual rules and, for instance, events from the past may appear to be happening in the present. **-timetable** *n.* schedule of times, *e.g.*, of working hours, trains, *etc.* [OE. *tima*]

tim'id *a.* diffident; lacking courage. **timid'ity** *n.* **-tim'idly** *adv.* **-tim'orous** *a.* timid. [L. *timidus*, fr. *timere,* fear]

tim'pani *n. pl.* orchestral kettle drums. (G. *tympanon*, drum]

tin *n.* malleable white metal; vessel of tin or tinned iron. *-v.t.* coat with tin; put in a tin, *esp.* for preserving (food). **-tinn'y** *a.* of sound, light and unmusical, like clash of tin. [OE.]

tinc'ture *n.* color, stain; solution of a medical substance. *-v.t.* color, imbue. [L. *tingere, tinct-*, dye]

tin'der *n.* dry easily-burning material used to catch a spark from flint and steel. [OE. *tynder-tendan*, kindle]

tine *n.* tooth, spike offork, antler, harrow, *etc.* [OE. *tind*]

tinge *v.t.* color or flavor slightly. *-n.* slight trace. [L. *tingere,* dye]

tingle *v.i.* vibrate; thrill; feel 'pins and needles' [var. of *tinkle*]

tink'er *n.* mender of pots and pans. *-v.i.* work in clumsy or amateur fashion. [fr. noise of his work]

tin'kle *v.i.* give out a series of light sounds like a small bell. *-v.t.* cause to do this. *-n.* sound or action of this. [imit.]

tin'sel *n.* thin metal plates, cord, *etc.*, for decoration; anything sham and showy. [F. *étincelle*, spark]

tint *n.* color; tinge. *-v.t.* dye, give a tint to. [L. *tingere*, dye]

tintinnabulation *n.* sound of bells. [L. *tintinnabuium*, bell]

ti'ny *a.* very small. [orig. uncertain]

tip *n.* slender or pointed end of anything; piece of metal, leather, *etc.*, protecting or softening a tip. *-v.t.* put a tip on. **tip'staff** *n.* sheriffs officer, who carried a tipped staff. **-tip'toe** *v.i.* walk on one's toes. **-tiptop'** *a.* of the best quality or highest degree. [of Teut. orig.]

tip *n.* small present of money; piece of useful private information. *-v.t.* give a tip to. **-tip'ster** *n.* one who sells tips about races. [orig. a *cant* word]

tip *v.t.* upset. *-v.i.* topple over. *-n.* place for tipping carts, emptying out rubbish, *etc.* **-tip'-cat** *n.* game in which a spindle of wood is struck into the air by hitting one of the pointed ends with a stick; the piece of wood struck. [orig. type. of unknown orig.]

tip *v.t.* touch lightly. *-n.* children's game in which a pursuer touches one of the others pursued, who then becomes the pursuer. [var. of *tap*]

tipp'et *n.* covering for the neck and shoulders. [dim. of *tip,* point (orig. the point of a hood)]

tip'ple *v.i.* take strong drink habitually to excess. *-v.t.* drink. *-n.* drink. **-tipp'ler** *n.* [orig. uncertain]

tip'sy *a.* drunk or partly drunk. **-tip'sy cake** *n.* wine-soaked cake with custard sauce. [fr. *tip*, upset]

tirade' *n.* long speech, generally vigorous and hostile; harangue. [It. *tirata*, volley]

tire *n.* and *v.* attire; rim of metal, rubber, *etc.*, round a wheel. *-v.t.* put one on. [attire]

tire *v.i.* become weary or fatigued. *-v.t.* fatigue. **-tire'some** *a.* wearisome, irritating. [OE. *tiorian*, exhaust]

ti'ro, tyro *n.* beginner, novice. [L. *raw* recruit]

tiss'ue *n.* fine woven fabric *esp.* of gold or silver; substance of an animal body, of a plant, *etc.* **-tiss'ue-paper** *n.* very thin paper. [F. *tissu*, woven]

tit *n.* in 'tit for tat,' giving like for like. [earlier *tip* for *tap*, blow for blow]

tit *n.* varieties of small birds, usually in combination, *e.g.* tomtit, bluetit; small horse. **-tit'bit'** *n.* toothsome morsel [ON. *tittr*, titmouse]

tit *n.* teat; (*sl.*) breast [F. *tette*]

Tita'nia (ti-ta'ni-a) *n.* queen of fairyland, wife of Oberon. [L.]

titan'ic (ti-) *a.* huge, gigantic. [G. *Titanes*, family of giants]

tithe (-TH) *n.* tenth part, *esp.* of agricultural produce paid as a tax. -*v.t.* exact tithes from. [OE. *teotha*, tenth]

tit'illate *v.t.* tickle, stimulate agreeably. - **titilla'tion** *n.* [L. *titillare*]

tit'ivate *v.i.* (*sl.*) to smarten up; to adorn. [orig. unknown]

ti'tle *n.* heading, name of a book; name, appellation; legal right or document proving it. **-tit'le deed** *n.* document confirming ownership. **-ti'tle page** *n.* page at beginning of book bearing title, author's name and publishers' imprint. [L. *titulus*]

tit'mouse *n.* small bird. [OE. *mase*]

titt'er *v.i.* giggle or laugh in a suppressed way. -*n.* such laugh. [imit.]

tit'tle *n.* whit, detail. [L. *titulus*, title, small stroke as part of a letter]

tit'tle-tat'tle *n.* gossip. -*v.i.* gossip. [redupl. of obs. *tittle*, prate]

tit'ular *a.* so in name or title only; held by virtue of a title. [*See* **title**]

to *prep.* towards, in the direction of, as far as; used to introduce a comparison, ratio, indirect object, infinitive mood, *etc.* -*adv.* to the required or normal state or position. **-to-do'** *n.* fuss, commotion. [OE.]

toad *n.* animal like a frog. **-toad'stool** *n.* fungus like a mushroom, but usually poisonous. **-toad'y** *n.* one who fawns or curries favor unworthily. -*v.i.* do this. **toad'-eater** *n.* sycophant. [OE. *tadige*]

toast *v.t.* brown at the fire; warm; drink the health of. -*n.* slice of bread browned at the fire; a health; person toasted. - **toast'master** *n.* one whose duty is to announce toasts at a banquet. [OF. *toster*, fr. L. *torrere, tort-*, parch]

tobacco *n.* plant of which the leaves are used for smoking; prepared leaves. **tobacc'onist** *n.* dealer in tobacco. [Sp. *taboco*]

tobog'gan *n.* sledge for sliding down a slope of snow or ice. -*v.i.* slide on one. [Canadian Ind. *tobakun*]

tocca'ta *n.* pious, organ composition designed to exhibit the player's technique, [It. *toccare*, touch]

toc'sin *n.* alarm rung on a bell. [F.]

today' *n.* this day; present time. -*adv.* on this day. [*to* and *day*]

toddle *v.i.* walk with unsteady short steps. -*n.* a toddling. **-todd'ler** *n.* little child. [orig. uncertain]

todd'y *n.* sweetened mixture of whiskey, hot water, *etc.* [Anglo-Ind.]

toe *n.* digit of the foot. -*v.t.* reach or touch with the toe. [OE. *ta*]

toff'ee *n.* sweetmeat made of boiled sugar, *etc.* [orig. uncertain]

to'ga *n.* mantle of a Roman citizen. [L.]

togeth'er *adv.* in company, simultaneously. [OE. *togoedere*]

togs *n. pl.* (*sl.*) clothes. [L. *toga*]

toil *v.i.* labor. -*n.* heavy work or task. **toil'some** *a.* **-toil'-worn** *a.* [OF. *touillier*, fr. L. *tudiculare*, stir]

toil'et *n.* process of dressing; articles used in this; manner of doing it, style of dress; dressing-table; cover for it; lavatory. [F. *toilette*]

toils *n. pl.* nets for catching game. [F. *toile*, fr. L. *tela*, cloth, web]

to'ken *n.* sign or object used as evidence; symbol. **-to'ken pay'ment,** nominal payment as symbol only. **-to'ken strike',** workmen's strike intended merely as a gesture. [OE. *tæn*]

tol'erate *v.i.* put up with. **-tolera'tion** *n.* **-tol'erable** *a.* **tolerably** *adv.* **tol'erant** *a.* disinclined to interfere with others ways or opinions. **-tol'erance** *n.* **tol'erantly** *adv.* [L. *tolerare*]

toll *n.* tax, *esp.* for the use of a bridge or road. **-toll gate.** [OE.]

toll *v.t.* make (a bell) ring slowly at regular intervals; announce a death thus. -*v.i.* ring thus. -*n.* action or sound of tolling. [obs. *toll*, draw, pull]

tomahawk *n.* fighting axe as used by Amer. Indians. -*v.t.* strike or kill with one. [N. Amer. Ind.]

toma'to *n.* plant with bright red yellow, fruit; the fruit, [Mex. *tomatl*]

tomb *n.* grave or monument over one. [G. *tymbos*, funeral mound]

tom'bola *n.* kind of lottery. [It.]

tom'boy *n.* romping boyish girl. [*Tom* and *boy*]

tom'-cat *n.* male cat. [Tom]

tome *n.* volume, large ponderous book,

[G. *tomos*]

tomfoolery *n.* clowning, buffoonery; trifling. [*Tom*]

tomm'y-gun *n.* light, short-barrelled quick-firing gun. [J. T. *Thompson*, inventor]

tomorr'ow *n.* day after to-day. *adv.* on the next day after this one. [*morrow*]

ton (tun) *n.* measure of weight, 20 cwt.; unit of a ship's carrying capacity. **tonn'age** *n.* carrying capacity; charge per ton; ships. [var. of *tun*]

ton'do *n.* round painting, carved relief, or other work of art.

tone *n.* quality of musical sound quality of voice, color, *etc.*; healthy condition. *-v.t.* give a tone to. **-ton'ic** *a.* relating to tone; improving bodily tone. *-n.* medicine to do this. **-ton'ic sol-fa'**, system of musical notation by means of syllables with dots and dashes, *etc.* [G. *tonos*, tension]

tongs (-z) *n. pl.* large pincers, *esp.* for handling coal, *etc.* [OE. *tang*]

tongue (tung) *n.* muscular organ inside the mouth, used for speech, taste, *etc.*; various things shaped like this; speech; language. [OE. *tunge*]

tonight' *n.* this night; the coming night. *-adv.* on this night. [*night*]

tonn'eau *n.* back of body of motorcar. [F. *cask*]

ton'sil *n.* gland at the side of the throat. **ton'sillitis** *n.* inflammation of the tonsils. [L. *tonsillce* pl.]

ton'sure *n.* shaving of part of the head as a religious or monastic practice; the part shaved. [L. *tondere, tons-*, shear]

ton'tine *n.* annuity paid to subscribers or the survivor(s). [*Tonti*, Italian banker]

too *adv.* in addition; in excess, more than enough; also. [stressed form of **to**]

tool *n.* implement or appliance for mechanical operations. *-v.t.* work on with a tool. [OE. *tol*]

toot *n.* sound of a horn. *-v.t.* and *i.* make it [Du. *tuiten*, blow a horn]

tooth *n.* **teeth** *pl.* ivory process of the jaw; anything resembling this. **-tooth'some** *a.* pleasant to eat. [OE. *toth*]

top *n.* highest part; platform on a ship's mast. *-v.t.* cut off, put on, pass, or reach, a top. **-top'hole** *a.* (*sl.*) first-rate **top'most** *a.* **-top'ping** *a.* (*sl.*) excellent. **top' se'cret** *n.* secret known only in high places. [OE.]

top *n.* toy which spins on a point. [orig. uncertain]

to'paz *n.* precious stone of various colors; humming bird. [G. *topazos*]

tope *v.i.* drink to excess habitually. **to'per** *n.* [F. *toper*, clinch a bargain (or 'wet'it)]

to'piary *a.* (of shrubs) shaped, made ornamental by cutting. [G. *topos*, place]

top'ic *n.* subject of a discourse or conversation. **-top'ical** *a.* of a topic; up-to-date, having news value. [G. *topos*, place]

topog'raphy *n.* description of a place; its features. **-topograph'ic** *a.* **-topograph'ically** *adv.* **-topog'rapher** *n.* [G. *topos*, place]

top'ple *v.i.* fall over. [top]

top'sy-turv'y *a.* upside down; in a state of confusion. [orig. uncertain]

toque *n.* woman's close-fitting brimless hat. [F.]

torch *n.* twist of bemp, *etc.*, soaked in tar or oil to burn as a portable light. **torch'light** *n.* **-torch'bearer** *n.* [F. torche]

toreador' *n.* bull-fighter, *esp.* one who fights on horseback. [Sp.]

tor'ment *n.* suffering or agony of body or mind. **-torment'** *v.t.* afflict; tease. **torment'or** *n.* [L. *tormentum*]

torna'do *n.* whirlwind; violent storm. [Sp. *tronada*, fr. *tronar*, to thunder]

torpe'do *n.* fish which gives out an electric discharge; cigar-shaped missile filled with explosives and propelling itself underwater by compressed air engines after discharge from a ship. *-v.t.* strike or sink with a torpedo. **-torpe'do-boat** *n.* (*usu.* destroyer) [L. = *numbness*; cramp-fish]

tor'pid *a.* sluggish, dormant. **-torpid'ity** *n.* **-tor'por** *n.* torpid state. [L. *torpere*, be torpid]

torque (tork) *n.* collar or like ornament of twisted gold or metal; in mechanics, rotating or twisting forces. **-torque'-rod** *n.* (motoring) rod fitted to live axle to prevent its twisting round with drive. **torque' tube** *n.* (motoring) tube enclosing propeller shaft. [L. *torquire*, twist]

torr'ent *n.* rushing stream. **-torren'tial** *a.* [L. *torrens, torrent-*, boil]

torr'id *a.* hot, scorching; dried up with heat. [L. *torrere*, burn or boil]

tor'sion *n.* twist. [L, *torquere*, twist]

tort *n.* breach of legal duty. [F.]

tort'ellini *n.* small, rounded pieces of pasta dough filled with cheese or chopped meat, served with tomato, cheese, or cream sauce.

tort'uous *a.* winding, twisting, not straightforward. [L. *torquere*, twist]

tor'toise *n.* four-footed reptile covered with a shell of horny plates. [Late L. *tortuca*]

tort'ure *n.* infliction of severe pain. -*v.t.* subject to torture. **-tort'urer** *n.* **tort'ure-chamber** *n.* [L. *torquere,* twist]

Tor'y *n.* political conservative or die-hard. [Ir. *toraidhe,* robber]

toss *v.t.* throw up or about. -*v.i.* be thrown, or fling oneself, about. -*n.* act of tossing. **-toss'pot** *n.* toper. [orig. uncertain]

tot *n.* very small thing; small quantity, *esp.* of a drink; tiny child. [orig. uncertain]

tot *v.t.* add up. -*v.i.* (with up) amount to. -*n.* addition sum. [orig. uncertain]

to'tal *n.* whole amount. -*a.* complete, entire. -*v.t.* add up; amount to. **-total'ity** *n.* **-totaliza'tor** *n.* machine which registers total **totalita'rian** *a.* of a government, in complete control of the nation's resources. (L. *totus,* all]

to'tem *n.* tribal badge or emblem, usually an animal. **-totem'ic** *a.* [N. Amer. Ind., hereditary emblem]

tatter *v.i.* walk unsteadily, begin to fall [orig. uncertain]

tou'can (too'-) *n.* S. American bird with very large beak. [Brazilian *tucana*]

touch (tuch) *v.t.* put the hand on, come into contact with; reach; move the feelings of (*sl.*) borrow from. -*v.i.* call; (with on) refer to. -*n.* a touching; slight blow, stroke, contact, amount, *etc.* **-touch' wood** *n.* tinder. **-touch'stone** *n.* stone for testing gold or silver. **-touch' paper** *n.* fuse for firing a charge. [F. *toucher*]

touch'y (tuch'-) *a.* over-sensitive, easily offended. [earlier *tetchy,* fr. OF. *entechio*]

tough (tuf) *a.* strong and pliable, not brittle; sturdy; difficult; needing effort to bite. **-tough'ness** *n.* **-tough'en** *v.t.* and *i.* [OE. *toh*]

toupee' *n.* false hair, wig. [F.]

tour *n.* a traveling round. -*v.t.* travel through. -*v.i.* travel. **-tour'ist** *n.* one who travels for pleasure. [F. fr. *tourner,* turn]

tournament *n.* a meeting for knightly contests; a meeting for games or athletic contests. **-tour'ney** *n.* a tournament. [F. *tournoyer,* fr. *tourner,* turn]

tourniquet *n.* bandage which can be tightened by twisting a crosspiece put through it to stop bleeding. [P.]

tou'sle *v.t.* disorder. [fr. obs, *touse*]

tout *v.i.* solicit custom (*usu.* in an undesirable fashion). -*n.* one who does this. [OE. *totian,* look out for]

tow *n.* hemp or flax fiber. [OE.]

tow *v.t.* drag at the end of a reopen; a towing, being towed; vessel in tow. **-tow'age** *n.* [OE. *togian,* draw]

tow'ard *a.* docile (also **tow'ardly**). **-towards'** (tordz) *prep.* in the direction of. (also **toward'**). [OE. *toweard*]

tow'el *n.* cloth for wiping off moisture after washing. **-tow'eling** *n.* material used for towels. [OF. *touaille*]

tow'er *n.* tall building or part of a building; fortress. -*v.i.* rise aloft, stand very high. [F. *tour,* fr. L. *turris*]

town *n.* collection of dwellings, *etc.* larger than a village. **-town'ship** *n.* division of a county. [OE. *tun,* homestead]

tox'ic *a.* poisonous, due to poison. **-toxi'city, toxication** *n.* **-toxicol'ogy** *n.* science of poisons. **-tox'in** *n.* poison, *usu.* of bacterial origin. [G. *taxikon,* arrow poison]

toy *n.* plaything. -*v.i.* act idly, trifle. [Du. *tuig,* tools]

trace *n.* chain or strap by which a horse pulls a vehicle; track left by anything; indication; minute quantity. -*v.t.* follow the course or track of, find out; make a plan of, draw. **-tra'cery** *n.* interlaced or network ornament. **-tra'cer bull'et** *n.* bullet that indicates its course by a smoke or fire trail. [L. *trahere, tract-,* draw]

trache'a *n.* windpipe. **-trache'al, trache'an** *a.* [L. *trachia*]

track *n.* mark or line of marks, left by the passage of anything; path; course. *v.t.* follow up the track of, *esp.* in hunting. [F. *trac*]

tract *n.* space of land, *etc.*, area. [L. *tractus,* a stretching out]

tract *n.* pamphlet, *esp.* a religious one. **tract'ate** *n.* treatise. [L. *tractare,* handle]

tract'able *a.* easy to manage, docile. [L. *tractare,* handle]

trac'tion *n.* action of drawing. **trac'tion-engine** *n.* steam or motor engine for drawing; steam-roller. **tract'or** *n.* self-propelling agricultural implement, *e.g.*, plow. **-tract'orfeed** *n.* in computer technology, the automatic movement of a continuous roll of edge-perforated paper through the platen of the printer. [L. *trahere, tract-,* draw]

trade *n.* commerce, traffic; practice of buying and selling; any profitable pursuit; those engaged in a trade. -*v.i.* engage in trade. -*v.t.* buy and sell, barter. **trade'mark** *n.* distinctive mark on a maker's goods. **-tra'der** *n.* **-trades'man** *n.* shopkeeper; mechanic. **-trade u'nion** *n.* society of workmen for protection of their interests. **-trade'wind** *n.* wind blowing constantly towards the equator in certain parts of the globe. [LG. *cognate* with tread]

tradi'tion *n.* body of beliefs, facts, *etc.*,

handed down from generation to generation without being reduced to writing; process of handing down. -**tradi′tional** *a.* -**tradi′tionally** *adv.* [L. *traditio* a handing over]

traduce′ *v.t.* slander, calumniate. **traducer** *n.* [L. *traducere*, lead across]

traffic *n.* passing to and fro of pedestrians, vehicles, *etc.*, in a road or street, *etc.*; trade. -*v.i.* trade. -**trafficker** *n.* trader. [F. *trafic*]

trag′edy (-j-) *n.* drama showing the ruin or downfall of the principal character, dealing with the sorrowful or terrible side of life; this type of drama. -**trag′ic** *a.* of, or in the manner of, tragedy; (journalism) disastrous; appalling. -**trag′ically** *adv.* -**trage′dian** *n.* player in tragedy; **tragicom′edy** *n.* play with both tragic and comic elements. [G. *tragoidia*- lit. 'goat-song']

trail *v.t.* drag behind one; follow the track of. -*v.i.* be drawn behind; hang loosely. *n.* thing that trails; back end of a guncarriage; track or trace. -**trail′er** *n.* road vehicle drawn by an automobile, *esp.* one that is designed to serve as a dwelling, office, *etc.* when parked; film scenes shown as preliminary advertisement for a cinema film. [OF. *trainer*, tow]

train *v.t.* cause to grow in a particular way; educate, instruct, exercise; aim (a gun). -*v.i.* follow a course of training, *esp.* to achieve physical fitness for athletics. *n.* trailing part of a dress; body of attendants; fuse or trail of powder to a mine; line of railway vehicles joined to a locomotive; collection of vehicles, *etc.*, *esp.* in military use. -**trainee′** *n.* person being trained. [F. *trainer*, drag]

train′-oil *n.* whale-oil. [earlier *train*, Du. *traan*, tear, exudation]

trait *n.* distinguishing characteristic. [F. = *line*, stroke, feature]

trait′or *n.* one who betrays or is guilty of treason. -**trait′orous** *a.* -**trait′orously** *adv.* [L. *traditor*, fr. *tradere*, hand over]

trajectory *n.* line of flight of a projectile. [L. *trajicere, traject-*, cast across]

tram *n.* mining wagon-road; line of rails; truck running on rails; car for passengers running on rails laid through streets. **tram′car** *n.* -**tram′way** *n.* rails for trams in a street. [of LG. orig.]

tramm′el *n.* net; anything that restrains or holds captive. -*v.t.* restrain. [orig. uncertain]

tramp *v.i.* walk heavily, travel on foot, *esp.* as a vagabond or for pleasure. -*v.t.* cross on foot. -*n.* an act of tramping; walk; vagabond; cargo-boat. -**tram′ple** *v.t.* tread under foot. [of Teut. orig.]

trampoline *n.* tough canvas sheet stretched horizontally with elastic cords, *etc.* over frame for gymnastic, acrobatic use. [It. *trampoline*, springboard]

trance (-a-) *n.* state of suspended consciousness, *esp.* from rapture or ecstasy; catalepsy. [F. *transe*; (orig. passage from life to death)]

tranche (-onsh) *n.* portion or instalment of a usually large sum of money, such as a loan borrowed by a government. [Fr., *slice*]

tran′quil (-ng-kw-) *a.* calm, quiet. **tran′quilly** *adv.* -**tranquil′ity, tranquill′ity** *n.* -**tranquil′ize, tranquillize** *v.t.* -**tranquil′izer, tranquillizer** *n.* one that tranquilizes; drug used to reduce anxiety. [L. *tranquillus*]

trans- prefix, across, through, beyond. [L.] -**transact′** *v.t.* carry on or through; conduct (an affair, *etc.*). -**transac′tion** *n.* -**transcend′** *v.t.* exceed, surpass. **transcend′ent** *a.* -**transcend′ence** *n.* **transcendent′al** *a.* surpassing experience; super-natural; abstruse. -**trancendent′alism** *n.* -**transcribe′** *v.t.* copy out. -**trans′cript** *n.* copy. -**trans′ept** *n.* transverse part of a cruciform church: either of its arms. -**transfer′** *v.t.* make over; move from one place to another. **trans′fer** *n.* a transferring or being transferred. -**trans′ferable** *a.* -**trans′ference** *n.* -**transfig′ure** *v.t.* alter the appearance of, glorify. -**transfigura′tion** *n.* -**transfix′** *v.t.* pierce. -**transform′** *v.t.* change the shape or character of. -**transforma′tion** *n.* -**transform′er** *n.* (*elec.*) apparatus for transforming voltage of alternating current. -**transfuse′** *v.t.* convey from one vessel to another, *esp.* of blood from a healthy person to an ill one. -**transfu′sion** *n.* -**transgress′** *v.t.* break (a law); sin. -**transgres′sion** *n.* **transgress′or** *n.* -**tranship′** *v.t.* move from one ship, train, *etc.*, to another. **tranship′ment** *n.* -**tran′sient** *a.* passing away. -**tran′sience** *n.* -**tran′sit** *n.* passage, crossing. -**transi′tion** *n.* change from one state to another. -**transi′tional** *a.* -**tran′sitory** *a.* transient. -**translate′** *v.t.* move (a bishop) from one see to another; turn from one language into another. -**transla′tion** *n.* -**transla′tor** *n.* -**translit′erate** *v.t.* write in the letters of another alpbabet. -**translitera′tion** *n.* -**translu′cent** *a.* letting light pass, semi-transparent-**translu′cent** *n.* **transmigrate** *v.i.* of the soul, to pass into another body. -**transmigra′tion** *n.*

transmit' *v.t.* send or cause to pass to another place, person, *etc.* -**transmis'sion** *n.* -**transmitt'er** *n.* apparatus for transmitting, *e.g*, radio communications. - **transmute'** *v.t.* change in form, properties, or nature. -**transmuta'tion** *n.* - **transpar'ent** *a.* letting light pass without distortion, that can be seen through distinctly; obvious. -**transpar'ence** *n.* - **transpar'ency** *n.* transparence; a picture made visible by a light behind it. - **transpar'ently** *adv.* -**transpire'** *v.t.* exhale. -*v.i.* exhale; come to be known. **transpira'tion** *n.* -**transplant'** *v.t.* move and plant again in another place. - **transplanta'tion** *n.* -**transport'** *v.t.* convey from one place to another; carry into banishment; enrapture. -**trans'port** *n.* means of conveyance; ships, vehicles, *etc.* used in transporting stores; ship so used. -**transpose'** *v.t.* change the order of, interchange; put music into a different key. - **transpo'sal** *n.* -**transposi'tion** *n.* - **transubstantia'tion** *n.* change in essence or substance. -**trans'verse** *a.* lying across, at right angles. -**transom** *n.* cross-piece; lintel. [corrupt. of F. *traversin*, crosspiece]

trap *n.* snare, contrivance for catching game, *etc.*; movable covering for an opening, *esp.* through a ceiling, *etc.*; two-wheeled carriage; arrangement of pipes to prevent escape of gas, *etc.* -*v.t.* catch, entrap. -**trap'door** *n.* door in a floor or roof. -**trapp'er** *n.* [OE. *troeppe*]

trap *v.t.* caparison. -**trapp'ings** *n. pl.* caparison; equipment, ornaments. [F. *drop*, cloth]

trapeze' horizontal bar suspended from two ropes. [L. *trapezium*]

trapezium *n.* quadrilateral figure with two sides only parallel. -**trape'zoid** *n.* quadrilateral with no parallel sides. [G. *trapeza*, table]

trash *n.* worthless refuse; rubbish. **trash'y** *a.* -**trash'iness** *n.* [orig. uncertain]

trau'ma *n.* wound, injury; shock. - **traumat'ic** *a.* [G. = *wound*]

trav'ail *v.i.* labor or be in labor. -*n.* toil; pains of childbirth. [F. = *work*]

trav'el *v.i.* journey. -*v.t.* journey through. -*n.* journeying. -*pl* .account of traveling. -**trav'eler** *n.* -**trav'elogue** *n.* travel talk or film. [var. of *travail*]

trav'erse *v.t.* cross, go through or over; oppose. [F. *traverser*]

trav'esty *n.* comic imitation. -*v.t.* ridicule by a travesty. [F. *travestir*, disguise]

trav'olator, trav'elator *n.* a moving pavement for transporting pedestrians, as in an airport. [fr. *travel* and *escalator*]

trawl *n.* net dragged along the bottom of the sea. -*v.i.* fish with one. -**trawl'er** *n.* trawling vessel. [OF. *trailler*, drag]

tray *n.* shallow flat receptacle used for holding or carrying small articles; any similar utensil of metal, plastic, wickerwork, *etc.* [OE. *trig*]

treachery *n.* deceit, betrayal. **treach'erous** *a.* -**treach'erously** *adv.* [F. *tricherie*, OF. *trecherie*, trickery]

trea'cle *n.* unrefined molasses, thick syrup. -**trea'cly** *a.* of, like treacle. [OF. *triacle*, antidote against venom]

tread *v.t.* set foot on. -*v.i.* walk. *n.* a treading; fashion of walking; upper surface of a step, tyre, *etc.* -**trea'dle** *n.* lever worked by the foot to turn a wheel. [OE. *tredan*]

trea'son *n.* treachery; breaking allegiance. -**trea'sonable** *a.* constituting treason. -**trea'sonous** *a.* [F. *trahison*, fr. L. *tradition* handing over]

treas'ure (trezh-) *n.* riches, stored wealth or valuables. -*v.t.* prize; store up. **treas'urer** *n.* official in charge of funds. **treas'ury** *n.* place for funds or treasure, *esp.* of a state; govt. dept. in charge of the public revenue. -**treas'ure trove** *n.* treasure found hidden with no evidence of the ownership. [G. *thesauros*]

treat *v.t.* deal with, act towards; apply remedies to. -*v.i.* negotiate. -*n.* entertainment, pleasure given. -**treat'ise** *n.* book on a given subject. -**treat'ment** *n.* [F. *traiter*, fr. L. *tractare*, handle]

treat'y *n.* contract between states. [OF. *traiter* fr. L. *tractare*]

tre'ble (treb'l) *a.* threefold. -*n.* soprano voice; part of music for it; singer with such voice. -*v.t.* and *i.* increase three-fold. **treb'ly** *adv.* [L. *triplus*]

tree *n.* large perennial plant with a woody trunk; beam. [OE. *treow*]

tree struc'ture *n.* (*compute.*) database format using master records, linked to several subordinate records, each of which is linked to only one master record.

tre'foil *n.* plant with leaves in three parts like the clover. [L. *trifolium*]

trek *v.i.* journey by bullock-wagon; journey overland. [Du. *trekken*, drag]

trellis *n.* lattice or grating of light bars fitted crosswise. -*v.t.* screen or supply with trellis. [F. *treillis*]

trem'ble *v.i.* quiver, shake. -*n.* a trembling. [L. *tremere*, quake]

tremen'dous *a.* causing fear or awe; vast, immense. [L. *tremere*, quake]

trem'olo *n.* (*mus.*) tremulous effect on a sustained note, a shake. [L. *tremere,* quake]

trem'or *n.* a trembling. **-trem'ulous** *a.* quivering easily; timorous. [L. *tremere,* quake]

trench *v.t.* cut grooves or ditches in. *-v.i.* infringe. *-n.* long narrow ditch, *esp.* as a shelter in war. **-trench'ant** *a.* cutting, incisive. **-trench'er** *n.* wooden plate. **trench'erman** *n.* hearty eater. [F. *trancher,* to cut]

trend *v.i.* have a general direction. *-n.* direction or tendency. **-trend'setter** *n.* person or thing that creates, or may create, a new fashion. **-trend'setting** *a.* **-trendy** *a.* very fashionable; faddish. [OE. *trendan*]

trepan' *v.t.* kidnap, ensnare. [F.]

trepan' *v.t.* (*surg.*) remove a small piece of the skull to relieve pressure on brain. [F., fr. G. *trypan,* bore]

trepang' *n.* sea-slug. [Malay. *tripang*]

trepidation *n.* state of alarm; trembling from fear. [L. *trepidatio*]

tres'pass *n.* wrongdoing; wrongful entering on another's land. *-v.i.* commit trespass. [OF. *trespasser,* pass across]

tress *n.* lock of hair. (F. *tresse*]

tres'tle (*-sl*) *n.* bar fixed on pairs of spreading legs and used as a support. [OF. *trestel,* fr. L. *transtrum,* crosspiece]

trews *n.* (tartan) trousers. [Ir. *trius*]

triangle *n.* plane figure with three angles and three sides; percussion instrument. **-triang'ular** *a.* [L. *triangulum*]

tribe *n.* race or subdivision of a race of people. **-tri'bal** *a.* [L. *tribus]*

tribulation *n.* misery, trouble, affliction. [L. *tribulare,* oppress]

trib'une *n.* popular leader; speaker's platform; bishop's throne. **-tribu'nal** *n.* lawcourt; bench of judges, *etc.* [L. *tribunus,* protector of the commons]

trib'ute *n.* tax paid by one state to another; speech or act of homage. **trib'utary** *a.* paying tribute; auxiliary. *n.* stream flowing into another. [L. *tributum*]

trice *v.t.* pull up and secure with a rope. *n.* in a trice, in one pull, in an instant. [Du. *trijsen,* to hoist]

trick *n.* stratagem; feat of skill or cunning; cards played in one round. *-v.t.* cheat. **-trick'ery** *n.* **-trick'ster** *n.* **trick'sy** *a.* sportive; deceptive; crafty. **trick'y** *a.* crafty; ticklish. [ONF. *trique*]

trick *v.t.* deck, attire. (Celt. orig.]

trickle *v.i.* flow slowly or in drops. [for *strickle,* fr. *strike,* in sense of flow]

tri- *prefix.* three. [L. fr. *tres,* or G. *treis,* three] **-tri'color** *a.* three colored. *-n.* tricolor flag, *esp.* the French one. **tri'cycle** *n.* vehicle like a bicycle, but with three wheels. **-tri'dent** *n.* three-pronged fork. **-trienn'ial** *a.* happening every, or lasting, three years.

tri'fle *n.* insignificant thing or matter; pudding of sponge-cake, whipped cream, *etc.* *-v.i.* act or speak idly. **-tri'ffing** *a.* unimportant. **-tri'fler** *n.* [OF. *trufle,* mockery]

trigg'er *n.* catch which releases a spring, *esp.* to fire a gun, *etc.* [earlier tricker, Du., *trekker,* fr. *trekken,* pull]

trigonom'etry *n.* branch of mathematics dealing with the relations of the sides and angles of triangles. **trigonomet'rical** *a.* **-trigonom'eter** *n.* [fr. G. *trigonon,* triangle]

trill *v.i.* sing with a quavering voice. sing lightly. *-n.* such singing. [It; *trillare,* of imit. orig.]

tril'ogy *n.* series of three related dramas or novels. [G. *trilogia,* series of three tragedies]

trim *v.t.* prune; adjust, put in good order. *-v.i.* shuffle, act as a timeserver. *n.* order, state of being trimmed. *a.* neat, smart; in good order. [OE. *trymman,* arrange, make firm]

trinitrotol'uene (*abbrev.* **TNT**) *n.* a high explosive. [nitric acid, toluene]

trin'ity *n.* state of being threefold; three persons of the Godhead. **-trinitar'ian** *n.* and *a.* [L. *trinitas*]

trink'et *n.* small ornament for the person. [orig. uncertain]

trio. *See* under **triple.**

trip *v.i.* run lightly, skip; stumble. *-v.t.* cause to stumble. *-n.* light step; stumble; journey, excursion. **-trip switch** *n.* electric switch arranged to interrupt a circuit suddenly and disconnect power from a running machine so that the machine is stopped. [OF. *triper,* dance]

tripe *n.* stomach of a ruminant animal prepared for food; (*sl.*) rubbish. [F. *entrails*]

trip'le *a.* threefold. *-v.t.* and *i.* treble. **trip'ly** *adv.* **-trip'let** *n.* three of a kind. **tri'o** *n.* group of three; music for three performers, *etc.* **-tri'partite** *a.* having three parts. **-trip'licate** *a.* three-fold. *v.t.* make threefold. *-n.* state of being triplicate; one of a set of three copies. **triplica'tion** *n.* **-tri'pod** *n.* stool or stand, *etc.*, with three feet. **-trip'tych** *n.* carving or picture in three compartments. **tri'reme** *n.* three-banked galley. [L. fr. *tres,* three]

tri'sect *v.t.* to divide into three (*usu.* equal) parts. -**trisection** *n.* [L. fr. *tres*, three, *secare, sectu*, to cut]
trite *a.* hackneyed; worn out. [L. *tritus*, to rub]
triturate *v.t.* rub to powder. -**trit'uration** *n.* [L. *tritus*, rubbed]
tri'umph *n.* great success, victory; exultation. -*v.i.* achieve great success or victory; exult. -**triumph'ant** *a.* -**triumph'al** *a.* [L. *triumphus*]
tri'umvir *n.* one of three men joined equally in an office. -**trium'virate** *n.* [L. back formation fr. L. *trium virorum*, of three men]
tri'une *a.* three in one; *pert.* to Trinity. *n.* (L. *tri-* and *unus*, one]
triv'et *n.* an iron bracket or stand for putting a pot or kettle on. [OE. *trefet* fr. L. *tripes, triped-*, tripod]
triv'ial *a.* commonplace, trifling. **triviality** *n.* (L. *trivialis*]
tro'chee *n.* metrical foot of a long followed by a short syllable. opposite of *iambus* (*q. v.*) **troch'aic** *a.* [G. *trochaikos*, fr. *trechein*, run]
trog'lodyte *n.* cave-dweller. [G. *troglodytes*]
troll *v.t.* pass (cup) round; sing heartily. [orig. uncertain]
troll *n.* diminutive supernatural being in Scandinavian mythology. [ON.]
troll'ey *n.* form of small truck; pole and wheel by which a tramcar collects power from overhead wire. -**trolley bus** *n.* an omnibus which is similarly powered. [orig. uncertain]
troll'op *n.* untidy woman, slut. [orig. uncertain]
trom'bone *n.* large brass wind-instrument of which one part slides in and out of the other. [It.]
troop *n.* crowd of persons or animals; unit of cavalry. -*pl.* soldiers. -*v.i.* move in a troop. -**troop'er** *n.* a cavalry-soldier; state policeman. [F. *troupe*]
tropaeo'lum *n.* kinds of trailing flowering plants of S. America. [G. *tropaion*, trophy]
trope *n.* (*rhet.*) figurative expression, as metaphor, *etc.* [G. *tropos*, fr. *trepein*, turn]
tro'phy *n.* memorial of a victory, in war, sport, the chase, *etc.* [F. *trophée*]
trop'ic *n.* either of two circles in the heavens or round the earth where the sun seems to turn at a solstice. -*pl.* hot regions between the tropics. -**trop'ical** *a.* [*trope*]
troposphere *n.* lowest layer of Earth's atmosphere bounded by stratosphere. [G. *trope*, turning, *sphaira*, sphere]
trot *v.i.* of a horse, move at medium pace, lifting the feet in diagonal pairs; of a person, *etc.*, run easily with short strides. -*n.* action of trotting; a brisk, steady pace. -**trott'er** *n.* horse which trots; *(sl.)* foot; pig, sheep's foot for eating. [F. *trotter*]
troth *n.* faith. [var. of *truth*]
trou'badour *n.* strolling minstrel of medieval Provence. [F.]
trou'ble (trub'l) *v.t.* disturb, afflict. -*v.i.* be agitated or disturbed. -*n.* disturbance, agitation; inconvenience; distress; confusion. -**troub'lous** *a.* -**troub'lesome** *a.* [F. *trouper*]
trough (trof) *n.* long open vessel; hollow between two waves. [OE. *trog*]
trounce *v.t.* beat severely, thrash. **trouncing** *n.* [orig. uncertain]
troupe *n.* company of actors, acrobats, *etc.* -**troup'er** *n.* [F.]
trou'sers *n. pl.* two-legged outer garment with legs reaching to the ankles. [earlier *trouse*, Gael. *triuohas*]
trou'sseau *n.* outfit of clothing, *esp.* for a bride. [F.]
trout *n.* freshwater fish esteemed as food. [OE. *truht*]
trow *v.i.* trust; believe. [OE. *treowian*, trust]
trow'el *n.* small tool like a spade for spreading mortar, lifting plants, *etc.* [Late L. *truella*, small ladle]
troy-weight *n.* system of weights used for gold and silver. [fr. weight used at *Troyes* fair (France)]
tru'ant *n.* one absent from duty without leave, *esp.* a child so absent from school. [F. *truand*, vagabond]
truce *n.* temporary cessation of fighting. [*pl.* of OE. *treow*, agreement]
truck *v.t.* and *i.* barter; exchange. -*n.* barter; payment of workmen in goods; (*colloq.*) rubbish. -**truck farm** *n.* small farm specializing in growing vegetables for market. [F. *troquer*]
truck *n.* open vehicle for heavy goods; kind of barrow; disk at a masthead. -*v.t.* transport by truck. -**truc'kle-bed** *n.* small bed on castors which could be pushed under a larger bed. -**truc'kle** *v.i.* cringe, fawn. [G. *trochileia*, pulley]
truc'ulent *a.* ferocious, inclined to fight, belligerent. [L. truculentus]
trudge *v.i.* walk laboriously. -*n.* laborious walk. [earlier truss, pack (off)]
true *a.* in accordance with facts; faithful;

exact, correct. **-truth** (-oo-) *n.* state of being true; something that is true. **-tru'ism** *n.* self-evident truth. **tru'ly** *adv.* **-truth'ful** *a.* **-truth'fully** *adv.* [OE. *treow*, faith]

truf'fle *n.* edible fungus growing underground. [OF. *truffe*]

trull *n.* drab, trollop. [cp. Ger. *trulle*]

trump *n.* trumpet; Jew's-harp. [F. *trompe*]

trump *n.* card of a suit temporarily ranking above the others. *-v.t.* take (a trick) with a trump. *-v.i.* trump up, get up, fabricate. [earlier *triumph*]

trum'pery *a.* showy, but worthless. *-n.* worthless finery. [F. *tromperie*, deceit]

trum'pet *n.* metal wind instrument like a horn. *-v.i.* blow a trumpet or make a sound like one. *-v.t.* proclaim. . [F. *trompette*]

truncate *v.t.* cut short. [L. *truncare*, truncate, fr. *truncus*, trunk]

truncheon *n.* short thick club or baton; staff of office. [F. *troncon*, dim. of *tronc*, trunk]

trund'le *v.t.* roll. [OE. *trendel*, ring]

trunk *n.* main stem of a tree; person's body without or excluding the head and limbs; box for clothes, *etc.*; elephant's or other proboscis. **-trunk line** *n.* main line of railway, canal, telephone, *etc.* **-trunk road** *n.* main road. [OF. *tronc*, L. *truncus*, trunk]

truss *v.t.* fasten up, tie up. *-n.* support; bundle (of hay, *etc.*). [F. *trousser*, pack]

trust *n.* confidence, firm belief, property held for another; state of being relied on; combination of producers to do away with competition and keep up prices. *-v.t.* rely on, believe in. **-trustee'** *n.* one legally holding property on another's behalf. **trustee'ship** *n.* **-trust'ful** *a.* **-trust'worthy** *a.* **-trust'y** *a.* [ON. *traust*]

truth. *See* **true.**

try *v.t.* test; conduct a judicial enquiry; attempt; cause to suffer. *-v.i.* attempt something, endeavor. *-n.* attempt. **-tri'al** *n.* **-try-sail** *n.* small fore-and-aft sail set with gaff, storm sail. [F. *trier*, to sift]

tryst *n.* appointment to meet. [OF. *tristre*, hunting station]

Tsar. *See* **Czar.**

tset'se *n.* small African fly carrying germ of sleeping-sickness. [Bechuana]

tub *n.* open wooden vessel like the bottom half of a barrel; bath. *-v.t.* and *i.* bathe. [Du. *tobbe*]

tube *n.* pipe, long narrow hollow cylinder. **-tu'bular** *a.* [L. *tubus*]

tu'ber *n.* swelling on the roots of certain plants, *e.g.*, potato. **-tu'berous** *a.* [L. *lump*]

tu'bercle *n.* granular small tumor in consumptive lungs, *etc.*, **-tuber'cular** *a.* **tuberculo'sis** *n.* disease, *esp.* of the lung, marked by the presence of tubercles and a characteristic bacillus, *esp.* consumption of the lungs. [L. *tuberculum*, dim. of *tuber*, lump]

tu'berose *n.* plant with tuberous root and sweet-scented, creamy flowers. [L. *tuberose*, tuberous]

tuck *v.t.* gather or stitch in folds; draw or roll together. *-n.* stitched fold; food, *esp.* dainties eaten by schoolboys. [orig. *tug*, OE. *tucian*, illtreat]

Tues'day *n.* third day of the week. [OE. *Tiwesdoeg*, day of *Tiw*, Teutonic god of war]

tuft *n.* bunch of feathers, threads, *etc.* knot; cluster. **-tuft-hunter** *n.* hanger-on of important persons. [F. *touffe*]

tug *v.t.* pull hard or violently. *-n.* violent pull; steamship used to tow other vessels. [orig. obscure]

tui'tion *n.* teaching. [L. *twitio*]

tu'lip *n.* plant of the lily family with bright bell-shaped flowers. [OF. *tulipe*, fr. Pers. *dulband*, turban]

tulle *n.* diaphanous silk fabric. [*Tulle*, France]

tum'ble *v.i.* fall; turn somersaults. *-v.t.* throw down; rumple. *-n.* fall; somersault. **-tum'bler** *n.* acrobat; round-bottomed drinking-glass; variety of pigeon. [OE. *tumbian*, dance]

tum'brel, tum'bril *n.* tip-cart; military cart for ammunition; open cart which carried French Revolution victims to guillotine. [OF. *tomber*, fall]

tu'mid *a.* swollen, distended. [L. *tumere*, to swell]

tu'mor *n.* abnormal growth on the body. [L. *tumere*, to swell]

tu'mulus *n.* burial mound. **-tu'mular** *a.* [L.]

tu'mult *n.* uproar, commotion; confusion of mind. **-tumult'uous** *a.* [L. *tumultus*, fr. *tumere*, swell]

tun *n.* large cask. [OE. *tunne*]

tun'dra *n.* flat, treeless, marshy plains of *n.* Russia and Siberia. [Lapp]

tune *n.* melody; concord; adjustment of a musical instrument. *-v.t.* put in tons. **tune'ful** *a.* **-tune'fully** *adv.* **-tu'ner** *n.* [var. of *tone*]

tung'sten *n.* rare metal with high melting-point. **-tung'stic** *a.* [Sw. *tung*, heavy, *sten*, stone]

tu'nic *n.* short military coat; garment of

similar shape. [L. *tunics*]
tunn'el *n.* artificial underground passage. *-v.t.* and *i.* make a tunnel (through). -**tunn'eler** *n.* [OF. *tonel*, dim. of ME. *tonne*, tun]
tunny *n.* large edible sea-fish of the mackerel family. [F. *then*]
tup *n.* male sheep; striking face of steam hammer. [ME. *tupe*]
tur'ban *n.* man's headdress made by coiling a length of material round a cap or the head. -**tur'banned** *a.* [Pers. *dulband*]
tur'bid *a.* muddy, thick. -**turbid'ity** *n.* [E. *turbare*, disturb]
tur'bine *n.* kind of water-wheel; rotary steam or gas engine. [F.]
tur'bot *n.* large flat-fish used as food. [F., fr. O. Sw. *tornbut*, thorn butt]
tur'bulent *a.* riotous, in commotion. [F. -L. *turbulentus*]
tureen' *n.* dish for soup. [earlier *terreen*, F. *terrine*, earthenware pot]
turf *n.* short grass with the earth bound to it by the matted roots; sod. *-v.t.* lay with turf. [OE. = *sod*, peat]
tur'gid *a.* bombastic; pompous, inflated. -**turgidity** *n.* [L. *turgidus*]
tur'key *n.* large bird reared for food. [*Turkey-cock*, orig. the guinea-fowl, the present bird being American]
tur'moil *n.* confusion and bustle; disturbance; agitation. [orig. uncertain]
turn *v.t.* make move round or rotate; shape on a lathe; change, reverse, alter position of, *etc.* *-v.i.* move round; change; become, *etc.* *-n.* act of turning; walk; rotation; part of a rotation; performance; inclination; *etc.* -**turn'er** *n.* -**turn'coat** *n.* one who deserts party on principles. **turn'key** *n.* jailer. -**turn'over** *n.* act of turning over; in business, amount of money changing hands; kind of pie with top flapped over. -**turn'pike** *n.* gate across a road where tolls are paid, toll gate; toll road, or one formerly maintained as one; main road. -**turn'stile** *n.* revolving gate for controlling admission of people. -**turn'table** *n.* revolving platform. [L. *tornare*, fr. *tornus*, lathe]
turn'ip *n.* plant with a round root used as a vegetable or fodder. [*turn* and OE. *næp*, L. *napus*]
turp'entine *n.* resin got from certain trees; oil or spirit made from this. [L. *terebinthina*, resin of the terebinth]
turp'itude *n.* baseness. [L. *turpitudo*]
tur'quoise *n.* opaque blue precious stone. [F. = *Turkish*]
turr'et *n.* small tower; revolving tower for a gun on a ship, tank or fort. [OF. *tourete*, dim. of *tour*, tower]
tur'tle *n.* common wild dove. [OE.]
tur'tle *n.* sea-tortoise; its shell. -**turn'tur'tle,** capsize. -**tur'tleneck** *n.* closefitting turnover collar; sweater with such a collar. [corrupt. of F. *tortue*, tortoise]
tusk *n.* long pointed tooth sticking out from a mouth. -**tusk'er** *n.* animal with tusks fully developed. [OE. *tux*]
tus'sle *n.* struggle. *-v.i.* [dial *touse*]
tuss'ock *n.* clump of grass. -**tuss'ocky** *a.* [for earlier *tush*, bush of hair]
tuss'ore *n.* strong, fawn-colored Indian or Chinese silk. [Hind. *tasar*]
tut *interj.* exclamation of impatience, *etc.* [imit.]
tu'telage *n.* guardianship. -**tu'telary** *a.* protecting. [L. *tutela*]
tu'tor *n.* person giving lessons privately, or to individuals in a college; guardian. **tutor'ial** *a.* [L., fr. *tueri*, *tut-*, see to]
tuxe'do *n.* semi-formal dinner jacket. [*Tuxedo Park*, N. Y.]
twaddle *n.* talk not worth listening to. *v.i.* utter twaddle. -**twadd'ler** *n.* [earlier *twattle*, var. of *tattle*]
twain *a.* two. *-n.* a pair, couple; two persons or things. [OE. *twegen*]
twang *n.* ringing sound as of plucked string. *-v.i.* and *t.* make, cause to make, such sound. [imit.]
tweak *v.t.* pinch and twist or pull. *-n.* act of tweaking. [OE. *twiccian*]
tweed *n.* rough-surfaced woolen cloth, usually of mixed colors. [for *tweel*, var. of *twill*]
tweez'ers *n. pl.* small forceps or pincers. [earlier *tweeses*, *pl.* of obs. *twee*, F. *étui*, case for instruments]
twelve *n.* and *a.* cardinal number, two more than ten. -**twelfth** *a.* ordinal number. -**twelve'month** *n.* year. [OE. *twelf*]
twent'y *n.* and *a.* cardinal number, twice ten. -**twent'ieth** *a.* ordinal number. [OE. *twentig*]
twice *adv.* two times. [OE. *twiges*]
twid'dle *v.t.* twirl, play with. [imit.]
twig *n.* small branch. [OE.]
twig *v.t.* and *i* (*sl.*) comprehend. [Gael. *tuig*]
twi'light *n.* half light after sunset or before dawn. [*twi-*, two]
twill *n.* fabric woven so as to have a surface of parallel diagonal ridges. *v.t.* weave thus. [OE. *twili*]

twin *n.* one of a pair, *esp.* of children born together. *-a.* being a twin. [OE. *twinn*, twofold]

twine *v.t.* and *i.* twist or coil round. *-n.* string. [OE. *twin*]

twinge *n.* momentary sharp pain; (fig.) qualm, as of conscience. [OE. *twengan v.*]

twin'kle *v.i.* shine with dancing or quivering light. *-n.* twinkling; flash; gleam of amusement in eyes or face. **-twink'ling** *n.* instant. [OE. *twinclian*]

twirl *v.t.* and *i.* turn or twist round quickly, spin round. [orig. uncertain]

twist *v.t.* and *i.* make or become spiral, by turning with one end fast. *-n.* a twisting; something twisted. [OE.]

twit *v.t.* taunt. [OE. *ætwitan*, blame]

twitch *v.i.* give a momentary sharp pull; jerk. *-v.t.* pull at thus. *-n.* such pull or jerk; spasmodic jerk. [OE. *twiccian*, pluck]

twitt'er *v.i.* of birds, utter a succession of tremulous sounds. *-n.* such succession of notes. [imit.]

two *n.* and *a.* cardinal number, one more than one. **-two-faced** *a.* having two faces; insincere. **-two'fold** *adv.* and *a.* [OE. *two*]

tycoon' *n.* title applied (by foreigners) to the former hereditary commanders-in-chief of the Japanese Army; important business man. [Jap. *taikum*, great prince]

tympanums *n.* ear-drum. **-tympan'ic** *a.* of or like a drum. [L. fr. G.]

type *n.* class; characteristic build; specimen, block bearing a letter used for printing; such pieces collectively; state of being set up for printing. *-v.t.* print with a typewriter. **-type'script**, typewritten copy. **-type'writer** *n.* keyed writing machine. **-ty'pist** *n.* **-typ'ical** *a.* **-typically** *adv.* **-typ'ify** *v.t.* serve as a type or model of **-typog'raphy** *n.* art of printing; style of printing.

typhoon' *n.* violent cyclonic hurricane. [Chin. *tai fung*, big wind]

ty'phus *n.* contagious fever. [G. *typhos*, vapour]

ty'rant *n.* oppressive or cruel ruler. **tyrann'ical** *a.* **-tyrann'ically** *adv.* **tyrann'icide** *n.* slayer of a tyrant; his deed. **-tyr'annize** *v.i.* **-tyr'annous** *a.* **tyr'anny** *n.* [G. *tyrannos*, absolute ruler]

U

ubiq'uity *n.* being everywhere at the same moment. **ubiquitous** *a.* [L. *ubique*, everywhere]

U'-boat *n.* German submarine. [Ger. *unterseeboot*, under-sea boat]

udd'er *n.* mammary gland or milk-bag of a cow, *etc.* [OE. *uder*]

ug'ly *a.* unpleasing or repulsive to the sight; ill-omened; threatening. **-ug'liness** *n.* [ON. *uggligr*, fr. *uggr*, fear]

uh'lan *n.* German light cavalryman. [Ger. fr. *Tatar*]

ukulele *n.* four-stringed guitar. [Hawaiian]

ul'cer *n.* open sore. **-ul'cerate** *v.i.* form an ulcer. *-v.t.* make ulcerous. **-ul'cerous** *a.* **-ulcera'tion** *n.* [L. *ulcus, ulcer-*]

ul'ster *n.* **ul'ster-man's, ul'ster-woman's,** long caped overcoat. [*Ulster*]

ulterior *a.* situated beyond; beyond what appears. [L., compar. of *ultra*, beyond, on the other side]

ultimate *a.* last, farthest. **-ult'imately** *adv.* **-ultima'tum** *n.* final proposal the rejection of which causes war. **-ult'imo** *adv.* in last month. [L. *ultimus*, superl. of *ultra*, beyond]

ultramarine' *a.* beyond the sea. *n.* blue pigment. **-ultramont'ane** *a.* south of or beyond the Alps; favorable to the absolute authority of the Pope. **ultrason'ics** *n.* science of waves beyond the frequency of sound. **-ultravi'olet** *a.* beyond the violet (of rays of the spectrum). [L. *ultra*, beyond]

umbel *n.* flower cluster in which a number of stalks, each bearing a flower, radiate from a common center. [L. *umbella*, dim. of *umbra*, a shade]

um'ber *n.* dark brown pigment. [It. *terra d' ombra*, shadow (earth)]

umbilical *a.* of the navel. **-umbil'icus** *n.* [L. *umbilicus*]

um'brage *n.* sense of injury, offense. **umbrage'ous** *a.* shady. [L. *umbra*, shadow]

umbrella *n.* a light folding circular cover of silk, *etc.*, on a steel framework, carried in the hand to protect against rain. [L. *umbra*, shadow]

um'pire *n.* person chosen to decide a question; person chosen to decide disputes and enforce the rules in a game. *-v.i.* act as umpire in. *-v.i.* act as umpire. [ME. *nomper*, fr. F. *non pair*, not equal (*i. e.*, odd man called in when arbitrators disagreed)]

ump'teen *n.* (*sl.*) indefinite number, quite a lot. [*umpty*, morse for dash]

un- *prefix.* makes compounds negativing the idea of the simple words, *e.g.*, **unarmed'** *a.* not armed. **-unfast'en** *v.t.* loosen or remove the fastening. **untruth'** *n.* lie. These are only given where the meaning or derivation cannot easily be found from the simple word. [OE.]

unan'imous *a.* of one mind, agreeing. -**unan'imously** *adv.* -**unanim'ity** *n.* [L. *unanimus -unus*, one, *animus*, mind]

unassum'ing *a.* modest, not bold or forward. [*an-* and L. *assumere*]

uncann'y *a.* weird, mysterious. -**uncann'iness** *n.* [OE. *can*, know]

un'cate *a.* hooked. -**un'ciform** *a.* hook-shaped. -**un'cinal** *a.* [L. *uncus*, hook]

unc'le (unk'l) *n.* brother of a father or mother; husband of an aunt. [F. *oncle*, fr. L. *avunculus*, uncle on mother's side]

uncon'scious *a.* not knowing, unaware; insensible. -*n.* hidden or repressed part of thought. [*un-* and L. *conscius*]

uncout *a.* clumsy, without ease or polish. -**uncouth'ly** *adv.* -**uncouth'ness** *n.* [OE. *uncuth*, unknown]

unction *n.* anointing; soothing words or thought; fervor of words or tone; imitation of this; affected enthusiasm. -**unc'tuous** *a.* full of unction; greasy. [L. *unctio*, fr. *ungere, unct-*, anoint]

un'der *prep.* below, beneath; bound by, included in; in the time of. -*adv.* in a lower place or condition -*a.* lower. **underbred'** *a.* ill-bred. -**und'er-carriage** *n.* landing structure of aircraft. **undercharge'** *v.t.* charge less than the proper amount. -*n.* too low a charge. **underhand'** *a.* unfair, sly. -**underhung'** *a.* with the lower part projecting beyond the upper. -**un'derling** *n.* subordinate. **underneath'** *adv.* below. -*prep.* under. **underpass'** *n.* road or passage for traffic or pedestrians which passes underneath a highway or railroad. -**undershirt'** *n.* collarless garment for wearing underneath a shirt. -**un'dershot** *a.* moved by water passing under. -**un'der strapper** *n.* underling, subordinate. -**un'dertow** *n.* current beneath surface moving in a different direction from surface current; back-wash; and numerous other compounds of *under* which need no explanation. [OE. *under*]

undergrad'uate *n.* university student who has not yet taken a degree. [*graduate*]

und'erground *a.* subterranean; secret - **go und'erground**, of a political organization, continue its activities in secret. -*n.* **underground railway**. [*ground*]

und'erstand *v.t.* see the meaning of, infer; take for granted. -*v. i.* be informed. -*p.p.* **understood**. -**understand'ing** *n.* intelligence. [OE. *understanan*]

under'study *v.t.* study an actor's part so as to be able to take his place in emergency. -*n.* one who does this. [*study*]

undertake' *v.t.* make oneself responsible for; enter upon a task, *etc.* [ME. *undertaken*]

un'dertaker *n.* one who undertakes; one who manages funerals. [*under* and *take*]

un'derwrite *v.t.* agree to pay, take up shares in, *e.g.*, in marine insurance, *etc.* [trans. of *subscriber*]

un'dulate *v.i.* move in waves or like waves. -**undula'tion** *n.* -**un'dulatory** *a.* [L. *unda*, wave]

undu'ly *adv.* too much, excessively, wrongly, improperly. [*due*]

unfrock' *v.t.* strip a monk, priest, of his gown, *i.e.*, his office. [*frock*]

ungain'ly *a.* awkward, uncouth, clumsy [ON. *gegn*, convenient]

un'guent *n.* an ointment. -**ung'uentary** *a.* [L. *unguentum*]

ung'ulate *a.* having hoofs. [L. *unguis*, nail]

unhinge' *v.t.* take from hinges; unbalance, *esp.* mentally. [*hinge*]

u'nicorn *n.* a fabulous animal like a horse, with a single long horn. [L. *unicorns*, fr. *cornu*, horn]

uni- *prefix* one. [L. *unus*, one]

u'niform *a.* not changing, unvarying; conforming to the same standard or rule. -*n.* uniform dress worn by members of the same body, *e.g.*, soldiers, nurses, *etc.* -**u'niformly** *adv.* -**uniform'ity** *n.* [L. *uniformis*]

unify *v.t.* bring to unity or uniformity. **unifica'tion** *n.* [Med. L. *unificare*]

u'nion *n.* joining into one; state of being joined; result of being joined; federation. combination of societies, *etc.*; trade union. -**u'nionist** *n.* supporter of union. **u'nionism** *n.* [F.]

unique' *a.* being the only one of its kind. [F. fr. L. *unicus*]

u'nison *n.* agreement, harmony; sounding at the same pitch. [L. *uni* and *sonus*]

u'nit *n.* single thing or person; standard quantity. -**unitar'ian** (-ir-) *n.* member of a Christian body that denies the doctrine of the Trinity. -**unitar'ianism** *n.* [L. *unus*]

unite' *v. t.* join into one, connect. -*v.i.* become one, combine. -**u'nity** *n.* state of being one; harmony. -**Uni'ted Nations Organization** organization founded in 1945 for maintaining peace and settling international difficulties by arbitration. [L. *unire, -itus*, to unite]

un'iverse *n.* whole of creation, all existing things. -**univer'sal** *a.* relating to all things or all men; applying to all members of a community. **-univer'sally** *adv.* **-universal'ity** *n.* [L. *universus*, lit. 'turned to one,' *unus*]

univers'ity *n.* educational institution for study, examination and conferment of degrees in all or most of the important branches of learning. [L. *universitas*]

unkempt' *a.* of rough or uncared-for appearance. [OE. *cemban*, comb]

unless' *conj.* if not, except when; save. [for *on less*]

unru'ly *a.* badly behaved, ungovernable; turbulent. [*rule*]

until' *prep.* up to the time of. *conj.* to the time that; with a negative, before. [*See* **till**]

un'to *prep.* to. [*See* **to**]

untouch'able *n.* Hindu below the caste level. *-a.* [*touch*]

untoward' *a.* inconvenient; inopportune. [arch. toward, propitious]

unwield'y *a.* large and cumbersome; difficult to handle. [*wield*]

up *adv.* in or to a higher position, a source, an activity, *etc.*; quite. *-prep.* to or towards the source, *etc.* **-up'ward** *a.* and *adv.* **-up'wards** *adv.* [OE.]

up- as *prefix* makes compounds mostly of obvious meaning, *e.g.*, **upbringing** *n.* bringing up. **-uphold'** *v.t.* hold up, support, *etc.* **upbraid'** *v.t.* scold, reproach; reprove severely. **-upbraid'ing** *n.* abuse, reproach. **-upbraid'ingly** *adv.* [orig. uncertain]

UPC *n.* machine-readable code using parallel bars to represent digits, used for labeling consumer products. [*U*niversal *P*roduct *C*ode]

uphol'sterer *n.* one who provides carpets, hangings, or covers chairs, *etc.* **upholst'er** *v. t.* to put coverings on, supply carpets, *etc.* **-upholst'ery** *n.* [earlier *upholder*, in ME. a broker]

up'link *n.* communications connection for the transmission of radio or other ground signals to an aircraft, satellite, or spacecraft.

upon' *prep.* on. [OE. *uppon*]

upp'er *a.* higher, situated above. *-n.* upper part of a boot or shoe. [up]

upp'ish *a.* self-assertive. [up]

up'right *a.* erect; honest, just. *-n.* thing standing upright, *e.g.*, post in a framework. [right]

up'roar *n.* tumult, disturbance. **uproar'ious** *a.* **-uproar'iously** *adv.* [Du. *oproer*, stirring up]

upset' *v.t.* overturned. overturned. *-n.* an upsetting; trouble. **-up'set price** *n.* price below which goods at auction may not be sold. [*set*]

up'shot *n.* outcome, conclusion, final result. [orig. *deciding shot*]

up'start *n.* one suddenly raised to wealth, power, *etc.* [*start*]

ura'nium *n.* hard white radioactive metal. [*Uranus*, planet]

urbane' *a.* polished, courteous. **urban'ity** *n.* **-ur'ban** *a.* relating to a town or city. [L. *urbanus*, of a city, urbs]

urch'in *n.* sea urchin; hedgehog; mischievous boy; boy or youngster. [F. *hérisson*, fr. L. *ericius*, hedgehog]

Ur'du *n.* Hindustani. [for *zaban-i-urdu*, language of the camp]

urge *v.t.* drive on; entreat or exhort earnestly. *-n.* strong impulse. **-ur'gent** *a.* pressing; needing attention at once; importunate. **-ur'gently** *adv.* **-ur'gency** *n.* (L. *urgere*]

urine *n.* fluid secreted by the kidneys. **u'ric** *a.* **-u'ric a'cid** *n.* **-u'rinate** *v.t.* discharge urine. **-u'rinal** *n.* place for urinating. [L. *urina*]

urn *n.* vase with a foot and usually a rounded body. [L. *urna*]

ur'sine *a.* of, like, a bear. [L. *ursus*, bear]

urtica'ria *n.* nettle-rash. (L. *urtica*, nettle]

us *pron.* obj. case of *we*. [OE.]

use *n.* employment, applications to a purpose; profit, serviceableness; need to employ; habit. **-use** *v.t.* employ, avail oneself of, accustom. **-u'sable** (-z-) *a.* **u'sage** (-s-) *n.* act of using; custom; customary way of using. **-use'ful** (-s-) *a.* **-use'fully** *adv.* **-usefulness** *n.* **use'less** *a.* **-use'lessly** *adv.* **-use'lessness** *n.* **-u'sual** (z) *a.* habitually. **-u'sually** *adv.* [L. *usus*, use]

u'ser friend'ly *a.* easy to use, learn, or understand; easily operated, *usu.* with computers.

ush'er *n.* doorkeeper, one showing people to seats, *etc.*; formerly an underteacher. *v.t.* introduce, announce. [F. *huissier*, fr. L. *ostiarius-stium*, door]

us'quebaugh (-kwi-baw) *n.* whiskey. [Ir. and Gael. *iusge*, water, *beatha*, life]

usurp' *v. t.* seize wrongfully. **-usurp'er** *n.* **-usurpa'tion** *n.* [L. *usurpare]*

u'sury (-z-) *n.* lending of money at excessive interest; such interest. **u'surer** *n.* **-usu'rious** *a.* [L. *usura*]

utensil *n.* vessel or implement, *esp.* in domestic use. [L. *utensilis*, fr. *uti*, use]

u'terus *n.* womb. **-u'terine** *a.* [L.]

util'ity *n.* usefulness; useful thing. *a.*

serviceable. **-utilita'rianism** *n.* doctrine that the morality of actions is to be tested by their utility, *esp.* that the greatest good of the greatest number should be the sole end of public action. **utilita'ria** *a.* **-u'tilize** *v. t.* make use of. **-utiliza'tion** *n.* [L. *utilitas*, fr. *uti*, use]

ut'most *a.* extreme, farthest. -*n.* one's best endeavor. [OE. *ut*, out]

Uto'pia *n.* imaginary state with perfect political, social, concerns or constitution. **-Uto'pian** *a.* visionary. [Sir T. More's imaginary country (in book published 1516), fr. G. *ou*, not, *topos*, place]

utt'er *a.* complete, total. **-utt'erly** *adv.* [OE. *uttera*, compar. of *ut*, out]

utt'er *v.t.* express, emit audibly; put in circulation. **-utt'erance** *n.* uttering; expression in words; spoken words. [ME. *uttren*, fr. *adv.* utter]

u'vula *n.* pendent fleshy part of the soft palate. **-u'vular** *a.* [Med. L.) of *uva*, bunch of grapes]

uxorious *a.* excessively fon one's wife. [L. *uxorius*, fr. *uxor*, wife]

V

vacate' *v.t.* quit, leave empty. **-va'cant** *a.* unoccupied; without thought, empty. **va'cantly** *adv.* **-va'cancy** *n.* emptiness; situation unoccupied. **-vaca'tion** *n.* act of vacating; scheduled period when school is suspended; period away from work or home for recreation. [L. *vacare*, be empty]

vaccinate (-ks-) *v.t.* inoculate with vaccine *esp*, as a protection against smallpox. **-vaccina'tion** *n.* **-vac'cinator** *n.* **-vac'cine** *n.* virus of cowpox. [L. *vacca*, cow]

va'cillate (vas'-) *v.i.* waver. **-vacilla'tion** *n.* [L. *vacillate*, vacillate]

vac'uum *n.* place devoid of matter; place from which air has been practically exhausted. **-vac'uous** *a.* vacant. **-vacu'ity** *n.* **-vac'uum clean'er,** suction cleaner for sweeping, dusting, *etc.* [L. *vacuus*, empty]

vademe'cum *n.* manual, pocket companion. [L. = go with me]

vag'abon *v.t.* having no fixed dwelling. -*n.* wanderer; idle scamp. **vag'abona** *n.* [L. *vagari*, wander]

vagar'y *n.* freak; unaccountable proceeding. *pl.* **vagar'ies.** (prob. fr. L. *vagare*, to wander]

va'grant *n.* tramp. -*a.* on tramp; wandering idly. **-va'grancy** *n.* [OF. *walcrer*, wander]

vague *a.* indefinite; not distinct; mentally unprecise. **-vague'ly** *adv.* **vague'ness** *n.* [L. *vagus*, wandering]

vain *a.* worthless, useless; conceited; foolish. **-va'nity** *n.* [L. *vanus*, empty]

vainglo'ry *n.* self-glorification from vanity. **-vainglo'rious** *a.* [*vain* and *glory*]

val'ance *n.* short curtain round a bedstead, above window-curtains, *etc.* **val'anced** *a.* [orig. uncertain]

vale *n.* valley. [L. *vallis*]

valedic'tion *n.* farewell. **-valedic'tory** *a.* [L. *valedicere, valedict-*, say farewell]

va'lences, va'lency *n.* combining power of element or atom. [L. *valere*, be strong]

val'entine *n.* picture, set of verses, *etc.*, sent to a sweetheart on the 14th February; sweetheart chosen on that day. [St. *Valentine*]

valer'ian *n.* flowering herb used in medicine. [F. *valériane*]

val'et *n.* manservant looking after his master's clothes, *etc.* [F.]

valetud'inary *a.* sickly. **-valetudina'rian** *n.* person obliged or disposed to live the life of an invalid. [L. *valetudinarius*, fr. *valetudo*, state of health]

Valhall'a *n.* in Scandinavian mythology, place of immortality for heroes slain in battle. [ON. *valr*, slain, *holl*, hall]

val'iant *a.* brave. [F. vaillant]

val'id *a.* sound; binding in law. **valid'ity** *n.* **-val'idate** *v. t.* [L. *validus*, strong]

valise' *n.* traveling bag. [F.]

vall'ey *n.* (**vall'eys** *pl.*) low area between hills. [F. *vallee*]

val'or (-er) *n.* personal bravery or courage. **-val'orous** *a.* [OF. *valour*]

val'ue *n.* worth, price; equivalent. -*v.t.* to estimate a value of; to care for. **- val'uable** *a.* capable of being valued; of great value. -*n.* a valuable thing. **valua'tion** *n.* **-val'ueless** *a.* **-val'uer** *n.* [L. *valere*, be worth]

valve *n.* device to control the passage of a fluid, gas, *etc.*, through a pipe; thermionic valve (*q.v.*). **-val'vular** *a.* [L. *valva*, leaf of folding door]

vamp *n.* upper leather of a shoe. -*v.t.* and *i.* (*mus.*) improvise an accompaniment. [OF. *avanpie* (*i.e. avant pied*) part of the shoe covering the front of foot]

vamp'ire *n.* blood-sucking animal, person, ghost *etc.*; (*sl.*) person who preys on others. **-vamp** *n.* (*sl.*) a flirt. (Slav. *vampir*]

van *n.* leading division of an army or fleet. **-van'guard** *n.* [F. *avant-garde*, fr. *avant*, in front]

van *n.* covered road or rail vehicle, *esp.* for goods. [short for *caravan*]

vandalism *n.* barbarous destruction of works of art, *etc.*; malicious destruction or defacement of property. **-vandal** *n.* **-vandalize** *v.t.* [L. *Vandalus*, Vandal]

vane *n.* weather cock. [OE. *fana*, flag]

vanill'a *n.* plant of the orchid kind; extract of this for flavoring. [Sp. *vainilla*, small pod]

van'ish *v.i.* disappear. [L. *evanescere*, fr. *vanus*, empty]

van'ity *n.* worthless pleasure or display; conceit of one's appearance, ability, *etc.* [L. *vanitas*, *-atis*]

van'quish *v. t.* conquer. [OF. *vainquir*, fr. L. *vincere*]

van'tage (va-) *n.* advantage, *esp.* in lawn tennis; condition favoring success. [AF. *vantage*]

vap'id *a.* flat, dull, insipid; savorless. **vapid'ity** *n.* [L. *vapidus*]

va'por (-er) *n.* gaseous form of a substance more familiar as liquid or solid; steam or mist; invisible moisture in the air. **-va'porize** *a.* turn into vapor, fine mist. **-va'porous** *a.* [L. *vapor*]

var'icose *a.* of a vein, morbidly dilated. [L. *varicosus-varix*, dilated vein]

var'let *n.* page, attendant; pert rascal. [OF. dim. of *vassal*]

var'nish *n.* resinous solution put on a surface to make it hard and shiny. *-v.t.* apply varnish to. [F. *vernis*]

var'y (var'-i) *v.t.* change. *-v.i.* be changed; become different. **-var'iable** *a.* **-variabil'ity** *n.* **-var'iance** *n.* state of discord. **-var'iant** *a.* different. *-n.* different form. **-varia'tion** *n.* **-var'iegate** *v.t.* diversify by patches of different colors. **variegation** *n.* **-vari'ety** *n.* state of being varied or various; varied assortment; sort or kind. **-var'ious** *a.* manifold, diverse, of several kinds. [L. *varius*, various]

vase *n.* vessel, jar. **-vas'cular** *a.* of, or having, vessels for conveying sap, blood, *etc.* [L. *vas*, with dim. *vasculum*]

Vas'eline *n.* brand of petroleum which is a transparent yellowish semi-solid substance used in ointments, pomades, as a lubricant, *etc.* [Trademark]

vass'al *n.* holder of land by feudal tenure; dependant. **-vass'alage** *n.* [F.]

vast (-a-) *a.* very large. **-vast'ly** *adv.* **vast'ness** *n.* [L. *vastus*]

vat *n.* large tub. [OE. *foet*, cask]

Vat'ican *n.* collection of buildings, including the palace of the Pope, at Rome; the papal authority. [L. *Mons Vaticanus*, a hill in Rome]

vaudeville *n.* popular song, light theatrical production interspersed with comic songs; variety concert. [from F. *Vau* (*Val*) *de Vire*, in Normandy]

vault *n.* arched roof; arched apartment; cellar. *-v.t.* build with an arched roof. [L. *voluta*, turned]

vault *v.i.* spring or jump with the hands resting on something. *-v.t.* jump over in this way. *-n.* such jump. [F. *volter*]

vaunt *v.i.* boast. *-v.t.* boast of. *-n.* boast. [F. *vanter*]

veal *n.* calf flesh used as food. [OF. *veel*, fr. L. *vitulus*, calf]

Ve'da *n.* one of the four sacred books of the Hindus written in old Sanskrit. **-Ve'dic** *a.* [Sanskr. *veda*, knowledge]

vedette' *n.* mounted sentinel. [F.]

veer *v.i.* change direction (*e.g.*, wind); change one's opinion. [F. *virer*]

veer *v.t.* (*naut.*) slacken or let out (rope). [Du *vieren*]

veg'etable (-j-) *a.* of, from, or concerned with, plants. *-n.* plant, *esp.* one used for food. **-vegeta'rian** *n.* one who does not eat meat. **-vegeta'rianism** *n.* **-veg'etate** *v.i.* live the life of a plant. **vegeta'tion** *n.* plants collectively; the plants growing in a place; process of plant growth. (L. *vegetus*, lively, flourishing]

ve'hement *a.* forcefully eager, impetuous. **-ve'hemently** *adv.* **-ve'hemence** *n.* (L. *vehemens*]

ve'hicle *n.* carriage, cart, or other conveyance on land; means of expression; liquid which serves as medium for medicinal substances, *etc.* **-vehic'ular** *a.* [L. *vehiculum*, fr. *vehere*, carry]

veil *n.* piece of material to cover the face and head; pretext. *-v.t.* cover with, or as with, a veil. [L. *velum*]

vein (van) *n.* tube in the body taking blood to the heart; rib of a leaf or insect's wing; fissure in rock filled with ore; streak. *-v.t.* mark with streaks. **-ve'nous** *a.* [L. *vena*]

veld (felt) *n.* (*S. Africa*) open country, thinly wooded grassland. [Du. *veld*, field]

vell'um *n.* parchment of calf skin prepared for writing on or bookbinding. [L. *vitulus*, calf. *See* **veal**]

velocipede (-os'-) *n.* early bicycle without pedals, moved by striking the feet on the ground. [F.]

velo'city *n.* speed, rate of speed. [L. *velax*, *veloc*, swift]

velours' *n.* kind of hatter's plush; fabric

resembling velvet. [F.]

vel'vet *n.* silk fabric with a thick, short pile. **-vel'vety** *a.* smoothly soft like velvet. **-velveteen'** *n.* cotton fabric resembling velvet. [L. *villus*, nap]

ve'nal *a.* guilty of taking, prepared to take, bribes. **-venal'ity** *n.* [L. *veaalis*, fr. *venum*, that which is for sale]

vend *v.t.* sell; peddle. **-vend'or** *n.* **vend'ible** *a.* [L. *vendere*]

vendetta' *n.* blood-feud. [It.]

veneer' *v.t.* to cover with a thin layer of finer wood. *-n.* such covering. [earlier *fineer*, Ger. *furnieren*]

ven'erable *a.* worthy of reverence; aged; hallowed by age. **-ven'erate** *v.t.* **- veneration** *n.* [L. *venerari*, worship]

vene'real *a.* from, or connected with, sexual intercourse. [L. *venereus*, fr. *venus*, *vener-*, love]

vene'tian-blind *n.* window blind of thin slats of wood, slanted to admit light and air. [*Venice*]

veng'eance *n.* revenge, retribution for wrong done. **-venge'ful** *a.* **-venge'fully** *adv.* [F. *veneer*, fr. L. *vindicate*]

ve'nial *a.* pardonable. **-venial'ity** *n.* [L. *venia*, pardon]

ven'ison *n.* flesh of deer as food. [F. *venaison*, L. *venatio*, hunting]

ven'om *n.* poison, *esp.* of a snake; spite. **ven'omous** *a.* [L. *venenum*]

vent *n.* small hole or outlet. *-v.t.* give outlet to (*e.g.*, air, one's feelings, *etc.*) [F.]

ventilate *v.t.* supply with fresh air; bring into discussion. **-vent'ilator** *n.* **ventila'tion** *n.* [L. *ventilare*, fan]

ventricle *n.* cavity or hollow in the body, *esp.* in the heart or brain. **-ventric'ular** *a.* [L. *venter*, belly]

ventril'oquist *n.* one who can so speak that the sounds seem to come from some other person or place. **-ventril'oquism** *n.* **-ventrilo'quial** *a.* [*ventricle*]

venture *n.* undertaking of a risk, speculation. *-v.t.* risk. *-v.i.* dare; have courage to do something or go somewhere. **-ven'turesome** *a.* **-vent'urous** *a.* [ME. *aventure*, adventure]

ven'ue *n.* district in which a case is tried; meeting place; scene (of some event). [Med. L. *vicinetum*, area from which a jury was summoned]

veracious *a.* truthful. **-vera'city** (-as'-) *n.* [L. *verax, verac-*]

veranda, verandah *n.* open gallery or portico at the side of a house. [Port. *veranda*]

verb *n.* part of speech which asserts or declares. **-verb'al** *a.* of, by, or relating to, words. **-verb'ally** *adv.* **-verba'tim** *adv.* word for word. **-verb'iage** *n.* excess of words. **-verbose'** *a.* wordy. **-verbos'ity** *n.* [L. *verbum*, word]

verbe'na *n.* kinds of fragrant plant including wild vervain. [L.]

verdant *a.* green. **-verd'ure** *n.* greenery. [OF. *verd*, green, fr. L. *viridis*]

ver'dict *n.* decision of a jury; opinion reached after examination of facts, *etc.* [OF. *veir dit*, true word]

verdigris *n.* green rust on copper. [OF. *vert de Grece*, Greek green]

verd'ure. *See* **verdant.**

verge *n.* edge, brink. **-ver'ger** *n.* bearer of a wand of office; usher in a church. [L. *virga*, wand]

verge *v.i.* be on the border of, come close to. [L. *vergere*, turn]

ver'ify *v.t.* prove or confirm the truth of. **-verifi'able** *a.* **-verifica'tion** *n.* **ver'itable** *a.* true, genuine. **-ver'itably** *adv.* **-ver'ity** *n.* truth. **-ver'ily** *adv.* truly. **-verisimil'tude** *n.* appearance of truth, likelihood. [L. *verus*, true]

ver'juice *n.* sour fruit juice: [F. *verjus*]

vermicell'i *n.* Italian pasta of flour, *etc.*, made in long thin tubes. [It.]

verm'icide *n.* substance to destroy worms. **-verm'iform** *a.* shaped like a worm. **-verm'ifuge** *n.* substance to drive out worms. [L. *vermis*, worm]

vermil'ion *n.* bright red color or pigment. *-a.* of this color. [L. *vermiculus*, dim. of *vermis*, worm]

ver'min *n.* injurious animals, parasites, *etc.* **-ver'minous** *a.* [L. *vermis*, worm]

ver'mouth *n.* liqueur of wormwood. [L. *vermis*, worm]

vernac'ular *a.* of language, idiom, *etc.*, of one's own country *n.* mother tongue; homely speech. [L. *vernaculus*, domestic]

vern'al *a.* of spring. [L. *ver*, spring]

vern'ier *n.* small sliding scale for obtaining fractional parts of the subdivisions of a graduated scale. [*Vernier*, F. mathematician (d. 1637)]

ver'onal *n.* hypnotic drug. [G.]

ver'satile *a.* capable of dealing with many subjects. **-versatil'ity** *n.* [F.]

verse *n.* line of poetry; short division of a poem or other composition. **-ver'sify** *v.t.* turn into verse. *-v.i.* to write verses. **versifica'tion** *n.* [OE. *fers*]

versed *a.* skilled; proficient. [F. *versé*]

ver'sion *n.* a translation; an account or

description. [L. *vertere*, translate]

ver'so *n.* back of an object; left-hand page. [L. *vertere, vers-*, turn]

ver'sus *prep.* against. [L.]

vert'ebra *n.* single section of a backbone. **-vert'ebrate** *a.* having a backbone. **-vert'ebral** *a.* [L.]

vert'ex *n.* **-vert'ices** *pl.* summit. [L. *vertex, -icis*, summit]

vert'ical *a.* upright; overhead. [fr. L. *vertere*, to turn]

verti'go *n.* giddiness. **-verti'ginous** *a.* dizzy. [L.]

ver'vain *n.* wild verbena, much used in ancient magic. [OF. *verveine*]

verve *n.* inspired enthusiasm; life, vigor, *esp.* in creative work, [F.]

ver'y *a.* true, real. *adv.* extremely, to a great extent. [OF. *verai*, true]

Ve'ry light *n.* colored flare fired from pistol to illuminate, or as signal. [Samuel *Very*, inventor]

ves'icle *n.* small blister, bubble, or cavity. **-vesic'ular** *a.* (L. *vesica*, bladder]

ves'pers *n.pl.* evening church service. [L. *vesper*, evening star]

vess'el *n.* any utensil or appliance for containing, *esp.* for liquids; ship. [OF. *vaissel*, fr. L. *vas*, vase]

vest *n.* sleeveless garment worn beneath s suit coat, waistcoat. *-v.t.* endow. *-v.i.* be in a person's authority. **-vest'ment** *n.* robe or official garment. **-vest'ry** *n.* room attached to a church for keeping vestments, holding meetings, *etc.* **-vest'ure** *n.* clothing, a covering. [L. *vestis*, garment]

Ves'ta *n.* Roman goddess of the home. **ves'ta** *n.* kind of match. **-ves'tal** *a.* pure, chaste, of Vesta. [L.]

vestibule *n.* entrance hall, passage, or space between outer and inner doors. [L. *vestibulum*, porch]

vest'ige *n.* trace or mark. [L. *vestigium*, footprint]

vetch *n.* plant of the bean family used for fodder, *esp.* the tare. [L. *vicia*]

vet'eran *n.* person who has served a long time, *esp.* a soldier with much service. [L. *veteranus*]

veterinary *a.* of, or for, the diseases of domestic animals. **-veterinar'ian** *n.* one skilled in the medical treatment of animals. *n.* [L. *veterinarius*]

ve'to *n.* power of rejecting a piece of legislation, or preventing it from coming into effect; any prohibition. *-v.t.* enforce a veto against; forbid with authority. [L. = *I forbid*]

vex *v.t.* annoy or distress. **-vexa'tion** *n.* **vexatious** *a.* **-vexed** *a.* annoyed; much discussed. [L. *vexare*, shake]

vi'able *a.* born alive, capable of living and growing; practicable. [L. *vita*, life]

vi'aduct *n.* bridge over a valley for road or rail. [L. *via*, way]

vi'al, phi'al *n.* small glass bottle for holding liquids. [G. *phiale*, flat vessel]

vi'ands *n.pl.* food. [F. *viande*]

vi'brate *v.i.* move to and fro rapidly and continuously, oscillate, quiver. *-v.t.* cause to do this. **-vibra'tion** *n.* **-vibra'tor** *n.* **vibra'tory** *a.* **-vi'brant** *a.* [L. *vibrare*, shake]

vic'ar *n.* clergyman; deputy. **-vic'arage** *n.* vicar's house. **-vicar'ial** *a.* **-vicar'ious** *a.* done or suffered by one person on behalf of another. **-vicar'iously** *adv.* [L. *vicarius*, substitute]

vice *n.* fault or blemish; evil or immoral habit or practice. **-vi'cious** *a.* **-vi'ciously** *adv.* [L. *vitium*]

vice - *prefix.* **-vicere'gent** *n.* holder of delegated authority. **-vice'roy** *n.* ruler acting for a king in a province or dependency. **-vicere'gal** *a.* **-vice'reine** *n.fem.* viceroy's wife. **-viceroy'alty** *n.* [L. = *in place of*]

vice ver'sa *adv.* other way round. [L.]

vicinity *n.* neighborhood. [L. *vicinitas vicinus*, neighborhood]

vicissitude *n.* change of fortune. *-pl.* ups and downs. [L. *vicissitude*]

victim *n.* person or animal killed as a sacrifice; one injured by accident or so that an object may be gained by another. **-vic'timize** *v.t.* make a victim of- **victimiza'tion** *n.* [L. *victima*]

vic'tor *n.* conqueror or winner. **-vic'tory** *n.* winning of a battle, *etc.* **-victor'ious** *a.* **-victor'iously** *adv.* [L.]

victo'ria *n.* light horse-carriage with folding hood. [Queen *Victoria*]

victual (vit'l) *n.* (*usu.* in *pl.*) food. *-v.t.* supply with food. *v.i.* obtain supplies [L. *victualia*, fr. *vivere, vict-*, live]

vid'eo *a.* relating to vision or the transmission or production of television image. *-n.* apparatus for recording television programs and viewing pre-recorded video tapes. **-vid'eophone** *n.* telephonic device in which there is both verbal and visual communication between parties. **vid'eo tape** *n.* magnetic tape on which to record images for use in the video machine. [L. *videre*, to see]

vie *v.i.* contend, enter into competition. [OF. *envier*, challenge]

view *n.* survey by eyes or mind; picture; scene; opinion; purpose, *-v.t.* took at, examine, survey. **-viewless** *a.* invisible [F. *vue*]

vig'il (-j-) *n.* a keeping awake, a watch; eve of a feast day. **-vig'ilant** *a.* **vig'ilance** *n.* [L. *vigilia,* watchfulness]

vignette' (vin-yet') *n.* illustration in a book not enclosed in a definite border; portrait showing only head and shoulders with the background shaded off; slight word-sketch. [F.]

vig'or (-ger) *n.* force, strength, activity. **vig'orous** *a.* **-vig'orously** *adv.* [L. *vigor- vigere,* be strong]

vi'king *n.* Northern sea-rover of the 8th–10th c. [ON. *vikingr,* or perh. fr. OE. *wicing,* fr. *wic,* camp]

vile *a.* base, mean, bad. **-vil'ify** *v.t.* speak ill of. **-vilifica'tion** *n.* [L. *vilis*]

vill'a *n.* country or suburban house. (L. *manor*]

vill'age *n.* assemblage of dwellings in the country. **-vill'ager** *n.* dweller in a village. [L. *villa,* manor]

vill'ain (-in) *n.* feudal serf (also **vill'ein**); scoundrel. **-vill'ainous** *a.* **-vill'ainy** *n.* [Low L. *villanus*]

vim *n.* (*sl.*) vigor, force, energy. [L. *vis.* strength]

vinaigrette' *n.* savory sauce, *esp.* for salads; small bottle of smelling salts. [F.]

vin'dicate *v.t.* establish the truth or merit of, clear of charges. **-vindica'tion** *n.* **-vin'dicator** *n.* **-vin'dicatory** *a.* **vindic'tive** *a.* revengeful; inspired by resentment. [L. *vindicate,* avenge]

vine *n.* climbing plant which bears grapes: **-vine'yard** *n.* vine farm, or plantation of vines. **-vi'nery** *n.* greenhouse for grapes. **-vi'nous** *a.* of, or due, to wine. **-vin'tage** *n.* gathering of the grapes; the yield; wine of a particular year. **-vint'ner** *n.* dealer in wine. [L. *vinum,* wine]

vine'gar *n.* an acid liquid got from wine and other alcoholic liquors. [F. *vinaigre,* fr. *aigre,* sour]

vi'ol *n.* medieval instrument like a violin. **-violin'** *n.* fiddle. **-vi'ola** *n.* tenor fiddle. **-violoncell'o** (-chel'-) *n.* large bass violin. **-violin'ist** *n.* **-violoncell'ist** *n.* [F. *viole;* It. *viola*]

vi'ola *n.* single-colored variety of pansy. [L. = *violet*]

vi'olate *v.t.* outrage, desecrate; infringe. **-viola'tion** *n.* **-vi'olator** *n.* [L. *violare, violate-*]

vi'olent *a.* of great force; marked by, or due to, extreme force of passion or fierceness. **-vi'olence** *n.* **-vi'olently** *adv.* [F.]

vi'olet *n.* plant with a small bluish purple flower; the flower; color of it. *-a* of this color. [L. *viola*]

vi'per *n.* venomous snake. [L. *vipera*]

vira'go *n.* abusive woman. [L.]

vir'gin *n.* girl or woman who has not had sexual intercourse with a man. *-a.* chaste unsullied; fresh, untilled (of land). **vir'ginal** *a.* *-n.* kind of harpsichord. **virgin'ity** *n.* [L. *virgo, virgin-*]

Vir'go *n.* the Virgin, 6th sign of the zodiac, which sun enters about 22nd August. [L.]

viridesc'ent *a.* greenish, turning green. **-viri'dity** *n.* freshness, greenness. [L. *viridis,* green]

vir'ile *a.* manly; strong; procreative. **vir'ility** *n.* [L. *virilis,* fr. vir, man]

virtu' *n.* artistic excellence, objects of art or antiquity collectively. [It. *virtu,* virtue]

vir'tue *n.* moral goodness; good quality; inherent power. **-vir'tual** *a.* so in effect though not in name. **-vir'tually** *adv.* **vir'tuous** *a.* morally good; chaste. **vir'tuously** *adv.* **-virtuo'so** *n.* one with special skill in a fine art. **-virtuos'ity** *n.* such a skill. [L. *virtus*]

vi'rus *n.* poison; disease, infection. **vir'ulent** *a.* poisonous; bitter, malignant. **virulently** *adv.* **-vir'ulence** *n.* [L.]

vi'sa *n.* endorsement on passport to show that it has been examined, [F.]

vis'age (-z-) *n.* face; expression. [F.]

vise *n.* appliance with a screwjaw for holding things while working on them. (F. *vis.,* screw]

vis'cera (vis-e-ra) *n. pl.* internal organs; entrails. **-vis'ceral** *a.* [L.]

viscid *a.* sticky, of a consistency like treacle. **-vis'cose** *n.* form of cellulose used in making rayon. **-vis'cous** *a.* viscid. **-viscid'ity** *n.* **-viscos'ity** *n.* [L. *viscum,* birdlime]

vis'count (vi-kownt) *n.* peer of rank next above a baron. **-viscount'ess** *fem.* (Of. *visconte,* vice-count]

vis'ion *n.* sight. **-vis'ionary** *a.* unpractical, dreamy. *-n.* one full of fancies. **-vis'ible** *a.* that can be seen. **visibil'ity** *n.* **-vis'ibly** *adv.* **-vis'ual** *a.* of sight. **-vis'ual dis'play u'nit** (*abbrev.* **VDU**) *n.* screen attached to a computer on which the information is displayed. **vis'ualize** *v.t.* make visible; form a mental image of. **-visualization** *n.* [L. *videre, vis-,* see]

vis'it *v.t.* go, or come, and see. *-n.* a visiting. **-vis'itor** *n.* **-vis'itant** *n.* visitor. -

visita'tion *n.* formal visit or inspection; affliction or plague. [vision]

vi'sor, vi'sard, viz'ard *n.* movable front part of a helmet covering the face. [F. *visière*, fr. *vis*, face]

vista *n.* view, *esp.* between trees. [It., fr. L. *videre*, see]

vi'tal *a.* necessary to, or affecting life. **vi'tally** *adv.* **-vital'ity** *n.* life, vigor. **vi'talize** *v.t.* give life to. [L. *vita*, life]

vitamin *n.* factor in certain foodstuffs regarded as essential to life and health. [L. *vita*, life]

vi'tiate (vish'-), *v.t.* spoil, deprive of efficacy. **-vitia'tion** *n.* [L. *vitiare*]

vit'treous *a.* of glass; glassy. **-vit'rify** *v.t.* and *i.* **-vitrifac'tion, vitrification** *n.* [L. *vitrum*, glass]

vit'riol *n.* sulfuric acid; caustic speech. **-vitriol'ic** *a.* [Low L. *vitreous*]

vituperate *v.t.* abuse in words, revile. *-v.i.* use abusive language. **vitupera'tion** *n.* **-vitu'perative** *a.* [L. *vituperate*, vituperate, fr. *vitium*, fault]

vivacious *a.* lively, animated, gay. **-viva'city** *n.* [L. *vivax, vivac-*, fr. *vivere*, live]

viva'rium *n.* place to keep living creatures. [L.]

vivid *a.* bright, intense; clear, lively, graphic. **-viv'idly** *adv.* **-viv'ify** *v.t.* animate, inspire. [L. *vividus*]

viviparous *a.* bringing forth young alive. [L. *vivus*, alive, *parere*, bring forth]

vivisection *n.* dissection or experiment on living bodies of animals, *etc.* **viv'isector** *n.* [L. *virus*, alive, *secare*, cut]

vix'en *n.* female fox; spiteful woman. **vix'enish** *a.* [OE. *fem.* of fox]

vizard. See **visor.**

viz'ier *n.* minister of state in a Muslim country. (Turk. *vezir*]

vocable *n.* word. **-vocab'ulary** *n.* list of words; stock of words used. [L. *vocabulum*, fr. *vocare*, call]

vo'cal *a.* of, with, or giving out, voice. **-vo'calist** *n.* singer. **-vo'cally** *adv.* **vo'calize** *v.t.* utter with the voice. **voca'tion** *n.* calling. **-voca'tive** *n.* in some languages, the case of nouns used in addressing a person. [L. *vox*, voice]

vocif'erate *v.t.* and *i.* shout. **-vocif'erous** *a.* shouting, noisy. **-vocifera'tion** *n.* [L. *vox*, voice]

vod'ka *n.* Russian spirit distilled from rye. [Russ. dim. of *voda*, water]

vogue *n.* fashion. [F.]

voice *n.* sound given out by a person in speaking or singing, *etc.*; quality of the sound; expressed opinion; share in a discussion; verbal forms proper to relation of subject and action. *-v.t.* give utterance to. **-voice'less** *a.* **-voice recogni'tion** *n.* (*compute.*) conversion of tones of human speech into analog waveforms and then into a digital form that can be processed by a computer system. [F. *voix*, fr. L. *vox*, voc-]

void *a.* empty. *-n.* empty space. *-v.t.* empty out. [OF. *voit*]

voile *n.* thin cotton fabric. [F.]

vol'atile *a.* evaporating quickly; lively. **volatil'ity** *n.* **-volat'ilize** *v.t.* and *i.* [L. *volatilis*, flying]

volca'no *n.* mountain with a hole through which lava, ashes, smoke, *etc.*, are discharged. **-volcan'ic** *a.* [L. *Vulcanus*, Vulcan (whose forge was supposed to be below Etna)]

vole *n.* kinds of small rodent, as water-vole, field-vole, *etc.* [for *vole-mousse*, fr. Norw. *voll*, field]

voli'tion (-ish'-) *n.* act or power of willing. **-voli'tional** *a.* [Med. L. *volitio*]

voll'ey *n.* simultaneous discharge of weapons or missiles; rush of oaths, questions, *etc.* in sport, kick, stroke at moving ball before it hits the ground. *-v.t.* discharge in a volley. *-v. i.* fly in a volley. **-voll'eyball** *n.* team game where a large ball is hit by hand over a high net. [F. *volée*, flight, orig. at tennis]

volt'age *n.* electromotive force measured in volts. **-volt** *n.* unit of electromotive power. [A. *Volta*, 1745-1827]

voluble *a.* with incessant or abundant speech. **-volubil'ity** *n.* **-vol'ubly** *adv.* [L. *volvere, volut-*, roll]

vol'ume *n.* book, or part of a book, bound; mass; bulk, space occupied. **-volu'minous** *a.* bulky, over ample. [L. *volumen*]

voluntary *a.* having, or done by, free will. *-n.* organ solo in a church service. **vol'untarily** *adv.* **-volunteer'** *n.* one who offers service, joins a force, *etc.*, of his own free will. *-v.i.* offer oneself. [L. *voluntas*, wish, will]

voluptuous *a.* of or contributing to the pleasures of the senses. **-volup'tuary** *n.* one given to luxury and sensual pleasures. [L. *voluptas*, pleasure]

vol'ute *n.* spiral scroll-like ornament found *esp.* in Ionic capitals; genus of shellfish like whelks. **-volu'ted, volution** *n.* whorl, spiral; convolution. [L. *volvere*, roll]

vom'it *v.t.* eject from the stomach through

the mouth. *-v.t.* be sick. *-n.* matter vomited. [L. *vomere*, vomit-]

voo'doo *n.* African black magic practiced in Haiti, *etc.*; one skilled in this. [W. Afr. *vodu*]

voracious *a.* greedy, ravenous. -**vora'city** *n.* **voraciously** *adv.* [L. *vorax, vorac*]

vor'tex *a.* **vortices** *pl.* whirlpool; whirling motion. [L.]

vo'tary *n.* one vowed to a service or pursuit. **-vo'taress** *fem.* **-vo'tive** *a.* given or consecrated by vow. [L. *votum*, vow]

vote *n.* formal expression of a choice; individual pronouncement, or right to give it, in a question or election; result of voting; that which is given or allowed by vote. *v.i.* give a vote. *-v.t.* grant or enact by vote. **-vo'ter** *n.* [L. *votum, vow*]

vouch *v.i.* vouch for, make oneself responsible for. *-v.t.* guarantee. **-vouch'er** *n.* document proving the correctness of an item in accounts. **-vouchsafe'** *v.i.* condescend to grant or do something. [OF. *vochier*]

vow *n.* solemn promise, *esp.* a religious one. *-v.t.* promise or threaten by vow, [F. *vœu*, fr. L. *vovere, vot-*]

vow'el *n.* vocal sound pronounced without stoppage or friction of the breath; letter standing for such sound. [F. *voyelle*, fr. L. *vocalis* (*littera*), vocal (letter)]

voy'age *n.* journey, *esp.* a long one, by water. *-v.i.* make a voyage. [F]

vulcanize *v.t.* treat (rubber) with sulfur at a high temperature. **-vul'canite** *n.* rubber so hardened. **-vulcanization** *n.* [*Vulcan*; *See* **volcano**]

vul'gar *a.* of the common people; common; coarse, not refined; offending against good taste. **-vulga'rian** *n.* vulgar fellow, *esp.* a rich one. **-vul'garly** *adv.* -**vul'garism** *n.* word or construction used only by the uneducated. **-vutgar'ity** *n.* -**vul'garize** *v.t.* make vulgar or too common. **-vulgariza'tion** *n.* **-vul'gar fractions** common fraction, as distinct from decimals. **-vul'gar tongue'**, vernacular. [L. *vulgaris*, fr. *vulgus*, common people]

Vul'gate *n.* 4th c. Latin version of the Bible made by St. Jerome [L. *vulgatus*]

vul'nerable *a.* not proof against wounds; offering an opening to criticism, *etc.* [L. *vulnerare*, wound]

vul'pine *a.* of foxes; foxy; crafty, cunning. [L. *vulpinus*, of the fox, *vulpes*]

vul'ture *n.* large bird which feeds on carrion. [L. *vultur*]

W

wab'ble. *See* **wobble.**

wad (wod) *n.* small pad of fibrous material, used *esp.* to pack charge in a gun; money, notes. *-v.t.* line, pad, stuff, *etc.*, with a wad. **-wadd'ing** *n.* stuffing. [orig. unknown]

wad'dle *v.i.* walk like a duck. [wade]

wade *v.i.* walk through something that hampers movement, *esp.* water. **-wa'der** *n.* person or bird that wades; high waterproof boot. [OE. *wadan*]

wad'i *n.* dry bed of a stream. [Arab.]

wafer *n.* thin cake or biscuit; the Host; disk of paste for fastening papers. *-v.t.* fasten with a wafer. **-waf'fle** *n.* kind of pancake. **-waffle-iron** *n.* [Du. *wafel*]

waft *v.t.* convey smoothly through air or water. *-n.* breath of wind, odor, *etc.* [orig. uncertain]

wag *v.t.* cause to move to and fro. *-v.i.* shake, swing. *-n.* merry fellow (orig. *waghalter*, rascal). **-wagg'ery** *n.* -**wagg'ish** *a.* **-wag'tail** *n.* small bird with a wagging tail. [OE. *wagian*]

wage *n.* payment for work done (*usu.* in *pl.*). *-v.t.* carry on. **-wa'ger** *n.* and *v.t.* and *i.* bet. [ONF. *wage*, for *gage*, pledge]

wag'gle *v.t.* wag. [fr. *wag*]

wag'on *n.* four-wheeled vehicle for heavy loads. **-wag'oner** *n.* **-wagonette'** *n.* four-wheeled horse carriage with lengthwise seats. [Du. *wagen*, carriage]

waif *n.* homeless person, *esp.* a child. **waifs and strays**, the homeless destitute; odds and ends. [ONF.]

wail *n., v.t.* and *i.* lament. [ON. *vœla]*

wain *n.* farm wagon. [OE. *wægn*]

wains'cot *n.* wooden lining of the walls of a room, *esp.* oak. *-v. t.* line thus. [LG. *wagenschot*]

waist *n.* part of the body between hips and ribs; various central parts. **waistcoat** *n.* sleeveless garment worn under a coat. [ME. *waste*, growth, fr. *wax*, grow]

wait *v.t.* await. *-v.i.* be expecting, attend; serve at table. *-n.* act of waiting; carol singer. **-wait'er** *n.* attendant on guests in restaurant, hotel, *etc.* **-wait'ress** *fem.* [ONF. *waitier*, lurk, lie in ambush]

waive *v.t.* forgo; renounce (a right, claim). (ONF. *waiver*, renounce]

wake *v.i.* rouse from sleep. *-v.t.* rouse from sleep; stir up. *-n.* watch by a dead person; holiday. **-wa'ken** *v.t.* wake. **wake'ful** *a.* [OE. *waccian]*

wake *n.* track left by a ship, airplane, *etc.*,

track. (Du. *wak*]
wake'-rob'in *n.* mild arum, cuckoopint. [*wake*]
wale, weal *n.* streak left by the blow of a stick or whip. [OE. *walu*]
walk (wawk) *v.i.* move on the feet at an ordinary pace; cross by walking. *-v.t.* cause to walk. *-n.* slowest gait of animals; occupation or career; path, *etc.* for walking; spell of walking for pleasure, *etc.* **-walk'er** *n.* **-walk'way** *n.* pedestrian passage, *usu.* suspended *e.g.* between buildings. [OE. *wealean*, roll]
Walk'man *n.* small portable cassette recorder with light headphones. [Trademark]
wall (wawl) *n.* structure of brick, stone, *etc.*, serving as a fence, side of a building, *etc.*; surface of one. *-v.t.* supply with a wall; block up with a wall. **-wall'flower** *n.* sweet smelling garden flower, often growing on walls. [L. *vallum*]
wall'a(h) *n.* man, agent. **-competition wallah**, Indian civil servant appointed by competitive examination. [Hind. *wale*, doer]
wall'aby *n.* small kangaroo. [Austral.]
wall'et (wol-) *n.* small bag; pocketbook for paper-money, *etc.* [var. of *wattle*]
walleyed (wawl-id) *a.* having eyes with pale irises. [ON. *vald-eygthr*]
wall'op *v.t.* beat, flog. *-n.* beating, blow; (*sl.*) draught beer. [ONF. *waloper*]
wall'ow *v.i.* roll in mire, water, *etc.* *-n.* act of wallowing. [OE. *wealwian*]
wal'nut (wawl-) *n.* large nut with a crinkled shell splitting easily into two halves; the tree. [OE. *wealh*, foreign]
wal'rus (wol-) *n.* large seal-like sea animal with long tusks. [Dan. *hvalros*]
waltz (wawlts) *n.* dance. *-v.i.* dance it. [Ger. *walzer-watzen,* roll]
wam'pum *n.* strings of shells, beads, used by N. American Indians as money. [N. Amer. Ind.]
wan (won) *a.* pale, sickly-complexioned, faint-looking. [OE. *wann*, lurid]
wand (wond) *n.* stick, usually straight and slender. [ON. *vondr*]
wand'er (won-) *v.i.* roam; ramble; deviate from one's path; be delirious. [OE. *wandrian*]
wander'lust *n.* travel urge. [Ger.]
wane *v.i.* and *n.* decline. [OE. *wanian*]
wang'le *v.t.* manipulate, manage in a skillful way. [orig. uncertain]
want (wont) *n., v.t.* and *i.* lack. [ON. *vant*]
want'on (won-) *a.* unrestrained; playful; dissolute; without motive. *-v.i.* frolic. *-n.* wanton person. [ME. *wanto-wen*]
wap''iti (wop-) *n.* large N. American deer. [N. Amer. Ind. *wapitik*]
war *n.* fighting between nations; state of hostility. *-v.i.* make war. **-war'fare** *n.* hostilities. **-war'like** *a.* **-war'monger** *n.* spreader of war propaganda. **war'paint** *n.* paint, adornments assumed by N. American Indians before battle. **war'ship** *n.* naval vessel of any type used in warfare. **-warr'ior** *n.* fighter. [ONF. *werre*, F. *guerre*]
war'ble (wor-) *v.i.* sing with trills. **warb'ler** *n.* [ONF. *werbler*]
ward (wawrd) *n.* guardianship; minor under care of a guardian; division of a city, or hospital, *etc.* *-pl.* indentations of the bead of a key or lock. *-v.t.* guard. **ward'er** *n.* prison keeper. **-ward'ress** *fem.* **-ward'ship** *n.* **-ward'robe** *n.* piece of furniture for hanging clothes in. **-ward'room** *n.* officers' mess on a warship. **-ward'en** *n.* president or governor. **-ward'enship** *n.* [OE. *weard*, ONF. *warder*, F. *garder*]
ware *n.* goods; articles collectively. **ware'house** *n.* store-house; large commercial establishment. [OE. *waru*]
ware *a.* on guard. *-v.t.* beware; keep clear of. **-wa'riness** *n.* suspicious care, caution. [OE. *woer*]
war'lock *n.* wizard, sorcerer. [OE. *waer,* truth, compact, *leogan*, to lie]
warm *a.* moderately hot; ardent. *-v.t.* and *i.* heat. **-warm'ly** *adv.* **warm'th** *n.* [OE. *wearm*]
warn *v.t.* caution, put on guard. **-warn'ing** *n.* [OE. warnian]
warp *n.* lengthwise threads in a loom; rope. *-v.t.* twist; move by a rope fastened to a buoy. *-v. i.* become twisted. [OE. *weorpan*, throw]
warr'ant *n.* authority; document giving authority. *-v.t.* authorize; guarantee. **warr'anty** *n.* justification, guarantee. [ONF. *warant*, F. *garant*]
warr'en *n.* ground occupied by rabbits. [ONF. *warenne*, F. *garenne*]
wart (wort) *n.* hard growth on the skin. **-wart'y** *a.* [OE. *wearte*]
war'y *a.* cautious; watchful; on the defensive. **-war'ily** *adv.* [fr. *ware*]
wash (wosh) *v.t.* clean with liquid; carry along with a rush of water; color lightly. *v.i.* wash oneself, stand washing. *-n.* an act of washing; clothes washed at one time; sweep of water, *esp.* set up by moving ship; thin coat of color. **-wash'er** *n.* one who or that which washes; ring put under a nut.

-wash'y *a.* diluted. **wash'out** *n.* (*sl.*) failure, ineffectual effort. **-wash-leather** *n.* akin to chamois leather. **-washstand** *n.* stand holding basin and waterjug. [OE. *wascan*]

wasp *n.* striped stinging insect resembling a bee. **-wasp'ish** *a.* irritable; spiteful. [OE. *wœsp, wœps*]

wass'ail *n.* drinking bout; liquor for it. *-v.i.* carouse. [OE. *wes heil*, be hale ('your health')]

waste *v.t.* expend uselessly, use extravagantly; lay desolate. *-v.i.* dwindle; pine away. *-a.* wasted; desert. *-n.* what is wasted; act of wasting; desert. **-wast'age** *n.* **-waste'ful** *a.* **-waste'fully** *adv.* **wast'er** *n.* **-waste'ful** *a.* **-waste'fully** *adv.* **-wast'er** *n.* **-wast'rel** *n.* useless person, profligate. [ONF. *waster*, F. *gâter*, fr. L. *vastare*, destroy]

watch (woch) *n.* state of being on the lookout; spell of duty; pocket clock. *-v.t.* observe closely; guard. *-v.i.* be on watch, be wakeful. **-watch'ful** *a.* **-watch'fully** *adv.* **-watch'man** *n.* **-watch'keeper** *n.* officer of the watch. **-watch'maker** *n.* **watch'word** *n.* rallying-cry. [OE. *wœcce*]

wat'er *n.* transparent tasteless liquid, the substance of rain, rivers, *etc.*, transparency of a gem. *-v.t.* put water on or into; cause to drink. *-v.i.* take in or obtain water. **-wat'ery** *a.* **-wat'er-bailiff** *n.* customs official who inspects vessels entering and leaving port; official in charge of fishing rights and prevention of poaching. **-wat'er-boat'man** *n.* kind of water-beetle. **-wat'ercress** *n.* moisture loving salad plant. **-wat'erfall** *n.* fall of water (river, stream) over a perpendicular drop. **-wat'erglass** *n.* solution (sodium silicate) for preserving eggs. **-wat'erlil'y** *n.* water-plant with floating leaves and large flowers. **-wat'er-logged** *a.* soaked, filled with water so as to be unseaworthy. **-wat'ermark** *n.* mark made in paper during manufacture and visible on holding the paper to the light. **wat'erproof** *a.* not letting water through. *-n.* waterproof garment. **-watertight** *a.* [OE. *wœter*]

watt (wot) *n.* unit of electric power. [J. *Watt*, engineer (d. 1819)]

wat'tle (wot-) *n.* hurdle of wicker. *-v.t.* make into basket-work. [OE. *watel*]

watt'le *n.* pendent skin of bird's throat; species of Australian, S. African, *etc.*, acacia. [orig. unknown]

waul, wawl *v.i.* cry as cat; squall. [imit.]

wave *v.i.* move to and fro; beckon; have an undulating shape. *-v.t.* move to and fro; give the shape of waves; express by waves. *-n.* act or gesture of waving; ridge and trough on water, *etc.*; vibration. **wa'vy** *a.* **-wa'vily** *adv.* [OE. *wafian*, brandish]

wa'ver *v.i.* hesitate, be irresolute. **wa'verer** *n.* [fr. *wave*]

wax *v.i.* grow, increase. [OE. *weaxan*]

wax *n.* yellow plastic material made by bees; this or similar substance used for sealing, making candles, *etc.* *-v.t.* put wax on. **-wax'works** *n. pl.* display of figures modelled in wax. [OE. *weax*, beeswax]

way *n.* track; direction; method. **way'farer** *n.* traveler, *esp.* on foot. **waylay'** *v.t.* lie in wait for. **-way'ward** *a.* capricious, perverse. **-way'wardly** *adv.* **-way'wardness** *n.* [OE. *weg*]

we *pron.* 1st person *pl.* pronoun. I and others. [OE.]

weak *a.* lacking strength. **-weak'ly** *a.* weak; sickly. **-weak'ly** *adv.* **-weak'en** *v.t.* and *i.* **-weak'ling** *n.* feeble creature. **-weak'ness** *n.* [ON. *vickr*]

weal *n.* well-being. [OE. *wela*]

weal. See **wale.**

weald *n.* open or wooded country; the Weald, formerly wooded, between the N. and S. Downs, England. [OE. *weald*]

wealth (welth) *n.* riches; abundance. **-wealth'y** *a.* [OE. *weld*]

wean *v.t.* accustom to food other than mother's milk. **-wean'ling** *n.* newly weaned child. [OE. *wenian*, accustom]

weap'on (wep'n) *n.* implement to fight with. [OE. *woepen*]

wear *v.t.* carry on the body; show consume. *-v.i.* last; become impaired by use. *-n.* act of wearing; impairment; things to wear. **-wear'er** *n.* **-wear'ing** *a.* exhausting. [OE. *woerian*]

wear'y *a.* tired. *-v.t.* and *i.* tire. **wear'ily** *adv.* **-wear'iness** *n.* **-wear'isome** *a.* [OE. *werig*]

weas'el (-z-) *n.* small animal related to the ferret, *etc.* [OE. *wesle*]

weath'er (weTH-) *n.* atmospheric conditions. *-a.* towards the wind. *-v.t.* affect by weather; sail to windward of, come safely through. **-weath'ercock** *n.* revolving vane to show which way the wind blows. **-weath'ered** *a.* (*archit.*) slightly inclined, to throw off water. [OE. *weder*]

weave *v.t.* form in texture or fabric by interlacing. *-v.i.* make by crossing threads, *etc.*, thread one's way (among). *n.* texture. **-weav'er** *n.* [OE. *wefan*]

web *n.* woven fabric; net spun by a spider; membrane between the toes of waterfowl.

[OE. *webb*]

wed *v.t.* marry; to unite closely. **-wedd'ing** *n.* marriage. **-wed'lock** *n.* marriage. [OE. *weddian*]

wedge *n.* piece of material sloping to an edge. -*v.t.* fasten or split with a wedge; stick by compression or crowding. [OE. *wecg*]

Wed'nesday *n.* fourth day of the week. [OE. *wodnesdoeg*, day of *Woden*, or Odin]

wee *a.* small, little, tiny. [ME. *we*, bit]

weed *n.* plant growing where it is not desired. -*v.t.* and *i.* pull out weeds. **-weed'y** *a.* [OE. *weod*, herb]

weeds *n.pl.* widow's mourning garments. [OE. *woed*, garment]

week *n.* period of seven days. **-week'ly** *a.* happening, done, *etc.*, once a week. **-week'ly** *adv.* once a week, (OE. *wicu*]

ween *v.i.* think, imagine. [OE. *wenan*]

weep *v.i.* shed tears. -*v.t.* lament. **-weep'ing-will'ow**, willow with drooping boughs. (OE. *wepan*]

wee'vil *n.* beetle harmful to grain, *etc.* [OE. *wifel*, beetle]

weft *n.* cross threads in weaving; woof [OE. *wefta*, fr. *wefan*, weave]

weigh *v.t.* find the weight of, raise, as in weigh anchor. -*v.i.* have weight. **weight** *n.* force exerted by the earth on a body; heavy mass; object of known mass for weighing; importance. -*v.t.* add a weight to. **-weight'y** *a.* **-weight'ily** *adv.* [OE. *wegan*, carry]

weir *n.* dam across a river. [OE. *wer*]

weird *a.* unearthly. [OE. *wyrd*, fate]

wel'come *a.* received gladly. -*n.* kindly greeting. -*v.t.* receive gladly or hospitably. [*well* and *come*]

weld *v.t.* unite (hot metal) by hammering or compressing; unite closely. -*n.* welded joint. [var. of *well*]

wel'fare *n.* well-being; prosperity. [*well* and *fare*]

wel'kin *n.* sky. [OE. *wolcen*, cloud]

well *adv.* in good manner or degree. -*a.* in good health; suitable. **-well-being** *n.* health and contentment; prosperity. **well-bred** *a.* polite, mannerly; (of horse) coming from good stock. **-well-favored** *a.* good-looking, handsome. **-well-nigh** *adv.* almost. **-well-off'** *a.* fortunate-**well-to-do** *a.* prosperous. [OE. *wel*]

well *n.* deep hole for water; spring. -*v.i.* flow out or up. [OE. *wiella*]

well'ingtons *n. pl.* knee-length rubber boots worn in wet weather. [Duke of *Wellington*]

Welsh *a.* of Wales. -*n.* language, or people, of Wales. [OE. *wcelisc*, foreign]

welsh, welch *v.t.* and *i.* (of bookmaker) abscond without paying debts. **-welsh'er** *n.* [uncertain]

welt *n.* seam; leather rim put on a boot-upper for the sole to be attached to; wale. -*v.t.* provide a shoe with a welt; thrash. [orig. uncertain]

welt'er *v.i.* roll or tumble. -*n.* turmoil. (M. Du. *welteren*]

wen *n.* tumor forming a permanent swelling beneath the skin. [OE.]

wench *n.* damsel. [OE. *wencel*, child]

wend *v.i.* go. [OE. *wendan*, turn]

went *v.i.*, *p.t.* of go. [*wend*]

wer'wolf, were'wolf *n.* human being able to turn into a wolf. [OE. *werwulf*, man-wolf]

Wes'leyan *a.* of Wesley or the Church founded by him. -*n.* member of that church. [J. *Wesley* (d. 1791)]

west *n.* part of the sky where the sun sets; part of a country, *etc.*, lying to this side. *a.* that is toward this region. *adv.* to the west. **-west'erly** *a.* **-west'ward** *a.* and *adv.* **-west'wards** *adv.* **-west'ern** *a.* [OE.]

wet *a.* having water or other liquid on a surface or being soaked in it; rainy. -*v.t.* make wet. -*n.* moisture, rain. **-wet' blankets** damping influence. **-wet nurse,** nurse who suckles a child not her own. [OE. *woot*]

weth'er (-TH-) *n.* castrated ram. [OE.]

whack *v.t.* hit, *esp.* with a stick. -*n.* such a blow. [imit.]

whale *n.* large fish-shaped sea animal. **whale-back** *n.* vessel with turtle-deck; vessel with upper deck of this type, used for carrying grain. **-whale'bone** *n.* springy substance from the upper jaw of certain whales. **-wha'ler** *n.* man or ship employed in hunting whales. [OF. *hwœl*]

wharf (hworf) *n.* quay for loading and unloading ships. **-wharf'age** *n.* accommodation or dues at a wharf. **-wharf'inger** *n.* **-wharf owner.** [OE. *hwerf*, shore]

what (hwot) *pron.* which thing? that which. -*a.* which. **-whatev'er** *pron.* anything which; of what kind it may be. **whatsoev'er** *a.* [OE. *hwcet*]

wheat *n.* cereal plant with thick four-sided seed-spikes, of which bread is chiefly made. **-wheat'en** *a.* [OE. *hwœte*]

wheat'ear *n.* small bird, one of the chats. [corrupt. of *white-arse*]

whee'dle *v.t.* and *i.* coax. [orig. uncertain]

wheel *n.* circular frame or disk with spokes revolving on an axle. -*v.t.* convey by wheeled apparatus or vehicles; cause to turn or change direction. *-v.i.* revolve; change direction. **-wheel'barrow** *n.* barrow with one wheel. **-wheel'wright** *n.* maker or repairer of wheels. [OE. *kweol*]

wheeze *v.i.* to breathe with difficulty and noise. *-n.* (*sl.*) joke; trick. **-wheez'y** *a.* [ON. *hvœsa*, hiss]

whelk *n.* shell-fish. [OE. *weoloc*]

whelm *v.t.* submerge, overbear, destroy. [orig. uncertain]

whelp *n.* pup or cub. *-v.i.* and *t.* produce whelps. [OE. *hwelp*]

when *adv.* at what time. *-conj.* at the time. **-whenev'er** *adv.* and *conj.* at whatever time. [OE. *hwænne*]

whence *adv.* from what place. [fr. *when*]

where *adv.* and *conj.* at what place. **whereas'** *conj.* considering that, while, on the contrary. **-where'fore** *adv.* why. *conj.* consequently. **-wherev'er** *adv.* at whatever place. **-where'withal** *n.* means; resources. [OE. *hwar*]

wherr'y *n.* light shallow boat or barge. [orig. unknown]

whet *v.t.* sharpen. **-whet'stone** *n.* stone for sharpening tools. [OE. *hwettan*]

wheth'er (-TH-) *a.* and *pron.* which of the two. *-conj.* introduces first of two alternatives, of which second may be expressed or implied. [OE. *hwœther*]

whey *n.* watery part of milk. **-whey'ey, whey'ish** *a.* [OE. *hwœg*]

which *a.* asks for a selection from alternatives. *-pron.* which person or thing; thing 'who.' [OE. *kwilc*]

whiff *v.t.* and *i.* and *n.* puff. [imit.]

while *n.* space of time. *-conj.* in the time that. *-v.t.* pass (*time*, usually idly). **whilst** *adv.* [OE. *hwil*]

whim *n.* caprice, fancy. **-whim'sical** *a.* delicately fanciful. **-whimsical'ity** *n.* [orig. uncertain]

whim'brel *n.* small curlew. [imit.]

whim'per *v.i.* cry or whine softly. **-whim'pering** *v.i.* cry or whine softly. **-whim'pering** *a.* such cry. [imit.]

whin' *n.* gorse, furze. **-whin'chat** *n.* small bird found among gorse, the stonechat. [of Scand. orig.]

whine *n.* long-drawn wail. *v.i.* make one. [OE. *hwinan*]

whinn'y *v.i.* neigh joyfully. *-n.* such neigh. [imit.]

whip *v.t.* apply a whip to; thrash; lash. *v.i.* dart. *-n.* lash attached to a stick for urging or punishing. **-whip'cord** *n.* thin hard cord. **-whip-hand** *n.* superiority, advantage. **-whipp'er-snapper** *n.* small child; insignificant person. [orig. uncertain]

whipp'et *n.* coursing dog like a small greyhound. [orig. uncertain]

whirl *v.t.* and *i.* swing rapidly round. *-n.* whirling movement. **-whirl'igig** *n.* spinning toy. **-whirl'pool** *n.* circular current. **-whirl'wind** *n.* wind whirling round a forward-moving axis. [ON. *hvirfill*, ring]

whir, whirr *n.* sound as of rapid beating or whirling. [imit.]

whisk *v.t.* and *i.* brandish, sweep, or beat lightly. *-n.* light brush; flapper; egg-beating implement. **-whisk'er** *n.* hair of a man's face. [of Teut. orig.]

whiskeys, whisk'y *n.* spirit distilled from various grains. [for *usquebaugh*, Ir. *uisge beatha*, water of life]

whisp'er *v.t.* and *i.* speak with rustling breath instead of voice. *-n.* such speech. [OE. *hwisprian*]

whist *n.* card game. [var. of *whisk*]

whis'tle (-sl) *n.* sound made by forcing the breath through rounded and nearly closed lips; any similar sound; instrument to make it. *-v.i.* make such sound. *-v.t.* utter or summon, *etc.*, by whistle. **-whis'tler** *n.* [OE. hwistle]

whit *n.* jot. [OE, *wiht*, thing]

white *a.* of the color of snow; pale; light in color. *-n.* color of snow; white pigment; white part. **-white-ant** *n.* termite. **white'bait** *n.* small edible fish. **-white drugs** *n.pl.* harmful narcotics; dope. **white elephant** *n.* useless or incongruous gift. **-White House** *n.* executive department of the U.S. government; official residence of the president of the U.S. in Washington D.C. **-white-line** *n.* safety line on road. **-white-livered** *a.* cowardly. **-whi'ten** *v.t.* and *i.* **-white'ness** *n.* **white-paper** *n.* government report on any recent investigation. **-white slave** *n.* woman or child abducted or sold for purposes of prostitution. **-white'smith** *n.* tinsmith. **-white'wash** *n.* liquid mixture for whitening. *-v.t.* apply this, clear of imputations. **-whi'ting** *n.* dried chalk; small sea-fish. **-whi'tish** *a.* [OE. *hwit*]

whith'er (-TH-) *adv.* to what place. **whithersoev'er** *adv.* [OE. *hwider*]

whit'low *n.* inflamed swelling on a finger. [orig. uncertain]

whit'tle *v.t.* cut or carve with a knife; pare away. [OE. *thwitan*, cut]

whiz *n.* violent hissing sound. *-v.i.* move with such sound; make it. [imit.]

who *pron.* (*obj.* whom) relative and interrogative pronoun, always referring to persons. **-whoev'er** *pron.* any one or everyone that. [OE. *hwa*]

whole (h-) *a.* complete; healthy; all. *-n.* complete thing or system. **-who'lly** *adv.* **-whole'meal** *a.* of flour which contains the whole of the grain. **whole'sale** *n.* sale of goods by large quantities. *-a.* dealing by wholesale; extensive. **-whole'saler** *n.* - **whole'some** *a.* producing a good effect, physically or morally. [OE. *hal,* hale, uninjured]

whoop *v.t.* and *i.* and *n.* about. - **whoop'ing-cough** *n.* disease marked by a whooping breath. [F. *houper*]

whore (h-) *n.* prostitute. [ON. *hora*]

whorl *n.* turn of a spiral; ring of leaves, *etc.* **-whorl'ed** *a.* [OE. *hweorfan,* turn]

whor'tleberry *n.* bilberry. [earlier *hurtleberry,* fr. OE. *hortan,* bilberries]

whose *pron. possess.* of who, which. [OE. *hwces-hwa,* who]

why *adv.* and *conj.* for what cause; wherefore. *-interj.* of surprise, *etc. -n.* the reason or purpose of anything. [OE. *hwi*]

wick *n.* strip or thread feeding the flame of a lamp or candle. [OE. *weoce*]

wick'ed *a.* evil, sinful. **-wick'edly** *adv.* - **wick'edness** *n.* [ME. *wikke,* feeble]

wick'er *n.* plaited osiers, *etc.*, for baskets. *-a.* **-wick'erwork** *n.* basketwork. [ME. *wikir,* osier]

wick'et *n.* small gate; in cricket, a set of three stumps and bails. [AF. *wiket,* F. *guiche*]

wide *a.* broad; far from the mark. **wi'den** *v.t.* and *i.* **-wide'ly** *adv.* **-width** *n.* **-wide'-awake'** *a.* alert. *-n.* kind of soft felt hat. [OE. *wid*]

wid'geon *n.* kind of wild duck. [orig. uncertain]

wid'ow *n.* woman whose husband is dead and who has not married again. *v.t.* make a widow of **-wid'ower** *n.* man whose wife has died and who has not married again. **-wid'owhood** *n.* [OE. *wydewa*]

wield *v.t.* hold and use. **-wield'y** *a.* manageable. [OE. *gewieldan,* govern]

wife *n.* wives *pl.* woman married to a man. **-wife'ly** *a.* [OE. *wif,* woman]

wig *n.* artificial hair for the head. [for *periwig* -O Du. *peruyk*]

wight *n.* American Indian's hut or tent. [N. Amer. Ind.]

wild *a.* not tamed or domesticated; not cultivated (as wildflowers); savage; excited, rash. **-wild'ly** *adv.* **-wild'ness** *n.* - **wil'derness** *a.* desert. **-wild fire** *n.* burning liquid used formerly in sea-fights, Greek fire. **-like wild'fire** *adv.* very quickly. [OE. *wilde*]

wile *n.* trick. **-wi'ly** *a.* artful. [OE. *wil*]

will *v. aux.* forms moods and tenses indicating intention or conditional result. *v.i.* have a wish. *-v.t.* wish intend, purpose; leave as a legacy. *-n.* faculty of deciding what one will do; purpose, wish; directions written for disposal of property after death. **-will'ing** *a.* ready; given cheerfully. - **will'ingly** *adv.* **-will'ingness** *n.* **-will'y-nill'y** *adv.* willing or unwilling. [OE. *willan*]

will-o'-the-wisp *n.* light flitting over marshes; elusive person or hope. [E. = *William* of the torch]

will'ow *n.* tree such as the weeping willow with long thin flexible branches; its wood. **-will'owy** *a.* lithe and slender. **will'ow patterns** famous pattern on china, *etc.*, illustrating a Chinese legend. [OE. *welig*]

wilt *v.i.* droop; fade; go limp. *-v.t.* make to wilt. [orig. uncertain]

wim'ple *n.* covering for head and extending round cheeks and neck, worn by nuns. [OE. *wimple*]

win *v.t.* get by labor or effort; reach; allure; be successful in. *-v.i.* be successful. - **winn'er** *n.* [OE. *gewinaan*]

wince *v.i.* flinch. *-n.* a flinching from pain, *etc.* IOF. *guenchir,* shrink]

win'cey *n.* cotton cloth with wool filling. **-winceyette'** *n.* cotton cloth. [orig. uncertain]

winch *n.* crank; windlass. [OE. *wince,* pulley]

Win'chester disk *n.* (*compute.*) system in which data are recorded on metal disks enclosed in scaled containers that are permanently mounted on the disk drive. also **hard drive.**

wind *n.* air in motion; breath. **-wind** *v.t.* sound by blowing. **-wind'fall** (-awl) *n.* fallen fruit; piece of good luck. - **wind'jamm'er** *n.* sailing ship. **-wind'mill** *n.* mill worked by sails. **-wind'pipe** *n.* passage from throat to lungs. **-wind'shield** *n.* in car, motor cycle, *etc.*, sheet of strong glass for protection in front of driver. - **wind'surfing** *n.* sport of sailing standing up on a sailboard that is equipped with a mast, sail, and wishbone boom; boardsailing. **-wind'y** *a.* exposed to winds; (*sl.*) timid, fearful. **-wind'ward** (-ord) *n.* side towards the wind. **-wind'flower** *n.* wood anemone. [OE.]

wind *v.i.* twine; vary from a direct course. *-v.t.* twist round, wrap; make ready for working by tightening a spring. **-wind'lass** *n.* machine which hauls or hoists by wrapping rope round an axle. [OE. *windan*]

win′dow *n.* hole in a wall (with or without glass), to admit light. [ON. *vindauge*, wind-eye]

wine *n.* fermented juice of the grape, or other fruit. **-wine box** *n.* wine sold in a cubic carton, having a plastic lining and a tap for dispensing. **-wine grow′er** *n.* a person engaged in cultivating vines in order to make wine. **-wine grow′ing** *n.* **wine press** *n.* apparatus for squeezing grapes in order to extract juice for wine making. **-wine tas′ting** *n.* an occasion for sampling a number of wines. **-wine tas′ter** *n.* [OE. *win*, fr. L. *vinum*]

wing *n.* limb a bird uses in flying; flight; lateral extension; plane. *v.t.* cross by flight; supply with wings; disable. *-v.i.* fly. [ON. *voengr*, wing]

wink *v.i.* close and open an eye; connive with (*at*). *-n.* an act of winking. [OE. *wincian*]

win′kle *n.* periwinkle. [OE. *wincle*]

winn′ow *v.t.* blow free of chaff. [OE. *winduian*, winnow]

win′some *a.* charming, attractive. [OE. *wynsum*, fr. *wynn*, joy]

win′ter *n.* fourth season. *-v.i.* pass the winter. *-v.t.* tend during winter. **-win′try** *a.* **-win′tergreen** *n.* evergreen plant; flavoring obtained from oil extracted from the plant. **-win′ter quarters** *n. pl.* quarters for troops during winter. [OE.]

wipe *v.t.* rub so as to clean. *-n.* a wiping. [OE. *wipian*]

wire *n.* metal drawn into the form of cord; (*coll.*) telegram. *-v.t.* provide, catch, fasten with, wire; send by telegraph. **wi′ry** *a.* like wire, tough. **-wire′less** *n.*, *a.* and *v.t.* telegraphy or telephony without connecting wires. **-wire′drawn** *a.* strained, over-subtle. **-wire′-pulling** *n.* use of influence behind the scenes. **-wire′tap** *v.t.* and *i.* make a connection to a telegraph or telephone wire in order to obtain information secretly. **-wire′tapper** *n.* [OE. wir]

wise *a.* sagacious; having intelligence and knowledge. **-wis′dom** *n.* **-wise′ly** *adv.* **-wis′dom tooth′**, large back-tooth cut in one's later 'teens. [OE. *wis*]

wise *n.* manner. [OE. *wise*]

wise′acre *n.* foolish pretender to wisdom. [Du. *wijssegger*, soothsayer]

wish *v.i.* have a desire. *-v.t.* desire. *-n.* desire or thing desired. **-wish′ful** *a.* **wish′ful think′ing,** beliefs colored by one's wishes. [OE. *wyscan*]

wisp *n.* twisted handful, usually of straw, *etc.* [orig. uncertain]

wisteria *n.* climbing plant with pale purple flowers. [C. *Wistar* (d. 1818)]

wist′ful *a.* longing. **-wist′fully** *adv.* **wist′fulness** *n.* [orig. uncertain]

wit *n.* sense; intellect; ingenuity in connecting amusingly incongrous ideas; person gifted with this power. **-witt′y** *a.* **-witt′ily** *adv.* **-witt′icism** *n.* witty remark. **-witt′ingly** *adv.* on purpose. [OE. *witt*, fr. *witan*, know]

witch *n.* woman said to be endowed with black-magical powers. **-witch′craft** *n.* **witch′ery** *n.* **-witch′ing** *a.* weird. **witch′-doc′tor** *n.* medicine-man, magician. [OE. *wicca*]

witch′-elm, wych′-elm *n.* variety of elm. **-witch′-hazel** *n.* **-witch′-alder** *n.* [OE. *wice*, bending, drooping]

with *prep.* in company or possession of, against; in relation to; through. **-withal′** *adv.* also, likewise. **-withdraw′** *v.t.* and *i.* draw back, retire. **-withdraw′al** *n.* **-withhold′** *v.t.* keep, hold back, restrain. **-within′** *prep.* and *adv.* in, inside. **-without′** *adv.* outside. *-prep.* lacking. -withstand *v.t.* oppose. [OE.]

withe, with′y *n.* tough, flexible twig, willow. [OE. *withthe*]

with′er *v.i.* fade. *-v.t.* cause to fade; blight. [var. of *weather*]

with′ers *n. pl.* ridge between a horse's shoulder-blades. [OE. *withre*, resistance]

wit′ness *n.* testimony; one who sees something; one who gives testimony. *-v.i.* give testimony. *-v.t.* see; attest; see and sign as having seen. [OE *witnes*, evidence]

wiz′ard *n.* sorcerer, magician. [*wise*]

wiz′ened *a.* shriveled, dried up, withered. [OE. *wisnian*, wither]

woad *n.* blue dye. [OE. *wad*]

wobb′le *v.i.* shake, be unsteady. *-n.* swaying movement. [L. Ger. *wabbeln*]

woe *n.* grief **-woe′begone** *a.* sorrowful. **-woe′ful** *a.* **-woe′fully** *adv.* [OE. wa]

wold. *See* **weald.**

wolf (woolf) *n.* wolves *pl.* wild beast allied to the dog. **-wolf's-bane** *n.* aconite. [OE. *wulf*]

wolf′ram *n.* ore containing iron, manganese and tungsten. **-wolf′ramite** *n.* important ore of tungsten. [Ger.]

wolverine *n.* rapacious N. American animal, the glutton, carcajou; its fur. (*wolf*]

wom′an (woo-) *n.* **wom′en** *pl.* adult human female; female sex. **-wom′anhood** *n.* **-wom′anly** *a.* **-wom′anish** *a.* **wom′ankind** *n.* [OE. *wifmann*, *wife-man*, female]

womb *n.* female organ of conception and gestation, the uterus. [OE. *wamb*, belly]

wom'bat *n.* Australian marsupial animal resembling the opossum. [native]

won'der (wun-) *n.* marvel; emotion excited by an amazing or unusual thing. *v.i.* feel this emotion. **-won'derful** *a.* **won'derfully** *adv.* **-won'drous** *a.* **won'drously** *adv.* **-won'derment** *n.* [OE. *wundor*]

wont *n.* custom. **-wont'ed** *a.* habitual. [OE. *gewun*, usual]

woo *v.t.* court, seek to marry. **-woo'er** *n.* **-woo'ing** *n.* and *a.* [OE. *wogian]*

wood *n.* tract of land with growing trees; substance of trees, timber. **-wood'en** *a.* **wood'y** *a.* **-wood'bine** *n.* honeysuckle. **wood'cock** *n.* bird like a snipe. **-wood'cut** *n.* engraving on wood. **-wood'land** *n.* woods, forest. **-wood'pecker** *n.* bird which searches tree-trunks for insects. **wood'man** *n.* forester. **-wood'craft** *n.* knowledge of woodland conditions. **wood'ruff** *n.* woodland plant with small white fragrant flowers. **-wood'winds** *n. pl.* clarinet, oboe, *etc.*, in an orchestra. [OE. *wudu*, forest]

woof *n.* threads that cross the warp in weaving, the weft. [OE. *owef*]

wool *n.* soft hair of the sheep and certain other animals. **-wool'en** *a.* **-wooll'y** *a.* [OE. *wull*]

word (wurd) *n.* single symbol used in speaking or writing, a unit of speech; information; promise. *-v.t.* express in words. **-word'y** *a.* **-word'ily** *adv.* **-word proc'essing** *v.t.* (*compute.*) recording and revising of words or phrases by machines to produce reports or documents. **-word proc'essing pro'gram** *n.* computer program to enable the processing of documents. [OE.]

work (wurk) *n.* labor; task; something made or accomplished. *-pl.* factory. *-v.t.* cause to operate; make, shape. *-v.i.* apply effort; labor; operate; ferment; be engaged in a trade, profession, *etc.* **-work'able** *a.* **-work'er** *n.* **-work'house** *n.* institution for paupers. **-work'man** *n.* manual worker. - **work'manship** *n.* skill of a workman; way a thing is finished, style. **-work'shop** *n.* place where things are made. **-work'top** *n.* a surface in a kitchen, often of heat resistant laminated plastic, that is used for food preparation. [OE. *woerc*]

world (wurld) *n.* universe; sphere of existence; mankind; society. **-world'ling** *n.* one given up to affairs of this world. **world'ly** *a.* engrossed in temporal pursuits. [OE. *weorold*]

worm (wurm) *n.* small limbless creeping creature, shaped like a snake; thread of a screw. *-v.i.* crawl. *-v.t.* work (oneself) in insidiously; extract (a secret) craftily. **worm'eaten** *a.* eaten by worms; old, out-of-date. [OE. *wyrm*, serpent]

worm'wood (wurm-) *n.* bitter herb; (*fig.*) bitterness. [OE. *wermod*]

worr'y (wur'i) *v.t.* seize or shake with teeth; trouble, harass. *-v.i.* be unduly concerned. *-n.* useless care or anxiety. **worry'ing** *a.* [OE. *wyrgan*, strangle]

worse (wurs) *a.* and *adv.* comparative of bad or badly. **-worst** *a.* and *adv.* superlative of bad or badly. **-wors'en** *v.t.* and *i.* [OE. *wiersa*]

wor'ship (wur-) *n.* reverence, adoration. *-v.t.* adore; love and admire. **wor'shipful** *a.* **-wor'shiper** *n.* [OE. *weorthscipe*, 'worth-ship']

wor'sted (wur-) *n.* woolen yarn. [fr. *Worstead*, in Norfolk, England]

wort *n.* plant, herb; infusion of malt before fermentation. [OE. *wyrt*]

worth (wurth) *a.* having value specified; meriting. *-n.* merit, value. **-wor'thy** (-TH-) *a.* **-wor'thily** *adv.* **-wor'thiness** *n.* - **worth'less** *a.* [OE. *weorth*]

wound *n.* injury, hurt by cut, stab, *etc.* *-v.t.* inflict a wound on; pain. **-wound'ing** *a.* [OE. *wund*]

wrack *n.* sea-weed, *esp.* the kind burned as kelp; wreckage. [var. of *wreck*]

wraith *n.* apparition of a person seen shortly before or after death. [ON. *vörthr*, guardian]

wran'gle (-ng-gi) *v. i.* quarrel or dispute noisily. *-n.* act of doing this. [ME. *wrangela*]

wrap *v.t.* cover, *esp.* by putting something round; put round. *-n.* loose garment; covering. **-wrapp'er** *n*; [earlier *wiap*, of uncertain orig.]

wrath *n.* anger. **-wrath'ful** *a.* - **wrath'fully** *adv.* **-wrathfulness** *n.* [OE. = *angry*]

wreak *v.t.* inflict (vengeance, *etc.*). [OE. *wrecan*, avenge]

wreath *n.* something twisted into ring form; garland. **-wreathe** *v.t.* surround; form into wreath; wind round. [OE. *wrath*, fillet]

wreck *n.* destruction of a ship by accident; wrecked ship; ruin; something ruined. *-v.t.* cause the wreck of. **-wreck'age** *n.* [OE. *wræc*, fr. *wrecan*, drive]

wren *n.* very small brown bird, allied to the goldcrest. [OE. *wrenna*]

wrench *n.* violent twist; tool for twisting or screwing. -*v.t.* twist; distort; seize forcibly. [OE. *wrenc*, trick]

wrest *v.t.* take by force; twist violently. *n.* tool for tuning a harp, *etc.* **-wres'tle** (-sl) *v.i.* contend by grappling and trying to throw down. **-wres'tler** *n.* [OE. *wræstan*]

wretch *n.* miserable creature. **-wretch'ed** *a.* miserable; worthless. **-wretch'edness** *n.* **-wretch'edly** *adv.* [OE. *wræcca*, outcast]

wrig'gle *v.t.* and *i.* move sinuously like a worm. -*n.* quick twisting movement. [fr. obs. *wrig*]

wright *n.* workman, maker, *e.g.*, wheelwright. [OE. *wyrhta*, worker]

wring *v.t.* twist, squeeze, compress; extort; pain. [OE. *wringan*]

wrin'kle (-ng-kl) *n.* slight ridge on a surface. -*v.t.* makes wrinkles in. -*v.i.* become wrinkled. [OE. *wrincle*]

wrist *n.* joint between the hand and the arm. **-wrist'let** *n.* band worn on the wrist. **-wrist-watch'** *n.* watch worn on wrist. [OE]

write *v.i.* mark paper, *etc.*, with the symbols which are used to represent words or sounds; compose; send a letter. *v.t.* set down in words; compose; communicate in writing. **-writ** *n.* a formal or legal document. **-wri'ter** *n.* penman; author. [OE. *writan*]

writhe *v.i.* twist or roll body about, as in pain; to squirm (with shame, *etc.*) [OE. *writhan*]

wrong *a.* not right or good or suitable. *n.* that which is wrong; harm; evil. -*v.t.* do wrong to. **-wrong'ly** *adv.* **-wrong'ful** *a.* **-wrong'fully** *adv.* [OE. *wrang*, injustice]

wroth *a.* angry. [fr. *wrath*]

wrought' *pa.t.* of *work.*

wrung' *p.p.* and *pp.* of **wring.**

wry *a.* turned to one side, distorted. **wry'neck** *n.* small bird which twists its neck thus. [OE. *wrigian*, twist]

wyandotte *n.* breed of domestic fowls. [name of Amer. Ind. tribe]

X

X-rays' *n. pl.* invisible short-wave rays used in surgery to take photographs of the bones, *etc.*, inside the human frame. [*X* = the unknown]

xanth'ic (zan-) *a.* yellowish. **-xanth'ism** *n.* a condition of skin, fur, or feathers in which yellow coloration predominates. [G. *xanthos*, yellow]

xantipp'e (zan-tip'-i) *n.* shrewish woman, scold. [wife of Socrates]

xen'on *n.* gaseous element of the atmosphere. [G. *zenos*, stranger]

xenopho'bia *n.* morbid fear of strangers. [G. *zenos*, stranger]

xo'anon *n.* primitive image of a god, carved, *esp.* originally, in wood, and supposed to have fallen from heaven. [G. *xuo*, scrape, smooth]

xy'lograph *n.* wood-engraving, impression from wood-block. **-xylog'raphy** *n.* wood-engraving. **-xylog'rapher** *n.* wood-engraver. **-xylograph'ic** *a. pert.* to xylography. [G. *xylon*, wood, *graphein*, write]

xy'loid *a.* woody, like wood. [G. *xylon*, wood, *eidos*, form]

xy'lonite (zi) *n.* celluloid.

xylophone *n.* musical instrument of wooden bars which vibrate when struck. [G. *xylon*, wood]

xy'lorimba (zi) *n.* large xylophone with an extended range of five octaves. [fr. *xylophone* and *marimba*]

Y

yacht (yot) *n.* light vessel for racing or pleasure. -*v.i.* cruise or race in a yacht. **yachts'man** *n.* [Du. *jacht*]

yahoo' *n.* brute in human form. [coined by Swift in *Gulliver's Travels*]

yak *n.* long-haired Tibetan ox. [Tibetan]

yam *n.* tropical plant with large edible tuber, the sweet potato. [Senegalese *nyami*, eat]

yam'mer *v.i.* talk in a sad voice, complain; talk continuously, *usu.* loudly. [OE. *geomar*, sad]

Yank'ee *n.* inhabitant of U.S.A. *esp.* of New England, or of the Northern States. -*a.* belonging to U.S.A. [orig. uncertain]

yap *n.* and *v.i.* bark (of small dog). [imit.]

yapp *n.* bookbinding with limp leather cover projecting over the edges. [*Yapp*, London bookseller]

yard *n.* unit of measure, 36 inches; that length of anything; spar slung across a ship's mast to extend sails. **-yard'arm** *n.* either half of a long slender beam or pole used to support a square sail. [OE. *gierd*, rod]

yard *n.* piece of enclosed ground around a building [OE. *geard*]

yarn *n.* spun thread of fiber prepared for weaving, knitting, *etc.*; tale. -*v. i.* tell a tale. [OE. *gearn*]

yash'mak *n.* veil worn by Muslim women. [Ar. *yashmaq*]
yaw *v.i.* fall off from a course in steering a ship. [orig. uncertain]
yawl *n.* small yacht, boat. [Du. *jol*]
yawn *v.i.* gape; open the mouth wide, *esp.* in sleepiness. *-n.* the act of yawning. [OE. *ganian*]
ye *pron.* you. [OE. *gea*]
year *n.* time taken by one revolution of the earth round the sun, about 365¼ days; twelve months. **-year'ling** *n.* animal one year old. **-year'ly** *adv.* every year, once a year. *-a.* happening, *etc.*, once a year. [OE. *gear*]
yearn (yern) *v.i.* feel a longing or desire. [OE. *giernan*]
yeast *n.* substance used as a fermenting agent, *esp.* in raising bread. **-yeast'y** *a.* frothy, fermenting. [OE. *gist*]
yell *v.i.* cry out in a loud shrill tone. *-n.* loud, shrill cry. [OE. *gellan*]
yell'ow *a.* of the color of lemons, gold, *etc.* *-n.* this color, *-a.* (*fig.*) envious, jealous. -(*coll.*) cowardly. **-yell'ow fever** *n.* acute infectious disease of tropical Amer. and W. Africa. **-yell'owhammer** *n.* yellow bunting. **-yell'ow press'** sensational journalism. **-yell'ow rain** *n.* a type of yellow precipitation described in parts of S.E. Asia and alleged by some to be evidence of chemical warfare. [OE. *geoly*]
yelp *v.s.* give a quick, shrill cry. *-n.* such cry. [OE. *gielpan*, boast]
yeo'man *n.* man owning and farming a small estate. **-yeo'manry** *n.* yeomen collectively; territorial cavalry force. [contra. of young man]
yes *interj.* affirms or consents, gives an affirmative answer. **-yes'man** *n.* servile person who never dares to disagree. [OE. *gese*]
yesterday *n.* day before today. [OE. *giestrandæg*]
yet *adv.* now, still; hitherto. *conj.* but, at the same time, nevertheless, however. [OE. *giet*]
yew *n.* evergreen tree with dark leaves; its wood. [OE. *iw*]
Yidd'ish *n.* Jewish dialect of corrupt Hebrew, German and other elements. [Ger. *jüdisch*, Jewish]
yield *v.t.* give or return as food; give up, surrender. *-v.i.* produce; surrender, give way. *-n.* amount produced; profit, or result. [OE. *gieldan*, pay]
yo'del *v.i.* warble in a falsetto tone. *-n.* falsetto warbling as practiced by Swiss mountaineers. [Ger. *jodeln*]
yo'ga *n.* Hindu discipline of deep meditation aiming at union of soul with God; exercises associated with this. **-yogi** *n.* devotee of yoga. [Sans. = *union*]
yog'urt, yogh'urt *n.* thick, custard-like preparation of curdled milk. [Turk. *yoghurt*]
yoke *n.* wooden bar put across the necks of two animals to hold them together and to which a plow, *etc.*, may be attached; various objects like a yoke in shape or use; bond or tie. *-v.t.* put a yoke on; couple, unite. [OE. *geoc*]
yo'kel *n.* rustic. [orig. unknown]
yolk *n.* yellow part of an egg. [OE. *geoloca*, fr. *geolu*, yellow]
yon *a.* that or those over there. **-yon'der** *a.* yon. *adv.* over there, in that direction. [OE. *geon*]
yore *n.* past. [OE. *geara-gear*, year]
you *pron.* plural of the 2nd person pron. but used also as a sing. (OE. *eow*]
young (yung) *a.* not far advanced in growth, life or existence, not yet old; vigorous. *-n.* offspring. **-young'ster** *n.* child, *esp.* lively boy. [OE. *geong*]
your *pron.* belonging to you. **-yours** *pron.* **-yourself** *pron.* [OE. *eower*]
youth *n.* state or time of being young; state before adult age; young person; young people. **-youth'ful** *a.* [OE. *geogoth*]
yule *n.* Christmas festival. **-yule-log** *n.* **-yule-tide** *n.* [OE. *geol*]
yuppie *n.* wealthy young person. *-a.* [fr. *y*oung *up*wardly-mobile *p*rofessional]

Z

za'ny *n.* clown. [It. Giovanni, John]
zeal *n.* fervor, keenness. **-zeal'ous** *a.* **-zeal'ously** *adv.* **-zeal'ot** *n.* fanatic. [G. *zeros*]
ze'bra *n.* striped animal like a horse, native of Africa. [Port.]
ze'bu *n.* domestic animal of Asia and eastern Africa, resembling ox, but with large hump. [F.]
Zen *n.* Japanese school of Buddhism teaching contemplation and meditation. *a.* [Jap.]
zena'na *n.* women's quarters in high-caste Indian houses. [Pers. *zanana*, fr. zan, woman]
zen'ith *n.* point of the heavens directly above an observer. [Arab. *samt*, a road]
zeph'yr (zefer) *n.* west wind; gentle breeze. [G. *zephyros*, west wind]

Zepp'elin *n.* German airship, used in World War I. [Count *Zeppelin*]

ze'ro *n.* nothing; figure 0; point on a graduated instrument from which positive and negative quantities are reckoned. **ze'ro hour** in military operations, time from which each item on the program is at an interval stated. [It., fr. Arab. *sifr*, cipher]

zest *n.* relish. **-zest'ful** *a.* **-zest'fully** *adv.* [F. = slice of lemon peel for flavoring]

zig'zag *n.* line bent by a series of angles. *-a.* forming a zigzag. *-adv.* with a zigzag course. *-v.i.* move along in a zigzag course. [F.]

zinc *n.* white metal. *-v.t.* coat with it [Ger. *zink*]

zinc'ograph, zinc'o *n.* design in relief on zinc plate; print made from this. *-v.t.* and *i.* etch on zinc, reproduce thus. **zincog'rapher** *n.* **-zincog'raphy** *n.* **zincograph'ic** *a.* [G. *zink*]

zing'aro *n.* gypsy. **-zing'ari** *pl.* [It.]

zinn'ia *n.* plant allied to the aster, with brightly colored flowers. [J. G. *Zinn* (d. 1759)]

Zi'on *n.* (hill in) ancient Jerusalem; Israel; the people of Israel; Christianity; paradise. **-Zi'onism** *n.* movement to found and support a Jewish homeland in Palestine. **-Zi'onist** *n.* advocate of this. [Heb. *tsiyon*, hill]

zip code *n.* five-figure number used in postal addresses designed to facilitate delivery of mail. [fr. *z*one *i*mprovement *p*lan]

zip'per *n.* quick-fastening device for clothes. [imit.]

zir'con *n.* mineral, Ceylon stone, varieties of which include jocinth and jargoon. **-zircon'ic** *a.* [Arab. *zarquin*]

zither(n) *n.* flat, stringed instrument with 29-42 strings. [Ger.]

zo'diac *n.* imaginary belt of the heavens outside which the sun, moon, and chief planets do not pass and divided crosswise into twelve equal areas (signs of the zodiac), each named after a constellation. **-zo'diacal** *a.* [G. *zodiakos*, fr. *zoon*, animal (the constellations being named mainly after animals)]

zom'bie *n.* African snake deity; in American voodooism, corpse given appearance of life by sorcery. [W. African *zambi*, fetish]

zone *n.* girdle; encircling band; any of the five belts into which the tropics and the arctic and antarctic circles divide the earth. **-zo'ning** *n.* town-planning according to zonal areas, residential, *etc.* [G.]

zool'ogy *n.* natural history of animals. **-zoolo'gical** *a.* **-zool'ogist** *n.*

zoo *n.* short for zoological gardens, place where wild animals are kept for show. **-zo'olite** *n.* fossil animal. **zo'ophyte** *n.* plant-like animal, *e.g.*, a sponge. [G. *zoos*, living]

Zoroas'trian, Zorathus'trian *a. pert.* to Persian religion of Zoroaster (Zorathustra). *-n.* adherent of this.

Zouave *n.* soldier of French-Algerian infantry, wearing a uniform of oriental type. [F.]

zy'gote *n.* fertilized egg cell. [G. *zygon*, yoke]

zymot'ic *a.* of, or caused by, fermentation; of a disease, due to multiplication of germs introduced into the body from outside. [G. *zimotikos*, fr. *zume*, leaven]

Abbreviations

A

a or **@** at; to
A1 first class
A ace, argon
A angstrom unit
AA Alcoholics Anonymous, anti-aircraft
AAA Agricultural Adjustment Administration, American Automobile Association
AAAL American Academy of Arts and Letters
AAAS American Association for the Advancement of Science
A and M agricultural and mechanical, ancient and modern
AAR against all risks
AAU Amateur Athletic Union
AAUP American Association of University Professors
AAUW American Association of University Women
AB able-bodied seaman, airman basic. Alberta. [*artium baccalaureus*] bachelor of arts
ABA American Bankers Association, American Bar Association, American Basketball Association, American Booksellers Association
abbr abbreviation
ABC American Bowling Congress, American Broadcasting Company, Australian Broadcasting Company
ABCD accelerated business collection and delivery
abd or **abdom** abdomen, abdominal
abl ablative
abn airborne
abr abridged, abridgment
abs absolute, abstract
ABS American Bible Society
abstr abstract
ac account, acre
Ac actinium
AC air-conditioning, alternating current, (ante Christum) before Christ
acad academic, academy
AC and U Association of Colleges and Universities
acc accusative
accel accelerando
acct account, accountant
accus accusative
ACE American Council on Education
ack acknowledge, acknowledgment
ACLU American Civil Liberties Union
ACP American College of Physicians
acpt acceptance
ACS American Chemical Society, American College of Surgeons
act active, actor, actual
ACT American College Test, Association of Classroom Teachers, Australian Capital Territory
actg acting
AD active duty, after date, [*anno domini*] in the year of our Lord
ADA American Dental Association, average daily attendance
ADC aide-de-camp. Air Defense Command
ADD American Dialect Dictionary
addn addition
addnl additional
ADF automatic direction finder
ADH antidiuretic hormone
ad int ad interim
ADIZ air defense identification zone
adj adjective, adjunct, adjustment, adjutant
ad loc (*ad locum*) to or at the place
adm administration, administrative
admin administration
admrx administratrix
ADP automatic data processing
adv advert. (*adversus*) against
ad val ad valorem
advt advertisement
AEC Atomic Energy Commission
AEF American Expeditionary Force
aeq (*aequalis*) equal
aero aeronautical, aeronautics
aet or **aetat** (*aetatis*) of age, aged
af affix
AF air force, audio frequency
AFB air force base
AFC American Football Conference, automatic frequency control
aff affirmative
afft affidavit
AFL-CIO American Federation of Labor and Congress of Industrial Organizations
aft afternoon
AFT American Federation of Teachers, automatic fine tuning

AFTRA American Federation of Television and Radio Artists
Ag (L. *argentum*) silver
AE adjutant general, attorney general
agcy agency
AGR advanced gas-cooled reactor
agr or **agric** agricultural, agriculture
agt agent
AH ampere-hour, (*anno hegiræ*) in the year of the Hegira (the flight of Mohammed from Mecca to Medina, 622 A.D.)
AHL American Hockey League
AI ad interim, artificial insemination, artificial intelligence
AID Agency for International Development
AIDS acquired immune (or immuno-) deficiency syndrome
AIM American Indian Movement
AK Alaska
aka also known as
AKC American Kennel Club
Al aluminium
AL Alabama, American League, American Legion
Ala Alabama
ALA American Library Association
alc alcohol
alk alkaline
allo allegro
alt alternate, altitude
Alta Alberta
alw allowance
Am America, American, americium
AM (*ante meridiem*) before midday, (*artium magister*) master of arts
AMA American Medical Association
Amer America, American
Amer Ind American Indian
Amn airman
amp ampere
amp hr ampere-hour
AMS Agricultural Marketing Service
AMU atomic mass unit
AMVETS American Veteran (of World War I)
AN airman (Navy)
ANA American Newspaper Association, American Nurses Association
anat anatomical, anatomy
Angl Anglican
anhyd anhydrous
ann annals, annual
annon anonymous
ANOVA analysis of variance
AO account of
AP additional premium, antipersonnel, Associated Press, author's proof
APB all points bulletin
APC armored personnel carrier
API air position indicator
APO army post office
appl applied
approx approximate, approximately
appt appoint, appointed, appointment
apptd appointed
Apr April
APR annual percentage rate
apt apartment, aptitude
aq aqua, aqueous
Ar argon
AR accounts receivable, acknowledgment of receipt, all risks, Arkansas
ARC American Red Cross
arch archaic, architect, architecture
Arch Archbishop
arg argent, argument
arith arithmetical
Ariz Arizona
Ark Arkansas
ARP air-raid precautions
arr arranged, arrival, arrive
art article, artificial
As arsenic
AS after sight, American Samoa, Anglo-Saxon
ASA American Standards Association
ASAP as soon as possible
asb asbestos
ASCAP American Society of Composers, Authors and Publishers
ASCU Association of State Colleges and Universities
ASE American Stock Exchange
ASEAN Association of Southeast Asian Nations
ASI airspeed indicator
ASL American Sign Language
ASR airport surveillance radar, air-sea rescue
assn association
assoc associate, associated, association
ASSR Autonomous Soviet Socialist Republic
asst assistant
Assyr Assyrian
astrol astrologer, astrology
astron astronomer, astronomy

ASV American Standard Version
Atl Atlantic
atm atmosphere, atmospheric
attn attention
atrib attributive, attributively
Au (*aurum*) gold
aud audit, auditor
Aug August
Aus Austria, Austrian, Australia, Australian
AUS Army of the United States
Austral Australia
auth authentic, authorized
auto automatic
av avenue, average, avoidupois
AV ad valorem, audiovisual, Authorized Version
AVC automatic volume control
avdp avoirdupois
ave avenue
avg average
AWACS airborne warning and control system
AYC American Youth Congress
AYD American Youth for Democracy
AZ Arizona

B

B boron
Ba barium
BA bachelor of arts
BAEd bachelor of arts in education
BAg bachelor of agriculture
bal balance
B and B bed-and-breakfast
b and w black and white
Bapt Baptist
bar barometer, barometric
BAr bachelor of architecture
Bart baronet
BBC British Broadcasting Corporation
bbl barrel, barrels
BC before Christ, British Columbia
BCD binary-coded decimal
BCh bachelor of chemistry
bcn beacon
BCSE Board of Civil Service Examiners
bd ft board foot
bdl or **bdle** bundle
bdrm bedroom
Be beryllium
BE bachelor of education, bachelor of engineering, bill of exchange
BEC Bureau of Employees' Compensation
BEd bachelor of education
BEF British Expeditionary Force
beg begin, beginning
Belg Belgian, Belgium
BEM British Empire Medal
BEngr bachelor of engineering
BFA bachelor of fine arts
BG or **B Gen** brigadier general
BH bill of health
bhd bulkhead
BHE Bureau of Higher Education
bhp bishop
BIA bachelor of industrial arts, Braille Institute of America, Bureau of Indian Affairs
bib Bible, biblical
biog biographer, biographical, biography
biol biologic, biological, biologist, biology
bk bank, book
Bk berkelium
bkg banking, bookkeeping, breakage
bkgd background
bks barracks
bkt basket, bracket
bl bale, barrel, block
BL Bachelor of law, bachelor of letters, bill of lading, breadth/length
bldg building
bldr builder
Blitt or **BLit** (*baccalaureus litterarum*) bachelor of letters, bachelor of literature
blk black, block, bulk
blvd boulevard
BMR basal metabolic rate
BNDD Bureau of Narcotics and Dangerous Drugs
BO back order, body odor, branch office, buyer's option
BOD biochemical oxygen demand, biological oxygen demand
bor borough
bot botanical, botanist, botany, bottle, bottom, bought
BP bills payable, blood pressure, blue print, boiling point
BPD barrels per day
bpi bits per inch, bytes per inch
Br Britain, British, bromine
BR bills receivable
brig brigade, brigadier
Brig Gen brigadier general
Brit Britain, British
brl barrel

bro brother, brothers
bros brothers
BS bachelor of science, balance sheet, bill of sale, British standard
BSA Boy Scouts of America
BSI British Standards Institution
bskt basket
Bt baronet
btry battery
Btu British thermal unit
bu bureau, bushel
bur bureau
bus business
BV Blessed Virgin
BW bacteriological warfare, biological warfare, black and white
BWI British West Indies
BYO bring your own

C

C carbon
ca circa
Ca calcium
CA California, chartered accountant, chief accountant
CAB Civil Aeronautics Board
CAD computer-aided design
CAF cost and freight
CAGS Certificate Advanced Graduate Study
CAI computer-aided instruction, computer-associated instruction
cal calendar, caliber, calorie, small calorie
Cal California, large calorie
calc calculate, calculated
Calif California
CAM computer-aided manufacturing
can canceled, cancellation
Can or **Canad** Canada, Canadian
canc canceled
C and F cost and freight
C and W country and western
cap capacity, capital, capitalize
CAP Civil Air Patrol
caps capitals, capsule
Capt captain
card cardinal
CAS certificate of advanced study
cat catalog, catalyst
cath cathedral, cathode
CATV community antenna television
caus causative
cav cavalry, cavity
Cb columbium
CBC Canadian Broadcasting Corporation
CBD cash before delivery
CBI computer-based instruction, Cumulative Book Index
CBS Columbia Broadcasting System
CBW chemical and biological warfare
cc cubic centimeter
CC carbon copy, chief clerk
CCF Cooperative Commonwealth Federation (of Canada)
cckw counterclockwise
CCTV closed-circuit television
CCU cardiac care unit, coronary care unit, critical care unit
ccw counterclockwise
cd candela
Cd cadmium
CD carried down, certificate of deposit, civil defense, (*corps diplomatique*) diplomatic corps
CDD certificate of disability for discharge
cdg commanding
CDR commander
CDT central daylight time
Ce cerium
ce chemical engineer, civil engineer
CEA College English Association, Council of Economic Advisors
CED Committee for Economic Development
cem cement
cent centigrade, central, centium, century
Cent Central
CENTO Central Treaty Organization
CEO chief executive officer
CER conditioned emotional response
cert certificate, certified
CETA Comprehensive Employment and Training Act
cf (*confer*) compare
Cf californium
CF carried forward, cost and freight, cystic fibrosis
CFI cost, freight, and insurance
cfm cubic feet per minute
cfs cubic feet per second
cg or **cgm** centigram
CG center of gravity, coast guard, commanding general
CGT (*Confederation Generale du Travail*) General Confederation of Labor
ch chain, chapter, church
CH clearinghouse, courthouse, customhouse
chan channel

chap chapter
chem chemical, chemist, chemistry
chg change, charge
chm chairman, checkmate
Chmn chairman
chron chronicle, chronological, chronology
Ci curie
CI certificate of insurance, cost and insurance
CIA Central Intelligence Agency
CID Criminal Investigation Department
cie (*compagnie*) company
CIF cost, insurance and freight
C in C commander in chief
CIP Cataloging in Publication
cir circle, circuit, circumference
circ circular
cit citation, cited, citizen
civ civil, civilian
CJ chief justice
ck cask, check
cl centiliter, class
Cl chlorine
CL center line, civil law, common law
cld called, cleared
Clev Cleveland
clin clinical
clk clerk
clr clear, clearance
CLU chartered life underwriter
cm centimeter, cumulative
Cm curium
CMA certified medical assistant
cmd command
cmdg commanding
cmdr commander
CMG Companion of the Order of St. Michael and St. George
cml commercial
CMSgt chief master sergeant
CN credit note
CNO chief of naval operations
CNS central nervous system
co company, county
Co cobalt
CO cash order, Colorado, commanding officer, conscientious objector
c/o care of
cod codex
COD cash on delivery
C of S chief of staff
col color, colored, column
col or coll collateral, college
Col colonel, Colorado
COL colonel, cost of living
collat collateral
colloq colloquial
Colo Colorado
comb combination, combined
comd command
comdg commanding
comdr commander
comdt commandant
COMECON Council for Mutual Economic Assistance
coml commercial
comm command, commerce, commission, committee, communication
commo Commodore
comp compare, complex
compd compound
comr commissioner
conc concentrate, concentrated
conf conference, confidential
Confed Confederate
cong congress, congressional
Conn Connecticut
consol consolidated
cont containing, contents, continent, continued
contd continued
contg containing
contrib contribution, contributor
CORE Congress of Racial Equality
corp corporal, corporation
corr correct, corrected, corresponding
cos cosine
COS cash on shipment, chief of staff
cp compare, coupon
CP candlepower, charter party, communist party
CPA certified public accountant
CPB Corporation for Public Broadcasting
CPCU chartered property and casualty underwriter
cpd compound
CPFF cost plus fixed fee
CPI consumer price index
Cpl corporal
CPO chief petty officer
CPOM master chief petty officer
CPOS senior chief petty officer
CPS characters per second, cycles per second
CPT captain
cpu central processing unit
Cr chromeum

CR carrier's risk, cathode ray
CRC Civil Rights Commission
cresc crescendo
crim criminal
crit critical, criticism, criticized
CRT cathode-ray tube
crust crystalline, crystallized
Cs cesium
CS capital stock, chief of staff, Christian Science, civil service
C/S cycles per second
CSA Confederate States of America
CSC Civil Service Commission
CSM command sergeant major
CST central standard time
ct carat, cent, count, county, court
CT central time, certificated teacher, Connecticut
CTC centralized traffic control
ctf certificate
ctg or **ctge** cartage
ctn carton
cto concerto
C to C center to center
ctr center, counter
cu cubic, cumulative
Cu (*cuprum*) copper
CU close-up
cum cumulative
cur currency, current
CV cardiovascular, curriculum vitae
cvt convertible
cw clockwise
CW chemical warfare, chief warrant officer
CWO cash with order, chief warrant officer
cwt hundred weight
CY calendar year
cyl cylinder
CYO Catholic Youth Organization
CZ Canal Zone

D

d deceased, penny
D Democrat, deuterium
da deka-
DA days after acceptance, deposit account, district attorney
DAB Dictionary of American Biography
dag dekagram
dal dekaliter
dam dekameter
DAR Daughters of the American Revolution
dat dative
DAV Disabled American Veterans
db debenture
db or **dB** decibel
DB daybook
DBE Dame Commander of the Order of the British Empire
dbl double
DBMS data base management system
DC direct current, District of Columbia
dd dated, delivered
DD days after date, demand draft, dishonorable discharge, due date
DDC Dewey Decimal Classification
DDD direct distance dialing
DDS doctor of dental science, doctor of dental surgery
DE Delaware
deb debenture
dec deceased, declaration, declared, decorative, decrease
Dec December
def defendant, defense, deferred, defined, definite
deg degree
del delegate, delegation, delete
Del Delaware
dely delivery
dem demonstrative, demurrage
Dem Democrat, Democratic
Den Denmark
dent dental, dentist, dentistry
dep depart, department, departure, deposit, depot, deputy
dept department
der or **deriv** derivation, derivative
DEW distant early warning
DF damage free, direction finder
DFC Distinguished Flying Cross
DFM Distinguished Flying Medal
dft defendant, draft
dg decigram
DG director general, (*Dei gratia*) by the grace of God
dia diameter
diag diagonal, diagram
dial dialect
diam diameter
dict dictionary
dim diminutive
dip diploma
dir director
disc discount

dist distance, district
distr distribute, distribution
div dividend, division
DJ disc jockey, district judge, doctor of jurisprudence
DJIA Dow Jones Industrial Average
dkg dekagram
dkl dekaliter
dkm dekameter
dl deciliter
DLitt or **DLit** (*doctor litterarum*) doctor of letters, doctor of literature
DLO dead letter office, dispatch loading only
dm decimeter
DM deutsche Mark
DMZ demilitarized zone
dn down
DNB Dictionary of National Biography
do ditto
DOA dead on arrival
DOB date of birth
doc document
DOD Department of Defense
DOE Department of Energy
dol dollar
DOM (*Deo optimo maximo*) to God, the best and greatest
DOS disk operating system
DOT Department of Transportation
doz dozen
DP data processing, dew point
DPH department of public health
dr dram
Dr doctor
DR dead reckoning
DSM Distinguished Service Medal
DSO Distinguished Service Order
DSP (*decessit sine prole*) died without issue
DST daylight time, double time
dup duplex, duplicate
DV (*Deo volente*) God willing
DW deadweight
dwt deadweight ton, pennyweight
DX distance
dy delivery, deputy, duty
Dy dysprosium
dynam dynamics
dz dozen

E

ea each
E and OE errors and omissions excepted
EB eastbound
eccl ecclesiastic, ecclesiastical
ECG electrocardiogram
ECM European Common Market
ecol ecological, ecology
econ economics, economist, economy
ed edited, edition, editor, education
EDP electronic data processing
EDT eastern daylight time
educ education, educational
EEC European Economic Community
EEG electroencephalogram, electroencephalograph
EENT eye, ear, nose, and throat
EEO equal employment opportunity
eff efficiency
EFT or **EFTS** electronic funds transfer (system)
e.g. (*exempli gratia*) for example
EHF extremely high frequency
EHP effective horsepower, electric horsepower
EHV extra high voltage
elec electric, electrical, electricity
elem elementary
elev elevation
ELF extremely low frequency
ELSS extravehicular life support system
EM electromagnetic, electron microscope
emer emeritus
emf electromotive force
emp emperor, empress
enc or **encl** enclosure
ENE east-northeast
eng engine, engineer, engineering
Eng England, English
ENS ensign
env envelope
EO executive order
EOM end of month
EP extended play
EPA Environmental Protection Agency
eq equal, equation
equip equipment
equiv equivalency, equivalent
Er erbium
Es einsteinium
ESE east-southeast
ESL English as a second language
esp especially
Esq esquire
est established, estimate, estimated
EST eastern standard time

esu electrostatic unit
ESV earth satellite vehicle
ET eastern time, extra-terrestrial
ETA estimated time of arrival
et al *et alii* (masc.), *et aliae* (fem.) or *et alia* (neut.) and others
etc et cetera, and the rest
ETD estimated time of departure
ETO European theater of operations
et seq (*et sequens*) and the following one
et ux (*et uxor*) and wife
Eu europium
Eur Europe, European
EVA extravehicular activity
ex example, exchange, excluding, executive, express, extra
exch exchange, exchanged
exec executive
exhbn exhibition
exor executor
expy expressway
ext extension, exterior, external

F

f Fahrenheit, farad, faraday, and the following one
F fluorine
FA field artillery, fielding average, football association
FAA Federal Aviation Administration, free of all average
fac facsimile, faculty
FADM fleet admiral
fam familiar, family
F and A fore and aft
FAO Food and Agriculture Organization of the United Nations
FAQ fair average quality
far farthing
FAS free alongside ship
fath fathom
FBI Federal Bureau of Investigation
FCA Farm Credit Administration
FCC Federal Communications Commission
fcp foolscap
FDA Food and Drug Administration
FDIC Federal Deposit Insurance Corporation
Fe (*ferrum*) iron
Feb February
fec (*fecit*) he made it
fed federal, federation
fem female, feminine
FERA Federal Emergency Relief Administration
ff folios, and the following ones, fortissimo
FHA Federal Housing Administration
fict fiction, fictitious
FIFO first in, first out
fig figurative, figuratively, figure
fin finance, financial, finish
FIO free in and out
fir firkin
fl florin (*floruit*) flourished
FL Florida
Fla Florida
fl oz fluid ounce
FLSA Fair Labor Standards Act
fm fathom
Fm fermium
FM field manual
FMB Federal Maritime Board
FMCS Federal Mediation and Conciliation Service
fn footnote
fo or fol folio
FO foreign office
FOB free on board
FOC free of charge
fp freezing point
FPA Foreign Press Association, free of particular average
FPC Federal Power Commission
fps feet per second, foot-pound-second, frames per second
fr father, franc, from
Fr francium
freq frequency
Fri Friday
FRS Federal Reserve System
frt freight
frwy freeway
FS Foreign Service
FSLIC Federal Savings and Loan Insurance Corporation
FSP Food Stamp Program
ft feet, foot
FTC Federal Trade Commission
fth fathom
ft lb foot-pound
fur furlong
fut future
fwd foreword, forward
FWD front-wheel drive
FX foreign exchange
FY fiaml year

FYI for your information
fz (*forzando, forzato*) accented

G

g acceleration of gravity, gram, gravity
Ga gallium, Georgia
GA general assembly, general average, Georgia
gal gallery, gallon
galv galvanized
GAO General Accounting Office
gar garage
GATT General Agreement on Tariffs and Trade
GAW guaranteed annual wage
gaz gazette
GB Great Britain
GCA ground-controlled approach
GCB Knight Grand Cross of the Bath
Gd gadolinium
GDR German Democratic Republic
Ge germanium
GE gilt edges
gen general, genitive, genus
Gen AF general of the air force
genl general
geog geographic, geographical, geography
geol geologic, geological, geology
geom geometric, geometrical, geometry
ger gerund
GGPA graduate grade-point average
GHQ general headquarters
gi gill
GI gastrointestinal, general issue, government issue
GM general manager, grand master, guided missile
GMT Greenwich mean time
GMW gram-molecular weight
gn guinea
GNI Gross national income
GNP gross national product
GO general order
GOP Grand Old Party (Republican)
gov government, governor
govt government
gp group
GP general practice
GPD gallons per day
GPH gallons per hour
GPM gallons per minute
GPO general post office, Government Printing Office
GPS gallons per second
gr grade, grain, gram, gravity, gross
grad graduate, graduated
gram grammar, grammatical
gro gross
gr wt gross weight
GSA General Services Administration, Girl Scouts of America
GSC general staff corps
GSO general staff officer
GSV guided space vehicle
GT gross ton
Gt Brit Great Britain
gtd guaranteed
gyn gynecology

H

ha hectare
hab corp habeas corpus
Hb hemoglobin
hc (*honoris case*) for the sake of honor
HC Holy Communion, House of Commons
HCF highest common factor
hd head
HD heavy duty
hdbk handbook
He helium
HE Her Excellency, His Excellency
HEW Department of Health, Education and Welfare
hf half
Hf hafnium
HF high frequency
hg hectogram
Hg (*hydrargyrum*) mercury
HH Her Highness, His Highness, His Holiness
HI Hawaii
Hind Hindustani
hist historian, historical, history
hl hectoliter
HL House of Lords
hld hold
HLS (*hoc loco situs*) laid in this place, holograph letter signed
hlt halt
hm hectometer
HM Her Majesty, Her Majesty's, His Majesty, His Majesty's
HMC Her Majesty's Customs, His Majesty's Customs
HMS Her Majesty's ship, His Majesty's ship

HN head nurse
Ho holmium
hon honor, honorable, honorary
hor horizontal
hort horticultural, horticulture
hosp hospital
HP high pressure, hire purchase, horsepower
HQ headquarters
hr hour
HR House of Representatives
HRH Her Royal Highness, His Royal Highness
hrzn horizon
HS high school
HSGT high-speed ground transport
HST Hawaiian standard time
ht height
HUD Department of Housing and Urban Development
HV high velocity, high-voltage
hvy heavy
HWM high-water mark
hwy highway
Hz hertz

I

Ia or **IA** Iowa
IAAF International Amateur Athletic Federation
IABA International Amateur Boxing Association
IAEA International Atomic Energy Agency
IALC instrument approach and landing chart
IATA International Air Transport Association
ib or **ibid** ibidem
IBM intercontinental ballistic missile
IBRD International Bank for Rmonstruction and Development
ICA International Cooperation Administration, International Cooperative Alliance
ICAO International Civil Aviation Organization
ICBM intercontinental ballistic missile
ICC Indian Claims Commission, International Chamber of Commerce, Interstate Commerce Commission
ICFM International Confederation of Free Trade Unions
ICJ International Court of Justice
ICRC International Committee of the Red Cross
ICU intensive care unit
id idem
ID Idaho, identification
i e (*id est*) that is
IFC International Finance Corporation
IG inspector general
illust or **illus** illustrated, illustration, illustrator
IL Illinois
ILO International Labor Organization
ILS instrument landing system
IMF International Monetary Fund
immun immunity, immunization
imp imperative, imperfect, import
in inch
In indium
IN Indiana
inc including, incorporated, increase
incl including, inclusive
incog incognito
ind independent, industrial, industry
Ind Indian, Indiana
inf infantry, infinitive
inq inquire
INRI (*Jesus Nazarenus Rex Iudaeorum*) Jesus of Nàzareth, King of the Jews
ins inches, insurance
INS Immigration and Naturalization Service
inti or **intnl** international
intrans intransitive
in trans (*in transitu*) in transit
intsv intensive
IOC International Olympic Committee
ipn inches per minute
IPPF International Planned Parenthood Federation
ips inches per second
iq (*idem quod*) the same as
Ir iridium
IR infrared, inland revenue, intelligence ratios, internal revenue
IRA Irish Republican Army
IRBM intermediate range ballistic missile
irreg irregular
IRS Internal Revenue Service
ISBN International Standard Book Number
ISC interstate commerce
ISSN international Standard Serial Number
ital italic, italicized

ITO International Trade Organization
IU international unit
IV intravenous, intravenously
IWW Industrial Workers of the World

J

j joule
JA joint account, judge advocate
JAG judge advocate general
Jan January
JBS John Birch Society
JCS joint chiefs of staff
jct junction
JD justice department, juvenile delinquent, (*juris doctor*) doctor of jurisprudence, doctor of law
JP justice of the peace
Jr junior
jt or **jnt** joint
jun junior
Jun June
junc junction
juv juvenile

K

k karat, kilogram
K (*kalium*) potassium, Kelvin
Kan or **Kans** Kansas
kb or **kbar** kilobar
KB kilobyte
KC Kansas City, King's Counsel, Knights of Columbus
kcal kilocalorie, kilogram calorie
KCB Knight Commander of the Order of the Bath
kc/s kilocycles per second
KD knocked down
kg kilogram
KG knight of the Order of the Garter
KGB (*Komitet Gosudarstvennoi Bezopasnosti*) (Soviet) State Security Committee
kHz kilohertz
KIA killed in action
KJV King James Version
KKK Ku Klux Klan
kl kiloliter
km kilometer
KMPS kilometers per second
kn knot
K of C Knights of Columbus
kph kilometers per hour
Kr Krypton
KS Kansas
kt karat, knight
kv kilovolt
kw kilowatt
kwhr or **kwh** kilowatt-hour
Ky or **KY** Kentucky

L

La lanthanum, Louisiana
LA law agent, Los Angeles, Louisiana
Lab Labrador
lam laminated
lang language
lat latitude
Lat Latin, Latvia
LAT local apparent time
lb (*libra*) pound
LB Labrador
lc lowercase
LC landing craft, letter of credit, Library of Congress
LCD lowest common denominator
LD lethal dose
LDC less developed country
ldg landing, loading
LDS Latter-day Saints
lect lecture, lecturer
leg legal, legislative, legislation
legis legislation, legislative, legislature
LF low frequency
lg large, long
LH left hand
Li lithium
LI Long Island
lib liberal, librarian
lieut lieutenant
LIFO last in, first out
lin lineal, linear
ling linguistics
liq liquid, liquor
lit liter, literal, literally, literary, literature
lith lithographic, lithography
ll lines
LL limited liability
LM Legion of Merit, lunar module
LMT local mean time
lndg landing
LNG liquefied natural gas
loc cit (*loco citato*) in the place cited
LP low pressure
LPG liquefied petroleum gas
LPGA Ladies Professional Golf Association
Lr lawrencium

LS (*locus sigilli*) place of the seal
LSS lifesaving station, life-support system
Lt lieutenant
LT long ton
LTC or **Lt Col** lieutenant colonel
Lt Comdr lieutenant commander
ltd limited
LTG or **Lt Gen** lieutenant general
lt gov lieutenant governor
LTJG lieutenant, junior grade
Lu lutetium
lub lubricant, lubricating
LVT landing vehicle, tracked
LWM low-water mark
LWV League of Women Voters
LZ landing zone

M

m much, meter (*mille*) thousand
M monsieur
ma or **mA** miliampere
MA Massachusetts, (*magister artium*) master of arts
MAD mutual assured destruction
MAE or **MA Ed** master of arts in education
mag magnesium, magnetism, magnitude
Maj major
Maj Gen major general
man manual
Man Manitoba
manuf manufacture, manufacturing
MAP modified American plan
mar maritime
Mar March
masc masculine
MASH mobile army surgical hospital
Mass Massachusetts
math mathematical, mathematician
metric matriculated, matriculation
max maximum
mb millibar
MB bachelor of medicine, Manitoba, megabyte
MBA master of business administration
mbd million barrels per day
MBE Member of the Order of the British Empire
MBS Mutual Broadcasting System
mc megacycle, millicurie
MC Member of Congress
mcf thousand cubic feet
mcg microgram
MCPO master chief petty officer
Md Maryland
MD Maryland, (*medicinae doctor*) doctor of medicine
mdse merchandise
MDT mountain daylight time
Me Maine, methyl
ME Maine
meas measure
mech mechanical, mechanics
med medicine, medieval, medium
Med Mediterranean
MEd master of education
met meteorological, meteorology, metropolitan
METO Middle East Treaty Organization
Mex Mexican, Mexico
MF medium frequency, mezzo forte, microfiche
mfd manufactured
mfg manufacturing
MFN most favored nation
mfr manufacturer
mg milligram
Mg magnesium
mgd million gallons per day
mgr manager, monseigneur, monsignor
mgt management
MH medal of honor, mobile home
MHz megahertz
mi mile, mileage, mill
MI Michigan, military intelligence
MIA missing in action
Mich Michigan
mid middle
midn midshipman
mil military, million
min minimum, minute
Minn Minnesota
misc miscellaneous
Miss Mississippi, mistress (unmarried woman)
Mk Mark
mks meter-kilogram-second
mktg marketing
Ml milliliter
MLA Member of the Legislative Assembly
MLD median lethal dose, minimum lethal dose
MLF multilateral force
Mlle mademoiselle
Mlles mademoiselles
mm millimeter

MM messieurs, mutatis mutandis
Mme madame
MN Minnesota
mo month
Mo Missouri, molybdenum
MO mail order, medical officer, Missouri, modus operandi, money order
mod moderate, modern, modification, modified, module, modulus
modif modification
mol molecular, molecule
MOL Manned Orbiting Laboratory
Mont Montana
MP melting point, member of parliament, metropolitan police, military police, military policeman
mpg miles per gallon
mph miles per hour
MR map reference, mentally retarded
Mr mister
mRNA messenger RNA
Mrs mistress (married woman)
ms millisecond
MS manuscript, master of science, military science, Mississippi, motorship, multiple sclerosis
Ms mistress (woman, marital status unmarked)
MSc master of science
msec millisecond
msg message
MSG master sergeant, monosodium glutamate
msgr monseigneur, monsignor
MSgt master sergeant
MSS manuscripts
MST mountain standard time
mt mount, mountain
MT Montana, mountain time
mtg meeting, mortgage
mtge mortgage
mun or **munic** municipal
mus museum, music, musical, musician
mv or **mV** millivolt
MV motor vessel
MVA Missouri Valley Authority
MW megawatt
MWe megawatts electric
mxd mixed

N

n neuter, neutron, north, northern, noun, number
N newton, nitrogen
Na (*natrium*) sodium
NA no account, North America, not applicable
NAACP National Association for the Advancement of Colored People
NAB New American Bible
NACU National Association of Colleges and Universities
NAMH National Association for Mental Health
NAS National Academy of Sciences, naval air station
NASA National Aeronautics and Space Administration
nat national native, natural
NATO North Atlantic Treaty Organization
naut nautical
Nb niobium
NB New Brunswick, northbound, nota bene
NBA National Basketball Association, National Boxing Association
NBC National Broadcasting Company
NBS National Bureau of Standards
NC no charge, no credit, North Carolina
NCAA National Collegiate Athletic Association
ncv no commercial value
Nd neodymium
ND North Dakota
N Dak North Dakota
Ne neon
NE Nebraska, New England, northeast
NEA National Education Association
Neb or **Nebr** Nebraska
NEB New English Bible
neg negative
nem con (*nemine contrudicente*) no one contradicting
nem diss (*nemine dissentiente*) no one dissenting
neut neuter
Nev Nevada
New Eng New England
NF Newfoundland, no funds
NFC National Football Conference
NFL National Football League
Nfld Newfoundland
NFS not for sale
ng nanogram
NG national guard, no good
NH New Hampshire
NHL National Hockey League
NHP nominal horsepower

Ni nickel
NIH National Institutes of Health
NJ New Jersey
NL National League, new line, (*non licet*) it is not permitted
NLF National Liberation Front
NLRB National Labor Relations Board
NLT night letter
NM nautical mile, New Mexico, no mark
N Mex New Mexico
NMI no middle initial
NMR nuclear magnetic resonance
NNE north-northeast
NNW north-northwest
no north, northern, (*numero*) number
No nobelium
nom nominative
non seq (*non sequitur*) it does not follow
NOP not otherwise provided for
Nor Norway, Norwegian
NORAD North American Air Defense Command
norm normal
nos numbers
NOS not otherwise specified
Nov November
Np neptunium
NPR National Public Radio
nr near
NRA National Recovery Administration, National Rifle Association
NRC National Research Council, Nuclear Regulatory Commission
NS new style, not specified, not sufficient, Nova Scotia
NSA National Security Agency
NSC National Security Council
NSW New South Wales
NT New Testament, Northern Territory, Northwest Territories
NTP normal temperature and pressure
nt wt or **n wt** net weight
NV Nevada, nonvoting
NW northwest
NWT Northwest Territories
NY New York
NYA National Youth Administration
NYC New York City
NYSE New York Stock Exchange
NZ New Zealand

O

o ohm
O Ohio, oxygen
o/a on or about
OAS Organization of American States
OAU Organization of African Unity
ob (*obit*) he died, she died
OBE Officer of the Order of the British Empire
obj object, objective
OCR optical character reader, optical character recognition
oct octavo
Oct October
OD on demand, overdose, overdrawn
OE Old English
OECD Organization for Economic Cooperation and Development
OED Oxford English Dictionary
OF outfield
off office, officer, official
offic official
OH Ohio
OHMS on Her Majesty's service, on His Majesty's service
OIT Office of International Trade
OK Oklahoma
Okla Oklahoma
OM order of merit
On or **ONT** Ontario
OP out of print
op cit (*opere citato*) in the work cited
OPEC Organization of Petroleum Exporting Countries
Opp opposite
opt optical, optician
OR Oregon, owner's risk
orch orchestra
ord order, ordinance
Oreg or **Ore** Oregon
org organic, organization, organized
orig original, originally, originator
Os osmium
OS old style, ordinary seaman, out of stock
OT occupational therapy, Old Testament, overtime
OTC over-the-counter
OTS officers' training school
OW one-way
Oxon (*Oxonia*) Oxford
oz (*onza*) ounce, ounces

P

p page, penny, peseta, peso
P phosphorus
Pa Pennsylvania, protactinium
PA particular average, Pennsylvania, per

annum, personal appearance, power of attorney, press agent, private account
p and h postage and handling
P and L profit and loss
par paragraph, parallel
part participle, particular
pass passenger, passive
pat patent
path or **pathol** pathological, pathology
PAU Pan American Union
PAYE pay as you earn, pay as you enter
payt payment
Pb (*plumbum*) lead
PB power brakes
PBS Public Broadcasting Service
PBX private branch exchange
PC Peace Corps, percent, percentage, personal computer, postcard
pct percent, percentage
pd paid
Pd palladium
PD per diem, police department
PDD past due date
PDT Pacific daylight time
PE physical education, printer's error, probable error
P/E price/earnings
pen peninsula
PEN International Association of Poets, Playwrights, Editors, Essayists and Novelists
Penn Pennsylvania
per period, person
perf perfect, perforated, performance
perh perhaps
perm permanent
perp perpendicular
pers person, personal, personnel
pert pertaining
pfd preferred
PGA Professional Golfers' Association
ph phase
PH public health, Purple Heart
phar pharmacy
pharm pharmaceutical, pharmacist, pharmacy
PhB (*philosophiae baccalaureus*) bachelor of philosophy
PhD (*philosophiae doctor*) doctor of philosophy
phon Phonetics
photog photographic, photography
phr phrase
phys physics
pinx (*pinxit*) he painted it, she painted it
pk park, peak, peck, pike
PK psychokinesis
pkg package
pkng packaging
pkt packet, pocket
pkwy parkway
pl place, plate, plural
PL partial loss, private line
plat plateau, platoon
plf plaintiff
PLO Palestine Liberation Organization
PLSS portable life-support system
pm phase modulation, premium
Pm promethium
PM paymaster, permanent magnet, police magistrate, postmaster, (*post meridien*) after midday, postmortem, prime minister, provost marshal
pmk postmark
pmt payment
PN promissory note
Po polonium
PO petty officer, postal order, post office, purchase order
POC port of call
POD pay on delivery, post office department
POE port of embarkation, port of entry
poly polytechnic
POO post office order
pop popular, population
por portrait
POR pay on return
Port Portugal, Portuguese
pos position, positive
poss possessive
pp pages, (*per procurationem*) by proxy
PP parcel post, past participle, postpaid, prepaid
ppd post paid, prepaid
ppm parts per million
PPS (*post postscriptum*) an additional postscript
ppt parts per thousand, parts per trillion
pptn precipitation
PQ previous question, Province of Quebec
pr pair, price, printed
Pr praseodymium
PR payroll, proportional representation, public relations
PRC People's Republic of China
prec preceding

pred predicate
pref preface, preferred, prefix
prem premium
prep preparatory, preposition
pres present, president
Presb Presbyterian
prev previous, previously
prf proof
prim primary, primitive
prin principal, principle
priv private, privately, privative
PRN (*pro re nata*) for the emergency, as needed
PRO public relations officer
prob probable, probably, probate, problem
proc proceedings
prod product, production
prof professional, professor
prom promontory
pron pronoun, pronounced, pronunciation
prop property, proposition, proprietor
pros prosody
Prot Protestant
prov province, provincial, provisional
PS (*postscriptum*) postscript
pseud pseudonym, pseudonymous
psi pounds per square inch
PST Pacific standard time
psych psychology
psychol psychologist, psychology
pt part, payment, pint, point, port
Pt platinum
PT Pacific time, part-time, physical therapy, physical training
pta peseta
PTA Parent-Teacher Association
ptg printing
PTO Parent-Teacher Organization, please turn over
Pu plutonium
pub public, publication, published, publisher, publishing
publ publication, published, publisher
PUD pickup and delivery
PVA polyvinyl acetate
PVC polyvinyl chloride
pvt private
PVT pressure, volume, temperature
PW prisoner of war
pwr power
pwt pennyweight
PX please exchange, post exchange

Q

q quart, quartile, quarto, query, question
QB queen's bench
QC quality control, queen's counsel
QED (*quod erat demonstrandum*) which was to be demonstrated
QEF (*quod erat faciendum*) which was to be done
QEI (*quod erat inveniendum*) which was to be found out
QMG quartermaster general
qp or **q pl** (*quantum placet*) as much as you please
qq questions
qr quarter, quire
qs (*quantum sufficit*) as much as suffices
qt quantity, quart
qtd quartered
qto quarto
qty quantity
qu or **ques** question
quad quadrant
qual qualitative, quality
quant quantitative
quar quarterly
Que Quebec
quot quotation
qv (*quod vide*) which see

R

r radius, repeat, Republican, ruble, rupee
R radical, registered trademark
Ra radium
RA regular army, Royal Academician, Royal Academy
RAAF Royal Australian Air Force
rad radical, radian, radiator, radio, radius, radix
RAF Royal Air Force
RAM random access memory
R & B rhythm and blues
R & D research and development
R & R rest and recreation, rest and recuperation
Rb rubidium
RBC red blood cells, red blood count
RBE relative biological effectiveness
RC Red Cross, Roman Catholic
RCAF Royal Canadian Air Force
RCMP Royal Canadian Mounted Police
RCN Royal Canadian Navy
rct recruit
rd road, rod, round

RD refer to drawer
RDA recommended daily allowance, recommended dietary allowance
RDF radio direction finder, radio direction finding
Re rhenium
rec receipt, record, recording, recreation
recd received
recip reciprocal, reciprocity
rec sec recording secretary
rect receipt, rectangle, rectangular, rectified
red reduce, reduction
ref reference, referred, refining, reformed, refunding
refl reflex, reflexive
refirig refrigerating, refrigeration
reg region, register, registered, registration, regular
regd registered
regt regiment
rel rerrelating, relative, released, religion, religious
relig religion
rep report, representative, republic
Rep Republican
repl replace, replacement
req request, require, required, requisition
reqd required
res research, reservation, reserve, residence, resolution
resp respective, respectively
retd retained, retired, returned
rev revenue, reverse, review, reviewed, revised, revision, revolution
Rev reverend
rf refunding
RF radio frequency
rh relative humidity
Rh rhodium
rhet rhetoric
RI refractive index, Rhode Island
RIP (*requiescat in pace*) may he rest in peace, may she rest in peace
rit ritardando
riv river
rm ream, room
RMS Royal Mail Service, Royal Mail Steamship
Rn radon
RN registered nurse, Royal Navy
rnd round
ROG receipt of goods
ROI return of investment
Rom Roman, Romance, Romania, Romanian
ROM read-only memory
ROP record of production
rot rotating, rotation
ROTC Reserve Officers Training Corps
RP Received Pronunciation, reply paid, reprint, reprinting
RPM revolutions per minute
RPO railways post office
RPS revolutions per second
rpt repeat, report
RR railroad
RS Royal Society
RSV Revised Standard Version
RSVP (*répondez s'il vous plait*) please reply
RSWC right side up with care
rt right
RT radiotelephone, room temperature
rte route
rtw ready-to-wear
Ru ruthenium
RV recreational vehicle
rwy or **ry** railway

S

s saint, schilling, senate, shilling, sine, singular, small, south, southern
S sulfur
SA Salvation Army, seaman apprentice, (*sine anno* without year) without dates, South Africa, South America, South Australia
SAC Strategic Air Command
SAE self-addressed envelope, stamped addressed envelope
SALT Strategic Arms Limitation Talks
SAM surface-to-air missile
S & M sadism and masochism
sanit sanitary, sanitation
SASE self-addressed stamped envelope
Sask Saskatchewan
sat saturate, saturated, saturation
Sat Saturday
satd saturated
S Aust South Australia
sb substantive
Sb (*stibium*) antimony
SBA Small Business Administration
SBN Standard Book Number
sc scale, scene, science, (*sculpsit*) he carved it, she carved it, he engraved it, she engraved it
SC scandium, Scots

SC small capitals, South Carolina, supreme court
sch school
sci science, scientific
SCP single-cell protein
SCPO senior chief petty officer
sct scout
SD South Dakota, special delivery, stage direction
SDA specific dynamic action
S Dak South Dakota
SDI Strategic Defense Initiative
SDR special drawing rights
Se selenium
SE southeast, Standard English, stock exchange
SEATO Southeast Asia Treaty Organization
sec second, secretary, (*secundum*) according to
sect section, sectional
secy secretary
sed sediment, sedimentation
sel selected, selection
sen senate, senator, senior
sep separate, separated
Sep September
sepd separated
Sept September
seq (*sequens*) the following
serg or **sergt** sergeant
serv service
sf or **sfz** sforzando
SF science fiction, sinking fund
SFC sergeant first class
SG sergeant, solicitor general, specific gravity
sgd signed
Sgt sergeant
Sgt Maj sergeant major
sh share
shipt shipment
shpt shipment
sht sheet
shtg shortage
Si silicon
SI (*Système International d' Unités*) International System of Units
SIDS sudden infant death syndrome
sig signal, signature, signor
SIG special interest group
Sigill (*sigillum*) seal
sin sine
sing singular
SJ Society of Jesus
SK Saskatchewan
sl slightly, slow
SL salvage loss, sea level, south latitude
SLBM submarine-launched ballistic missile
sld sailed, sealed, sold
SLR single lens reflex
Sm samarium
SMaj sergeant major
SMSgt senior master sergeant
SMV slow-moving vehicle
Sn (*stannum*) tin
SNG substitute natural gas, synthetic natural gas
so south, southern
SO seller's option, strikeout
soc social, society
sociol sociologist, sociology
soln solution
soph sophomore
sp species, specific, specimen, spelling
SP self-propelled, shore patrol
SPCA Society for the Prevention of Cruelty to Animals
SPCC Society for the Prevention of Cruelty to Children
spec special, specifically
specif specific, specifically
sp gr specific gravity
SPOT satellite positioning and tracking
SPQR (*senatus populusque Romanus*) the senate and the people of Rome
sq squadron, square
Sr senior, señor, sister, strontium
Sra señora
SRO standing room only
Srta señorita
SS saints, same size, Social Security, steamship
SSA Social Security Administration
SSE south-southeast
SSG or **SSgt** staff sergeant
SSM staff sergeant major
SSW south-southwest
st stanza, state, street
St saint, stratus
ST short ton, single throw, standard time
sta station, stationary
stat (*statim*) immediately
stbd starboard
std standard
Ste (*sainte*) saint (*fem.*)
ster or **stg** sterling

stge storage
stk stock
STOL short takeoff and landing
stor storage
STP standard temperature and pressure
STV subscription television
sub subaltern, subtract, suburb
subj subject, subjunctive
suff sufficient, suffix
Sun Sunday
supp or **suppl** supplement, supplementary
supr supreme
supt superintendent
sur surface
surg surgeon, surgery, surgical
surv survey, surveying, surveyor
sv sailing vessel, saves, (*sub verbo or* sub voce) under the word
svgs savings
sw switch
SW shortwave, southwest
sym symbol, symmetrical
syn synonym, synonymous
syst system

T

T tritium
Ta tantalum
TA teaching assistant
TAC Tactical Air Command
tan tangent
tb tablespoon, tablespoonful
Tb terbium
TB trial balance, tubercle bacillus
tbs or **tbsp** tablespoon, tablespoonful
Tc technetium
tchr teacher
TD touchdown, Treasury Department
TDN total digestible nutrients
TE tellurium
tech technical, technically, technician, technological, technology
TEFL teaching English as a foreign language
tel telegram, telegraph, telephone
teleg telegraphy
temp temperance, temperature, template, temporal, temporary
Tenn Tennessee
TESL teaching English as a second language
TESOL Teachers of English to speakers of Other Languages
Test Testament
Tex Texas
TG transformational grammar, type genus
Th thorium, Thursday
Thurs or **Thu** Thursday
Ti titanium
tk tank, truck
tkt ticket
TL total loss, truckload
TLC tender loving care
TLO total loss only
tlr tailor, trailer
Tm thulium
TM trademark, transcendental meditation
TMO telegraph money order
tn ton, town, train
TN Tennessee, true north
tng training
tnpk turnpike
topog topography
tot total
tpk or **tpke** turnpike
tps townships, troops
tr translated, translator, transpose
trans transaction, transitive, translated, translation, translator
transl translated, translation
transp transportation
trib tributary
trop tropic, tropical
ts tensile strength
tsp teaspoon, teaspoonsful
TT telegraphic transfer, Trust Territories
Tu Tuesday
TU trade union, transmission unit
TUC Trades Union Congress
Tues or **Tue** Tuesday
TV television, terminal velocity, transvestite
TX Texas

U

U university, uranium
UAE United Arab Emirates
UAR United Arab Republic
UC undercharge, uppercase
ugt urgent
UHF ultrahigh frequency
UK United Kingdom
ult ultimate, ultimo
UN United Nations
unan unanimous
UNESCO United Nations Educational, Scientific, and Cultural Organization

UNICEF United Nations International Children's Emergency Fund
univ universal, university
UNRWA United Nations Relief and Works Agency
uns unsymmetrical
UPC Universal Product Code
UPI United Press International
USA United States Army, United States of America
USAF United States Air Force
USCG United States Coast Guard
USDA United States Department of Agriculture
USIA United States Information Agency
USM United States Mail
USMC United States Maritime Corps, United States Marine Corps,
USN United States Navy
USO United Service Organizations
USPS United States Postal Service
USS United States ship
USSR Union of Soviet Socialist Republics
usu usual, usually
UT Universal time, Utah
util utility
UV ultraviolet
UW underwriter
ux wife
UXB unexploded bomb

V

v vector, verb, versus, very, volt, voltage, vowel
V vanadium
Va Virginia
VA Veterans Administration, vice admiral, Virginia, visual aid, volt-ampere
vac vacuum
VADM vice admiral
val value, valued
var variant, variety, various
VAT value-added tax
vb verb, verbal
VC veterinary corps, vice-chancellor, vice-consul, Victoria Cross, Vietcong
VD vapor density, venereal disease
VDT video display terminal
VDU visual display unit
veg vegetable
vel vellum, velocity
vert vertebrate, vertical
VFD volunteer fire department
VG very good, vicar-general
VHF very high frequency
vi verb intransitive
VI Virgin Islands, viscosity index, volume indicator
vic vicinity
Vic Victoria
vil village
vis visibility, visual
VISTA Volunteers in Service to America
viz videlicet
VLF very low frequency
VOA Voice of America
voc vocational, vocative
vocab vocabulary
vol volcano, volume, volunteer
VOLAR volunteer army
VOM volt ohm meter
VP variable pitch, various places, verb phrase, vice president
VRM variable rate mortgage
vs verse, versus
VS veterinary surgeon
vss verses, versions
V/STOL vertical short takeoff and landing
Vt Vermont
VT vacuum tube, variable time, Vermont
VTOL vertical takeoff and landing
VTR video tape recorder, video tape recording
VU volume unit
Vulg Vulgate
vv verses, vice versa

W

W (*Wolfram*) tungsten
WA Washington, Western Australia
war warrant
W Aust Western Australia
WC water closet, without charge
Wed Wednesday
WFTU World Federation of Trade Unions
WH watt-hour
WHA World Hockey Association
whf wharf
WHO World Health Organization
whr watt-hour
whs or **whse** warehouse
whsle wholesale
wi when issued
WI West Indies, Wisconsin
WIA wounded in action

wid widow, widower
wk week, work
wkly weekly
WL waterline, wavelength
WNW west-northwest
WO warrant officer
w/o without
W/O water-in-oil
WOC without compensation
WP without prejudice
WPM words per minute
wpn weapon
WR warehouse receipt
WRAC Women's Royal Army Corps
WRAF Women's Royal Air Force
WRNS Women's Royal Naval Service
wrnt warrant
WSW west-southwest
wt weight
WT watertight, wireless telegraphy
WV or **W Va** West Virginia
WVS Women's Voluntary Services
WW warehouse warrant, with warrants, world war
w/w wall-to-wall
WY or **Wyo** Wyoming

X

x cross, ex, experimental, extra
XC ex coupon
XD or **x div** ex dividend
Xe xenon
XI or **x in** or **x int** ex interest
XL extra large, extra long

Y

y yard, year, yen
Y ytrium
Yb ytterbium
YB yearbook
yd yard
YO year old
YOB year of birth
yr year, younger, your
yrbk yearbook
Yug Yugoslavia

Z

z zero, zone
Zn zinc
ZPG zero population growth
zr zirconium

The United States: States and Their Capital Cities

State	*Abbreviations*	*Capital*
Alabama	Ala., AL	Montgomery
Alaska	AK	Juneau
Arizona	Ariz., AZ	Phoenix
Arkansas	Ark., AR	Little Rock
California	Calif. CA	Sacramento
Colorado	Colo., CO	Denver
Connecticut	Conn., CT	Hartford
Delaware	Del., DE	Dover
Florida	Fla., FL	Tallahassee
Georgia	Ga., GA	Atlanta
Hawaii	HI	Honolulu
Idaho	ID	Boise
Illinois	Ill., IL	Springfield
Indiana	Ind., IN	Indianapolis
Iowa	IA	Des Moines
Kansas	Kans., KS	Topeka
Kentucky	Ky., KY	Frankfort
Louisiana	La., LA	Baton Rouge
Maine	Me., ME	Augusta
Maryland	Md., MD	Annapolis
Massachusetts	Mass., MA	Boston
Michigan	Mich., MI	Lansing
Minnesota	Minn., MN	St. Paul
Mississippi	Miss., MS	Jackson
Missouri	Mo., MO	Jefferson City
Montana	Mont., MT	Helena
Nebraska	Nebr., NE	Lincoln
Nevada	Ne., NV	Carson City
New Hampshire	N.H., NH	Concord
New Jersey	N.J., NJ	Trenton
New Mexico	N. Mex., NM	Santa Fe
New York	N.Y., NY	Albany
North Carolina	N.C., NC	Raleigh
North Dakota	N.D., ND	Bismarck

Ohio	OH	Columbus
Oklahoma	Okla., OK	Oklahoma City
Oregon	Oreg., OR	Salem
Pennsylvania	Pa., PA	Harrisburg
Rhode Island	R.I., RI	Providence
South Carolina	S.C, SC	Columbia
South Dakota	S.D., SD	Pierre
Tennessee	Tenn., TN	Nashville
Texas	Tex., TX	Austin
Utah	UT	Salt Lake City
Vermont	Vt., VT	Montpelier
Virginia	Va., VA	Richmond
Washington	Wash., WA	Olympia
West Virginia	W. Va., WV	Charleston
Wisconsin	Wis., WI	Madison
Wyoming	Wyo., WY	Cheyenne

Weights and Measures

Measurement of Mass or Weight

avoirdupois		*metric equivalent*
	1 grain (gr.)	= 4.8 mg
	1 dram (dr.)	= 1.772 g
16 drams	= 1 ounce (oz.)	= 28.3495 g
16 oz. (=7000gr.)	= 1 pound (lb.)	= 0.4536 kg
100 lb	= 1 short hundredweight	= 45.3592 kg
112 lb	= 1 long hundredweight	= 50.8024 kg
2000 lb	= 1 short ton	= 0.9072 tonnes
2,240 lb	= 1 long ton	= 1.01605 tonnes

metric		*avoirdupois equivalent*
	1 milligram (mg)	= 0.015 gr.
10 mg	= 1 centigram (cg)	= 0.154 gr.
10 cg	= 1 decigram (dg)	= 1.543 gr.
10 dg	= 1 gram (g)	= 15.43 gr. = 0.035 oz.
1g	= 1 decagrain (dag)	= 0.353 oz.
10 dag	= 1 hectogram (hg)	= 3.527 oz.
10 hg	= 1 kilogram (kg)	= 2.205 lb.
1000 kg	= 1 tonne (metric ton)	= 0.984 (long) ton
		= 2204.62 lb

Troy Weight

		metric equivalent
	1 grain	= 0.065 g
4 grains	= 1 carat of gold or silver	= 0.2592 g
6 carats	= 1 pennyweight (dwt.)	= 1.5552 g
20 dwt.	= 1 ounce (oz.)	= 31.1035 g
12 oz.	= 1 pound (lb.)	= 373.242 g
25 lb	= 1 quarter (qr.)	= 9.331 kg
100 lb	= 1 hundredweight (cwt.)	= 37.324 kg
20 cwt.	= 1 ton of gold or silver	= 746.48 kg

'Note: the grain troy is the same as the grain avoirdupois, but the pound troy contains 5760 grains, the pound avoirdupois 7000 grains. Jewels are not weighed by this measure.

Linear Measure

				metric equivalent
	1 inch (in.)			= 25.4 mm
12 in.	= 1 foot (ft.)			= 0.305 m
3 ft.	= 1 yard (yd.)			= 0.914 m
2 yds.	= 6 ft.	= 1 fathom (fm.)		= 1.829 m
5.5 yds.	= 16.5 ft.	= 1 rod		= 5.029 m
4 rod	= 22 yds.	= 66 ft.	= 1 chain	= 20.12 m
10 chain	= 220 yds.	= 660 ft.	= 1 furlong (fur.)	= 0.201 km
8 fur.	= 1760 yds.	= 5280 ft.	= 1 (statute) mile (m.)	= 1.609 km
3m.	= 1 league			= 4.827 km

metric

	1 millimeter (mm)	= 0.0394 in.
10 mm	= 1 centimeter (cm)	= 0.3937 in.
10 cm	= 1decimeter (dm)	= 3.937 in.
10 cim	= 1 meter (m)	= 39.37 in.
10 m	= 1 decameter (dam)	= 10.94 yds.
10 dam	= 1 hectometer (hm)	= 109.4 yds.
10 hm	= 1 kilometer (km)	= 0.621 m.

Surveyor's Measure

Surveyor's Linear Units

			metric equivalent
	1 link	= 7.92 in.	= 20.117 cm
25 links	= 1 rod	= 5.50 yds.	= 5.029 m
100 links	= 1 chain	= 22 yds.	= 20.12 m
10 chains	= 1 furlong (fur.)	= 220 yds.	= 0.201 m
80 chains	= 8 fur.	= 1 mile (m.)	= 1.609 km

Surveyor's Square units

metric equivalent

100 x 100 links or 10,000 sq.	= 1 sq. chain	= 484 sq. yds.	= 404.7 m^2 links
4 x 4 poles or 16 sq. poles	= 1 sq. chain		
22 x 22 yds. or 484 sq. yds.	= 1 sq. chain		
100,000 sq. links or 10 sq. chains	= 1 acre	= 4840 sq. yds.	= 0.4047 ha

Square Measure

		metric equivalent
	1 square inch (sq. in.)	= 6.4516 cm^2
144 sq. in.	= 1 square foot (sq. ft.)	= 0.0929 m^2
9 sq. ft.	= 1 square yard (sq. yd.)	= 0.8361 m^2
301/4 sq. yds.	= 1 square perch	= 25.29 m^2
40 sq. perch	= 1 rood	= 0. 10 1 2 ha
4 roods or 4840 sq. yds.	= 1 acre	= 04.047 ha
640 acres	= 1 square mile (sq. m.)	= 2.5900 km^2

metric units

	1 square millimeter (mm^2)	= 0.0016 sq. in.
100 mm^2	= 1 square centimeter (cm^2)	= 0.1550 sq. in.
100 cm^2	= 1 square decimeter (dm^2)	= 15.5000 sq. in.
100 dm^2	= 1square meter (m^2)	= 10.7639 sq. ft. (= 1.1959 sq. yds.)
100 m^2	= 1 square decameter (dam^2)	= 1076.3910 sq. ft.
100 dam^2	= 1 square hectometer (hm^2)*	= 0.0039 sq. m.
100 hm^2	= 1 square kilometer (km^2)	= 0.3861 sq. m.

Note:* The **square hectometer is also known as a *hectare* (ha).
The hectare can be sub-divided into ares:

metric units

100 m^2	= 1 are	= 119.59 sq. yds.
1000 m^2	= 10 ares = 1 dekare	= 1195.9 sq. yds.
10 000 m^2	= 100 ares= 1 hectare	= 2.471 acres

Cubic Measure

		metric equivalent
	1 cubic inch (cu. in.)	= 16.39 cm^3
1728 cu. in.	= 1 cubic foot (cu. ft.)	= 0.0283 m^3
27 cu. ft.	= I cubic yard (cu. yd.)	= 0.7646 m^3

metric units

1000 cubic millimeters (mm^3)	= 1cubic centimeter (cm^3)	= 0.0610 cu. in.
1000 cubic centimeters (cm^3)	= 1cubic decimeter (dm^3)	= 610 cu. in.
1000 cubic decimeters (dm^3)	= 1cubic meter (m^3)	= 35.3147 cu. ft.

The stere is also used, in particular as a unit of measurement for timber:

1 cubic meter	= 1 stere	35.3147cu. ft.
10 decisteres	= 1 stere	35.3147 cu. ft.
10 steres	= 1 decastere	353.1467 cu. ft. (=13.0795 cu. yds.)

Liquid Measure

		metric equivalent
4 fl. oz.	= 1 gill	= $118.291 cm^3$
4 gills	= 1 pint (pt.)	= $473.163 cm^3$
2pt.	= 1 quart (qt.)	= 0.946 1
4 qt.	= 1 gallon (gal.)	= 3.785 1

U.S. and British Equivalents

U.S.	*British*
1 fluid ounce	1.0408 fl. oz.
1 pint	0.8327 pt.
1 gallon	0.8327 gal.

metric units		
10 milliliters (ml)	= 1 centiliter (cl)	= 0.0211 pt.
10 cl	= 1 decaliter (dl)	= 0.211 pt.
10 dl	= 1 liter (1)	= 2.11 pt.
		(= 0.264 gal.)
101	= 1 decaliter (dal)	= 2.64 gal.
10 dal	= 1 hectoliter (hl)	= 26.4 gal.
10 hl	= 1 kiloliter (kl)	= 264.0 gal.

Temperature

Equations for Conversion

°Fahrenheit = $(9/5 \times x°C) + 32$
°Centigrade = $5/9 \times (x°F - 32)$
°Kelvin = $x°C + 273.15$

Some Equivalents

	Centigrade	*Fahrenheit*
Normal temperature of the human body	36.9°C	98.4°F
Freezing point	0°C	32°F
Boiling point	100°C	212°F

Table of Equivalents

Fahrenheit	*Centigrade*	*Centigrade*	*Fahrenheit*
100°C	212°F	30°C	86°F
90°C	194°F	20°C	68°F
80°C	176°F	10°C	50°F
70°C	158°F	0°C	32°F
60°C	140°F	–10°C	14°F
50°C	122°F	–20°C	4°F
40°C	104°F	–30°C	–22°F